Routing TCP/IP
Volume II

Jeff Doyle, CCIE #1919 and Jennifer DeHaven Carroll, CCIE #1402

Cisco Press

Cisco Press
201 West 103rd Street
Indianapolis, IN 46290 USA

Routing TCP/IP

Volume II

Jeff Doyle and Jennifer DeHaven Carroll

Copyright © 2001 Cisco Systems, Inc.

Published by:
Cisco Press
201 West 103rd Street
Indianapolis, IN 46290 USA

Printed in the United States of America 3 4 5 6 7 8 9 0

Third Printing   October 2002

Library of Congress Cataloging-in-Publication Number: 98-86516

ISBN: 1-57870-089-2

Warning and Disclaimer

This book is designed to provide information about the TCP/IP. Every effort has been made to make this book as complete and as accurate as possible, but no warranty or fitness is implied.

The information is provided on an "as is" basis. The authors, Cisco Press, and Cisco Systems, Inc. shall have neither liability nor responsibility to any person or entity with respect to any loss or damages arising from the information contained in this book or from the use of the discs or programs that may accompany it.

The opinions expressed in this book belong to the author and are not necessarily those of Cisco Systems, Inc.

Feedback Information

At Cisco Press, our goal is to create in-depth technical books of the highest quality and value. Each book is crafted with care and precision, undergoing rigorous development that involves the unique expertise of members from the professional technical community.

Readers' feedback is a natural continuation of this process. If you have any comments regarding how we could improve the quality of this book, or otherwise alter it to better suit your needs, you can contact us through e-mail at feedback@ciscopress.com. Please make sure to include the book title and ISBN in your message.

We greatly appreciate your assistance.

Publisher	John Wait
Editor-In-Chief	John Kane
Cisco Representative	Anthony Wolfenden
Cisco Press Program Manager	Sonia Torres Chavez
Cisco Marketing Communications Manager	Tom Geitner
Cisco Marketing Program Manager	Edie Quiroz
Executive Editor	Brett Bartow
Acquisitions Editor	Amy Lewis
Production Manager	Patrick Kanouse
Development Editor	Christopher Cleveland
Production Editor	Marc Fowler
Copy Editor	Keith Cline
Technical Editors	Pete Moyer, Henry Benjamin, Mike Penning
Team Coordinator	Tammi Ross
Book Designer	Gina Rexrode
Cover Designer	Louisa Adair
Compositor	Octal Publishing, Inc.
Indexer	Tim Wright
Proofreader	Gayle Johnson

CISCO SYSTEMS

Corporate Headquarters
Cisco Systems, Inc.
170 West Tasman Drive
San Jose, CA 95134-1706
USA
http://www.cisco.com
Tel: 408 526-4000
       800 553-NETS (6387)
Fax: 408 526-4100

European Headquarters
Cisco Systems Europe
11 Rue Camille Desmoulins
92782 Issy-les-Moulineaux
Cedex 9
France
http://www-europe.cisco.com
Tel: 33 1 58 04 60 00
Fax: 33 1 58 04 61 00

Americas Headquarters
Cisco Systems, Inc.
170 West Tasman Drive
San Jose, CA 95134-1706
USA
http://www.cisco.com
Tel: 408 526-7660
Fax: 408 527-0883

Asia Pacific Headquarters
Cisco Systems Australia,
Pty., Ltd
Level 17, 99 Walker Street
North Sydney
NSW 2059 Australia
http://www.cisco.com
Tel: +61 2 8448 7100
Fax: +61 2 9957 4350

Cisco Systems has more than 200 offices in the following countries.
Addresses, phone numbers, and fax numbers are listed on the
Cisco Web site at www.cisco.com/go/offices

Argentina • Australia • Austria • Belgium • Brazil • Bulgaria • Canada • Chile • China • Colombia • Costa
Rica • Croatia • Czech Republic • Denmark • Dubai, UAE • Finland • France • Germany • Greece • Hong
Kong • Hungary • India • Indonesia • Ireland • Israel • Italy • Japan • Korea • Luxembourg • Malaysia
Mexico • The Netherlands • New Zealand • Norway • Peru • Philippines • Poland • Portugal • Puerto Rico
Romania • Russia • Saudi Arabia • Scotland • Singapore • Slovakia • Slovenia • South Africa • Spain
Sweden • Switzerland • Taiwan • Thailand • Turkey • Ukraine • United Kingdom • United States • Venezuela
Vietnam • Zimbabwe

Trademark Acknowledgments

All terms mentioned in this book that are known to be trademarks or service marks have been appropriately capitalized. Cisco Press or Cisco Systems, Inc. cannot attest to the accuracy of this information. Use of a term in this book should not be regarded as affecting the validity of any trademark or service mark.

About the Authors

Jeff Doyle, CCIE #1919, is a Professional Services Consultant with Juniper Networks, Inc. in Denver, Colorado. Specializing in IP routing protocols and MPLS Traffic Engineering, Jeff has helped design and implement large-scale Internet service provider networks throughout North America, Europe, and Asia. Jeff has also lectured on advanced networking technologies at service provider forums such as the North American Network Operators' Group (NANOG) and the Asia Pacific Regional Internet Conference on Operational Technologies (APRICOT). Prior to joining Juniper Networks, Jeff was a Senior Network Systems Consultant with International Network Services. Jeff can be contacted at jeff@juniper.net.

Jennifer DeHaven Carroll, is a principal consultant with Lucent technologies and is a Cisco Certified Internetwork Expert (CCIE # 1402). She has planned, designed, and implemented many large networks over the past 13 years. She has also developed and taught theory and Cisco implementation classes on all IP routing protocols. Jenny can be reached at jennifer.carroll@ieee.org.

About the Technical Reviewers

Henry Benjamin, CCIE #4695, CCNA, CCDA, B. Eng., is a Cisco certified Internet Expert and an IT Network Design Engineer for Cisco Systems, Inc. He has more than eight years of experience in Cisco networks, including planning, designing, and implementing large IP networks running IGRP, EIGRP, and OSPF. Currently Henry is working for the IT design team internally at Cisco in Sydney, Australia. Henry holds a Bachelor of Engineering degree from Sydney University.

Peter J. Moyer, CCIE #3286, is a Professional Services Consultant for Juniper Networks, where he designs and implements large-scale ISP networks. In addition to his consulting work, Peter has developed and delivered advanced IP training courses and IP network design seminars to Juniper customers and partners. He has presented at networking conferences on such advanced topics as MPLS. Before joining Juniper, Peter was a Senior Network Consultant for International Network Services (INS), where he designed and implemented large-scale enterprise networks. Peter holds a Bachelor of Science degree in Computer and Information Science from the University of Maryland.

Dedications

Jeff Doyle: This book is dedicated to my wife, Sara, and my children, Anna, Carol, James, and Katherine. They are my refuge, and they keep me sane, humble, and happy.

Jennifer DeHaven Carroll: To my husband, Mike, and son, Mitchell, who continue to encourage me.

Acknowledgments

Jeff Doyle: An author of a technical book is just a front man for a small army of brilliant, dedicated people. This book is certainly no exception. At the risk of sounding like I'm making an Academy Award acceptance speech, I would like to thank a number of those people.

First and foremost, I would like to thank Jenny Carroll, whose efforts as a technical editor on *Volume I* were amazing. Not only has Jenny again contributed her technical expertise to this second volume as a technical editor, but when I became hopelessly behind schedule, she stepped in as a coauthor, at my request, and wrote the last two chapters. Neither volume would be what they are without her invaluable advice and attention to detail.

I would also like to thank Pete Moyer, my friend and associate, who came aboard as a technical editor for this second volume. Pete has had a profound influence on my life beyond this project, and I will always be indebted to him.

My gratitude goes to Laurie McGuire and Chris Cleveland for their expert guidance as development editors. They have made the book a better book and me a better writer.

Thanks to Brett Bartow and all the folks at Cisco Press for their enormous patience with me as I struggled to finish the book and let deadline after deadline slip. They continued to show me great kindness throughout the project when I'm sure they would have preferred to bash me on the head with a copy of my first book.

Finally, I would like to thank you, good reader, for making the first book such a success and for waiting so patiently for me to finish this second volume. I hope the book proves to be worth the wait.

Jennifer DeHaven Carroll: I'd like to thank Jeff Doyle for giving me the opportunity to contribute to his books. It has been fun and challenging.

Contents at a Glance

Table of Contents

Introduction

Since the publication of *Volume I* of *Routing TCP/IP*, many volumes have been added to the Cisco Press CCIE Professional Development series. And the CCIE program itself has expanded to include various areas of specialization. Yet the IP routing protocols remain the essential foundation on which the CCIE candidate must build his or her expertise. If the foundation is weak, the house will tumble.

I stated in the introduction to *Volume I* that "...as internetworks grow in size and complexity, routing issues can become at once both large and subtle." Scalability and management of growth continues to be a central theme in this second volume, as we move beyond the interior gateway protocols to examine both interautonomous system routing and more exotic routing issues such as multicasting and IPv6.

My objective in this book is not only to help you walk away from the CCIE lab exam with one of those valued and valuable numbers after your name, but also to help you develop the knowledge and skills to live up to the CCIE title. As with the first volume, I want to make CCIEs, not people who can pass the CCIE lab. In this vein, you will find in this book more information than you will need to pass the lab, but certainly all of the material is important in your career as a recognized internetworking expert.

When I earned my CCIE, the lab still consisted mostly of AGS+ routers. Certainly the lab and the nature of the exam have changed substantially since that ancient time. If anything, the lab is more difficult now. Another addition to the CCIE program has been the recertification requirement. Even before I took the recertification exam for the first time, people were telling me how much *Volume I* had helped them prepare for the test—particularly for IS-IS, a protocol that few outside of service provider environments are exposed to. I have therefore written this second volume with not only CCIE candidates in mind, but also existing CCIEs who need to review for their recertification. The chapters on multicasting and IPv6 are directed to this audience.

I have endeavored to follow the same structure that I followed in *Volume I*, in which a protocol is introduced in generic terms, followed by examples of configuring the protocol using Cisco IOS Software, and finally by examples of Cisco IOS Software tools for troubleshooting the protocol. In the case of BGP and IP multicast, this structure is far too lengthy for a single chapter and therefore spans multiple chapters.

I hope you learn as much from reading this book as I have from writing it.

Icons Used in This Book

Router

Bridge

Hub

DSU/CSU

Catalyst switch

Multilayer switch

ATM switch

ISDN switch

Communication server

Gateway

Access server

PC

PC with software

Sun Workstation

Mac

Terminal

File server

Web server

CiscoWorks Workstation

Printer

Laptop

IBM mainframe

Front-End Processor

Cluster Controller

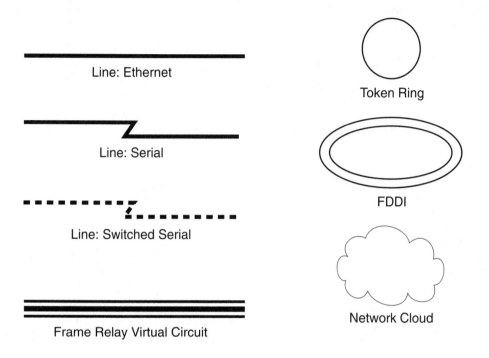

Line: Ethernet

Line: Serial

Line: Switched Serial

Frame Relay Virtual Circuit

Token Ring

FDDI

Network Cloud

Command Syntax Conventions

The conventions used to present command syntax in this book are the same conventions used in the IOS Command Reference. The Command Reference describes these conventions as follows:

- Vertical bars (|) separate alternative, mutually exclusive elements.
- Square brackets [ ] indicate optional elements.
- Braces { } indicate a required choice.
- Braces within brackets [{ }] indicate a required choice within an optional element.

- **Boldface** indicates commands and keywords that are entered literally as shown. In actual configuration examples and output (not general command syntax), boldface indicates commands that are manually input by the user (such as a **show** command).
- *Italics* indicates arguments for which you supply actual values.

PART I

Exterior Gateway Protocols

This chapter covers the following key topics:

- **The Origins of EGP**—This section discusses the history of the development of the Exterior Gateway Protocol, presented in RFC 827 (1982).

- **Operation of EGP**—This section explores the fundamental mechanics of EGP with a focus on EGP topology issues, EGP functions, and EGP message formats.

- **Shortcomings of EGP**—This section explores some of the reasons why EGP is no longer pursued as a viable external gateway protocol solution.

- **Configuring EGP**—This section presents four separate case studies—EGP stub gateway, EGP core gateway, indirect neighbors, and default routes—to demonstrate different types of EGP configuration.

- **Troubleshooting EGP**—This section examines how to interpret an EGP neighbor table and presents a case study on the slow convergence speed of an EGP network to show why EGP is no longer a popular option.

CHAPTER 1

Exterior Gateway Protocol

The first question knowledgeable readers will (and should) ask is "Why kill a few trees publishing a chapter about an obsolete protocol such as the Exterior Gateway Protocol (EGP)?" After all, EGP has been almost universally replaced by the Border Gateway Protocol (BGP). This question has two answers.

First, although EGP is rarely used these days, it is still occasionally encountered. As of this writing, for instance, you can still find EGP in a few U.S. military internetworks. As a CCIE, you should understand EGP for such rare encounters.

Second, this chapter serves as something of a history lesson. Examining the motives for developing an external gateway protocol and the shortcomings of the original external protocol provides a prologue for the following two chapters. BGP will make more sense to you if you are familiar with the roots from which it evolved.

The Origins of EGP

In the early 1980s, the routers (gateways) that made up the ARPANET (predecessor of the modern Internet) ran a distance vector routing protocol known as the *Gateway-to-Gateway Protocol* (GGP). Every gateway knew a route to every reachable network, at a distance measured in gateway hops. As the ARPANET grew, its architects foresaw the same problem that administrators of many growing internetworks encounter today: Their routing protocol did not scale well.

Eric Rosen, in RFC 827[1], chronicles the scalability problems:

- With all gateways knowing all routes, "the overhead of the routing algorithm becomes excessively large." Whenever a topology change occurs, the likelihood of which increases with the size of the internetwork, all gateways have to exchange routing information and recalculate their tables. Even when the internetwork is in a steady state, the size of the routing tables and routing updates becomes an increasing burden.

- As the number of GGP software implementations increases, and the hardware platforms on which they are implemented become more diverse, "it becomes impossible to regard the Internet as an integrated communications system." Specifically, maintenance and troubleshooting become "nearly impossible."

- As the number of gateways grows, so does the number of gateway administrators. As a result, resistance to software upgrades increases: "[A]ny proposed change must be made in too many different places by too many different people."

The solution proposed in RFC 827 was that the ARPANET be migrated from a single internetwork to a system of interconnected, autonomously controlled internetworks. Within each internetwork, known as an autonomous system (AS), the administrative authority for that AS is free to manage the internetwork as it chooses. In effect, the concept of autonomous systems broadens the scope of internetworking and adds a new layer of hierarchy. Where there was a single internetwork—a network of networks—there is now a network of autonomous systems, each of which is itself an internetwork. And just as a network is identified by an IP address, an AS is identified by an autonomous system number. An AS number is a 16-bit number assigned by the same addressing authority that assigns IP addresses.

NOTE   Also like IP addresses, some AS numbers are reserved for private use. These numbers range from 64512 to 65535. See RFC 1930 (www.isi.edu/in-notes/rfc1930.txt) for more information.

Chief among the choices the administrative authority of each AS is free to make is the routing protocol that its gateways run. Because the gateways are interior to the AS, their routing protocols are known as interior gateway protocols (IGPs). Because GGP was the routing protocol of the ARPANET, it became by default the first IGP. However, interest in the more modern (and simpler) Routing Information Protocol (RIP) was building in 1982, and it was expected that this and other as-yet-unplanned protocols would be used in many autonomous systems. These days, GGP has been completely replaced by RIP, RIP-2, Interior Gateway Routing Protocol (IGRP), Enhanced IGRP (EIGRP), Open Shortest Path First (OSPF), and Integrated Intermediate System-to-Intermediate System (IS-IS).

Each AS is connected to other autonomous systems via one or more exterior gateways. RFC 827 proposed that the exterior gateways share routing information between each other by means of a protocol known as the EGP. Contrary to popular belief, although EGP is a distance vector protocol, it is not a routing protocol. It has no algorithm for choosing an optimal path between networks; rather, it is a common language that exterior gateways use to exchange reachability information with other exterior gateways. That reachability information is a simple list of major network addresses (no subnets) and the gateways by which they can be reached.

Operation of EGP

Version 1 of EGP was proposed in RFC 827. Version 2, slightly modified from version 1, was proposed in RFC 888[2], and the formal specification of EGPv2 is given in RFC 904[3].

EGP Topology Issues

EGP messages are exchanged between EGP neighbors, or *peers*. If the neighbors are in the same AS, they are *interior neighbors*. If they are in different autonomous systems, they are *exterior neighbors*. EGP has no function that automatically discovers its neighbors; the addresses of the neighbors are manually configured, and the messages they exchange are unicast to the configured addresses.

RFC 888 suggests that the time-to-live (TTL) of EGP messages be set to a low number, because an EGP message should never travel farther than to a single neighbor. However, nothing in the EGP functionality requires EGP neighbors to share a common data link. For example, Figure 1-1 shows two EGP neighbors separated by a router that speaks only RIP. Because EGP messages are unicast to neighbors, they can cross router boundaries. Therefore, Cisco routers set the TTL of EGP packets to 255.

Figure 1-1   *EGP Neighbors Do Not Have to Be Connected to the Same Network*

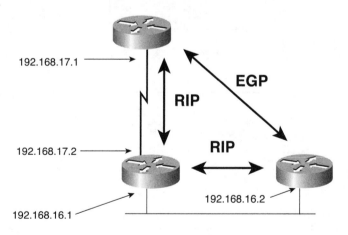

EGP gateways are either core gateways or stub gateways. Both gateway types can accept information about networks in other autonomous systems, but a stub gateway can send only information about networks in its own AS. Only core gateways can send information they have learned about networks in autonomous systems other than their own.

To understand why EGP defines core and stub gateways, it is necessary to understand the architectural limitations of EGP. As previously mentioned, EGP is not a routing protocol. Its updates list only reachable networks, without including enough information to determine shortest paths or to prevent routing loops. Therefore, the EGP topology must be built with no loops.

Figure 1-2 shows an EGP topology. There is a single core AS to which all other autonomous systems (stub autonomous systems) must attach. This two-level tree topology is very similar to the two-level topology requirements of OSPF, and its purpose is the same. Recall from *Routing TCP/IP, Volume I* that interarea OSPF routing is essentially distance vector, and therefore vulnerable to routing loops. Requiring all traffic between nonbackbone OSPF areas to traverse the backbone area reduces the potential for routing loops by forcing a loop-free interarea topology. Likewise, requiring all EGP reachability information between stub autonomous systems to traverse the core AS reduces the potential for routing loops in the EGP topology.

Figure 1-2   *To Prevent Routing Loops, Only Core Gateways Can Send Information Learned from One AS to Another AS*

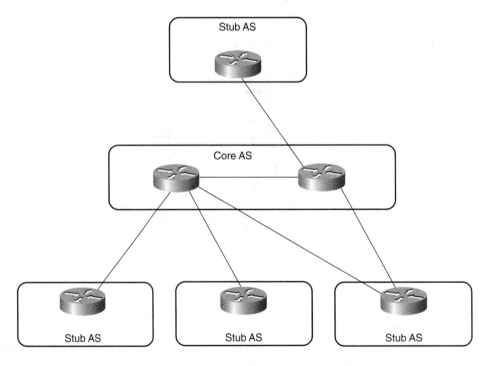

EGP Functions

EGP consists of the following three mechanisms:

- Neighbor Acquisition Protocol
- Neighbor Reachability Protocol
- Network Reachability Protocol

These three mechanisms use ten message types to establish a neighbor relationship, maintain the neighbor relationship, exchange network reachability information with the neighbor, and notify the neighbor of procedural or formatting errors. Table 1-1 lists all of the EGP message types and the mechanism that uses each message type.

Table 1-1   *EGP Message Types*

Message Type	Mechanism
Neighbor Acquisition Request	Neighbor Acquisition
Neighbor Acquisition Confirm	Neighbor Acquisition
Neighbor Acquisition Refuse	Neighbor Acquisition
Neighbor Cease	Neighbor Acquisition
Neighbor Cease Acknowledgment	Neighbor Acquisition
Hello	Neighbor Reachability
I-Heard-You	Neighbor Reachability
Poll	Network Reachability
Update	Network Reachability
Error	All functions

The following sections discuss the details of each of the three EGP mechanisms; the section "EGP Message Formats" in this chapter covers the specific details of the messages.

Neighbor Acquisition Protocol

Before EGP neighbors can exchange reachability information, they must establish that they are compatible. This function is performed by a simple two-way handshake in which one neighbor sends a Neighbor Acquisition Request message, and the other neighbor responds with a Neighbor Acquisition Confirm message.

None of the RFCs specify how two EGP neighbors initially discover each other. In practice, an EGP gateway learns of its neighbor by manual configuration of the neighbor's IP address. The gateway then unicasts an Acquisition Request message to the configured neighbor. The message states a *Hello interval*, the minimum interval between Hello messages that the gateway is willing to accept from the neighbor, and a *Poll interval*, the minimum interval that the gateway is willing to be polled by the neighbor for routing updates. The neighbor's responding Acquisition Confirm message will contain its own values for the same two intervals. If the neighbors agree on the values, they are ready to exchange network reachability information.

When a gateway first learns of a neighbor, it considers the neighbor to be in the Idle state. Before sending the first Acquisition Request, the gateway transitions the neighbor to the *Acquire* state; when the gateway receives an Acquisition Confirm, it transitions the neighbor to the Down state.

NOTE   See RFC 904 for a complete explanation of the EGP finite state machine.

A gateway can refuse to accept a neighbor by responding with a Neighbor Acquisition Refuse message rather than an Acquisition Confirm message. The Refuse message can include a reason for the refusal, such as a lack of table space, or it can refuse for an unspecified reason.

A gateway can also break an established neighbor relationship by sending a Neighbor Cease message. As with the Refuse message, the originating gateway has the option of including a reason for the Cease or leaving the reason unspecified. A neighbor receiving a Neighbor Cease message responds with a Neighbor Cease Acknowledgment.

The last case of a Neighbor Acquisition procedure is a case in which a gateway sends an Acquisition Request but the neighbor does not respond. RFC 888 suggests retransmitting the Acquisition message "at a reasonable rate, perhaps every 30 seconds or so." Cisco's EGP implementation does not just repeat unacknowledged messages over a constant period. Rather, it retransmits an unacknowledged Acquisition message 30 seconds after the original transmission. It then waits 60 seconds before the next transmission. If no response is received within 30 seconds of the third transmission, the gateway transitions the neighbor state from Acquire to Idle (see Example 1-1). The gateway remains in the Idle state for 300 seconds (5 minutes) and then transitions to Acquire and starts the process all over.

Notice in Example 1-1 that each EGP message has a sequence number. The sequence number allows EGP message pairs (such as Neighbor Acquisition Request/Confirm, Request/Refusal, and Cease/Cease-Ack pairs) to be identified. The next section, "Network Reachability Protocol," details how the sequence numbers are used.

When two EGP gateways become neighbors, one is the *active* neighbor and one is the *passive* neighbor. Active gateways always initiate the neighbor relationship by sending Neighbor Acquisition Requests. Passive gateways do not send Acquisition Requests; they only respond to them. The same is true for Hello/I-Heard-You message pairs, described in the following section: The active neighbor sends the Hello, and the passive neighbor responds with an I-Heard-You (I-H-U). A passive gateway can initiate a Neighbor Cease message, however, to which the active gateway must reply with a Cease Acknowledgement message.

Example 1-1 **debug ip egp transactions** *Command Output Displays EGP State Transitions*

```
Shemp#debug ip egp transactions
EGP debugging is on
Shemp#
EGP: 192.168.16.2 going from IDLE to ACQUIRE
EGP: from 192.168.16.1 to 192.168.16.2, version=2, asystem=1, sequence=0
     Type=ACQUIRE, Code=REQUEST, Status=0 (UNSPECIFIED), Hello=60, Poll=180
EGP: from 192.168.16.1 to 192.168.16.2, version=2, asystem=1, sequence=0
     Type=ACQUIRE, Code=REQUEST, Status=0 (UNSPECIFIED), Hello=60, Poll=180
EGP: from 192.168.16.1 to 192.168.16.2, version=2, asystem=1, sequence=0
     Type=ACQUIRE, Code=REQUEST, Status=0 (UNSPECIFIED), Hello=60, Poll=180
EGP: 192.168.16.2 going from ACQUIRE to IDLE
EGP: 192.168.16.2 going from IDLE to ACQUIRE
EGP: from 192.168.16.1 to 192.168.16.2, version=2, asystem=1, sequence=0
     Type=ACQUIRE, Code=REQUEST, Status=0 (UNSPECIFIED), Hello=60, Poll=180
EGP: from 192.168.16.1 to 192.168.16.2, version=2, asystem=1, sequence=0
     Type=ACQUIRE, Code=REQUEST, Status=0 (UNSPECIFIED), Hello=60, Poll=180
EGP: from 192.168.16.1 to 192.168.16.2, version=2, asystem=1, sequence=0
     Type=ACQUIRE, Code=REQUEST, Status=0 (UNSPECIFIED), Hello=60, Poll=180
EGP: 192.168.16.2 going from ACQUIRE to IDLE
```

A core gateway, which can be a neighbor of routers in several other autonomous systems, might be the active gateway of one neighbor adjacency and the passive gateway of another neighbor adjacency. Cisco's EGP implementation uses the AS numbers as the determining factor: The neighbor whose AS number is lower will be the active neighbor.

Neighbor Reachability Protocol

After a gateway has acquired a neighbor, it maintains the neighbor relationship by sending periodic Hello messages. The neighbor responds to each Hello with an I-H-U message. RFC 904 does not specify a standard period between Hellos; Cisco uses a default period of 60 seconds, which can be changed with the command **timers egp**.

When three Hello/I-H-U message pairs have been exchanged, the neighbor state changes from Down to Up (see Example 1-2). The neighbors can then exchange network reachability information, as described in the next section.

If an active neighbor sends three sequential messages without receiving a response, the neighbor state transitions to Down. The gateway sends three more Hellos at the normal Hello interval; if there is still no response, the state changes to Cease. The gateway sends three Neighbor Cease messages at 60-second intervals. If the neighbor responds to any of the messages with a Cease Acknowledgment, or does not respond at all, the gateway transitions the neighbor state to Idle and waits 5 minutes before transitioning back to Acquire and attempting to reacquire the neighbor. Example 1-3 shows this sequence of events.

Example 1-2 **debug ip egp transactions** *Command Output Displays Two-Way Handshake Success and EGP State Transitions*

```
EGP: 192.168.16.2 going from IDLE to ACQUIRE
EGP: from 192.168.16.1 to 192.168.16.2, version=2, asystem=1, sequence=2
     Type=ACQUIRE, Code=REQUEST, Status=1 (ACTIVE-MODE), Hello=60, Poll=180
EGP: from 192.168.16.2 to 192.168.16.1, version=2, asystem=2, sequence=2
     Type=ACQUIRE, Code=CONFIRM, Status=2 (PASSIVE-MODE), Hello=60, Poll=180
EGP: 192.168.16.2 going from ACQUIRE to DOWN
EGP: from 192.168.16.1 to 192.168.16.2, version=2, asystem=1, sequence=2
     Type=REACH, Code=HELLO, Status=2 (DOWN)
EGP: from 192.168.16.2 to 192.168.16.1, version=2, asystem=2, sequence=2
     Type=REACH, Code=I-HEARD-YOU, Status=2 (DOWN)
EGP: from 192.168.16.1 to 192.168.16.2, version=2, asystem=1, sequence=2
     Type=REACH, Code=HELLO, Status=2 (DOWN)
EGP: from 192.168.16.2 to 192.168.16.1, version=2, asystem=2, sequence=2
     Type=REACH, Code=I-HEARD-YOU, Status=2 (DOWN)
EGP: from 192.168.16.1 to 192.168.16.2, version=2, asystem=1, sequence=2
     Type=REACH, Code=HELLO, Status=2 (DOWN)
EGP: from 192.168.16.2 to 192.168.16.1, version=2, asystem=2, sequence=2
     Type=REACH, Code=I-HEARD-YOU, Status=2 (DOWN)
EGP: 192.168.16.2 going from DOWN to UP
```

Example 1-3 *The Neighbor at 192.168.16.2 Has Stopped Responding. The Interval Between Each of the Unacknowledged EGP Messages Is 60 Seconds*

```
Shemp#
EGP: from 192.168.16.1 to 192.168.16.2, version=2, asystem=1, sequence=2
     Type=REACH, Code=HELLO, Status=1 (UP)
EGP: from 192.168.16.2 to 192.168.16.1, version=2, asystem=2, sequence=2
     Type=REACH, Code=I-HEARD-YOU, Status=1 (UP)
EGP: from 192.168.16.1 to 192.168.16.2, version=2, asystem=1, sequence=2
     Type=REACH, Code=HELLO, Status=1 (UP)
EGP: from 192.168.16.1 to 192.168.16.2, version=2, asystem=1, sequence=2
     Type=POLL, Code=0, Status=1 (UP), Net=192.168.16.0
EGP: from 192.168.16.1 to 192.168.16.2, version=2, asystem=1, sequence=3
     Type=REACH, Code=HELLO, Status=1 (UP)
EGP: 192.168.16.2 going from UP to DOWN
EGP: from 192.168.16.1 to 192.168.16.2, version=2, asystem=1, sequence=3
     Type=REACH, Code=HELLO, Status=2 (DOWN)
EGP: from 192.168.16.1 to 192.168.16.2, version=2, asystem=1, sequence=3
     Type=REACH, Code=HELLO, Status=2 (DOWN)
EGP: from 192.168.16.1 to 192.168.16.2, version=2, asystem=1, sequence=3
     Type=REACH, Code=HELLO, Status=2 (DOWN)
EGP: 192.168.16.2 going from DOWN to CEASE
EGP: from 192.168.16.1 to 192.168.16.2, version=2, asystem=1, sequence=3
     Type=ACQUIRE, Code=CEASE, Status=5 (HALTING)
EGP: from 192.168.16.1 to 192.168.16.2, version=2, asystem=1, sequence=3
     Type=ACQUIRE, Code=CEASE, Status=1 (ACTIVE-MODE)
EGP: from 192.168.16.1 to 192.168.16.2, version=2, asystem=1, sequence=3
     Type=ACQUIRE, Code=CEASE, Status=1 (ACTIVE-MODE)
EGP: 192.168.16.2 going from CEASE to IDLE
```

Example 1-4 shows another example of a dead neighbor, except this time a core gateway (192.168.16.2) in the passive mode is discovering the dead neighbor (192.168.16.1).

Example 1-4   *Neighbor 192.168.16.1 Has Stopped Responding. The* **debug** *Messages Are Taken from 192.168.16.2, a Gateway in Passive Mode*

```
Moe#
EGP: from 192.168.16.1 to 192.168.16.2, version=2, asystem=1, sequence=1
     Type=REACH, Code=HELLO, Status=1 (UP)
EGP: from 192.168.16.2 to 192.168.16.1, version=2, asystem=2, sequence=1
     Type=REACH, Code=I-HEARD-YOU, Status=1 (UP)
EGP: from 192.168.16.2 to 192.168.16.1, version=2, asystem=2, sequence=1
     Type=POLL, Code=0, Status=1 (UP), Net=192.168.16.0
EGP: from 192.168.16.2 to 192.168.16.1, version=2, asystem=2, sequence=2
     Type=POLL, Code=0, Status=1 (UP), Net=192.168.16.0
EGP: 192.168.16.1 going from UP to DOWN
EGP: 192.168.16.1 going from DOWN to CEASE
EGP: from 192.168.16.2 to 192.168.16.1, version=2, asystem=2, sequence=3
     Type=ACQUIRE, Code=CEASE, Status=5 (HALTING)
EGP: from 192.168.16.2 to 192.168.16.1, version=2, asystem=2, sequence=3
     Type=ACQUIRE, Code=CEASE, Status=2 (PASSIVE-MODE)
EGP: from 192.168.16.2 to 192.168.16.1, version=2, asystem=2, sequence=3
     Type=ACQUIRE, Code=CEASE, Status=2 (PASSIVE-MODE)
EGP: 192.168.16.1 going from CEASE to IDLE
```

When the gateway does not receive a Hello within the 60-second Hello interval, it tries to "wake up" its neighbor. Because a gateway in passive mode cannot send Hellos, it sends a Poll message. The gateway then waits for one Poll interval. (Cisco's default Poll interval is 180 seconds, or 3 minutes.) If no response is received, it sends another Poll and waits another Poll interval. If there still is no response, the gateway changes the neighbor state to Down and then immediately to Cease. As in Example 1-3, three Cease messages are sent and the neighbor state is changed to Idle.

Network Reachability Protocol

When the neighbor state is Up, the EGP neighbors can begin exchanging reachability information. Each gateway periodically sends a Poll message to its neighbor, containing some sequence number. The neighbor responds with an Update message that contains the same sequence number and a list of reachable networks. Example 1-5 shows how Cisco's IOS Software uses the sequence numbers.

Example 1-5   *EGP Neighbors Poll Each Other Periodically for Network Reachability Updates*

```
EGP: from 192.168.16.1 to 192.168.16.2, version=2, asystem=1, sequence=120
        Type=REACH, Code=HELLO, Status=1 (UP)
EGP: from 192.168.16.2 to 192.168.16.1, version=2, asystem=2, sequence=120
        Type=REACH, Code=I-HEARD-YOU, Status=1 (UP)
EGP: from 192.168.16.1 to 192.168.16.2, version=2, asystem=1, sequence=120
        Type=REACH, Code=HELLO, Status=1 (UP)
EGP: from 192.168.16.2 to 192.168.16.1, version=2, asystem=2, sequence=120
        Type=REACH, Code=I-HEARD-YOU, Status=1 (UP)
EGP: from 192.168.16.1 to 192.168.16.2, version=2, asystem=1, sequence=120
        Type=POLL, Code=0, Status=1 (UP), Net=192.168.16.0
EGP: from 192.168.16.2 to 192.168.16.1, version=2, asystem=2, sequence=120
        Type=UPDATE, Code=0, Status=1 (UP), IntGW=2, ExtGW=1, Net=192.168.16.0
        Network 172.17.0.0 via 192.168.16.2 in 0 hops
        Network 192.168.17.0 via 192.168.16.2 in 0 hops
        Network 10.0.0.0 via 192.168.16.2 in 3 hops
        Network 172.20.0.0 via 192.168.16.4 in 0 hops
        Network 192.168.18.0 via 192.168.16.3(e) in 3 hops
        Network 172.16.0.0 via 192.168.16.3(e) in 3 hops
        Network 172.18.0.0 via 192.168.16.3(e) in 3 hops
EGP: 192.168.16.2 updated 7 routes
EGP: from 192.168.16.2 to 192.168.16.1, version=2, asystem=2, sequence=3
        Type=POLL, Code=0, Status=1 (UP), Net=192.168.16.0
EGP: from 192.168.16.1 to 192.168.16.2, version=2, asystem=1, sequence=3
        Type=UPDATE, Code=0, Status=1 (UP), IntGW=1, ExtGW=0, Net=192.168.16.0
        Network 172.19.0.0 via 192.168.16.1 in 0 hops
EGP: from 192.168.16.1 to 192.168.16.2, version=2, asystem=1, sequence=121
        Type=REACH, Code=HELLO, Status=1 (UP)
EGP: from 192.168.16.2 to 192.168.16.1, version=2, asystem=2, sequence=121
        Type=REACH, Code=I-HEARD-YOU, Status=1 (UP)
```

Every Hello/I-H-U pair exchanged between neighbors contains the same sequence number until a Poll is sent. The Poll/Update pair also uses the same sequence number. After the Update has been received, the active neighbor increments the sequence number. In Example 1-5, the sequence number is 120 through the Poll/Update, and it then is incremented to 121. Notice that both neighbors send a Poll; in this example, the Poll from the passive neighbor (192.168.16.2) has an entirely different sequence number (3). A neighbor always responds with an Update containing the same sequence number as the Poll.

The default polling interval used by Cisco's IOS Software is 180 seconds and can be changed with the command **timers egp**. Normally, a gateway sends an Update only when it is polled; however, this means a topology change might go unannounced for up to 3 minutes. EGP provides for this eventuality by allowing a gateway to send one *unsolicited* Update—that is, an Update that is not in response to a Poll—each Poll interval. Cisco, however, does not support unsolicited Updates.

NOTE	The **timers egp** command is also used to change the Hello interval. The format of the command is **timers egp** *hello polltime*.

Both the Poll and the Update messages include the address of a source network. For example, the Poll and Update messages in Example 1-5 show a source network of 192.168.16.0. The source network is the network from which all reachability information is measured—that is, all networks requested or advertised can be reached via a router attached to the source network. Although this network is usually the network to which the two neighbors are both attached, it is more accurately the network about which the Poll is requesting information, and the network about which the Update is supplying information. EGP is a purely classful protocol, and the source network—as well as the network addresses listed in the Updates—are always major class network addresses, and never subnets.

Following the source network address is a list of one or more routers and the networks that can be reached via those routers. The common characteristic of the routers on the list is that they are all attached to the source network. If a router on the list is not the EGP gateway that originated the Update, the router is an *indirect* or *third-party* neighbor.

Figure 1-3 illustrates the concept of indirect EGP neighbors. One router, Moe, is a core gateway and is peered with three other gateways.

The debug messages in Example 1-5 are taken from Shemp, the router in AS1. Notice in the Update originated by Moe (192.168.16.2) that three networks are listed as reachable via Moe, but also, four networks are listed as reachable via Larry (192.168.16.4) and Curly (192.168.16.3). These two routers are Shemp's indirect neighbors, via Moe. Joe, in AS3, is not an indirect neighbor, because it is not attached to the source network. Its networks are merely advertised as being reachable via Moe.

The advertisement of indirect neighbors saves bandwidth on a common link, but more importantly, indirect neighbors increase efficiency by eliminating an unnecessary router hop. In Figure 1-3, for example, Shemp is not peered with any router other than Moe. In fact, Larry is not even speaking EGP, but is advertising its networks to Moe via RIP. Moe is performing a sort of "preemptive redirect" by informing Shemp of better next-hop routers than itself.

In fact, it is possible for an EGP Update to contain indirect neighbors only—that is, the originator might not include itself as a next hop to any network. In this scenario, the originator is a *route server*. It has learned reachability information from an IGP or from static routes, and it advertises this information to EGP neighbors without itself performing any packet-forwarding functions.

Figure 1-3   *Indirect EGP Neighbors*

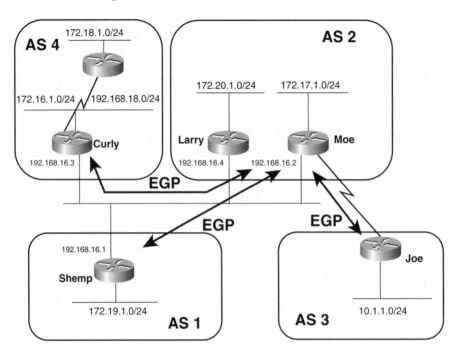

From the perspective of an EGP gateway, a neighbor is either an *interior gateway* or an *exterior gateway*. A neighbor is an interior gateway if it is in the same AS, and it is an exterior gateway if it is in a different AS. In Figure 1-3, all the EGP gateways see all their neighbors as external gateways. If Larry were speaking EGP and peered with Moe, those two routers would see each other as interior gateways.

An EGP Update message includes two fields for describing whether the routers in its list are interior or exterior gateways (see the following section, "EGP Message Formats"). Looking at the first Update message in Example 1-5, you can see these fields just before the source network: IntGW=2 and ExtGW=1. The sum of these two fields tells how many routers are listed in the Update. All the interior gateways specified are listed first; therefore, if IntGW=2 and ExtGW=1, the first two routers listed are interior gateways and the last router listed is an exterior gateway. If you compare the Update message from 192.168.16.2 in Example 1-5 with Figure 1-3, you will see that the three networks reachable via Curly are listed last in the Update and are marked as exterior—that is, they are reachable via a gateway exterior to Moe. Because stub gateways cannot advertise networks outside of their own AS, only Updates from core gateways can include exterior gateways.

The EGP Update message associates a distance with each network it lists. The distance field is 8 bits, so the distance can range from 0 to 255. RFC 904 does not specify how the distance is to be interpreted, however, other than that 255 is used to indicate unreachable networks. Nor does the RFC define an algorithm for using the distance to calculate shortest inter-AS paths. Cisco chooses to interpret the distance as hops, as shown in Example 1-5. The default rules are very basic:

- A gateway advertises all networks within its own AS as having a distance of 0.

- A gateway advertises all networks within an AS other than its own as having a distance of 3.

- A gateway indicates that a network has become unreachable by giving it a distance of 255.

For example, you can see in Example 1-5 and Figure 1-3 that although network 172.20.0.0 is one router hop away from Moe, Moe is advertising the network with a distance of 0—the same distance as network 172.17.0.0, which is directly attached. Network 10.0.0.0 is also one router hop away, and network 172.18.0.0 is two hops away, but both are in different autonomous systems and are therefore advertised with a distance of 3. The point is that the distance used by EGP is virtually useless for determining the best path to a network.

Example 1-6 shows the routing table of Shemp and the route entries resulting from the Update in Example 1-5.

Example 1-6   *Shemp's Routing Table*

```
Shemp#show ip route
Codes: C - connected, S - static, I - IGRP, R - RIP, M - mobile, B - BGP
       D - EIGRP, EX - EIGRP external, O - OSPF, IA - OSPF inter area
       E1 - OSPF external type 1, E2 - OSPF external type 2, E - EGP
       i - IS-IS, L1 - IS-IS level-1, L2 - IS-IS level-2, * - candidate default

Gateway of last resort is not set

E    10.0.0.0 [140/4] via 192.168.16.2, 00:00:52, Ethernet0
C    192.168.16.0 is directly connected, Ethernet0
E    192.168.17.0 [140/1] via 192.168.16.2, 00:00:52, Ethernet0
E    192.168.18.0 [140/4] via 192.168.16.3, 00:00:52, Ethernet0
E    172.20.0.0 [140/1] via 192.168.16.4, 00:00:52, Ethernet0
E    172.16.0.0 [140/4] via 192.168.16.3, 00:00:52, Ethernet0
E    172.17.0.0 [140/1] via 192.168.16.2, 00:00:52, Ethernet0
E    172.18.0.0 [140/4] via 192.168.16.3, 00:00:52, Ethernet0
     172.19.0.0 255.255.255.0 is subnetted, 1 subnets
C       172.19.1.0 is directly connected, Loopback0
Shemp#
```

There are two points of interest in the routing table. First, notice that the EGP entries have an administrative distance of 140. This is higher than the administrative distance of any IGP (with the exception of External EIGRP), so a router will always choose an IGP route over an EGP advertisement of the same network.

Second, notice that the distances to each of the EGP-advertised networks are one higher than the distances shown in the Update of Example 1-5. Cisco's EGP process increments the distance by one, just as a RIP routing algorithm does.

EGP Message Formats

EGP uses five different formats to encode the ten message types shown in Table 1-1. All the messages have a common header, as shown in Figure 1-4.

Figure 1-4   *EGP Message Header*

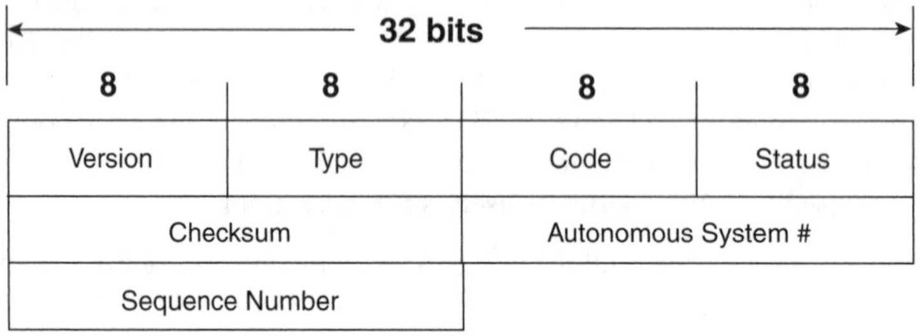

```
|←————————————————— 32 bits —————————————————→|

      8           8           8           8

| Version  |   Type    |    Code    |  Status   |

|       Checksum       |  Autonomous System #   |

|   Sequence Number    |
```

The fields in the EGP message header are defined as follows:

- **Version**—Specifies the current EGP version number. If this number in a received message does not agree with the receiver's version number, the message is rejected. The version number of all current EGP implementations is 2.

- **Type**—Specifies which of the five message formats follows the header. Table 1-2 (which appears after this list) shows the ten EGP message types and the type number used by each.

- **Code**—Specifies the subtype. For example, if type = 5, the code specifies whether the message is a Hello or an I-Heard-You.

- **Status**—Varies according to the message type (as with the Code field). For example, a Neighbor Acquisition message can use the status to indicate whether it is active or passive, whereas a Neighbor Reachability message can use the Status field to indicate an Up or Down state.

- **Checksum**—The one's complement of the one's complement sum of the EGP message. This is the same error-checking algorithm used by IP, TCP, and UDP.

- **Autonomous System Number**—Specifies the AS of the message's originator.

- **Sequence Number**—Synchronizes message pairs (as described previously in this chapter). For example, an Update should always contain the same sequence number as the Poll to which it is responding.

Table 1-2   *EGP Message Types*

Type	Message
3	Neighbor Acquisition Request
3	Neighbor Acquisition Confirm
3	Neighbor Acquisition Refuse
3	Neighbor Cease
3	Neighbor Cease Acknowledgment
5	Hello
5	I-Heard-You
2	Poll
1	Update
8	Error

The Neighbor Acquisition Message (EGP Message Type 3)

Neighbor Acquisition messages are EGP message type 3. Table 1-3 shows the codes used to indicate the EGP message. Table 1.4, taken from RFC 904, shows the possible values of the Status field and the reasons a particular status might be used.

Table 1-3   *Codes Used with Message Type 3*

Code	Message
0	Neighbor Acquisition Request
1	Neighbor Acquisition Confirm
2	Neighbor Acquisition Refuse
3	Neighbor Cease
4	Neighbor Cease Acknowledgment

Figure 1-5 shows the format of the Neighbor Acquisition message. The Hello Interval and Poll Interval fields are present only in the Neighbor Acquisition Request (code 0) and Neighbor Acquisition Confirm (code 1) messages. All other Neighbor Acquisition messages are identical to the message header, with no other fields included.

Table 1-4   *Status Numbers Used with Message Type 3*

Status	Description	Use
0	Unspecified	When nothing else fits
1	Active mode	Request/Confirm only
2	Passive mode	Request/Confirm only
3	Insufficient resources	1. Out of table space 2. Out of system resources
4	Administratively prohibited	1. Unknown autonomous system 2. Use another gateway
5	Going down	1. Operator initiated stop 2. Abort timeout
6	Perimeter problem	1. Nonsense polling parameters 2. Unable to assume compatible mode
7	Protocol violation	Invalid command or response received in this state

Figure 1-5   *The Neighbor Acquisition Message*

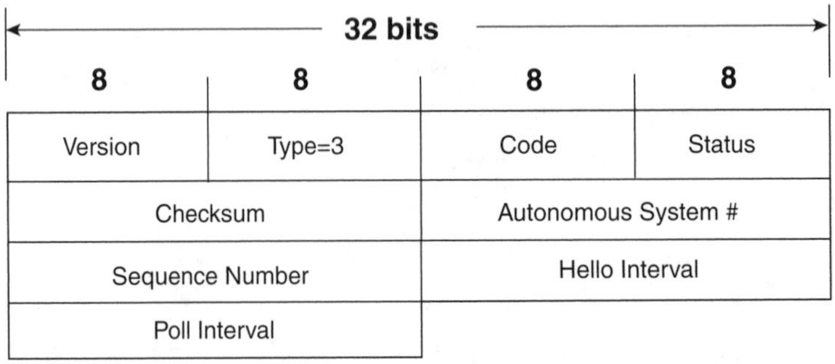

- **Hello interval**—The minimum interval, in seconds, between Hellos that the originator is willing to accept. The Cisco default Hello interval is 60 seconds and can be changed with the command **timers egp**.

- **Poll interval**—The minimum interval, in seconds, between Polls that the originator is willing to accept. The Cisco default Poll interval is 180 seconds and can be changed with the command **timers egp**.

The Neighbor Reachability Message (EGP Message Type 5)

The Neighbor Reachability message (see Figure 1-6) is the EGP header, with Type = 5. No additional fields are included, because all necessary information is carried in the Code (see Table 1-5) and Status (see Table 1-6) fields.

Figure 1-6   *The Neighbor Reachability Message*

8	8	8	8
Version	Type=5	Code	Status
Checksum		Autonomous System #	
Sequence Number			

Table 1-5   *Codes Used with Message Type 5*

Code	Message
0	Hello
1	I-Heard-You

Table 1-6   *Status Numbers Used with Message Types 5 and 2*

Status	Description
0	Indeterminate
1	Up state
2	Down state

The Poll Message (EGP Message Type 2)

The only field that is added to the EGP header to create the Poll message (see Figure 1-7) is the IP Source Network, the network about which reachability information is being requested. The IP address encoded in this field is always a major Class A, B, or C network. The Code field is always 0, and the Status numbers used are the same as those described in Table 1-6. (RFC 888 shows the Status field as unused in the Poll and Error messages.)

Figure 1-7   *The Poll Message*

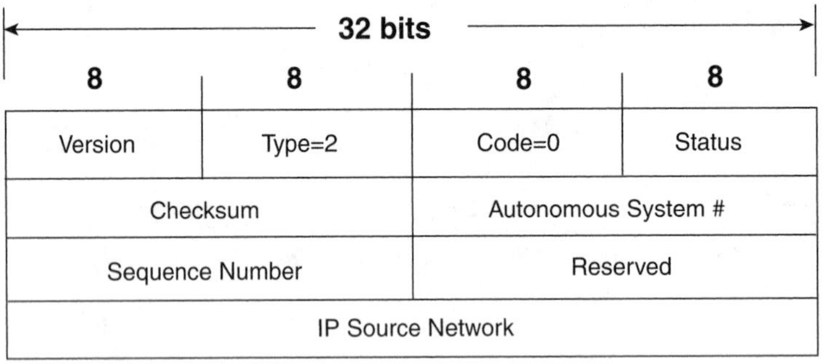

32 bits			
8	8	8	8
Version	Type=2	Code=0	Status
Checksum		Autonomous System #	
Sequence Number		Reserved	
IP Source Network			

The Update Message (EGP Message Type 1)

As with the Poll message, the Code field of the Update is always 0. Table 1-7 shows the possible values of the Status field, which is the same as the values of Table 1-6 with the exception of the Unsolicited value.

Table 1-7   *Status Numbers Used with Message Type 1*

Status	Description
0	Indeterminate
1	Up state
2	Down state
128	Unsolicited

The most significant bit of the Status field is the Unsolicited bit; if the bit is set (giving the field a value of 128), the Update is unsolicited. The Unsolicited bit can be used in combination with any of the other Status values.

The Update message includes a four-level hierarchy of lists. Figure 1-8 shows the format of the Update message and how the hierarchy of lists is organized.

At the highest level of the hierarchy is a list of all the routers that are directly attached to the source network. The number of gateways on the list is specified by the sum of the # of Interior Gateways and the # of Exterior Gateways fields.

At the next level, interior gateways are distinguished from exterior gateways. All interior gateways, including the originator, are listed first. If there are any exterior gateways, they are listed after the interior gateways.

Figure 1-8   *The Update Message*

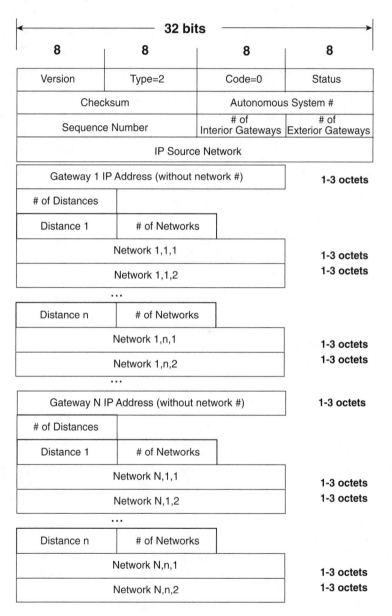

At the third layer of the hierarchy, each listed gateway has a list of distances. As with the interior and exterior gateways, a field specifies the number of distances on the list.

Finally, for each listed distance there is a list of networks that can be reached at that distance and via that gateway. A field is included to specify the number of networks on the list.

The complete descriptions for the fields of the Update message format are as follows:

- **# of Interior Gateways**—Specifies the number of interior gateways on the list.

- **# of Exterior Gateways**—Specifies the number of exterior gateways following the list of interior gateways. The sum of this field and the # of Interior Gateways, shown as N in Figure 1-8, is the total number of gateways listed in the Update.

- **IP Source Network**—Specifies the network about which reachability information is being supplied. That is, all networks listed in the Update are reachable via a gateway attached to this network. The IP address encoded in this field is always a major Class A, B, or C network.

- **Gateway IP Address**—Specifies the address of a gateway attached to the source network. Only the host portion of the major Class A, B, or C address is listed; as a result, the length of the field is variable from 1 octet for a Class C address to 3 octets for a Class A address. The network portion of the address is already known from the IP Source Network field.

- **# of Distances**—Specifies the total number of distances being advertised under the listed gateway.

- **Distance**—Specifies a particular distance advertised under the listed gateway.

- **# of Networks**—Specifies the total number of networks advertised under the listed distance of the listed gateway.

- **Network**—Specifies the IP address of the network being advertised. In Figure 1-8, each network is shown as belonging to a particular gateway, a particular distance, and a particular order in the network list. Like the Gateway IP Address field, the Network field is variable. Unlike the Gateway IP Address field, the Network field lists the network portion rather than the host portion of a major Class A, B, or C address.

The Error Message (EGP Message Type 8)

A gateway can send an Error message (see Figure 1-9) at any time to notify a sender of a bad EGP message or an invalid field value. The Code field of the error message is always 0, and the Status is one of the values described in Table 1-7.

NOTE RFC 888 shows the Status field in the Error message (like in the Poll message) as unused. RFC 904 specifies the uses shown in Table 1-7.

Figure 1-9 *The Error Message*

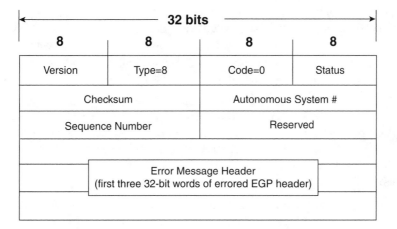

The originator of the Error message can use an arbitrary value as the sequence number. Table 1-8, which is taken from RFC 904, describes the possible values of the Reason field. The Error message header is the first 12 octets of the EGP message that prompted the Error message.

Table 1-8 *Values of the Reason Field of the Error Message*

Reason Field Value	Description	Use
0	Unspecified	When nothing else fits.
1	Bad EGP header format	1. Bad message length. 2. Invalid Type, Code, or Status field.
2	Bad EGP Data field format	1. Nonsense polling rates (Request/Confirm). 2. Invalid Update message format. 3. Response IP Network Address field does not match command (Update).
3	Reachability info unavailable	No information available on the network specified in the IP Network Address field (Poll).
4	Excessive polling rate	1. Two or more Hello messages received within the Hello interval. 2. Two or more Poll messages received within the Poll interval. 3. Two or more Request messages received within some (reasonably short) interval.
5	No response	No Update received for the Poll within some (reasonably long) interval.

Shortcomings of EGP

The fundamental problem with EGP is its inability to detect routing loops. Because there is an upper boundary on the distance EGP uses (255), you might be tempted to say that counting to infinity is at least a rudimentary loop-detection mechanism. It is, but the high limit combined with the typical Poll interval makes counting to infinity useless. Given a default Poll interval of 180 seconds, EGP peers could take almost 13 hours to count to infinity.

As a result, EGP must be run on an engineered loop-free topology. Although that was not a problem in 1983, when EGP was intended merely to connect stub gateways to the ARPANET backbone, the creators of EGP already foresaw that such a limited topology would soon become inadequate. The autonomous systems making up the Internet would need to evolve into a less structured mesh, in which many autonomous systems could serve as transit systems for many other autonomous systems.

With the advent of the NSFnet, the limitations of EGP became more pronounced. Not only were there now multiple backbones, but there were acceptable use policies concerning what traffic could traverse what backbone. Because EGP cannot support sophisticated policy-based routing, interim solutions had to be engineered[4].

Another major problem with EGP is its inability to adequately interact with IGPs to determine a shortest route to a network in another AS. For example, EGP distances do not reliably translate into RIP hop counts. If the EGP distance causes the hop count to exceed 15, RIP declares the network unreachable. Other shortcomings of EGP include its susceptibility to failures when attempting to convey information on a large number of networks, and its vulnerability to intentionally or unintentionally inaccurate network information.

Last but certainly not least, EGP can be mind-numbingly slow to advertise a network change. The section "Troubleshooting EGP" includes an example in which a network in an EGP-connected AS becomes unreachable. As the example demonstrates, almost an hour passes before a gateway four hops away determines that the network has gone down.

Several attempts were made to create an EGPv3, but none were successful. In the end, EGP was abandoned in favor of an entirely new inter-AS protocol, BGP. As a result, Exterior Gateway Protocol is now not only the name of a protocol, but the name of a class of protocols, giving rise to the notion of an EGP named EGP. Nonetheless, the legacy of EGP is still with us today in the form of autonomous systems and inter-AS routing.

Configuring EGP

You can configure EGP on a router in four basic steps:

Step 1 Specify the router's AS with the command **autonomous-system**.

Step 2 Start the EGP process and specify the neighbor's AS with the command **router egp**.

Step 3   Specify the EGP neighbors with the **neighbor** command.

Step 4   Specify what networks are to be advertised by EGP.

The first three steps are demonstrated in the first case study, along with several approaches to Step 4.

Case Study: An EGP Stub Gateway

Figure 1-10 shows an EGP stub gateway in AS 65502, connected to a core gateway in AS 65501. The IGP of the stub AS is RIP.

Figure 1-10   *EGP Stub Gateway Advertises the Interior Networks of AS 65502 to the Core Gateway*

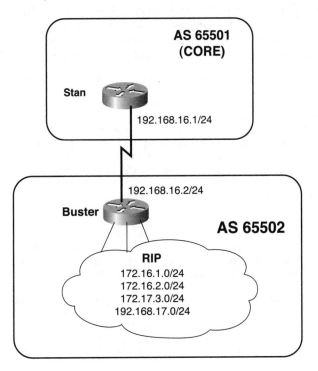

Example 1-7 shows the initial configuration of the stub gateway.

Example 1-7 *Stub Gateway Configuration for Figure 1-10*

```
autonomous-system 65502
!
router rip
 redistribute connected
 redistribute egp 65501 metric 5
 network 172.16.0.0
!
router egp 65501
 neighbor 192.168.16.1
```

Notice that the *local AS* (LAS) is specified by the **autonomous-system** statement, and the *far AS* (FAS) is specified by the **router egp** statement. An EGP process cannot be configured until the LAS is configured. The EGP process is told where to find its peer by the **neighbor** statement. Buster's routing table (see Example 1-8) contains both EGP route entries learned from the core gateway and RIP entries learned from the interior neighbors.

Example 1-8 *Buster's Routing Table Shows Entries Learned from the EGP Neighbor and from the Interior RIP Neighbors*

```
Buster#show ip route
Codes: C - connected, S - static, I - IGRP, R - RIP, M - mobile, B - BGP
       D - EIGRP, EX - EIGRP external, O - OSPF, IA - OSPF inter area
       E1 - OSPF external type 1, E2 - OSPF external type 2, E - EGP
       i - IS-IS, L1 - IS-IS level-1, L2 - IS-IS level-2, * - candidate default

Gateway of last resort is not set

E    10.0.0.0 [140/4] via 192.168.16.1, 00:02:12, Serial3
C    192.168.16.0 is directly connected, Serial3
R    192.168.17.0 [120/1] via 172.16.1.2, 00:00:05, Ethernet0
E    192.168.19.0 [140/4] via 192.168.16.1, 00:02:13, Serial3
E    192.168.20.0 [140/4] via 192.168.16.1, 00:02:13, Serial3
E    192.168.21.0 [140/4] via 192.168.16.1, 00:02:13, Serial3
E    192.168.22.0 [140/4] via 192.168.16.1, 00:02:13, Serial3
     172.16.0.0 255.255.255.0 is subnetted, 2 subnets
C       172.16.1.0 is directly connected, Ethernet0
R       172.16.2.0 [120/1] via 172.16.1.2, 00:00:05, Ethernet0
R    172.17.0.0 [120/1] via 172.16.1.2, 00:00:05, Ethernet0
Buster#
```

The EGP-learned routes are being redistributed into RIP with a metric of 5 (see Example 1-9).

Example 1-9 *Routing Table from a Router Interior to AS 65502 Shows the Redistributed EGP Routes*

```
Charlie#show ip route
Codes: C - connected, S - static, I - IGRP, R - RIP, M - mobile, B - BGP
       D - EIGRP, EX - EIGRP external, O - OSPF, IA - OSPF inter area
       E1 - OSPF external type 1, E2 - OSPF external type 2, E - EGP
       i - IS-IS, L1 - IS-IS level-1, L2 - IS-IS level-2, * - candidate default

Gateway of last resort is not set

R    10.0.0.0 [120/5] via 172.16.1.1, 00:00:13, Ethernet0
R    192.168.16.0 [120/1] via 172.16.1.1, 00:00:13, Ethernet0
C    192.168.17.0 is directly connected, Ethernet3
R    192.168.19.0 [120/5] via 172.16.1.1, 00:00:13, Ethernet0
R    192.168.20.0 [120/5] via 172.16.1.1, 00:00:13, Ethernet0
R    192.168.21.0 [120/5] via 172.16.1.1, 00:00:13, Ethernet0
R    192.168.22.0 [120/5] via 172.16.1.1, 00:00:13, Ethernet0
     172.16.0.0 255.255.255.0 is subnetted, 2 subnets
C       172.16.1.0 is directly connected, Ethernet0
C       172.16.2.0 is directly connected, Ethernet1
     172.17.0.0 255.255.255.0 is subnetted, 1 subnets
C       172.17.3.0 is directly connected, Ethernet2
Charlie#
```

Notice that directly connected networks are also being redistributed into RIP. This
configuration is necessary to advertise network 192.168.16.0 into the LAS; split horizon
prevents Stan from advertising the network to Buster via EGP. An alternative configuration
is to add a **network 192.168.16.0** statement to the RIP configuration, along with a **passive-
interface** statement to keep RIP broadcasts off of the inter-AS link.

As Buster's EGP configuration stands so far, network information is being received from
the core, but no interior networks are being advertised to the core (see Example 1-10).

Example 1-10 *Stan's Routing Table Shows That None of the Interior Networks from AS 65502 Are Being Learned
from Buster*

```
Stan#show ip route
Codes: C - connected, S - static, I - IGRP, R - RIP, M - mobile, B - BGP
       D - EIGRP, EX - EIGRP external, O - OSPF, IA - OSPF inter area
       E1 - OSPF external type 1, E2 - OSPF external type 2, E - EGP
       i - IS-IS, L1 - IS-IS level-1, L2 - IS-IS level-2, * - candidate default

Gateway of last resort is not set

E    10.0.0.0 [140/4] via 192.168.18.2, 00:01:56, Serial1
C    192.168.16.0 is directly connected, Serial0
C    192.168.18.0 is directly connected, Serial1
E    192.168.19.0 [140/1] via 192.168.18.2, 00:01:57, Serial1
E    192.168.20.0 [140/4] via 192.168.18.2, 00:01:57, Serial1
E    192.168.21.0 [140/4] via 192.168.18.2, 00:01:57, Serial1
E    192.168.22.0 [140/1] via 192.168.18.2, 00:01:57, Serial1
Stan#
```

One option for configuring EGP to advertise the interior networks is to add a **redistribute rip** statement. However, there are hazards associated with mutual redistribution. The danger is more pronounced when there are topological loops or multiple redistribution points, but even a simple design like the one in Figure 1-10 can be vulnerable to route feedback. For safety, route filters should always be used with mutual redistribution configurations to ensure that no interior network addresses are accepted from the exterior gateway, and no exterior addresses are advertised to the exterior gateway. The problems associated with mutual redistribution are introduced in *Routing TCP/IP, Volume I* and are discussed in further detail in Chapter 2, "Introduction to Border Gateway Protocol 4," and Chapter 3, "Configuring and Troubleshooting Border Gateway Protocol 4," of this book.

A better approach to configuring EGP to advertise interior networks is to use the **network** statement. When used with EGP or BGP, the **network** statement has a different function from when used with an IGP configuration. For example, the **network 172.16.0.0** statement under Buster's RIP configuration instructs the router to enable RIP on any interface that has an IP address in the major network 172.16.0.0. When used in conjunction with an inter-AS protocol, the **network** statement tells the protocol what network addresses to advertise. Example 1-11 shows Buster's configuration to advertise all the networks in AS 65502.

Example 1-11 *Buster Configuration to Advertise All Networks in AS 65502*

```
autonomous-system 65502
!
router rip
 redistribute connected
 redistribute egp 65501 metric 5
 network 172.16.0.0
!
router egp 65501
 network 172.16.0.0
 network 172.17.0.0
 network 192.168.17.0
 neighbor 192.168.16.1
```

Example 1-12 shows Stan's routing table after the **network** statements have been added to Buster's EGP configuration.

The advantage of using the **network** statement under EGP rather than redistribution is somewhat akin to the advantage of using static routes rather than a dynamic routing protocol: Both allow precise control over network reachability. In the case of EGP, the precision is limited by EGP's classfulness. Although you can keep a major network "private" by not specifying it in a **network** statement, the same cannot be said of individual subnets. Refer back to Example 1-8, which shows that Buster's routing table contains subnets 172.16.1.0/24 and 172.16.2.0/24. Reexamining the EGP Update message format in Figure 1-8, you will recall that the Update carries only the major class portion of the IP network: the first octet of a Class A network, the first two octets of a Class B network, and the first three octets of a Class C network. Therefore, the **network** statement under EGP can specify only major networks.

Example 1-12 *Buster Is Now Advertising the Interior Networks of AS 65502 to Stan*

```
Stan#show ip route
Codes: C - connected, S - static, I - IGRP, R - RIP, M - mobile, B - BGP
       D - EIGRP, EX - EIGRP external, O - OSPF, IA - OSPF inter area
       E1 - OSPF external type 1, E2 - OSPF external type 2, E - EGP
       i - IS-IS, L1 - IS-IS level-1, L2 - IS-IS level-2, * - candidate default

Gateway of last resort is not set

E    10.0.0.0 [140/4] via 192.168.18.2, 00:00:27, Serial1
C    192.168.16.0 is directly connected, Serial0
E    192.168.17.0 [140/1] via 192.168.16.2, 00:01:38, Serial0
C    192.168.18.0 is directly connected, Serial1
E    192.168.19.0 [140/1] via 192.168.18.2, 00:00:27, Serial1
E    192.168.20.0 [140/4] via 192.168.18.2, 00:00:27, Serial1
E    192.168.21.0 [140/4] via 192.168.18.2, 00:00:27, Serial1
E    192.168.22.0 [140/1] via 192.168.18.2, 00:00:27, Serial1
E    172.16.0.0 [140/1] via 192.168.16.2, 00:01:39, Serial0
E    172.17.0.0 [140/1] via 192.168.16.2, 00:01:39, Serial0
Stan#
```

Case Study: An EGP Core Gateway

By definition, an EGP core gateway can peer with multiple neighbors within multiple far autonomous systems and can pass network information from one FAS to another FAS. Because of this, the configuration of a core gateway differs slightly. Figure 1-11 shows a core router, Stan, which is peered with a router in a FAS (Buster) and a router within its LAS (Ollie).

Figure 1-11 *Core Router Stan Must Peer with Both Remote Neighbor Buster and Local Neighbor Ollie*

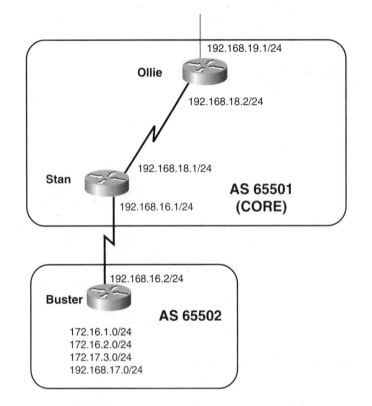

Example 1-13 demonstrates the EGP configuration of Stan in Figure 1-11 .

Example 1-13 *Core Gateway Configuration for Network Topology in Figure 1-11*

```
autonomous-system 65501
!
router egp 0
 network 192.168.16.0
 neighbor any
```

The LAS is still specified with the **autonomous-system** command, but the FAS is not specified by the **router egp** command. Instead, an AS number of 0 is used to specify any AS. Likewise, neighbors are specified with a **neighbor any** command, to respond to any neighbor that sends Acquisition messages. The **neighbor any** command implicitly configures neighbors, whereas the **neighbor** command explicitly configures neighbors. Core gateways can have explicitly configured neighbors, but the implicit **neighbor any** makes life simpler when there are a large number of neighbors, as might be expected at a core gateway.

Of course, at least one neighbor must have an explicit neighbor configuration; two neighbors cannot discover each other if they both have a **neighbor any** command. Example 1-14 shows the configuration for the neighbor Ollie in Figure 1-11.

Example 1-14 *Neighbor Configuration for Ollie in the Network Topology of Figure 1-11*

```
autonomous-system 65501
!
router egp 0
 network 192.168.19.0
 neighbor 192.168.18.1
 neighbor any
```

Although Ollie still picks up its external neighbors with the **neighbor any** command, Stan's address is explicitly configured. If it were not, Stan and Ollie would be unaware of each other's existence.

With the configuration in Example 1-14, the core gateway will pass reachability information about networks external to its own AS to every other external AS. The core gateway will not, however, pass information about the networks in its own AS. You can see in Buster's routing table of Example 1-8, for instance, that there is no entry for network 192.168.18.0. If the interior networks are to be advertised, Stan must have a **network** statement for each network to be advertised. The only **network** statement shown is for 192.168.16.0, which allows Ollie to receive information about that network. Look again at Buster's routing table. Notice that there is an entry for network 192.168.19.0. This entry is the result of the **network 192.168.19.0** statement in Ollie's configuration in Example 1-14.

What happens if a core should not peer with every EGP-speaking neighbor? In Figure 1-12, the three routers in AS 65506 are all running EGP, but Stan should peer with only Spanky and Buckwheat. Alfalfa should peer with Ollie. Of course, the core administrator could trust the administrator of AS 65506 to set up the correct peering with **neighbor** statements, but trust is seldom good enough in inter-AS routing.

Figure 1-12 *Spanky and Buckwheat Must Peer Only with Stan, Whereas Alfalfa Must Peer Only with Ollie*

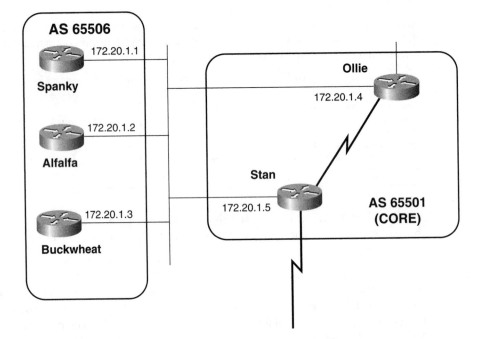

In this example, all three gateways in AS 65506 have **neighbor** statements for both Stan and Ollie. To regulate the peering, an access list is used with the **neighbor any** statement, as demonstrated in the configuration for Stan in Example 1-15.

Example 1-15 *Regulating Peering with Access Lists Using the **neighbor any** Command*

```
autonomous-system 65501
!
router egp 0
 network 192.168.16.0
 neighbor any 10
!
access-list 10 deny 172.20.1.2
access-list 10 permit any
```

In Example 1-15, the **neighbor any** statement contains a reference to access list 10, which denies Alfalfa (172.20.1.2) and permits all other neighbors. A similar configuration at Ollie denies Spanky and Buckwheat and permits all other neighbors. Example 1-16 shows the results of this configuration.

Example 1-16 *The **show ip egp** Command Displays Information About EGP Neighbors*

```
Stan#show ip egp
Local autonomous system is 65501

 EGP Neighbor     FAS/LAS  State       SndSeq RcvSeq Hello  Poll j/k Flags
*192.168.18.2     65501/65501 UP    10      3      4    60    180   4 Temp, Act
*192.168.16.2     65502/65501 UP  3:20     39     39    60    180   4 Temp, Act
*172.20.1.1       65506/65501 UP     4      2      2    60    180   4 Temp, Act
*172.20.1.3       65506/65501 UP    10      4      4    60    180   4 Temp, Act
Stan#

Ollie#show ip egp
Local autonomous system is 65501

 EGP Neighbor     FAS/LAS  State       SndSeq RcvSeq Hello  Poll j/k Flags
*192.168.18.1     65501/65501 UP     9      4      3    60    180   4 Perm, Pass
*172.20.1.2       65506/65501 UP    13      5      5    60    180   4 Temp, Act
Ollie#
```

Using the **show ip egp** command with Stan and Ollie shows that Ollie is peered with Alfalfa and Stan is peered with Spanky and Buckwheat.

NOTE   The details of the fields displayed by the **show ip egp** command are discussed in the section "Troubleshooting EGP." For now, the addresses of the neighbors are of interest.

Case Study: Indirect Neighbors

In Figure 1-13, three stub gateways (Groucho, Harpo, and Chico) are connected to the core gateway named Ollie. Groucho and Harpo, in separate autonomous systems, share a common Ethernet and can therefore be configured as indirect or third-party neighbors.

Figure 1-13 *EGP Indirect Neighbors*

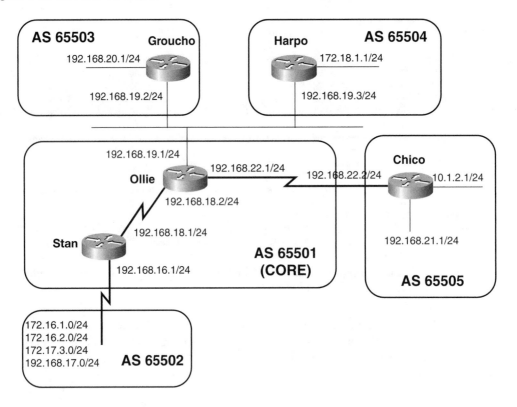

Groucho and Harpo cannot exchange EGP information directly, but they can route packets directly to each other if Ollie advertises them as indirect neighbors. Example 1-17 shows the configuration for Ollie.

Example 1-17 *Advertising Indirect EGP Neighbors to One Another Enables the Routing of Packets Between Indirect EGP Neighbors*

```
autonomous-system 65501
!
router egp 0
 network 192.168.19.0
 network 192.168.22.0
 network 192.168.18.0
 neighbor 192.168.19.3
 neighbor 192.168.19.3 third-party 192.168.19.2
 neighbor 192.168.19.2

 neighbor 192.168.19.2 third-party 192.168.19.3
 neighbor 192.168.18.1
 neighbor any
```

In the configuration in Example 1-17, Groucho and Harpo are explicitly configured as neighbors. Following the **neighbor** statements for the two routers are **neighbor third-party** statements. These entries specify the neighbor in question and then specify that gateway's indirect neighbor on the shared Ethernet. Notice that Chico, which is not on the shared Ethernet, falls under the **neighbor any** statement. Example 1-18 shows the core gateway's indirect neighbors recorded as Third Party.

Example 1-18 *Displaying Core Gateway Indirect Neighbors*

```
Ollie#show ip egp
Local autonomous system is 65501

  EGP Neighbor      FAS/LAS    State    SndSeq RcvSeq Hello  Poll j/k Flags
*192.168.19.3      65504/65501 UP 5TE       8    249     60   180   4 Perm, Act
*192.168.19.2      65503/65501 UP 5TE       8   3177     60   180   4 Perm, Act
*192.168.18.1      65501/65501 UP 5TE       9   3192     60   180   4 Perm, Pass
*192.168.22.2      65505/65501 UP 5TE       5   3170     60   180   4 Temp, Act
  EGP Neighbor      Third Party
*192.168.19.3      192.168.19.2
*192.168.19.2      192.168.19.3
Ollie#
```

Ollie's EGP neighbor table indicates that Groucho and Harpo (192.168.19.2 and 192.168.19.3, respectively) have been configured as indirect neighbors of each other.

Harpo's routing table (see Example 1-19) shows the results of the indirect neighbor configuration. Rather than pointing to the core gateway as the next hop to network 192.168.20.0 in AS 65503, the next hop points directly to Groucho (192.168.19.2).

Example 1-19 *Routing Table Displays Next-Hop Routes to Indirect Neighbors*

```
Harpo#show ip route
Codes: C - connected, S - static, I - IGRP, R - RIP, M - mobile, B - BGP
       D - EIGRP, EX - EIGRP external, O - OSPF, IA - OSPF inter area
       E1 - OSPF external type 1, E2 - OSPF external type 2, E - EGP
       i - IS-IS, L1 - IS-IS level-1, L2 - IS-IS level-2, * - candidate default

Gateway of last resort is not set

E    10.0.0.0 [140/4] via 192.168.19.1, 00:02:21, Ethernet0
E    192.168.16.0 [140/4] via 192.168.19.1, 00:02:21, Ethernet0
E    192.168.17.0 [140/4] via 192.168.19.1, 00:02:21, Ethernet0
E    192.168.18.0 [140/1] via 192.168.19.1, 00:02:21, Ethernet0
C    192.168.19.0 is directly connected, Ethernet0
E    192.168.20.0 [140/4] via 192.168.19.2, 00:02:21, Ethernet0
E    192.168.21.0 [140/4] via 192.168.19.1, 00:02:22, Ethernet0
E    192.168.22.0 [140/1] via 192.168.19.1, 00:02:22, Ethernet0
E    172.16.0.0 [140/4] via 192.168.19.1, 00:02:22, Ethernet0
E    172.17.0.0 [140/4] via 192.168.19.1, 00:02:22, Ethernet0
     172.18.0.0 255.255.255.0 is subnetted, 1 subnets
C       172.18.1.0 is directly connected, Loopback0
Harpo#
```

Harpo's routing table in Example 1-19 shows that network 192.168.20.0 is directly reachable via next hop 192.168.19.2. Without the indirect neighbor configuration, Harpo would have to use 192.168.19.1 as the next hop.

Case Study: Default Routes

EGP can be configured to advertise a default route in addition to more specific routes. If an AS has only a single exterior gateway, a default route is usually more efficient than a full list of exterior routes. Memory and processing cycles are conserved on the router, and bandwidth is saved on the link.

To advertise a default route into AS 65502, as illustrated previously in Figure 1-13, you configure Stan as demonstrated in Example 1-20.

Example 1-20 *Advertising a Default Route*

```
router egp 0
 network 192.168.16.0
 neighbor any
 default-information originate
 distribute-list 20 out Serial0
!
access-list 20 permit 0.0.0.0
```

The **default-information originate** command is used to generate the default route. Unlike in other protocols, when the command is used with EGP, there are no optional statements. Notice, too, that a route filter has been added, which permits only the default route to be advertised out of Stan's S0 interface to AS 65502. Without this filter, the default and all more-specific networks would be advertised. Example 1-21 shows the results of the configuration.

Example 1-21 *192.168.20.1 Is Reachable as a Result of the Default Route*

```
Buster#show ip route
Codes: C - connected, S - static, I - IGRP, R - RIP, M - mobile, B - BGP
       D - EIGRP, EX - EIGRP external, O - OSPF, IA - OSPF inter area
       E1 - OSPF external type 1, E2 - OSPF external type 2, E - EGP
       i - IS-IS, L1 - IS-IS level-1, L2 - IS-IS level-2, * - candidate default

Gateway of last resort is 192.168.16.1 to network 0.0.0.0

C    192.168.16.0 is directly connected, Serial3
R    192.168.17.0 [120/1] via 172.16.1.2, 00:00:20, Ethernet0
     172.16.0.0 255.255.255.0 is subnetted, 2 subnets
C       172.16.1.0 is directly connected, Ethernet0
R       172.16.2.0 [120/1] via 172.16.1.2, 00:00:21, Ethernet0
R    172.17.0.0 [120/1] via 172.16.1.2, 00:00:21, Ethernet0
E*   0.0.0.0 0.0.0.0 [140/4] via 192.168.16.1, 00:00:46, Serial3
```

Example 1-21 *192.168.20.1 Is Reachable as a Result of the Default Route (Continued)*

```
Buster#ping 192.168.20.1
Type escape sequence to abort.
Sending 5, 100-byte ICMP Echos to 192.168.20.1, timeout is 2 seconds:
!!!!!
Success rate is 100 percent (5/5), round-trip min/avg/max = 64/66/76 ms
Buster#
```

The routing table of AS 65502's exterior gateway shows that the core gateway is advertising only a default route, by which all the exterior networks in Figure 1-13 are reached.

Troubleshooting EGP

The earlier section "Shortcomings of EGP" discussed several reasons why EGP cannot be used in complex inter-AS topologies. An unexpected benefit is that by forcing a simple topology, EGP is easy to troubleshoot.

As with any routing protocol, the first step in troubleshooting EGP is examining the routing tables. If a required route is missing or an unwanted route is present, the routing tables should lead you to the source of the problem. Because the EGP metrics have very little meaning, using the routing tables for troubleshooting is greatly simplified in comparison with other routing protocols.

When examining EGP configurations, remember that the gateway must have some sort of **neighbor** statement—either explicit or **neighbor any**—for every neighbor. Understanding the use of the **network** statement, and how it differs from the **network** statement used with IGPs, is also important.

The **debug ip egp transactions** command, used several times in the "Operation of EGP" section, is a very useful troubleshooting tool. The output of this command reveals all the important information in all the EGP messages being exchanged between neighbors.

Interpreting the Neighbor Table

An examination of the EGP neighbor table using **show ip egp** will tell you about the state and configuration of a gateway's neighbors. Example 1-18 displayed the output of this command; Example 1-22 shows some additional output from the **show ip egp** command that examines Stan's neighbor table.

Example 1-22 **show ip egp** *Command Output Displays Information Useful for Troubleshooting EGP Peers*

```
Stan#show ip egp
Local autonomous system is 65501

 EGP Neighbor     FAS/LAS    State   SndSeq RcvSeq Hello  Poll j/k Flags
*192.168.18.2   65501/65501 UP  2:08   3227     43    60   180   4 Temp, Act
*192.168.16.2   65502/65501 UP  6d17   3233   3233    60   180   4 Temp, Act
Stan#
```

You can see in Stan's neighbor table that neighbor 192.168.18.2 is an interior neighbor, because the FAS and LAS are the same (65501). The state of the neighbor is shown, as is its uptime. Whereas 192.168.18.2 has been up for just over 2 hours, 192.168.16.2 has been up for 6 days and 17 hours. The present sequence number being used by the gateway for each neighbor is shown, as is the present sequence number being used by the neighbor.

After the Hello and Poll intervals, the number of neighbor reachability messages that have been received in the past four Hello intervals is recorded. This number is used to determine whether a neighbor should be declared Up or Down, based on two values known as the *j* and *k* thresholds. The *j* threshold specifies the number of neighbor reachability messages that must be received during four Hello intervals before a Down neighbor is declared Up. The *k* threshold specifies the minimum number of neighbor reachability messages that must be received within four Hello intervals to prevent an Up neighbor from being declared Down. The thresholds, shown in Table 1-9, differ for active and passive neighbors.

Table 1-9   *EGP* j *and* k *Thresholds*

Threshold	Active	Passive	Description
j	3	1	Neighbor Up threshold
k	1	4	Neighbor Down threshold

The next field (Flags) in Example 1-22 specifies whether the neighbor is permanent or temporary. Permanent neighbors are neighbors that have been explicitly configured with a **neighbor** statement, whereas temporary neighbors have been implicitly peered under the **neighbor any** statement. In Example 1-22, you can see that both of Stan's neighbors are temporary; this fits with the configuration of Stan discussed earlier, in which there is a single **neighbor any** statement. Comparing Example 1-22 with Example 1-18, you might find it interesting that although Stan sees Ollie (192.168.18.2) as a temporary neighbor, Ollie sees Stan (192.168.18.1) as a permanent neighbor. An examination of Ollie's configuration in Example 1-23 shows why.

Example 1-23 *Neighbor Configuration of Router Ollie*

```
autonomous-system 65501
!
router egp 0
 network 192.168.19.0
 network 192.168.22.0
 network 192.168.18.0
 neighbor 192.168.19.3
 neighbor 192.168.19.3 third-party 192.168.19.2
 neighbor 192.168.19.2
 neighbor 192.168.19.2 third-party 192.168.19.3
 neighbor 192.168.18.1
 neighbor any
```

The explicit **neighbor 192.168.18.1** causes Ollie to classify Stan as a permanent neighbor.

The last field indicates whether the local router is the active or the passive neighbor. Example 1-22 shows that Stan is the active neighbor for both of its peer relationships, so you would expect Ollie to show that it is the passive neighbor. Example 1-18 bears out this assumption and also indicates that Ollie is the active neighbor for all of its other peer relationships. This is also to be expected, because AS 65501 is lower than the other AS numbers.

Case Study: Converging at the Speed of Syrup

A distinct characteristic of EGP is that nothing happens quickly. The neighbor acquisition process is slow, and the advertisement of network changes is almost glacial. As a result, you might sometimes mistakenly assume that there is a problem where none exists (except for the problematic nature of EGP itself). For example, suppose users in AS 65503 of Figure 1-13 complain that they cannot reach network 172.17.0.0 in AS 65502. When you examine Groucho's routing table, there is a route to 172.17.0.0 (see Example 1-24), but a ping to a known address on that network fails. You might be led to believe that traffic to the network is being misrouted, or *black holed*.

A clue to the problem is shown in Ollie's routing table (see Example 1-25). Notice that a new update for network 172.17.0.0 has not been received in more than 16 minutes, but the route entry for the network is still valid and is still being advertised to Ollie's neighbors.

Example 1-24 *Groucho in Figure 1-13 Has a Route to 172.17.0.0, but the Network Is Unreachable*

```
Groucho#show ip route
Codes: C - connected, S - static, I - IGRP, R - RIP, M - mobile, B - BGP
       D - EIGRP, EX - EIGRP external, O - OSPF, IA - OSPF inter area
       E1 - OSPF external type 1, E2 - OSPF external type 2, E - EGP
       i - IS-IS, L1 - IS-IS level-1, L2 - IS-IS level-2, * - candidate default

Gateway of last resort is 192.168.19.1 to network 0.0.0.0

E    10.0.0.0 [140/4] via 192.168.19.1, 00:01:23, Ethernet0
E    192.168.16.0 [140/4] via 192.168.19.1, 00:01:23, Ethernet0
E    192.168.17.0 [140/4] via 192.168.19.1, 00:01:23, Ethernet0
C    192.168.19.0 is directly connected, Ethernet0
C    192.168.20.0 is directly connected, Loopback0
E    192.168.21.0 [140/4] via 192.168.19.1, 00:01:24, Ethernet0
E    192.168.22.0 [140/1] via 192.168.19.1, 00:01:24, Ethernet0
E    172.16.0.0 [140/4] via 192.168.19.1, 00:01:24, Ethernet0
E    172.17.0.0 [140/4] via 192.168.19.1, 00:01:24, Ethernet0
E    172.18.0.0 [140/4] via 192.168.19.1, 00:01:24, Ethernet0
E*   0.0.0.0 0.0.0.0 [140/4] via 192.168.19.1, 00:01:24, Ethernet0

Groucho#ping 172.17.3.1
Type escape sequence to abort.
Sending 5, 100-byte ICMP Echos to 172.17.3.1, timeout is 2 seconds:
.....
Success rate is 0 percent (0/5)
Groucho#
```

Example 1-25 *New Network Updates Are Not Being Advertised*

```
Ollie#show ip route
Codes: C - connected, S - static, I - IGRP, R - RIP, M - mobile, B - BGP
       D - EIGRP, EX - EIGRP external, O - OSPF, IA - OSPF inter area
       N1 - OSPF NSSA external type 1, N2 - OSPF NSSA external type 2
       E1 - OSPF external type 1, E2 - OSPF external type 2, E - EGP
       i - IS-IS, L1 - IS-IS level-1, L2 - IS-IS level-2, * - candidate default
       U - per-user static route, o - ODR

Gateway of last resort is not set

E    10.0.0.0/8 [140/1] via 192.168.22.2, 00:01:20, Serial1
E    192.168.16.0/24 [140/1] via 192.168.18.1, 00:01:13, Serial0
E    192.168.17.0/24 [140/4] via 192.168.18.1, 00:16:14, Serial0
C    192.168.18.0/24 is directly connected, Serial0
C    192.168.19.0/24 is directly connected, Ethernet0
E    192.168.20.0/24 [140/1] via 192.168.19.2, 00:02:06, Ethernet0
E    192.168.21.0/24 [140/1] via 192.168.22.2, 00:01:21, Serial1
C    192.168.22.0/24 is directly connected, Serial1
E    172.16.0.0/16 [140/4] via 192.168.18.1, 00:01:13, Serial0
E    172.17.0.0/16 [140/4] via 192.168.18.1, 00:16:14, Serial0
E    172.18.0.0/16 [140/1] via 192.168.19.3, 00:01:59, Ethernet0
Ollie#
```

Stan has not included network 172.17.0.0 in the past five update messages to Ollie. There is no black hole problem here; network 172.17.0.0 has just become unreachable due to a disconnected Ethernet interface on a router in AS 65502. EGP will not declare a route down until it has failed to receive six consecutive updates for the route. Couple this with an update interval of 180 seconds, and you will see that EGP will take 18 minutes to declare a route down. Only then will it stop including the network in its own updates. In the internetwork of Figure 1-13, 54 minutes will pass between the time the exterior gateway of AS 65502 declares network 172.17.0.0 down and the time Groucho declares the network down!

End Notes

[1]Eric Rosen, "RFC 827: EXTERIOR GATEWAY PROTOCOL (EGP)" (Work in Progress)
[2]Linda J. Seamonson and Eric C. Rosen, "RFC 888: 'STUB' EXTERIOR GATEWAY PROTOCOL" (Work in Progress)
[3]D.L. Mills, "RFC 904: Exterior Gateway Protocol Formal Specification" (Work in Progress)
[4]J. Rekhter, "RFC 1092: EGP and Policy Based Routing in the New NSFNET Backbone" (Work in Progress)

Looking Ahead

This chapter has explored both the motives for inventing an inter-AS routing protocol and the reasons why EGP has proven inadequate in that role. Chapter 2 introduces the protocol that has replaced EGP, the Border Gateway Protocol, and examines its operation. Table 1-10 summarizes the commands used in this chapter.

Table 1-10   *Chapter 1 Command Review*

Command	What It Does
autonomous-system *local-as*	Specifies the local autonomous system in which the EGP router resides
debug ip egp transactions	Displays information about EGP message exchanges and state changes
default-information originate	Causes EGP to advertise a default route
neighbor *ip-address*	Specifies the IP address of an EGP neighbor
neighbor any [*access-list-number* | *name*]	Tells EGP to attempt to peer with any router that initiates the Neighbor Acquisition Protocol
neighbor any third-party *ip-address* [**internal** | **external**]	Configures an indirect EGP neighbor
neighbor *ip-address* **third-party** *third-party-ip-address* [**internal** | **external**]	Configures EGP to send updates regarding indirect neighbors

continues

Table 1-10   *Chapter 1 Command Review (Continued)*

Command	What It Does
network *network-number*	Specifies networks in the IGP routing table that should be advertised to EGP peers
router egp *remote-as*	Configures an EGP routing process
router egp 0	Configures an EGP core gateway process
show ip egp	Displays information about the EGP connections and neighbors
timers egp *hello polltime*	Sets the EGP Hello and Poll intervals to a value different from the default

Review Questions

You can find the answers to the Review Questions in Appendix D, "Answers to Review Questions."

1   What is the current version of EGP?

_____

_____

_____

2   What is an EGP interior neighbor? An EGP exterior neighbor?

_____

_____

_____

3   What is the primary difference between an EGP stub gateway and an EGP core gateway?

_____

_____

_____

4   Why does EGP use the concept of a core, or backbone, AS?

_____

_____

_____

5 What is the difference between an active EGP neighbor and a passive EGP neighbor?

_____

_____

_____

6 What is the purpose of an EGP Poll message?

_____

_____

_____

7 What is an indirect, or third-party, neighbor?

_____

_____

_____

8 How does EGP use its metrics to calculate the best path to a destination?

_____

_____

_____

Configuration Exercises

You can find the answers to the Configuration Exercises in Appendix E, "Answers to Configuration Exercises."

1 Autonomous System 65531 in Figure 1-14 is a core AS.

Figure 1-14 *The Internetwork for Configuration Exercise 1*

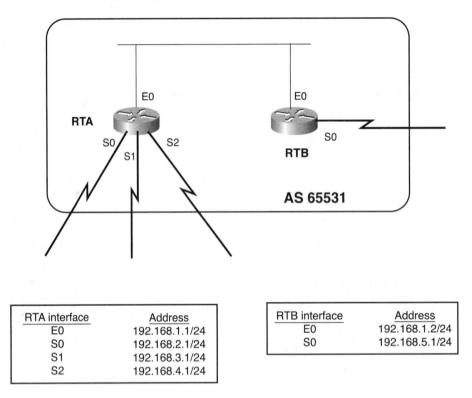

RTA interface	Address
E0	192.168.1.1/24
S0	192.168.2.1/24
S1	192.168.3.1/24
S2	192.168.4.1/24

RTB interface	Address
E0	192.168.1.2/24
S0	192.168.5.1/24

Configure EGP on RTA and RTB, with the following constraints:

— The data link interior to the AS is not advertised to any exterior neighbor.

— RTA advertises the network attached to its S1 interface to RTB; with this exception, no other inter-AS link is advertised between RTA and RTB.

— RTA and RTB advertise a default route to their exterior neighbors, in addition to networks learned from other autonomous systems. Neither gateway advertises a default route to its internal neighbor.

2 Example 1-26 shows the route table of RTC in Figure 1-15.

Example 1-26 *The Route Table of RTC in Figure 1-15*

```
RTC#show ip route
Codes: C - connected, S - static, I - IGRP, R - RIP, M - mobile, B - BGP
       D - EIGRP, EX - EIGRP external, O - OSPF, IA - OSPF inter area
       E1 - OSPF external type 1, E2 - OSPF external type 2, E - EGP
       i - IS-IS, L1 - IS-IS level-1, L2 - IS-IS level-2, * - candidate default
```

continues

Example 1-26 *The Route Table of RTC in Figure 1-15 (Continued)*

```
Gateway of last resort is not set

I    192.168.105.0 [100/8976] via 192.168.6.2, 00:01:00, Serial1
I    192.168.110.0 [100/8976] via 192.168.6.2, 00:01:00, Serial1
I    192.168.100.0 [100/8976] via 192.168.10.2, 00:01:00, Serial2
I    192.168.120.0 [100/8976] via 192.168.10.2, 00:01:01, Serial2
C    192.168.2.0 is directly connected, Serial0
C    192.168.6.0 is directly connected, Serial1
C    192.168.10.0 is directly connected, Serial2
RTC#
```

Figure 1-15 *The Internetwork for Configuration Exercise 2*

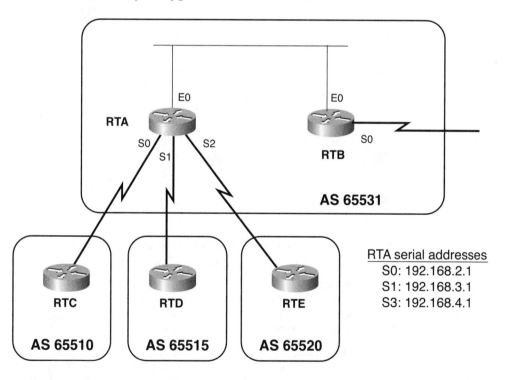

Using redistribution, configure RTC to advertise all EGP-learned networks into AS 65510, and all internal networks except 192.168.105.0 to the core AS. Protect against route feedback by ensuring that none of the networks internal to AS 65510 are advertised back via EGP. The process ID in this configuration is the same as the local AS number.

3 Example 1-27 shows the route table of RTD in Figure 1-15.

Example 1-27 *The Route Table of RTD in Figure 1-15*

```
RTD#show ip route
Codes: C - connected, S - static, I - IGRP, R - RIP, M - mobile, B - BGP
       D - EIGRP, EX - EIGRP external, O - OSPF, IA - OSPF inter area
       E1 - OSPF external type 1, E2 - OSPF external type 2, E - EGP
       i - IS-IS, L1 - IS-IS level-1, L2 - IS-IS level-2, * - candidate default

Gateway of last resort is not set

C    192.168.3.0 is directly connected, Serial0
C    192.168.7.0 is directly connected, Serial1
R    192.168.230.0 [120/1] via 192.168.7.2, 00:00:14, Serial1
R    192.168.200.0 [120/2] via 192.168.7.2, 00:00:15, Serial1
R    192.168.220.0 [120/1] via 192.168.7.2, 00:00:15, Serial1
R    192.168.210.0 [120/2] via 192.168.7.2, 00:00:15, Serial1
RTD#
```

Configure RTD with the following parameters:

— Only 192.168.220.0 and 192.168.230.0 are to be advertised to AS 65531.

— No routing protocol is redistributed into EGP.

— EGP is redistributed into the IGP of AS 65515.

— 192.168.3.0 is advertised into AS 65515 with a metric of 1.

— 192.168.100.0, from RTC, is advertised into AS 65515 with a metric of 1.

— 192.168.120.0, from RTC, is advertised into AS 65515 with a metric of 3.

— All other routes are advertised into AS 65515 with a metric of 5.

4 Example 1-28 shows the route table of RTE in Figure 1-15.

Example 1-28 *The Route Table of RTE in Figure 1-15*

```
RTE#show ip route
Codes: C - connected, S - static, I - IGRP, R - RIP, M - mobile, B - BGP
       D - EIGRP, EX - EIGRP external, O - OSPF, IA - OSPF inter area
       N1 - OSPF NSSA external type 1, N2 - OSPF NSSA external type 2
       E1 - OSPF external type 1, E2 - OSPF external type 2, E - EGP
       i - IS-IS, L1 - IS-IS level-1, L2 - IS-IS level-2, * - candidate default
       U - per-user static route, o - ODR

Gateway of last resort is not set

O    192.168.125.0/28 [110/74] via 192.168.130.6, 00:01:03, Serial1
C    192.168.4.0/24 is directly connected, Serial0
     192.168.225.0/28 is subnetted, 1 subnets
```

continues

Example 1-28 *The Route Table of RTE in Figure 1-15 (Continued)*

```
O E2    192.168.225.160 [110/50] via 192.168.130.18, 00:01:04, Ethernet0
        192.168.215.0/24 is variably subnetted, 3 subnets, 3 masks
O         192.168.215.161/32 [110/65] via 192.168.130.6, 00:01:04, Serial1
O E2    192.168.215.192/26 [110/50] via 192.168.130.18, 00:01:04, Ethernet0
O E1    192.168.215.96/28 [110/164] via 192.168.130.6, 00:01:04, Serial1
        192.168.130.0/24 is variably subnetted, 7 subnets, 4 masks
D         192.168.131.192/27 [90/2195456] via 192.168.130.6, 00:16:49, Serial1
D         192.168.131.96/27 [90/409600] via 192.168.130.18, 00:16:49, Ethernet0
O         192.168.131.97/32 [110/11] via 192.168.130.18, 00:01:05, Ethernet0
D         192.168.131.64/27 [90/409600] via 192.168.130.18, 00:15:01, Ethernet0
D         192.168.131.8/30 [90/2195456] via 192.168.130.6, 00:16:49, Serial1
C         192.168.131.4/30 is directly connected, Serial1
C         192.168.131.16/28 is directly connected, Ethernet0
RTE#
```

Configure RTE with the following parameters:

— No IGP is redistributed into EGP.

— EGP is not redistributed into any IGP.

— All the internal networks of AS 65520 are advertised to AS 65531.

— The internal routers of AS 65520 can forward packets to any network advertised by RTA.

— All process IDs are the same as the AS number.

— All OSPF interfaces are in area 0.

5 In Figure 1-16, AS 65525 has been added to the internetwork of the previous exercises. RTF's Ethernet interface has an IP address of 192.168.1.3/24.

Figure 1-16 *The Internetwork for Configuration Exercise 5*

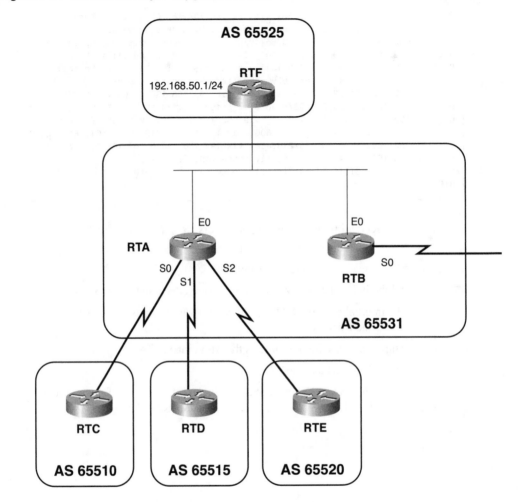

Configure this router to peer only with RTB and make any necessary configuration changes to support third-party neighbors.

Troubleshooting Exercise

You can find the answer to the Troubleshooting Exercise in Appendix F, "Answers to Troubleshooting Exercises."

1 In Figure 1-17, router RTG has been added to the internetwork.

Figure 1-17 *The Internetwork for Troubleshooting Exercise 1*

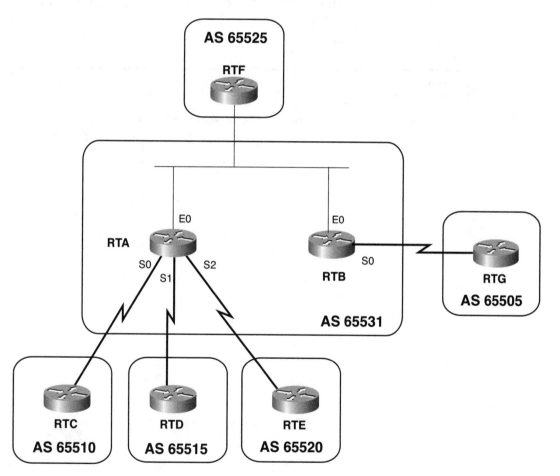

Although it is peering with RTB and exchanging reachability information, there is a configuration error. Based on the information in Example 1-29, what is the error?

Example 1-29 *The EGP Tables of RTB and RTG in Figure 1-17*

```
RTB#show ip egp
Local autonomous system is 65531

 EGP Neighbor      FAS/LAS  State    SndSeq RcvSeq Hello  Poll j/k Flags
*192.168.1.1     65531/65531 UP      4      2      6     60   180   2 Perm, Pass
*192.168.1.3     65525/65531 UP      4      2      492   60   180   2 Perm, Pass
*192.168.5.2     65505/65531 UP      3      2      33    60   180   3 Temp, Pass
 EGP Neighbor      Third Party
*192.168.1.1       192.168.1.3(e)
*192.168.1.3       192.168.1.1
RTB#
```

```
RTG#show ip egp
Local autonomous system is 65505

 EGP Neighbor      FAS/LAS  State    SndSeq RcvSeq Hello  Poll j/k Flags
*192.168.5.1     65505/65505 UP      9      36     3     60   180   4 Perm, Act
RTG#
```

This chapter covers the following key topics:

- **Classless Interdomain Routing**—This section introduces CIDR and discusses both its advantages and its shortcomings.

- **Who Needs BGP?**—This section examines several inter-AS scenarios, with an eye to where BGP is necessary and where it is not.

- **BGP Basics**—This section discusses the fundamentals of the Border Gateway Protocol, including message types and path attributes.

- **IBGP and IGP Synchronization**—This section presents the issues surrounding synchronization between IBGP and the IGP within an AS, why synchronization is required by default, and how synchronization problems can be avoided.

- **Managing Large-Scale BGP Peering**—This section presents four tools for controlling large-scale BGP implementations.

- **BGP Message Formats**—This section examines the details of the various BGP messages.

CHAPTER 2

Introduction to Border Gateway Protocol 4

Border Gateway Protocol (BGP) is a particularly important topic for any CCIE, and you can expect your knowledge of it to be thoroughly challenged in the CCIE lab.

You learned in Chapter 1, "Exterior Gateway Protocol," that the architects of the ARPANET began recognizing in the early 1980s that autonomous systems, and an inter-AS reachability protocol, were necessary to maintain manageability of the fast-growing Internet. Their original solution, Exterior Gateway Protocol (EGP), was adequate for the backbone-based ARPANET, but from the beginning, the architects understood the necessity of moving to a meshed inter-AS topology. They further understood that EGP was not capable of efficiently routing in such an environment because of its inability to detect loops, its very slow convergence time, and its lack of tools to support routing policies.

Attempts were made to enhance EGP, but in the end, an entirely new inter-AS protocol, a true routing protocol rather than a mere reachability protocol such as EGP, was called for. That inter-AS routing protocol, first introduced in 1989 in RFC 1105[1], is BGP. The first version of BGP was updated exactly one year later in RFC 1163[2]. BGP was upgraded again in 1991 in RFC 1267[3], and with this third modification, it became customary to refer to the three versions as BGP-1, BGP-2, and BGP-3, respectively.

The current version of BGP, BGP-4, was introduced in 1995 in RFC 1771[4]. BGP-4 differs significantly from the earlier versions. The most important difference is that BGP-4 is classless, whereas the earlier versions are classful. The motive for this fundamental change goes to the very heart of the reason exterior gateway protocols exist at all: to keep routing within the Internet both manageable and reliable. Classless interdomain routing (CIDR)— originally introduced in RFC 1517[5] in 1993, finalized in RFC 1519[6] in the same year as a standard proposal, and amended by RFC 1520[7]—was created for this purpose, and BGP-4 was created to support CIDR.

Classless Interdomain Routing

The invention of autonomous systems and exterior routing protocols solved the early scalability problems on the Internet in the 1980s. However, by the early 1990s the Internet was beginning to present a different set of scalability problems, including the following:

- Explosion of the Internet routing tables. The exponentially growing routing tables were becoming increasingly unmanageable both by the routers of the time and the people who managed them. The mere size of the tables was burden enough on Internet resources, but day-to-day topological changes and instabilities added heavily to the load.

- Depletion of the Class B address space. In January 1993, 7133 of the 16,382 available Class B addresses had been assigned; at 1993 growth rates, the entire Class B address space would be depleted in less than 2 years (as cited in RFC 1519).

- The eventual exhaustion of the entire 32-bit IP address space.

Classless interdomain routing provides a short-term solution to the first two problems. Another short-term solution is network address translation (NAT), discussed in Chapter 4, "Network Address Translation." These solutions were intended to buy the Internet architects enough time to create a new version of IP with enough address space for the foreseeable future. That initiative, known as IP Next Generation (IPng), resulted in the creation of IPv6, with a 128-bit address format. IPv6, discussed in Chapter 8, "IP Version 6," is the long-term solution to the third problem. Interestingly, CIDR and NAT have been so successful that few people place as much urgency on the migration to IPv6 as they once did.

CIDR is merely a politically sanctioned address summarization scheme that takes advantage of the hierarchical structure of the Internet. So before discussing CIDR further, a review of summarization and classless routing, and a look at the modern Internet, are in order.

A Summarization Summary

Summarization or *route aggregation* (discussed extensively in *Routing TCP/IP, Volume I*) is the practice of advertising a contiguous set of addresses with a single, less-specific address. Basically, summarization/route aggregation is accomplished by reducing the length of the subnet mask until it masks only the bits common to all the addresses being summarized. In Figure 2-1, for example, the four subnets (172.16.100.192/28, 172.16.100.208/28, 172.16.100.224/28, and 172.16.100.240/28) are summarized with the single aggregate address 172.16.100.192/26.

Many networkers who view summarization as a difficult topic are surprised to learn that they use summarization daily. What is a subnet address, after all, other than a summarization of a contiguous group of host addresses? For example, the subnet address 192.168.5.224/27 is the aggregate of host addresses 192.168.5.224/32 through 192.168.5.255/32. (The "host address" 192.168.5.224/32 is, of course, the address of the data link itself.) The key characteristic of a summary address is that its mask is shorter than the masks of the addresses it is summarizing. The ultimate summary address is the default address, 0.0.0.0/0, commonly written as just 0/0. As the /0 indicates, the mask has shrunk until no network bits remain—the address is the aggregate of all IP addresses.

Figure 2-1   *Route Aggregation*

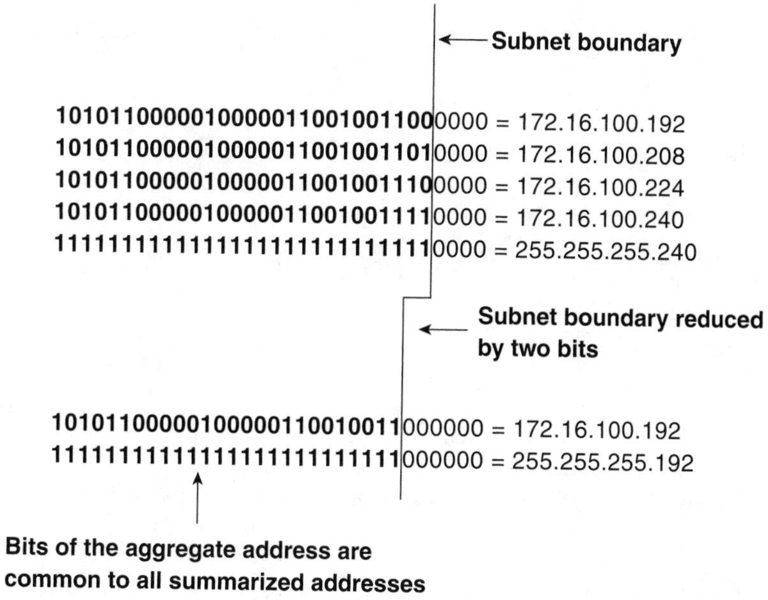

◄——**Subnet boundary**

1010110000010000011001001100|0000 = 172.16.100.192
1010110000010000011001001101|0000 = 172.16.100.208
1010110000010000011001001110|0000 = 172.16.100.224
1010110000010000011001001111|0000 = 172.16.100.240
1111111111111111111111111111|0000 = 255.255.255.240

◄—— **Subnet boundary reduced by two bits**

10101100000100000110010011|000000 = 172.16.100.192
11111111111111111111111111|000000 = 255.255.255.192

Bits of the aggregate address are common to all summarized addresses

Summarization can also cross class boundaries. For example, the four Class C networks (192.168.0.0, 192.168.1.0, 192.168.2.0, and 192.168.3.0) can all be summarized with the aggregate address 192.168.0.0/22. Notice that the aggregate, with its 22-bit mask, is no longer a legal Class C address. Therefore, to support the aggregation of major class network addresses, the routing environment must be classless.

Classless Routing

Classless routing features two aspects:

- Classlessness can be a characteristic of a routing protocol.
- Classlessness can be a characteristic of a router.

Classless routing protocols carry, as part of the routing information, a description of the network portion of each advertised address. The network portion of a network address is commonly referred to as the *address prefix*. An address prefix can be described by including an address mask, a length field that indicates how many bits of the address are prefix bits, or by including only the prefix bits in the update (see Figure 2-2). The classless IP routing protocols are RIP-2, EIGRP, OSPF, Integrated IS-IS, and BGP-4.

Figure 2-2   *Advertising an Address Prefix with a Classless Routing Protocol*

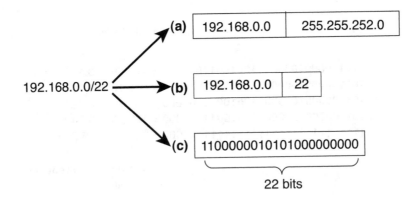

A classful router records destination addresses in its routing table as major class networks and subnets of those networks. When it performs a route lookup, it first looks up the major class network address and then tries to find a match in its list of subnets under that major address. A classless router ignores address classes and merely attempts a "longest match." That is, for any given destination address, it chooses the route that matches the most bits of the address. Take the routing table of Example 2-1, for instance, which shows several variably subnetted IP networks. If the router is classless, it attempts to find the longest match for each destination address.

Example 2-1   *A Routing Table Containing Several Variably Subnetted IP Networks*

```
Cleveland#show ip route
Codes: C - connected, S - static, I - IGRP, R - RIP, M - mobile, B - BGP
       D - EIGRP, EX - EIGRP external, O - OSPF, IA - OSPF inter area
       E1 - OSPF external type 1, E2 - OSPF external type 2, E - EGP
       i - IS-IS, L1 - IS-IS level-1, L2 - IS-IS level-2, * - candidate default

Gateway of last resort is 192.168.2.130 to network 0.0.0.0

O E2 192.168.125.0 [110/20] via 192.168.2.2, 00:11:19, Ethernet0
O    192.168.75.0 [110/74] via 192.168.2.130, 00:11:19, Serial0
O E2 192.168.8.0 [110/40] via 192.168.2.18, 00:11:19, Ethernet1
     192.168.1.0 is variably subnetted, 3 subnets, 3 masks
O E1    192.168.1.64 255.255.255.192
           [110/139] via 192.168.2.134, 00:11:20, Serial1
O E1    192.168.1.0 255.255.255.128
           [110/139] via 192.168.2.134, 00:00:34, Serial1
O E2    192.168.1.0 255.255.255.0
           [110/20] via 192.168.2.2, 00:11:20, Ethernet0
     192.168.2.0 is variably subnetted, 4 subnets, 2 masks
C       192.168.2.0 255.255.255.240 is directly connected, Ethernet0
C       192.168.2.16 255.255.255.240 is directly connected, Ethernet1
C       192.168.2.128 255.255.255.252 is directly connected, Serial0
```

Example 2-1   *A Routing Table Containing Several Variably Subnetted IP Networks (Continued)*

```
C        192.168.2.132 255.255.255.252 is directly connected, Serial1
O E2 192.168.225.0 [110/20] via 192.168.2.2, 00:11:20, Ethernet0
O E2 192.168.230.0 [110/20] via 192.168.2.2, 00:11:21, Ethernet0
O E2 192.168.198.0 [110/20] via 192.168.2.2, 00:11:21, Ethernet0
O E2 192.168.215.0 [110/20] via 192.168.2.2, 00:11:21, Ethernet0
O E2 192.168.129.0 [110/20] via 192.168.2.2, 00:11:21, Ethernet0
O E2 192.168.131.0 [110/20] via 192.168.2.2, 00:11:21, Ethernet0
O E2 192.168.135.0 [110/20] via 192.168.2.2, 00:11:21, Ethernet0
O*E2 0.0.0.0 0.0.0.0 [110/1] via 192.168.2.130, 00:11:21, Serial0
O E2 192.168.0.0 255.255.0.0 [110/40] via 192.168.2.18, 00:11:22, Ethernet1
Cleveland#
```

If the router receives a packet with a destination address of 192.168.1.75, several entries in the routing table match the address: 192.168.0.0/16, 192.168.1.0/24, 192.168.1.0/25, and 192.168.1.64/26. The entry 192.168.1.64/26 is chosen (see Example 2-2) because it matches 26 bits of the destination address—the longest match.

Example 2-2   *A Packet with a Destination Address of 192.168.1.75 Is Forwarded Out Interface S1*

```
Cleveland#show ip route 192.168.1.75
Routing entry for 192.168.1.64 255.255.255.192
  Known via "ospf 1", distance 110, metric 139, type extern 1
  Redistributing via ospf 1
  Last update from 192.168.2.134 on Serial1, 06:46:52 ago
  Routing Descriptor Blocks:
  * 192.168.2.134, from 192.168.7.1, 06:46:52 ago, via Serial1
      Route metric is 139, traffic share count is 1
```

A packet with a destination address of 192.168.1.217 will not match 192.168.1.64/26, nor will it match 192.168.1.0/25. The longest match for this address is 192.168.1.0/24, as demonstrated in Example 2-3.

Example 2-3   *The Router Cannot Match 192.168.1.217 to a More-Specific Subnet, So It Matches the Network Address 192.168.1.0/24*

```
Cleveland#show ip route 192.168.1.217
Routing entry for 192.168.1.0 255.255.255.0
  Known via "ospf 1", distance 110, metric 20, type extern 2, forward metric 10
  Redistributing via ospf 1
  Last update from 192.168.2.2 on Ethernet0, 06:48:18 ago
  Routing Descriptor Blocks:
  * 192.168.2.2, from 10.2.1.1, 06:48:18 ago, via Ethernet0
      Route metric is 20, traffic share count is 1
```

The longest match that can be made for destination address 192.168.5.3 is the aggregate address 192.168.0.0/16, as demonstrated in Example 2-4.

Example 2-4 *Packets Destined for 192.168.5.3 Do Not Match a More-Specific Subnet or Network, and Therefore Match the Supernet 192.168.0.0/16*

```
Cleveland#show ip route 192.168.5.3
Routing entry for 192.168.0.0 255.255.0.0, supernet
  Known via "ospf 1", distance 110, metric 139, type extern 1
  Redistributing via ospf 1
  Last update from 192.168.2.18 on Ethernet1, 06:49:26 ago
  Routing Descriptor Blocks:
  * 192.168.2.18, from 192.168.7.1, 06:49:26 ago, via Ethernet1
      Route metric is 139, traffic share count is 1
```

Finally, a destination address of 192.169.1.1 will not match any of the network entries in the routing table, as demonstrated in Example 2-5. However, packets with this destination address are not dropped, because the routing table of Example 2-1 contains a default route. The packets are forwarded to next-hop router 192.168.2.130.

Example 2-5 *No Match Is Found in the Routing Table for 192.169.1.1; Packets Destined for This Address Are Forwarded to the Default Address, Out Interface S0*

```
Cleveland#show ip route 192.169.1.1
% Network not in table
```

Beginning with IOS 11.3, Cisco routers are classless by default. Prior to this release, the IOS defaults were classful. You can change the default with the **ip classless** command.

The routing table in Example 2-1 and the associated examples demonstrates another characteristic of longest-match routing. Namely, a route to an aggregate address does not necessarily point to every member of the aggregate. Figure 2-3 shows the vectors of the routes in Examples 2-2 through 2-5.

Figure 2-3 *The Vectors of Routes in the Routing Table of Example 2-1*

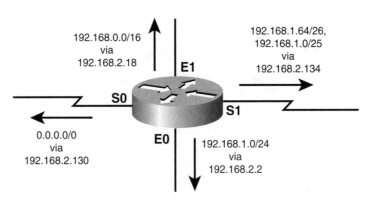

You can consider network 192.168.1.0/24 an aggregate of all its subnets; Figure 2-3 shows that the route to this network address directs packets out interface E0. Yet routes to two of its subnets, 192.168.1.0/25 and 192.168.1.64/26, point out a different interface, S1.

NOTE   In fact, 192.168.1.64/26 is itself a member of 192.168.1.0/25. The fact that there are distinct routes for these two addresses, both pointing out S1, hints that they are advertised by separate routers somewhere upstream.

Likewise, 192.168.1.0/24 is a member of the aggregate 192.168.0.0/16, but the route to that less-specific address is out E1. The least-specific route, 0.0.0.0/0, which is an aggregate of all other addresses, is out S0. Because of longest-match routing, packets to subnets 192.168.1.64/26 and 192.168.1.0/25 are forwarded out S1, whereas packets to other subnets of network 192.168.1.0/24 are forwarded out E0. Packets with destination addresses beginning with 192.168, other than 192.168.1, are forwarded out E1, and packets whose destination addresses do not begin with 192.168 are forwarded out S0.

Summarization: The Good, the Bad, and the Asymmetric

Summarization is a great tool for conserving network resources, from the amount of memory required to store the routing table to the amount of network bandwidth and router horsepower necessary to transmit and process routing information. Summarization also conserves network resources by "hiding" network instabilities.

For example, the network in Figure 2-4 has a flapping route—a route that, due to a bad physical connection or router interface, keeps transitioning down and up and down again.

Without summarization, every time subnet 192.168.1.176/28 goes up or down, the information must be conveyed to every router in the corporate internetwork. Each of those routers, in turn, must process the information and adjust its routing table accordingly. If router Nashville advertises all the upstream routes with the aggregate address 192.168.1.128/25, however, changes to any of the more-specific subnets are not advertised past that router. Nashville is the aggregation point; the aggregate continues to be stable even if some of its members are not.

The price to be paid for summarization is a reduction in routing precision. In Example 2-6, interface S1 of the router in Figure 2-3 has failed, causing the routes learned from the neighbor on that interface to become invalid. Instead of dropping packets that would normally be forwarded out S1, however, such as a packet with a destination address of 192.168.1.75, the packet now matches the next-best route, 192.168.1.0/24, and is forwarded out interface E0. (Compare this to Example 2-2.)

Figure 2-4 *A Flapping Route Can Destabilize the Entire Network*

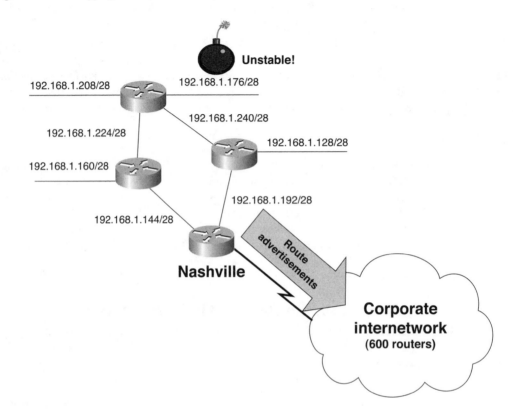

Example 2-6 *A Failed Route Can Lead to Inaccurate Packet Forwarding*

```
Cleveland#
%LINEPROTO-5-UPDOWN: Line protocol on Interface Serial1, changed state to down
%LINK-3-UPDOWN: Interface Serial1, changed state to down
Cleveland#show ip route 192.168.1.75
Routing entry for 192.168.1.0 255.255.255.0
  Known via "ospf 1", distance 110, metric 20, type extern 2, forward metric 10
  Redistributing via ospf 1
  Last update from 192.168.2.2 on Ethernet0, 00:00:20 ago
  Routing Descriptor Blocks:
  * 192.168.2.2, from 10.2.1.1, 00:00:20 ago, via Ethernet0
      Route metric is 20, traffic share count is 1

Cleveland#
```

This imprecision may or may not be a problem, depending on what the rest of the internetwork looks like. Continuing with the example, suppose the next-hop router 192.168.2.2 still has a route entry to 192.168.1.64/26 via the router Cleveland, either because the internetwork has not yet converged or because the route was statically entered. In this case, a routing loop occurs. On the other hand, some router reachable via Cleveland's E0 interface may have a "back door" route to subnet 192.168.1.64/26 that should be used only if the primary route, via Cleveland's S1, becomes invalid. In this second case, the route to 192.168.1.0/24 has been designed as a backup route, and the behavior shown in Example 2-6 is intentional.

Figure 2-5 shows an internetwork in which a loss of routing precision can cause a different sort of problem. Here, routing domain 1 is connected to routing domain 2 by routers in San Francisco and Atlanta. What defines these domains is unimportant for the example. What is important is that all the networks in domain 1 can be summarized with the address 172.16.192.0/18, and all the networks in domain 2 can be summarized with the address 172.16.128.0/18.

Figure 2-5   *When Multiple Routers Are Advertising the Same Aggregate Addresses, Loss of Routing Precision Can Become a Problem*

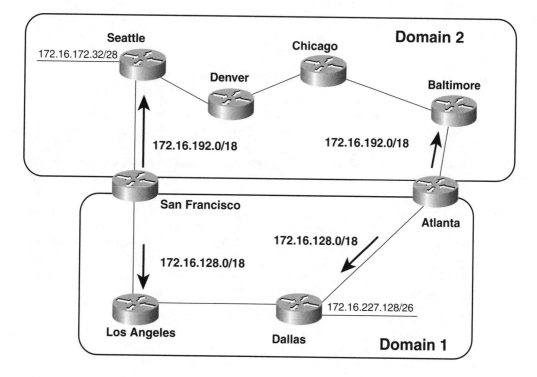

Rather than advertise individual subnets, Atlanta and San Francisco advertise the summary addresses into the two domains. If a host on Dallas' subnet 172.16.227.128/26 sends a packet to a host on Seattle's subnet 172.16.172.32/28, the packet most likely is routed to Atlanta, because that is the closest router advertising domain 2's summary route. Atlanta forwards the packet into domain 2, and it arrives at Seattle. When the host on subnet 172.16.172.32/28 sends a reply, Seattle forwards that packet to San Francisco—the closest router advertising the summary route 172.16.192.0/18.

The problem here is that the traffic between the two subnets has become asymmetric: Packets from 172.16.227.128/26 to 172.16.172.32/28 take one path, whereas packets from 172.16.172.32/28 to 172.16.227.128/26 take a different path. Asymmetry occurs because the Dallas and Seattle routers do not have complete routes to each other's subnets. They have only routes to the routers advertising the summaries and must forward packets based on those routes. In other words, the summarization at San Francisco and Atlanta has hidden the details of the internetworks behind those routers.

Asymmetric traffic can be undesirable for several reasons. First, internetwork traffic patterns become unpredictable, making baselining, capacity planning, and troubleshooting more problematic. Second, link usage can become unbalanced. The bandwidth of some links can become saturated, while other links are underutilized. Third, a distinct variation can occur in the delay times of outgoing traffic and incoming traffic. This delay variation can be detrimental to some delay-sensitive applications such as voice and live video.

The Internet: Still Hierarchical After All These Years

Although the Internet has grown away from the single-backbone architecture of the ARPANET described in Chapter 1, it retains a certain hierarchical structure. At the lowest level, Internet subscribers connect to an Internet service provider (ISP). In many cases, that ISP is one of many small providers in the local geographic area (called *local* ISPs). For example, there are presently almost 200 ISPs in Colorado's 303 area code. These local ISPs in turn are the customers of larger ISPs that cover an entire geographic region such as a state or a group of adjacent states. These larger ISPs are called *regional service providers*. Examples in Colorado are CSD Internet and Colorado Supernet. The regional service providers, in turn, connect to large ISPs with high-speed (DS-3 or OS-3 or better) backbones spanning a national or global area. These largest providers are the *network service providers* and include companies such as MCI/WorldCom (UUNET), SprintNet, Cable & Wireless, Concentric Network, and PSINet. More commonly, these various providers are referred to as Tier III, Tier II, and Tier I providers, respectively.

Figure 2-6 shows how these different types of ISPs are interrelated. In each case, a subscriber—whether an end user or a lower-level service provider—connects to a higher-level service provider at that ISP's *Point of Presence* (POP). A POP is just a nearby router to which the subscriber can connect via dialup or a dedicated local loop. At the highest level, the network service providers interconnect via *network access points* (NAPs). A NAP is a LAN or switch—typically Ethernet, FDDI, or ATM—across which different providers can exchange routes and data traffic.

Figure 2-6   *ISP/NAP Hierarchy*

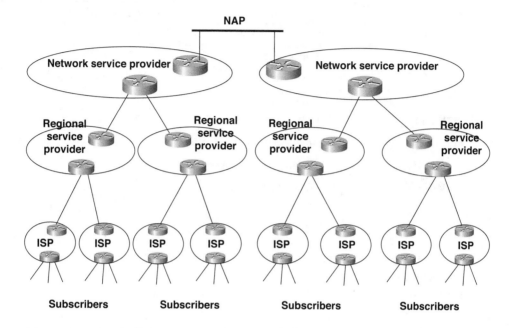

As Table 2-1 shows, some NAPs are known by names such as Commercial Internet Exchange (CIX), Federal Internet Exchange (FIX), and Metropolitan Area Exchange (MAE—originally called Metropolitan Area Ethernets, a creation of Metropolitan Fiber Systems, Inc.). CIX, FIX, and MAE-East were early experiments to connect backbones; based on the experience gained from these connection points, the National Science Foundation implemented the first four NAPs in 1994 as part of the decommissioning of the NSFnet.

Table 2-1   *Well-Known Network Access Points in the United States*

NAP	Location	Maintained By
New York NAP*	Pennsauken, New Jersey	Sprint
Chicago NAP*	Chicago, Illinois	Ameritech and Bellcore
San Francisco NAP*	San Francisco, California	Pacific Bell
Big East NAP	Bohemia, New York	ICS Network Systems
MAE-West	San Jose, California	MCI/WorldCom
MAE-East*	Washington, DC	MCI/WorldCom
MAE-LA	Los Angeles, California	MCI/WorldCom

continues

Table 2-1 *Well-Known Network Access Points in the United States (Continued)*

NAP	Location	Maintained By
MAE-Houston	Houston, Texas	MCI/WorldCom
MAE-Dallas	Dallas, Texas	MCI/WorldCom
MAE-New York	New York City, New York	MCI/WorldCom
MAE-Chicago	Chicago, Illinois	MCI/WorldCom
FIX-East	College Park, Maryland	University of Maryland
FIX-West	Moffett Field, California	NASA Ames Research Center
CIX	Santa Clara, California	Wiltel
Digital PAIX	Palo Alto, California	Digital Equipment Corporation

*One of the original four NSF NAPs

In addition to the major NAPs shown in Table 2-1, where the NSPs come together, there are many smaller NAPs. These usually interconnect smaller regional providers. Examples of regional NAPs are Seattle Internet eXchange (SIX) and the New Mexico network access point.

In conjunction with the formation of the NAPs, the NSF funded the Routing Arbiter (RA) project. One of the duties of the RA is to promote Internet stability and manageability. To this end, the RA proposed a database (the RADB, or Routing Arbiter Database) of routes (topology) and policies (preferred paths) from the service providers. The database is maintained at NAPs on a *route server*, a UNIX workstation or server running BGP. Rather than peering with every other router at the NAP, each provider's router peers with only the route server. Routes and policies are communicated to the server, which uses a sophisticated database language called RIPE-181 to process and maintain the information. The appropriate routes are then passed to the other routers.

Although the route server speaks BGP and processes routes, it does not perform packet forwarding. Instead, its updates inform routers of the best next-hop router that is directly reachable across the NAP. You are already familiar with this concept from the discussion in Chapter 1 of EGP third-party neighbors. By making one-to-many peering feasible rather than many-to-many peering, route servers increase the stability, manageability, and throughput of traffic through the NAPs.

The NAPs and the RA project proved that the competing network service providers could cooperate to provide manageable connectivity and stability to the Internet. As a result, the NSF ceased funding of the route servers and NAPs on January 1, 1997, and turned the operations over to the commercial interests. Although publicly funded Internet research continues with such projects as Internet2, GigaPOPs, and the very high-speed Backbone Network Service (vBNS), the present Internet can be considered a commercial operation.

A result of the transition to commercial control of the Internet is that the topology of the modern Internet is far from the tidy picture drawn by the preceding paragraphs. The largest service providers, driven by financial, competitive, and policy interests, generally choose to peer directly rather than peer through route servers. The peering also takes place at many levels, rather than just at the top level shown in Figure 2-6.

When two or more service providers agree to share routes across a NAP, either directly or through a route server, they enter into a *peering agreement*. A peering agreement may be established directly between two providers (a *bilateral* peering agreement) or between a group of similar-sized providers (a *multilateral* peering agreement, or MLPA). Traffic patterns play a major role in determining the financial nature of the agreement. If the traffic between the peering partners is reasonably balanced in both directions, money usually does not exchange hands. The peering is equitable for the two partners. However, if the traffic is heavier in one direction than in the other across the peering point, as is the case when a small provider peers with a larger provider, the small provider usually must pay for the peering privilege. The rationale here is that the small provider benefits more from the peering than the larger provider.

Another factor muddling the Internet picture is the location of peering points. NAPs in which many providers come together, such as the ones listed in Table 2-1, are *public* peering sites. In addition to these public sites, service providers have created hundreds of smaller NAPs at sites where they find themselves co-located with other service providers. The peering agreements at such sites are usually *private* agreements between two or a few providers. Private peering is encouraged because it helps relieve congestion at the national NAPs, adds to route diversity, and can decrease delay for some traffic.

Another fact hinting that real life is not as tidy as Figure 2-6 suggests is that many national and regional service providers also sell local Internet access, in direct competition with the local ISPs. The "starting point" of the route traces in Example 2-7, for example, is a dial-in POP belonging to Concentric Network—a backbone provider. Regional service providers also frequently have a presence at the backbone NAPs. They might connect to one or more network service providers across the NAP, or they might connect to other regional service providers across the NAP, bypassing any network service provider.

The route traces in Example 2-7 show a little of the Internet backbone structure. Both traces originated from a Concentric Network POP in Denver. In the first trace, the packets traverse Concentric Network's backbone to MAE-East, where they connect to the BBN Planet backbone (lines 3 and 4). The packets traverse BBN Planet's backbone to a Tier II NAP shared by BBN and US West in Minneapolis (lines 10 and 11) and then are passed to the US West destination.

Example 2-7   *Route Traces from a Concentric Network POP in Denver*

```
--- traceroute to www.uswest.com (205.215.207.54),
    30 hops max, 18 byte packets

  1 (  207.155.168.5)  ts003e01.den-co.concentric.net  174 ms
  2 (  207.155.168.1)  rt001e0102.den-co.concentric.net.168.155.207.IN-ADDR.ARPA
162 ms
  3 (  207.88.24.29)   us-dc-wash-core1-a1-0d12.rtr.concentric.net  385 ms
  4 (  192.41.177.2)   maeeast2.bbnplanet.net  225 ms
  5 (      4.0.1.93)   p2-2.vienna1-nbr2.bbnplanet.net  232 ms
  6 (     4.0.3.130)   p3-1.nyc4-nbr2.bbnplanet.net  222 ms
  7 (      4.0.5.26)   p1-0.nyc4-nbr3.bbnplanet.net  223 ms
  8 (     4.0.3.121)   p2-1.chicago1-nbr1.bbnplanet.net  235 ms
  9 (      4.0.5.89)   p10-0-0.chicago1-br1.bbnplanet.net  239 ms
 10 (      4.0.2.18)   h1-0.minneapol1-cr1.bbnplanet.net  258 ms
 11 (   4.0.246.254)   h1-0.uswest-mn.bbnplanet.net  260 ms
 12 (207.225.159.221)  207.225.159.221  249 ms
 13 ( 205.215.207.54)  www.uswc.uswest.net  258 ms

--- traceroute to www.rmi.net (166.93.8.30),
    30 hops max, 18 byte packets

  1 (  207.155.168.5)  ts003e01.den-co.concentric.net  152 ms
  2 (  207.155.168.1)  rt001e0102.den-co.concentric.net.168.155.207.IN-ADDR.ARPA
161 ms
  3 (   207.88.24.21)  207.88.24.21  190 ms
  4 (   207.88.0.253)  us-ca-scl-core1-f9-0.rtr.concentric.net  189 ms
  5 (   207.88.0.178)  207.88.0.178  206 ms
  6 ( 144.228.207.73)  sl-gw18-chi-5-1-0-T3.sprintlink.net  210 ms
  7 ( 144.232.0.217)   sl-bb11-chi-3-3.sprintlink.net  216 ms
  8 ( 144.232.0.174)   sl-bb5-chi-4-0-0.sprintlink.net  211 ms
  9 (  144.232.8.85)   sl-bb7-pen-5-1-0.sprintlink.net  225 ms
 10 (  144.232.5.53)   sl-bb10-pen-1-3.sprintlink.net  236 ms
 11 (  144.232.5.62)   sl-nap1-pen-4-0-0.sprintlink.net  228 ms
 12 (  192.157.69.13)  p219.t3.ans.net  263 ms
 13 ( 140.223.60.209)  f1-1.t60-6.Reston.t3.ans.net  264 ms
 14 (  140.223.65.17)  h12-1.t64-0.Houston.t3.ans.net  286 ms
 15 (  140.223.25.14)  h13-1.t80-1.St-Louis.t3.ans.net  283 ms
 16 (  140.223.25.29)  h14-1.t24-0.Chicago.t3.ans.net  292 ms
 17 (   140.223.9.18)  h14-1.t96-0.Denver.t3.ans.net  309 ms
 18 ( 140.222.96.122)  f1-0.c96-10.Denver.t3.ans.net  313 ms
 19 (  207.25.224.14)  h1-0.enss3191.t3.ans.net  306 ms
 20 (  166.93.46.246)  166.93.46.246  305 ms
 21 (   166.93.8.30)   www.rmi.net  285 ms
```

The packets in the second trace take a pretty thorough tour of the United States before arriving at their destination, a few miles from their origination. First, they follow Concentric's backbone through a router in California (line 4) and then to the Chicago NAP, where they connect to the Sprint backbone (line 6). The packets are routed to the New York NAP in Pennsauken, New Jersey, where they are passed to the ANS backbone (lines 11 and 12). They then visit routers in Reston, Houston, St. Louis, and Chicago (again), and finally arrive back in Denver.

Like the packets in the last trace, we have taken a rather lengthy and circuitous route to get back to the topic at hand, CIDR.

CIDR: Reducing Routing Table Explosion

Given the somewhat hierarchical structure of the Internet, you can see how the structure lends itself to an address summarization scheme. At the top layers, large blocks of contiguous Class C addresses are assigned by the Internet Assigned Numbers Authority (IANA) to the various addressing authorities around the globe, known as the *regional IP registries*. Currently, there are three regional registries. The regional registry for North and South America, the Caribbean, and sub-Saharan Africa is the American Registry for Internet Numbers (ARIN). ARIN also is responsible for assigning addresses to the global network service providers. The regional registry for Europe, the Middle East, northern Africa, and parts of Asia (the area of the former Soviet Union) is the Resèaux IP Europèens (RIPE). The regional registry for the rest of Asia and the Pacific nations is the Asia Pacific Network Information Center (APNIC).

NOTE	ARIN was spun off of the InterNIC (run by Network Solutions, Inc.) in 1997 to separate the management of IP addresses and domain names.

Table 2-2 shows the original scheme for assigning Class C addresses to the regions these registries serve, although some of the allocations are now outdated. As Example 2-8 demonstrates, the blocks labeled "Others" are now being assigned. The regional registries, in turn, assign portions of these blocks to the large service providers or to local IP registries. Generally, the blocks assigned at this level are no smaller than 32 contiguous Class C addresses (and are usually larger). Concentric Network has been assigned the block 207.155.128.0/17, for example, which includes the equivalent of 128 contiguous Class C addresses (see Example 2-8).

Table 2-2   *CIDR Address Allocation by Geographic Region*

Region	Address Range
Multiregional	192.0.0.0–193.255.255.255
Europe	194.0.0.0–195.255.255.255
Others	196.0.0.0–197.255.255.255

continues

Table 2-2   *CIDR Address Allocation by Geographic Region (Continued)*

Region	Address Range
North America	198.0.0.0–199.255.255.255
Central/South America	200.0.0.0–201.255.255.255
Pacific Rim	202.0.0.0–203.255.255.255
Others	204.0.0.0–205.255.255.255
Others	206.0.0.0–207.255.255.255

Example 2-8   *When a WHOIS Is Performed on the Address 207.155.128.5 from Example 2-7, the Address Is Shown as Part of a /17 CIDR Block Assigned to Concentric Network*

```
--- looking up 207.155.128.5
--- performing WHOIS on "207.155.128.5", please wait...
--- contacting host whois.arin.net
--- smart query on "207.155.128"

Concentric Research Corp. (NETBLK-CONCENTRIC-CIDR)
    10590 N. Tantau Ave.
    Cupertino, CA  95014

    Netname: CONCENTRIC-CIDR
    Netblock: 207.155.128.0 - 207.155.255.255
    Maintainer: CRC

    Coordinator:
        DNS and IP ADMIN   (DIA-ORG-ARIN)   hostmaster@CONCENTRIC.NET
        (408) 342-2800
Fax- (408) 342-2810

    Domain System inverse mapping provided by:

    NAMESERVER3.CONCENTRIC.NET    206.173.119.72
    NAMESERVER2.CONCENTRIC.NET    207.155.184.72
    NAMESERVER1.CONCENTRIC.NET    207.155.183.73
    NAMESERVER.CONCENTRIC.NET     207.155.183.72

    Record last updated on 13-Feb-97.
    Database last updated on 29-Jan-99 16:12:40 EDT.
```

The service providers receiving these blocks assign them in smaller blocks to their subscribers. If those subscribers are themselves ISPs, they can again break their blocks into smaller blocks. The obvious advantage of assigning these blocks of Class C addresses, called *CIDR blocks*, comes when the blocks are summarized back up the hierarchy. For more information on how addresses are assigned throughout the Internet, see RFC 2050 (www.isi.edu/in-notes/rfc2050.txt).

To illustrate, suppose Concentric Network assigns to one of its subscribers a portion of its 207.155.128.0/17 block, consisting of 207.155.144.0/20. If that subscriber is an ISP, it may assign a portion of that block, say 207.155.148.0/22, to one of its own subscribers. That subscriber advertises its /22 (read "slash twenty-two") block back to its ISP. That ISP in turn summarizes all of its subscribers to Concentric Network with the single aggregate 207.155.144.0/20, and Concentric Network summarizes its subscribers into the NAPs to which it is attached with the single aggregate 207.155.128.0/17.

The advertisement of a single aggregate to the higher-level domain is obviously preferable to advertising possibly hundreds of individual addresses. But an equally important benefit is the stability such a scheme adds to the Internet. If the state of a network in a low-level domain changes, that change is felt only up to the first aggregation point and no further.

Table 2-3 shows the different sizes of CIDR blocks, their equivalent size in Class C networks, and the number of hosts each block can represent.

Table 2-3   *CIDR Block Sizes*

CIDR Block Prefix Size	Number of Equivalent Class C Addresses	Number of Possible Host Addresses
/24	1	254
/23	2	510
/22	4	1022
/21	8	2046
/20	16	4094
/19	32	8190
/18	64	16,382
/17	128	32,766
/16	256	65,534
/15	512	131,070
/14	1024	262,142
/13	2048	524,286

CIDR: Reducing Class B Address Space Depletion

The depletion of Class B addresses was due to an inherent flaw in the design of the IP address classes. A Class C address provides 254 host addresses, whereas a Class B address provides 65,534 host addresses. That's a wide gap. Before CIDR, if your company needed 500 host addresses, a Class C address would not have served your needs. You probably would have requested a Class B address, even though you would be wasting 65,000 host addresses. With CIDR, your needs can be met with a /23 block. The host addresses that would have otherwise been wasted have been conserved.

Difficulties with CIDR

Although CIDR has proven successful in slowing both the growth of Internet routing tables and the depletion of Class B addresses, it also has presented some problems for the users of CIDR blocks.

The first problem is one of portability. If you have been given a CIDR block, the addresses are most likely part of a larger block assigned to your ISP. Suppose, however, that your ISP is not living up to your expectations or contractual agreements, or you have just gotten a more attractive offer from another ISP. A change of ISPs most likely means you must re-address. It's unlikely that an ISP will allow a subscriber to keep its assigned block when the subscriber moves to a new provider. Aside from an ISP's being unwilling to give away a portion of its own address space, regional registries strongly encourage the return of address space when a subscriber changes ISPs.

For an end user, re-addressing carries varying degrees of difficulty. The process is probably the easiest for those who use private address space within their routing domain and network address translation (see Chapter 4) at the edges of the domain. In this case, only the "public-facing" addresses have to be changed, with minimal impact on the internal users. At the other extreme are end users who have statically assigned public addresses to all their internal network devices. These users have no choice but to visit every device in the network to re-address.

Even if the end user is using the CIDR block throughout the domain, the pain of re-addressing can be somewhat reduced by the use of DHCP (or BOOTP). In this case, the DHCP scopes must be changed and users must reboot, but only some statically addressed network devices, such as servers and routers, must be individually re-addressed.

The problem is much amplified if you are an ISP rather than an end user and you want to change your upstream service provider. Not only must your own internetwork be renumbered, but so must any of your subscribers to whom you have assigned a portion of your CIDR block.

CIDR also presents a problem to anyone who wants to connect to multiple service providers. Multihoming (discussed in more depth later in this chapter) is used for redundancy so that an end user or ISP is not vulnerable to the failure of a single upstream service provider. The trouble is that if your addresses are taken from one ISP's block, you must advertise those addresses to the second provider.

Figure 2-7 shows what can happen. Here, the subscriber has a /23 CIDR block that is part of ISP1's larger /20 block. When the subscriber attaches to ISP2, he wants to ensure that traffic from the Internet can reach him through either ISP1 or ISP2. To make this happen, he must advertise his /23 block through ISP2. The trouble arises when ISP2 advertises the /23 block to the rest of the world. Now all the routers "out there" have a route to 205.113.48.0/20 advertised by ISP1 and a route to 205.113.50.0/23 advertised by ISP2. Any packets destined for the subscriber are forwarded on the more-specific route, and as a result, almost all traffic from the Internet to the subscriber is routed through ISP2—including traffic from sources that are geographically much closer to the subscriber through ISP1.

Figure 2-7   *Incoming Internet Traffic Matches the Most-Specific Route*

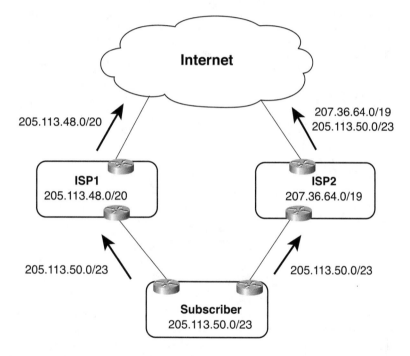

In Figure 2-7, it is even possible for the 205.113.50.0/23 route to be advertised into ISP1 from the Internet. This shouldn't happen, because most ISPs set route filters to prevent their own routes from reentering their domain. However, there are no guarantees that ISP1 is filtering properly. If the more-specific route should leak in from the Internet, traffic from ISP1's other subscribers could traverse the Internet and ISP2 to 205.113.50.0/23 rather than take the more-direct path.

For the subscriber to be multihomed, ISP1 must advertise the more-specific route in addition to its own CIDR block (see Figure 2-8). Most service providers will not agree to this arrangement, because it means "punching a hole" in their own CIDR block (sometimes called *address leaking*). In addition to reducing the overall effectiveness of CIDR, advertising a more-specific route of its own CIDR block carries an administrative burden for the ISP.

Figure 2-8 *ISP1 "Punches a Hole" in Its CIDR Block*

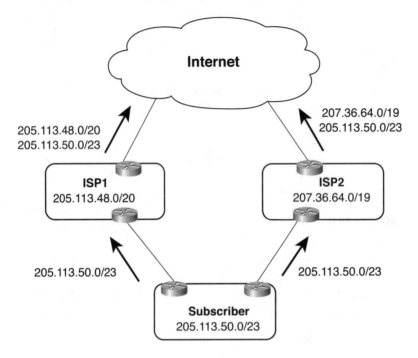

Although Figures 2-7 and 2-8 show ISP1 as having only a single connection to the Internet, in most cases an ISP has many connections to higher-level providers and at NAPs. At each of these connections, the provider must reconfigure its router to advertise the more-specific route in addition to the CIDR block, and possibly must modify all its incoming route filters. Administration is also complicated by the fact that ISP1 and ISP2 have to closely coordinate their efforts to ensure that the subscriber's /23 block is advertised correctly. Because ISP1 and ISP2 are competitors, either or both might be resistant to working so closely together.

Even if the subscriber in Figure 2-8 can get ISP1 and ISP2 to agree to advertise its own /23 block, there is another obstacle. Some Tier I providers accept only prefixes of /19 or smaller, to control the backbone-level routing tables. If ISP1 or ISP2 or both get their Internet connectivity from one of these network service providers, they cannot advertise the subscriber's /23. The practice of filtering any CIDR addresses with a prefix larger than /19 has become so well-known that a /19 prefix is commonly referred to as a *globally routable* address. The implication here is that if you advertise a longer CIDR prefix, say a /21 or /22, your prefix might not be advertised to all parts of the Internet. Remember that any parts of the Internet that do not know how to reach you are essentially unreachable by you.

NOTE   Many Tier I providers have relaxed their /19 rules recently in response to increased subscriber complaints.

A possible solution for the multihomed subscriber in Figure 2-8 is to obtain a *provider-independent* address space (also known as a *portable* address space). That is, the subscriber can apply for a block that is not a part of either ISP1's or ISP2's CIDR block; both ISPs can advertise the subscriber's block without interference with their own address space. Since the formation of ARIN, obtaining a provider-independent block is somewhat easier than it was under the InterNIC. Although ARIN strongly encourages you to seek an address space first from your provider and second from your provider's provider, obtaining a provider-independent address space from ARIN is a last resort. However, you still face difficulties.

First, if you want to multihome, it is likely that your present address space was obtained from your original ISP. Changing to a provider-independent address space means renumbering, with all the difficulties already discussed. (Of course, if you obtained your IP address space in the pre-CIDR days, you are already provider-independent, making the question moot.)

Second, the registries assign address space based on justified need, not on long-term predicted need. This policy means that you probably will be allocated "just enough" space to fit your present needs and a three-month predicted need. From there, you have to justify a further allocation by proving that you are efficiently using the original space. For example, ARIN requires proof of address utilization by one of two means: the use of the Shared WHOIS Project (SWIP) or the use of a Referral WHOIS Server (RWHOIS). SWIP, most commonly used, is the practice of adding WHOIS information to a SWIP template and e-mailing it to ARIN. To use RWHOIS, you establish an RWHOIS server on your premises that ARIN can access for WHOIS information. In both cases, the WHOIS information establishes proof that you have efficiently used, and are approaching exhaustion of, your present address space.

Of course, you still have a problem if you cannot justify obtaining a globally routable (/19) address space. The bottom line is that CIDR allocation rules make multihoming a difficult problem for small subscribers and ISPs. The following section discusses multihoming in more detail, along with some alternative topologies.

Who Needs BGP?

Not as many internetworks need BGP as you might think. A common misconception is that whenever an internetwork must be broken into multiple routing domains, BGP should be run between the domains. BGP is certainly an option, but why complicate matters by unnecessarily adding another routing protocol to the mix?

Take, for example, a multinational corporate network consisting of 3000 routers and perhaps 150,000 users. Figure 2-9 shows how such a huge internetwork might be constructed. The entire network is routed with OSPF and is divided into eight geographic OSPF routing domains for easier manageability. Although the illustration shows only the backbone areas for each OSPF domain, each of the domains is divided into multiple OSPF areas that also correspond to geographic subregions.

Figure 2-9   *Even a Very Large Internetwork Can Be Built Using Only Multiple IGP Domains*

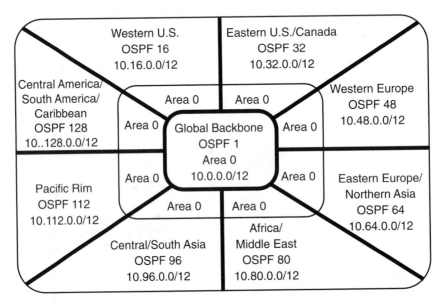

BGP can be used to provide connectivity between the multiple OSPF domains, but it is unnecessary. Instead, each of the eight OSPF backbone areas redistributes into a single global backbone. The global backbone is another OSPF domain, consisting of a single OSPF area. Although this core consists of high-end routers to handle the packet-switching load, the load on these routers from routing tables and OSPF processing is actually very small. Because of the way the entire internetwork is addressed, each of the eight OSPF domains advertises only a single aggregate route to the global backbone. In fact, aggregation is fundamental to making this design work. There are, presumably, such a large number of subnets in such an internetwork that without aggregation OSPF would "choke" trying to process them all. The result would be very poor performance and possible router failures.

The hierarchical construction of the physical topology and the address space are two of the three factors contributing to the simplicity of the internetwork in Figure 2-9. The third factor is a common administrative body for the entire internetwork. Having a single administration means that routing policies are imposed equally and consistently throughout. In this case, the routing policy dictates the address range used in each OSPF area and that all OSPF processes interconnect through OSPF 1 only.

NOTE　　A routing policy is just a designed and configured process for controlling the traffic patterns within an internetwork by controlling routes and their characteristics. Redistribution, route filters, and route maps are the most common tools for implementing routing policies with Cisco IOS Software.

Of course, in real life, few corporations the size of the one depicted in Figure 2-9 have the luxury of being designed "from the ground up" in such a coordinated, logical fashion. Many, if not most, large internetworks have evolved from smaller internetworks that have been merged as divisions and corporations have merged. The result is that different network administrators have made different design choices for the various parts of the internetwork; when the parts are merged, the first order of business is basic interoperability.

The second order of business might be the enforcement of routing policies. Some traffic from some domains of the internetwork to other domains may be required to always prefer certain links or routes, for example, or perhaps only certain routes should be advertised between domains. In most cases, the necessary policies can still be implemented with redistribution between IGPs and tools such as route filters and route maps. You should implement BGP only when a sound engineering reason compels you to do so, such as when the IGPs do not provide the tools necessary to implement the required routing policies or when the size of the routing tables cannot be controlled with summarization. BGP proves useful, for instance, when many different IGPs are used in the domains. Here, BGP might be simpler to implement than attempting to redistribute among all the IGPs.

When considering whether BGP is necessary in an internetwork design, keep in mind why exterior routing protocols were invented in the first place. Exterior routing protocols are used to route between autonomous systems—that is, between internetwork domains under different administrative authorities. In a single corporate internetwork, even a large one with different domains under different local administrations, there is usually enough of a centralized authority to impose routing policy using the tools available with interior routing protocols. When separate autonomous systems must interconnect, however, BGP might be called for.

The majority of the cases calling for BGP involve Internet connectivity—either between a subscriber and an ISP or (more likely) between ISPs. Yet even when interconnecting autonomous systems, BGP might be unnecessary. The remainder of this section examines typical inter-AS topologies and demonstrates where BGP is and is not needed.

A Single-Homed Autonomous System

Figure 2-10 shows a subscriber attached by a single connection to an ISP. BGP, or any other type of routing protocol, is unnecessary in this topology. If the single link fails, no routing decision needs to be made, because no alternative route exists. A routing protocol accomplishes nothing. In this topology, the subscriber adds a static default route to the border router and redistributes the route into his AS.

Figure 2-10 *Static Routes Are All That Is Needed in This Single-Homed Topology*

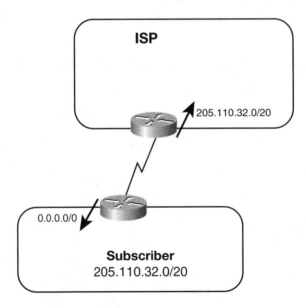

The ISP similarly adds a static route pointing to the subscriber's address range and advertises that route into its AS. Of course, if the subscriber's address space is a part of the ISP's larger address space, the route advertised by the ISP's router goes no farther than the ISP's own AS. "The rest of the world" reaches the subscriber by routing to the ISP's advertised address space, and the more-specific route to the subscriber is picked up only within the ISP's AS.

An important principle to remember when working with inter-AS traffic is that each physical link actually represents two logical links: one for incoming traffic and one for outgoing traffic (see Figure 2-11).

Figure 2-11 *Each Physical Link Between Autonomous Systems Represents Two Logical Links, Carrying Incoming and Outgoing Packets*

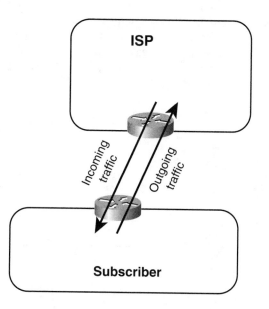

The routes you advertise in each direction influence the traffic separately. Avi Freedman, who has written many excellent articles on ISP issues, calls a route advertisement a promise to carry packets to the address space represented in the route. In Figure 2-10, the subscriber's router is advertising a default route into the local AS—a promise to deliver packets to any destination for which there is not a more-specific route. And the ISP's router, advertising a route to 205.110.32.0/20, is promising to deliver traffic to the subscriber's AS. The outgoing traffic from the subscriber's AS is the result of the default route, and the incoming traffic to the subscriber's AS is the result of the route advertised by the ISP's router. This concept might seem somewhat trivial and obvious at this point, but it is very important to keep in mind as you examine more-complex topologies.

The obvious vulnerability of the topology in Figure 2-10 is that the entire connection is made up of single points of failure. If the single data link fails, if a router or one of its interfaces fails, if the configuration of one of the routers fails, if a process within the router fails, or if one of the routers' all-too-human administrators makes a mistake, the subscriber's entire Internet connectivity can be lost. What is lacking in this picture is *redundancy*.

Multihoming to a Single Autonomous System

Figure 2-12 shows an improved topology, with redundant links to the same provider. How the incoming and outgoing traffic is manipulated across these links depends on how the two links are used. For example, a typical setup when multihoming to a single provider is for one of the links to be a primary, dedicated Internet access link—say, a T1—and for the other link to be used only for backup. In such a scenario, the backup link is likely to be some lower-speed connection.

Figure 2-12 *Multihoming to a Single Autonomous System*

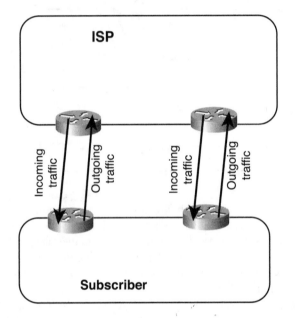

When the redundant link is used only for backup, there is again no call for BGP. The routes can be advertised just as they were in the single-homed scenario, except that the routes associated with the backup link have the distances set high so that they are used only if the primary link fails.

Example 2-9 shows what the configurations of the routers carrying the primary and secondary links might look like.

Example 2-9 *Primary and Secondary Link Configurations for Multihoming to a Single Autonomous System*

```
Primary Router
router ospf 100
 network 205.110.32.0 0.0.15.255 area 0
 default-information originate metric 10
!
ip route 0.0.0.0 0.0.0.0 205.110.168.108

Backup Router
router ospf 100
 network 205.110.32.0 0.0.15.255 area 0
 default-information originate metric 100
!
ip route 0.0.0.0 0.0.0.0 205.110.168.113 150
```

In this configuration, the backup router has a default route whose administrative distance is set to 150 so that it is in the routing table only if the default route from the primary router is unavailable. Also, the backup default is advertised with a higher metric than the primary default route to ensure that the other routers in the OSPF domain prefer the primary default route. The OSPF metric type of both routes is E2, so the advertised metrics remain the same throughout the OSPF domain. This consistency ensures that the metric of the primary default route remains lower than the metric of the backup default route in every router, regardless of the internal cost to each border router. Example 2-10 shows the default routes in a router internal to the OSPF domain.

Example 2-10 *The First Display Shows the Primary External Route; the Second Display Shows the Backup Route Being Used After the Primary Route Has Failed*

```
Phoenix#show ip route 0.0.0.0
Routing entry for 0.0.0.0 0.0.0.0, supernet
  Known via "ospf 1", distance 110, metric 10, candidate default path
  Tag 1, type extern 2, forward metric 64
  Redistributing via ospf 1
  Last update from 205.110.36.1 on Serial0, 00:01:24 ago
  Routing Descriptor Blocks:
  * 205.110.36.1, from 205.110.36.1, 00:01:24 ago, via Serial0
      Route metric is 10, traffic share count is 1

Phoenix#show ip route 0.0.0.0
Routing entry for 0.0.0.0 0.0.0.0, supernet
  Known via "ospf 1", distance 110, metric 100, candidate default path
  Tag 1, type extern 2, forward metric 64
  Redistributing via ospf 1
  Last update from 205.110.38.1 on Serial1, 00:00:15 ago
  Routing Descriptor Blocks:
  * 205.110.38.1, from 205.110.38.1, 00:00:15 ago, via Serial1
      Route metric is 100, traffic share count is 1
```

Although a primary/backup design satisfies the need for redundancy, it does not efficiently use the available bandwidth. A better design is to use both paths, with each providing backup for the other in the event of a link or router failure. In this case, the configuration used in both routers is as indicated in Example 2-11.

Example 2-11 *Configuration for Load Sharing When Multihomed to the Same AS*

```
router ospf 100
 network 205.110.32.0 0.0.15.255 area 0
 default-information originate metric 10 metric-type 1
!
ip route 0.0.0.0 0.0.0.0 205.110.168.108
```

The static routes in both routers have equal administrative distances, and the default routes are advertised with equal metrics (10). Notice that the default routes are now advertised with an OSPF metric type of E1. With this metric type, each of the routers in the OSPF domain takes into account the internal cost of the route to the border routers in addition to the cost of the default routes themselves. As a result, every router chooses the closest exit point when choosing a default route (see Figure 2-13).

Figure 2-13 *Border Routers Advertising a Default Route with a Metric of 10 and an OSPF Metric Type of E1*

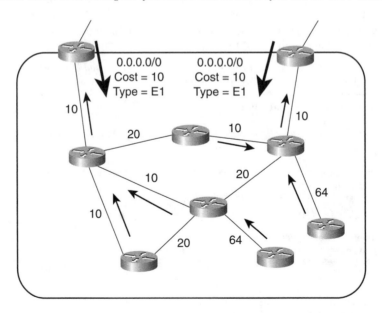

In most cases, advertising default routes into the AS from multiple exit points, and summarizing address space out of the AS at the same exit points, is sufficient for good internetwork performance. The one consideration is whether asymmetric traffic patterns will become a concern. If the geographical separation between the two (or more) exit points is large enough for delay variations to become significant, you might have a need for better control of the routing. You might now consider BGP.

Suppose, for example, that the two exit routers depicted in Figure 2-12 are located in Los Angeles and London. You might want all your exit traffic destined for the Eastern Hemisphere to use the London router and all your exit traffic for the Western Hemisphere to use the Los Angeles router. Remember that the incoming route advertisements influence your outgoing traffic. If the provider advertises routes into your AS via BGP, your internal routers have more-accurate information about external destinations. BGP also provides the tools for setting routing policies for the external destinations.

Similarly, outgoing route advertisements influence your incoming traffic. If internal routes are advertised to the provider via BGP, you have influence over which routes are advertised at which exit point, and also tools for influencing (to some degree) the choices the provider makes when sending traffic into your AS.

When considering whether to use BGP, carefully weigh the benefits gained against the cost of added routing complexity. You should use BGP only when you can realize an advantage in traffic control. Consider the incoming and outgoing traffic separately. If it is only important to control your incoming traffic, use BGP to advertise routes to your provider while still advertising only a default route into your AS.

On the other hand, if it is only important to control your outgoing traffic, use BGP only to receive routes from your provider. Consider carefully the ramifications of accepting routes from your provider. "Taking full BGP routes" means that your provider advertises to you the entire Internet routing table. As of this writing, that is approximately 88,000 route entries, as shown in Example 2-12. To store and process a table of this size, you need a reasonably powerful router and at least 64 MB of memory (although 128 MB is recommended). On the other hand, you can easily implement a simple default routing scheme with a low-end router and a moderate amount of memory.

Example 2-12 *This Full Internet Routing Table Summary Shows 57,624 BGP Entries*

```
route-server>show ip route summary
Route Source    Networks    Subnets    Overhead    Memory (bytes)
connected       0           1          56          144
static          2           1          168         432
bgp 65000       76302       11967      4943064     12847416
    External: 88269 Internal: 0 Local: 0
internal        779                                906756
Total           77083       11969      4943288     13754748
route-server>
```

NOTE The routing table summary in Example 2-12 is taken from a publicly accessible route server at route-server.ip.att.net. Another server to which you can Telnet is route-server.cerf.net. The number of BGP entries varies somewhat in each, but all indicate a similar size.

"Taking partial BGP routes" is a compromise between taking full routes and accepting no routes at all. As the name implies, partial routes are some subset of the full Internet routing table. For example, a provider might advertise only routes to its other subscribers, plus a default route to reach the rest of the Internet. The following section presents a scenario in which taking partial routes proves useful.

Another consideration is that when running BGP, a subscriber's routing domain must be identified with an autonomous system number. Like IP addresses, autonomous system numbers are limited and are assigned only by the regional address registries when there is a justifiable need. And like IP addresses, a range of autonomous system numbers is reserved for private use: the AS numbers 64512 to 65535. With few exceptions, subscribers that are connected to a single service provider (either single or multihomed) use an autonomous system number out of the reserved range. The service provider filters the private AS number out of the advertised BGP path.

Although the topology in Figure 2-12 is an improvement over the topology in Figure 2-10 because redundant routers and data links have been added, it still entails a single point of failure: the ISP itself. If the ISP loses connectivity to the rest of the Internet, so does the subscriber. And if the ISP suffers a major internal outage, the single-homed subscriber also suffers.

Multihoming to Multiple Autonomous Systems

Figure 2-14 shows a topology in which a subscriber has homed to more than one service provider. In addition to the advantages of multihoming already described, this subscriber is protected from losing Internet connectivity as the result of a single ISP failure.

For a small corporation or a small ISP, there are substantial obstacles to multihoming to multiple service providers. You already have seen the problems involved if the subscriber's address space is a part of one of the service providers' larger address space:

- The originating provider must be persuaded to "punch a hole" in his CIDR block.

- The second provider must be persuaded to advertise an address space that belongs to a different provider.

- Both providers must be willing to closely coordinate the advertisement of the subscriber's address space.

- If the subscriber's address space is smaller than a /19 (which a small subscriber's space is likely to be), some backbone providers might not accept the route.

Figure 2-14 *Multihoming to Multiple Autonomous Systems*

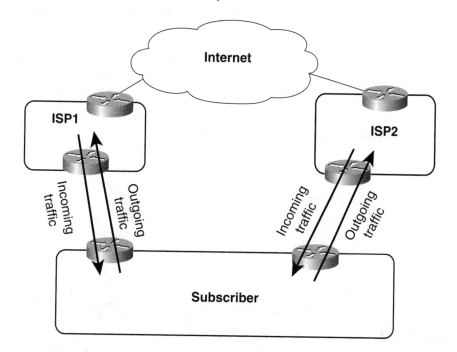

The best candidates for multihoming to multiple providers are corporations and ISPs that are large enough to qualify for a provider-independent address space (or who already have one) and a public autonomous system number.

The subscriber in Figure 2-14 could still forego BGP. One option is to use one ISP as a primary Internet connection and the other as a backup only; another option is to default route to both providers and let the routing chips fall where they may. If a subscriber has gone to the expense of multihoming and contracting with multiple providers, however, neither of these solutions is likely to be acceptable. BGP is the preferred option in this scenario.

Again, incoming and outgoing traffic should be considered separately. For incoming traffic, the most reliability is realized if all internal routes are advertised to both providers. This setup ensures that all destinations within the subscriber's AS are completely reachable via either ISP. Even though both providers are advertising the same routes, there are cases in which incoming traffic should prefer one path over another. BGP provides the tools for communicating these preferences.

For outgoing traffic, the routes accepted from the providers should be carefully considered. If full routes are accepted from both providers, the best route for every Internet destination is chosen. In some cases, however, one provider might be a preferred for full Internet connectivity, whereas the other provider is preferred for only some destinations. In this case, full routes can be taken from the preferred provider and partial routes can be taken from the other provider. For example, you might want to use the secondary provider, only to reach its other subscribers and for backup to your primary Internet provider (see Figure 2-15). The secondary provider sends its customer routes, and the subscriber configures a default route to the secondary ISP to be used if the connection to the primary ISP fails.

Figure 2-15 *ISP1 Is the Preferred Provider for Most Internet Connectivity; ISP2 Is Used Only to Reach Its Other Customers' Internetworks and for Backup Internet Connectivity*

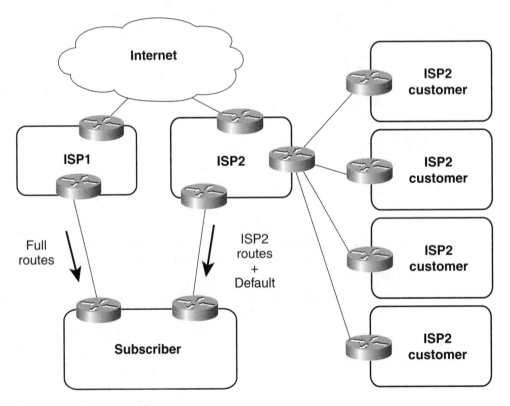

Notice that the full routes sent by ISP1 probably include the customer routes of ISP2. Because the same routes are received from ISP2, however, the subscriber's routers normally prefer the shorter path through ISP2. If the link to ISP2 fails, the subscriber uses the longer paths through ISP1 and the rest of the Internet to reach ISP2's customers.

Similarly, the subscriber normally uses ISP1 to reach all destinations other than ISP2's customers. If some or all of those more-specific routes from ISP1 are lost, however, the subscriber uses the default route through ISP2.

If router CPU and memory limitations prohibit taking full routes, partial routes from both providers are an option. Each provider might send its own customer routes, and the subscriber points default routes to both providers. In this scenario, some routing accuracy is traded for a savings in router hardware.

In yet another partial-routes scenario, each ISP might send its customer routes and also the customer routes of its upstream provider. In Figure 2-16, for example, ISP1 is connected to Sprint, and ISP2 is connected to MCI. The partial routes sent to the subscriber by ISP1 consist of all of ISP1's customer routes and all of Sprint's customer routes. The partial routes sent by ISP2 consist of all of ISP2's customer routes and all of MCI's customer routes. The subscriber points to default routes at both providers. Because of the size of the two backbone service providers, the subscriber has enough routes to make efficient routing decisions on a large number of destinations. At the same time, the partial routes are still significantly smaller than a full Internet routing table.

Figure 2-16 *The Subscriber Is Taking Partial Routes from Both ISPs, Consisting of Each ISP's Customer Routes and the Customer Routes of Their Respective Upstream Providers*

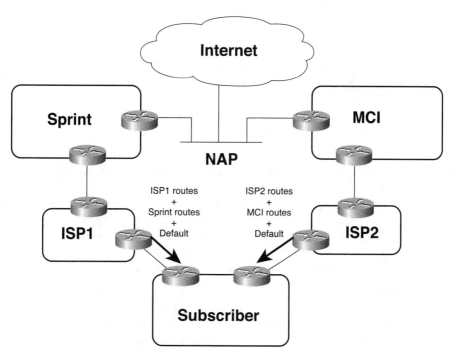

The remainder of this chapter (after two short cautionary sections) examines the operation of BGP and the tools it provides for setting preferences and policies for both incoming and outgoing traffic.

A Note on "Load Balancing"

The principal benefits of multihoming are redundancy and, to a lesser extent, increased bandwidth. Increased bandwidth does not mean that both links are used with equal efficiency. You should not expect the traffic load to be balanced 50/50 across the two links; one of the ISPs will almost always be "better connected" than the other ISP. The ISP itself or its upstream provider might have better routers, better physical links, or more NAP connections than the other ISP, or one ISP might just be topologically closer to more of the destinations to which your users regularly connect.

That is not to say that you cannot, through the expenditure of considerable time and effort, manipulate route preferences to fairly evenly balance your route traffic across the two links. The problem is that you probably actually degrade your Internet performance by forcing some traffic to take a less-optimal route for the sake of so-called load balancing. All you really accomplish, in most cases, is an evening out of the utilization numbers of your two ISP links. Do not be too concerned if 75 percent of your traffic uses one link while only 25 percent of your traffic uses the other link. Multihoming is for redundancy and increased routing efficiency, not load balancing.

BGP Hazards

Creating a BGP peering relationship involves an interesting combination of trust and mistrust. The BGP peer is in another AS, so you must trust the network administrator on that end to know what he or she is doing. At the same time, if you are smart, you will take every practical measure to protect yourself in the event that a mistake is made on the other end. When you're implementing a BGP peering connection, paranoia is your friend.

Recall the earlier description of a route advertisement as a promise to deliver packets to the advertised destination. The routes you advertise directly influence the packets you receive, and the routes you receive directly influence the packets you transmit. In a good BGP peering arrangement, both parties should have a complete understanding of what routes are to be advertised in each direction. Again, incoming and outgoing traffic must be considered separately. Each peer should ensure that he is transmitting only the correct routes and should use route filters or other policy tools such as AS_PATH filters, described in Chapter 3, to ensure that he is receiving only the correct routes.

Your ISP might show little patience with you if you make mistakes in your BGP configuration, but the worst problems can be attributed to a failure on both sides of the peering arrangement. Suppose, for example, that through some misconfiguration you advertise 207.46.0.0/16 to your ISP. On the receiving side, the ISP does not filter out this incorrect route, allowing it to be advertised to the rest of the Internet. This particular CIDR block belongs to Microsoft, and you have just claimed to have a route to that destination. A significant portion of the Internet community could decide that the best path to Microsoft is through your domain. You will receive a flood of unwanted packets across your Internet connection and, more importantly, you will have black-holed traffic that should have gone to Microsoft. They will be neither amused nor understanding.

Figure 2-17 shows another example of a BGP routing mistake. This same internetwork was shown in Figure 2-15, but here the customer routes that the subscriber learned from ISP2 have been inadvertently advertised to ISP1.

Figure 2-17 *This Subscriber Is Advertising Routes Learned from ISP2 into ISP1, Inviting Packets Destined for ISP2 and Its Customers to Transit His Domain*

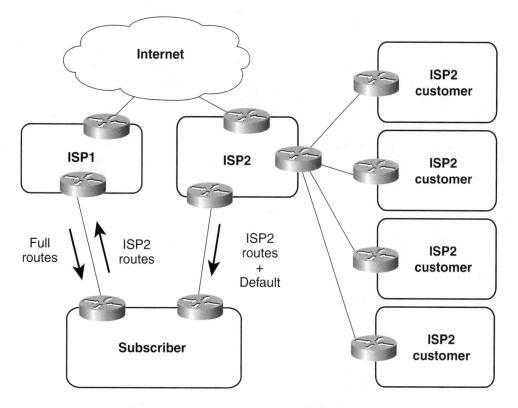

In all likelihood, ISP1 and its customers will see the subscriber's domain as the best path to ISP2 and its customers. In this case, the traffic is not black-holed, because the subscriber does indeed have a route to ISP2. The subscriber has become a transit domain for packets from ISP1 to ISP2, to the detriment of its own traffic. And because the routes from ISP2 to ISP1 still point through the Internet, the subscriber has caused asymmetric routing for ISP2.

The point of this section is that BGP, by its very nature, is designed to allow communication between autonomously controlled systems. A successful and reliable BGP peering arrangement requires an in-depth understanding of not only the routes to be advertised in each direction, but also the routing policies of each of the involved parties.

BGP Basics

Like EGP, BGP forms a unique, unicast-based connection to each of its BGP-speaking peers. To increase the reliability of the peer connection, BGP uses TCP (port 179) as its underlying delivery mechanism. The update mechanisms of BGP are also somewhat simplified by allowing the TCP layer to handle such duties as acknowledgment, retransmission, and sequencing. Because BGP rides on TCP, a separate point-to-point connection to each peer must be established.

BGP is a distance vector protocol in that each BGP node relies on downstream neighbors to pass along routes from their routing table; the node makes its route calculations based on those advertised routes and passes the results to upstream neighbors. However, other distance vector protocols quantify the distance with a single number, representing hop count or, in the case of IGRP and EIGRP, a sum of total interface delays and lowest bandwidth. In contrast, BGP uses a list of AS numbers through which a packet must pass to reach the destination (see Figure 2-18). Because this list fully describes the path a packet must take, BGP is called a *path vector* routing protocol to contrast it with traditional distance vector protocols. The list of AS numbers associated with a BGP route is called the *AS_PATH* and is one of several *path attributes* associated with each route. Path attributes are described fully in a subsequent section.

Figure 2-18 *BGP Determines the Shortest Loop-Free Inter-AS Path from a List of AS Numbers Known as the AS_PATH Attribute*

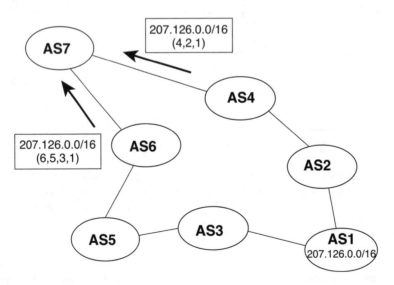

Recall from Chapter 1 that EGP is not a true routing protocol because it does not have a fully developed algorithm for calculating the shortest path and it cannot detect route loops. In contrast, the AS_PATH attribute qualifies BGP as a routing protocol on both counts. First, the shortest inter-AS path is very simply determined by the least number of AS numbers. In Figure 2-18, AS7 is receiving two routes to 207.126.0.0/16. One of the routes has four AS hops, and the other has three hops. AS7 chooses the shortest path, (4,2,1).

Route loops also are very easily detected with the AS_PATH attribute. If a router receives an update containing its local AS number in the AS_PATH, it knows that a routing loop has occurred. In Figure 2-19, AS7 has advertised a route to AS8. AS8 advertises the route to AS9, which advertises it back to AS7. AS7 sees its own number in the AS_PATH and does not accept the update, thereby avoiding a potential routing loop.

Figure 2-19 *If a BGP Router Sees Its Own AS Number in the AS_PATH of a Route from Another AS, It Rejects the Update*

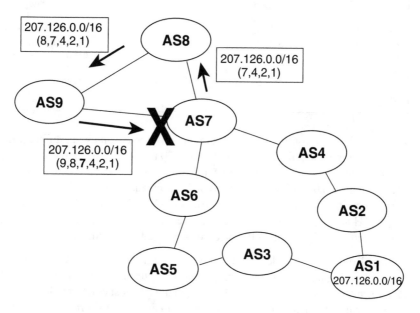

BGP does not show the details of the topologies within each AS. Because BGP sees only a tree of autonomous systems, it can be said that BGP takes a higher view of the Internet than IGP, which sees only the topology within an AS. And because this higher view is not really compatible with the view seen by IGPs, Cisco routers maintain a separate routing table to hold BGP routes. Example 2-13 demonstrates a typical BGP routing table viewed with the **show ip bgp** command.

Example 2-13 *The* **show ip bgp** *Command Displays the BGP Routing Table*

```
route-server>show ip bgp
BGP table version is 4639209, local router ID is 12.0.1.28
Status codes: s suppressed, d damped, h history, * valid, > best, i - internal
Origin codes: i - IGP, e - EGP, ? - incomplete

   Network          Next Hop         Metric LocPrf Weight Path
*  3.0.0.0          192.205.31.225                      0 7018 701 80 i
*                   192.205.31.161                      0 7018 701 80 i
*>                  192.205.31.33                       0 7018 701 80 i
*                   192.205.31.97                       0 7018 701 80 i
*  4.0.0.0          192.205.31.225                      0 7018 1 i
*                   192.205.31.161                      0 7018 1 i
*>                  192.205.31.33                       0 7018 1 i
*                   192.205.31.97                       0 7018 1 i
*  6.0.0.0          192.205.31.226                      0 7018 568 721 1455 i
*                   192.205.31.225                      0 7018 568 721 1455 i
*                   192.205.31.161            0 7018 701 6113 568 721 1455 i
*>                  192.205.31.34                       0 7018 568 721 1455 i
*                   192.205.31.33                       0 7018 568 721 1455 i
*                   192.205.31.97             0 7018 1239 568 721 1455 i
*  9.2.0.0/16       192.205.31.225                      0 7018 1 1673 1675 i
*                   192.205.31.161                      0 7018 701 1673 1675 i
 --More--
```

Although the BGP routing table in Example 2-13 looks somewhat different from the AS-internal routing table displayed with the **show ip route** command, the same elements exist. The table shows destination networks, next-hop routers, and a measure by which the shortest path can be selected. The **Metric**, **LocPrf**, and **Weight** columns are discussed later in this section, but what is of interest now is the **Path** column. This column lists the AS_PATH attributes for each network. Notice that each AS_PATH ends in an **i**, indicating that the path terminates at an IGP according to the **Origin codes** legend.

Notice also that for each destination network, multiple next hops are listed. Unlike the AS-internal routing table, which lists only the routes currently being used, the BGP table lists all known paths. A > following the * (valid) in the leftmost column indicates which path the router is currently using. This best path is the one with the shortest AS_PATH. When multiple routes have equivalent paths, as in the table of Example 2-13, the router must have some criteria for deciding which path to choose. That decision process is covered later in this section.

When there are parallel, equal-cost paths to a particular destination, as in Example 2-13, Cisco's implementation of EBGP by default selects only one path—in contrast to other IP routing protocols, in which the default is to load balance across up to four paths. As with the other IP routing protocols, the **maximum-paths** command is used to change the default maximum number of parallel paths in the range from one to six. Note that load balancing works only with EBGP. IBGP can use only one link.

The neighbor with which a BGP speaker peers can be either in a different AS or in the same AS. If the neighbor's AS differs, the neighbor is an *external peer* and the BGP is called *external BGP* (EBGP). If the neighbor is in the same AS, the neighbor is an *internal peer* and the BGP is called *internal BGP* (IBGP). A unique set of issues must be confronted when configuring IBGP; those issues are discussed in the section "IBGP and IGP Synchronization."

When two neighbors first establish a BGP peer connection, they exchange their entire BGP routing tables. After that, they exchange incremental, partial updates—that is, they exchange routing information only when something changes, and only information about what changed. Because BGP does not use periodic routing updates, the peers must exchange keepalive messages to ensure that the connection is maintained. The Cisco default keepalive interval is 60 seconds (RFC 1771 does not specify a standard keepalive time); if three intervals (180 seconds) pass without a peer receiving a keepalive message, the peer declares its neighbor down. You can change these intervals with the **timers bgp** command.

BGP Message Types

Before establishing a BGP peer connection, the two neighbors must perform the standard TCP three-way handshake and open a TCP connection to port 179. TCP provides the fragmentation, retransmission, acknowledgment, and sequencing functions necessary for a reliable connection, relieving BGP of those duties. All BGP messages are unicast to the one neighbor over the TCP connection.

BGP uses four message types:

- Open
- Keepalive
- Update
- Notification

This section describes how these messages are used; for a complete description of the message formats and the variables of each message field, see the section "BGP Message Formats."

Open Message

After the TCP session is established, both neighbors send Open messages. Each neighbor uses this message to identify itself and to specify its BGP operational parameters. The Open message includes the following information:

- **BGP version number**—This specifies the version (2, 3, or 4) of BGP that the originator is running. Unless a router is set to run an earlier version with the **neighbor version** command, it defaults to BGP-4. If a neighbor is running an earlier version of BGP, it rejects the Open message specifying version 4; the BGP-4 router then changes to BGP-3 and sends another Open message specifying this version. This negotiation continues until both neighbors agree on the same version.

- **Autonomous system number**—This is the AS number of the originating router. It determines whether the BGP session is EBGP (if the AS numbers of the neighbors differ) or IBGP (if the AS numbers are the same).

- **Hold time**—This is the maximum number of seconds that can elapse before the router must receive either a Keepalive or an Update message. The hold time must be either 0 seconds (in which case, Keepalives must not be sent) or at least 3 seconds; the default Cisco hold time is 180 seconds. If the neighbors' hold times differ, the smaller of the two times becomes the accepted hold time.

- **BGP identifier**—This is an IP address that identifies the neighbor. The Cisco IOS determines the BGP Identifier in exactly the same way as it determines the OSPF router ID: The numerically highest loopback address is used; if no loopback interface is configured with an IP address, the numerically highest IP address on a physical interface is selected.

- **Optional parameters**—This field is used to advertise support for such optional capabilities as authentication, multiprotocol support, and route refresh.

Keepalive Message

If a router accepts the parameters specified in its neighbor's Open message, it responds with a Keepalive. Subsequent Keepalives are sent every 60 seconds by Cisco default, or a period equal to one-third the agreed-upon hold time.

Update Message

The Update message advertises feasible routes, withdrawn routes, or both. The Update message includes the following information:

- **Network Layer Reachability Information (NLRI)**—This is one or more (Length, Prefix) tuples that advertise IP address prefixes and their lengths. If 206.193.160.0/19 were being advertised, for example, the Length portion would specify the /19 and the Prefix portion would specify 206.193.160.

- **Path Attributes**—The path attributes, described in a later section of the same name, are characteristics of the advertised NLRI. The attributes provide the information that allows BGP to choose a shortest path, detect routing loops, and determine routing policy.

- **Withdrawn Routes**—These are (Length, Prefix) tuples describing destinations that have become unreachable and are being withdrawn from service.

Note that although multiple prefixes might be included in the NLRI field, each update message describes only a single BGP route (because the path attributes describe only a single path, but that path might lead to multiple destinations). This, again, emphasizes that BGP takes a higher view of an internetwork than an IGP, whose routes always lead to a single destination IP address.

Notification Message

The Notification message is sent whenever an error is detected and always causes the BGP connection to close. The section "BGP Message Formats" includes a list of possible errors that can cause a Notification message to be sent.

An example of the use of a Notification message is the negotiation of a BGP version between neighbors. If, after establishing a TCP connection, a BGP-3 speaker receives an Open message specifying version 4, the router responds with a Notification message stating that the version is not supported. The connection is closed, and the neighbor attempts to reestablish a connection with BGP-3.

The BGP Finite State Machine

The stages of a BGP connection establishment and maintenance can be described in terms of a finite state machine. Figure 2-20 and Table 2-4 show the complete BGP finite state machine and the input events that can cause a state transition.

Figure 2-20 *The BGP Finite State Machine*

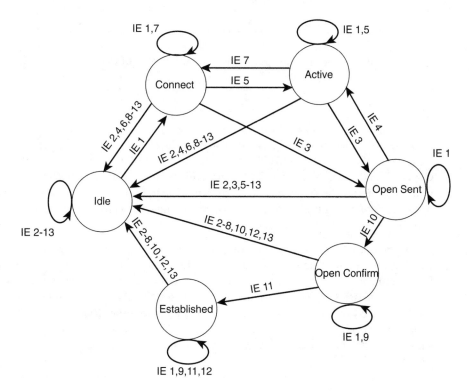

Table 2-4 *The Input Events (IE) of Figure 2-20*

IE	Description
1	BGP Start
2	BGP Stop
3	BGP Transport connection open
4	BGP Transport connection closed
5	BGP Transport connection open failed
6	BGP Transport fatal error
7	ConnectRetry timer expired
8	Hold timer expired
9	Keepalive timer expired
10	Receive Open message
11	Receive Keepalive message
12	Receive Update message
13	Receive Notification message

The following sections provide a brief description of each of the six states illustrated in Figure 2-20.

Idle State

BGP always begins in the Idle state, in which it refuses all incoming connections. When a Start event (IE 1) occurs, the BGP process initializes all BGP resources, starts the ConnectRetry timer, initializes a TCP connection to the neighbor, listens for a TCP initialization from the neighbor, and changes its state to Connect. The Start event is caused by an operator configuring a BGP process or resetting an existing process, or by the router software resetting the BGP process.

An error causes the BGP process to transition to the Idle state. From there, the router may automatically try to issue another Start event. However, limitations should be imposed on how the router does this—constantly trying to restart in the event of persistent error conditions causes flapping. Therefore, after the first transition back to the Idle state, the router sets the ConnectRetry timer and cannot attempt to restart BGP until the timer expires. Cisco's initial ConnectRetry time is 60 seconds. The ConnectRetry time for each subsequent attempt is twice the previous time, meaning that consecutive wait times increase exponentially.

Connect State

In this state, the BGP process is waiting for the TCP connection to be completed. If the TCP connection is successful, the BGP process clears the ConnectRetry timer, completes initialization, sends an Open message to the neighbor, and transitions to the OpenSent state. If the TCP connection is unsuccessful, the BGP process continues to listen for a connection to be initiated by the neighbor, resets the ConnectRetry timer, and transitions to the Active state.

If the ConnectRetry timer expires while in the Connect state, the timer is reset, another attempt is made to establish a TCP connection with the neighbor, and the process stays in the Connect state. Any other input event causes a transition to Idle.

Active State

In this state, the BGP process is trying to initiate a TCP connection with the neighbor. If the TCP connection is successful, the BGP process clears the ConnectRetry timer, completes initialization, sends an Open message to the neighbor, and transitions to OpenSent. The Hold timer is set to 4 minutes.

If the ConnectRetry timer expires while BGP is in the Active state, the process transitions back to the Connect state and resets the ConnectRetry timer. It also initiates a TCP connection to the peer and continues to listen for connections from the peer. If the neighbor is attempting to establish a TCP session with an unexpected IP address, the ConnectRetry timer is reset, the connection is refused, and the local process stays in the Active state. Any other input event (except a start event, which is ignored in the Active state) causes a transition to Idle.

OpenSent State

In this state, an Open message has been sent, and BGP is waiting to hear an Open from its neighbor. When an Open message is received, all its fields are checked. If errors exist, a Notification message is sent and the state transitions to Idle.

If no errors exist in the received Open message, a Keepalive message is sent and the Keepalive timer is set. The Hold time is negotiated, and the smaller value is agreed upon. If the negotiated Hold time is zero, the Hold and Keepalive timers are not started. The peer connection is determined to be either internal or external, based on the peer's AS number, and the state is changed to OpenConfirm.

If a TCP disconnect is received, the local process closes the BGP connection, resets the ConnectRetry timer, begins listening for a new connection to be initiated by the neighbor, and transitions to Active. Any other input event (except a start event, which is ignored) causes a transition to Idle.

OpenConfirm State

In this state, the BGP process waits for a Keepalive or Notification message. If a Keepalive is received, the state transitions to Established. If a Notification is received, or a TCP disconnect is received, the state transitions to Idle.

If the Hold timer expires, an error is detected, or a Stop event occurs, a Notification is sent to the neighbor and the BGP connection is closed, changing the state to Idle.

Established State

In this state, the BGP peer connection is fully established and the peers can exchange Update, Keepalive, and Notification messages. If an Update or Keepalive message is received, the Hold timer is restarted (if the negotiated hold time is nonzero). If a Notification message is received, the state transitions to Idle. Any other event (again, except for the Start event, which is ignored) causes a Notification to be sent and the state to transition to Idle.

Path Attributes

A *path attribute* is a characteristic of an advertised BGP route. Some path attributes are familiar, such as the destination IP address and the next-hop router, because they are a common characteristic of all routes. Others, such as the ATOMIC_AGGREGATE, are unique to BGP and might be unfamiliar. In addition to providing the information necessary for basic routing functionality, the path attributes are what allow BGP to set and communicate routing policy.

Each path attribute falls into one of four categories:

- Well-known mandatory
- Well-known discretionary
- Optional transitive
- Optional nontransitive

From the names of these four categories, you can see that two subclasses exist and that each subclass has its own subclass. First, an attribute is either *well-known*, meaning that it must be recognized by all BGP implementations, or it is *optional*, meaning that the BGP implementation is not required to support the attribute.

Well-known attributes are either *mandatory*, meaning that they must be included in all BGP Update messages, or they are *discretionary*, meaning that they may or may not be sent in a specific Update message.

If an optional attribute is *transitive*, a BGP process should accept the path in which it is included, even if it doesn't support the attribute, and it should pass the path on to its peers.

If an optional attribute is *nontransitive*, a BGP process that does not recognize the attribute can quietly ignore the Update in which it is included and not advertise the path to its other peers.

Table 2-5 lists the path attributes, and following sections describe the use of each attribute. Chapter 3, "Configuring and Troubleshooting Border Gateway Protocol 4," demonstrates the configuration, filtering, and manipulation of the path attributes.

Table 2-5   *Path Attributes**

Attribute	Class
ORIGIN	Well-known mandatory
AS_PATH	Well-known mandatory
NEXT_HOP	Well-known mandatory
LOCAL_PREF	Well-known discretionary
ATOMIC_AGGREGATE	Well-known discretionary
AGGREGATOR	Optional transitive
COMMUNITY	Optional transitive
MULTI_EXIT_DISC (MED)	Optional nontransitive
ORIGINATOR_ID	Optional nontransitive
CLUSTER_LIST	Optional nontransitive

*Actually, there are a few more attributes besides the ones listed in Table 2-5; however, they are neither specified in RFC 1771 nor supported by Cisco, so they are beyond the scope of this book.

The ORIGIN Attribute

ORIGIN is a well-known mandatory attribute that specifies the origin of the routing update. When BGP has multiple routes, it uses the ORIGIN as one factor in determining the preferred route. It specifies one of the following origins:

- **IGP**—The Network Layer Reachability Information (NLRI) was learned from a protocol internal to the originating AS. An IGP origin gets the highest preference of the ORIGIN values. BGP routes are given an origin of IGP if they are learned from an IGP routing table via the **network** statement, as described in Chapter 3.

- **EGP**—The NLRI was learned from the Exterior Gateway Protocol. EGP is preferred second to IGP.

- **Incomplete**—The NLRI was learned by some other means. Incomplete is the lowest-preferred ORIGIN value. Incomplete does not imply that the route is in any way faulty, only that the information for determining the origin of the route is incomplete. Routes that BGP learns through redistribution carry the incomplete origin attribute, because there is no way to determine the original source of the route.

The AS_PATH Attribute

AS_PATH is a well-known mandatory attribute that uses a sequence of AS numbers to describe the inter-AS path, or route, to the destination specified by the NLRI. When a BGP speaker originates a route—when it advertises NLRI about a destination within its own AS—it adds its AS number to the AS_PATH. As subsequent BGP speakers advertise the route to external peers, they *prepend* their own AS numbers to the AS_PATH (see Figure 2-21). The result is that the AS_PATH describes all the autonomous systems it has passed through, beginning with the most recent AS and ending with the originating AS.

Figure 2-21 *AS Numbers Are Prepended (Added to the Front of) the AS_PATH*

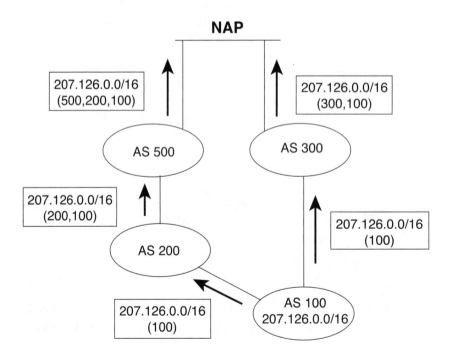

Note that a BGP router adds its AS number to the AS_PATH only when an Update is sent to a neighbor in another AS. That is, an AS number is prepended to the AS_PATH only when the route is being advertised between EBGP peers. If the route is being advertised between IBGP peers—peers within the same autonomous system—no AS number is added.

Usually, having multiple instances of the same AS number on the list would make no sense and would defeat the purpose of the AS_PATH attribute. In one case, however, adding multiple instances of a particular AS number to the AS_PATH proves useful. Remember that outgoing route advertisements directly influence incoming traffic. Normally, the route from the NAP to AS 100 in Figure 2-21 passes through AS 300 because the AS_PATH of that route is shorter. But what if the link to AS 200 is AS 100's preferred path for incoming traffic? The links along the (500,200,100) path might all be DS3, for example, whereas the links along the (300,100) path are only DS1. Or perhaps AS 200 is the primary provider, and AS 300 is only the backup provider. Outgoing traffic is sent to AS 200, so it is desired that incoming traffic follow the same path.

AS 100 can influence its incoming traffic by changing the AS_PATH of its advertised route (see Figure 2-22). By adding multiple instances of its own AS number to the list sent to AS 300, AS 100 can make routers at the NAP think that the (500,200,100) path is the shorter path. The procedure of adding extra AS numbers to the AS_PATH is called *AS path prepending.*

Figure 2-22 *AS 100 Has Begun the AS_PATH Advertised to AS 300 with Multiple Instances of Its Own AS Number*

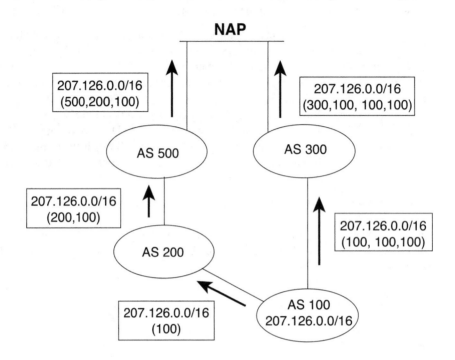

The other function of the AS_PATH attribute, as discussed earlier in the chapter, is loop avoidance. The mechanism is very simple: If a BGP router receives a route from an external peer whose AS_PATH includes its own AS number, the router knows that the route has looped. Such a route is dropped.

The NEXT_HOP Attribute

As the name implies, this well-known mandatory attribute describes the IP address of the next-hop router on the path to the advertised destination. The IP address described by the BGP NEXT_HOP attribute is not always the address of a neighboring router. The following rules apply:

- If the advertising router and receiving router are in different autonomous systems (external peers), the NEXT_HOP is the IP address of the advertising router's interface.

- If the advertising router and the receiving router are in the same AS (internal peers), and the NLRI of the update refers to a destination within the same AS, the NEXT_HOP is the IP address of the neighbor that advertised the route.

- If the advertising router and the receiving router are internal peers and the NLRI of the update refers to a destination in a different AS, the NEXT_HOP is the IP address of the external peer from which the route was learned.

Figure 2-23 illustrates the first rule. Here, the advertising router and receiving router are in different autonomous systems. The NEXT_HOP is the interface address of the external peer. So far, this behavior is the same as would be expected of any routing protocol.

Figure 2-23 *If a BGP Update Is Advertised via EBGP, the NEXT_HOP Attribute Is the IP Address of the External Peer*

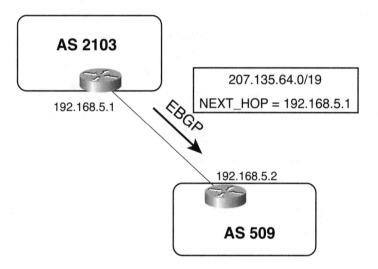

Figure 2-24 illustrates the second rule. This time, the advertising router and the receiving router are in the same AS, and the destination being advertised is also in the AS. The NEXT_HOP associated with the NLRI is the IP address of the originating router.

Figure 2-24   *If a BGP Update Is Advertised via IBGP, and the Advertised Destination Is in the Same AS, the*
NEXT_HOP Attribute Is the IP Address of the Originating Router

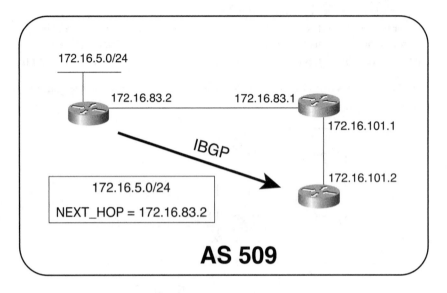

Notice that the advertising router and the receiving router do not share a common data link,
but the IBGP TCP connection is passed through an IGP-speaking router. This is discussed
in more detail in the section "Internal BGP"; for now, the important point is that the
receiving router must perform a recursive route lookup (recursive lookups are discussed in
Routing TCP/IP, Volume I) to send a packet to the advertised destination. First, it looks up
the destination 172.16.5.30; that route indicates a next hop of 172.16.83.2. Because that IP
address does not belong to one of the router's directly connected subnets, the router must
then look up the route to 172.16.83.2. That route, learned via the IGP, indicates a next hop
of 172.16.101.1. The packet can now be forwarded. This example is very important for
understanding the dependency of IBGP on the IGP.

Figure 2-25 illustrates the third rule. Here, a route has been learned via EBGP and is then
passed to an internal peer. Because the destination is in a different AS, the NEXT_HOP of
the route passed across the IBGP connection is the interface of the external router from
which the route was learned.

Figure 2-25 *If a BGP Update Is Advertised via IBGP, and the Advertised Destination Is in a Different AS, the NEXT_HOP Attribute Is the IP Address of the External Peer from Which the Route Was Learned*

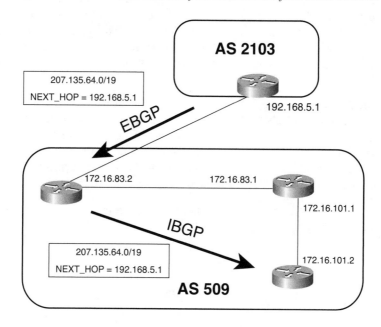

In Figure 2-25, the IBGP peer must perform a recursive route lookup to forward a packet to 207.135.64.0/19. However, a potential problem exists. The network 192.168.5.0, to which the next-hop address belongs, is not part of AS 509. Unless the AS border router advertises the network into AS 509, the IGP—and hence the internal peers—will not know about this network. And if the network is not in the routing tables, the next-hop address for 207.135.64.0/19 is unreachable, and packets for that destination are dropped. In fact, although the route to 207.135.64.0/19 is installed in the internal peer's BGP table, it is not installed in the IGP routing table, because the next-hop address is invalid for that router.

The first solution to the problem is, of course, to ensure that the external network linking the two autonomous systems is known to the internal routers. Although you could use static routes, the practical method is to run the IGP in passive mode on the external interfaces. In some cases, this might be undesirable. The second solution is to use a configuration option to cause the AS border router in AS 509 to set its own IP address in the NEXT_HOP attribute, in place of the IP address of the external peer. The internal peers would then have a next-hop router address of 172.16.83.2, which is known to the IGP. This configuration option, called **next-hop-self**, is demonstrated in Chapter 3.

The LOCAL_PREF Attribute

LOCAL_PREF is short for local preference. This well-known discretionary attribute is used only in updates between internal BGP peers; it is not passed to other autonomous systems. The attribute is used to communicate a BGP router's degree of preference for an advertised route. If an internal BGP speaker receives multiple routes to the same destination, it compares the LOCAL_PREF attributes of the routes. The route with the highest LOCAL_PREF is selected.

Figure 2-26 demonstrates how the LOCAL_PREF attribute is used. AS 2101 is taking routes from two ISPs, but ISP1 is the preferred service provider. The router connected to ISP1 advertises the routes from that provider with a LOCAL_PREF of 200, and the router connected to ISP2 advertises the routes from that provider with a LOCAL_PREF of 100 (the default value). All internal peers, including the router attached to ISP2, prefer the routes learned from ISP1 over routes to the same destinations learned from ISP2.

Figure 2-26 *The LOCAL_PREF Attribute Communicates a Degree of Preference to Internal Peers, with the Higher Value Preferred*

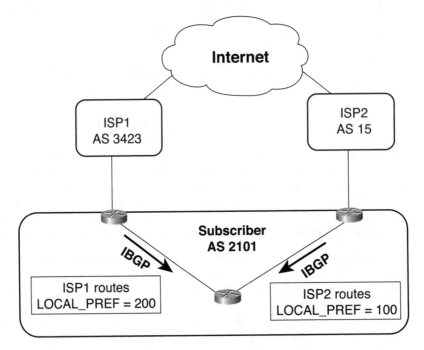

The MULTI_EXIT_DISC Attribute

The LOCAL_PREF attribute affects only traffic leaving the AS. To influence incoming traffic, the MULTI_EXIT_DISC attribute, known as the MED for short, is used. This optional nontransitive attribute is carried in EBGP updates and allows an AS to inform another AS of its preferred ingress points. If all else is equal, an AS receiving multiple routes to the same destination compare the MEDs of the routes. Unlike LOCAL_PREF, in which the largest value is preferred, the lowest MED value is preferred. This is because MED is considered a metric, and with a metric the lowest value—the lowest distance—is preferred.

NOTE   In BGP-2 and BGP-3, the MULTI_EXIT_DISC attribute is called the INTER_AS metric.

Figure 2-27 shows how you can use the MED. Here, a subscriber is dual-homed to a single ISP. AS 525 prefers that its incoming traffic use the DS-3 link, with the DS-1 link used only for backup. The MED in the updates passing across the DS-3 link is set to 0 (the default), and the MED in the updates passing across the DS-1 link is set to 100. If nothing else differs in the two routes, the ISP prefers the DS-3 link, with the lower MED.

Notice that within the ISP, IBGP is being used between the routers. The MEDs from AS 525 are passed between these internal peers so that they both know which route to prefer. However, MEDs are not passed beyond the receiving AS. If the ISP advertises 206.25.160.0/19 to another AS, for example, it does not pass along the MED set by the originating AS. This means that MEDs are used only to influence traffic between two directly connected autonomous systems; to influence route preferences beyond the neighboring AS, the AS_PATH attribute must be manipulated, as shown earlier in this section.

MEDs also are not compared if two routes to the same destination are received from two different autonomous systems. If the ISP in Figure 2-27 receives advertisements of 206.25.160.0/19 not only from AS 525 but also from another AS, for example, the MEDs from the two autonomous systems are not compared. MEDs are meant only for a single AS to demonstrate a degree of preference when it has multiple ingress points.

Figure 2-27   *The Lower MED Associated with Routes Passed Over the DS-3 Link Causes the ISP to Prefer This Link*

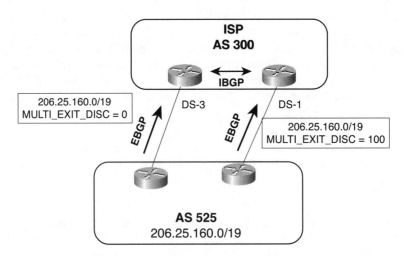

The ATOMIC_AGGREGATE and AGGREGATOR Attributes

A BGP-speaking router can transmit overlapping routes to another BGP speaker. Overlapping routes are nonidentical routes that point to the same destination. For example, the routes 206.25.192.0/19 and 206.25.128.0/17 are overlapping. The first route is included in the second route, although the second route also points to other more-specific routes besides 206.25.192.0/19.

When making a best-path decision, a router always chooses the more-specific path. When advertising routes, however, the BGP speaker has several options for dealing with overlapping routes:

- Advertise both the more-specific and the less-specific route
- Advertise only the more-specific route
- Advertise only the nonoverlapping part of the route
- Aggregate the two routes and advertise the aggregate
- Advertise the less-specific route only
- Advertise neither route

Earlier, this chapter emphasized that when summarization (route aggregation) is performed, some route information is lost and routing can become less precise. When aggregation is performed in a BGP-speaking router, the information that is lost is path detail. Figure 2-28 illustrates this loss of path detail.

Figure 2-28 *Aggregating BGP Routes Results in the Loss of Path Information*

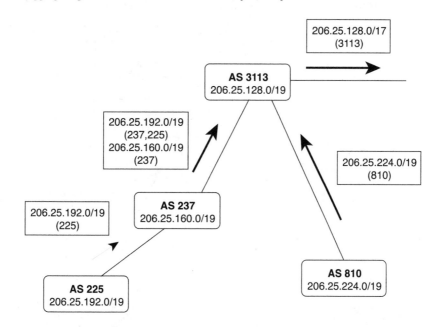

AS 3113 is advertising an aggregate address representing addresses in several autonomous systems. Because that AS is originating the aggregate, it includes only its own number in the AS_PATH. The path information to some of the more-specific prefixes represented by the aggregate is lost.

ATOMIC_AGGREGATE is a well-known discretionary attribute that is used to alert downstream routers that a loss of path information has occurred. Any time a BGP speaker summarizes more-specific routes into a less-specific aggregate (the fifth option in the preceding list), and path information is lost, the BGP speaker must attach the ATOMIC_AGGREGATE attribute to the aggregate route. Any downstream BGP speaker that receives a route with the ATOMIC_AGGREGATE attribute cannot make any NLRI information of that route more specific, and when advertising the route to other peers, the ATOMIC_AGGREGATE attribute must remain attached.

When the ATOMIC_AGGREGATE attribute is set, the BGP speaker has the option of also attaching the AGGREGATOR attribute. This optional transitive attribute provides information about where the aggregation was performed by including the AS number and the IP address of the router that originated the aggregate route (see Figure 2-29). Cisco's implementation of BGP inserts the BGP router ID as the IP address in the attribute.

Figure 2-29   *The ATOMIC_AGGREGATE Attribute Indicates That a Loss of Path Information Has Occurred, and the AGGREGATOR Attribute Indicates Where the Aggregation Occurred*

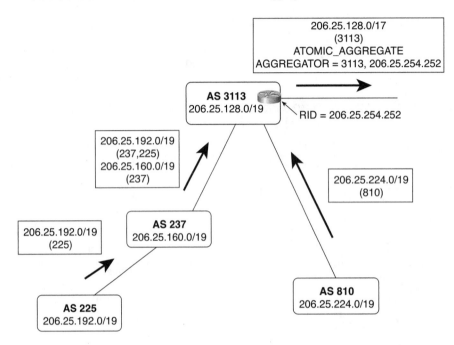

The COMMUNITY Attribute

COMMUNITY is an optional transitive attribute that is designed to simplify policy enforcement. Originally a Cisco-specific attribute, it is now standardized in RFC 1997[8]. The COMMUNITY attribute identifies a destination as a member of some community of destinations that share one or more common properties. For example, an ISP might assign a particular COMMUNITY attribute to all of its customers' routes. The ISP can then set its LOCAL_PREF and MED attributes based on the COMMUNITY value rather than on each individual route.

The COMMUNITY attribute is a set of four octet values. RFC 1997 specifies that the first two octets are the autonomous system and the last two octets are an administratively defined identifier, giving a format of AA:NN. The default Cisco format, on the other hand, is NN:AA. You can change this default to the RFC 1997 format with the command **ip bgp-community new-format**.

Suppose, for example, a route from AS 625 has a COMMUNITY identifier of 70. The COMMUNITY attribute, in the AA:NN format, is 625:70 and is represented in hex as a concatenation of the two numbers: 0x02710046, where 625 = 0x0271 and 70 = 0x0046. The RFCs use the hex representation, but COMMUNITY attribute values are represented on Cisco routers in decimal. For example, 625:70 is 40960070 (the decimal equivalent of 0x2710046).

The community values from 0 (0x00000000) to 65535 (0x0000FFFF) and from 4294901760 (0xFFFF0000) to 4294967295 (0xFFFFFFFF) are reserved. Out of this reserved range, several well-known communities are defined:

- **INTERNET**—The Internet community does not have a value; all routes belong to this community by default. Received routes belonging to this community are advertised freely.

- **NO_EXPORT (4294967041, or 0xFFFFFF01)**—Routes received carrying this value cannot be advertised to EBGP peers or, if a confederation is configured, the routes cannot be advertised outside of the confederation. (Confederations are defined in a later section, "Managing Large-Scale BGP Peering.")

- **NO_ADVERTISE (4294967042, or 0xFFFFFF02)**—Routes received carrying this value cannot be advertised at all, to either EBGP or IBGP peers.

- **LOCAL_AS (4294967043, or 0xFFFFFF03)**—RFC 1997 calls this attribute NO_EXPORT_SUBCONFED. Routes received carrying this value cannot be advertised to EBGP peers, including peers in other autonomous systems within a confederation.

Chapter 3 provides examples of using communities to help enforce routing policies.

The ORIGINATOR_ID and CLUSTER_LIST Attributes

ORIGINATOR_ID and CLUSTER_LIST are optional, nontransitive attributes used by route reflectors, which are described in the section " Managing Large-Scale BGP Peering." Both attributes are used to prevent routing loops. The ORIGINATOR_ID is a 32-bit value created by a route reflector. The value is the router ID of the originator of the route in the local AS. If the originator sees its RID in the ORIGINATOR_ID of a received route, it knows that a loop has occurred, and the route is ignored.

CLUSTER_LIST is a sequence of route reflection cluster IDs through which the route has passed. If a route reflector sees its local cluster ID in the CLUSTER_LIST of a received route, it knows that a loop has occurred, and the route is ignored.

Administrative Weight

Administrative weight is a Cisco-specific BGP parameter that applies only to routes within an individual router. It is not communicated to other routers. The weight is a number between 0 and 65,535 that can be assigned to a route; the higher the weight, the more preferable the route. When choosing a best path, the BGP decision process considers weight above all other route characteristics except specificity. By default, all routes learned from a peer have a weight of 0, and all routes generated by the local router have a weight of 32,768.

Administrative weights can be set for individual routes, or for routes learned from a specific neighbor. For example, peer A and peer B might be advertising the same routes to a BGP speaker. By assigning a higher weight to the routes received from peer A, the BGP speaker prefers the routes through that peer. This preference is entirely local to the single router; weights are not included in the BGP updates or in any other way communicated to the BGP speaker's peers.

AS_SET

The AS_PATH attribute has been presented so far as consisting of an ordered sequence of AS numbers that describes the path to a particular destination. There are actually two types of AS_PATH:

- **AS_SEQUENCE**—This is the ordered list of AS numbers, as previously described.
- **AS_SET**—This is an unordered list of the AS numbers along a path to a destination.

These two types are distinguished in the AS_PATH attribute with a type code, as described in the section "BGP Message Formats."

NOTE   There are, in fact, four types of AS_PATH. See the section "Confederations" for details on the other two types: AS_CONFED_SEQUENCE and AS_CONFED_SET.

Recall that one of the major benefits of the AS_PATH is loop prevention. If a BGP speaker sees its own AS number in a received route from an external peer, it knows that a loop has occurred and ignores the route. When aggregation is performed, however, as in Figure 2-28, some AS_PATH detail is lost. As a result, the potential for a loop increases.

Suppose, for example, AS 810 in Figure 2-28 has an alternate connection to another AS (see Figure 2-30). The aggregate from AS 3113 is advertised to AS 6571, and from there back to AS 810.

Because the AS numbers "behind" the aggregation point are not included in the AS_PATH, AS 810 does not detect the potential loop. Next, suppose a network within AS 810, such as 206.25.225.0/24, fails. The routers within that AS will match the aggregate route from AS 6571, and a loop occurs.

Figure 2-30 *The Loss of Path Detail When Aggregating Can Cause Inter-AS Routing Loops*

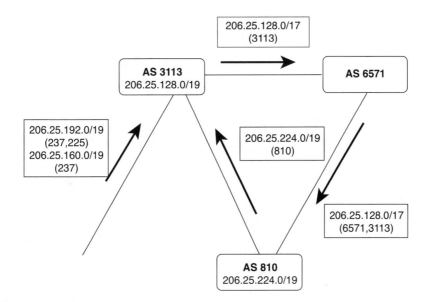

If you think about it, the loop-prevention function of the AS_PATH does not require that the AS numbers be included in any particular order. All that is necessary is that a receiving router be able to recognize whether its own AS number is a part of the AS_PATH. This is where AS_SET comes in.

When a BGP speaker creates an aggregate from NLRI learned from other autonomous systems, it can include all those AS numbers in the AS_PATH as an AS_SET. For example, Figure 2-31 shows the network of Figure 2-28 with an AS_SET added to the aggregate route.

The aggregating router still begins an AS_SEQUENCE, so receiving routers can trace the path back to the aggregator, but an AS_SET is included to prevent routing loops. In this example, you also can see why the AS_SET is an unordered list. Behind the aggregator in AS 3113 are branching paths to the autonomous systems in which the aggregated routes reside. There is no way for an ordered list to describe these separate paths.

When an AS_SET is included in an AS_PATH, the ATOMIC_AGGREGATE does not have to be included with the aggregate. The AS_SET serves to notify downstream routers that aggregation has occurred and includes more information than the ATOMIC_AGGREGATE.

Figure 2-31 *Including an AS_SET in the AS_PATH of an Aggregate Route Restores the Loop Avoidance That Was Lost in the Aggregation*

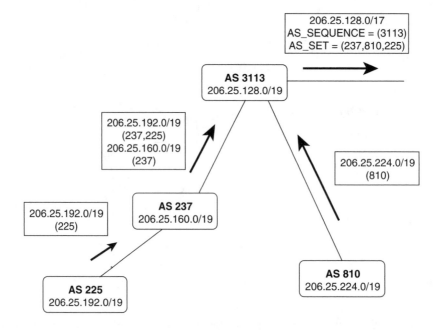

Like most options in life, AS_SET involves a trade-off. You already understand that one of the advantages of route summarization is route stability. If a network that belongs to the aggregate fails, the failure is not advertised beyond the aggregation point. If an AS_SET is included with the aggregate's AS_PATH, this stability is reduced. If the link to AS 225 in Figure 2-31 fails, for example, the AS_SET changes; this change is advertised beyond the aggregation point.

The BGP Decision Process

The BGP Routing Information Database (RIB) consists of three parts:

- **Adj-RIBs-In**—Stores unprocessed routing information that has been learned from updates received from peers. The routes contained in Adj-RIBs-In are considered feasible routes.

- **Loc-RIB**—Contains the routes that the BGP speaker has selected by applying its local routing policies to the routes contained in Adj-RIBs-In.

- **Adj-RIBs-Out**—Contains the routes that the BGP speaker advertises to its peers.

These three parts of the Routing Information Database may be three distinct databases, or the RIB may be a single database with pointers to distinguish the three parts.

The BGP decision process selects routes by applying local routing policies to the routes in the Adj-RIBs-In and by entering the selected or modified routes into the Loc-RIB and Adj-RIBs-Out. The decision process entails three phases:

- Phase 1 calculates the degree of preference for each feasible route. It is invoked whenever a router receives a BGP Update from a peer in a neighboring AS containing a new route, a changed route, or a withdrawn route. Each route is considered separately, and a nonnegative integer is derived that indicates the degree of preference for that route.

- Phase 2 chooses the best route out of all the available routes to a particular destination and installs the route in the Loc-RIB. It is invoked only after phase 1 has been completed.

- Phase 3 adds the appropriate routes to the Adj-RIBs-Out for advertisement to peers. It is invoked after the Loc-RIB has changed, and only after phase 2 has been completed. Route aggregation, if it is to be performed, happens during this phase.

Barring a routing policy that dictates otherwise, phase 2 always selects the most specific route to a particular destination out of all feasible routes to that destination. It is important to note that if the address specified by the route's NEXT_HOP attribute is unreachable, the route is not selected. This fact has particular ramifications for internal BGP, as described in the section "IBGP and IGP Synchronization."

You should have an appreciation by now of the multiple attributes that can be assigned to a BGP route to enforce routing policy within a single router, to internal peers, to adjacent autonomous systems, and beyond. A sequence and rules are needed for considering these attributes, especially when a router must select among multiple, equally specific routes to the same destination. The following criteria are used to break ties:

1 Prefer the route with the highest administrative weight. This is a Cisco-specific function, because BGP administrative weight is a Cisco parameter.

2 If the weights are equal, prefer the route with the highest LOCAL_PREF value.

3 If the LOCAL_PREF values are the same, prefer the route that was originated locally on the router. That is, prefer a route that was learned from an IGP on the same router.

4 If the LOCAL_PREF is the same, and no route was locally originated, prefer the route with the shortest AS_PATH.

5 If the AS_PATH length is the same, prefer the path with the lowest origin code. IGP is lower than EGP, which is lower than Incomplete.

6 If the origin codes are the same, prefer the route with the lowest MULTI_EXIT_DISC value. This comparison is done only if the AS number is the same for all the routes being considered.

7 If the MED is the same, prefer EBGP routes over confederation EBGP routes, and prefer confederation EBGP routes over IBGP routes.

8   If the routes are still equal, prefer the route with the shortest path to the BGP NEXT_HOP. This is the route with the lowest IGP metric to the next-hop router.

9   If the routes are still equal, they are from the same neighboring AS, and BGP multipath is enabled with the **maximum-paths** command, install all the equal-cost routes in the Loc-RIB.

10   If multipath is not enabled, prefer the route with the lowest BGP router ID.

Route Dampening

Route flaps are a leading contributor to instability on the Internet—and, for that matter on any internetwork. Flaps occur when a valid route is declared invalid and then declared valid again. The problem is evident: Every time the state of a route changes, the change must be advertised throughout the internetwork, and each router must make the appropriate recalculations. Both bandwidth and CPU resources are consumed.

NOTE

You might occasionally hear the term *route oscillation* used interchangeably with *route flapping,* but the terms differ. Oscillations are periodic; flaps are not.

Most people quickly name unstable physical links or failing router interfaces as leading causes of route flapping, and they are right. But another common cause of route flaps, possibly the most common of all, is humans. Technicians tinkering in the telco central office or in your wiring closet can certainly cause outages leading to flaps, but don't forget the inexperienced network administrator innocently configuring or troubleshooting his router. Perhaps he is repeatedly adding and deleting a route, changing the state of an interface, or clearing a BGP session. If the resulting route changes are communicated to his ISP, his careless work can affect the entire Internet.

How bad can the effects of an instability be? Consider a single somewhat overloaded or underpowered BGP router. An upstream connection becomes unstable, causing many routes to flap simultaneously. The router cannot handle the changes, and it fails. Now downstream routers have to process not only the original flapping routes, but also all the now-unreachable routes originated from the failed router. The effects can snowball, cascading throughout the internetwork, possibly causing more routers to fail. It is not pretty.

You already have seen how route aggregation helps to hide instabilities. If a member route of the aggregate fails, the aggregate itself does not change. Packets destined for the failed route continue to be forwarded to the aggregate address; the originator of the aggregate has knowledge of the invalid route and drops the packets.

But aggregation is not always possible. For instance, an ISP's subscriber might have a provider-independent IP address. Because the address is outside of the provider's address block, the subscriber's address must be advertised independently of the provider's aggregate. And as you learned in the discussion on multihoming, aggregation also cannot be used when a subscriber is multihomed to multiple providers.

Even if an ISP can provide a stable route to the rest of the Internet by aggregating its subscribers' routes, the aggregate does not contribute to stability within the ISP's own AS. A route flap still affects all routers behind the aggregation point.

Route dampening is a method created to stop unstable routes from being forwarded throughout an internetwork. It does not prevent a router from accepting unstable routes, but it does prevent it from forwarding them. Although route dampening has been around for some time, it has only recently been formalized in an RFC, RFC 2439 (www.isi.edu/in-notes/tr.rfc2439.txt).

A router using route dampening assigns to each route a dynamic figure of merit that reflects the route's degree of stability. When a route flaps, it is assigned a *penalty*; the more it flaps, the more penalties accumulate. There is also a time period called the *half-life*. The penalty is decreased at a rate that reduces it to half at the end of each half-life. If the penalty value exceeds a predefined threshold, known as the *suppress limit*, the route is suppressed—that is, it is no longer advertised. The route continues to be suppressed until the half-life reduces the penalties to less than another threshold called the *reuse limit*. At that time, the route is advertised again. Alternatively, the route's penalties can be manually cleared; such a clearing proves useful in cases in which the instability has been rectified and immediate reuse of the route is required.

Unless the suppress limit is set unusually low, a single flap does not cause the route to be suppressed. The half-life eventually reduces the penalty to zero. If a route flaps enough for its penalties to increase faster than the half-life reduces them, however, it will exceed the suppress limit. Although penalties can continue to accumulate while the route is suppressed, the route cannot be suppressed beyond a period known as the *maximum suppress limit*. This ensures that a route that has flapped perhaps dozens of times in a short period does not accumulate such a high penalty that it remains suppressed indefinitely.

The Cisco defaults for the various route-dampening variables are as follows:

- **Penalty**—1000 per flap
- **Suppress limit**—2000
- **Reuse limit**—750
- **Half-life**—15 minutes
- **Maximum suppress time**—60 minutes, or 4 times the half-life

Examples of configuring and using route dampening on Cisco routers are found in the case study "Route Dampening" in Chapter 3.

IBGP and IGP Synchronization

With very few exceptions, interior BGP—BGP between peers in the same AS—is used only in multihomed scenarios. IBGP allows edge routers to share NLRI and associated attributes, to enforce a systemwide routing policy. IBGP also is the means by which an edge router in a transit AS passes routes learned from an external peer to other edge routers for advertisement to their external peers.

You might be tempted to think that in some cases IBGP could be used as an IGP. For instance, an ISP's AS is mostly connected to other autonomous systems by EBGP, and mostly carries transit traffic. Why not run IBGP only within the AS, and have a single consistent routing protocol? The problem is that for full connectivity, every IBGP router must peer with every other IBGP router—that is, the IBGP internetwork must be *fully meshed*. This section explains why an IGP is necessary to support IBGP and why synchronization between IGP and IBGP is important. Fully meshed IBGP is used for two reasons:

- To prevent BGP routing loops within an AS
- To ensure that all routers along the path of a BGP route know how to forward packets to the destination

When routes are advertised via IBGP, they are by definition advertised within the same AS. As a result, the AS_PATH does not change. In fact, the local AS number is not added to the AS_PATH until the route is advertised to an EBGP peer. As a result, the IBGP routes do not have the loop protection that EBGP routes have. To protect against loops, BGP does not advertise routes that have been learned from an IBGP peer to another IBGP peer.

Figure 2-32 illustrates what happens when IBGP peers are not fully meshed. Here, IBGP peering sessions have been configured between Seattle and Tacoma and between Tacoma and Spokane. You can see that Seattle and Tacoma are exchanging NLRI about their local networks, as are Spokane and Tacoma. But Seattle and Spokane are not learning each other's NLRI.

Figure 2-33 shows how full reachability is achieved by creating fully meshed IBGP peers. Note that Seattle and Spokane are peers, even though no direct data link exists between them. The TCP session that BGP uses passes through Tacoma but is logically a point-to-point session between Seattle and Spokane. This is an important point, because for the TCP session to be established, Seattle and Spokane must have knowledge of the addresses of the data links interconnecting them.

Figure 2-32 *In a Partially Meshed IBGP Environment, Full NLRI Is Not Advertised, Because Routes Learned from One IBGP Peer Are Not Forwarded to Another IBGP Peer*

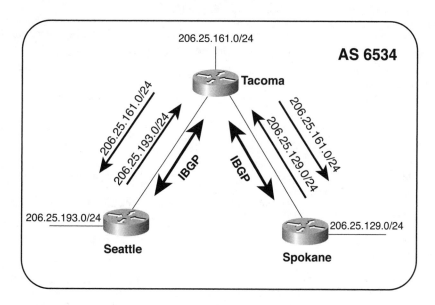

Figure 2-33 *In a Fully Meshed IBGP Environment, Every IBGP Router Is Peered with Every Other IBGP Router, and Full NLRI Is Exchanged*

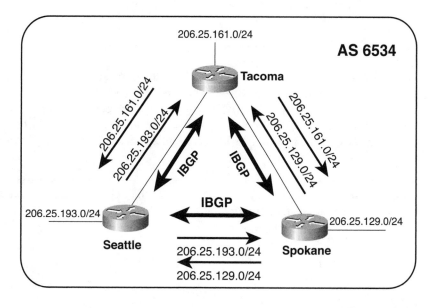

At first, ensuring that the data link addresses are known seems simple enough—the addresses at each router must be included in the BGP **network** statements (discussed in Chapter 3). However, it is not always that simple.

Example 2-14 shows Seattle's BGP routing table and its IGP routing table. For the router to forward packets, the destination must be in the IGP routing table.

Example 2-14 *Although Several Routes Exist in the BGP Routing Table, They Are Not Automatically Entered into the Router's IGP Routing Table*

```
Seattle#show ip bgp
BGP table version is 7, local router ID is 206.25.193.1
Status codes: s suppressed, * valid, > best, i - internal
Origin codes: i - IGP, e - EGP, ? - incomplete

   Network          Next Hop        Metric LocPrf Weight Path
*> 192.168.1.0      0.0.0.0              0         32768 i
*  i                192.168.1.1          0    100      0 i
*>i192.168.2.0      192.168.1.1          0    100      0 i
*>i206.25.161.0     192.168.1.1          0    100      0 i
*> 206.25.193.0     0.0.0.0              0         32768 i

Seattle#show ip route
Codes: C - connected, S - static, I - IGRP, R - RIP, M - mobile, B - BGP
       D - EIGRP, EX - EIGRP external, O - OSPF, IA - OSPF inter area
       E1 - OSPF external type 1, E2 - OSPF external type 2, E - EGP
       i - IS-IS, L1 - IS-IS level-1, L2 - IS-IS level-2, * - candidate default

Gateway of last resort is not set

C    206.25.193.0 is directly connected, Loopback0
C    192.168.1.0 is directly connected, Serial0
Seattle#
```

As you can see from the output in Example 2-14, the BGP table contains several routes, including the addresses of the Seattle-Tacoma and Spokane-Tacoma data links (192.168.1.0/24 and 192.168.2.0/24). But only Seattle's directly connected links are entered in the IGP routing table. Notice also that Spokane's network 206.25.129.0/24 is not even in the BGP table, indicating that Seattle and Spokane are not peering correctly.

NOTE Notice the weight of the directly connected links in the BGP table as compared to the weights of the routes learned from Tacoma.

Example 2-14 illustrates the problem of *synchronization*. The rule of synchronization states the following:

> Before a route learned from an IBGP neighbor is entered into the IGP routing table or is advertised to a BGP peer, the route must first be known via IGP.

In the internetwork of Figure 2-33, the BGP routes cannot be entered into the IGP routing table because no IGP is running on the routers, and synchronization requires that the routes be known via IGP before they can be entered.

To understand why the rule of synchronization exists, consider the network shown in Figure 2-34. In this case, IBGP is not used as the interior gateway protocol. Instead, a legitimate IGP (OSPF) is used. Salt Lake and Provo are connected to two separate autonomous systems, and they advertise the EBGP-learned routes with each other over an IBGP connection. The TCP session for this IBGP connection passes through Orem and Ogden.

Figure 2-34 *This Internetwork Runs Partially-Meshed IBGP Between Salt Lake and Provo and Uses OSPF as Its IGP*

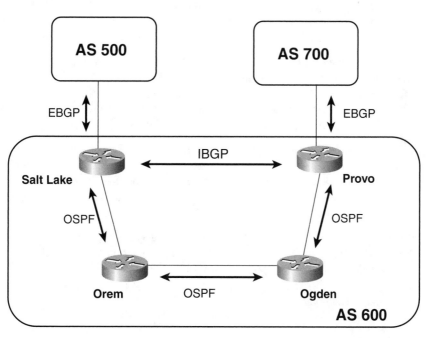

Next, suppose Salt Lake learns a route to 196.223.18.0/24 from AS 500 and advertises the route over the IBGP connection to Provo, using a next-hop-self policy to change the NEXT_HOP attribute to its own router ID. Provo then advertises the route to AS 700. Routers in AS 700 now begin forwarding packets destined for 196.223.18.0/24 to Provo. (Remember that a route advertisement is a promise to deliver packets.) Here is where things go wrong. Provo does a route lookup for 196.223.18.0/24 and sees that the network is reachable via Salt Lake. It then does a lookup for Salt Lake's IP address and sees that it is reachable via the next-hop router, Ogden. So the packet destined for 196.223.18.0/24 is forwarded to Ogden. But the external routes are shared between Salt Lake and Provo via IBGP; the OSPF routers have no knowledge of the external routes. Therefore, when the packet is forwarded to Ogden, that router does a route lookup and does not find an entry for 196.223.18.0/24. The router drops the packet and all subsequent packets for that address. Traffic for the network 196.223.18.0/24 is black-holed.

Of course, if the OSPF routers in Figure 2-34 know about the external routes, the situation just described will not happen. Ogden will know that 196.223.18.0/24 is reachable via Salt Lake and will forward the packet correctly. Synchronization prevents packets from being black-holed within a transit AS by an IGP with insufficient information.

When Provo receives the advertisement for 196.223.18.0/24 from Salt Lake, it adds the route to its BGP table. It then checks its IGP routing table to see whether an entry exists for the route. If not, Provo knows that the route is unknown to the IGP, and it cannot advertise the route. If and when the IGP makes an entry in the routing table for 196.223.18.0/24 (that is, when the IGP knows of the route), Provo's BGP route is synchronized with the IGP route, and the router is free to begin advertising the route to its BGP peers.

Returning to the example of Figure 2-33 and Example 2-14, you can now see why synchronization is preventing the fully meshed IBGP from working properly. Tacoma is stuck in a Catch-22. It is receiving routes from Seattle and Spokane, but it cannot enter the routes in its IGP routing table or advertise them, because the routes are not in the IGP routing table already. There is no IGP to put them there.

Synchronization is a somewhat antiquated feature of BGP that assumes redistribution of routes into the IGP. As this example shows, however, with fully meshed IBGP, all routers can know all necessary BGP routes through BGP alone. Synchronization, in this case, stands in the way of keeping BGP routes within BGP and using IGP only for establishing IBGP connectivity.

Luckily, Cisco routers have the option of disabling synchronization. Example 2-15 shows Seattle's BGP and IGP routing tables after synchronization is turned off. Tacoma has forwarded the routes from Spokane, and packets are forwarded correctly.

Example 2-15 *Seattle Has Full NLRI In Its BGP and IGP Routing Tables After Synchronization Is Disabled on the Three Routers Shown in Figure 2-33*

```
Seattle#show ip bgp
BGP table version is 11, local router ID is 206.25.193.1
Status codes: s suppressed, * valid, > best, i - internal
Origin codes: i - IGP, e - EGP, ? - incomplete

   Network          Next Hop          Metric LocPrf Weight Path
*> 192.168.1.0      0.0.0.0                0         32768 i
```

continues

Example 2-15 *Seattle Has Full NLRI In Its BGP and IGP Routing Tables After Synchronization Is Disabled on the Three Routers Shown in Figure 2-33 (Continued)*

```
* i                    192.168.1.1          0    100      0 i
*>i192.168.2.0         192.168.1.1          0    100      0 i
* i                    192.168.2.1          0    100      0 i
*>i206.25.129.0        192.168.2.1          0    100      0 i
*>i206.25.161.0        192.168.1.1          0    100      0 i
*> 206.25.193.0        0.0.0.0              0           32768 i

Seattle#show ip route
Codes: C - connected, S - static, I - IGRP, R - RIP, M - mobile, B - BGP
       D - EIGRP, EX - EIGRP external, O - OSPF, IA - OSPF inter area
       E1 - OSPF external type 1, E2 - OSPF external type 2, E - EGP
       i - IS-IS, L1 - IS-IS level-1, L2 - IS-IS level-2, * - candidate default

Gateway of last resort is not set

C    206.25.193.0 is directly connected, Loopback0
B    206.25.129.0 [200/0] via 192.168.2.1, 00:07:34
C    192.168.1.0 is directly connected, Serial0
B    192.168.2.0 [200/0] via 192.168.1.1, 00:07:42
B    206.25.161.0 [200/0] via 192.168.1.1, 00:07:43

Seattle#ping 206.25.129.1
Type escape sequence to abort.
Sending 5, 100-byte ICMP Echos to 206.25.129.1, timeout is 2 seconds:
!!!!!
Success rate is 100 percent (5/5), round-trip min/avg/max = 4/5/8 ms
Seattle#
```

The moral of the story is that for IBGP to work correctly, one of two configuration options must be performed:

- The external routes must be redistributed into the IGP to ensure that the IGP can synchronize with BGP. The drawback to this approach is that if you are taking a large number of routes from BGP, such as a full Internet routing table, you are placing a huge processing and memory burden on the IGP routers. In the majority of cases, routers cannot handle this burden and will fail. In fact, several large-scale outages have resulted from full BGP routes being inadvertently redistributed into OSPF or IS-IS. In one incident, a major provider was down for 19 hours.

- The IBGP routers must be fully meshed, and synchronization must be disabled. Every router then has knowledge of the external routes via BGP, and disabling synchronization allows the routes to be entered into the routing table without having to first inform the IGP. The drawback to this approach is that in an AS where there are more than a few IBGP routers, peering every router with every other router becomes an administrative challenge. Nonetheless, this is the approach that is almost always used when dealing with Internet routes. Two tools for controlling the full IBGP mesh requirement, route reflectors and confederations, are presented in the next section.

Chapter 3 offers several examples of IBGP configurations. It also revisits the drawbacks to the two configuration options and demonstrates some partial solutions to them.

Managing Large-Scale BGP Peering

The preceding section pointed out that when an AS becomes large, attempting to create fully meshed IBGP peers can be daunting. This is just one of the problems that emerges when you attempt to work with BGP on a large scale. BGP features four tools that can simplify the management of large numbers of BGP peers:

- Peer groups
- Communities
- Route reflectors
- Confederations

The first two tools help simplify the management of routing policies between multiple peers, either internal or external. The second two tools simplify the management of IBGP among large numbers of peers.

Peer Groups

Often in large BGP internetworks, policies on a router apply to multiple peers. The same attributes might be set in the updates going to several peers, for example, or the same filter might be used on routes coming from several peers. In such cases, you can simplify configuration and management by adding peers that share common policies to a *peer group*.

A peer group is defined on a Cisco router with a name and a set of routing policies. Peers are then added to the peer group. Any changes that must be made to the policies can then be made for the group rather than for each individual peer. Peer groups also prove useful for improving performance on a router. Instead of repeatedly consulting the policy database for each update sent to each peer, the router can consult the policy database once, create a single update, and then send copies of it to all the peers in the group.

At times, additional policies might apply to one or more members of a peer group. In such a case, you can apply the additional policies to the appropriate neighbors in addition to the common policies of the group.

Communities

Whereas peer groups apply policies to a group of routers, communities apply policies to a group of routes. A router adds a route to a preconfigured community by setting its COMMUNITY attribute to some value that identifies it as a member of the community. Neighboring routers can then apply their policies, such as filtering or redistribution policies, to the routes based on the value of the COMMUNITY attribute. The COMMUNITY attribute, which can be set to a well-known value or to some value defined by the network administrator, is described more fully in the section "The COMMUNITY Attribute," earlier in this chapter.

You can set more than one COMMUNITY attribute for a single route. A router receiving a route with multiple COMMUNITY attributes has the option of setting policies based on all those attributes or on some subset of the attributes. When routes containing COMMUNITY attributes are aggregated, the aggregate inherits all the COMMUNITY attributes of all the routes.

Route Reflectors

Route reflectors are useful when an AS contains a large number of IBGP peers. (For more information, see RFC 1966 at www.isuedu/in-notes/rfc1771.txt.) Unless EBGP routes are redistributed into the autonomous system's IGP, all IBGP peers must be fully meshed. For every *n* routers, there will be $n(n - 1)/2$ IBGP connections in the AS. For example, Figure 2-35 shows six fully meshed IBGP routers, hardly a large number of routers; even here, however, 15 IBGP connections are needed.

Figure 2-35 *Fully Meshed IBGP Peers*

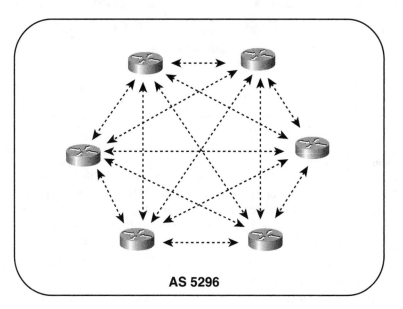

AS 5296

Route reflectors offer an alternative to fully meshed IBGP peers. A router is configured as a route reflector (RR), and other IBGP routers, known as *clients*, peer with the RR only, rather than with every other IBGP router (see Figure 2-36). As a result, the number of peering sessions is reduced from $n(n-1)/2$ to $n-1$. A router reflector and its clients are known collectively as a *cluster.*

Figure 2-36 *IBGP Clients in a Route Reflection Cluster Peer Only with the Route Reflector, Reducing the Number of Necessary IBGP Connections*

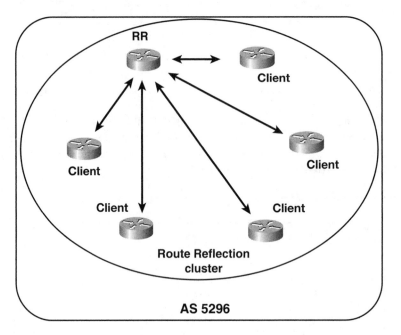

Route reflectors work by relaxing the rule that IBGP peers cannot advertise routes learned from other IBGP peers. In the internetwork of Figure 2-36, for example, the route reflector learns routes from each of its clients. Unlike other IBGP routers, the RR can advertise these routes to its other clients and to nonclient peers. In other words, the routes from one IBGP client are reflected from the RR to the other clients. To avoid possible routing loops or other routing errors, the route reflector cannot change the attributes of the routes it receives from clients.

A client router in a route reflection cluster can peer with external neighbors, but the only internal neighbor it can peer with is a route reflector in its cluster or other clients in the cluster. However, the RR itself can peer with both internal and external neighbors outside of the cluster and can reflect their routes to its clients (see Figure 2-37).

Figure 2-37 *Route Reflection Cluster Peering Relationships*

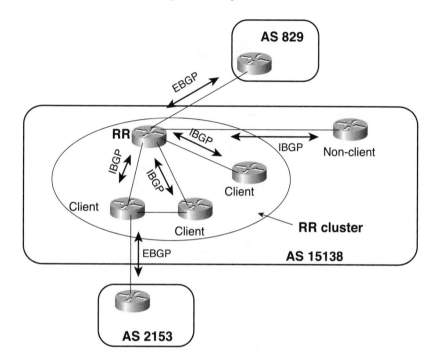

If an RR receives multiple routes to the same destination, it uses the normal BGP decision process to select the best path. RFC 1966 defines three rules that the RR uses to determine who the route is advertised to, depending on how the route was learned:

- If the route was learned from a nonclient IBGP peer, it is reflected to clients only.

- If the route was learned from a client, it is reflected to all nonclients and clients, except for the originating client.

- If the route was learned from an EBGP peer, it is reflected to all clients and nonclients.

The route reflector functionality has to be supported only on the route reflector itself. From the clients' perspectives, they are merely peering with an internal neighbor. This is an attractive feature of route reflectors, because routers with relatively basic BGP implementations can still be clients in a route reflection cluster.

The concept of route reflectors is similar to that of route servers, discussed earlier in this chapter. The primary purpose of both devices is to reduce the number of required peering sessions by providing a single peering point for multiple neighbors. The neighbors then depend on the one device to learn their routes. The difference between route reflectors and route servers is that route reflectors are also routers, whereas route servers are not.

A single RR, like a single route server, introduces a single point of failure into a system. If the RR fails, the clients lose their only source of NLRI. Therefore, for redundancy, a cluster can have more than one RR (see Figure 2-38). The clients have physical connections to each of the route reflectors, and they peer to each. If one of the RRs fails, the clients still have a connection to the other RR and do not lose reachability information.

Figure 2-38 *A Cluster Can Have Multiple Route Reflectors for Redundancy*

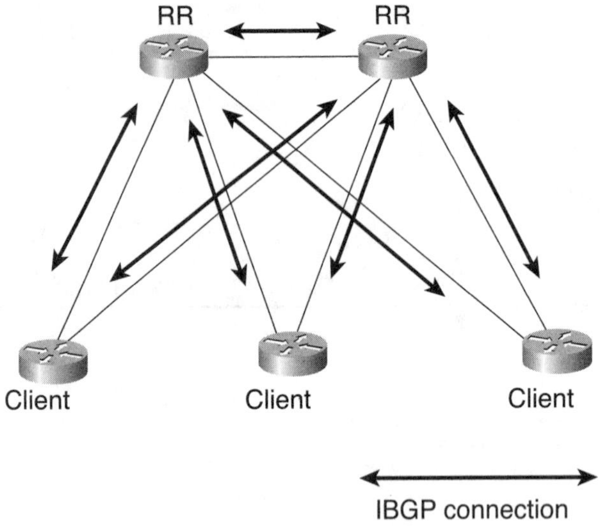

NOTE Although it is possible for a client to have a physical link to only one RR and still peer to multiple RRs, this setup defeats the purpose of having redundancy. The client is still vulnerable to the failure of the single RR to which it is physically connected.

An AS also can have multiple clusters. Figure 2-39 shows an AS with two clusters. Each cluster has redundant route reflectors, and the clusters themselves are interconnected redundantly.

Because clients do not know they are clients, a route reflector can itself be a client of another route reflector. As a result, you can build "nested" route reflection clusters (see Figure 2-40).

Figure 2-39 *Multiple Route Reflection Clusters Can Be Created Within a Single Autonomous System*

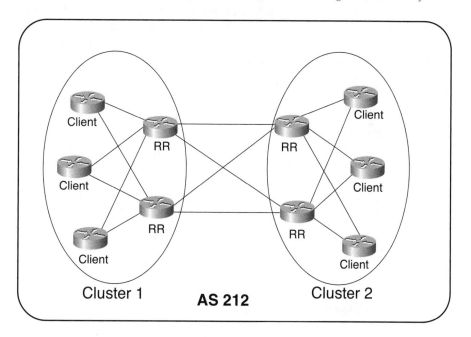

Figure 2-40 *A Route Reflector Can Be the Client of Another Route Reflector*

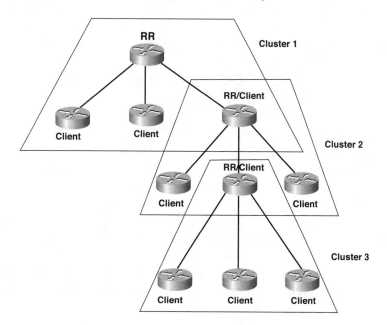

Although clients cannot peer with routers outside of their own cluster, they can peer with each other. As a result, a route reflection cluster can be fully meshed (see Figure 2-41). When the clients are fully meshed, the route reflector is configured so that it does not reflect routes from one client to another. Instead, it reflects only routes from clients to its nonclient peers, and routes from nonclient peers to clients.

Figure 2-41 *A Route Reflection Cluster Can Be Fully Meshed*

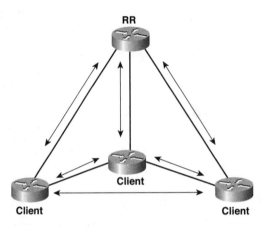

Recall from the discussion in the section "IBGP and IGP Synchronization" that BGP cannot forward a route learned from one internal peer to another internal peer, because the AS_PATH attribute does not change within an AS, and routing loops could result. Note, however, that a route reflector is a BGP router in which this rule has been relaxed. To prevent routing loops, route reflectors use two BGP path attributes: ORIGINATOR_ID and CLUSTER_LIST.

ORIGINATOR_ID is an optional, nontransitive attribute that is created by the route reflector. The ORIGINATOR_ID is the router ID of the originator of a route within the local AS. A route reflector does not advertise a route back to the originator of the route; nonetheless, if the originator receives an update with its own RID, the update is ignored.

Each cluster within an AS must be identified with a unique 4-octet *cluster ID*. If the cluster contains a single route reflector, the cluster ID is the router ID of the route reflector. If the cluster contains multiple route reflectors, each RR must be manually configured with a cluster ID.

CLUSTER_LIST is an optional, nontransitive attribute that tracks cluster IDs the same way that the AS_PATH attribute tracks AS numbers. When an RR reflects a route from a client to a nonclient, it appends its cluster ID to the CLUSTER_LIST. If the CLUSTER_LIST is empty, the RR creates one. When an RR receives an update, it checks the CLUSTER_LIST. If it sees its own cluster ID in the list, it knows that a routing loop has occurred and ignores the update.

Confederations

Confederations are another way to control large numbers of IBGP peers. A confederation is an AS that has been subdivided into a group of subautonomous systems, known as *member autonomous systems* (see Figure 2-42). The BGP speakers within the confederation speak IBGP to peers in the same member AS and EBGP to peers in other member autonomous systems. The confederation is assigned a *confederation ID*, which is represented to peers outside of the confederation as the AS number of the entire confederation. External peers do not see the internal structure of the confederation; rather, they see a single AS. In Figure 2-42, AS 9184 is the confederation ID.

Figure 2-42 *A Typical Confederation*

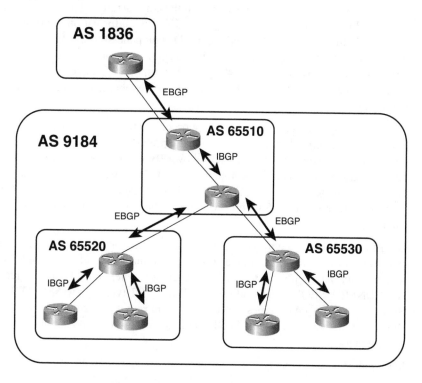

You are very familiar with the concept of subdividing entities for better manageability. IP subnets are subdivisions of IP networks, and VLSM subdivides subnets. Similarly, autonomous systems are subdivisions of large internetworks (such as the Internet). Confederations are subdivisions of autonomous systems.

The section "AS_SET" described two types of AS_PATH attributes: AS_SEQUENCE and AS_SET. Confederations add two more types to the AS_PATH:

- **AS_CONFED_SEQUENCE**—This is an ordered list of AS numbers along a path to a destination. It is used in exactly the same way as the AS_SEQUENCE, except that the AS numbers in the list belong to autonomous systems within the local confederation.

- **AS_CONFED_SET**—This is an unordered list of AS numbers along a path to a destination. It is used in exactly the same way as the AS_SET, except that the AS numbers in the list belong to autonomous systems within the local confederation.

Because the AS_PATH attribute is used in updates between the member autonomous systems, loop avoidance is preserved. From the perspective of a BGP router within a member AS, all peers in other member autonomous systems are external neighbors.

When an update is sent to a peer external to the confederation, the AS_CONFED_SEQUENCE and AS_CONFED_SET information is stripped from the AS_PATH attribute, and the confederation ID is prepended to the AS_PATH. Because of this, external peers see the confederation as a single AS rather than as a collection of autonomous systems. As Figure 2-42 shows, it is common practice to use AS numbers from the reserved range 64512 to 65535 to number the member autonomous systems within a confederation.

When choosing a route, the BGP decision process remains the same, with one addition: EBGP routes external to the confederation are preferred over EBGP routes to member autonomous systems, which are preferred over IBGP routes. Another difference between confederations and standard autonomous systems is the way in which some attributes are handled. Attributes such as NEXT_HOP and MED can be advertised unchanged to EBGP peers in another member AS within the confederation, and the LOCAL_PREF attribute also can be sent.

Unlike route reflector environments in which only the route reflector itself has to support route reflection, all routers within a confederation must support the confederation functionality. This support is necessary because all routers must be able to recognize the AS_CONFED_SEQUENCE and AS_CONFED_SET types in the AS_PATH attribute. Because these AS_PATH types are removed from routes advertised out of the confederation, however, routers in other autonomous systems do not have to support confederations.

In very large autonomous systems, you can use confederations and route reflectors together. You can configure one or more RR clusters within one or more member autonomous systems for even more optimal control of IBGP peers.

BGP Message Formats

BGP messages are carried within TCP segments using TCP port 179. The maximum message size is 4096 octets, and the minimum size is 19 octets. All BGP messages have a common header (see Figure 2-43). Depending on the message type, a data portion might or might not follow the header.

Figure 2-43 *The BGP Message Header*

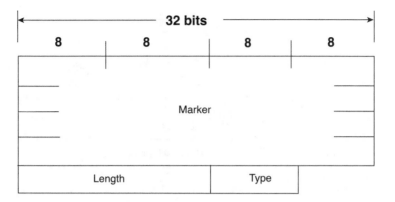

Marker is a 16-octet field that is used to detect loss of synchronization between BGP peers and to authenticate messages when authentication is supported. If the message type is Open or if the Open message contains no authentication information, the Marker field is set to all 1s. Otherwise, the value of the marker can be predicted by some computation as part of the authentication process.

Length is a 0-octet field that indicates the total length of the message, including the header, in octets.

Type is a 0-octet field specifying the message type. Table 2-6 indicates the possible type codes.

Table 2-6   *BGP Type Codes*

Code	Type
1	Open
2	Update
3	Notification
4	Keepalive

The Open Message

The Open message, whose format is shown in Figure 2-44, is the first message sent after a TCP connection has been established. If a received Open message is acceptable, a Keepalive message is sent to confirm the Open. After the Open has been confirmed, the BGP connection is in the Established state and Update, Keepalive, and Notification messages can be sent.

Figure 2-44 *The BGP Open Message Format*

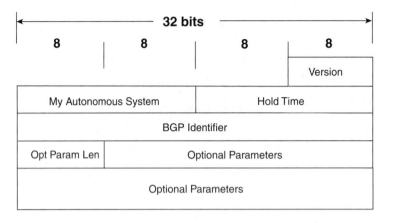

The BGP Open message contains the following fields:

- **Version**—A 1-octet field specifying the BGP version running on the originator.

- **My Autonomous System**—A 2-octet field specifying the AS number of the originator.

- **Hold Time**—A 2-octet number indicating the number of seconds the sender proposes for the hold time. A receiver compares the value of the Hold Time field and the value of its configured hold time and accepts the smaller value or rejects the connection. The hold time must be either 0 or at least 3 seconds.

- **BGP Identifier**—The router ID of the originator. A Cisco router sets its router ID as either the highest IP address of any of its loopback interfaces or, if no loopback interface is configured, the highest IP address of any of its physical interfaces.

- **Optional Parameters Length**—A 1-octet field indicating the total length of the following Optional Parameters field, in octets. If the value of this field is zero, no Optional Parameters field in included in the message.

- **Optional Parameters**—A variable-length field containing a list of optional parameters. Each parameter is specified by a 1-octet type field, a 1-octet length field, and a variable-length field containing the parameter value.

The Update Message

The Update message, whose format is shown in Figure 2-45, is used to advertise a single feasible route to a peer, or to withdraw multiple unfeasible routes, or both.

Figure 2-45 *The BGP Update Message Format*

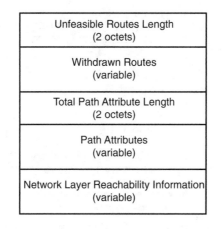

| Unfeasible Routes Length (2 octets) |
| Withdrawn Routes (variable) |
| Total Path Attribute Length (2 octets) |
| Path Attributes (variable) |
| Network Layer Reachability Information (variable) |

The BGP Update message contains the following fields:

- **Unfeasible Routes Length**—A 2-octet field indicating the total length of the following Withdrawn Routes field, in octets. A value of zero indicates that no routes are being withdrawn and that no Withdrawn Routes field is included in the message.

- **Withdrawn Routes**—A variable-length field containing a list of routes to be withdrawn from service. Each route in the list is described with a (Length, Prefix) tuple in which the Length is the length of the prefix and the Prefix is the IP address prefix of the withdrawn route. If the Length part of the tuple is zero, the Prefix matches all routes.

- **Total Path Attribute Length**—A 2-octet field indicating the total length of the following Path Attribute field, in octets. A value of zero indicates that attributes and NLRI are not included in this message.

- **Path Attributes**—A variable-length field listing the attributes associated with the NLRI in the following field. Each path attribute is a variable-length triple of (Attribute Type, Attribute Length, Attribute Value). The Attribute Type part of the triple is a 2-octet field consisting of four flag bits, four unused bits, and an Attribute Type code (see Figure 2-46).

- **Network Layer Reachability Information**—A variable-length field containing a list of (Length, Prefix) tuples. The Length indicates the length in bits of the following prefix, and the Prefix is the IP address prefix of the NLRI. A Length value of zero indicates a prefix that matches all IP addresses.

Figure 2-46 *The Attribute Type Part of the Path Attributes Field*

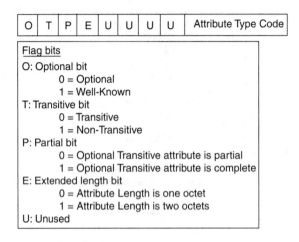

Table 2-7 shows the most common Attribute Type codes and the possible Attribute Values for each Attribute Type.

Table 2-7 *Attribute Types and Associated Attribute Values**

Attribute Type Code	Attribute Type	Attribute Value Code	Attribute Value
1	ORIGIN	0	IGP
		1	EGP
		2	Incomplete
2	AS_PATH	1	AS_SET
		2	AS_SEQUENCE
		3	AS_CONFED_SET
		4	AS_CONFED_SEQUENCE
3	NEXT_HOP	0	Next-hop IP address
4	MULTI_EXIT_DISC	0	4-octet MED
5	LOCAL_PREF	0	4-octet LOCAL_PREF
6	ATOMIC_AGGREGATE	0	None
7	AGGREGATOR	0	AS number and IP address of aggregator
8	COMMUNITY	0	4-octet community identifier
9	ORIGINATOR_ID	0	4-octet router ID of originator
10	CLUSTER_LIST	0	Variable-length list of cluster IDs

*Other attribute types exist, but they are proprietary to non-Cisco vendors and are therefore beyond the scope of this book.

The Keepalive Message

Keepalive messages are exchanged on a period one-third the hold time, but not less than 1 second. If the negotiated hold time is 0, Keepalives are not sent.

The Keepalive message consists of only the 19-octet BGP message header, with no additional data.

The Notification Message

Notification messages, whose format is shown in Figure 2-47, are sent when an error condition is detected. The BGP connection is closed immediately after the message is sent.

Figure 2-47 *The BGP Notification Message Format*

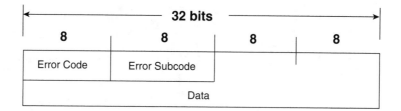

The BGP Notification message contains the following fields:

- **Error Code**—A 1-octet field indicating the type of error.

- **Error Subcode**—A 1-octet field providing more-specific information about the error. Table 2-8 shows the possible error codes and associated error subcodes.

- **Data**—A variable-length field used to diagnose the reason for the error. The contents of the Data field depend on the error code and subcode.

Table 2-8   *BGP Notification Message Error Codes and Error Subcodes*

Error Code	Error	Error Subcode	Subcode Detail
1	Message Header Error	1	Connection not synchronized
		2	Bad message length
		3	Bad message type

continues

Table 2-8 *BGP Notification Message Error Codes and Error Subcodes (Continued)*

Error Code	Error	Error Subcode	Subcode Detail
2	Open Message Error	1	Unsupported version number
		2	Bad peer AS
		3	Bad BGP identifier
		4	Unsupported optional parameter
		5	Authentication failure
		6	Unacceptable hold time
3	Update Message Error	1	Malformed attribute list
		2	Unrecognized well-known attribute
		3	Missing well-known attribute
		4	Attribute flags error
		5	Attribute length error
		6	Invalid ORIGIN attribute
		7	AS routing loop
		8	Invalid NEXT_HOP attribute
		9	Optional attribute error
		10	Invalid network field
		11	Malformed AS_PATH
4	Hold Timer Expired	0	—
5	Finite State Machine Error	0	—
6	Cease	0	—

End Notes

[1]K. Lougheed and Y. Rekhter, "RFC 1105: A Border Gateway Protocol (BGP)" (Work in Progress)

[2]K. Lougheed and Y. Rekhter, "RFC 1163: A Border Gateway Protocol (BGP)" (Work in Progress)

[3]K. Lougheed and Y. Rekhter, "RFC 1267: A Border Gateway Protocol 3 (BGP-3)" (Work in Progress)

[4]Y. Rekhter and T. Li, "RFC 1771: A Border Gateway Protocol 4 (BGP-4)" (Work in Progress)

[5]Internet Engineering Steering Group, R. Hinden, Editor, "RFC 1517: Applicability Statement for the Implementation of Classless Inter-Domain Routing (CIDR)" (Work in Progress)

[6]V. Fuller et al., "RFC 1519: Classless Inter-Domain Routing (CIDR): An Address Assignment and Aggregation Strategy" (Work in Progress)

[7]Y. Rekhter and C. Topolcic, "RFC 1520: Exchanging Routing Information Across Provider Boundaries in the CIDR Environment" (Work in Progress)

[8]R. Chandra and P. Traina, "RFC 1997: BGP Communities Attribute" (Work in Progress)

Looking Ahead

Now that you have had a good look at the basics of BGP and related concepts, Chapter 3 shows you how to configure and troubleshoot BGP on Cisco routers. In addition to configuring BGP, you learn how to set routing policies and how to redistribute BGP and IGPs.

Recommended Reading

Halabi, B., and D. McPherson, *Internet Routing Architectures, Second Edition.* Indianapolis, Indiana: Cisco Press; 2000.

This book is considered by many as the definitive text on BGP-4.

Stewart J.W. III. *BGP4: Inter-Domain Routing in the Internet.* Reading, Massachusetts: Addison Wesley Longman; 1999.

Although not Cisco-specific, Stewart's book is a handy, concise overview of BGP.

Review Questions

1 What is the most important difference between BGP-4 and earlier versions of BGP?

_____

_____

_____

2 What two problems was CIDR developed to alleviate?

_____

_____

_____

3 What is the difference between classful and classless IP routers?

_____

_____

_____

4 What is the difference between classful and classless IP routing protocols?

_____

_____

_____

5 Given the addresses 172.17.208.0/23, 172.17.210.0/23, 172.17.212.0/23, and 172.17.214.0/23, summarize the addresses with a single aggregate, using the longest possible address mask.

_____

_____

_____

6 What is an address prefix?

_____

_____

_____

7 The routing table in Example 2-16 is taken from a classless router. To what next-hop address does the router forward packets with each of the following destination addresses?

172.20.3.5

172.20.1.67

172.21.255.254

172.16.50.50

172.16.0.224

172.16.51.50

172.17.40.1

172.17.41.1

172.30.1.1

Example 2-16 *The Routing Table for Review Question 7*

```
Stratford#show ip route
Codes: C - connected, S - static, I - IGRP, R - RIP, M - mobile, B - BGP
       D - EIGRP, EX - EIGRP external, O - OSPF, IA - OSPF inter area
       E1 - OSPF external type 1, E2 - OSPF external type 2, E - EGP
       i - IS-IS, L1 - IS-IS level-1, L2 - IS-IS level-2, * - candidate default

Gateway of last resort is not set

     172.20.0.0 is variably subnetted, 6 subnets, 2 masks
D       172.20.0.0 255.255.0.0 [90/409600] via 172.20.5.2, 00:01:50, Ethernet0
D       172.20.2.0 255.255.255.0
           [90/409600] via 172.20.6.2, 00:01:50, Ethernet1
D       172.20.3.0 255.255.255.0
           [90/5401600] via 172.20.6.2, 00:01:50, Ethernet1
C       172.20.5.0 255.255.255.0 is directly connected, Ethernet0
C       172.20.6.0 255.255.255.0 is directly connected, Ethernet1
C       172.20.7.0 255.255.255.0 is directly connected, Ethernet2
     172.16.0.0 is variably subnetted, 3 subnets, 2 masks
D       172.16.50.0 255.255.255.0
           [90/409600] via 172.20.6.2, 00:01:50, Ethernet1
D       172.16.0.0 255.255.255.0
           [90/460800] via 172.20.6.2, 00:01:51, Ethernet1
D       172.16.0.0 255.255.0.0 [90/409600] via 172.20.7.2, 00:01:51, Ethernet2
     172.17.0.0 is subnetted (mask is 255.255.255.0), 1 subnets
D       172.17.40.0 [90/2841600] via 172.20.7.2, 00:01:52, Ethernet2
D    172.16.0.0 (mask is 255.240.0.0) [90/409600] via 172.20.5.2, 00:01:52, Ethernet0
Stratford#
```

8 Explain how summarization helps hide network instabilities.

_____

_____

_____

9 Explain how summarization can cause asymmetric traffic patterns.

_____

_____

_____

10 Is asymmetric traffic undesirable?

_____

_____

_____

11 What is a NAP?

_____

_____

_____

12 What is a route server?

_____

_____

_____

13 What is a provider-independent address space, and why can it be advantageous to have one?

_____

_____

_____

14 Why can it be a problem to have a /21 provider-independent address space?

_____

_____

_____

15 What is a routing policy?

_____

_____

_____

16 What is the underlying protocol that BGP uses to reliably connect to its neighbors?

_____

_____

_____

17 What are the four BGP message types, and how is each one used?

_____

_____

_____

18 In what state or states can BGP peers exchange Update messages?

_____

_____

_____

19 What is NLRI?

_____

_____

_____

20 What is a path attribute?

_____

_____

_____

21 What are the four categories of BGP path attributes?

_____

_____

_____

22 What is the purpose of the AS_PATH attribute?

_____

_____

_____

23 What are the different types of AS_PATH?

_____

_____

_____

24 What is the purpose of the NEXT_HOP attribute?

_____

_____

_____

25 What is the purpose of the LOCAL_PREF attribute?

_____

_____

_____

26 What is the purpose of the MULTI_EXIT_DISC attribute?

_____

_____

_____

27 What attribute or attributes are useful if a BGP speaker originates an aggregate route?

_____

_____

_____

28 What is a BGP administrative weight?

_____

_____

_____

29 Given an EBGP route and an IBGP route to the same destination, which route will a BGP router prefer?

_____

_____

_____

30 A router has two IBGP routes to the same destination. Path A has a LOCAL_PREF of 300 and three AS numbers in the AS_PATH. Path B has a LOCAL_PREF of 200 and two AS numbers in the AS_PATH. Assuming no other differences, which path will the router choose?

_____

_____

_____

31 What is route dampening?

_____

_____

_____

32 Define the penalty, suppress limit, reuse limit, and half-life as they apply to route dampening.

_____

_____

_____

33 What is IGP synchronization, and why is it important?

_____

_____

_____

34 Under what circumstances can you safely disable IGP synchronization?

_____

_____

_____

35 What is a BGP peer group?

_____

_____

_____

36 What is a BGP community?

_____

_____

_____

37 What is a route reflector? What is a route reflection client? What is a route reflection cluster?

_____

_____

_____

38 What is the purpose of the ORIGINATOR_ID and the CLUSTER_LIST path attributes?

_____

_____

_____

39 What is a BGP confederation?

_____

_____

_____

40 Can route reflectors be used within confederations?

_____

_____

_____

41 What is the purpose of the **next-hop-self** function? Are there any reasonable alternatives to using this function?

_____

_____

_____

This chapter covers the following key topics:

- **Basic BGP Configuration**—This section provides a series of case studies for BGP configuration, including peering BGP routers, injecting IBGP routes into BGP, injecting BGP routes into an IGP, IBGP without an IGP, IBGP over an IGP, EBGP multihop, and aggregate routes.

- **Managing BGP Connections**—This section examines a variety of commands and tools that are available for making BGP connections more manageable from both an administrative and a maintenance standpoint.

- **Routing Policies**—This section discusses resetting BGP connections and provides a series of case studies covering filtering routes by network layer reachability information (NLRI), by AS_PATH, and with route maps; administrative weight; administering distances and backdoor routes; using the LOCAL_PREF and MULTI_EXIT_DISC attributes; prepending the AS_PATH; route tagging; and route dampening.

- **Large-Scale BGP**—This section provides a series of case studies for large-scale BGP design, including BGP peer groups, BGP communities, private AS numbers, BGP confederations, and route reflectors.

Configuring and Troubleshooting Border Gateway Protocol 4

Many newcomers to BGP approach the protocol with trepidation. The source of this sentiment is the fact that BGP implementations are much more rare than IGP implementations. Outside of ISPs, most network administrators deal with BGP far less than with IGPs, if at all. Even when BGP is used, the configurations in small ISPs and non-ISP subscribers are usually pretty basic. Because most networking professionals lack in-depth experience with the protocol, it is often viewed as mysterious or intimidating.

You learned in Chapter 2, "Introduction to Border Gateway Protocol 4," that BGP itself is a relatively simple protocol. Certainly it is less complex than EIGRP, OSPF, or Integrated IS-IS. The complexity of BGP is not in the protocol, but in the scenarios in which it is used and the powerful tools associated with it. If an AS is not multihomed, or has only basic routing policies, BGP is usually unnecessary.

This chapter begins with basic BGP configurations and then presents some examples of using BGP to set routing policies—rules for sending and receiving route advertisements. Configuring BGP in large autonomous systems is covered last.

The configuration options available to BGP are so numerous that troubleshooting cannot be demonstrated adequately in just a few case studies. Therefore, this chapter presents troubleshooting issues in parallel with many configuration options and cases.

Basic BGP Configuration

This section presents the essential steps for configuring a BGP process and the most commonly used techniques for controlling BGP. For the great majority of BGP implementations, the information presented in this section is all that you need.

Case Study: Peering BGP Routers

A BGP session between routers is configured in two steps:

Step 1   Establish the BGP process and specify the local AS number with the **router bgp** command.

Step 2   Specify a neighbor and the neighbor's AS number with the **neighbor remote-as** command.

Figure 3-1 shows two routers in different autonomous systems. The structure of the BGP configuration for these routers differs from EGP configuration. Recall from Chapter 1, "Exterior Gateway Protocol," that the **router egp** command specifies the remote AS, and the **autonomous-system** command specifies the local AS. In contrast, **router bgp** specifies the local AS. Each neighbor's AS is specified with the **neighbor remote-as** command. This difference is significant. Whereas only core EGP routers can peer with more than one remote AS (with the **router egp 0** command), any BGP process can peer with any number of remote autonomous systems. The EGP requirement for stub autonomous systems connected through a core AS is eliminated; autonomous systems can be meshed fully under BGP.

Figure 3-1 *An EBGP Session Is Established Between Taos and Vail*

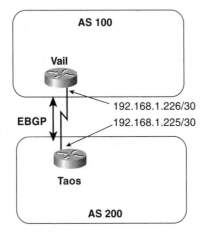

Example 3-1 shows the EBGP configurations for the Taos and Vail routers in Figure 3-1.

Example 3-1 *EBGP Configurations for Routers in Figure 3-1*

```
Taos
router bgp 200
 neighbor 192.168.1.226 remote-as 100
```
```
Vail
router bgp 100
 neighbor 192.168.1.225 remote-as 200
```

Example 3-2 shows the information Vail has recorded about Taos. Much of the information in this screen is particularly useful for troubleshooting. Appendix A, "The **show ip bgp neighbors** Display," provides a complete description of all the fields displayed by the **show ip bgp neighbors** command.

Example 3-2   **show ip bgp neighbors** *Command Output Contains Details About the Peer Connection with a Neighbor*

```
Vail#show ip bgp neighbors
BGP neighbor is 192.168.1.225,  remote AS 200, external link
 Index 1, Offset 0, Mask 0x2
  BGP version 4, remote router ID 192.168.1.225
  BGP state = Established, table version = 1, up for 19:32:02
  Last read 00:00:03, hold time is 180, keepalive interval is 60 seconds
  Minimum time between advertisement runs is 30 seconds
  Received 1175 messages, 0 notifications, 0 in queue
  Sent 1175 messages, 0 notifications, 0 in queue
  Prefix advertised 0, suppressed 0, withdrawn 0
  Connections established 1; dropped 0
  Last reset never
  0 accepted prefixes consume 0 bytes
  0 history paths consume 0 bytes
 Connection state is ESTAB, I/O status: 1, unread input bytes: 0
 Local host: 192.168.1.226, Local port: 11025
 Foreign host: 192.168.1.225, Foreign port: 179

Enqueued packets for retransmit: 0, input: 0  mis-ordered: 0 (0 bytes)

Event Timers (current time is 0x45FDF2C):
Timer          Starts   Wakeups          Next
Retrans         1176        0            0x0
TimeWait           0        0            0x0
AckHold         1175      885            0x0
SendWnd            0        0            0x0
KeepAlive          0        0            0x0
GiveUp             0        0            0x0
PmtuAger           0        0            0x0
DeadWait           0        0            0x0

iss: 4072889888  snduna: 4072912224  sndnxt: 4072912224     sndwnd:  16004
irs: 4121607729  rcvnxt: 4121630065  rcvwnd:       16004  delrcvwnd:    380

SRTT: 300 ms, RTTO: 607 ms, RTV: 3 ms, KRTT: 0 ms
minRTT: 4 ms, maxRTT: 340 ms, ACK hold: 200 ms
Flags: higher precedence, nagle

Datagrams (max data segment is 1460 bytes):
Rcvd: 2220 (out of order: 0), with data: 1175, total data bytes: 22335
Sent: 2077 (retransmit: 0), with data: 1175, total data bytes: 22335
Vail#
```

The first line of output in Example 3-2 shows the address of Taos (192.168.1.225), its AS number (200), and the type of BGP connection to the router (external). The third line displays the BGP version used between Vail and Taos, and Taos' router ID. The fourth line begins by showing the state of the BGP finite state machine. The table version is incremented whenever the BGP routing table changes; in Example 3-2, no changes have taken place since the connection to Taos was established, so the table version is still 1. Uptime shows the time since the present peer connection was established. In Example 3-2, Taos has been peered continuously for 19 hours, 32 minutes, and 2 seconds.

Also of interest are the details of the underlying TCP connection. Example 3-2 highlights these lines. The lines show that the TCP connection state is Established, that Vail is originating BGP messages from TCP port 11025, and that the destination port at Taos is 179. The source port can be especially important when you are capturing packets on a link carrying more than one BGP session.

In Figure 3-2, another router is added to AS 100. Because they are in the same AS, Vail and Aspen are internal neighbors.

Figure 3-2   *IBGP Is Spoken Between Vail and Aspen*

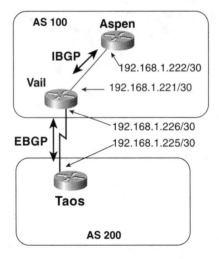

Example 3-3 shows the configuration for Vail.

Example 3-3   *Configuration for Vail Router in Figure 3-2*

```
router bgp 100
 neighbor 192.168.1.222 remote-as 100
 neighbor 192.168.1.225 remote-as 200
```

Example 3-4 shows Aspen being configured. BGP debugging is used to observe the peer session being created. The figure shows that the time from the creation of the BGP configuration (18:24:13) to the beginning of the BGP peer negotiation (18:24:33) is 20 seconds; the TCP connection is established during this interval. BGP then transitions from Idle to Active, and the entire negotiation lasts approximately 10 seconds.

Example 3-4 The **debug ip bgp events** *Command Displays the States of the BGP Finite State Machine as Aspen Peers with Vail*

```
Aspen#debug ip bgp events
BGP events debugging is on
Aspen#conf t
Enter configuration commands, one per line.  End with CNTL/Z.
Aspen(config)#router bgp 100
Aspen(config-router)#neighbor 192.168.1.221 remote-as 100
Aspen(config-router)#^Z
Aspen#
18:24:13: %SYS-5-CONFIG_I: Configured from console by console
Aspen#
18:24:33: BGP: 192.168.1.221 went from Idle to Active
18:24:41: BGP: 192.168.1.221 went from Active to OpenSent
18:24:42: BGP: 192.168.1.221 went from OpenSent to OpenConfirm
18:24:42: BGP: 192.168.1.221 went from OpenConfirm to Established
18:24:43: BGP: 192.168.1.221 computing updates, neighbor version 0, table version
n 1, starting at 0.0.0.0
18:24:43: BGP: 192.168.1.221 update run completed, ran for 0ms, neighbor version
 0, start version 1, throttled to 1, check point net 0.0.0.0
Aspen#
```

Example 3-5 shows a portion of Aspen's neighbor information.

Example 3-5 *Aspen's Neighbor Information Shows That Vail's Router ID Is from One of Its Physical Interfaces*

```
Aspen#show ip bgp neighbors
BGP neighbor is 192.168.1.221,  remote AS 100, internal link
 Index 1, Offset 0, Mask 0x2
  BGP version 4, remote router ID 192.168.1.226
  BGP state = Established, table version = 1, up for 00:03:46
  Last read 00:00:46, hold time is 180, keepalive interval is 60 seconds
  Minimum time between advertisement runs is 5 seconds
  Received 6 messages, 0 notifications, 0 in queue
  Sent 6 messages, 0 notifications, 0 in queue
  Prefix advertised 0, suppressed 0, withdrawn 0
  Connections established 1; dropped 0
  Last reset never
  0 accepted prefixes consume 0 bytes
  0 history paths consume 0 bytes
 Connection state is ESTAB, I/O status: 1, unread input bytes: 0
 Local host: 192.168.1.222, Local port: 179
 Foreign host: 192.168.1.221, Foreign port: 11000
```

Notice that Vail's router ID is 192.168.1.226, the address of its interface to Taos. The rules for selecting a BGP router ID are identical to the rules for selecting an OSPF router ID:

- The router chooses the numerically highest IP address on any of its loopback interfaces.

- If no loopback interfaces are configured with IP addresses, the router chooses the numerically highest IP address on any of its physical interfaces. The interface from which the router ID is taken does not have to be running BGP.

Because Vail does not have a loopback interface configured, the router chose the numerically highest IP address on a physical interface. Using addresses associated with loopback interfaces has two advantages:

- The loopback interface is more stable than any physical interface. It is active when the router boots up, and it fails only if the entire router fails.

- The network administrator has more leeway in assigning predictable or recognizable addresses as the router IDs.

Cisco's BGP continues to use a router ID learned from a physical interface, even if the interface subsequently fails or is deleted. Therefore, the stability of a loopback interface is only a minor advantage. The primary benefit is the capability to control the router ID, making it easily distinguishable from other IP addresses.

Example 3-6 shows how to configure Vail with a unique router ID.

Example 3-6 *Configuring Vail with a Unique Router ID*

```
interface loopback 0
 ip address 192.168.255.254 255.255.255.255
!
router bgp 100
 neighbor 192.168.1.222 remote-as 100
 neighbor 192.168.1.225 remote-as 200
```

Just configuring a loopback address on a working BGP router does not change the router ID, however. The command **clear ip bgp** (discussed in more detail in the section "Configuring Routing Policies") must be issued at Vail to clear all of its BGP sessions. A second look at Aspen's neighbor information in Example 3-7 shows that Vail's router ID is now its loopback 0 address.

Another point of interest in Example 3-7, when compared to Example 3-5, is the table version. After Vail's session is reset, the table version is incremented to 2. The change also is reflected in the **Connections established; dropped** field. These fields should not change often; if they do, it might indicate an unstable neighbor.

Example 3-7 *Vail's Router ID, After a Loopback Address Is Configured and Its BGP Sessions Are Reset, Is Its Loopback Address*

```
Aspen#show ip bgp neighbors
BGP neighbor is 192.168.1.221,  remote AS 100, internal link
  Index 1, Offset 0, Mask 0x2
  BGP version 4, remote router ID 192.168.255.254
  BGP state = Established, table version = 2, up for 00:00:42
    Last read 00:00:42, hold time is 180, keepalive interval is 60 seconds
    Minimum time between advertisement runs is 5 seconds
    Received 37 messages, 0 notifications, 0 in queue
    Sent 37 messages, 0 notifications, 0 in queue
    Prefix advertised 0, suppressed 0, withdrawn 0
  Connections established 2; dropped 1
    Last reset 00:00:51, due to Peer closed the session
    0 accepted prefixes consume 0 bytes
    0 history paths consume 0 bytes
Connection state is ESTAB, I/O status: 1, unread input bytes: 0
Local host: 192.168.1.222, Local port: 179
Foreign host: 192.168.1.221, Foreign port: 11003
```

You also can set the router ID of a BGP speaker manually, overriding both the physical and loopback interface addresses. The command for doing so is **bgp router-id**. For example, the configuration in Example 3-8 sets the BGP router ID of Vail to 1.1.3.2.

Example 3-8 *Setting the BGP Router ID Manually*

```
interface loopback 0
 ip address 192.168.255.254 255.255.255.255
!
router bgp 100
 bgp router-id 1.1.3.2
 neighbor 192.168.1.222 remote-as 100
 neighbor 192.168.1.225 remote-as 200
```

The **bgp router-id** command can prove useful in situations where loopback interfaces are needed for other reasons, such as OSPF router IDs or SNMP functions, but the IP addresses on the interfaces differ from what you desire for the BGP router ID.

Case Study: Injecting IGP Routes into BGP

Chapter 2 emphasizes that at an AS border, outgoing route advertisements affect incoming traffic, and incoming route advertisements affect outgoing traffic. As a result, outgoing and incoming advertisements should be considered separately. This section begins the discussion of BGP route advertisements by examining basic methods of injecting routes into BGP.

Figure 3-3 shows that AS 200 uses EIGRP as its IGP. Taos must advertise three addresses to its EBGP peer: 192.168.200.0/24 is learned via EIGRP, 192.168.100.0/24 is directly attached to Taos, and 192.168.1.216/30 is connecting Taos and AngelFire. Whereas the first two addresses are full class C addresses, the last is a subnet. Other subnets of 192.168.1.0 appear outside of AS 200, so the subnet only, not the major network address, must be advertised.

Figure 3-3 *AS 200 Is Using EIGRP as Its IGP*

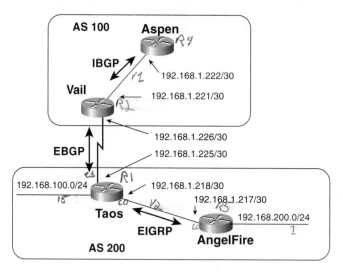

Example 3-9 shows a "first-pass" configuration of Taos.

Example 3-9 *Taos' Basic EIGRP and BGP Configuration*

```
router eigrp 200
 passive-interface Serial0
 network 192.168.1.0
 network 192.168.100.0
!
router bgp 200
 redistribute eigrp 200
 neighbor 192.168.1.226 remote-as 100
```

Example 3-10 shows the results in Vail's BGP table. All EIGRP networks have been advertised over the EBGP link. Notice in the configuration that no metric was specified with the **redistribute** command. As a result, the metric of each route defaults to the EIGRP metric, as shown in Taos' routing table in Example 3-11. The directly connected networks have a metric of 0, and 192.168.200.0/24 has a metric of 409600. You can change this default method of selecting a metric with the **default-metric** command.

NOTE   The BGP metric is the MULTI_EXIT_DISC. The use and manipulation of this attribute is demonstrated in the section "Case Study: Using the MULTI_EXIT_DISC Attribute."

Example 3-10 *Taos Advertised 192.168.100.0/24 and 192.168.200.0/24 Correctly, but the Subnet 192.168.1.216/30 Was Summarized to the Major Network*

```
Vail#show ip bgp
BGP table version is 15, local router ID is 192.168.255.254
Status codes: s suppressed, d damped, h history, * valid, > best, i - internal
Origin codes: i - IGP, e - EGP, ? - incomplete

   Network          Next Hop         Metric LocPrf Weight Path
*> 192.168.1.0      192.168.1.225    281600           0 200 ?
*> 192.168.100.0    192.168.1.225         0           0 200 ?
*> 192.168.200.0    192.168.1.225    409600           0 200 ?
Vail#
```

Example 3-11 *Taos' Routing Table Shows That the EIGRP Metrics Are the Same as the Metrics in Vail's BGP Table*

```
Taos#show ip route
Codes: C - connected, S - static, I - IGRP, R - RIP, M - mobile, B - BGP
       D - EIGRP, EX - EIGRP external, O - OSPF, IA - OSPF inter area
       N1 - OSPF NSSA external type 1, N2 - OSPF NSSA external type 2
       E1 - OSPF external type 1, E2 - OSPF external type 2, E - EGP
       i - IS-IS, L1 - IS-IS level-1, L2 - IS-IS level-2, * - candidate default
       U - per-user static route, o - ODR
       T - traffic engineered route

Gateway of last resort is not set

D    192.168.200.0/24 [90/409600] via 192.168.1.217, 00:52:09, Ethernet0
     192.168.1.0/24 is variably subnetted, 3 subnets, 2 masks
D       192.168.1.0/24 is a summary, 00:52:11, Null0
C       192.168.1.224/30 is directly connected, Serial0
C       192.168.1.216/30 is directly connected, Ethernet0
C    192.168.100.0/24 is directly connected, Ethernet1
Taos#
```

The two major networks in AS 200 are advertised correctly, but you can see in Example 3-9 that the subnet 192.168.1.216/30 has been summarized to the major network. The reason for this is that BGP-4, although it is classless, by default summarizes at network boundaries. In the internetwork of Figure 3-3, this summarization presents no problem. Vail is directly connected to the other two subnets of 192.168.1.0 and therefore knows the two more-specific routes. As the network grows and other subnets of that network are used on other routers, however, the summary can cause incorrect routing. To turn off BGP's automatic summarization, configure Taos as in Example 3-12.

Example 3-12 *Taos Configuration to Turn Off BGP Automatic Summarization*

```
router eigrp 200
 passive-interface Serial0
 network 192.168.1.0
 network 192.168.100.0
!
router bgp 200
 redistribute eigrp 200
 neighbor 192.168.1.226 remote-as 100
 no auto-summary
```

Example 3-13 shows the results in Vail's BGP table. The subnets of 192.168.1.0 are now being advertised. However, the major network 192.168.1.0 is still being advertised in addition to the subnets. Another look at Taos' routing table in Example 3-11 shows why. EIGRP also performs automatic route summarization and has entered a summary route to Null0 in the routing table. BGP is picking up this route in addition to the subnets and is advertising it to Vail.

Example 3-13 *Vail's BGP Table, After BGP Auto-Summarization Is Turned Off at Taos*

```
Vail#show ip bgp
BGP table version is 17, local router ID is 192.168.255.254
Status codes: s suppressed, d damped, h history, * valid, > best, i - internal
Origin codes: i - IGP, e - EGP, ? - incomplete

   Network          Next Hop            Metric LocPrf Weight Path
*> 192.168.1.0      192.168.1.225       281600         0 200 ?
*> 192.168.1.216/30 192.168.1.225            0         0 200 ?
*> 192.168.1.224/30 192.168.1.225            0         0 200 ?
*> 192.168.100.0    192.168.1.225            0         0 200 ?
*> 192.168.200.0    192.168.1.225       409600         0 200 ?
Vail#
```

To turn off EIGRP auto-summarization for the Taos router, you use the same **no auto-summary** command as demonstrated in Example 3-14.

Example 3-14 *Taos Configuration to Turn Off EIGRP Automatic Summarization*

```
router eigrp 200
 passive-interface Serial0
 network 192.168.1.0
 network 192.168.100.0
 no auto-summary
!
router bgp 200
 redistribute eigrp 200
 neighbor 192.168.1.226 remote-as 100
 no auto-summary
```

Example 3-15 shows the resulting BGP table at Vail.

Example 3-15 *Vail's BGP Table After EIGRP Auto-Summarization Is Turned Off at Taos*

```
Vail#show ip bgp
BGP table version is 20, local router ID is 192.168.255.254
Status codes: s suppressed, d damped, h history, * valid, > best, i - internal
Origin codes: i - IGP, e - EGP, ? - incomplete

   Network          Next Hop          Metric LocPrf Weight Path
*> 192.168.1.216/30 192.168.1.225          0             0 200 ?
*> 192.168.1.224/30 192.168.1.225          0             0 200 ?
*> 192.168.100.0    192.168.1.225          0             0 200 ?
*> 192.168.200.0    192.168.1.225     409600             0 200 ?
Vail#
```

The advantage of using redistribution to inject routes into BGP is that internal changes can be advertised with few or no changes to the BGP configuration. If a network is added or removed within the EIGRP domain of AS 200, the change is automatically advertised to Vail. However, advertising every IGP route is also the major disadvantage of IGP-to-BGP redistribution. For example, the administrators of autonomous systems 100 and 200 might or might not want subnet 192.168.1.224/30 advertised from Taos to Vail, as it is in Example 3-15. If the subnet should not be advertised, a route filter must be used. Later in this chapter, the section "Routing Policies" demonstrates, through several case studies, various options for configuring route filters.

Route filters are almost always necessary when redistributing an IGP's routes into BGP. By default, every route known by the IGP is redistributed. The administrator of the AS might want to advertise only a subset of the IGP routes, and so must filter the others. Or, perhaps a multihomed AS should not be a transit for any of its neighboring autonomous systems. Route filters must be used to prevent external routes learned from one AS from being advertised to other autonomous systems. Then there is the problem of route feedback, in which external routes received from EBGP are advertised into an IGP and then are redistributed from that IGP back into EBGP. At a minimum, best practice dictates that route filters should be used to ensure that only the correct routes are redistributed. In actual practice, redistribution of IGP prefixes into BGP is rarely used because of this lack of precise control.

An alternative to redistributing IGP routes into BGP is to use the **network** command. As discussed in Chapter 1, this command functions differently under EGP and BGP than it does under an IGP. When used with an IGP, the **network** command specifies the address of an interface or group of interfaces on which the routing protocol will be enabled. When used with EGP and BGP, **network** specifies an IP prefix to be advertised. For each prefix specified with the command, BGP looks into the routing table. If an entry in the table exactly matches the **network** prefix, that prefix is entered into the BGP table and advertised.

Example 3-16 shows the configuration for Taos using the **network** command rather than redistribution.

Example 3-16 *Configuring Taos with the* **network** *Command*

```
router eigrp 200
 passive-interface Serial0
 network 192.168.1.0
 network 192.168.100.0
 !
router bgp 200
 network 192.168.1.216 mask 255.255.255.252
 network 192.168.100.0
 network 192.168.200.0
 neighbor 192.168.1.226 remote-as 100
```

The major networks 192.168.100.0 and 192.168.200.0 are specified alone. For the subnet 192.168.1.216, a mask is also specified. Subnets and masks can be specified only under BGP-4; under EGP or earlier versions of BGP, all of which are classful, only major networks can be specified.

Notice that the **no auto-summary** command is not used under either EIGRP or BGP in this configuration. Because no redistribution is taking place, turning off auto-summarization is unnecessary. Example 3-17 shows the result of the configuration.

Example 3-17 *Vail's BGP Table After Taos Is Reconfigured Using the BGP* **network** *Command*

```
Vail#show ip bgp
BGP table version is 36, local router ID is 192.168.255.254
Status codes: s suppressed, d damped, h history, * valid, > best, i - internal
Origin codes: i - IGP, e - EGP, ? - incomplete

   Network          Next Hop        Metric LocPrf Weight Path
*> 192.168.1.216/30 192.168.1.225        0             0 200 i
*> 192.168.100.0    192.168.1.225        0             0 200 i
*> 192.168.200.0    192.168.1.225   409600             0 200 i
Vail#
```

Unlike in Example 3-15, subnet 192.168.1.224/30 is not advertised, because it was not specified with a **network** command. The administrator has more control than with redistribution, and no filtering is necessary. Comparing Example 3-15 and Example 3-17, notice that the ORIGIN codes differ. Whereas the redistributed routes in Example 3-15 are tagged with a **?**, indicating an ORIGIN of "incomplete," the routes in Example 3-17 are tagged with an **i**, indicating an ORIGIN of IGP. This tagging can make a difference in some circumstances because the BGP decision process, discussed in Chapter 2, gives a higher preference to ORIGIN code 1 (IGP) than to code 3 (incomplete).

A maximum of 200 addresses can be specified with the **network** command. If you must advertise more addresses across a BGP connection, you must use redistribution.

Case Study: Injecting BGP Routes into an IGP

Prefixes that are learned from an EBGP neighbor are automatically added to the routing table. In Figure 3-4, for instance, AS 300 is advertising two routes: 192.168.250.0/24 and 192.168.1.212/30. AS 300's IGP, and the configuration of router Tahoe, are unimportant to this example. The important observations are that the prefixes advertised by Tahoe to its external BGP peer are displayed in the Taos routing table as reachable and that pings to a destination in AS 300 are successful (see Example 3-18). An extended ping is used because the subnet of Taos' serial interface, 192.168.1.224/30, is not advertised. The BGP-learned routes are tagged in the routing table with a **B**.

Figure 3-4   *AS 300 Has Been Added to the Topology Presented in Figure 3-3*

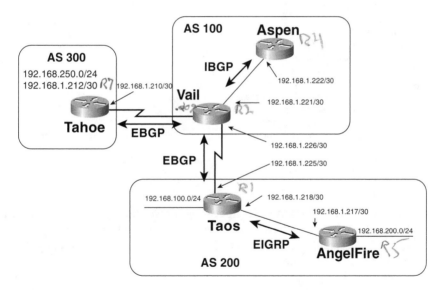

Example 3-18 *A Ping to an Address in AS 300 of Figure 3-4 Is Successful*

```
Taos#show ip route
Codes: C - connected, S - static, I - IGRP, R - RIP, M - mobile, B - BGP
       D - EIGRP, EX - EIGRP external, O - OSPF, IA - OSPF inter area
       N1 - OSPF NSSA external type 1, N2 - OSPF NSSA external type 2
       E1 - OSPF external type 1, E2 - OSPF external type 2, E - EGP
       i - IS-IS, L1 - IS-IS level-1, L2 - IS-IS level-2, * - candidate default
```

continues

Example 3-18 *A Ping to an Address in AS 300 of Figure 3-4 Is Successful (Continued)*

```
          U - per-user static route, o - ODR
          T - traffic engineered route
Gateway of last resort is not set
D    192.168.200.0/24 [90/409600] via 192.168.1.217, 00:25:37, Ethernet0
B    192.168.250.0/24 [20/0] via 192.168.1.226, 16:18:12
     192.168.1.0/24 is variably subnetted, 4 subnets, 2 masks
D       192.168.1.0/24 is a summary, 00:25:43, Null0
C       192.168.1.224/30 is directly connected, Serial0
C       192.168.1.216/30 is directly connected, Ethernet0
B       192.168.1.212/30 [20/0] via 192.168.1.226, 16:18:12
C    192.168.100.0/24 is directly connected, Ethernet1

Taos#ping
Protocol [ip]:
Target IP address: 192.168.250.1
Repeat count [5]:
Datagram size [100]:
Timeout in seconds [2]:
Extended commands [n]: y
Source address or interface: 192.168.100.1
Type of service [0]:
Set DF bit in IP header? [no]:
Validate reply data? [no]:
Data pattern [0xABCD]:
Loose, Strict, Record, Timestamp, Verbose[none]:
Sweep range of sizes [n]:
Type escape sequence to abort.
Sending 5, 100-byte ICMP Echos to 192.168.250.1, timeout is 2 seconds:
!!!!!
Success rate is 100 percent (5/5), round-trip min/avg/max = 8/64/112 ms
Taos#
```

Although the networks of AS 300 are reachable from Taos, the BGP routes must be advertised into EIGRP before the networks are reachable from AS 200's interior routers. One way to accomplish this is with redistribution at Taos, as demonstrated by the configuration in Example 3-19.

Example 3-19 *Advertising the BGP Routes into EIGRP*

```
router eigrp 200
 redistribute bgp 200 metric 10000 100 255 1 1500
 passive-interface Serial0
 network 192.168.1.0
 network 192.168.100.0
!
router bgp 200
 network 192.168.1.216 mask 255.255.255.252
 network 192.168.100.0
 network 192.168.200.0
 neighbor 192.168.1.226 remote-as 100
```

Example 3-20 shows that AS 300's prefixes are advertised to AngelFire and that the destinations are reachable. However, many of the same concerns about redistribution exist for inbound routes as for outbound routes. Redistribution picks up every BGP route, but the administrator might want only a subset of the BGP routes to be redistributed. In such a case, route filters are again required to suppress the unwanted routes.

CAUTION   Another vitally important reason exists for not redistributing BGP routes into an IGP. A full Internet routing table consists of more than 80,000 prefixes, and an IGP process will "choke" trying to process so many routes. Redistribution of a full Internet table, or even a large partial table, will inevitably cause a major network crash. The redistribution examples shown in this chapter can be useful in an enterprise network with limited prefixes, but you should never use a BGP-to-IGP redistribution on an Internet-facing router.

Example 3-20 *Taos Has Redistributed Its BGP-Learned Routes into EIGRP*

```
AngelFire#show ip route
Codes: C - connected, S - static, I - IGRP, R - RIP, M - mobile, B - BGP
       D - EIGRP, EX - EIGRP external, O - OSPF, IA - OSPF inter area
       N1 - OSPF NSSA external type 1, N2 - OSPF NSSA external type 2
       E1 - OSPF external type 1, E2 - OSPF external type 2, E - EGP
       i - IS-IS, L1 - IS-IS level-1, L2 - IS-IS level-2, * - candidate default
       U - per-user static route, o - ODR

Gateway of last resort is not set

D    192.168.100.0/24 [90/409600] via 192.168.1.218, 01:14:22, Ethernet0/0
     192.168.1.0/24 is variably subnetted, 4 subnets, 2 masks
D       192.168.1.224/30 [90/2195456] via 192.168.1.218, 01:16:44, Ethernet0/0
C       192.168.1.216/30 is directly connected, Ethernet0/0
D EX    192.168.1.212/30 [170/307200] via 192.168.1.218, 00:03:55, Ethernet0/0
D EX 192.168.250.0/24 [170/307200] via 192.168.1.218, 00:03:55, Ethernet0/0
C    192.168.200.0/24 is directly connected, Ethernet0/1

AngelFire#ping 192.168.250.1

Type escape sequence to abort.
Sending 5, 100-byte ICMP Echos to 192.168.250.1, timeout is 2 seconds:
!!!!!
Success rate is 100 percent (5/5), round-trip min/avg/max = 4/8/12 ms
AngelFire#
```

For more control over which routes are advertised into AS 200, you can use static routes, as demonstrated in Example 3-21.

Example 3-21 *Controlling Routes Advertised into AS 200 via Static Routes*

```
router eigrp 200
 redistribute static metric 10000 100 255 1 1500
 passive-interface Serial0
 network 192.168.1.0
 network 192.168.100.0
!
router bgp 200
 network 192.168.1.216 mask 255.255.255.252
 network 192.168.100.0
 network 192.168.200.0
 neighbor 192.168.1.226 remote-as 100
!
ip route 192.168.250.0 255.255.255.0 Serial0
```

In this configuration, only 192.168.250.0/24 is advertised into the AS. As Example 3-22 shows, AngelFire has no knowledge of subnet 192.168.1.212/30. Using static routes in the configuration has the added benefit of protecting AS 200 from instabilities. If network 192.168.250.0 flaps in AS 300, the changes are not advertised any further into AS 200 than Taos.

Example 3-22 *Subnet 192.168.1.212/30 Is Not Advertised to AngelFire*

```
AngelFire#show ip route
Codes: C - connected, S - static, I - IGRP, R - RIP, M - mobile, B - BGP
       D - EIGRP, EX - EIGRP external, O - OSPF, IA - OSPF inter area
       N1 - OSPF NSSA external type 1, N2 - OSPF NSSA external type 2
       E1 - OSPF external type 1, E2 - OSPF external type 2, E - EGP
       i - IS-IS, L1 - IS-IS level-1, L2 - IS-IS level-2, * - candidate default
       U - per-user static route, o - ODR

Gateway of last resort is not set

D    192.168.100.0/24 [90/409600] via 192.168.1.218, 00:14:33, Ethernet0/0
     192.168.1.0/24 is variably subnetted, 3 subnets, 2 masks
D       192.168.1.224/30 [90/2195456] via 192.168.1.218, 00:14:33, Ethernet0/0
C       192.168.1.216/30 is directly connected, Ethernet0/0
D EX 192.168.250.0/24 [170/307200] via 192.168.1.218, 00:11:17, Ethernet0/0
C    192.168.200.0/24 is directly connected, Ethernet0/1

AngelFire#ping 192.168.250.1

Type escape sequence to abort.
Sending 5, 100-byte ICMP Echos to 192.168.250.1, timeout is 2 seconds:
!!!!!
Success rate is 100 percent (5/5), round-trip min/avg/max = 4/7/8 ms
AngelFire#
```

Of course, in a single-homed AS, such as AS 200 in Figure 3-4, little reason exists to advertise any external routes into the AS at all. Unless there is a need to advertise specific routes into the AS, a default route suffices, as demonstrated by Example 3-23.

Example 3-23 *Configuring a Default Route in a Single-Homed AS*

```
router eigrp 200
 redistribute static metric 10000 100 255 1 1500
 passive-interface Serial0
 network 192.168.1.0
 network 192.168.100.0
!
router bgp 200
 network 192.168.1.216 mask 255.255.255.252
 network 192.168.100.0
 network 192.168.200.0
 neighbor 192.168.1.226 remote-as 100
!
ip classless
ip route 0.0.0.0 0.0.0.0 Serial0
```

In the configuration in Example 3-23, Taos generates a default route and advertises it to all EIGRP speakers; however, you also can configure BGP to generate a default route. To advertise a default from Vail to its BGP neighbors, use the configuration in Example 3-24.

Example 3-24 *Configuring a Default Route to BGP Neighbors*

```
router bgp 100
 network 0.0.0.0
 neighbor 192.168.1.210 remote-as 300
 neighbor 192.168.1.222 remote-as 100
 neighbor 192.168.1.225 remote-as 200
!
ip route 0.0.0.0 0.0.0.0 Null0
```

A default route to the Null0 interface is created statically, and the route is advertised with the **network** command. The assumption with the configuration in Example 3-24 is that Vail has full routing information. All packets are forwarded to Vail; any destination address that cannot be matched to a more-specific route matches the static route and is dropped.

In some design cases, a default should be sent to some neighbors, but not to others. To send a default from Vail to Taos, but not to any of Vail's other neighbors, use the configuration in Example 3-25.

Example 3-25 *Configuring a Default Route to Specific BGP Neighbors*

```
router bgp 100
 neighbor 192.168.1.210 remote-as 300
 neighbor 192.168.1.222 remote-as 100
 neighbor 192.168.1.225 remote-as 200
 neighbor 192.168.1.225 default-originate
```

The BGP **neighbor default-originate** command is similar to the OSPF **default-information-originate always** command in that a default is advertised whether the router actually has a default route or not. Notice in the configuration that the static route from the preceding configuration is no longer present; however, a route to 0.0.0.0/0 is still advertised to Taos, as Example 3-26 shows. Example 3-26 also shows the routing table of Tahoe. You can see that, unlike Taos, Tahoe does not have an entry for 0.0.0.0/0.

Example 3-26 *A Default Route Has Been Advertised to Taos, But Not to Tahoe*

```
Taos#show ip route
Codes: C - connected, S - static, I - IGRP, R - RIP, M - mobile, B - BGP
       D - EIGRP, EX - EIGRP external, O - OSPF, IA - OSPF inter area
       N1 - OSPF NSSA external type 1, N2 - OSPF NSSA external type 2
       E1 - OSPF external type 1, E2 - OSPF external type 2, E - EGP
       i - IS-IS, L1 - IS-IS level-1, L2 - IS-IS level-2, * - candidate default
       U - per-user static route, o - ODR
       T - traffic engineered route

Gateway of last resort is 192.168.1.226 to network 0.0.0.0

D    192.168.200.0/24 [90/409600] via 192.168.1.217, 02:06:34, Ethernet0
B    192.168.250.0/24 [20/0] via 192.168.1.226, 00:46:03
     192.168.1.0/24 is variably subnetted, 4 subnets, 2 masks
D       192.168.1.0/24 is a summary, 02:06:34, Null0
C       192.168.1.224/30 is directly connected, Serial0
C       192.168.1.216/30 is directly connected, Ethernet0
B       192.168.1.212/30 [20/0] via 192.168.1.226, 00:46:04
C    192.168.100.0/24 is directly connected, Ethernet1
B*   0.0.0.0/0 [20/0] via 192.168.1.226, 00:47:03
Taos#


Tahoe#show ip route
Codes: C - connected, S - static, I - IGRP, R - RIP, M - mobile, B - BGP
       D - EIGRP, EX - EIGRP external, O - OSPF, IA - OSPF inter area
       E1 - OSPF external type 1, E2 - OSPF external type 2, E - EGP
       i - IS-IS, L1 - IS-IS level-1, L2 - IS-IS level-2, * - candidate default

Gateway of last resort is not set

B    192.168.100.0 [20/0] via 192.168.1.209, 00:48:26
     192.168.1.0 255.255.255.252 is subnetted, 3 subnets
B       192.168.1.216 [20/0] via 192.168.1.209, 00:48:26
```

Example 3-26 *A Default Route Has Been Advertised to Taos, But Not to Tahoe (Continued)*

```
C        192.168.1.208 is directly connected, Serial0
C        192.168.1.212 is directly connected, Serial1
C    192.168.250.0 is directly connected, Ethernet0
B    192.168.200.0 [20/0] via 192.168.1.209, 00:48:27
Tahoe#
```

The advertisement of a default route to a BGP neighbor does not suppress the more-specific routes. In Example 3-26, you can see that the routes from AS 300 are still present in Taos' routing table. In some cases, this can be desirable. For example, an ISP might send to a customer the routes to all of its other customers (a partial Internet table), as well as a default to the rest of the Internet. Such a case is useful when multihomed to the same ISP. The customer network can then make best-path choices to the ISP's customers and use the default route for all other external destinations.

If only the default is to be sent, you must use a route filter to suppress all more-specific routes. The configuration in Example 3-27, using the **neighbor distribute-list** command, is just one way to filter BGP routes. The section "Routing Policies" demonstrates other techniques.

Example 3-27 *Filtering BGP Routes with the **neighbor distribute-list** Command*

```
router bgp 100
 neighbor 192.168.1.210 remote-as 300
 neighbor 192.168.1.222 remote-as 100
 neighbor 192.168.1.225 remote-as 200
 neighbor 192.168.1.225 default-originate
 neighbor 192.168.1.225 distribute-list 1 out
!
access-list 1 permit 0.0.0.0
access-list 1 deny any
```

Case Study: IBGP without an IGP

In Figure 3-5, another router is added to AS 100; it connects to another AS via EBGP. AS 100 is now a transit AS, carrying traffic that neither originates nor terminates in AS 100.

Figure 3-5 *AS 100 Is Running IBGP to Carry the Transit Traffic Between AS 400 and the Other Two Autonomous Systems*

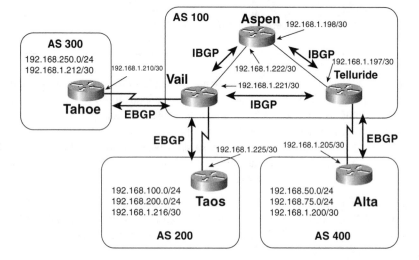

To carry the transit traffic, the interior routers in AS 100 are fully meshed with IBGP, as shown in the configurations in Example 3-28.

Example 3-28 *Configuring the Interior Routers in AS 100 to Be Fully Meshed with IBGP*

```
Vail
router bgp 100
 no synchronization
 network 192.168.1.208 mask 255.255.255.252
 network 192.168.1.224 mask 255.255.255.252
 neighbor 192.168.1.197 remote-as 100
 neighbor 192.168.1.210 remote-as 300
 neighbor 192.168.1.222 remote-as 100
 neighbor 192.168.1.225 remote-as 200

Aspen
router bgp 100
 no synchronization
 network 192.168.1.196 mask 255.255.255.252
 network 192.168.1.220 mask 255.255.255.252
 neighbor 192.168.1.197 remote-as 100
 neighbor 192.168.1.221 remote-as 100

Telluride
router bgp 100
 no synchronization
```

Example 3-28 *Configuring the Interior Routers in AS 100 to Be Fully Meshed with IBGP (Continued)*

```
  network 192.168.1.204 mask 255.255.255.252
  neighbor 192.168.1.198 remote-as 100
  neighbor 192.168.1.205 remote-as 400
  neighbor 192.168.1.221 remote-as 100
```

Example 3-29 shows Alta's routing table; a few pings demonstrate that the destinations in AS 200 and AS 300 are reachable.

Example 3-29 *Routes from AS 200 and AS 300 Have Been Passed Across the IBGP Connections in AS 100 to AS 400*

```
Alta#show ip route
Codes: C - connected, S - static, I - IGRP, R - RIP, M - mobile, B - BGP
       D - EIGRP, EX - EIGRP external, O - OSPF, IA - OSPF inter area
       E1 - OSPF external type 1, E2 - OSPF external type 2, E - EGP
       i - IS-IS, L1 - IS-IS level-1, L2 - IS-IS level-2, * - candidate default
Gateway of last resort is not set
B    192.168.100.0 [20/0] via 192.168.1.206, 02:02:59
C    192.168.75.0 is directly connected, Ethernet1
C    192.168.50.0 is directly connected, Ethernet0
     192.168.1.0 255.255.255.252 is subnetted, 8 subnets
B       192.168.1.224 [20/0] via 192.168.1.206, 02:02:59
C       192.168.1.200 is directly connected, Ethernet2
C       192.168.1.204 is directly connected, Serial0
B       192.168.1.196 [20/0] via 192.168.1.206, 02:03:30
B       192.168.1.216 [20/0] via 192.168.1.206, 02:02:59
B       192.168.1.220 [20/0] via 192.168.1.206, 02:03:30
B       192.168.1.208 [20/0] via 192.168.1.206, 02:02:59
B       192.168.1.212 [20/0] via 192.168.1.206, 02:02:59
B    192.168.250.0 [20/0] via 192.168.1.206, 02:02:59
B    192.168.200.0 [20/0] via 192.168.1.206, 02:03:00

Alta#ping 192.168.250.1
Type escape sequence to abort.
Sending 5, 100-byte ICMP Echos to 192.168.250.1, timeout is 2 seconds:
!!!!!
Success rate is 100 percent (5/5), round-trip min/avg/max = 4/5/8 ms

Alta#ping 192.168.200.1
Type escape sequence to abort.
Sending 5, 100-byte ICMP Echos to 192.168.200.1, timeout is 2 seconds:
!!!!!
Success rate is 100 percent (5/5), round-trip min/avg/max = 8/9/12 ms
Alta#
```

Remember the following important points when configuring IBGP as shown in Figure 3-5:

- Synchronization must be turned off.
- Every IBGP router must be peered with every other IBGP router.
- All networks and subnets connecting the IBGP routers must be known.

In the configurations in Example 3-28, you can see that synchronization is disabled with the command **no synchronization**. Recall from Chapter 2 that the rule of synchronization states that a router cannot advertise IBGP routes to an EBGP peer unless the routes are known by the IGP. In other words, BGP must be synchronized with the IGP. Neither redistribution nor **network** statements cause a route to be advertised that is not in the routing table.

The rule of synchronization is circumvented if IBGP-learned routes are entered into the routing table. The redistribution or **network** statements could match an IBGP route in the routing table and advertise it, even though the IGP does not know about the route. Therefore, when synchronization is enabled, IBGP routes are not entered into the routing table.

Example 3-30 shows what happens at Aspen when synchronization is enabled. The BGP table shows that the router has learned all the routes advertised by its IBGP peers, but the routing table shows that none of the routes have been entered. Although Aspen has no EBGP peers, forwarding is affected. If Telluride forwards a packet destined for 192.168.250.1, for example, Aspen does not have an entry for that destination in its routing table and will drop the packet.

Example 3-30 *When Synchronization Is Enabled, IBGP-Learned Routes Are Not Entered into the Routing Table*

```
Aspen#show ip bgp
BGP table version is 3, local router ID is 192.168.1.222
Status codes: s suppressed, d damped, h history, * valid, > best, i - internal
Origin codes: i - IGP, e - EGP, ? - incomplete
   Network          Next Hop          Metric LocPrf Weight Path
*> 192.168.1.196/30 0.0.0.0                0            32768 i
*  i192.168.1.200/30 192.168.1.205         0    100      0 400 i
*  i192.168.1.204/30 192.168.1.197         0    100      0 i
*  i192.168.1.208/30 192.168.1.221    0   100      0 i
*  i192.168.1.212/30 192.168.1.210         0    100      0 300 i
*  i192.168.1.216/30 192.168.1.225         0    100      0 200 i
*> 192.168.1.220/30 0.0.0.0                0            32768 i
*  i192.168.1.224/30 192.168.1.221         0    100      0 i
*  i192.168.50.0    192.168.1.205          0    100      0 400 i
*  i192.168.75.0    192.168.1.205          0    100      0 400 i
*  i192.168.100.0   192.168.1.225          0    100      0 200 i
*  i192.168.200.0   192.168.1.225     409600    100      0 200 i
*  i192.168.250.0   192.168.1.210          0    100      0 300 i

Aspen#show ip route
Codes: C - connected, S - static, I - IGRP, R - RIP, M - mobile, B - BGP
       D - EIGRP, EX - EIGRP external, O - OSPF, IA - OSPF inter area
       N1 - OSPF NSSA external type 1, N2 - OSPF NSSA external type 2
       E1 - OSPF external type 1, E2 - OSPF external type 2, E - EGP
       i - IS-IS, L1 - IS-IS level-1, L2 - IS-IS level-2, * - candidate default
       U - per-user static route, o - ODR
       T - traffic engineered route
```

Example 3-30 *When Synchronization Is Enabled, IBGP-Learned Routes Are Not Entered into the Routing Table (Continued)*

```
Gateway of last resort is not set

     192.168.1.0/30 is subnetted, 2 subnets
C       192.168.1.196 is directly connected, Ethernet1
C       192.168.1.220 is directly connected, Ethernet0
Aspen#
```

In Example 3-31, synchronization is disabled at Aspen, and the IBGP routes are entered into the routing table.

NOTE   If you turn off synchronization on a working BGP process, you must reset the BGP connections with the **clear ip bgp *** command before the changes will take effect. The use of this command is explained more completely in the section "Resetting BGP Connections."

Example 3-31 *Aspen's IBGP Routes Are Entered into the Routing Table When Synchronization Is Disabled*

```
Aspen#show ip route
Codes: C - connected, S - static, I - IGRP, R - RIP, M - mobile, B - BGP
       D - EIGRP, EX - EIGRP external, O - OSPF, IA - OSPF inter area
       N1 - OSPF NSSA external type 1, N2 - OSPF NSSA external type 2
       E1 - OSPF external type 1, E2 - OSPF external type 2, E - EGP
       i - IS-IS, L1 - IS-IS level-1, L2 - IS-IS level-2, * - candidate default
       U - per-user static route, o - ODR
       T - traffic engineered route

Gateway of last resort is not set

B    192.168.75.0/24 [200/0] via 192.168.1.205, 00:01:00
B    192.168.200.0/24 [200/409600] via 192.168.1.225, 00:01:00
B    192.168.250.0/24 [200/0] via 192.168.1.210, 00:01:00
B    192.168.50.0/24 [200/0] via 192.168.1.205, 00:01:00
     192.168.1.0/30 is subnetted, 8 subnets
B       192.168.1.224 [200/0] via 192.168.1.221, 00:01:50
B       192.168.1.200 [200/0] via 192.168.1.205, 00:01:00
B       192.168.1.204 [200/0] via 192.168.1.197, 00:01:52
C       192.168.1.196 is directly connected, Ethernet1
B       192.168.1.216 [200/0] via 192.168.1.225, 00:01:01
C       192.168.1.220 is directly connected, Ethernet0
B       192.168.1.208 [200/0] via 192.168.1.221, 00:01:50
B       192.168.1.212 [200/0] via 192.168.1.210, 00:01:01
B    192.168.100.0/24 [200/0] via 192.168.1.225, 00:01:02
Aspen#
```

You can observe in Figure 3-5 and in the configurations for the routers in AS 100 that each of the three routers is peered with the other two routers. The reason for this is that a router does not pass routes learned from one IBGP peer to another IBGP peer. Vail, for instance, learns the addresses of AS 400 from its IBGP session with Telluride. If this session did not exist, Vail would not learn the routes from Aspen. Aspen also learns routes from Vail and Telluride over the respective IBGP connections to those peers. If Aspen did not learn the routes, it would not be able to forward packets between Telluride and Vail.

When an EBGP-learned route is advertised to an IBGP peer, the next-hop address of the route is unchanged. Observe in Aspen's BGP table in Example 3-30 that the next-hop address of all the routes to destinations in other autonomous systems is the interface address of the router that originated the EBGP route. For example, the next-hop address of the route to 192.168.200.0/24 is 192.168.1.225, Taos' interface. These next-hop addresses are entered into the routing table. As a result, all the IBGP routers must know how to reach the next-hop addresses. In the configurations for Figure 3-5, Vail and Telluride both have **network** statements for the subnet addresses of the links to their EBGP peers. These statements exist solely so that the IBGP peers know how to reach the next-hop addresses on those links.

Aspen also has **network** statements for its two data links. These exist so that Telluride knows how to reach the next-hop address 192.168.1.221 at Vail, and so that Vail knows how to reach the next-hop address 192.168.1.197 at Telluride. These addresses are also important for the formation of the IBGP peering session between Vail and Telluride. Although the logical connection is between these two routers, as shown in Figure 3-5, the TCP connection that the IBGP session uses passes through Aspen. If Vail and Telluride do not know how to find each other, the TCP connection cannot be established.

The location of these **network** statements is also important. If the statement **network 192.168.1.220 mask 255.255.255.252** was at Vail rather than at Aspen, for example, the subnet would not be advertised past Aspen, and Telluride would not know how to reach next-hop address 192.168.1.221.

The rule that next-hop addresses of EBGP routes do not change when advertised to IBGP peers does not apply in the opposite direction. If a router advertises an IBGP-learned route to an EBGP peer, the next-hop address is the interface of the advertising router. This is true even if the route was originally an EBGP-learned route. Compare the next-hop addresses of the routes in Aspen's BGP table in Example 3-31 with the next-hop addresses of the routes in Alta's BGP table, shown in Example 3-32. Notice that Aspen shows the next-hop address for 192.168.250.0/24 as 192.168.1.210, at Tahoe. Yet Alta's next-hop address for the same route is 192.168.1.206, at Telluride. In fact, every EBGP-learned route at Alta has the same next-hop address.

Example 3-32 *The Next-Hop Address for an EBGP-Learned Route Is Always the Address of the EBGP Peer That Advertised the Route*

```
Alta#show ip bgp
BGP table version is 102, local router ID is 192.168.75.1
Status codes: s suppressed, * valid, > best, i - internal
Origin codes: i - IGP, e - EGP, ? - incomplete

   Network          Next Hop          Metric LocPrf Weight Path
*> 192.168.1.196/30 192.168.1.206                       0 100 i
*> 192.168.1.200/30 0.0.0.0               0       32768 i
*> 192.168.1.204/30 192.168.1.206        0           0 100 i
*> 192.168.1.208/30 192.168.1.206                    0 100 i
*> 192.168.1.212/30 192.168.1.206                    0 100 300 i
*> 192.168.1.216/30 192.168.1.206                    0 100 200 i
*> 192.168.1.220/30 192.168.1.206                    0 100 i
*> 192.168.1.224/30 192.168.1.206                    0 100 i
*> 192.168.50.0     0.0.0.0              0       32768 i
*> 192.168.75.0     0.0.0.0              0       32768 i
*> 192.168.100.0    192.168.1.206                    0 100 200 i
*> 192.168.200.0    192.168.1.206                    0 100 200 i
*> 192.168.250.0    192.168.1.206                    0 100 300 i
Alta#
```

You can override the rule that the next-hop address of an EBGP route does not change when advertised to an IBGP peer by using the **neighbor next-hop-self** command. Example 3-33 demonstrates the use of the **neighbor next-hop-self** command in the configurations for Vail and Telluride in AS 100.

Example 3-33 *Forcing the Next-Hop Address of an EBGP Route to Change When Advertised to an IBGP Peer*

```
Vail
router bgp 100
 no synchronization
 neighbor 192.168.1.197 remote-as 100
 neighbor 192.168.1.197 next-hop-self
 neighbor 192.168.1.210 remote-as 300
 neighbor 192.168.1.222 remote-as 100
 neighbor 192.168.1.222 next-hop-self
 neighbor 192.168.1.225 remote-as 200
```

```
Telluride
router bgp 100
 no synchronization
 neighbor 192.168.1.198 remote-as 100
 neighbor 192.168.1.198 next-hop-self
 neighbor 192.168.1.205 remote-as 400
 neighbor 192.168.1.221 remote-as 100
 neighbor 192.168.1.221 next-hop-self
```

Notice in Example 3-33 that at both routers, the **network** statements of the previous configurations have been removed. Because both routers now advertise their EBGP-learned routes with their own addresses as the next hop, the **network** statements are no longer needed. Example 3-34 shows Aspen's BGP table after the reconfiguration.

Example 3-34 *Vail and Telluride Now Advertise Themselves As the Next Hops for the EBGP-Learned Routes They Send to Aspen*

```
Aspen#show ip bgp
BGP table version is 35, local router ID is 192.168.1.222
Status codes: s suppressed, d damped, h history, * valid, > best, i - internal
Origin codes: i - IGP, e - EGP, ? - incomplete

   Network          Next Hop         Metric LocPrf Weight Path
*> 192.168.1.196/30 0.0.0.0              0            32768 i
*>i192.168.1.200/30 192.168.1.197        0    100        0 400 i
*>i192.168.1.212/30 192.168.1.221        0    100        0 300 i
*>i192.168.1.216/30 192.168.1.221        0    100        0 200 i
*> 192.168.1.220/30 0.0.0.0              0            32768 i
*>i192.168.50.0     192.168.1.197        0    100        0 400 i
*>i192.168.75.0     192.168.1.197        0    100        0 400 i
*>i192.168.100.0    192.168.1.221        0    100        0 200 i
*>i192.168.200.0    192.168.1.221   409600    100        0 200 i
*>i192.168.250.0    192.168.1.221        0    100        0 300 i
Aspen#
```

This section serves to demonstrate several fundamental concepts about the behavior of IBGP. However, the approach taken to demonstrate those concepts is certainly not standard. Although you can find many discussions in the routing newsgroups about using IBGP in an AS without an IGP, in practice you rarely, if ever, find such an implementation. For example, this section shows a configuration in which a **network** statement is used so that internal routers know how to reach external next-hop addresses. "Real-life" IBGP implementations use either the **next-hop-self** function or run an IGP in passive mode on the external interfaces. A third option occasionally encountered is to redistribute connected interfaces into the IGP on AS border routers, but this can be a heavy-handed approach and is generally frowned upon.

More importantly, an IGP makes the TCP sessions over which IBGP rides, and therefore IBGP itself, more robust. The following section begins to expose you to more-realistic BGP configurations.

Case Study: IBGP Over an IGP

In Figure 3-6, the routers within AS 100 have been reconfigured. In this topology, OSPF is running as the autonomous system's IGP, and IBGP runs only between Vail and Telluride.

Figure 3-6   *OSPF Is Added to the Routers in AS 100*

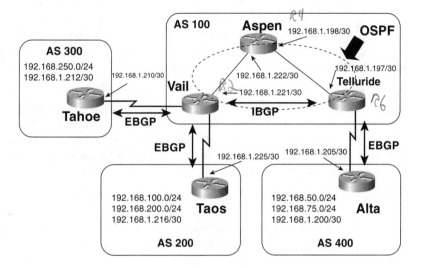

Example 3-35 shows the configurations of the three routers in AS 100.

Example 3-35 *Configurations for Vail, Aspen, and Telluride in AS 100*

```
Vail
router ospf 100
 redistribute bgp 100 subnets
 network 192.168.1.221 0.0.0.0 area 0
!
router bgp 100
 neighbor 192.168.1.197 remote-as 100
 neighbor 192.168.1.197 next-hop-self
 neighbor 192.168.1.210 remote-as 300
 neighbor 192.168.1.225 remote-as 200

Aspen
router ospf 100
 network 192.168.1.0 0.0.0.255 area 0

Telluride
router ospf 100
 redistribute bgp 100 subnets
 network 192.168.1.197 0.0.0.0 area 0
!
router bgp 100
 neighbor 192.168.1.205 remote-as 400
 neighbor 192.168.1.221 remote-as 100
 neighbor 192.168.1.221 next-hop-self
```

In the BGP configurations, synchronization is enabled and EBGP routes are redistributed into OSPF. (Synchronization enabled is the default, so no command appears in the configuration.) These two configuration steps are integral to the correct operation of the IBGP link. The redistribution serves the same purpose as the IBGP links to Aspen in the preceding case study. If Aspen receives a packet originated in AS 400 and destined for AS 200, and it does not know the route, it drops the packet.

Synchronization serves as insurance that the redistribution works correctly. If the route to 192.168.100.0/24 is not redistributed into OSPF at Vail, for instance, it will not show up in Telluride's routing table. Telluride knows about the route from the IBGP connection, but because the route is not in its routing table, the router cannot advertise the route to Alta. No traffic to that destination is forwarded from AS 400 to AS 100. If there is an alternative path from AS 400 to AS 200 (not shown in Figure 3-6), that path can be used.

Example 3-36 shows Telluride's BGP table and routing table, and Example 3-37 shows Alta's routing table. Notice from Telluride's configuration that no routes are redistributed from OSPF into BGP, and no BGP **network** commands are used. All necessary routes are already in Telluride's BGP table, and these are the routes that are advertised to Alta. The routes in Telluride's routing table serve only to satisfy the requirements of synchronization.

Example 3-36 *The BGP and Routing Tables of Telluride in Figure 3-6*

```
Telluride#show ip bgp
BGP table version is 9, local router ID is 192.168.1.206
Status codes: s suppressed, d damped, h history, * valid, > best, i - internal
Origin codes: i - IGP, e - EGP, ? - incomplete
   Network          Next Hop         Metric LocPrf Weight Path
*> 192.168.1.200/30 192.168.1.205         0              0 400 i
*>i192.168.1.212/30 192.168.1.221         0    100       0 300 i
*>i192.168.1.216/30 192.168.1.221         0    100       0 200 i
*> 192.168.50.0     192.168.1.205         0              0 400 i
*> 192.168.75.0     192.168.1.205         0              0 400 i
*>i192.168.100.0    192.168.1.221         0    100       0 200 i
*>i192.168.200.0    192.168.1.221    409600    100       0 200 i
*>i192.168.250.0    192.168.1.221         0    100       0 300 i

Telluride#show ip route
Codes: C - connected, S - static, I - IGRP, R - RIP, M - mobile, B - BGP
       D - EIGRP, EX - EIGRP external, O - OSPF, IA - OSPF inter area
       N1 - OSPF NSSA external type 1, N2 - OSPF NSSA external type 2
       E1 - OSPF external type 1, E2 - OSPF external type 2, E - EGP
       i - IS-IS, L1 - IS-IS level-1, L2 - IS-IS level-2, * - candidate default
       U - per-user static route, o - ODR
       T - traffic engineered route

Gateway of last resort is not set

B    192.168.75.0/24 [20/0] via 192.168.1.205, 15:16:37
O E2 192.168.200.0/24 [110/1] via 192.168.1.198, 15:15:38, Ethernet0
O E2 192.168.250.0/24 [110/1] via 192.168.1.198, 15:15:38, Ethernet0
```

Example 3-36 *The BGP and Routing Tables of Telluride in Figure 3-6 (Continued)*

```
B      192.168.50.0/24 [20/0] via 192.168.1.205, 15:16:38
       192.168.1.0/30 is subnetted, 6 subnets
B        192.168.1.200 [20/0] via 192.168.1.205, 15:16:38
C        192.168.1.204 is directly connected, Serial0
C        192.168.1.196 is directly connected, Ethernet0
O E2     192.168.1.216 [110/1] via 192.168.1.198, 15:15:38, Ethernet0
O        192.168.1.220 [110/20] via 192.168.1.198, 15:18:22, Ethernet0
O E2     192.168.1.212 [110/1] via 192.168.1.198, 15:15:38, Ethernet0
O E2 192.168.100.0/24 [110/1] via 192.168.1.198, 15:15:39, Ethernet0
Telluride#
```

Example 3-37 *Alta's Routing Table in Figure 3-6*

```
Alta#show ip route
Codes: C - connected, S - static, I - IGRP, R - RIP, M - mobile, B - BGP
       D - EIGRP, EX - EIGRP external, O - OSPF, IA - OSPF inter area
       E1 - OSPF external type 1, E2 - OSPF external type 2, E - EGP
       i - IS-IS, L1 - IS-IS level-1, L2 - IS-IS level-2, * - candidate default
Gateway of last resort is not set
B      192.168.100.0 [20/0] via 192.168.1.206, 15:34:05
C      192.168.75.0 is directly connected, Ethernet1
C      192.168.50.0 is directly connected, Loopback0
       192.168.1.0 255.255.255.252 is subnetted, 4 subnets
C        192.168.1.200 is directly connected, Ethernet2
C        192.168.1.204 is directly connected, Serial0
B        192.168.1.216 [20/0] via 192.168.1.206, 15:33:37
B        192.168.1.212 [20/0] via 192.168.1.206, 15:33:37
B      192.168.250.0 [20/0] via 192.168.1.206, 15:34:05
B      192.168.200.0 [20/0] via 192.168.1.206, 15:34:05
```

The topology of Figure 3-6 contains a major vulnerability. If Aspen or one of its links fails, AS 400 is isolated from the rest of the internetwork. In Figure 3-7, a link is added between Vail and Telluride for redundancy, and a second IBGP session is established over the link.

Figure 3-7 *A New Link and a Second IBGP Session Are Added Between Vail and Telluride for Redundancy*

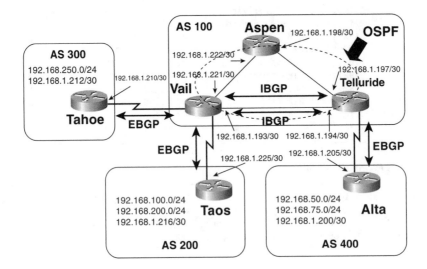

Example 3-38 shows the configurations of Vail and Telluride.

Example 3-38 *Configurations for Vail and Telluride in AS 100*

```
Vail
router ospf 100
 redistribute bgp 100 subnets
 network 192.168.1.193 0.0.0.0 area 0
 network 192.168.1.221 0.0.0.0 area 0
!
router bgp 100
 neighbor 192.168.1.194 remote-as 100
 neighbor 192.168.1.194 next-hop-self
 neighbor 192.168.1.197 remote-as 100
 neighbor 192.168.1.197 next-hop-self
 neighbor 192.168.1.210 remote-as 300
 neighbor 192.168.1.225 remote-as 200
```
```
Telluride
router ospf 100
 redistribute bgp 100 subnets
 network 192.168.1.194 0.0.0.0 area 0
 network 192.168.1.197 0.0.0.0 area 0
!
router bgp 100
 neighbor 192.168.1.193 remote-as 100
 neighbor 192.168.1.193 next-hop-self
 neighbor 192.168.1.205 remote-as 400
 neighbor 192.168.1.221 remote-as 100
 neighbor 192.168.1.221 next-hop-self
```

Example 3-39 shows the resulting BGP table at Telluride. All the routes learned from Vail indicate two next-hop addresses, representing the two IBGP connections. A **>** indicates the path currently being used. If the link fails, the other link is used.

Example 3-39 *Telluride's Routing Table Shows Alternative Paths for the Routes from Vail*

```
Telluride#show ip bgp
BGP table version is 17, local router ID is 192.168.255.253
Status codes: s suppressed, d damped, h history, * valid, > best, i - internal
Origin codes: i - IGP, e - EGP, ? - incomplete

   Network          Next Hop          Metric LocPrf Weight Path
*> 192.168.1.200/30 192.168.1.205          0             0 400 i
*>i192.168.1.212/30 192.168.1.193          0    100      0 300 i
* i                 192.168.1.221          0    100      0 300 i
*>i192.168.1.216/30 192.168.1.193          0    100      0 200 i
* i                 192.168.1.221          0    100      0 200 i
*> 192.168.50.0     192.168.1.205          0             0 400 i
*> 192.168.75.0     192.168.1.205          0             0 400 i
*>i192.168.100.0    192.168.1.193          0    100      0 200 i
* i                 192.168.1.221          0    100      0 200 i
*>i192.168.200.0    192.168.1.193     409600    100      0 200 i
* i                 192.168.1.221     409600    100      0 200 i
*>i192.168.250.0    192.168.1.193          0    100      0 300 i
* i                 192.168.1.221          0    100      0 300 i
Telluride#
```

Although the configuration illustrated in Figure 3-7 provides redundancy, the failover can be slow. By default, the BGP keepalive interval is 60 seconds and the hold time is 180 seconds, as shown in Example 3-40. Potentially, 180 seconds could pass before BGP detects a failed IBGP connection and switches to the other link. You can improve the failover time by resetting the BGP keepalive and hold times with the **timers bgp** command. For example, **timers bgp 3 9** sets the keepalive interval to 3 seconds and the hold time to 9 seconds.

Example 3-40 *The Default BGP Keepalive Time Is 60 Seconds, and the Default Hold Time Is 180 Seconds*

```
Telluride#show ip bgp neighbor 192.168.1.193
BGP neighbor is 192.168.1.193,  remote AS 100, internal link
  Index 2, Offset 0, Mask 0x4
   NEXT_HOP is always this router
   BGP version 4, remote router ID 192.168.255.254
   BGP state = Established, table version = 14, up for 00:01:30
   Last read 00:00:31, hold time is 180, keepalive interval is 60 seconds
   Minimum time between advertisement runs is 5 seconds
   Received 6 messages, 0 notifications, 0 in queue
   Sent 5 messages, 0 notifications, 0 in queue
   Prefix advertised 3, suppressed 0, withdrawn 0
   Connections established 1; dropped 0
```

continues

Example 3-40 *The Default BGP Keepalive Time Is 60 Seconds, and the Default Hold Time Is 180 Seconds (Continued)*

```
Last reset 00:02:51, due to User reset
3 accepted prefixes consume 96 bytes
0 history paths consume 0 bytes
--More--
```

Figure 3-8 shows a better way to add redundancy. Instead of creating two IBGP sessions over the alternative paths, a single IBGP session is created between the loopback interfaces of the routers. OSPF takes care of finding the best path for the IBGP session and reroutes the session much faster if a link fails.

Figure 3-8 *A Single IBGP Session Is Established Between Vail's and Telluride's Loopback Interfaces*

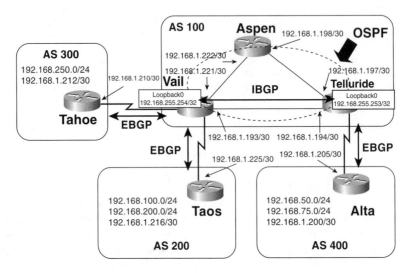

Example 3-41 shows the configurations of Vail and Telluride for the setup in Figure 3-8.

Example 3-41 *Configuring a Single IBGP Session Between the Loopback Interfaces of Vail and Telluride*

```
Vail
interface Loopback0
 ip address 192.168.255.254 255.255.255.255
!
router ospf 100
 redistribute bgp 100 subnets
 network 192.168.1.193 0.0.0.0 area 0
 network 192.168.1.221 0.0.0.0 area 0
 network 192.168.255.254 0.0.0.0 area 0
!
router bgp 100
 neighbor 192.168.1.210 remote-as 300
```

Example 3-41 *Configuring a Single IBGP Session Between the Loopback Interfaces of Vail and Telluride (Continued)*

```
 neighbor 192.168.1.225 remote-as 200
 neighbor 192.168.255.253 remote-as 100
 neighbor 192.168.255.253 update-source Loopback0
 neighbor 192.168.255.253 next-hop-self

Telluride
interface Loopback0
 ip address 192.168.255.253 255.255.255.255
!
router ospf 100
 redistribute bgp 100 subnets
 network 192.168.1.194 0.0.0.0 area 0
 network 192.168.1.197 0.0.0.0 area 0
 network 192.168.255.253 0.0.0.0 area 0
!
router bgp 100
 neighbor 192.168.1.205 remote-as 400
 neighbor 192.168.255.254 remote-as 100
 neighbor 192.168.255.254 update-source Loopback0
 neighbor 192.168.255.254 next-hop-self
```

The significant difference in these configurations, beyond the obvious creation of loopback addresses, is the **neighbor update-source** statement. This command causes the BGP messages to be sourced from the IP address of the loopback interface rather than from the physical interface the message is sent on. Without it, the TCP source of the TCP sessions would be the outgoing interface address. The end points of the TCP sessions would not match and would therefore not come up. Also important is the additional **network** statement under OSPF, advertising the loopback address. Without it, the address is unreachable, and the IBGP session is not created. Example 3-42 shows Telluride's BGP table after the reconfiguration.

Example 3-42 *The Next-Hop Address of the Routes from Vail Is Vail's Loopback Address*

```
Telluride#show ip bgp
BGP table version is 7, local router ID is 192.168.255.253
Status codes: s suppressed, d damped, h history, * valid, > best, i - internal
Origin codes: i - IGP, e - EGP, ? - incomplete

   Network          Next Hop          Metric LocPrf Weight Path
*> 192.168.1.200/30 192.168.1.205          0             0 400 i
*>i192.168.1.212/30 192.168.255.254        0    100      0 300 i
*>i192.168.1.216/30 192.168.255.254        0    100      0 200 i
*> 192.168.50.0     192.168.1.205          0             0 400 i
*> 192.168.75.0     192.168.1.205          0             0 400 i
*>i192.168.100.0    192.168.255.254        0    100      0 200 i
*>i192.168.200.0    192.168.255.254   409600    100      0 200 i
*>i192.168.250.0    192.168.255.254        0    100      0 300 i
Telluride#
```

CAUTION	The examples in this section use BGP-to-IGP redistribution to better demonstrate basic IBGP behavior. However, it is worth noting one more time that if you are receiving a large number of routes from an external BGP peer, redistribution into your IGP can be very dangerous. In a topology such as the one in Figure 3-8, the safe approach is to configure a full IBGP mesh—IBGP sessions between the loopback interfaces of all three routers in AS 100. Aspen then learns the necessary information for packet forwarding directly from BGP, and no redistribution is necessary.

Case Study: EBGP Multihop

Just as you can establish an IBGP session between loopback interfaces, as demonstrated in the preceding case study, you also can establish EBGP sessions between loopback interfaces. Figure 3-9 shows such a session. Here, the end points of the EBGP session between Telluride and Alta are loopback interfaces.

Figure 3-9   *An EBGP Session Is Established Between Telluride's and Alta's Loopback Interfaces*

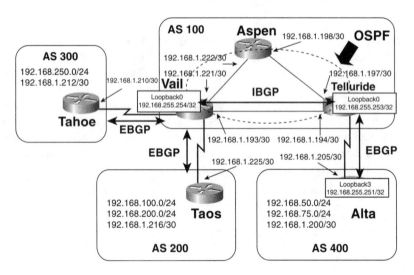

Example 3-43 shows the preliminary configuration of the two routers in Figure 3-9.

Example 3-43 *Configuring an EBGP Session Between the Loopback Interfaces for Telluride and Alta*

```
Telluride
router bgp 100
  network 192.168.1.204 mask 255.255.255.252
  neighbor 192.168.255.251 remote-as 400
  neighbor 192.168.255.251 update-source Loopback0
```

Example 3-43 *Configuring an EBGP Session Between the Loopback Interfaces for Telluride and Alta (Continued)*

```
  neighbor 192.168.255.254 remote-as 100
  neighbor 192.168.255.254 update-source Loopback0
  neighbor 192.168.255.254 next-hop-self
!
ip route 192.168.255.251 255.255.255.255 192.168.1.205
```

Alta
```
router bgp 400
  network 192.168.50.0
  network 192.168.75.0
  network 192.168.1.200 mask 255.255.255.252
  neighbor 192.168.255.253 remote-as 100
  neighbor 192.168.255.253 update-source Loopback3
  no auto-summary
!
ip route 192.168.255.253 255.255.255.255 192.168.1.206
```

Notice that static routes have been added to each router. These routes are necessary so that each router knows how to find the address of its neighbor's loopback interface to begin the TCP session. In the preceding case study, adding a **network** statement under OSPF performed the same function. In this scenario, no IGP runs between the routers, so static routes are used. When troubleshooting IBGP, keep in mind that the IBGP routers must know how to find their peers *before* an IBGP session can be established and BGP routes can be exchanged. If two IBGP neighbors are not peering, one of the first things you should check is whether the routers know how to reach each other.

Unfortunately, the neighbors do not peer with the configurations shown. Example 3-44 offers a hint about the problem. The highlighted line indicates that the neighbors are not directly connected. You already know this; the addresses of the loopback interfaces are indeed not directly connected, which is why the static routes are required. However, the fact that BGP points this out is significant.

Example 3-44 **show ip bgp neighbors** *Output Shows That the EBGP Connection to Alta Is Not Established*

```
Telluride#show ip bgp neighbor 192.168.255.251
BGP neighbor is 192.168.255.251,  remote AS 400, external link
  Index 1, Offset 0, Mask 0x2
    BGP version 4, remote router ID 0.0.0.0
    BGP state = Idle, table version = 0
    Last read 00:00:11, hold time is 180, keepalive interval is 60 seconds
    Minimum time between advertisement runs is 30 seconds
    Received 0 messages, 0 notifications, 0 in queue
    Sent 0 messages, 0 notifications, 0 in queue
    Prefix advertised 0, suppressed 0, withdrawn 0
    Connections established 0; dropped 0
    Last reset never
```

continues

Example 3-44 show ip bgp neighbors *Output Shows That the EBGP Connection to Alta Is Not Established (Continued)*

```
    0 accepted prefixes consume 0 bytes
    0 history paths consume 0 bytes
    External BGP neighbor not directly connected.
    No active TCP connection
Telluride
```

The significance is that although you can create IBGP across multiple router hops, EBGP neighbors by default must be directly connected. In Figure 3-9, the packets sourced from Alta's loopback interface must be routed to its serial interface. At Telluride, the packet must be routed from its serial interface to its loopback interface. In other words, the TCP packets must cross two router hops between the loopback interfaces.

The **neighbor ebgp-multihop** command enables you to override the default one-hop EBGP limit by changing the TTL of EBGP packets from the default value of 1. Example 3-45 shows the neighbor configurations using the **neighbor ebgp-multihop** command to change the TTL of the EBGP packets to 2.

Example 3-45 *Using the **neighbor ebgp-multihop** Command Overrides the Default One-Hop EBGP Limit for Alta and Telluride*

```
Telluride
router bgp 100
 network 192.168.1.204 mask 255.255.255.252
 neighbor 192.168.255.251 remote-as 400
 neighbor 192.168.255.251 ebgp-multihop 2
 neighbor 192.168.255.251 update-source Loopback0
 neighbor 192.168.255.254 remote-as 100
 neighbor 192.168.255.254 update-source Loopback0
 neighbor 192.168.255.254 next-hop-self
!
ip route 192.168.255.251 255.255.255.255 192.168.1.205
```
```
Alta
router bgp 400
 network 192.168.50.0
 network 192.168.75.0
 network 192.168.1.200 mask 255.255.255.252
 neighbor 192.168.255.253 remote-as 100
 neighbor 192.168.255.253 ebgp-multihop 2
 neighbor 192.168.255.253 update-source Loopback3
 no auto-summary
!
ip route 192.168.255.253 255.255.255.255 192.168.1.206
```

Example 3-46 shows the result of the configuration change. The EBGP session is established, and the output indicates the new hop limit.

Example 3-46 show ip bgp neighbors *Output Shows That the EBGP Connection to Alta Is Established*

```
Telluride#show ip bgp neighbor 192.168.255.251
BGP neighbor is 192.168.255.251,  remote AS 400, external link
 Index 1, Offset 0, Mask 0x2
  BGP version 4, remote router ID 192.168.255.251
  BGP state = Established, table version = 9, up for 00:04:44
  Last read 00:00:14, hold time is 180, keepalive interval is 60 seconds
  Minimum time between advertisement runs is 30 seconds
  Received 9 messages, 0 notifications, 0 in queue
  Sent 11 messages, 0 notifications, 0 in queue
  Prefix advertised 4, suppressed 0, withdrawn 0
  Connections established 1; dropped 0
  Last reset 00:25:59, due to User reset
  3 accepted prefixes consume 96 bytes
  0 history paths consume 0 bytes
  External BGP neighbor may be up to 2 hops away
 Connection state is ESTAB, I/O status: 1, unread input bytes: 0
 Local host: 192.168.255.253, Local port: 11001
 Foreign host: 192.168.255.251, Foreign port: 179
```

Unlike IBGP, which is normally configured between loopback interfaces, the majority of EBGP sessions are configured between directly connected interfaces. Therefore, **ebgp-multihop** is not frequently required. An example of where EBGP between loopback interfaces can be useful is when two external neighbors are directly connected with multiple links (such as multiple ATM or Frame Relay virtual circuits) for redundancy, but only a single EBGP session is desired. If the link being used by EBGP fails, the session can be rerouted over an alternative link.

Case Study: Aggregate Routes

Autonomous system 100 in Figure 3-10 contains eight Class C network addresses, all of which can be summarized with the aggregate address 192.168.192.0/21. Stowe is learning the internal networks via EIGRP and is advertising the aggregate to Sugarbush via EBGP.

There are two ways to create an aggregate address under BGP. The first is to create a static entry in the routing table for the aggregate address and then advertise it with the **network** command. The second way is to use the **aggregate-address** command.

Figure 3-10 *All the Internal Networks of AS 100 Can Be Aggregated into the Single Address 192.168.192.0/21*

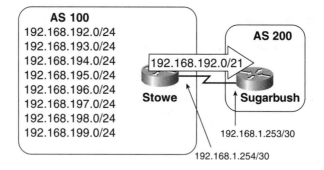

Aggregation Using Static Routes

Example 3-47 demonstrates a configuration for Stowe using a static entry aggregate address advertised with the **network** command.

Example 3-47 *Creating an Aggregate Address Under BGP Using a Static Entry Advertised with the **network** Command*

```
router eigrp 100
  network 192.168.199.0
!
router bgp 100
  network 192.168.192.0 mask 255.255.248.0
  neighbor 192.168.1.253 remote-as 200
!
ip classless
ip route 192.168.192.0 255.255.248.0 Null0
```

The static route is pointed at the Null interface because the aggregate itself is not a legitimate end destination. It merely represents the more-specific routes in Stowe's routing table. Packets whose destination addresses belong to one of AS 100's Class C addresses match the aggregate address in routers external to AS 100 and are forwarded to Stowe. At that router, the packet is matched to the more-specific address and forwarded to the correct internal next-hop router. If for some reason the more-specific Class C address is not in Stowe's routing table, the packet is forwarded to the Null interface and dropped.

Example 3-48 shows the BGP tables of Stowe and Sugarbush. Only the aggregate address exists in Stowe's BGP table; that router's BGP configuration has not entered any other address.

Example 3-48 *The BGP Tables of Stowe and Sugarbush Both Contain Only the Aggregate Route*

```
Stowe#show ip bgp
BGP table version is 2, local router ID is 192.168.199.2
Status codes: s suppressed, d damped, h history, * valid, > best, i - internal
Origin codes: i - IGP, e - EGP, ? - incomplete

   Network          Next Hop           Metric LocPrf Weight Path
*> 192.168.192.0/21 0.0.0.0                 0            32768 i
Stowe#
```
```
Sugarbush#show ip bgp
BGP table version is 18, local router ID is 172.17.3.1
Status codes: s suppressed, d damped, h history, * valid, > best, i - internal
Origin codes: i - IGP, e - EGP, ? - incomplete

   Network          Next Hop           Metric LocPrf Weight Path
*> 192.168.192.0/21 192.168.1.254           0          0 100 i
Sugarbush#
```

Suppressing More-Specific Routes

In a simple topology such as the one in Figure 3-10, this first method normally suffices. As the topology and the routing policies grow more complex, however, the options available with the **aggregate-address** command make that method more useful. The remainder of this case study examines the **aggregate-address** command and its options.

For the aggregate specified by the **aggregate-address** command to be advertised, at least one of the more-specific addresses belonging to the aggregate must be entered into the BGP table either through redistribution or the **network** command. Example 3-49 demonstrates a configuration for Stowe using the **aggregate-address** command and redistribution.

Example 3-49 *Creating an Aggregate Address Under BGP Using the* **aggregate-address** *Command*

```
router eigrp 100
 network 192.168.199.0
!
router bgp 100
 aggregate-address 192.168.192.0 255.255.248.0 summary-only
 redistribute eigrp 100
 neighbor 192.168.1.253 remote-as 200
```

Example 3-50 shows the resulting BGP tables at Stowe and Sugarbush. Stowe's table looks quite different than it did in Example 3-48—all the more-specific routes are included. However, Sugarbush's table looks the same. Only the aggregate address is advertised.

Example 3-50 *Stowe's BGP Table Includes All the More-Specific Routes; Only the Aggregate Is Advertised to Sugarbush*

```
Stowe#show ip bgp
BGP table version is 23, local router ID is 192.168.199.2
Status codes: s suppressed, d damped, h history, * valid, > best, i - internal
Origin codes: i - IGP, e - EGP, ? - incomplete

   Network          Next Hop          Metric LocPrf Weight Path
s> 192.168.192.0    192.168.199.1     2297856         32768 ?
*> 192.168.192.0/21 0.0.0.0                           32768 i
s> 192.168.193.0    192.168.199.1     2297856         32768 ?
s> 192.168.194.0    192.168.199.1     2297856         32768 ?
s> 192.168.195.0    192.168.199.1     2297856         32768 ?
s> 192.168.196.0    192.168.199.1     2297856         32768 ?
s> 192.168.197.0    192.168.199.1     2297856         32768 ?
s> 192.168.198.0    192.168.199.1     2297856         32768 ?
s> 192.168.199.0    0.0.0.0                 0         32768 ?
Stowe#
```

```
Sugarbush#show ip bgp
BGP table version is 2, local router ID is 172.17.3.1
Status codes: s suppressed, d damped, h history, * valid, > best, i - internal
Origin codes: i - IGP, e - EGP, ? - incomplete

   Network          Next Hop          Metric LocPrf Weight Path
*> 192.168.192.0/21 192.168.1.254                    0 100 i
Sugarbush#
```

The keys to the left of the more-specific routes in Stowe's BGP table indicate that the routes have been suppressed. This suppression results from the **summary-only** option used with the **aggregate-address** command. Without that option, both the aggregate and the more-specific routes are advertised.

Advertising Aggregate and More-Specific Routes

Advertising both the aggregate and the more-specific routes makes no sense in the simple topology of Figure 3-10. But Figure 3-11 shows a scenario in which such a scheme can be desirable. Here, AS 100 is multihomed to AS 200. AS 200 needs the full routes from AS 100 to set routing policy, but it must send only the aggregate to AS 300.

Although the more-specific routes of AS 100 are advertised, they are sent to AS 200 with a COMMUNITY attribute of NO_EXPORT. As Chapter 2 discusses, routes carrying this attribute cannot be advertised to EBGP peers. As a result, AS 200 knows the routes but does not advertise them to AS 300. Only the aggregate, which does not carry the COMMUNITY NO_EXPORT attribute, is advertised to AS 300. Example 3-51 shows the configuration for Stowe. The configuration for Mammoth is similar and appears later in this section.

Figure 3-11 *AS 100 Is Multihomed to AS 200*

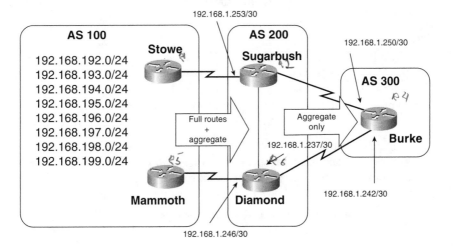

Example 3-51 *Configuring Stowe to Advertise Both the Aggregate and the More-Specific Routes*

```
router eigrp 100
 network 192.168.199.0
!
router bgp 100
 aggregate-address 192.168.192.0 255.255.248.0
 redistribute eigrp 100
 neighbor 192.168.1.253 remote-as 200
 neighbor 192.168.1.253 send-community
 neighbor 192.168.1.253 route-map COMMUNITY out
!
ip classless
!
access-list 101 permit ip host 192.168.192.0 host 255.255.248.0
!
route-map COMMUNITY permit 10
 match ip address 101
 set community none
!
route-map COMMUNITY permit 20
 set community no-export
```

The **summary-only** keyword has been removed from the **aggregate-address** command, so
both the aggregate and the more-specific routes are advertised to AS 200. The **neighbor
192.168.1.253 send-community** command specifies that the COMMUNITY attribute
is sent to Sugarbush. The **neighbor 192.168.1.253 route-map COMMUNITY out**
command filters outgoing BGP routes through a route map named COMMUNITY. If the

route map matches the update to access list 101, no COMMUNITY attribute is set. If the route does not match access list 101, the route is given a COMMUNITY attribute of NO_EXPORT.

The usage of access list 101 might be new to you. Normally, the first address specified in an extended IP access list is the source address, and the second address is the destination. In this application, however, the first address is the route prefix, and the second address is the prefix's mask. The reason such an odd access list is necessary is because the exact prefix must be identified. If **access-list 1 permit 192.168.192.0 0.0.7.255** were used, it would match both the aggregate 192.168.192.0/21 and the more-specific route 192.168.192.0/24.

Example 3-52 shows Sugarbush's BGP table, and you can see that it contains both the aggregate route and the more-specific routes. Additionally, the command **show ip bgp community no-export** is used to display the routes with the NO_EXPORT COMMUNITY attribute. All routes from Stowe except for the aggregate are listed.

Example 3-52 *Sugarbush's BGP Table Contains Both the Aggregate Route and the More-Specific Routes; All the Routes from Stowe Except for the Aggregate Have the NO_EXPORT COMMUNITY Attribute*

```
Sugarbush#show ip bgp
BGP table version is 30, local router ID is 172.17.3.1
Status codes: s suppressed, d damped, h history, * valid, > best, i - internal
Origin codes: i - IGP, e - EGP, ? - incomplete

   Network          Next Hop         Metric LocPrf Weight Path
* i192.168.192.0    192.168.1.237    2297856    100      0 100 ?
*>                  192.168.1.254    2297856             0 100 ?
* i192.168.192.0/21 192.168.1.237               100      0 100 i
*>                  192.168.1.254                        0 100 i
* i192.168.193.0    192.168.1.237    2297856    100      0 100 ?
*>                  192.168.1.254    2297856             0 100 ?
* i192.168.194.0    192.168.1.237    2297856    100      0 100 ?
*>                  192.168.1.254    2297856             0 100 ?
* i192.168.195.0    192.168.1.237    2297856    100      0 100 ?
*>                  192.168.1.254    2297856             0 100 ?
* i192.168.196.0    192.168.1.237    2297856    100      0 100 ?
*>                  192.168.1.254    2297856             0 100 ?
* i192.168.197.0    192.168.1.237    2297856    100      0 100 ?
*>                  192.168.1.254    2297856             0 100 ?
*>i192.168.198.0    192.168.1.237          0    100      0 100 ?
*                   192.168.1.254    2681856             0 100 ?
* i192.168.199.0    192.168.1.237    2681856    100      0 100 ?
*>                  192.168.1.254          0             0 100 ?

Sugarbush#show ip bgp community no-export
BGP table version is 10, local router ID is 172.17.3.1
Status codes: s suppressed, d damped, h history, * valid, > best, i - internal
Origin codes: i - IGP, e - EGP, ? - incomplete
```

Example 3-52 *Sugarbush's BGP Table Contains Both the Aggregate Route and the More-Specific Routes; All the Routes from Stowe Except for the Aggregate Have the NO_EXPORT COMMUNITY Attribute (Continued)*

```
   Network          Next Hop          Metric LocPrf Weight Path
*> 192.168.192.0    192.168.1.254     2297856             0 100 ?
*> 192.168.193.0    192.168.1.254     2297856             0 100 ?
*> 192.168.194.0    192.168.1.254     2297856             0 100 ?
*> 192.168.195.0    192.168.1.254     2297856             0 100 ?
*> 192.168.196.0    192.168.1.254     2297856             0 100 ?
*> 192.168.197.0    192.168.1.254     2297856             0 100 ?
*  192.168.198.0    192.168.1.254     2681856             0 100 ?
*> 192.168.199.0    192.168.1.254           0             0 100 ?
Sugarbush#
```

Example 3-53 shows Burke's BGP table. No routes except the aggregate have been advertised.

Example 3-53 *Burke's BGP Table Contains Only the Aggregate Route*

```
Burke#show ip bgp
BGP table version is 15, local router ID is 172.21.1.1
Status codes: s suppressed, * valid, > best, i - internal
Origin codes: i - IGP, e - EGP, ? - incomplete

   Network          Next Hop          Metric LocPrf Weight Path
*> 192.168.192.0/21 192.168.1.249                       0 200 100 i
*                   192.168.1.241                       0 200 100 i
Burke#
```

Mammoth produces the same advertisements as Stowe. For demonstration purposes, a different configuration (Example 3-54) is used to arrive at the same results. At Mammoth, an IP prefix list is used rather than an access list.

Example 3-54 *Configuration for Mammoth in Figure 3-11*

```
router eigrp 100
 network 192.168.198.0
!
router bgp 100
 aggregate-address 192.168.192.0 255.255.248.0
 redistribute eigrp 100
 neighbor 192.168.1.246 remote-as 200
 neighbor 192.168.1.246 send-community
 neighbor 192.168.1.246 route-map COMMUNITY out
!
ip classless
ip route 192.168.255.251 255.255.255.255 192.168.1.205
!
```

continues

Example 3-54 *Configuration for Mammoth in Figure 3-11 (Continued)*

```
!
ip prefix-list AGGREGATE seq 5 permit 192.168.192.0/21
!
route-map COMMUNITY permit 10
 match ip address prefix-list AGGREGATE
 set community none
!
route-map COMMUNITY permit 20
 set community no-export
```

Like route maps, prefix lists are identified by a name rather than by a number. In Example 3-54, the prefix list is named AGGREGATE. The lines of the list are distinguished by a sequence number (**seq**) that identifies each line's place in a multiple-line list and makes editing the list easier. If you do not type a sequence number when you enter a line, Cisco IOS Software enters it automatically, in the order that you enter the lines. Following the **permit | deny** keyword, a prefix and the prefix length are specified.

The prefix list shown in Mammoth's configuration in Example 3-54 matches 192.168.192.0/21 exactly. However, you can also add an option that matches a range of prefixes. For example, the command **ip prefix-list AGGREGATE seq 5 permit 192.168.192.0/21 ge 24** matches all prefixes whose first 21 bits match 192.168.192.0 and whose length is greater than or equal to 24 bits. This line would match all the more-specific routes in AS 100. A keyword of **le**, on the other hand, is used to match prefixes whose lengths are less than or equal to the specified number of bits.

The BGP table at Diamond looks very similar to the one at Sugarbush; the more-specific routes and the aggregate are entered. In addition to the aggregate from Sugarbush, Burke's BGP table in Example 3-53 shows that the aggregate is also advertised by Diamond. Example 3-55 shows the aggregate and one of the more-specific routes from Diamond's BGP table in greater detail. You can see that the aggregate does not have any COMMUNITY attributes (although it does, as an aggregate, have the **ATOMIC_AGGREGATE** and **AGGREGATOR** attributes set), and the more-specific route does.

Example 3-55 *A Closer Look at Two of the Routes from Diamond's BGP Table Shows the Attributes of Each*

```
Diamond# show ip bgp 192.168.192.0 255.255.248.0
BGP routing table entry for 192.168.192.0/21, version 59
Paths: (2 available, best #1)
  Advertised to non peer-group peers:
    192.168.1.238 192.168.1.242
  100, (aggregated by 100 192.168.198.2)
    192.168.1.245 from 192.168.1.245 (192.168.198.2)
      Origin IGP, localpref 100, valid, external, atomic-aggregate, best, ref 2
  100, (aggregated by 100 192.168.199.2)
```

Example 3-55 *A Closer Look at Two of the Routes from Diamond's BGP Table Shows the Attributes of Each (Continued)*

```
      192.168.1.238 from 192.168.1.238 (192.168.1.253)
        Origin IGP, localpref 100, valid, internal, not synchronized, atomic-aggregate,
    ref 2
    Diamond#

    Diamond#show ip bgp 192.168.199.0
    BGP routing table entry for 192.168.199.0/24, version 58
    Paths: (2 available, best #1, not advertised to EBGP peer)
      Advertised to non peer-group peers:
        192.168.1.238
      100
        192.168.1.245 from 192.168.1.245 (192.168.198.2)
          Origin incomplete, metric 2681856, localpref 100, valid, external, best, ref 2
          Community: no-export
      100
        192.168.1.238 from 192.168.1.238 (192.168.1.253)
          Origin incomplete, metric 0, localpref 100, valid, internal, not synchronized,
    ref 2
    Diamond#
```

Advertising Aggregate and Selected More-Specifics

The previous scenarios send the more-specific routes of AS 100 to AS 200 so that AS 200 can implement routing policy. That is, AS 200 uses the routes to set routing preferences for sending traffic to AS 100. AS 100 also can influence its incoming traffic by manipulating its outgoing advertisements. For example, advertising 192.168.193.0/24 over the Stowe/Sugarbush link and not over the Mammoth/Diamond link causes incoming traffic to use the Stowe/Sugarbush link. An administrator might want to implement such a policy if the AS is geographically diverse. For instance, Stowe might be in Vermont and Mammoth in California. The administrator might want incoming traffic to use the ingress point closest to the destination, to minimize internal routing.

For this demonstration, the following routing policies are implemented in AS 100 of Figure 3-11:

- 192.168.192.0/24, 192.168.193.0/24, and 192.168.194.0/24 are advertised over the Stowe/Sugarbush link.

- 192.168.196.0/24, 192.168.197.0/24, and 192.168.198.0/24 are advertised over the Mammoth/Diamond link.

- 192.168.195.0/24 and 192.168.199.0/24 are not advertised at all.

- An aggregate route is advertised over both links for backup so that if either link fails, all incoming traffic is routed to the remaining link.

To suppress a subset of the aggregated routes, the **suppress-map** option is used with the
aggregate-address command. The listed policies are implemented at Stowe and Mammoth
with the configurations in Example 3-56. The COMMUNITY route maps and the EIGRP
configurations do not change from the preceding section and so are not shown for
simplicity.

Example 3-56 *Suppressing Selected Prefixes with the* **suppress-map** *Option of the* **aggregate-address** *Command*

```
Stowe
router bgp 100
 aggregate-address 192.168.192.0 255.255.248.0 suppress-map VERMONT
 redistribute eigrp 100
 neighbor 192.168.1.253 remote-as 200
 neighbor 192.168.1.253 send-community
 neighbor 192.168.1.253 route-map COMMUNITY out
!
access-list 1 permit 192.168.195.0 0.0.0.255
access-list 1 permit 192.168.196.0 0.0.3.255
!
route-map VERMONT permit 10
 match ip address 1

Mammoth
router bgp 100
 aggregate-address 192.168.192.0 255.255.248.0 suppress-map CALIFORNIA
 redistribute eigrp 100
 neighbor 192.168.1.246 remote-as 200
 neighbor 192.168.1.246 send-community
 neighbor 192.168.1.246 route-map COMMUNITY out
!
ip prefix-list SUPPRESSEDROUTES seq 5 permit 192.168.192.0/22 le 24
ip prefix-list SUPPRESSEDROUTES seq 10 permit 192.168.199.0/24
!
route-map CALIFORNIA permit 10
 match ip address prefix-list SUPPRESSEDROUTES
```

Stowe's configuration uses a route map named VERMONT to determine the routes to be
suppressed. The route map in turn uses access list 1 to identify the appropriate routes. The
access list permits the prefix 192.168.195.0/24 and also all prefixes whose first 22 bits
match 192.168.196.0/22. All other prefixes match the implicit "deny any" at the end of the
access list and so are not suppressed.

NOTE   The logic of route maps sometimes seems a bit tortured. In this case, a route that is denied
by the access list is "denied from being suppressed"; that is, the route is permitted to be
advertised. Routes that are permitted by the access list, on the other hand, are "permitted to
be suppressed" and so are not advertised.

Mammoth's configuration uses a route map named CALIFORNIA to determine the routes to be suppressed. Mammoth again uses a prefix list rather than an access list to identify the appropriate routes. Sequence 5 of the prefix list permits all prefixes whose first 22 bits match 192.168.192.0/22 and whose length is less than or equal to 24. Sequence 10 of the prefix list permits the prefix 192.168.199.0/24. Advertisements of routes with these permitted prefixes are suppressed; all other routes are implicitly denied by the prefix list and so are not suppressed.

Example 3-57 shows the resulting BGP tables at Sugarbush and Diamond. Sugarbush forwards packets destined for 192.168.193.0/24 to Stowe (192.168.1.254), for example, whereas packets destined for 192.168.196.0/24 are forwarded to Diamond (192.168.1.237). Diamond, in turn, routes the packets destined for 192.168.196.0/24 to Mammoth (192.168.1.245). Both Stowe and Mammoth are advertising the aggregate; if the link to either router fails, the packets that normally would be forwarded across that link will match the aggregate from the remaining link.

Example 3-57 *These BGP Tables Show That Stowe and Mammoth Have Advertised Different Subsets of the More-Specific Routes in AS 100, Whereas Both Still Advertise the Aggregate*

```
Sugarbush#show ip bgp
BGP table version is 79, local router ID is 192.168.1.253
Status codes: s suppressed, d damped, h history, * valid, > best, i - internal
Origin codes: i - IGP, e - EGP, ? - incomplete

   Network          Next Hop         Metric LocPrf Weight Path
*> 192.168.192.0    192.168.1.254    2297856           0 100 ?
* i192.168.192.0/21 192.168.1.237            100       0 100 i
*>                  192.168.1.254                      0 100 i
*> 192.168.193.0    192.168.1.254    2297856           0 100 ?
*> 192.168.194.0    192.168.1.254    2297856           0 100 ?
*>i192.168.196.0    192.168.1.237    2297856    100    0 100 ?
*>i192.168.197.0    192.168.1.237    2297856    100    0 100 ?
*>i192.168.198.0    192.168.1.237          0    100    0 100 ?
Sugarbush#
```

```
Diamond#show ip bgp
BGP table version is 137, local router ID is 172.18.1.1
Status codes: s suppressed, d damped, h history, * valid, > best, i - internal
Origin codes: i - IGP, e - EGP, ? - incomplete

   Network          Next Hop         Metric LocPrf Weight Path
* i192.168.192.0    192.168.1.238    2297856    100    0 100 ?
*> 192.168.192.0/21 192.168.1.245                      0 100 i
* i                 192.168.1.238            100       0 100 i
* i192.168.193.0    192.168.1.238    2297856    100    0 100 ?
* i192.168.194.0    192.168.1.238    2297856    100    0 100 ?
*> 192.168.196.0    192.168.1.245    2297856           0 100 ?
*> 192.168.197.0    192.168.1.245    2297856           0 100 ?
*> 192.168.198.0    192.168.1.245          0           0 100 ?
Diamond#
```

Changing the Attributes of the Aggregate

Yet another option that you can use with the **aggregate-address** command is the **attribute-map** option. This option enables you to change the attributes of the aggregate route. Notice in Example 3-57, for instance, that all the more-specific routes have an ORIGIN attribute of Incomplete, because the routes are redistributed into BGP from EIGRP. The aggregates have an origin of IGP, however, because they originated within the BGP processes of Stowe and Mammoth. Suppose the administrator wants AS 200 to use the Mammoth/Diamond link for all traffic following the aggregate route and to use the Stowe/Sugarbush link only for backup. The BGP decision process, as discussed in Chapter 2, chooses an ORIGIN of IGP over an ORIGIN of Incomplete when considering two routes to the same destination. If Stowe changes the ORIGIN of its aggregate to Incomplete, the routers in AS 200 will prefer the Mammoth/Diamond link. Example 3-58 shows the configuration for Stowe.

Example 3-58 *Stowe Changes Its Aggregate ORIGIN to Incomplete*

```
router eigrp 100
 network 192.168.199.0
!
router bgp 100
 aggregate-address 192.168.192.0 255.255.248.0 attribute-map ORIGIN suppress-map
VERMONT
 redistribute eigrp 100
 neighbor 192.168.1.253 remote-as 200
 neighbor 192.168.1.253 send-community
 neighbor 192.168.1.253 route-map COMMUNITY out
!
access-list 1 permit 192.168.195.0 0.0.0.255
!
access-list 101 permit ip host 192.168.192.0 host 255.255.248.0
!
route-map ORIGIN permit 10
 set origin incomplete
!
route-map COMMUNITY permit 10
 match ip address 101
 set community none
!
route-map COMMUNITY permit 20
 set community no-export
!
route-map VERMONT permit 10
 match ip address 1
```

Example 3-59 shows the resulting BGP table at Sugarbush. Before the reconfiguration, Sugarbush preferred the aggregate learned via EBGP over the aggregate learned via IBGP (see Example 3-57). However, the ORIGIN attribute has a higher priority in the decision process than IBGP/EBGP, so the IBGP route from Diamond, with an ORIGIN of IGP, is now preferred.

Example 3-59 *The Aggregate Advertised by Stowe (192.168.1.254) Now Has an ORIGIN of Incomplete; the Aggregate Advertised by Diamond and Originated by Mammoth Is the Preferred Route*

```
Sugarbush#show ip bgp
BGP table version is 17, local router ID is 192.168.1.253
Status codes: s suppressed, d damped, h history, * valid, > best, i - internal
Origin codes: i - IGP, e - EGP, ? - incomplete

   Network          Next Hop          Metric LocPrf Weight Path
*> 192.168.192.0    192.168.1.254     2297856               0 100 ?
*>i192.168.192.0/21 192.168.1.237            100          0 100 i
*                   192.168.1.254                         0 100 ?
*> 192.168.193.0    192.168.1.254     2297856               0 100 ?
*> 192.168.194.0    192.168.1.254     2297856               0 100 ?
*>i192.168.196.0    192.168.1.237     2297856    100       0 100 ?
*>i192.168.197.0    192.168.1.237     2297856    100       0 100 ?
*>i192.168.198.0    192.168.1.237           0    100       0 100 ?
Sugarbush#
```

Interestingly, the reconfiguration also affects the routing in AS 300, as demonstrated in Example 3-60. The preferred route at Sugarbush is the IBGP route; synchronization is enabled, so the IBGP route is not advertised to EBGP peer Burke. As a result, Burke learns the aggregate only from Diamond.

Example 3-60 *Only Diamond Advertises the Aggregate to Burke*

```
Burke#show ip bgp
BGP table version is 3, local router ID is 172.21.1.1
Status codes: s suppressed, * valid, > best, i - internal
Origin codes: i - IGP, e - EGP, ? - incomplete

   Network          Next Hop          Metric LocPrf Weight Path
*> 192.168.192.0/21 192.168.1.241                         0 200 100 i
Burke#
```

Using AS_SET with Aggregates

Figure 3-12 shows a modified version of the internetwork shown in Figure 3-11, including a change in the source of the aggregate address. Here, both AS 100 and AS 200 advertise the full routes of AS 100 to AS 300 and AS 400, without an aggregate.

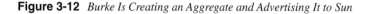

Figure 3-12 *Burke Is Creating an Aggregate and Advertising It to Sun*

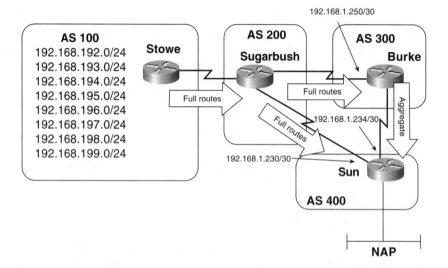

Router Burke, in AS 300, suppresses the more-specific addresses of AS 100 and sends an aggregate to Sun in AS 400. Burke's configuration in Example 3-61 is similar to configurations you have encountered already in this case study.

Example 3-61 *Burke Is Configured to Suppress Specific Addresses of AS 100 and Send an Aggregate to Sun in AS 400*

```
router bgp 300
 aggregate-address 192.168.192.0 255.255.248.0 summary-only
 neighbor 192.168.1.234 remote-as 400
 neighbor 192.168.1.234 next-hop-self
 neighbor 192.168.1.249 remote-as 200
 neighbor 192.168.1.249 distribute-list 1 out
!
access-list 1 deny    192.168.192.0
access-list 1 permit any
```

One difference between the Burke configuration in Example 3-61 and the previous configurations is the **neighbor distribute-list** command. This command implements a route filter and operates in the same way as **distribute-list** commands discussed in *TCP/IP Routing, Volume I*. In this case, the filter prevents the aggregate from being advertised back to Sugarbush.

Example 3-62 shows the BGP table at Sun. As expected, the table includes the more-specific routes from Sugarbush and the aggregate route from Burke. Of interest in this case study is the AS_PATH associated with the aggregate. The AS_SEQUENCE of the AS_PATH attribute of an aggregate begins with the AS in which the aggregate was originated. Burke originated the aggregate, so the AS_SEQUENCE includes only AS 300. The aggregate actually points to destinations in AS 100; like any summarization, the aggregate has caused a loss of routing information.

Example 3-62 *The AS_PATH of the Aggregate from Burke Includes Only AS 300, the AS in Which the Aggregate Was Originated*

```
Sun#show ip bgp
BGP table version is 20, local router ID is 192.168.1.234
Status codes: s suppressed, d damped, h history, * valid, > best, i - internal
Origin codes: i - IGP, e - EGP, ? - incomplete

   Network          Next Hop         Metric LocPrf Weight Path
*> 192.168.192.0    192.168.1.229                      0 200 100 ?
*> 192.168.192.0/21 192.168.1.233                      0 300 i
*> 192.168.193.0    192.168.1.229                      0 200 100 ?
*> 192.168.194.0    192.168.1.229                      0 200 100 ?
*> 192.168.195.0    192.168.1.229                      0 200 100 ?
*> 192.168.196.0    192.168.1.229                      0 200 100 ?
*> 192.168.197.0    192.168.1.229                      0 200 100 ?
*> 192.168.198.0    192.168.1.229                      0 200 100 ?
*> 192.168.199.0    192.168.1.229                      0 200 100 ?
Sun#
```

In Example 3-63, Burke sets the ATOMIC_AGGREGATE and AGGREGATOR attributes in the aggregate to indicate that a loss of information has occurred.

Example 3-63 *The Aggregate from Burke Has the ATOMIC_AGGREGATE and AGGREGATOR (aggregated by 300 192.168.1.250) Attributes Set to Indicate a Loss of Path Information*

```
Sun#show ip bgp 192.168.192.0 255.255.248.0
BGP routing table entry for 192.168.192.0/21, version 23
Paths: (1 available, best #1)
  Advertised to non peer-group peers:
    192.168.1.229
  300, (aggregated by 300 192.168.1.250)
    192.168.1.233 from 192.168.1.233 (192.168.1.250)
      Origin IGP, localpref 100, valid, external, atomic-aggregate, best, ref 2
Sun#
```

In the case of the topology in Figure 3-12, the loss of path information causes a problem. Unlike Burke, Sun does not have a route filter in place to prevent the aggregate from being advertised to Sugarbush. Because Sugarbush does not see its own AS number in the AS_PATH of the aggregate from Sun, it enters the aggregate into its BGP table, as demonstrated in Example 3-64.

Example 3-64 *Sugarbush Accepts the Aggregate Route from Sun Because It Does Not Find Its Own AS Number in the Route's AS_PATH*

```
Sugarbush#show ip bgp
BGP table version is 19, local router ID is 172.20.1.1
Status codes: s suppressed, d damped, h history, * valid, > best, i - internal
Origin codes: i - IGP, e - EGP, ? - incomplete

   Network          Next Hop          Metric LocPrf Weight Path
*> 192.168.192.0    192.168.1.254     2297856            0 100 ?
*> 192.168.192.0/21 192.168.1.230                        0 400 300 i
*> 192.168.193.0    192.168.1.254     2297856            0 100 ?
*> 192.168.194.0    192.168.1.254     2297856            0 100 ?
*> 192.168.195.0    192.168.1.254     2297856            0 100 ?
*> 192.168.196.0    192.168.1.254     2297856            0 100 ?
*> 192.168.197.0    192.168.1.254     2297856            0 100 ?
*> 192.168.198.0    192.168.1.254     2681856            0 100 ?
*> 192.168.199.0    192.168.1.254           0            0 100 ?
Sugarbush#
```

If one of the more-specific routes from AS 100 becomes invalid, Sugarbush should drop any packets destined for that network. With the aggregate in place, however, the packets will instead be matched to the aggregate route. Suppose, for example, that the interface to network 192.168.197.0/24 in AS 100 fails. Stowe advertises the fact, and the route to that destination is removed from all BGP tables. Next, Sugarbush receives a packet with a destination address of 192.168.197.5. Not finding the more-specific address, the router matches the destination to the aggregate and forwards the packet to Sun. Sun again finds no more-specific address, matches the aggregate, and forwards the packet to Burke. Burke, as the originator of the aggregate, has no more-specific address and drops the packet. The packet to an invalid destination has been unnecessarily forwarded across two extra router hops before being correctly discarded. The problem would be even worse if Sugarbush were advertising an aggregate to Burke. In this case, instead of the packet's being dropped later than necessary, it loops until its TTL expires.

To remedy the problem, Burke can advertise an AS_SET in addition to the AS_SEQUENCE as part of the AS_PATH attribute by adding the **as-set** keyword to the **aggregate-address** statement. As discussed in Chapter 2, the AS_SET is an unordered list of the AS numbers along the path to the more-specific addresses that make up the aggregate. Unlike the AS_SEQUENCE, the AS_SET is not used to determine a shortest path; rather, its only purpose is to restore the loop-detection functionality lost in the aggregation.

Example 3-65 shows the configuration for Burke to advertise the AS_SET.

Example 3-65 *Configuring Burke to Advertise the AS_SET*

```
router bgp 300
 aggregate-address 192.168.192.0 255.255.248.0 as-set summary-only
 neighbor 192.168.1.234 remote-as 400
 neighbor 192.168.1.234 next-hop-self
 neighbor 192.168.1.249 remote-as 200
 neighbor 192.168.1.249 distribute-list 1 out
!
access-list 1 deny    192.168.192.0
access-list 1 permit any
```

Example 3-66 shows the resulting BGP table at Sun. All the AS numbers on the path to the more-specific addresses are included in the AS_PATH of the aggregate. When the aggregate is advertised to Sugarbush, that router recognizes its AS number of 200 in the AS_PATH and does not accept the route.

Example 3-66 *When Burke Is Configured to Include the AS_SET in the AS_PATH Attribute, All the AS Numbers on the Path to the Aggregated Addresses Are Included*

```
Sun#show ip bgp
BGP table version is 10, local router ID is 172.21.1.1
Status codes: s suppressed, d damped, h history, * valid, > best, i - internal
Origin codes: i - IGP, e - EGP, ? - incomplete
   Network          Next Hop           Metric LocPrf Weight Path
*> 192.168.192.0    192.168.1.229               0 200 100 ?
*> 192.168.192.0/21 192.168.1.233               0 300 200 100 ?
*> 192.168.193.0    192.168.1.229               0 200 100 ?
*> 192.168.194.0    192.168.1.229               0 200 100 ?
*> 192.168.195.0    192.168.1.229               0 200 100 ?
*> 192.168.196.0    192.168.1.229               0 200 100 ?
*> 192.168.197.0    192.168.1.229               0 200 100 ?
*> 192.168.198.0    192.168.1.229               0 200 100 ?
*> 192.168.199.0    192.168.1.229               0 200 100 ?
Sun#
```

It is important to know that when the AS_SET is advertised, the aggregate route inherits all the attributes of the aggregated routes. In the case of Figure 3-12, the AS_PATH of all the more-specific routes is (300,200,100). As a result, the AS_SET appears in Sun's BGP table as an ordered sequence, indistinguishable from the AS_SEQUENCEs.

Figure 3-13 shows a different topology. A new AS has been added, and network 192.168.197.0/24 has been moved from AS 100 to the new AS 500. Burke still receives the same routes, but now not all AS_PATH attributes match. As a result, the AS_SET is now advertised as the unordered sequence shown in Example 3-67.

Figure 3-13 *Network 192.168.197.0/24 Is Moved from AS 100 to AS 500; Burke Can No Longer Represent the AS_SET as an Ordered Set*

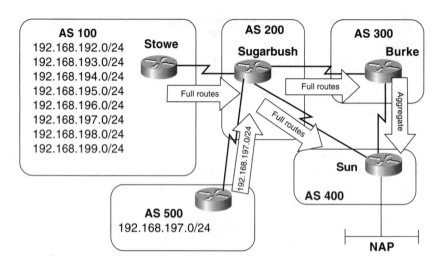

Example 3-67 *The AS_SET Is Now Displayed in Sun's BGP Table as an Unordered Set, Distinguishable from the Ordered AS_SEQUENCEs*

```
Sun#show ip bgp
BGP table version is 35, local router ID is 172.21.1.1
Status codes: s suppressed, d damped, h history, * valid, > best, i - internal
Origin codes: i - IGP, e - EGP, ? - incomplete

   Network          Next Hop         Metric LocPrf Weight Path
*> 192.168.192.0    192.168.1.229                       0 200 100 ?
*> 192.168.192.0/21 192.168.1.233                       0 300 {200,100,500} ?
*> 192.168.193.0    192.168.1.229                       0 200 100 ?
*> 192.168.194.0    192.168.1.229                       0 200 100 ?
*> 192.168.195.0    192.168.1.229                       0 200 100 ?
*> 192.168.196.0    192.168.1.229                       0 200 100 ?
*> 192.168.197.0    192.168.1.229                       0 200 500 i
*> 192.168.198.0    192.168.1.229                       0 200 100 ?
*> 192.168.199.0    192.168.1.229                       0 200 100 ?
Sun#
```

Basing an Aggregate on Selected More-Specific Routes

In some situations, you might want to advertise an aggregate with the AS_SET but do not want the aggregate to inherit all the attributes of all the aggregated routes. In Figure 3-14, Sugarbush receives all the routes from AS 100 and AS 500 and advertises an aggregate to Burke.

Figure 3-14 *For Sugarbush to Advertise the Aggregate with an AS_SET, the Aggregate Must Not Inherit the NO_EXPORT COMMUNITY Attribute from 192.168.197.0/24*

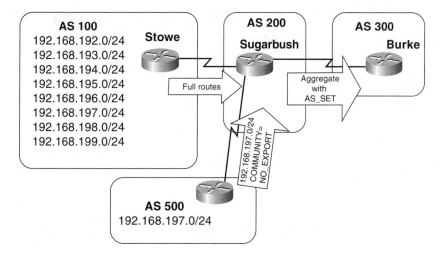

The problem with the setup in Figure 3-14 is that AS 500 is advertising 192.168.197.0/24 with the COMMUNITY attribute of NO_EXPORT. When Sugarbush uses the AS_SET option, the aggregate inherits the NO_EXPORT attribute, as demonstrated in Example 3-68. Note that the NO_EXPORT attribute is given to the aggregate locally, not added to the advertisement of the aggregate. As a result, Sugarbush acts on the attribute and does not advertise the aggregate route.

Example 3-68 *The* **show ip bgp community no-export** *Command Displays All Routes with the NO_EXPORT COMMUNITY Attribute; in This Case, the Aggregate Route Has Inherited the Attribute from One of the Aggregated Addresses, 192.168.197.0/24*

```
Sugarbush#show ip bgp community no-export
BGP table version is 19, local router ID is 172.20.1.1
Status codes: s suppressed, d damped, h history, * valid, > best, i - internal
Origin codes: i - IGP, e - EGP, ? - incomplete

   Network          Next Hop         Metric LocPrf Weight Path
*> 192.168.192.0/21 0.0.0.0                          32768 {100,500} ?
s> 192.168.197.0    192.168.1.1           0              0 500 i
Sugarbush#
```

The last option of the **aggregate-address** command to be discussed, **advertise-map**, enables you to choose the routes upon which to base the aggregate. In the case of the internetwork in Figure 3-14, if Sugarbush does not consider 192.168.197.0/24 when forming the aggregate, the aggregate does not inherit that route's attributes. Example 3-69 shows the configuration for Sugarbush using the **advertise-map** option of the **aggregate-address** command.

Example 3-69 *Configuring Sugarbush to Choose the Routes Upon Which to Base the Aggregate*

```
router bgp 200
 aggregate-address 192.168.192.0 255.255.248.0 as-set summary-only advertise-map
ALLOW_ROUTE
 neighbor 192.168.1.1 remote-as 500
 neighbor 192.168.1.250 remote-as 300
 neighbor 192.168.1.254 remote-as 100
 !
access-list 1 deny   192.168.197.0
access-list 1 permit any
 !
route-map ALLOW_ROUTE permit 10
 match ip address 1
```

The **advertise-map** option in the configuration in Example 3-69 points to a route map named ALLOW_ROUTE, which identifies the more-specific routes on which the aggregate is based. The route map in turn points to access list 1, which rejects 192.168.197.0 and permits all other routes. Because Sugarbush now ignores 192.168.197.0/24 when forming the aggregate, the aggregate route does not inherit the NO_EXPORT attribute, as demonstrated in Example 3-70.

Example 3-70 *After Sugarbush Is Reconfigured with the **advertise-map** Option, the Aggregate Route No Longer Has the NO_EXPORT Attribute*

```
Sugarbush#show ip bgp community no-export
BGP table version is 18, local router ID is 172.20.1.1
Status codes: s suppressed, d damped, h history, * valid, > best, i - internal
Origin codes: i - IGP, e - EGP, ? - incomplete

   Network          Next Hop         Metric LocPrf Weight Path
s> 192.168.197.0    192.168.1.1           0               0 500 i
Sugarbush#
```

Limiting the more-specific prefixes on which an aggregate is based can present some vulnerabilities. In the network of Figure 3-14 and the associated configurations, suppose the link between Stowe and Sugarbush fails. The aggregate is based only on the prefixes from AS 100 and so is no longer advertised. As a result, the destinations within AS 500 are no longer reachable from AS 300 and beyond.

Managing BGP Connections

Cisco IOS offers several features to help in the management of BGP peer connections. The first is the **neighbor description** statement. Like the **description** statement that can be entered under an interface configuration, this statement has no functional impact on the router. Rather, it adds an informational text string to the configuration. You already have encountered many configuration options that apply to a BGP neighbor, and you will encounter several more in the remaining sections of this chapter. When the BGP configuration becomes elaborate, the **neighbor description** helps provide a reminder of who and where each neighbor is. Example 3-71 demonstrates the use of the **neighbor description** statement.

Example 3-71 *The* **neighbor description** *Command Helps Alleviate Confusion with Elaborate BGP Configurations*

```
router bgp 200
 aggregate-address 192.168.192.0 255.255.248.0 as-set summary-only
 neighbor 192.168.1.1 remote-as 500
 neighbor 192.168.1.1 description ******T1 to Sun, Ckt. ID 54.HCGS.123456
 neighbor 192.168.1.237 remote-as 200
 neighbor 192.168.1.237 description ****Ethernet to Diamond, Interface E0
 neighbor 192.168.1.250 remote-as 300
 neighbor 192.168.1.250 description ****T1 to Burke, Ckt. ID 54.HCGS.654321
 neighbor 192.168.1.254 remote-as 100
 neighbor 192.168.1.254 description ****56K to Stowe, Ckt. ID 54.DWDA.987654
```

The description can contain any useful information you want to add, up to 80 characters. This example includes the link type, the name of the neighboring router, and, where appropriate, the circuit ID.

Two BGP neighbors also can authenticate each other with a password using the **neighbor password** statement. In the configuration in Example 3-72, the password **noT4U2n0** has been entered for the neighbor 192.168.1.253.

Example 3-72 *BGP Neighbor Authentication*

```
service password-encryption
!
router bgp 100
 redistribute eigrp 100
 neighbor 192.168.1.253 remote-as 200
 neighbor 192.168.1.253 description ****56K to Sugarbush, Ckt. ID 54.DWDA.987654
 neighbor 192.168.1.253 password 7 14191D3F5831782574
```

Notice also that the **service password-encryption** option has been entered into the router's global configuration, causing the password to be encrypted when the configuration is displayed, for added privacy.

The passwords between different neighbor connections can differ, or they can all be the same. You also can apply a common password to a peer group rather than to individual neighbors by specifying the peer group name in place of an IP address. For each BGP connection, however, the two neighbors must have the same password.

The IOS uses MD5 authentication when a BGP neighbor password is configured. MD5 is a one-way *message digest* or *secure hash* function produced by RSA Data Security, Inc. It also is occasionally referred to as a *cryptographic checksum*, because it works in somewhat the same way as an arithmetic checksum. MD5 computes a 128-bit hash value from a plain-text message of arbitrary length (in this case, a BGP message) and a password. This "fingerprint" is transmitted along with the message. The receiver, knowing the same password, calculates its own hash value. If nothing in the message has changed, the receiver's hash value should match the sender's value transmitted with the message. The hash value is impossible to decipher (without a huge amount of computing power) without knowing the password so that an unauthorized router cannot, either maliciously or by accident, peer with a router running neighbor authentication.

Other options available for the neighbor connection are the **neighbor advertisement-interval** and **neighbor version** commands. The first command changes the default BGP update-interval to a specified interval between 0 and 600 seconds. If a large number of routes must be exchanged across a link, using this command to increase the period between advertisements can reduce the impact on the link's available bandwidth. You should not change the advertisement interval, however, unless you fully understand the consequences, such as possible reduced reconvergence times.

The **neighbor version** command is useful if a neighbor cannot support the default BGP-4. Rather than have the version 4 router negotiate down to the neighbor's supported version, you can configure the router to speak a specific version to a specific neighbor. As a result, the time necessary to establish a BGP connection is reduced. If both neighbors speak version 4, you gain nothing with this command, and its use is unnecessary.

The BGP decision process implemented in the Cisco IOS takes into consideration the length of the AS_PATH attribute when choosing between multiple routes to the same destination. However, RFC 1771 does not include this step. As a result, a Cisco BGP speaker occasionally is peered with another vendor's router that does not consider the AS_PATH length. If this situation creates the potential for inconsistent routing decisions, you can instruct the Cisco router to ignore the AS_PATH length in its decision process with the command **bgp bestpath as-path ignore**.

In some policy situations, you might want to limit the number of prefixes a router is allowed to accept from a neighbor. For example, you might know that only a certain number of prefixes should be advertised from a particular AS. Any number above this probably indicates a configuration mistake by that autonomous system's administrator. Or perhaps there is a service agreement in place in which you agree to accept only a finite number of prefixes; to advertise a larger number, the administrator of the neighboring AS must first get your approval. To enforce such a policy, you can use the **neighbor maximum-prefix** command. Consider the configuration in Example 3-73.

Example 3-73 *Limiting the Number of Prefixes That a Router Is Allowed to Accept from a Neighbor*

```
router bgp 100
 redistribute eigrp 100
 neighbor 192.168.1.253 remote-as 200
 neighbor 192.168.1.253 maximum-prefix 300
```

The router in Example 3-73 is configured to accept a maximum of 300 prefixes from neighbor 192.168.1.253. If the limit is exceeded, the router closes the BGP session with the neighbor, and the session cannot be reestablished until you issue the **clear ip bgp 192.168.1.253** command.

Perhaps breaking the peering session might be too severe a consequence for exceeding the maximum prefixes, but you still want to be notified when it happens. The configuration in Example 3-74 does not close the session, but instead causes the router to generate a log message.

Example 3-74 *Configuring the Router to Generate a Log Message When a Neighbor Exceeds the Number of Prefixes That Can Be Sent*

```
router bgp 100
 redistribute eigrp 100
 neighbor 192.168.1.253 remote-as 200
 neighbor 192.168.1.253 maximum-prefix 300 warning-only
```

A log message is generated when the neighbor's advertised prefix exceeds 75 percent of the maximum—in this case, at 225 prefixes. You can change that default percentage. The configuration in Example 3-75 generates a log message when the neighbor's advertised prefixes exceed 90 percent of the maximum.

Example 3-75 *Configuring the Router to Generate a Log Message When a Neighbor Exceeds 90 Percent of the Number of Prefixes That Can Be Sent*

```
router bgp 100
 redistribute eigrp 100
 neighbor 192.168.1.253 remote-as 200
 neighbor 192.168.1.253 maximum-prefix 300 90 warning-only
```

On occasion, you might need to temporarily disconnect a peer but not want to delete its neighbor configuration. The configuration in Example 3-76 uses the **neighbor shutdown** command to disconnect the neighbor 192.168.1.237.

Example 3-76 *Temporarily Disconnecting a Neighbor Connection*

```
aggregate-address 192.168.192.0 255.255.248.0 as-set summary-only
 neighbor 192.168.1.1 remote-as 500
 neighbor 192.168.1.1 description ******T1 to Sun, Ckt. ID 54.HCGS.123456
 neighbor 192.168.1.237 remote-as 200
 neighbor 192.168.1.237 description ****Ethernet to Diamond, Interface E0
 neighbor 192.168.1.237 shutdown
 neighbor 192.168.1.250 remote-as 300
 neighbor 192.168.1.250 description ****T1 to Burke, Ckt. ID 54.HCGS.654321
 neighbor 192.168.1.254 remote-as 100
 neighbor 192.168.1.254 description ****56K to Stowe, Ckt. ID 54.DWDA.987654
```

The **neighbor shutdown** command in Example 3-76 closes the TCP port 179 connection to a specified neighbor, similar to the way the **shutdown** command disables a single interface. When the **show ip bgp neighbor** command is issued, the neighbor is indicated as administratively shut down.

Finally, you can use the **timers bgp** command to change the default BGP keepalive and hold time intervals of 60 seconds and 180 seconds. The argument can be made that reducing these intervals speeds the detection of an unreliable neighbor, but the real solution to such a problem is to eliminate the causes of the neighbor's unreliability. A change of the default intervals with this command applies to every neighbor, not just a single neighbor. Even if a neighbor has different default keepalive and hold time intervals, the intervals that are used are dynamically negotiated as part of the peering process. Therefore, under normal circumstances, there should be very few reasons to use this command.

Routing Policies

Webster's Dictionary defines a *policy* as "a high-level overall plan embracing the general goals and acceptable procedures." A *routing policy* is a plan that defines how routes are accepted on a router and how routes are advertised. The goal that the policy embraces is the correct forwarding or suppressing of IP packets. *Acceptable procedures* means that the routing policy is implemented with the least-negative impact possible on the CPU and memory resources of the router, the bandwidth resources of the connected links, and the policies of neighboring routers.

NOTE   The term *routing policies* used in this section and throughout this chapter should not be confused with the Cisco feature known as Policy Routes. These special versions of static routes, implemented with the command **ip policy route-map**, are discussed in *Routing TCP/IP, Volume I*, Chapter 14, "Route Maps."

Routing policies are always important, but especially so in a BGP environment. By its very nature, BGP interconnects autonomous systems, and neighboring autonomous systems probably are not under your administrative control. You must plan BGP routing policies very carefully. You must fully understand which packets should be forwarded to which neighbors, which packets should be accepted from those neighbors, and under what circumstances those packets are forwarded and received. When a complete routing plan is developed, you are ready to design the configuration that enables the policy. This stage requires that you completely understand the BGP configuration options available to you. A lab can prove very useful at this stage, to test the design and verify your assumptions before the design is implemented on a production network. Only after a configuration has been completely designed, understood, and validated should you implement it.

A mistake at any one of these steps can have serious consequences in your internetwork and can result in unhappy users, unhappy customers, unhappy service providers, and unhappy managers. Because of the potential for disruption of traffic across significant portions of the Internet, many service providers discontinue BGP peering with customers who frequently misconfigure their policies. The economic impact of being denied BGP peering— particularly if the customer is itself a service provider—can be severe. No other IP routing protocol offers policy features as powerful as those of BGP, and no other protocol carries as great a potential for getting you into trouble as does BGP.

This section demonstrates the available options for configuring routing policies under BGP. You already have been exposed to some of the most fundamental tools for configuring routing policy. If you read *Volume I* and have read all of this volume up to this point, you know how to configure any of the IP routing protocols to advertise selected routes and how to redistribute routes from one protocol to another. You also know how to use route filters and route maps and how to manipulate the administrative distances and metrics of the various IP routing protocols. You understand the hazards of having more than one path into and out of an area, a routing domain, or an AS, and you know some strategies for avoiding those hazards. In this chapter, you have encountered several brief examples of some BGP-specific tools, such as manipulating the ORIGIN and COMMUNITY attributes and filtering NLRI from a single neighbor.

Finally, you understand that outbound route advertisements affect incoming traffic and that inbound route advertisements affect outgoing traffic. When designing a routing policy, it is vitally important that you consider the advertised routes and received routes separately and design both an *inbound* and an *outbound* routing policy.

Resetting BGP Connections

When a BGP speaker's configuration is changed, it is often necessary to reset the connections to the affected neighbors for the change to take effect. The Cisco IOS Software Command Summary lists the following circumstances under which you must reset a BGP connection:

- Additions or changes to BGP-related access lists
- Changes to BGP-related weights
- Changes to BGP-related distribution lists
- Changes in the BGP-related timer's specifications
- Changes to the BGP administrative distance
- Changes to BGP-related route maps

All the items on this list affect a route's BGP routing policy in some way, and this is a hint about why resets are required. If you are changing routing policy, you do not want the policies to take effect "on the fly." Rather, you want to fully configure the new policy and only then implement the policy. Allowing each statement of a routing policy to take effect as you enter it can cause routing loops, black holes, security breaches, or other equally nasty results.

You can reset connections with the command **clear ip bgp**, issued from IOS Exec mode. You can apply the reset to a specific neighbor, a peer group, or to all the router's neighbors. To reset a connection to a specific neighbor, the neighbor's IP address is specified. To reset a connection to neighbor 192.168.1.253, for example, the command is **clear ip bgp 192.168.1.253**. To reset a connection to all members of a peer group named subscribers, the command is **clear ip bgp subscribers**. And to reset all of a router's BGP connections, the command is **clear ip bgp ***.

You should clear only the connections that are actually affected by the changes you make. When a connection is reset, a Cease notification message is sent to the neighbor, the BGP session is closed, the TCP session is closed, and all caches are invalidated. A new BGP session is then begun. While this process takes place, service is disrupted to and from the connection. Resetting all connections when only one or two are affected by the new configuration can have serious consequences in a production environment.

Cisco provides an alternative to a full reset, called *soft reconfiguration*. Rather than completely tearing down and reestablishing a TCP and BGP connection, soft reconfiguration merely triggers updates to cause new routing policies to take effect. A soft reset can be triggered for outbound only, inbound only, or both. Outbound soft reconfiguration is used when the policies affecting outbound traffic are changed. Inbound soft reconfiguration is used when the policies affecting inbound traffic are changed. Like a "hard" reset, you can specify a single neighbor, a peer group, or all BGP connections.

Suppose, for example, that you change the policy on a BGP router that affects the outbound traffic to neighbor 192.168.1.253. To trigger updates to that neighbor under the new policy, the command is **clear ip bgp 192.168.1.253 soft out**.

Inbound soft reconfiguration is used when you change the policies concerning inbound traffic. Beginning with Cisco IOS Software Release 12.1, dynamic soft reconfiguration is supported for inbound routes. Prior to that version, however, you must first add a **neighbor soft-reconfiguration inbound** statement to the BGP configuration before inbound soft reconfiguration can be used. The command **clear ip bgp soft in** is then used for every neighbor that sends traffic affected by the new inbound policies. Suppose you change the inbound routing policies on router Stowe in Figure 3-14, and the policies affect traffic received from neighbor 192.168.1.253. Example 3-77 shows what Stowe's BGP configuration will look like.

Example 3-77 *Configuring a Neighbor for Soft Inbound Reconfiguration*

```
router bgp 100
 redistribute eigrp 100
 neighbor 192.168.1.253 remote-as 200
 neighbor 192.168.1.253 soft-reconfiguration inbound
```

When the **neighbor soft-reconfiguration inbound** statement is added, the router begins storing updates from the specified neighbor. These updates are unmodified by any existing inbound policies so that the router can correctly apply the new policies when soft reconfiguration is triggered. After the new inbound policies are configured for Stowe in the example shown, the command **clear ip bgp 192.168.1.253 soft in** is entered from Exec mode. The router then uses the stored, unmodified updates to implement the new inbound policies.

Soft reconfiguration also can be triggered for both inbound and outbound policies at the same time. For instance, the command **clear ip bgp 192.168.1.253 soft**, with no **in** or **out** keyword, sends updates to neighbor 192.168.1.253 and also applies inbound policies to the stored updates from that neighbor.

The obvious drawback to using inbound soft reconfiguration is that memory is required to store the updates. If the neighbor is advertising a large number of routes, or if updates from many neighbors are being stored, the impact on the local router's memory can be significant. You can avoid this load on memory. When inbound BGP routing policies are changed on a router, its neighbors can send an outbound soft reconfiguration. The local router, receiving the updates from its neighbors, then applies the new inbound policies. You should use inbound soft reconfiguration only if you cannot send, or arrange to have sent, an outbound soft reconfiguration from the affected neighbors. You might find inbound soft reconfiguration necessary if the policy change affects the traffic from many neighbors, and if you must apply the policy change to all neighbors simultaneously. In either case, you must carefully weigh the impact on local memory.

Case Study: Filtering Routes by NLRI

Route filters are at the heart of almost any routing policy. After all, if you have an inbound and an outbound routing policy, what you are most likely defining is which routes a router accepts and which routes a router advertises.

The first and simplest of the route filters available to BGP are defined by the **distribute-list** command. This route filter is defined for each neighbor or peer group and points to an access list that defines the prefixes, or NLRI, on which the filter will act.

The internetwork in Figure 3-15 is used for this and the following two case studies.

Figure 3-15 *AS 30 Is Multihomed to Different Transit Autonomous Systems*

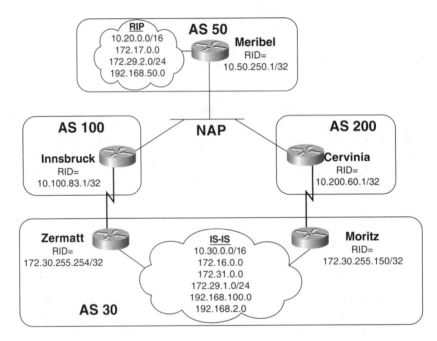

The IGP of AS 50 is RIP, and the IGP of AS 30 is Integrated IS-IS. AS 100 and AS 200 are transit autonomous systems. Example 3-78 shows the preliminary configurations of the five routers in Figure 3-15.

Example 3-78 *Filtering Routes by NLRI: Initial Router Configurations*

```
Zermatt
interface Loopback0
 ip address 172.30.255.254 255.255.255.255
 ip router isis
!
router isis
 net 30.5678.1234.defa.00
 redistribute bgp 30 metric 0 metric-type internal level-2
!
```

Example 3-78 *Filtering Routes by NLRI: Initial Router Configurations (Continued)*

```
router bgp 30
 redistribute isis level-2
 neighbor 10.100.83.1 remote-as 100
 neighbor 10.100.83.1 ebgp-multihop 2
 neighbor 10.100.83.1 update-source Loopback0
 no auto-summary
 !
ip classless
ip route 10.100.83.1 255.255.255.255 Serial1.906
```

Moritz
```
interface Loopback0
 ip address 172.30.255.150 255.255.255.255
 ip router isis
 !
router isis
 net 30.1234.5678.abcd.00
 redistribute bgp 30 metric 0 metric-type internal level-2
 !
router bgp 30
 redistribute isis level-2
 neighbor 10.200.60.1 remote-as 200
 neighbor 10.200.60.1 ebgp-multihop 2
 neighbor 10.200.60.1 update-source Loopback0
 no auto-summary
 !
ip route 10.200.60.1 255.255.255.255 Serial1.803
```

Innsbruck
```
interface Loopback0
 ip address 10.100.83.1 255.255.255.255
 !
router bgp 100
 neighbor 10.50.250.1 remote-as 50
 neighbor 10.50.250.1 ebgp-multihop 2
 neighbor 10.50.250.1 update-source Loopback0
 neighbor 10.200.60.1 remote-as 200
 neighbor 10.200.60.1 ebgp-multihop 2
 neighbor 10.200.60.1 update-source Loopback0
 neighbor 172.30.255.254 remote-as 30
 neighbor 172.30.255.254 ebgp-multihop 2
 neighbor 172.30.255.254 update-source Loopback0
 no auto-summary
 !
ip classless
ip route 10.50.250.1 255.255.255.255 Ethernet0
ip route 10.200.60.1 255.255.255.255 Ethernet0
ip route 172.30.255.254 255.255.255.255 Serial1.609
```

continues

Example 3-78 *Filtering Routes by NLRI: Initial Router Configurations (Continued)*

```
Cervinia
interface Loopback0
 ip address 10.200.60.1 255.255.255.255
!
router bgp 200
 neighbor 10.50.250.1 remote-as 50
 neighbor 10.50.250.1 ebgp-multihop 2
 neighbor 10.50.250.1 update-source Loopback0
 neighbor 10.100.83.1 remote-as 100
 neighbor 10.100.83.1 ebgp-multihop 2
 neighbor 10.100.83.1 update-source Loopback0
 neighbor 172.30.255.150 remote-as 30
 neighbor 172.30.255.150 ebgp-multihop 2
 neighbor 172.30.255.150 update-source Loopback0
 no auto-summary
!
ip classless
ip route 10.50.250.1 255.255.255.255 Ethernet0/0
ip route 10.100.83.1 255.255.255.255 192.168.4.2
ip route 172.30.255.150 255.255.255.255 Serial0/1.308
```

```
Meribel
interface Loopback0
 ip address 10.50.250.1 255.255.255.255
!
router rip
 redistribute bgp 50 metric 1
 network 10.0.0.0
!
router bgp 50
 redistribute rip
 neighbor 10.100.83.1 remote-as 100
 neighbor 10.100.83.1 ebgp-multihop 2
 neighbor 10.100.83.1 update-source Loopback0
 neighbor 10.200.60.1 remote-as 200
 neighbor 10.200.60.1 ebgp-multihop 2
 neighbor 10.200.60.1 update-source Loopback0
 no auto-summary
!
ip classless
ip route 10.100.83.1 255.255.255.255 Ethernet0
ip route 10.200.60.1 255.255.255.255 Ethernet0
```

Notice that Figure 3-15 shows no IP addresses for any of the data links. All the BGP sessions are configured between router IDs, defined by the loopback interfaces of the routers, so the data link addresses are irrelevant to this example. Also important in these configurations are the static routes, which tell the routers how to find their neighbors' router IDs. Without the static routes, the BGP sessions cannot be established.

CAUTION   This case study and some of the following case studies use mutual redistribution between the IGP and BGP to easily demonstrate the application of routing policy. Once again, keep in mind that in practice, mutual distribution is usually a bad idea. And more importantly, if many prefixes are involved, redistribution from BGP to any IGP is *always* a bad idea.

AS 30 in Figure 3-15 is multihomed for redundancy but should not be a transit AS. That is, no traffic passing between AS 100 and AS 200 should cross AS 30. Innsbruck's BGP table in Example 3-79 shows that as the configurations stand, this policy is not in effect. One of the next-hop routers that Innsbruck shows for the destinations within AS 50 is Zermatt (172.30.255.254). The reason for this is that Meribel advertises those addresses to both Cervinia and Innsbruck. Cervinia advertises the addresses to Moritz, which redistributes the addresses into IS-IS. Zermatt then learns the addresses from its IS-IS neighbor within AS 30, redistributes them into BGP, and advertises them to Innsbruck.

Example 3-79 *Innsbruck Shows Zermatt as a Feasible Next Hop to the Destinations Within AS 50*

```
Innsbruck#show ip bgp
BGP table version is 21, local router ID is 10.100.83.1
Status codes: s suppressed, d damped, h history, * valid, > best, i - internal
Origin codes: i - IGP, e - EGP, ? - incomplete
   Network          Next Hop          Metric LocPrf Weight Path
*  10.20.0.0/16     172.30.255.254       20            0 30 ?
*                   10.200.60.1                        0 200 50 ?
*>                  10.50.250.1           0            0 50 ?
*  10.30.0.0/16     10.50.250.1                        0 50 200 30 ?
*>                  172.30.255.254       20            0 30 ?
*                   10.200.60.1                        0 200 30 ?
*  10.50.250.1/32   172.30.255.254       20            0 30 ?
*                   10.200.60.1                        0 200 50 ?
*>                  10.50.250.1           0            0 50 ?
*> 10.200.60.1/32   10.50.250.1           0            0 50 ?
*  172.16.0.0       10.50.250.1                        0 50 200 30 ?
*>                  172.30.255.254       20            0 30 ?
*                   10.200.60.1                        0 200 30 ?
*  172.17.0.0       172.30.255.254       20            0 30 ?
*                   10.200.60.1                        0 200 50 ?
*>                  10.50.250.1           1            0 50 ?
*  172.29.0.0       172.30.255.254       20            0 30 ?
*                   10.200.60.1                        0 200 50 ?
*>                  10.50.250.1           1            0 50 ?
*  172.29.1.0/24    10.50.250.1                        0 50 200 30 ?
*>                  172.30.255.254       20            0 30 ?
*                   10.200.60.1                        0 200 30 ?
*> 172.30.255.150/32 172.30.255.254      30            0 30 ?
*  172.30.255.254/32 10.50.250.1                       0 50 200 30 ?
*>                  10.200.60.1                        0 200 30 ?
*  172.31.0.0       10.50.250.1                        0 50 200 30 ?
```

continues

Example 3-79 *Innsbruck Shows Zermatt as a Feasible Next Hop to the Destinations Within AS 50 (Continued)*

```
    *>                      172.30.255.254      20            0 30 ?
    *                       10.200.60.1                        0 200 30 ?
    *   192.168.2.0/30      10.50.250.1                        0 50 200 30 ?
    *>                      10.200.60.1                        0 200 30 ?
    *> 192.168.2.4/30       172.30.255.254      20            0 30 ?
    *   192.168.50.0        172.30.255.254      20            0 30 ?
    *                       10.200.60.1                        0 200 50 ?
    *>                      10.50.250.1          1             0 50 ?
    *   192.168.100.0       10.50.250.1                        0 50 200 30 ?
    *>                      172.30.255.254      20            0 30 ?
    *                       10.200.60.1                        0 200 30 ?
Innsbruck#
```

If Innsbruck loses its connection to the NAP, it will forward packets destined for AS 50 to
Zermatt, making AS 30 a transit AS. To prevent this, an outbound policy is implemented at
both Zermatt and Moritz, allowing only addresses interior to AS 30 to be advertised.
Example 3-80 shows the BGP configuration for Zermatt.

Example 3-80 *Implementing an Outbound Policy at Zermatt to Allow Only Addresses Interior to AS 30 to Be
Advertised*

```
router bgp 30
 redistribute isis level-2
 neighbor 10.100.83.1 remote-as 100
 neighbor 10.100.83.1 ebgp-multihop 2
 neighbor 10.100.83.1 update-source Loopback0
 neighbor 10.100.83.1 distribute-list 1 out
 no auto-summary
!
access-list 1 permit 192.168.100.0
access-list 1 permit 10.30.0.0
access-list 1 permit 192.168.2.0
access-list 1 permit 172.29.1.0
access-list 1 permit 172.31.0.0
access-list 1 permit 172.16.0.0
```

Only the parts of Zermatt's configuration relevant to the example are shown.

Moritz's **distribute-list** configuration is identical, except for the neighbor reference. At
both routers, access list 1 allows all the interior routes and denies all other routes.

Another problem shown in Example 3-79 is that Innsbruck lists not only Meribel
(10.50.250.1) as a next hop for the destinations within AS 50, but also Cervinia
(10.200.60.1). The same double entry exists in the BGP table of Cervinia, which shows
both Meribel and Innsbruck as next-hop routers for the AS 50 addresses. The problem is
caused by the fact that Innsbruck and Cervinia are peered not only with Meribel, but also
with each other.

This problem does not cause any sort of routing dysfunction—if Meribel withdraws a route, the withdrawal is advertised between Cervinia and Innsbruck also. The problem is more a matter of aesthetics and clarity. An invalid route should not exist in the BGP table.

To correct the problem, Example 3-81 provides the BGP configuration for Innsbruck.

Example 3-81 *Eliminating Redundant Next-Hop Routers in Innsbruck's BGP Configuration*

```
router bgp 100
  neighbor 10.50.250.1 remote-as 50
  neighbor 10.50.250.1 ebgp-multihop 2
  neighbor 10.50.250.1 update-source Loopback0
  neighbor 10.200.60.1 remote-as 200
  neighbor 10.200.60.1 ebgp-multihop 2
  neighbor 10.200.60.1 update-source Loopback0
  neighbor 10.200.60.1 distribute-list 1 out
  neighbor 172.30.255.254 remote-as 30
  neighbor 172.30.255.254 ebgp-multihop 2
  neighbor 172.30.255.254 update-source Loopback0
  no auto-summary
!
access-list 1 deny    10.20.0.0
access-list 1 deny    192.168.50.0
access-list 1 deny    172.29.0.0
access-list 1 deny    172.17.0.0
access-list 1 permit any
```

Cervinia has an identical route filter configured for Innsbruck. The filter blocks the advertisement of the AS 50 addresses on the BGP connection between Innsbruck and Cervinia. A point of interest in this configuration is the third line of the access list. Figure 3-15 indicates that subnet 172.29.2.0/24 resides in AS 50, but the access list filters for the network 172.29.0.0. This is because RIP, a classful protocol, does not redistribute the subnet to BGP at Meribel. Rather, it summarizes to the major network address. Subnet 172.29.1.0/24 resides in AS 30; IS-IS is classless and therefore redistributes the subnet into BGP at Zermatt and Moritz. Innsbruck's access list has no effect on this subnet advertisement, because the third line must have an exact match to the major network address.

Finally, Example 3-79 shows that some of the AS 30 addresses, such as 192.168.100.0, are being advertised to Innsbruck from Meribel. This problem is similar to the preceding one— Cervinia advertises the routes to Meribel, which then advertises them to Innsbruck. Example 3-82 shows the configuration for Innsbruck to block all incoming routes from Meribel except the ones that are interior to AS 50.

Example 3-82 *Configuring Innsbruck to Block Incoming Routes from Mirabel Except Those Interior to AS 50*

```
router bgp 100
 neighbor 10.50.250.1 remote-as 50
 neighbor 10.50.250.1 ebgp-multihop 2
 neighbor 10.50.250.1 update-source Loopback0
 neighbor 10.50.250.1 distribute-list 2 in
 neighbor 10.200.60.1 remote-as 200
 neighbor 10.200.60.1 ebgp-multihop 2
 neighbor 10.200.60.1 update-source Loopback0
 neighbor 10.200.60.1 distribute-list 1 out
 neighbor 172.30.255.254 remote-as 30
 neighbor 172.30.255.254 ebgp-multihop 2
 neighbor 172.30.255.254 update-source Loopback0
 no auto-summary
!
access-list 1 deny    10.20.0.0
access-list 1 deny    192.168.50.0
access-list 1 deny    172.29.0.0
access-list 1 deny    172.17.0.0
access-list 1 permit any
access-list 2 permit 10.20.0.0
access-list 2 permit 192.168.50.0
access-list 2 permit 172.29.0.0
access-list 2 permit 172.17.0.0
```

Example 3-83 shows the resulting BGP table at Innsbruck. Comparing it to the table in
Example 3-79, you can readily see that the table is much smaller and that it now makes
much more sense.

Example 3-83 *Innsbruck's BGP Table After the Route Filters Have Been Added*

```
Innsbruck#show ip bgp
BGP table version is 12, local router ID is 10.100.83.1
Status codes: s suppressed, d damped, h history, * valid, > best, i - internal
Origin codes: i - IGP, e - EGP, ? - incomplete

   Network          Next Hop          Metric LocPrf Weight Path
*> 10.20.0.0/16     10.50.250.1            0             0 50 ?
*  10.30.0.0/16     10.200.60.1                          0 200 30 ?
*>                  172.30.255.254        20             0 30 ?
*> 10.50.250.1/32   10.50.250.1            0             0 50 ?
*  172.16.0.0       10.200.60.1                          0 200 30 ?
*>                  172.30.255.254        20             0 30 ?
*> 172.17.0.0       10.50.250.1            1             0 50 ?
*> 172.29.0.0       10.50.250.1            1             0 50 ?
*  172.29.1.0/24    10.200.60.1                          0 200 30 ?
*>                  172.30.255.254        20             0 30 ?
*  172.31.0.0       10.200.60.1                          0 200 30 ?
*>                  172.30.255.254        20             0 30 ?
```

Example 3-83 *Innsbruck's BGP Table After the Route Filters Have Been Added (Continued)*

```
*> 192.168.2.0/30   10.200.60.1                      0 200 30 ?
*> 192.168.50.0     10.50.250.1          1           0 50 ?
*  192.168.100.0    10.200.60.1                      0 200 30 ?
*>                  172.30.255.254       20          0 30 ?
Innsbruck#
```

Case Study: Filtering Routes by AS_PATH

In the face of a large number of advertised addresses, filtering by NLRI can quickly become unwieldy or completely impractical. Only a few addresses are being advertised in Figure 3-15, yet the access lists shown in the previous section are already somewhat lengthy.

A common factor in the examples in the preceding section is that in each case, the access lists are used to identify all the addresses within a single AS. In such situations, it is easier to filter on the AS number instead of enumerating each interior address in an access list. The **ip as-path access-list** command defines a variant of an access list that identifies AS numbers. Just as an access list identifying NLRI is called by the **neighbor distribute-list** command, the AS_PATH access list is called by the **neighbor filter-list** command.

The AS_PATH access list uses a powerful text-parsing tool known as *regular expressions*, or *regex* for short. Regular expressions are commonly used in such programming languages as Perl, Expect, awk, and Tcl, in search engines, and in UNIX utilities such as *egrep*. Regular expressions use a string of characters, all of which are either *metacharacters* or *literals*, to find matches in text. In the case of AS_PATH access lists, they are used to find matches in the AS_PATH attributes of BGP updates.

Literals are regular characters that describe what to match. Metacharacters describe how the match is made. For example, the regex ^[4-7] matches any string of text that begins with a number between 4 and 7. In this expression, 4 and 7 are the literals. The metacharacters in the expression are ^, [], and -. The caret indicates the beginning of a line: "The string begins with the following." The brackets indicate a group of characters known as a *character class*: "Anything within the brackets." The hyphen indicates a range: "Anything in the sequence from the first literal to the last literal." Table 3-1 summarizes the most common metacharacters, and Appendix B, "A Regular-Expression Tutorial," contains a short tutorial on the use of regular expressions. If you are not experienced with regular expressions, read Appendix B before continuing with this section.

Other metacharacters, and some of the metacharacters shown in the table, match more than what is indicated. For the sake of simplicity, only the metacharacters and the matches relevant to AS_PATH access lists are listed.

Table 3-1 *Regular-Expression Metacharacters Relevant to AS_PATH Access Lists*

Metacharacter	What It Matches
.	Any single character, including white space.
[]	Any character listed between the brackets.
[^]	Any character except those listed between the brackets. (The caret is placed before the sequence of literals.)
-	(Hyphen.) Any character in the range between the two literals separated by the hyphen.
?	Zero or one instance of the character or pattern.
*	Zero or more instances of the character or pattern.
+	One or more instances of the character or pattern.
^	Start of a line.
$	End of a line.
|	Either of the literals separated by the metacharacter.
_	(Underscore.) A comma, the beginning of the line, the end of the line, or a space.

In the preceding section, the routers Zermatt and Moritz were configured to advertise only routes to addresses interior to AS 30. All other routes were filtered, to prevent AS 100 or AS 200 from attempting to use AS 30 as a transit AS. To implement the filter, all the AS 30 addresses were individually listed in an access list. Example 3-84 shows the configuration for Zermatt using an AS_PATH access list to achieve the same results as in the preceding case study.

Example 3-84 *Configuring Zermatt to Advertise Only Routes to Addresses Interior to AS 30 Using an AS_PATH Access List*

```
router bgp 30
 redistribute isis level-2
 neighbor 10.100.83.1 remote-as 100
 neighbor 10.100.83.1 ebgp-multihop 2
 neighbor 10.100.83.1 update-source Loopback0
 neighbor 10.100.83.1 filter-list 1 out
 no auto-summary
!
ip as-path access-list 1 permit ^$
```

Moritz's configuration has an identical AS_PATH access list. The regular expression here uses two metacharacters—the first matches the beginning of a line, and the second matches the end of a line. No literals are included. The regex matches AS_PATHs that include no AS numbers. The only routes in Zermatt's BGP table in Example 3-85 that have empty

AS_PATHs are to the destinations interior to AS 30. They match the AS_PATH list statement and are permitted. Like other access lists, the AS_PATH list has an implicit "deny any" at the end; all the other routes in Example 3-85 match this implicit deny and are not advertised.

Example 3-85 *The Only Empty AS_PATHs in Zermatt's BGP Table Are Those of Routes to Addresses Within AS 30*

```
Zermatt#show ip bgp
BGP table version is 109, local router ID is 172.30.255.254
Status codes: s suppressed, * valid, > best, i - internal
Origin codes: i - IGP, e - EGP, ? - incomplete

   Network          Next Hop         Metric LocPrf Weight Path
*> 10.20.0.0/16     10.100.83.1                        0 100 50 ?
*> 10.30.0.0/16     192.168.2.1          20        32768 ?
*> 10.50.250.1/32   10.100.83.1                        0 100 50 ?
*> 172.16.0.0       192.168.2.1          20        32768 ?
*> 172.17.0.0       10.100.83.1                        0 100 50 ?
*> 172.29.0.0       10.100.83.1                        0 100 50 ?
*> 172.29.1.0/24    192.168.2.1          20        32768 ?
*> 172.30.255.150/32 192.168.2.1         30        32768 ?
*> 172.31.0.0       192.168.2.1          20        32768 ?
*> 192.168.2.4/30   192.168.2.1          20        32768 ?
*> 192.168.50.0     10.100.83.1                        0 100 50 ?
*> 192.168.100.0    192.168.2.1          20        32768 ?
Zermatt#
```

Also in the preceding case study, routers Innsbruck and Cervinia were configured to accept routes from Meribel only if the advertised addresses are interior to AS 50. Additionally, these two routers should not advertise to each other routes learned from Meribel. Example 3-86 shows Innsbruck's configuration using AS_PATH access lists to accomplish the same goals.

Example 3-86 *Configuring Innsbruck Using AS_PATH Access Lists to Accept Routes from Meribel if They Are Interior to AS 50*

```
router bgp 100
 neighbor 10.50.250.1 remote-as 50
 neighbor 10.50.250.1 ebgp-multihop 2
 neighbor 10.50.250.1 update-source Loopback0
 neighbor 10.50.250.1 filter-list 2 in
 neighbor 10.200.60.1 remote-as 200
 neighbor 10.200.60.1 ebgp-multihop 2
 neighbor 10.200.60.1 update-source Loopback0
 neighbor 10.200.60.1 filter-list 1 out
 neighbor 172.30.255.254 remote-as 30
 neighbor 172.30.255.254 ebgp-multihop 2
 neighbor 172.30.255.254 update-source Loopback0
 no auto-summary
```

continues

Example 3-86 *Configuring Innsbruck Using AS_PATH Access Lists to Accept Routes from Meribel if They Are Interior to AS 50 (Continued)*

```
!
ip as-path access-list 1 deny _50_
ip as-path access-list 1 permit .*
ip as-path access-list 2 permit ^50$
```

List 1 is applied to outgoing updates to Cervinia. The first statement of this list denies any update that includes the AS number 50 anywhere in its AS_PATH. The metacharacters before and after the 50 ensure that this number alone is matched. If the metacharacters were left out, the statement would match not only 50, but also such numbers as 500, 5000, 350, and so on. The regex of the second statement says, "Match any character, and match zero or more occurrences of that character." In other words, match anything. This is the AS_PATH access list version of a "permit any." The result of these two lines is that Innsbruck does not advertise to Cervinia any routes learned from Meribel but advertises all other routes to Cervinia.

List 2 is applied to incoming updates from Meribel. The regex of the one line reads, "Match the beginning of the line, followed by 50, followed by the end of the line." In other words, match AS_PATHs that include the AS number 50 and nothing else. Those routes are permitted. Any routes that Meribel advertises that it learned from another AS will have more than the number 50 in the AS_PATH. These routes are denied by the implicit "deny" at the end of the list.

For the topology in Figure 3-15, Cervinia's AS_PATH access lists are identical to those shown for Innsbruck. In Figure 3-16, however, the topology has been modified. Here, AS 125 is added and serves as a transit between AS 200 and AS 50. If Meribel loses its link to the NAP, traffic into and out of AS 50 should traverse AS 125 and AS 200. With the AS_PATH access lists shown in the preceding example, list 1 denies any routes whose AS_PATH includes the AS number 50. This includes routes to AS 50 learned from router Oberstdorf, which have an AS_PATH of (125,50). As a result, Innsbruck cannot learn these routes from Cervinia and take advantage of the alternate route into AS 50.

Figure 3-16 *AS 125 Provides an Alternate Path to AS 50*

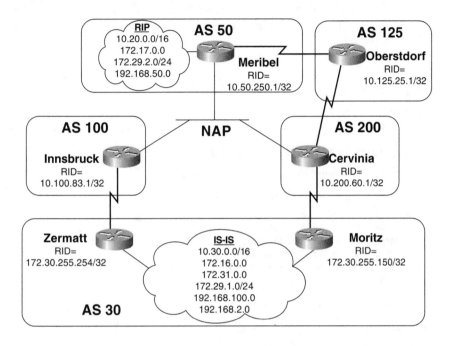

To remedy the situation, Example 3-87 shows the configuration for Cervinia.

Example 3-87 *Configuring Cervinia to Accommodate AS 125 as a Transit AS to AS 50*

```
router bgp 200
 neighbor 10.50.250.1 remote-as 50
 neighbor 10.50.250.1 ebgp-multihop 2
 neighbor 10.50.250.1 update-source Loopback0
 neighbor 10.50.250.1 filter-list 2 in
 neighbor 10.100.83.1 remote-as 100
 neighbor 10.100.83.1 ebgp-multihop 2
 neighbor 10.100.83.1 update-source Loopback0
 neighbor 10.100.83.1 filter-list 1 out
 neighbor 10.125.25.1 remote-as 125
 neighbor 10.125.25.1 ebgp-multihop 2
 neighbor 10.125.25.1 update-source Loopback0
 neighbor 172.30.255.150 remote-as 30
 neighbor 172.30.255.150 ebgp-multihop 2
 neighbor 172.30.255.150 update-source Loopback0
 no auto-summary
!
ip as-path access-list 1 deny ^50$
ip as-path access-list 1 permit .*
ip as-path access-list 2 permit ^50$
```

In Example 3-87, the first statement of list 1 denies AS_PATHs that contain only the AS number 50, not all AS_PATHs that contain 50, as in the preceding example. Routes that Cervinia learns directly from Meribel are denied, whereas routes to AS 50 learned from Oberstdorf are permitted.

Case Study: Filtering with Route Maps

You also can implement route filters with route maps. The route map can use either access lists, to filter by NLRI, or AS_PATH access lists, to filter by the AS_PATH attribute.

Example 3-88 shows a possible configuration for Zermatt in Figure 3-15.

Example 3-88 *Configuring Zermatt to Filter Routes with a Route Map*

```
router bgp 30
 redistribute isis level-2
 neighbor 10.100.83.1 remote-as 100
 neighbor 10.100.83.1 ebgp-multihop 2
 neighbor 10.100.83.1 update-source Loopback0
 neighbor 10.100.83.1 route-map Innsbruck out
 no auto-summary
!
access-list 1 permit 192.168.100.0
access-list 1 permit 10.30.0.0
access-list 1 permit 192.168.2.0
access-list 1 permit 172.29.1.0
access-list 1 permit 172.31.0.0
access-list 1 permit 172.16.0.0
!
route-map Innsbruck permit 10
 match ip address 1
```

Access list 1 is the same list that is used in the case study "Filtering Routes by NLRI," in which the access list is called by the **neighbor distribute-list** command. In this case, the **neighbor route-map** command refers outgoing routes to a route map named Innsbruck, which in turn uses the **match ip address** command to call the access list. The route map permits any routes permitted by the access list and denies the rest.

A route map also can call an AS_PATH access list, as demonstrated in the configuration for Zermatt in Example 3-89.

The configuration for Zermatt in Example 3-89 is the same as in Example 3-88, except the **match as-path** command is used rather than the **match ip address** command. The AS_PATH access list is the same one as is used in the case study "Filtering Routes by AS_PATH." Routes with an empty AS_PATH attribute—routes originating in AS 30—are permitted, and all other routes are denied.

Example 3-89 *Configuring Zermatt with a Route Map to Call an AS_PATH Access List*

```
router bgp 30
 redistribute isis level-2
 neighbor 10.100.83.1 remote-as 100
 neighbor 10.100.83.1 ebgp-multihop 2
 neighbor 10.100.83.1 update-source Loopback0
 neighbor 10.100.83.1 route-map Innsbruck out
 no auto-summary
!
ip as-path access-list 1 permit ^$
!
route-map Innsbruck permit 10
 match as-path 1
```

Route maps can filter incoming as well as outgoing BGP updates. In the preceding case study, router Innsbruck filters incoming routes from Meribel and accepts only those routes that have an AS_PATH attribute of 50, with no other numbers in the list. The router also filters outgoing routes to Cervinia and allows only those routes that do not have AS 30 in their AS_PATH. Using route maps for the same purpose, Example 3-90 shows the configuration for Innsbruck.

Example 3-90 *Configuring Innsbruck to Filter Routes with a Route Map*

```
router bgp 100
 neighbor 10.50.250.1 remote-as 50
 neighbor 10.50.250.1 ebgp-multihop 2
 neighbor 10.50.250.1 update-source Loopback0
 neighbor 10.50.250.1 route-map Meribel in
 neighbor 10.200.60.1 remote-as 200
 neighbor 10.200.60.1 ebgp-multihop 2
 neighbor 10.200.60.1 update-source Loopback0
 neighbor 10.200.60.1 route-map Cervinia-to-Meribel out
 neighbor 172.30.255.254 remote-as 30
 neighbor 172.30.255.254 ebgp-multihop 2
 neighbor 172.30.255.254 update-source Loopback0
 no auto-summary
!
ip as-path access-list 1 deny _50_
ip as-path access-list 1 permit .*
ip as-path access-list 2 permit ^50$
!
route-map Meribel permit 10
 match as-path 2
!
route-map Cervinia-to-Meribel permit 10
 match as-path 1
```

Using route maps rather than distribute lists or filter lists can prove useful when you must configure many route filters on a single router. Because route maps use names rather than numbers, an intuitive name can make such a configuration a little easier to decipher. In Example 3-88 and Example 3-89, naming the route map Innsbruck very clearly identifies what neighbor the route map concerns. In Example 3-90, the names identify paths through neighbors.

The major reason for using route maps, however, is their power not only to identify particular routes with **match** statements, but also to change their attributes with **set** statements. The next five case studies demonstrate the use of route maps to implement more-complex routing policies. Respectively, the five case studies demonstrate methods for influencing route preferences:

- Within a single router (multiple BGP routes to the same destination)
- Within a single router (multiple routes to the same destination from different routing protocols)
- Within the local autonomous system
- Within neighboring autonomous systems
- Within autonomous systems beyond the neighboring autonomous systems

Case Study: Administrative Weights

Frequently, a BGP router is presented with multiple routes to the same destination. Although BGP has default methods for choosing among these routes, you might need to override these defaults on occasion to implement a routing policy. Although the RFCs do not provide for methods to influence route preferences within a single router, Cisco's IOS Software does.

The first of these Cisco-specific tools is *administrative weight*. Each route is assigned a weight, which is a number between 0 and 65,535. Given multiple routes to the same destination, the router prefers the route with the highest weight. By default, BGP routes originated by the router are given a weight of 32,768, and routes learned from neighbors are given a weight of 0.

Given multiple routes to the same destination, administrative weight overrides all other factors in the BGP decision process. But administrative weight is also local to the router. That is, it is not advertised to any neighboring BGP speakers. Therefore, the assigned weight of a route on one router does not have any bearing on the preference of the route in other routers.

In Figure 3-17, the connectivity of AS 30 has been improved. Zermatt and Moritz are each multihomed to AS 100 and AS 200 for added redundancy. Each router receives routes to the addresses in AS 50 from Innsbruck and from Cervinia. Recall from the discussion of the BGP decision process in Chapter 2 that when selecting a preferred route from multiple same-destination routes, if all other attributes are equal, BGP selects the route from the neighbor with the lowest router ID. This means that both Zermatt and Moritz in Figure 3-17 will use Innsbruck to reach the destinations in AS 50, because its router ID is lower than Cervinia, as demonstrated by the output in Example 3-91. Zermatt and Moritz show that the destinations within AS 50 are reachable via either Innsbruck (10.100.83.1) or Cervinia (10.200.60.1). Both routers have marked the routes from Innsbruck as the best routes, because Innsbruck's router ID is lower.

Figure 3-17 *Zermatt and Moritz Are Multihomed for Redundancy*

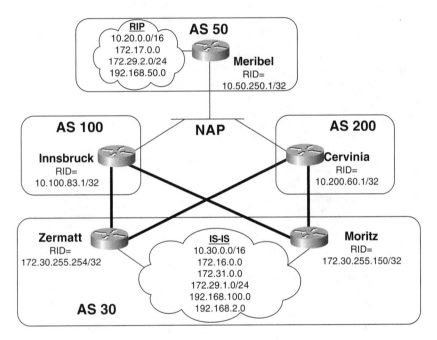

Example 3-91 *BGP Tables of Zermatt and Moritz in Figure 3-17*

```
Zermatt# show ip bgp
BGP table version is 34, local router ID is 172.30.255.254
Status codes: s suppressed, * valid, > best, i - internal
Origin codes: i - IGP, e - EGP, ? - incomplete

   Network          Next Hop          Metric LocPrf Weight Path
*  10.20.0.0/16     10.200.60.1                        0 200 50 ?
*>                  10.100.83.1                        0 100 50 ?
*> 10.30.0.0/16     192.168.2.1           20       32768 ?
*  10.50.250.1/32   10.200.60.1                        0 200 50 ?
*>                  10.100.83.1                        0 100 50 ?
```

continues

Example 3-91 *BGP Tables of Zermatt and Moritz in Figure 3-17 (Continued)*

```
*> 10.100.83.1/32    10.200.60.1                        0 200 50 ?
*> 10.200.60.1/32    10.100.83.1                        0 100 50 ?
*> 172.16.0.0        192.168.2.1           20       32768 ?
*  172.17.0.0        10.200.60.1                        0 200 50 ?
*>                   10.100.83.1                        0 100 50 ?
*  172.29.0.0        10.200.60.1                        0 200 50 ?
*>                   10.100.83.1                        0 100 50 ?
*> 172.29.1.0/24     192.168.2.1           20       32768 ?
*> 172.30.255.150/32 192.168.2.1           30       32768 ?
*> 172.31.0.0        192.168.2.1           20       32768 ?
*> 192.168.2.4/30    192.168.2.1           20       32768 ?
*  192.168.50.0      10.200.60.1                        0 200 50 ?
*>                   10.100.83.1                        0 100 50 ?
*> 192.168.100.0     192.168.2.1           20       32768 ?
Zermatt#
```

```
Moritz#show ip bgp
BGP table version is 33, local router ID is 172.30.255.150
Status codes: s suppressed, * valid, > best, i - internal
Origin codes: i - IGP, e - EGP, ? - incomplete

   Network          Next Hop         Metric LocPrf Weight Path
*> 10.20.0.0/16     10.100.83.1                        0 100 50 ?
*                   10.200.60.1                        0 200 50 ?
*> 10.30.0.0/16     192.168.2.5           20       32768 ?
*> 10.50.250.1/32   10.100.83.1                        0 100 50 ?
*                   10.200.60.1                        0 200 50 ?
*> 10.100.83.1/32   10.200.60.1                        0 200 50 ?
*> 10.200.60.1/32   10.100.83.1                        0 100 50 ?
*> 172.16.0.0       192.168.2.5           20       32768 ?
*> 172.17.0.0       10.100.83.1                        0 100 50 ?
*                   10.200.60.1                        0 200 50 ?
*> 172.29.0.0       10.100.83.1                        0 100 50 ?
*                   10.200.60.1                        0 200 50 ?
*> 172.29.1.0/24    192.168.2.5           20       32768 ?
*> 172.30.255.254/32 192.168.2.5          30       32768 ?
*> 172.31.0.0       192.168.2.5           20       32768 ?
*> 192.168.2.0/30   192.168.2.5           20       32768 ?
*> 192.168.50.0     10.100.83.1                        0 100 50 ?
*                   10.200.60.1                        0 200 50 ?
   Network          Next Hop         Metric LocPrf Weight Path
*> 192.168.100.0    192.168.2.5           20       32768 ?
Moritz#
```

To spread out the traffic load more evenly, Zermatt should use the link to Innsbruck to reach AS 50, and only use the link to Cervinia as a backup. Moritz should use the link to Cervinia, and only use Innsbruck as a backup. Both routers implement this policy by manipulating the weights of the routes, as demonstrated in Example 3-92.

Example 3-92 *Configuring Zermatt and Moritz to Follow Route Policies by Manipulating Route Weights*

```
Zermatt
router bgp 30
 redistribute isis level-2
 neighbor 10.100.83.1 remote-as 100
 neighbor 10.100.83.1 ebgp-multihop 2
 neighbor 10.100.83.1 update-source Loopback0
 neighbor 10.100.83.1 filter-list 1 out
 neighbor 10.100.83.1 weight 50000
 neighbor 10.200.60.1 remote-as 200
 neighbor 10.200.60.1 ebgp-multihop 2
 neighbor 10.200.60.1 update-source Loopback0
 neighbor 10.200.60.1 filter-list 1 out
 neighbor 10.200.60.1 weight 20000
 no auto-summary

Moritz
router bgp 30
 redistribute isis level-2
 neighbor 10.100.83.1 remote-as 100
 neighbor 10.100.83.1 ebgp-multihop 2
 neighbor 10.100.83.1 update-source Loopback0
 neighbor 10.100.83.1 filter-list 1 out
 neighbor 10.100.83.1 weight 20000
 neighbor 10.200.60.1 remote-as 200
 neighbor 10.200.60.1 ebgp-multihop 2
 neighbor 10.200.60.1 update-source Loopback0
 neighbor 10.200.60.1 filter-list 1 out
 neighbor 10.200.60.1 weight 50000
 no auto-summary
```

The configurations in Example 3-92 use the **neighbor weight** command to assign weights to routes according to which neighbor advertises the routes. Zermatt assigns a weight of 50000 to routes learned from Innsbruck (10.100.83.1) and a weight of 20000 to routes learned from Cervinia (10.200.60.1). Moritz does just the opposite. As a result, the two routers prefer the routes with the higher weight, and will use the alternative paths only if the preferred route becomes invalid, as demonstrated by the output in Example 3-93.

Example 3-93 *Zermatt and Moritz Designate the Routes with the Highest Weight as "Best"; the Locally Originated Routes Continue to Have a Default Weight of 32768*

```
Zermatt#show ip bgp
BGP table version is 104, local router ID is 172.30.255.254
Status codes: s suppressed, * valid, > best, i - internal
Origin codes: i - IGP, e - EGP, ? - incomplete

   Network          Next Hop            Metric LocPrf Weight Path
*> 10.20.0.0/16     10.100.83.1                       50000 100 50 ?
*                   10.200.60.1                       20000 200 50 ?
```

continues

Example 3-93 *Zermatt and Moritz Designate the Routes with the Highest Weight as "Best"; the Locally Originated Routes Continue to Have a Default Weight of 32768 (Continued)*

```
*> 10.30.0.0/16      192.168.2.1          20       32768 ?
*> 10.50.250.1/32    10.100.83.1                   50000 100 50 ?
*                    10.200.60.1                   20000 200 50 ?
*> 10.100.83.1/32    10.200.60.1                   20000 200 50 ?
*> 10.200.60.1/32    10.100.83.1                   50000 100 50 ?
*> 172.16.0.0        192.168.2.1          20       32768 ?
*> 172.17.0.0        10.100.83.1                   50000 100 50 ?
*                    10.200.60.1                   20000 200 50 ?
*> 172.29.0.0        10.100.83.1                   50000 100 50 ?
*                    10.200.60.1                   20000 200 50 ?
*> 172.29.1.0/24     192.168.2.1          20       32768 ?
*> 172.30.255.150/32 192.168.2.1          30       32768 ?
*> 172.31.0.0        192.168.2.1          20       32768 ?
*> 192.168.2.4/30    192.168.2.1          20       32768 ?
*> 192.168.50.0      10.100.83.1                   50000 100 50 ?
*                    10.200.60.1                   20000 200 50 ?
*> 192.168.100.0     192.168.2.1          20       32768 ?
Zermatt#
```

```
Moritz#show ip bgp
BGP table version is 20, local router ID is 172.30.255.150
Status codes: s suppressed, * valid, > best, i - internal
Origin codes: i - IGP, e - EGP, ? - incomplete

   Network           Next Hop             Metric LocPrf Weight Path
*  10.20.0.0/16      10.100.83.1                  20000 100 50 ?
*>                   10.200.60.1                  50000 200 50 ?
*> 10.30.0.0/16      192.168.2.5          20      32768 ?
*  10.50.250.1/32    10.100.83.1                  20000 100 50 ?
*>                   10.200.60.1                  50000 200 50 ?
*> 10.100.83.1/32    10.200.60.1                  50000 200 50 ?
*> 10.200.60.1/32    10.100.83.1                  20000 100 50 ?
*> 172.16.0.0        192.168.2.5          20      32768 ?
*  172.17.0.0        10.100.83.1                  20000 100 50 ?
*>                   10.200.60.1                  50000 200 50 ?
*  172.29.0.0        10.100.83.1                  20000 100 50 ?
*>                   10.200.60.1                  50000 200 50 ?
*> 172.29.1.0/24     192.168.2.5          20      32768 ?
*> 172.30.255.254/32 192.168.2.5          30      32768 ?
*> 172.31.0.0        192.168.2.5          20      32768 ?
*> 192.168.2.0/30    192.168.2.5          20      32768 ?
*  192.168.50.0      10.100.83.1                  20000 100 50 ?
*>                   10.200.60.1                  50000 200 50 ?
*> 192.168.100.0     192.168.2.5          20      32768 ?
Moritz#
```

The **neighbor weight** command is useful if the weights for all routes learned from a particular neighbor are to be the same. Sometimes, however, different weights must be assigned to routes from the same neighbor. One way to implement a policy requiring this

is with the **neighbor filter-list weight** command. Like the **neighbor filter-list** command
used for route filtering, this command references an AS_PATH access list to identify routes
according to the details of their AS_PATH attribute. However, although a particular
neighbor can have at most one **neighbor filter-list in** and one **neighbor filter-list out**
command, multiple instances of the **neighbor filter-list weight** command might be
assigned to a single neighbor. You can configure the **neighbor filter-list** and the **neighbor
filter-list weight** command for the same neighbor; although the commands look very
similar, their purposes and effects differ significantly.

Figure 3-18 depicts the same topology as in Figure 3-17, but another AS has been connected
to the NAP. Both Innsbruck and Cervinia advertise the routes from AS 50 and AS 75 to both
Zermatt and Moritz. A new routing policy is established, requiring Moritz to use Cervinia
to reach the destinations within AS 75 and Innsbruck to reach the destinations within AS 50.

Figure 3-18 *AS 75 Has Been Connected to the NAP*

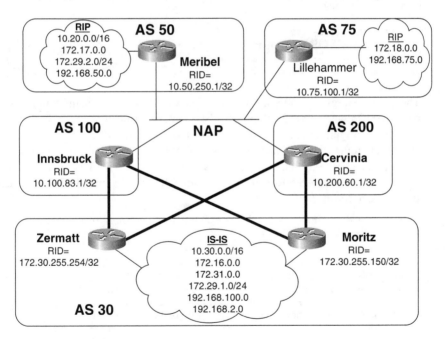

Example 3-94 shows the configuration for Moritz using the **neighbor filter-list weight**
command.

Example 3-94 *Configuring Moritz to Prefer Cervinia as the Next-Hop Router to AS 75 via the* **neighbor filter-list weight** *Command*

```
router bgp 30
 redistribute isis level-2
 neighbor 10.100.83.1 remote-as 100
 neighbor 10.100.83.1 ebgp-multihop 2
 neighbor 10.100.83.1 update-source Loopback0
 neighbor 10.100.83.1 filter-list 1 out
 neighbor 10.100.83.1 filter-list 2 weight 40000
 neighbor 10.100.83.1 filter-list 3 weight 60000
 neighbor 10.200.60.1 remote-as 200
 neighbor 10.200.60.1 ebgp-multihop 2
 neighbor 10.200.60.1 update-source Loopback0
 neighbor 10.200.60.1 filter-list 1 out
 neighbor 10.200.60.1 filter-list 2 weight 60000
 neighbor 10.200.60.1 filter-list 3 weight 40000
 no auto-summary
!
ip as-path access-list 1 permit ^$
ip as-path access-list 2 permit _75$
ip as-path access-list 3 permit _50$
```

The regular expression _75$ in list 2 identifies AS_PATHs that end in 75 and will match the paths (100,75) and (200,75). Similarly, list 3 matches paths that end in 50. Under the neighbor configuration for Innsbruck (10.100.83.1), routes to AS 75 are given a weight of 40000, and routes to AS 50 are given a weight of 60000. Under the neighbor configuration for Cervinia (10.200.60.1), the opposite is true. Routes to AS 75 are given a weight of 60000, and routes to AS 50 are given a weight of 40000. Example 3-95 shows the resulting BGP table at Moritz.

Example 3-95 *Cervinia Is the Preferred Next-Hop Router to Reach AS 75, and Innsbruck Is the Preferred Next-Hop Router to Reach AS 50*

```
Moritz#show ip bgp
BGP table version is 19, local router ID is 172.30.255.150
Status codes: s suppressed, * valid, > best, i - internal
Origin codes: i - IGP, e - EGP, ? - incomplete
   Network          Next Hop          Metric LocPrf Weight Path
*> 10.20.0.0/16     10.100.83.1                     60000 100 50 ?
*                   10.200.60.1                     40000 200 50 ?
*> 10.30.0.0/16     192.168.2.5          20         32768 ?
*> 10.50.250.1/32   10.100.83.1                     60000 100 50 ?
*                   10.200.60.1                     40000 200 50 ?
*> 10.100.83.1/32   10.200.60.1                     40000 200 50 ?
*> 10.200.60.1/32   10.100.83.1                     60000 100 50 ?
*> 172.16.0.0       192.168.2.5          20         32768 ?
*> 172.17.0.0       10.100.83.1                     60000 100 50 ?
*                   10.200.60.1                     40000 200 50 ?
*  172.18.0.0       10.100.83.1                     40000 100 75 i
```

Example 3-95 *Cervinia Is the Preferred Next-Hop Router to Reach AS 75, and Innsbruck Is the Preferred Next-Hop Router to Reach AS 50 (Continued)*

```
*>                      10.200.60.1                     60000 200 75 i
*> 172.29.0.0           10.100.83.1                     60000 100 50 ?
*                       10.200.60.1                     40000 200 50 ?
*> 172.29.1.0/24        192.168.2.5          20         32768 ?
*> 172.30.255.254/32 192.168.2.5            30         32768 ?
*> 172.31.0.0           192.168.2.5          20         32768 ?
*> 192.168.2.0/30       192.168.2.5          20         32768 ?
*> 192.168.50.0         10.100.83.1                     60000 100 50 ?
*                       10.200.60.1                     40000 200 50 ?
*  192.168.75.0         10.100.83.1                     40000 100 75 i
*>                      10.200.60.1                     60000 200 75 i
*> 192.168.100.0        192.168.2.5          20         32768 ?
Moritz#
```

If you use both the **neighbor weight** command and the **neighbor filter-list weight** command under the same neighbor configuration, the **neighbor filter-list weight** command takes precedence. Any routes from the peer whose weights are not set by **neighbor filter-list weight** have their weights set by the **neighbor weight** command.

You also can manipulate the weight with the **neighbor route-map** command. Example 3-96 shows the configuration for Moritz using route maps to achieve the same results as the configuration in Example 3-94.

Example 3-96 *Configuring Moritz to Prefer Cervinia as the Next-Hop Router to AS 75 via Route Maps*

```
router bgp 30
 redistribute isis level-2
 neighbor 10.100.83.1 remote-as 100
 neighbor 10.100.83.1 ebgp-multihop 2
 neighbor 10.100.83.1 update-source Loopback0
 neighbor 10.100.83.1 route-map Innsbruck in
 neighbor 10.100.83.1 filter-list 1 out
 neighbor 10.200.60.1 remote-as 200
 neighbor 10.200.60.1 ebgp-multihop 2
 neighbor 10.200.60.1 update-source Loopback0
 neighbor 10.200.60.1 route-map Cervinia in
 neighbor 10.200.60.1 filter-list 1 out
 no auto-summary
!
ip as-path access-list 1 permit ^$
ip as-path access-list 2 permit _75$
ip as-path access-list 3 permit _50$
!
route-map Innsbruck permit 10
 match as-path 2
 set weight 40000
!
```

continues

Example 3-96 *Configuring Moritz to Prefer Cervinia as the Next-Hop Router to AS 75 via Route Maps (Continued)*

```
route-map Innsbruck permit 20
 match as-path 3
 set weight 60000
!
route-map Cervinia permit 10
 match as-path 2
 set weight 60000
!
route-map Cervinia permit 20
 match as-path 3
 set weight 40000
```

When route maps are used to set weights, only the AS_PATH can be matched; individual IP addresses cannot be matched with the **match ip address** command. You also can use weight-setting route maps in the same neighbor configuration as **neighbor filter-list weight** and **neighbor weight** commands. Weight-setting route maps take precedence over either of the other two commands.

Case Study: Administrative Distances and Backdoor Routes

The other Cisco-specific tool for manipulating preferences on a single router is *administrative distance*. Whereas administrative weight influences preference among multiple routes to the same destination that have been learned from different BGP peers, administrative distance influences preference among multiple routes to the same destination that have been learned from different routing protocols. This means that whereas the effects of administrative weights are seen in the BGP table, the effects of administrative distances are seen in the IP routing table.

Normally, an administrative distance is assigned to a route according to the protocol or source from which the route is learned. The lower the distance, the more preferable the route. Table 3-2 shows the default administrative distances for the various protocols. You can see that within an AS, if a router learns routes to the same destination from RIP and OSPF, the OSPF route is preferred because its distance (110) is lower than that of the RIP route (120).

EBGP has a default distance of 20, lower than any of the IGPs. At first, this might seem like a problem in internetworks such as the one in Figure 3-18. When Zermatt advertises one of the AS 30 internal addresses to Innsbruck, the address is passed to Cervinia, which can pass it back to Moritz. Moritz, hearing the route via EBGP, prefers it over the IS-IS route to the same destination, because the IS-IS route has a distance of 115. In fact, this doesn't happen, because of the basic BGP loop-avoidance mechanism. Moritz observes the 30 in the AS_PATH of the route from Cervinia and drops the route.

Table 3-2   *Cisco Default Administrative Distances*

Route Source	Administrative Distance
Connected interface	0
Static route	1
EIGRP summary route	5
External BGP	20
EIGRP	90
IGRP	100
OSPF	110
IS-IS	115
RIP	120
EGP	140
External EIGRP	170
Internal BGP	200
Local BGP	200
Unknown	255

When a static route refers to an interface rather than a next-hop address, the destination is considered to be a directly connected network.

On the other hand, IBGP does not add an AS number to the AS_PATH. So a route learned from an IGP and then passed to an IBGP peer within a single AS could cause routing loops or black holes. For this reason, the distance of IBGP routes is 200, higher than that of any IGP. An IGP-learned route is always preferred over an IBGP route to the same destination.

Local BGP routes are those originated on the local router as the result of using the BGP **network** command. Like IBGP routes, they have a default administrative distance of 200 so that they are not preferred over IGP routes.

Chapter 13, "Route Filtering," of *Volume I* includes a case study demonstrating how to manipulate the default distances of IGP routes. To change the default distances of BGP, you use the **distance bgp** command. This command sets the distances for EBGP, IBGP, and local BGP routes, respectively. The configuration in Example 3-97 changes the IBGP administrative distance to 95, making the IBGP routes preferred over all IGP routes to the same destination, except EIGRP routes.

Example 3-97 *Changing the IBGP Administrative Distance to 95 to Make IBGP Routes Preferred Over All IGP Routes Except EIGRP*

```
router bgp 30
 neighbor 10.200.60.1 remote-as 200
 neighbor 10.200.60.1 ebgp-multihop 2
 neighbor 10.200.60.1 update-source Loopback0
 distance bgp 20 95 200
```

Unlike IGPs, there is seldom a good reason for changing the default BGP distances for all routes. However, there is a situation is which the distances of some BGP routes should be changed. In Figure 3-19, a private link is added between routers Meribel and Lillehammer, and the routers speak RIP across the link. This link is used as a *back door*. That is, some traffic between AS 50 and AS 75 should be sent over the private backdoor route rather than across the public NAP. Perhaps AS 50 and AS 75 have a business partnership, and they want some of their communications to pass over their private link rather than the public Internet.

Figure 3-19 *A Private Backdoor Link Has Been Added Between AS 50 and AS 75, Allowing the IGP Processes of Those Autonomous Systems to Communicate Directly Rather Than Through the EBGP Sessions*

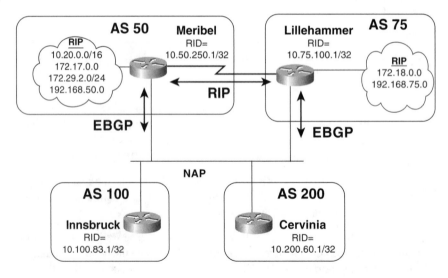

In this example, traffic between 172.17.0.0 in AS 50 and 172.18.0.0 in AS75 should travel across the backdoor link and use the NAP route only if the backdoor route fails. The problem is the administrative distance. Lillehammer, for instance, learns the route to 172.17.0.0 from Meribel via both RIP across the backdoor link and EBGP across the NAP link. EBGP has a distance of 20 and RIP has a distance of 120, so the EBGP route is preferred, as indicated in the output in Example 3-98.

Example 3-98 *Lillehammer Learns the Route to 172.17.0.0 via Both RIP and EBGP; the EBGP Route, with an Administrative Distance of 20, Is Preferred*

```
Lillehammer#show ip route
Codes: C - connected, S - static, I - IGRP, R - RIP, M - mobile, B - BGP
       D - EIGRP, EX - EIGRP external, O - OSPF, IA - OSPF inter area
       N1 - OSPF NSSA external type 1, N2 - OSPF NSSA external type 2
       E1 - OSPF external type 1, E2 - OSPF external type 2, E - EGP
       i - IS-IS, L1 - IS-IS level-1, L2 - IS-IS level-2, * - candidate default
       U - per-user static route, o - ODR
       T - traffic engineered route

Gateway of last resort is not set

C    192.168.75.0/24 is directly connected, Ethernet2
B    172.17.0.0/16 [20/1] via 10.50.250.1, 00:01:24
B    172.16.0.0/16 [20/0] via 10.100.83.1, 00:01:22
C    172.18.0.0/16 is directly connected, Ethernet1
     172.29.0.0/16 is variably subnetted, 2 subnets, 2 masks
B       172.29.1.0/24 [20/0] via 10.100.83.1, 00:01:22
B       172.29.0.0/16 [20/1] via 10.50.250.1, 00:01:24
B    172.31.0.0/16 [20/0] via 10.100.83.1, 00:01:22
     192.168.4.0/29 is subnetted, 1 subnets
C       192.168.4.0 is directly connected, Ethernet0
     10.0.0.0/8 is variably subnetted, 7 subnets, 2 masks
B       10.30.0.0/16 [20/0] via 10.100.83.1, 00:01:22
B       10.20.0.0/16 [20/0] via 10.50.250.1, 00:01:24
C       10.21.0.0/16 is directly connected, Serial1.507
C       10.75.100.1/32 is directly connected, Loopback0
S       10.100.83.1/32 is directly connected, Ethernet0
S       10.50.250.1/32 is directly connected, Ethernet0
S       10.200.60.1/32 is directly connected, Ethernet0
B    192.168.50.0/24 [20/1] via 10.50.250.1, 00:01:27
B    192.168.100.0/24 [20/0] via 10.100.83.1, 00:01:25
Lillehammer#
```

One solution is to use the BGP **network** command, as demonstrated in Example 3-99.

Example 3-99 *Using the **network** Command to Cause the EBGP-Discovered Routes to Be Treated as Local BGP Routes*

```
Lillehammer
router rip
 redistribute bgp 75
 network 10.0.0.0
 network 172.18.0.0
 network 192.168.75.0
!
router bgp 75
 network 172.17.0.0
```

continues

Example 3-99 *Using the* **network** *Command to Cause the EBGP-Discovered Routes to Be Treated as Local BGP Routes (Continued)*

```
  network 172.18.0.0
  network 192.168.75.0
  neighbor 10.50.250.1 remote-as 50
  neighbor 10.50.250.1 ebgp-multihop 2
  neighbor 10.50.250.1 update-source Loopback0
  neighbor 10.100.83.1 remote-as 100
  neighbor 10.100.83.1 ebgp-multihop 2
  neighbor 10.100.83.1 update-source Loopback0
  neighbor 10.200.60.1 remote-as 200
  neighbor 10.200.60.1 ebgp-multihop 2
  neighbor 10.200.60.1 update-source Loopback0

Meribel
router rip
 redistribute bgp 50 metric 1
 network 10.0.0.0
 !
router bgp 50
 network 172.18.0.0
 redistribute rip
 neighbor 10.75.100.1 remote-as 75
 neighbor 10.75.100.1 ebgp-multihop 2
 neighbor 10.75.100.1 update-source Loopback0
 neighbor 10.100.83.1 remote-as 100
 neighbor 10.100.83.1 ebgp-multihop 2
 neighbor 10.100.83.1 update-source Loopback0
 neighbor 10.200.60.1 remote-as 200
 neighbor 10.200.60.1 ebgp-multihop 2
 neighbor 10.200.60.1 update-source Loopback0
 no auto-summary
```

In the configurations in Example 3-99, the **network** commands cause the EBGP-discovered routes to be treated as local BGP routes. Network 172.17.0.0 is advertised to Lillehammer via EBGP, for instance, and is entered into the routing table. The command **network 172.17.0.0** is added to Lillehammer's BGP configuration, even though 172.17.0.0 is not really a local route. Because the address is in the routing table, the **network** command matches it and makes it a local route.

The logic sounds quite strange, but it works. By first being an EBGP route, 172.17.0.0 is changed into a local BGP route with the **network** command. Because 172.17.0.0 is now considered a local route at Lillehammer, it is assigned an administrative distance of 200. The RIP route to 172.17.0.0 now has a lower distance and becomes the preferred route, as indicated in the output in Example 3-100.

Example 3-100 *By Causing Lillehammer to Treat the EBGP Route to 172.17.0.0 as a Local BGP Route with an Administrative Distance of 200, the RIP Route to That Network Becomes the Preferred Route*

```
Lillehammer#show ip route
Codes: C - connected, S - static, I - IGRP, R - RIP, M - mobile, B - BGP
       D - EIGRP, EX - EIGRP external, O - OSPF, IA - OSPF inter area
       N1 - OSPF NSSA external type 1, N2 - OSPF NSSA external type 2
       E1 - OSPF external type 1, E2 - OSPF external type 2, E - EGP
       i - IS-IS, L1 - IS-IS level-1, L2 - IS-IS level-2, * - candidate default
       U - per-user static route, o - ODR
       T - traffic engineered route

Gateway of last resort is not set

C    192.168.75.0/24 is directly connected, Ethernet2
R    172.17.0.0/16 [120/2] via 10.21.1.1, 00:00:06, Serial1.507
B    172.16.0.0/16 [20/0] via 10.200.60.1, 00:00:36
C    172.18.0.0/16 is directly connected, Ethernet1
     172.29.0.0/16 is variably subnetted, 2 subnets, 2 masks
B       172.29.1.0/24 [20/0] via 10.200.60.1, 00:00:36
B       172.29.0.0/16 [20/1] via 10.50.250.1, 00:00:24
B    172.31.0.0/16 [20/0] via 10.200.60.1, 00:00:36
     192.168.4.0/29 is subnetted, 1 subnets
C       192.168.4.0 is directly connected, Ethernet0
     10.0.0.0/8 is variably subnetted, 7 subnets, 2 masks
B       10.30.0.0/16 [20/0] via 10.200.60.1, 00:00:36
B       10.20.0.0/16 [20/0] via 10.50.250.1, 00:00:24
C       10.21.0.0/16 is directly connected, Serial1.507
C       10.75.100.1/32 is directly connected, Loopback0
S       10.100.83.1/32 is directly connected, Ethernet0
S       10.50.250.1/32 is directly connected, Ethernet0
S       10.200.60.1/32 is directly connected, Ethernet0
B    192.168.50.0/24 [20/1] via 10.50.250.1, 00:00:25
B    192.168.100.0/24 [20/0] via 10.200.60.1, 00:00:37
Lillehammer#
```

Although the administrative distances have been manipulated correctly, this configuration has a problem. By using the **network** command to convert an EBGP route into a local route, the local BGP router now advertises the route in its own EBGP updates. Lillehammer, for example, now advertises 172.17.0.0 in its EBGP updates to its peers across the NAP. Because Meribel's BGP process learns the route to 172.17.0.0 from redistribution, it advertises the route with an ORIGIN of Incomplete. But Lillehammer, because of the **network** statement, advertises the route with an ORIGIN of IGP. As a result, Cervinia and Innsbruck choose Lillehammer as the best next hop to 172.17.0.0, as demonstrated in the output in Example 3-101. External traffic to 172.17.0.0 is forwarded to Lillehammer, which forwards the traffic across the backdoor link. Only traffic between 172.17.0.0 and 172.18.0.0 is supposed to use the backdoor link; all other traffic should use the NAP.

Example 3-101 *Cervinia Shows Lillehammer (10.75.100.1) as the Best Next Hop to Network 172.17.0.0, Causing*
the Backdoor Link Between Lillehammer and Meribel to Become a Transit Network for All External
Traffic to 172.17.0.0

```
Cervinia#show ip bgp 172.17.0.0
BGP routing table entry for 172.17.0.0/16, version 474
Paths: (3 available, best #2, advertised over EBGP)
  100 75
    10.100.83.1 from 10.100.83.1
      Origin IGP, localpref 100, valid, external
  75
    10.75.100.1 from 10.75.100.1 (192.168.75.1)
      Origin IGP, metric 2, localpref 100, valid, external, best
  50
    10.50.250.1 from 10.50.250.1
      Origin incomplete, metric 1, localpref 100, valid, external
Cervinia#
```

Example 3-102 shows the solution to this problem via the **network backdoor** command,
another Cisco-specific tool.

Example 3-102 *Restricting External Traffic from the Backdoor Link Between Lillehammer and Meribel*

```
Lillehammer
router rip
 redistribute bgp 75
 network 10.0.0.0
 network 172.18.0.0
 network 192.168.75.0
!
router bgp 75
 network 172.17.0.0 backdoor
 network 172.18.0.0
 network 192.168.75.0
 neighbor 10.50.250.1 remote-as 50
 neighbor 10.50.250.1 ebgp-multihop 2
 neighbor 10.50.250.1 update-source Loopback0
 neighbor 10.100.83.1 remote-as 100
 neighbor 10.100.83.1 ebgp-multihop 2
 neighbor 10.100.83.1 update-source Loopback0
 neighbor 10.200.60.1 remote-as 200
 neighbor 10.200.60.1 ebgp-multihop 2
 neighbor 10.200.60.1 update-source Loopback0

Meribel
router rip
 redistribute bgp 50 metric 1
 network 10.0.0.0
!
router bgp 50
 network 172.18.0.0 backdoor
```

Example 3-102 *Restricting External Traffic from the Backdoor Link Between Lillehammer and Meribel (Continued)*

```
 redistribute rip
 neighbor 10.75.100.1 remote-as 75
 neighbor 10.75.100.1 ebgp-multihop 2
 neighbor 10.75.100.1 update-source Loopback0
 neighbor 10.100.83.1 remote-as 100
 neighbor 10.100.83.1 ebgp-multihop 2
 neighbor 10.100.83.1 update-source Loopback0
 neighbor 10.200.60.1 remote-as 200
 neighbor 10.200.60.1 ebgp-multihop 2
 neighbor 10.200.60.1 update-source Loopback0
 no auto-summary
```

The **network backdoor** command has the same effect as the **network** command: The EBGP route is treated as a local BGP route, and the administrative distance is changed to 200. The difference is that the address specified by the **network backdoor** command is not advertised to EBGP peers. In the case of network 172.17.0.0, the new configurations result in the same routing table at Lillehammer shown in Example 3-100. But Cervinia's BGP table no longer contains a route to that network from Lillehammer.

Case Study: Using the LOCAL_PREF Attribute

The LOCAL_PREF attribute is used to set preferences among multiple routes to the same destination. Unlike administrative weight, the LOCAL_PREF is not limited to a single router. Rather, it is communicated to IBGP peers. The attribute is not communicated to EBGP peers—hence the name *local preference*.

A route's LOCAL_PREF attribute can be any number between 0 and 4,294,967,295; the higher the number, the more preferable the route. By default, all routes advertised to IBGP peers have a LOCAL_PREF of 100. This default value can be changed with the **ip default local-preference** command. You can change the LOCAL_PREF attribute of individual routes by using a route map and the command **set local-preference**.

In Figure 3-20, AS 30 is multihomed to a single AS. For redundancy, links are added between Zermatt and Moritz and between Innsbruck and Saalbach; IBGP is run on each of these links.

Routing policy in AS 30 requires that all outgoing traffic to AS 75 must use the Moritz-Saalbach link, and all outgoing traffic to AS 50 must use the Zermatt-Innsbruck link. In each case, the other link should be used only if the preferred link is unavailable. Example 3-103 shows the configurations of Zermatt and Moritz.

Figure 3-20 *AS 30 Is Multihomed to a Single Autonomous System*

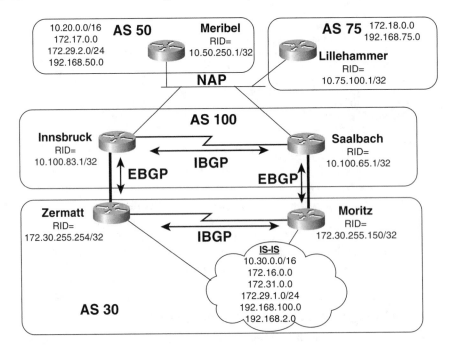

Example 3-103 *Influencing Route Preferences with the LOCAL_PREF Attribute*

```
Zermatt
router isis
 net 30.5678.1234.defa.00
 default-information originate
!
router bgp 30
 redistribute isis level-2
 neighbor 10.100.83.1 remote-as 100
 neighbor 10.100.83.1 ebgp-multihop 2
 neighbor 10.100.83.1 update-source Loopback0
 neighbor 10.100.83.1 route-map PREF in
 neighbor 10.100.83.1 filter-list 1 out
 neighbor 172.30.255.150 remote-as 30
 neighbor 172.30.255.150 ebgp-multihop 2
 neighbor 172.30.255.150 update-source Loopback0
 neighbor 172.30.255.150 next-hop-self
 no auto-summary
!
ip route 10.100.83.1 255.255.255.255 Serial1.906
ip route 172.30.255.150 255.255.255.255 Serial1.908
 !
```

Example 3-103 *Influencing Route Preferences with the LOCAL_PREF Attribute (Continued)*

```
ip as-path access-list 1 permit ^$
ip as-path access-list 2 permit _50$
!
route-map PREF permit 10
 match as-path 2
 set local-preference 200
!
route-map PREF permit 20
```

Moritz
```
router isis
 net 30.1234.5678.abcd.00
 default-information originate
!
router bgp 30
 redistribute isis level-2
 neighbor 10.100.65.1 remote-as 100
 neighbor 10.100.65.1 ebgp-multihop 2
 neighbor 10.100.65.1 update-source Loopback0
 neighbor 10.100.65.1 route-map PREF in
 neighbor 10.100.65.1 filter-list 1 out
 neighbor 172.30.255.254 remote-as 30
 neighbor 172.30.255.254 ebgp-multihop 2
 neighbor 172.30.255.254 update-source Loopback0
 neighbor 172.30.255.254 next-hop-self
 no auto-summary
!
ip route 10.100.65.1 255.255.255.255 Serial1.803
ip route 172.30.255.254 255.255.255.255 Serial1.809
!
ip as-path access-list 1 permit ^$
ip as-path access-list 2 permit _75$
!
route-map PREF permit 10
 match as-path 2
 set local-preference 300
!
route-map PREF permit 20
```

Each router links the incoming routes from its EBGP peer to a route map named PREF. Sequence 10 of this route map identifies the AS_PATH of the incoming routes. Incoming routes at Zermatt whose AS_PATH ends in a 50 are assigned a LOCAL_PREF of 200. Incoming routes at Moritz whose AS_PATH ends in a 75 are assigned a LOCAL_PREF of 300. Any routes that are not matched at sequence 10 are permitted by sequence 20 and get the default value of 100.

NOTE   In practice, the two routers would probably assign the same LOCAL_PREF values. The values differ in this example only so that the influence of each route map is more easily observed.

Example 3-104 shows the results in the BGP tables of the two routers.

Example 3-104 *Zermatt Sets a LOCAL_PREF of 200 for Routes to Destinations Within AS 50, and Moritz Sets a LOCAL_PREF of 300 for Routes to Destinations Within AS 75*

```
Zermatt#show ip bgp
BGP table version is 20, local router ID is 172.30.255.254
Status codes: s suppressed, * valid, > best, i - internal
Origin codes: i - IGP, e - EGP, ? - incomplete
   Network          Next Hop          Metric LocPrf Weight Path
*> 10.20.0.0/16     10.100.83.1                200      0 100 50 ?
*> 10.30.0.0/16     192.168.2.1          20         32768 ?
*  i                172.30.255.150       20    100      0 ?
*> 10.50.250.1/32   10.100.83.1                200      0 100 50 ?
*> 10.75.100.1/32   10.100.83.1                100      0 100 75 ?
*> 10.100.65.1/32   10.100.83.1                200      0 100 50 ?
*>i10.100.83.1/32   172.30.255.150             100      0 100 50 ?
*> 172.16.0.0/16    192.168.2.1          20         32768 ?
*  i                172.30.255.150       20    100      0 ?
*> 172.17.0.0       10.100.83.1                200      0 100 50 ?
*  172.18.0.0       10.100.83.1                         0 100 75 i
*>i                 172.30.255.150             300      0 100 75 i
*> 172.29.0.0       10.100.83.1                200      0 100 50 ?
*> 172.29.1.0/24    192.168.2.1          20         32768 ?
*  i                172.30.255.150       20    100      0 ?
*> 172.31.0.0       192.168.2.1          20         32768 ?
*  i                172.30.255.150       20    100      0 ?
*>i192.168.2.0/30   172.30.255.150       20    100      0 ?
*> 192.168.2.4/30   192.168.2.1          20         32768 ?
*> 192.168.50.0     10.100.83.1                200      0 100 50 ?
*  192.168.75.0     10.100.83.1                         0 100 75 i
*>i                 172.30.255.150             300      0 100 75 i
*> 192.168.100.0    192.168.2.1          20         32768 ?
*  i                172.30.255.150       20    100      0 ?
Zermatt#
```

```
Moritz#show ip bgp
BGP table version is 25, local router ID is 172.30.255.150
Status codes: s suppressed, * valid, > best, i - internal
Origin codes: i - IGP, e - EGP, ? - incomplete
   Network          Next Hop          Metric LocPrf Weight Path
*  10.20.0.0/16     10.100.65.1                         0 100 50 ?
*>i                 172.30.255.254             200      0 100 50 ?
*> 10.30.0.0/16     192.168.2.5          20         32768 ?
*  i                172.30.255.254       20    100      0 ?
```

Example 3-104 *Zermatt Sets a LOCAL_PREF of 200 for Routes to Destinations Within AS 50, and Moritz Sets a LOCAL_PREF of 300 for Routes to Destinations Within AS 75 (Continued)*

```
 *   10.50.250.1/32   10.100.65.1                         0 100 50 ?
 *>i                  172.30.255.254         200          0 100 50 ?
 *   10.75.100.1/32   10.100.65.1                         0 100 75 ?
 *>i                  172.30.255.254         100          0 100 75 ?
 *>i10.100.65.1/32    172.30.255.254         200          0 100 50 ?
 *> 10.100.83.1/32    10.100.65.1                         0 100 50 ?
 *> 172.16.0.0/16     192.168.2.5        20           32768 ?
 *  i                 172.30.255.254     20  100          0 ?
 *   172.17.0.0       10.100.65.1                         0 100 50 ?
 *>i                  172.30.255.254         200          0 100 50 ?
 *> 172.18.0.0        10.100.65.1            300          0 100 75 i
 *   172.29.0.0       10.100.65.1                         0 100 50 ?
 *>i                  172.30.255.254         200          0 100 50 ?
 *> 172.29.1.0/24     192.168.2.5        20           32768 ?
 *  i                 172.30.255.254     20  100          0 ?
 *> 172.31.0.0        192.168.2.5        20           32768 ?
 *  i                 172.30.255.254     20  100          0 ?
 *> 192.168.2.0/30    192.168.2.5        20           32768 ?
 *>i192.168.2.4/30    172.30.255.254     20  100          0 ?
 *   192.168.50.0     10.100.65.1                         0 100 50 ?
 *>i                  172.30.255.254         200          0 100 50 ?
 *> 192.168.75.0      10.100.65.1            300          0 100 75 i
 *> 192.168.100.0     192.168.2.5        20           32768 ?
 *  i                 172.30.255.254     20  100          0 ?
Moritz#
```

Notice the fundamental difference between the configurations in Example 3-103 and the IS-IS configurations from several of the earlier examples. Here, BGP routes are not distributed into the IS-IS domain. Instead, each router advertises a default address. When sending traffic to an external destination, the interior routers forward packets to the nearest default address—either Zermatt or Innsbruck. Those routers then forward the packets to either their respective EBGP peer or to the IBGP peer across the redundant link, depending on the LOCAL_PREF attribute of the external route.

Eliminating the redistribution of BGP into IS-IS is not done on a whim; it is required for this topology and this routing policy. If Moritz redistributes the EBGP route to 172.18.0.0 into IS-IS, for example, the route is advertised across the IS-IS domain to Zermatt. Zermatt accepts the route and redistributes it back into BGP, entering it into its own BGP table. Because Zermatt enters the route into its BGP table, the route is considered locally originated and is given a weight of 32768. Administrative weight overrules LOCAL_PREF, and Zermatt sees the best route to 172.17.0.0 as through the IS-IS domain rather than across the direct link to Moritz.

Case Study: Using the MULTI_EXIT_DISC Attribute

The MULTI_EXIT_DISC attribute, or MED, is used to influence the routing decisions in neighboring autonomous systems. The MED is also known as the *external metric*, and in fact is labeled as "metric" in the BGP table. Like LOCAL_PREF, the MED is a 4-octet number and therefore can be any number from 0 to 4294967295.

When a BGP speaker learns a route from a peer, it can pass the route's MED to any IBGP peers, but not to EBGP peers. As a result, the MED has relevance only between neighboring autonomous systems. If router Zermatt in Figure 3-20 advertises 172.16.0.0 with a certain MED to Innsbruck, Innsbruck can advertise the MED to Saalbach. When Innsbruck and Saalbach advertise the route to their EBGP peers in AS 50 and AS 75, however, they cannot include the MED in the route.

The MED is a relatively weak attribute. In the BGP decision process, the weights, LOCAL_PREFs, AS_PATH lengths, and ORIGINs of multiple routes to the same destination are all considered before MED. If all of those variables are equal, however, the route with the lowest MED is chosen.

TIP   It can be a bit confusing to remember that the highest LOCAL_PREF is preferred, but the lowest MED is preferred. Another term for MED is *metric*, and another term for metric is *distance*. So remember "highest preference, shortest distance."

You can manipulate the MED with the **set metric** command under a route map. In Figure 3-20, AS 30 wants AS 100 to send incoming traffic to network 172.16.0.0 via the Saalbach-Moritz link. Traffic to network 172.31.0.0 should be sent across the Innsbruck-Zermatt link. AS 100 is free to send other traffic across either link. Example 3-105 shows the configurations of Zermatt and Moritz.

Example 3-105 *Configuring Zermatt and Moritz to Manipulate the MED Attribute*

```
Zermatt
router bgp 30
 redistribute isis level-2
 neighbor 10.100.83.1 remote-as 100
 neighbor 10.100.83.1 ebgp-multihop 2
 neighbor 10.100.83.1 update-source Loopback0
 neighbor 10.100.83.1 route-map PREF in
 neighbor 10.100.83.1 route-map MED out
 neighbor 10.100.83.1 filter-list 1 out
 neighbor 172.30.255.150 remote-as 30
 neighbor 172.30.255.150 ebgp-multihop 2
 neighbor 172.30.255.150 update-source Loopback0
 neighbor 172.30.255.150 next-hop-self
 !
```

Example 3-105 *Configuring Zermatt and Moritz to Manipulate the MED Attribute (Continued)*

```
access-list 1 permit 172.31.0.0
access-list 2 permit any
!
route-map MED permit 10
 match ip address 1
 set metric 100
!
route-map MED permit
 match ip address 2
 set metric 200
```

Moritz
```
router bgp 30
 redistribute isis level-2
 neighbor 10.100.65.1 remote-as 100
 neighbor 10.100.65.1 ebgp-multihop 2
 neighbor 10.100.65.1 update-source Loopback0
 neighbor 10.100.65.1 route-map PREF in
 neighbor 10.100.65.1 route-map MED out
 neighbor 10.100.65.1 filter-list 1 out
 neighbor 172.30.255.254 remote-as 30
 neighbor 172.30.255.254 ebgp-multihop 2
 neighbor 172.30.255.254 update-source Loopback0
 neighbor 172.30.255.254 next-hop-self
 no auto-summary
!
access-list 1 permit 172.16.0.0
access-list 2 permit any
!
route-map MED permit 10
 match ip address 1
 set metric 100
!
route-map MED permit 20
 match ip address 2
 set metric 200
```

Each router links the outgoing routes to its EBGP peer to a route map named MED.
Sequence 10 of this route map references access list 1 and assigns a MED to matching
routes. Zermatt gives the route to 172.31.0.0 a MED of 100, and Moritz gives the route to
172.16.0.0 a MED of 100. Any routes that do not match the access list in sequence 10 are
permitted in sequence 20 and are assigned a MED of 200. Example 3-106 shows the results
in Innsbruck's BGP table.

Example 3-106 *Innsbruck Forwards Packets Destined for 172.16.0.0 to Saalbach (10.100.65.1) and Packets Destined for 172.31.0.0 to Zermatt (172.30.255.254) Based on the Lower Metrics of These Paths*

```
Innsbruck#show ip bgp 172.16.0.0
BGP routing table entry for 172.16.0.0/16, version 10
Paths: (2 available, best #2)
  Advertised to non peer-group peers:
    10.50.250.1 10.75.100.1
  30
    172.30.255.254 from 172.30.255.254 (172.30.255.254)
      Origin incomplete, metric 200, localpref 100, valid, external, ref 2
  30
    10.100.65.1 from 10.100.65.1 (10.100.65.1)
      Origin incomplete, metric 100, localpref 100, valid, internal, best, ref 2

Innsbruck#show ip bgp 172.31.0.0
BGP routing table entry for 172.31.0.0/16, version 26
Paths: (2 available, best #1)
  Advertised to non peer-group peers:
    10.50.250.1 10.75.100.1
  30
    172.30.255.254 from 172.30.255.254 (172.30.255.254)
      Origin incomplete, metric 100, localpref 100, valid, external, best, ref 2
  30
    10.100.65.1 from 10.100.65.1 (10.100.65.1)
      Origin incomplete, metric 200, localpref 100, valid, internal, ref 2
Innsbruck#
```

Normally, the MEDs of multiple routes to the same destination are compared only when the routes originate from the same AS. After all, the purpose of the MED is to allow an AS to communicate its preferences for incoming traffic when multiple links exist to a neighboring AS. Comparing the preferences of two different autonomous systems usually makes no sense. On occasion, however, exceptions apply.

Figure 3-21 again shows a backdoor link between AS 50 and AS 75. As in the case study "Administrative Distances and Backdoor Routes," the networks 172.17.0.0 and 172.18.0.0 are advertised via RIP over the backdoor link and are used for private communication between the two autonomous systems.

The **network backdoor** command was used so that AS 75 would not advertise 172.17.0.0 and AS 50 would not advertise 172.18.0.0. But in this example, AS 50 and AS 75 want the routers in AS 100 to use the backdoor link as a secondary route. If Meribel's interface to the NAP fails, for example, Innsbruck and Saalbach should send packets destined for 172.17.0.0 to Lillehammer, to be forwarded across the backdoor to AS 50. This requires Meribel and Lillehammer to advertise networks that do not exist in their own AS and to clearly identify the routes as backup routes. In this situation, because routes to the same destination are being originated by routers in different autonomous systems, comparing MEDs from different autonomous systems can make sense.

Figure 3-21 *The Backdoor Route Between AS 50 and AS 75 Should Also Be Used as a Backup Route*

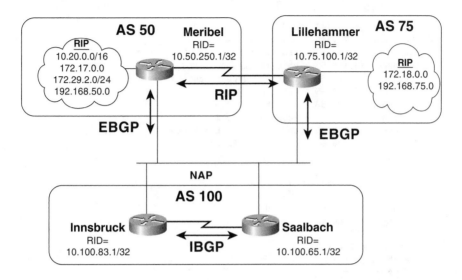

Two commands are relevant to the circumstances of Figure 3-21. The first is **set metric-type internal**. This command, used as part of a route map, sets the MED of a BGP route to the same metric as the IGP route to the same destination. For instance, Meribel's RIP route to 172.17.0.0 is one hop. Lillehammer's RIP route to the same destination, learned across the backdoor link, is two hops. The **set metric-type internal** command causes those routers' BGP routes advertising the network to inherit those metrics. As a result, the routers in AS 100 prefer Meribel's route, with a MED of 1, over Lillehammer's route to the same destination, with a MED of 2.

The second relevant command is used on the receiving side—in Figure 3-21, on the routers in AS 100. The command **bgp always-compare-med** tells a router to compare the MED of multiple routes to the same destination, even if the routes originate in different autonomous systems. Using these two commands, Example 3-107 presents the configurations of Meribel, Lillehammer, and Saalbach.

Example 3-107 *The Configurations of Meribel, Lillehammer, and Saalbach in Figure 3-21, Allowing Saalbach to Compare MED Values from Different Autonomous Systems*

```
Meribel
router bgp 50
 network 172.17.0.0
 network 172.18.0.0
 redistribute rip
 neighbor 10.75.100.1 remote-as 75
 neighbor 10.75.100.1 ebgp-multihop 2
```

continues

Example 3-107 *The Configurations of Meribel, Lillehammer, and Saalbach in Figure 3-21, Allowing Saalbach to Compare MED Values from Different Autonomous Systems (Continued)*

```
 neighbor 10.75.100.1 update-source Loopback0
 neighbor 10.75.100.1 distribute-list 2 in
 neighbor 10.100.65.1 remote-as 100
 neighbor 10.100.65.1 ebgp-multihop 2
 neighbor 10.100.65.1 update-source Loopback0
 neighbor 10.100.65.1 route-map MED out
 neighbor 10.100.83.1 remote-as 100
 neighbor 10.100.83.1 ebgp-multihop 2
 neighbor 10.100.83.1 update-source Loopback0
 neighbor 10.100.83.1 route-map MED out
no auto-summary
!
ip as-path access-list 1 permit ^$
!
access-list 2 permit 192.168.75.0
access-list 2 permit 172.18.0.0
!
route-map MED permit 10
 match as-path 1
 set metric-type internal

Lillehammer
router bgp 75
 network 172.17.0.0
 network 172.18.0.0
 network 192.168.75.0
 neighbor 10.50.250.1 remote-as 50
 neighbor 10.50.250.1 ebgp-multihop 2
 neighbor 10.50.250.1 update-source Loopback0
 neighbor 10.50.250.1 distribute-list 2 in
 neighbor 10.100.65.1 remote-as 100
 neighbor 10.100.65.1 ebgp-multihop 2
 neighbor 10.100.65.1 update-source Loopback0
 neighbor 10.100.65.1 route-map MED out
 neighbor 10.100.83.1 remote-as 100
 neighbor 10.100.83.1 ebgp-multihop 2
 neighbor 10.100.83.1 update-source Loopback0
 neighbor 10.100.83.1 route-map MED out
!
ip as-path access-list 1 permit ^$
!
access-list 2 permit 10.20.0.0
access-list 2 permit 172.17.0.0
access-list 2 permit 172.29.0.0
access-list 2 permit 192.168.50.0
!
route-map MED permit 10
 match as-path 1
 set metric-type internal
```

continues

Example 3-107 *The Configurations of Meribel, Lillehammer, and Saalbach in Figure 3-21, Allowing Saalbach to Compare MED Values from Different Autonomous Systems (Continued)*

```
Saalbach
router bgp 100
 no synchronization
 bgp always-compare-med
 neighbor 10.50.250.1 remote-as 50
 neighbor 10.50.250.1 ebgp-multihop 2
 neighbor 10.50.250.1 update-source Loopback0
 neighbor 10.50.250.1 filter-list 2 in
 neighbor 10.75.100.1 remote-as 75
 neighbor 10.75.100.1 ebgp-multihop 2
 neighbor 10.75.100.1 update-source Loopback0
 neighbor 10.100.83.1 remote-as 100
 neighbor 10.100.83.1 ebgp-multihop 2
 neighbor 10.100.83.1 update-source Loopback0
 neighbor 10.100.83.1 next-hop-self
 neighbor 10.100.83.1 filter-list 1 in
 neighbor 172.30.255.150 remote-as 30
 neighbor 172.30.255.150 ebgp-multihop 2
 neighbor 172.30.255.150 update-source Loopback0
 no auto-summary
```

Notice that in Meribel's configuration a **network** statement is used for 172.17.0.0, even though the network is being redistributed into BGP. This statement is necessary to fix the ORIGIN of the route to IGP, because a **network** statement is used for the route at Lillehammer. Without it, the ORIGIN of the route from Meribel would be Incomplete. ORIGIN has a higher priority than MED in the BGP decision process, meaning that the Lillehammer route would be preferred at AS 100, even with its higher MED.

Another important detail in Meribel's configuration is the distribute list filtering incoming NLRI from Lillehammer. This filter permits the route to 192.168.75.0 and 172.18.0.0 and denies all other routes. Of particular importance is the fact that the route to 172.17.0.0 advertised by Lillehammer is denied by this filter. Otherwise, the EBGP route, with an administrative distance of 20, would take precedence over Meribel's RIP route, causing a routing loop.

Example 3-108 shows the resulting BGP table at Saalbach. Meribel's route to 172.17.0.0, with a MED of 1, is preferred over Lillehammer's route, with a MED of 2. 172.18.0.0 is directly attached to Lillehammer, so the local metric and the resulting MED from that router are 0. After being advertised via RIP to Meribel, the local metric at that router is 1, which is also reflected in that MED of Meribel's route. If either of the preferred routes fails, the alternate route is chosen, and traffic to that destination uses the backdoor link.

Example 3-108 *The MEDs for the Routes to 172.17.0.0 and 172.18.0.0 Match the Internal RIP Metrics of AS 50 and AS 75*

```
Saalbach#show ip bgp
BGP table version is 54, local router ID is 10.100.65.1
Status codes: s suppressed, d damped, h history, * valid, > best, i - internal
Origin codes: i - IGP, e - EGP, ? - incomplete

   Network          Next Hop         Metric LocPrf Weight Path
*> 10.20.0.0/16     10.50.250.1           0             0 50 ?
*> 10.21.0.0/16     10.50.250.1           0             0 50 ?
*  i10.30.0.0/16    10.100.83.1         200    100      0 30 ?
*>                  172.30.255.150      200             0 30 ?
*> 10.50.250.1/32   10.50.250.1           0             0 50 ?
*> 10.75.100.1/32   10.50.250.1           0             0 50 ?
*> 10.100.83.1/32   10.50.250.1           0             0 50 ?
*> 172.16.0.0       172.30.255.150      100             0 30 ?
*> 172.17.0.0       10.50.250.1           1             0 50 i
*                   10.75.100.1           2             0 75 i
*  172.18.0.0       10.50.250.1           1             0 50 i
*>                  10.75.100.1           0             0 75 i
*> 172.29.0.0       10.50.250.1           1             0 50 ?
*  i172.29.1.0/24   10.100.83.1         200    100      0 30 ?
*>                  172.30.255.150      200             0 30 ?
*>i172.31.0.0       10.100.83.1         100    100      0 30 ?
*                   172.30.255.150      200             0 30 ?
*> 192.168.50.0     10.50.250.1           1             0 50 ?
*> 192.168.75.0     10.75.100.1           0             0 75 i
*  i192.168.100.0   10.100.83.1         200    100      0 30 ?
*>                  172.30.255.150      200             0 30 ?
Saalbach#
```

Innsbruck's configuration and BGP table are not shown in this example, but they are similar.

Case Study: Prepending the AS_PATH

The MULTI_EXIT_DISC attribute can influence the incoming traffic from neighboring autonomous systems, but it cannot influence the routing decisions of more-remote autonomous systems.

Figure 3-22 repeats a topology encountered in an earlier case study. Looking at the BGP table of Meribel in Example 3-109, you can see that the router has duplicate, equal-cost paths to the destinations within AS 30. Because all other values are equal, Meribel's BGP decision process has chosen Innsbruck as the next-hop router for all traffic to AS 30 based on Innsbruck's lower router ID. As a result, the Cervinia-Moritz link does not get used at all for traffic from AS 50 to AS 30; available bandwidth is poorly utilized.

Figure 3-22 *Dual, Equal-Cost Paths Exist Between AS 50 and AS 30*

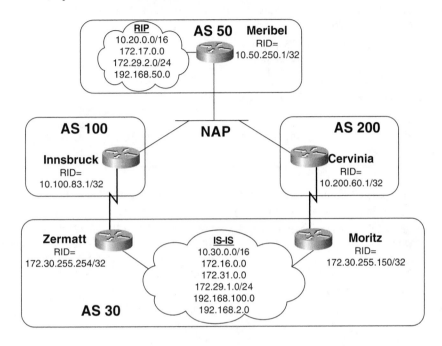

Example 3-109 *Meribel's BGP Table Shows the Dual Paths to the Destinations Within AS 30; Innsbruck Is Chosen as the Best Path for All the Destinations Because Its Router ID (10.100.83.1) Is Lower Than Cervinia's (10.200.60.1)*

```
Meribel#show ip bgp
BGP table version is 18, local router ID is 10.50.250.1
Status codes: s suppressed, d damped, h history, * valid, > best, i - internal
Origin codes: i - IGP, e - EGP, ? - incomplete
   Network          Next Hop            Metric LocPrf Weight Path
*> 10.20.0.0/16     0.0.0.0                  0         32768 ?
*  10.30.0.0/16     10.200.60.1                        0 200 30 ?
*>                  10.100.83.1                        0 100 30 ?
*> 10.50.250.1/32   0.0.0.0                  0         32768 ?
*> 10.100.65.1/32   0.0.0.0                  0         32768 ?
*> 10.100.83.1/32   0.0.0.0                  0         32768 ?
*> 10.200.60.1/32   0.0.0.0                  0         32768 ?
*  172.16.0.0       10.200.60.1                        0 200 30 ?
*>                  10.100.83.1                        0 100 30 ?
*> 172.17.0.0       10.20.1.1                1         32768 i
*> 172.29.0.0       10.20.1.1                1         32768 ?
*  172.29.1.0/24    10.200.60.1                        0 200 30 ?
*>                  10.100.83.1                        0 100 30 ?
*> 172.30.255.150/32 10.100.83.1                       0 100 30 ?
```

continues

Example 3-109 *Meribel's BGP Table Shows the Dual Paths to the Destinations Within AS 30; Innsbruck Is Chosen as the Best Path for All the Destinations Because Its Router ID (10.100.83.1) Is Lower Than Cervinia's (10.200.60.1) (Continued)*

```
*> 172.30.255.254/32 10.200.60.1                    0 200 30 ?
*  172.31.0.0        10.200.60.1                    0 200 30 ?
*>                   10.100.83.1                    0 100 30 ?
*> 192.168.2.0/30    10.200.60.1                    0 200 30 ?
*> 192.168.2.4/30    10.100.83.1                    0 100 30 ?
*> 192.168.50.0      10.20.1.1              1       32768 ?
*  192.168.100.0     10.200.60.1                    0 200 30 ?
*>                   10.100.83.1                    0 100 30 ?
Meribel#
```

AS 30 cannot influence the routing decisions of AS 50 with MEDs, because the two autonomous systems are not directly connected neighbors. But AS 30 can influence the routing decisions of AS 50 by modifying the AS_PATH of the routes it advertises by using the **set as-path prepend** command. Suppose AS 30 wants AS 50 to forward all traffic destined for 172.16.0.0 and 172.31.0.0 to Cervinia and wants traffic to 10.30.0.0, 172.29.1.0/24, and 192.168.100.0 forwarded to Innsbruck. Example 3-110 shows the configuration for Zermatt and Moritz.

Example 3-110 *Configuring Zermatt and Moritz for AS Path Prepending*

```
Zermatt
router bgp 30
 no synchronization
 redistribute isis level-2
 neighbor 10.100.83.1 remote-as 100
 neighbor 10.100.83.1 ebgp-multihop 2
 neighbor 10.100.83.1 update-source Loopback0
 neighbor 10.100.83.1 route-map PATH out
 neighbor 10.100.83.1 filter-list 1 out
 no auto-summary
!
ip as-path access-list 1 permit ^$
!
access-list 3 permit 172.31.0.0
access-list 3 permit 172.16.0.0
!
route-map PATH permit 10
 match ip address 3
 set as-path prepend 30
!
route-map PATH permit 20
```

```
Moritz
router bgp 30
 no synchronization
 redistribute isis level-2
```

Example 3-110 *Configuring Zermatt and Moritz for AS Path Prepending (Continued)*

```
 neighbor 10.200.60.1 remote-as 200
 neighbor 10.200.60.1 ebgp-multihop 2
 neighbor 10.200.60.1 update-source Loopback0
 neighbor 10.200.60.1 route-map PATH out
 neighbor 10.200.60.1 filter-list 1 out
 no auto-summary
!
ip as-path access-list 1 permit ^$
!
access-list 3 permit 192.168.100.0
access-list 3 permit 10.30.0.0
access-list 3 permit 172.29.1.0
!
route-map PATH permit 10
 match ip address 3
 set as-path prepend 30
!
route-map PATH permit 20
```

Each router filters outgoing packets through a route map named PATH. Statement 10 of the route map uses access list 3 to identify certain roues by their NLRI; matching routes have an AS number of 30 added to their AS_PATH. Note that this number is in addition to the AS number 30 normally added to the AS_PATH. Routes that are not matched by access list 3 are permitted by statement 20 of the route map.

Example 3-111 shows the resulting BGP table at Meribel. The prepended routes are now longer than the routes from the preferred path, and the router chooses the routes with the shorter AS_PATHs.

Example 3-111 *Meribel's BGP Table Shows the Prepended AS_PATHs from Zermatt and Moritz; the Router Chooses the Paths with the Shorter AS_PATH*

```
Meribel#show ip bgp
BGP table version is 70, local router ID is 10.50.250.1
Status codes: s suppressed, d damped, h history, * valid, > best, i - internal
Origin codes: i - IGP, e - EGP, ? - incomplete
   Network          Next Hop         Metric LocPrf Weight Path
*> 10.20.0.0/16     0.0.0.0               0         32768 ?
*  10.30.0.0/16     10.200.60.1                         0 200 30 30 ?
*>                  10.100.83.1                         0 100 30 ?
*> 10.50.250.1/32   0.0.0.0               0         32768 ?
*> 10.100.65.1/32   0.0.0.0               0         32768 ?
*> 10.100.83.1/32   0.0.0.0               0         32768 ?
*> 10.200.60.1/32   0.0.0.0               0         32768 ?
*> 172.16.0.0       10.200.60.1                         0 200 30 ?
*                   10.100.83.1                         0 100 30 30 ?
*> 172.17.0.0       10.20.1.1             1         32768 i
*> 172.29.0.0       10.20.1.1             1         32768 ?
```

continues

Example 3-111 *Meribel's BGP Table Shows the Prepended AS_PATHs from Zermatt and Moritz; the Router Chooses the Paths with the Shorter AS_PATH (Continued)*

```
*   172.29.1.0/24    10.200.60.1                          0 200 30 30 ?
*>                   10.100.83.1                          0 100 30 ?
*> 172.30.255.150/32 10.100.83.1                          0 100 30 ?
*> 172.30.255.254/32 10.200.60.1                          0 200 30 ?
*> 172.31.0.0        10.200.60.1                          0 200 30 ?
*                    10.100.83.1                          0 100 30 30 ?
*> 192.168.2.0/30    10.200.60.1                          0 200 30 ?
*> 192.168.2.4/30    10.100.83.1                          0 100 30 ?
*> 192.168.50.0      10.20.1.1              1         32768 ?
*  192.168.100.0     10.200.60.1                          0 200 30 30 ?
*>                   10.100.83.1                          0 100 30 ?
Meribel#
```

You should use AS_PATH prepending with great caution. If you do not fully understand the effects your configuration will have, unexpected or broken routing can result. Suppose, for example, the command **set as-path prepend 30 30** is used in Moritz's configuration. This command adds two instances of the AS number 30 to the AS_PATH rather than one. Examining the effects on the route to 10.30.0.0, Cervinia in Figure 3-22 receives the route from Moritz with an AS_PATH of (30,30,30) and a route from Meribel to the same destination with an AS_PATH of (50,100,30). Because the routes have the same AS_PATH length, Cervinia chooses the route with the lowest next-hop address: Meribel's. The original intention was to affect the routing at AS 50 only, but this configuration also has caused AS 200 to choose a longer path to the destination.

It is also important when prepending to always use the AS number of the prepending router's AS. If another AS number is used, and an AS using that number is encountered by the advertised route, that AS will not accept the route.

Case Study: Route Tagging

A route tag field can be thought of as a sort of "pocket" in a routing update for transporting information across a routing domain. The information represented by the tag has no relevance to the routing protocol itself, and the routing protocol does not act on the tag in any way. Tags are useful when a route is redistributed from protocol A into protocol B and then redistributed back into protocol A at some other point. The tag field within the transit routing protocol's updates allows protocol A to send information to its peers on the other side of the transit domain. Usually, this information is inconsistent or meaningless to the transit routing protocol.

RIP-2, EIGRP, Integrated IS-IS, OSPF, and BGP support route tags. RIP-1 and IGRP do not. Chapter 14 of *Volume I* introduces route tagging and presents examples of its use. This case study obviously concentrates on the use of tags in a BGP environment.

Figure 3-23 depicts an environment in which route tags are useful. AS 1300 provides transit for the inter-AS traffic of several autonomous systems. Each route of the three outlying autonomous systems is advertised via EBGP to one of the three border routers in AS 1300. The route is redistributed into OSPF, redistributed back into BGP at the other two border routers, and then advertised to their EBGP peers.

NOTE   A configuration such as the one depicted here, with BGP redistributed into an IGP, can find applications in some large enterprise networks. As stated several times throughout this chapter, however, you should never redistribute BGP routes into an IGP in a service provider AS or in an AS in which large numbers of BGP prefixes are being received.

Figure 3-23 *AS 1300 Is a Transit AS for the Other Three Autonomous Systems*

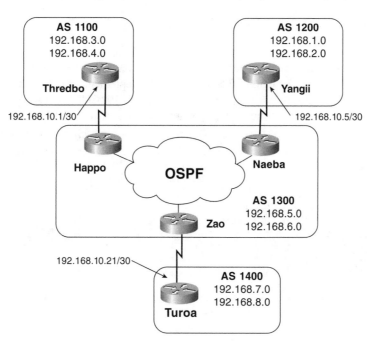

The problem with the topology in Figure 3-23 is that the BGP processes of the three outlying autonomous systems must share their routing information through OSPF, which has no understanding of BGP path attributes. As a result, path information is lost. Example 3-112 shows the BGP table at router Turoa. You can see that all routes appear to be originated by AS 1300. If AS 1400 has an alternate path to AS 1100 or AS 1200, it cannot make an accurate routing decision because of this information loss.

Example 3-112 *The AS_PATH Information of the Routes from AS 1100 and AS 1200 Has Not Been Preserved Across the OSPF Domain in AS 1300; as a Result, All Routes Learned from AS 1300 Appear to Have Been Originated by That AS*

```
Turoa#show ip bgp
BGP table version is 44, local router ID is 192.168.8.1
Status codes: s suppressed, d damped, h history, * valid, > best, i - internal
Origin codes: i - IGP, e - EGP, ? - incomplete

   Network          Next Hop          Metric LocPrf Weight Path
*> 192.168.1.0      192.168.10.22          1             0 1300 ?
*> 192.168.2.0      192.168.10.22          1             0 1300 ?
*> 192.168.3.0      192.168.10.22          1             0 1300 ?
*> 192.168.4.0      192.168.10.22          1             0 1300 ?
*> 192.168.5.0      192.168.10.22         20             0 1300 ?
*> 192.168.6.0      192.168.10.22         20             0 1300 ?
*> 192.168.7.0      0.0.0.0                0         32768 i
*> 192.168.8.0      0.0.0.0                0         32768 i
*> 192.168.10.0     192.168.10.22        192             0 1300 ?
Turoa#
```

BGP can use the route tag field in the OSPF packets to convey AS_PATH information across the OSPF domain. In fact, Cisco's BGP implementation does this automatically. Example 3-113 shows the details of Zao's route to 192.168.1.0 in AS 1200, across the OSPF domain. Notice the tag field, which is marked with a 1200.

Example 3-113 *When Router Naeba Redistributed Its EBGP Route to 192.168.1.0 into OSPF, It Wrote the AS_PATH of the Route into the External Route Tag Field of the OSPF AS-External LSA; You Can See the Tag in the Route Entry at Zao, on the Other Side of the OSPF Domain*

```
Zao#show ip route 192.168.1.0
Routing entry for 192.168.1.0/24
  Known via "ospf 1300", distance 110, metric 1
  Tag 1200, type extern 2, forward metric 128
  Redistributing via ospf 1300, bgp 1300
  Advertised by bgp 1300 match internal external 2
  Last update from 192.168.10.18 on Serial1.503, 00:13:33 ago
  Routing Descriptor Blocks:
  * 192.168.10.18, from 192.168.10.13, 00:13:33 ago, via Serial1.503
      Route metric is 1, traffic share count is 1
Zao#
```

See Chapter 9, "Open Shortest Path First," of *Volume I* for more details on the format and use of the OSPF AS-External LSA.

When IGP routes are redistributed into BGP, however, the BGP process does not automatically assume that the IGP's tag field contains AS_PATH information. You must configure the process to recover the AS_PATH information. One way to recover the

AS_PATH information from the tags of redistributed routes is with the **set as-path tag** command. Example 3-114 shows the configuration for Zao using the **set as-path tag** command.

Example 3-114 *Configuring Zao to Recover AS_PATH Information from the Tags of Redistributed Routes*

```
router ospf 1300
 redistribute bgp 1300
 network 192.168.10.0 0.0.0.255 area 0
!
router bgp 1300
 redistribute ospf 1300 match internal external 2 route-map GET_TAG
 neighbor 192.168.10.21 remote-as 1400
!
route-map GET_TAG permit 10
 set as-path tag
```

The **redistribute ospf** statement under the BGP configuration references a route map named GET_TAG, which sets the AS_PATH attribute of the redistributed routes to the value in the OSPF tag field. Example 3-115 shows that as a result, Turoa's BGP table now contains accurate AS_PATH information to the routes in AS 1100 and AS 1200.

Example 3-115 *Turoa's BGP Table Now Contains Accurate AS_PATH Information*

```
Turoa#show ip bgp
BGP table version is 148, local router ID is 192.168.8.1
Status codes: s suppressed, d damped, h history, * valid, > best, i - internal
Origin codes: i - IGP, e - EGP, ? - incomplete

   Network          Next Hop            Metric LocPrf Weight Path
*> 192.168.1.0      192.168.10.22            1             0 1300 1200 ?
*> 192.168.2.0      192.168.10.22            1             0 1300 1200 ?
*> 192.168.3.0      192.168.10.22            1             0 1300 1100 ?
*> 192.168.4.0      192.168.10.22            1             0 1300 1100 ?
*> 192.168.5.0      192.168.10.22           20             0 1300 ?
*> 192.168.6.0      192.168.10.22           20             0 1300 ?
*> 192.168.7.0      0.0.0.0                   0         32768 i
*> 192.168.8.0      0.0.0.0                   0         32768 i
*> 192.168.10.0     192.168.10.22          192             0 1300 ?
Turoa#
```

No configuration is required at Happo or Naeba for Zao to pick up AS_PATH information from the OSPF tag field with the **set as-path tag** command. However, the only information that is entered into the tag field automatically is the AS_PATH. Notice in Example 3-115 that the routes from AS 1100 and AS 1200 are marked with an ORIGIN of Incomplete. Routers Thredbo and Yangii use the BGP **network** command to advertise their interior routes with an ORIGIN of IGP, but Happo and Naeba do not enter that information into the OSPF tag. The ORIGIN code that Turoa sees is Incomplete as a result of the route's being redistributed from OSPF into BGP at Zao.

This might or might not be a problem, depending on whether Turoa has alternative routes to AS 1100 and AS 1200, and whether the ORIGIN of the routes might influence the BGP decision process. Cisco offers an alternative configuration, called an *automatic tag*, which enters not only the AS_PATH information but also the ORIGIN code. The automatic tag is set with the **set automatic-tag** command, and the route map containing the command is called from the BGP process with the **table-map** command. Unlike the **set as-path tag** command, which is configured on routers redistributing routes from an IGP into BGP, the **set automatic-tag** command is configured on the routers redistributing routes from BGP into an IGP.

All three AS 1300 routers in Figure 3-23 will be configured the same for setting automatic tags. Example 3-116 shows the configuration for Naeba.

Example 3-116 *Configuring Naeba to Enter AS_PATH Information and ORIGIN Code*

```
router ospf 1300
 redistribute bgp 1300
 network 192.168.0.0 0.0.255.255 area 0
!
router bgp 1300
 table-map SET_TAG
 redistribute ospf 1300 match internal external 2
 neighbor 192.168.10.5 remote-as 1200
!
ip as-path access-list 1 permit .*
!
route-map SET_TAG permit 10
 match as-path 1
 set automatic-tag
```

Example 3-117 shows the resulting BGP table at Turoa. You can see that it looks almost identical to the table in Example 3-115, but the routes from AS 1100 and AS 1200 now correctly reflect an ORIGIN attribute of IGP.

Another use for route tags is to identify certain groups of routes, perhaps for filtering. In Figure 3-23, routers Naeba and Happo might be configured to tag some subset of their EBGP routes before redistributing them into OSPF. Zao, retrieving the routes from the OSPF domain, could then identify the routes by their common tag instead of having to filter by NLRI. Recall from Chapter 2 that the BGP COMMUNITY attribute also is designed to identify routes in a common group. In the topology of Figure 3-23, however, the COMMUNITY attribute cannot be communicated across the OSPF domain. For an example of using tags for this purpose, see "Case Study: Route Tagging," in Chapter 14 of *Volume I*.

Finally, you can use tagging only when an IGP is redistributed into BGP. When the **network** command is used, the BGP route is considered locally originated and therefore does not inherit any of the attributes, including tags, of the IGP route.

Example 3-117 *Turoa's BGP Table Now Contains Not Only the Correct AS_PATH Information, But Also the Correct ORIGIN*

```
Turoa#show ip bgp
BGP table version is 228, local router ID is 192.168.8.1
Status codes: s suppressed, d damped, h history, * valid, > best, i - internal
Origin codes: i - IGP, e - EGP, ? - incomplete

   Network          Next Hop          Metric LocPrf Weight Path
*> 192.168.1.0      192.168.10.22          1             0 1300 1200 i
*> 192.168.2.0      192.168.10.22          1             0 1300 1200 i
*> 192.168.3.0      192.168.10.22          1             0 1300 1100 i
*> 192.168.4.0      192.168.10.22          1             0 1300 1100 i
*> 192.168.5.0      192.168.10.22         20             0 1300 ?
*> 192.168.6.0      192.168.10.22         20             0 1300 ?
*> 192.168.7.0      0.0.0.0                0         32768 i
*> 192.168.8.0      0.0.0.0                0         32768 i
*> 192.168.10.0     192.168.10.22        192             0 1300 ?
Turoa#
```

Case Study: Route Dampening

Route dampening, as discussed in Chapter 2, is a process that can assign a penalty to a flapping route. If the route accumulates enough penalties, the route is suppressed—that is, it is not advertised—for a certain period of time. By default, a route is assigned a penalty value of 1000 for each flap. If the value of the route's accumulated penalties exceeds 2000, the route is suppressed until the penalty value drops below 750. These upper and lower thresholds are the *suppress limit* and the *reuse limit*. The accumulated penalty is reduced every 5 seconds, at a rate such that the penalty is reduced by half every 15 minutes. You can see that this rate, known as the *half-life*, is exponential. If the penalty is 3000, it is reduced by 1500 over 15 minutes; if the penalty is 300, it is reduced by 150 over 15 minutes. There is also a maximum time the route can be suppressed, known as the *maximum suppress limit*. By default, this limit is four times the half-life, or 60 minutes.

Route dampening is enabled under the BGP process configuration with the command **bgp dampening**. If you want to change the default values, the syntax is **bgp dampening** *half-life reuse suppress max-suppress*.

Figure 3-24 shows a topology in which one router, Colorado, is homed to five other autonomous systems. If the routes advertised by any of the remote autonomous systems flaps, Colorado must advertise the change to all other EBGP peers. Although this may not be much of a burden on the sample topology, imagine the effects if Colorado has 150 EBGP peers rather than the five shown. A regularly flapping route could cause a heavy processing burden on that hub router.

Figure 3-24 *If a Route in Any of the "Spoke" Autonomous Systems Flaps, the "Hub" Router, Colorado, Must Send an Update to All of Its EBGP Peers Advertising the Change*

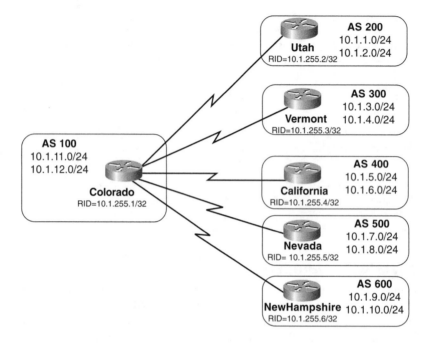

Example 3-118 provides the BGP configuration for Colorado.

Example 3-118 *Configuring Colorado to Send Updates to EBGP Peers to Advertise Changes When a Route Flaps*

```
router bgp 100
 bgp dampening
 network 10.1.11.0 mask 255.255.255.0
 network 10.1.12.0 mask 255.255.255.0
 neighbor 10.1.255.2 remote-as 200
 neighbor 10.1.255.2 ebgp-multihop 2
 neighbor 10.1.255.2 update-source Loopback2
 neighbor 10.1.255.3 remote-as 300
 neighbor 10.1.255.3 ebgp-multihop 2
 neighbor 10.1.255.3 update-source Loopback2
 neighbor 10.1.255.4 remote-as 400
 neighbor 10.1.255.4 ebgp-multihop 2
 neighbor 10.1.255.4 update-source Loopback2
 neighbor 10.1.255.5 remote-as 500
 neighbor 10.1.255.5 ebgp-multihop 2
 neighbor 10.1.255.5 update-source Loopback2
 neighbor 10.1.255.6 remote-as 600
 neighbor 10.1.255.6 ebgp-multihop 2
 neighbor 10.1.255.6 update-source Loopback2
 no auto-summary
```

Example 3-119 shows Colorado's BGP table. Notice that 10.1.4.0/24 is marked with a **d**, indicating that it has been dampened, or suppressed. 10.1.7.0/24 has been marked with an **h**. This means that there is a history of flapping; that is, although the route has not accumulated a large-enough penalty to be suppressed, it does have a penalty.

Example 3-119 *Two Routes, 10.1.4.0/24 and 10.1.7.0/24, Have Accumulated Penalties; the First Has Accumulated More than 2000 and Has Been Dampened*

```
Colorado#show ip bgp
BGP table version is 756, local router ID is 10.1.255.1
Status codes: s suppressed, d damped, h history, * valid, > best, i - internal
Origin codes: i - IGP, e - EGP, ? - incomplete
   Network          Next Hop          Metric LocPrf Weight Path
*> 10.1.1.0/24      10.1.255.2             0             0 200 i
*> 10.1.2.0/24      10.1.255.2             0             0 200 i
*> 10.1.3.0/24      10.1.255.3             0             0 300 i
*d 10.1.4.0/24      10.1.255.3             0             0 300 i
*> 10.1.5.0/24      10.1.255.4             0             0 400 i
*> 10.1.6.0/24      10.1.255.4             0             0 400 i
h  10.1.7.0/24      10.1.255.5             0             0 500 i
*> 10.1.8.0/24      10.1.255.5             0             0 500 i
*> 10.1.9.0/24      10.1.255.6             0             0 600 i

*> 10.1.10.0/24     10.1.255.6             0             0 600 i
*> 10.1.11.0/24     0.0.0.0                0         32768 i
*> 10.1.12.0/24     0.0.0.0                0         32768 i
```

The unstable routes are readily apparent in the BGP table of Example 3-119 because there are not very many entries. What about a table with thousands of BGP entries, however? Finding unstable routes by looking for a **d** or **h** could be impractical. Two commands make finding these routes easier: **show ip bgp flap-statistics** and **show ip bgp dampened-paths**. As the names imply, the first command shows all routes that have flapped and how many times a route has flapped. The second command shows only those routes that have been suppressed. Example 3-120 shows these commands used at Colorado; notice that for suppressed routes, both outputs indicate when the route is expected to be advertised again. This time is contingent on the route's not being assigned further penalties. Note that flap statistics are recorded only if BGP dampening is configured. You cannot use the command **show ip bgp flap-statistics** to check for unstable routes on a router that is not running the dampening process.

Example 3-120 *You Can Display Only Those Routes in the BGP Table That Have Flapped, or Only Those Routes That Have Been Suppressed*

```
Colorado#show ip bgp flap-statistics
BGP table version is 756, local router ID is 10.1.255.1
Status codes: s suppressed, d damped, h history, * valid, > best, i - internal
Origin codes: i - IGP, e - EGP, ? - incomplete
```

continues

Example 3-120 *You Can Display Only Those Routes in the BGP Table That Have Flapped, or Only Those Routes That Have Been Suppressed (Continued)*

```
    Network         From             Flaps Duration Reuse    Path
*d 10.1.4.0/24      10.1.255.3       3     00:15:52 00:19:40 300
 h 10.1.7.0/24      10.1.255.5       2     00:20:49          500

Colorado#show ip bgp dampened-paths
BGP table version is 757, local router ID is 10.1.255.1
Status codes: s suppressed, d damped, h history, * valid, > best, i - internal
Origin codes: i - IGP, e - EGP, ? - incomplete

    Network         From             Reuse    Path
*d 10.1.4.0/24      10.1.255.3       00:19:2 300 i
```

Looking at the details of a route shows you not only the statistics displayed in Example 3-120, but also the accumulated penalties. In Example 3-121, you can see that the route to 10.1.4.0/24 has a penalty of 1815; the half-life decay process has reduced the penalty below the suppress threshold of 2000, but not yet to the reuse threshold of 750. That second threshold is expected to be reached in 19 minutes and 10 seconds.

Example 3-121 *If an Unstable Route Is Specified with the* **show ip bgp** *Command, the Route's Penalty Value Displays*

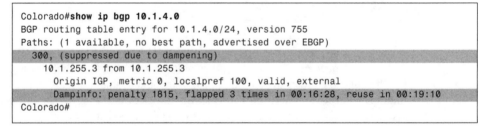

```
Colorado#show ip bgp 10.1.4.0
BGP routing table entry for 10.1.4.0/24, version 755
Paths: (1 available, no best path, advertised over EBGP)
  300, (suppressed due to dampening)
    10.1.255.3 from 10.1.255.3
      Origin IGP, metric 0, localpref 100, valid, external
      Dampinfo: penalty 1815, flapped 3 times in 00:16:28, reuse in 00:19:10
Colorado#
```

In some cases, you might want to put a suppressed route back into service before the reuse limit is reached. The administrator in AS 300 might have assured you that the cause of the flaps of subnet 10.1.4.0/24 has been identified and eliminated, for instance, and now he wants traffic to resume. Two commands are available: **clear ip bgp flap-statistics** and **clear ip bgp dampening**. These two commands have the same effect of clearing all penalties for a route or for all routes (depending on whether a route is specified with the command), but the second command clears only those routes that have been suppressed. The **clear ip bgp flap-statistics** also enables you to identify a group of routes by their AS path, either by specifying a filter list or by using a regular expression. For example, the command **clear ip bgp flap-statistics regexp _30_** clears the flap statistics for all routes that have the AS number 30 in their AS_PATH attribute. This command proves useful if AS 30 is a transit AS, and a bad link has caused all destinations reachable through that AS to accumulate penalties.

Large-Scale BGP

Large-scale BGP is something of a subjective term. You decide when your BGP topology grows large enough to justify the use of the tools discussed in this section. As a rule, however, peer groups and communities are used in moderate-sized to larger internetworks. Route reflectors can also be found in moderate-sized and larger internetworks, but confederations generally are found only in the largest of BGP topologies, such as that of a large ISP. The following case studies discuss each of these tools.

Case Study: BGP Peer Groups

The preceding case study presented a BGP topology in Figure 3-24 in which an autonomous system is multihomed to several other autonomous systems. Suppose, however, that the router Colorado has 150 EBGP peers rather than five. In addition to the standard configuration, each neighbor connection has an outgoing and an incoming route filter. So for each neighbor, there are five BGP configuration statements:

- A **neighbor remote-as** statement
- A **neighbor ebgp-multihop** statement, because the connections are between loopback addresses
- A **neighbor update-source** statement, for the same reason
- A **neighbor filter-list out** statement
- A **neighbor filter-list in** statement

For 150 EBGP peers, this translates into 750 configuration statements.

When the same routing policies are applied to many BGP peers, a router's BGP configuration can be greatly simplified by designating the peers as members of a single peer group. Most of the configuration options and routing policies that otherwise would be defined for each neighbor can instead be defined once, for the peer group. A peer group is relevant only to the router on which it is defined and is not communicated to the router's peers. You follow three steps to create a peer group:

Step 1 Designate the peer group name.

Step 2 Designate the routing policies and configuration options common to all members of the peer group.

Step 3 Designate the neighbors that belong to the peer group.

The configuration in Example 3-122 creates a peer group named CLIENTS on the router Colorado in Figure 3-24.

Example 3-122 *Creating a Peer Group, CLIENTS, on the Router Colorado*

```
router bgp 100
 network 10.1.11.0 mask 255.255.255.0
 network 10.1.12.0 mask 255.255.255.0
 neighbor CLIENTS peer-group
 neighbor CLIENTS ebgp-multihop 2
 neighbor CLIENTS update-source Loopback2
 neighbor CLIENTS filter-list 2 in
 neighbor CLIENTS filter-list 1 out
 neighbor 10.1.255.2 remote-as 200
 neighbor 10.1.255.2 peer-group CLIENTS
 neighbor 10.1.255.3 remote-as 300
 neighbor 10.1.255.3 peer-group CLIENTS
 neighbor 10.1.255.4 remote-as 400
 neighbor 10.1.255.4 peer-group CLIENTS
 neighbor 10.1.255.5 remote-as 500
 neighbor 10.1.255.5 peer-group CLIENTS
 neighbor 10.1.255.6 remote-as 600
 neighbor 10.1.255.6 peer-group CLIENTS
 no auto-summary
!
 ip as-path access-list 1 permit ^$
 ip as-path access-list 2 permit ^[2-6]00$
```

The **neighbor CLIENTS peer-group** statement creates the peer group, and the next four statements define options and policies common to all members of the group. The EBGP neighbors are then designated as usual with **neighbor remote-as**, and a single statement is added designating the neighbor as a member of the peer group CLIENTS.

By consolidating shared options and policies, peer groups can significantly shorten a BGP configuration. Returning to the scenario in which Colorado has 150 EBGP peers, if all the peers are members of peer group CLIENTS, the configuration is reduced from 750 statements to 305. The configuration also becomes much easier to interpret. All options are configured in one place, and all that is necessary is to know which neighbors are members of which peer group.

When all the members of a peer group belong to the same AS, you can shorten the configuration even more by specifying the common AS under the peer group configuration. All the members could be EBGP peers in the same remote AS, but in most cases a large number of peers in the same AS will be IBGP peers. In Figure 3-25, routers NewMexico and Idaho have been added as IBGP peers of Colorado.

Figure 3-25 *Two IBGP Peers Have Been Added to AS 100*

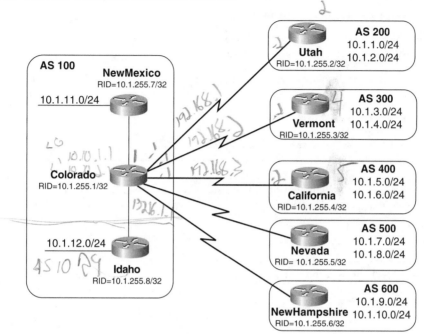

Example 3-123 shows the configuration for Colorado.

Example 3-123 *Configuring Colorado with a Peer Group for Its Internal Peers*

```
router bgp 100
 no synchronization
 network 10.1.11.0 mask 255.255.255.0
 network 10.1.12.0 mask 255.255.255.0
 neighbor CLIENTS peer-group
 neighbor CLIENTS ebgp-multihop 2
 neighbor CLIENTS update-source Loopback2
 neighbor CLIENTS filter-list 2 in
 neighbor CLIENTS filter-list 1 out
 neighbor LOCAL peer-group
 neighbor LOCAL remote-as 100
 neighbor LOCAL next-hop-self
 neighbor LOCAL filter-list 3 out
 neighbor 10.1.255.2 remote-as 200
 neighbor 10.1.255.2 peer-group CLIENTS
 neighbor 10.1.255.3 remote-as 300
 neighbor 10.1.255.3 peer-group CLIENTS
 neighbor 10.1.255.4 remote-as 400
 neighbor 10.1.255.4 peer-group CLIENTS
```

continues

Example 3-123 *Configuring Colorado with a Peer Group for Its Internal Peers (Continued)*

```
 neighbor 10.1.255.5 remote-as 500
 neighbor 10.1.255.5 peer-group CLIENTS
 neighbor 10.1.255.6 remote-as 600
 neighbor 10.1.255.6 peer-group CLIENTS
 neighbor 10.1.255.7 peer-group LOCAL
 neighbor 10.1.255.8 peer-group LOCAL
 no auto-summary
 !
ip as-path access-list 1 permit ^$
ip as-path access-list 2 permit ^[2-6]00$
ip as-path access-list 3 permit ^[246]00$
```

NewMexico and Idaho have been added to the peer group LOCAL. Their common AS number is specified under the peer group configuration, as is a common outgoing routing policy.

NOTE   AS_PATH list 3 permits any route from AS 200, 400, or 600. Routes from AS 300 and AS 500 are implicitly denied, as are local routes originated from Colorado.

Incoming routing policies that are defined for a single peer group member take precedence over incoming routing policies defined for the peer group. Suppose, for example, that Colorado should accept only subnet 10.1.5.0/24 from EBGP peer California, but all other peer group policies and options apply. Example 3-124 shows the new configuration for Colorado.

Example 3-124 *Applying a Routing Policy to a Single Neighbor in a Peer Group*

```
router bgp 100
 no synchronization
 network 10.1.11.0 mask 255.255.255.0
 network 10.1.12.0 mask 255.255.255.0
 neighbor CLIENTS peer-group
 neighbor CLIENTS ebgp-multihop 2
 neighbor CLIENTS update-source Loopback2
 neighbor CLIENTS filter-list 2 in
 neighbor CLIENTS filter-list 1 out
 neighbor LOCAL peer-group
 neighbor LOCAL remote-as 100
 neighbor LOCAL next-hop-self
 neighbor LOCAL filter-list 3 out
 neighbor 10.1.255.2 remote-as 200
 neighbor 10.1.255.2 peer-group CLIENTS
 neighbor 10.1.255.3 remote-as 300
 neighbor 10.1.255.3 peer-group CLIENTS
```

Example 3-124 *Applying a Routing Policy to a Single Neighbor in a Peer Group (Continued)*

```
 neighbor 10.1.255.4 remote-as 400
 neighbor 10.1.255.4 peer-group CLIENTS
 neighbor 10.1.255.4 distribute-list 10 in
 neighbor 10.1.255.5 remote-as 500
 neighbor 10.1.255.5 peer-group CLIENTS
 neighbor 10.1.255.6 remote-as 600
 neighbor 10.1.255.6 peer-group CLIENTS
 neighbor 10.1.255.7 peer-group LOCAL
 neighbor 10.1.255.8 peer-group LOCAL
 no auto-summary
!
ip as-path access-list 1 permit ^$
ip as-path access-list 2 permit ^[2-6]00$
ip as-path access-list 3 permit ^[246]00$
access-list 10 permit 10.1.5.0
```

Distribute list 10 has been added to the neighbor configuration for California (10.1.255.4). Although Colorado's configuration defines California as a member of the CLIENTS peer group, the distribute list overrides the incoming filter list 2 for that peer.

You can display details about the peer groups defined on a router with the command **show ip bgp peer-groups**, as demonstrated in Example 3-125. You also can use the command to observe the details of a single peer group, by specifying the name of the group at the end of the command.

Example 3-125 *The* **show ip bgp peer-groups** *Command Displays Details About a Router's Peer Groups*

```
Colorado#show ip bgp peer-group
BGP neighbor is CLIENTS, peer-group leader
 Index 1, Offset 0, Mask 0x2
  BGP version 4
  Minimum time between advertisement runs is 5 seconds
  Incoming update AS path filter list is 2
  Outgoing update AS path filter list is 1

BGP neighbor is LOCAL, peer-group leader,  remote AS 100
 Index 0, Offset 0, Mask 0x0
  NEXT_HOP is always this router
  BGP version 4
  Minimum time between advertisement runs is 5 seconds
  Outgoing update AS path filter list is 3
Colorado#
```

Case Study: BGP Communities

Whereas peer groups enable you to apply common policies to a group of neighbors, communities enable you to apply policies to a group of routes. A community is a route attribute and therefore is communicated from one BGP speaker to another.

You follow three steps to configure a community attribute:

Step 1 Use a route map to identify the routes in which the attribute is to be set.

Step 2 Use the **set community** command to set the attribute.

Step 3 Use the **neighbor send-community** command to specify the neighbors to which the attribute is sent.

In Figure 3-26, AS 100 is connected across a NAP to AS 2000. A routing policy in AS 2000 states that subnet 10.2.2.0/24 should be advertised to AS 100, but not to any of the EBGP peers connected to Colorado. To implement this policy, the NO_EXPORT community attribute is used. This attribute allows a route to be advertised throughout a neighboring AS but does not allow that AS to advertise the route to other autonomous systems. Example 3-126 shows router Austria's configuration.

Figure 3-26 *Network Topology for BGP Communities Case Study*

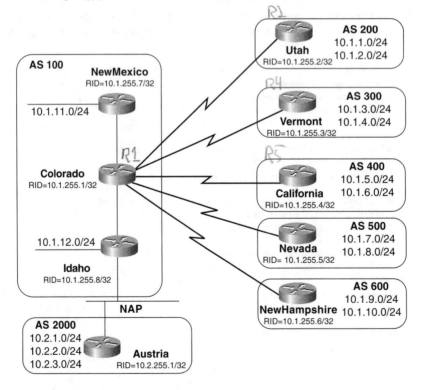

Example 3-126 *Restricting a Subnet in AS 2000 from Being Advertised Beyond AS 100*

```
router bgp 2000
 network 10.2.1.0 mask 255.255.255.0
 network 10.2.2.0 mask 255.255.255.0
 network 10.2.3.0 mask 255.255.255.0
 neighbor 10.1.255.8 remote-as 100
 neighbor 10.1.255.8 ebgp-multihop 2
 neighbor 10.1.255.8 update-source Loopback0
 neighbor 10.1.255.8 send-community
 neighbor 10.1.255.8 route-map AUSTRIA out
 no auto-summary
!
access-list 1 permit 10.2.2.0
!
route-map AUSTRIA permit 10
 match ip address 1
 set community no-export
!
route-map AUSTRIA permit 20
```

Example 3-127 shows the results of the configuration in Example 3-126. Colorado's BGP table includes the route to 10.2.2.0/24, indicating that Idaho has advertised the route to its IBGP peers. But Nevada's BGP table does not contain the route; Colorado has honored the NO_EXPORT attribute and has suppressed the route to its EBGP peers.

Example 3-127 *The Route to 10.2.2.0 Has the NO_EXPORT Community Attribute Set, So Colorado Does Not Advertise the Route to Its EBGP Peers Such as Nevada*

```
Colorado#show ip bgp 10.2.2.0
BGP routing table entry for 10.2.2.0/24, version 42
Paths: (1 available, best #1, not advertised to EBGP peer)
  2000
    10.1.255.8 from 10.1.255.8
      Origin IGP, metric 0, localpref 100, valid, internal, best
      Community: no-export
Colorado#

Nevada#show ip bgp 10.2.2.0
% Network not in table
Nevada#
```

Of course, an autonomous system would not be truly autonomous if another AS could tell it what to do. Suppose AS 100 wants to override the NO_EXPORT attribute set by Austria and advertise 10.2.2.0/24 to Colorado's EBGP peers. Example 3-128 shows the configuration for Idaho to implement such a policy.

Example 3-128 *Configuring Idaho to Delete Communities Advertised by AS 2000*

```
router bgp 100
 no synchronization
 network 10.1.12.0 mask 255.255.255.0
 neighbor 10.1.255.1 remote-as 100
 neighbor 10.1.255.1 update-source Loopback0
 neighbor 10.1.255.1 next-hop-self
 neighbor 10.1.255.1 route-map IDAHO out
 neighbor 10.1.255.7 remote-as 100
 neighbor 10.1.255.7 update-source Loopback0
 neighbor 10.2.255.1 remote-as 2000
 neighbor 10.2.255.1 ebgp-multihop 2
 neighbor 10.2.255.1 update-source Loopback0
 no auto-summary
!
access-list 1 permit 10.2.2.0
!
route-map IDAHO permit 10
 match ip address 1
 set community none
!
route-map IDAHO permit 20
```

The **set community none** statement in Idaho's configuration does not set a community attribute; rather, it deletes existing community attributes. That is why no **neighbor send-community** statement is necessary in this configuration. Example 3-129 shows the results at Colorado and Nevada.

Example 3-129 *Colorado No Longer Sees a NO_EXPORT Community Attribute for the Route to 10.2.2.0/24 and Advertises the Route to Its EBGP Peers*

```
Colorado#show ip bgp 10.2.2.0
BGP routing table entry for 10.2.2.0/24, version 90
Paths: (1 available, best #1, advertised over EBGP)
  2000
    10.1.255.8 from 10.1.255.8
      Origin IGP, metric 0, localpref 100, valid, internal, best
Colorado#
```

```
Nevada#show ip bgp 10.2.2.0
BGP routing table entry for 10.2.2.0 255.255.255.0, version 325
Paths: (1 available, best #1)
  100 2000
    10.1.255.1 from 10.1.255.1
      Origin IGP, valid, external, best
Nevada#
```

The NO_ADVERTISE community attribute sends the same message as NO_EXPORT—it tells routers to not advertise the route to any peers. The difference is that NO_ADVERTISE is sent to IBGP peers rather than EBGP peers. Suppose that Idaho in Figure 3-26 wants to advertise subnets 10.2.1.0/24 and 10.2.3.0/24 to Colorado but does not want that peer to advertise the routes to any of its own IBGP or EBGP peers. Example 3-130 shows the configuration for Idaho.

Example 3-130 *Setting the NO_ADVERTISE Community at Idaho for Selected Prefixes*

```
router bgp 100
 no synchronization
 network 10.1.12.0 mask 255.255.255.0
 neighbor 10.1.255.1 remote-as 100
 neighbor 10.1.255.1 update-source Loopback0
 neighbor 10.1.255.1 next-hop-self
 neighbor 10.1.255.1 send-community
 neighbor 10.1.255.1 route-map IDAHO out
 neighbor 10.1.255.7 remote-as 100
 neighbor 10.1.255.7 update-source Loopback0
 neighbor 10.2.255.1 remote-as 2000
 neighbor 10.2.255.1 ebgp-multihop 2
 neighbor 10.2.255.1 update-source Loopback0
 no auto-summary
!
ip as-path access-list 2 permit ^2000$
!
access-list 1 permit 10.2.2.0
!
route-map IDAHO permit 10
 match ip address 1
 set community none
!
route-map IDAHO permit 20
 match as-path 2
 set community no-advertise
!
route-map IDAHO permit 30
```

Recall that Austria is configured to advertise 10.2.2.0/24 with the NO_EXPORT community and the other two subnets of AS 2000 with no community attributes. Idaho has now completely reversed that policy. Subnet 10.2.2.0/24 has no community attribute, and the subnets 10.2.1.0/24 and 10.2.3.0/24 have the NO_ADVERTISE attribute, preventing them from being advertised outside of AS 100. Example 3-131 shows the results of this configuration.

Example 3-131 *Colorado Has Knowledge of All Three Routes from AS 2000 But Advertises Only 10.2.2.0/24 to Its Peers*

```
Colorado#show ip bgp regexp 2000
BGP table version is 138, local router ID is 10.1.255.1
Status codes: s suppressed, d damped, h history, * valid, > best, i - internal
Origin codes: i - IGP, e - EGP, ? - incomplete

   Network          Next Hop            Metric LocPrf Weight Path
*>i10.2.1.0/24      10.1.255.8               0    100      0 2000 i
*>i10.2.2.0/24      10.1.255.8               0    100      0 2000 i
*>i10.2.3.0/24      10.1.255.8               0    100      0 2000 i
Colorado#
```
```
Nevada#show ip bgp regexp 2000
BGP table version is 355, local router ID is 10.1.255.5
Status codes: s suppressed, * valid, > best, i - internal
Origin codes: i - IGP, e - EGP, ? - incomplete

   Network          Next Hop            Metric LocPrf Weight Path
*> 10.2.2.0/24      10.1.255.1                              0 100 2000 i
Nevada#
```

NOTE   Example 3-131 also shows yet another way to use the **show ip bgp** command. Here, a regular expression is used to display all routes that have a 2000 in their AS_PATH.

A community attribute called LOCAL_AS is something of a hybrid of the NO_EXPORT and NO_ADVERTISE attributes. This attribute is used in conjunction with BGP confederations, in which subautonomous systems are configured within an AS. A route with a LOCAL_AS attribute can be advertised to peers in other subautonomous systems within a confederation but cannot be advertised outside of the AS that forms the confederation.

The well-known community attributes that have been demonstrated so far are acted upon automatically by a BGP speaker. However, you also can configure community attributes that have only the meaning you define. You can designate communities in two ways:

- The decimal format, using a number between 1 and 4294967200
- The AA:NN format, in which AA is a 16-bit AS number between 1 and 65535 and NN is an arbitrary 16-bit number between 1 and 65440

In Figure 3-26, each of the "client" autonomous systems of AS 100 has two subnets. Suppose AS 100 applies a certain policy to one of the two subnets of each client AS and a different policy to the other subnet. The policies could be applied by using a lengthy access list at Colorado to identify each route by its NLRI (remember the scenario in which there are not five client autonomous systems, but 150). Another way is to have each client AS assign each subnet to one of two predetermined communities. For example, each client could assign one subnet to community 5 and the other to community 10. The configuration in Example 3-132 shows what Utah's configuration might look like.

Example 3-132 *Assigning Subnets to Communities in Utah*

```
router bgp 200
 network 10.1.1.0 mask 255.255.255.0
 network 10.1.2.0 mask 255.255.255.0
 neighbor 10.1.255.1 remote-as 100
 neighbor 10.1.255.1 ebgp-multihop 2
 neighbor 10.1.255.1 update-source Loopback0
 neighbor 10.1.255.1 send-community
 neighbor 10.1.255.1 route-map UTAH out
 no auto-summary
!
access-list 1 permit 10.1.1.0
access-list 2 permit 10.1.2.0
!
route-map UTAH permit 10
 match ip address 1
 set community 5
!
route-map UTAH permit 20
 match ip address 2
 set community 10
```

All the other EBGP peers of Colorado have similar configurations, as demonstrated in Example 3-133. In addition to making it much easier for Colorado to identify the routes for each policy, this approach gives the administrators of the client autonomous systems the leeway to decide which route is used for which policy.

Example 3-133 *Each of the Routes Advertised by Colorado's EBGP Peers Is a Member of Either Community 5 or Community 10*

```
Colorado#show ip bgp community 5
BGP table version is 60, local router ID is 10.1.255.1
Status codes: s suppressed, d damped, h history, * valid, > best, i - internal
Origin codes: i - IGP, e - EGP, ? - incomplete

   Network          Next Hop         Metric LocPrf Weight Path
*> 10.1.1.0/24      10.1.255.2            0             0 200 i
*> 10.1.3.0/24      10.1.255.3            0             0 300 i
*> 10.1.5.0/24      10.1.255.4            0             0 400 i
*> 10.1.7.0/24      10.1.255.5            0             0 500 i
*> 10.1.9.0/24      10.1.255.6            0             0 600 i
```

continues

Example 3-133 *Each of the Routes Advertised by Colorado's EBGP Peers Is a Member of Either Community 5 or Community 10 (Continued)*

```
Colorado#show ip bgp community 10
BGP table version is 60, local router ID is 10.1.255.1
Status codes: s suppressed, d damped, h history, * valid, > best, i - internal
Origin codes: i - IGP, e - EGP, ? - incomplete

   Network          Next Hop          Metric LocPrf Weight Path
*> 10.1.2.0/24      10.1.255.2             0             0 200 i
*> 10.1.4.0/24      10.1.255.3             0             0 300 i
*> 10.1.6.0/24      10.1.255.4             0             0 400 i
*> 10.1.8.0/24      10.1.255.5             0             0 500 i
*> 10.1.10.0/24     10.1.255.6             0             0 600 i
Colorado#
```

A *community list* is used to identify routes by their community attributes. This list is a special adaptation of an access list: There are possibly multiple lines in the list, each of which has a "permit" or "deny" action. The list is identified by a number between 1 and 99, and there is an implicit "deny any" at the end. In the configuration in Example 3-134, Colorado uses community lists to assign LOCAL_PREF attributes to routes according to their community.

NOTE   Such a policy might be used if the client autonomous systems were multihomed to AS 100. For simplicity, such a topology is not shown in this example.

Example 3-134 *Using Community Lists to Assign LOCAL_PREF Attributes to Routes According to Their Community Values*

```
router bgp 100
 no synchronization
 network 10.1.11.0 mask 255.255.255.0
 network 10.1.12.0 mask 255.255.255.0
 neighbor CLIENTS peer-group
 neighbor CLIENTS ebgp-multihop 2
 neighbor CLIENTS update-source Loopback2
 neighbor CLIENTS next-hop-self
 neighbor CLIENTS send-community
 neighbor CLIENTS route-map COMM_PREF in
 neighbor LOCAL peer-group
 neighbor LOCAL remote-as 100
 neighbor LOCAL next-hop-self
 neighbor 10.1.255.2 remote-as 200

 neighbor 10.1.255.2 peer-group CLIENTS
 neighbor 10.1.255.3 remote-as 300
```

Example 3-134 *Using Community Lists to Assign LOCAL_PREF Attributes to Routes According to Their Community Values (Continued)*

```
 neighbor 10.1.255.3 peer-group CLIENTS
 neighbor 10.1.255.4 remote-as 400
 neighbor 10.1.255.4 peer-group CLIENTS
 neighbor 10.1.255.5 remote-as 500
 neighbor 10.1.255.5 peer-group CLIENTS
 neighbor 10.1.255.6 remote-as 600
 neighbor 10.1.255.6 peer-group CLIENTS
 neighbor 10.1.255.7 peer-group LOCAL
 neighbor 10.1.255.8 peer-group LOCAL
 no auto-summary
!
ip community-list 1 permit 5
ip community-list 2 permit 10
!
route-map COMM_PREF permit 10
 match community 1
 set local-preference 150
!
route-map COMM_PREF permit 20
 match community 2
 set local-preference 200
```

Incoming routes from the members of peer group CLIENTS are sent to a route map named COMM_PREF. Sequence 10 of the route map uses community list 1 to identify routes with a community of 5 and assigns them a LOCAL_PREF of 150. Sequence 20 uses community list 2 to identify routes with a community of 10 and assigns them a LOCAL_PREF of 200. Example 3-135 shows the results in Colorado's BGP table.

Example 3-135 *The Routes Belonging to Community 5 as Shown in Example 3-131 Have Been Assigned a LOCAL_PREF of 150, and the Routes Belonging to Community 10 Have Been Assigned a LOCAL_PREF of 200*

```
Colorado#show ip bgp
BGP table version is 16, local router ID is 10.1.255.1
Status codes: s suppressed, d damped, h history, * valid, > best, i - internal
Origin codes: i - IGP, e - EGP, ? - incomplete

   Network          Next Hop         Metric LocPrf Weight Path
*> 10.1.1.0/24      10.1.255.2            0    150      0 200 i
*> 10.1.2.0/24      10.1.255.2            0    200      0 200 i
*> 10.1.3.0/24      10.1.255.3            0    150      0 300 i
*> 10.1.4.0/24      10.1.255.3            0    200      0 300 i
*> 10.1.5.0/24      10.1.255.4            0    150      0 400 i
*> 10.1.6.0/24      10.1.255.4            0    200      0 400 i
*> 10.1.7.0/24      10.1.255.5            0    150      0 500 i
*> 10.1.8.0/24      10.1.255.5            0    200      0 500 i
*> 10.1.9.0/24      10.1.255.6            0    150      0 600 i
```

continues

Example 3-135 *The Routes Belonging to Community 5 as Shown in Example 3-131 Have Been Assigned a LOCAL_PREF of 150, and the Routes Belonging to Community 10 Have Been Assigned a LOCAL_PREF of 200 (Continued)*

```
*> 10.1.10.0/24     10.1.255.6          0     200     0 600 i
*>i10.1.11.0/24     10.1.255.7          0     100     0 i
*>i10.1.12.0/24     10.1.255.8          0     100     0 i
*>i10.2.1.0/24      10.1.255.8          0     100     0 2000 i
*>i10.2.2.0/24      10.1.255.8          0     100     0 2000 i
*>i10.2.3.0/24      10.1.255.8          0     100     0 2000 i
Colorado#
```

RFC 1997 and RFC 1998, which describe the BGP community attribute, specify the use of the AA:NN format. By default, Cisco IOS uses the older, decimal format. To use the newer format, you add the command **ip bgp-community new-format** to the global router configuration. When entering communities in this format, you can type the community directly in the AA:NN format, in hexadecimal, or in decimal. For example, any of the following three entries specify the community 400:50 (AS 400, number 50):

- **set community 400:50**

- **set community 0x1900032**

- **set community 26214450**

All these commands specify a 32-bit number in which the first 16 bits is 400 in decimal and the second 16 bits is 50 in decimal. Regardless of which of the three commands are used, the community displays in the router configuration file and the BGP tables as 400:50.

Example 3-136 shows the configuration for Utah using this format.

Example 3-136 *Configuring Utah to Display Communities in the AA:NN Format*

```
router bgp 200
 network 10.1.1.0 mask 255.255.255.0
 network 10.1.2.0 mask 255.255.255.0
 neighbor 10.1.255.1 remote-as 100
 neighbor 10.1.255.1 ebgp-multihop 2
 neighbor 10.1.255.1 update-source Loopback0
 neighbor 10.1.255.1 send-community
 neighbor 10.1.255.1 route-map UTAH out
 no auto-summary
!
ip bgp-community new-format
!
access-list 1 permit 10.1.1.0
access-list 2 permit 10.1.2.0
!
route-map UTAH permit 10
 match ip address 1
 set community 200:5
!
```

Example 3-136 *Configuring Utah to Display Communities in the AA:NN Format (Continued)*

```
route-map UTAH permit 20
 match ip address 2
 set community 200:10
```

Just as there are standard and extended access lists, there are also standard and extended community lists. And like IP access lists, standard community lists are numbered 1 through 99, and extended community lists are numbered 100 through 199. The difference between the two community list types is that extended lists enable you to use regular expressions to specify the community (very useful when using the AA:NN format). To implement the same LOCAL_PREF policy at Colorado as previously described, but using the AA:NN format, enter the configuration for Colorado as shown in Example 3-137.

Example 3-137 *Using Extended Community Lists*

```
router bgp 100
 no synchronization
 network 10.1.11.0 mask 255.255.255.0
 network 10.1.12.0 mask 255.255.255.0
 neighbor CLIENTS peer-group
 neighbor CLIENTS ebgp-multihop 2
 neighbor CLIENTS update-source Loopback2
 neighbor CLIENTS next-hop-self
 neighbor CLIENTS send-community
 neighbor CLIENTS route-map COMM_PREF in
 neighbor LOCAL peer-group
 neighbor LOCAL remote-as 100
 neighbor LOCAL next-hop-self
 neighbor 10.1.255.2 remote-as 200
 neighbor 10.1.255.2 peer-group CLIENTS
 neighbor 10.1.255.3 remote-as 300
 neighbor 10.1.255.3 peer-group CLIENTS
 neighbor 10.1.255.4 remote-as 400
 neighbor 10.1.255.4 peer-group CLIENTS
 neighbor 10.1.255.5 remote-as 500
 neighbor 10.1.255.5 peer-group CLIENTS
 neighbor 10.1.255.6 remote-as 600
 neighbor 10.1.255.6 peer-group CLIENTS
 neighbor 10.1.255.7 peer-group LOCAL
 neighbor 10.1.255.8 peer-group LOCAL
 no auto-summary
!
ip community-list 101 permit .*:5
ip community-list 102 permit .*:10
!
route-map COMM_PREF permit 10
 match community 101
 set local-preference 150
!
```

continues

Example 3-137 *Using Extended Community Lists (Continued)*

```
route-map COMM_PREF permit 20
 match community 102
 set local-preference 200
```

The configuration in Example 3-137 is identical to Colorado's previous configuration in Example 3-134, except that extended community lists are used. If standard community lists were used, a separate line would be needed to match each community from each AS, as demonstrated in Example 3-138.

Example 3-138 *Using Standard Community Lists*

```
ip community-list 1 permit 200:5
ip community-list 1 permit 300:5
ip community-list 1 permit 400:5
ip community-list 1 permit 500:5
ip community-list 1 permit 600:5
```

With the extended community lists, a match is specified with a single line. The regular expression .* matches any AS number, and the **5** matches the common part of the community number.

Example 3-139 displays the routes matching community lists 101 and 102 at Colorado. The combination of community list and **show ip bgp community-list** commands becomes very useful in large-scale BGP implementations, which might have tens of thousands of BGP route entries. Finding routes with particular community attributes becomes a simple matter of entering a community list and then displaying the routes that match the list.

Example 3-139 *The* **show ip bgp community-list** *Command Displays BGP Routes Matching a Specified Community List*

```
Colorado#show ip bgp community-list 101
BGP table version is 19, local router ID is 10.1.255.1
Status codes: s suppressed, d damped, h history, * valid, > best, i - internal
Origin codes: i - IGP, e - EGP, ? - incomplete

   Network          Next Hop          Metric LocPrf Weight Path
*> 10.1.1.0/24      10.1.255.2             0    150      0 200 i
*> 10.1.3.0/24      10.1.255.3             0    150      0 300 i
*> 10.1.5.0/24      10.1.255.4             0    150      0 400 i
*> 10.1.7.0/24      10.1.255.5             0    150      0 500 i
*> 10.1.9.0/24      10.1.255.6             0    150      0 600 I

Colorado#show ip bgp community-list 102
BGP table version is 19, local router ID is 10.1.255.1
Status codes: s suppressed, d damped, h history, * valid, > best, i - internal
Origin codes: i - IGP, e - EGP, ? - incomplete
```

Example 3-139 *The* **show ip bgp community-list** *Command Displays BGP Routes Matching a Specified Community List (Continued)*

```
   Network          Next Hop        Metric LocPrf Weight Path
*> 10.1.2.0/24      10.1.255.2          0    200      0 200 i
*> 10.1.4.0/24      10.1.255.3          0    200      0 300 i
*> 10.1.6.0/24      10.1.255.4          0    200      0 400 i
*> 10.1.8.0/24      10.1.255.5          0    200      0 500 i
*> 10.1.10.0/24     10.1.255.6          0    200      0 600 i
Colorado#
```

A route can have multiple community attributes. Suppose router Austria in Figure 3-26 advertises all of its subnets to Idaho with a community of 2000:100. At Idaho, the routes from Austria are also to be made members of community 100:2000. Example 3-140 shows the configuration for Idaho.

Example 3-140 *Configuring Idaho to Add an Additional Community Value to the Routes from Austria*

```
router bgp 100
 no synchronization
 network 10.1.12.0 mask 255.255.255.0
 neighbor 10.1.255.1 remote-as 100
 neighbor 10.1.255.1 update-source Loopback0
 neighbor 10.1.255.1 next-hop-self
 neighbor 10.1.255.1 send-community
 neighbor 10.1.255.1 route-map IDAHO out
 neighbor 10.1.255.7 remote-as 100
 neighbor 10.1.255.7 update-source Loopback0
 neighbor 10.1.255.7 next-hop-self
 neighbor 10.2.255.1 remote-as 2000
 neighbor 10.2.255.1 ebgp-multihop 2
 neighbor 10.2.255.1 update-source Loopback0
 no auto-summary
!
ip as-path access-list 2 permit ^2000$
!
route-map IDAHO permit 10
 match as-path 2
 set community 6555600 additive
!
route-map IDAHO permit 20
```

This configuration presents two points of interest. First, the community set by statement 10 of route map IDAHO is 6555600. The command **ip bgp-community new-format** is supported in IOS 12.0 and later; router Idaho is running IOS 11.0 and therefore does not understand the AA:NN format. However, a quick calculation reveals that the decimal number 6555600 is equivalent to the 32-bit number 100:2000 (or 0x6407d0). Colorado, which is running IOS 12.0, correctly interprets this 32-bit number in the AA:NN format. The important point here is that although the community attribute can be represented in AA:NN, decimal, or hex format, it is still in reality a 32-bit number.

The other point of interest is the keyword **additive** used with the **set community** command. If the command **set community 6555600** is used without the **additive** keyword Idaho replaces the existing community attribute of any matching routes with the community 100:2000. In this case, the goal is to add an additional community, not replace the community sent by Austria. Example 3-141 shows the results at Colorado.

Example 3-141 *The Community Attribute 2000:100 Is Added by Austria, and the Community Attribute 100:2000 Is Added by Idaho*

```
Colorado#show ip bgp 10.2.1.0
BGP routing table entry for 10.2.1.0/24, version 49
Paths: (1 available, best #1, advertised over EBGP)
  2000
    10.1.255.8 from 10.1.255.8
      Origin IGP, metric 0, localpref 100, valid, internal, best
      Community: 100:2000 2000:100
Colorado#
```

When a route has multiple communities, community lists and match statements are used slightly differently. The statement **ip community-list 1 permit 2000:100** matches any route that has 2000:100 as one of its communities. On the other hand, the statement **ip community-list 1 permit 2000:100 100:2000** matches any route that has either or both communities. If you want to match only those routes that are members of both communities 2000:100 and 100:2000, no more and no less, the **exact-match** keyword is used in the matching statement, as demonstrated in Example 3-142. With this keyword, routes that have only 2000:100 or 100:2000, and routes that have both communities but also have other communities, are not matched.

Example 3-142 *The **exact-match** Keyword Returns Routes That Exactly Match the Specified Community List*

```
Colorado#conf t
Enter configuration commands, one per line.  End with CNTL/Z.
Colorado(config)#ip community-list 10 permit 2000:100 100:2000
Colorado(config)#^Z
Colorado#
%SYS-5-CONFIG_I: Configured from console by console
Colorado#show ip bgp community-list 10 exact-match
BGP table version is 52, local router ID is 10.1.255.1
Status codes: s suppressed, d damped, h history, * valid, > best, i - internal
Origin codes: i - IGP, e - EGP, ? - incomplete

   Network          Next Hop          Metric LocPrf Weight Path
*>i10.2.1.0/24     10.1.255.8             0    100      0 2000 i
*>i10.2.2.0/24     10.1.255.8             0    100      0 2000 i
*>i10.2.3.0/24     10.1.255.8             0    100      0 2000 i
Colorado#
```

If a route can be assigned multiple community attributes, there should also be a way to remove some community attributes without removing them all, as the **set community none** statement does. This is the job of the **set comm-list delete** command.

In the previous configurations, the routes to the subnets in AS 2000 of Figure 3-26 have the community attributes 2000:100 and 100:2000. At AS 400, the community 100:2000 should be retained, but not the community 2000:100. Example 3-143 shows the configuration for California.

Example 3-143 *Configuring California to Selectively Delete Community Values*

```
router bgp 400
 network 10.1.5.0 mask 255.255.255.0
 network 10.1.6.0 mask 255.255.255.0
 neighbor 10.1.255.1 remote-as 100
 neighbor 10.1.255.1 ebgp-multihop 2
 neighbor 10.1.255.1 update-source Loopback0
 neighbor 10.1.255.1 send-community
 neighbor 10.1.255.1 route-map DROP_COMM in
!
ip bgp-community new-format
!
ip community-list 1 permit 2000:100
!
route-map DROP_COMM permit 10
 set comm-list 1 delete
```

The route map DROP_COMM refers to community list 1 and deletes the community specified by the list. Example 3-144 shows the results. In a previous configuration, you saw that multiple community attributes can be specified in a single community list line. When the list is being used by the **set comm-list delete** command, however, each line of the list can specify only a single community. Therefore, if you want to delete the communities 2000:100, NO_EXPORT, and 300:5 from routes, you must configure a community list with three separate lines.

Example 3-144 *No Matches Can Be Found in California's BGP Table for Routes with Both 2000:100 and 100:2000 Community Attributes, But the Routes from AS 2000 All Have Single Community Attributes of 100:2000*

```
California#show ip bgp community 2000:100 100:2000 exact-match
California#show ip bgp community 100:2000 exact-match
BGP table version is 16, local router ID is 10.1.255.4
Status codes: s suppressed, d damped, h history, * valid, > best, i - internal
Origin codes: i - IGP, e - EGP, ? - incomplete

   Network          Next Hop          Metric LocPrf Weight Path
*> 10.2.1.0/24      10.1.255.1                    0 100 2000 i
*> 10.2.2.0/24      10.1.255.1                    0 100 2000 i
*> 10.2.3.0/24      10.1.255.1                    0 100 2000 i
California#
```

Case Study: Private AS Numbers

You are familiar with private IP addresses, as specified by RFC 1918. These addresses, in the range 10.0.0.0–10.255.255.255, 172.16.0.0–172.31.255.255, and 192.168.0.0–192.168.255.255, are designed to help alleviate the depletion of IP addresses. When an internetwork has a need for IP addresses, but the addresses do not need to be known publicly (that is, they do not need to be reachable from the Internet), you can use private addresses rather than public addresses. Because anyone can use any private IP address, the addresses are not unique and must never be advertised into the public Internet.

Private AS numbers also exist, and like private IP addresses, they are designed to alleviate the depletion of public AS numbers. AS numbers 64512 to 65535 are reserved for private use. If a BGP-speaking subscriber is homed to a single ISP, the subscriber can and is encouraged to use a private AS number.

For example, previous case studies have depicted the autonomous systems connected to router Colorado in Figure 3-26 as "client" autonomous systems of AS 100. AS 2000, connected across a NAP to AS 100, represents the public Internet. AS 100 might be an ISP and the connected autonomous systems its subscribers, or AS 100 might be the publicly connected part of a large corporate internetwork, and the other autonomous systems its private divisions. Whatever the case, the five "client" autonomous systems in Figure 3-26 are reachable only across the NAP and through AS 100. The only reason they have individual AS numbers is so that EBGP can be used to connect them to AS 100; AS 100 can advertise their routes to the Internet without including their AS numbers. Figure 3-27 shows the same internetwork as Figure 3-26, but here the "client" autonomous systems use AS numbers out of the private pool.

Remember that like private IP addresses, private AS numbers must not be advertised to the Internet, because they are not unique. Example 3-145 shows that without further configuration, the AS numbers of AS 100's clients are advertised across the NAP to router Austria.

Figure 3-27 *The Autonomous Systems Attached to Colorado Use Private AS Numbers*

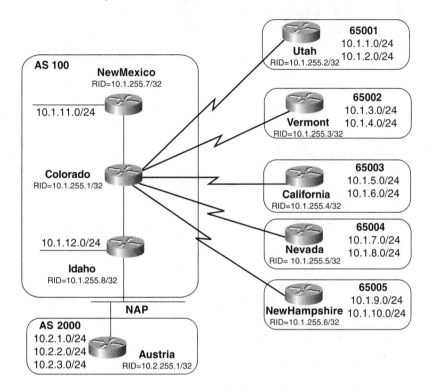

Example 3-145 *Austria's BGP Table Shows Private AS Numbers in the AS_PATHs of Some of the Routes from AS 100; if Austria Is Part of the Public Internet, Connected to AS 100 Across a NAP, These AS Numbers Must Not Be Included in the AS_PATHs*

```
Austria#show ip bgp
BGP table version is 189, local router ID is 10.2.255.1
Status codes: s suppressed, d damped, h history, * valid, > best, i - internal
Origin codes: i - IGP, e - EGP, ? - incomplete

   Network          Next Hop            Metric LocPrf Weight Path
*> 10.1.1.0/24      10.1.255.8                      0 100 65001 i
*> 10.1.2.0/24      10.1.255.8                      0 100 65001 i
*> 10.1.3.0/24      10.1.255.8                      0 100 65002 i
*> 10.1.4.0/24      10.1.255.8                      0 100 65002 i
*> 10.1.5.0/24      10.1.255.8                      0 100 65003 i
*> 10.1.6.0/24      10.1.255.8                      0 100 65003 i
*> 10.1.7.0/24      10.1.255.8                      0 100 65004 i
*> 10.1.8.0/24      10.1.255.8                      0 100 65004 i
```

continues

Example 3-145 *Austria's BGP Table Shows Private AS Numbers in the AS_PATHs of Some of the Routes from AS 100; if Austria Is Part of the Public Internet, Connected to AS 100 Across a NAP, These AS Numbers Must Not Be Included in the AS_PATHs (Continued)*

```
*> 10.1.9.0/24      10.1.255.8                        0 100 65005 i
*> 10.1.10.0/24     10.1.255.8                        0 100 65005 i
*> 10.1.11.0/24     10.1.255.8                        0 100 i
*> 10.1.12.0/24     10.1.255.8           0            0 100 i
*> 10.2.1.0/24      0.0.0.0             0        32768 i
*> 10.2.2.0/24      0.0.0.0             0        32768 i
*> 10.2.3.0/24      0.0.0.0             0        32768 i
Austria#
```

In Example 3-146, Idaho is configured to prevent the private AS numbers from being advertised across the NAP.

Example 3-146 *Filtering Private AS Numbers*

```
router bgp 100
 no synchronization
 network 10.1.12.0 mask 255.255.255.0
 neighbor 10.1.255.1 remote-as 100
 neighbor 10.1.255.1 update-source Loopback0
 neighbor 10.1.255.1 next-hop-self
 neighbor 10.1.255.1 send-community
 neighbor 10.1.255.7 remote-as 100
 neighbor 10.1.255.7 update-source Loopback0
 neighbor 10.1.255.7 next-hop-self
 neighbor 10.2.255.1 remote-as 2000
 neighbor 10.2.255.1 ebgp-multihop 2
 neighbor 10.2.255.1 update-source Loopback0
 neighbor 10.2.255.1 remove-private-AS
 no auto-summary
```

The **neighbor remove-private-AS** command is reasonably self-explanatory. It removes private AS numbers from the AS_PATH of routes before advertising them to the specified neighbor. In Example 3-147, you can see that all the AS_PATH attributes of all the routes advertised from Idaho to Austria now contain only AS 100. The routers within AS 100 still have the full path information for the client autonomous systems and can forward packets to the correct destination AS. In this regard, advertising the client subnets as if they are part of AS 100 is a form of summarization at the autonomous system level.

Example 3-147 *After the* **neighbor remove-private-AS** *Command Has Been Added to Idaho's BGP Configuration, the Private AS Numbers of AS 100's Client Autonomous Systems Are Hidden from Austria*

```
Austria#show ip bgp
BGP table version is 214, local router ID is 10.2.255.1
Status codes: s suppressed, d damped, h history, * valid, > best, i - internal
Origin codes: i - IGP, e - EGP, ? - incomplete

   Network          Next Hop          Metric LocPrf Weight Path
*> 10.1.1.0/24      10.1.255.8                          0 100 i
*> 10.1.2.0/24      10.1.255.8                          0 100 i
*> 10.1.3.0/24      10.1.255.8                          0 100 i
*> 10.1.4.0/24      10.1.255.8                          0 100 i
*> 10.1.5.0/24      10.1.255.8                          0 100 i
*> 10.1.6.0/24      10.1.255.8                          0 100 i
*> 10.1.7.0/24      10.1.255.8                          0 100 i
*> 10.1.8.0/24      10.1.255.8                          0 100 i
*> 10.1.9.0/24      10.1.255.8                          0 100 i
*> 10.1.10.0/24     10.1.255.8                          0 100 i
*> 10.1.11.0/24     10.1.255.8                          0 100 i
*> 10.1.12.0/24     10.1.255.8          0               0 100 i
*> 10.2.1.0/24      0.0.0.0             0           32768 i
*> 10.2.2.0/24      0.0.0.0             0           32768 i
*> 10.2.3.0/24      0.0.0.0             0           32768 i
Austria#
```

Case Study: BGP Confederations

BGP confederations make large transit autonomous systems more manageable by enabling the administrator to break the AS into subautonomous systems. The subdivided AS itself becomes the confederation, and the subautonomous systems are the member autonomous systems. Autonomous systems outside of the confederation see the entire confederation as a single AS and do not see the member autonomous systems. Because the member autonomous systems are hidden from the outside, they may use either public or private AS numbers, although best practice suggests using private AS numbers.

The advantage of confederations is that they sharply reduce the number of IBGP peering sessions. IBGP is used normally within each member AS, but a special version of EBGP known as *confederation EBGP* is run between the autonomous systems. No IBGP sessions are configured from a BGP speaker in one AS to a BGP speaker in another AS within the confederation.

Figure 3-28 shows an example of a confederation. AS 1200 has been subdivided into three confederation autonomous systems: AS 65533, AS 65534, and AS 65535. From the perspective of outside autonomous systems, such as AS 1000 and AS 1500, the confederation is a single autonomous system: AS 1200. These external autonomous systems have no knowledge of the confederation member autonomous systems.

Figure 3-28 *AS 1200 Is a BGP Confederation; Although It Consists of Several Subautonomous Systems, the Neighboring Autonomous Systems See the Confederation Only as AS 1200*

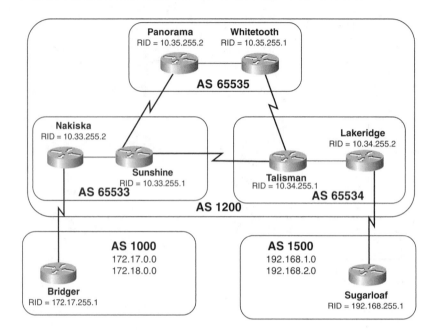

Confederation EBGP is run between Panorama and Sunshine, between Sunshine and Talisman, and between Talisman and Whitetooth. Example 3-148 shows the configuration for Talisman.

Example 3-148 *Configuring Talisman as a Confederation Router*

```
router ospf 65534
 network 10.34.0.0 0.0.255.255 area 65534
 network 10.255.0.0 0.0.255.255 area 0
!
router bgp 65534
 no synchronization
 bgp confederation identifier 1200
 bgp confederation peers 65533 65535
 neighbor Confed peer-group
 neighbor Confed ebgp-multihop 2
 neighbor Confed update-source Loopback
 neighbor Confed next-hop-self
 neighbor MyGroup peer-group
 neighbor MyGroup remote-as 65534
 neighbor MyGroup update-source Loopback0
 neighbor 10.33.255.1 remote-as 65533
 neighbor 10.33.255.1 peer-group Confed
```

Example 3-148 *Configuring Talisman as a Confederation Router (Continued)*

```
neighbor 10.34.255.2 peer-group MyGroup
neighbor 10.35.255.1 remote-as 65535
neighbor 10.35.255.1 peer-group Confed
```

Talisman is configured so that its local AS is 65534. Its peer connections to Whitetooth and Sunshine are set up like any other EBGP session, and the connection to Lakeridge is IBGP. The **bgp confederation identifier** command tells the router that it is a member of a confederation and the confederation ID. The **bgp confederation peers** command lists the member autonomous systems to which Talisman is connected. This command tells the BGP process that the EBGP connection is confederation EBGP rather than normal EBGP.

A confederation may run BGP only, a common IGP throughout the entire confederation, or different IGPs within each member AS. In Figure 3-28, all the routers within AS 1200 run OSPF. The OSPF permits local communication within the confederation and tells the BGP processes how to find their various neighbors. In the configuration in Example 3-148, no routes are redistributed between OSPF and BGP at any router. Subsequent configuration examples do not show the OSPF configuration.

Example 3-149 shows configurations of Lakeridge and Sugarloaf.

Example 3-149 *Configuring EBGP Between Confederation Router Lakeridge and External Router Sugarloaf*

```
Lakeridge
router bgp 65534
 no synchronization
 bgp confederation identifier 1200
 neighbor 10.34.255.1 remote-as 65534
 neighbor 10.34.255.1 update-source Loopback0
 neighbor 10.34.255.1 next-hop-self
 neighbor 192.168.255.1 remote-as 1500
 neighbor 192.168.255.1 ebgp-multihop 2
 neighbor 192.168.255.1 update-source Loopback0

Sugarloaf
router bgp 1500
 network 192.168.1.0
 network 192.168.2.0
 neighbor 10.34.255.2 remote-as 1200
 neighbor 10.34.255.2 ebgp-multihop 2
 neighbor 10.34.255.2 update-source Loopback0
```

At Lakeridge, the **bgp confederation peers** command is not used because Lakeridge is not running confederation EBGP. It does, however, have a normal EBGP connection to Sugarloaf. Notice that from the perspective of Sugarloaf, Lakeridge is in AS 1200, not AS 65534. Sugarloaf, being outside of the confederation, has no knowledge of the member autonomous systems.

Confederation EBGP is something of a hybrid between normal BGP and IBGP. Specifically, within a confederation, the following applies:

- The NEXT_HOP attribute of routes external to the confederation is preserved throughout the confederation.

- MULTI_EXIT_DISC attributes of routes advertised into a confederation are preserved throughout the confederation.

- LOCAL_PREF attributes of routes are preserved throughout the entire confederation, not just within the member AS in which they are assigned.

- The AS numbers of the member autonomous systems are added to the AS_PATH within the confederation but are not advertised outside of the confederation. By default, the member AS numbers are listed in the AS_PATH as AS_PATH attribute type 4, AS_CONFED_SEQUENCE. If the **aggregate-address** command is used within the confederation, the **as-set** keyword causes member AS numbers behind the aggregation point to be listed as AS_PATH attribute type 3, AS_CONFED_SET.

- The confederation AS numbers in an AS_PATH are used for loop avoidance but are not considered when choosing a shortest AS_PATH within the confederation.

Most of these characteristics are due to the fact that from the outside, the confederation appears to be a single autonomous system. The following discussion provides examples of each of these characteristics.

In Figure 3-28, the routes in AS 1000 are advertised from Bridger to Nakiska with a NEXT_HOP attribute of 172.17.255.1. This attribute is preserved when the routes are advertised via IBGP from Nakiska to Sunshine. If Sunshine were connected to Talisman with a normal EBGP connection, Sunshine would change the NEXT_HOP of the routes to 10.33.255.1 before advertising them to Talisman. Because the connection is confederation EBGP, however, the original NEXT_HOP attribute is preserved. As a result, Lakeridge could have route entries for 172.17.0.0 and 172.18.0.0 with a next-hop address of 172.17.255.1. Lakeridge's connection to Sugarloaf is normal EBGP, so the routes are advertised to Sugarloaf with a NEXT_HOP attribute of 10.34.255.2.

The **neighbor next-hop-self** command is used throughout the confederation of Figure 3-28 so that all next-hop addresses are known via the IGP. You can observe these commands in the configurations of Talisman and Lakeridge.

Bridger is configured to advertise its routes with a MED of 50, and Nakiska is configured to set the LOCAL_PREF of the same routes to 200. You can observe the results in Example 3-150. In a normal EBGP session, Sunshine would not advertise the MED that originated in AS 1000, or the LOCAL_PREF that should only have relevance within AS65533. Because the confederation is seen from the outside as a single AS, however, these values must be consistent throughout the confederation.

Example 3-150 *The Routes from AS 1000 Have a MED of 50 and a LOCAL_PREF of 200 at Lakeridge; These Values Were Preserved Across the Confederation EBGP Connection from Sunshine*

```
Lakeridge#show ip bgp
BGP table version is 28, local router ID is 10.34.255.2
Status codes: s suppressed, * valid, > best, i - internal
Origin codes: i - IGP, e - EGP, ? - incomplete

   Network          Next Hop         Metric LocPrf Weight Path
*>i172.17.0.0       10.33.255.1          50    200      0 (65533) 1000 i
*>i172.18.0.0       10.33.255.1          50    200      0 (65533) 1000 i
*> 192.168.1.0      192.168.255.1         0             0 1500 i
*> 192.168.2.0      192.168.255.1         0             0 1500 i
Lakeridge#
```

You also can see in Example 3-150 that AS 65533 is included in the AS_PATH of the routes to the networks in AS 1000. The AS_CONFED_SEQUENCE is shown in parentheses for two reasons. First, it is not advertised outside of the confederation, as demonstrated in Example 3-151. Second, it is used only for loop avoidance within the confederation, not for path selection.

Example 3-151 *Sugarloaf Sees the Confederation in Figure 3-28 as a Single Autonomous System and Does Not See the Member Autonomous Systems; the AS_CONFED_SEQUENCE, Shown in Parentheses in Example 3-150, Is Replaced with the Confederation ID 1200*

```
Sugarloaf#show ip bgp
BGP table version is 32, local router ID is 192.168.255.1
Status codes: s suppressed, d damped, h history, * valid, > best, i - internal
Origin codes: i - IGP, e - EGP, ? - incomplete

   Network          Next Hop         Metric LocPrf Weight Path
*> 172.17.0.0       10.34.255.2                         0 1200 1000 i
*> 172.18.0.0       10.34.255.2                         0 1200 1000 i
*> 192.168.1.0      0.0.0.0               0         32768 i
*> 192.168.2.0      0.0.0.0               0         32768 i
Sugarloaf#
```

In the BGP tables of Whitetooth and Panorama displayed in Example 3-152, you can observe a consequence of the fact that member AS numbers do not influence the path selection process. Both routers have two paths to each of the destinations in AS 1000 and AS1500—one via its IBGP neighbor, and one via its confederation EBGP neighbor. Whitetooth, for instance, has two paths to network 172.17.0.0. The AS_PATH of one is (65534, 65533, 1000) and the other is (65533, 1000). Clearly the latter AS_PATH is shorter, but the member AS numbers are ignored. As a result, the two paths are seen as equivalent: (1000). All else being equal, the BGP decision process chooses normal EBGP routes over confederation EBGP routes and confederation EBGP routes over IBGP routes. In Example 3-152, the choice is between a confederation EBGP route and an IBGP route.

Notice in the BGP tables of the two routers that the confederation EBGP path is chosen in every instance.

Example 3-152 *The AS_CONFED_SEQUENCE, Shown in Parentheses in the Whitetooth and Panorama BGP Tables, Are Not Considered When Choosing a Shortest AS_PATH Within an AS Confederation*

```
Whitetooth#show ip bgp
BGP table version is 9, local router ID is 10.35.255.1
Status codes: s suppressed, d damped, h history, * valid, > best, i - internal
Origin codes: i - IGP, e - EGP, ? - incomplete

   Network          Next Hop         Metric LocPrf Weight Path
*> 172.17.0.0       10.34.255.1          50    200      0 (65534 65533) 1000 i
*  i                10.33.255.1          50    200      0 (65533) 1000 i
*> 172.18.0.0       10.34.255.1          50    200      0 (65534 65533) 1000 i
*  i                10.33.255.1          50    200      0 (65533) 1000 i
*> 192.168.1.0      10.34.255.1           0    100      0 (65534) 1500 i
*  i                10.33.255.1           0    100      0 (65533 65534) 1500 i
*> 192.168.2.0      10.34.255.1           0    100      0 (65534) 1500 i
*  i                10.33.255.1           0    100      0 (65533 65534) 1500 i
Whitetooth#
```

```
Panorama#show ip bgp
BGP table version is 5, local router ID is 10.35.255.2
Status codes: s suppressed, d damped, h history, * valid, > best, i - internal
Origin codes: i - IGP, e - EGP, ? - incomplete

   Network          Next Hop         Metric LocPrf Weight Path
*  i172.17.0.0       10.34.255.1          50    200      0 (65534 65533) 1000 i
*>                   10.33.255.1          50    200      0 (65533) 1000 i
*  i172.18.0.0       10.34.255.1          50    200      0 (65534 65533) 1000 i
*>                   10.33.255.1          50    200      0 (65533) 1000 i
*  i192.168.1.0      10.34.255.1           0    100      0 (65534) 1500 i
*>                   10.33.255.1           0    100      0 (65533 65534) 1500 i
*  i192.168.2.0      10.34.255.1           0    100      0 (65534) 1500 i
*>                   10.33.255.1           0    100      0 (65533 65534) 1500 i
Panorama#
```

In the topology of Figure 3-28, ignoring the member AS numbers presents no problem. Consider the topology in Figure 3-29, however, where everything is identical except the BGP router IDs in AS 65534 and AS 65535, which have been swapped. This change might seem innocent enough, but consider the effect that it has on the BGP decision process at Sunshine. The routes to the networks in AS 1500 are being advertised by both Talisman and Panorama. The AS_PATH lengths are the same because the member AS numbers are ignored, and both neighbors are confederation EBGP peers. Both Talisman and Panorama use the **neighbor next-hop-self** command, so the IGP path to the next-hop address of both routes is the same. The tiebreaker becomes the lowest neighboring router ID, which is Panorama. Sunshine therefore chooses the path through AS 65535 via Panorama rather than the more-direct path via Talisman, as demonstrated in Example 3-153.

Figure 3-29 *The Router IDs of the Routers in AS 65534 and AS 65535 Have Been Swapped*

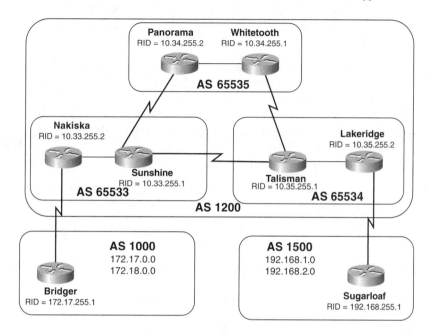

Example 3-153 *Sunshine Has Chosen Suboptimal Paths to the Networks in AS 1500 Based on Panorama's Lower Router ID*

```
Sunshine#show ip bgp
BGP table version is 17, local router ID is 10.33.255.1
Status codes: s suppressed, d damped, h history, * valid, > best, i - internal
Origin codes: i - IGP, e - EGP, ? - incomplete

   Network          Next Hop         Metric LocPrf Weight Path
*>i172.17.0.0       10.33.255.2          50    200      0 1000 i
*>i172.18.0.0       10.33.255.2          50    200      0 1000 i
*>  192.168.1.0     10.34.255.2           0    100      0 (65535 65534) 1500 i
*                   10.35.255.1           0    100      0 (65534) 1500 i
*>  192.168.2.0     10.34.255.2           0    100      0 (65535 65534) 1500 i
*                   10.35.255.1           0    100      0 (65534) 1500 i
Sunshine#
```

Little can be done to remedy the problems in the topology of Figure 3-29. Attempting to filter routes or manipulate administrative weights will make the configurations highly complex, defeating one of the reasons for creating a confederation in the first place. Attempting to manipulate the route choices with LOCAL_PREF or MED attributes is fraught with hazards, because the attributes are advertised throughout the confederation; with the loops in the topology, the attributes can affect route choices in unintended locations.

You must design confederations so that problems such as those presented by the topology in Figure 3-29 do not arise. A common design technique takes its cue from OSPF, in which all areas must interconnect through a single backbone area, eliminating the possibility of inter-area loops.

Figure 3-30 shows the same routers as in the earlier illustrations, but the member autonomous systems have been redesigned. AS 65000 is a backbone autonomous system, and all the other autonomous systems must interconnect through it. The result is that the path from any nonbackbone AS to any other nonbackbone AS is the same distance. The connections between AS 65000 and AS 65535 demonstrate that it is still possible to have redundant connections, but not between nonbackbone autonomous systems. BGP's loop-avoidance mechanism prevents the possibility of suboptimal inter-AS paths.

Figure 3-30 *AS 65000 Is a Backbone AS in the Confederation; All Other Areas Interconnect Through It, Making the AS_PATHs Between All Nonbackbone Autonomous Systems the Same Length*

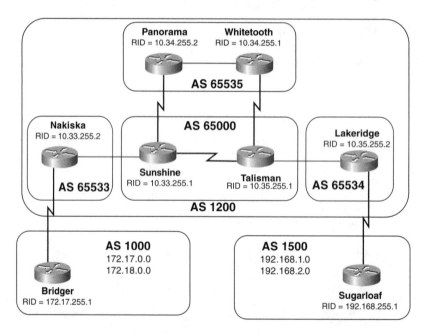

Another advantage of a loop-free topology such as the one in Figure 3-30 is that the MED attribute can be used between member autonomous systems. To understand why MEDs are safe in this topology, look first at the topology in Figure 3-31. This is similar to the confederation in Figure 3-28, except that AS 65534 has redundant connections to AS 65535. Suppose MEDs are used so that AS 65535 prefers the Whitetooth/Lakeridge link over the Panorama/Talisman link for traffic destined for AS 1500. Correct results can be achieved between these two autonomous systems, but the problem is that the MEDs are also forwarded from AS 65534 to AS 65533. Depending on how the latter AS is configured to handle MEDs, and which MEDs are sent by Talisman, AS 65533 could again choose a suboptimal route.

Figure 3-31 *MED Attributes Are Forwarded Throughout a Confederation; if AS 65534 Uses MEDs to Influence the Preferences of AS 65535, AS 65533 Will Also Receive the MEDs*

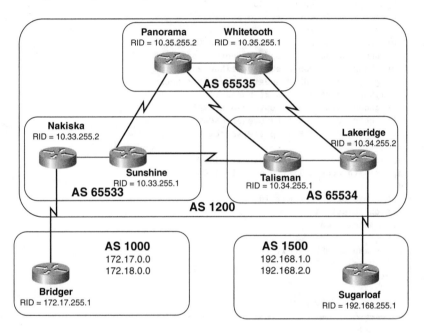

In Figure 3-30, AS 65000 can safely send MEDs to AS 65535. The only path AS 65535 has to other nonbackbone autonomous systems is through the backbone. A route that includes 65000 in its AS_PATH is not accepted by Sunshine or Talisman, so MEDs sent from those routers to AS 65535 are not seen by other member autonomous systems.

By default, Panorama and Whitetooth in Figure 3-30 prefer confederation EBGP routes over IBGP routes. So Panorama sends all traffic destined for the networks in AS 1000 and AS 1500 to Sunshine; Whitetooth sends all traffic for the same destinations to Talisman. MEDs can be used so that AS 65535 sends all traffic destined for the networks in AS 1000 across the Panorama/Sunshine link and all traffic destined for the networks in AS 1500 across the Whitetooth/Talisman link. Example 3-154 shows the configurations of Sunshine and Talisman.

Example 3-154 *Configuring Sunshine and Talisman to Send MEDs to AS 65535*

```
Sunshine
router bgp 65000
 no synchronization
 bgp confederation identifier 1200
 bgp confederation peers 65533 65535
 neighbor 10.33.255.2 remote-as 65533
 neighbor 10.33.255.2 ebgp-multihop 2
 neighbor 10.33.255.2 update-source Loopback0
 neighbor 10.34.255.2 update-source Loopback0
 neighbor 10.34.255.2 ebgp-multihop 2
 neighbor 10.34.255.2 update-source Loopback0
 neighbor 10.34.255.2 next-hop-self
 neighbor 10.34.255.2 route-map SETMED out
 neighbor 10.35.255.1 remote-as 65000
 neighbor 10.35.255.1 update-source Loopback0
!
ip as-path access-list 1 permit _1000_
ip as-path access-list 2 permit _1500_
!
route-map SETMED permit 10
 match as-path 1
 set metric 100
!
route-map SETMED permit 20
 match as-path 2
 set metric 200
!
route-map SETMED permit 30

Talisman
router bgp 65000
 no synchronization
 bgp confederation identifier 1200
 bgp confederation peers 65534 65535
 neighbor 10.33.255.1 remote-as 65000
 neighbor 10.34.255.1 remote-as 65535
 neighbor 10.34.255.1 ebgp-multihop 2
 neighbor 10.34.255.1 update-source Loopback0
 neighbor 10.34.255.1 next-hop-self
 neighbor 10.34.255.1 route-map SETMED out
 neighbor 10.35.255.2 remote-as 65534
 neighbor 10.35.255.2 ebgp-multihop 2
 neighbor 10.35.255.2 update-source Loopback0
!
ip as-path access-list 1 permit _1500_
ip as-path access-list 2 permit _1000_
!
route-map SETMED permit 10
 match as-path 1
 set metric 100
!
```

Example 3-154 *Configuring Sunshine and Talisman to Send MEDs to AS 65535 (Continued)*

```
route-map SETMED permit 20
 match as-path 2
 set metric 200
!
route-map SETMED permit 30
```

Sunshine sets to 100 the MED for all routes whose AS_PATH includes 1000; the MED for all routes whose AS_PATH includes 1500 is set to 200. Talisman does just the opposite. Example 3-155 shows before-and-after views of Panorama's BGP table. In the first table, the router prefers the confederation EBGP paths for all destinations. In the second table, the MEDs have been changed so that Panorama sends traffic destined for the networks of AS 1500 across the IBGP link to Whitetooth, which forwards the traffic across its preferred confederation EBGP link.

Example 3-155 *Panorama's BGP Table, Before and After the Routers in AS 65000 Are Configured to Send MED Attributes*

```
Panorama#show ip bgp
BGP table version is 34, local router ID is 10.35.2.1
Status codes: s suppressed, d damped, h history, * valid, > best, i - internal
Origin codes: i - IGP, e - EGP, ? - incomplete

   Network          Next Hop         Metric LocPrf Weight Path
* i172.17.0.0       10.35.255.1           0    100      0 (65000 65533) 1000 i
*>                  10.33.255.1           0    100      0 (65000 65533) 1000 i
* i172.18.0.0       10.35.255.1           0    100      0 (65000 65533) 1000 i
*>                  10.33.255.1           0    100      0 (65000 65533) 1000 i
* i192.168.1.0      10.35.255.1           0    100      0 (65000 65534) 1500 i
*>                  10.33.255.1           0    100      0 (65000 65534) 1500 i
* i192.168.2.0      10.35.255.1           0    100      0 (65000 65534) 1500 i
*>                  10.33.255.1           0    100      0 (65000 65534) 1500 i
Panorama#

Panorama#show ip bgp
BGP table version is 47, local router ID is 10.35.2.1
Status codes: s suppressed, d damped, h history, * valid, > best, i - internal
Origin codes: i - IGP, e - EGP, ? - incomplete

   Network          Next Hop         Metric LocPrf Weight Path
* i172.17.0.0       10.35.255.1         200    100      0 (65000 65533) 1000 i
*>                  10.33.255.1         200    100      0 (65000 65533) 1000 i
* i172.18.0.0       10.35.255.1         200    100      0 (65000 65533) 1000 i
*>                  10.33.255.1         200    100      0 (65000 65533) 1000 i
*>i192.168.1.0      10.35.255.1         100    100      0 (65000 65534) 1500 i
*                   10.33.255.1         200    100      0 (65000 65534) 1500 i
*>i192.168.2.0      10.35.255.1         100    100      0 (65000 65534) 1500 i
*                   10.33.255.1         200    100      0 (65000 65534) 1500 i
Panorama#
```

In Figure 3-32, two subnets local to the confederation are added: 10.33.5.0/24 in AS 65533, and 10.35.5.0/24 in AS 65535. Sunshine and Talisman are reconfigured to apply the same routing policies to these two subnets as are applied to the external networks. That is, MEDs are set so that AS 65535 sends traffic destined for 10.33.5.0/24 across the Panorama/Sunshine link and traffic destined for 10.35.5.0/24 across the Whitetooth/Talisman link.

Figure 3-32 *Local Subnets Are Added to AS 65533 and AS 65535*

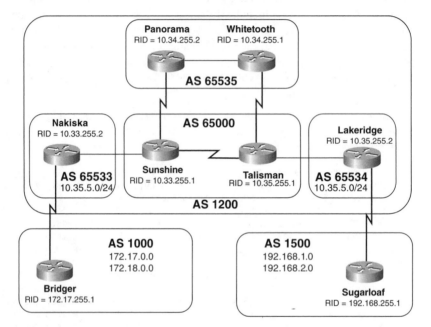

You can see in Panorama's BGP table in Example 3-156 that the policies are not having the desired effect. The MEDs are correctly configured, but the router is still preferring its confederation EBGP path for both subnets rather than preferring the IBGP path, with its lower MED, for traffic to 10.35.5.0/24. The reason for this behavior is that by default, the MED of a confederation-interior route (signified by the absence of any exterior AS numbers in the AS_PATH) is not considered in the BGP decision process.

Example 3-156 *Panorama Is Choosing Paths to Confederation-Exterior Destinations Based on the Lowest MED, But the MED Is Not Considered When Choosing Confederation-Interior Paths*

```
Panorama#show ip bgp
BGP table version is 127, local router ID is 10.35.2.1
Status codes: s suppressed, d damped, h history, * valid, > best, i - internal
Origin codes: i - IGP, e - EGP, ? - incomplete
```

Example 3-156 *Panorama Is Choosing Paths to Confederation-Exterior Destinations Based on the Lowest MED, But the MED Is Not Considered When Choosing Confederation-Interior Paths (Continued)*

```
    Network           Next Hop          Metric LocPrf Weight Path
  * i10.33.5.0/24     10.35.255.1          200    100      0 (65000 65533) i
  *>                  10.33.255.1          100    100      0 (65000 65533) i
  *> 10.35.5.0/24     10.33.255.1          200    100      0 (65000 65534) i
  * i                 10.35.255.1          100    100      0 (65000 65534) i
  *> 172.17.0.0       10.33.255.1          100    100      0 (65000 65533) 1000 i
  *> 172.18.0.0       10.33.255.1          100    100      0 (65000 65533) 1000 i
  *>i192.168.1.0      10.35.255.1          100    100      0 (65000 65534) 1500 i
  *                   10.33.255.1          200    100      0 (65000 65534) 1500 i
  *>i192.168.2.0      10.35.255.1          100    100      0 (65000 65534) 1500 i
  *                   10.33.255.1          200    100      0 (65000 65534) 1500 i
Panorama#
```

The command **bgp deterministic-med** tells the BGP process to compare MEDs when choosing paths to confederation-interior destinations. Example 3-157 shows the configuration for Panorama using the **bgp deterministic-med** command.

Example 3-157 *Configuring Panorama to Compare MEDs When Choosing Paths to Confederation-Interior Destinations*

```
router bgp 65535
 no synchronization
 bgp confederation identifier 1200
 bgp confederation peers 65000
 bgp deterministic-med
 neighbor 10.33.255.1 remote-as 65000
 neighbor 10.33.255.1 ebgp-multihop 2
 neighbor 10.33.255.1 update-source Loopback0
 neighbor 10.34.255.1 remote-as 65535
 neighbor 10.34.255.1 update-source Loopback0
```

Example 3-158 shows the results of configuring Panorama with the **bgp deterministic-med** command. Panorama now uses the path with the lowest MED, whether the path is interior or exterior to the member AS. You can obtain similar results by using the **bgp always-compare-med** command, discussed in an earlier case study. The difference is that this command, unlike **bgp deterministic-med**, compares the MEDs of paths to the same destination regardless of whether the MEDs are advertised from the same AS. In a backbone-based confederation such as the one in Figure 3-32, this is not an issue, because no AS has a path to more than one neighboring AS.

Example 3-158 *Panorama Is Considering the MED When Choosing Both Confederation-Interior and Confederation-Exterior Routes*

```
Panorama#show ip bgp
BGP table version is 10, local router ID is 10.35.2.1
Status codes: s suppressed, d damped, h history, * valid, > best, i - internal
Origin codes: i - IGP, e - EGP, ? - incomplete

   Network          Next Hop         Metric LocPrf Weight Path
*> 10.33.5.0/24     10.33.255.1         100    100      0 (65000 65533) i
* i                 10.35.255.1         200    100      0 (65000 65533) i
*>i10.35.5.0/24     10.35.255.1         100    100      0 (65000 65534) i
*                   10.33.255.1         200    100      0 (65000 65534) i
*> 172.17.0.0       10.33.255.1         100    100      0 (65000 65533) 1000 i
*> 172.18.0.0       10.33.255.1         100    100      0 (65000 65533) 1000 i
*>i192.168.1.0      10.35.255.1         100    100      0 (65000 65534) 1500 i
*                   10.33.255.1         200    100      0 (65000 65534) 1500 i
*>i192.168.2.0      10.35.255.1         100    100      0 (65000 65534) 1500 i
*                   10.33.255.1         200    100      0 (65000 65534) 1500 i
Panorama#
```

You can use yet another command to accomplish the same goals: **bgp bestpath med confed**. This command has the same effect as **bgp deterministic-med**, with one difference. If a route has an external AS number in its AS_PATH, and other routes to the same destination have only confederation AS numbers in their AS_PATHs, the router picks the confederation-internal path with the lowest MED and ignores the path with the external AS number. However, such a situation should be very rare. The existence of two routes to the same destination, one indicating that the destination is inside the confederation and another that the destination is outside, is probably evidence of a misconfiguration or a poor design.

Case Study: Route Reflectors

Route reflectors are another way to reduce the number of IBGP peer connections in a large AS. The use of route reflectors has two advantages over confederations:

- All routers in a confederation must understand and support confederations. But only the route reflectors themselves must understand route reflection; the client routers see their connection to the RR as just another IBGP connection.

- Route reflection is simpler to implement, both in terms of the commands needed and in terms of topology issues.

On the other hand, you might want to take advantage of the sorts of controls available with EBGP to manage a large AS. In this case, confederations are a better choice. This case study shows the possibility of using both.

Figure 3-33 shows a modification of AS 65533 in Figure 3-32. Fortress is a route reflector, and Nakiska and Marmot are the clients.

Figure 3-33 *Network Topology with Route Reflectors: Fortress Is a Route Reflector, Nakiska, and Marmot Are
Clients*

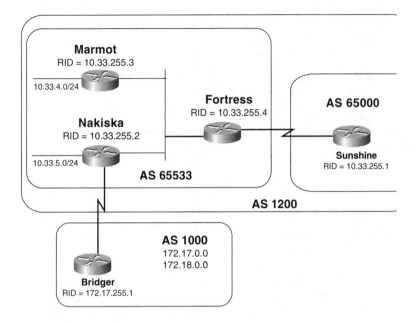

Example 3-159 shows the configuration of the three routers.

Example 3-159 *Configuring Fortress as the Route Reflector and Nakiska and Marmot as Clients*

```
Fortress
router bgp 65533
 no synchronization
 bgp confederation identifier 1200
 bgp confederation peers 65000
 neighbor 10.33.255.1 remote-as 65000
 neighbor 10.33.255.1 ebgp-multihop 2
 neighbor 10.33.255.1 update-source Loopback0
 neighbor 10.33.255.2 remote-as 65533
 neighbor 10.33.255.2 update-source Loopback0
 neighbor 10.33.255.2 route-reflector-client
 neighbor 10.33.255.2 next-hop-self
 neighbor 10.33.255.3 remote-as 65533
 neighbor 10.33.255.3 update-source Loopback0
 neighbor 10.33.255.3 route-reflector-client
 neighbor 10.33.255.3 next-hop-self
```

continues

Example 3-159 *Configuring Fortress as the Route Reflector and Nakiska and Marmot as Clients (Continued)*

```
Nakiska
router bgp 65533
 no synchronization
 bgp confederation identifier 1200
 network 10.33.5.0 mask 255.255.255.0
 neighbor 10.33.255.4 remote-as 65533
 neighbor 10.33.255.4 update-source Loopback0
 neighbor 10.33.255.4 next-hop-self
 neighbor 172.17.255.1 remote-as 1000
 neighbor 172.17.255.1 ebgp-multihop 2
 neighbor 172.17.255.1 update-source Loopback0
```

```
Marmot
router bgp 65533
 no synchronization
 bgp confederation identifier 1200
 network 10.33.4.0 mask 255.255.255.0
 neighbor 10.33.255.4 remote-as 65533
 neighbor 10.33.255.4 update-source Loopback0
 neighbor 10.33.255.4 next-hop-self
```

Nakiska and Marmot have normal IBGP configurations, except that they peer only with the RR, not with each other. Nakiska also peers with Bridger, a router outside of the route reflection cluster. The only command added to Fortress, to make it a route reflector, is a **neighbor route-reflector-client** statement for each of its clients. This statement implements the relaxed IBGP rules necessary for route reflection discussed in Chapter 2; namely, that IBGP routes learned from one client are advertised to the other clients and to IBGP peers outside the cluster, and that IBGP routes learned from IBGP peers outside the cluster are advertised to clients.

Example 3-160 shows the entry for 10.33.5.0/24 in Marmot's BGP table. The ORIGINATOR_ID and CLUSTER_LIST attributes, added by the RR, are indicated on the last line. The ORIGINATOR_ID is added by the RR and indicates the client that advertises the route; the originator of the route to 10.33.5.0/24 is Nakiska (10.33.255.2). This attribute ensures that routes do not loop within the cluster. If Fortress receives this NLRI in an update, it recognizes Nakiska's router ID in the attribute and ignores the route. The attribute is optional nontransitive, so a router does not have to support or understand the attribute to participate in a route reflection cluster, although some loop protection will be lost.

Like the ORIGINATOR_ID, the CLUSTER_LIST is a loop-prevention measure. A 4-octet cluster ID identifies the cluster, and the RR adds this number to the CLUSTER_LIST. If the RR receives an update with its own cluster ID in the CLUSTER_LIST, it knows a loop has occurred and it ignores the route. This function proves important when the path passes through multiple route reflection clusters. The CLUSTER_LIST of the route in Figure 3-33

Example 3-160 *Marmot's BGP Entry for Subnet 10.33.5.0/24 Indicates the ORIGINATOR_ID and CLUSTER_LIST Attributes Added to the Route by the Route Reflector*

```
Marmot#show ip bgp 10.33.5.0
BGP routing table entry for 10.33.5.0 255.255.255.0, version 16
Paths: (1 available, best #1)
  Local
    10.33.255.2 (metric 11) from 10.33.255.4 (10.33.255.2)
      Origin IGP, metric 0, localpref 100, valid, internal, best
      Originator : 10.33.255.2, Cluster list: 10.33.255.4
Marmot#
```

is 10.33.255.4, Fortress' router ID. By default, the RR enters its own BGP RID in the CLUSTER_LIST. To specify a cluster ID other than the RR's RID, you use the **bgp cluster-id** command. You can specify a cluster ID as a number between 1 and 4294967295 or in dotted decimal format.

If you configure more than one route reflector in a cluster, you must use the **bgp cluster-id** command to ensure that all RRs are identifying themselves as members of the same cluster. In Figure 3-34, router Norquay is added and is configured as a second RR to add redundancy to the cluster.

Figure 3-34 *Norquay Is Added to the Route Reflection Cluster for Redundancy*

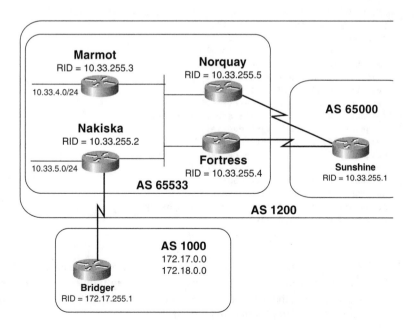

Example 3-161 shows the configurations of Fortress and Norquay.

Example 3-161 *Configuring Fortress and Norquay as Route Reflectors*

```
Fortress
router bgp 65533
 no synchronization
 bgp cluster-id 33
 bgp confederation identifier 1200
 bgp confederation peers 65000
 neighbor 10.33.255.1 remote-as 65000
 neighbor 10.33.255.1 ebgp-multihop 2
 neighbor 10.33.255.1 update-source Loopback0
 neighbor 10.33.255.2 remote-as 65533
 neighbor 10.33.255.2 update-source Loopback0
 neighbor 10.33.255.2 route-reflector-client
 neighbor 10.33.255.2 next-hop-self
 neighbor 10.33.255.3 remote-as 65533
 neighbor 10.33.255.3 update-source Loopback0
 neighbor 10.33.255.3 route-reflector-client
 neighbor 10.33.255.3 next-hop-self
 neighbor 10.33.255.5 remote-as 65533
 neighbor 10.33.255.5 update-source Loopback0
 neighbor 10.33.255.5 next-hop-self

Norquay
router bgp 65533
 no synchronization
 bgp cluster-id 33
 bgp confederation identifier 1200
 bgp confederation peers 65000
 neighbor 10.33.255.1 remote-as 65000
 neighbor 10.33.255.1 ebgp-multihop 2
 neighbor 10.33.255.1 update-source Loopback0
 neighbor 10.33.255.2 remote-as 65533
 neighbor 10.33.255.2 route-reflector-client
 neighbor 10.33.255.2 update-source Loopback0
 neighbor 10.33.255.2 next-hop-self
 neighbor 10.33.255.3 remote-as 65533
 neighbor 10.33.255.3 route-reflector-client
 neighbor 10.33.255.3 update-source Loopback0
 neighbor 10.33.255.3 next-hop-self
 neighbor 10.33.255.4 remote-as 65533
 neighbor 10.33.255.4 update-source Loopback0
 neighbor 10.33.255.4 next-hop-self
```

Both RRs are configured with a cluster ID of 33. They peer with each other via standard
IBGP and with the route reflection clients using the **neighbor route-reflector-client**
statement. As a result, the two RRs reflect routes to the clients, but IBGP rules prevent them
from advertising the IBGP routes to each other.

The only change to the client configurations is the addition of an IBGP configuration for Norquay, as shown in Example 3-162.

Example 3-162 *Clients Nakiska and Marmot Peer to Both Fortress and Norquay*

```
Nakiska
router bgp 65533
 no synchronization
 bgp confederation identifier 1200
 network 10.33.5.0 mask 255.255.255.0
 neighbor 10.33.255.4 remote-as 65533
 neighbor 10.33.255.4 update-source Loopback0
 neighbor 10.33.255.4 next-hop-self
 neighbor 10.33.255.5 remote-as 65533
 neighbor 10.33.255.5 update-source Loopback0
 neighbor 10.33.255.5 next-hop-self
 neighbor 172.17.255.1 remote-as 1000
 neighbor 172.17.255.1 ebgp-multihop 2
 neighbor 172.17.255.1 update-source Loopback0

Marmot
router bgp 65533
 no synchronization
 bgp confederation identifier 1200
 network 10.33.4.0 mask 255.255.255.0
 neighbor 10.33.255.4 remote-as 65533
 neighbor 10.33.255.4 update-source Loopback0
 neighbor 10.33.255.4 next-hop-self
 neighbor 10.33.255.5 remote-as 65533
 neighbor 10.33.255.5 update-source Loopback0
 neighbor 10.33.255.5 next-hop-self
```

Example 3-163 shows the resulting entry in Marmot's BGP table for subnet 10.33.5.0/24. Where there was a single path to the destination in Example 3-160, there are now two. The paths are entirely equal; because the router is not configured to use both paths with the **maximum-paths** command, the router chooses the route from 10.33.255.4, the lowest next-hop address.

Example 3-163 *Marmot Is Receiving Routes from RRs Fortress and Norquay*

```
Marmot#show ip bgp 10.33.5.0
BGP routing table entry for 10.33.5.0 255.255.255.0, version 2
Paths: (2 available, best #1)
  Local
    10.33.255.2 (metric 11) from 10.33.255.4 (10.33.255.2)
      Origin IGP, metric 0, localpref 100, valid, internal, best
      Originator : 10.33.255.2, Cluster list: 0.0.0.33
  Local
    10.33.255.2 (metric 11) from 10.33.255.5 (10.33.255.2)
      Origin IGP, metric 0, localpref 100, valid, internal
      Originator : 10.33.255.2, Cluster list: 0.0.0.33
Marmot#
```

The route reflectors of Example 3-161 belong to the same cluster, as indicated by the shared cluster ID. However, the route reflectors could also belong to separate clusters, and the configurations of the clients, in Example 3-162, would not change. Key to this concept is the fact that the clients do not know that they are clients. This approach, peering clients with redundant route reflectors in multiple clusters rather than in the same cluster, is used in many current route reflection designs.

Although route reflection clients can have EBGP connections, as Nakiska does in Figure 3-34, clients normally should not have any IBGP neighbors except the route reflector. This means that the connections between clusters must be made between the route reflectors, not between clients, because clients do not examine the CLUSTER_LIST attribute of received routes. An intercluster loop would not be detected by a client. The RRs are peered via standard IBGP and obey all the IBGP rules. The only additional information passed between the RRs is the CLUSTER_LIST attribute, to prevent loops. The route reflectors within an AS must be fully meshed with all other route reflectors in the AS and with all other AS-interior routers that do not belong to a cluster, as shown in Figure 3-35.

Figure 3-35 *The Links Interconnecting Clusters Must Be Between Route Reflectors, Not Between Clients*

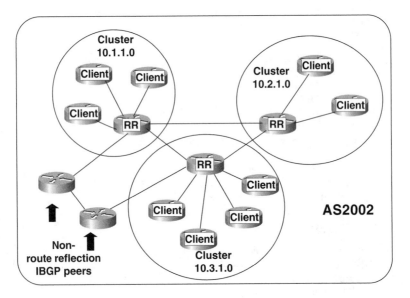

The rule that clients must peer only to their RRs has two exceptions. First, a client itself can be a route reflector for another cluster. This allows "nesting" of route reflection clusters, or the creation of a hierarchy of clusters, as illustrated in Figure 2-40 of Chapter 2.

The second exception is when there is a full IBGP mesh among the clients, as shown in Figure 2-41 of Chapter 2. Fully meshing the clients provides some increased robustness. When such a design is used, you should configure the route reflector with the command **no**

bgp client-to-client reflection. Routes are then communicated between the fully meshed clients under normal IBGP rules, and the RR does not reflect routes from one client to another. It does, however, continue to reflect routes from clients to peers outside of the cluster, and from peers outside of the cluster to clients.

Looking Ahead

This chapter concludes this book's examination of exterior gateway protocols. Subsequent chapters examine advanced IP routing issues, including network address translation, multicast routing, and quality of service. Case studies that involve an exterior gateway protocol in later chapters use BGP.

Recommended Reading

Halabi, S. *Internet Routing Architectures, Second Edition*. Indianapolis, Indiana: Cisco Press; 2000.

This book is considered the definitive text on BGP-4 using Cisco IOS Software.

Command Summary

Table 3-3 provides a list and description of the commands discussed in this chapter.

Table 3-3 *Command Summary*

Command	Description
aggregate-address *address mask* [**as-set**] [**summary-only**] [**suppress-map** *map-name*] [**advertise-map** *map-name*] [**attribute-map** *map-name*]	Creates an aggregate entry in the BGP routing table.
auto-summary	Enables the automatic summarization of subnets to their major network addresses.
bgp always-compare-med	Allows the comparison of MED attributes of routes to the same destination but advertised by peers in different autonomous systems.
bgp bestpath as-path ignore	Tells the BGP process to ignore the AS_PATH length in the BGP decision process.
bgp bestpath med confed	Enables the comparison of MED attributes of routes advertised by confederation EBGP peers.
bgp client-to-client reflection	Enables route reflection between IBGP peers.

continues

Table 3-3 *Command Summary (Continued)*

Command	Description
bgp cluster-id *cluster-id*	Sets the cluster ID of a BGP route reflection cluster.
bgp confederation identifier *autonomous-system*	Specifies the confederation ID (the AS number seen by confederation-exterior peers).
bgp confederation peers *autonomous-system* [*autonomous-system*]	Lists the member autonomous systems of a router's confederation EBGP peers.
bgp dampening [*half-life reuse suppress max-suppress-time*] [**route-map** *map*]	Enables route dampening and changes route dampening defaults.
bgp default local-preference *value*	Changes the default LOCAL_PREF value from 100.
bgp deterministic-med	Enables the comparison of the MED attributes of routes advertised by confederation EBGP peers in the same neighboring member AS.
bgp log-neighbor-changes	Enables logging of neighbor resets.
clear ip bgp {**|address|peer-group-name*} [**soft** [**in** | **out**]]	Resets one or more BGP peer connections.
clear ip bgp dampening [*address mask*]	Clears BGP dampening information and unsuppresses suppressed routes.
clear ip bgp flap-statistics [{**regexp** *regexp*}]|{**filter-list** *list*}|{*address mask*}	Clears BGP flap statistics.
clear ip bgp peer-group *peer-group-name*	Removes all members of a peer group.
default-information originate	Causes a router to advertise the default address 0.0.0.0 to its BGP peers.
default-metric *number*	Sets the default metric (MED) that a BGP router adds to the routes advertised to EBGP peers.
distance bgp *external-distance internal-distance local-distance*	Changes the default administrative distances of BGP routes.
ip as-path access-list *access-list-number* {**permit** | **deny**} *regexp*	Defines an access list that examines the AS_PATH attributes of BGP routes.
ip bgp-community new-format	Displays community attributes in the AA:NN format.
ip community-list *community-list-number* {**permit** | **deny**} *community-number*	Defines an access list that identifies BGP routes by their COMMUNITY attributes.

Table 3-3   *Command Summary (Continued)*

Command	Description
ip prefix-list *prefix-list-name* [**seq** *sequence-number*]{**permit**|**deny**} {*ip-prefix/length*}[**ge** | **le**]*min/max-length*	Defines an access list that examines the NLRI prefix and length advertised in a route.
match as-path *path-list-number*	Creates a call to an AS_PATH access list.
match community-list *community-list-number* [**exact**]	Creates a call to a COMMUNITY access list.
neighbor {*ip-address*|*peer-group-name*} **advertisement-interval** *seconds*	Changes the default minimum advertisement interval for routing updates to BGP peers.
neighbor {*ip-address*|*peer-group-name*} **default-originate** [**route-map** *map-name*]	Causes a router to advertise the default address 0.0.0.0 to the specified neighbor or peer group.
neighbor {*ip-address* | *peer-group-name*} **description** *text*	Associates a descriptive text string with a neighbor's configuration.
neighbor {*ip-address* | *peer-group-name*} **distribute-list** {*access-list-number* | **prefix-list** *prefix-list-name*} {**in** | **out**}	Filters routes to or from a neighbor or peer group by NLRI.
neighbor {*ip-address* | *peer-group-name*} **ebgp-multihop** *hops*	Changes the default TTL of packets carrying BGP messages to neighbors.
neighbor {*ip-address* | *peer-group-name*} **filter-list** *access-list-number* {**in** | **out** | **weight** *weight*}	Filters incoming or outgoing BGP routes by AS_PATH, or sets the weight of incoming routes.
neighbor {*ip-address*|*peer-group-name*} **maximum-prefix** *maximum* [*threshold*][**warning-only**]	Sets a maximum number of NLRI prefixes that can be advertised by a neighbor or peer group.
neighbor {*ip-address*|*peer-group-name*} **next-hop-self**	Causes a BGP router to advertise its own address as the NEXT_HOP attribute of EBGP-learned routes advertised to IBGP peers.
neighbor {*ip-address*|*peer-group-name*} **password** *string*	Enables MD5 authentication between peers.
neighbor *ip-address* **peer-group** *peer-group-name*	Assigns a neighbor to a peer group.
neighbor *peer-group-name* **peer-group**	Creates a peer group.
neighbor {*ip-address* | *peer-group-name*} **prefix-list** *prefix-list-name* {**in**|**out**}	Filters routes to or from a neighbor based on NLRI as identified by a prefix list.
neighbor {*ip-address* | *peer-group-name*} **remote-as** *as-number*	Adds a neighbor to the BGP neighbor table and identifies the neighbor as EBGP or IBGP.

continues

Table 3-3 *Command Summary (Continued)*

Command	Description
neighbor {*ip-address* | *peer-group-name*} **route-map** *map-name* {**in**|**out**}	References a route map for setting policy for routes to or from a neighbor or peer group.
neighbor *ip-address* **route-reflector-client**	Configures a router as a route reflector and identifies a neighbor as a route reflection client.
neighbor {*ip-address*|*peer-group-name*} **send-community**	Identifies a neighbor to which COMMUNITY attributes are to be sent.
neighbor {*ip-address*|*peer-group-name*} **shutdown**	Disables a neighbor or peer group.
neighbor {*ip-address*|*peer-group-name*} **soft-reconfiguration inbound**	Enables the router to store incoming, unmodified updates from a neighbor for inbound soft reconfiguration.
neighbor {*ip-address*|*peer-group-name*} **timers** *keepalive holdtime*	Changes the default keepalive and holdtime intervals for a neighbor.
neighbor {*ip-address* | *peer-group-name*} **update-source** *interface*	Identifies the interface IP address from which IBGP updates are to be sourced.
neighbor {*ip-address* | *peer-group-name*} **version** *version*	Sets the BGP process to a single version.
neighbor {*ip-address* | *peer-group-name*} **weight** *weight*	Assigns a weight to routes received from a neighbor.
network *network-number* [**mask** *network-mask*]	Specifies a network to be advertised by the BGP process.
network *network-address* **backdoor**	Sets the administrative distance of the specified EBGP route to 200 and disables EBGP advertisement of the route.
network *address mask* **weight** *weight* [**route-map** *map-name*]	Assigns a weight to the route to the identified destination.
router bgp *autonomous-system*	Enables a BGP process on a router and specifies the local AS number.
set as-path {**tag** | **prepend** *as-path-string*}	Sets the AS_PATH of an identified route to the redistributed tag, or prepends the AS_PATH with a specified string of one or more AS numbers.
set comm-list *community-list-number* **delete**	Removes the community attributes identified by the called community list from an identified route.
set community {*community-number* [**additive**]} | **none**	Sets a community attribute in an identified route.

Table 3-3   *Command Summary (Continued)*

Command	Description
set dampening *half-life reuse suppress max-suppress-time*	Changes the default dampening factors for an identified route.
set metric-type internal	Sets the value of an identified route's MED attribute to match the IGP metric of the next hop.
set origin {**igp** | **egp** *autonomous-system* | **incomplete**}	Changes the ORIGIN attribute of an identified route.
set weight *weight*	Sets the weight of an identified route.
show ip bgp [*network*][*network-mask*][**longer-prefixes**]	Displays entries in the BGP table.
show ip bgp cidr-only	Displays entries in the BGP table with non-natural (classless) network masks.
show ip bgp community {*community-name* | *community-number*} [**exact**]	Displays entries in the BGP table with the specified community attribute.
show ip bgp community-list *community-list-number* [**exact**]	Displays entries in the BGP table that are permitted by the specified community list.
show ip bgp dampened-paths	Displays dampened (suppressed) paths.
show ip bgp filter-list *access-list-number*	Displays entries in the BGP table that match the specified access list.
show ip bgp flap-statistics [{**regexp** *regexp*} | {**filter-list** *list-number*} | {*address mask* [**longer-prefix**]}]	Displays the flap statistics of one or more entries in the BGP table.
show ip bgp inconsistent-as	Displays any entries in the BGP table with multiple paths to the same destination but with inconsistent AS_PATH attributes.
show ip bgp neighbors [*address*][**received-routes** | **routes** | **advertised-routes** | {**paths** *regex*} | **dampened-routes**]	Displays information about the TCP and BGP connections to neighbors.
show ip bgp paths	Displays all BGP paths in the database.
show ip bgp peer-group [*peer-group-name*][**summary**]	Displays information about characteristics shared by a peer group.
show ip bgp regexp *regexp*	Displays entries in the BGP table whose AS_PATH attributes match the specified regular expression.

continues

Table 3-3   *Command Summary (Continued)*

Command	Description
show ip bgp summary	Displays summary information about all BGP connections.
synchronization	Enables synchronization between BGP and the local IGP.
table-map *route-map-name*	Enables a call to a route map to modify the metric or tag values of a route being entered into the IGP routing table.
timers bgp *keepalive holdtime*	Changes the default keepalive and holdtime intervals for the entire BGP process.

Configuration Exercises

Table 3-4 shows the routers and addresses used for configuration exercises 1 through 13.

Table 3-4   *Routers/Addresses for Configuration Exercises 1–13*

Autonomous System	Router	Interface	IP Address/Mask
1	R1	L0	10.255.255.1/32
		S0	192.168.100.1/30
		E0	192.168.100.5/30
		E1	192.168.100.13/30
	R2	L0	10.255.255.2/32
		S0	192.168.100.9/30
		S1	192.168.100.57/30
		E0	192.168.100.6/30
		E1	192.168.100.17/30
	R3	L0	10.255.255.3/32
		S0	192.168.100.25/30
		E0	192.168.100.18/30
		E1	192.168.100.21/30
	R4	L0	10.255.255.4/32
		S0	192.168.100.29/30
		S1	192.168.100.33/30
		E0	192.168.100.22/30
		E1	192.168.100.14/30

Table 3-4   *Routers/Addresses for Configuration Exercises 1–13 (Continued)*

Autonomous System	Router	Interface	IP Address/Mask
2	R5	S0	192.168.100.2 /30
		E0	192.168.1.129/26
	R6	S0	192.168.100.10/30
		E0	192.168.1.130/26
3	R7	L0	10.255.255.7/32
		S0	192.168.100.26/30
		S1	192.168.100.41/30
		E0	192.168.100.37/30
		E1	172.16.1.1/24
4	R8	L0	10.255.255.8/32
		S0	192.168.100.30/30
		S1	192.168.100.45/30
		E0	192.168.100.38/30
		E1	172.16.2.1/24
5	R9	L0	10.255.255.9/32
		S0	192.168.100.42/30
		E0	192.168.9.1/24
		E1	192.168.150.1/24
	R10	L0	10.255.255.10/32
		S0	192.168.100.46/30
		E0	192.168.10.1/24
		E1	192.168.100.53/30
		E2	192.168.150.2/24
	R11	L0	10.255.255.11/32
		S0	192.168.100.34/30
		E0	192.168.100.54/30
		E1	192.168.11.1/24
6	R12	L0	192.168.255.1/32
		S0	192.168.100.58/30
		E0	192.168.16.83/27

Table 3-4 lists the autonomous systems, routers, interfaces, and addresses used in configuration exercises 1 through 13. All interfaces of the routers are shown. For each exercise, if the table indicates that the router has a loopback interface, that interface should be the source of all IBGP connections. EBGP connections should always be between physical interface addresses, unless otherwise specified in an exercise. Hint: Draw the internetwork, based on the subnets listed in the table, before attempting the exercises.

1 AS 1 in Table 3-4 is a transit AS, and the IGP is OSPF. Area 0 spans the entire AS. No networks internal to the AS are advertised outside of the AS. None of the subnets over which EBGP is run should be advertised into AS 1. Write BGP configurations for the routers in AS 1, putting all internal neighbors in a peer group called LOCAL. For R3 only, EBGP peering should be performed between loopback interfaces. Authenticate all IBGP connections with the password **ExeRCise1**.

_____

_____

_____

2 AS 2 in Table 3-4 is a stub (nontransit) AS, and its IGP is EIGRP. Configure the routers in AS 2 to speak EBGP to any external peers and to redistribute any EIGRP routes into BGP. Redistribute BGP-learned routes into EIGRP. Implement any necessary filters to prevent incorrect routes from being redistributed.

_____

_____

_____

3 Networks 192.168.1.0, 192.168.2.0, 192.168.3.0, 192.168.4.0, and 192.168.5.0 exist within AS 2. The administrator of this AS wants the neighboring AS to prefer R5 when sending traffic to 192.168.1.0 and 192.168.3.0. The neighboring AS should prefer R6 when sending traffic to 192.168.2.0 and 192.168.4.0. In each case, the less-preferred link serves as a backup to the more-preferred link. 192.168.5.0 is a private network and must not be advertised to any EBGP peer. Modify the configurations written in Exercise 2 to implement this policy.

_____

_____

_____

4 Configure the EBGP neighbors of R5 and R6 to advertise a default route to AS 2. No other routes are to be advertised.

_____

_____

_____

5 The administrator of AS 2's neighboring AS disagrees with part of the policy set in Exercise 2. He wants all routers in his AS to send traffic destined for 192.168.3.0 to R6, with R5 as a backup. All traffic destined for 192.168.4.0 should be sent to R5, with R6 as a backup. The rest of the policy set in Exercise 2 is acceptable. Write configurations to implement this policy.

_____

_____

_____

6 AS 3 in Table 3-4 is a stub AS, and AS 4 is a transit AS. The IGP of both autonomous systems is OSPF, and the internal interfaces of R7 and R8 are both in area 0. Write BGP and OSPF configurations for R7 and R8, advertise the internal addresses shown in Table 3-4 to all EBGP peers, and ensure that routers in the OSPF domains can reach any external destination. Do not redistribute routes in either direction. Also, ensure that the BGP router ID of R7 is 192.168.3.254.

_____

_____

_____

7 Modify the configurations of Exercise 6 so that R7 and R8 speak OSPF across the link directly connecting them; remove BGP from the link. Traffic between subnets 172.16.3.0/24 and 172.16.4.0/24 should prefer this direct link and should use any EBGP links only as backup. Traffic between the other addresses internal to AS 3 and AS 4 should use the EBGP links and should use the direct link only as a backup. Additionally, traffic from other autonomous systems can use the direct link as a backup route. If an EBGP link to AS 4 fails, for example, the neighboring AS can send traffic destined for AS 4 to AS 3, to be forwarded to AS 4 across the direct link.

_____

_____

_____

8 AS 5 in Table 3-4 is a transit AS, and its IGP is IS-IS. The Level 2 area 47.0001 spans the entire AS. The internal networks are 192.168.9.0, 192.168.10.0, 192.168.11.0, and 192.168.12.0. Write IS-IS and BGP configurations for R9, R10, and R11. Ensure that all external routes are known by the routers in the IS-IS domain and that all internal networks are advertised to all EBGP peers. Do not redistribute IS-IS routes into BGP.

_____

_____

_____

9 Modify the configurations written in Exercise 8 so that network 192.168.12.0 is known only by AS 4, and no other autonomous system.

_____

_____

_____

10 Modify the configurations written in Exercise 9 so that AS 3 and AS 4 prefer the path through AS 1 to reach network 192.168.11.0.

_____

_____

_____

11 The networks internal to AS 6 in Table 3-4 are 192.168.16.0, 192.168.17.0, 192.168.18.0, and 192.168.19.0. Write a BGP configuration for R12 that advertises these networks to the neighboring AS and that also advertises a summary route for the networks. The neighboring AS should advertise only the summary to other autonomous systems.

_____

_____

_____

12 Modify the most recent configuration you wrote for R12's EBGP neighbor so that the neighbor does not accept prefixes that do not belong to the aggregate being advertised by R12, does not accept prefixes longer than 24 bits, and does not accept more than five prefixes.

_____

_____

_____

13 Example 3-164 shows a BGP configuration for R7 in Table 3-4. The internal prefixes shown in Table 3-4 are advertised by OSPF.

Example 3-164 *BGP Configuration of Router R7*

```
router bgp 3
 redistribute ospf 1
 neighbor NEIGHBORS peer-group
 neighbor NEIGHBORS ebgp-multihop 2
 neighbor NEIGHBORS update-source Loopback0
 neighbor NEIGHBORS route-map EX13 out
 neighbor 10.255.255.8 remote-as 4
 neighbor 10.255.255.8 peer-group NEIGHBORS
 neighbor 10.255.255.9 remote-as 5
 neighbor 10.255.255.9 peer-group NEIGHBORS
 neighbor 10.255.255.3 remote-as 1
 neighbor 10.255.255.3 peer-group NEIGHBORS
 no auto-summary
!
ip classless
ip as-path access-list 1 permit ^1 2$
!
access-list 1 permit 172.16.1.0
access-list 2 permit 172.16.3.0
!
route-map EX13 permit 10
 match ip address 1
 set as-path prepend 2
!
route-map EX13 permit 20
 match ip address 2
 set as-path prepend 1
!
route-map EX13 permit 30
 match as-path 1
 set as-path prepend 4 5
!
route-map EX13 deny 40
```

Explain the effects of route map EX13.

_____

_____

_____

14 Router R1 in Figure 3-36 is a route reflector for routers R2, R3, and R4 and is connected to those neighbors via Frame Relay PVCs. Write a BGP configuration for R1 that provides full connectivity for the networks attached to the four routers. The cluster ID is 6500.

Figure 3-36 *The Route Reflection Cluster for Configuration Exercise 14*

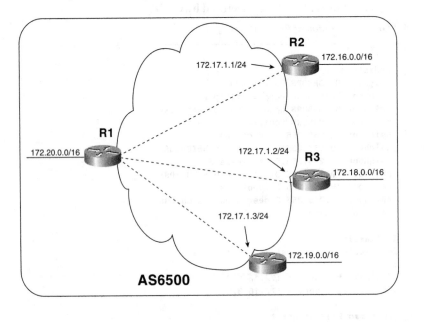

Troubleshooting Exercises

Figure 3-37 shows the internetwork diagram for Troubleshooting Exercises 1 through 6.

Figure 3-37 *The Internetwork for Troubleshooting Exercises 1 through 6*

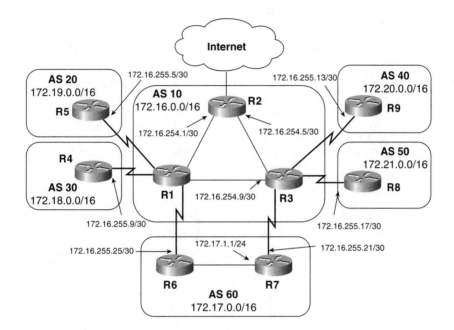

1 Example 3-165 shows the BGP configuration of router R2 in Figure 3-37.

Example 3-165 *BGP Configuration of Router R2*

```
router bgp 10
 no synchronization
 network 0.0.0.0
 neighbor 172.16.254.2 remote-as 10
 neighbor 172.16.254.2 next-hop-self
 neighbor 172.16.254.6 remote-as 10
 neighbor 172.16.254.6 next-hop-self
 no auto-summary
!
ip classless
ip route 0.0.0.0 0.0.0.0 Ethernet10
```

Example 3-166 shows the BGP table and routing table for R2. Although there are routes to the destinations in the autonomous systems shown in Figure 3-37, pings to those destinations fail. Why?

Example 3-166 *The BGP and Routing Tables of R2 in Figure 3-37*

```
R2#show ip bgp
BGP table version is 7, local router ID is 10.1.1.1
Status codes: s suppressed, d damped, h history, * valid, > best, i - internal
Origin codes: i - IGP, e - EGP, ? - incomplete
   Network          Next Hop          Metric LocPrf Weight Path
*> 0.0.0.0          0.0.0.0                0          32768 i
*>i172.17.0.0       172.16.255.21          0    100      0 60 i
*>i172.18.0.0       172.16.255.9           0    100      0 30 i
*>i172.19.0.0       172.16.255.5           0    100      0 20 i
*>i172.20.0.0       172.16.255.13          0    100      0 40 i
*>i172.21.0.0       172.16.255.17          0    100      0 50 i

R2#show ip route
Codes: C - connected, S - static, I - IGRP, R - RIP, M - mobile, B - BGP
       D - EIGRP, EX - EIGRP external, O - OSPF, IA - OSPF inter area
       E1 - OSPF external type 1, E2 - OSPF external type 2, E - EGP
       i - IS-IS, L1 - IS-IS level-1, L2 - IS-IS level-2, * - candidate default

Gateway of last resort is 0.0.0.0 to network 0.0.0.0

     10.0.0.0 255.255.255.0 is subnetted, 1 subnets
C       10.1.1.0 is directly connected, Ethernet11
B    172.20.0.0 [200/0] via 172.16.255.13, 00:01:15
B    172.21.0.0 [200/0] via 172.16.255.17, 00:01:16
     172.16.0.0 255.255.255.252 is subnetted, 2 subnets
C       172.16.254.0 is directly connected, Ethernet12
C       172.16.254.4 is directly connected, Ethernet13
B    172.17.0.0 [200/0] via 172.16.255.21, 00:01:16
B    172.18.0.0 [200/0] via 172.16.255.9, 00:00:59
B    172.19.0.0 [200/0] via 172.16.255.5, 00:00:59
S*   0.0.0.0 0.0.0.0 is directly connected, Ethernet10
R2#ping 172.17.1.1
Type escape sequence to abort.
Sending 5, 100-byte ICMP Echos to 172.17.1.1, timeout is 2 seconds:
.....
Success rate is 0 percent (0/5)
R2#
```

_____

_____

_____

2 Example 3-167 shows **debug** output from routers R1 and R5 in Figure 3-37. What problem do the messages indicate?

Example 3-167 **debug** *Output from R1 and R5 in Figure 3-37*

```
R1#debug ip bgp
BGP debugging is on
R1#
BGP: 172.16.255.5 open active, local address 172.16.255.6
BGP: 172.16.255.5 sending OPEN, version 4
BGP: 172.16.255.5 received NOTIFICATION 2/2 (peer in wrong AS) 2 bytes 000A
BGP: 172.16.255.5 closing

R5#
6d08h: BGP: 172.16.255.6 open active, delay 28272ms
6d08h: BGP: 172.16.255.6 open active, local address 172.16.255.5
6d08h: BGP: 172.16.255.6 sending OPEN, version 4
6d08h: BGP: 172.16.255.6 OPEN rcvd, version 4
6d08h: BGP: 172.16.255.6 bad OPEN, remote AS is 10, expected 30
6d08h: BGP: 172.16.255.6 sending NOTIFICATION 2/2 (peer in wrong AS) 2 bytes 000A
6d08h: BGP: 172.16.255.6 remote close, state CLOSEWAIT
6d08h: BGP: 172.16.255.6 closing
```

_____

_____

_____

3 Example 3-168 shows the BGP tables of R1 and R3 in Figure 3-37. The first table indicates that 172.17.0.0/24 can be reached either via R6 (172.16.255.25) or R3 (172.16.254.9). Which path is R1 using, and why?

Example 3-168 *BGP Tables from R1 and R3 in Figure 3-37*

```
R1#show ip bgp
BGP table version is 8, local router ID is 172.20.7.1
Status codes: s suppressed, * valid, > best, i - internal
Origin codes: i - IGP, e - EGP, ? - incomplete

   Network          Next Hop         Metric LocPrf Weight Path
*>i0.0.0.0          172.16.254.1          0    100      0 i
*  i172.17.0.0      172.16.254.9          0    100      0 60 i
*>                  172.16.255.25         0             0 60 i
*> 172.18.0.0       172.16.255.9          0             0 30 i
*> 172.19.0.0       172.16.255.5          0             0 20 i
*>i172.20.0.0       172.16.254.9          0    100      0 40 i
*>i172.21.0.0       172.16.254.9          0    100      0 50 i
R1#
```

continues

Example 3-168 *BGP Tables from R1 and R3 in Figure 3-37 (Continued)*

```
R3#show ip bgp
BGP table version is 5, local router ID is 172.16.255.22
Status codes: s suppressed, d damped, h history, * valid, > best, i - internal
Origin codes: i - IGP, e - EGP, ? - incomplete

    Network          Next Hop         Metric LocPrf Weight Path
* i0.0.0.0          172.16.254.5          0    100      0 i
* i172.17.0.0       172.16.254.10         0    100      0 60 i
*>                  172.16.255.21         0             0 60 i
* i172.18.0.0       172.16.254.10         0    100      0 30 i
* i172.19.0.0       172.16.254.10         0    100      0 20 i
*> 172.20.0.0       172.16.255.13         0             0 40 i
*> 172.21.0.0       172.16.255.17         0             0 50 i
R3#
```

4 Example 3-169 shows the BGP and IGP configurations for R1, R3, R6, and R7 in Figure 3-37.

Example 3-169 *BGP and IGP Configurations for Routers R1, R3, R6, and R7*

```
R1
router bgp 10
 neighbor 172.16.254.1 remote-as 10
 neighbor 172.16.254.1 next-hop-self
 neighbor 172.16.254.9 remote-as 10
 neighbor 172.16.254.9 next-hop-self
 neighbor 172.16.255.5 remote-as 20
 neighbor 172.16.255.9 remote-as 30
 neighbor 172.16.255.25 remote-as 60
```

```
R3
router bgp 10
 neighbor 172.16.254.5 remote-as 10
 neighbor 172.16.254.5 next-hop-self
 neighbor 172.16.254.10 remote-as 10
 neighbor 172.16.254.10 next-hop-self
 neighbor 172.16.255.13 remote-as 40
 neighbor 172.16.255.17 remote-as 50
 neighbor 172.16.255.21 remote-as 60
 neighbor 172.16.255.21 next-hop-self
```

```
R6
router eigrp 60
```

Example 3-169 *BGP and IGP Configurations for Routers R1, R3, R6, and R7 (Continued)*

```
 redistribute bgp 60 metric 1000 100 255 1 1500
 network 172.17.0.0
!
router bgp 60
 network 172.17.0.0
 neighbor 172.16.255.26 remote-as 10
```

R7
```
router eigrp 60
 redistribute bgp 60 metric 1000 100 255 1 1500
 network 172.17.0.0
!
router bgp 60
 network 172.17.0.0
 neighbor 172.16.255.22 remote-as 10
```

Example 3-168 shows the BGP tables for R1 and R3. For each of the following destinations, what next-hop address does R6 use? Explain why R6 uses the addresses you name.

Destinations:

172.20.7.102

172.18.58.35

10.53.12.6

_____

_____

_____

5 Example 3-170 shows the BGP configurations for R1 and R3 in Figure 3-37.

Example 3-170 *BGP Configurations for Routers R1 and R3*

```
R1
router bgp 10
no synchronization
aggregate-address 172.16.0.0 255.255.248.0 summary-only
neighbor 172.16.254.1 remote-as 10
neighbor 172.16.254.1 next-hop-self
neighbor 172.16.254.9 remote-as 10
neighbor 172.16.254.9 next-hop-self
neighbor 172.16.255.5 remote-as 20
neighbor 172.16.255.9 remote-as 30
neighbor 172.16.255.25 remote-as 60
```

continues

Example 3-170 *BGP Configurations for Routers R1 and R3 (Continued)*

```
R3
router bgp 10
 no synchronization
 aggregate-address 172.16.0.0 255.255.248.0 summary-only
 neighbor 172.16.254.5 remote-as 10
 neighbor 172.16.254.5 next-hop-self
 neighbor 172.16.254.10 remote-as 10
 neighbor 172.16.254.10 next-hop-self
 neighbor 172.16.255.13 remote-as 40
 neighbor 172.16.255.17 remote-as 50
 neighbor 172.16.255.21 remote-as 60
 neighbor 172.16.255.21 next-hop-self
```

The objective is to suppress all the more-specific routes and advertise only an aggregate. R8's BGP table, in Example 3-171, still shows the more-specific routes. What is wrong?

Example 3-171 *The BGP Table of R8 in Figure 3-37*

```
R8#show ip bgp
BGP table version is 163, local router ID is 172.21.1.1
Status codes: s suppressed, * valid, > best, i - internal
Origin codes: i - IGP, e - EGP, ? - incomplete

   Network          Next Hop         Metric LocPrf Weight Path
*> 0.0.0.0          172.16.255.18                      0 10 i
*> 172.17.0.0       172.16.255.18                      0 10 60 i
*> 172.18.0.0       172.16.255.18                      0 10 30 i
*> 172.19.0.0       172.16.255.18                      0 10 20 i
*> 172.20.0.0       172.16.255.18                      0 10 40 i
*> 172.21.0.0       0.0.0.0               0         32768 i
R8#
```

_____

_____

_____

6 Packets from AS 60 destined for any of the other autonomous systems shown in Figure 3-37 should be forwarded across the link between R6 and R1. The link between R7 and R3 should be used only as a backup for this traffic, although packets destined for the Internet can still use this link. To implement this policy, R3 should advertise only the default route and the aggregate 172.16.0.0/13. R1 should advertise the more-specific routes. Example 3-172 shows the configurations for R1, R3, R6, and R7.

Example 3-172 *Configurations for Routers R1, R3, R6, and R7*

```
R1
router bgp 10
no synchronization
neighbor 172.16.254.1 remote-as 10
neighbor 172.16.254.1 next-hop-self
neighbor 172.16.254.9 remote-as 10
neighbor 172.16.254.9 next-hop-self
neighbor 172.16.255.5 remote-as 20
neighbor 172.16.255.9 remote-as 30
neighbor 172.16.255.25 remote-as 60
```

```
R3
router bgp 10
 no synchronization
 aggregate-address 172.16.0.0 255.248.0.0 summary-only
 neighbor 172.16.254.5 remote-as 10
 neighbor 172.16.254.5 next-hop-self
 neighbor 172.16.254.10 remote-as 10
 neighbor 172.16.254.10 next-hop-self
 neighbor 172.16.255.13 remote-as 40
 neighbor 172.16.255.17 remote-as 50
 neighbor 172.16.255.21 remote-as 60
 neighbor 172.16.255.21 next-hop-self
```

```
R6
redistribute bgp 60 metric 1000 100 255 1 1500
 network 172.17.0.0
!
router bgp 60
 network 172.17.0.0
 neighbor 172.16.255.26 remote-as 10
```

```
R7
router eigrp 60
 redistribute bgp 60 metric 1000 100 255 1 1500
 network 172.17.0.0
!
router bgp 60
 network 172.17.0.0
 neighbor 172.16.255.22 remote-as 10
```

Example 3-173 shows R7's routing table. Has the objective been accomplished? If not, why not?

Example 3-173 *R7's Routing Table for Troubleshooting Exercise 6*

```
R7#show ip route
Codes: C - connected, S - static, I - IGRP, R - RIP, M - mobile, B - BGP
       D - EIGRP, EX - EIGRP external, O - OSPF, IA - OSPF inter area
```

continues

Example 3-173 *R7's Routing Table for Troubleshooting Exercise 6 (Continued)*

```
           N1 - OSPF NSSA external type 1, N2 - OSPF NSSA external type 2
           E1 - OSPF external type 1, E2 - OSPF external type 2, E - EGP
           i - IS-IS, L1 - IS-IS level-1, L2 - IS-IS level-2, * - candidate default
           U - per-user static route, o - ODR
           T - traffic engineered route

Gateway of last resort is 172.16.255.22 to network 0.0.0.0

      172.17.0.0/24 is subnetted, 3 subnets
C        172.17.1.0 is directly connected, Ethernet0
D        172.17.3.0 [90/409600] via 172.17.1.2, 09:18:50, Ethernet0
C        172.17.2.0 is directly connected, Ethernet1
      172.16.0.0/30 is subnetted, 1 subnets
C        172.16.255.20 is directly connected, Serial0
D EX 172.19.0.0/16 [170/2611200] via 172.17.1.2, 00:19:08, Ethernet0
D EX 172.18.0.0/16 [170/2611200] via 172.17.1.2, 00:19:08, Ethernet0
B*   0.0.0.0/0 [20/0] via 172.16.255.22, 00:18:37
B    172.16.0.0/13 [20/0] via 172.16.255.22, 00:18:09
R7#
```

7 Reexamine Figure 3-19 and Example 3-98 and the associated discussion. Meribel advertises its local route 172.17.0.0 to its EBGP peers with an ORIGIN of Incomplete, whereas Lillehammer advertises the route back to Meribel with an ORIGIN of IGP. Will this cause Meribel to prefer the route from Lillehammer, thereby causing a routing loop?

8 Example 3-174 shows the configuration for the router named Colorado in Figure 3-24.

Example 3-174 *Configuration for Router Colorado in Figure 3-24*

```
router bgp 100
 network 10.1.11.0 mask 255.255.255.0
 network 10.1.12.0 mask 255.255.255.0
 neighbor CLIENTS peer-group
 neighbor CLIENTS ebgp-multihop 2
 neighbor CLIENTS update-source Loopback2
 neighbor CLIENTS filter-list 2 in
 neighbor CLIENTS filter-list 1 out
```

Example 3-174 *Configuration for Router Colorado in Figure 3-24 (Continued)*

```
neighbor 10.1.255.2 remote-as 200
neighbor 10.1.255.2 peer-group CLIENTS
neighbor 10.1.255.3 remote-as 300
neighbor 10.1.255.3 peer-group CLIENTS
neighbor 10.1.255.4 remote-as 400
neighbor 10.1.255.4 peer-group CLIENTS
neighbor 10.1.255.5 remote-as 500
neighbor 10.1.255.5 peer-group CLIENTS
neighbor 10.1.255.6 remote-as 600
neighbor 10.1.255.6 peer-group CLIENTS
 no auto-summary
!
ip classless
ip route 10.1.255.2 255.255.255.255 Serial0/1.305
ip route 10.1.255.3 255.255.255.255 Serial0/1.306
ip route 10.1.255.4 255.255.255.255 Serial0/1.307
ip route 10.1.255.5 255.255.255.255 Serial0/1.308
!
ip as-path access-list 1 permit ^$
ip as-path access-list 2 permit ^[2-6]00$
```

All router IDs shown in Figure 3-24 are configured on loopback interfaces, and no routing protocol other than BGP is running on any of the routers. Assuming that all the links shown in the figure are functioning properly, are all the other five routers EBGP peers of Colorado? If not, why not?

_____

_____

_____

9 Refer to the configuration shown in Troubleshooting Exercise 8 for router Colorado in Figure 3-24. What will be the result of removing the **no auto-summary** statement from the configuration?

_____

_____

_____

10 Refer again to the configuration shown in Troubleshooting Exercise 8. What routes does the incoming route filter permit?

_____

_____

_____

11 Refer to Figure 3-24 and the configuration for router Colorado in Troubleshooting Exercise 8. What subnets, other than those local to its own AS or the inter-AS links, can a host on subnet 10.1.3.0/24 ping?

_____

_____

_____

Advanced IP Routing Issues

This chapter covers the following key topics:

- **Operation of NAT**—This section discusses the basics of network address translation, including fundamental concepts and terminology, and typical NAT applications.

- **NAT Issues**—This section examines some potential problems that you might encounter with NAT. Solutions to many of the problems, either through Cisco IOS Software functionality or through design techniques, are identified.

- **Configuring NAT**—This section presents case studies demonstrating how Cisco IOS Software is configured to perform typical NAT functions.

- **Troubleshooting NAT**—This section examines various methods and tools for troubleshooting Cisco NAT.

Network Address Translation

Network address translation (NAT) is a function by which IP addresses within a packet are replaced with different IP addresses. This function is most commonly performed by either routers or firewalls. This chapter, of course, focuses on NAT within routers.

NOTE   The acronym NAT is used interchangeably to mean *network address translation* and *network address translator* (software that runs the NAT function).

Operation of NAT

NAT is described in RFC 1631.[1] The original intention of NAT was, like classless interdomain routing (CIDR), to slow the depletion of available IP address space by allowing many private IP addresses to be represented by some smaller number of public IP addresses. Since that time, users have found NAT to be a useful tool for network migrations and mergers, server load sharing, and creating "virtual servers." This section examines all these applications, but first describes the basics of NAT functionality and terminology.

Basic NAT Concepts

Figure 4-1 depicts a simple NAT function. Device A has an IP address that belongs to the private range specified by RFC 1918, whereas device B has a public IP address. When device A sends a packet to device B, the packet passes through a router that is running NAT. The NAT replaces device A's private address (192.168.2.23) in the source address field with a public address (203.10.5.23) that can be routed across the Internet, and forwards the packet. When device B sends a reply to device A, the destination address of the packet is 203.10.5.23. This packet again passes through the NAT router, and the destination address is replaced with device A's private address.

Figure 4-1 *The NAT Router Replaces the Private Address of Device A (192.168.2.23) with a Publicly Routable Address (203.10.5.23)*

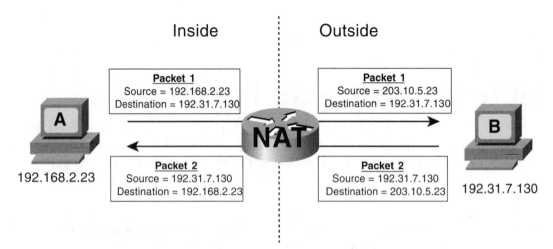

NAT is transparent to the end systems involved in the translation. In Figure 4-1, device A knows only that its IP address is 192.168.2.23; it is unaware of the 203.10.5.23 address. Device B, on the other hand, thinks the address of device A is 203.10.5.23; it knows nothing about the 192.168.2.23 address. That address is "hidden" from device B.

NAT can hide addresses in both directions. In Figure 4-2, NAT is performed on the addresses of both device A and device B. Device A thinks device B's address is 172.16.80.91, when in fact device B's real address is 192.31.7.130. You can see that the NAT router is translating both the source and destination addresses in both directions to support this address scheme.

Cisco NAT devices divide their world into the *inside* and the *outside*. Typically the inside is a private enterprise or ISP, and the outside is the public Internet or an Internet-facing service provider. Additionally, a Cisco NAT device classifies addresses as either *local* or *global*. A local address is an address that is seen by devices on the inside, and a global address is an address that is seen by devices on the outside. Given these four terms, an address may be one of four types:

- **Inside local (IL)**—Addresses assigned to inside devices. These addresses are not advertised to the outside.

- **Inside global (IG)**—Addresses by which inside devices are known to the outside.

- **Outside global (OG)**—Addresses assigned to outside devices. These addresses are not advertised to the inside.

- **Outside local (OL)**—Addresses by which outside devices are known to the inside.

Figure 4-2   *The NAT Router Is Translating Both the Source and Destination Addresses in Both Directions*

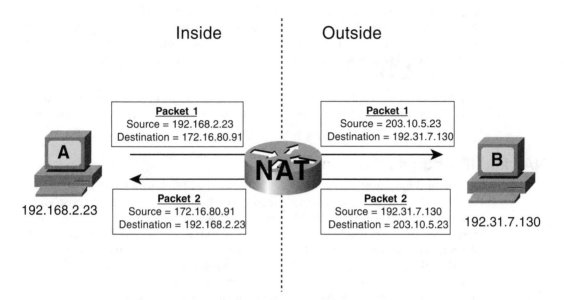

In Figure 4-2, device A is on the inside and device B is on the outside. 192.168.2.23 is an inside local address, and 203.10.5.23 is an inside global address. 172.16.80.91 is an outside local address, and 192.31.7.130 is an outside global address.

IG addresses are mapped to IL addresses, and OL addresses are mapped to OG addresses. The NAT device tracks these mappings in an *address translation table*. Example 4-1 shows the address translation table for the NAT router in Figure 4-2. This table contains three entries. Reading the entries from the bottom up, the first entry maps OL address 172.16.80.91 to the OG address 192.31.7.130. The next entry maps the IG address 203.10.5.23 to the IL address 192.168.2.23. These two entries are static, created when the router was configured to translate the specified addresses. The last (top) entry maps the inside addresses to the outside addresses. This entry is dynamic and was created when device A first sent a packet to device B.

Example 4-1   *The Address Translation Table of the NAT Router in Figure 4-2*

```
NATrouter#show ip nat translations
Pro Inside global     Inside local      Outside local     Outside global
--- 203.10.5.23       192.168.2.23      172.16.80.91      192.31.7.130
--- 203.10.5.23       192.168.2.23      ...               ...
... ...               ...               172.16.80.91      192.31.7.130
NATrouter#
```

As the preceding paragraph demonstrates, a NAT entry may be *static* or *dynamic*. Static entries are one-to-one mappings of local addresses and global addresses. That is, a unique local address is mapped to a unique global address. Dynamic entries may be many-to-one or one-to-many. A many-to-one mapping means that many addresses can be mapped to a single address. In a one-to-many mapping, a single address can be mapped to one of several available addresses.

The following sections describe several common applications of NAT and demonstrate more clearly how static NAT and the various implementations of dynamic NAT operate.

NAT and IP Address Conservation

The original mission of NAT was to slow the depletion of IP addresses, and this is the focus of RFC 1631. The core assumption of the concept is that only some of an enterprise's hosts will be connected to the Internet at any one time. Some devices (print servers and DHCP servers, for example) never require connectivity outside of the enterprise at all. As a result, the enterprise can be addressed out of the private RFC 1918 address space, and a significantly smaller number of uniquely assigned public addresses are placed in a pool on a NAT at the edge of the enterprise, as demonstrated in Figure 4-3. The non-unique private addresses are IL addresses, and the public addresses are IG addresses.

Figure 4-3   *In This NAT Design, a Pool of Public IP Addresses Serves a Private Address Space 8 Times as Large*

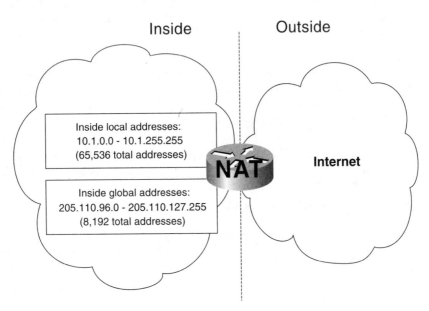

Inside   Outside

Inside local addresses:
10.1.0.0 - 10.1.255.255
(65,536 total addresses)

Inside global addresses:
205.110.96.0 - 205.110.127.255
(8,192 total addresses)

NAT

Internet

When an inside device sends a packet to the Internet, the NAT dynamically selects a public address from the inside global address pool and maps it to the device's inside local address. This mapping is entered into the NAT table. For instance, Example 4-2 shows that three inside devices from the enterprise in Figure 4-3—10.1.1.1.20, 10.1.197.64, and 10.1.63.148— have sent packets through the NAT. Three addresses from the IG pool— 205.110.96.2, 205.110.96.3, and 205.110.96.1, respectively—have been mapped to the IL addresses.

Example 4-2 *Three Addresses from the Inside Local Address Space in Figure 4-3 Have Been Dynamically Mapped to Three Addresses from the Inside Global Address Pool*

```
NATrouter#show ip nat translations
Pro Inside global      Inside local      Outside local      Outside global
--- 205.110.96.2       10.1.1.20         ---                ---
--- 205.110.96.3       10.1.197.64       ---                ---
--- 205.110.96.1       10.1.63.148       ---                ---
NATrouter#
```

The destination address of any packet from an outside device responding to the inside device is the IG address. Therefore, the original mapping must be held in the NAT table for some length of time to ensure that all packets of a particular connection are translated consistently. Holding an entry in the NAT table for some period also reduces subsequent lookups when the same device regularly sends packets to the same or multiple outside destinations.

When an entry is first placed into the NAT table, a timer is started; the period of the timer is the *translation timeout*. Each time the entry is used to translate the source or destination address of a subsequent packet, the timer is reset. If the timer expires, the entry is removed from the NAT table and the dynamically assigned address is returned to the pool. Cisco's default translation timeout is 86,400 seconds (24 hours); you can change this with the command **ip nat translation timeout**.

NOTE   The default translation timeout varies according to protocol. Table 4-3, later in this chapter, displays these values.

This particular NAT application is a many-to-one application, because for each IG address in the pool, many IL addresses could be mapped to it. In the case of Figure 4-3, an 8-to-1 relationship exists. This is a familiar concept—telcos use it when they design switches and trunks that can handle only a portion of their total subscribers, and airlines use it when they overbook flights. Think of it as statistically multiplexing IL addresses to IG addresses. The risk, as with telcos and airlines, is in underestimating peak usage periods and running out of capacity.

No restrictions apply to the ratio of the size of the local address space and the size of the address pool. In Figure 4-3, the IL range and/or the IG range can be made larger or smaller to fit specific requirements. For example, the IL range 10.0.0.0/8, comprising more than 16 million addresses, can be mapped to a four-address pool of 205.110.96.1–205.110.96.4 or smaller. The real limitation is not the number of possible addresses in the specified IL range, but the number of actual devices using addresses in the range. If only four devices are using addresses out of the 10.0.0.0/8 range, no more than four addresses are needed in the pool. If there are 500,000 devices on the inside, you need a bigger pool.

When an address from the dynamic pool is in the NAT table, it is not available to be mapped to any other address. If all the pool addresses are used up, subsequent inside packets attempting to pass through the NAT router cannot be translated and are dropped. Therefore, it is important to ensure that the NAT pool is large enough, and that the translation timeout is small enough, so that the dynamic address pool never runs dry.

Almost all enterprises have some systems, such as mail, Web, and FTP servers, that must be accessible from the outside. The addresses of these systems must remain the same; otherwise outside hosts will not know from one time to the next how to reach them. Therefore, you cannot use dynamic NAT with these systems; their IL addresses must be statically mapped to IG addresses. The IG addresses used for static mapping must not be included in the dynamic address pool; although the IG address is permanently entered into the NAT table, the same address can still be chosen from the dynamic pool, creating an address ambiguity.

The NAT technique described in this section can be very useful for scaling a growing enterprise. Rather than repeatedly requesting more address space from the addressing authorities or the ISP, you can move the existing public addresses into the NAT pool and renumber the inside devices from a private address space. Depending on the size of the organization and the structure of its existing address allocations, you can perform the renumbering as a single project or as an incremental migration.

NAT and ISP Migration

One of the drawbacks of CIDR, as discussed in Chapter 2, "Introduction to Border Gateway Protocol 4," is that it can increase the difficulty of changing Internet service providers. If you have been assigned an address block that belongs to ISP1, and you want to change to ISP2, you almost always have to return ISP1's addresses and acquire a new address range from ISP2. This return can mean a painful and costly re-addressing project within your enterprise.

TIP   It cannot be overemphasized that the pain and expense of an address migration is sharply reduced when the addressing scheme is well designed in the first place.

Suppose you are a subscriber of ISP1, which has a CIDR block of 205.113.48.0/20, and the ISP has assigned you an address space of 205.113.50.0/23. You then decide to switch your Internet service to ISP2, which has a CIDR block of 207.36.64.0/19. ISP2 assigns you a new address space of 207.36.76.0/23. Instead of renumbering your inside systems, you can use NAT (see Figure 4-4). The 205.113.50.0/23 address space has been returned to ISP1, but you continue to use this space for the IL addresses. Although the addresses are from the public address space, you can no longer use them to represent your internetwork to the public Internet. You use the 207.36.76.0/23 space from ISP2 as the IG addresses and map (statically or dynamically) the IL addresses to these IG addresses.

Figure 4-4   *This Enterprise Has an Inside Local Address Space That Belongs to ISP1 But Is a Subscriber of ISP2. It Uses NAT to Translate the IL Addresses to IG Addresses Assigned Out of ISP2's CIDR Block*

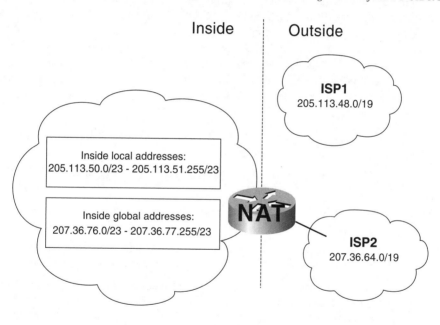

The danger in using a scheme such as this is in the possibility that any of the inside local addresses might be leaked to the public Internet. If this were to happen, the leaked address would conflict with ISP1, which has legal possession of the addresses. If ISP2 is using appropriately paranoid route filtering, such a mistake should not cause leakage to the Internet. As Chapter 2 emphasized, however, you should *never* make the assumption that an AS-external peer is filtering properly. Therefore, you must take extreme care to ensure that all the IL addresses are translated before packets are allowed into ISP2.

Another problem arising from this scheme is that ISP1 will probably reassign the 205.113.50.0/23 range to another customer. That customer is then unreachable to you. Suppose, for example, that a host on your network wants to send a packet to newbie@ISP1.com. DNS translates the address of that destination as 205.113.50.100, so the host uses that address. Unfortunately, that address is interpreted as belonging to your local internet and is either misrouted or is dropped as unreachable.

The moral of the story is that the migration scheme described in this section is very useful on a temporary basis, to reduce the complexity of the immediate move. Ultimately, however, you should still re-address your internet with private addresses.

NAT and Multihomed Autonomous Systems

Another shortcoming of CIDR is that multihoming to different service providers becomes more difficult. Figure 4-5 recaps the problem as discussed in Chapter 2. A subscriber is multihomed to ISP1 and ISP2 and has a CIDR block that is a subset of ISP1's block. To establish correct communication with the Internet, both ISP1 and ISP2 must advertise the subscriber's specific address space of 205.113.50.0/23. If ISP2 does not advertise this address, all the subscriber's incoming traffic passes through ISP1. And if ISP2 advertises 205.113.50.0/23, whereas ISP1 advertises only its own CIDR block, all the subscriber's incoming traffic matches the more-specific route and passes through ISP2. This poses several problems:

- ISP1 must "punch a hole" in its CIDR block, which probably means modifying the filters and policies on many routers.

- ISP2 must advertise part of a competitor's address space, an action that both ISPs are likely to find objectionable.

- Advertising the subscriber's more-specific address space represents a small reduction in the effectiveness of CIDR in controlling the size of Internet routing tables.

- Some national service providers do not accept prefixes longer than /19, meaning the subscriber's route through ISP2 will be unknown to some portion of the Internet.

Figure 4-6 shows ways that NAT can help solve the problem of CIDR in a multihomed environment. Translation is configured on the router connecting to ISP2, and the IG address pool is a CIDR block assigned by ISP2. ISP2 no longer advertises an ISP1 address space, so it is no longer necessary for ISP1 to advertise the subscriber's more-specific aggregate. Hosts within the subscriber's enterprise can access the Internet either by selecting the closest edge router or by some established policy. The IL address of the hosts' packets will be the same, no matter which router they pass through; if packets are sent to ISP2, however, the address is translated. So from the perspective of the Internet, the source addresses of packets from the subscriber vary according to which ISP has forwarded the packets.

Figure 4-5 *Because the Multihomed Subscriber's CIDR Block Is a Subset of ISP1's CIDR Block, Both ISP1 and ISP2 Must Advertise the More-Specific Aggregate*

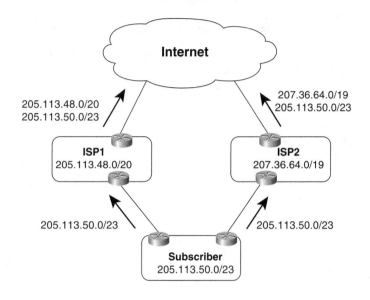

Figure 4-6 *NAT Is Used to Resolve the CIDR Problem Depicted in Figure 4-5*

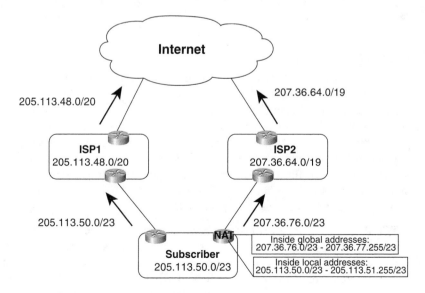

Figure 4-7 shows a more efficient design. NAT is implemented on both edge routers and the CIDR blocks from each ISP become the IG address pools of the respective NATs. The IL addresses are from the private 10.0.0.0 address space. This enterprise can change ISPs with relative ease, needing only to reconfigure the IG address pools when the ISP changes.

Figure 4-7   *The IL Addresses of This Enterprise Have No Relationship to Any ISP; All ISP CIDR Blocks Are Assigned to NAT Inside Global Address Pools*

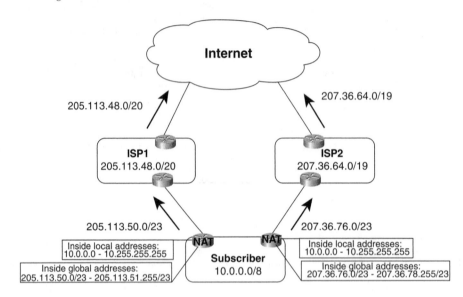

Port Address Translation

The many-to-one applications of NAT discussed so far have involved a statistical multiplexing of a large range of addresses into a smaller pool of addresses. However, there is a one-to-one mapping of individual addresses. When an address from an inside global pool is mapped to an inside local address, for instance, that IG address cannot be mapped to any other address until the first mapping is cleared. However, there is a specialized function of NAT that allows many addresses to be mapped to a single address at the same time. Cisco calls this function *port address translation* (PAT). The same function is known in other circles as *network address and port translation* (NAPT) or *IP masquerading*. It is also sometimes referred to as *address overloading*.

A TCP/IP session is not identified as a packet exchange between two IP addresses, but as an exchange between two IP sockets. A socket is an (address, port) *tuple*. For example, a Telnet session might consist of a packet exchange between 192.168.5.2, 23 and 172.16.100.6, 1026. PAT translates both the IP address and the port. Packets from different addresses can be translated to a common address, but to different ports of that address, and therefore can share the same address. Figure 4-8 shows how PAT works.

Figure 4-8   *By Translating Both the IP Address and the Associated Port, PAT Allows Many Hosts to Simultaneously Use a Single Global Address*

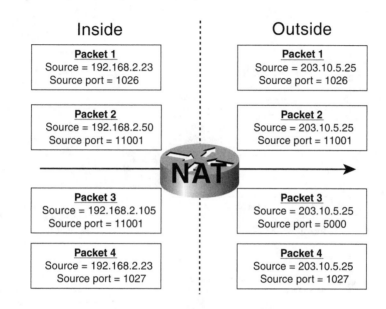

Four packets with inside local addresses arrive at the NAT. Notice that packets 1 and 4 are from the same address but different source ports. Packets 2 and 3 are from different addresses but have the same source port. The source addresses of all four packets are translated to the same inside global address, but the packets remain unique because they each have a different source port. By translating ports, approximately 32,000 different inside local sockets can be translated to a single inside global address. As a result, PAT is a very useful application for small office/home office (SOHO) installations, where several devices might share a single assigned address on a single connection to an ISP.

NAT and TCP Load Distribution

You can use NAT to represent multiple, identical servers as having a single address. In Figure 4-9, devices on the outside reach a server at address 206.35.91.10. In actuality, there are four mirrored servers on the inside, and the NAT distributes sessions among them in a round-robin fashion. Notice that the destination addresses of packets 1 through 4, each from a different source, are translated to servers 1 through 4. Packet 5, representing a session from yet another source, is translated to server 1.

Obviously, the accessible contents of the four servers in Figure 4-9 must be identical. A host accessing the server farm might hit server 2 at one time and server 4 another time. It must appear to the host that it has hit the same server on both occasions.

Figure 4-9   *TCP Packets Sent to a Server Farm, Represented by the Single Address 206.35.91.10, Are Translated Round-Robin to the Actual Addresses of the Four Identical Servers*

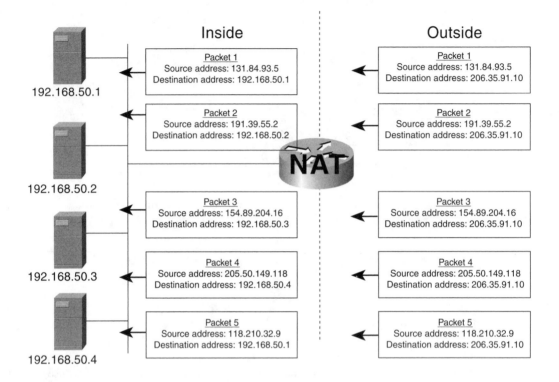

This scheme is similar to DNS-based load sharing, in which a single name is resolved round-robin to several IP addresses. The disadvantage of DNS-based load sharing is that when a host receives the name/address resolution, the host caches it. Future sessions are sent to the same address, reducing the effectiveness of the load sharing. NAT-based load sharing performs a translation only when a new TCP connection is opened from the outside, so the sessions are more likely to be distributed evenly. In NAT TCP load balancing, non-TCP packets pass through the NAT untranslated.

It is important to note that NAT-based load balancing, like DNS-based load balancing, is not robust. NAT has no way to know when one of the servers goes down, so it continues to translate packets to that address. As a result, a failed or offline server can cause some traffic to the server farm to be black-holed.

NAT and Virtual Servers

NAT also can allow the distribution of services to different addresses, while giving the appearance that the services are all reachable at one address (see Figure 4-10).

Figure 4-10 *You Can Configure NAT to Translate Incoming Packets to Different Addresses Based on the Destination Port*

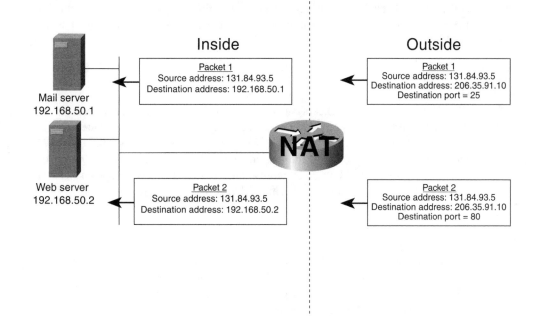

In Figure 4-10, the enterprise has a mail server at the local address 192.168.50.1 and an HTTP server at the local address 192.168.50.2. Both servers have a global address of 206.35.91.10. When a host from the outside sends a packet to the inside, the NAT examines the destination port in addition to the destination address. In Figure 4-10, a host has sent a packet to 206.35.91.10 with a destination port of 25, indicating mail. The NAT translates this packet's destination address to the mail server's, 192.168.50.1. A second packet from the same host has a destination port of 80, indicating HTTP. The NAT translates this packet's destination address to the Web server's, 192.168.50.2.

NAT Issues

Although the general applications of NAT presented so far are straightforward, the underlying functions of NAT can be less so, because of the following two factors:

- The general processing of IP and TCP headers
- The nature of some specific protocols and applications

Changing the content of an IP address or TCP port can change the meaning of some of the other fields, especially the checksum. And many protocols and applications carry the IP address or information based on the IP address within their data fields. Changing an IP address in the header could change the meaning of the encapsulated data, possibly breaking the application. This section examines the most common issues surrounding the operation of NAT.

Header Checksums

The checksum of an IP packet is calculated over the entire header. Therefore, if the source or destination IP address or both change, the checksum must be recalculated. The same is true of the checksum in the TCP header. This number is calculated over the TCP header and data, and also over a pseudo-header that includes the source and destination IP addresses. Therefore, if an IP address or a port number changes, the TCP checksum must also change. Cisco's NAT performs these checksum recalculations.

Fragmentation

Recall from the section "NAT and Virtual Servers" that you can use NAT to translate to different local addresses based on the destination port. A packet with a destination port of 25 can be translated to a particular IL address, for example, whereas a packet with some other destination port numbers can be translated to other addresses. However, what if the packet destined for port 25 becomes fragmented at some point in the network before it reaches the NAT? The TCP or UDP header, containing the source and destination port numbers, is in the first fragment only. If that fragment is merely translated and forwarded, the NAT has no way to tell whether the subsequent fragments must be translated.

IP makes no guarantees that packets are delivered in order. So it's quite possible that the first fragment might not even arrive at the NAT before later fragments. You must design NAT to handle such eventualities.

Cisco's NAT keeps stateful information about fragments. If a first fragment is translated, information is kept so that subsequent fragments are translated the same way. If a fragment arrives before the first fragment, the NAT has no choice but to hold the fragment until the first fragment arrives and can be examined.

Encryption

Cisco's NAT can change the IP address information carried within the data fields of many applications, as you will see shortly. If the data fields are encrypted, however, NAT has no way of reading the data. Therefore, for NAT to function, neither the IP addresses nor any information derived from them (such as the TCP header checksum) can be encrypted.

Another concern is virtual private networks (VPNs) using, for example, IPSec. With certain modes of IPSec, if an IP address is changed in an IPSec packet, the IPSec becomes meaningless and the VPN is broken. When any sort of encryption is used, you must place the NAT on the secure side rather than in the encrypted path.

Security

Some view NAT as a part of a security plan, because it hides the details of the inside network. A translated host may appear on the Internet one day with one address and on another day with a different address. But this should be considered very weak security at best. Although NAT might slow an attacker who wants to hit a particular host, forcing him to play a sort of shell game with IP addresses, it will not stop any determined and knowledgeable aggressor. And worse, NAT does nothing to prevent such common attacks as denial of service or session hijacking.

Protocol-Specific Issues

NAT should be transparent to the end systems that send packets through it. However, many applications—both commercial applications and applications that are part of the TCP/IP protocol suite—use the IP addresses. Information within the data field may be based on an IP address, or an IP address itself may be carried in the data field. If NAT translates an address in the IP header without being aware of the effects on the data, the application breaks.

Table 4-1 lists the applications that Cisco's NAT implementation supports. For the applications listed as carrying IP address information in the application data, NAT is aware of those applications and makes the appropriate corrections to the data. Note that the table is current as of this writing. If you are implementing NAT, you should check the Cisco Web site or TAC for application support that might have been added recently.

Table 4-1   *IP Traffic Types/Applications Supported by Cisco NAT*

Traffic Types/Applications Supported
Any TCP/UDP traffic that does not carry source and/or destination IP addresses in the application data stream
HTTP
TFTP
Telnet
archie
finger
NTP

continues

Table 4-1 *IP Traffic Types/Applications Supported by Cisco NAT (Continued)*

Traffic Types/Applications Supported (Continued)
NFS
rlogin, rsh, rcp
Traffic Types/Applications Supported with IP Addresses in Their Data Stream
ICMP
FTP (including PORT and PASV)
NetBIOS over TCP/IP (datagram, name, and session services)
Progressive Networks' RealAudio
White Pines' CuSeeMe
Xing Technologies' StreamWorks
DNS A and PTR queries and responses
H.323/NetMeeting [12.0(1)/12.0(1)T and later]
VDOLive [11.3(4)/11.3(4)T and later]
Vxtreme [11.3(4)/11.3(4)T and later]
IP Multicast [12.0(1)T] (source address translation only)
Traffic Types/Applications Not Supported
Routing table updates
DNS zone transfers
BOOTP
talk, ntalk
SNMP
NetShow

Table 4-1 is taken directly from the Cisco white paper "Cisco IOS Network Address Translation (NAT) Packaging Update," available at www.cisco.com.

ICMP

Some ICMP messages include the IP header of the packet that caused the message to be generated. Table 4-2 lists these message types. Cisco's NAT checks the listed message types; if IP information in the message matches a translated IP address in the header, the NAT also translates the IP information. Additionally, the checksum in the ICMP header is corrected in the same way it is corrected for TCP and UDP.

Table 4-2   *ICMP Message Types That Carry IP Header Information in the Message Body*

Message	Type Number
Destination Unreachable	3
Source Quench	4
Redirect	5
Time Exceeded	11
Parameter Problem	12

DNS

One of the core functions of any TCP/IP internetwork, and especially of the Internet, is the Domain Name System (DNS). If systems cannot get DNS queries and responses across a NAT, DNS can become complicated. Figure 4-11 shows ways you can implement DNS servers around a NAT that cannot translate DNS packets.

The NAT in Figure 4-11 translates in both directions—outside hosts are made to appear to the inside as if they are on the 10.0.0.0 network, and inside hosts are made to appear to the outside as if they are on the 204.13.55.0 network. DNS servers reside on both the inside and the outside, and each contains resource records that map names to the addresses appropriate for its side of the NAT.

Figure 4-11   *If NAT Does Not Support DNS, Name Servers Must Be Implemented on Both Sides of the NAT, Reflecting the Name-to-Address Mappings Appropriate for That Side of the NAT*

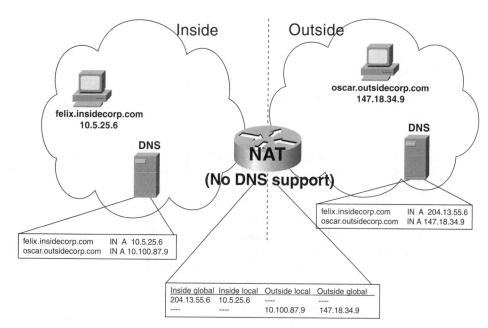

A problem with this approach is the difficulty of maintaining inconsistent resource records on the two DNS servers. A more serious problem is that the NAT mappings must be static, to match the mappings in the DNS resource records. Pooled NAT does not work, because the mappings change dynamically. A better approach, and one that is supported by Cisco's implementation of NAT, is to have the NAT support translation of DNS queries.

Although a detailed examination of DNS operations is beyond the scope of this book, a short review of the key concepts will help you understand where DNS can coexist with NAT and where it cannot. You are familiar with the structure of domain names; for example, the name *cisco.com* describes a second-level domain (*cisco*) under the top-level domain *com*. All the IP namespace is organized in a tree structure, with host names connected to increasingly higher-level domains, until all domains meet at the root.

NOTE   An excellent text on DNS is Paul Albitz and Cricket Liu's *DNS and BIND* (O'Reilly and Associates, 1992).

Name servers store information about some part of the domain namespace. The information in a particular name server may be for an entire domain, some portion of a domain, or even multiple domains. The portion of the namespace for which a server contains information is the server's *zone*.

DNS servers are either *primary* or *secondary* servers. A primary DNS server acquires its zone information from files stored locally in the host on which the server is running and is said to be *authoritative* for its zone. A secondary DNS server acquires its zone information from a primary DNS server. It does this by downloading the zone files of the primary in a process called a *zone transfer*.

Because a zone transfer is a file transfer, a NAT cannot parse the address information out of the file. Even if it could, zone files are often very large, which would put a significant performance burden on the NAT device. Therefore, a primary and secondary DNS server for the same zone cannot be located on opposite sides of a NAT, because the information in zone files will not be translated during a zone transfer.

The information within zone files is made up of entries called *resource records* (RR). There are several types of resource records, such as Start-of-Authority (SOA) records, specifying the authoritative server for the domain; Canonical Name (CNAME) records, for recording aliases; Mail Exchange (MX) records, specifying mail servers for a domain; and Windows Internet Name Server (WINS) records, used in some Windows NT name servers. The two RRs of importance to NAT are Address (A) records, which map host names to IP addresses, and Pointer (PTR) records, which map IP addresses to names. When a host must find an IP address for a particular name, its DNS resolver queries a DNS server's A records. If the host wants to find a name that goes with a particular IP address (a reverse lookup), it queries the server's PTR records.

Figure 4-12 shows the format of a DNS message, which carries both the queries from hosts and the responses from servers. The header, like most headers, is a group of fields carrying information for the management and processing of the message. The header information significant to NAT includes a bit specifying whether the message is a query or a response, and fields specifying the number of RRs contained in each of the other four sections.

Figure 4-12 *The DNS Message Format*

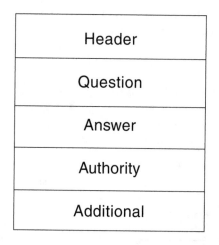

The Question section is a group of fields that, as the name clearly indicates, asks a question of the server. Among other things, the question may contain a name to which the server must try to match an address out of its A records, or the question may contain an address to which the server must try to match a name from its PTR records. Every DNS message contains a question, and a message never contains more than one question.

The Answer section contains RRs that, of course, answer the question. The answer may list one or many RRs, or none at all. The Authority and Additional sections contain information that is supplemental to the answer, and may also be empty.

When a DNS packet passes through a Cisco NAT, the Question, Answer, and Additional sections are examined. If the message is a query for an IP address to match a name, no addresses are yet included, and the Answer and Additional sections are empty, so no translation takes place. The response to the query, however, contains one or more A RRs in the Answer section and possibly in the Additional section. NAT searches its table for a match to the address in these records and translates the addresses in the message if it finds a match. If it does not find a match, the message is dropped.

If the DNS message is a query for a name to match a known IP address (a reverse lookup), NAT examines its table for a match to the address in the Question section. Again, either a match is found and the address is translated, or the message is dropped. The response to the query contains one or more PTR RRs in the Answer section and possibly in the Additional section, and the addresses in these records also are either translated or the message is dropped.

In summary, remember the following two facts when working with DNS and NAT:

- DNS A and PTR queries can cross a Cisco NAT, so a host on one side of a NAT can query a DNS server on the other side of the NAT.

- DNS zone transfers cannot cross a Cisco NAT, so primary and secondary DNS servers for the same zone cannot reside on opposite sides of the NAT.

FTP

The File Transfer Protocol (FTP) is something of an unusual application protocol in that it uses two connections (see Figure 4-13). The control connection is initiated by the host and is used to exchange FTP commands with the server. The data connection is initiated by the server and is used for the actual file transfer.

Figure 4-13 *An FTP Session Consists of Two Separate TCP Connections; the Host Initiates the Control Connection, and the Server Initiates the Data Connection*

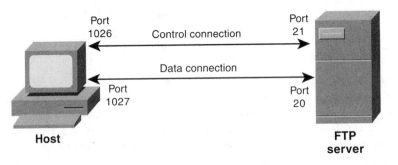

The sequence of events for setting up an FTP session and transferring a file is as follows:

1 The FTP server performs a passive open (that is, begins listening for a connection request) on TCP port 21, the control port.

2 The host selects ephemeral (temporary) ports for the control connection and for the data connection. In Figure 4-13, these are ports 1026 and 1027, respectively.

3 The host performs a passive open on the data port.

4 The host performs an active open for the control connection, creating a TCP connection between its control port (1026 in Figure 4-13) and the server's port 21.

5 To transfer the file, the host sends a **PORT** command across the control connection, telling the server to open a data connection on the host's data port (1027 in Figure 4-13).

6 The server performs an active open for the data connection, creating a TCP connection between its port 20 and the host's data port.

7 The requested file is transferred across the data connection.

This sequence of events presents a problem for some secured networks. Specifically, it is a common security practice to configure a firewall or access list to disallow the initiation of connections from the outside to random ports. This is done by looking for a cleared ACK or RST bit in the TCP header, indicating a connection request. You can see that when the FTP server tries to establish a connection to the host's ephemeral port across such a firewall, the connection is denied.

NOTE   The **established** keyword tells a Cisco access list to look for a cleared ACK or RST bit in the TCP header.

To overcome this difficulty, the host can issue a **PASV** command rather than a **PORT** command to open the data connection. This command asks the server to passively open a data port and to inform the host of the port number. The host then performs the active open of the data connection to the server port. Because the connection request is outgoing through the firewall rather than incoming, the connection is not blocked.

The significance of all this to NAT is that the **PORT** and **PASV** commands carry not only the port numbers but also the IP addresses. If the messages cross a NAT, these addresses must be translated. To make matters worse, the IP address is encoded in ASCII in its dotted-decimal form. This means that the IP address in the FTP message is not of a fixed length, as it would be if it were a 32-bit binary representation. For example, the address 10.1.5.4 is eight ASCII characters (including the dots), whereas 204.192.14.237 is 14 ASCII characters. So when the address is translated, the message size can change.

If the size of the translated FTP message remains the same, the Cisco NAT recalculates only the TCP checksum (in addition to any operations performed on the IP header). If the translation results in a smaller message, the NAT pads the message with ACSII zeros to make it the same size as the original message.

The problem becomes more complicated if the translated message is larger than the original message, because the TCP sequence and acknowledgment numbers are based directly on the length of the TCP segments. Cisco's NAT keeps a table to track the changes in SEQ and ACK numbers. When an FTP message is translated, an entry is made into the table containing the source and destination IP addresses and ports, the initial sequence number, the delta for the sequence numbers, and a time stamp. This information is used to correctly adjust the SEQ and ACK numbers in the FTP messages. It can be deleted after the FTP connection is closed.

SMTP

Simple Mail Transfer Protocol (SMTP) messages normally contain domain names, not IP addresses. However, they can use IP addresses rather than names when requesting mail transfers. Therefore, Cisco NAT examines the appropriate fields within SMTP messages and makes translations when IP addresses are found.

Unlike SMTP, which is used for uploading mail and for transferring mail between servers, the Post Office Protocol (POP) and the Internet Message Access Protocol (IMAP) are used only for downloading messages from a mail server to a client. Both protocols use only host names, never IP addresses, within the message bodies. Therefore, these protocols do not require special examination when crossing a NAT.

SNMP

Simple Network Management Protocol (SNMP) uses a rich and widely varying set of Management Information Bases (MIBs) to manage a wide variety of networking devices. In addition to the many Internet-standard MIB groups, a vast number of private MIBs have been created for the management of vendor-specific devices.

You can deduce from this very basic description that many MIBs can contain one or more IP addresses. Because of the many messages, formats, and variables possible with SNMP, NAT cannot easily examine the contents of an SNMP message for IP addresses. Therefore, NAT does not support the translation of IP addresses within SNMP messages.

Routing Protocols

IP routing protocols present something of the same problem presented by SNMP. There are many IP routing protocols, each with its own packet formats and its own operational characteristics. Therefore, NAT cannot translate IP routing protocol packets. A NAT router can run a routing protocol on the inside interfaces and a routing protocol on the outside interfaces, but no routing protocol packets should transit a NAT boundary in which the advertised addresses change, either through a single protocol or by redistribution. This restriction does not present much of a problem, because NAT routers will be located on the edge of a routing domain, and therefore can usually use a default address or a small set of summary addresses.

Traceroute

Route tracing utilities can vary somewhat. Some, such as Cisco's **trace** command, use ICMP packets. Others, such as tracert under Microsoft Windows 95, use UDP packets. But the basic functionality is the same: Packets are sent to a destination with an incrementally increasing TTL, and the addresses of the intermediate systems sending ICMP Time Exceeded error messages are recorded. You saw in the earlier section on ICMP that Time Exceeded messages are translated by Cisco NAT, so routes can be traced through NAT.

The NAT in Figure 4-14 is translating in both directions. The router jerry.insidenet.com has an IP address of 10.1.16.50 and is translated to an IG address of 204.13.55.6. The device berferd.outsidenet.com has an address of 147.18.34.9 and is translated to an OL address of 10.2.1.3. Therefore, the OL address is the address by which jerry knows berferd.

Figure 4-14 *NAT Is Translating in Both Directions*

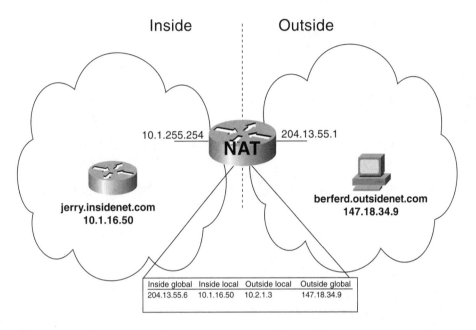

When jerry performs a trace to berferd, the destination is 10.2.1.3. Example 4-3 shows that the first hop is the NAT router. The NAT then translates the destination address to 147.18.34.9 and the source address to 204.13.55.6 and forwards the packet out its outside interface. When berferd receives the trace packet, which is sent to a bogus port, it responds with an ICMP Port Unreachable error packet. That packet has a destination of 204.13.55.6 and a source of 147.18.34.9. NAT translates these addresses to a destination of 10.1.16.50 and a source of 10.2.1.3, which is what jerry receives. Therefore, the trace is successful, but the inside device sees only the outside local address.

Example 4-3 *A Trace from jerry.insidenet.com to berferd.outsidenet.com in Figure 4-14 Shows That the Trace Is Successful, and NAT "Hides" the Outside Global Address from the Inside*

```
Jerry#trace berferd.outsidenet.com

Type escape sequence to abort.
Tracing the route to berferd.outsidenet.com (10.2.1.3)

  1 10.1.255.254 8 msec 8 msec 4 msec
  2 berferd.outsidenet.com (10.2.1.3) 12 msec *  8 msec
Jerry#
```

Configuring NAT

The first step in configuring NAT is to designate the inside and outside interfaces. Beyond that, the configuration depends on whether you are configuring static NAT or dynamic NAT. For static NAT, you just create the appropriate mapping entries in the NAT table. For dynamic NAT, you create a pool of addresses to be used in the translation and create access lists to identify the addresses to be translated. A single command then ties the pool and the access list together.

This section demonstrates the most common configuration techniques for NAT in its most common uses.

Case Study: Static NAT

In Figure 4-15, the inside network is addressed out of the 10.0.0.0 address space. Two of the devices, hosts A and C, must be able to communicate with the outside world. Those two devices are translated to the public addresses 204.15.87.1/24 and 204.15.87.2/24.

Example 4-4 shows the configuration to implement NAT at Mazatlan.

Figure 4-15 *The Inside Local Addresses of Devices A and C Are Statically Translated to Inside Global Addresses by the NAT Process in Router Mazatlan*

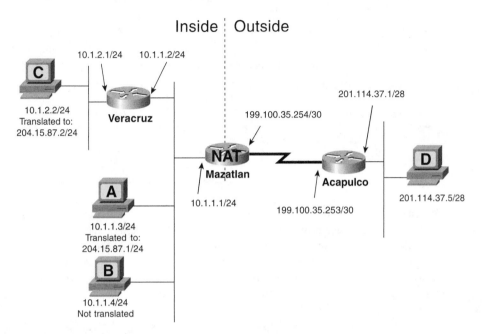

Example 4-4 *Implementing Static NAT at Router Mazatlan in Figure 4-15*

```
interface Ethernet0
 ip address 10.1.1.1 255.255.255.0
 ip nat inside
!
interface Serial1
 no ip address
 encapsulation frame-relay
!
interface Serial1.705 point-to-point
 ip address 199.100.35.254 255.255.255.252
 ip nat outside
 frame-relay interface-dlci 705
!
router ospf 100
 network 10.1.1.1 0.0.0.0 area 0
 default-information originate
!
ip nat inside source static 10.1.2.2 204.15.87.2
ip nat inside source static 10.1.1.3 204.15.87.1
!
ip route 0.0.0.0 0.0.0.0 199.100.35.253
!
```

The router's E0 interface is designated as being on the inside with the **ip nat inside** command, and the Frame Relay subinterface S1.705 is designated as being on the outside with the **ip nat outside** command.

Next, the inside local addresses are mapped to inside global addresses with the **ip nat inside source static** commands. There are two of these commands, one for host C and one for host A. Example 4-5 shows the resulting NAT table.

Example 4-5 *The IL Addresses of Hosts C and A Are Statically Translated into IG Addresses*

```
Mazatlan#show ip nat translations
Pro Inside global     Inside local     Outside local     Outside global
--- 204.15.87.2       10.1.2.2         ---               ---
--- 204.15.87.1       10.1.1.3         ---               ---
Mazatlan#
```

When host A or C sends a packet to the outside, Mazatlan sees the source address in its NAT table and makes the appropriate translation. The router Acapulco has a route (in this case, a static route) to network 204.15.87.0 and has no knowledge of the 10.0.0.0 network. Therefore, Acapulco and host D can respond to packets from hosts A and C. If host B or router Veracruz sends a packet to host D, the packet is forwarded, but without any translation; when D responds to the untranslated IL address, Acapulco has no route and drops the packet, as demonstrated in Example 4-6.

Example 4-6 *When Host D in Figure 4-15 Responds to the Untranslated IL Address of Host B, Acapulco Has No Route to 10.0.0.0 and Drops the Packet*

```
Acapulco#debug ip icmp
ICMP packet debugging is on
Acapulco#
1d00h: ICMP: dst (10.1.1.4) host unreachable sent to 201.114.37.5
1d00h: ICMP: dst (10.1.1.4) host unreachable sent to 201.114.37.5
1d00h: ICMP: dst (10.1.1.4) host unreachable sent to 201.114.37.5
1d00h: ICMP: dst (10.1.1.4) host unreachable sent to 201.114.37.5
1d00h: ICMP: dst (10.1.1.4) host unreachable sent to 201.114.37.5
```

Outside global addresses can also be statically translated into outside local addresses. Suppose, for example, that the administrator of the inside network in Figure 4-15 wants host D to "appear" to be a part of the inside network—say, with an address of 10.1.3.1. Example 4-7 shows the NAT configuration for Mazatlan.

Example 4-7 *Configuring Mazatlan to Statically Translate Outside Global Addresses to Outside Local Addresses*

```
ip nat inside source static 10.1.1.3 204.15.87.1
ip nat inside source static 10.1.2.2 204.15.87.2
ip nat outside source static 201.114.37.5 10.1.3.1
```

The router's NAT configuration remains the same, except for the addition of the **ip nat outside source static** command, which in this case maps the OG address 201.114.37.5 to the OL address 10.1.3.1. Example 4-8 shows the resulting NAT table.

Example 4-8   *An OG-to-OL Mapping Is Added to the NAT Table by the Additional Command at Mazatlan*

```
Mazatlan#show ip nat translations
Pro Inside global     Inside local      Outside local     Outside global
--- 204.15.87.2       10.1.2.2          - - -             - - -
--- 204.15.87.1       10.1.1.3          - - -             - - -
--- ---               - - -             10.1.3.1          201.114.37.5
Mazatlan#
```

Although this case study has involved only static mappings, some dynamic mapping occurs after traffic has passed between host A and host D, and between host C and host D, as illustrated by Example 4-9. In each case, the inside mappings are automatically mapped to the outside mappings.

Example 4-9   *The Inside Addresses of Hosts A and C Have Been Automatically Mapped to the Outside Addresses of Host D*

```
Mazatlan#show ip nat translations
Pro Inside global     Inside local      Outside local     Outside global
--- 204.15.87.2       10.1.2.2          - - -             - - -
--- 204.15.87.1       10.1.1.3          - - -             - - -
--- ---               - - -             10.1.3.1          201.114.37.5
--- 204.15.87.1       10.1.1.3          10.1.3.1          201.114.37.5
--- 204.15.87.2       10.1.2.2          10.1.3.1          201.114.37.5
Mazatlan#
```

It is important to understand that this configuration does nothing to prevent a host on the inside from sending packets to host D's OG address rather than the OL address. In Figure 4-16, host A can successfully ping host D at either its OL address (10.1.3.1) or its OG address (201.114.37.5).

In fact, debugging output from host C in Example 4-10 reveals a bit more detail about the behavior of this network. Host C pings host D on its OG address, but the source address of the reply packets is host D's OL address. The ICMP Echo Request packet to destination 201.114.37.5 has passed through the NAT unchanged, but the ICMP Echo Reply packet, with a source address of 201.114.37.5, is translated by the NAT to the OL address.

Figure 4-16 *Host A Can Send Packets to Either the OL or OG Address of Host D*

```
Microsoft(R) Windows 98
   (C)Copyright Microsoft Corp 1981-1998.

C:\WINDOWS>ping 10.1.3.1

Pinging 10.1.3.1 with 32 bytes of data:

Reply from 10.1.3.1: bytes=32 time=13ms TTL=253
Reply from 10.1.3.1: bytes=32 time=6ms TTL=253
Reply from 10.1.3.1: bytes=32 time=6ms TTL=253
Reply from 10.1.3.1: bytes=32 time=6ms TTL=253

Ping statistics for 10.1.3.1:
    Packets: Sent = 4, Received = 4, Lost = 0 (0% loss),
Approximate round trip times in milli-seconds:
    Minimum = 6ms, Maximum =  13ms, Average =   7ms

C:\WINDOWS>ping 201.114.37.5

Pinging 201.114.37.5 with 32 bytes of data:

Reply from 201.114.37.5: bytes=32 time=5ms TTL=253
Reply from 201.114.37.5: bytes=32 time=4ms TTL=253
Reply from 201.114.37.5: bytes=32 time=4ms TTL=253
Reply from 201.114.37.5: bytes=32 time=5ms TTL=253

Ping statistics for 201.114.37.5:
    Packets: Sent = 4, Received = 4, Lost = 0 (0% loss),
Approximate round trip times in milli-seconds:
    Minimum = 4ms, Maximum =  5ms, Average =   4ms

C:\WINDOWS>
```

Example 4-10 *Although Host C Sends Pings to 201.114.37.5, NAT Causes the Replies to Have a Source Address of 10.1.3.1*

```
HostC#debug ip icmp
ICMP packet debugging is on
HostC#ping 201.114.37.5

Type escape sequence to abort.
Sending 5, 100-byte ICMP Echos to 201.114.37.5, timeout is 2 seconds:
!!!!!
Success rate is 100 percent (5/5), round-trip min/avg/max = 8/12/20 ms
HostC#
ICMP: echo reply rcvd, src 10.1.3.1, dst 10.1.2.2
ICMP: echo reply rcvd, src 10.1.3.1, dst 10.1.2.2
ICMP: echo reply rcvd, src 10.1.3.1, dst 10.1.2.2
ICMP: echo reply rcvd, src 10.1.3.1, dst 10.1.2.2
ICMP: echo reply rcvd, src 10.1.3.1, dst 10.1.2.2
HostC#
```

TIP	If you're recreating these examples in a lab, Example 4-10 reveals a useful trick. Host C is actually a Cisco router with IP routing disabled (**no ip routing**) and an **ip default-gateway** command pointing to Veracruz's locally attached interface. As Example 4-10 demonstrates, this setup enables you to use the IOS's extensive debugging tools to observe network behavior from a host's perspective.

If the administrator of the inside network wants to prevent traffic from being sent to OG addresses, he must implement a filter, as shown in Example 4-11.

Example 4-11 *Implementing a Filter to Prevent Traffic of the Inside Network from Being Sent to OG Addresses*

```
interface Ethernet0
 ip address 10.1.1.1 255.255.255.0
 ip access-group 101 in
 ip nat inside
!
interface Serial1
 no ip address
 encapsulation frame-relay
!
interface Serial1.705 point-to-point
 ip address 199.100.35.254 255.255.255.252
 ip nat outside
 frame-relay interface-dlci 705
!
router ospf 100
 network 10.1.1.1 0.0.0.0 area 0
 default-information originate
!
ip nat inside source static 10.1.1.3 204.15.87.1
ip nat inside source static 10.1.2.2 204.15.87.2
ip nat outside source static 201.114.37.5 10.1.3.1
!
ip route 0.0.0.0 0.0.0.0 199.100.35.253
!
access-list 101 permit ip any host 10.1.3.1
!
```

Notice that an incoming filter is used on interface E0. The filtering must take place before the address translation; an outgoing filter on S1.705 would have no way to differentiate the already translated destination address. Figure 4-17 shows the results of the filter; host A can still reach host D on its OL address, but packets to the OG address are blocked.

Figure 4-17 *After the Filter Is Implemented on Mazatlan, Inside Hosts Can Only Reach Host D via Its OL Address*

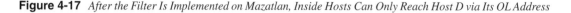

```
Microsoft(R) Windows 98
   (C)Copyright Microsoft Corp 1981-1998.

C:\WINDOWS>ping 10.1.3.1

Pinging 10.1.3.1 with 32 bytes of data:

Reply from 10.1.3.1: bytes=32 time=14ms TTL=253
Reply from 10.1.3.1: bytes=32 time=6ms TTL=253
Reply from 10.1.3.1: bytes=32 time=6ms TTL=253
Reply from 10.1.3.1: bytes=32 time=6ms TTL=253

Ping statistics for 10.1.3.1:
    Packets: Sent = 4, Received = 4, Lost = 0 (0% loss),
Approximate round trip times in milli-seconds:
    Minimum = 6ms, Maximum =  14ms, Average =  8ms

C:\WINDOWS>ping 201.114.37.5

Pinging 201.114.37.5 with 32 bytes of data:

Reply from 10.1.1.1: Destination net unreachable.
Reply from 10.1.1.1: Destination net unreachable.
Reply from 10.1.1.1: Destination net unreachable.
Reply from 10.1.1.1: Destination net unreachable.

Ping statistics for 201.114.37.5:
    Packets: Sent = 4, Received = 4, Lost = 0 (0% loss),
Approximate round trip times in milli-seconds:
    Minimum = 0ms, Maximum =  0ms, Average =  0ms

C:\WINDOWS>
```

The **debug** output in Example 4-10 and Example 4-6 emphasizes the fact that NAT does not, by itself, guarantee that private or illegal IP addresses do not leak into the public Internet. Wise administrators filter for the private Class A, B, and C addresses on interfaces connected to ISPs. Wise ISPs do the same on interfaces connected to their subscribers.

A difficulty with the various configurations shown in this case study so far is that very few "real-life" devices will use IP addresses to reach other devices. Names are almost always used. Therefore, DNS servers must have the correct IP addresses relevant to their side of the NAT. In Figure 4-18, DNS servers are placed on the inside and outside networks. DNS1 might have the following name-to-address mappings:

```
HostA.insidenet.com    IN   A    10.1.1.3
HostB.insidenet.com    IN   A    10.1.1.4
HostC.insidenet.com    IN   A    10.1.2.2
```

Here, all hosts have local addresses (local to the inside network). DNS2 might have the following name-to-address mapping:

```
HostD.outsidenet.com   IN   A    201.114.37.5
```

These entries all map to global addresses. DNS1 is authoritative for inside.net, and DNS2 is authoritative for outside.net. Example 4-12 shows the NAT configuration for Mazatlan.

Figure 4-18 *DNS1 Is Authoritative for the Inside Network, and DNS2 Is Authoritative for the Outside Network*

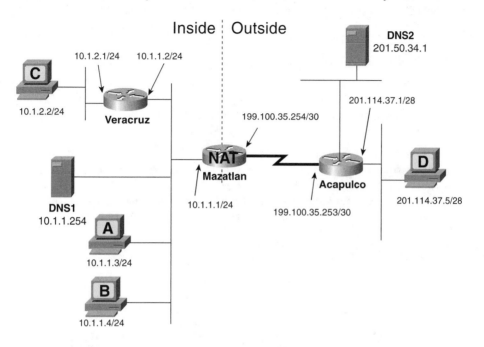

Example 4-12 *Mazatlan's NAT Configuration, Supporting DNS1 and DNS2 in Figure 4-18*

```
ip nat inside source static 10.1.1.3 204.15.87.1
ip nat inside source static 10.1.2.2 204.15.87.2
ip nat inside source static 10.1.1.4 204.15.87.3
ip nat inside source static 10.1.1.254 204.15.87.254
ip nat outside source static 201.114.37.5 10.1.3.1
ip nat outside source static 201.50.34.1 10.1.3.2
```

In addition to the three inside hosts and one outside host, the configuration in Example 4-12 has entries for the two DNS servers. If host A wants to send a packet to host D, it sends a DNS query to DNS1 for the address of HostD.outsidenet.com. DNS1 then queries DNS2, which returns an address of 201.114.37.5. When this DNS message passes through the NAT, the address is translated to 10.1.3.1, and DNS1 passes this address on to host A. Host A then sends packets to this address, and the NAT translates the source and destination addresses of the packets.

If host D wants to speak to a host on the inside network, the opposite happens. Host D might query DNS2 for the address of HostC.insidenet.com, prompting DNS2 to query DNS1. DNS1 responds with an address of 10.1.2.2, which is translated to 204.15.87.2 by the NAT and passed to host D by DNS2. Again, when packets are exchanged between host D and host C, the NAT translates the source and destination addresses.

Case Study: Dynamic NAT

The problem with the configurations of the preceding case study is one of scalability. What if, instead of the four inside devices shown in Figure 4-18, there are 60 or 6000? Maintaining static NAT mappings, like maintaining static route entries, quickly becomes an administrative burden as the network grows.

The inside network in Figure 4-19 uses 10.1.1.0–10.1.2.255 for its IL address space and has been assigned the public address space 204.15.86.0/23 by its ISP. This public address space is used as a pool from which IG addresses are dynamically selected for mapping to the IL addresses. To make things more manageable and predictable, the space 10.1.1.0/24 is mapped to 204.15.86.0/24, and 10.1.2.0/24 is mapped to 204.15.87.0/24.

Figure 4-19 *The Inside Network Has a Large Range of IL and IG Addresses*

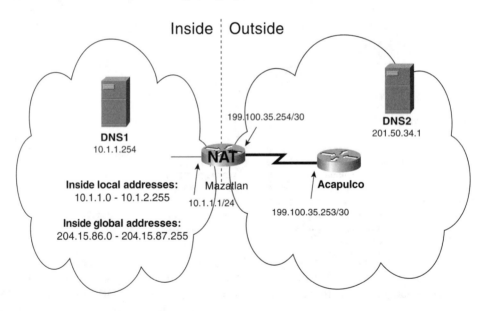

The **ip nat pool** command creates a pool of addresses and gives it a name. The pool is then designated as an IG pool and is linked to an IL address range with the command **ip nat inside source list**. Example 4-13 shows the configuration for Mazatlan.

Example 4-13 *Mazatlan Is Configured to Dynamically Assign IG Addresses from an Address Pool*

```
interface Ethernet0
 ip address 10.1.1.1 255.255.255.0
 ip nat inside
!
interface Serial1
 no ip address
 encapsulation frame-relay
!
interface Serial1.705 point-to-point
 ip address 199.100.35.254 255.255.255.252
 ip nat outside
 frame-relay interface-dlci 705
!
router ospf 100
 network 10.1.1.1 0.0.0.0 area 0
 default-information originate
!
ip nat pool PoolOne 204.15.86.1 204.15.86.254 netmask 255.255.255.0
ip nat pool PoolTwo 204.15.87.1 204.15.87.253 netmask 255.255.255.0
ip nat inside source list 1 pool PoolOne
ip nat inside source list 2 pool PoolTwo
ip nat inside source static 10.1.1.254 204.15.87.254
!
ip route 0.0.0.0 0.0.0.0 199.100.35.253
!
access-list 1 permit 10.1.1.0 0.0.0.255
access-list 2 permit 10.1.2.0 0.0.0.255
!
```

Two pools are created, named PoolOne and PoolTwo. PoolOne is assigned an address range of 204.15.86.1–204.15.86.254. PoolTwo is assigned an address range of 204.15.87.1– 204.15.87.253. Notice that the address ranges exclude the network addresses and the broadcast addresses; the **netmask** portion of the commands acts as a sanity check, ensuring that such addresses as 204.15.87.255 are not mapped. An alternative to using the **netmask** keyword is the **prefix-length.** For example:

```
ip nat pool PoolTwo 204.15.87.1 204.15.87.253 prefix-length 24
```

has the same effect as the command with the **netmask 255.255.255.0** keyword. Because of these commands, you can assign a range such as 204.15.86.0–204.15.86.255, and the "0" and "255" host addresses will not be mapped. However, it is good practice to configure only the actual pool addresses to avoid confusion.

Notice also that PoolTwo does not include the address 204.15.87.254. This address is statically assigned to DNS1 and so is left out of the pool. Any time an outside device must be able to initiate a session to an inside device, as in the case of DNS1, there must be a statically assigned address. If its IG address were dynamic, outside devices would have no way of knowing to which address to send packets.

Next, access lists are used to identify the addresses to be translated. In Mazatlan's configuration, access list 1 identifies the IL range 10.1.1.0–10.1.1.255, and access list 2 identifies the IL range 10.1.2.0–10.1.2.255.

Last, the IL addresses are linked to the correct pool. For example, the statement **ip nat inside source list 1 pool PoolOne** says that an IP address sourced from the inside (that is, IL addresses) and matching the range specified in access list 1 is to be translated to an IG address taken from PoolOne.

Example 4-14 shows Mazatlan's NAT table just after the dynamic NAT configuration is added. You can see that the only mapping in the table is the static entry for DNS1.

Example 4-14 *When Mazatlan's Dynamic NAT Is First Configured, No Entries Reside in the NAT Table Except for the Single Static Entry*

```
Mazatlan#show ip nat translations
Pro Inside global     Inside local      Outside local     Outside global
--- 204.15.87.254     10.1.1.254        ---               ---
Mazatlan#
```

Example 4-15 shows the NAT table after several inside devices have originated traffic to the outside. The IG addresses are allocated from each pool numerically, beginning with the lowest available number.

Example 4-15 *Dynamic IL-to-IG Mappings Are Entered into the NAT Table as Inside Devices Send Packets to the Outside*

```
Mazatlan#show ip nat translations
Pro Inside global     Inside local      Outside local     Outside global
--- 204.15.86.4       10.1.1.3          ---               ---
--- 204.15.86.3       10.1.1.83         ---               ---
--- 204.15.86.2       10.1.1.239        ---               ---
--- 204.15.86.1       10.1.1.4          ---               ---
--- 204.15.87.3       10.1.2.164        ---               ---
--- 204.15.87.2       10.1.2.57         ---               ---
--- 204.15.87.1       10.1.2.2          ---               ---
--- 204.15.87.254     10.1.1.254        ---               ---
Mazatlan#
```

Occasionally, a network administrator might want the host portion of the IG address to match the host portion of the IL address to which it is mapped. To accomplish this, the keywords **type match-host** are added to the end of the statement defining the pool, as demonstrated in Example 4-16.

Example 4-16 *Configuring the Host Portion of the IG Address to Match the Host Portion of the IL Address to Which It Is Mapped*

```
ip nat pool PoolOne 204.15.86.1 204.15.86.254 netmask 255.255.255.0 type match-host
ip nat pool PoolTwo 204.15.87.1 204.15.87.253 netmask 255.255.255.0 type match-host
ip nat inside source list 1 pool PoolOne
ip nat inside source list 2 pool PoolTwo
ip nat inside source static 10.1.1.254 204.15.87.254
!
ip route 0.0.0.0 0.0.0.0 199.100.35.253
!
access-list 1 permit 10.1.1.0 0.0.0.255
access-list 2 permit 10.1.2.0 0.0.0.255
```

Example 4-17 shows the resulting NAT table. Comparing it with the table in Example 4-15, you can see that all the same IL addresses have been translated. Instead of selecting IG addresses from their respective pools sequentially, however, IG addresses are selected with matching host portions.

Example 4-17 *The Host Portions of the IG Addresses Match the Host Portions of the IL Addresses to Which They Are Mapped*

```
Mazatlan#show ip nat translations
Pro Inside global     Inside local     Outside local     Outside global
--- 204.15.86.4       10.1.1.4         ---               ---
--- 204.15.86.3       10.1.1.3         ---               ---
--- 204.15.86.83      10.1.1.83        ---               ---
--- 204.15.86.239     10.1.1.239       ---               ---
--- 204.15.87.2       10.1.2.2         ---               ---
--- 204.15.87.57      10.1.2.57        ---               ---
--- 204.15.87.164     10.1.2.164       ---               ---
--- 204.15.87.254     10.1.1.254       ---               ---
Mazatlan#
```

By default, the dynamic entries are held in the NAT table for 86,400 seconds (24 hours). You can change this time with the command **ip nat translation timeout** to any time between 0 and 2,147,483,647 seconds (approximately 68 years). The timeout period begins when a translation is first made and is reset each time a packet is translated by the mapping. While a pool address is mapped to an address in the NAT table, it cannot be mapped to any other address. If the timeout period elapses with no new "hits" to the mapping, the entry is removed from the table, and the pool address is returned to the pool and becomes available. If you use 0 seconds or the keyword **never** with the **ip nat translation timeout** command, the mapping is never removed from the NAT table.

The translation timeout for each entry appears with the **show ip nat translations verbose** command, as demonstrated in Example 4-18. The **ip nat translations verbose** command shows how long ago the mapping was entered into the NAT table, how long ago the mapping was last used to translate an address, and the time remaining before the end of the timeout period. You can use the Flags field to indicate translation types other than dynamic. In Example 4-18, for instance, the last entry is shown to be a static translation.

Example 4-18 *The **show ip nat translations verbose** Command Reveals Details About the Translation Timeout Periods for Each Mapping*

```
Mazatlan#show ip nat translations verbose
Pro Inside global     Inside local      Outside local      Outside global
--- 204.15.86.4        10.1.1.3          ---                ---
    create 00:31:55, use 00:31:55, left 23:28:04, flags: none
--- 204.15.86.3        10.1.1.83         ---                ---
    create 00:32:19, use 00:32:19, left 23:27:40, flags: none
--- 204.15.86.2        10.1.1.239        ---                ---
    create 00:33:38, use 00:33:38, left 23:26:21, flags: none
--- 204.15.86.1        10.1.1.4          ---                ---
    create 00:34:25, use 00:00:05, left 23:59:54, flags: none
--- 204.15.87.3        10.1.2.164        ---                ---
    create 00:31:02, use 00:31:02, left 23:28:57, flags: none
--- 204.15.87.2        10.1.2.57         ---                ---
    create 00:34:10, use 00:34:10, left 23:25:49, flags: none
--- 204.15.87.1        10.1.2.2          ---                ---
    create 00:35:04, use 00:35:04, left 23:24:55, flags: none
--- 204.15.87.254      10.1.1.254        ---                ---
    create 03:59:32, use 03:59:32, flags: static
Mazatlan#
```

The translation timeout period is important when the range of IL addresses is larger than the pool of IG addresses. Consider the configuration in Example 4-19.

Example 4-19 *1022 IL Addresses Share a Pool of 254 IG Addresses*

```
ip nat pool GlobalPool 204.15.86.1 204.15.86.254 prefix-length 24
ip nat inside source list 1 pool GlobalPool
!
access-list 1 permit 10.1.0.0 0.0.3.255
```

Here, 1022 possible IL addresses—10.1.0.1 through 10.1.3.254—are translated using a pool of 254 available IG addresses. That means that when the NAT table contains 254 mapping entries, no more available IG addresses exist. Any packets with IL addresses that have not already been mapped are dropped. The designer of such an addressing scheme is gambling that only a fraction of the total users in the network will need outside access. With each mapping remaining in the NAT table for 24 hours, however, the chances of using up all available IG addresses increase substantially. By reducing the translation timeout, the designer can reduce this likelihood.

Case Study: A Network Merger

NAT is useful for preventing possible address conflicts between internetworks. The previous two case studies demonstrate the connection of internetworks using private address space to an internetwork using public addresses. The publicly addressed internetwork might be some other enterprise, or it might be the Internet. The bottom line is that the private RFC 1918 addresses must be translated because they are not unique. Across the Internet, many enterprises use the same addresses in their internetworks, and these addresses are "hidden" by NAT.

You also can use the configurations of the previous case studies in situations where the inside network is addressed out of the public address space but the addresses were not assigned by an addressing authority. For example, the inside network's address space might be 171.68.0.0/16. When connected to the Internet, NAT is required, because this address space is assigned to another company. Allowing these untranslated packets onto the Internet will cause routing conflicts.

Another situation in which address conflicts might arise is the merger of two previously separate internetworks. In Figure 4-20, Surf Corporation and Sand, Inc. have formed a corporate merger to form Surf n' Sand Enterprises. Part of the merger is the connection of their two internetworks. Unfortunately, when the two internetworks were first constructed, the designers both chose to use the 10.0.0.0 address space. As a result, many devices in Surf Corp.'s internetwork have the same addresses as devices in Sand, Inc.'s internetwork.

Figure 4-20 *Two Internetworks with Many Duplicate Addresses Must Be Connected*

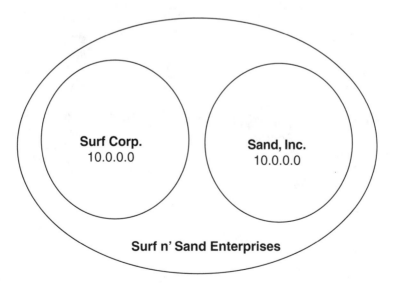

The best solution is to re-address the new internetwork. Address schemes are frequently designed poorly, however, making re-addressing a major project. In the Surf n' Sand internetwork, for instance, all the devices have manually configured IP addresses rather than addresses assigned by DHCP. NAT can serve as an interim solution to connect the internetworks until the re-addressing project can be completed.

NOTE   Note that in this application, NAT should always be considered an interim solution. It is bad practice to allow address conflicts to exist within an internetwork indefinitely.

The Surf n' Sand administrator first applies to his ISP or an addressing authority to acquire a public address space and is assigned the CIDR block 206.100.160.0/19. This block is then split in half. 206.100.160.0/20 is assigned to the former Sand internetwork, and 206.100.176.0/20 is assigned to the former Surf internetwork. An assumption is made here that although the 10.0.0.0 network is capable of supporting more than 16 million host addresses, in reality there are not more hosts in either network than can be serviced out of the /20 address space.

The routers Cozumel and Guaymas in Figure 4-21 connect the two internetworks with the configurations in Example 4-20.

Figure 4-21   *NAT Is Used at the Boundaries of the Two Internetworks to Correct the Address Conflicts*

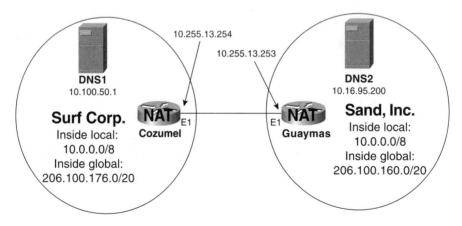

Example 4-20 *NAT Configurations for Routers Cozumel and Guaymas in Figure 4-21*

```
Cozumel
interface Ethernet0
 ip address 10.100.85.1 255.255.255.0
 ip nat inside
!
interface Ethernet1
 ip address 10.255.13.254 255.255.255.248
 ip nat outside
!
router ospf 1
 redistribute static
 network 10.100.85.1 0.0.0.0 area 18
!
ip nat pool Surf 206.100.176.2 206.100.191.254 prefix-length 20
ip nat inside source list 1 pool Surf
ip nat inside source static 10.100.50.1 206.100.176.1
!
ip route 206.100.160.0 255.255.240.0 10.255.13.253
!
access-list 1 deny   10.255.13.254
access-list 1 permit any
```

```
Guaymas
interface Ethernet0
 ip address 10.16.95.1 255.255.255.0
 ip nat inside
!
interface Ethernet1
 ip address 10.255.13.253 255.255.255.248
 ip nat outside
!
interface Serial1
 no ip address
 encapsulation frame-relay
!
interface Serial1.508 point-to-point
 ip address 10.18.3.253 255.255.255.0
 ip nat inside
 frame-relay interface-dlci 508
!
router eigrp 100
 redistribute static metric 1000 100 255 1 1500
 passive-interface Ethernet1
 network 10.0.0.0
 no auto-summary
!
ip nat pool Sand 206.100.160.2 206.100.175.254 prefix-length 20
ip nat inside source list 1 pool Sand
ip nat inside source static 10.16.95.200 206.100.160.1
!
```

continues

Example 4-20 *NAT Configurations for Routers Cozumel and Guaymas in Figure 4-21 (Continued)*

```
ip route 206.100.176.0 255.255.240.0 10.255.13.254
!
access-list 1 deny   10.255.13.253
access-list 1 permit 10.0.0.0
!
```

The DNS servers are crucial to this design. In the NAT configurations, each server has a static IL-to-IG mapping. Suppose a device in the Sand internetwork, Beachball.sand.com, wants to send a packet to Snorkel.surf.com in the Surf internetwork. Suppose further that both devices have an IP address of 10.1.2.2. The following sequence of events occurs:

1 Host Beachball queries DNS2 for the address of Snorkel.surf.com.

2 DNS2 queries DNS1, which is authoritative for the surf.com domain. The query has a source address of 10.16.95.200 and a destination address of 206.100.176.1. The query is forwarded to Guaymas, which is advertising a route into EIGRP for 206.100.176.0/20.

3 Guaymas translates the source address from 10.16.95.200 to 206.100.160.1, based on the static NAT entry, and forwards the packet to Cozumel.

4 Cozumel translates the destination address from 206.100.176.1 to 10.100.50.1, based on the static NAT entry, and forwards the query to DNS1.

5 DNS1 responds to the query, indicating that Snorkel.surf.com has an IP address of 10.1.2.2. The response message has a source address of 10.100.50.1 and a destination address of 206.100.160.1. The response is forwarded to Cozumel, which is advertising a route into OSPF for 206.100.160.0/20.

6 Cozumel translates the source address of the DNS response to 206.100.176.1. NAT also finds the address 10.1.2.2 in the Answer field of the message; the address matches access list 1 and is translated to an address from the pool named Surf. For this example, the address is 206.100.176.3. The mapping is entered into the NAT table, and the response is forwarded to Guaymas.

7 Guaymas translates the destination of the DNS response to 10.16.95.200 and forwards the message to DNS1.

8 DNS1 informs Beachball that the IP address of Snorkel.surf.com is 206.100.176.3.

9 Beachball sends a packet to Snorkel with a source address of 10.1.2.2 and a destination address of 206.100.176.3. Again, the packet is forwarded to Guaymas.

10 At Guaymas, the source address matches access list 1, and an address is selected from the pool named Sand. For this example, the address is 206.100.160.2. The source address is translated, the mapping is entered into the NAT table, and the packet is forwarded to Cozumel.

11 Cozumel finds that the destination address of 206.100.176.3 is mapped in its NAT table to 10.1.2.2 and makes the translation to that IL address. The packet is forwarded to Snorkel.

12 Snorkel sends a packet in response. The source address is 10.1.2.2, and the destination address is 206.100.160.2. The packet is forwarded to Cozumel.

13 Cozumel translates the packet's source address to 206.100.176.3 and forwards the packet to Guaymas.

14 Guaymas translates the packet's destination address to 10.1.2.2 and forwards the packet to Beachball.

By following this example, you can see that although two devices have the same IP address, neither is aware of the other's true address. The key to making all this work is the routing configurations of Cozumel and Guaymas. Neither router leaks information about the 10.0.0.0 network to the other. Nothing in either configuration allows a packet with a destination address within the 10.0.0.0 network to be forwarded to the other router, with the exception of packets destined for the directly connected 10.255.13.248/29 subnet. Access list 1 is configured so that packets sourced from either router's E1 interface are not translated.

NOTE   Troubleshooting Exercise 3 asks you to consider this access list configuration further.

Another detail of interest in Example 4-20 is that there is more than one inside interface at Guaymas. Multiple inside interfaces are quite acceptable.

One topic of importance that is not readily evident in the configuration concerns the coordination of the NAT translation timeout period and the DNS cache Time-To-Live (TTL) period. When a DNS server receives a resource record from another DNS server, it caches the record so that it can respond directly to subsequent queries for the same record. In the example in this case study, DNS2 will cache the A RR that maps Snorkel.surf.com to IP address 206.100.176.3. DNS2 can then respond to subsequent requests for Snorkel's IP address without again querying DNS1. This cached RR has a TTL period associated with it and is flushed when the TTL expires. The DNS TTL period must be shorter than the NAT translation timeout period.

Suppose, for example, that the NAT translation timeout expires on the 10.1.2.2-to-206.100.176.3 mapping, and the IG address is returned to the pool. 206.100.176.3 is then mapped to a different IL address within the Surf internetwork, but DNS2 still has an RR mapping Snorkel.surf.com to 206.100.176.3. If a device in the Sand internetwork queries DNS2 for Snorkel's address, DNS2 responds with obsolete information, and packets are sent to the wrong host.

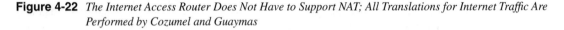

A final note on this design concerns Internet access. You can easily accomplish Internet access by adding an access router to the subnet between Cozumel and Guaymas (see Figure 4-22). The source addresses of packets from both the Surf and Sand internetworks already are translated to valid public addresses; all that is needed is for default routes to be added to Cozumel and Guaymas, pointing to the Internet access router.

Figure 4-22 *The Internet Access Router Does Not Have to Support NAT; All Translations for Internet Traffic Are Performed by Cozumel and Guaymas*

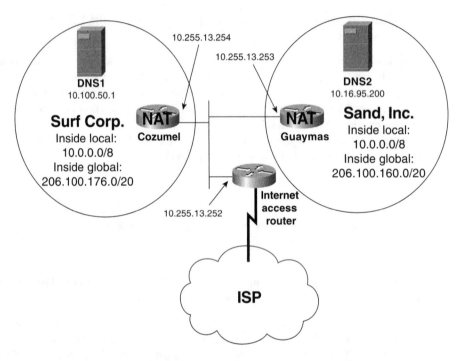

Case Study: ISP Multihoming with NAT

The section "NAT and Multihomed Autonomous Systems" earlier in this chapter demonstrated ways you can employ NAT to overcome the problem of multihoming to different ISPs with different CIDR blocks. The subscriber in Figure 4-7 is multihomed, and each ISP sees packets with source addresses belonging to its own address space. Neither ISP receives packets from the subscriber with source addresses belonging to the other ISP's block of addresses.

Based on the NAT case studies you have already seen, you can easily write configurations for the two NAT routers shown in Figure 4-7. But what about a situation in which a single router is multihomed to both ISPs, as shown in Figure 4-23? Montego is receiving full BGP routes from both ISPs, so it can choose the best provider to any destination. When a packet is forwarded to ISP1, the packet must have a source address from the 205.113.50.0/23 block assigned by ISP1; when a packet is forwarded to ISP2, it must have a source address from the 207.36.76.0/23 block assigned by ISP2.

Figure 4-23 *ISP1 and ISP2 Have Each Assigned a CIDR Block to JamaicaNet; When Packets Are Forwarded to an ISP, They Must Have the Correct Source Address for That ISP*

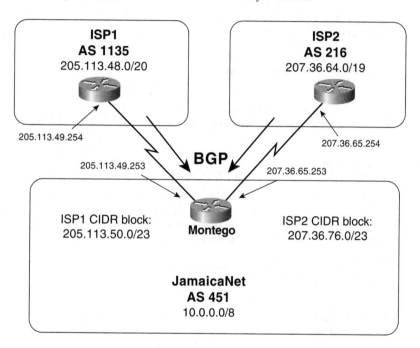

Example 4-21 shows Montego's configuration for using different address pools on different interfaces.

Example 4-21 *Montego's Configuration in Figure 4-23*

```
interface Ethernet0
 ip address 10.1.1.1 255.255.255.0
 ip nat inside
!
interface Ethernet1
 ip address 10.5.1.1 255.255.255.0
 ip nat inside
!
interface Serial1
 no ip address
 encapsulation frame-relay
!
```

continues

Example 4-21 *Montego's Configuration in Figure 4-23 (Continued)*

```
interface Serial1.708 point-to-point
 description PVC to ISP1
 ip address 205.113.49.253 255.255.255.252
 ip nat outside
 frame-relay interface-dlci 708
!
interface Serial1.709 point-to-point
 description PVC to ISP2
 ip address 207.36.65.253 255.255.255.252
 ip nat outside
 frame-relay interface-dlci 709
!
router ospf 10
 network 10.0.0.0 0.255.255.255 area 10
 default-information originate always
!
router bgp 451
 neighbor 205.113.49.254 remote-as 1135
 neighbor 207.36.65.254 remote-as 216
!
ip nat pool ISP1 205.113.50.1 205.113.51.254 prefix-length 23
ip nat pool ISP2 207.36.76.1 207.36.77.254 prefix-length 23
ip nat inside source route-map ISP1_MAP pool ISP1
ip nat inside source route-map ISP2_MAP pool ISP2
!
access-list 1 permit 10.0.0.0 0.255.255.255
access-list 2 permit 207.36.65.254
!
route-map ISP1_MAP permit 10
 match ip address 1
 match interface Serial1.708
!
route-map ISP2_MAP permit 10
 match ip address 1
 match ip next-hop 2
!
```

The address blocks assigned by the ISPs are specified in the pools ISP1 and ISP2. The significant feature of this NAT configuration is that the **ip nat inside source** statements make calls to route maps rather than access lists. By using route maps, you can specify not only the IL address, but also the interface or the next-hop address to which the packet is to be forwarded. ISP1_MAP specifies packets that have a source address belonging to the 10.0.0.0 network (as identified by access list 1) and which are to be forwarded out interface s1.708 to ISP1. ISP2_MAP also specifies packets from 10.0.0.0 that are to be forwarded to the next-hop address 207.36.65.254 to ISP2.

NOTE	Normally, either the **match interface** or the **match ip next-hop** command is used in both route maps for consistency. Both commands are used here for demonstration purposes.

For example, an inside device with an address of 10.1.2.2 sends a packet with a destination address of 137.19.1.1. The packet is forwarded to Montego, because that router is advertising a default route into JamaicaNet via OSPF. Montego does a route lookup and determines that the best route to the destination is via ISP2, out S1.709 and with a next-hop address of 207.36.65.254. The first **ip nat inside source** statement checks this information against route map ISP1_MAP. Although the source address matches, the egress interface does not. The second **ip nat inside source** statement checks the information against route map ISP2_MAP. Here both the source address and the next-hop address match, so the source address is translated to an address out of the ISP2 pool.

Example 4-22 shows Montego's NAT table after some traffic has passed to the ISPs. Because an IL address can be mapped to an address from more than one pool, the address mappings are extended mappings, showing the protocol type and the port number. Extended mapping is discussed in more detail in the case study "Port Address Translation."

Example 4-22 *Montego's NAT Table Shows That the IG Address Chosen for Translation Depends on the ISP to Which the Packet Is to Be Forwarded*

```
Montego#show ip nat translations
Pro Inside global     Inside local     Outside local      Outside global
udp 207.36.76.2:4953  10.1.2.2:4953    137.19.1.1:69      137.19.1.1:69
udp 205.113.50.2:2716 10.1.1.2:2716    171.35.100.4:514   171.35.100.4:514
tcp 205.113.50.1:11009 10.5.1.2:11009  205.113.48.1:23    205.113.48.1:23
tcp 207.36.76.1:11002 10.1.1.2:11002   198.15.61.1:23     198.15.61.1:23
tcp 205.113.50.3:11007 10.1.2.2:11007  171.35.18.1:23     171.35.18.1:23
tcp 207.36.76.2:11008 10.1.2.2:11008   207.36.64.1:23     207.36.64.1:23
Montego#
```

Of interest in the NAT table in Example 4-22 are the three entries for the IL address 10.1.2.2. The UDP traffic and one of the TCP sessions went to a destination via ISP2. The IG address to which the IL address is mapped is 207.36.76.2. The other TCP session was sent via ISP1 and so was mapped to 205.113.50.3. These entries demonstrate that the pool from which the IG address is chosen changes, even for the same source address, depending on where the packet is forwarded.

Figure 4-24 shows DNS servers for the three autonomous systems. The servers in ISP1 and ISP2 must access Ochee, the DNS server authoritative for JamaicaNet. This means that Ochee must have static NAT entries to addresses in both CIDR blocks. Statically mapping an IL address to more than one IG address is normally not allowed, because the mappings are ambiguous. In this case, ambiguity is not a problem because the same NAT is doing both mappings. When Montego routes Ochee's DNS queries and responses to DNS1 or DNS2, the appropriate translations are made.

Figure 4-24 *The DNS Server Ochee Must Have a Static IL-to-IG Mapping So That It Can Be Queried by DNS1 and DNS2*

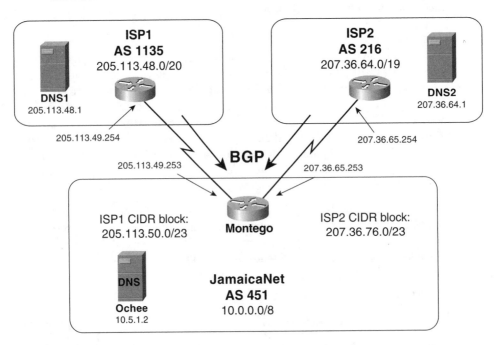

To allow static NAT mappings of one IL address to multiple IG addresses, the keyword **extendable** is added to the end of the mapping statements. Example 4-23 shows the NAT configuration for Montego.

Example 4-23 *NAT Configuration for Montego to Allow Static NAT Mappings of One IL Address to Multiple IG Addresses*

```
ip nat pool ISP1 205.113.50.2 205.113.51.254 prefix-length 23
ip nat pool ISP2 prefix-length 23
 address 207.36.76.1 207.36.76.99
 address 207.36.76.101 207.36.77.254
ip nat inside source route-map ISP1_MAP pool ISP1
ip nat inside source route-map ISP2_MAP pool ISP2
ip nat inside source static 10.5.1.2 207.36.76.100 extendable
ip nat inside source static 10.5.1.2 205.113.50.1 extendable
!
access-list 1 permit 10.0.0.0 0.255.255.255
access-list 2 permit 207.36.65.254
!
route-map ISP1_MAP permit 10
 match ip address 1
 match interface Serial1.708
```

Example 4-23 *NAT Configuration for Montego to Allow Static NAT Mappings of One IL Address to Multiple IG Addresses (Continued)*

```
!
route-map ISP2_MAP permit 10
 match ip address 1
 match ip next-hop 2
```

From the perspective of DNS1, Ochee's address is 205.113.50.1. Notice that NAT pool ISP1 is modified to exclude this address from the pool. From the perspective of DNS2, Ochee's address is 207.36.76.100. This address is taken from the middle of the 207.36.76.0/23 block rather than from one end or the other, making pool ISP2 discontiguous. The pool is modified in the configuration to specify two ranges of addresses: those before Ochee's address, and those after Ochee's address.

You configure a discontiguous range of addresses by first naming the pool and specifying the prefix length or netmask. The configuration prompt then enables you to enter a list of ranges. Example 4-24 shows the configuration steps for pool ISP2, including the prompts.

Example 4-24 *Configuring a NAT Pool for a Discontiguous Range of Addresses*

```
Montego(config)#ip nat pool ISP2 prefix-length 23
Montego(config-ipnat-pool)#address 207.36.76.1 207.36.76.99
Montego(config-ipnat-pool)#address 207.36.76.101 207.36.77.254
```

Port Address Translation

At the opposite extreme from the multihomed NAT router in the preceding case study is the SOHO (small office, home office) router connecting a few devices to the Internet. Instead of acquiring separate public addresses for each device, port address translation (PAT) allows all the SOHO devices to share a single IG address.

PAT allows *overloading*, or the mapping of more than one IL address to the same IG address. To accomplish this, the NAT entries in the routing table are *extended* entries—the entries track not only the relevant IP addresses, but also the protocol types and ports. By translating both the IP address and the port number of a packet, up to 65535 IL addresses could theoretically be mapped to a single IG address (based on the 16-bit port number).

NOTE   Each NAT entry uses approximately 160 bytes of memory, so 65535 entries would consume more than 10 MB of memory and large amounts of CPU power. Nowhere near this number of addresses are mapped in practical PAT configurations.

Cisco's NAT attempts to preserve BSD semantics, mapping an IL port number to the same IG port number whenever possible. A different IG port number is used only when the port number associated with the IL address is already being used in another mapping.

Figure 4-25 shows three devices connected to an ISP.

Figure 4-25 *Barbados Uses PAT to Map the Addresses of the Three Inside Hosts to the Single Serial Interface Address*

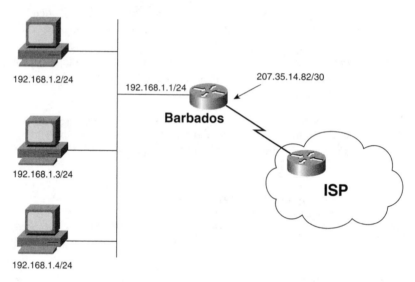

The access router has a single public IP address assigned by the ISP on its serial interface, as demonstrated in the configuration in Example 4-25.

Example 4-25 *Enabling PAT on Router Barbados in Figure 4-25*

```
interface Ethernet0
 ip address 192.168.1.1 255.255.255.0
 ip nat inside
!
interface Serial0
 ip address 207.35.14.82 255.255.255.252
 ip nat outside
!
ip nat inside source list 1 interface Serial0 overload
!
ip route 0.0.0.0 0.0.0.0 Serial0
!
access-list 1 permit 192.168.1.0 0.0.0.255
!
```

PAT is enabled with the **overload** keyword. Although the **ip nat inside source** command could reference an address pool, in this case it just references the interface on which the IG address is configured. As usual, the access list identifies the IL addresses.

Example 4-26 shows the NAT table in the access router after a few packets have passed through it. Most of the IG ports match the IL ports, but notice that there are two instances in which an IL socket has a port number that has already been used (192.168.1.2:11000 and 192.168.1.2:11001). As a result, the NAT has chosen an unused port for these sockets that does not match the IL port.

Example 4-26 *Different IL Addresses Have Been Mapped to Different Ports of the Same IG Address*

```
Barbados#show ip nat translations
Pro Inside global       Inside local       Outside local       Outside global
tcp 207.35.14.82:11011 192.168.1.3:11011  191.115.37.2:23     191.115.37.2:23
tcp 207.35.14.82:5000  192.168.1.2:11000  191.115.37.2:23     191.115.37.2:23
udp 207.35.14.82:3749  192.168.1.2:3749   135.88.131.55:514   135.88.131.55:514
tcp 207.35.14.82:11000 192.168.1.4:11000  191.115.37.2:23     191.115.37.2:23
tcp 207.35.14.82:11002 192.168.1.2:11002  118.50.47.210:23    118.50.47.210:23
udp 207.35.14.82:9371  192.168.1.2:9371   135.88.131.55:514   135.88.131.55:514
icmp 207.35.14.82:7428 192.168.1.3:7428   135.88.131.55:7428 135.88.131.55:7428
tcp 207.35.14.82:5001  192.168.1.2:11001  135.88.131.55:23    135.88.131.55:23
tcp 207.35.14.82:11001 192.168.1.4:11001  135.88.131.55:23    135.88.131.55:23
Barbados#
```

Case Study: TCP Load Balancing

Figure 4-26 shows a topology similar to the one in the PAT case study. Here the three inside devices are not hosts, however, but are identical servers with mirrored content. The intent is to create a "virtual server" with an address of 199.198.5.1; that is, from the outside there appears to be a single server at that IG address. In reality, the router Barbados is configured to perform round-robin translations to the three IL addresses.

Figure 4-26 *The Three Inside Devices Are Identical Servers with Mirrored Content, Which from the Outside Appear to Be a Single Server*

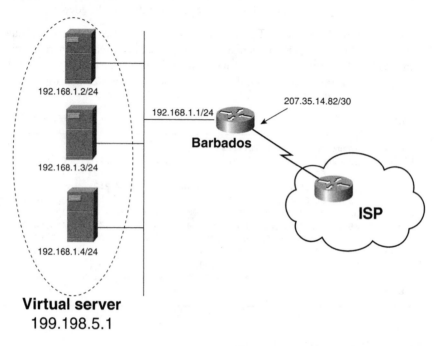

Virtual server
199.198.5.1

Example 4-27 shows the configuration for Barbados.

Example 4-27 *Barbados' NAT Configuration Evenly Distributes the TCP Load to the Three Identical Servers; Outside Devices See Only a Single Inside Global Address*

```
interface Ethernet0
 ip address 192.168.1.1 255.255.255.0
 ip nat inside
!
interface Serial0
 ip address 207.35.14.82 255.255.255.252
 ip nat outside
!
ip nat pool V-Server 192.168.1.2 192.168.1.4 prefix-length 24 type rotary
ip nat inside destination list 1 pool V-Server
!
ip route 0.0.0.0 0.0.0.0 Serial0
!
access-list 1 permit 199.198.5.1
!
```

Instead of translating an IL address as most of the previous case studies have demonstrated, this configuration translates the IG address. The address pool V-Server contains a list of the available IL addresses, and the keywords **type rotary** cause a round-robin assignment of the pool addresses. The access list, as usual, identifies the address to be translated—in this case, the single destination address 199.198.5.1.

Example 4-28 shows the resulting NAT table after four outside devices have sent TCP traffic to the virtual server. You can observe that the first three connections (reading from the bottom up) were allocated sequentially from the lowest IL address in the pool to the highest. Only three addresses are available in the pool, so the fourth connection is again mapped to the lowest IL address.

Example 4-28 *The TCP Connections to the Virtual Server Address 199.198.5.1 Are Balanced Across the Three Real Server Addresses*

```
Barbados#show ip nat translations
Pro Inside global      Inside local      Outside local      Outside global
tcp 199.198.5.1:23     192.168.1.2:23    203.1.2.3:11003    203.1.2.3:11003
tcp 199.198.5.1:23     192.168.1.4:23    135.88.131.55:11002 135.88.131.55:11002
tcp 199.198.5.1:23     192.168.1.3:23    118.50.47.210:11001 118.50.47.210:11001
tcp 199.198.5.1:23     192.168.1.2:23    191.115.37.2:11000 191.115.37.2:11000
Barbados#
```

Case Study: Service Distribution

You also can use NAT to create a virtual server in which connections are distributed by TCP or UDP services rather than by TCP connection. The internetwork in Figure 4-27 is very similar to that in Figure 4-26, except that the servers are not identical. Rather, different servers offer different services. From the outside, all three servers appear to be a single server with the address 199.198.5.1.

Figure 4-27 *Three Inside Devices That Offer Different Services Appear to Be a Single Server from the Outside*

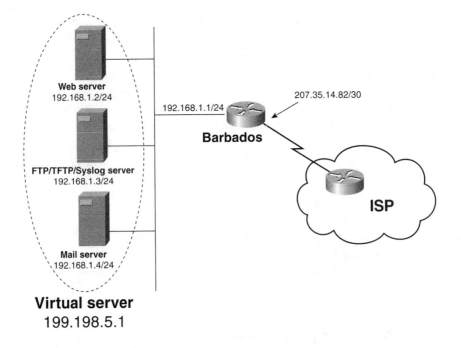

Virtual server
199.198.5.1

Example 4-29 shows the NAT configuration in Barbados.

Example 4-29 *The NAT Configuration in Barbados Translates the Virtual IG Address According to the TCP or UDP Port Associated with the Address*

```
interface Ethernet0
 ip address 192.168.1.1 255.255.255.0
 ip nat inside
!
interface Serial0
 ip address 207.35.14.82 255.255.255.252
 ip nat outside
!
ip nat inside source static tcp 192.168.1.4 25 199.198.5.1 25 extendable
ip nat inside source static udp 192.168.1.3 514 199.198.5.1 514 extendable
ip nat inside source static udp 192.168.1.3 69 199.198.5.1 69 extendable
ip nat inside source static tcp 192.168.1.3 21 199.198.5.1 21 extendable
ip nat inside source static tcp 192.168.1.3 20 199.198.5.1 20 extendable
ip nat inside source static tcp 192.168.1.2 80 199.198.5.1 80 extendable
!
ip route 0.0.0.0 0.0.0.0 Serial0
!
```

No address pools or access lists are here; instead, the configuration is a series of simple IL-to-IG mappings. The difference between these statements and the static statements you saw earlier is that TCP or UDP is specified, as are the source and destination ports. The **extendable** keyword is used, because the same address—this time, the IG address—appears in more than one statement. You do not have to type the keyword: Cisco IOS Software adds it automatically. In order, the statements map SMTP (TCP port 25), syslog (UDP port 514), TFTP (UDP port 69), FTP (TCP ports 20 and 21), and HTTP (TCP port 80).

Example 4-30 shows the NAT table just after Barbados is configured; the only entries are the static entries.

Example 4-30 *Before Any Dynamic Translations Occur, Barbados' NAT Table Contains Only the Static Mappings of IL Sockets to IG Sockets*

```
Barbados#show ip nat translations
Pro Inside global      Inside local      Outside local      Outside global
udp 199.198.5.1:514    192.168.1.3:514   - - -              - - -
udp 199.198.5.1:69     192.168.1.3:69    - - -              - - -
tcp 199.198.5.1:80     192.168.1.2:80    - - -              - - -
tcp 199.198.5.1:21     192.168.1.3:21    - - -              - - -
tcp 199.198.5.1:20     192.168.1.3:20    - - -              - - -
tcp 199.198.5.1:25     192.168.1.4:25    - - -              - - -
Barbados#
```

Example 4-31 shows the NAT table after some traffic has passed through Barbados. Notice that among all the dynamic mappings, only two OG addresses appear. Yet the sessions have been mapped to different IL addresses, depending on the port associated with the IG address.

Example 4-31 *UDP and TCP Packets Are Mapped to Different IL Addresses, Depending on Their Associated Port Numbers*

```
Barbados#show ip nat translations
Pro Inside global      Inside local      Outside local          Outside global
udp 199.198.5.1:514    192.168.1.3:514   - - -                  - - -
tcp 199.198.5.1:25     192.168.1.4:25    207.35.14.81:11003     207.35.14.81:11003
udp 199.198.5.1:69     192.168.1.3:69    - - -                  - - -
tcp 199.198.5.1:80     192.168.1.2:80    - - -                  - - -
tcp 199.198.5.1:21     192.168.1.3:21    - - -                  - - -
tcp 199.198.5.1:20     192.168.1.3:20    - - -                  - - -
tcp 199.198.5.1:25     192.168.1.4:25    - - -                  - - -
tcp 199.198.5.1:20     192.168.1.3:20    191.115.37.2:1027      191.115.37.2:1027
tcp 199.198.5.1:21     192.168.1.3:21    191.115.37.2:1026      191.115.37.2:1026
tcp 199.198.5.1:80     192.168.1.2:80    191.115.37.2:1030      191.115.37.2:1030
udp 199.198.5.1:69     192.168.1.3:69    191.115.37.2:1028      191.115.37.2:1028
udp 199.198.5.1:514    192.168.1.3:514   207.35.14.81:1029      207.35.14.81:1029
Barbados#
```

Troubleshooting NAT

Cisco NAT enables you to do a lot, and the configurations are straightforward. If it does not work, you can spot a few common causes by asking the following questions:

- Do the dynamic pools contain the correct range of addresses?
- Is there any overlap between dynamic pools?
- Is there any overlap between addresses used for static mapping and the addresses in the dynamic pools?
- Do the access lists specify the correct addresses to be translated? Are any addresses left out? Are any addresses included that should not be included?
- Are the correct inside and outside interfaces specified?

One of the most common problems with a new NAT configuration is not NAT itself, but routing. Remember that you are changing a source or destination address in a packet; after the translation, does the router know what to do with the new address?

Another problem can be timeouts. If a translated address is cached in some system after the dynamic entry has timed out of the NAT table, packets can be sent to the wrong address, or the destination may seem to have disappeared. Besides the **ip nat translation timeout** command already discussed, you can change several other default timeouts. Table 4-3 lists all the keywords you can use with the **ip nat translation** command and the default values of the timeout periods. You can change all the defaults within a range of 0–2,147,483,647 seconds.

Table 4-3 *Dynamic NAT Table Timeout Values*

ip nat translation	Default Period (in Seconds)	Description
timeout	86,400 (24 hours)	Timeout for all non-port-specific dynamic translations
dns-timeout	60	Timeout for DNS connections
finrst-timeout	60	Timeout after TCP FIN or RST flags are seen (closing a TCP session)
icmp-timeout	60	Timeout for ICMP translations
port-timeout tcp	60	Timeout for TCP port translations
port-timeout udp	60	Timeout for UDP port translations
syn-timeout	60	Timeout after TCP SYN flag is seen, and no further session packets
tcp-timeout	86,400 (24 hours)	Timeout for TCP translations (non-port-specific)
udp-port	300 (5 minutes)	Timeout for UDP translations (non-port-specific)

Theoretically, there is no limit on the number of mappings that the NAT table can hold. Practically, memory and CPU or the boundaries of the available addresses or ports place a limit on the number of entries. Each NAT mapping uses approximately 160 bytes of memory. In the rare case where the entries must be limited either for performance or policy reasons, you can use the **ip nat translation max-entries** command.

Another useful command for troubleshooting is **show ip nat statistics**, as demonstrated in Example 4-32. This command displays a summary of the NAT configuration, as well as counts of active translation types, hits to an existing mapping, misses (causing an attempt to create a mapping), and expired translations. For dynamic pools, the type of pool, the total available addresses, the number of allocated addresses, the number of failed allocations, and the number of translations using the pool (refcount) appear.

Example 4-32 **show ip nat statistics** *Displays Many Useful Details for Analyzing and Troubleshooting Your NAT Configuration*

```
StCroix#show ip nat statistics
Total active translations: 3 (2 static, 1 dynamic; 3 extended)
Outside interfaces:
  Serial0, Serial1.708, Serial1.709
Inside interfaces:
  Ethernet0, Ethernet1
Hits: 980  Misses: 43
Expired translations: 54
Dynamic mappings:
-- Inside Source
access-list 1 interface Serial0 refcount 0
StCroix#
```

Finally, you can manually clear dynamic NAT entries from the NAT table. This action can prove useful if you need to get rid of a particular offending entry without waiting for the timeout to expire, or if you need to clear the entire NAT table to reconfigure an address pool. Note that Cisco IOS Software does not allow you to change or delete an address pool while addresses from the pool are mapped in the NAT table. The **clear ip nat translations** command clears entries; you can specify a single entry by the global and local address or by TCP and UDP translations (including ports), or you can use an asterisk (*) to clear the entire table. Of course, only dynamic entries are cleared; the command does not remove static entries.

End Note

[1]Egevang, K.B., and P. Francis. "RFC 1631: The IP Network Address Translator (NAT)" (Work in Progress)

Looking Ahead

You have seen that NAT aids in a more efficient use of available network addresses. The next chapter, "Introduction to IP Multicast Routing," discusses how multicast routing protocols can make more efficient use of network resources when groups of devices must share common information.

Command Summary

Table 4-4 provides a list and description of the commands discussed in this chapter

Table 4-4   *Command Summary*

Command	Description
clear ip nat translations {*	[**inside** [**tcp** {**inside** [*global-ip* [*global-port*] *local-ip* [*local-port*]}	**udp** {**inside**[*global-ip* [*global-port*] *local-ip* [*local-port*]}]	[**inside** *global-ip local-ip*][**outside** *local-ip global-ip*]	Clears dynamic entries from the NAT table.
ip nat {**inside**	**outside**}	Designates the inside and outside interfaces; traffic originating from or destined for the interface is examined by the NAT.
ip nat inside destination list {*access-list-number\name*} **pool** *name*	Enables translation of inside destination addresses.
ip nat inside source {**list** {*access-list-number\name*} **pool** *name* [**overload**]	**static** *local-ip global-ip*}	Enables translation of inside source addresses.
ip nat outside source {**list** {*access-list-number\name*} **pool** *name*	**static** *global-ip local-ip*}	Enables translation of outside source addresses.
ip nat pool name *start-ip end-ip* {**netmask** *netmask*	**prefix-length** *prefix-length*} **type** {**rotary**	**match-host**}	Defines a pool of addresses to be used for address translation.
ip nat translation max-entries *entries*	Sets a limit on the number of entries allowed in the NAT table.
ip nat translation {**timeout**	**udp-timeout**	**dns-timeout**	**tcp-timeout**	**finrst-timeout**	**icmp-timeout**	**syn-timeout**	**port-timeout**{**tcp**	**udp**}} *seconds*	Changes the default period after which a dynamic entry is removed from the NAT table and the address is returned to the pool.
show ip nat statistics	Displays NAT statistics.
show ip nat translations [**verbose**]	Displays the NAT table.

Configuration Exercises

Refer to Figure 4-28 for Configuration Exercises 1–5.

Figure 4-28 *The Internetwork for Configuration Exercises 1–5*

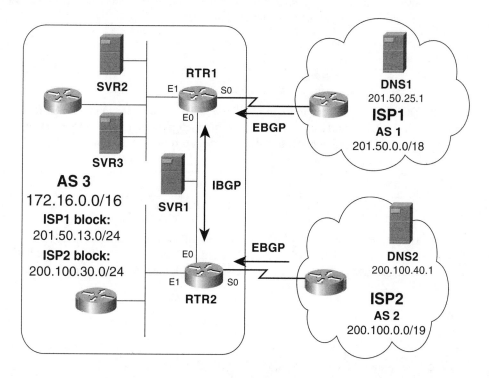

1   ISP1 in Figure 4-28 has assigned the address block 201.50.13.0/24 to AS 3. ISP2 has
    assigned the address block 200.100.30.0/24 to AS 3. RTR1 and RTR2 are accepting
    full BGP routes from the ISP routers but do not transmit any routes to the ISPs. They
    run IBGP between them and OSPF on all Ethernet interfaces. No routes are
    redistributed between BGP and OSPF. The addresses of the router interfaces are as
    follows:

    RTR1, E0: 172.16.3.1/24

    RTR1, E1: 172.16.2.1/24

    RTR1, S0: 201.50.26.13/30

    RTR2, E0: 172.16.3.2/24

    RTR2, E1: 172.16.1.1/24

    RTR2, S0: 200.100.29.241/30

SVR1 is the DNS server authoritative for AS 3; its address is 172.16.3.3. DNS1 reaches SVR1 at 201.50.13.1, whereas DNS2 reaches the same server at 200.100.30.254. Write routing and NAT configurations for RTR1 and RTR2, translating inside addresses appropriately for each ISP's assigned address block. Any inside device must be able to reach either ISP, but no packets can leave AS 3 with a private source address under any circumstance.

_____

_____

_____

2   The address of SVR2 in Figure 4-28 is 172.16.2.2, and the address of SVR3 is 172.16.2.3. Modify the configurations of Configuration Exercise 1 so that devices within ISP1's AS connect to the servers round-robin at the address 201.50.13.3.

_____

_____

_____

3   HTTP packets sent to 200.100.30.50 from ISP2 are sent to SVR2 in Figure 4-28. SMTP packets sent to 200.100.30.50 from ISP2 are sent to SVR3. Modify the configurations of the previous exercises to implement these translations.

_____

_____

_____

4   Five outside devices in Figure 4-28, 201.50.12.67–201.50.12.71, must appear to devices within AS 3 as having addresses 192.168.1.1–192.168.1.5, respectively. Add the appropriate NAT configurations to the previously created configurations.

_____

_____

_____

5   Devices in AS 3 of Figure 4-28 with addresses in the 172.16.100.0/24 subnet should all appear to have the IG address 200.100.30.75 when sending packets to ISP2. Modify the configurations of the previous exercises to accommodate this.

_____

_____

_____

6 In Figure 4-29, redundant links have been added so that RTR1 and RTR2 each have connections to both ISPs, and each accept full BGP routes from both ISPs. The address of RTR1, S1 is 200.100.29.137/30, and the address of RTR2, S1 is 201.50.26.93/30. Write configurations for the two routers, ensuring that all features added in the previous exercises still work correctly.

Figure 4-29 *The Internetwork for Configuration Exercise 6*

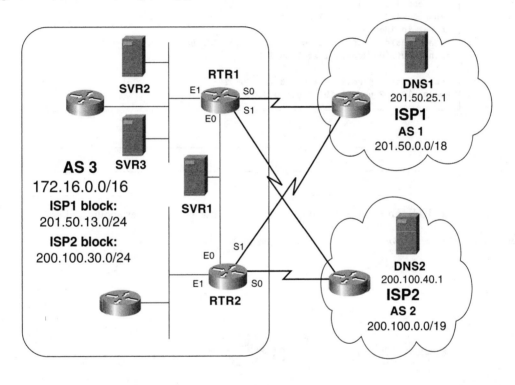

Troubleshooting Exercises

1 Identify the mistake in the configuration in Example 4-33.

Example 4-33 *Configuration for Troubleshooting Exercise 1*

```
ip nat pool EX1 192.168.1.1 192.168.1.254 netmask 255.255.255.0 type match-host
ip nat pool EX1A netmask 255.255.255.240
 address 172.21.1.33 172.21.1.38
 address 172.21.1.40 172.21.1.46
ip nat inside source list 1 pool EX1
ip nat inside source static 10.18.53.210 192.168.1.1
ip nat outside source list 2 pool EX1A
!
access-list 1 permit 10.0.0.0 0.255.255.255
access-list 2 permit 192.168.2.0 0.0.0.255
```

_____

_____

_____

2 RTR1 in Figure 4-30 connects two internetworks with overlapping addresses.

Figure 4-30 *The Internetwork for Troubleshooting Exercise 2*

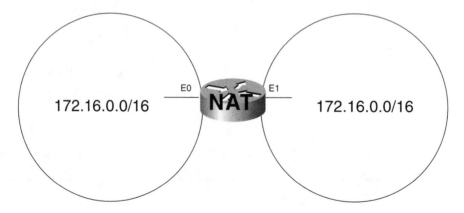

NAT is implemented on the router as configured in Example 4-34, but devices cannot communicate across the router. What is wrong?

_____

_____

_____

Example 4-34 *Configuration for Troubleshooting Exercise 2*

```
interface Ethernet0
 ip address 172.16.10.1 255.255.255.0
 ip nat inside
!
interface Ethernet1
 ip address 172.16.255.254 255.255.255.0
 ip nat outside
!
router ospf 1
 redistribute static metric 10 metric-type 1 subnets
 network 10.0.0.0 0.255.255.255 area 0
!
ip nat translation timeout 500
ip nat pool NET1 10.1.1.1 10.1.255.254 netmask 255.255.0.0
ip nat pool NET2 192.168.1.1 192.168.255.254 netmask 255.255.0.0
ip nat inside source list 1 pool NET1
ip nat outside source list 1 pool NET2
!
ip classless
!
ip route 10.1.0.0 255.255.0.0 Ethernet0
ip route 192.168.0.0 255.255.0.0 Ethernet1
!
access-list 1 permit 172.16.0.0 0.0.255.255
```

3 Refer to the configurations of Cozumel and Guaymas in Figure 4-21. If the first line of access list 1 in both configurations is removed, what is the result? Can Guaymas and Cozumel still ping each other?

_____

_____

_____

- **Requirements for IP Multicast**—This section explains the basic concepts of IP multicasting and examines the functions necessary for efficient multicasting, such as addressing and signaling.

- **Multicast Routing Issues**—This section describes the issues common to all IP multicast routing protocols.

- **Operation of the Distance Vector Multicast Routing Protocol (DVMRP)**—This section describes the operation of DVMRP.

- **Operation of Multicast OSPF (MOSPF)**—This section describes the operation of MOSPF.

- **Operation of Core-Based Trees (CBT)**—This section describes the operation of CBT.

- **Introduction to Protocol Independent Multicast (PIM)**—This section examines the basic PIM functions shared by both PIM-DM and PIM-SM.

- **Operation of Protocol Independent Multicast, Dense Mode (PIM-DM)**—This section describes the operation of PIM-DM.

- **Operation of Protocol Independent Multicast, Sparse Mode (PIM-SM)**—This section describes the operation of PIM-SM.

CHAPTER 5

Introduction to IP Multicast Routing

Multicasting is the process of sending data to a group of receivers. It might be argued that unicasting and broadcasting are subsets of multicasting. In the case of unicasting, there is only a single member of the group; in the case of broadcasting, all possible receivers are members of the group. This chapter demonstrates why such an argument is valid only on a conceptual level; in networking, at least, distinct differences exist between multicasting, unicasting, and broadcasting.

The delivery of radio and television programming is commonly called "broadcasting," but in reality it is multicasting. A transmitter sends data on a certain frequency, and some group of receivers acquires the data by tuning in to that frequency. The frequency is, in this sense, a multicast address. All receivers within the range of the transmission are capable of receiving the signal, but only those who listen to the correct frequency actually receive it.

The signal range brings up another important concept: Radio and television transmissions have *scope*—they are limited by the power of the transmitter. Receivers outside the scope of the transmission cannot receive the signal. You will see in this chapter that IP multicast networks also can have scope.

You have already had some exposure to IP multicasting in *Volume I*. RIP-2, EIGRP, and OSPF all employ multicasting for efficiency in communicating routing information. Applications can use multicasting for exactly the same reason—to increase network efficiency and conserve network resources. Figure 5-1 depicts a set of IP hosts. One of the hosts is a source (S) of data that must be delivered to a group (G) of receivers. There is more than one receiver, but the group does not contain all possible receivers.

Figure 5-1 *The Source Must Deliver the Same Data to Multiple Receivers*

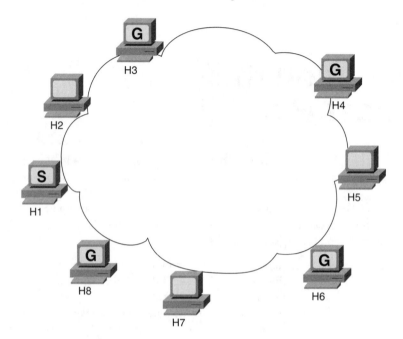

One approach is for the source to use a replicated unicast. That is, the source creates a separate packet containing identical data for each destination host in the group. Each packet is then unicast to a specific host, as shown in Figure 5-2.

If there are only a few destinations, this scheme works fine. In fact, many "multicast" applications in use today actually utilize replicated unicast. As the number of recipients grows into the hundreds or thousands, however, the burden on the host to create and send so many copies of the same data also increases. More importantly, the host's interface, directly connected medium, directly connected router, and slow WAN links all become potential bottlenecks. There are also problems if the data is delay-sensitive and cannot be contained in a single packet. If all the copies of packet number 2 must wait for all the copies of packet number 1 to be queued and sent, the queuing delay can introduce unacceptable gaps in the data stream.

Figure 5-2   *Unicasting the Same Data to Multiple Receivers Places a Burden on the Source*

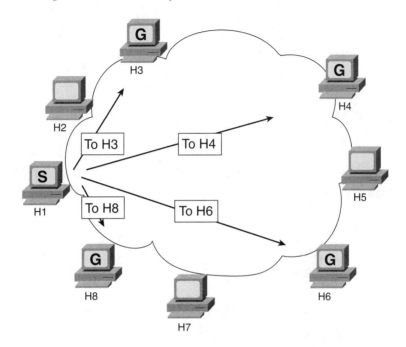

Another possible approach to multicasting is to broadcast the data as depicted in Figure 5-3. This removes the burden from the source and its local facilities, which now have to send only a single copy of each packet, but it can extend the burden to the other hosts in the network. Each host must accept a copy of the broadcasted packet and process the packet. It is only at the higher layers, or possibly within the application itself, that disinterested hosts recognize that the packet is to be discarded. If the number of hosts in the receiving group is small in relation to the total number of hosts in the network, this processing burden can again be unacceptable.

NOTE	When there are relatively few group members in relation to the total number of hosts in a multicast domain, the domain is *sparsely populated*. You will encounter this concept again later in this chapter.

Another difficulty with broadcasting is that IP routers do not forward packets to broadcast destinations. If the cloud in Figure 5-3 is a routed internetwork rather than a single broadcast medium, broadcast packets cannot reach the remote hosts. Directed broadcasts could be used, but that may be the worst possible solution. Not only would all hosts receive the packet, but also the source would again be burdened with having to replicate packets.

Figure 5-3 *Broadcasting Data Can Place a Burden on the Rest of the Network*

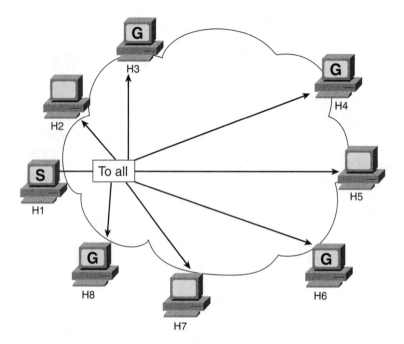

Multicasting allows the source to send a single packet to a single multicast destination address, thus removing the processing burden of replicating packets. Any receiver that is listening for the multicast address can receive the packet, removing the need for disinterested hosts to process an unwanted packet. And unlike broadcast packets, multicast-aware routers can forward multicast packets.

Many aspects of IP multicasting are not covered in this chapter. This book is concerned only with IP routing, so the primary focus of this chapter is on IP multicast routing. Other topics are touched upon only as they pertain to routing. For a complete treatment of IP multicast, have a look at the references cited at the end of the chapter in "Recommended Reading."

Requirements for IP Multicast

IP multicast is not a new concept; Steve Deering wrote the first RFC on multicast host requirements in 1986.[1] But it is only in the past few years that interest in multicasting has really taken off, as enterprises present increasing demands for one-to-many and many-to-many communications.

Examples of one-to-many applications include video and audio feeds for distance learning or company news, software distribution, network-based entertainment programs, news and stock updates, and database or Web site replication. The classic many-to-many application is conferencing, including video, audio, and shared whiteboards. Multiplayer games are another many-to-many application, although most corporations would be loath to include them on a wish list. As the use of such group-based applications increases, the efficiency and performance advantages of multicast over broadcast and replicated unicast for packet delivery become more attractive.

You must make a variety of protocol choices when implementing IP multicast. Because of this, multicast is presently found primarily in enterprise networks where a single administrative authority can make the design choices. As the popularity of multicasting grows, however, customers are increasing their pressure on ISPs to support multicast across the Internet. Interest in multicast within ISPs is also growing as more and more replicated unicast traffic is sent across the Internet, eating up more and more bandwidth. Although corporations have been interested in multicast for some time, the "killer app" that will finally bring IP multicast to maturity will be entertainment over the Internet.

Multicast has been researched for some time on a subset of the Internet known as the Multicast Backbone, or MBone. ISPs are also beginning to offer multicast services to their customers, such as UUNET's UUcast. However, ubiquitous availability of multicast services across the entire Internet must await further research and development of inter-AS protocols such as Multiprotocol BGP (MBGP) and Border Gateway Multicast Protocol (BGMP). Presently, no IP multicast routing protocols exist that support routing policies comparable to those supported by BGP. Until adequate tools for enforcing policy are introduced, it is unlikely that multicasting will find wide Internet acceptance.

The three basic requirements for supporting multicast across a routed internetwork are as follows:

- There must be a set of addresses by which multicast groups are identified.
- There must be a mechanism by which hosts can join and leave groups.
- There must be a routing protocol that allows routers to efficiently deliver multicast traffic to group members without overtaxing network resources.

This section examines the basics of each of these requirements; subsequent sections examine the details of the various protocols that are currently available to meet the requirements.

Multicast IP Addresses

The IANA has set aside Class D IP addresses for use as multicast addresses. According to the first octet rule, as described in Chapter 2, "TCP/IP Review," of *Volume I*, the first four bits of a Class D address are always 1110, as shown in Figure 5-4. Finding the minimum and maximum 32-bit numbers within this constraint, the range of Class D addresses is 224.0.0.0–239.255.255.255.

Figure 5-4   *Class D Addresses Are in the Range 224.0.0.0–239.255.255.255*

Rule	Minimums and maximums	Decimal range
Class A: First bit is always 0.	**0**0000000 = 0 **0**1111111 = 127	1 - 126* ** 0 and 127 are reserved.*
Class B: First two bits are always 10.	**10**000000 = 128 **10**111111 = 191	128 - 191
Class C: First three bits are always 110.	**110**00000 = 192 **110**11111 = 223	192 - 223
Class D: First four bits are always 1110.	**1110**0000 = 224 **1110**1111 = 239	224 - 239

Unlike the Class A, B, and C address ranges, the Class D range is "flat"—that is, subnetting is not used, as demonstrated by Figure 5-5. Therefore, with 28 variable bits, 2^{28} (more than 268 million) multicast groups can be addressed out of the Class D space.

Figure 5-5   *Unlike Class A, B, and C IP Addresses, Class D Addresses Do Not Have a Network Portion and a Host Portion*

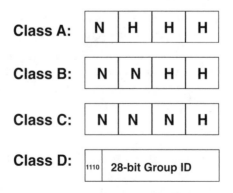

A multicast group is defined by its multicast IP address; groups may be permanent or transient. *Permanent* refers to the fact that the group has a permanently assigned address, not that members are permanently assigned to the group. In fact, hosts are free to join or leave any group. Transient groups are, as you might guess, groups that do not have a permanent existence—like a videoconference group. An unreserved address is assigned to the group and is relinquished when the group ceases to exist.

Table 5-1 shows some of the well-known addresses assigned to permanent groups by the IANA. You have encountered most of these addresses before, when you studied the routing protocols to which they are assigned. For example, you know that on a multiaccess network, OSPF DRothers send updates to the OSPF DR and BDR at 224.0.0.6; the DR sends packets to the DRothers at 224.0.0.5.

Table 5-1   *Some Well-Known Reserved Multicast Addresses*

Address	Group
224.0.0.1	All systems on this subnet
224.0.0.2	All routers on this subnet
224.0.0.4	DVMRP routers
224.0.0.5	All OSPF routers
224.0.0.6	OSPF designated routers
224.0.0.9	RIP-2 routers
224.0.0.10	EIGRP routers
224.0.0.13	PIM routers
224.0.0.15	CBT routers
224.0.1.39	Cisco-RP-Announce
224.0.1.40	Cisco-RP-Discovery

The IANA reserves all the addresses in the range 224.0.0.0–224.255.255.255 for routing protocols and other network maintenance functions. Multicast routers do not forward packets with a destination address from this range. There are also addresses outside of this range that are reserved for open and commercial groups; for example, 224.0.1.1 is reserved for the Network Time Protocol (NTP), 224.0.1.8 is assigned to SUN NIS+, and 224.0.6.0–224.0.6.127 are assigned to the Cornell ISIS Project. Yet another reserved range is 239.0.0.0–239.255.255.255. The use of this last group of addresses is discussed in the section "Multicast Scoping" later in this chapter. For a complete list of reserved Class D addresses, see Appendix C, "Reserved Multicast Addresses," or RFC 1700.

A group member's network interface card (NIC) also must be multicast-aware. When a host joins a group, the NIC determines a predictable MAC address. To accomplish this, all multicast-aware Ethernet, Token Ring, and FDDI NICs use the reserved IEEE 802 address 0100.5E00.0000 to determine a unique multicast MAC. It is significant that the eighth bit of this address is 1; that bit, in the 802 format, is the Individual/Group (I/G) bit. When set, it indicates that the address is a multicast address.

Multicasting Over Ethernet and FDDI

Ethernet and FDDI interfaces map the lower 23 bits of the group IP address onto the lower 23 bits of the reserved MAC address to form a multicast MAC address, as shown in Figure 5-6. Here, the Class D IP address 235.147.18.23 is used to create the MAC address 0100.5E13.1217.

Figure 5-6   *Multicast MAC Addresses on Ethernet and FDDI Networks Are Created by Concatenating the Last 23 Bits of the IP Address with the First 25 Bits of the MAC Address 0100.5E00.0000*

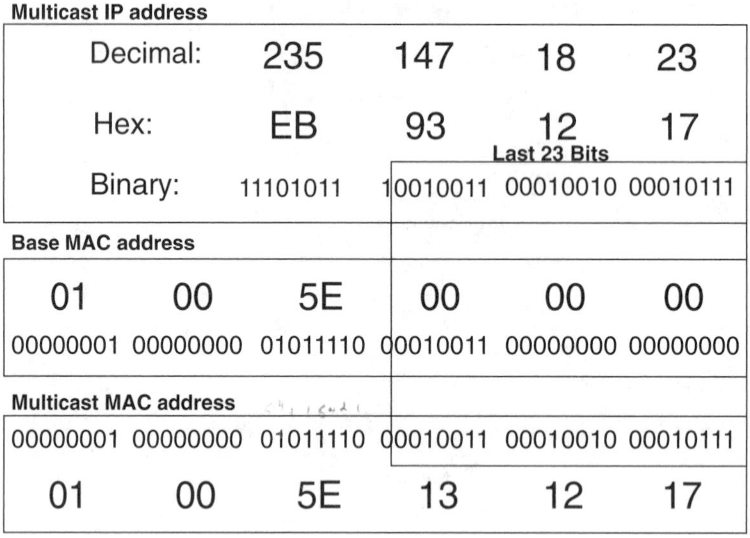

You already have encountered a couple of these addresses. Recall that in Chapter 9, "Open Shortest Path First," of *Volume I*, it was briefly explained that the All OSPF Routers address 224.0.0.5 uses a MAC address of 0100.5E00.0005, and the All OSPF Designated Routers address 224.0.0.6 uses the MAC address 0100.5E00.0006. Now you know why.

Because only the last 23 bits of the IP address are mapped to the MAC address, the resulting multicast MAC address is not universally unique. For example, the IP address 225.19.18.23 will produce the very same MAC address, 0100.5E13.1217, as 235.147.18.23. In fact, calculating the ratio of the total number of Class D addresses (2^{28}) to the number of possible MAC addresses under the reserved prefix (2^{23}) reveals that 32 different Class D IP addresses can be mapped to every possible MAC address!

The IETF's position is that the odds of two or more group addresses existing on the same LAN producing the same MAC address are acceptably remote. On the rare occasion that such a conflict does arise, the members of the two groups on the LAN will receive each other's traffic. In most of these cases, each group's packets will be destined for different port numbers or possibly have different application layer authentication schemes; each group's members will discard the other group's packets at the transport layer or above.

The benefits of this predictable MAC approach are twofold:

- A multicast source or router on the local network has to deliver only a single frame to the multicast MAC address in order for all group members on the LAN to receive it.

- Because the MAC address is always known if the group address is known, there is no need for an ARP process.

Multicasting Over Token Ring

Multicast over Token Ring networks is treated differently. Token Ring specifies *functional* or *function-dependent* MAC addresses to reach stations running such common TR functions as Active Monitor, Ring Parameter Server, and Ring Error Monitor. The first bit of the first octet of the TR MAC address is the I/G address, which indicates whether the address is unicast (I/G=0) or broadcast/multicast (I/G=1). The second bit is the Universal/Local (U/L) bit, which indicates whether the address is a manufacturer burned-in address (U/L=0) or a locally administered address (U/L=1). Additionally, the first bit of the third octet is the Functional Address Indicator (FAI). The job of the FAI is to distinguish functional addresses (I/G=1, U/L=1, FAI=0) from locally administered group address (I/G=1, U/L=1, FAI=1). A specific functional address is created by setting one, and only one, of the 31 remaining bits after the FAI. So, for example, the functional address of the Active Monitor is C000.0000.0001 and a bridge is reached at C000.0000.0100. Because only one of the 31 bits can be set, there are 31 available functional addresses. This rule has consequences for IP multicast.

Token Ring MAC addresses use the *little-endian* format, in which each octet is read from right to left; Ethernet uses the *big-endian* format, in which each octet is read from left to right. Therefore, the Ethernet multicast MAC address of 0100.5E13.1217 would be read by Token Ring as 8000.7AC8.48E6. The FAI in this TR address is 0, but more than one of the following 31 bits is set to 1. Therefore, Token Ring interprets the address as an illegal functional address.

NOTE   FDDI also uses the little-endian format, but it does not use functional addresses such as Token Ring and therefore supports the same mapping scheme as Ethernet.

Because IP addresses cannot be mapped into Token Ring addresses as they are into Ethernet addresses, another method must be found to resolve this issue. Currently, there are two methods for addressing TR frames carrying IP multicast packets:[2]

- Just use the broadcast address FFFF.FFFF.FFFF for all frames carrying multicast packets.

- Use a single reserved functional address, C000.0004.0000.

Cisco routers default to the first method and support the second method with the command **ip multicast use-functional** configured on TR interfaces.

Both of these methods have drawbacks. The first method is inefficient, delivering multicast packets to all stations on the ring and relying on upper-layer protocols to accept or reject the packets. The second method can be used only if the TR NICs on all stations on the ring recognize the functional address. Not all NICs do. Another problem with the second method is that TR NICs that recognize a functional address send an interrupt to the station's CPU. If there is even moderate IP multicast traffic on the ring, and especially if there is multicast traffic for several different groups all mapped to the one functional address, host performance will suffer. Because of these limitations, Token Ring is a poor choice for supporting IP multicast.

Group Membership Concepts

Before a host can join a group, it (or its user) must know what groups are available to be joined, and how to join them. Various mechanisms are available for advertising multicast groups, such as online "TV Guides," or Web-based schedules such as the one shown in Figure 5-7.

Figure 5-7   *One Way of Locating Multicast Groups Is Through Web-Based Announcements, Such as This Schedule of MBone Sessions at www.cilea.it/MBone/browse.htm*

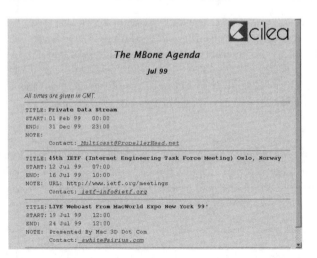

There are also tools that utilize such protocols as Session Description Protocol (SDP) and Session Advertisement Protocol (SAP) to describe multicast events and advertise those descriptions. Figure 5-8 shows an example of an application that uses these protocols. A user also may learn of a multicast session by invitation, such as via a simple e-mail.

Figure 5-8   *Applications Such as Multikit Listen for SDP and SAP and Display the Multicast Sessions Advertised by Those Protocols*

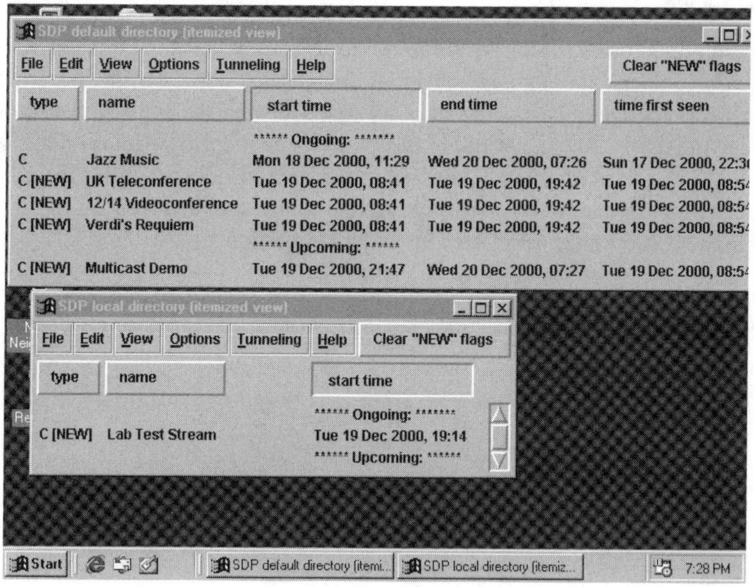

A detailed discussion of these mechanisms is beyond the scope of this book. This section presumes that hosts have somehow learned of a multicast group, and it examines the issues around joining and leaving the group. After examining these issues, you will see how they are handled by the Internet Group Management Protocol (IGMP), the de facto protocol for managing IP multicast groups on individual subnets.

Joining and Leaving a Group

Interestingly, the source of a multicast session does not have to be a member of the multicast group to which it is sending traffic. In fact, the source typically does not even know what hosts, if any, are members of the group. Receivers are free to join and leave groups at any time. This again fits the earlier analogy of a radio or television signal; audience members can tune in or tune out at any time, and the originating station has no direct way of knowing who is listening.

If the source and all group members share a common LAN, no other protocols are required. The source sends packets to a multicast IP (and MAC) address, and the group members "tune in" to this address. But sending multicast traffic over a routed internetwork becomes more complicated. Every router could merely forward all multicast packets onto every LAN, in case there are group members on the LAN, but this partially circumvents the goal of multicasting, which is to conserve network resources. If no group members are on the LAN, bandwidth and processing is wasted not only on that subnet, but also on all data links and routers leading to it.

Therefore, a router must have some means to learn whether a connected network includes group members, and if so, members of what group. When a router becomes aware of a multicast session, it can query all of its attached subnets for hosts that want to join the receiving group. The query might be addressed to the "all systems on this subnet" address of 224.0.0.1, or it might be addressed to the specific address of the group for which it is querying. If one or more hosts respond, the router can then forward the session's packets onto the appropriate subnet, as illustrated in Figure 5-9.

Figure 5-9   *Multicast Group Member Discovery*

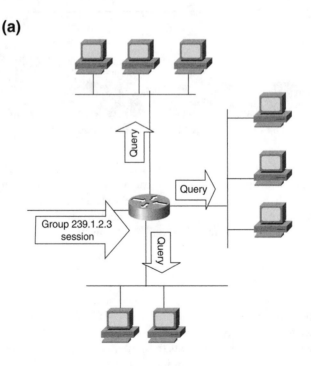

(b)

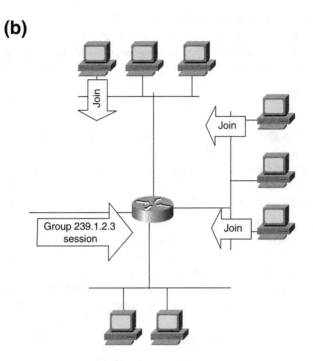

(c)

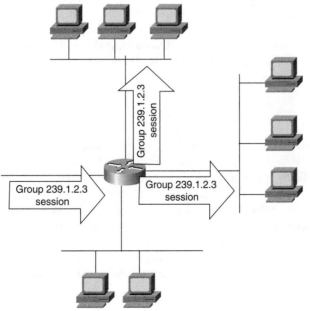

The router can periodically resend queries to the subnet. If there are still group members on the subnet, they will respond to all queries to let the router know they are still active in the group. If no hosts respond, the router assumes that all hosts on the subnet have left the group, and it ceases forwarding the group's packets onto the subnet.

Join Latency

A problem with the scheme described so far is that if a host knows of a group it wants to join, it is not always practical for the host to wait for a router to query for the group. To reduce this wait time, a host could send a message to the router requesting a join, without waiting for a query. Upon receiving the join request, the router immediately forwards the multicast traffic onto the subnet.

This procedure has benefits for more than just the local subnet. In the section "Multicast Routing Concepts" later in this chapter, you will see that having hosts initiate the join can help make multicast routing protocols more efficient. If a router has no group members on any of its attached subnets, and the subnets are not transit networks for multicast traffic to other routers, the router itself can request that upstream neighbors not forward multicast traffic to it. The result is that the traffic streams do not enter parts of the network in which there are no group members. If the router then receives a join request on one of its attached subnets, it can send a request upstream to begin receiving the relevant data stream.

The trade-off of this scheme is that if a host sends a join request to its local router, and then has to wait for the router to request the appropriate traffic from its upstream neighbors, the *join latency* is increased. Join latency is the period between the time a host sends a join request and the time the host actually begins receiving group traffic. Of course, if there are already other group members on the subnet when the host decides to join, the join latency will be practically zero. The host has no reason to send a join request to the router; it can just begin listening to the packets that are already being forwarded onto its subnet for the other group members.

Leave Latency

Allowing a host to explicitly notify its local router when it leaves a group can increase efficiency as well. Rather than having to wait for no hosts to respond to its queries before it implicitly concludes that there are no group members on a subnet, the router can actively determine whether there are remaining members. Upon receiving a leave notification from a host, the router immediately sends a query onto the subnet, asking whether there are any remaining members. If no one responds, the router concludes that there are no more members and can cease forwarding packets for the group onto that subnet. The result is a decreased *leave latency*, which is the period between the time the last group member on a subnet leaves the group and the time the router stops forwarding group traffic onto the subnet.

Host-initiated group leaves also improve routing protocol efficiency. If a router knows that it no longer has any group members on any of its subnets, it can "prune" itself from the multicast tree. The sooner a router determines that there are no group members, the sooner it can prune itself.

Decreased join and leave latencies also can improve the overall quality of a multicast network. There could be a large suite of multicast groups known to a host. Low join and leave latencies mean that the end user can easily "channel surf" through the available groups in the same way that users casually flip through radio and television channels.

Group Maintenance

The message that a host sends to a router to indicate that it wants to join a group is known as a *report*. A host can use several possible destination addresses when sending a report:

- The report can be unicast to the router that sent the query. The problem here is that there may be more than one router attached to the subnet that is tracking the group. All concerned routers must hear the report.

- The report can be sent to the "all routers on this subnet" address of 224.0.0.2. However, you will see shortly that it is useful for other group members on the subnet to also hear the report.

- To ensure that other group members hear the report, it can be sent to the "all systems on this subnet" address of 224.0.0.1. This method reduces the efficiency of multicasting, however, by forcing all multicast-capable hosts on the subnet, not just the group members, to process the report beyond Layer 2.

- The report can be sent to the group address. This method ensures that all group members on the subnet, and any routers listening for members of the group, hear the report. The NICs of hosts that are not members of the group reject the reports based on their Layer 2 address.

If all group members on a subnet respond to a query, bandwidth is unnecessarily wasted. After all, the router needs to know only that there is at least one member of the group on the subnet; it does not need to know exactly how many there are, or who they are. Another problem with all group members responding to a query is the possibility of collisions if all members respond at once. Backing off and retransmitting consumes more network and host resources. If many group members are on the subnet, there is an increased probability that multiple collisions will occur before everyone sends his report.

Sending reports to the group address eliminates multiple reports on a subnet. When a query is received, each group member starts a timer based on a random value. The member does not send a report until the timer expires. Because the timers are random, it is much more likely that one member's timer will expire before the other timers. This member sends a report, and because the report is sent to the group address, all other members hear it. These other members, hearing the report, cancel their timers and do not send a report of their own.

As a result, only one report is generally sent on the subnet. One report per subnet is all the router needs.

Multiple Routers on a Network

The possibility was raised in the preceding section that multiple routers might be attached to a subnet, all of which need to know whether group members are present. Figure 5-10 shows an example. Two routers are attached to the subnet, both of which receive the same multicast stream from the same source over different routes. If one router or route fails, the group members can continue to receive their multicast session from the other router. Under normal circumstances, however, it is inefficient for both routers to forward the same data stream onto the subnet.

Figure 5-10   *Two Routers Receive the Same Multicast Session, but Only One Forwards It onto the Subnet*

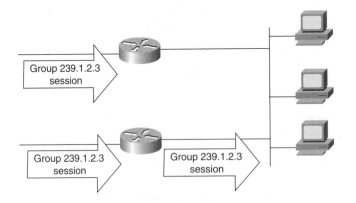

The routers are aware of each other because of their routing protocols. So one way to ensure that only one router forwards the session onto the subnet is to add a designated router, or *querier*, function to the multicast routing protocol. The querier is responsible for forwarding the multicast stream. The other router or routers only listen, and they begin forwarding the stream only if the querier fails.

The problem with allowing the routing protocol to elect a querier is that multiple IP multicast routing protocols are available. If the two routers in Figure 5-10 are running incompatible protocols, their respective querier election processes will not detect each other; each will decide that it is the querier, and both will forward the data stream.

The local group management protocol, however, is independent of the routing protocols. The routers have to run this common protocol to query group members, so it makes sense to give the querier function to the group management protocol. This guarantees that the routers are speaking a common language on the subnet and can agree on which is responsible for forwarding the session.

Internet Group Management Protocol (IGMP)

Regardless of which of the several routing protocols is used in a multicast internetwork, IGMP is always the "language" spoken between hosts and routers. All hosts that want to join multicast groups, and all routers with interfaces on subnets containing multicast hosts, must implement IGMP. It is a control protocol like ICMP, sharing some functional similarities. Like ICMP, it is responsible for managing higher-level data exchanges. IGMP messages are encapsulated in IP headers like ICMP (with a protocol number of 2), but unlike ICMP, the messages are limited to the local data link. This is guaranteed both by the IGMP implementation rules, which require that a router never forward an IGMP message, and by always setting the TTL in the IP header to 1.

There are two current versions of IGMP: IGMPv1 is described in RFC 1112,[3] and IGMPv2 is described in RFC 2236.[4] Cisco IOS Software Release 11.1 and all later versions support IGMPv2 by default; however, many host TCP/IP implementations still support only version 1 (Windows NT 4.0 with service packs previous to SP4, for example). For this reason, the default can be changed with the **ip igmp version** command.

This next section discusses IGMPv2 and then presents its differences with IGMPv1. IGMPv3 has also been proposed,[5] although IOS does not currently support it. However, version 3 is briefly discussed in this section with the expectation that Cisco IOS Software may support it in the near future.

IGMPv2 Host Functions

Hosts running IGMPv2 use three types of messages:

- Membership Report messages
- Version 1 Membership Report messages
- Leave Group messages

Membership Report messages are sent to indicate that a host wants to join a group. The messages are sent when a host first joins a group, and sometimes in response to a Membership Query from a local router.

When a host first learns of a group and wants to join, it does not wait for the local router to send a query. As you will learn in the sections on the various multicast routing protocols, the router may not—in fact, most likely does not—have any knowledge of the particular group the host wants to join, and therefore does not query for members. If the host had to wait for a query, it might never get the opportunity to join. Instead, when the host first joins a group, it sends an unsolicited Membership Report for the group.

Multicast sessions are identified in the routers by a (source, group) pair of addresses, where source is the address of the session's originator and group is the Class D group address. If the local multicast router does not already have knowledge of the multicast session the host wants to join, it sends a request upstream toward the source. The data stream is received, and the router begins forwarding the stream onto the subnet of the host that requested membership.

The destination address of the Membership Report message's IP header is the group address, and the message itself also contains the group address. To ensure that the local router receives the unsolicited Membership Report, the host sends one or two duplicate reports separated by a short interval. RFC 2236 recommends an interval of 10 seconds.

IGMPv2 hosts support IGMPv1 Membership Reports for backward compatibility. The mechanisms that IGMPv2 uses to detect and support IGMPv1 hosts and routers on its subnet are discussed in the section "IGMPv1 Versus IGMPv2."

The local router periodically polls the subnet with queries. Each query contains a value called the Max Response Time, which is normally 10 seconds (specified in units of tenths of a second). When a host receives a query, it sets a delay timer to a random value between 0 and the Max Response Time. If the timer expires, the host responds to the query with one Membership Report for each group to which it belongs.

NOTE   All multicast-enabled devices are members of the "all systems on this subnet" group, represented by the group address 224.0.0.1. Because this is a default, hosts do not send Membership Reports for this group.

Because the destination of the Membership Report is the group address, other group members that might be on the subnet hear the report in addition to the router. If the host receives a Membership Report for a group before its delay timer expires, it does not send a Membership Report for that group. In this way, the router is informed of the presence of at least one group member on the subnet, without all members flooding the subnet with reports.

When a host leaves a group, it notifies the local router with a Leave Group message. The message contains the address of the group being left, but unlike Membership Report messages, the Leave Group message is addressed to the "all routers on this subnet" address of 224.0.0.2. This is because only the multicast routers on the subnet need to know that the host is leaving; other group members do not.

RFC 2236 recommends that a Leave Group message be sent only if the leaving member was the last host to send a Membership Report in response to a query. As the next section explains, the local router always responds to a Leave Group message by querying for remaining group members. If group members other than the "last responder" leave quietly, the router continues forwarding the session and does not send a query. As a result, a little bandwidth is saved. However, this behavior is not required. If the designer of a multicast application does not want to include a state variable to remember whether this host was the last to respond to a query, the application can always send a Leave Group message when it leaves a group.

IGMPv2 Router Functions

The only type of IGMP message sent by routers is a query. Within IGMPv2, there are two subtypes of queries:

- General Query
- Group-Specific Query

The General Query is the message with which the router polls each of its subnets to discover whether group members are present and to detect when there are no members of a group left on a subnet. By default, the queries are sent every 60 seconds; the default can be changed to any value between 0 and 65,535 seconds with the command **ip igmp query-interval**.

As described in the preceding section, the query also contains a value called the Max Response Time. This value specifies the maximum amount of time the host has to respond to a query with a Membership Report. By default, the Max Response Time is 10 seconds; you can use the command **ip igmp query-max-response-time** to change it. The value is carried in the message in an 8-bit field and is expressed in units of tenths of a second (although the value is specified with **ip igmp query-max-response-time** in units of seconds). For example, the default 10 seconds is expressed within the message as 100 tenths of a second. Therefore, the range that can be specified is 0 to 255 tenths, or 0 to 25.5 seconds.

The General Query message is sent to the "all systems on this subnet" address of 224.0.0.1 and does not contain a reference to any specific group. As a result, the single message polls for reports from members of any and all groups that might be active on the subnet. The router tracks known groups and the interfaces attached to subnets with active members, as shown in the output in Example 5-1.

Example 5-1   *The show ip igmp groups Command Displays the IP Multicast Groups of Which the Router Is Aware*

```
Gold#show ip igmp groups
IGMP Connected Group Membership
Group Address    Interface        Uptime    Expires   Last Reporter
224.0.1.40       Serial0/1.306    3d01h     never     0.0.0.0
228.0.5.3        Ethernet0/0      00:09:07  00:02:55  172.16.1.254
239.1.2.3        Ethernet0/0      1d08h     00:02:53  172.16.1.23

Gold#
```

If a Cisco multicast router does not hear a Membership Report on a particular subnet for a group within 3 times the query interval (3 minutes by default), the router declares that no active members of the group are on the subnet. This covers the eventuality of a lone group member being disconnected or otherwise not following the IGMPv2 rules for leaving a group.

NOTE

This differs from RFC 2236, which specifies twice the query interval plus one Max Response Time interval.

The normal way that a host leaves a group is by sending a Leave Group message. When a router receives a Leave Group message, it must determine whether any remaining members of that group are on the subnet. To do this, the router issues a Group-Specific Query, which differs from a General Query in that it contains the group address, and it also uses the group address as its destination address.

If the Group-Specific Query were to become lost or corrupted, a remaining group member on the subnet might not send a report. As a result, the router would incorrectly conclude that there are no group members on the subnet and stop forwarding the session packets. To protect against this eventuality, the router sends two Group-Specific Queries, separated by a 1-second interval.

When a multicast-enabled router first becomes active on a subnet, it assumes that it is the *querier*—the router responsible for sending all General and Group-Specific Queries to the subnet—and immediately sends a General Query.

NOTE

RFC 2236 recommends sending multiple queries; however, Cisco's IGMPv2 sends only one.

This action serves both to quickly discover the group members active on the subnet and to alert other multicast routers that may be on the subnet. When there are multiple routers, the rule for electing the querier is simple: The router with the lowest IP address is the querier. So when the existing router on the subnet hears the General Query from the new router, it checks the source address. If the address is lower than its own IP address, it relinquishes the role of querier to the new router. If its own IP address is lower, it continues sending queries. When the new router receives one of these queries, it sees that the old router has a lower IP address and becomes a nonquerier.

If the nonquerier does not hear queries from the querier within a certain period of time, known as the *Other Querier Present Interval*, it concludes that the querier is no longer present and assumes that role. Cisco IOS Software has a default Other Querier Present Interval of twice the Query Interval, or 120 seconds; you can change this with the command **ip igmp query-timeout**.

IGMPv1

The important differences between IGMPv1 and IGMPv2 are as follows:

- IGMPv1 has no Leave Group message, meaning that there is a longer period between the time the last host leaves a group and the time the router stops forwarding the group traffic.

- IGMPv1 has no Group-Specific Query. This follows from the fact that there is no Leave Group message.

- IGMPv1 does not specify a Max Response Time in its query messages. Instead, hosts have a fixed Max Response Time of 10 seconds.

- IGMPv1 has no querier election process. Instead, it relies on the IP multicast routing protocol to elect a designated router on the subnet. Because different protocols use different election mechanisms, it is possible under IGMPv1 to have more than one querier on a subnet.

The section "IGMP Message Format" illustrates how these differences affect the fields in IGMPv1 and IGMPv2 messages.

In some cases, IGMPv1 and IGMPv2 implementations might exist on the same subnet:

- Some group members might run IGMPv1 while others run IGMPv2.

- Some group members might run IGMPv2 while the router runs IGMPv1.

- The router might run IGMPv2 while some group members run IGMPv1.

- One router might run IGMPv1 while another router on the subnet runs IGMPv2.

RFC 2236 describes several mechanisms that allow IGMPv2 to adapt in these situations. If there is a mixture of version 1 and version 2 members on the same subnet, the version 2 members treat both version 1 and version 2 Membership Reports the same when determining whether to suppress their own Membership Reports. That is, if a version 2 member hears a query from the router and subsequently hears a version 1 Membership Report for its group before its own delay timer expires, it does not send a Membership Report. Version 1 hosts, on the other hand, ignore version 2 messages. Therefore, if a version 2 Membership Report is sent for a group first, the version 1 member also sends a report when its delay timer expires. This does not cause problems for the version 2 host, and this is important for the version 2 router so that it is aware of the presence of version 1 group members.

If a host is running version 2 and the local router is running version 1, the IGMPv1 router ignores the version 2 messages. So when a version 2 host receives a version 1 query, it responds with version 1 Membership Reports. The IGMPv1 query also does not specify a Max Response Time, so the IGMPv2 host uses the fixed version 1 period of 10 seconds. The host may or may not send Leave Group messages in the presence of version 1 routers; the IGMPv1 router does not recognize Leave Group messages, and ignores them.

If a version 2 router receives a version 1 Membership Report, it treats all members of the group as if they are running version 1. The router ignores Leave Group messages and hence does not send Group-Specific Queries that the version 1 members would ignore. Instead, it sets a timer, known as the *Old Host Present Timer* (as shown in Example 5-2). The period of the timer is the same value as the Group Membership Interval. Whenever a new version 1 Membership Report is received, the timer is reset; if the timer expires, the router concludes that no more version 1 members of the group are on the subnet and reverts to version 2 messages and procedures.

NOTE   As described earlier, the Group Membership Interval is the period of time that the router waits to hear a Membership Report before declaring that no members are on a subnet. Cisco's default is three times the Query Interval.

Example 5-2   *This Multicast Router Is Receiving IGMPv2 Membership Reports for Group 239.1.2.3 and IGMPv1 Membership Reports for Group 228.0.5.3. The Version 1 Reports Cause the Router to Set an Old Host Present Timer for That Group*

```
Gold#debug ip igmp
IGMP debugging is on
Gold#
IGMP: Send v2 Query on Ethernet0/0 to 224.0.0.1
IGMP: Received v2 Report from 172.16.1.23 (Ethernet0/0) for 239.1.2.3
IGMP: Received v1 Report from 172.16.1.254 (Ethernet0/0) for 228.0.5.3
IGMP: Starting old host present timer for 228.0.5.3 on Ethernet0/0
IGMP: Send v2 Query on Ethernet0/0 to 224.0.0.1
IGMP: Received v2 Report from 172.16.1.23 (Ethernet0/0) for 239.1.2.3
IGMP: Received v1 Report from 172.16.1.254 (Ethernet0/0) for 228.0.5.3
IGMP: Starting old host present timer for 228.0.5.3 on Ethernet0/0
```

Notice in Example 5-2 that the router continues to send version 2 General Queries. The only significant difference between these queries and version 1 queries is that the Max Response Time is nonzero. The field in which this value is carried is unused in version 1, and the version 1 host ignores it. As a result, the host interprets version 2 queries as version 1 queries.

Another point of interest in Example 5-2 is that the Old Host Present timer is set only for group 228.0.5.3. The router treats only this group as an IGMPv1 group. Group 239.1.2.3, on the same interface, is treated as a version 2 group.

If version 1 and version 2 routers exist on the same subnet, the version 1 router will not participate in the querier election process. Because of this, it is important that the version 2 router behaves as a version 1 router for consistency. There is no automatic conversion to version 1; the version 2 router must be manually configured with the **ip igmp version 1** command.

IGMPv3

Because IGMPv3 is still under development and is not yet supported, this section does not examine it in the detail that the first two versions are examined. Instead, this section summarizes the major features that this version will add if and when it comes into general use.

The primary addition to IGMPv3 is the inclusion of a Group-and-Source-Specific Query. This allows a group to be identified not only by group address, but also by source address. The Membership Report and Group Leave messages are modified so that they also can make this identification.

When a group has many sources (a many-to-many group), the IGMPv3 router can perform source filtering based on the requests of group members. For example, a particular member may want to receive group traffic from only certain specified sources, or it may want to receive traffic from all sources except certain specified sources. The member can express these wants in a Membership Report with *Include* or *Exclude* filter requests. If no member on a particular subnet wants to receive traffic from a particular source, the router does not forward that source's traffic onto the subnet.

IGMP Message Format

IGMPv2 uses a single message format, as shown in Figure 5-11. The IP header encapsulating the message indicates a protocol number of 2. Because the IGMP message must not leave the local subnet on which it was originated, the TTL is always set to 1. Additionally, IGMPv2 messages carry the IP Router Alert option that informs routers to "examine this packet more closely."[6]

Figure 5-11 *The IGMPv2 Message Format*

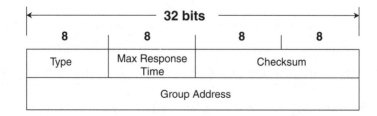

The fields for the IGMPv2 message are defined as follows:

- *Type* describes one of four message types:
  - Membership Query (0x11) is used by the multicast router to discover the presence of group members on a subnet. A General Membership Query message sets the Group Address field to 0.0.0.0, whereas a Group-Specific Query sets the field to the address of the group being queried.

— Version 2 Membership Report (0x16) is sent by a group member to inform the router that at least one group member is present on the subnet.

— Version 1 Membership Report (0x12) is used by IGMPv2 hosts for backward compatibility with IGMPv1.

— Leave Group (0x17) is sent by a group member if it was the last member to send a Membership Report, to inform the router that it is leaving the group.

- *Max Response Time* is set only in query messages. In all other message types, the field is set to 0x00. This field specifies a period, in units of 1/10 second, during which at least one group member must respond with a Membership Report message.

- *Checksum* is the 16-bit one's complement of the one's complement sum of the IGMP message. This is the standard checksum algorithm used by TCP/IP.

- *Group Address* is set to 0.0.0.0 in General Query messages and is set to the group address in Group-Specific messages. Membership Report messages carry the address of the group being reported in this field; Group Leave messages carry the address of the group being left in this field.

Figure 5-12 shows the format of an IGMPv1 message.

Figure 5-12 *The IGMPv1 Message Format*

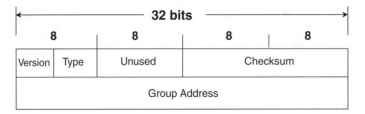

The only differences in the IGMPv1 format from IGMPv2 are as follows:

- The first octet is split into a 4-bit Version field and a 4-bit Type field.

- The second octet, which is the Max Response Time in version 2, is unused. This field is set to 0x00.

Another difference is that the Router Alert option is not set in the IP header of IGMPv1 messages.

IGMPv1 defines just two message types:

- Host Membership Query (Type 1)

- Host Membership Report (Type 2)

The Version field is always set to 1. As a result, you can see that the combined Version and Type field is 0x11 for a Host Membership Query message, which is the same value as the

8-bit Type field of an IGMPv2 Membership Query. The combined Version and Type fields of the Host Membership Report is 0x12, whereas the Type field of the IGMPv2 Membership Report is 0x16.

Cisco Group Membership Protocol (CGMP)

A fundamental design principle of IP multicast is that traffic should be delivered only to destinations that want to receive the traffic. You have seen how Class D addressing and its associated MAC addressing help meet this goal at the data link layer, and how IGMP allows routers to determine whether they should deliver sessions to particular subnets. You will see in subsequent sections how IP multicast routing protocols extend this principle across internetworks, delivering multicast sessions only to those routers that have group members on their attached subnets.

What about a switched network, however, such as the one shown in Figure 5-13? Large office buildings and campuses abound with such networks. The Ethernet switches, which are really just high-powered, high-port-density transparent bridges, limit unicast traffic by learning what MAC addresses are associated with what ports. They can then filter and forward frames based on this information. But broadcast traffic is forwarded to every port of every switch. A large network such as the one depicted in Figure 5-13 is normally broken into several virtual LANS (VLANs) to control the scope of the broadcast traffic. However, it is not unusual to find "flat" switched networks this large—one big subnet, or broadcast domain.

Figure 5-13 *Unless This Switched Campus Network Is Divided into Multiple VLANs, It Comprises a Single Broadcast Domain. That Is, the Router Port Defines a Layer 3 Subnet, and Any Broadcast Frame Is Transmitted Out of All 384 Switch Ports*

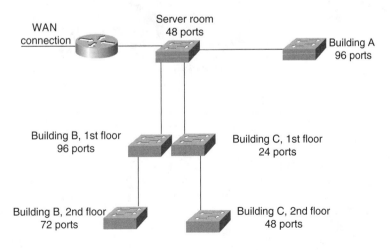

Just as broadcast frames are forwarded to every port within a broadcast domain, so too are frames carrying IP multicast packets. After all, a broadcast domain is nothing more than a multicast group to which all hosts belong. Figure 5-14 illustrates the problem. Three group members are attached to a 24-port switch. An IGMP Membership Report is sent to the router, and the router begins forwarding the appropriate multicast session onto the subnet. Because IGMP is a Layer 3 protocol, the Ethernet switch has no easy way to determine what ports the group members are on. As a result, the multicast traffic is forwarded to all 23 ports (discounting the source port).

Figure 5-14 *One of the Three Group Members Sends an IGMP Membership Report, Joining Multicast Group A (a). When the Router Forwards the Multicast Session, the Switch Replicates the Frames to All Ports Except the Source Port (b)*

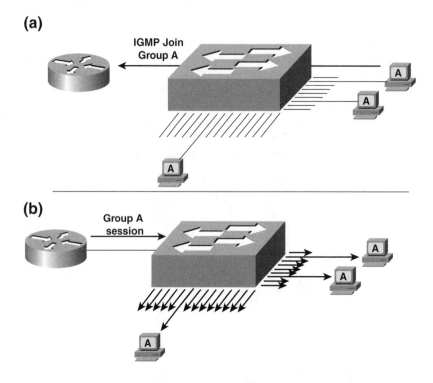

Obviously, the preferable behavior is for the switch to forward the multicast session only out of those ports to which the group members are attached. If this can be accomplished, switching is not only more efficient, but also is the preferable way to implement LANs that carry multicast sessions. For example, a videoconferencing multicast stream uses approximately 1 Mbps of bandwidth, and an MPEG II video stream can use approximately 4 Mbps. If these sessions can be limited to the group members' ports, network and host resources can be conserved.

Cisco Group Membership Protocol (CGMP) is designed to do exactly that—distribute multicast sessions only to those switch ports on which group members are located. Before examining the operation of CGMP, the next section takes a brief look at some other solutions for regulating switched multicast traffic.

Alternative Multicast Control Methods on Switched Networks

There are three methods besides CGMP for constraining multicast traffic in switched environments, all of which are supported by Cisco Catalyst software:

- Manual configuration of switched multicast trees
- GMRP
- IGMP Snooping

Because none of these three solutions has any direct bearing on routing, only an overview is provided in this section. Have a look at Cisco's *Catalyst Switch Software Documentation* on CCO for more details and complete configuration instructions.

Manual configuration of switched multicast trees just means that you make static entries into the switch's bridging table. Cisco Catalyst switches call this table the *content addressable memory* (CAM) table. Suppose that the group members in Figure 5-13 are on switch ports 2/3, 2/4, and 2/19, the router is on port 1/1, and the group address is 239.0.5.10. This IP address gives the group a multicast MAC address of 0100.5E00.050A. The command for manually entering this information into the Catalyst CAM table is as follows:

```
set cam permanent 01-00-5e-00-05-0a 2/3-4,2/19
set multicast router 1/1
```

The preceding adds the entry to the CAM table and writes it to the switch's NVRAM; the entry can be removed only with the **clear cam** or **clear config** command. Alternatively, the **static** keyword can be used rather than the **permanent** keyword. In that case, the entry is not written to NVRAM and is removed if the switch is reset.

The second command is optional. It informs the switch of the port on which the multicast router is located, further limiting the scope of the multicast traffic within the switch.

There are several limitations to using manual configuration. The two most obvious are that it is not dynamic, and it does not scale. If another group member joins on a different port, a group member leaves, or a different group is added to the switch, the information must be manually configured. For anything other than small, fixed groups, manual configuration is not practical.

Another limitation is that manual configuration cannot be used across VLAN boundaries. If the group 239.0.5.10 is on VLAN 1, for example, and VLAN 2 also exists on the switch, none of the members of 239.0.5.10 can be in the second VLAN—they must all reside in the same VLAN.

Another technique is to use GARP Multicast Registration Protocol (GMRP), an open protocol defined in the IEEE 802.1p standard that enables MAC-layer multicast group addresses to be dynamically registered and deregistered in the switch. GMRP is enabled on the switch with the command **set gmrp enable**; no configuration is required on the router. As the IEEE 802.1p standard suggests, GMRP is strictly a Layer 2 protocol.

The third technique is IGMP Snooping, enabled on the Catalyst switch with the command **set igmp enable**. With this option, the switch software examines IGMP messages and, as a result, knows the location of both multicast routers and group members. Unlike the proprietary CGMP, IGMP Snooping is supported by several switch manufacturers, making it a better choice for multivendor switched networks; however, detection of IGMP messages means that every IP packet must be examined. When this is implemented in software, the result can be a significant degradation of switch performance. You should use IGMP Snooping only if all the switches in the multicast network can implement the function in hardware, using specialized application-specific integrated circuits (ASICs) that can examine the IP packets at line rate. For example, this is supported on Cisco Catalyst switches with NetFlow Feature Card II (NFFC II).

Operation of CGMP

Although both Cisco routers and Cisco switches must be configured to run CGMP, only the routers produce CGMP packets. The CGMP process on switches only reads the packets. There are two types of CGMP packets:

- *Join* packets are sent by the router to tell the switch to add one or more members to a multicast group.

- *Leave* packets are sent by the router to tell the switch to remove one or more members from a multicast group, or to delete the group altogether.

These two packet types have an identical format, and the destination of the packets is always the reserved MAC address 0100.0cdd.dddd. CGMP-enabled switches listen for this address.

The essential information in both packets is one or more pairs of MAC addresses:

- Group Destination Address (GDA)
- Unicast Source Address (USA)

When a CGMP router comes online, it makes itself known to the switch by sending a CGMP Join packet with the GDA set to zero (0000.0000.0000) and the USA set to its own MAC address. The CGMP-speaking switch now knows that a multicast router is attached to the port on which it received the packet. The router repeats the packet every 60 seconds as a keepalive.

When a host wants to join a group, it sends an IGMP Membership Report message, as illustrated in Part A of Figure 5-15. The switch, following normal IEEE 802.1 procedures, enters the host's MAC address into its CAM table.

Figure 5-15 *When a Cisco Router Receives an IGMP Membership Report on a CGMP Interface (a), It Sends a CGMP Join Packet Telling the Switch to Map the Host MAC Address to the Group MAC Address (b)*

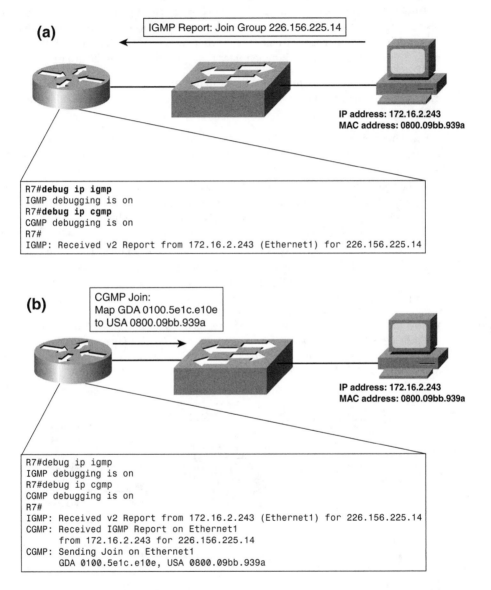

NOTE   The Catalyst's CAM table is a bridging table that records the MAC addresses it has heard and the ports on which they were heard.

When the router receives the IGMP Membership Report, it sends a CGMP Join packet with the GDA set to the group MAC address and the USA set to the host's MAC address, as illustrated in Part B of Figure 5-15. The switch is now aware of the multicast group, and because the switch knows the port on which the host is located, it can add that port to the group. When the router sends frames to the group MAC address, the switch forwards a copy of the frame out all ports (except the router port) associated with the group.

As long as group members remain on the switched network, the router sends IGMP queries every 60 seconds, which the switch forwards to the members. The switch forwards the IGMP reports, sent in reply to the queries, to the router.

When a host sends an IGMPv2 Leave message, the message is forwarded to the router, as illustrated in Part A of Figure 5-16. The router sends two IGMP Group-Specific Queries, which the switch forwards to all group ports. If another member responds to the Group-Specific Query, the router sends a CGMP Leave packet to the switch with the GDA set to the group MAC address and the USA set to the leaving member's MAC address, as illustrated in Part B of Figure 5-16. This packet tells the switch to delete just the leaving member's port from the group. If no members respond to the Group-Specific Query, the router concludes that no members are left on the segment. In this case, it sends a CGMP Leave packet to the switch with the GDA set to the group MAC address and the USA set to zero, as illustrated in Part C of Figure 5-16. This packet tells the switch to remove the group itself from the CAM table.

Figure 5-16 *When a Router Receives an IGMP Leave Message on a CGMP Interface (a), It Queries to Learn Whether There Are Other Members Left on the Subnet (b). If Other Members Respond, It Sends a CGMP Leave Packet to the Switch, Removing Just the Leaving Member. If No Members Respond, the Router Sends a CGMP Leave Message to the Switch, Removing the Entire Group (c)*

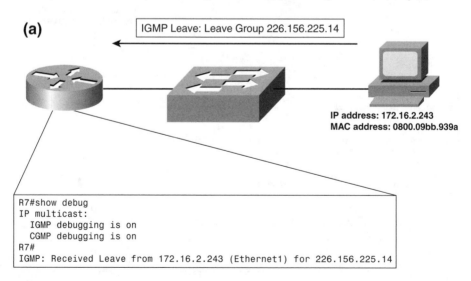

(b)

IGMP Group-Specific Query:
Anyone else on Group 226.156.225.14 ?

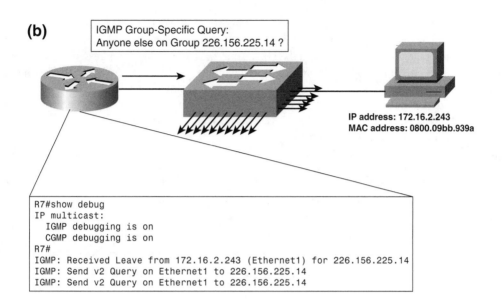

IP address: 172.16.2.243
MAC address: 0800.09bb.939a

```
R7#show debug
IP multicast:
  IGMP debugging is on
  CGMP debugging is on
R7#
IGMP: Received Leave from 172.16.2.243 (Ethernet1) for 226.156.225.14
IGMP: Send v2 Query on Ethernet1 to 226.156.225.14
IGMP: Send v2 Query on Ethernet1 to 226.156.225.14
```

(c)

CGMP Leave:
Delete GDA 0100.5e1c.e10e

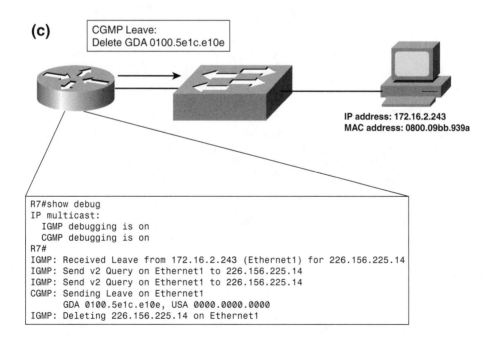

IP address: 172.16.2.243
MAC address: 0800.09bb.939a

```
R7#show debug
IP multicast:
  IGMP debugging is on
  CGMP debugging is on
R7#
IGMP: Received Leave from 172.16.2.243 (Ethernet1) for 226.156.225.14
IGMP: Send v2 Query on Ethernet1 to 226.156.225.14
IGMP: Send v2 Query on Ethernet1 to 226.156.225.14
CGMP: Sending Leave on Ethernet1
       GDA 0100.5e1c.e10e, USA 0000.0000.0000
IGMP: Deleting 226.156.225.14 on Ethernet1
```

Table 5-2 summarizes the various possible values of the GDA and USA in CGMP packets, and the meaning of each. Only the last two Leave packets have not been discussed. A Leave with the GDA set to zero and the USA set to the router's MAC address signals the switch to remove all groups and ports associated with the router port from the CAM. This message is sent if the router's CGMP function has been disabled on that port. A Leave with both the GDA and the USA set to zero tells all switches receiving the message to delete all groups and associated ports from the CAM. This message is sent as the result of a **clear ip cgmp** command entered at the router.

Table 5-2   *CGMP Packets*

Type	GDA	USA	Function
Join	Zero	Router MAC	Identifies the port as a multicast router port.
Join	Group MAC	Member MAC	Identifies the multicast group and adds the member's port to the group.
Leave	Group MAC	Member MAC	Removes the member port from the specified group.
Leave	Group MAC	Zero	Removes the group from the CAM.
Leave	Zero	Router MAC	Removes all groups and ports bound for the router's port from the CAM.
Leave	Zero	Zero	Removes all groups from all switches.

CGMP Packet Format

The source MAC address of frames carrying CGMP packets is the MAC address of the originating router, and the destination MAC address is the reserved multicast address 0100.0cdd.dddd. Only routers originate CGMP packets. Within the frame, the packet is encapsulated in a SNAP header. The OUI field of the SNAP header is 0x00000c, and the type field is 0x2001.

Figure 5-17 shows the format of the CGMP packet.

Figure 5-17 *The CGMP Packet Format*

The fields of the CGMP packet are defined as follows:

- *Version* is always set to 0x1 to signify version 1.

- *Type* specifies whether the packet is a Join (0x0) or Leave (0x1).

- *Reserved* is always set to 0 (0x0000).

- *Count* specifies how many GDA/USA pairs the packet carries.

- *GDA* is the Group Destination Address. When the field is nonzero, it specifies the MAC address of a multicast group. When the field is set to zero (0000.0000.0000), it specifies all possible groups.

- *USA* is the Unicast Source Address. When the field is nonzero, it may specify the MAC address of the originating router or the MAC address of a group member. When it is zero, it specifies all group members and the originating router.

Multicast Routing Issues

Currently, five IP multicast routing protocols are in various stages of development and deployment:

- Distance Vector Multicast Routing Protocol (DVMRP)

- Multicast OSPF (MOSPF)

- Core-Based Trees (CBT)

- Protocol-Independent Multicast, Dense Mode (PIM-DM)
- Protocol-Independent Multicast, Sparse Mode (PIM-SM)

The particulars of each of these protocols are examined in subsequent sections, along with their individual advantages and disadvantages. Although Cisco IOS Software does not support all five of the protocols, a study of each will help you better understand the rationale behind the support or nonsupport of each. Of the five, Cisco IOS Software supports PIM-DM and PIM-SM. There is also just enough support of DVMRP to allow PIM networks to connect to DVMRP networks. These five protocols are multicast IGPs. Multicasting across AS boundaries is discussed in Chapter 7, "Large-Scale IP Multicast Routing."

The five IP multicast routing protocols differ significantly from each other, but like the unicast routing protocols, they also share many characteristics. This section presents the general issues surrounding the design of any multicast routing protocol.

Multicast Forwarding

Like any other router, the two fundamental functions of a multicast router are route discovery and packet forwarding. This section addresses the unique requirements of multicast forwarding, and the next section looks at the requirements for multicast route discovery.

Unicast packet forwarding involves forwarding a packet toward a certain destination. Unless certain policies are configured, a unicast router is uninterested in the source of the packet. The packet is received, the destination IP address is examined, a longest-match route lookup is performed, and the packet is forwarded out a single interface toward the destination.

Instead of forwarding packets toward a destination, multicast routers forward packets away from a source. This distinction may sound trifling at first glance, but it is actually essential to correct multicast packet forwarding. A multicast packet is originated by a single source but is destined for a group of destinations. At a particular router, the packet arrives on some incoming interface, and copies of the packet may be forwarded out multiple outgoing interfaces.

If a loop exists so that one or more of the forwarded packets makes its way back to the incoming interface, the packet is again replicated and forwarded out the same outgoing interfaces. The result can be a *multicast storm*, in which packets continue to loop and be replicated until the TTL expires. It is the replication that makes a multicast storm potentially so much more severe than a simple unicast loop. Therefore, all multicast routers must be aware of the source of the packet and must only forward packets away from the source.

A useful and commonly used terminology is that of *upstream* and *downstream*. Multicast packets should always flow downstream from the source to the destinations, never upstream toward the source. To ensure this behavior, each multicast router maintains a multicast forwarding table in which (source, group) or (S, G) address pairs are recorded. Packets from a particular source and destined for a particular group should always arrive on an upstream interface and be forwarded out one or more downstream interfaces. By definition, an upstream interface is closer to the source than any downstream interface, as illustrated by Figure 5-18. If a router receives a multicast packet on any interface other than the upstream interface for that packet's source, it quietly discards the packet.

Figure 5-18 *By Identifying Upstream and Downstream Interfaces in Relation to Each Multicast Source, Routers Avoid Multicast Routing Loops*

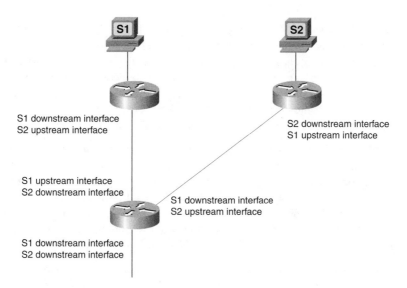

Of course, the router needs some mechanism for determining the upstream and downstream interfaces for a given (S, G). This is the job of the multicast routing protocol.

Multicast Routing

The function of a unicast routing protocol is to find the shortest path to a particular destination. This determination might be made from the advertisements of neighboring routers (distance vector) or from a shortest path tree calculated from a topological database (link state). The end result in both cases is an entry in the routing or forwarding table indicating the interface to forward packets out, and possibly a next-hop router. The cited interface is, from the perspective of the unicast routing protocol, the downstream interface on the path to the destination—the closest interface to the destination.

In contrast, the function of a multicast routing protocol is to determine the upstream interface—the closest interface to the source. Because multicast routing protocols concern themselves with the shortest path to the source, rather than the shortest path to the destination, the procedure of forwarding multicast packets is known as *reverse path forwarding*.

The easiest way for a multicast routing protocol to determine the shortest path to a source is to consult the unicast forwarding table. However, as the last section pointed out, multicast packets are forwarded based on the information in a separate multicast forwarding table. The reason for this is that the router must record not only the upstream interface for the source of a particular (S, G) pair, but also the downstream interfaces associated with the group.

The simplest way to forward packets would be to merely declare all interfaces except the upstream interface to be downstream interfaces. This approach, known as *reverse path broadcasting* (RPB), has obvious shortcomings. As the name implies, packets are effectively broadcast to all subnets on the routed internetwork. Group members probably exist on only a subset of the subnets—probably a small subset. Flooding a copy of every multicast packet onto every subnet not only defeats the objective of multicasting to deliver packets only to interested receivers, but also actually defeats the purpose of routing itself.

A slightly improved procedure is *truncated reverse path broadcast* (TRPB). When a router discovers, via IGMP, that one of its attached subnets has no group members, and there are no next-hop routers on the subnet, the router stops sending multicast traffic onto the subnet. In keeping with the arboreal terminology, such a nontransit subnet is a *leaf network.* Although TRPB helps conserve resources on leaf networks, it is really little improvement over RPB. Interrouter links, on which bandwidth is more likely to be at a premium, continue to carry multicast traffic whether they need to or not.

So the second function of a multicast routing protocol is to determine the actual downstream interfaces associated with an (S, G) pair. When all routers have determined their upstream and downstream interfaces for a particular source and group, a multicast tree has been established (see Figure 5-19). The root of the tree is the source's directly connected router, and the branches lead to all subnets on which group members reside. No branches lead to "empty" subnets"—subnets with no members of the associated group. The forwarding of packets only out interfaces leading to group members is called *reverse path multicast* (RPM).

Multicast trees last only for the duration of the multicast session. And because members can join and leave the group throughout the lifetime of the session, the structure of the tree is dynamic. The third function of a multicast routing protocol is to manage the tree, "grafting" branches as members join the group and "pruning" branches as members leave the group. The next three sections discuss issues surrounding this third function.

Figure 5-19 *The Paths Leading from the Multicast Source to All Group Members' Subnets Form a Multicast Tree*

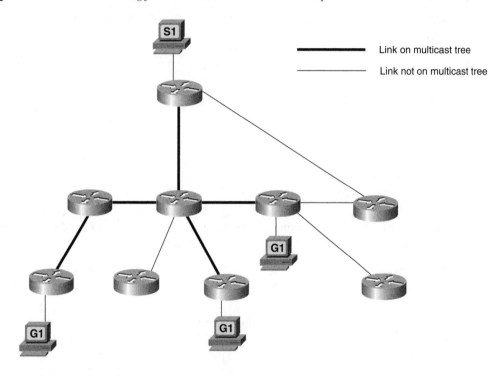

Sparse Versus Dense Topologies

A dense topology is one in which there are many multicast group members relative to the total number of hosts in an internetwork. Sparse topologies have few group members relative to the total number of hosts. Sparse does not mean that there are few hosts. A sparse topology might mean there are 2,000 members of a group, for example, spread among 100,000 total hosts.

No specific numeric ratios delineate sparse and dense topologies. It is safe to say, however, that dense topologies are usually found in switched LAN and campus environments, and sparse topologies usually involve WANs. What is important is that multicast routing protocols are designed to work best in one or the other topology and are designated as either *dense mode* protocols or *sparse mode* protocols. Table 5-3 shows the class to which each of the five multicast routing protocols belongs.

Table 5-3   *Dense Mode and Sparse Mode Multicast Routing Protocols*

Protocol	Dense Mode	Sparse Mode
DVMRP	X	
MOSPF	X	
PIM-DM	X	
PIM-SM		X
CBT		X

Implicit Joins Versus Explicit Joins

As was previously observed, members may join or leave a group at any time during the lifetime of a multicast session, and as a result, the multicast tree can change dynamically. It is the job of the multicast routing protocol to manage this changing tree, adding branches as members join and pruning branches as members leave.

The multicast routing protocol may accomplish this task by using either an *implicit* or *explicit* join strategy. Implicit joins are sender-initiated, whereas explicit joins are receiver-initiated.

Multicast routing protocols that maintain their trees by implicit joins are commonly called *broadcast-and-prune* or *flood-and-prune* protocols. When a sender first initiates a session, each router in the internetwork uses reverse path broadcasting to forward the packets out every interface except the upstream interface. As a result, the multicast session initially reaches every router in the internetwork. When a router receives the multicast traffic, it uses IGMP to determine whether there are any group members on its directly connected subnets. If there are not, and there are no downstream routers to which the traffic must be forwarded, the router sends a poison-reverse message called a *prune message* to its upstream neighbor. That upstream neighbor then stops forwarding the session traffic to the pruned router. If the neighbor also has no group members on its subnets, and all downstream routers have pruned themselves from the tree, that router also sends a prune message upstream. The result is that the multicast tree is eventually pruned of all branches that do not lead to routers with attached group members. Figure 5-20 illustrates the broadcast-and-prune technique.

Figure 5-20 *Broadcast-and-Prune Protocols First Use RPB to Forward a Multicast Session to All Parts of the Internetwork (a). Routers with No Connection to Group Members Then Prune Themselves from the Tree (b) so That the Resulting Tree Only Reaches Routers with Group Members (c)*

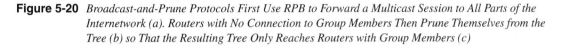

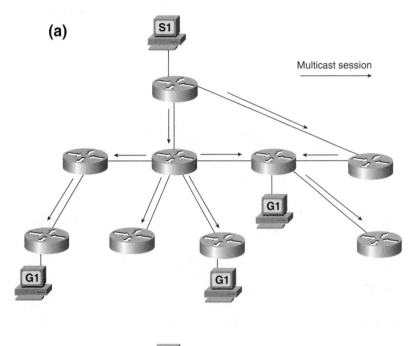

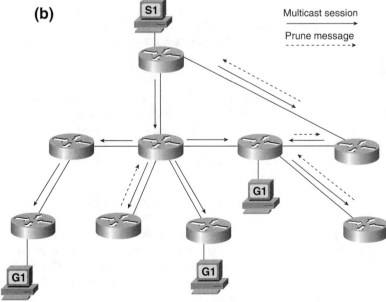

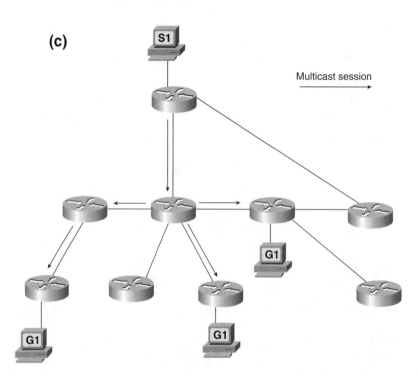

For every (S, G) pair in its forwarding table, every router in the internetwork maintains state for each of its downstream interfaces. The state is either *forward* or *prune*. The prune state has a timer associated with it, and when the timer expires, the session traffic is again forwarded to neighbors on that interface. Each neighbor once again checks for group members and floods the traffic to its own downstream neighbors. If new group members are discovered, the traffic continues to be accepted. Otherwise, a new prune message is sent upstream.

The broadcast-and-prune technique is better suited to dense topologies than to sparse ones. The initial flooding to all routers, the periodic reflooding as prune states expire, and the maintenance of prune states all contribute to a waste of network resources when many or most branches are pruned. There is also a strong element of illogic in the maintenance of prune state, requiring routers that are not participating in the multicast tree to remember that they are not a part of the tree.

A better technique for sparse topologies is the explicit join, in which the routers with directly attached group members initiate the join. When a group member signals its router, via IGMP, that it wants to join a group, the router sends a message upstream toward the source, indicating the join. In contrast to a prune message, this message can be thought of as a *graft* message; the router sending the message is grafting itself onto the tree. If all of a router's group members leave, and the router has no downstream neighbors active on the group, the router prunes itself from the tree.

Because traffic is never forwarded to any router that does not explicitly request the traffic, network resources are conserved. And because prune state is not kept by nonparticipating routers, overall memory is conserved. As a result, explicit joins scale better in sparse topologies. The argument can be made, of course, that explicit joins always scale better, regardless of whether the topology is sparse or dense. Table 5-4 shows which of the five multicast routing protocols use implicit joins and which use explicit joins.

Table 5-4   *Implicit Join and Explicit Join Protocols*

Protocol	Implicit Join	Explicit Join
DVMRP	X	
MOSPF		X
PIM-DM	X	
PIM-SM		X
CBT		X

Source-Based Trees Versus Shared Trees

Some multicast routing protocols construct separate multicast trees for every multicast source. These trees are *source-based* trees, because they are rooted at the source. The multicast trees that have been presented in previous sections have been source-based trees.

You have learned that multicast trees can change during the lifetime of a multicast session as members join and leave the group, and that it is the responsibility of the multicast routing protocol to dynamically adapt the tree to these changes. However, some parts of the tree might not change. Figure 5-21 shows two multicast trees superimposed onto the same internetwork. Notice that although the trees have different sources and different members, their paths pass through at least one common router.

Shared trees take advantage of the fact that many multicast trees can share a single router within the network. Rather than root each tree at its source, the tree is rooted at a shared router called (depending on the protocol) the *rendezvous point* (RP) or *core*. The RP is predetermined and strategically located in the internetwork. When a source begins a multicast session, it registers with the RP. It may be up to the source's directly connected router to determine the shortest path to the RP, or it may be up to the RP to find the shortest path to each source. Explicit joins are used to build trees from routers with attached group members to the RP. Rather than the (S, G) pair recorded for source-based trees, the shared trees use a (*, G) state. This state reflects that fact that the RP is the root of the tree to the group and that there may be many sources upstream of the RP. More importantly, a separate (S, G) pair must be recorded for each distinct source on a source-based tree. Shared trees, on the other hand, record only a single (*, G) for each group.

Figure 5-21 *These Two Multicast Trees Have Different Shapes, but They Both Pass Through the Single Router RP*

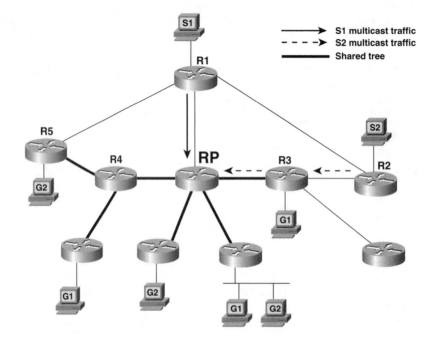

The impact of the (S, G) entries can be demonstrated with a few simple calculations. Suppose in some source-tree, flood-and-prune multicast domain, there are 200 multicast groups and an average of 30 sources per group. Each router must record 30 (S, G) entries for each group, or 30 * 200 = 6000 entries. If there are 150 sources in each of the 200 groups, the entries increase to 150 * 200 = 30,000.

NOTE   Keep in mind that with interactive multicast applications, many group members (receivers) are also sources (senders).

In contrast, shared tree routers record a single (*, G) entry for each group. So if there are 200 groups in a shared-tree multicast domain, the RP records 200 (*, G) entries. Most significantly, this number does not vary with the number of sources. Another way of stating these facts is that source-based trees scale on an order of $(S^G * G^N)$, and shared trees scale on an order of (G^N), where G^N is the number of groups in the multicast domain and S^G is the number of sources per group. Impact is greatly reduced on non-RP routers also, because they do not keep state for groups for which they do not forward packets. These routers record a single (*, G) entry for each active downstream group.

This scalability means that shared trees are generally preferable in sparse topologies. As usual, however, there are trade-offs. First, the path from the source through the RP may not be the optimum path to every group member for every group. Reexamining Figure 5-21, notice that a member of group 2 is attached to router R5. The optimal path from the source S2 to this group member is R2-R1-R5. But the source traffic must reach the RP first, so the path taken is R2-R3-RP-R4-R5. RPs must be chosen carefully to minimize suboptimal paths. Another drawback is that the RP can become a bottleneck when there are multiple high-bandwidth multicast sessions. Because of both suboptimal paths and RP congestion, latency can become a problem in poorly designed shared tree internetworks. The RP also represents a single point of failure. Finally, shared trees can be difficult to debug.

Table 5-5 shows which multicast routing protocols use source-based trees and which use shared trees. Comparing this table with Table 5-4, you can see that although MOSPF uses explicit joins, it also uses source-based trees. The converse situation is never true—a protocol using shared trees must always use explicit joins, because it has no other way to maintain loop-free trees.

Table 5-5   *Source-Based Tree and Shared Tree Protocols*

Protocol	Source-Based Trees	Shared Trees
DVMRP	X	
MOSPF	X	
PIM-DM	X	
PIM-SM		X
CBT		X

Multicast Scoping

You have seen in the preceding discussions of multicast routing issues that although multicast routing certainly uses fewer network resources than other strategies, such as replicated unicast or simple flooding, it can still be wasteful in some circumstances. This is particularly true of broadcast-and-prune protocols when used in sparse topologies. In some instances, a multicast source and all group members can be found close together in relation to the size of the entire internetwork. In such a case, a mechanism that limits the multicast traffic to the general area on the internetwork in which the members are located would help conserve resources. There also may be cases in which, for security or other policy reasons, the extent of the multicast traffic must be limited.

When multicast traffic is confined to "islands," the traffic is *scoped*. Put another way, multicast scoping is the practice of putting boundaries on the reach of multicast traffic.

TTL Scoping

One method for establishing boundaries to limit the scope of multicast traffic is to set a special filter on outgoing interfaces that checks the TTL value of all multicast packets. Only packets whose TTL value, after the normal decrement performed by the router, exceeds a configured threshold are forwarded. All other multicast packets are dropped.

Figure 5-22 shows an example. On this router, a multicast packet arrives on interface E2 with a TTL of 13. The router decrements the packet's TTL to 12. Interface E0 has a multicast TTL threshold of 0, which is the default; no multicast packets are blocked based on their TTL. Therefore, a copy of the packet is forwarded out E0. Likewise, a copy of the packet is forwarded out interface E1, because its TTL threshold is set to 5, which is less than the packet's TTL. However, the packet is not forwarded out E3. That interface's TTL threshold is 30, meaning that only packets whose TTL value is greater than 30 can be forwarded.

Figure 5-22 *Multicast Packets Are Forwarded Only Out Downstream Interfaces Whose TTL Threshold Is Less Than the Outgoing Packet's TTL*

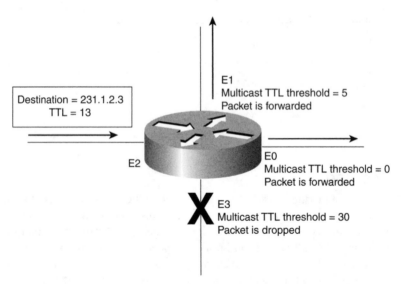

TTL scoping has been used on the MBone for some time. The MBone is constructed of regional multicast networks connected through the Internet by IP-over-IP tunnels. Table 5-6 shows typical TTL thresholds used to restrict multicast traffic in the MBone. If you want some traffic to stay within a single site—high-bandwidth real-time video, for example— you configure the source application to send packets with a TTL no higher than 15.

Table 5-6   *MBone TTL Thresholds*

TTL Value	Restriction
0	Restricted to the same host
1	Restricted to the same subnet
15	Restricted to the same site
63	Restricted to the same region
127	Worldwide
191	Worldwide limited bandwidth
255	Unrestricted

TTL scoping has several shortcomings. First, it is inflexible. An interface's TTL threshold applies to all multicast packets. If you want some multicast sessions to pass the threshold and others to be restricted by it, the separate applications sourcing the sessions must be manipulated. This leads to the second problem: Users must be trusted to set the TTLs in their multicast applications correctly. If a session is sourced with a too-high TTL, it will pass outside the boundary you have set.

Another problem with TTL scoping is that it is difficult to implement in all but the simplest topologies. As your multicast internetwork grows in both scale and complexity, predicting the correct thresholds to contain and pass the correct sessions becomes a challenge.

Finally, TTL scoping can cause inefficiencies with broadcast-and-prune protocols. Figure 5-23 demonstrates the problem. The internetwork is a multicast site, and the boundary router has a TTL threshold of 8 configured on the interfaces leading to other parts of the internetwork. The multicast source is generating a session in which the TTL of all packets is set to 8, in keeping with local policy, to limit its traffic to the multicast site. There are no group members anywhere along the left branch of the tree, so those routers should prune themselves all the way back to the source's directly connected router. In fact, you can see that one router has sent a prune message upstream to its neighbor.

The problem is with the boundary router and its configured TTL filter. When the multicast packets reach this router, the packets are discarded at both downstream interfaces, because the packets' TTL values are less than the TTL threshold. This is expected behavior. However, the packet discards also mean that no IGMP queries for group members take place. Without the queries, the router does not send a prune message back upstream. As a result, multicast traffic continues to be forwarded unnecessarily through all the routers leading to the boundary router.

Figure 5-23   *The TTL Multicast Filter at the Boundary Router Is Preventing It from Sending a Prune Message Upstream*

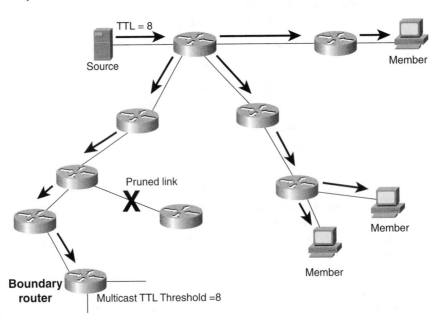

Administrative Scoping

Administrative scoping, described in RFC 2365,[7] takes a different approach to bounding multicast traffic. Rather than filter on TTL values, a range of Class D addresses is reserved for scoping. Filtering on these group addresses can then set boundaries. The reserved range of multicast addresses is 239.0.0.0–239.255.255.255.

The administratively scoped address space can be further subdivided in a hierarchical manner. For example, RFC 2365 suggests using the range 239.255.0.0/16 for local or site scope and the range 239.192.0.0/14 for organizationwide scope. An enterprise is, however, free to utilize the address space in any way it sees fit. In this regard, the reserved Class D range is similar to the RFC 1918 addresses reserved for private use. And like those addresses, the administratively scoped multicast address space is nonunique. Therefore, it is important to set filters for 239.0.0.0–239.255.255.255 so that none of the addresses in that range leak into the public Internet.

You have encountered both TTL scoping and address-based scoping already in this chapter and elsewhere in this book. Recall that the TTL for IGMP and OSPF packets is always set to 1 to prevent the packets from being forwarded by any receiving router. In this way, the scope is set to the local subnet. Similarly, routers do not to forward packets whose addresses are in the range 224.0.0.0–224.0.0.255. This range, which includes all the addresses shown in Table 5-1, is also scoped to the local subnet.

Operation of the Distance Vector Multicast Routing Protocol (DVMRP)

DVMRP uses the broadcast-and-prune method to build a separate source-based tree for every multicast source. It uses a variant of RIP to discover the shortest path to the source—hence the name *Distance Vector* Multicast Routing Protocol. Each multicast tree is maintained dynamically by pruning and grafting branches as group members leave and join the group.

DVMRP uses seven packet types:

- DVMRP Probe
- DVMRP Report
- DVMRP Prune
- DVMRP Graft
- DVMRP Graft Acknowledgement
- DVMRP Ask Neighbors2
- DVMRP Neighbors2

All the packets have a destination address of 224.0.0.4, the reserved All DVMRP Routers address (see Table 5-1). The uses of the various packet types are described in the following sections, and the section "DVMRP Packet Formats" gives a detailed description of the packet formats.

There are several versions of DVMRP. Version 1 is described in RFC 1075,[8] and version 3, the most recent version, is described in an Internet draft.[9] This chapter describes version 3 of the protocol. You should be aware that earlier versions of DVMRP vary significantly both in functionality and in packet formats. While an effort is made in this section to note differences between DVMRPv3 and some earlier versions, coverage of all the differences would make the section unacceptably long and complex. In this section, "DVMRP" is understood to mean DVMRPv3 unless otherwise noted. If you are working with an earlier version or have an interest in the differences, you should read RFC 1075, the relevant *mgated* documentation, or the software documentation of the router supporting the earlier version.

NOTE   Most routers running DVMRP are found on the MBone, and most of those run a version of *mrouted* or *mgated*.

Cisco IOS Software does not support a full implementation of DVMRP; however, it does support connectivity to a DVMRP network such as the MBone.

Neighbor Discovery and Maintenance

The first task when a DVMRP router comes online is to discover its neighbors using Probe packets. Each Probe packet contains the following information:

- A set of flags describing the originating router's DVMRP capabilities. These flags are used to determine backward compatibility with earlier versions of the protocol.

- A generation ID, which is used to detect a change in a neighbor state.

- A list the addresses of neighbors from which the originating router has received probes.

Out of all this information, the most fundamental is the list of neighbor addresses. When a DVMRP router receives a Probe packet, it records the address of the originating router and the interface on which the probe was received. Recall that the receiving router never forwards any packet with a destination address from the 224.0.0.0/24 range. Both because the Probe packet has a destination address of 224.0.0.4, and because it is originated with a TTL of 1, the receiving DVMRP router knows that the originator is a directly connected neighbor. When the router sends its own probes, it lists all the neighbor addresses it has learned on the subnet on which the probe is sent. When a router sees its own IP interface address in a neighbor's probe, it knows that two-way communication is established with the neighbor.

After a neighbor has been discovered, probes also are used as keepalives. Probes are sent at 10-second intervals, and a neighbor is declared dead if a probe is not received from it within 35 seconds.

Earlier versions of DVMRP do not use Probe packets. Instead, they discover neighbors upon reception of route advertisement messages from their neighbors.

During the neighbor discovery process, earlier versions of DVMRP would, when discovering more than one router on a subnet with group members, select a designated router. The designated router, which is the only router that sends multicast session packets and IGMP queries onto the subnet, is the router with the lowest IP address on that subnet. DVMRPv3 determines a designated router through the IGMPv2 querier election process rather than by reading the source IP addresses of received route advertisement messages.

As you learned previously, a broadcast-and-prune multicast routing protocol must store prune states. If the router is restarted, however, it cannot know what prunes have been sent or received. It may also be slow to reestablish multicast forwarding if it has to wait for the next regularly scheduled route update. The generation ID, a nondecreasing 32-bit number derived from some changing reference such as a time-of-day clock, is designed to alleviate these problems. When a DVMRP router restarts, its generation ID changes. When neighbors detect this changed number in the router's Probe messages, they flush all prune information previously received from the router. They also immediately send a copy of their routing table to the neighbor. Multicast data will again flow to the restarted router due to the cleared prune information, and the router must again prune itself or remain a part of the tree.

The DVMRP Routing Table

The primary purpose of the DVMRP routing table is to determine, for each multicast source, the upstream interface for that source. As explained earlier in the chapter, this process is important for loop avoidance; if a packet is received from a source on any interface other than the upstream interface—the interface closest to the source—the packet must be discarded.

DVMRP uses a variant of RIP to advertise the complete routing table plus all directly connected multicast-enabled subnets. The routes are advertised in DVMRP Report messages, sent to every neighbor using the All DVMRP Routers address 224.0.0.4. Route updates are sent every 60 seconds, known as the *Route Report Interval*. The exception to this rule occurs when a new neighbor is discovered by the probe process. In this case, the routing table is immediately unicast to the new neighbor. Flash updates also can be used to shorten reconvergence times.

If a route is not updated within 140 seconds, the *route expiration time*, the route is put into holddown for two report intervals (120 seconds). During this time, the route is advertised with a metric of infinity; when the holddown time expires, the route is removed from the routing table.

The metric associated with each route is hop count, with infinity defined as 32 hops. However, a route may have a metric in the range of 1 through 63. The metric values 1 through 31 indicate reachable sources; the values 33 through 63 are used to indicate *route dependencies*.

For pruning to work correctly, a DVMRP router must be aware of the downstream neighbors that depend on it to forward packets from particular multicast sources. For each source network, a downstream router signals a route dependency to an upstream router by sending a poison reverse route to the upstream router. The poison reverse route contains a metric that is the advertised metric plus infinity. Suppose, for example, that router A advertises network 172.16.1.0/24 to router B, with a hop count of 3. Router B determines that router A is the upstream router toward this subnet. Router B must signal to router A that it is dependent on router A for multicast traffic from sources on this subnet. Therefore, router B advertises 172.16.1.0/24 to router A with a metric of 35 (3 + 32). Router A recognizes this advertisement as a route dependency.

Yet another function of the DVMRP routing table is the selection of a *designated forwarder*. When multiple upstream routers are connected to a multiaccess network, as in Figure 5-24, only the designated forwarder forwards multicast packets downstream. This prevents multiple copies of the same packets from being forwarded onto the multiaccess network. When two or more routers on a multiaccess network exchange routes, they can tell which of the routers is closest to the source. That router is the designated forwarder for that source network. In Figure 5-24, upstream router B would be the designated forwarder for the source shown, because it is only one router hop from the source; upstream router A is two hops away. If the routers are an equal distance from the source, the router with the numerically lower IP address on the shared network becomes the designated forwarder.

Figure 5-24 *When Multiple Upstream Routers to a Source Are Connected to the Same Data Link, a Designated Forwarder Is Elected*

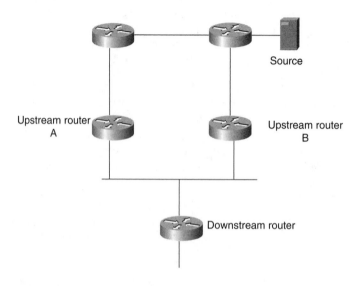

DVMRP Packet Forwarding

When a router first receives a multicast packet from a particular source, an *RPF check* is performed, using the routing table, to verify that the packet arrived on the upstream interface for the packet's source. If the packet arrived on any other interface, it is dropped. If the packet did arrive on the upstream interface, the (S, G) pair is recorded in a forwarding table, and a copy of the packet is forwarded to all downstream dependent neighbors. The router also uses IGMP to query for group members on each of its leaf networks—that is, networks with no neighbors. A copy is forwarded to any leaf networks that contain group members.

If there are no downstream dependent neighbors, and no leaf networks with group members, the router sends a prune message to the upstream router. If the upstream router also has no local group members, and if it has received a prune message from all of its downstream dependent neighbors, it sends a prune message of its own to its upstream neighbor. In this way, the multicast tree is dynamically pruned until only branches leading to active group members remain.

A prune message contains a *prune lifetime*, which indicates how long an upstream router should hold a prune state before resuming the forwarding of packets from the source in question to the pruned router. The default prune lifetime is 2 hours. If the router receiving a prune is itself sending a prune upstream, the prune lifetime is set to the minimum of either 2 hours or the remaining lifetimes of any downstream prunes received for the same (S, G) pair.

As discussed previously, a host can signal its desire to join a multicast group at any time by sending an IGMP membership report message to its local router. If that router has previously pruned itself from the tree delivering packets from that group, it must now graft itself back onto the tree. The router does this by sending a DVMRP Graft message upstream. Grafts are sent hop by hop upstream until an active branch of the multicast tree is found.

If a router sends a graft message and does not begin receiving traffic for the requested group, it must have a mechanism by which it knows whether the source has stopped transmitting, or the graft has been lost. Therefore, at each hop, an upstream router acknowledges the receipt of a Graft message by sending a Graft Ack message to its downstream neighbor. The originator of the graft also sets a *Graft Retransmission* timer; if a Graft Ack is not received before the timer expires, another Graft message is sent, and the timer is reset. The initial period of the Graft Retransmission timer is 5 seconds, and subsequent periods are calculated using a binary exponential backoff algorithm.

DVMRP Message Formats

The IP header of a DVMRP packet specifies protocol number 2. Note that this is the same protocol number used by IGMP, a legacy of DVMRP's beginnings as a subset of that protocol. This section describes DVMRPv3 formats; for a description of earlier formats, see RFC 1075 or other appropriate documentation.

DVMRP Message Header

Figure 5-25 shows the format of the DVMRP header, which begins every DVMRP message.

Figure 5-25 *The DVMRP Message Header*

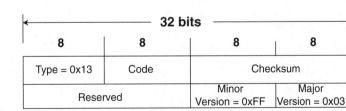

The fields for the DVMRP message are described as follows:

- *Type* is the IGMP type number, which is set to 0x13 for all DVMRP messages. RFC 1075 specifies a separate 4-bit Version field and 4-bit Type field in this position, in which the version is 0x1 and the type is 0x3. Note that the resulting 8 bits of the version 1 header is 0x13, the same as version 3, making version 3 backward-compatible. The actual DVMRPv3 version is specified in the Major Version field.

- *Checksum* is a standard IP-style checksum, using a 16-bit one's complement of the one's complement of the DVMRP message.

- *Minor Version* and *Major Version* are set to 0xFF and 0x03, respectively, for all DVMRPv3 messages.

- *Code* specifies the DVMRPv3 message type. Table 5-7 shows the possible values of the code field and the corresponding message types.

Table 5-7 *DVMRP Message Types by Code Value*

Code	DVMRP Message Types
1	Probe
2	Report
3	Ask Neighbors
4	Neighbors
5	Ask Neighbors 2
6	Neighbors 2
7	Prune
8	Graft
9	Graft Ack

The Ask Neighbors (code 3) and Neighbors (code 4) messages are obsoleted by the Ask Neighbors 2 (code 5) and Neighbors 2 (code 6) messages. None of these messages have yet been discussed; they are used by such diagnostic commands as **mrinfo** and **mstat**. They are discussed in this context in the troubleshooting section of Chapter 6, "Configuring and Troubleshooting IP Multicast Routing."

DVMRP Probe Message Format

DVMRP Probe messages serve four functions:

- They allow routers to locate each other by listing all DVMRP-speaking routers detected by the originating router on the originating interface.

- They provide a means for DVMRP routers to communicate their capabilities to each other.

- They enable the selection of a designated forwarder when there are multiple paths to a downstream group member.

- They provide a keepalive function by being transmitted every 10 seconds. If a probe is not heard from a neighbor within 35 seconds, the neighbor is declared dead.

Figure 5-26 shows the format of the probe message.

Figure 5-26 *The DVMRP Probe Message*

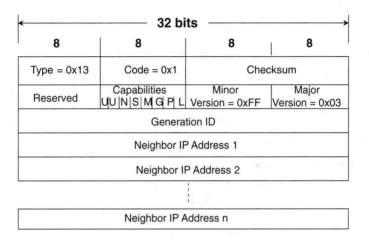

The fields for the DVMRP Probe message are described as follows:

- *Capabilities* uses eight of the reserved bits in the header for capability flags. The Probe message is the only DVMRP message to modify the header fields. Table 5-8 lists the capabilities flags and their meanings. If the flag is set to 1, the corresponding capability is supported by the originating router.

Table 5-8 *DVMRP Capabilities Flags*

Bit	Flag	Capability
0	L	This router is a leaf router.
1	P	This router understands pruning.
2	G	This router sends Generation IDs.
3	M	This router handles Mtrace requests.
4	S	This router supports the DVMRP MIB.
5	N	This router understands netmasks appended to Prune, Graft, and Graft Ack messages.
6, 7	U	Unused.

- *Generation ID* is a nondecreasing 32-bit number used for detecting when a router has restarted, without having to wait for an entire report interval to pass. When a change in the generation ID is detected, any prune information from the originating router is declared invalid and is flushed. If the prune information has been sent upstream, a Graft message is sent. The result of this process is that the restarted router is treated as a new router on multicast trees, and the broadcast-and-prune process is begun anew.

- *Neighbor Address* lists the neighbors from whom the originating router has received Probe messages on the originating interface.

DVMRP Route Report Message Format

Route Report messages, depicted in Figure 5-27, are sent every 60 seconds. The Route Report consists of a list of one or more netmasks, and for each netmask, a list of one or more source network addresses and associated metrics corresponding to the netmask. Although the lengths of the source networks in Figure 5-27 are all 3 octets, in reality the lengths may vary, as described in this section.

Figure 5-27 *DVMRP Route Report Message Format*

32 bits			
8	8	8	8
Type = 0x13	Code = 0x2	Checksum	
Reserved		Minor Version = 0xFF	Major Version = 0x03
Mask 1			Source Net 11
Source Net 11 (cont.)...		Metric 11	Source Net 12
Source Net 12 (cont.)...		Metric 12	Source Net 13
Source Net 13 (cont.)...		Metric 13	Mask 2
Mask 2 (cont.)		Source Net 21	
Source Net 21 (cont.)...	Metric 21	Source Net 22	
Source Net 22 (cont.)...	Metric 22	∎ ∎ ∎	

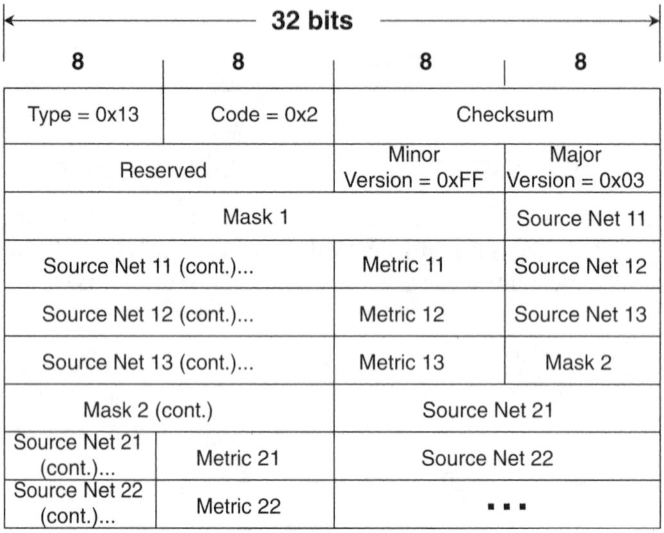

The fields for the DVMRP Route Report Message are defined as follows:

- *Mask* is a netmask. The first octet of the netmask is always assumed to be 255, so only the last 3 octets are included in the Mask field. Note that this assumption means that DVMRP routes can never be aggregated into addresses with a prefix length less than 8.

- *Source Net* is a source network address whose prefix length corresponds to the netmask preceding it. The length of the Source Net field varies according to the netmask. For example, if the netmask field is 255.0.0, the field is describing a mask of 255.255.0.0 (remembering that the first octet is assumed to be 255). The Source Net fields following such a netmask are all 2 octets, corresponding to the prefix length specified.

A default route is specified with a netmask of 0.0.0 and a 1-octet source net of 0. DVMRP routers always interpret this as 0.0.0.0/0, not 0.0.0.0/8.

- *Metric* is the sum of the interface metrics between the router originating the report and the source network. The metric is a hop count, with 32 signifying infinity. However, the full range of the metric value is 1–63. As described in the section "The DVMRP Routing Table," a router signals a dependency to an upstream router by advertising a poison reverse route in which the metric is the received metric plus infinity (32). Therefore, metric values between 33 and 63 indicate a downstream dependency.

DVMRP Prune Message Format

Figure 5-28 shows the format of the Prune message.

Figure 5-28   *The DVMRP Prune Message Format*

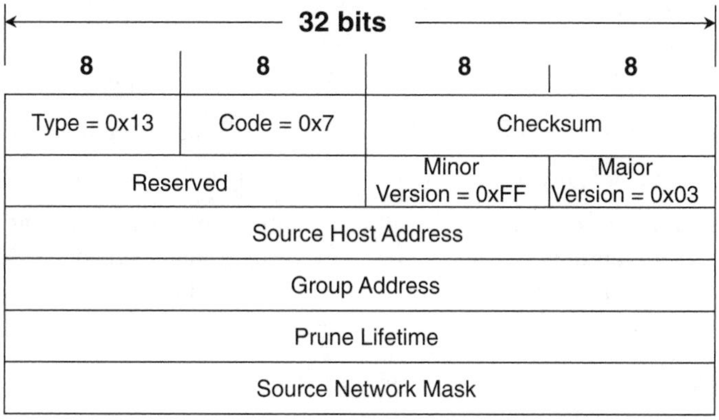

The fields for the DVMRP Prune message are defined as follows:

- *Source Host Address* is the IP address of the originating host.
- *Group Address* is the IP address of the group to be pruned.
- *Prune Lifetime* is the time, in seconds, that the upstream neighbor is to keep the prune. This value is either the minimum remaining lifetime of all downstream prunes received for the group address or, if there are no downstream prunes, the default prune lifetime of 2 hours.
- *Source Network Mask* is the netmask of the source network of the group to be pruned. This field is optional, and it is included only if the upstream neighbor has indicated in its Probe messages that it understands netmasks.

DVMRP Graft Message Format

Figure 5-29 shows the format of the Graft message.

Figure 5-29 *The DVMRP Graft Message Format*

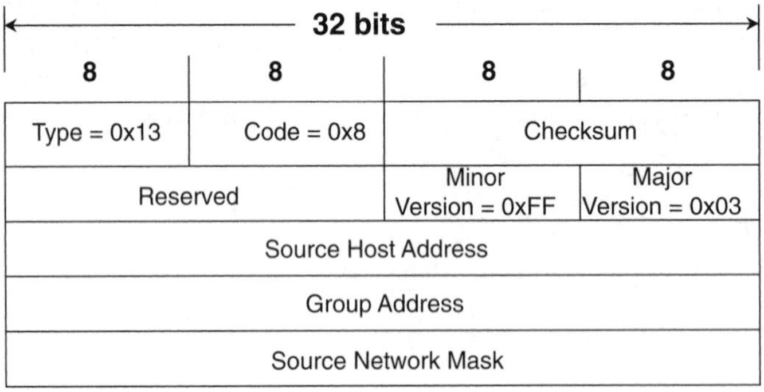

The fields for the DVMRP Graft message are defined as follows:

- *Source Host Address* is the IP address of the originating host.

- *Group Address* is the IP address of the group to be grafted.

- *Source Network Mask* is the netmask of the source network of the group to be grafted. This field is optional, and it is included only if the upstream neighbor has indicated in its Probe messages that it understands netmasks.

DVMRP Graft Acknowledgement Message Format

Figure 5-30 shows the format of the Graft Acknowledgement message. With the exception of the Code field in the header, the format is identical to that of the Graft message that it is acknowledging.

Figure 5-30   *The DVMRP Graft Acknowledgement Message Format*

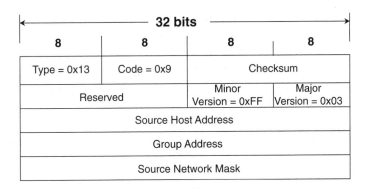

DVMRP Ask Neighbors 2 Message Format

The DVMRP Ask Neighbors 2 message is one of two messages (along with the Neighbors 2 message, discussed in the following section) that are used for troubleshooting. The "2" distinguishes the message from the obsolete Ask Neighbors message. The Ask Neighbors 2 message, shown in Figure 5-31, is unicast to a specified destination. When a router receives an Ask Neighbors 2 message, it should respond by unicasting a Neighbors 2 message to the originator. As the figure shows, the message is merely the DVMRP header with the code set to 0x5.

Figure 5-31   *The DVMRP Ask Neighbors 2 Message Format*

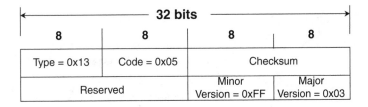

DVMRP Neighbors 2 Message Format

A DVMRP router in response to an Ask Neighbors 2 message sends the Neighbors 2 message, shown in Figure 5-32. The message is unicast to the originator of the Ask Neighbors 2 message. The message indicates the sender's DVMRP capabilities and lists the addresses of the sender's logical interfaces. For each interface listed, the DVMRP parameters for the interface are specified, and the DVMRP neighbors known on that interface are listed.

Figure 5-32 *The DVMRP Neighbors 2 Message Format*

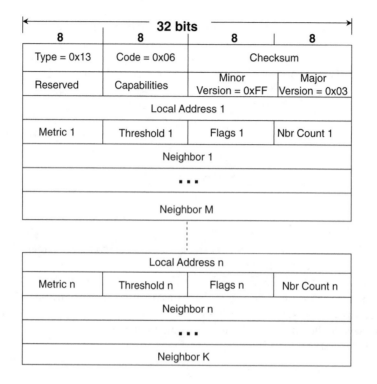

The fields for the DVMRP Neighbors 2 message are defined as follows:

- *Capabilities* specifies the DVMRP capabilities of the originating router. The field is the same as the Capabilities field of the Prune message, and its values are shown in Table 5-8.

- *Local Address* is the address of an interface on the router. If the interface is down or disabled, a single neighbor entry is associated with the interface, and the neighbor entry has an address of 0.0.0.0.

- *Metric* specifies the DVMRP metric of the interface.

- *Threshold* specifies the administrative scoping threshold of the interface.

- *Neighbor Count* specifies the number of neighbors listed for this interface.

- *Neighbor* is the IP address of a DVMRP neighbor known on this interface.

- *Flags* is a series of bits describing operational parameters of the interface. Table 5-9 lists the bits of this field and what flag each bit represents.

Table 5-9   *Interface Flags in the Neighbor 2 Message*

Bit	Flag	Description
0	Tunnel	Neighbor reached via tunnel
1	Source Route	Tunnel uses IP source routing
2	Reserved	No longer used
3	Reserved	No longer used
4	Down	Operational status down
5	Disabled	Administrative status down
6	Querier	Querier for interface
7	Leaf	No downstream neighbors on this interface

Operation of Multicast OSPF (MOSPF)

Multicast OSPF (MOSPF) offers an improvement over DVMRP in two aspects. First, it is a link-state protocol, whereas DVMRP is distance vector. That difference carries with it all the usual advantages of link state over distance vector: better convergence properties, better loop avoidance, and less periodic control traffic. The second improvement is that MOSPF is more scalable in a dense environment. This is partly due to its link-state algorithms, but also to the fact that MOSPF uses explicit joins rather than implicit joins via flood-and-prune.

Multicast OSPF is not a separate protocol from OSPF, but rather is an extension of that protocol, as indicated by the name of the RFC describing it.[10] Three extensions to OSPF are defined to support multicast. First, a new LSA is defined, called *the Group Membership LSA*. Group Membership LSAs are LSA type 6.

The Options field is extended to include a flag, called the MC bit, which is used to indicate support for IP multicast. The Options field, described in Chapter 9 of *Volume I*, is carried in OSPF Hello and Database Description packets and in all LSAs. The implication of the MC bit is that OSPF and MOSPF routers can be intermixed in the same internetwork, with the MOSPF routers using the MC bit to indicate their multicast support. Routers with mismatched MC bits still become adjacent. However, only neighbors whose MC bits are set in their Database Description packets exchange Group Membership LSAs during their database synchronization process. And only LSAs with the MC bit set are used in the calculation of multicast shortest-path trees.

Finally, the rtype field of the Router LSA is extended to include a flag called the W bit. This flag indicates that the originating router is a wildcard multicast receiver. Wildcard multicast receivers are defined in the section "Inter-Area MOSPF."

Just as unicast OSPF uses a Dijkstra-based SPF algorithm to calculate shortest-path trees to unicast destinations, MOSPF calculates trees from multicast sources to multicast destinations. Both unicast trees and multicast trees are calculated from the same link-state database. A difference, however, is that whereas the unicast SPF trees are rooted at source routers, multicast SPF trees are rooted at source multicast subnets.

MOSPF Basics

The best place to begin describing MOSPF is at a local multiaccess medium to which a group member is attached. Like unicast OSPF, MOSPF elects a designated router and a backup designated router. All attached MOSPF routers should run IGMP on the local link to discover group members, but only the DR sends IGMP membership queries and listens for IGMP membership reports.

Recall from Table 5-4 that MOSPF uses explicit joins. When a group member sends an IGMP message indicating that it wants to join a group, the MOSPF DR creates an entry in its *local group database*. The local group database entry records the group and the attached network on which the group member resides. For example, the router in Figure 5-33 has three attached subnets, and there are three multicast group members on two of those subnets. Two of the group members, on separate subnets, belong to the same group. The router has to know only the groups and subnets on which the groups have members; it does not need to know each individual group member.

Figure 5-33 *The Local Group Database Records Attached Groups and the Subnets on Which the Group Members Reside*

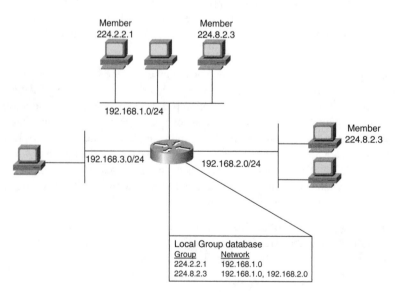

The DR then originates a Group Membership LSA for each attached group. The LSA specifies the group address and the originating router ID and lists all the router's attached networks on which members of the group reside. In some cases, the router itself may run multicast applications that make it a group member. The LSA includes a Type field in which the router can indicate that it is advertising itself as a group member.

The LSA is then flooded throughout the originating router's area. The Group Membership (type 6) LSA is similar to a Network (type 2) LSA in two regards:

- Like a Network LSA, only a designated router originates a Group Membership LSA.

- Like a Network LSA, a Group Membership LSA only has area-wide scope. That is, the LSA is not flooded outside of the originating router's area.

The objective of the LSA flooding is to ensure that all MOSPF routers in an area have a copy of all Group Membership LSAs originated in the area. As with unicast OSPF, all MOSPF routers in an area must have identical link-state databases. The only difference between an OSPF link-state database and an MOSPF database in a given area is the inclusion of the type 6 LSAs.

With synchronized databases, every MOSPF router in an area can calculate the same shortest path tree. The tree is rooted at the source network and has branches extending to every network containing a group member. However, the tree is not calculated immediately. Instead, it is calculated "on-demand," when the first multicast packet for the group arrives. This makes sense, because although the synchronized routers know where all destinations are, they may not yet know where the source is.

The SPF calculation knows where all routers with attached group members are based on the Group Membership LSAs. And it knows where the source is located based on the source and destination addresses of the first arriving packet for the group. The regular unicast Router and Network LSAs whose MC bits are set are then used to calculate the least-cost paths from the source to each destination.

The great advantage of the Group Membership LSA-based explicit joins, coupled with the on-demand SPF calculation, is that routers already know the location of the destination networks before the calculation is performed. So unlike flood-and-prune protocols such as DVMRP, packets are never forwarded to all parts of the routing domain. You might say that the MOSPF tree comes "prepruned."

Based on the results of the SPF calculation, entries are made into each router's multicast forwarding table. The shortest-path tree is loop-free, and every router knows which interface is the upstream interface and which interfaces are downstream interfaces. Therefore, no RPF check is required, as it is with DVMRP. The forwarding table entry for a particular (S, G) pair indicates what upstream neighbor a matching packet should be received from and what downstream neighbors the packet must be forwarded to. The local group database also is used to make entries into the forwarding table for locally attached networks containing group members.

Keep in mind a few caveats about MOSPF. First, although unicast OSPF supports equal-cost multipath, MOSPF does not. The MOSPF shortest-path tree describes a single path between the source and all networks containing group members.

Second, if OSPF and MOSPF routers coexist on the same multiaccess network, care must be taken to ensure that the MOSPF router is elected the DR. If an OSPF router becomes the DR, no Group Membership LSAs are originated for any group members on the network, and consequently no multicast packets for the group are forwarded to the network.

Finally, an MOSPF router must clear its entire forwarding table and recalculate its shortest-path trees if the topology within the MOSPF domain changes. Therefore, it is important that the domain be as stable as possible.

Inter-Area MOSPF

The preceding section described how MOSPF behaves when the source and all group members are within the same area. Emphasis was placed on the fact that a Group Membership LSA is not flooded outside of its originating area. So what happens when group members are in one or more areas different from the source?

You know from Chapter 9 of *Volume I* that inter-area OSPF communications is managed by Area Border Routers (ABRs). ABRs are members of the backbone area and one or more nonbackbone areas. They learn all the destinations within each attached area via Router and Network LSAs, just as any other router in the area does. ABRs then create Network Summary (type 3) LSAs, which advertise the destinations in one attached area into the ABR's other attached areas. Like type 1 and type 2 LSAs, type 3 LSAs are never flooded outside of the area in which they are originated. When an ABR receives a Network Summary LSA across the backbone area from another ABR, it creates its own Network Summary LSA to advertise that information into its attached nonbackbone areas. Figure 5-34 illustrates conceptually how ABRs use types 1, 2, and 3 LSAs.

Figure 5-34 *Unicast OSPF ABRs Use Network Summary LSAs to Advertise Destinations Learned from One Attached Area into Other Attached Areas*

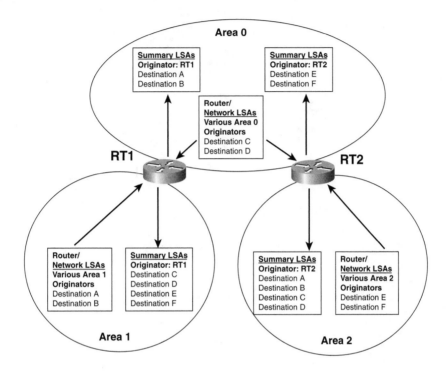

MOSPF ABRs are perversely called *inter-area multicast forwarders*. There are both similarities and differences with the way unicast ABRs operate. An inter-area multicast forwarder knows what groups have members in each of its attached nonbackbone areas based on the Group Membership LSAs it has received in those areas. For each known group, the forwarder creates a new Group Membership LSA and floods the LSA into the backbone, as illustrated in Figure 5-35. So far, this behavior is very similar to the way an ABR uses type 3 LSAs to summarize information learned from type 1 and type 2 LSAs into the backbone.

Figure 5-35 *Inter-Area Multicast Forwarders Use Group Membership LSAs to Advertise the Presence of Group Members in Their Nonbackbone Areas to the Backbone Area*

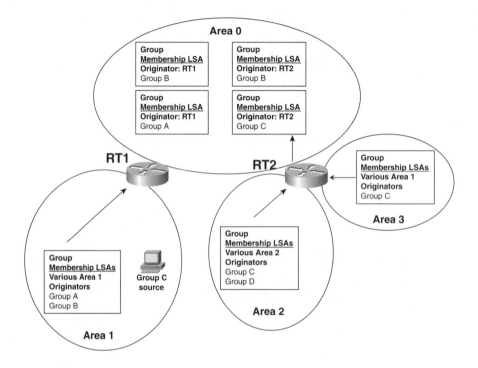

Here the similarity to unicast ABRs ends. Unlike the way in which type 3 LSAs are used, an inter-area multicast forwarder does not send type 6 LSAs into a nonbackbone area to advertise the presence of groups outside the area. In Figure 5-35, for example, RT1 receives the type 6 LSA originated by RT2, advertising group C, but it does not create a type 6 LSA to advertise group C into area 1.

The result is that an SPF tree is calculated in the backbone for each group, and the tree's branches extend to the inter-area multicast forwarder of each area containing group members. The nonbackbone areas have no knowledge of group members outside of their own area.

If the source for group C in Figure 5-35 is located in area 1, however, how do its packets reach members in areas 2 and 3? The answer is a *wildcard multicast receiver.* These devices advertise themselves by setting the W bit in the rtype field of their Router LSAs. Within an area, multicast traffic is always forwarded to all wildcard multicast receivers. In nonbackbone areas, an inter-area multicast forwarder (a multicast ABR) is always a wildcard multicast receiver.

When the source for group C in Figure 5-35 originates a group C packet, the packet is forwarded to RT1, the wildcard multicast receiver for area 1. RT1 also is a member of the backbone area, and so has calculated a shortest-path tree to all inter-area multicast forwarders whose attached areas contain members of group C. Seeing that RT2 is advertising group C members, the packet is forwarded to that router across the backbone. RT2, as a member of areas 2 and 3, has calculated separate SPF trees for group C in each area and forwards copies of the packet to the group C destinations.

NOTE	If there were any group C members in area 1, a copy of the packet would, of course, be forwarded over the local SPF tree to those members in addition to being forwarded to RT1.

Note that wildcard multicast receivers are unnecessary in the backbone area for intradomain traffic. For every group in the MOSPF domain, an SPF tree is calculated in area 0. The branches of the tree lead either to group members located in that area or to inter-area multicast forwarders attached to other areas. So if a source is located in the backbone area, its packets can be forwarded along the correct tree.

Inter-AS MOSPF

RFC 1584 provides for the routing of multicast packets into and out of an MOSPF domain. You know from Chapter 9 of *Volume I* that a router redistributing routes into an OSPF domain from some other routing protocol is called an Autonomous System Boundary Router (ASBR). An ASBR uses AS-External (type 5) LSAs to advertise destinations outside of the OSPF domain and ASBR Summary (type 4) LSAs to advertise their own location. These LSAs are flooded into all areas of the OSPF domain, with the exception of stub areas.

A router that connects an MOSPF domain to some other multicast routing domain (most likely DVMRP presently, and possibly some multicast EGP in the future) is called an *inter-AS multicast forwarder*. These routers behave very similarly to inter-area multicast forwarders. To forward multicast packets to destinations outside of the MOSPF domain, inter-AS multicast forwarders set the W bit in their Router LSAs and become wildcard multicast forwarders. When the routers are forwarding packets into the MOSPF domain from external sources, they become "proxy sources," with their external link serving as the root for the group's SPF tree.

Like ASBRs, inter-AS multicast forwarders can be located in any area. Notice, however, that wildcard multicast forwarding capability is signaled by the W bit of type 1 LSAs, and type 1 LSAs are not flooded outside of an area. If the inter-AS forwarder is located in area 0, this is not a problem; the inter-area multicast forwarders already pull all multicast traffic to the backbone. If the inter-AS forwarder is located in a nonbackbone area, however, that area's inter-area forwarder also must become a wildcard forwarder for the backbone area. Therefore, it is recommended that inter-AS multicast forwarders be located only in area 0.

It is also recommended that inter-AS forwarders be placed carefully within the MOSPF domain. Because all multicast traffic within the domain is forwarded to these routers, links leading to the routers can easily become congested.

MOSPF Extension Formats

This section describes only the formats of the multicast extensions to OSPF. For a complete description of all OSPF packets and LSAs, see Chapter 9 of *Volume I*.

Group Membership LSA Format

The Group Membership LSA carries the standard LSA header and has a type number of 6. Figure 5-36 shows the format for the Group Membership LSA. Only MOSPF-designated routers originate Group Membership LSAs. Notice in the format that no metric is associated with this LSA.

Figure 5-36 *The MOSPF Group Membership LSA Format*

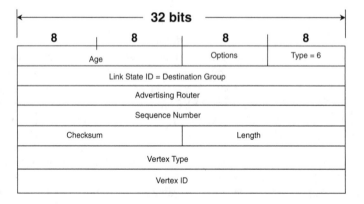

The fields for the Group Membership LSA are defined as follows:

- *Link State ID* carries the address of the multicast group being advertised.
- *Advertising Router* is always the router ID of the MOSPF designated router on the multiaccess network, because only the DR can originate type 6 LSAs.

- *Vertex Type* specifies whether the destination is a router (type = 1) or a transit network (type = 2). Type 1 is specified if the originating router is running some application that requires it to be a member of a multicast group. Transit network just refers to the originating router's directly connected network over which packets must pass to reach the attached group members.
- *Vertex ID* is the originating router's router ID.

Extended Router LSA Format

Figure 5-37 shows the format of a Router (type 1) LSA that has been extended to support MOSPF. The format is identical to the format shown in Figure 9.55 of *Volume I*, with the exception of the addition of the W bit in the rtype field. The W bit is set by inter-area and inter-AS multicast forwarders to indicate to other MOSPF routers in an area that they are wildcard multicast forwarders.

Figure 5-37 *The Router LSA Format, with the W Bit Added to the rtype Field for MOSPF Support*

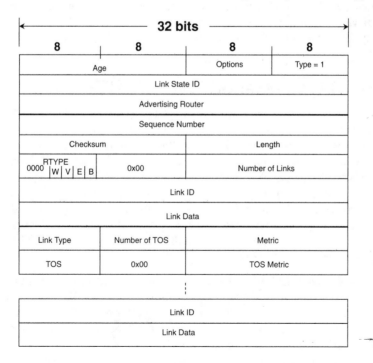

Extended Options Field Format

The Options field, shown in Figure 5-38, is a part of all OSPF Hello and Database Description packets and a part of the header of all LSAs. The other flags of this field are described in Chapter 9 of *Volume I*, but the pertinent flag for this chapter is the MC bit. When set, this bit indicates that the originating router is multicast-capable.

Figure 5-38 *The Options Field Format*

The MC bit in Hello packets does little more than signal multicast capability. Two routers will still become adjacent, even if one sets the MC bit and the other does not. The real use of the MC bit comes into play with the Database Description packets and with LSAs.

During database synchronization, an MOSPF router will send the type 6 LSAs in its database to its neighbor only if the neighbor's DD packets have the MC bit set. Likewise, only LSAs with the MC bit set are used in the MOSPF SPF calculation.

Operation of Core-Based Trees (CBT)

DVMRP and MOSPF have two limitations in common. First, they are both dense-mode protocols and do not scale well in sparse topologies. That is, when there are few group members relative to the total number of hosts in an internetwork, and the group members are widespread across the internetwork, both DVMRP and MOSPF consume an unacceptable amount of network resources to reach those group members. Much of that resource consumption is in the overhead necessary to calculate and hold state for individual trees rooted at each source. Second, both protocols are limited to a single unicast routing protocol for determining multicast trees—DVMRP to its own RIP-based protocol, and MOSPF to OSPF. Core-Based Trees (CBT), on the other hand, is a protocol-independent, sparse-mode, shared-tree protocol.

Protocol-independent means that CBT can use any underlying unicast routing protocol to find sources and other CBT routers and build its trees. Besides adding flexibility, overhead is reduced by using the existing routing protocols instead of adding another one just for multicast. And CBT trees are rooted at *core* CBT routers rather than at source networks. The cores can be located anywhere within an internetwork, and many group trees can be rooted at the one core, making the protocol more suitable for sparse multicast topologies.

There are currently three versions of CBT. CBTv2, described in RFC 2189,[11] obsoletes CBTv1. There is also a proposed CBTv3. All three versions are experimental, and none have seen widespread deployment. Indicative of this experimental status, neither CBTv2 nor CBTv3 is backward-compatible with its preceding version. This chapter focuses exclusively on CBTv2; when the term "CBT" is used, it refers to that version of the protocol.

CBT Basics

CBT uses nine message types:

- JOIN_REQUEST
- JOIN_ACK
- ECHO_REQUEST
- ECHO_REPLY
- QUIT_NOTIFICATION
- FLUSH_TREE
- Candidate Core Advertisement
- Bootstrap message
- HELLO

With a single exception discussed in the section "CBT Designated Routers," all CBT messages are sent to the reserved multicast address 224.0.0.15 (see Table 5-1). The messages are transmitted with a TTL of 1, which means all CBT information is passed hop by hop through the multicast domain. The format of each message type is detailed in the section "CBT Message Formats."

Like the other IP multicast routing protocols, CBT is informed that an attached host wants to join a group via IGMP Membership Report messages. CBT uses explicit joins, so when a CBT router must forward packets for a particular group, it must first graft itself to that group's multicast tree. The router first examines its unicast routing table for the location of the core for the particular group and then forwards a JOIN_REQUEST message upstream on the path toward the core. The message contains three important pieces of information:

- The multicast group address
- The address of the core
- The address of the originator

NOTE	How the router knows where to find the core is the topic of the following section, unsurprisingly titled "Finding the Core."

When the next-hop router receives the JOIN_REQUEST message, it examines the group address and the core address. Based on this information, the router establishes that it is one of the following:

- The core router

- Attached to the group's multicast tree (an *on-tree* router)

- Neither the core nor an on-tree router

If the router is either the core or an on-tree router, it sends a JOIN_ACK message to the originator of the JOIN_REQUEST, indicating that the originator has successfully joined the tree. The router adds the interface on which the JOIN_REQUEST was received to its forwarding table entry for the group and begins forwarding packets on the interface.

If the router is neither the core nor on the group tree, it must also join the tree. The router consults its own unicast routing table for the location of the core and forwards a copy of the JOIN_REQUEST message upstream. It also begins a *transient join state*, in which the group, the interface on which the JOIN_REQUEST was received, and the interface on which the JOIN_REQUEST was transmitted is recorded. A timer is started, and if a JOIN_ACK is not received within 7.5 seconds (the *transient timeout* period), the transient join state is deleted, and the join is considered unsuccessful.

In CBT parlance, the upstream interface toward the core is the *parent interface*, and the downstream interface toward the group member is the *child interface*. Likewise, an upstream neighbor is a parent router, and a downstream neighbor is a child router. Once a tree is established by the reception of a JOIN_ACK, a child router sends an ECHO_REQUEST message to its parent router every 60 seconds. The ECHO_REQUEST message contains only the address of the originating child router. The parent router responds with an ECHO_REPLY message, which lists all groups for which the parent router forwards packets on that link.

If an ECHO_REPLY is not heard within 70 seconds, the parent router is declared unreachable. Likewise, a particular group is declared invalid if it has not been listed in an ECHO_REPLY in the past 90 seconds. The child router then sends a QUIT_NOTIFICATION upstream to the parent router and a FLUSH_TREE downstream to each of its own child routers. The FLUSH_TREE lists all group addresses that have become invalid, and the receiving child routers flush all information about the listed groups from the forwarding tables. The child routers then send the appropriate FLUSH_TREE messages to their own children. The process continues until all branches of the tree downstream of the failed router are deleted.

The QUIT_NOTIFICATION message also is used for pruning. If a router learns via IGMP Leave Group messages that it no longer has any attached members of a particular group, it sends a QUIT_NOTIFICATION message to its parent router, listing the group address to be pruned. If that parent, in turn, has no attached members of the group and no other child interfaces for the group, it too sends a QUIT_NOTIFICATION upstream. The branch continues to be pruned back to either an active on-tree router or to the core.

Finding the Core

The obvious prerequisite for CBT routers to build trees to the core is for the routers to know what router is the core. One way to meet this requirement is for all routers to be preconfigured with the address of the core router for each group. This approach may be fine for small multicast internetworks, and it offers good network control, but the administrative requirements certainly do not scale to larger internetworks.

Another way is to use the bootstrap mechanism. Using this method, a set of routers within the CBT domain are configured as *candidate core* routers. These routers exchange Candidate Core messages, and one of them is elected a bootstrap router (BST) based on a priority or, if all priorities are equal, the router with the highest IP address. The other candidate core routers then unicast Candidate Core messages to the BSR every 60 seconds as a keepalive. Based on these Candidate Core messages, the BSR assembles a *candidate core set* (CC-set) and advertises the set to all CBT routers in the domain via Bootstrap messages. When a router is asked to join a group via IGMP, it runs a hash algorithm against the CC-set and determines the correct core router for the group.

The same bootstrap protocol is used by both CBT and PIM-SM. Because this chapter places a closer focus on the latter protocol, the bootstrap mechanism is summarized here and is described in greater detail in the section "Protocol-Independent Multicast, Sparse Mode (PIM-SM)."

CBT Designated Routers

CBT uses HELLO messages to elect a designated router on multiaccess networks. The rationale for using a CBT DR is the same as that for DVMRP-designated forwarders and MOSPF DRs. Because CBT does not use an RPF check when forwarding packets, a DR is especially important for preventing loops when there are multiple upstream paths to the core, as in Figure 5-39.

Each CBT interface is configured with a preference value between 0 and 255, and this value is carried in the HELLO message. A value between 1 and 254 indicates that the router is eligible to become the DR, with the lower number indicating a higher preference—that is, a router with a preference of 10 is "more eligible" than a router with a preference of 20. A preference of 0 indicates that the router is the DR.

When a CBT router first becomes active on a multiaccess link, it sends two HELLO messages in succession to advertise its presence and its preference value. The router then listens for HELLOs, with one of the following three results:

- A HELLO with a lower preference value is heard from another router on the network.
- All HELLOs heard on the network have a higher preference value.
- No other HELLOs are heard on the network.

Figure 5-39 *CBT Elects a Designated Router on Multiaccess Networks to Manage Multiple Upstream Paths to the Core*

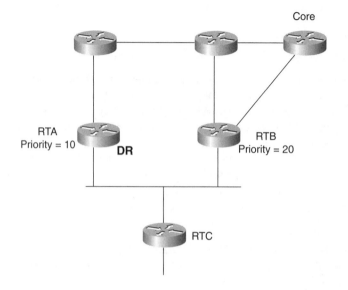

In the first case, the new router knows that the router with the lower preference value is elected as the DR. In the other two cases, the new router assumes the role of DR and advertises that fact by setting the preference to 0 in its HELLOs. If all HELLOs have equal preference values, the router with the lowest IP address is elected as the DR.

In steady state, the DR sends a HELLO every 60 seconds both as an advertisement of its status and as a keepalive. The DR also sends a HELLO in response to a HELLO from a new router. Other routers do not send HELLOs or respond to HELLOs from new routers.

In some cases, the elected DR may not be on the path to the core. Suppose that RTA in Figure 5-39 is elected as the DR, but RTB is the best next-hop router to the core. In this case, when RTC forwards a JOIN_REQUEST to RTA, RTA unicasts the JOIN_REQUEST back across the multiaccess link to RTB. This redirection occurs only with JOIN_REQUESTs; when RTB sends a JOIN_ACK, the message is sent directly to RTC.

Member and Nonmember Sources

You might have noticed that so far nothing has been said about how sources deliver their traffic to the core. In many multicast applications, a sender also is a group member. CBT takes advantage of this fact, so a sender that is also a group member—a *member source*—can reach the core by virtue of the fact that its directly connected router is on-tree. Figure 5-40 illustrates this concept. Here, the host labeled SG1 is a member source of group 1. Because the host is a group member, its local router has already joined the CBT tree for group 1. Therefore, when SG1 sources packets for group 1, the local router can forward the packets up the tree.

Figure 5-40 *SG1 Is a Member Source for Group 1. Its Local Router Has Joined the Group 1 Tree and Forwards Packets up the Tree Toward the Source*

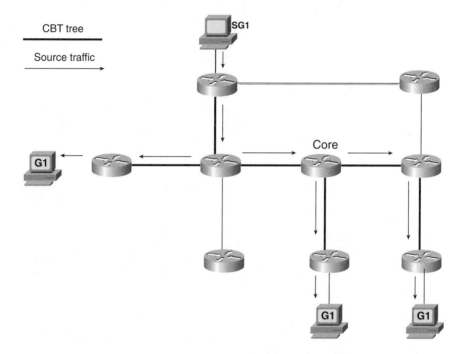

A fundamental characteristic of CBT is described in this behavior. Namely, CBT uses *bidirectional trees*. In other words, multicast traffic can not only travel downstream on the tree from the core to group members, but it also can travel upstream on the tree from a member source to the core. This is in contrast to the other shared-tree protocol, PIM-SM, which uses unidirectional trees.

Of course, not all sources are group members. Therefore, CBT also must have a mechanism for accommodating these *nonmember sources*. The mechanism is a simple IP-in-IP tunnel, as shown in Figure 5-41. Here, the same host is originating multicast traffic for group 1, but the host itself is not a member of the group. When its local router receives the traffic, it creates a tunnel to the core (assuming the router is running CBT and therefore knows the address of the core). The multicast traffic is then unicast to the core, which passes the traffic onto the group tree.

Figure 5-41 *If the Source Host Is Not a Group Member, Its Local CBT Router Encapsulates the Source Traffic in an IP-in-IP Tunnel and Unicasts the Traffic to the Core*

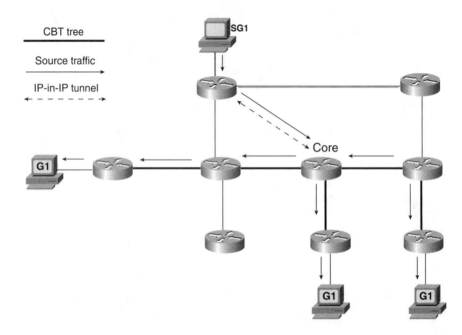

CBT Message Formats

CBT messages are encapsulated in IP headers with a protocol number of 7. With the unicast exceptions documented earlier in this section, the packets are transmitted with a destination address of 224.0.0.15 and a TTL of 1. Figure 5-42 shows the format of the common header shared by all CBT messages.

Figure 5-42 *The CBT Message Header Format*

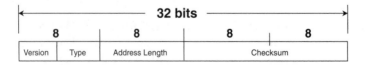

The fields for the CBT message header are defined as follows:

- *Version* specifies the CBT version number. This section has dealt exclusively with version 2, although there is an obsolete version 1 and a proposed version 3.

- *Type* specifies the message type. Table 5-10 shows the type numbers used by the various CBT messages.

Table 5-10 *CBT Message Types*

Type	Message
0	HELLO
1	JOIN_REQUEST
2	JOIN_ACK
3	QUIT_NOTIFICATION
4	ECHO_REQUEST
5	ECHO_REPLY
6	FLUSH_TREE
7	Bootstrap
8	Candidate Core Advertisement

- *Address Length* specifies the length, in bytes, of the unicast or multicast addresses carried in the relevant messages.

- *Checksum* is a standard one's complement of the one's complement sum of the entire CBT message.

CBT HELLO Message Format

HELLOs, the format of which is illustrated in Figure 5-43, are used to elect designated routers on multiaccess networks. They also are sent by a DR every 60 seconds as a keepalive.

Figure 5-43 *The CBT HELLO Message Format*

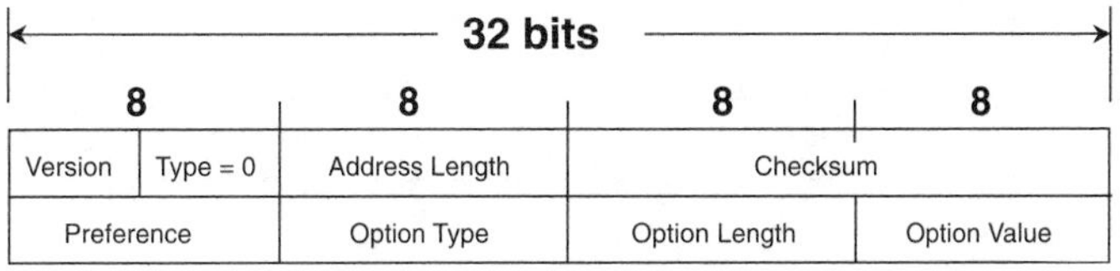

The fields for the CBT HELLO message are defined as follows:

- *Preference* is a value between 0 and 255. Values from 1 to 254 indicate the "degree of eligibility" of the originating router to become the DR. The lower the preference value, the higher the eligibility. An advertised value of 0 indicates that the HELLO was originated by the DR. When a router first becomes active on a network, it triggers a DR election (even if there is an existing DR) by sending two HELLOs containing its preference. Any router whose preference value is higher (less eligible) does not respond. A router with a lower preference value (more eligible) responds with a HELLO containing its own preference value. The new router either becomes the DR if it does not receive a responding HELLO, or it implicitly acknowledges another router with a lower preference as the DR by ceasing to send HELLOs.

- *Option Type* specifies the type of option in the Option Value field. CBTv2 defines only a single option, the *border router* (BR), which has not been previously defined in this section. A BR is a router connecting the CBT domain to another multicast routing domain. HELLOs originated by BRs have an Option Type of 0.

- *Option Length* specifies the length of the Option Value field in bytes. HELLOs originated by BRs have an Option Length of 0.

- *Option Value* is a variable-length field carrying the option value. HELLOs originated by BRs have an Option Value of 0.

CBT JOIN_REQUEST Message Format

Routers that, as the result of an IGMP Membership Report, want to be grafted onto a CBT tree for a particular group originate JOIN_REQUEST messages, the format of which is illustrated by Figure 5-44.

Figure 5-44 *The CBT JOIN_REQUEST Message Format*

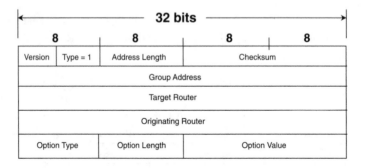

The fields for the CBT JOIN_REQUEST message are defined as follows:

- *Group Address* is the multicast address of the group to be joined.

- *Target Router* is the address of the core router for the group.

- *Originating Router* is the address of the router that originated the message.

- *Option Type*, *Option Length*, and *Option Value* are the same fields defined for the HELLO message.

CBT JOIN_ACK Message Format

Core routers or on-tree routers in response to JOIN_REQUEST messages send JOIN_ACK messages, the format of which is illustrated by Figure 5-45. They are sent to the originator of the JOIN_REQUEST to indicate a successful join to the group tree.

Figure 5-45 *The CBT JOIN_ACK Message Format*

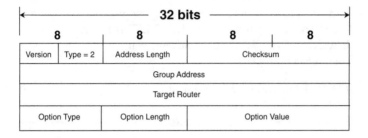

The fields for the CBT JOIN_ACK message are defined as follows:

- *Group Address* is the multicast address of the group being joined.

- *Target Router* is the address of the router to which the JOIN_ACK is being sent. This is the address found in the Originating Router field of the JOIN_REQUEST message to which this message is responding.

- *Option Type*, *Option Length*, and *Option Value* are the same fields defined for the HELLO message.

CBT QUIT_NOTIFICATION Message Format

QUIT_NOTIFICATION messages, the format of which is illustrated by Figure 5-46, are sent to parent (directly upstream) routers to request a prune from a particular group tree. A router originates a QUIT_NOTIFICATION when it no longer has any downstream interfaces for a particular group, either as the result of received IGMP Leave Group messages, Query timeouts, or QUIT_NOTIFICATION messages received from its own child (directly downstream) routers.

Figure 5-46 *The CBT QUIT_NOTIFICATION Message Format*

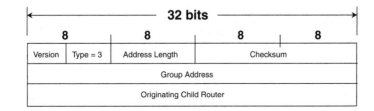

The fields for the CBT QUIT_NOTIFICATION message are defined as follows:

- *Group Address* is the multicast address of the group being quit.
- *Originating Child Router* is the address of the router originating the message.

CBT ECHO_REQUEST Message Format

A child router is responsible for maintaining the link to the parent router. To accomplish this, the child router sends an ECHO_REQUEST message every 60 seconds. As Figure 5-47 shows, the ECHO_REQUEST message consists of only a header and the address of the originating child router.

Figure 5-47 *The CBT ECHO_REQUEST Message Format*

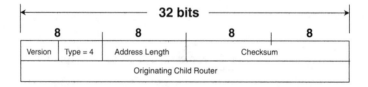

CBT ECHO_REPLY Message Format

Parent routers send ECHO_REPLY messages, the format of which is illustrated by Figure 5-48, in response to ECHO_REQUEST messages from child routers. The two message types together form a keepalive mechanism for the link between parent and child routers.

Figure 5-48 *The CBT ECHO_REPLY Message Format*

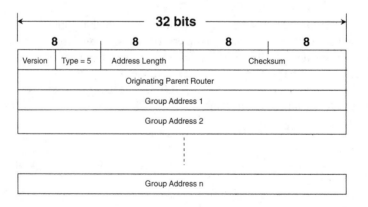

The fields for the CBT ECHO_REPLY message are defined as follows:

- *Originating Parent Router* is the address of the message originator.
- *Group Address* is one or more fields listing the multicast group addresses for which the parent router is forwarding packets on the link to the child router.

CBT FLUSH_TREE Message Format

The FLUSH_TREE message, the format of which is illustrated by Figure 5-49, is sent downstream to child routers when a CBT router loses connection with a parent router. Child routers receiving a FLUSH_TREE clear the forwarding information for all groups listed in the message.

Figure 5-49 *The CBT FLUSH_TREE Message Format*

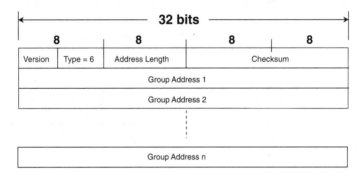

Group Address is one or more fields listing the multicast group addresses to which the originating parent router has lost contact and for which the receiving child router should clear forwarding state.

Introduction to Protocol Independent Multicast (PIM)

If you are a CCIE candidate, studying the previous sections on protocols not supported or only partially supported (in the case of DVMRP) by Cisco may strike you as a poor investment of time. Yet each protocol offers lessons in what is desirable about a multicast routing protocol and what is not.

DVMRP shares the characteristic of unicast distance vector protocols of being very simple to implement—little more is required than to just turn it on. But this simplicity comes at the expense of high overhead, creating serious scaling problems in anything other than small, high-bandwidth networks densely populated with group members.

MOSPF brings its link-state advantages to the table, but at the cost of increased design complexity. Its use of explicit joins eliminates DVMRP's topsy-turvy rule that routers not forwarding for a particular group must remember (hold state) that they are not forwarding packets for that group. The result is a reduced impact on network resources. Yet MOSPF's source-based trees still make the protocol unsuitable for topologies sparsely populated with group members. Given the limited increase in scalability, many, if not most, network designers are unwilling to pay the cost of MOSPF's more-complex topological requirements.

DVMRP is "self-contained," in that it uses its own built-in protocol to locate the unicast addresses necessary for the creation and maintenance of multicast trees. In this sense it is completely independent of any underlying unicast routing protocol, but the price of this independence is the consumption of network resources to gather information that probably already exists in the unicast routing table.

NOTE   This cost is not as high as it might seem. As the section "PIM-DM Basics" explains, costs also are associated with running a flood-and-prune protocol without a built-in unicast component.

MOSPF, on the other hand, is a multicast extension of a unicast protocol. So while MOSPF eliminates the redundancy of a separate unicast protocol, it cannot run independently of OSPF.

CBT introduces true protocol independence. It consults the existing unicast routing table for unicast destinations, without regard for what protocol is used to maintain that table. CBT also is scalable to sparse topologies, although core placement must be carefully planned to minimize suboptimal paths and traffic bottlenecks. At this time, CBT is stuck in a Catch-22: The interest in the protocol for real-world applications is limited by its lack of maturity, and the protocol lacks maturity because of its limited use in the real world. CBT is unlikely to move into mainstream acceptance unless and until its designers can introduce significant advantages over the currently favored and more versatile PIM-SM.

PIM is the only IP multicast routing protocol fully supported by Cisco IOS. (DVMRP is supported only to the degree that PIM can connect to a DVMRP network.)

Like CBT, and as its name asserts, PIM is protocol-independent. That is, it uses the unicast routing table to locate unicast addresses, without regard for how the table learned the addresses.

There is a standard list of PIM message formats. Some messages are used only by PIM-DM, some are used only by PIM-SM, and some are shared. All message formats, including those used only by PIM-DM, are described at the end of the section "Protocol Independent Multicast, Sparse Mode (PIM-SM)."

The current version of PIM is PIMv2. Version 1 of the protocol encapsulates its messages in IP packets with protocol number 2 (IGMP) and uses the multicast address 224.0.0.2. PIMv2, which is supported beginning with Cisco IOS Software Release 11.3(2)T, uses its own protocol number of 103 and the reserved multicast address 224.0.0.13. When a PIMv2 router peers with a PIMv1 router, it automatically sets that interface to PIMv1.

Operation of Protocol Independent Multicast, Dense Mode (PIM-DM)

As of this writing, no RFC describes PIM-DM. It is, however, described in an Internet draft.[12] Beyond the common message formats, you are likely to find more similarities between PIM-DM and DVMRP than between PIM-DM and PIM-SM.

PIM-DM Basics

PIM-DM uses five PIMv2 messages:

- Hello
- Join/Prune
- Graft
- Graft-Ack
- Assert

PIMv2 routers use Hello messages to discover neighbors. When a PIMv2 router (either PIM-DM or PIM-SM) becomes active, it periodically sends a Hello message on every interface on which PIM is configured. PIMv1 routers have the same functionality, except that they use Query messages. The Hello (or Query) messages contain a *holdtime*, which specifies the maximum time the neighbor should wait to hear a subsequent message before declaring the originating router dead. Both the PIMv2 Hello interval and the PIMv1 Query interval are 30 seconds in Cisco IOS Software by default. They can be changed on a per-interface basis with the command **ip pim query-interval**. The holdtime is set automatically to 3.5 times the Hello/Query interval.

Example 5-3 shows a **debug** capture of PIM messages being sent and received. Notice that the router has both PIMv1 and PIMv2 neighbors, as indicated by the **Hello** and **Router-Query** keywords. Notice also that the router is sending Hellos on interface E0 but is receiving neither Hellos nor Queries on the interface, indicating that there are no PIM neighbors on that subnet.

Example 5-3 *Router Steel Is Querying for Neighbors on Interfaces E0, E1, and S1.708. It Is Hearing from Neighbors on E1 and S1.708*

```
Steel#debug ip pim
PIM debugging is on
Steel#
PIM: Received v2 Hello on Ethernet1 from 172.16.6.3
PIM: Received Router-Query on Serial1.708 from 172.16.2.242
PIM: Send v2 Hello on Ethernet1
PIM: Send v2 Hello on Ethernet0
PIM: Send Router-Query on Serial1.708  (dual PIMv1v2)
PIM: Received v2 Hello on Ethernet1 from 172.16.6.3
PIM: Received Router-Query on Serial1.708 from 172.16.2.242
PIM: Send v2 Hello on Ethernet1
PIM: Send v2 Hello on Ethernet0
PIM: Send Router-Query on Serial1.708  (dual PIMv1v2)
PIM: Received v2 Hello on Ethernet1 from 172.16.6.3
```

In Example 5-4, the **debug ip packet detail** command is used (linked to an access list to filter uninteresting packets) to get a closer look at the PIM messages. Here, you can see that the PIMv2 messages are sent to 224.0.0.13 and use protocol number 103, whereas the PIMv1 messages are sent to 224.0.0.2 and use protocol number 2.

Example 5-4 *This **debug** Capture Shows the Multicast Destination Addresses and the Protocol Numbers Used by PIMv1 and PIMv2*

```
Steel#debug ip packet detail 101
IP packet debugging is on (detailed) for access list 101
Steel#
IP: s=172.16.6.3 (Ethernet1), d=224.0.0.13, len 38, rcvd 0, proto=103
IP: s=172.16.2.241 (local), d=224.0.0.2 (Serial1.708), len 35, sending
broad/multicast, proto=2
IP: s=172.16.2.242 (Serial1.708), d=224.0.0.2, len 32, rcvd 0, proto=2
IP: s=172.16.6.1 (local), d=224.0.0.13 (Ethernet1), len 30, sending broad/multicast,
proto=103
IP: s=172.16.5.1 (local), d=224.0.0.13 (Ethernet0), len 30, sending broad/multicast,
proto=103
IP: s=172.16.6.3 (Ethernet1), d=224.0.0.13, len 38, rcvd 0, proto=103
IP: s=172.16.2.241 (local), d=224.0.0.2 (Serial1.708), len 35, sending
broad/multicast, proto=2
IP: s=172.16.2.242 (Serial1.708), d=224.0.0.2, len 32, rcvd 0, proto=2
IP: s=172.16.6.1 (local), d=224.0.0.13 (Ethernet1), len 30, sending broad/multicast,
proto=103
IP: s=172.16.5.1 (local), d=224.0.0.13 (Ethernet0), len 30, sending broad/multicast,
proto=103
```

In Example 5-5, the command **show ip pim neighbor** is used to observe the resulting PIM neighbor table.

Example 5-5   *The PIM Neighbor Table Records the Neighbors Heard from in Example 5-3*

```
Steel#show ip pim neighbor
PIM Neighbor Table
Neighbor Address  Interface      Uptime    Expires   Ver  Mode
172.16.6.3        Ethernet1      01:57:22  00:01:29  v2   Dense   (DR)
172.16.2.242      Serial1.708    04:55:56  00:01:05  v1   Dense
Steel#
```

When a source begins sending multicast packets, PIM-DM uses flood-and-prune to build the multicast tree. As each PIM-DM router receives a multicast packet, the router adds an entry to its multicast forwarding table. Ultimately, the packets are flooded to all leaf routers—that is, all routers that have no downstream PIM neighbors. If a leaf router receives a multicast packet for which it has no attached group members, the router must prune itself from the multicast tree. It does this by sending a Prune message to the upstream neighbor toward the source. The destination address of the Prune message is 224.0.0.13, and the address of the upstream router is encoded within the message. If that upstream neighbor has no attached members of the packet's group, and either has no other downstream neighbors or has received prunes from all of its downstream neighbors, it sends a Prune message to its own upstream neighbor toward the source.

Referring back to the bulleted list of PIMv2 message types earlier in this section, you will see that there is no "Prune" message type. Instead, there is a Join/Prune. This is a single message type that has separate fields for listing groups to be joined and groups to be pruned. This section continues to use "Prune message" and "Join message" for clarity, but you should be aware that a Prune message is actually a Join/Prune with a group address listed in the prune section. Likewise, a Join message is a Join/Prune message with a group address in the Join field.

Example 5-6 shows a forwarding table entry for multicast group 239.70.49.238. You can observe the (S, G) pair, showing the source to be 172.16.1.1. The router has consulted its unicast routing table for the upstream interface to the source, which is S1.708, and the upstream neighbor toward the source, which is 172.16.2.242. That information is entered into the multicast forwarding table and is used for the RPF check. As with DVMRP, if a packet with a source address of 172.16.1.1 and a destination address of 239.70.49.238 arrives on any interface other than S1.708, the RPF check fails and the packet is dropped.

NOTE   Example 5-6 does not show all the information in the forwarding table pertaining to this group; some information has been deleted for clarity. Chapter 6 presents the forwarding table in more detail.

Example 5-6 *The show ip mroute Command Displays the Multicast Forwarding Table*

```
Steel#show ip mroute 239.70.49.238
IP Multicast Routing Table
Flags: D - Dense, S - Sparse, C - Connected, L - Local, P - Pruned
       R - RP-bit set, F - Register flag, T - SPT-bit set, J - Join SPT
Timers: Uptime/Expires
Interface state: Interface, Next-Hop or VCD, State/Mode

 (172.16.1.1, 239.70.49.238), 01:56:27/00:02:59, flags: CT
   Incoming interface: Serial1.708, RPF nbr 172.16.2.242
   Outgoing interface list:
     Ethernet1, Prune/Dense, 01:40:23/00:00:39
     Ethernet0, Forward/Dense, 00:00:46/00:00:00

Steel#
```

Associated with the (S, G) entry are two timers. The first timer indicates how long the entry has been in the table. The second timer indicates the expiration time of the entry. If a multicast packet is not forwarded for this (S, G) within 2 minutes and 59 seconds, the entry is deleted.

NOTE   Cisco IOS Software uses an expiration timer of 2.5 minutes, whereas the Internet Draft recommends an expiration timer of 3.5 minutes.

There are also two flags associated with the entry in Example 5-6. The first flag (C) indicates that there is a group member on a directly connected subnet of the router. The second flag (T) indicates that the router is an active member of the *shortest path tree* (SPT)—in CBT parlance, it is "on-tree."

NOTE   PIM calls source-based trees shortest path trees, and shared trees *rendezvous point trees* (RPTs). SPT is a descriptive name, because as you will see in a subsequent section, these trees sometime traverse a shorter path to the source than do the RPTs.

Two interfaces appear on the outgoing interface list in Example 5-6. The first interface, E1, is in prune state and dense mode. Therefore, you know that the downstream neighbor on this interface has sent a Prune message. The timers show that the interface has been up for 1 hour, 40 minutes, and 23 seconds, and that the prune state expires in 39 seconds. When a Prune message is received, a 210-second expiration timer is started. The prune state is maintained until the timer expires, at which time the state is changed to "forward" and packets are again forwarded downstream. It is up to the downstream router to again send a Prune message to its upstream neighbor; this behavior is the same as what you saw for DVMRP.

The second interface, E0, is in forward state. Recall from Example 5-3 that the router is sending Hellos on E0 but is receiving no Hellos from neighbors on that interface. Based on that information and the information in Example 5-6, you know that the router is forwarding on E0 because there is a group member on that subnet. Example 5-7 confirms this conclusion. Notice in Example 5-6 that there is an uptime associated with the interface, but no expiration time. This is because there is no neighbor state to expire. Instead, the router deletes the interface from the forwarding table when IGMP tells it that there are no longer group members on the subnet, or when the expiration timer shown in Example 5-7 reaches 0.

Example 5-7 *The* **show ip igmp group** *Command Displays the Connected Group Members Recorded in the IGMP Membership Table*

```
Steel#show ip igmp group 239.70.49.238
IGMP Connected Group Membership
Group Address    Interface          Uptime    Expires   Last Reporter
239.70.49.238    Ethernet0          01:52:23  00:02:34  172.16.5.2
Steel#
```

Example 5-8 shows the forwarding table of the next router upstream toward the source. RPF checks are performed for (172.16.1.1, 239.70.49.238) against interface S1.803 and upstream neighbor 172.16.2.254, and there is only one downstream interface. Comparing the flag for this entry against the flags in Example 5-6, you can see that this router is on the shortest path tree but that it has no directly connected group members.

Example 5-8 *The Flags for This Entry Indicate That the Router Is on the SPT but That It Has No Directly Connected Group Members*

```
Nickel#show ip mroute 239.70.49.238
IP Multicast Routing Table
Flags: D - Dense, S - Sparse, C - Connected, L - Local, P - Pruned
       R - RP-bit set, F - Register flag, T - SPT-bit set
Timers: Uptime/Expires

 (172.16.1.1/32, 239.70.49.238), uptime 02:05:23, expires 0:02:58, flags: T
  Incoming interface: Serial1.803, RPF neighbor 172.16.2.254
  Outgoing interface list:
    Serial1.807, Forward state, Dense mode, uptime 02:05:24, expires 0:02:34

Nickel#
```

NOTE   The output in Example 5-8 is formatted slightly differently from the preceding forwarding table. This is due to a different Cisco IOS Software Release. However, you can readily see that the information is the same.

Moving upstream again, Example 5-9 shows another forwarding table for the group. The flags again indicate "Connected," but what is connected in this instance is not a group member. Notice that the incoming interface, E0/0, shows an RPF neighbor address of 0.0.0.0. This indicates that the connected device is the source for the group.

Example 5-9   *This Router Is Connected to the Source 172.16.1.1, as Indicated by the RPF Neighbor Address of 0.0.0.0*

```
Bronze#show ip mroute 239.70.49.238
IP Multicast Routing Table
Flags: D - Dense, S - Sparse, C - Connected, L - Local, P - Pruned
       R - RP-bit set, F - Register flag, T - SPT-bit set, J - Join SPT
Timers: Uptime/Expires
Interface state: Interface, Next-Hop, State/Mode

 (172.16.1.1/32, 239.70.49.238), 02:10:43/00:02:59, flags: CT
  Incoming interface: Ethernet0/0, RPF nbr 0.0.0.0
  Outgoing interface list:
    Serial0/1.305, Prune/Dense, 02:10:43/00:01:28
    Serial0/1.308, Forward/Dense, 02:10:43/00:00:00

Bronze#
```

Example 5-9 also shows two outgoing interfaces (172.16.1.1, 239.70.49.238). One is in forwarding state, and the other is in prune state. Like all flood-and-prune protocols, PIM-DM must maintain prune state for all interfaces. The reason for this requirement is so that a router that has pruned itself from a multicast tree can graft itself back onto the tree when necessary.

For example, Example 5-10 shows a router's entry for (172.16.1.1, 239.70.49.238) in which there are no attached group members and no downstream neighbors. As a result, the outgoing interface list is null. The P flag indicates that the router has sent a Prune message to the upstream neighbor 172.16.2.246. If a connected host now sends an IGMP message requesting a join to the group, the router sends a PIM Graft message upstream toward the source. But the only way the router knows the address of the group's source is via the initial flood of multicast packets. Hence, prune state must be maintained as shown in the example.

Example 5-10 *This Router Has a Null Outgoing Interface List for the (S,G) Pair (172.16.1.1, 239.70.49.238) and So Has Pruned Itself from That Source Tree*

```
Lead#show ip mroute 239.70.49.238
IP Multicast Routing Table
Flags: D - Dense, S - Sparse, C - Connected, L - Local, P - Pruned
       R - RP-bit set, F - Register flag, T - SPT-bit set
Timers: Uptime/Expires
Interface state: Interface, Next-Hop, State/Mode

 (172.16.1.1/32, 239.70.49.238), 02:32:42/0:00:17, flags: PT
  Incoming interface: Serial1.605, RPF nbr 172.16.2.246
  Outgoing interface list: Null

Lead#
```

The Graft message is unicast to the upstream neighbor on the group tree. When the upstream router receives the Graft message, it adds the interface on which the message was received to its outgoing interface list. The interface is put into forward state, and a Graft Ack message is immediately unicast to the new downstream neighbor. If the router is already forwarding packets to other downstream neighbors, nothing else must be done. If the router has also pruned itself from the tree, however, it too must send a Graft to its upstream neighbor. When a router sends a Graft message, it waits 3 seconds for a Graft Ack. If the acknowledgement is not received within that time, the router retransmits the Graft message.

This PIM-DM flood-and-prune mechanism is very similar to that of DVMRP; however, there is one significant difference. Recall from the section "The DVMRP Routing Table" that DVMRP signals route dependencies to upstream neighbors using a poison reverse mechanism. The dependency tells an upstream DVMRP router that a particular downstream router is depending on it to forward packets from a particular source. All this can happen even before the source begins forwarding packets, because of DVMRP's built-in routing protocol. As a result, in some topologies DVMRP can limit the scope of its flooding. PIM-DM does not have this capability, because it does not have a built-in routing protocol. Therefore, PIM-DM always floods to the entire PIM domain. The protocol designers state the following in the specification:

We choose to accept the additional overhead in favor of the simplification and flexibility gained by not depending on a specific type of topology discovery protocol.

Prune Overrides

Another advantage of DVMRP's downstream dependency mechanism is apparent during the prune process. In Figure 5-50, a single router has multiple downstream neighbors. The upstream router, Mercury, is flooding a group's multicast packets onto the LAN connecting the three routers. Copper has a null outgoing interface list and therefore sends a Prune to

Mercury. Silver, however, has an attached group member and therefore wants to receive the multicast traffic.

Figure 5-50 *Copper Has Sent a Prune Message for (172.16.1.1, 238.70.49.238) Because Its Outgoing Interface List for That (S, G) Pair Is Empty. But Silver Has a Member of the Group and Wants to Continue Receiving the Traffic*

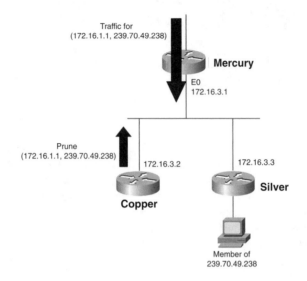

If the three routers are running DVMRP, there is no problem. Mercury knows its downstream dependencies for the group's source, and it knows it has received a Prune only from Copper, so it continues to forward traffic for Silver.

Suppose, however, that the routers in Figure 5-50 are running PIM-DM. Mercury certainly knows that it has two neighbors, based on the Hello messages, but nothing in the Hello messages describe dependencies. So when Copper sends a Prune message, Mercury does not know whether or not to prune the LAN interface.

PIM-DM circumvents this problem with a process called *prune override*. Copper sends the Prune message to Mercury, but Mercury's address is encoded in the message itself. The IP packet carrying the message is addressed to the *ALL PIM Routers* address 224.0.0.13. When Mercury receives the message, it does not immediately prune the interface. Instead, it sets a 3-second timer. At the same time, Silver also has received the Prune message because of the multicast destination address. It sees that the Prune is for a group it wants to continue receiving, and that the message has been sent to its upstream neighbor forwarding the group traffic. So Silver sends a Join message to Mercury, as illustrated by Figure 5-51. The result is that Silver overrides the Prune sent by Copper. As long as Mercury receives a Join before its 3-second timer expires, no interruption in traffic occurs.

Figure 5-51 *Silver Overrides Copper's Prune with a Join Message*

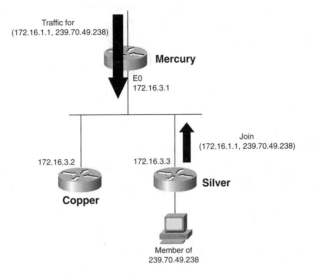

Example 5-11 shows a prune override in action. Debugging is used to capture PIM activity on Mercury in Figures 5-50 and 5-51. The first message shows that a Prune (a Join/Prune message with 239.70.49.238 listed in its Prune field) has been received on interface E0 from Copper (172.16.3.2) for the (S, G) pair (172.16.1.1, 239.70.49.238). Notice that the first line indicates that the message is "to us." This is an indicator that Mercury has recognized its own address encoded in the message.

Example 5-11 *The Router Mercury in Figure 5-51 Has Received a Prune from Copper (172.16.3.2). Silver (172.16.3.3) Then Sends a Join, Overriding Copper's Prune*

```
Mercury#debug ip pim
PIM debugging is on
Mercury#
PIM: Received Join/Prune on Ethernet0 from 172.16.3.2, to us
PIM: Prune-list: (172.16.1.1/32, 239.70.49.238)
PIM: Schedule to prune Ethernet0 for (172.16.1.1/32, 239.70.49.238)
PIM: Received Join/Prune on Ethernet0 from 172.16.3.3, to us
PIM: Join-list: (172.16.1.1/32, 239.70.49.238)
PIM: Add Ethernet0/172.16.3.3 to (172.16.1.1/32, 239.70.49.238), Forward state
```

The second and third lines show that Mercury has scheduled the (S, G) entry to be pruned from interface E0. That is, the 3-second timer has started. On the fourth line, Mercury has received a Join from Silver (172.16.3.3). On lines 5 and 6, E0 has been put into forward state for the (S, G) pair. Copper's Prune has been overridden.

Unicast Route Changes

When a topology changes, the unicast routing table also changes. And if the unicast route changes affect the route to a source, PIM-DM must also change. An obvious case would be one in which a topology change results in a different previous-hop router on the path to a source.

When a source's RPF router changes, PIM-DM first sends a Prune message to the old router. A Graft message is then sent to the new RPF router to build the new tree.

PIM-DM-Designated Routers

PIM-DM elects a designated router on multiaccess networks. The protocol itself does not need a DR, but recall that IGMPv1 does not have a querier process and relies on the routing protocol to elect a DR to manage IGMP queries. This is the role of the PIM-DM (and PIM-SM) designated router.

The DR election process is quite simple. As you already know, every PIM-DM router sends a PIMv2 Hello message or a PIMv1 Query message every 30 seconds for neighbor discovery. On multiaccess networks, the PIM-DM router with the highest IP address becomes the DR, as illustrated by the output in Example 5-12. The other routers monitor the DR's Hello packets; if none are heard within 105 seconds, the DR is declared dead, and a new DR is elected.

Example 5-12 *The PIM Neighbor Table of Mercury in Example 5-11 Indicates That Silver, with the Highest Attached IP Address of 172.16.3.3, Is the Designated Router*

```
Mercury#show ip pim neighbor
PIM Neighbor Table
Neighbor Address   Interface        Uptime     Expires    Ver   Mode
172.16.3.3         Ethernet0        2d23h      00:01:17   v1v2  Dense    (DR)
172.16.3.2         Ethernet0        2d23h      00:01:21   v1    Dense
172.16.2.250       Serial1.503      09:15:11   00:01:17   v1    Dense
Mercury#
```

PIM Forwarder Election

In Figure 5-52, both Mercury and Copper have a route to source 172.16.1.1. They also have downstream interfaces to a member of group 239.70.49.238 that are connected to a common multiaccess network. Both Mercury and Copper are receiving copies of the same multicast packets from the source, but it would obviously be inefficient for both routers to forward the packets onto the same network.

Figure 5-52 *Both Copper and Mercury Are Receiving Copies of the Multicast Packets Sent by Source 172.16.1.1, but Only One Router Should Forward the Packets onto Subnet 172.16.3.0/24*

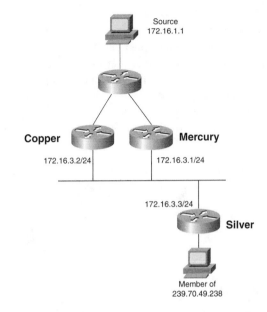

To prevent such a situation, PIM routers select a single *forwarder* on the shared network. Recall that DVMRP has a similar function, the designated forwarder. DVMRP-designated forwarders are selected as part of the route exchange across the multiaccess network. Because PIM does not have its own routing protocol, however, it instead uses Assert messages to select the forwarder.

When a router receives a multicast packet on an outgoing multiaccess interface, it sends an Assert message on the network. The Assert message includes the source and group address, the metric of the unicast route to the source, and the metric preference (in Cisco terms, the administrative distance) of the unicast protocol used to discover the route. The routers producing the duplicate packets compare the messages and determine the forwarder based on the following criteria:

- The router advertising the lowest metric preference (administrative distance) is the forwarder. The routers would advertise only different metric preferences if their routes to the source have been discovered via different unicast routing protocols.

- If the metric preferences are equal, the router advertising the lowest metric is the forwarder. In other words, if the routers are running the same unicast routing protocol, the router metrically closest to the source becomes the forwarder.

- If both the metric preferences and the metrics are equal, the forwarder is the router with the highest IP address on the network.

The forwarder continues forwarding group traffic onto the multiaccess network. The other routers stop forwarding that group's traffic and remove the multiaccess interface from their outgoing interface list.

When the multicast source in Figure 5-52 first begins sending packets to group 239.70.49.238, for example, both Copper and Mercury receive copies of the packets, and both routers forward the packets onto subnet 172.16.3.0/24, as illustrated in Part A of Figure 5-53. When Copper receives a packet from Mercury for (172.16.1.1, 239.70.49.238) on its Ethernet interface, it sees that the interface is on the outgoing interface list for that (S, G) pair. As a result, it sends an Assert message on the subnet. When Mercury receives a multicast packet from Copper on the same interface, it takes the same action, as illustrated in Part B of Figure 5-53.

Figure 5-53 *When Copper and Mercury Detect Packets for (172.16.1.1, 239.70.49.238) on Their Downstream Multiaccess Interfaces, They Originate Assert Messages to Determine the Forwarder for the Group*

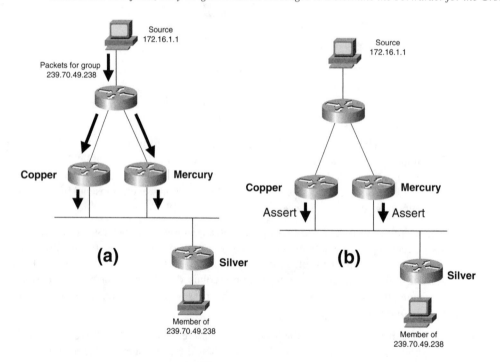

Example 5-13 shows Silver's unicast routing table and its multicast forwarding table. The unicast table indicates equal-cost OSPF paths to the source 172.16.1.1 via either Copper (172.16.3.2) or Mercury (172.16.3.1). Because routes are OSPF, they have an equal administrative distance of 110. And because both routes have an OSPF cost of 74, the forwarder is the router with the highest IP address.

Example 5-13 *Silver's Unicast Routing Table Shows Two Next-Hop Routers to the Subnet of Source 172.16.1.1. The Multicast Routing Table Shows That the Next-Hop Router with the Highest IP Address Has Been Chosen as the Forwarder*

```
Silver#show ip route
Codes: C - connected, S - static, I - IGRP, R - RIP, M - mobile, B - BGP
       D - EIGRP, EX - EIGRP external, O - OSPF, IA - OSPF inter area
       N1 - OSPF NSSA external type 1, N2 - OSPF NSSA external type 2
       E1 - OSPF external type 1, E2 - OSPF external type 2, E - EGP
       i - IS-IS, L1 - IS-IS level-1, L2 - IS-IS level-2, * - candidate default
       U - per-user static route, o - ODR
       T - traffic engineered route
Gateway of last resort is not set
     172.16.0.0/16 is variably subnetted, 8 subnets, 2 masks
O       172.16.2.252/30 [110/138] via 172.16.3.1, 00:02:16, Ethernet1
                        [110/138] via 172.16.3.2, 00:02:16, Ethernet1
O       172.16.2.248/30 [110/74] via 172.16.3.1, 00:02:16, Ethernet1
O       172.16.2.244/30 [110/74] via 172.16.3.2, 00:02:16, Ethernet1
                        [110/74] via 172.16.3.1, 00:02:16, Ethernet1
O       172.16.2.240/30 [110/138] via 172.16.3.1, 00:02:16, Ethernet1
O       172.16.2.236/30 [110/74] via 172.16.3.1, 00:02:16, Ethernet1
C       172.16.5.0/24 is directly connected, Ethernet0
O       172.16.1.0/24 [110/84] via 172.16.3.1, 00:02:16, Ethernet1
                      [110/84] via 172.16.3.2, 00:02:16, Ethernet1
C       172.16.3.0/24 is directly connected, Ethernet1
Silver#

Silver#show ip mroute 172.16.1.1 239.70.49.238
IP Multicast Routing Table
Flags: D - Dense, S - Sparse, C - Connected, L - Local, P - Pruned
       R - RP-bit set, F - Register flag, T - SPT-bit set, J - Join SPT
Timers: Uptime/Expires
Interface state: Interface, Next-Hop or VCD, State/Mode

(172.16.1.1, 239.70.49.238), 00:02:02/00:02:59, flags: CT
  Incoming interface: Ethernet1, RPF nbr 172.16.3.2
  Outgoing interface list:
    Ethernet0, Forward/Dense, 00:01:50/00:00:00

Silver#
```

Operation of Protocol Independent Multicast, Sparse Mode (PIM-SM)

You learned earlier how shared trees are more scalable in sparsely populated multicast internetworks, and how they can even be used in densely populated internetworks. The discussion may have left you with the impression that shared multicast trees are always preferable over source-based trees. Such is not the case.

Figure 5-54 shows a situation in which a source-based tree might be preferred over a shared tree. In this topology, the source and destination are closer to each other than they are to the core router at which the shared tree is rooted. A source-based tree directly between the source and destination is preferable, if only the associated overhead could be reduced.

Figure 5-54 *A Source-Based Tree Might Be Preferable to the Shared Tree in This Internetwork*

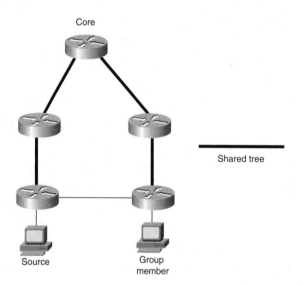

Unlike CBT, PIM-SM supports both shared and source-based trees, which is the primary reason it is presently the multicast routing protocol of choice in most modern internetworks.

PIM-SM is described in RFC 2362.[13]

PIM-SM Basics

PIM-SM uses seven PIMv2 messages:

- Hello
- Bootstrap
- Candidate-RP-Advertisement
- Join/Prune
- Assert
- Register
- Register-Stop

Notice that three of the messages (Hello, Join/Prune, and Assert) also are used by PIM-DM. There are four messages unique to PIM-SM, just as there are two messages (Graft and Graft-Ack) used only by PIM-DM.

Several functions are common to PIM-SM and PIM-DM:

- Neighbor discovery through exchange of Hello messages
- Recalculation of the RPF interface when the unicast routing table changes
- Election of a designated router on multiaccess networks
- The use of Prune Overrides on multiaccess networks
- Use of Assert messages to elect a designated forwarder on multiaccess networks

These functions are all described in the PIM-DM section and so are not described again here.

Unlike PIM-DM, PIM-SM uses explicit joins, making the creation of both shared and source-based multicast trees more efficient.

Finding the Rendezvous Point

As you have already learned, a shared tree is rooted at a router somewhere in the multicast internetwork rather than at the source. CBT calls this router the *core*, and PIM-SM calls it the *rendezvous point* (RP). Before a shared tree can be established, the joining routers must know how to find the RP. The router can learn the address of the RP in three ways:

- The RP address can be statically configured on all routers.
- An open-standard bootstrap protocol can be used to designate and advertise the RP.
- The Cisco-proprietary Auto-RP protocol can be used to designate and advertise the RP.

The use of all three methods is demonstrated in Chapter 6.

As with static routes, statically configuring RP addresses on all routers has the advantage of providing very specific control of the internetwork, but at the cost of high administrative overhead. Static RP configuration is generally only feasible on small multicast internetworks.

The Bootstrap Protocol

The bootstrap protocol, first supported in Cisco IOS Software Release 11.3T, is essentially the same protocol used by CBT to advertise core routers, with a few changes in message names and formats. To run the bootstrap protocol, *candidate bootstrap routers* (C-BSRs) and *candidate rendezvous points* (C-RPs) are administratively designated in the internetwork. Typically, the same set of routers is configured as both C-BSRs and C-RPs. The

C-BSRs and C-RPs identify themselves by means of an IP address, which is typically configured to be the address of a loopback interface.

The first step is for a bootstrap router (BSR) to be elected from the C-BSRs. Each C-BSR is assigned a priority between 0 and 255 (the default is 0) and a BSR IP address. When a router is configured as a candidate BSR, it sets a bootstrap timer to 130 seconds and listens for a Bootstrap message.

Bootstrap messages advertise the originator's priority and BSR IP address. When a C-BSR receives a Bootstrap message, it compares the originator's priority with its own priority. If the originator has a higher priority, the receiver resets its bootstrap timer and continues to listen. If the receiver's priority is higher, it declares itself the BSR and begins sending Bootstrap messages every 60 seconds. If the priorities are equal, the higher BSR IP address is the tiebreaker.

If a C-BSR's 130-second bootstrap timer expires, the router assumes that there is no BSR, declares itself the BSR, and begins sending Bootstrap messages every 60 seconds.

Bootstrap messages use the All_PIM_Routers destination address of 224.0.0.13 and have a TTL of 1. When a PIM router receives a Bootstrap message, it sends a copy out all interfaces except the one on which the message was received. This procedure not only ensures that the Bootstrap messages are flooded throughout the multicast domain, it also ensures that every PIM router receives a copy and thus knows which router is the BSR.

A C-RP is configured with an RP IP address and a priority between 0 and 255. The router can be configured to be a candidate RP for only certain multicast groups, or it can be the C-RP for all groups. When the BSR is known by reception of Bootstrap messages, the C-RP begins unicasting Candidate-RP-Advertisement messages to the BSR. These messages contain the originator's RP address, the group addresses for which the originator is a candidate RP, and its priority.

The BSR compiles the C-RPs, their respective priorities, and their corresponding groups into an *RP-Set*, and it advertises the RP-Set throughout the PIM domain in Bootstrap messages. Also included in the Bootstrap message is an 8-bit hash-mask. Again, all PIM routers receive the Bootstrap messages because of the destination address 224.0.0.13.

When a router must join a shared tree as the result of receiving either an IGMP message or a PIM Join message, it examines the RP-Set learned from the BSR via Bootstrap messages.

- If there is only one C-RP for the group, that router is selected as the RP.

- If there are multiple C-RPs for the group, each with different priorities, the router with the lowest priority number is chosen as the RP.

- If there are multiple C-RPs for the group with equally low priorities, a hash function is run. The input of the function is the group prefix, the hash-mask, and the C-RP address, and the output is some numeric value. The C-RP with the highest resulting value becomes the RP.

- If the hash function returns the same value for more than one C-RP, the C-RP with the highest IP address becomes the RP.

NOTE   The hash function, if you must know, is as follows:

$$Value(G,M,C) = (1103515245 * ((11035515245 * (G\&M) + 12345) \text{ XOR } C) + 12345) \bmod 2^{31}$$

where:

G = Group prefix

M = Hash-mask

C = C-RP address

This set of procedures ensures that all routers in the domain select the same RP for the same group. The only reason the hash function is necessary is to incorporate the hash-mask, which allows some number of consecutive group addresses to be mapped to the same RP. The use of the hash-mask is demonstrated in Chapter 6.

The Auto-RP Protocol

Auto-RP was first supported in Cisco IOS Software Release 11.1(6). It was developed by Cisco to provide automatic discovery of the RP before the bootstrap protocol was specified for PIM-SM. As with bootstrap, candidate RPs (C-RPs) are designated in the PIM-SM domain and are identified by designated IP addresses, usually the address of a loopback interface. One or more *RP mapping agents*, routers that play a role similar to BSRs, also are designated. The four major differences from the bootstrap protocol are as follows:

- Auto-RP is Cisco proprietary and usually cannot be used in multivendor topologies. However, some other vendors now support Auto-RP.

- RP mapping agents are designated rather than elected from a set of candidates as BSRs are.

- RP mapping agents map groups to RPs instead of advertising an RP-Set and distributing the selection process throughout the domain.

- Rather than the multicast address 224.0.0.13 used by bootstrap and understood by all PIM routers, Auto-RP uses two reserved multicast addresses: 224.0.1.39 and 224.0.1.40.

When a Cisco PIM-SM router is configured to be a candidate RP for one or more groups, it advertises itself and the groups for which it is a C-RP in *RP-Announce* messages. These messages are multicast every 60 seconds to the reserved Cisco-RP-Announce address 224.0.1.39. The configured mapping agents for the domain listen for this address. From all the received RP-Announce messages, the mapping agent selects an RP for a group based on the numerically highest IP address of all the group's C-RPs.

The RP mapping agent then advertises the complete list of group-to-RP mappings in *RP-Discovery* messages. These messages are sent every 60 seconds to the reserved Cisco-RP-Discovery address 224.0.1.40. All Cisco PIM-SM routers listen for this address and thus learn the correct RP to use for each known group.

PIM-SM and Shared Trees

The major difference between a shared tree route entry and a source-based or SPT route entry is that the shared tree entry is not source-specific—in keeping with the fact that many sources share the same tree. Therefore, the entry is a (*, G) pair, where the asterisk is a wildcard representing any and all source addresses sending to the group G.

When a PIM-SM DR receives an IGMP Membership Report from a host requesting a join to a multicast group, it first checks to see whether there is already an entry in the multicast table for the group. If there is an entry for the group, the interface on which the IGMP message was received is added to the entry as an outgoing interface. No other action is necessary.

If no entry exists, a (*, G) entry is created for the group, and the outgoing interface is added. The router then looks up the group-to-RP mapping for this group (as demonstrated in Example 5-14), the unicast routing table is consulted for the route to the specified RP, and the upstream interface to the RP is added to the incoming (RPF) interface.

Example 5-14 *The* **show ip pim rp mapping** *Command Displays a Router's Group-to-RP Mappings. Here, All Multicast Groups Are Mapped to the RP 172.16.224.1*

```
Iron#show ip pim rp mapping
PIM Group-to-RP Mappings

Group(s): 224.0.0.0/4, Static
    RP: 172.16.224.1 (?)
Iron#
```

Example 5-15 shows an example of a (*, G) route entry at router Iron in Figure 5-55.

Example 5-15 *This (*, G) Entry Indicates That the Upstream Neighbor on the Shared Tree for Group 236.82.134.23 Is 172.16.224.1, Reachable Out Interface S1.708, and That the RP for the Group Is 172.16.224.1. The Flags Associated with the Entry Indicate Sparse Mode and That There Is a Connected Member (on Interface E0)*

```
Iron#show ip mroute 236.82.134.23
IP Multicast Routing Table
Flags: D - Dense, S - Sparse, C - Connected, L - Local, P - Pruned
       R - RP-bit set, F - Register flag, T - SPT-bit set, J - Join SPT
Timers: Uptime/Expires
Interface state: Interface, Next-Hop or VCD, State/Mode

(*, 236.82.134.23), 00:08:58/00:02:59, RP 172.16.224.1, flags: SC
  Incoming interface: Serial1.708, RPF nbr 172.16.2.242
  Outgoing interface list:
    Ethernet0, Forward/Sparse, 00:08:59/00:02:47

Iron#
```

Figure 5-55 *Router Brass Is the RP for This PIM-SM Domain. Its RP Address, 172.16.224.1, Is Configured on Its Loopback Interface*

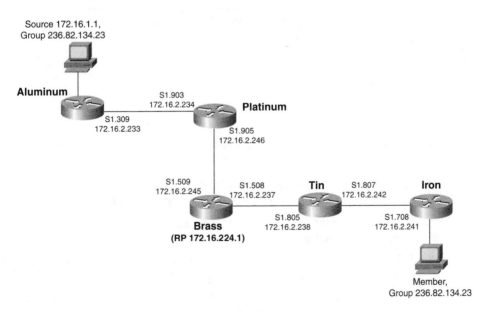

The router then sends a Join/Prune message out the upstream interface to 224.0.0.13, as illustrated by Figure 5-56. The message includes the address of the group to be joined and the address of the RP. The prune section of the message is empty. Two flags also are set—the wildcard bit (WC-bit) and the RP-tree bit (RPT-bit):

- The WC-bit = 1 indicates that the join address is an RP address rather than a source address.

- The RPT-bit = 1 indicates that the message is being propagated along a shared tree to the RP.

Figure 5-56 *A Join/Prune Message Is Multicast Hop by Hop to the RP*

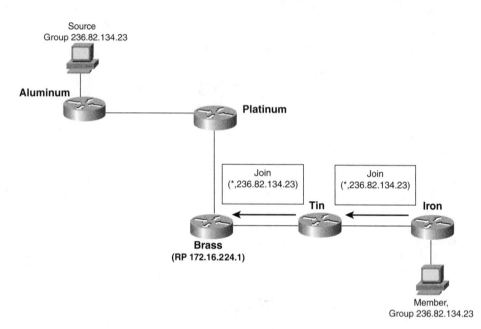

When the upstream router receives the Join/Prune, one of four situations and associated actions holds true:

- The router is not the RP, and it is on the shared tree. The router adds the interface on which it received the Join/Prune to the outgoing interface list for the group.

- The router is not the RP, and it is not on the tree. The router creates a (*, G) entry and sends its own Join/Prune upstream toward the RP.

- The router is the RP, and it has an entry for the group. The router adds the interface on which it received the Join/Prune to the outgoing interface list for the group.

- The router is the RP, and it has no entry for the group. The router creates a (*, G) entry and adds the receiving interface to the outgoing interface list for the group.

The implication of the last bullet is that a group does not have to have a source for a tree to be built from members of the RP.

Once the shared tree is established, routers periodically send Join/Prune messages to upstream neighbors as a keepalive. The Join/Prune lists all route entries for which the destination neighbor is the previous-hop router. The default period is 60 seconds. This can be changed with the Cisco IOS Software command **ip pim message-interval**. The holdtime is 3 times the Join/Prune interval, or 3 minutes by default, and it is advertised in the Join/Prune message. If a PIM-SM router does not hear a Join/Prune for a known group from a downstream neighbor within the holdtime, it prunes the downstream router from the outgoing interface list of the group entry. Example 5-16 shows the entry for group 236.82.134.23 in router Tin of Figure 5-55. The outgoing interface to router Iron, S1.805, indicates that the interface will be pruned if a Join/Prune is not received from Iron within 2 minutes, 11 seconds.

Example 5-16 *The Entry for Group 236.82.134.23 at Tin in Figure 5-55 Shows the Remaining Holdtime Associated with Downstream Router Iron. Notice That There Is No C Flag Set for This Entry, Because Tin Has No Directly Connected Group Members*

```
Tin#show ip mroute 236.82.134.23
IP Multicast Routing Table
Flags: D - Dense, S - Sparse, C - Connected, L - Local, P - Pruned
       R - RP-bit set, F - Register flag, T - SPT-bit set
Timers: Uptime/Expires

(*, 236.82.134.23), 00:09:39/0:02:56, RP 172.16.224.1, flags: S
  Incoming interface: Serial1.805, RPF neighbor 172.16.2.237
  Outgoing interface list:
    Serial1.807, Forward state, Sparse mode, uptime 00:09:39, expires 0:02:11

Tin#
```

Pruning occurs in the same manner. When a router wants to prune itself from a shared tree because it no longer has any directly connected group members or downstream neighbors, it sends a Join/Prune message out the RPF interface to the upstream neighbor. The group and RP address are listed in the Prune section, and the WC-bit and RPT-bit are set. The upstream router then removes the receiving interface from the outgoing interface list for the group. If that router has no more downstream neighbors and no connected group members, it also prunes itself.

NOTE   The Prune Override mechanism, as described in the PIM-DM section, is used to ensure that downstream neighbors on multiaccess networks are not inadvertently pruned.

Source Registration

The fundamental concept of shared trees, mentioned several times already, is that the multicast tree is rooted at a core or rendezvous point rather than at the source. The question arises, then, of how the source delivers multicast packets to the RP for delivery over the branches of the tree. Recall that CBT resolves the question by using bidirectional trees—packets can flow both down a branch from the core and up the branch toward the core. The source's directly connected router joins the shared tree to the core and then sends its traffic up the branch to the core. The problem with bidirectional trees is that it is very hard to ensure a loop-free topology, because RPF checks cannot be performed when there is no distinct "upstream" and "downstream."

Unlike CBT, PIM-SM uses RPF checks. Therefore, its trees must be unidirectional—that is, traffic can flow only down tree branches from the RP. The unidirectional traffic ensures a clearly defined incoming or RPF interface. If traffic flows only from the RP outward, however, how does a source deliver its multicast traffic to the RP?

When a PIM-SM router first receives a multicast packet from a directly connected source, it looks in its group-to-RP mappings to find the correct RP for the destination group, as demonstrated in the output in Example 5-17. This step is the same as when a member signals a group join with an IGMP message.

Example 5-17 *The Group-to-RP Mapping of Router Aluminum in Figure 5-55. Compare This to Example 5-14; Iron Has a Static RP Napping, Whereas Aluminum Has Learned the RP Address Dynamically*

```
Aluminum#show ip pim rp mapping
PIM Group-to-RP Mappings

Group(s) 224.0.0.0/4, uptime: 00:02:39, expires: 00:02:17
    RP 172.16.224.1 (?), PIMv2 v1
    Info source: 172.16.2.245 (?)
Aluminum#
```

After the group's RP is determined, the router encapsulates the multicast packet in a PIM Register message and sends the message to the RP. Instead of multicasting, the Register message is unicast to the RP address, as illustrated by Figure 5-57.

When the RP receives the Register message, the multicast packet is decapsulated. If the multicast routing table already has an entry for the group, copies of the multicast packet are forwarded out all interfaces on the outgoing interface list, as illustrated by Figure 5-58.

Figure 5-57 *The First Multicast Packet Is Encapsulated in a PIM Register Message and Is Unicast to the RP*

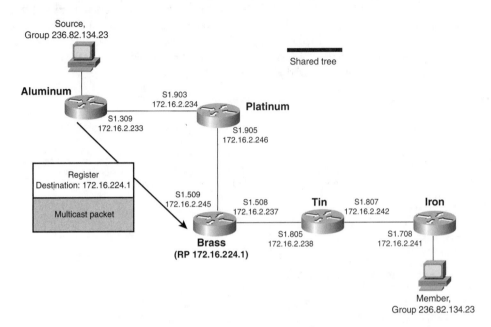

Figure 5-58 *The Multicast Packet Is Removed from the Register Message and Is Forwarded Out All Interfaces on the Group's Outgoing Interface List*

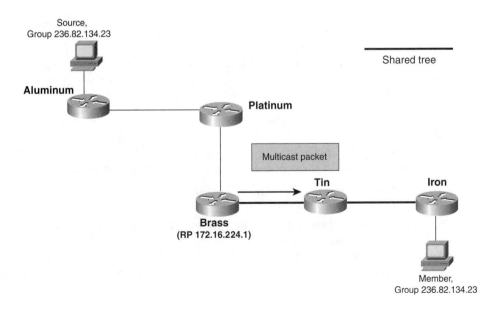

If there is a significant amount of multicast traffic to be sent to the RP, it is inefficient to continue encapsulating the packets in Register messages to get them to the RP. Therefore, the RP creates an (S, G) entry in its multicast table and initiates an SPT to the source DR by multicasting a Join/Prune message, as illustrated by Figure 5-59. In this message, the source address is included, WC-bit = 0, and RPT-bit = 0 to indicate that the path is a source-based SPT rather than a shared RPT.

Figure 5-59 *The RP Creates a Source-Based, Shortest Path Tree to the Source's DR*

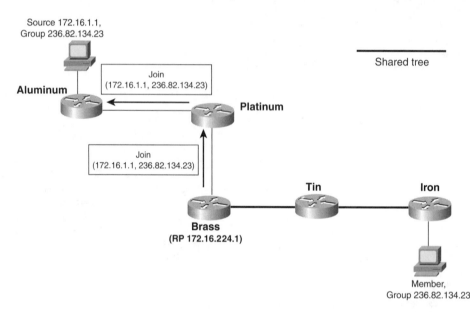

Once the SPT is established and the RP is receiving the group traffic over that tree, it sends a Register Stop message to the source's DR to tell the router to stop sending the multicast packets in Register messages, as illustrated by Figure 5-60.

If there are no group members when the source begins sending multicast traffic to the RP, the RP does not build an SPT. Instead, it just sends a Register Stop to the source's DR, telling it to stop sending the encapsulated multicast packets in Register messages. The RP has a (*, G) entry for the group, and when a member joins, the RP can then initiate the SPT.

A mechanism known as *Register Suppression* helps protect against the DR continuing to send packets to a failed RP. When a DR receives a Register Stop, it starts a 60-second *Register-Suppression* timer. When the timer expires, the router again sends its multicast packets to the RP in Register messages. However, 5 seconds before this occurs, the DR sends a Register message with a flag set, called the Null-Register bit, and with no encapsulated packets. If this message triggers a Register Stop from the RP, the Register-Suppression timer is reset.

Figure 5-60 *The RP Sends a Register Stop Message to Stop the Register Messages. The Source's Multicast Packets Are Now Sent to the RP Over the SPT*

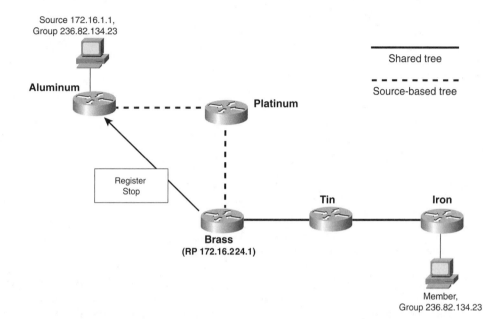

The debug messages in Example 5-18 show the sequence of events that occurs when router Aluminum begins sending multicast traffic to group 236.82.134.23. In this particular case, no members have yet joined the group. As a result, the RP (Brass) immediately sends a Register Stop message to Aluminum in response to the Register.

Example 5-18 *This RP Has No Members for Group 236.82.134.23. As a Result, It Immediately Replies to the Register Message from Aluminum (172.16.2.233) with a Register Stop Message. Notice That Both Messages Are Unicast Rather Than Multicast*

```
Brass#debug ip pim 236.82.134.23
PIM debugging is on
Brass#
PIM: Received Register on Serial1.509 from 172.16.2.233 for 172.16.1.1, group
236.82.134.23
PIM: Send Register-Stop to 172.16.2.233 for 172.16.1.1, group 236.82.134.23
```

Example 5-19 shows the route entry for the group. Notice that there are both (*, G) and (S, G) entries for the group. The (*, G) entry shows a null incoming interface and an RPF neighbor of 0.0.0.0, indicating that this router is the root of the shared tree. The (S, G) entry shows that router Platinum (172.16.2.246), the upstream neighbor toward the source, is the RPF neighbor. There are no interfaces on the outgoing interface list, so the entry is pruned.

Example 5-19 *The Routing Entry for Group 236.82.134.23 at the RP. No Members Have Joined the Group*

```
Brass#show ip mroute 236.82.134.23
IP Multicast Routing Table
Flags: D - Dense, S - Sparse, C - Connected, L - Local, P - Pruned
       R - RP-bit set, F - Register flag, T - SPT-bit set, J - Join SPT
Timers: Uptime/Expires
Interface state: Interface, Next-Hop or VCD, State/Mode

(*, 236.82.134.23), 00:07:38/00:02:59, RP 172.16.224.1, flags: S
  Incoming interface: Null, RPF nbr 0.0.0.0
  Outgoing interface list:
    Serial1.509, Forward/Sparse, 00:03:06/00:02:50

(172.16.1.1, 236.82.134.23), 00:07:38/00:01:21, flags: P
  Incoming interface: Serial1.509, RPF nbr 172.16.2.246
  Outgoing interface list: Null

Brass#
```

Example 5-20 shows the route entries for the group at Aluminum, the source's DR. Here, the (*, G) entry also exists, with the Ethernet interface connecting to the source in the outgoing interface list. The incoming interface list is null. The (S, G) entry shows the same Ethernet interface on the incoming interface list. The entries have two flags in common: One flag indicates that the source is directly connected; the other (F) indicates that the router must send a Register message for the group traffic.

Example 5-20 *The Corresponding Route Entry at the Source's DR Shows a Pruned SPT Entry*

```
Aluminum#show ip mroute 236.82.134.23
IP Multicast Routing Table
Flags: D - Dense, S - Sparse, C - Connected, L - Local, P - Pruned
       R - RP-bit set, F - Register flag, T - SPT-bit set, J - Join SPT
Timers: Uptime/Expires
Interface state: Interface, Next-Hop, State/Mode

(*, 236.82.134.23), 00:15:30/00:02:59, RP 172.16.224.1, flags: SJCF
  Incoming interface: Null, RPF nbr 0.0.0.0
  Outgoing interface list:
    Ethernet0/0, Forward/Sparse, 00:15:23/00:02:28

(172.16.1.1/32, 236.82.134.23), 00:00:29/00:02:30, flags: PCFT
  Incoming interface: Ethernet0/0, RPF nbr 0.0.0.0
  Outgoing interface list: Null

Aluminum#
```

The T flag on the (S, G) entry indicates that the entry represents an SPT, and the P entry indicates that there are no interfaces on the outgoing interface list. If there were an RPF neighbor, the router would send a Prune message to it for the group.

The final flag of interest is the J flag on the (*, G) entry. This flag indicates that the router switches to the SPT when a packet is received on the shared tree. Just how PIM-SM routers switch from shared trees to SPTs is the subject of the following section.

The debug messages in Example 5-21 show the sequence of events that occurs when the host attached to router Iron joins the group. The Join/Prune message, which was generated by Iron and multicast hop by hop to the RP, is received from Tin. The interface to Tin is added to the (*, G) entry; the interface is also added to the (S, G) entry, because the SPT to Aluminum will be used. Next, an SPT Join message is sent to Aluminum.

Example 5-21 *These* **debug** *Messages Show the Member Attached to Router Iron Joining Group 236.82.134.23*

```
Brass#debug ip pim 236.82.134.23
PIM debugging is on
Brass#
PIM: Received v2 Join/Prune on Serial1.508 from 172.16.2.238, to us
PIM: Join-list: (*, 236.82.134.23) RP 172.16.224.1, RPT-bit set, WC-bit set, S-bit
set
PIM: Add Serial1.508/172.16.2.241 to (*, 236.82.134.23), Forward state
PIM: Add Serial1.508/172.16.2.241 to (172.16.1.1/32, 236.82.134.23)
PIM: Building Join/Prune message for 236.82.134.23
PIM: For 172.16.2.246, Join-list: 172.16.1.1/32
PIM: Send periodic Join/Prune to 172.16.2.246 (Serial1.509)
```

Example 5-22 shows the resulting route entries at the RP, and Example 5-23 shows the resulting route entries at the source's DR.

Example 5-22 *When a Group Member Joins, Its Interface Is Added to the (*, G) Entry. It Also Is Added to the (S, G) Entry Because of the SPT to Aluminum*

```
Brass#show ip mroute 236.82.134.23
IP Multicast Routing Table
Flags: D - Dense, S - Sparse, C - Connected, L - Local, P - Pruned
       R - RP-bit set, F - Register flag, T - SPT-bit set, J - Join SPT
Timers: Uptime/Expires
Interface state: Interface, Next-Hop or VCD, State/Mode

(*, 236.82.134.23), 00:29:58/00:03:05, RP 172.16.224.1, flags: S
  Incoming interface: Null, RPF nbr 0.0.0.0
  Outgoing interface list:
    Serial1.509, Forward/Sparse, 00:29:58/00:02:52
    Serial1.508, Forward/Sparse, 00:24:36/00:03:05

(172.16.1.1, 236.82.134.23), 00:24:54/00:02:59, flags: T
  Incoming interface: Serial1.503, RPF nbr 172.16.2.246
  Outgoing interface list:
    Serial1.508, Forward/Sparse, 00:24:36/00:02:35

Brass#
```

Example 5-23 *The Interface Toward the RP Has Been Added to the Outgoing Interface List of Aluminum's (S, G) Entry, and the Entry Is No Longer in Prune State*

```
Aluminum#show ip mroute 236.82.134.23
IP Multicast Routing Table
Flags: D - Dense, S - Sparse, C - Connected, L - Local, P - Pruned
       R - RP-bit set, F - Register flag, T - SPT-bit set, J - Join SPT
Timers: Uptime/Expires
Interface state: Interface, Next-Hop, State/Mode

(*, 236.82.134.23), 00:00:47/00:02:59, RP 172.16.224.1, flags: SJCF
  Incoming interface: Serial0/1.309, RPF nbr 172.16.2.245
  Outgoing interface list:
    Ethernet0/0, Forward/Sparse, 00:00:01/00:02:58

(172.16.1.1/32, 236.82.134.23), 00:00:47/00:02:59, flags: CFT
  Incoming interface: Ethernet0/0, RPF nbr 0.0.0.0
  Outgoing interface list:
    Serial0/1.309, Forward/Sparse, 00:00:34/00:02:58

Aluminum#
```

PIM-SM and Shortest Path Trees

In Figure 5-61, router Lead has been added to the PIM-SM domain, and Lead has a group member attached. Under basic shared-tree rules, Lead would join the shared tree rooted at Brass. It is obvious in the illustration, however, that the direct link to Aluminum is a more efficient path for the multicast packets from the source to Lead's group member.

You already have seen how PIM-SM can build an SPT between the RP and the source DR. The protocol also allows SPTs to be built all the way from a router with attached group members to the source DR, to alleviate inefficiencies in topologies, such as the one in Figure 5-61.

Example 5-24 shows Lead building an SPT after its group member requests a join via IGMP. First, the router sends a Join to the RP (out S1.605), as expected. When the multicast packets begin arriving, the router can observe the IP address of the source. Consulting its unicast routing table, it sees that the source IP address is reachable via a different interface (S1.603) than the interface to the RP. Lead sends a Join to Aluminum, and an SPT is built directly between those two routers. When Lead begins receiving the multicast traffic for (172.16.1.1, 236.82.134.23) over the SPT, it sends a Prune message to the RP removing itself from the shared tree.

Figure 5-61   *The Direct Link Between Lead and Aluminum Is a More Efficient Route for Multicast Packets to Lead's Attached Group Member Than the Aluminum-Platinum-Brass-Lead Path*

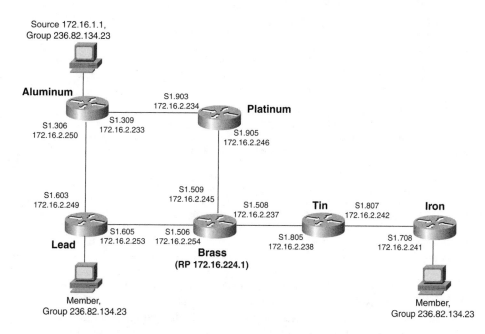

Example 5-24   *Lead Joins the Shared RPT. After It Begins Receiving the Multicast Traffic, It Joins the SPT Directly from the Source DR and Prunes Itself from the RPT*

```
Lead#debug ip pim 236.82.134.23
PIM debugging is on
Lead#
PIM: Check RP 172.16.224.1 into the (*, 236.82.134.23) entry
PIM: Send v2 Join on Serial1.605 to 172.16.2.254 for (172.16.224.1/32,
236.82.134.23), WC-bit, RPT-bit, S-bit
PIM: Building batch join message for 236.82.134.23
PIM: Send Join on Serial1.603 to 172.16.2.250 for (172.16.1.1/32, 236.82.134.23),
S-bit
PIM: Send v2 Prune on Serial1.605 to 172.16.2.254 for (172.16.1.1/32,
236.82.134.23), RPT-bit, S-bit
Lead#
```

Example 5-25 shows the multicast route entries for group 236.82.134.23 at Lead. The (*, G) entry for the shared tree still exists, and it continues to exist as long as the router has members or downstream neighbors for the group. Notice, however, that the (S, G) entry indicates a different incoming interface and a different RPF neighbor.

Example 5-25 *Lead's Route Entries for Group 236.82.134.23 Show That the Router Has Switched from the RPT to the SPT*

```
Lead#show ip mroute 236.82.134.23
IP Multicast Routing Table
Flags: D - Dense, S - Sparse, C - Connected, L - Local, P - Pruned
       R - RP-bit set, F - Register flag, T - SPT-bit set, J - Join SPT
Timers: Uptime/Expires
Interface state: Interface, Next-Hop or VCD, State/Mode

(*, 236.82.134.23), 00:26:26/00:02:58, RP 172.16.224.1, flags: SJC
  Incoming interface: Serial1.605, RPF nbr 172.16.2.254
  Outgoing interface list:
    Ethernet0, Forward/Sparse, 00:26:26/00:02:12

(172.16.1.1, 236.82.134.23), 00:26:26/00:02:36, flags: CJT
  Incoming interface: Serial1.603, RPF nbr 172.16.2.250
  Outgoing interface list:
    Ethernet0, Forward/Sparse, 00:26:26/00:02:12

Lead#
```

Example 5-26 shows the route entries for Aluminum, and Example 5-27 shows the route entries for Brass. You can observe that Aluminum is forwarding on SPT trees to both Lead and Brass. At Brass, the interface to Lead is not in the outgoing interface list of the (S, G) entry, because the RP is not forwarding to that router.

Example 5-26 *Aluminum's Multicast Route Entry for Group 236.82.134.23, Showing an SPT to Both Lead and Brass*

```
Aluminum#show ip mroute 236.82.134.23
IP Multicast Routing Table
Flags: D - Dense, S - Sparse, C - Connected, L - Local, P - Pruned
       R - RP-bit set, F - Register flag, T - SPT-bit set, J - Join SPT
Timers: Uptime/Expires
Interface state: Interface, Next-Hop, State/Mode

(*, 236.82.134.23), 00:08:17/00:02:59, RP 172.16.224.1, flags: SJCF
  Incoming interface: Serial0/1.309, RPF nbr 172.16.2.234
  Outgoing interface list:
    Ethernet0/0, Forward/Sparse, 00:07:33/00:02:30

(172.16.1.1/32, 236.82.134.23), 00:08:17/00:02:59, flags: CFT
  Incoming interface: Ethernet0/0, RPF nbr 0.0.0.0
  Outgoing interface list:
    Serial0/1.309, Forward/Sparse, 00:08:07/00:02:48
    Serial0/1.306, Forward/Sparse, 00:06:55/00:02:59

Aluminum#
```

Example 5-27 *Brass's Route Entries for Group 236.82.134.23. The Interface to Lead (S1.506) Remains on the Outgoing Interface List of the (*, G) Entry but Is Not on the Outgoing Interface List of the (S, G) Entry*

```
Brass#show ip mroute 236.82.134.23
IP Multicast Routing Table
Flags: D - Dense, S - Sparse, C - Connected, L - Local, P - Pruned
       R - RP-bit set, F - Register flag, T - SPT-bit set, J - Join SPT
Timers: Uptime/Expires
Interface state: Interface, Next-Hop or VCD, State/Mode

(*, 236.82.134.23), 00:13:13/00:03:20, RP 172.16.224.1, flags: S
  Incoming interface: Null, RPF nbr 0.0.0.0
  Outgoing interface list:
    Serial1.508, Forward/Sparse, 00:13:04/00:03:20
    Serial1.509, Forward/Sparse, 00:12:30/00:02:18
    Serial1.506, Forward/Sparse, 00:11:52/00:02:33

(172.16.1.1, 236.82.134.23), 00:13:14/00:02:59, flags: T
  Incoming interface: Serial1.509, RPF nbr 172.16.2.246
  Outgoing interface list:
    Serial1.508, Forward/Sparse, 00:13:05/00:02:49

Brass#
```

RFC 2362 specifies that a router should switch from the RPT to an SPT when "the data rate is high." What, then, constitutes a high data rate? The answer is rather arbitrary. It might depend on the cumulative available bandwidth across the route, the congestion along the route, the performance of the routers, or any number of other factors. You, as the network administrator, must make the determination based on the unique characteristics of your own internetwork.

Cisco uses a simple default. Cisco routers join the SPT immediately after receiving the first packet on the shared tree for a given (S, G). This default can be changed with the command **ip pim spt-threshold**, in which the threshold for switching to the SPT is specified in kilobits per second (the default represents 0 Kbps). The router measures the arrival rate of packets once every second. If packets for either any group or a specified group arrive at a rate exceeding the threshold, the router switches. When a router switches to the SPT, it monitors the arrival rate on the source tree. If the group's rate falls below the configured threshold for more than 60 seconds, the router attempts to switch back to the shared tree for that group.

The keyword **infinity** also can be used with the command to prevent a router from ever switching to the SPT.

Interestingly, a router switches to an SPT even if the shortest route to the source is through the RP. In the previous examples, router Iron stayed on the RPT. The reason is that, to simplify the introduction to PIM-SM tree behavior, the statement **ip pim spt-threshold infinity** was added to Iron's configuration. Example 5-28 displays Iron's route entry for group 236.82.134.23. The command is then removed from the router's configuration, and the route is observed again. You can see that the router, after the SPT threshold is set back to the default, immediately switched to the SPT. The route entries at the RP remain as they appear in Example 5-27, because the interface toward Iron is already on the outgoing interface list of the (S, G) entry.

Example 5-28 *Iron's Entries for Group 236.82.134.23, Before and After the SPT Switching Threshold Has Been Reset to the Default*

```
Iron#show ip mroute 236.82.134.23
IP Multicast Routing Table
Flags: D - Dense, S - Sparse, C - Connected, L - Local, P - Pruned
       R - RP-bit set, F - Register flag, T - SPT-bit set, J - Join SPT
Timers: Uptime/Expires
Interface state: Interface, Next-Hop or VCD, State/Mode
(*, 236.82.134.23), 00:00:57/00:02:59, RP 172.16.224.1, flags: SC
  Incoming interface: Serial1.708, RPF nbr 172.16.2.242
  Outgoing interface list:
    Ethernet0, Forward/Sparse, 00:00:57/00:02:02

Iron#conf t
Enter configuration commands, one per line.  End with CNTL/Z.
Iron(config)#no ip pim spt-threshold infinity
Iron(config)#^Z
Iron#
2d01h: %SYS-5-CONFIG_I: Configured from console by console

Iron#show ip mroute 236.82.134.23
IP Multicast Routing Table
Flags: D - Dense, S - Sparse, C - Connected, L - Local, P - Pruned
       R - RP-bit set, F - Register flag, T - SPT-bit set, J - Join SPT
Timers: Uptime/Expires
Interface state: Interface, Next-Hop or VCD, State/Mode

(*, 236.82.134.23), 00:01:23/00:02:59, RP 172.16.224.1, flags: SJC
  Incoming interface: Serial1.708, RPF nbr 172.16.2.242
  Outgoing interface list:
    Ethernet0, Forward/Sparse, 00:01:23/00:02:34

(172.16.1.1, 236.82.134.23), 00:00:11/00:02:59, flags: CJT
  Incoming interface: Serial1.708, RPF nbr 172.16.2.242
  Outgoing interface list:
    Ethernet0, Forward/Sparse, 00:00:12/00:02:47

Iron#
```

In Example 5-28 and in several previous figures, a J flag is associated with either the (*, G) entry, the (S, G) entry, or both. This is the Join SPT flag. When associated with a (*, G) entry, it indicates that traffic flowing down the shared tree exceeds the SPT threshold. If the SPT has not already been joined, it will be following the next received group packet. When associated with an (S, G) entry, the J flag indicates that the SPT has been joined because the RPT traffic has exceeded the SPT threshold.

Table 5-11 lists and describes all the flags that may be associated with an mroute. This list is taken directly from the Cisco IOS Software Command Reference.

Table 5-11 *mroute Flags*

Flag	Description
D-Dense	Entry is operating in dense mode.
S-Sparse	Entry is operating in sparse mode.
C-Connected	A member of the multicast group is present on the directly connected interface.
L-Local	The router itself is a member of the group.
P-Pruned	The route has been pruned.
R-RP-bit set	Indicates that the (S, G) entry is pointing toward the RP. This is typically prune state along the shared tree for a particular source.
F-Register flag	Indicates that the software is registering for a multicast source.
T-SPT-bit set	Indicates that packets have been received on the shortest path tree.
J-Join SPT	For (*, G) entries, indicates that the rate of traffic flowing down the shared tree is exceeding the SPT-Threshold set for the group. (The default SPT-Threshold setting is 0 Kbps.) When the J-Join SPT flag is set, the next (S, G) packet received down the shared tree triggers an (S, G) join in the direction of the source, thereby causing the router join the source tree.
	For (S, G) entries, indicates that the entry was created because the SPT-Threshold for the group was exceeded. When the J-Join SPT flag is set for (S, G) entries, the router monitors the traffic rate on the source tree and attempts to switch back to the shared tree for this source if the traffic rate on the source tree falls below the group's SPT-Threshold for more than 1 minute.

PIMv2 Message Formats

PIMv2 messages are encapsulated in IP packets with a protocol number of 103. Except for the cases in which the messages are unicast, the IP destination address is the reserved multicast address 224.0.0.13, and the TTL is set to 1. Both the multicast address and the TTL ensure that the messages are forwarded only to neighboring routers.

Although version 2 is the current version, PIMv1 is still common. That version uses an IP protocol number of 2, making it a subset of the IGMP protocol. Version 1 uses a multicast address of 224.0.0.2.

Cisco IOS supports PIMv2 beginning with 11.3(2)T. It provides backward compatibility with PIMv1 by automatically switching to that version on any interface on which a version neighbor is detected. An interface also can be manually set to PIMv1 or PIMv2 with the **ip pim version** command.

For the sake of space, only PIMv2 message formats are covered in this book. For PIMv1 formats, refer to the appropriate Internet drafts.

You will notice that several message types have field labels that refer to encoded addresses. For more information on the encoding formats and details of these fields, see section 4.1 of RFC 2362.

All *Reserved* fields in the following messages are set to all zeros and are ignored upon receipt.

PIMv2 Message Header Format

All PIM messages have a standard header, shown in Figure 5-62.

Figure 5-62 *The PIMv2 Message Header*

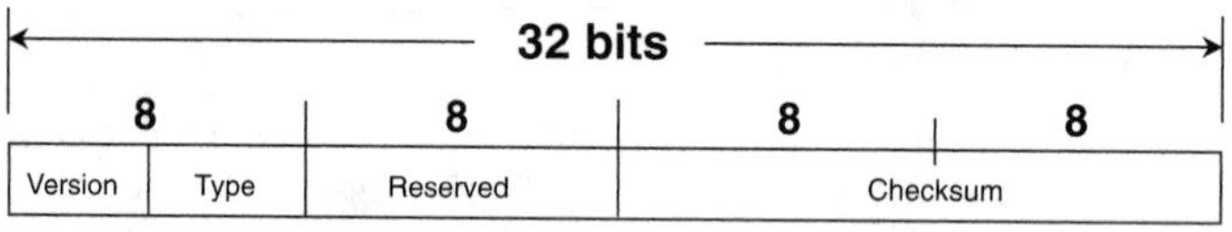

The fields for the PIMv2 message header are defined as follows:

- *Version* specifies the version number. The current version number is 2, although PIMv1 is still in common usage.

- *Type* specifies the type of PIM message encapsulated behind the header. Table 5-12 lists the PIMv2 message types.

Table 5-12 *PIMv2 Message Types*

Type	Message
0	Hello
1	Register (used in PIM-SM only)
2	Register-Stop (used in PIM-SM only)
3	Join/Prune
4	Bootstrap (used in PIM-SM only)
5	Assert
6	Graft (used in PIM-DM only)
7	Graft-Ack (used in PIM-DM only)
8	Candidate-RP-Advertisement (used in PIM-SM only)

- *Checksum* is a standard IP-style checksum, using a 16-bit one's complement of the one's complement of the PIM message, excluding the data portion of the Register message.

PIMv2 Hello Message Format

PIMv2 Hello messages, the format of which is illustrated in Figure 5-63, are used for neighbor discovery and neighbor keepalives. The messages are sent every 30 seconds by default, and the period can be changed with the command **ip pim query-interval**.

Figure 5-63   *The PIMv2 Hello Message Format*

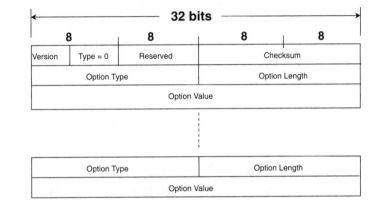

The fields for the PIMv2 Hello message are defined as follows:

- *Option Type* specifies the type of option in the Option Value field. Presently, only Option Type 1 is used. This specifies that the Option Value field is a holdtime. Values 2 through 16 are reserved.

- *Option Length* specifies the length, in bytes, of the Option Value field. When the Option Value is a holdtime (Option Type = 1), the Option Length is 2.

- *Option Value* is a variable-length field carrying the value of whatever option is specified by the Option Type. Holdtime (Option Type = 1, Option Length =2) is the time that a router waits to hear a Hello message from a PIM neighbor before declaring the neighbor dead. The holdtime is 3.5 times the Hello interval.

The format shows that multiple option TLVs (type/length/value) can be carried in a single Hello message.

PIMv2 Register Message Format

Register messages, the format of which is illustrated in Figure 5-64, used only by PIM-SM, are unicast from the source's DR to the RP, and they carry the initial multicast packets from the source. That is, Register messages are used to tunnel multicast traffic from the source to the RP when an SPT has not yet been established from the source's DR to the RP.

Figure 5-64   *The PIMv2 Register Message Format*

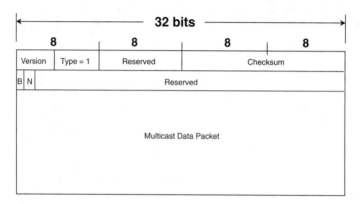

The fields for the PIMv2 Register message are defined as follows:

- *Checksum*, in Register messages, is calculated only on the message header. The data packet portion is excluded.

- *B* is the Border bit. The bit is set to 0 if the originator is a DR with a directly connected source. The bit is set to 1 if the source is a PIM Multicast Border Router (PMBR). PMBRs, and other interdomain multicast issues, are discussed in Chapter 7.

- *N* is the Null-Register bit. A DR that is probing the RP before expiring its local Register-Suppression timer sets this bit to 1.

- *Multicast Data Packet* is a single packet from the source that is being tunneled to the RP in the Register message.

PIMv2 Register Stop Message Format

The Register Stop message, the format of which is illustrated in Figure 5-65, is sent by an RP to a DR originating Register messages. The packet is used in one of two situations:

- The RP is receiving the sourced multicast packets over the SPT and no longer needs to receive them encapsulated in Register messages.

- There are no group members, either directly attached or over SPTs or RPTs, for the RP to forward the packets to.

Figure 5-65 *The PIMv2 Register Stop Message Format*

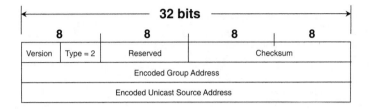

The fields for the PIMv2 Register Stop message are defined as follows:

- *Encoded Group Address* is the multicast group IP address for which the receiver should stop sending Register messages.

- *Encoded Unicast Source Address* is the IP address of the multicast source. This field can also specify the wildcard source for (*, G) entries by setting the address to all zeros.

PIMv2 Join/Prune Message Format

Join/Prune messages, the format of which is illustrated in Figure 5-66, are sent upstream to either RPs or sources and are used to join and prune both RPTs and SPTs. The message consists of a list of one more multicast groups. For each multicast address, there is a list of one or more source addresses. Together, these lists specify all (S, G) and (*, G) entries to be joined or pruned.

Figure 5-66 *The PIMv2 Join/Prune Message Format*

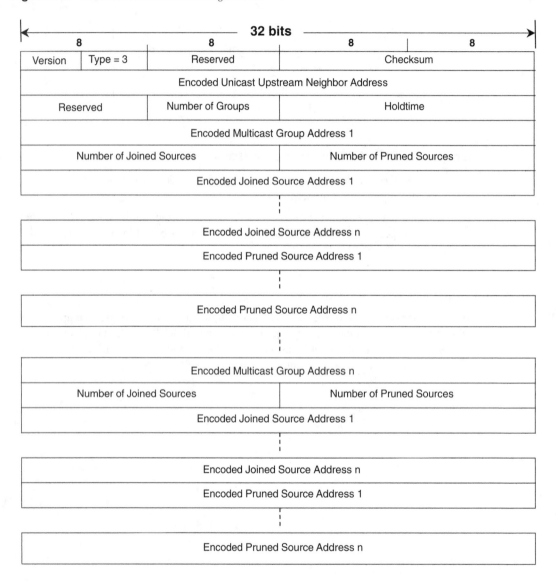

The fields for the PIMv2 Join/Prune message are defined as follows:

- *Encoded Unicast Upstream Neighbor Address* is the IP address of the RPF or upstream neighbor to which the message is being sent.

- *Number of Groups* specifies the number of multicast groups contained in the message.

- *Encoded Multicast Group Address* specifies an IP address of a multicast group.

- *Number of Joined Sources* specifies the number of Encoded Joined Source Addresses listed under this multicast group address.

- *Number of Pruned Sources* specifies the number of Encoded Pruned Source Addresses listed under this multicast group address.

- *Encoded Joined Source Address* specifies the source address for an (S, G) pair or a wildcard for a (*, G) pair. The two wildcards in a (*, *, RP) triple (described in Chapter 7) can also be specified in this field. In addition to the source address, three flags are encoded into this field:

  — *S* is the Sparse bit. The bit is set to 1 for PIM-SM and is used for version 1 compatibility.

  — *W* is the wildcard (WC) bit. If it's set to 1, the Encoded Joined Source Address represents the wildcard in a (*, G) or (*, *, RP) entry. When it's set to 0, the Encoded Joined Source Address represents the source address in an (S, G) entry. When a join is sent to an RP, the W bit must be set to 1.

  — *R* is the RPT bit. When the bit is set to 1, the join is sent to the RP. When the bit is set to 0, the join is sent to the source.

- *Encoded Pruned Source Address* specifies the address of a pruned source. The encoding is the same as for the Encoded Joined Source Address field, and the S, W, and R bits apply to the pruned address as they do to the joined address.

PIMv2 Bootstrap Message Format

Bootstrap messages, the format of which is illustrated in Figure 5-67, are originated by bootstrap routers (BSRs) every 60 seconds and are flooded throughout a PIM-SM domain to ensure that all routers determine the same RPs for the same groups. The message contains a list of one or more multicast group addresses. For each of these group addresses, there is a list of Candidate RPs (C-RPs) and their priorities. This list is the RP-Set for that group. Receiving routers use a common algorithm to determine, from the list of C-RPs, the RP for the group. The algorithm is designed to ensure that all routers in the PIM domain derive the same RP address. Bootstrap messages also are used to elect a BSR, as described in the section "The Bootstrap Protocol."

Figure 5-67 *The PIMv2 Bootstrap Message Format*

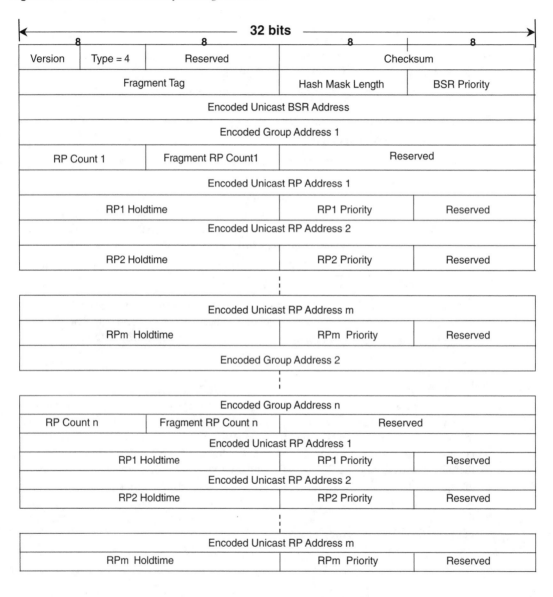

The fields for the PIMv2 Boostrap message are defined as follows:

- *Fragment Tag* is used when a Bootstrap message must be divided into fragments because the message length exceeds the maximum packet size. The fragment tag is a randomly generated number that is assigned to all fragments of the same message. That is, all fragments of any unique Bootstrap message will have the same number in the Fragment Tag field.

- *Hash Mask Length* describes the mask to be used in the hash algorithm. The length of the mask is set using the **ip pim bsr-candidate** command.

- *BSR Priority* is a number between 0 and 255 that specifies the priority of the originating candidate BSR. The C-BSR with the highest priority becomes the BSR. This priority is set using the **ip pim bsr-candidate** command.

- *Encoded Unicast BSR Address* is the IP address of the domain's BSR.

- *Encoded Group Address* specifies an IP address of a multicast group.

- *RP Count* specifies the number of C-RPs listed for the given multicast group—that is, the size of the RP-Set. The description of the size of the RP-Set is important, because if the Bootstrap message is fragmented and one of the fragments is lost, the determination of the RP may become inconsistent across the PIM domain. Therefore, if the number of RPs in the received RP-Set does not match the RP count, the entire set is discarded.

- *Fragment RP Count* specifies the number of C-RPs included in this fragment for this group.

- *Encoded Unicast RP Address* is the IP address of a C-RP.

- *RP Holdtime* is the time a BSR should wait to hear a Candidate-RP-Advertisement message from a C-RP before deleting the C-RP from the RP-Set. The holdtime is 150 seconds.

- *RP Priority* is a number between 0 and 255 used in the RP selection algorithm. The "highest" priority is 0.

The PIMv2 Assert Message Format

The PIMv2 Assert message, the format of which is illustrated in Figure 5-68, is used to elect a designated forwarder on multiaccess networks. When a PIM router receives a multicast packet on an interface that is on the outgoing interface for the packet's group, the router assumes that there must be another router connected to that data link forwarding for the group. The router sends an Assert so that other routers sharing the multiaccess network can decide which of them will forward packets for the group.

Figure 5-68 *The PIMv2 Assert Message Format*

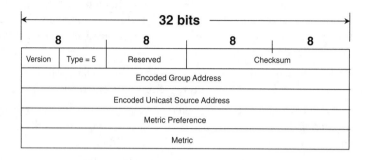

The fields for the PIMv2 Assert message are defined as follows:

- *Encoded Group Address* is the multicast IP destination address of the packet that triggered the Assert.

- *Encoded Unicast Source Address* is the IP source address of the multicast packet that triggered the Assert.

- *Metric Preference* is a preference value assigned to the unicast routing protocol that provided the route to the source. This value is used in the same way an administrative distance is used, to provide a consistent metric when comparing routes from diverse routing protocols.

- *Metric* is the metric associated with the route to the source in the originator's unicast routing table.

The PIMv2 Graft Message Format

A PIM-DM router sends a PIMv2 Graft message to its upstream neighbor to request a rejoin to a previously pruned tree. The format of the message is the same as the Join/Prune message shown in Figure 5-66, except that the Type = 6.

The PIMv2 Graft-Ack Message Format

A PIM-DM router sends a Graft-Ack message to a downstream neighbor in response to a Graft message. The format of the Graft-Ack message is the same as the Join/Prune message shown in Figure 5-66, except that the Type = 7.

The Candidate-RP-Advertisement Message Format

Candidate RPs (C-RPs) periodically unicast Candidate-RP-Advertisement messages to BSRs. The BSR uses the information in the message to build its RP-Set, which is in turn advertised to all PIM-SM routers in the domain within Bootstrap messages. Figure 5-69 shows the format of the Candidate-RP-Advertisement message.

Figure 5-69 *The Candidate-RP-Advertisement Message Format*

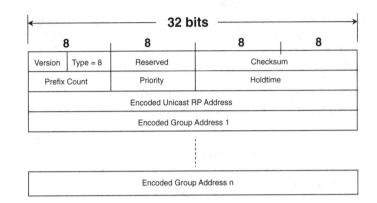

The fields for the Candidate-RP-Advertisement message are defined as follows:

- *Prefix Count* specifies the number of multicast group addresses included in the message. If the originator is a C-RP for all multicast groups in the domain, the Prefix Count is 0.

- *Priority* is a number between 0 and 255, specifying the priority of the originating C-RP. This number is used in the algorithm for selecting an RP. Priorities are represented inverse to the value of the priority number; 0 is the highest priority, and 255 is the lowest.

- *Holdtime* specifies the amount of time the message is valid.

- *Encoded Unicast RP Address* is the C-RP address. This address is the IP address of one of the router's interfaces; typically, the address of a loopback interface is used.

- *Encoded Group Address* specifies one or more multicast group addresses for which the originator is a candidate RP.

End Notes

[1]Steve E. Deering, "RFC 988: Host Extensions for IP Multicasting," RFC 988, July 1986. This RFC has since been obsoleted; the most recent version is RFC 1112.

[2]Tomas Pusateri, "RFC 1469: IP Multicast over Token-Ring Local Area Networks," (Work in Progress). This document actually recommends three methods of supporting IP multicast, but the third is not used.

[3]Steve Deering, "RFC 1112: Host Extensions for IP Multicasting," August 1989. A now-obsolete "IGMPv0" is described in RFC 988.

[4]William C. Fenner, "RFC 2236: Internet Group Management Protocol, Version 2," (Work in Progress).

[5]Brad Cain, Steve Deering, Ajit Thyagarajan, "Internet Group Management Protocol, Version 3," <draft-ietf-idmr-igmp-v3-01.txt>, February 1999.

[6]Dave Katz, "RFC 2113: IP Router Alert Option," (Work in Progress).

[7]David Meyer, "RFC 2365: Administratively Scoped IP Multicast," (Work in Progress).

[8]D. Waitzman, C. Partridga, and S. Deering, "RFC 1075: Distance Vector Multicast Routing Protocol," (Work in Progress).

[9]Thomas Pusateri, "Distance Vector Multicast Routing Protocol," draft-ietf-idmr-dvmrp-v3-09, September 1999.

[10]John Moy, "RFC 1584: Multicast Extensions to OSPF," (Work in Progress).

[11]Tony Ballardie, "RFC 2189: Core Based Trees (CBT version 2) Multicast Routing," (Work in Progress).

[12]Stephen Deering et al., "Protocol Independent Multicast Version 2 Dense Mode Specification," draft-ietf-pim-v2-dm-03.txt, March 1999.

[13]Deborah Estrin et al., "RFC 2362: Protocol Independent Multicast-Sparse Mode (PIM-SM): Protocol Specification," (Work in Progress).

Looking Ahead

Of all the IP routing protocols examined in the two volumes of this book, the multicast protocols are the most unfamiliar to the most people. Although this chapter provides a reasonable overview of the five protocols and the relevant supporting protocols, it is by no means exhaustive. There is much more to IP multicast that cannot be covered within the confines of this book; for more extensive coverage, refer to "Recommended Reading."

Now that you have some understanding of how the five protocols work, Chapter 6 provides Cisco-specific examples of how to configure and troubleshoot IP multicast routing.

You can think of the protocols covered in this chapter as multicast IGPs. All the protocols operate within a single multicast domain. In Chapter 7, you examine the protocols used for inter-AS multicast routing.

Recommended Reading

Beau Williamson, *Developing IP Multicast Networks*. Indianapolis, IN, Cisco Press, 2000.

Command Summary

Table 5-13 lists and describes the commands discussed in this chapter.

Table 5-13 *Command Summary*

Command	Description
clear ip cgmp [*type number*]	Causes a CGMP Leave message to be sent, clearing all multicast group entries from the caches of receiving Catalyst switches.
debug ip igmp	Displays IGMP messages received and sent, as well as IGMP-host-related events.
debug ip *packet* [*access-list-number* | **detail**]	Displays IP packets received and sent. The optional access list is used to filter uninteresting packets from the display.
debug ip pim [*group*]	Displays PIM messages received and sent, as well as PIM-related events.
ip igmp query-interval *seconds*	Changes the interval at which IGMP queries are sent from the default 60 seconds.
ip igmp query-max-response-time *seconds*	Changes the Max Response Time advertised in IGMP queries from the default 10 seconds.
ip igmp query-timeout *seconds*	Changes the default time the router waits to hear an IGMP query from the DR or querier before taking over as the DR or querier. The default is 2 times the query interval.
ip igmp version {**1** | **2**}	Sets the IGMP version on an interface. The default is 2.
ip multicast use-functional	Enables the mapping of IP multicast addresses to the Token Ring functional address 0xC000.0004.0000.
ip pim bsr-candidate *type number hash-mask-length* [*priority*]	Configures the router to announce itself as a C-BSR.
ip pim message-interval *seconds*	Changes the interval at which sparse-mode Join-Prune messages are sent from the default 60 seconds.
ip pim query-interval *seconds*	Changes the interval at which PIMv2 Hello or PIMv1 Router Query messages are sent from the default 30 seconds.
ip pim spt-threshold {*kbps* | **infinity**} [**group-list** *access-list-number*]	Specifies the receive rate at which a PIM-SM router switches from the RPT to the SPT. The default is to switch after the first multicast packet is received.

continues

Table 5-13 *Command Summary (Continued)*

Command	Description
ip pim version [**1** | **2**]	Sets an interface to use PIMv1 or PIMv2. The default is 2.
show ip igmp groups [*group-name* | *group-address* | *type number*]	Displays the list of multicast groups for which there are directly connected members, learned via IGMP.
show ip mroute [*group-name* | *group-address*] [*source*] [**summary**] [**count**] [**active** *kbps*]	Displays the contents of the IP multicast routing table.
show ip pim neighbor [*type number*]	Displays the list of neighbors discovered by PIMv1 Router Query messages or PIMv2 Hellos.
show ip pim rp [*group-name* | *group-address* | **mapping**]	Displays the active RPs associated with multicast groups or mroutes.
show ip route [*address* [*mask*] [**longer-prefixes**]] | [*protocol* [*process-id*]]	Displays routes in the unicast IP routing table.

Review Questions

1 Give several reasons why replicated unicast is not a practical substitution for true multicast in a large network.

_____

_____

_____

2 What range of addresses is reserved for IP multicast?

_____

_____

_____

3 How many subnets can be created from a single Class D prefix?

_____

_____

_____

4 In what way do routers treat packets with destination addresses in the range 224.0.0.1–224.0.0.255 differently from other multicast addresses?

_____

_____

_____

5 Write the Ethernet MAC addresses that correspond to the following IP addresses:

(a) 239.187.3.201

(b) 224.18.50.1

(c) 224.0.1.87

_____

_____

_____

6 What multicast IP address or addresses are represented by the MAC address 0100.5E06.2D54?

_____

_____

_____

7 Why is Token Ring a poor medium for delivering multicast packets?

_____

_____

_____

8 What is join latency?

_____

_____

_____

9 What is leave latency?

_____

_____

_____

10 What is a multicast DR (or querier)?

_____

_____

_____

11 What device sends IGMP Query messages?

_____

_____

_____

12 What device sends IGMP Membership Report messages?

_____

_____

_____

13 How is an IGMP Membership Report message used?

_____

_____

_____

14 What is the functional difference between a General IGMP Query and a Group-Specific IGMP Query?

_____

_____

_____

15 Is IGMPv2 compatible with IGMPv1?

_____

_____

_____

16 What IP protocol number signifies IGMP?

_____

_____

_____

17 What is the purpose of the Cisco Group Membership Protocol (CGMP)?

_____

_____

_____

18 What is the advantage of using IP Snooping rather than CGMP? What is the possible disadvantage?

_____

_____

_____

19 What devices send CGMP messages: routers, Ethernet switches, or both?

_____

_____

_____

20 What is Reverse Path Forwarding?

_____

_____

_____

21 How many hosts constitute a dense topology, and how many hosts constitute a sparse topology?

_____

_____

_____

22 What is the primary advantage of explicit joins over implicit joins?

_____

_____

_____

23 What is the primary structural difference between a source-based multicast tree and a shared multicast tree?

_____

_____

_____

24 What is multicast scoping?

_____

_____

_____

25 What are the two methods of IP multicast scoping?

_____

_____

_____

26 From the perspective of a multicast router, what is meant by upstream and what is meant by downstream?

_____

_____

_____

27 What is an RPF check?

_____

_____

_____

28 What is a prune? What is a graft?

_____

_____

_____

29 What is a prune lifetime? What happens when a prune lifetime expires?

_____

_____

_____

30 What is a route dependency? How does DVMRP signal a route dependency?

_____

_____

_____

31 Is DVMRP a dense-mode protocol or a sparse-mode protocol?

_____

_____

_____

32 Is MOSPF a dense-mode protocol or a sparse-mode protocol?

_____

_____

_____

33 What is the name and type number of the LSA used exclusively by MOSPF?

_____

_____

_____

34 Can an MOSPF router establish an adjacency with an OSPF router that does not support MOSPF?

_____

_____

_____

35 Define the following MOSPF router types:

(a) Interarea multicast forwarder

(b) Inter-AS multicast forwarder

(c) Wildcard multicast receiver

_____

_____

_____

36 Is CBT a dense-mode protocol or a sparse-mode protocol?

_____

_____

_____

37 What are a CBT parent router and a CBT child router?

_____

_____

_____

38 Describe the two ways a CBT DR can deliver packets from a source to the core and the circumstances under which each method is used.

_____

_____

_____

39 What is a PIM prune override?

_____

_____

_____

40 What is a PIM forwarder? How is a forwarder selected?

_____

_____

_____

41 What criteria does PIM use to select a DR?

_____

_____

_____

42 What is a PIM SPT? What is a PIM RPT?

_____

_____

_____

43 What two mechanisms are available for Cisco routers to automatically discover PIM-SM RPs?

_____

_____

_____

44 Of the mechanisms in Question 43, which should be used in multivendor router topologies?

_____

_____

_____

45 What is a C-RP?

_____

_____

_____

46 What is a BSR?

_____

_____

_____

47 What is an RP mapping agent?

_____

_____

_____

48 What is the difference between an (S, G) mroute entry and a (*, G) mroute entry?

_____

_____

_____

49 What is the major drawback with a bidirectional CBT tree between the source and core, as opposed to a PIM-SM unidirectional tree from the RP to the source?

_____

_____

_____

50 What is PIM-SM source registration?

_____

_____

_____

51 When does a Cisco router switch from a PIM-SM RPT to an SPT?

_____

_____

_____

- **Configuring IP Multicast Routing**—This section presents the basics of configuring both PIM-DM and PIM-SM using Cisco IOS Software and presents case studies to further understand the configuration of these protocols.

- **Troubleshooting IP Multicast Routing**—This section examines some of the tools available for troubleshooting IP multicast with Cisco IOS Software and provides some troubleshooting tips.

CHAPTER 6

Configuring and Troubleshooting IP Multicast Routing

You examined various IP multicast routing protocols in Chapter 5, "Introduction to IP Multicast Routing," and you learned that the protocol of choice for Cisco and for most router vendors presently is PIM, whether dense mode or sparse mode. Now that you have an understanding of the basics of PIM operation, this chapter looks at the procedures to configure and troubleshoot both PIM-DM and PIM-SM using Cisco IOS Software.

Configuring IP Multicast Routing

Before you can configure a particular IP multicast routing protocol, you must set up the router for general, protocol-neutral multicast routing.

NOTE "Protocol-independent" would be a better term than "protocol-neutral," but it would cause confusion in light of PIM.

Example 6-1 shows a configuration containing some of the commands you might use. Out of all the commands shown, **ip multicast-routing** is the only required one. Just as the default (and therefore hidden) **ip routing** enables unicast IP routing, this command enables the support of all IP multicast routing functions.

Example 6-1 *The Command **ip multicast-routing** Is Required to Enable Multicast Routing Support; Other Commands in This Basic Configuration Might Be Required by Specific Implementations*

```
version 12.1
!
hostname Stovepipe
!
ip multicast-routing
ip dvmrp route-limit 20000
!
interface Ethernet0
 ip address 172.17.1.1 255.255.255.0
 ip igmp version 1
!
```

continues

Example 6-1 *The Command* **ip multicast-routing** *Is Required to Enable Multicast Routing Support; Other Commands in This Basic Configuration Might Be Required by Specific Implementations (Continued)*

```
interface Ethernet1
 ip address 172.17.2.1 255.255.255.0
 ip cgmp
!
interface Serial0
 ip address 172.18.1.254 255.255.255.252
 no ip mroute-cache
!
interface TokenRing0
 ip address 172.16.2.1 255.255.255.0
 ip multicast use-functional
 ring-speed 16
!
interface TokenRing1
 ip address 172.16.1.1 255.255.255.0
 ring-speed 16
```

Of some interest in this configuration is the fact that there are no commands evident enabling Internet Group Management Protocol (IGMP). When IP multicast routing is enabled on the router, IGMPv2 is automatically enabled on the LAN interfaces. The only IGMP command in this configuration is **ip igmp version** on interface E0, changing the default to IGMPv1. Table 6-1 lists all the IGMP commands that change the default values in a given interface. Other IGMP commands are demonstrated later in this chapter.

Table 6-1 *IGMP Interface Commands*

Command	Default Value	Description
ip igmp query-interval *seconds*	60	The frequency at which the router queries for group members on the interface.
ip igmp query-max-response-time *seconds*	10	The Max-Response-Time value advertised in IGMP query messages, telling hosts how long the router waits before deleting the group. The command is valid only for IGMPv2.
ip igmp query-timeout *seconds*	2x query interval	The time the router waits to hear a query from another router before taking over as the querier.
ip igmp version {1 | 2}	2	Sets the interface to either IGMPv1 or IGMPv2.

The configuration of interface E1 in Example 6-1 includes the **ip cgmp** command, which causes Cisco Group Management Protocol (CGMP) messages to be originated for an attached Catalyst switch. Another option is **ip cgmp proxy**, which can be used when there are other routers on the subnet that are not CGMP-capable. This command tells the router to advertise those non-CGMP routers in its CGMP messages. If you configure a Cisco router as a CGMP proxy, you must ensure that that router is elected as the IGMP querier.

The next command of interest in Example 6-1 is **no ip mroute-cache** on S0. This command disables fast switching of IP multicast packets in the same way that **no ip route-cache** disables fast switching of unicast IP packets. You would disable the fast switching of multicast IP packets for the same reasons you would disable fast switching of unicast packets—for example, to enable per-packet load sharing across parallel paths rather than per-destination load sharing.

The configuration of interface TO0 includes the **ip multicast use-functional** command, whereas the configuration of TO1 does not. The result is that TO0 maps multicast IP packets to the Token Ring functional address 0xC000.0004.0000. TO1, on the other hand, maps multicast IP addresses to the broadcast address 0xFFFF.FFFF.FFFF.

Case Study: Configuring Protocol-Independent Multicast, Dense Mode (PIM-DM)

After you have enabled IP multicast routing on a Cisco router, you can very simply enable PIM-DM by adding the command **ip pim dense-mode** to all the router's interfaces. Figure 6-1 shows a simple PIM-DM topology, and Example 6-2 shows the configuration of router Porkpie. The other router configurations are similar to that of Porkpie.

Two important considerations when configuring PIM-DM are reflected in Example 6-2. The first and most obvious is that a unicast routing protocol—in this case, OSPF—must be running. Without it, PIM has no mechanism for determining the Reverse Path Forwarding (RPF) interface. The second consideration can be observed by comparing the configuration in Example 6-2 with the topology diagram in Figure 6-1. When configuring PIM, the protocol should be enabled on every interface. Otherwise, you run the risk of inadvertent RPF failures.

Figure 6-1 *This Topology Is Used to Demonstrate Basic PIM-DM Functionality*

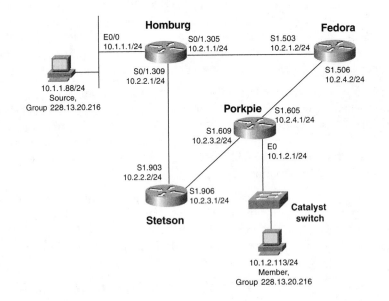

Example 6-2 *The* **ip pim dense-mode** *Command Enables PIM-DM on an Interface*

```
hostname Porkpie
!
ip multicast-routing
!
interface Ethernet0
 ip address 10.1.2.1 255.255.255.0
 ip pim dense-mode
 ip cgmp
!
interface Serial1
 no ip address
 encapsulation frame-relay
 no ip mroute-cache
!
interface Serial1.605 point-to-point
 description PVC to Fedora
 ip address 10.2.4.1 255.255.255.0
 ip pim dense-mode
 no ip mroute-cache
 frame-relay interface-dlci 605
!
interface Serial1.609 point-to-point
 description PVC to Stetson
 ip address 10.2.3.2 255.255.255.0
```

Example 6-2 *The* **ip pim dense-mode** *Command Enables PIM-DM on an Interface (Continued)*

```
 ip pim dense-mode
 no ip mroute-cache
 frame-relay interface-dlci 609
!
router ospf 1
 network 10.0.0.0 0.255.255.255 area 0
!
```

Example 6-3 shows Porkpie's mroute entry for group 228.13.20.216 after source 10.1.1.88 has begun transmitting, and after member 10.1.2.113 has joined. The PIM-DM section of Chapter 5 showed only the (S, G) mroute entry in its examples for the sake of clarity. In reality, a (*, G) entry is created in addition to the (S, G). The (*, G) entry is not part of PIM-DM specification and is not used for packet forwarding. Rather, Cisco IOS Software creates the entry as a "parent" data structure of (S, G). All interfaces connected to PIM neighbors, and all interfaces with directly connected group members, are added to the outgoing interface list of the (*, G) entry. The incoming interface list of this entry, when only PIM-DM is running, is always empty. The incoming and outgoing interfaces in the (S, G) entry are then taken from this list.

NOTE   Cisco IOS Software Release 12.1 was released during the initial writing of this chapter and was installed on the demonstration routers. As a result, you will notice some differences in the field formats of commands such as **show ip mroute** and **show ip route** from earlier chapters.

Example 6-3 *Porkpie's mroute Entry for Group 228.13.20.21*

```
Porkpie#show ip mroute 228.13.20.216
IP Multicast Routing Table
Flags: D - Dense, S - Sparse, C - Connected, L - Local, P - Pruned
       R - RP-bit set, F - Register flag, T - SPT-bit set, J - Join SPT
       M - MSDP created entry, X - Proxy Join Timer Running
       A - Advertised via MSDP
Outgoing interface flags: H - Hardware switched
Timers: Uptime/Expires
Interface state: Interface, Next-Hop or VCD, State/Mode

(*, 228.13.20.216), 20:06:06/00:02:59, RP 0.0.0.0, flags: DJC
  Incoming interface: Null, RPF nbr 0.0.0.0
  Outgoing interface list:
    Ethernet0, Forward/Dense, 20:05:25/00:00:00
    Serial1.609, Forward/Dense, 00:03:32/00:00:00
    Serial1.605, Forward/Dense, 00:03:32/00:00:00
```

continues

Example 6-3 *Porkpie's mroute Entry for Group 228.13.20.21 (Continued)*

```
(10.1.1.88, 228.13.20.216), 00:03:21/00:02:59, flags: CT
  Incoming interface: Serial1.605, RPF nbr 10.2.4.2
  Outgoing interface list:
    Ethernet0, Forward/Dense, 00:03:21/00:00:00
    Serial1.609, Prune/Dense, 00:03:21/00:00:03

Porkpie#
```

In Example 6-3, you can see that E0, S1.609, and S1.605 are on the (*, G) outgoing interface list. S1.605 is then entered as the RPF interface in the (S, G) entry, and packets are being forwarded out E0. S1.609 is also on the outgoing list, but is pruned.

As discussed in Chapter 5, PIM (and any other multicast protocol that uses RPF checks) can have only one incoming interface. Example 6-4 shows Porkpie's unicast routing table. There are two equal-cost paths to source subnet 10.1.1.0/24, so PIM breaks the tie by choosing the interface to the neighbor with the numerically higher IP address as the RPF interface. In Example 6-4, this address is 10.2.4.2 on interface S1.605. A look back at Example 6-3 verifies that this interface is on the incoming interface list.

Example 6-4 *Porkpie's Unicast Routing Table*

```
Porkpie#show ip route
Codes: C - connected, S - static, I - IGRP, R - RIP, M - mobile, B - BGP
       D - EIGRP, EX - EIGRP external, O - OSPF, IA - OSPF inter area
       N1 - OSPF NSSA external type 1, N2 - OSPF NSSA external type 2
       E1 - OSPF external type 1, E2 - OSPF external type 2, E - EGP
       i - IS-IS, L1 - IS-IS level-1, L2 - IS-IS level-2, ia - IS-IS inter area
       * - candidate default, U - per-user static route, o - ODR
       P - periodic downloaded static route

Gateway of last resort is not set

     10.0.0.0/24 is subnetted, 6 subnets
O       10.2.1.0 [110/128] via 10.2.4.2, 00:15:07, Serial1.605
C       10.1.2.0 is directly connected, Ethernet0
O       10.2.2.0 [110/128] via 10.2.3.1, 00:15:07, Serial1.609
O       10.1.1.0 [110/138] via 10.2.4.2, 00:15:07, Serial1.605
                 [110/138] via 10.2.3.1, 00:15:07, Serial1.609
C       10.2.3.0 is directly connected, Serial1.609
C       10.2.4.0 is directly connected, Serial1.605
Porkpie#
```

In Figure 6-2, another router has been added to the internetwork. This router, Bowler, is connected to the Ethernet switch and so is sharing a multiaccess link with Porkpie. The rules for IGMP queriers, PIM-designated routers, and PIM forwarders discussed in Chapter 5 all come into play here:

- The router with the lowest IP address becomes the IGMPv2 querier.

- The router with the highest IP address becomes the PIM-designated router. The DR is important only when IGMPv1 is running on the subnet.

- The PIM forwarder is the router whose route to the source has the lowest administrative distance. If the administrative distances are equal, the router whose route to the source has the lowest metric is the forwarder. If both the administrative distances and the metrics are equal, the router with the highest IP address is the forwarder.

Figure 6-2   *Router Bowler Has Joined the Internetwork of Figure 6-1; Bowler, Porkpie, and the Group Member Are Connected to a Multiaccess Network Through the Catalyst Switch*

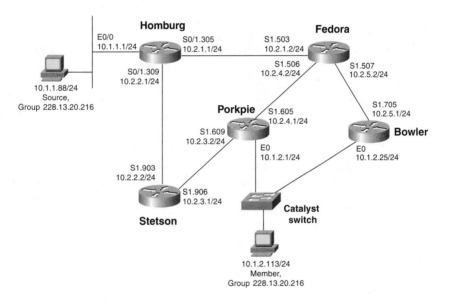

Example 6-5 shows that the IGMPv2 querier and PIM-designated router rules have been applied. Porkpie (10.1.2.1) has the lower IP address on the subnet, so it is the IGMP querier. Bowler (10.2.1.25) has the higher IP address, so it is the designated router. Porkpie and Bowler are both running IGMPv2, so the DR has no importance here.

Example 6-5   *Porkpie (10.1.2.1) Is the IGMP Querier, but Bowler Is the PIM Designated Route*

```
Bowler#show ip igmp interface ethernet 0
Ethernet0 is up, line protocol is up
  Internet address is 10.1.2.25/24
  IGMP is enabled on interface
  Current IGMP version is 2
  CGMP is enabled on interface
  IGMP query interval is 60 seconds
```

continues

Example 6-5 *Porkpie (10.1.2.1) Is the IGMP Querier, but Bowler Is the PIM Designated Route (Continued)*

```
      IGMP querier timeout is 120 seconds
      IGMP max query response time is 10 seconds
      Last member query response interval is 1000 ms
      Inbound IGMP access group is not set
      IGMP activity: 6 joins, 2 leaves
      Multicast routing is enabled on interface
      Multicast TTL threshold is 0
      Multicast designated router (DR) is 10.1.2.25 (this system)
      IGMP querying router is 10.1.2.1
      No multicast groups joined
Bowler#
```

Example 6-6 shows the unicast routes to source subnet 10.1.1.0/24 at both Porkpie and Bowler. Knowing that the internetwork of Figure 6-2 is running OSPF exclusively, it comes as no surprise that both routes have an administrative distance of 110. You also can readily see that both routes have an OSPF cost of 138. Therefore, the PIM forwarder for (10.1.1.88, 228.13.20.216) on the attached subnet 10.1.2.0/24 is the router with the highest IP address: Bowler. Example 6-7 proves it. Comparing Porkpie's (S, G) entry with the one in Example 6-3, notice that interface E0 has now been pruned. Bowler's E0 interface is in forward mode, indicating that it is now forwarding the group traffic onto the subnet.

Example 6-6 *The Unicast Routes to Source Subnet 10.1.1.0/24 in Porkpie and Bowler Have Equal Administrative Distances and Metrics; Therefore, the Router with the Highest IP Address Will Be the PIM Forwarder for Subnet 10.1.2.0/24*

```
Porkpie#show ip route 10.1.1.0
Routing entry for 10.1.1.0/24
  Known via "ospf 1", distance 110, metric 138, type intra area
  Redistributing via ospf 1
  Last update from 10.2.3.1 on Serial1.609, 01:01:30 ago
  Routing Descriptor Blocks:
  * 10.2.4.2, from 10.1.1.1, 01:01:30 ago, via Serial1.605
      Route metric is 138, traffic share count is 1
    10.2.3.1, from 10.1.1.1, 01:01:30 ago, via Serial1.609
      Route metric is 138, traffic share count is 1

Porkpie#
```

```
Bowler#show ip route 10.1.1.0
Routing entry for 10.1.1.0/24
  Known via "ospf 1", distance 110, metric 138, type intra area
  Redistributing via ospf 1
  Last update from 10.2.5.2 on Serial1.705, 01:02:22 ago
  Routing Descriptor Blocks:
  * 10.2.5.2, from 10.1.1.1, 01:02:22 ago, via Serial1.705
      Route metric is 138, traffic share count is 1

Bowler#
```

Example 6-7 *Comparing the mroutes for (10.1.1.88, 228.13.20.216) Shows that Bowler Is Now the Forwarder for the Group onto Subnet 10.1.2.0/24*

```
Porkpie#show ip mroute 228.13.20.216
IP Multicast Routing Table
Flags: D - Dense, S - Sparse, C - Connected, L - Local, P - Pruned
       R - RP-bit set, F - Register flag, T - SPT-bit set, J - Join SPT
       M - MSDP created entry, X - Proxy Join Timer Running
       A - Advertised via MSDP
Outgoing interface flags: H - Hardware switched
Timers: Uptime/Expires
Interface state: Interface, Next-Hop or VCD, State/Mode

(*, 228.13.20.216), 23:51:13/00:02:59, RP 0.0.0.0, flags: DJC
  Incoming interface: Null, RPF nbr 0.0.0.0
  Outgoing interface list:
    Serial1.609, Forward/Dense, 03:48:39/00:00:00
    Serial1.605, Forward/Dense, 03:48:39/00:00:00
    Ethernet0, Forward/Dense, 01:18:18/00:00:00

(10.1.1.88, 228.13.20.216), 00:03:06/00:02:53, flags: PCT
  Incoming interface: Serial1.605, RPF nbr 10.2.4.2
  Outgoing interface list:
    Serial1.609, Prune/Dense, 00:03:06/00:00:18
    Ethernet0, Prune/Dense, 00:03:06/00:02:53

Porkpie#
```

```
Bowler#show ip mroute 228.13.20.216
IP Multicast Routing Table
Flags: D - Dense, S - Sparse, C - Connected, L - Local, P - Pruned
       R - RP-bit set, F - Register flag, T - SPT-bit set, J - Join SPT
       M - MSDP created entry, X - Proxy Join Timer Running
       A - Advertised via MSDP
Outgoing interface flags: H - Hardware switched
Timers: Uptime/Expires
Interface state: Interface, Next-Hop or VCD, State/Mode

(*, 228.13.20.216), 01:47:12/00:02:59, RP 0.0.0.0, flags: DJC
  Incoming interface: Null, RPF nbr 0.0.0.0
  Outgoing interface list:
    Ethernet0, Forward/Dense, 01:26:34/00:00:00
    Serial1.705, Forward/Dense, 01:47:12/00:00:00

(10.1.1.88, 228.13.20.216), 01:27:43/00:02:59, flags: CTA
  Incoming interface: Serial1.705, RPF nbr 10.2.5.2
  Outgoing interface list:
    Ethernet0, Forward/Dense, 01:26:34/00:00:00

Bowler#
```

Interestingly, Porkpie is querying for group members on the subnet, while Bowler is forwarding the multicast packets for group 228.13.20.216. Reviewing the rules for IGMPv2 in Chapter 5, there is no conflict. Queries from Porkpie result in IGMP Membership Reports from the group member, addressed to the group address. Bowler hears the Membership Report and begins forwarding the group traffic. If the member wants to leave the group, it sends IGMP Leave messages addressed to the All Multicast Routers address 224.0.0.2, as illustrated by Example 6-8, which are also heard by Bowler.

Example 6-8 *Although Porkpie (10.1.2.1) Is the IGMP Querier, Bowler Still Hears the IGMP Leave Message from the Attached Group Member; as the Forwarder for This Group, It Deletes the Interface from the Outgoing Interface List for the Group*

```
Bowler#debug ip igmp
IGMP debugging is on
Bowler#
IGMP: Received Leave from 10.1.2.113 (Ethernet0) for 228.13.20.216
IGMP: Received v2 Query from 10.1.2.1 (Ethernet0)
IGMP: Received v2 Query from 10.1.2.1 (Ethernet0)
IGMP: Deleting 228.13.20.216 on Ethernet0
Bowler#
```

Referring back to Example 6-5, **show ip igmp interface** shows that Bowler's E0 is using the default IGMP query interval of 60 seconds and the default IGMP querier timeout interval of 120 seconds. Porkpie is using the same defaults. The debugging messages with time stamps in Example 6-9 show these timers in action. The first three messages show Porkpie faithfully sending an IGMP query every 60 seconds. But then something happens and the queries stop. The fourth and fifth messages show that at 120 seconds, Bowler takes over as querier and immediately sends a query of its own. Subsequent queries are then sent at 60-second intervals. The last two messages show that Porkpie has returned and is again sending queries. Because that router has a lower IP address, Bowler recognizes Porkpie as the querier and goes silent.

Example 6-9 *Debugging Is Used to Show What Happens When the IGMP Querier Fails and Then Returns*

```
Bowler#debug ip igmp
IGMP debugging is on
Bowler#
*Mar  5 23:41:36.318: IGMP: Received v2 Query from 10.1.2.1 (Ethernet0)
*Mar  5 23:42:36.370: IGMP: Received v2 Query from 10.1.2.1 (Ethernet0)
*Mar  5 23:43:36.422: IGMP: Received v2 Query from 10.1.2.1 (Ethernet0)
*Mar  5 23:45:36.566: IGMP: Previous querier timed out, v2 querier for Ethernet0 is
this system
*Mar  5 23:45:36.570: IGMP: Send v2 Query on Ethernet0 to 224.0.0.1
*Mar  5 23:46:05.602: IGMP: Send v2 Query on Ethernet0 to 224.0.0.1
*Mar  5 23:47:05.654: IGMP: Send v2 Query on Ethernet0 to 224.0.0.1
*Mar  5 23:48:05.706: IGMP: Send v2 Query on Ethernet0 to 224.0.0.1
```

Example 6-9 *Debugging Is Used to Show What Happens When the IGMP Querier Fails and Then Returns (Continued)*

```
*Mar  5 23:48:36.698: IGMP: Received v2 Query from 10.1.2.1 (Ethernet0)
*Mar  5 23:49:36.742: IGMP: Received v2 Query from 10.1.2.1 (Ethernet0)
Bowler#
```

Remember from Chapter 5 that PIM sends hellos to its neighbors by default every 30 seconds, and the holdtime is 3.5 times the hello interval. If a hello is not heard from a neighbor within the holdtime, the neighbor is declared dead. This final example begins with both Bowler and Porkpie online and with Bowler forwarding packets onto the Ethernet for group 228.13.20.216. Example 6-10 shows what happens when Bowler fails.

Example 6-10 *Porkpie Takes Over as PIM Forwarder for Group 228.13.20.216 After Failing to Hear Any PIM Hellos from Bowler for the Prescribed Holdtime*

```
Porkpie#debug ip pim 228.13.20.216
PIM debugging is on
Porkpie#
PIM: Neighbor 10.1.2.25 (Ethernet0) timed out
PIM: Changing DR for Ethernet0, from 10.1.2.25 to 10.1.2.1 (this system)
PIM: Building Graft message for 228.13.20.216, Serial1.609: no entries
PIM: Building Graft message for 228.13.20.216, Serial1.605: no entries
PIM: Building Graft message for 228.13.20.216, Ethernet0: no entries
Porkpie#
```

Porkpie has not heard a hello from Bowler within the holdtime, and it knows that it must take over the PIM forwarder duties. It assumes the role of the DR and sends PIM Graft messages to its neighbors. Comparing Porkpie's entry for (10.1.1.88, 228.13.20.216) in Example 6-11 with that at the top of Example 6-7, Porkpie is now forwarding the multicast packets onto the Ethernet whereas it had pruned the interface before becoming the forwarder. Notice also that the pruned flag, present in the entry in Example 6-7, is no longer in the entry in Example 6-11.

Example 6-11 *After the Failure of Bowler, Porkpie Is Forwarding Group Traffic onto the Ethernet*

```
Porkpie#show ip mroute 228.13.20.216
IP Multicast Routing Table
Flags: D - Dense, S - Sparse, C - Connected, L - Local, P - Pruned
       R - RP-bit set, F - Register flag, T - SPT-bit set, J - Join SPT
       M - MSDP created entry, X - Proxy Join Timer Running
       A - Advertised via MSDP
Outgoing interface flags: H - Hardware switched
Timers: Uptime/Expires
Interface state: Interface, Next-Hop or VCD, State/Mode

(*, 228.13.20.216), 1d01h/00:02:59, RP 0.0.0.0, flags: DJC
  Incoming interface: Null, RPF nbr 0.0.0.0
```

continues

Example 6-11 *After the Failure of Bowler, Porkpie Is Forwarding Group Traffic onto the Ethernet (Continued)*

```
        Outgoing interface list:
          Serial1.609, Forward/Dense, 05:16:35/00:00:00
          Serial1.605, Forward/Dense, 05:16:35/00:00:00
          Ethernet0, Forward/Dense, 00:06:14/00:00:00

      (10.1.1.88, 228.13.20.216), 00:23:10/00:02:59, flags: CT
        Incoming interface: Serial1.605, RPF nbr 10.2.4.2
        Outgoing interface list:
          Serial1.609, Prune/Dense, 00:23:10/00:01:44
          Ethernet0, Forward/Dense, 00:06:14/00:00:00

    Porkpie#
```

Configuring Protocol-Independent Multicast, Sparse Mode (PIM-SM)

It is probably obvious to you, after seeing the configuration statement for enabling PIM-DM on an interface, how PIM-SM is enabled. It is accomplished, quite simply, by using the **ip pim sparse-mode** command. This much of the configuration of PIM-SM is uninteresting and requires no standalone examples. The unique requirement of PIM-SM, and the more interesting aspect of its configuration, is the identification of the rendezvous points (RPs). You learned in Chapter 5 that RPs can be statically configured, or they can be dynamically discovered using either Cisco's Auto-RP or the open-standard bootstrap protocol. The following case studies demonstrate all three methods.

Case Study: Statically Configuring the RP

Figure 6-3 is the same internetwork you have been observing in this chapter, but now the routers are configured to run PIM-SM. Stetson has been chosen as the RP, and all routers are statically configured with that information. The illustration shows that Stetson's RP address is 10.224.1.1. This address can exist on any interface, as long as it is advertised by the unicast routing protocol so that the other routers know how to reach it. In practice, you should use the loopback interface. A minor reason for this is so that the RP address can be more easily managed, but the major reason is so that the RP address is not linked to any physical interface that might fail. This is the same reason that the loopback interface is recommended for IBGP peering endpoints.

Figure 6-3   *The Internetwork Is Now Running PIM-SM, with the RP Located at 10.224.1.1*

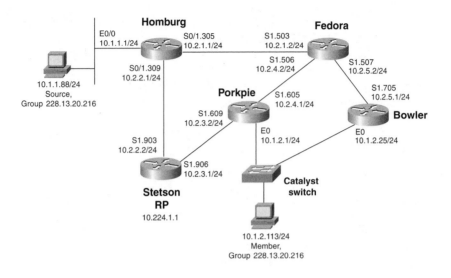

Example 6-12 shows Bowler's configuration. Notice that the interfaces that were
configured for dense mode are now configured for sparse mode.

Example 6-12 *The Configuration of Bowler in Figure 6-3*

```
hostname Bowler
!
ip multicast-routing
!
interface Ethernet0
 ip address 10.1.2.25 255.255.255.0
 ip pim sparse-mode
 ip cgmp
!
interface Serial1
 no ip address
 encapsulation frame-relay
!
interface Serial1.705 point-to-point
 description PVC to Fedora
 ip address 10.2.5.1 255.255.255.0
 ip pim sparse-mode
 no ip mroute-cache
 frame-relay interface-dlci 705
!
router ospf 1
 network 10.0.0.0 0.255.255.255 area 0
!
ip pim rp-address 10.224.1.1
!
```

The other point of interest in Example 6-12 is the command **ip pim rp-address 10.224.1.1**, which tells the router where to find the RP. When statically configuring the RP, all routers with attached group sources or members must have such a statement, in order for them to know where the RP is. Note that Stetson's loopback interface does not itself have to have PIM running on it, as indicated in Example 6-13. No PIM functionality is required of the interface, other than providing the RP address. That address is advertised to the internetwork by OSPF. However, the **ip pim rp-address 10.224.1.1** statement is present in the configuration, even though there are no attached sources or group members. The reason for this statement on this router, of course, is so that the router knows that it is the RP. In practice, it is wise to statically configure the RP address on all routers in the internetwork. It won't hurt if it isn't needed, and it prevents an accidentally missing statement where it is needed.

Example 6-13 *The Configuration of Stetson, the RP, in Figure 6-3*

```
hostname Stetson
!
ip multicast-routing
!
interface Loopback0
 ip address 10.224.1.1 255.255.255.255
!
interface Serial1
 no ip address
 encapsulation frame-relay
!
interface Serial1.903 point-to-point
 description PVC to R3
 ip address 10.2.2.2 255.255.255.0
 ip pim sparse-mode
 frame-relay interface-dlci 903
!
interface Serial1.906 point-to-point
 description PVC to 906
 ip address 10.2.3.1 255.255.255.0
 ip pim sparse-mode
 frame-relay interface-dlci 906
!
router ospf 1
 network 10.0.0.0 0.255.255.255 area 0
!
ip pim rp-address 10.224.1.1
```

In the PIM-DM section, you compared the mroute entries for group 228.13.20.216 in Porkpie and Bowler. The significance of the entries is that the routers share an Ethernet subnet with a group member, so issues such as IGMP querying and PIM forwarding arise. Example 6-14 again compares the two routers' mroute entries for the group. The entries here appear a little more ambiguous than the dense-mode entries in Example 6-7. For example, Porkpie's (*, G) entry shows E0 on the outgoing interface list and in forwarding state. The outgoing interface list of its (S, G) entry is empty. At Bowler, however, E0 is on the incoming interface list of the (*, G) entry, and the entry's outgoing interface list is empty. And E0 is on the outgoing interface list of the (S, G) entry and in forwarding state. What router is actually forwarding the group packets?

Example 6-14 *Comparing the mroute Entries for Group 228.13.20.216 at Porkpie and Bowler*

```
Porkpie#show ip mroute 228.13.20.216
IP Multicast Routing Table
Flags: D - Dense, S - Sparse, C - Connected, L - Local, P - Pruned
       R - RP-bit set, F - Register flag, T - SPT-bit set, J - Join SPT
       M - MSDP created entry, X - Proxy Join Timer Running
       A - Advertised via MSDP
Outgoing interface flags: H - Hardware switched
Timers: Uptime/Expires
Interface state: Interface, Next-Hop or VCD, State/Mode

(*, 228.13.20.216), 1d22h/00:02:59, RP 10.224.1.1, flags: SJC
  Incoming interface: Serial1.609, RPF nbr 10.2.3.1
  Outgoing interface list:
    Ethernet0, Forward/Sparse, 02:36:43/00:02:31

(10.1.1.88, 228.13.20.216), 03:08:42/00:02:02, flags: PCRT
  Incoming interface: Serial1.609, RPF nbr 10.2.3.1
  Outgoing interface list: Null

Porkpie#
```

```
Bowler#show ip mroute 228.13.20.216
IP Multicast Routing Table
Flags: D - Dense, S - Sparse, C - Connected, L - Local, P - Pruned
       R - RP-bit set, F - Register flag, T - SPT-bit set, J - Join SPT
       M - MSDP created entry, X - Proxy Join Timer Running
       A - Advertised via MSDP
Outgoing interface flags: H - Hardware switched
Timers: Uptime/Expires
Interface state: Interface, Next-Hop or VCD, State/Mode

(*, 228.13.20.216), 1d00h/00:02:59, RP 10.224.1.1, flags: SJPC
  Incoming interface: Ethernet0, RPF nbr 10.1.2.1
  Outgoing interface list: Null

(10.1.1.88, 228.13.20.216), 02:38:20/00:02:59, flags: CT
  Incoming interface: Serial1.705, RPF nbr 10.2.5.2
  Outgoing interface list:
    Ethernet0, Forward/Sparse, 02:37:36/00:02:12

Bowler#
```

You know what router is forwarding the group packets if you carefully studied PIM-SM procedures in Chapter 5. First, you know that Bowler is the DR, because its IP address on subnet 10.1.2.0/24 is higher. You can verify the DR with the **show ip pim interface** command, as demonstrated in Example 6-15.

Example 6-15 *The PIM Designated Router on Subnet 10.1.2.0/24 is Bowler (10.1.2.25)*

```
Porkpie#show ip pim interface

Address          Interface       Version/Mode    Nbr   Query   DR
                                                 Count Intvl
10.1.2.1         Ethernet0       v2/Sparse        1     30     10.1.2.25
10.2.4.1         Serial1.605     v2/Sparse        1     30     0.0.0.0
10.2.3.2         Serial1.609     v2/Sparse        1     30     0.0.0.0
Porkpie#
```

When a host first requests a join to a group, the DR joins the shared RP tree (RPT). Examining Bowler's unicast routing table in Example 6-16, the route from Bowler to the RP is through Porkpie, via subnet 10.1.2.0/24. You now know why Porkpie's E0 interface is on the outgoing interface list of the (*, G) entry. This entry represents the RPT linking Bowler to Stetson. Bowler's (*, G) entry has an empty outgoing interface list and a pruned flag set because it is the endpoint of the RPT branch.

Example 6-16 *The Shortest Route to the RP from Bowler Is Across Its Connected Ethernet to Porkpie*

```
Bowler#show ip route 10.224.1.1
Routing entry for 10.224.1.1/32
  Known via "ospf 1", distance 110, metric 75, type intra area
  Redistributing via ospf 1
  Last update from 10.1.2.1 on Ethernet0, 01:03:56 ago
  Routing Descriptor Blocks:
  * 10.1.2.1, from 10.224.1.1, 01:03:56 ago, via Ethernet0
      Route metric is 75, traffic share count is 1

Bowler#
```

Next, you know that by default after the first multicast packet is received, a PIM-SM router with an attached member will try to switch to the shortest path tree (SPT) to the source, whether that path leads through the RP or not. Bowler's unicast routing table shows that the shortest route to source subnet 10.1.1.0/24 is through Fedora, as indicated in Example 6-17. Looking again at the mroutes in Example 6-14, Bowler's (S, G) entry indicates that Fedora, at 10.2.5.2, is the upstream or RPF neighbor. E0 is on the entry's outgoing interface list and in forward state, because packets are of course being forwarded to the group member. Porkpie is not forwarding packets for this group, so its (S, G) entry has an empty outgoing interface list and a pruned flag.

Example 6-17 *Bowler's Shortest Path to Source Subnet 10.1.1.0/24 Is Through Fedora, Out Interface S1.705*

```
Bowler#show ip route 10.1.1.0
Routing entry for 10.1.1.0/24
  Known via "ospf 1", distance 110, metric 138, type intra area
  Redistributing via ospf 1
  Last update from 10.2.5.2 on Serial1.705, 01:17:30 ago
  Routing Descriptor Blocks:
  * 10.2.5.2, from 10.1.1.1, 01:17:30 ago, via Serial1.705
      Route metric is 138, traffic share count is 1

Bowler#
```

You also can use debugging to see how the multicast packets are being forwarded. Example 6-18 shows that Bowler is receiving the multicast packets for group 228.13.20.216 from source 10.1.1.88, via Fedora on interface S1.705. The packets are being forwarded out interface E0 to the connected group member.

Example 6-18 *Using Debugging to Capture IP Multicast Packets (mpackets), You Can Observe That Bowler Is Receiving Packets for (10.1.1.88, 228.13.20.216) on Interface S1.705 and Forwarding Them Out Interface E0*

```
Bowler#debug ip mpacket 228.13.20.216
IP multicast packets debugging is on for group 228.13.20.216
Bowler#
IP: s=10.1.1.88 (Serial1.705) d=228.13.20.216 (Ethernet0) len 573, mforward
IP: s=10.1.1.88 (Serial1.705) d=228.13.20.216 (Ethernet0) len 573, mforward
IP: s=10.1.1.88 (Serial1.705) d=228.13.20.216 (Ethernet0) len 573, mforward
IP: s=10.1.1.88 (Serial1.705) d=228.13.20.216 (Ethernet0) len 573, mforward
IP: s=10.1.1.88 (Serial1.705) d=228.13.20.216 (Ethernet0) len 573, mforward
IP: s=10.1.1.88 (Serial1.705) d=228.13.20.216 (Ethernet0) len 573, mforward
IP: s=10.1.1.88 (Serial1.705) d=228.13.20.216 (Ethernet0) len 573, mforward
IP: s=10.1.1.88 (Serial1.705) d=228.13.20.216 (Ethernet0) len 573, mforward
IP: s=10.1.1.88 (Serial1.705) d=228.13.20.216 (Ethernet0) len 573, mforward
```

Using the same debugging command at Porkpie also presents interesting results, as demonstrated in Example 6-19. The debug messages show that the router is not receiving packets for group 228.13.20.216 from either the RP or Fedora. Rather, it is receiving the packets that Bowler is forwarding onto the Ethernet subnet 10.1.2.0/24. Porkpie's mroute entries in Example 6-14 show the RPF interface for the group to be S1.609. Because the packets are being received on E0, the RPF check fails, and the packets are dropped.

Example 6-19 *Porkpie Is Not Forwarding Any Packets for Group 228.13.20.216*

```
Porkpie#debug ip mpacket 228.13.20.216
IP multicast packets debugging is on for group 228.13.20.216
Porkpie#
IP: s=10.1.1.88 (Ethernet0) d=228.13.20.216 len 583, not RPF interface
```

continues

Example 6-19 *Porkpie Is Not Forwarding Any Packets for Group 228.13.20.216 (Continued)*

```
IP: s=10.1.1.88 (Ethernet0) d=228.13.20.216 len 583, not RPF interface
IP: s=10.1.1.88 (Ethernet0) d=228.13.20.216 len 583, not RPF interface
IP: s=10.1.1.88 (Ethernet0) d=228.13.20.216 len 583, not RPF interface
IP: s=10.1.1.88 (Ethernet0) d=228.13.20.216 len 583, not RPF interface
IP: s=10.1.1.88 (Ethernet0) d=228.13.20.216 len 583, not RPF interface
IP: s=10.1.1.88 (Ethernet0) d=228.13.20.216 len 583, not RPF interface
IP: s=10.1.1.88 (Ethernet0) d=228.13.20.216 len 583, not RPF interface
IP: s=10.1.1.88 (Ethernet0) d=228.13.20.216 len 583, not RPF interface
```

So much of this example, as shown so far, depends on the fact that a Cisco router switches to the group's SPT after receiving the first multicast packet. You learned in Chapter 5 that you can change this default with the **ip pim spt-threshold** command. A threshold can be specified in kilobits per second, and the router will not switch to the SPT until the arrival rate of the group's packets exceeds the threshold. Alternatively, you can use the **infinity** keyword, and the router will never switch to the SPT. It is enlightening to see what happens when **ip pim spt-threshold infinity** is added to the configuration of Bowler in Figure 6-3.Example 6-20 shows the resulting mroute entries at Porkpie and Bowler after Bowler's reconfiguration. Bowler's RPT passes out its E0 interface, across subnet 10.1.2.0/24, and through Porkpie. So Porkpie must now forward packets from the RP. But Bowler's E0 interface also is its RPF interface for the group, and a PIM router cannot forward a group's packets out that group's RPF interface. This is simply a multicast version of the split-horizon rule, which states that packets are not forwarded out the interface they arrived on. As a result, Bowler's (*, G) now sports a pruned flag. Porkpie is now forwarding the packets to the group member. Interestingly, even though Porkpie has assumed the forwarding duties because Bowler must use the RPT, Porkpie itself is under no such constraints and has switched to an SPT through Fedora rather than through the RP.

Example 6-20 *After Bowler Is Configured to Never Switch to the SPT, the Forwarding Duties for Group 228.13.20.216 Pass to Porkpie*

```
Porkpie#show ip mroute 228.13.20.216
IP Multicast Routing Table
Flags: D - Dense, S - Sparse, C - Connected, L - Local, P - Pruned
       R - RP-bit set, F - Register flag, T - SPT-bit set, J - Join SPT
       M - MSDP created entry, X - Proxy Join Timer Running
       A - Advertised via MSDP
Outgoing interface flags: H - Hardware switched
Timers: Uptime/Expires
Interface state: Interface, Next-Hop or VCD, State/Mode

(*, 228.13.20.216), 00:45:09/00:02:59, RP 10.224.1.1, flags: SJC
  Incoming interface: Serial1.609, RPF nbr 10.2.3.1
  Outgoing interface list:
    Ethernet0, Forward/Sparse, 00:44:11/00:02:54
```

Example 6-20 *After Bowler Is Configured to Never Switch to the SPT, the Forwarding Duties for Group 228.13.20.216 Pass to Porkpie (Continued)*

```
(10.1.1.88, 228.13.20.216), 00:44:30/00:02:59, flags: CT
  Incoming interface: Serial1.605, RPF nbr 10.2.4.2
  Outgoing interface list:
    Ethernet0, Forward/Sparse, 00:44:11/00:02:24

Porkpie#
```

```
Bowler#show ip mroute 228.13.20.216
IP Multicast Routing Table
Flags: D - Dense, S - Sparse, C - Connected, L - Local, P - Pruned
       R - RP-bit set, F - Register flag, T - SPT-bit set, J - Join SPT
       M - MSDP created entry, X - Proxy Join Timer Running
       A - Advertised via MSDP
Outgoing interface flags: H - Hardware switched
Timers: Uptime/Expires
Interface state: Interface, Next-Hop or VCD, State/Mode

(*, 228.13.20.216), 00:45:31/00:02:07, RP 10.224.1.1, flags: SPC
  Incoming interface: Ethernet0, RPF nbr 10.1.2.1
  Outgoing interface list: Null

Bowler#
```

At times, you may need to assign different groups to different RPs. Typically this is done as the number of groups in the multicast domain grows, and you need to divide the RP duties to decrease the memory and CPU demands placed on any one router. Figure 6-4 shows the same internetwork you have been observing throughout this section, but now Fedora has also been designated as an RP, with an address of 10.244.1.2. With access lists, you can configure multiple RPs and specify what groups should use what RP.

Figure 6-4 *Both Stetson and Fedora Are Rendezvous Points; Access Lists Are Used in Conjunction with the Static RP Addresses to Tell Each Router in the Domain Which RP to Use for a Particular Group*

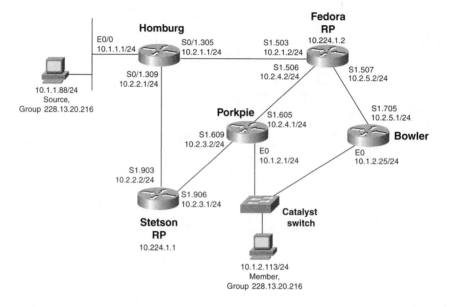

For example, consider the configuration in Example 6-21.

Example 6-21 *Bowler's RP Filtering Configuration*

```
ip pim rp-address 10.224.1.1 10
ip pim rp-address 10.224.1.2 5
!
access-list 5 permit 239.0.0.0 0.255.255.255
access-list 5 permit 228.13.20.0 0.0.0.255
access-list 10 permit 224.2.127.254
access-list 10 permit 230.253.0.0 0.0.255.255
```

Access list 5 specifies the groups that are permitted to use RP 10.224.1.2 (Fedora), and access list 10 specifies the groups that are allowed to use RP 10.224.1.1 (Stetson). Any group whose address does not match one of these two access lists will not have an RP assigned, and therefore cannot join either shared tree. This configuration is added to Bowler, and Example 6-22 shows the results. A quick examination shows that the groups listed (which are active groups on the router) have been mapped to an RP according to the constraints of access lists 5 and 10.

Example 6-22 *The* **show ip pim rp** *Command Displays the Groups Active on a Router and the RP to Which They Are Mapped*

```
Bowler#show ip pim rp
Group: 239.255.255.254, RP: 10.224.1.2, v2, uptime 01:20:13, expires 00:02:08
Group: 228.13.20.216, RP: 10.224.1.2, v2, uptime 01:19:30, expires never
Group: 224.2.127.254, RP: 10.224.1.1, v2, uptime 01:20:05, expires never
Group: 230.253.84.168, RP: 10.224.1.1, v2, uptime 01:20:06, expires 00:01:48
Bowler#
```

Case Study: Configuring Auto-RP

In a stable PIM domain, static configuration of the RP is straightforward. As new routers are added, they are configured with the location of the RP or RPs. Static RP configuration becomes a problem under two circumstances:

- The address of the RP must be changed, either on the existing RP or because a new RP is being installed. The network administrator must change the static configurations on all PIM routers, which in a large domain can involve significant downtime.

- The RP fails. A statically configured PIM domain cannot easily handle a failover to an alternate RP.

Therefore, in all but the smallest PIM domains, the use of one of the two automatic RP discovery mechanisms, Auto-RP or bootstrap, is recommended for both ease of management and better redundancy. This case study demonstrates Auto-RP, and a following case study demonstrates the bootstrap protocol.

As discussed in Chapter 5, Auto-RP is a Cisco-proprietary protocol developed before the bootstrap protocol was proposed as part of PIMv2. Auto-RP must be used with any Cisco IOS Software Release prior to Release 11.3, in which PIMv2 is first supported.

Two steps are required to configure basic Auto-RP:

1 All candidate-RPs must be configured.

2 All mapping agents must be configured.

Candidate RPs (C-RPs) are configured by the **ip pim send-rp-announce** command. When you enter this command, you specify the interface from which the router takes its RP address, and a TTL value that is added to the advertisement messages. The TTL provides scoping so that packets do not travel outside the boundaries of the domain. When a router is configured as a candidate RP, it begins sending RP-Announce messages to the reserved address 224.0.1.39 every 60 seconds.

The mapping agent listens for RP-Announce messages from the C-RPs and selects the RPs. It then advertises the RPs to the rest of the PIM domain in RP-Discovery messages, sent to the reserved address 224.0.1.40 every 60 seconds.

Figure 6-5 shows a sample topology. Here, routers Stetson and Fedora are candidate RPs with addresses 10.224.1.1 and 10.224.1.2, respectively. Porkpie is the mapping agent, with an identifying address of 10.224.1.3.

Figure 6-5 *Stetson and Fedora Are Candidate RPs, and Porkpie Is the Mapping Agent*

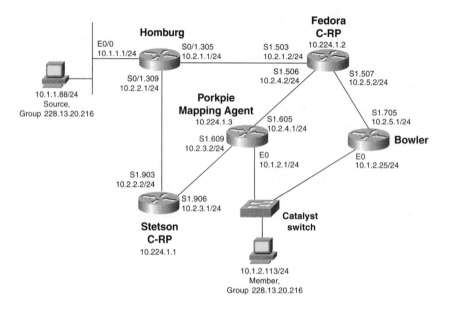

Example 6-23 shows the relevant parts of Fedora's configuration.

Example 6-23 *Configuring Fedora as a Candidate RP*

```
interface Loopback0
 ip address 10.224.1.2 255.255.255.255
!
ip pim send-rp-announce Loopback0 scope 5
```

Stetson's configuration is similar. The RP address is taken from interface L0, and the **scope** keyword sets the TTL of the originated RP-Announce messages.

Example 6-24 shows the configuration establishing Porkpie as a mapping agent.

Example 6-24 *Establishing Porkpie as a Mapping Agent*

```
interface Loopback0
 ip address 10.224.1.3 255.255.255.255
 ip pim sparse-mode
!
ip pim send-rp-discovery Loopback0 scope 5
```

Again, L0 is used to derive the mapping agent address, and the TTL is set to 5. In the configuration in Example 6-24, notice that PIM-SM must be configured on the loopback interface. This must be performed on the mapping agents; if you fail to enable PIM-SM on the interface first, you will get an error message like the one in Example 6-25.

Example 6-25 *Failing to Enable PIM-SM on a Mapping Agent's Loopback Interface Results in an Error Message*

```
Porkpie(config)#ip pim send-rp-discovery Loopback0 scope 5
Non PIM interface ignored in accepted command.
Porkpie(config)#
```

The resulting configuration statement will look like the following:

```
ip pim send-rp-discovery scope 5
```

The interface specified was not accepted, and as a result, the mapping agent does not work. Unlike mapping agents, PIM does not have to be configured on the loopback interface of a C-RP. Of course, on both mapping agents and C-RPs, PIM-SM must still be configured on all physical interfaces connected to PIM neighbors.

When a Cisco router is first configured with PIM-SM, it begins listening for the address 224.0.1.40. If changes have to be made to either the C-RPs or the mapping agents, the changes are automatically advertised by the changed device, and the routers throughout the domain learn of the change. Perhaps the most important feature, however, is that you can configure multiple RPs for any or all groups. The mapping agent chooses the RP for a group based on the highest RP address. If that RP fails, the mapping agent selects the next-highest qualifying RP and advertises that.

Example 6-26 shows an example of an RP failover. Here, **debug ip pim auto-rp** is used to display all Auto-RP activity. You can see that Porkpie, the mapping agent in Figure 6-5, is receiving RP-Announce messages from both Stetson (10.224.1.1) and Fedora (10.224.1.2). Because Fedora has the higher IP address, it is being advertised to the domain as the RP for all multicast groups (224.0.0.0/4). After the first reception of RP-Announce messages from Fedora, that router fails. When Porkpie has not heard another RP-Announce message from Fedora within 180 seconds (3 times the announcement interval), it declares the RP dead, selects Stetson as the new RP, and begins advertising the new RP. That sequence of events is highlighted at the bottom of the Debug messages.

Example 6-26 *Debugging Is Used to Observe an RP Failover at the Mapping Agent in Figure 6-5*

```
Porkpie#debug ip pim auto-rp
PIM Auto-RP debugging is on
Porkpie#
Auto-RP: Received RP-announce, from 10.224.1.1, RP_cnt 1, ht 181
Auto-RP: Update (224.0.0.0/4, RP:10.224.1.1), PIMv2 v1
Auto-RP: Received RP-announce, from 10.224.1.1, RP_cnt 1, ht 181
Auto-RP: Update (224.0.0.0/4, RP:10.224.1.1), PIMv2 v1
```

continues

Example 6-26 *Debugging Is Used to Observe an RP Failover at the Mapping Agent in Figure 6-5 (Continued)*

```
Auto-RP: Received RP-announce, from 10.224.1.2, RP_cnt 1, ht 181
Auto-RP: Update (224.0.0.0/4, RP:10.224.1.2), PIMv2 v1
Auto-RP: Received RP-announce, from 10.224.1.2, RP_cnt 1, ht 181
Auto-RP: Update (224.0.0.0/4, RP:10.224.1.2), PIMv2 v1
Auto-RP: Build RP-Discovery packet
Auto-RP:  Build mapping (224.0.0.0/4, RP:10.224.1.2), PIMv2 v1,
Auto-RP: Send RP-discovery packet on Loopback0 (1 RP entries)
Auto-RP: Send RP-discovery packet on Serial1.605 (1 RP entries)
Auto-RP: Send RP-discovery packet on Serial1.609 (1 RP entries)
Auto-RP: Send RP-discovery packet on Ethernet0 (1 RP entries)
Auto-RP: Received RP-announce, from 10.224.1.1, RP_cnt 1, ht 181
Auto-RP: Update (224.0.0.0/4, RP:10.224.1.1), PIMv2 v1
Auto-RP: Received RP-announce, from 10.224.1.1, RP_cnt 1, ht 181
Auto-RP: Update (224.0.0.0/4, RP:10.224.1.1), PIMv2 v1
Auto-RP: Build RP-Discovery packet
Auto-RP:  Build mapping (224.0.0.0/4, RP:10.224.1.2), PIMv2 v1,
Auto-RP: Send RP-discovery packet on Loopback0 (1 RP entries)
Auto-RP: Send RP-discovery packet on Serial1.609 (1 RP entries)
Auto-RP: Send RP-discovery packet on Ethernet0 (1 RP entries)
Auto-RP: Received RP-announce, from 10.224.1.1, RP_cnt 1, ht 181
Auto-RP: Update (224.0.0.0/4, RP:10.224.1.1), PIMv2 v1
Auto-RP: Received RP-announce, from 10.224.1.1, RP_cnt 1, ht 181
Auto-RP: Update (224.0.0.0/4, RP:10.224.1.1), PIMv2 v1
Auto-RP: Build RP-Discovery packet
Auto-RP:  Build mapping (224.0.0.0/4, RP:10.224.1.2), PIMv2 v1,
Auto-RP: Send RP-discovery packet on Loopback0 (1 RP entries)
Auto-RP: Send RP-discovery packet on Serial1.609 (1 RP entries)
Auto-RP: Send RP-discovery packet on Ethernet0 (1 RP entries)
Auto-RP: Received RP-announce, from 10.224.1.1, RP_cnt 1, ht 181
Auto-RP: Update (224.0.0.0/4, RP:10.224.1.1), PIMv2 v1
Auto-RP: Received RP-announce, from 10.224.1.1, RP_cnt 1, ht 181
Auto-RP: Update (224.0.0.0/4, RP:10.224.1.1), PIMv2 v1
Auto-RP: Mapping (224.0.0.0/4, RP:10.224.1.2) expired,
Auto-RP: Build RP-Discovery packet
Auto-RP:  Build mapping (224.0.0.0/4, RP:10.224.1.1), PIMv2 v1,
Auto-RP: Send RP-discovery packet on Loopback0 (1 RP entries)
Auto-RP: Send RP-discovery packet on Serial1.609 (1 RP entries)
Auto-RP: Send RP-discovery packet on Ethernet0 (1 RP entries)
Porkpie#
```

In Example 6-27, the **show ip pim rp** command is used at Bowler to display the groups that router is receiving for, and the RP that the group is mapped to. The first display is taken before Fedora fails, and shows that all groups are mapped to its RP address. The second display, taken after Fedora fails and the mapping agent advertises the new RP, shows that all groups are now mapped to Stetson.

Example 6-27 *Before Fedora Fails, All of Bowler's Groups Are Mapped to That RP (10.224.1.2); After the Failure, Bowler's Groups Are Remapped, Based on Information from the Mapping Agent, to Stetson (10.224.1.1)*

```
Bowler#show ip pim rp
Group: 239.255.255.254, RP: 10.224.1.2, v2, v1, uptime 00:08:07, expires 00:04:26
Group: 228.13.20.216, RP: 10.224.1.2, v2, v1, uptime 00:08:08, expires 00:04:26
Group: 224.2.127.254, RP: 10.224.1.2, v2, v1, uptime 00:08:07, expires 00:04:26
Group: 230.253.84.168, RP: 10.224.1.2, v2, v1, uptime 00:08:07, expires 00:04:26
Bowler#

Bowler#show ip pim rp
Group: 239.255.255.254, RP: 10.224.1.1, v2, v1, uptime 00:03:46, expires 00:02:56
Group: 228.13.20.216, RP: 10.224.1.1, v2, v1, uptime 00:03:46, expires 00:02:56
Group: 224.2.127.254, RP: 10.224.1.1, v2, v1, uptime 00:03:46, expires 00:02:56
Group: 230.253.84.168, RP: 10.224.1.1, v2, v1, uptime 00:03:46, expires 00:02:56
Bowler#
```

To change the 60-second default interval at which a C-RP sends RP-Announce messages, add the **interval** keyword to the **ip pim send-rp-announce** command. For example, the following causes Fedora to send RP-Announce messages every 10 seconds:

```
ip pim send-rp-announce Loopback0 scope 5 interval 10
```

The holdtime, the interval a mapping agent waits to hear an RP-Announce message from a C-RP, is always 3 times the announcement interval. So the result of the preceding command is to shorten the failover time of Fedora to 30 seconds, at the cost of 6 times as many RP-Announce messages originated by the router.

A C-RP advertises, in its RP-Announce messages, the groups for which it can act as the RP. The default is to announce 224.0.0.0/4, which represents all multicast groups. As with static RPs in the preceding case study, however, you will sometimes want to map different groups to different RPs. Suppose, for example, you want all groups 224.0.0.0 through 231.255.255.255 (224.0.0.0/5) to be mapped to Stetson, and all groups 232.0.0.0 through 239.255.255.255 (232.0.0.0/5) to be mapped to Fedora. The C-RP configurations of those two routers then look like Example 6-28.

Example 6-28 *Configuring Stetson and Fedora as C-RPs*

```
Stetson
ip pim send-rp-announce Loopback0 scope 5 group-list 20
!
access-list 20 permit 224.0.0.0 7.255.255.255
```
```
Fedora
ip pim send-rp-announce Loopback0 scope 5 group-list 30
!
access-list 30 permit 232.0.0.0 7.255.255.255
```

The **group-list** keyword ties the **ip pim send-rp-announce** statement to an access list. The access list then describes the groups for which router can become the RP. Example 6-29 shows the results at Bowler, after mapping agent Porkpie has advertised the RPs according to the constraints in their RP-Announce messages. 239.255.255.254 is mapped to Fedora, while the other three groups, all of whose addresses fall within the 224.0.0.0/5 range, are mapped to Stetson.

Example 6-29 *Bowler's Group-to-RP Mappings, Showing the Constraints Configured at Stetson and Fedora*

```
Bowler#show ip pim rp
Group: 239.255.255.254, RP: 10.224.1.2, v2, v1, uptime 00:04:25, expires 00:02:56
Group: 228.13.20.216, RP: 10.224.1.1, v2, v1, uptime 00:11:05, expires 00:03:57
Group: 224.2.127.254, RP: 10.224.1.1, v2, v1, uptime 00:11:05, expires 00:03:57
Group: 230.253.84.168, RP: 10.224.1.1, v2, v1, uptime 00:11:05, expires 00:03:57
Bowler#
```

Suppose you also want groups 228.13.0.0 through 228.13.255.255 to be mapped to Fedora. The configuration for router Fedora would then look like Example 6-30.

Example 6-30 *Configuring Fedora as the C-RP for Groups 228.13.0.0 through 228.13.255.255*

```
ip pim send-rp-announce Loopback0 scope 5 group-list 30
!
access-list 30 permit 232.0.0.0 7.255.255.255
access-list 30 permit 228.13.0.0 0.0.255.255
```

Example 6-31 shows the result at Bowler. Note that Stetson's configuration has not changed. That C-RP is announcing 224.0.0.0/5 as its permitted group range, which includes 228.13.0.0/16. The mapping agent now has two C-RPs for groups in the 228.13.0.0/16 range and has chosen Fedora because its IP address is higher.

Example 6-31 *Multicast Group 228.13.20.216, Which Was Mapped to RP 10.224.1.1 in Example 6-29, Is Now Mapped to RP 10.224.1.2*

```
Bowler#show ip pim rp
Group: 239.255.255.254, RP: 10.224.1.2, v2, v1, uptime 00:01:43, expires 00:04:16
Group: 228.13.20.216, RP: 10.224.1.2, v2, v1, uptime 00:01:43, expires 00:04:16
Group: 224.2.127.254, RP: 10.224.1.1, v2, v1, uptime 00:36:05, expires 00:02:47
Group: 230.253.84.168, RP: 10.224.1.1, v2, v1, uptime 00:36:05, expires 00:02:47
Bowler#
```

Several variants of the **show ip pim rp** command enable you to observe group-to-RP mappings. The command in its basic form, as used in the previous few examples, shows you only the active groups on a router and the RP to which each group address is matched. To observe the full range of groups that may be matched to an RP, use **show ip pim rp mapping**, as demonstrated in Example 6-32.

Example 6-32 *Through the Reception of RP-Discovery Messages from the Mapping Agent 10.224.1.3, Bowler Has Mapped Three Ranges of Multicast Group Addresses to Two Different RPs*

```
Bowler#show ip pim rp mapping
PIM Group-to-RP Mappings

Group(s) 224.0.0.0/5
  RP 10.224.1.1 (?), v2v1
    Info source: 10.224.1.3 (?), via Auto-RP
        Uptime: 01:14:37, expires: 00:02:42
Group(s) 228.13.0.0/16
  RP 10.224.1.2 (?), v2v1
    Info source: 10.224.1.3 (?), via Auto-RP
        Uptime: 00:43:15, expires: 00:02:37
Group(s) 232.0.0.0/5
  RP 10.224.1.2 (?), v2v1
    Info source: 10.224.1.3 (?), via Auto-RP
        Uptime: 00:43:15, expires: 00:02:41
Bowler#
```

A similar command is **show ip pim rp mapping in-use**, as demonstrated in Example 6-33. In addition to the information displayed in Example 6-32, the group ranges that are currently in use on the router are displayed. Notice that the output in both Example 6-32 and 6-33 displays the source of the mapping agent, 10.224.1.3. This information proves useful when there are multiple mapping agents.

Example 6-33 *The **in-use** Keyword Displays the Group Address Ranges That Are Currently in Use on the Router*

```
Bowler#show ip pim rp mapping in-use
PIM Group-to-RP Mappings

Group(s) 224.0.0.0/5
  RP 10.224.1.1 (?), v2v1
    Info source: 10.224.1.3 (?), via Auto-RP
        Uptime: 01:21:24, expires: 00:02:50
Group(s) 228.13.0.0/16
  RP 10.224.1.2 (?), v2v1
    Info source: 10.224.1.3 (?), via Auto-RP
        Uptime: 00:50:02, expires: 00:02:49
Group(s) 232.0.0.0/5
  RP 10.224.1.2 (?), v2v1
    Info source: 10.224.1.3 (?), via Auto-RP
        Uptime: 00:50:02, expires: 00:02:48

RPs in Auto-RP cache that are in use:
Group(s): 224.0.0.0/5,   RP: 10.224.1.1
Group(s): 232.0.0.0/5,   RP: 10.224.1.2
Group(s): 228.13.0.0/16,   RP: 10.224.1.2
Bowler#
```

On occasion, you may want to know what RP a particular group address will be mapped to, before that address is active on a router. Suppose, for example, you want to know what RP the group 235.1.2.3 will be mapped to at Bowler. For this, you use the **show ip pim rp-hash** command, as demonstrated in Example 6-34. The result shows that group 235.1.2.3 will be mapped to RP 10.224.1.2. The result is consistent with the access list constraints configured previously.

Example 6-34 *The Command* **show ip pim rp-hash** *Enables You to Determine to Which RP a Particular Group Will Be Mapped*

```
Bowler#show ip pim rp-hash 235.1.2.3
  RP 10.224.1.2 (?), v2v1
    Info source: 10.224.1.3 (?), via Auto-RP
        Uptime: 00:55:48, expires: 00:02:00
Bowler#
```

You can prevent your mapping agents from accepting unauthorized routers that may have been inadvertently or intentionally configured as C-RPs by setting up an RP announcement filter. Example 6-35 demonstrates a sample configuration for Porkpie.

Example 6-35 *Configuring Porkpie with an RP Announcement Filter*

```
ip pim rp-announce-filter rp-list 1 group-list 11
ip pim send-rp-discovery Loopback0 scope 5
!
access-list 1 permit 10.224.1.2
access-list 1 permit 10.224.1.1
access-list 11 permit 224.0.0.0 15.255.255.255
```

The configuration in Example 6-35 establishes an RP announcement filter to accept only the C-RPs specified in access list 1, and to accept groups advertised by those C-RPs only if they are specified in access list 11. In this configuration, access list 1 permits Stetson and Fedora and permits those routers to be C-RPs for all multicast groups.

Throughout this case study, Stetson and Fedora in Figure 6-5 have been the C-RPs and Porkpie has been the mapping agent for the sake of clarity. In practice, however, it makes little sense to configure multiple C-RPs for redundancy but configure only a single mapping agent. If the mapping agent fails, no RPs are advertised to the domain, and PIM-SM fails. A more real-life approach would be to make Stetson and Fedora both C-RPs and mapping agents. The nature of Auto-RP ensures that both mapping agents will derive and advertise the same RPs, and if one router fails, the other is still in service to advertise RPs to the domain.

Case Study: Configuring Sparse-Dense Mode

A slight "cheat" was used in the examples of the preceding case study. Examining Figure 6-5, notice that the C-RPs are directly connected to the mapping agent, and the mapping agent is directly connected to Bowler. In Figure 6-6, Homburg is now configured as the Auto-RP mapping agent. This topology gives rise to an interesting dilemma: Homburg advertises the RPs to all routers in RP-Discovery messages, using the reserve address 224.0.1.40. All PIM-SM routers listen for this address. In a sparse-mode environment, however, multicast packets must initially be forwarded on shared trees. That means the routers listening for 224.0.1.40 must notify their RP that they want to join that group, in order to receive the RP-Discovery messages. But how do the routers know where the RP is if they have not yet received the RP-Discovery messages?

Figure 6-6   *Homburg Is Now the Mapping Agent*

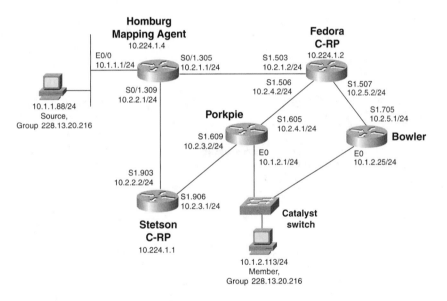

The same Catch-22 would apply to the C-RPs if they were not directly connected to the mapping agent. The mapping agent must receive RP-Announce messages from the C-RPs in order to select an RP, and to do this, it must join group 224.0.1.39. It cannot join this group, however, if it does not know where the RPs are, and it cannot know where the RPs are unless it receives RP-Announce messages.

PIM sparse-dense mode was created to overcome this problem. When an interface is configured in this mode, it uses sparse mode if an RP is known for the group. If no RP is known, it uses dense mode. In the case of 224.0.1.39 and 224.0.1.40, the groups are assumed to be in dense mode. Example 6-36 shows the sparse-dense mode configuration for Homburg.

Example 6-36 *PIM Sparse-Dense Mode Configuration for Router Homburg*

```
hostname Homburg
!
ip multicast-routing
!
interface Loopback0
 ip address 10.224.1.4 255.255.255.0
 ip pim sparse-mode
!
interface Ethernet0/0
 ip address 10.1.1.1 255.255.255.0
 ip pim sparse-dense-mode
 no ip mroute-cache
!
interface Serial0/1
 no ip address
 encapsulation frame-relay
 no ip mroute-cache
!
interface Serial0/1.305 point-to-point
 description PVC to R5
 ip address 10.2.1.1 255.255.255.0
 ip pim sparse-dense-mode
 no ip mroute-cache
 frame-relay interface-dlci 305
!
interface Serial0/1.309 point-to-point
 description PVC to R9
 ip address 10.2.2.1 255.255.255.0
 ip pim sparse-dense-mode
 no ip mroute-cache
 frame-relay interface-dlci 309
!
router ospf 1
 network 10.0.0.0 0.255.255.255 area 0
!
ip pim send-rp-discovery Loopback0 scope 5
!
```

The command **ip pim sparse-dense-mode** is used on all the physical interfaces, and it is configured similarly on all physical interfaces of all routers in the topology of Figure 6-6. The loopback interface is only in sparse mode, because it is needed only as the mapping agent address and never must make any sparse/dense determinations. Interface E0/0 could also be put into sparse mode, because it does not face any downstream routers and would not have to make sparse/dense decisions. However, it is good practice to place all interfaces in sparse-dense mode for consistency. In fact, it is commonly advised to use this mode in all modern PIM domains as long as all routers support the mode.

Example 6-37 shows the multicast routing table on Homburg after the reconfiguration. Notice that the entries for (*, 224.0.1.39) and (*, 224.0.1.40) have D flags, indicating that they are operating in dense mode. All other (*, G) entries are flagged as sparse.

Example 6-37 *The Flags Associated with (*,224.0.1.39) and (*,224.0.1.40) in Homburg's mroute Table Show That Those Groups Are Operating in Dense Mode*

```
Homburg#show ip mroute
IP Multicast Routing Table
Flags: D - Dense, S - Sparse, C - Connected, L - Local, P - Pruned
       R - RP-bit set, F - Register flag, T - SPT-bit set, J - Join SPT
Timers: Uptime/Expires
Interface state: Interface, Next-Hop, State/Mode
(*, 228.13.20.216), 00:20:42/00:02:59, RP 10.224.1.2, flags: SJCF
  Incoming interface: Serial0/1.305, RPF nbr 10.2.1.2
  Outgoing interface list:
    Ethernet0/0, Forward/Sparse-Dense, 00:20:42/00:02:43
(10.1.1.88/32, 228.13.20.216), 00:20:42/00:02:59, flags: CFT
  Incoming interface: Ethernet0/0, RPF nbr 0.0.0.0
  Outgoing interface list:
    Serial0/1.305, Forward/Sparse-Dense, 00:20:04/00:02:47
(*, 224.2.127.254), 00:20:34/00:02:59, RP 10.224.1.2, flags: SJCF
  Incoming interface: Serial0/1.305, RPF nbr 10.2.1.2
  Outgoing interface list:
    Ethernet0/0, Forward/Sparse-Dense, 00:20:34/00:02:42
(10.1.1.88/32, 224.2.127.254), 00:20:34/00:02:56, flags: CFT
  Incoming interface: Ethernet0/0, RPF nbr 0.0.0.0
  Outgoing interface list:
    Serial0/1.305, Forward/Sparse-Dense, 00:20:06/00:02:44
(*, 224.0.1.39), 00:20:32/00:00:00, RP 0.0.0.0, flags: DJCL
  Incoming interface: Null, RPF nbr 0.0.0.0
  Outgoing interface list:
    Ethernet0/0, Forward/Sparse-Dense, 00:20:32/00:00:00
    Serial0/1.305, Forward/Sparse-Dense, 00:20:32/00:00:00
    Serial0/1.309, Forward/Sparse-Dense, 00:20:32/00:00:00
(10.224.1.1/32, 224.0.1.39), 00:20:32/00:02:27, flags: CLT
  Incoming interface: Serial0/1.309, RPF nbr 10.2.2.2
  Outgoing interface list:
    Ethernet0/0, Forward/Sparse-Dense, 00:20:32/00:00:00
    Serial0/1.305, Forward/Sparse-Dense, 00:20:32/00:00:00

(10.224.1.2/32, 224.0.1.39), 00:19:54/00:02:05, flags: CLT
  Incoming interface: Serial0/1.305, RPF nbr 10.2.1.2
  Outgoing interface list:
    Ethernet0/0, Forward/Sparse-Dense, 00:19:54/00:00:00
    Serial0/1.309, Forward/Sparse-Dense, 00:19:54/00:02:08

(*, 224.0.1.40), 00:20:13/00:00:00, RP 0.0.0.0, flags: DJCL
  Incoming interface: Null, RPF nbr 0.0.0.0
  Outgoing interface list:
    Ethernet0/0, Forward/Sparse-Dense, 00:20:14/00:00:00
```

continues

Example 6-37 *The Flags Associated with (*,224.0.1.39) and (*,224.0.1.40) in Homburg's mroute Table Show That Those Groups Are Operating in Dense Mode (Continued)*

```
    Serial0/1.305, Forward/Sparse-Dense, 00:20:14/00:00:00
    Serial0/1.309, Forward/Sparse-Dense, 00:20:14/00:00:00

(10.224.1.4/32, 224.0.1.40), 00:20:06/00:02:48, flags: CLT
  Incoming interface: Loopback0, RPF nbr 0.0.0.0
  Outgoing interface list:
    Ethernet0/0, Forward/Sparse-Dense, 00:20:06/00:00:00
    Serial0/1.305, Forward/Sparse-Dense, 00:20:06/00:00:00
    Serial0/1.309, Forward/Sparse-Dense, 00:20:06/00:00:00

Homburg#
```

Besides the two Auto-RP groups, sometimes you might want to have some groups operating in sparse mode and others operating in dense mode. By using the **ip pim send-rp-announce group-list** command at the C-RPs, as demonstrated in the preceding case study, you can regulate what groups are mapped to the RP, and hence operate in sparse mode. Any groups not mapped to an RP will operate in dense mode.

Case Study: Configuring the Bootstrap Protocol

When PIMv2 was first described in RFC 2117, the bootstrap protocol was specified as the mechanism for automatic RP discovery. Cisco first supported PIMv2 in Cisco IOS Software Release 11.3T, and the bootstrap protocol is included in that support.

The two steps to configure bootstrap are very similar to the two steps for configuring Auto-RP:

1 All candidate RPs must be configured.

2 All candidate bootstrap routers (C-BSRs) must be configured.

Figure 6-7 shows the same PIM topology used in the preceding two case studies, but now it is running bootstrap rather than Auto-RP. Stetson and Fedora are again the C-RPs, but now they are also C-BSRs in keeping with a more robust design, providing failover for both the RP and BSR function.

Figure 6-7   *Stetson and Fedora Serve as Both Candidate RPs and Candidate BSRs*

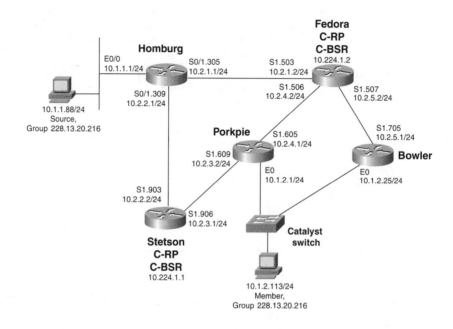

Example 6-38 shows the relevant configurations of Stetson and Fedora.

Example 6-38 *Configuring Routers Stetson and Fedora as Both Candidate RPs and Candidate BSRs*

```
Stetson
interface Loopback0
 ip address 10.224.1.1 255.255.255.255
!
ip pim bsr-candidate Loopback0 0
ip pim rp-candidate Loopback0
```
```
Fedora
interface Loopback0
 ip address 10.224.1.2 255.255.255.255
!
ip pim bsr-candidate Loopback0 0
ip pim rp-candidate Loopback0
```

The command **ip pim bsr-candidate** sets the router as a C-BSR and specifies that the BSR address is to be taken from interface L0. The **0** at the end of the command specifies the hash-mask length, which is 0 by default on Cisco routers. Use of the hash-mask is demonstrated later in this case study. The command **ip pim rp-candidate** sets the router as a C-RP and specifies that the RP address also is to be taken from interface L0.

First, a BSR must be elected from the available C-BSRs. The C-BSRs send Bootstrap messages throughout the PIM domain, with the destination address 224.0.0.13, that contain the originator's BSR address and priority. In the configuration so far, the default priority of 0 and the default hash-mask length of 0 remain unchanged, and therefore equal, on both C-BSRs. As a result, the higher BSR address is used as a tiebreaker. Fedora's BSR address (10.224.1.2) is higher than Stetson's (10.224.1.1), so Fedora is the BSR. Example 6-39 confirms the fact. By using **show ip pim bsr-router** on any router in the domain, you can observe not only the active BSR, but also the BSR's address, uptime, priority, hash-mask length, and holdtime.

Example 6-39 *The* **show ip pim bsr-router** *Command Displays the PIMv2 Domain's BSR*

```
Bowler#show ip pim bsr-router
PIMv2 Bootstrap information
  BSR address: 10.224.1.2 (?)
  Uptime:      00:17:35, BSR Priority: 0, Hash mask length: 0
  Expires:     00:01:56
Bowler#
```

When the C-RPs receive the Bootstrap messages and determine the address of the BSR, they unicast their Candidate-RP-Advertisement messages to the BSR. These messages contain the C-RP's address and priority. The BSR collects the C-RPs into an RP-Set, which is then included in its Bootstrap messages. This is where bootstrap diverges sharply from Auto-RP: Unlike the Auto-RP mapping agent, the BSR does not select RPs. The PIMv2 routers receive the Bootstrap messages, and they select the RP. The algorithm used to make the selection ensures that all routers select the same RPs for the same groups.

Example 6-40 shows the group-to-RP mappings at Bowler. You can see that the RP is Stetson, which is elected RP because of its lower RP address. (The C-RP priorities in this example are equal.)

Example 6-40 *The Active Groups at Bowler Are All Mapped to Stetson. Unlike Auto-RP, the C-RP with the Lowest RP Address Is Elected as the RP*

```
Bowler#show ip pim rp
Group: 239.255.255.254, RP: 10.224.1.1, v2, uptime 00:25:16, expires 00:02:40
Group: 228.13.20.216, RP: 10.224.1.1, v2, uptime 00:25:16, expires 00:02:40
Group: 224.2.127.254, RP: 10.224.1.1, v2, uptime 00:25:16, expires 00:02:40
Group: 230.253.84.168, RP: 10.224.1.1, v2, uptime 00:25:16, expires 00:02:40
Bowler#
```

Example 6-41 shows the complete group address range that is mapped to the RP. Compare this display to that of Example 6-33; of particular interest here is that the mapping is shown to be derived from bootstrap, and that the router knows all the C-RPs from the RP-Set.

Example 6-41 *Bowler Indicates That It Is Aware of Both Stetson and Fedora as C-RPs*

```
Bowler#show ip pim rp mapping
PIM Group-to-RP Mappings

Group(s) 224.0.0.0/4
  RP 10.224.1.1 (?), v2
    Info source: 10.224.1.2 (?), via bootstrap
         Uptime: 00:29:07, expires: 00:02:30
  RP 10.224.1.2 (?), v2
    Info source: 10.224.1.2 (?), via bootstrap
         Uptime: 00:29:07, expires: 00:02:17
Bowler#
```

The default behavior of both the BSR and the RP can be changed. In Example 6-39, for instance, the BSR is Fedora because its IP address is higher. If you want Stetson to be the BSR, with Fedora acting only as a backup in case Stetson fails, you can change Stetson's priority to something higher than the default of 0. To change Stetson's priority to 100, you need to configure Stetson as in Example 6-42.

Example 6-42 *Configuring Stetson with a Priority of 100 to Make It the BSR*

```
interface Loopback0
 ip address 10.224.1.1 255.255.255.255
!
ip pim bsr-candidate Loopback0 0 100
ip pim rp-candidate Loopback0
```

Example 6-43 shows the results of the new configuration. Bowler now shows Stetson as the BSR, with a priority of 100. Fedora assumes that role only if Stetson fails.

Example 6-43 *Stetson (10.224.1.1), with a Priority of 100, Has Become the BSR*

```
Bowler#show ip pim bsr-router
PIMv2 Bootstrap information
  BSR address: 10.224.1.1 (?)
  Uptime:      00:10:27, BSR Priority: 100, Hash mask length: 0
  Expires:     00:02:02
Bowler#
```

As with Auto-RP, you also can use access lists to distribute the RP duties among multiple RPs. Suppose, for example, that you want Fedora to be the RP for any groups whose addresses are in the 228.13.0.0/16 range, and Stetson to be the RP for all other groups. You use the configurations in Example 6-44.

Example 6-44 *Distributing RP Duties Between Fedora and Stetson*

```
Stetson
interface Loopback0
 ip address 10.224.1.1 255.255.255.255
!
ip pim bsr-candidate Loopback0 0 100
ip pim rp-candidate Loopback0 group-list 20
!
access-list 20 deny   228.13.0.0 0.0.255.255
access-list 20 permit any
```

```
Fedora
interface Loopback0
 ip address 10.224.1.2 255.255.255.255
!
ip pim bsr-candidate Loopback0 0
ip pim rp-candidate Loopback0 group-list 10
!
access-list 10 permit 228.13.0.0 0.0.255.255
```

Example 6-45 shows the results of these configurations. The BSR advertises the constraints in its Bootstrap messages, and Bowler maps its groups to the RPs based on those constraints. Of course, these configurations are not advised in a real internetwork. If one RP fails, the other can no longer assume a backup role. A more practical implementation would use access lists to distribute groups among multiple C-RPs, with at least two C-RPs for each group range created by the access lists.

Example 6-45 *After the Access Lists Are Added to Constrain the RP Mappings at Stetson and Fedora, Bowler Has Mapped Group 228.13.20.216 to Fedora and the Other Groups to Stetson*

```
Bowler#show ip pim rp mapping
PIM Group-to-RP Mappings

Group(s) 224.0.0.0/4
  RP 10.224.1.1 (?), v2
    Info source: 10.224.1.1 (?), via bootstrap
        Uptime: 00:07:25, expires: 00:02:26
Group(s) 228.13.0.0/16
  RP 10.224.1.2 (?), v2
    Info source: 10.224.1.1 (?), via bootstrap
        Uptime: 00:07:25, expires: 00:02:54

Bowler#show ip pim rp
Group: 239.255.255.254, RP: 10.224.1.1, v2, uptime 00:07:30, expires 00:02:52
Group: 228.13.20.216, RP: 10.224.1.2, v2, uptime 00:07:30, expires 00:03:32
Group: 224.2.127.254, RP: 10.224.1.1, v2, uptime 00:07:30, expires 00:02:52
Group: 230.253.84.168, RP: 10.224.1.1, v2, uptime 00:07:30, expires 00:02:52
Bowler#
```

A better way to distribute the RP duties when using PIMv2 bootstrap is to use the hash-mask. The hash-mask is a 32-bit number assigned to the BSR, and it is used in a somewhat similar fashion to a standard IP address mask. The BSR advertises the hash-mask in its Bootstrap messages, and the receiving routers run a hash algorithm that assigns a consecutive number of group addresses to one C-RP and then assigns the next group of addresses to the next C-RP.

If the hash-mask is 30 bits, for example, it masks the first 30 bits of all IP multicast addresses. The last 2 bits describe a range of four group addresses that will be assigned to an RP. So the addresses 225.1.1.0, 225.1.1.1, 225.1.1.2, and 225.1.1.3 are all part of one range and are assigned to one RP. The addresses 225.1.1.4, 225.1.1.5, 225.1.1.6, and 225.1.1.7 belong to the next range and are assigned to another RP. This "bundling" of group addresses continues throughout the entire IP multicast address range and across all available C-RPs. The result is that the IP multicast group addresses have been evenly distributed among the C-RPs. The mask gives you the flexibility to decide how many consecutive addresses are bundled into a single range so that related addresses are more likely to share the same RP. If the mask is 26 bits, for instance, 64 consecutive addresses are assigned to each range.

The hash-mask length is specified as part of the **ip pim bsr-candidate** command. As you have observed in previous examples in this case study, the default mask length is 0, meaning that there is a single bundle of group addresses spanning the entire range of the IP multicast address space. Example 6-46 shows the configurations to assign a hash-mask length of 30 for both Stetson and Fedora in Figure 6-7.

Example 6-46 *Assigning a Hash-Mask Length of 30 to Routers Stetson and Fedora*

```
Stetson
interface Loopback0
 ip address 10.224.1.1 255.255.255.255
!
ip pim bsr-candidate Loopback0 30
ip pim rp-candidate Loopback0
```
```
Fedora
interface Loopback0
 ip address 10.224.1.2 255.255.255.255
!
ip pim bsr-candidate Loopback0 30
ip pim rp-candidate Loopback0
```

In Example 6-47, the **show ip pim rp-hash** command is used to demonstrate the results. Beginning with 231.1.1.0, you can see that it and the next three consecutive group addresses are mapped to Fedora. Continuing the sequence, the next four addresses are mapped to Stetson. Across the entire range of IP multicast addresses, there should be a 50-50 distribution between the two RPs.

Example 6-47 *The Hash Algorithm Distributes Group Addresses Evenly Among the Available C-RPs*

```
Bowler#show ip pim rp-hash 231.1.1.0
  RP 10.224.1.2 (?), v2
    Info source: 10.224.1.2 (?), via bootstrap
        Uptime: 07:22:14, expires: 00:02:29
Bowler#show ip pim rp-hash 231.1.1.1
  RP 10.224.1.2 (?), v2
    Info source: 10.224.1.2 (?), via bootstrap
        Uptime: 07:22:19, expires: 00:02:24
Bowler#show ip pim rp-hash 231.1.1.2
  RP 10.224.1.2 (?), v2
    Info source: 10.224.1.2 (?), via bootstrap
        Uptime: 07:22:22, expires: 00:02:21
Bowler#show ip pim rp-hash 231.1.1.3
  RP 10.224.1.2 (?), v2
    Info source: 10.224.1.2 (?), via bootstrap
        Uptime: 07:22:28, expires: 00:02:15
Bowler#show ip pim rp-hash 231.1.1.4
  RP 10.224.1.1 (?), v2
    Info source: 10.224.1.2 (?), via bootstrap
        Uptime: 07:22:31, expires: 00:02:13
Bowler#show ip pim rp-hash 231.1.1.5
  RP 10.224.1.1 (?), v2
    Info source: 10.224.1.2 (?), via bootstrap
        Uptime: 07:22:35, expires: 00:02:10
Bowler#show ip pim rp-hash 231.1.1.6
  RP 10.224.1.1 (?), v2
    Info source: 10.224.1.2 (?), via bootstrap
        Uptime: 07:22:38, expires: 00:02:06
Bowler#show ip pim rp-hash 231.1.1.7
  RP 10.224.1.1 (?), v2
    Info source: 10.224.1.2 (?), via bootstrap
        Uptime: 07:22:43, expires: 00:02:02
```

Case Study: Multicast Load Sharing

At times, you may want to balance multicast traffic over parallel equal-cost paths, either to more fully utilize available bandwidth or to prevent a single path from becoming congested by heavy multicast traffic. But the RPF check prevents multicast load balancing directly over physical links.

The problem is illustrated in Figure 6-8, where the same PIM topology used in the previous case studies is repeated, except that Bowler is removed and Homburg is both the Auto-RP mapping agent and the RP.

Figure 6-8   *Two Equal-Cost Paths Exist between the Multicast Source and the Group Member*

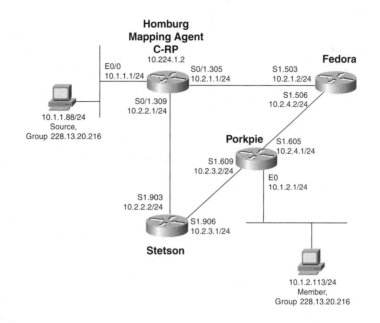

There are two equal-cost paths from the multicast source attached to Homburg and the group member attached to Porkpie: One path transits Fedora; the other transits Stetson. The problem exists because RPF must have only one incoming interface to work correctly. That means that if Fedora is chosen as the RPF neighbor, and group traffic arrives from Stetson, that traffic will not arrive on the RPF interface and will be dropped. Likewise, if Stetson is chosen as the RPF neighbor, traffic arriving from Fedora will fail the RPF check and be dropped. RPF requires all traffic to arrive on the same upstream interface.

The way to get around this problem is to use a tunnel, as shown in Figure 6-9. The tunnel is built between the loopback interfaces of Homburg and Porkpie, and all multicast traffic from the source to the group member is sent to this virtual tunnel interface rather than to either physical link. The multicast packets are then encapsulated and forwarded as regular IP packets. At this point, the encapsulated packets can be balanced across the two links, using either the default per-destination balancing or the optional per-packet balancing, as described in *Volume I*.

NOTE	Per-packet load balancing is achieved by turning off fast switching or its equivalent with the command **no ip route-cache** on the necessary interfaces.

Figure 6-9 *To Load Balance Over the Equal-Cost Paths, a Tunnel Is Created Between Homburg and Porkpie*

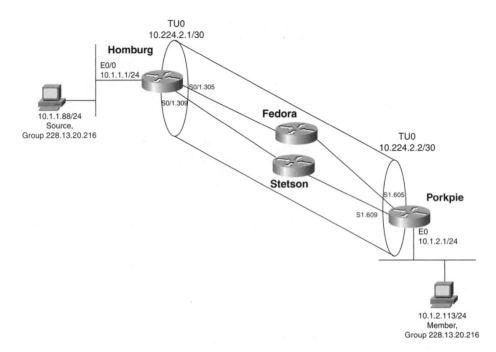

When the packets arrive at Porkpie, it does not matter whether they were received from Fedora or from Stetson, because their destination is the egress of the tunnel. At the virtual tunnel interface, the encapsulation is removed. From the perspective of the PIM process at Porkpie, the multicast packets appear to have all been received on the same interface, TU0, and to have been received from the same upstream neighbor, Homburg.

Example 6-48 shows the configurations of Homburg and Porkpie.

Example 6-48 *Configuring a Tunnel Between Homburg and Porkpie to Load Balance Over Equal-Cost Paths*

```
Homburg
hostname Homburg
!
ip multicast-routing
!
interface Loopback0
 ip address 10.224.1.4 255.255.255.0
 ip pim sparse-mode
!
interface Tunnel0
 ip address 10.224.2.1 255.255.255.252
 ip pim sparse-dense-mode
```

Example 6-48 *Configuring a Tunnel Between Homburg and Porkpie to Load Balance Over Equal-Cost Paths (Continued)*

```
 tunnel source Loopback0
 tunnel destination 10.224.1.3
!
interface Ethernet0/0
 ip address 10.1.1.1 255.255.255.0
 ip pim sparse-dense-mode
!
interface Serial0/1
 no ip address
 encapsulation frame-relay
!
interface Serial0/1.305 point-to-point
 description PVC to R5
 ip address 10.2.1.1 255.255.255.0
 frame-relay interface-dlci 305
!
interface Serial0/1.309 point-to-point
 description PVC to R9
 ip address 10.2.2.1 255.255.255.0
 frame-relay interface-dlci 309
!
router ospf 1
 passive-interface Tunnel0
 network 10.0.0.0 0.255.255.255 area 0
!
ip pim send-rp-announce Loopback0 scope 5
ip pim send-rp-discovery scope 5
```

Porkpie
```
hostname Porkpie
!
ip multicast-routing
!
interface Loopback0
 ip address 10.224.1.3 255.255.255.255
!
interface Tunnel0
 ip address 10.224.2.2 255.255.255.252
 ip pim sparse-dense-mode
 tunnel source Loopback0
 tunnel destination 10.224.1.4
!
interface Ethernet0
 ip address 10.1.2.1 255.255.255.0
 ip pim sparse-dense-mode
 ip cgmp
!
interface Serial1
 no ip address
```

continues

Example 6-48 *Configuring a Tunnel Between Homburg and Porkpie to Load Balance Over Equal-Cost Paths (Continued)*

```
 encapsulation frame-relay
 !
interface Serial1.605 point-to-point
 description PVC to R5
 ip address 10.2.4.1 255.255.255.0
 frame-relay interface-dlci 605
 !
interface Serial1.609 point-to-point
 description PVC to R9
 ip address 10.2.3.2 255.255.255.0
 frame-relay interface-dlci 609
 !
router ospf 1
 passive-interface Tunnel0
 network 10.0.0.0 0.255.255.255 area 0
```

On both routers, the tunnel interface is configured with a source of the router's loopback interface and a destination of the other router's loopback interface. The tunnel is using generic route encapsulation (GRE) and is given an IP address so that the virtual interface appears to the routing processes to be a physical IP interface. Finally, PIM is enabled on the tunnel interfaces. Notice that PIM is not enabled on any of the subinterfaces connecting to Stetson and Fedora. And on those two routers, multicasting is not enabled at all. Example 6-49 shows that, with these configurations, Porkpie has established a PIM adjacency with Homburg over the tunnel.

Example 6-49 *Porkpie Shows Homburg as a Neighbor Across the GRE Tunnel*

```
Porkpie#show ip pim neighbor
PIM Neighbor Table
Neighbor Address  Interface        Uptime    Expires   Ver  Mode
10.224.2.1        Tunnel0          04:09:21  00:01:11  v1   Sparse-Dense
Porkpie#
```

There is a further RPF problem to be solved, however. When Porkpie receives packets from source 10.1.1.88, it checks the unicast routing table for the upstream neighbor. Example 6-50 shows what the router finds.

Example 6-50 *The Unicast Routing Table Still Shows 10.2.3.1 or 10.2.4.2 as the Next-Hop Addresses to Reach 10.1.1.88*

```
Porkpie#show ip route 10.1.1.88
Routing entry for 10.1.1.0/24
  Known via "ospf 1", distance 110, metric 138, type intra area
  Redistributing via ospf 1
  Last update from 10.2.3.1 on Serial1.609, 01:13:30 ago
  Routing Descriptor Blocks:
```

Example 6-50 *The Unicast Routing Table Still Shows 10.2.3.1 or 10.2.4.2 as the Next-Hop Addresses to Reach 10.1.1.88 (Continued)*

```
  * 10.2.3.1, from 10.224.1.4, 01:13:30 ago, via Serial1.609
      Route metric is 138, traffic share count is 1
    10.2.4.2, from 10.224.1.4, 01:13:30 ago, via Serial1.605
      Route metric is 138, traffic share count is 1

Porkpie#
```

Porkpie's OSPF configuration has interface TU0 in passive mode to ensure that no unicast traffic crosses the tunnel—only multicast. Unfortunately, this means that OSPF still sees either Stetson (10.2.3.1) or Fedora (10.2.4.2) as the next hop toward 10.1.1.88. So when packets from 10.1.1.88 arrive on the tunnel interface, the RPF check fails, as demonstrated in Example 6-51.

Example 6-51 *The RPF Check Fails for Packets Arriving Over the Tunnel from 10.1.1.88 Because the Unicast Routing Table Does Not Show TU0 As an Upstream Interface to That Address*

```
Porkpie#debug ip mpacket
IP multicast packets debugging is on
Porkpie#
IP: s=10.1.1.88 (Tunnel0) d=228.13.20.216 len 569, not RPF interface
IP: s=10.1.1.88 (Tunnel0) d=228.13.20.216 len 569, not RPF interface
IP: s=10.1.1.88 (Tunnel0) d=228.13.20.216 len 569, not RPF interface
IP: s=10.1.1.88 (Tunnel0) d=228.13.20.216 len 569, not RPF interface
IP: s=10.1.1.88 (Tunnel0) d=228.13.20.216 len 569, not RPF interface
IP: s=10.1.1.88 (Tunnel0) d=228.13.20.216 len 569, not RPF interface
IP: s=10.1.1.88 (Tunnel0) d=228.13.20.216 len 569, not RPF interface
IP: s=10.1.1.88 (Tunnel0) d=228.13.20.216 len 569, not RPF interface
IP: s=10.1.1.88 (Tunnel0) d=228.13.20.216 len 569, not RPF interface
IP: s=10.1.1.88 (Tunnel0) d=228.13.20.216 len 569, not RPF interface
```

To overcome this second RPF problem, a static multicast route is used. Static mroutes are similar to static unicast routes in that they override any dynamic route entries. The difference is that static mroutes are not used for any forwarding. Instead, they are used to statically configure the RPF interface for a source, overriding the information in the unicast routing table. The command **ip mroute** is used along with an IP address and mask to specify an address or range of addresses. An RPF interface or RPF neighbor address also is specified, just as a static unicast route specifies either an outgoing interface or a next-hop neighbor. Example 6-52 shows the configuration for Porkpie with the static mroute.

Example 6-52 *Configuring Porkpie with a Static mroute*

```
hostname Porkpie
!
ip multicast-routing
!
```

continues

Example 6-52 *Configuring Porkpie with a Static mroute (Continued)*

```
interface Loopback0
 ip address 10.224.1.3 255.255.255.255
!
interface Tunnel0
 ip address 10.224.2.2 255.255.255.252
 ip pim sparse-dense-mode
 tunnel source Loopback0
 tunnel destination 10.224.1.4
!
interface Ethernet0
 ip address 10.1.2.1 255.255.255.0
 ip pim sparse-dense-mode
 ip cgmp
!
interface Serial1
 no ip address
 encapsulation frame-relay
!
interface Serial1.605 point-to-point
 description PVC to R5
 ip address 10.2.4.1 255.255.255.0
 frame-relay interface-dlci 605
!
interface Serial1.609 point-to-point
 description PVC to R9
 ip address 10.2.3.2 255.255.255.0
 frame-relay interface-dlci 609
!
router ospf 1
 passive-interface Tunnel0
 network 10.0.0.0 0.255.255.255 area 0
!
ip mroute 10.1.1.88 255.255.255.255 Tunnel0
```

Example 6-53 again uses debugging to verify that the multicast packets are now passing the RPF check at Porkpie and are being forwarded to the group member.

Example 6-53 *Packets from Source 10.1.1.88 Arriving on the Tunnel Interface Are Now Passing the RPF Check and Are Being Forwarded*

```
Porkpie#debug ip mpacket
IP multicast packets debugging is on
Porkpie#
IP: s=10.1.1.88 (Tunnel0) d=228.13.20.216 (Ethernet0) len 569, mforward
IP: s=10.1.1.88 (Tunnel0) d=228.13.20.216 (Ethernet0) len 569, mforward
IP: s=10.1.1.88 (Tunnel0) d=228.13.20.216 (Ethernet0) len 569, mforward
IP: s=10.1.1.88 (Tunnel0) d=228.13.20.216 (Ethernet0) len 569, mforward
IP: s=10.1.1.88 (Tunnel0) d=228.13.20.216 (Ethernet0) len 569, mforward
IP: s=10.1.1.88 (Tunnel0) d=228.13.20.216 (Ethernet0) len 569, mforward
IP: s=10.1.1.88 (Tunnel0) d=228.13.20.216 (Ethernet0) len 569, mforward
```

Example 6-53 *Packets from Source 10.1.1.88 Arriving on the Tunnel Interface Are Now Passing the RPF Check and Are Being Forwarded (Continued)*

```
IP: s=10.1.1.88 (Tunnel0) d=228.13.20.216 (Ethernet0) len 569, mforward
IP: s=10.1.1.88 (Tunnel0) d=228.13.20.216 (Ethernet0) len 569, mforward
IP: s=10.1.1.88 (Tunnel0) d=228.13.20.216 (Ethernet0) len 569, mforward
```

Example 6-54 shows the mroute entries for group 228.13.20.216. You can readily observe that Homburg is receiving multicast traffic from 10.1.1.88 on its E0/0 interface and forwarding the traffic on the tunnel. Porkpie is receiving the traffic on the tunnel and forwarding to the group member on its E0 interface.

Example 6-54 *The mroute Entries for (10.1.1.88, 228.13.20.216) Indicate That the Traffic for That Group Is Being Forwarded Over the GRE Tunnel*

```
Homburg#show ip mroute 228.13.20.216
IP Multicast Routing Table
Flags: D - Dense, S - Sparse, C - Connected, L - Local, P - Pruned
       R - RP-bit set, F - Register flag, T - SPT-bit set, J - Join SPT
Timers: Uptime/Expires
Interface state: Interface, Next-Hop, State/Mode

(*, 228.13.20.216), 04:48:39/00:02:59, RP 10.224.1.4, flags: SJC
  Incoming interface: Null, RPF nbr 0.0.0.0
  Outgoing interface list:
    Tunnel0, Forward/Sparse-Dense, 01:35:18/00:02:01
    Ethernet0/0, Forward/Sparse-Dense, 04:48:39/00:02:59

(10.1.1.88/32, 228.13.20.216), 01:41:09/00:02:59, flags: CT
  Incoming interface: Ethernet0/0, RPF nbr 0.0.0.0
  Outgoing interface list:
    Tunnel0, Forward/Sparse-Dense, 01:35:19/00:02:01

Homburg#
```

```
Porkpie#show ip mroute 228.13.20.216
IP Multicast Routing Table
Flags: D - Dense, S - Sparse, C - Connected, L - Local, P - Pruned
       R - RP-bit set, F - Register flag, T - SPT-bit set, J - Join SPT
       M - MSDP created entry, X - Proxy Join Timer Running
       A - Advertised via MSDP
Outgoing interface flags: H - Hardware switched
Timers: Uptime/Expires
Interface state: Interface, Next-Hop or VCD, State/Mode

(*, 228.13.20.216), 00:56:23/00:02:59, RP 10.224.1.4, flags: SJC
  Incoming interface: Tunnel0, RPF nbr 10.224.2.1, Mroute
  Outgoing interface list:
    Ethernet0, Forward/Sparse-Dense, 00:56:23/00:02:58
```

continues

Example 6-54 *The mroute Entries for (10.1.1.88, 228.13.20.216) Indicate That the Traffic for That Group Is Being Forwarded Over the GRE Tunnel (Continued)*

```
(10.1.1.88, 228.13.20.216), 00:13:37/00:02:59, flags: CJT
  Incoming interface: Tunnel0, RPF nbr 10.224.2.1, Mroute
  Outgoing interface list:
    Ethernet0, Forward/Sparse-Dense, 00:13:37/00:02:58

Porkpie#
```

Troubleshooting IP Multicast Routing

Your primary weapon when attacking problems in IP multicast internetworks is a solid understanding of the IP multicast protocols. Without that, no number of troubleshooting tools will help you wend your way through the often confusing, sometimes complex behaviors of IP multicast to the root of a particular problem. And understanding a single protocol is not enough. You also must understand how PIM, IGMP, and unicast routing all interact.

If you have been closely following the troubleshooting sections of each chapter of both *Volume I* and this volume, you should by now have a well-developed grasp of the approaches and techniques necessary for resolving problems in routed internetworks. So rather than present further case studies illustrating troubleshooting techniques, this section demonstrates the use of the several specialized tools provided for analyzing multicast internets.

Throughout this chapter, you have seen various **show** and **debug** commands that are useful for observing the behavior of IP multicast routing on Cisco routers. Table 6-2 lists the **show** commands available to you, and Table 6-3 lists the important multicast **debug** commands. Just as **show ip route** is the primary source of information when troubleshooting IP unicast routing, **show ip mroute** is the primary source of information when troubleshooting IP multicast routing.

Table 6-2 *Important **show** Commands for Troubleshooting IP Multicast*

Command	Description
show ip igmp groups [*group-name* | *group-address* | *type number*]	Displays the addresses of groups that have members on the router's interfaces.
show ip igmp interface [*type number*]	Displays relevant details of the IGMP-enabled interface.
show ip mcache [*group* [*source*]]	Displays the multicast contents of the fast-switching cache.
show ip mroute [*group-name* | *group-address*] [*source*] [**summary**] [**count**] [**active** *kbps*]	Displays the contents of the multicast routing table.

Table 6-2   *Important **show** Commands for Troubleshooting IP Multicast (Continued)*

show ip pim bsr	Displays information about PIM bootstrap routers.
show ip pim interface [*type number*] [**count**]	Displays relevant details of PIM-enabled interfaces.
show ip pim neighbor [*type number*]	Displays PIM neighbors.
show ip pim rp [*group-name*	*group-address*	**mapping**]	Displays the known RPs, and the groups mapped to the RPs.
show ip pim rp-hash *group*	Displays the RP for the group specified.
show ip rpf {*source-address*	*name*}	Displays details of how the router is determining RPF information.

Table 6-3   *Important **debug** Commands for Troubleshooting IP Multicast*

Command	Description
debug ip icmp [*hostname*	*group_address*]	Displays IGMP protocol activity.
debug ip mcache [*hostname*	*group_address*]	Displays multicast caching operations.
debug ip mpacket [*standard_access_list*	*extended_access_list*] [*hostname*	*group_address*][**detail**]	Displays multicast packets transiting the router.
debug ip mrouting [*hostname*	*group_address*]	Displays multicast routing table activity.
debug ip pim [*hostname*	*group_address*][**auto-rp**][**bsr**]	Displays PIM activity and events.

Using mrinfo

The **mrinfo** command enables you to observe a router's multicast connections and the details of those connections. The command is a part of the tools originally made available as part of *mrouted* for testing routers in the MBone. Therefore, the command is very useful in multivendor domains. Take, for example, the topology in Figure 6-10.

Figure 6-10 *This Topology Is Used Throughout the Troubleshooting Examples*

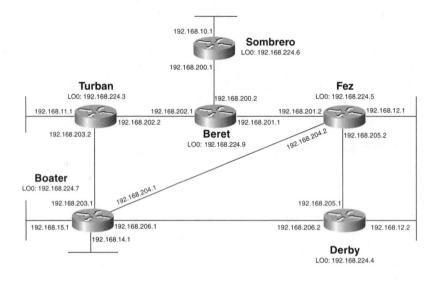

In Example 6-55, **mrinfo** is used at router Sombrero. The first line of the output shows the address used as the source of the query, the Cisco IOS Software version running on the router, and a number of flags. Table 6-4 lists the possible flags and their meanings. The next two lines of output show multicast interfaces on the router and any peers that the router may have. On the second line, Sombrero's interface 192.168.10.1 has no peers, indicated by the 0.0.0.0. The 1/0 indicates that the interface has a metric of 1 and that there is no TTL threshold set. PIM is running on the interface, the router is an IGMP querier for the attached subnet, and the subnet is a leaf network (that is, no multicast traffic will transit the network to another multicast router). The third line shows that Sombrero's interface 192.168.200.1 has a peer at address 192.168.200.2 (router Beret), the metric of the interface is 1, there is no TTL threshold, and PIM is running.

Example 6-55 *The IP Multicast Connection Information for Sombrero in Figure 6-10*

```
Sombrero#mrinfo
192.168.10.1 [version  12.1] [flags: PMA]:
   192.168.10.1 -> 0.0.0.0 [1/0/pim/querier/leaf]
   192.168.200.1 -> 192.168.200.2 [1/0/pim]

Sombrero#
```

Table 6-4   *Flags Associated with the* **mrinfo** *Command*

Flag	Definition
P	Prune-capable
M	**mtrace**-capable
S	SNMP-capable
A	Auto-RP-capable

The true usefulness of **mrinfo**, however, is that you can use the command to query other routers in the domain. In Example 6-56, the command is used at Sombrero to query Boater, by specifying one of Boater's IP addresses (in this case, its loopback address). Note that the flags indicate that SNMP is enabled on this router, whereas it is not on Sombrero. The router has five multicast-enabled interfaces, two of which are on leaf networks and three of which have PIM peers. A check of Figure 6-10 shows that this information is accurate.

Example 6-56 **mrinfo** *Is Used at Sombrero to Query Boater About Its Multicast Peers*

```
Sombrero#mrinfo 192.168.224.7
192.168.224.7 [version  12.1] [flags: PMSA]:
  192.168.14.1 -> 0.0.0.0 [1/0/pim/querier/leaf]
  192.168.15.1 -> 0.0.0.0 [1/0/pim/querier/leaf]
  192.168.203.1 -> 192.168.203.2 [1/0/pim]
  192.168.206.1 -> 192.168.206.2 [1/0/pim]
  192.168.204.1 -> 192.168.204.2 [1/0/pim]

Sombrero#
```

In Example 6-57, routers Derby and Fez are queried. These two routers share an Ethernet connection, and comparing the results of the queries shows that Derby (192.168.224.4) is the IGMP querier on that subnet.

Example 6-57 *Derby (192.168.224.4) and Fez (192.168.224.5) Are Queried from Sombrero*

```
Sombrero#mrinfo 192.168.224.4
192.168.224.4 [version  12.1] [flags: PMA]:
  192.168.12.2 -> 192.168.12.1 [1/0/pim/querier]
  192.168.205.1 -> 192.168.205.2 [1/0/pim]
  192.168.206.2 -> 192.168.206.1 [1/0/pim]

Sombrero#mrinfo 192.168.224.5
192.168.224.5 [version  12.1] [flags: PMA]:
  192.168.12.1 -> 192.168.12.2 [1/0/pim]
  192.168.205.2 -> 192.168.205.1 [1/0/pim]
  192.168.204.2 -> 192.168.204.1 [1/0/pim]
  192.168.201.2 -> 192.168.201.1 [1/0/pim]

Sombrero#
```

Using mtrace and mstat

Another useful tool is the **mtrace** command, which enables you to trace the RPF path from a specified destination to a specified source. Like **mrinfo**, **mtrace** is a UNIX-based MBone tool and can be used in multivendor domains. And also like **mrinfo**, you can issue the command from any router in the domain—you do not have to be on any router along the RPF path.

When the command is issued, you specify a source address and a destination address. A trace request is sent to the destination, which then uses a unicast trace to the source. The first-hop router on the path toward the source unicasts the results of the trace to the querying router.

Example 6-58 shows an example where a request is issued at Sombrero to trace the RPF path from Derby's 192.168.12.2 interface to Turban's 192.168.11.1 interface. Remember, because this is a reverse-path trace, Turban's interface is the source and Derby's interface is the destination. The output begins at the destination address and displays each intermediate router until the source is reached. The number of hops from the source is indicated, as is the multicast protocol used on that hop.

Example 6-58 mtrace *Is Used to Examine the RPF Path from Destination 192.168.12.2 to Source 192.168.11.1*

```
Sombrero#mtrace 192.168.11.1 192.168.12.2
Type escape sequence to abort.
Mtrace from 192.168.11.1 to 192.168.12.2 via RPF
From source (?) to destination (?)
Querying full reverse path...
 0   192.168.12.2
-1   192.168.12.2 PIM  [192.168.11.0/24]
-2   192.168.206.1 PIM  [192.168.11.0/24]
-3   192.168.203.2 PIM  [192.168.11.0/24]
-4   192.168.11.1
Sombrero#
```

Aside from the obvious use of isolating multicast routing failures, **mtrace** has an additional use of enabling you to examine multicast behavior before you turn up live multicast traffic on your internetwork. Notice in Figure 6-10 that no multicast sources or group members are indicated. Suppose you are going to turn up a multicast source attached to Boater, with an address of 192.168.14.35. This source will originate multicast traffic for group 235.100.20.18, and there will be group members at addresses 192.168.12.15, 192.168.10.8, and 192.168.11.102. Example 6-59 shows the results.

Example 6-59 mtrace *Can Be Used to Test the RPF for Source, Destination, and Group Addresses That Do Not Yet Exist in the Multicast Domain*

```
Sombrero#mtrace 192.168.14.35 192.168.12.15 235.100.20.18
Type escape sequence to abort.
Mtrace from 192.168.14.35 to 192.168.12.15 via group 235.100.20.18
From source (?) to destination (?)
```

Example 6-59 mtrace *Can Be Used to Test the RPF for Source, Destination, and Group Addresses That Do Not Yet Exist in the Multicast Domain (Continued)*

```
Querying full reverse path...
 0  192.168.12.15
-1  192.168.201.2 PIM  [192.168.14.0/24]
-2  192.168.204.1 PIM  [192.168.14.0/24]
-3  192.168.14.35

Sombrero#mtrace 192.168.14.35 192.168.10.8 235.100.20.18
Type escape sequence to abort.
Mtrace from 192.168.14.35 to 192.168.10.8 via group 235.100.20.18
From source (?) to destination (?)
Querying full reverse path...
 0  192.168.10.8
-1  192.168.10.1 PIM  [192.168.14.0/24]
-2  192.168.200.2 PIM  [192.168.14.0/24]
-3  192.168.202.2 PIM  [192.168.14.0/24]
-4  192.168.203.1 PIM  [192.168.14.0/24]
-5  192.168.14.35

Sombrero#mtrace 192.168.14.35 192.168.11.102 235.100.20.18
Type escape sequence to abort.
Mtrace from 192.168.14.35 to 192.168.11.102 via group 235.100.20.18
From source (?) to destination (?)
Querying full reverse path...
 0  192.168.11.102
-1  192.168.202.2 PIM  [192.168.14.0/24]
-2  192.168.203.1 PIM  [192.168.14.0/24]
-3  192.168.14.35
Sombrero#
```

The traces in Example 6-59 specify the multicast group along with the source and destination addresses. Although the RPF path would normally be the same for all groups, specifying the group can prove useful in situations where scoping or RP filtering affects the path taken. When no group is specified, as in Example 6-58, the group address 224.2.0.1 (the MBone audio group address) is used by default.

mstat is an adaptation of **mtrace** and provides not only a trace of the path from a source to a group destination, but also provides statistics about the path. Example 6-60 shows an example where a trace is again requested from source 192.168.14.35 to destination 192.168.10.8 for group 235.100.20.18. Comparing the output in Example 6-60 to the output for the same trace in Example 6-59, you can see that **mstat** provides not only packet statistics but also a more detailed view of the entire path.

Example 6-60 mstat *Provides a More-Detailed Trace of Group Traffic from a Source to a Destination*

```
Sombrero#mstat 192.168.14.35 192.168.10.8 235.100.20.18
Type escape sequence to abort.
Mtrace from 192.168.14.35 to 192.168.10.8 via group 235.100.20.18
```

continues

Example 6-60 mstat *Provides a More-Detailed Trace of Group Traffic from a Source to a Destination (Continued)*

```
From source (?) to destination (?)
Waiting to accumulate statistics......
Results after 10 seconds:

   Source           Response Dest    Packet Statistics For     Only For Traffic
192.168.14.35        192.168.200.1    All Multicast Traffic     From 192.168.14.35
   ¦          __/    rtt 47   ms    Lost/Sent = Pct  Rate      To 235.100.20.18
   v        /        hop 27   ms    -------------------        -------------------
192.168.14.1
192.168.203.1    ?
   ¦        ^        ttl   0
   v        ¦        hop 5    ms    0/0 = --%       0 pps     0/0 = --% 0 pps
192.168.203.2
192.168.202.2    ?
   ¦        ^        ttl   1
   v        ¦        hop 7    ms    0/0 = --%       0 pps     0/0 = --% 0 pps
192.168.202.1
192.168.200.2    ?
   ¦        ^        ttl   2
   v        ¦        hop 4    ms    0/0 = --%       0 pps     0/0 = --% 0 pps
192.168.200.1
192.168.10.1     ?
   ¦        \__      ttl   3
   v        \        hop 0    ms        0           0 pps         0     0 pps
192.168.10.8         192.168.200.1
   Receiver          Query Source
```

Reading from bottom to top, the display in Example 6-60 shows the query source and response destination, which in this example are both 192.168.200.1 (Sombrero). Notice that there is an ASCII representation of arrows, showing that Sombrero has sent the query to 192.168.10.1 (in this case, its own interface). The reverse path is then traced to the interface on Boater to which the source would be attached, and the response to the query is then sent to Sombrero. At the far left of the display, ASCII arrows also indicate the path multicast traffic will take from the source to the destination. At each hop, the **ttl** and **hop** statistics can be a little misleading. **ttl** actually shows the number of hops from that point to the source, whereas **hops** shows the delay (in milliseconds) between hops. Notice that the round-trip time (**rtt**) is indicated below the response destination. Statistics are then shown for all multicast traffic and for the (S, G) pair specified in the command. The first statistic compares the number of packets dropped to the number of packets sent. The second statistic shows the total traffic rate in packets per second. In Example 6-59, all these statistics are zero, of course, because no traffic has passed from the source to the destination. In fact, the source and destination do not even exist yet.

In Example 6-61, the proposed hosts have been installed, the source is generating traffic, and the group member has joined. You can now observe the packet-per-second rates and the drop statistics. An important point to keep in mind when using **mstat** is that the delay times between routers are valid only if the routers' clocks are synchronized.

Example 6-61 *The Same* **mstat** *Command Is Used After Multicast Traffic Has Begun Between the Source and Destination*

```
Sombrero#mstat 192.168.14.35 192.168.10.8 235.100.20.18
Type escape sequence to abort.
Mtrace from 192.168.14.35 to 192.168.10.8 via group 235.100.20.18
From source (?) to destination (?)
Waiting to accumulate statistics......
Results after 10 seconds:

    Source          Response Dest    Packet Statistics For      Only For Traffic
192.168.14.35       192.168.200.1     All Multicast Traffic      From 192.168.14.35
    ¦          __/    rtt 48   ms    Lost/Sent = Pct  Rate       To 235.100.20.18
    v         /       hop 48   ms    --------------------        --------------------
192.168.14.1
192.168.203.1    ?
    ¦         ^        ttl   0
    v         ¦        hop 10   ms    0/82 = 0%       8 pps    0/81 = --%  8 pps
192.168.203.2
192.168.202.2    ?
    ¦         ^        ttl   1
    v         ¦        hop 6    ms    0/82 = 0%       8 pps    0/81 = 0%   8 pps
192.168.202.1
192.168.200.2    ?
    ¦         ^        ttl   2
    v         ¦        hop 4    ms    0/82 = 0%       8 pps    0/81 = 0%   8 pps
192.168.200.1
192.168.10.1     ?
    ¦         \__      ttl   3
    v         \        hop 0    ms        82          8 pps        81     8 pps
192.168.10.8       192.168.200.1
  Receiver          Query Source

Sombrero#
```

Example 6-62 shows what the display might look like if the clocks are not in sync. The trace information and packet rates are still valid, but the delay times for the individual hops are obviously nonsensical. Also in Example 6-62, you can see that one packet has been lost on the hop between Turban and Beret. This may or may not represent a problem; the only way to know is to run several iterations of **mstat** and observe whether the packet loss is consistent. If so, further investigation using debugging may be required.

Example 6-62 *If the Routers' Clocks Are Not Synchronized, the Delays Shown for the Router Hops Are Meaningless*

```
Sombrero#mstat 192.168.14.35 192.168.10.8 228.13.20.216
Type escape sequence to abort.
Mtrace from 192.168.14.35 to 192.168.10.8 via group 228.13.20.216
From source (?) to destination (?)
Waiting to accumulate statistics......
Results after 10 seconds:
  Source            Response Dest     Packet Statistics For     Only For Traffic
192.168.14.35      192.168.200.1       All Multicast Traffic      From 192.168.14.35
     ¦          __/   rtt 44    ms    Lost/Sent = Pct  Rate     To 228.13.20.216
     v         /      hop 44    ms    --------------------      --------------------
192.168.14.1
192.168.203.1     ?
     ¦        ^       ttl   0
     v        ¦       hop -222  s      0/82 = 0%     8 pps      0/81 = 0%  8 pps
192.168.203.2
192.168.202.2     ?
     ¦        ^       ttl   1
     v        ¦       hop 113   s      1/82 = 1%     8 pps      1/81 = 1%  8 pps
192.168.202.1
192.168.200.2     ?
     ¦        ^       ttl   2
     v        ¦       hop 108   s      0/80 = 0%     8 pps      0/80 = 0%  8 pps
192.168.200.1
192.168.10.1      ?
     ¦        \__     ttl   3
     v         \      hop 0     ms        80         8 pps          80     8 pps
192.168.10.8      192.168.200.1
  Receiver        Query Source
```

Lastly, you may encounter a situation in which **mstat** shows a negative number of lost packets such as, **-3/85**. The "negative packet loss" in fact represents a packet gain. In other words, extra packets have been received. This may signify a loop and warrants further investigation.

Looking Ahead

You now have a good grasp of the basics of configuring IP multicast routing. As with unicast routing, however, as the multicast domain grows you are presented with problems of scalability and control. Chapter 7, "Large-Scale IP Multicast Routing," introduces you to tools and strategies for addressing the problems of large-scale multicast routing, from scoping domains to interdomain multicasting.

Configuration Exercises

1 What global Cisco IOS Software command is required to enable IP multicast routing?

_____

_____

_____

2 Show the commands that enable PIM on an interface in dense mode, sparse mode, and sparse-dense mode.

_____

_____

_____

3 Show the command to statically specify an RP with an address of 172.18.20.4.

_____

_____

_____

4 Write the configuration statements necessary to statically map groups 239.1.2.3 and 228.1.8.0 through 228.1.8.255 to RP 192.168.15.5, and group 239.6.7.8 to RP 192.168.20.10. Map all other groups to RP 192.168.25.1.

_____

_____

_____

5 All router interfaces shown in Figure 6-11 are running in sparse-dense mode. Show the relevant configurations in order for R1 to be the RP for only groups whose addresses begin with 226.13.0.0/24. R2 should only be the RP for groups whose addresses begin with 239.0.0.0/8. R3 is the mapping agent; ensure that the mapping agent will recognize only R1 and R2 as RPs, and only for the specified groups. All Auto-RP messages should have a TTL of 20.

Figure 6-11 *The Topology for Configuration Exercises 5–8*

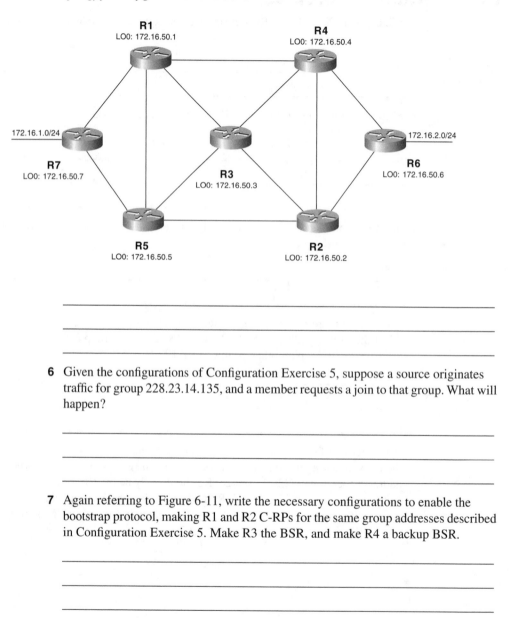

6   Given the configurations of Configuration Exercise 5, suppose a source originates
    traffic for group 228.23.14.135, and a member requests a join to that group. What will
    happen?

7   Again referring to Figure 6-11, write the necessary configurations to enable the
    bootstrap protocol, making R1 and R2 C-RPs for the same group addresses described
    in Configuration Exercise 5. Make R3 the BSR, and make R4 a backup BSR.

8 Write configurations for the topology in Figure 6-11 that allow multicast load balancing between source 172.16.1.75 and group member 172.16.2.100. Use unnumbered addressing on the tunnel interfaces, referencing E0, and assume the IGP is advertising those addresses.

_____

_____

_____

9 Examine the configurations of Homburg and Porkpie shown in the case study "Multicast Load Sharing." Each router is running OSPF in passive mode on the tunnel interfaces. Why?

_____

_____

_____

10 What is the purpose of the command **ip pim spt-threshold 100 group-list 25**?

_____

_____

_____

Troubleshooting Exercises

1 What is the output of Example 6-63 telling you?

Example 6-63 *The Output for Troubleshooting Exercise 1*

```
R1#
Turban#debug ip mpacket
IP multicast packets debugging is on
R1#
IP: s=192.168.14.35 (Serial0/1.307) d=228.13.20.216 len 573, mrouting disabled
IP: s=192.168.14.35 (Serial0/1.307) d=228.13.20.216 len 573, mrouting disabled
IP: s=192.168.14.35 (Serial0/1.307) d=228.13.20.216 len 573, mrouting disabled
IP: s=192.168.14.35 (Serial0/1.307) d=228.13.20.216 len 573, mrouting disabled
IP: s=192.168.14.35 (Serial0/1.307) d=228.13.20.216 len 573, mrouting disabled
IP: s=192.168.14.35 (Serial0/1.307) d=228.13.20.216 len 573, mrouting disabled
IP: s=192.168.14.35 (Serial0/1.307) d=228.13.20.216 len 573, mrouting disabled
IP: s=192.168.14.35 (Serial0/1.307) d=228.13.20.216 len 573, mrouting disabled
IP: s=192.168.14.35 (Serial0/1.307) d=228.13.20.216 len 573, mrouting disabled
IP: s=192.168.14.35 (Serial0/1.307) d=228.13.20.216 len 573, mrouting disabled
```

continues

Example 6-63 *The Output for Troubleshooting Exercise 1 (Continued)*

```
IP: s=192.168.14.35 (Serial0/1.307) d=228.13.20.216 len 573, mrouting disabled
IP: s=192.168.14.35 (Serial0/1.307) d=228.13.20.216 len 573, mrouting disabled
IP: s=192.168.14.35 (Serial0/1.307) d=228.13.20.216 len 573, mrouting disabled
```

_____

_____

_____

  2 What is the output of Example 6-64 telling you?

Example 6-64 *The Output for Troubleshooting Exercise 2*

```
R2#
IP: s=192.168.13.5 (Ethernet0) d=227.134.14.26 len 583, not RPF interface
IP: s=192.168.13.5 (Ethernet0) d=227.134.14.26 len 583, not RPF interface
IP: s=192.168.13.5 (Ethernet0) d=227.134.14.26 len 583, not RPF interface
IP: s=192.168.13.5 (Ethernet0) d=227.134.14.26 len 583, not RPF interface
IP: s=192.168.13.5 (Ethernet0) d=227.134.14.26 len 583, not RPF interface
IP: s=192.168.13.5 (Ethernet0) d=227.134.14.26 len 583, not RPF interface
IP: s=192.168.13.5 (Ethernet0) d=227.134.14.26 len 583, not RPF interface
IP: s=192.168.13.5 (Ethernet0) d=227.134.14.26 len 583, not RPF interface
IP: s=192.168.13.5 (Ethernet0) d=227.134.14.26 len 583, not RPF interface
```

_____

_____

_____

  3 What is the output of Example 6-65 telling you?

Example 6-65 *The Output for Troubleshooting Exercise 3*

```
R3#debug ip mpacket
IP multicast packets debugging is on
R3#
IP: s=172.16.3.50 (Serial0.405) d=224.0.1.40 (Serial0.407) len 52, mforward
IP: s=172.16.3.50 (Ethernet0) d=224.0.1.40 len 62, not RPF interface
IP: s=172.16.3.50 (Ethernet0) d=224.0.1.39 len 62, not RPF interface
IP: s=172.16.3.50 (Serial0.405) d=224.0.1.39 (Serial0.407) len 52, mforward
```

_____

_____

_____

4 In Figure 6-12, which of the four routers is the PIM-designated router?

Figure 6-12 *The Topology for Troubleshooting Exercises 4, 5, and 6*

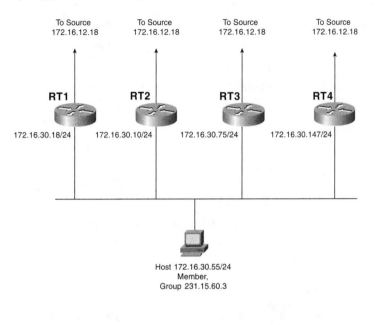

5 In Figure 6-12, which router is sending IGMPv2 queries to the group member?

6 Table 6-5 shows the unicast routes to source 172.16.12.18 in Figure 6-12. Which router is the PIM forwarder?

Table 6-5 *Unicast Routes to 172.16.12.18 in Figure 6-12*

Router	Next Hop	Protocol	Metric
R1	172.16.50.5	OSPF	35
R2	172.16.51.80	EIGRP	307200
R3	172.16.13.200	EIGRP	2297856
R4	172.16.44.1	OSPF	83

---

7 Example 6-66 shows an RPF trace taken from the PIM domain in Figure 6-10, which is running RIP-2 as its unicast IGP. Does this trace indicate a possible problem?

Example 6-66 *The* **mtrace** *for Troubleshooting Exercise 7*

```
Sombrero#mtrace 192.168.14.35 192.168.10.8 235.1.2.3
Type escape sequence to abort.
Mtrace from 192.168.14.35 to 192.168.10.8 via group 235.1.2.3
From source (?) to destination (?)
Querying full reverse path...
 0  192.168.10.8
-1  192.168.10.1 PIM  [192.168.14.0/24]
-2  192.168.200.2 PIM  [192.168.14.0/24]
-3  192.168.201.2 PIM  [192.168.14.0/24]
-4  192.168.204.1 PIM  [192.168.14.0/24]
-5  192.168.14.35
Sombrero#
```

- **Multicast Scoping**—This section examines the reasons for limiting the scope of IP multicast traffic, and the implementation of the two methods for multicast scoping: TTL scoping and administrative scoping.

- **Case Study: Multicasting Across Non-Multicast Domains**—This case study introduces techniques for passing IP multicast traffic across routers that do not support IP multicast.

- **Connecting to DVMRP Networks**—This section demonstrates strategies for connecting Cisco routers to DVMRP networks, and what parts of DVMRP are and are not supported by Cisco IOS Software.

- **Inter-AS Multicasting**—This section introduces the issues and problems specific to routing IP multicast traffic between autonomous systems and discusses the operation of MBGP and MSDP as solutions to some of the problems.

- **Case Study: Configuring MBGP**—This case study demonstrates the configuration of Multiprotocol BGP.

- **Case Study: Configuring MSDP**—This case study demonstrates the configuration of MSDP.

- **Case Study: MSDP Mesh Groups**—This case study demonstrates the configuration of MSDP mesh groups.

- **Case Study: Anycast RP**—This case study demonstrates the configuration of Anycast RP.

- **Case Study: MSDP Default Peers**—This case study demonstrates the configuration of MSDP default peers.

CHAPTER 7

Large-Scale IP Multicast Routing

The preceding two chapters explained the present state of IP multicast routing protocols and the basics of configuring Cisco IOS Software for multicast routing. As with unicast protocols, however, you must take additional measures as your multicast domain grows to maintain stability, scalability, and controllability. This chapter examines some of the techniques and protocols available to you to accomplish those objectives.

Multicast Scoping

A primary consideration when working with large-scale multicast domains is controlling the scope of the domain. You have read the discussion of the subject in Chapter 5, "Introduction to IP Multicast Routing," and you know that there are two methods of scoping multicast domains:

- TTL scoping
- Administrative scoping

With TTL scoping, the TTL value of multicast packets is set in such a way that the packets can travel only a certain distance before the TTL is decremented to 0 and the packet is discarded. You can add some granularity to this rough method by setting boundaries on interfaces with the **ip multicast ttl-threshold** command. For example, an interface might be configured with **ip multicast ttl-threshold 5**. Only packets with TTL values greater than 5 are forwarded out of this interface. Any packets with TTL values of 5 or below are dropped. Table 7-1 shows an example of TTL scoping values. The values in this table, which is a repeat of Table 5-6, are a set of TTL values suggested for use with the MBone.

In Chapter 6, "Configuring and Troubleshooting IP Multicast Routing," you encountered several commands, such as the commands for enabling Auto-RP candidate RPs and mapping agents, that enable you to set the TTL values of the protocol messages for TTL scoping. You will encounter more commands in this chapter with the same option. However, you saw in Chapter 5 that TTL scoping lacks flexibility—a TTL boundary at an interface applies to all multicast packets. This is fine for an absolute boundary, but at times you will want some packets to be blocked and others to be forwarded.

Table 7-1   *MBone TTL Thresholds*

TTL Value	Restriction
0	Restricted to same host
1	Restricted to same subnet
15	Restricted to same site
63	Restricted to same region
127	Worldwide
191	Worldwide limited bandwidth
255	Unrestricted

For this purpose, administrative scoping provides much more flexibility. Administrative scoping is just a procedure in which the multicast group address range 224.0.0.0–239.255.255.255 is partitioned in such a way that certain ranges of addresses are assigned certain scopes. Various domain boundaries can then be created by filtering on these address ranges. Administrative scoping is the subject of RFC 2365[1], and Table 7-2 shows the partitions that RFC suggests. You have already seen how the link-local scope of 224.0.0.0/24 is used. Packets with multicast addresses in this range—such as IGMP (224.0.0.1 and 224.0.0.2), OSPF (224.0.0.5 and 224.0.0.6), EIGRP (224.0.0.10), and PIM (224.0.0.13)—are never forwarded by a router and thus are restricted to the scope of the data link on which they were originated.

Table 7-2   *RFC 2365 Administrative Partitions*

Prefix	Scope
224.0.0.0/24	Link-local scope
224.0.1.0–238.255.255.255	Global scope
239.0.0.0/10	Unassigned
239.64.0.0/10	Unassigned
239.128.0.0/10	Unassigned
239.192.0.0/14	Organization-local scope
239.255.0.0/16	Unassigned

Adding the **ip multicast boundary** command to an interface creates an administrative boundary. The command just references an IP access list, which specifies the group address range to be permitted or denied at the interface, as demonstrated in Example 7-1.

Example 7-1 *Adding the* **ip multicast boundary** *Command to an Interface Creates an Administrative Boundary*

```
interface Ethernet0
 ip address 10.1.2.3 255.255.255.0
  ip multicast boundary 10
!
interface Ethernet1
 ip address 10.83.15.5 255.255.255.0
 ip multicast boundary 20
!
access-list 10 deny   239.192.0.0 0.3.255.255
access-list 10 permit 224.0.0.0 15.255.255.255
access-list 20 permit 239.135.0.0 0.0.255.255
access-list 20 deny   224.0.0.0 15.255.255.255
```

Interface E0 marks a boundary at which organization-local packets, as defined in Table 7-2, are blocked, while global-scoped packets are passed. The boundary at E1 permits packets whose destination addresses fall within the 239.135.0.0/16 range and denies all other multicast packets. This address range falls within an undefined range in Table 7-2 and therefore has been given some special meaning by the local network administrator.

Case Study: Multicasting Across Non-Multicast Domains

One challenge you will face is connecting diverse multicast domains across domains in which multicast is not supported. This may certainly be the case when multicasting is required in only certain areas of a large routing domain. You would not want to enable multicast on every router in the unicast domain just to provide connectivity to a relatively small number of multicast routers. A second and very common example is connecting multicast domains across the decidedly unicast Internet.

In Figure 7-1, two PIM domains are separated by a unicast-only IP domain. The unicast domain might be the backbone of an enterprise network, or it might be the Internet itself. The important point is that the two multicast domains must have connectivity across it. The solution is a simple one: Create a tunnel between the two routers that can carry the PIM traffic.

Figure 7-1 *PIM Domains Separated by a Unicast-Only IP Domain*

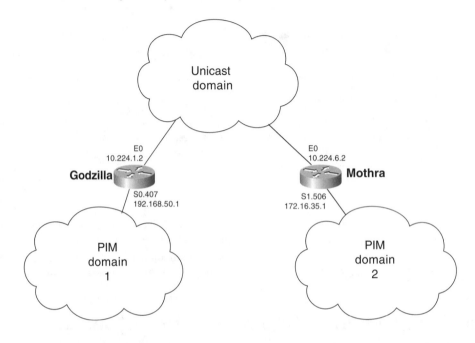

Example 7-2 shows the tunnel configurations of the two routers depicted in Figure 7-1.

Example 7-2 *Configuring Godzilla and Mothra to Provide Connectivity Between the Multicast Domains Through the Unicast-Only Domain*

```
Godzilla
interface Tunnel0
 ip unnumbered Ethernet0
 ip pim sparse-dense-mode
 tunnel source Ethernet0
 tunnel destination 10.224.6.2
!
interface Ethernet0
 ip address 10.224.1.2 255.255.255.0
!
interface Serial0.407 point-to-point
 description PVC to R7
 ip address 192.168.50.1 255.255.255.0
 ip pim sparse-dense-mode
 frame-relay interface-dlci 407
!
router ospf 1
 passive-interface Tunnel0
 network 10.0.0.0 0.255.255.255 area 0
 network 192.168.0.0 0.0.255.255 area 0
```

Example 7-2   *Configuring Godzilla and Mothra to Provide Connectivity Between the Multicast Domains Through the Unicast-Only Domain (Continued)*

```
!
ip mroute 172.16.0.0 255.255.0.0 Tunnel0
```

Mothra
```
interface Tunnel0
 ip unnumbered Ethernet0
 ip pim sparse-dense-mode
 tunnel source Ethernet0
 tunnel destination 10.224.1.2
!
interface Ethernet0
 ip address 10.224.6.2 255.255.255.0
!
interface Serial1.506 point-to-point
 description PVC to R6
 ip address 172.16.35.1 255.255.255.0
 ip pim sparse-dense-mode
 frame-relay interface-dlci 506
!
router ospf 1
 passive-interface Tunnel0
 network 0.0.0.0 255.255.255.255 area 0
!
ip mroute 192.168.0.0 255.255.0.0 Tunnel0
```

You already have seen a tunnel used in Chapter 6 to provide for load sharing across equal-cost paths. The configuration here is similar. The tunnel source is the Ethernet interface on each router, but PIM is not configured on that physical interface—only on the tunnel. GRE encapsulation, the default tunnel mode, is used. OSPF is configured to run passively on TU0 to ensure that no unicast traffic traverses the tunnel. Finally, static multicast routes are configured, referencing all possible source addresses from the opposite domain and showing their upstream interface as TU0. Recall from Chapter 6 that this route is necessary to prevent RPF failures. Without it, RPF checks would use the OSPF routes and determine the upstream interface to be the routers' E0 interfaces. As a result, all packets arriving on TU0 would fail the RPF check.

NOTE   If the DVMRP routers do not support GRE encapsulation, you can use IP-in-IP.

Example 7-3 shows the results of the configuration.

Example 7-3   *A PIM Adjacency Is Formed Across the GRE Tunnel*

```
Godzilla#show ip pim neighbor
PIM Neighbor Table
Neighbor Address  Interface        Uptime     Expires    Ver  Mode
192.168.50.2      Serial0.407      01:08:51   00:01:27   v2
172.16.35.1       Tunnel0          01:03:31   00:01:16   v2
Godzilla#
```
```
Mothra#show ip pim neighbor
PIM Neighbor Table
Neighbor Address  Interface        Uptime     Expires    Ver  Mode
172.16.35.2       Serial1.506      01:10:06   00:01:42   v2
192.168.50.1      Tunnel0          01:04:33   00:01:15   v2
Mothra#
```

Connecting to DVMRP Networks

You might, on occasion, have to connect your PIM router to a DVMRP router. This is not necessarily a large-scale multicast issue—routers that can speak only DVMRP can be encountered in an internetwork of any size. However, the most likely circumstance is when you are connecting to the MBone.

When you configure an interface on a Cisco router to run PIM, it listens for DVMRP Probe messages. When Probes are heard, as demonstrated in the output in Example 7-4, Cisco IOS Software automatically enables DVMRP on the interface. No special configuration is required. PIM routes are advertised to the DVMRP neighbor in DVMRP Report messages. DVMRP Report messages learned from the neighbor are kept in a separate DVMRP routing table shown in Example 7-5, but it is still PIM on the Cisco router that makes the multicast forwarding decisions. DVMRP Graft messages are sent and received normally, but it is the handling of Prunes and Probes that makes the Cisco IOS Software implementation of DVMRP different from a full implementation.

Example 7-4   *This Router Is Receiving DVMRP Probe Messages on Interface E0 from Neighbor 10.224.1.1*

```
Godzilla#debug ip dvmrp detail
DVMRP debugging is on
Godzilla#
DVMRP: Received Probe on Ethernet0 from 10.224.1.1
DVMRP: Aging routes, 0 entries expired
DVMRP: Received Probe on Ethernet0 from 10.224.1.1
DVMRP: Aging routes, 0 entries expired
DVMRP: Received Probe on Ethernet0 from 10.224.1.1
DVMRP: Aging routes, 0 entries expired
```

Example 7-5 *The* **show ip dvmrp route** *Command Displays DVMRP-Specific Route Information*

```
Godzilla#show ip dvmrp route
DVMRP Routing Table - 7 entries
10.224.2.0/24 [0/1] uptime 00:04:21, expires 00:02:38
    via 10.224.1.1, Ethernet0, [version mrouted 3.255] [flags: GPM]
10.224.3.0/24 [0/1] uptime 00:04:21, expires 00:02:38
    via 10.224.1.1, Ethernet0, [version mrouted 3.255] [flags: GPM]
10.224.4.0/24 [0/1] uptime 00:04:21, expires 00:02:38
    via 10.224.1.1, Ethernet0, [version mrouted 3.255] [flags: GPM]
10.224.5.0/24 [0/1] uptime 00:04:21, expires 00:02:38
    via 10.224.1.1, Ethernet0, [version mrouted 3.255] [flags: GPM]
10.224.6.0/24 [0/1] uptime 00:04:21, expires 00:02:38
    via 10.224.1.1, Ethernet0, [version mrouted 3.255] [flags: GPM]
172.16.70.0/24 [0/1] uptime 00:04:21, expires 00:02:38
    via 10.224.1.1, Ethernet0, [version mrouted 3.255] [flags: GPM]
192.168.50.0/24 [0/1] uptime 00:04:21, expires 00:02:38
    via 10.224.1.1, Ethernet0, [version mrouted 3.255] [flags: GPM]
```

The first difference between a full implementation of DVMRP and a Cisco IOS Software-based implementation of DVMRP is the handling of Probes. As already mentioned, the detection of Probe messages is how a Cisco router discovers DVMRP neighbors. Suppose, however, that the DVMRP neighbor is on a multiaccess network, and more than one Cisco router is attached to the same network. If one of the Cisco routers were to originate a Probe, the neighboring Cisco routers would mistakenly assume the originator is a DVMRP router rather than a PIM router, as illustrated by Figure 7-2. Therefore, Cisco routers listen for Probe messages but do not originate them.

Figure 7-2 *If the Top Cisco Router Were to Generate a DVMRP Probe Message, the Bottom Cisco Router Would Mistakenly Record the Originator as a DVMRP Neighbor; Therefore, Cisco Routers Do Not Generate DVMRP Probes*

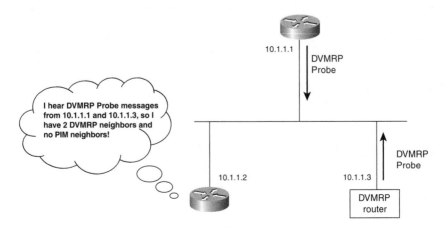

The second difference is the handling of Prune messages. Recall from the DVMRP discussion in Chapter 5 that a DVMRP router is required to maintain state for each downstream neighbor. If a downstream neighbor sends a Prune message, only that neighbor's state is pruned. Traffic is still forwarded on the interface unless all DVMRP neighbors send a Prune. This addresses the situation in which there are multiple downstream neighbors on a multiaccess network, and it prevents a Prune from one neighbor causing an unwanted Prune from another neighbor.

NOTE   Also recall from Chapter 5 that PIM-DM uses a Prune override mechanism to address this problem, instead of requiring the maintenance of neighbor states.

However, Cisco routers do not maintain DVMRP neighbor state. Therefore, to avoid the problem of one downstream neighbor's Prunes pruning traffic needed by another downstream neighbor, Cisco routers ignore DVMRP Prune messages received on multiaccess interfaces. On point-to-point interfaces, Prunes are received and processed normally, because by definition there can be only one downstream neighbor. Cisco routers send Prune messages normally on both multiaccess and point-to-point interfaces on which there are DVMRP neighbors.

The difficulty, as this approach stands, should be apparent to you. If DVMRP routers connected across a multiaccess network to upstream Cisco routers cannot prune themselves, the Cisco routers forward unwanted multicast traffic into the DVMRP domain. The solution to the difficulty is, once again, tunnels.

In Figure 7-3, a Cisco router is connected to two DVMRP routers across a multiaccess network. By creating tunnels to each of the DVMRP routers, Cisco IOS Software sees the DVMRP neighbors as connected via point-to-point links rather than a multiaccess link. The Cisco router then accepts prunes.

Figure 7-3   *Tunnels Are Used to Create Point-to-Point Connections to the DVMRP Routers Across the
Multiaccess Network, so DVMRP Pruning Works Correctly*

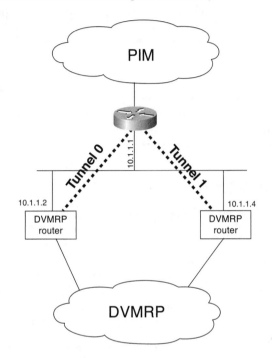

Example 7-6 shows the configuration for the Cisco router in Figure 7-3.

Example 7-6   *Configuring the Cisco Router in Figure 7-3 to Accept Prunes via Point-to-Point Links*

```
interface Tunnel0
 ip unnumbered Ethernet0
 ip pim sparse-dense-mode
 tunnel source Ethernet0
 tunnel destination 10.1.1.2
 tunnel mode dvmrp
!
interface Tunnel1
 no ip address
 ip pim sparse-dense-mode
 tunnel source Ethernet0
 tunnel destination 10.1.1.4
 tunnel mode dvmrp
!
interface Ethernet0
 ip address 10.1.1.1 255.255.255.0
```

The only significant difference from the earlier tunnel configurations you have seen is that the tunnel mode is set to DVMRP rather than the default GRE. As with the earlier tunnel configurations, PIM is configured on the tunnels but not on the physical interface. If there were also Cisco PIM routers on the multiaccess network, just configure PIM on the Ethernet interface so that the DVMRP routers connect over the tunnels and the PIM routers connect over the Ethernet.

NOTE   Remember that if multicast sources are reachable via the DVMRP routers, you must configure static mroutes to avoid RPF failures.

Inter-AS Multicasting

A challenge facing any multicast routing protocol (or any unicast routing protocol, for that matter) is scaling efficiently to the set of hosts requiring delivery of packets. You have seen how dense mode protocols such as PIM-DM and DVMRP do not scale well; by definition, the protocols assume that most hosts in the multicast domain are group members. PIM-SM, being a sparse mode protocol, scales better because it assumes most hosts in the multicast domain are not group members. Yet the assumption of both dense mode and sparse mode protocols is that they span a single domain. In other words, all the IP multicast routing protocols you have examined so far can be considered multicast IGPs.

How, then, can multicast packets be delivered across AS boundaries while maintaining the autonomy of each AS?

The PIM-SM Internet Draft begins to address the issue by defining a PIM Multicast Border Router (PMBR). The PMBR resides at the edge of a PIM domain and builds special branches to all RPs in the domain, as illustrated in Figure 7-4. Each branch is represented by a (*,*,RP) entry, where the two wildcard components represent all source and group addresses that map to that RP. When an RP receives traffic from a source, it forwards the traffic to the PMBR, which then forwards the traffic into the neighboring domain. The PMBR depends on the neighboring domain to send it prunes for any unwanted traffic, and the PMBR then sends prunes to the RP.

The shortcoming of the PMBR concept is this flood-and-prune behavior. In fact, PMBRs were proposed primarily to connect PIM-SM domains to DVMRP domains. Because of the poor scalability inherent in the approach, Cisco IOS Software does not support PMBRs.

Figure 7-4   *A PIM Multicast Border Router Forms Multicast Branches to Each RP in Its Domain Called (*, *, RP) Branches. RPs Forward All Source Traffic to the PMBR Along These Branches*

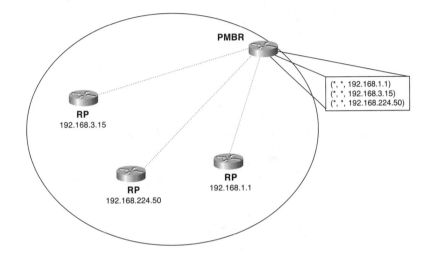

Accepting that PIM-SM is the de facto standard IP multicast routing protocol, the question of how to route multicast traffic between autonomous systems can be reduced to a question of how to route between PIM-SM domains. Two issues must be addressed:

- When a source is in one domain and group members are in other domains, RPF procedures must remain valid.

- To preserve autonomy, a domain cannot rely on an RP in another domain.

PIM-SM is protocol-independent, so the first issue seems easy enough to resolve. Just as PIM uses the unicast IGP routes to determine RPF interfaces within a domain, it can use BGP routes to determine RPF interfaces to sources in other autonomous systems. When moving traffic between domains, however, you may want your multicast traffic to use different links from your unicast traffic, as shown in Figure 7-5. If a multicast packet arrives on link A, and BGP indicates that the unicast route to the packet's source is via link B, the RPF check fails. Static mroutes could be used to prevent RPF problems, but they are obviously not practical on a large scale. Instead, BGP must be extended so that it can indicate whether an advertised prefix is to be used for unicast routing, multicast RPF checks, or both.

Figure 7-5   *Inter-AS Traffic Engineering Requirements May Dictate That Multicast Traffic Pass Over a Link Separate from Unicast Traffic*

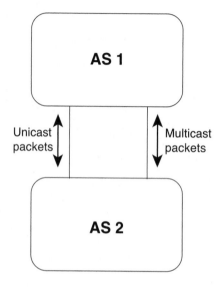

As it happens, PIM can take advantage of existing extensions to BGP. The extended version of BGP is called *Multiprotocol BGP* (MBGP) and is described in RFC 2283.[2] Although the extensions were created to allow BGP to carry reachability information for protocols such as IPv6 and IPX, the widespread application of MBGP is to advertise multicast sources. As a result, the "M" in MBGP is frequently and inaccurately thought to represent "multicast" rather than "multiprotocol."

The most common application of MBGP is for peer connections at NAPs among service providers that have agreed to exchange multicast traffic. As Figure 7-6 shows, the autonomous systems may be peered for unicast traffic but must share a separate peering point for multicast traffic. Some prefixes will be advertised over both the unicast and multicast NAPs, so MBGP is used to differentiate multicast RPF paths from unicast paths.

NOTE   Multicast NAPs are usually some nonswitched medium such as FDDI, as depicted in Figure 7-6.

Figure 7-6   *MBGP Is Used When Separate Peering Points Are Required for Multicast and Unicast*

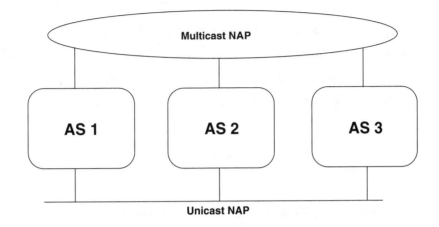

The second inter-AS PIM issue (to preserve autonomy, a domain cannot rely on an RP in another domain) stems from the fact that an AS does not want to depend on an RP that it does not control. If each AS places its own RPs, however, there must be a protocol that each RP can use to share its source information with other RPs across AS boundaries and in turn discover sources known by other RPs, as illustrated in Figure 7-7. That protocol is the *Multicast Source Discovery Protocol* (MSDP).[3]

Figure 7-7   *Multicast Source Discovery Protocol Is Spoken Between RPs and Allows Each RP to Discover Sources Known by Other RPs*

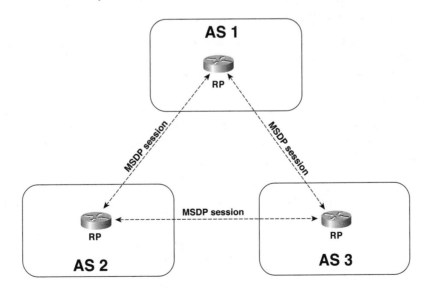

The following two sections describe the MBGP extensions and the operation of MSDP.

Multiprotocol Extensions for BGP (MBGP)

RFC 2283 extends BGP for multiprotocol support by defining two new attributes:

- Multiprotocol Reachable NLRI, or MP_REACH_NLRI (type 14)
- Multiprotocol Unreachable NLRI, or MP_UNREACH_NLRI (type 15)

NOTE   See Chapter 2, Table 2-7, for a more complete list of BGP attribute type codes.

Both attributes are optional, nontransitive. Recall from Chapter 2, "Introduction to Border Gateway Protocol 4," that this means BGP speakers are not required to support the attributes, and BGP speakers that do not support the attributes do not pass them to their peers.

The MP_REACH_NLRI attribute advertises feasible routes, and MP_UNREACH_NLRI withdraws feasible routes. The Network Layer Reachability Information (NLRI) contained in the attributes is the protocol-specific destination information. When MBGP is used for IP multicast, the NLRI is always an IPv4 prefix describing one or more multicast sources. Remember that PIM routers do not use this information for packet forwarding but only for determining the RPF interface toward a particular source. These two new attributes provide the capability of signaling to a BGP peer whether a particular prefix is to be used for unicast routing, multicast RPF, or both.

The MP_REACH_NLRI consists of one or more [Address Family Information, Next Hop Information, NLRI] triples. The MP_UNREACH_NLRI consists of one or more [Address Family Information, Unfeasible Routes Length, Withdrawn Routes] triples.

NOTE   The complete format of the MP_REACH_NLRI is more complicated than is indicated here—some fields are irrelevant to IP multicast. For a complete description, see RFC 2283.

The Address Family Information consists of an Address Family Identifier (AFI) and a Subsequent AFI (Sub-AFI). The AFI for IPv4 is 1, so it is always set to 1 for IP multicast.

The sub-AFI describes whether the NLRI is to be used for unicast routing only, multicast RPF information only, or both, as documented in Table 7-3.

Table 7-3   *Subsequent Address Family Identifiers*

Sub-AFI	Description
1	Unicast route information only
2	Multicast RPF information only
3	Prefix can be used for both unicast routing information and multicast RPF information

Operation of Multicast Source Discovery Protocol (MSDP)

The purpose of MSDP is, as the name states, to discover multicast sources in other PIM domains. The advantage of running MSDP is that your own RPs exchange source information with RPs in other domains; your group members do not have to be directly dependent on another domain's RP.

NOTE   You will see in some subsequent case studies how MSDP can prove useful for sharing source information within a single domain, too.

MSDP uses TCP (port 639) for its peering connections. As with BGP, using point-to-point TCP peering means that each peer must be explicitly configured. When a PIM DR registers a source with its RP as illustrated in Figure 7-8, the RP sends a Source Active (SA) message to all of its MSDP peers.

The SA contains the following:

- The address of the multicast source
- The group address to which the source is sending
- The IP address of the originating RP

Each MSDP peer that receives the SA floods the SA to all of its own peers downstream from the originator. In some cases, such as the RPs in AS 6 and AS 7 of Figure 7-8, an RP may receive a copy of an SA from more than one MSDP peer. To prevent looping, the RP consults the BGP next-hop database to determine the next hop toward the SA's originator. If both MBGP and unicast BGP are configured, MBGP is checked first, and then unicast BGP. That next-hop neighbor is the *RPF peer* for the originator, and SAs received from the originator on any interface other than the interface to the RPF peer are dropped. The SA flooding process is, therefore, called *peer RPF flooding*. Because of the peer RPF flooding mechanism, BGP or MBGP must be running in conjunction with MSDP.

Figure 7-8   *RPs Advertise Sources to Their MSDP Neighbors with Source Active Messages*

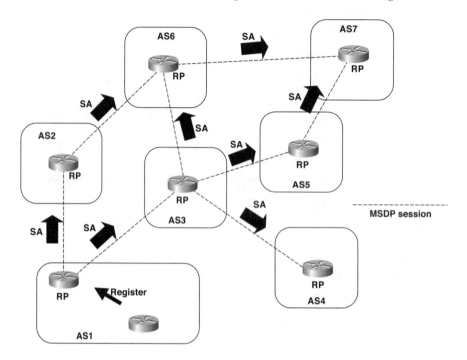

When an RP receives an SA, it checks to see whether there are any members of the SA's group in its domain by checking to see whether there are interfaces on the group's (*, G) outgoing interface list. If there are no group members, the RP does nothing. If there are group members, the RP sends an (S, G) join toward the source. As a result, a branch of the source tree is constructed across AS boundaries to the RP. As multicast packets arrive at the RP, they are forwarded down its own shared tree to the group members in the RP's domain. The members' DRs then have the option of joining the RPT tree to the source using standard PIM-SM procedures.

The originating RP continues to send periodic SAs for the (S, G) every 60 seconds for as long as the source is sending packets to the group. When an RP receives an SA, it has the option to cache the message. Suppose, for example, that an RP receives an SA for (172.16.5.4, 228.1.2.3) from originating RP 10.5.4.3. The RP consults its mroute table and finds that there are no active members for group 228.1.2.3, so it passes the SA message to its peers downstream of 10.5.4.3 without caching the message. If a host in the domain then sends a join to the RP for group 228.1.2.3, the RP adds the interface toward the host to the outgoing interface list of its (*, 224.1.2.3) entry. Because the previous SA was not cached, however, the RP has no knowledge of the source. Therefore, the RP must wait until the next SA message is received before it can initiate a join to the source.

If, on the other hand, the RP is caching SAs, the router will have an entry for (172.16.5.4, 228.1.2.3) and can join the source tree as soon as a host requests a join. The trade-off here is that in exchange for reducing the join latency, memory is consumed caching SA messages that may or may not be needed. If the RP belongs to a very large MSDP mesh, and there are large numbers of SAs, the memory consumption can be significant.

By default, Cisco IOS Software does not cache SAs. You can enable caching with the command **ip msdp cache-sa-state**. To help alleviate possible memory stress, you can link the command to an extended access list that specifies what (S, G) pairs to cache.

If an RP has an MSDP peer that is caching SAs, you can reduce the join latency at the RP without turning on caching by using *SA Request* and *SA Response* messages. When a host requests a join to a particular group, the RP sends an SA Request message to its caching peer(s). If a peer has cached source information for the group in question, it sends the information to the requesting RP with an SA Response message. The requesting RP uses the information in the SA Response but does not forward the message to any other peers. If a noncaching RP receives an SA Request, it sends an error message back to the requestor.

To enable a Cisco router to send SA Request messages, use the **ip msdp sa-request** command to specify the IP address or name of a caching peer. You can use the command multiple times to specify multiple caching peers.

MSDP Message Formats

MSDP messages are carried in TCP segments. When two routers are configured as MSDP peers, the router with the higher IP address listens on TCP port 639, and the router with the lower IP address attempts an active connect to port 639.

The MSDP messages use a TLV (Type/Length/Value) format and may be one of five types, shown in Table 7-4. The following sections detail the format of each message type.

Table 7-4   *MSDP Message Types*

Type	Message
1	Source Active
2	Source Active Request
3	Source Active Response
4	Keepalive
5	Notification

Source Active TLV

When an MSDP RP receives a PIM Register message from an IP multicast source, it sends a Source Active message to its peers. Figure 7-9 shows the MSDP Source Active TLV format. SA messages are subsequently sent every 60 seconds until the source is no longer active. Multiple (S, G) entries can be advertised by a single SA.

Figure 7-9   *The MSDP Source Active TLV Format*

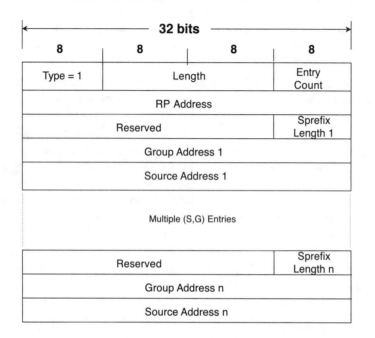

The fields for the MSDP Source Active TLV format are defined as follows:

- *Entry Count* specifies the number of (S, G) entries being advertised by the specified RP address.

- *RP Address* is the IP address of the originating RP.

- *Reserved* is set to all zeroes.

- *Sprefix Length* specifies the prefix length of the associated source address. This length is always 32.

- *Group Address* is the multicast IP address to which the associated source is sending multicast packets.

- *Source Address* is the IP address of the active source.

Source Active Request TLV

SA Request Messages, the format of which is shown in Figure 7-10, are used to request (S, G) information from MSPD peers that are caching SA state. SA Request messages should be sent only to caching peers (noncaching peers will return an error notification) and are sent only by RPs that are explicitly configured to do so.

Figure 7-10 *The MSDP Source Active Request TLV Format*

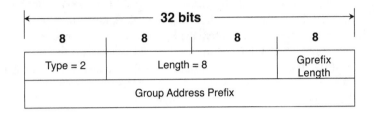

The fields for the MSDP Source Active Request TLV format are defined as follows:

- *Gprefix Length* specifies the length of the group address prefix.

- *Group Address Prefix* specifies the group address for which source information is requested.

Source Active Response TLV

SA Response messages, the format of which is shown in Figure 7-11, are sent by a caching peer in response to an SA Request message. They provide the requesting peer the source address and RP address associated with the specified group address. The format is the same as the SA message.

Figure 7-11 *The MSPD Source Active Response TLV Format*

Keepalive TLV

The active side (the peer with the lower IP address) of an MSDP connection tracks the passive side of the connection with a 75-second Keepalive timer. If no MSDP message is received from the passive side before the Keepalive timer expires, the active peer resets the TCP connection. If an MSDP message is received, the timer is reset. If the passive peer has no other MSDP messages to send, it sends a Keepalive message to prevent the active peer from resetting the connection. As Figure 7-12 shows, the Keepalive message is a simple 24-bit TLV consisting of a type and length field.

Figure 7-12 *The MSDP Keepalive TLV Format*

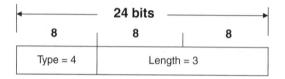

Notification TLV

A Notification message is sent when an error is detected. Figure 7-13 shows the Notification message format.

Figure 7-13 *The MSDP Notification TLV Format*

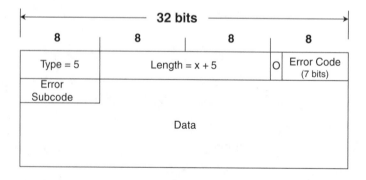

The fields for the MSDP Notification TLV format are defined as follows:

- *Length* = $x + 5$ is the length of the TLV, where x is the length of the data field and 5 is the first 5 octets.

- *O* is the *open bit*. If this bit is cleared, the connection must be closed upon receipt of the Notification. Table 7-5 shows the states of the O bit for different error subcodes. MC indicates *must close*; the O bit is always cleared. CC indicates *can close*; the O bit might be cleared.

- *Error code* is a 7-bit unsigned integer indicating the Notification type. Table 7-5 lists the error codes.

- *Error Subcode* is an 8-bit unsigned integer that may offer more details about the error code. If the error code has no subcode, this field is zero. Table 7-5 shows the possible error subcodes associated with the error codes.

- *Data* is a variable-length field containing information specific to the error code and error subcode. The various data fields are not covered in this chapter; see the MSDP Internet Draft for more information on the possible contents of this field.

Table 7-5 *MSDP Error Codes and Subcodes*

Error Code	Error Code Description	Error Subcode	Error Subcode Description	O-Bit State
1	Message header error	0	Unspecific	MC
		2	Bad message length	MC
		3	Bad message type	CC
2	SA Request error	0	Unspecific	MC
		1	Does not cache SA	MC
		2	Invalid group	MC
3	SA message/ SA response error	0	Unspecific	MC
		1	Invalid entry count	CC
		2	Invalid RP address	MC
		3	Invalid group address	MC
		4	Invalid source address	MC
		5	Invalid sprefix length	MC
		6	Looping SA (self is RP)	MC
		7	Unknown encapsulation	MC
		8	Administrative scope boundary violated	MC
4	Hold timer expired	0	Unspecific	MC
5	Finite state machine error	0	Unspecific	MC
		1	Unexpected message type FSM error	MC
6	Notification	0	Unspecific	MC
7	Cease	0	Unspecific	MC

Case Study: Configuring MBGP

Figure 7-14 depicts three autonomous systems. AS 200 is advertising unicast prefixes 172.16.226.0/24 and 172.16.227.0/24 to transit AS 100 and is used for normal inter-AS routing. AS 200 also has several multicast sources. These are hosts at 172.16.224.1 and 172.16.225.50. Additionally, several multicast sources are on subnet 172.16.227.0/24, and that prefix is advertised not only as a unicast prefix but also as a multicast source prefix.

Figure 7-14 *AS 200 Is Advertising Several Prefixes and Addresses; Some Are Unicast, Some Are Multicast, and One Is Both*

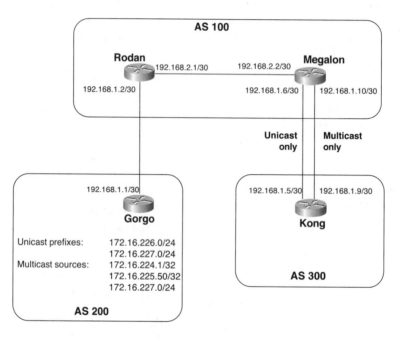

Example 7-7 shows the configurations of Gorgo and Rodan in Figure 7-14.

Example 7-7 *The MBGP Configurations of Gorgo and Rodan in Figure 7-14*

```
Gorgo
router bgp 200
 no synchronization
 network 172.16.226.0 mask 255.255.255.0
 network 172.16.227.0 mask 255.255.255.0
 neighbor 192.168.1.2 remote-as 100
 no auto-summary
 !
 address-family ipv4 multicast
 neighbor 192.168.1.2 activate
```

Example 7-7 *The MBGP Configurations of Gorgo and Rodan in Figure 7-14 (Continued)*

```
 network 172.16.224.1 mask 255.255.255.255
 network 172.16.225.50 mask 255.255.255.255
 network 172.16.227.0 mask 255.255.255.0
 exit-address-family

Rodan
router bgp 100
 no synchronization
 neighbor 192.168.1.1 remote-as 200
 neighbor 192.168.254.2 remote-as 100
 neighbor 192.168.254.2 update-source Loopback0
 neighbor 192.168.254.2 next-hop-self
 !
 address-family ipv4 multicast
 neighbor 192.168.1.1 activate
 neighbor 192.168.254.2 activate
 neighbor 192.168.254.2 next-hop-self
 exit-address-family
```

The unicast portion of both routers' BGP configurations is no different from the configurations you observed in Chapter 3, "Configuring and Troubleshooting Border Gateway Protocol 4." Neighbors and their AS numbers are identified, as are the two unicast prefixes that Gorgo is to advertise into AS 100.

NOTE   This chapter assumes you are already familiar with unicast BGP configuration. If some of the IBGP tools such as **next-hop-self** and **update-source** are not clear to you, you are encouraged to review Chapter 3.

MBGP is activated with the **address-family ipv4 multicast** command. Recall from the section "Multiprotocol Extensions for BGP (MBGP)" that MBGP uses two new route attributes—MP_REACH_NLRI and MP_UNREACH_NLRI—and that the attributes' Address Family Indicator (AFI) code for IPv4 is 1. The **multicast** keyword sets the attributes' Sub-AFI to multicast. Following the **address-family** command, MBGP is configured very similarly to unicast BGP. MBGP neighbors are identified, and the prefixes to be advertised as multicast are identified. The **activate** keyword is used to show that MBGP is to be activated for that neighbor. The peer's AS number is specified only under BGP, not MBGP. Notice that IBGP configurations, such as **next-hop-self**, are used under MBGP just as they are with BGP. You also can configure policies separately for MBGP neighbors. The final command, **exit-address-family**, is entered automatically by Cisco IOS Software to mark the end of the MBGP configuration stanzas.

Enabling **address-family ipv4 multicast** implicitly enables the **address-family ipv4 unicast** command. Although the command is never displayed in the configuration, it is applied to the unicast BGP configuration. Its result is that the prefixes specified under that configuration section are given the MP_REACH_NLRI attribute and are assigned a unicast Sub-AFI. Notice that the prefix 172.16.227.0/24 appears in Gorgo's configuration under both BGP and MBGP. This prefix is then advertised as both unicast and multicast (Sub-AFI = 3).

In Example 7-8, the **show ip bgp ipv4** command is used to show the results of the configurations. First the **unicast** keyword is used, and then the **multicast** keyword is used, and the prefixes whose Sub-AFI matches the keyword are displayed. Notice again that 172.16.227.0/24 is included in both displays because it has been configured as both a unicast and a multicast prefix.

NOTE   The output of **show ip bgp ipv4 unicast** is the same as the output of **show ip bgp**.

Example 7-8   *The* **show ip bgp ipv4** *Command Displays Prefixes According to Their Sub-AFI Values*

```
Rodan#show ip bgp ipv4 unicast
BGP table version is 7, local router ID is 192.168.254.1
Status codes: s suppressed, d damped, h history, * valid, > best, i - internal
Origin codes: i - IGP, e - EGP, ? - incomplete

   Network          Next Hop          Metric LocPrf Weight Path
*> 172.16.226.0/24  192.168.1.1            0             0 200 i
*> 172.16.227.0/24  192.168.1.1            0             0 200 i

Rodan#show ip bgp ipv4 multicast
BGP table version is 10, local router ID is 192.168.254.1
Status codes: s suppressed, d damped, h history, * valid, > best, i - internal
Origin codes: i - IGP, e - EGP, ? - incomplete

   Network          Next Hop          Metric LocPrf Weight Path
*> 172.16.224.1/32  192.168.1.1            0             0 200 i
*> 172.16.225.50/32 192.168.1.1            0             0 200 i
*> 172.16.227.0/24  192.168.1.1            0             0 200 i
Rodan#
```

The configurations of Megalon and Kong from Figure 7-14 are a bit more complicated, because separate links are used for unicast BGP and for MBGP. Example 7-9 shows the configurations for these two routers.

Example 7-9   *Configuring Megalon and Kong to Use Separate Data Links for Multicast and Unicast*

```
Megalon
router bgp 100
 no synchronization
 no bgp default ipv4-unicast
 neighbor 192.168.1.5 remote-as 300
 neighbor 192.168.1.5 activate
 neighbor 192.168.1.9 remote-as 300
 neighbor 192.168.254.1 remote-as 100
 neighbor 192.168.254.1 update-source Loopback0
 neighbor 192.168.254.1 activate
 neighbor 192.168.254.1 next-hop-self
 no auto-summary
 !
 address-family ipv4 multicast
 neighbor 192.168.1.9 activate
 neighbor 192.168.254.1 activate
 exit-address-family
```

```
Kong
router bgp 300
 no synchronization
 no bgp default ipv4-unicast
 neighbor 192.168.1.6 remote-as 100
 neighbor 192.168.1.6 activate
 neighbor 192.168.1.10 remote-as 100
 no auto-summary
 !
 address-family ipv4 multicast
 neighbor 192.168.1.10 activate
 exit-address-family
```

The MBGP configurations show that only the 192.168.1.8/30 subnet is used for MBGP peering, and there are some new commands under the unicast BGP section. Remember that when the **address-family ipv4 multicast** command is invoked, the **address-family ipv4 unicast** command is invoked automatically and implicitly. In the case of subnet 192.168.1.8/30, unicast BGP traffic is unwanted. Therefore, the command **no ip default ipv4-unicast** is used to prevent this automatic behavior. Then, the **neighbor activate** command is used to explicitly enable unicast BGP on the desired links. Notice that the 192.168.2.1/30 and 192.168.1.4/30 subnets are activated for unicast, but the 192.168.1.8/30 subnet is not. This link has only the AS number specified under BGP so that peering can occur.

Example 7-10 shows the results of the configurations in Example 7-9. The output here looks similar to that in Example 7-8, in that the unicast and multicast prefixes are correctly classified. In this case, however, the next-hop address of the unicast prefixes is 192.168.1.6, and the next-hop address (RPF neighbor) of the multicast prefixes is 192.168.1.10.

Example 7-10 *AS 300 Has Received the Prefixes Advertised by AS 200, Using the Correct Next-Hop Addresses for the Unicast-Only and Multicast-Only Links Between Kong and Megalon*

```
Kong#show ip bgp ipv4 unicast
BGP table version is 7, local router ID is 10.254.254.1
Status codes: s suppressed, d damped, h history, * valid, > best, i - internal
Origin codes: i - IGP, e - EGP, ? - incomplete

   Network          Next Hop            Metric LocPrf Weight Path
*> 172.16.226.0/24  192.168.1.6                          0 100 200 i
*> 172.16.227.0/24  192.168.1.6                          0 100 200 i

Kong#show ip bgp ipv4 multicast
BGP table version is 10, local router ID is 10.254.254.1
Status codes: s suppressed, d damped, h history, * valid, > best, i - internal
Origin codes: i - IGP, e - EGP, ? - incomplete

   Network          Next Hop            Metric LocPrf Weight Path
*> 172.16.224.1/32  192.168.1.10                         0 100 200 i
*> 172.16.225.50/32 192.168.1.10                         0 100 200 i
*> 172.16.227.0/24  192.168.1.10                         0 100 200 i
Kong#
```

Example 7-11 shows the practical application of BGP versus MBGP advertisements. Using the 172.16.227.0/24 prefix, which is advertised both as unicast and multicast, a route lookup is performed for 172.16.227.1. The display shows that the route carries a next-hop address of 192.168.1.6, which is the unicast-only link in Figure 7-14. Next, an RPF lookup is performed on the same address. That lookup returns a next-hop address of 192.168.1.10, the multicast-only link. So the same address references two different links, depending on the function for which the address is being used.

Example 7-11 *An IP Route Lookup for 172.16.227.1 Shows the Next Hop to Be 192.168.1.6, but an RPF Lookup of the Same Address Shows a Next Hop of 192.168.1.10*

```
Kong#show ip route 172.16.227.1
Routing entry for 172.16.227.0/24
  Known via "bgp 300", distance 20, metric 0
  Tag 100, type external
  Last update from 192.168.1.6 04:10:21 ago
  Routing Descriptor Blocks:
  * 192.168.1.6, from 192.168.1.6, 04:10:21 ago
      Route metric is 0, traffic share count is 1
      AS Hops 2

Kong#show ip rpf 172.16.227.1
RPF information for ? (172.16.227.1)
  RPF interface: Serial1
  RPF neighbor: ? (192.168.1.10)
  RPF route/mask: 172.16.227.0/24
```

Example 7-11 *An IP Route Lookup for 172.16.227.1 Shows the Next Hop to Be 192.168.1.6, but an RPF Lookup of the Same Address Shows a Next Hop of 192.168.1.10 (Continued)*

```
RPF type: mbgp
RPF recursion count: 0
Doing distance-preferred lookups across tables
Kong#
```

It is worth emphasizing one last time that MBGP does not affect the forwarding of multicast traffic. Further configuration is needed in a situation such as the parallel links depicted in Figure 7-14 to force multicast traffic over the multicast-only link. MBGP just allows the dissemination of RPF information across AS boundaries.

Case Study: Configuring MSDP

Figure 7-15 again shows the routers from the preceding case study. Here, the four routers are also RPs for their respective autonomous systems, and the illustration shows their RP addresses.

Figure 7-15 *MSDP Sessions Are Configured Between the Four RPs*

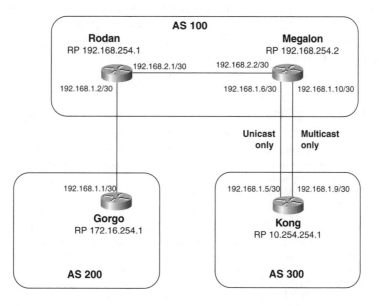

MSDP is enabled quite simply with the command **ip msdp peer**, specifying the peer's IP address. Example 7-12 shows the MSDP configurations for the four routers in Figure 7-15.

Example 7-12 *Configuring MSDP Sessions Between the Four RPs in Figure 7-15*

```
Gorgo
ip msdp peer 192.168.1.2

Kong
ip msdp peer 192.168.1.10

Rodan
ip msdp peer 192.168.1.1
ip msdp peer 192.168.254.2 connect-source Loopback0

Megalon
ip msdp peer 192.168.254.1 connect-source Loopback0
ip msdp peer 192.168.1.9
```

The peering between Gorgo and Rodan, and between Kong and Megalon, is quite straightforward. Each has only a single link over which to peer, so the session is configured between the two physical interface addresses. Between Rodan and Megalon, however, the peering is between loopback addresses. As with IBGP peering, MSDP sessions between loopback interfaces provide more resiliency. If the link shown between Rodan and Megalon in Figure 7-15 should fail, and if there is another path between the routers (not shown in the illustration), the TCP session can be rerouted. By default, the source address of the TCP packets carrying the MSDP session is the address of the originating physical interface. For peering to an address that is not part of a directly connected subnet, the **connect-source** option is used to change the default source address.

Example 7-13 displays the status of Megalon's two MSDP sessions using the **show ip msdp peer** command. Such expected information as the state of the connection, uptime, and messages sent/received appears.

Example 7-13 *The* **show ip msdp peer** *Command Displays the Status of MSDP Peering Sessions*

```
Megalon#show ip msdp peer
MSDP Peer 192.168.254.1 (?), AS 100
Description:
  Connection status:
    State: Up, Resets: 0, Connection source: Loopback0 (192.168.254.2)
    Uptime(Downtime): 3d22h, Messages sent/received: 5683/5677
    Output messages discarded: 0
    Connection and counters cleared 3d22h    ago
  SA Filtering:
    Input filter: none, route-map: none
    Output filter: none, route-map: none
  SA-Requests:
    Input filter: none
    Sending SA-Requests to peer: disabled
  Peer ttl threshold: 0
  Input queue size: 0, Output queue size: 0
```

Example 7-13 *The* **show ip msdp peer** *Command Displays the Status of MSDP Peering Sessions (Continued)*

```
MSDP Peer 192.168.1.9 (?), AS 300
Description:
  Connection status:
    State: Up, Resets: 0, Connection source: none configured
    Uptime(Downtime): 3d22h, Messages sent/received: 5674/5694
    Output messages discarded: 0
    Connection and counters cleared 3d22h    ago
  SA Filtering:
    Input filter: none, route-map: none
    Output filter: none, route-map: none
  SA-Requests:
    Input filter: none
    Sending SA-Requests to peer: disabled
  Peer ttl threshold: 0
  Input queue size: 0, Output queue size: 0
Megalon#
```

Example 7-13 also shows fields for displaying filters that might have been configured for
SA and SA Request messages. You have several options for filtering at an MSDP router to
control and scope MSDP activity. You can do the following:

- Control the local sources that are allowed to register with the RP.

- Control the SA messages the RP sends to and receives from its MSDP peers.

- Control the SA Request messages the RP sends to and receives from its peers.

Other options for larger-scale MSDP environments are the addition of descriptions for each
peer and configurable TTL values for the MSDP messages. Example 7-14 shows a more
elaborate configuration for router Megalon in Figure 7-15.

NOTE   The configuration shown here is for demonstration purposes only. No argument is made as
to the practicality of the configuration.

Example 7-14 *A More-Complex MSDP Configuration*

```
ip pim rp-address 192.168.254.2
ip msdp peer 192.168.254.1 connect-source Loopback0
ip msdp description 192.168.254.1 Rodan in AS 100
ip msdp sa-filter out 192.168.254.1 list 101
ip msdp filter-sa-request 192.168.254.1 list 1
ip msdp sa-request 192.168.254.1
ip msdp ttl-threshold 192.168.254.1 5
```

continues

Example 7-14 *A More-Complex MSDP Configuration (Continued)*

```
ip msdp peer 192.168.1.9
ip msdp description 192.168.1.9 Kong in AS 300
ip msdp sa-filter in 192.168.1.9 list 101
ip msdp sa-filter out 192.168.1.9 list 103
ip msdp sa-request 192.168.1.9
ip msdp ttl-threshold 192.168.1.9 2
ip msdp cache-sa-state list 101
ip msdp redistribute list 102
!
access-list 1 permit 229.50.0.0 0.0.255.255
access-list 101 permit ip 10.254.0.0 0.0.255.255 224.0.0.0 31.255.255.255
access-list 102 permit ip 192.168.224.0 0.0.0.255 224.0.0.0 31.255.255.255
access-list 103 permit ip 172.16.0.0 0.0.255.255 230.0.0.0 0.255.255.255
access-list 103 permit ip 192.168.224.0 0.0.0.255 224.0.0.0 31.255.255.255
```

The two statements enabling MSDP to Rodan and Kong, as shown in Example 7-12, remain. But added to the configuration is a text description for each peer, using the **ip msdp description** command. The description always appears directly after the **ip msdp peer** command for a specific peer, and it is obviously useful when there are large numbers of MSDP peers.

SA caching is enabled with **ip msdp cache-sa-state**, and in this configuration, an optional access list is referenced. Access list 101 specifies that Megalon will cache only SA messages for (S, G) pairs whose source address begins with 10.254.0.0/16. The group can be any multicast address (224.0.0.0/3).

An **ip msdp sa-request** statement is entered for each of the two peers to further reduce join latency. If the router receives a join message for a particular group, it sends an SA Request message to the two neighbors. The assumption here, as previously discussed, is that the two neighbors are configured to cache SA messages.

SA Requests to Rodan (192.168.254.1) are further restricted with the **ip msdp filter-sa-request** command. This filter references access list 1, which allows only 229.50.0.0/16. The result is that Megalon will request only source information from Rodan for groups whose addresses fall under prefix 229.50.0.0/16.

Next, Megalon is configured to send only SA messages for a subset of the possible sources that might send PIM-SM Register messages to it. The **ip msdp redistribute** statement references access list 102, which in turn permits source prefixes of 192.168.224.0/24 and group address prefixes of 224.0.0.0/3 (all multicast groups). Any source can still register with the RP, within the limits of the RP's PIM-SM configuration, but only those sources whose first 24 address bits are 192.168.224 are advertised in SA messages.

The forwarding of SA messages to MSDP peers is regulated with the **ip msdp sa-filter out** command. This filter applies to all SA messages, whether locally originated or received from another MSDP peer, whereas the **ip msdp redistribute** command applies only to

locally originated SA messages. Megalon has two of these statements. For neighbor
Rodan (192.168.254.1), only messages from source prefix 10.254.0.0/16 are forwarded, as
specified by access list 101. Megalon sends to Kong (192.168.1.9) only SA messages that
are permitted by access list 103. This access list permits messages whose source prefix is
172.16.0.0/16 and whose group addresses belong to 230.0.0.0/8, or sources whose prefix is
192.168.224.0/24 originating packets for any multicast group.

You can also filter incoming SA messages with the **ip msdp sa-filter in** command. Using
this command, Megalon accepts SA messages from Kong only if the (S, G) pair is permitted
by access list 101. Notice that this is the same constraint that is placed on outgoing SA
messages to Rodan.

Finally, the TTL values of the MSDP messages are regulated with the **ip msdp ttl-
threshold** command. The TTL of messages sent to Rodan is set to 5, whereas the TTL of
messages sent to Kong is set to 2.

Example 7-15 shows the results of this configuration. Compare this display with the display
in Example 7-13, and you can see the descriptions, filters, and TTL thresholds that have
changed.

Example 7-15 *This Display Reflects the Changes Made to Megalon's MSDP Configuration*

```
Megalon#show ip msdp peer
MSDP Peer 192.168.254.1 (?), AS 100
Description: Rodan in AS 100
  Connection status:
    State: Up, Resets: 0, Connection source: Loopback0 (192.168.254.2)
    Uptime(Downtime): 4d14h, Messages sent/received: 6624/6617
    Output messages discarded: 0
    Connection and counters cleared 4d14h    ago
  SA Filtering:
    Input filter: none, route-map: none
    Output filter: 101, route-map: none
  SA-Requests:
    Input filter: 1
    Sending SA-Requests to peer: enabled
  Peer ttl threshold: 5
  Input queue size: 0, Output queue size: 0
MSDP Peer 192.168.1.9 (?), AS 300
Description: Kong in AS 300
  Connection status:
    State: Up, Resets: 0, Connection source: none configured
    Uptime(Downtime): 4d14h, Messages sent/received: 6614/6634
    Output messages discarded: 0
    Connection and counters cleared 4d14h    ago
  SA Filtering:
    Input filter: 101, route-map: none
    Output filter: 102, route-map: none
  SA-Requests:
    Input filter: none
    Sending SA-Requests to peer: enabled
```

continues

Example 7-15 *This Display Reflects the Changes Made to Megalon's MSDP Configuration (Continued)*

```
  Peer ttl threshold: 2
  Input queue size: 0, Output queue size: 0
Megalon#
```

In addition to access lists, you can link incoming and outgoing SA filters to route maps for even better granularity of control and application of policy. You also can use route maps in conjunction with MSDP redistribution, as well as AS path access lists.

Case Study: MSDP Mesh Groups

In the preceding case study, routers Rodan and Megalon are RPs in the same AS. Large multicast domains can frequently have many RPs to share the workload or to localize multicast trees. Although MSPD has been presented so far as a tool for sharing inter-AS source information, it also proves useful when there are multiple RPs in a single domain, and sources always register to certain RPs but members throughout the domain must find any source.

Every RP in the domain commonly has an MSDP peering session to every other RP in the domain, for redundancy and robustness. Figure 7-16 shows an example. The four RPs in the illustration are in the same AS, and each is peered to the other three. The four routers may or may not be directly connected and are probably physically remote from each other.

Figure 7-16 *A Full MSDP Mesh Exists Between These Four Routers*

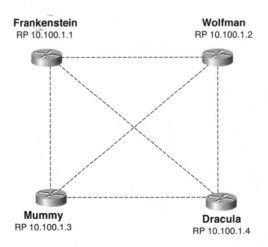

Frankenstein
RP 10.100.1.1

Wolfman
RP 10.100.1.2

Mummy
RP 10.100.1.3

Dracula
RP 10.100.1.4

Example 7-16 shows the configurations of the four routers in Figure 7-16.

Example 7-16 *Configuring MSDP on the Four Routers in Figure 7-16*

```
Frankenstein
ip pim rp-address 10.100.1.1
ip msdp peer 10.100.1.3 connect-source Loopback0
ip msdp description 10.100.1.3 to Mummy
ip msdp peer 10.100.1.2 connect-source Loopback0
ip msdp description 10.100.1.2 to Wolfman
ip msdp peer 10.100.1.4 connect-source Loopback0
ip msdp description 10.100.1.4 to Dracula

Wolfman
ip pim rp-address 10.100.1.2
ip msdp peer 10.100.1.1 connect-source Loopback0
ip msdp description 10.100.1.1 to Frankenstein
ip msdp peer 10.100.1.3 connect-source Loopback0
ip msdp description 10.100.1.3 to Mummy
ip msdp peer 10.100.1.4 connect-source Loopback0
ip msdp description 10.100.1.4 to Dracula

Mummy
ip pim rp-address 10.100.1.3
ip msdp peer 10.100.1.1 connect-source Loopback0
ip msdp description 10.100.1.1 to Frankenstein
ip msdp peer 10.100.1.2 connect-source Loopback0
ip msdp description 10.100.1.2 to Wolfman
ip msdp peer 10.100.1.4 connect-source Loopback0
ip msdp description 10.100.1.4 to Dracula

Dracula
ip pim rp-address 10.100.1.4
ip msdp peer 10.100.1.1 connect-source Loopback0
ip msdp description 10.100.1.1 to Frankenstein
ip msdp peer 10.100.1.2 connect-source Loopback0
ip msdp description 10.100.1.2 to Wolfman
ip msdp peer 10.100.1.3 connect-source Loopback0
ip msdp description 10.100.1.3 to Mummy
```

The problem with the configuration as it stands is that an SA message generated by one router is flooded by all the other routers, causing large numbers of peer RPF flooding failures and resulting MSDP notification messages. If every RP has an MSDP connection to every other RP, however, no flooding is necessary. Every RP receives a copy of every SA directly from the originator. To remedy the flooding problem, an MSDP mesh group is built.

An MSDP mesh group is a set of fully meshed MSDP peers such as the ones shown in Figure 7-16, but no transiting of SA messages takes place. That is, when an RP receives an SA from a peer, it does not forward the message to any other peer.

Mesh groups are configured with the **ip msdp mesh-group** command. The group is given an arbitrary name (so that one RP can belong to more than one mesh group, if necessary), and the members of the mesh group are specified. The configurations in Example 7-17 add the RPs in Figure 7-16 to a mesh group named Boogeymen.

Example 7-17 *Adding the RPs in Figure 7-16 to Mesh Group Boogeymen*

```
Frankenstein
ip pim rp-address 10.100.1.1
ip msdp peer 10.100.1.3 connect-source Loopback0
ip msdp description 10.100.1.3 to Mummy
ip msdp peer 10.100.1.2 connect-source Loopback0
ip msdp description 10.100.1.2 to Wolfman
ip msdp peer 10.100.1.4 connect-source Loopback0
ip msdp description 10.100.1.4 to Dracula
ip msdp mesh-group Boogeymen 10.100.1.3
ip msdp mesh-group Boogeymen 10.100.1.2
ip msdp mesh-group Boogeymen 10.100.1.4

Wolfman
ip pim rp-address 10.100.1.2
ip msdp peer 10.100.1.1 connect-source Loopback0
ip msdp description 10.100.1.1 to Frankenstein
ip msdp peer 10.100.1.3 connect-source Loopback0
ip msdp description 10.100.1.3 to Mummy
ip msdp peer 10.100.1.4 connect-source Loopback0
ip msdp description 10.100.1.4 to Dracula
ip msdp mesh-group Boogeymen 10.100.1.1
ip msdp mesh-group Boogeymen 10.100.1.3
ip msdp mesh-group Boogeymen 10.100.1.4

Mummy
ip pim rp-address 10.100.1.3
ip msdp peer 10.100.1.1 connect-source Loopback0
ip msdp description 10.100.1.1 to Frankenstein
ip msdp peer 10.100.1.2 connect-source Loopback0
ip msdp description 10.100.1.2 to Wolfman
ip msdp peer 10.100.1.4 connect-source Loopback0
ip msdp description 10.100.1.4 to Dracula
ip msdp mesh-group Boogeymen 10.100.1.1
ip msdp mesh-group Boogeymen 10.100.1.2
ip msdp mesh-group Boogeymen 10.100.1.4

Dracula
ip pim rp-address 10.100.1.4
ip msdp peer 10.100.1.1 connect-source Loopback0
ip msdp description 10.100.1.1 to Frankenstein
ip msdp peer 10.100.1.2 connect-source Loopback0
ip msdp description 10.100.1.2 to Wolfman
ip msdp peer 10.100.1.3 connect-source Loopback0
ip msdp description 10.100.1.3 to Mummy
```

Example 7-17 *Adding the RPs in Figure 7-16 to Mesh Group Boogeymen (Continued)*

```
ip msdp mesh-group Boogeymen 10.100.1.1
ip msdp mesh-group Boogeymen 10.100.1.2
ip msdp mesh-group Boogeymen 10.100.1.3
```

Case Study: Anycast RP

Designers of large, geographically diverse PIM-SM domains must often wrestle with the dilemma of where to most efficiently place the RPs. PIM-SM allows only a single group-to-RP mapping, which presents several problems in large domains:[4]

- Possible traffic bottlenecks
- Lack of scalable register decapsulation (when using shared trees)
- Slow failover when an active RP fails
- Possible suboptimal forwarding of multicast packets
- Dependence on remote RPs

You read in Chapters 5 and 6 about different schemes for alleviating some of these problems, such as the hashing algorithm used with the PIMv2 bootstrap protocol and Auto-RP filtering. None of these tools offer a completely acceptable solution. Anycast RP is a method of allowing the mapping of a single group to multiple RPs. The RPs can be distributed throughout the domain, and all use the same RP address. As a result, a "virtual RP" is created. MSDP is fundamental to the creation of a virtual RP.

NOTE   Generically, anycasting means that packets can be sent to a single address, and one of several devices can respond to the address.

Figure 7-17 shows an example where the same routers from the preceding case study are used, but all four routers are running Auto-RP and are announcing an RP address of 10.100.254.1. Source DRs within the domain know of just the one RP address and register with the closest physical RP. Normally, this causes partitioning of the PIM domain. Using an MSDP mesh group, however, the anycast RPs can exchange source information within the group.

Figure 7-17 *The Four Routers Form a Virtual RP, Announcing a Single RP Address of 10.100.254.1, and Using MSDP to Exchange Information About Sources That Have Registered to Each Router*

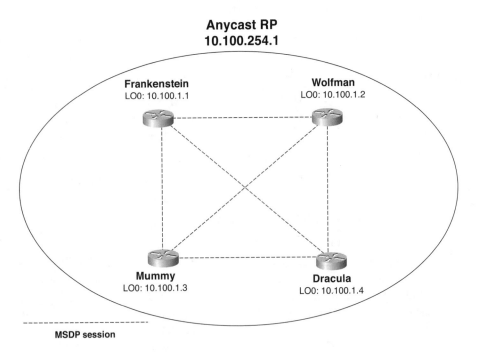

The unicast routing protocol of each anycast RP advertises the common RP address. From the perspective of source and group DRs, there is just a single RP at this address, with several routes to it. A DR chooses the shortest route, which in reality leads to the nearest anycast RP. If the anycast RP fails, the unicast protocol announces the route to the RP as unfeasible. The DR sees only the unfeasible route and chooses the next-best route, which in reality leads to the next-nearest anycast RP. As a result, RP failover is linked to and almost as fast as the unicast reconvergence time.

The MSDP peering takes place as before, between the LO0 interfaces; however, another loopback interface is used to configure the RP address that the routers announce. Normally, MSDP uses the RP address in its SA messages. Because all four routers are announcing the same RP address, MSDP must be configured to use a unique address in its SA messages. The **ip msdp originator-id** command accomplishes this. Example 7-18 shows the relevant configurations of the four routers, using mesh groups and **ip msdp originator-id**.

Example 7-18 *Configuring Frankenstein, Wolfman, Mummy, and Dracula for Anycast RP*

```
Frankenstein
interface Loopback0
 ip address 10.100.1.1 255.255.255.255
!
interface Loopback5
 ip address 10.100.254.1 255.255.255.255
 ip pim sparse-dense-mode
!
router ospf 1
 router-id 10.100.1.1
 network 0.0.0.0 255.255.255.255 area 0
!
router bgp 6500
 bgp router-id 10.100.1.1
 neighbor Boogeymen peer-group
 neighbor Boogeymen remote-as 6500
 neighbor Boogeymen update-source Loopback0
 neighbor 10.100.1.2 peer-group Boogeymen
 neighbor 10.100.1.3 peer-group Boogeymen
 neighbor 10.100.1.4 peer-group Boogeymen
 !
 address-family ipv4 multicast
 neighbor 10.100.1.2 activate
 neighbor 10.100.1.3 activate
 neighbor 10.100.1.4 activate
 exit-address-family
!
ip pim send-rp-announce Loopback5 scope 20
ip pim send-rp-discovery Loopback5 scope 20
ip msdp peer 10.100.1.3 connect-source Loopback0
ip msdp description 10.100.1.3 to Mummy
ip msdp peer 10.100.1.2 connect-source Loopback0
ip msdp description 10.100.1.2 to Wolfman
ip msdp peer 10.100.1.4 connect-source Loopback0
ip msdp description 10.100.1.4 to Dracula
ip msdp mesh-group Boogeymen 10.100.1.3
ip msdp mesh-group Boogeymen 10.100.1.2
ip msdp mesh-group Boogeymen 10.100.1.4
ip msdp cache-sa-state
ip msdp originator-id Loopback0

Wolfman
interface Loopback0
 ip address 10.100.1.2 255.255.255.255
!
interface Loopback5
 ip address 10.100.254.1 255.255.255.255
 ip pim sparse-dense-mode
```

continues

Example 7-18 *Configuring Frankenstein, Wolfman, Mummy, and Dracula for Anycast RP (Continued)*

```
!
router ospf 1
 router-id 10.100.1.2
 network 0.0.0.0 255.255.255.255 area 0
!
router bgp 6500
 bgp router-id 10.100.1.2
 neighbor Boogeymen peer-group
 neighbor Boogeymen remote-as 6500
 neighbor Boogeymen update-source Loopback0
 neighbor 10.100.1.1 peer-group Boogeymen
 neighbor 10.100.1.3 peer-group Boogeymen
 neighbor 10.100.1.4 peer-group Boogeymen
 !
 address-family ipv4 multicast
 neighbor 10.100.1.1 activate
 neighbor 10.100.1.3 activate
 neighbor 10.100.1.4 activate
 exit-address-family
 !
ip pim send-rp-announce Loopback5 scope 20
ip pim send-rp-discovery Loopback5 scope 20
ip msdp peer 10.100.1.1 connect-source Loopback0
ip msdp description 10.100.1.1 to Frankenstein
ip msdp peer 10.100.1.3 connect-source Loopback0
ip msdp description 10.100.1.3 to Mummy
ip msdp peer 10.100.1.4 connect-source Loopback0
ip msdp description 10.100.1.4 to Dracula
ip msdp mesh-group Boogeymen 10.100.1.1
ip msdp mesh-group Boogeymen 10.100.1.3
ip msdp mesh-group Boogeymen 10.100.1.4
ip msdp cache-sa-state
ip msdp originator-id Loopback0
```

Mummy
```
interface Loopback0
 ip address 10.100.1.3 255.255.255.255
!
interface Loopback5
 ip address 10.100.254.1 255.255.255.255
 ip pim sparse-dense-mode
!
router ospf 1
 router-id 10.100.1.3
 network 0.0.0.0 255.255.255.255 area 0
!
router bgp 6500
 bgp router-id 10.100.1.3
 neighbor Boogeymen peer-group
 neighbor Boogeymen remote-as 6500
 neighbor Boogeymen update-source Loopback0
```

Example 7-18 *Configuring Frankenstein, Wolfman, Mummy, and Dracula for Anycast RP (Continued)*

```
 neighbor 10.100.1.1 peer-group Boogeymen
 neighbor 10.100.1.2 peer-group Boogeymen
 neighbor 10.100.1.4 peer-group Boogeymen
 !
 address-family ipv4 multicast
 neighbor 10.100.1.1 activate
 neighbor 10.100.1.2 activate
 neighbor 10.100.1.4 activate
 exit-address-family
ip pim send-rp-announce Loopback5 scope 20
ip pim send-rp-discovery Loopback5 scope 20
ip msdp peer 10.100.1.1 connect-source Loopback0
ip msdp description 10.100.1.1 to Frankenstein
ip msdp peer 10.100.1.2 connect-source Loopback0
ip msdp description 10.100.1.2 to Wolfman
ip msdp peer 10.100.1.4 connect-source Loopback0
ip msdp description 10.100.1.4 to Dracula
ip msdp mesh-group Boogeymen 10.100.1.1
ip msdp mesh-group Boogeymen 10.100.1.2
ip msdp mesh-group Boogeymen 10.100.1.4
ip msdp cache-sa-state
ip msdp originator-id Loopback0
```

Dracula
```
interface Loopback0
 ip address 10.100.1.4 255.255.255.255
 !
interface Loopback5
 ip address 10.100.254.1 255.255.255.255
 ip pim sparse-dense-mode
 !
router ospf 1
 router-id 10.100.1.4
 network 0.0.0.0 255.255.255.255 area 0
 !
router bgp 6500
 bgp router-id 10.100.1.4
 neighbor Boogeymen peer-group
 neighbor Boogeymen remote-as 6500
 neighbor Boogeymen update-source Loopback0
 neighbor 10.100.1.1 peer-group Boogeymen
 neighbor 10.100.1.2 peer-group Boogeymen
 neighbor 10.100.1.3 peer-group Boogeymen
 !
 address-family ipv4 multicast
 neighbor 10.100.1.1 activate
 neighbor 10.100.1.2 activate
 neighbor 10.100.1.3 activate
 exit-address-family
```

continues

Example 7-18 *Configuring Frankenstein, Wolfman, Mummy, and Dracula for Anycast RP (Continued)*

```
!
ip pim send-rp-announce Loopback5 scope 20
ip pim send-rp-discovery Loopback5 scope 20
ip msdp peer 10.100.1.1 connect-source Loopback0
ip msdp description 10.100.1.1 to Frankenstein
ip msdp peer 10.100.1.2 connect-source Loopback0
ip msdp description 10.100.1.2 to Wolfman
ip msdp peer 10.100.1.3 connect-source Loopback0
ip msdp description 10.100.1.3 to Mummy
ip msdp mesh-group Boogeymen 10.100.1.1
ip msdp mesh-group Boogeymen 10.100.1.2
ip msdp mesh-group Boogeymen 10.100.1.3
ip msdp cache-sa-state
ip msdp originator-id Loopback0
```

In Example 7-18, each of the four routers is configured as both an Auto-RP candidate RP and a mapping agent. You also can use static mapping or PIMv2 bootstrap with anycast RP. All four routers in this example are configured to cache SA messages.

Interface LO5 is used on each router to configure the virtual RP address, whereas LO0 is the endpoint of the MSDP sessions. Notice in the configurations that the Auto-RP commands reference LO5, whereas the **ip msdp originator-id** command references LO0. This is vital, because MSDP must have unique IP addresses at the endpoints of its peering sessions.

The OSPF and BGP stanzas are shown for an important reason. Recall that OSPF and BGP use the highest IP address configured on any loopback interface as its router ID. Unfortunately, the IP address on LO5 is higher on each router than the IP address on LO0. As a result, the OSPF and BGP processes on each router would by default use a router ID of 10.100.254.1. One of many undesirable results would be the thrashing of the OSPF databases as each router's LSAs try to override the other routers' LSAs. One solution is to always use a virtual RP address that is numerically lower than any other loopback address, but there are obvious impracticalities in this and some large vulnerabilities to inadvertent configuration mistakes. A better solution, used in this example, is to force each router to use its unique LO0 address with the **router-id** statement under the OSPF and BGP configurations.

Notice also that the LO0 interfaces are not running PIM. These interfaces are unnecessary to PIM functionality, and serve only to provide router-specific IP addresses for MSDP peering.

Case Study: MSDP Default Peers

If an AS is a stub or nontransit AS, and particularly if the AS is not multihomed, there is little or no reason to run BGP to its transit AS. A static default route at the stub AS, and a static route pointing to the stub prefixes at the transit AS, is generally sufficient. But what if the stub AS is also a multicast domain and its RP must peer with an RP in the neighboring domain? The overview of the MSDP operation explained that MSDP depends on the BGP next-hop database for its peer RPF checks.

You can disable this dependency on BGP with the **ip msdp default-peer** command. MSDP just accepts all SA messages from default peers. Figure 7-18 shows a simple example. Here, the stub AS is peered to the transit AS by a single link. RPF checks are not necessary, because there is only one path and therefore no possibility of loops.

Figure 7-18 *BGP Is Typically Not Run Between a Stub AS and Its Transit AS, but This Can Cause a Problem for MSDP*

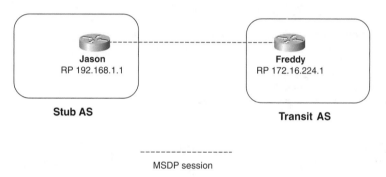

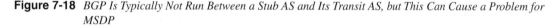

Example 7-19 shows the MSDP configuration of the two routers.

Example 7-19 *MSDP Configurations for Routers Jason and Freddy*

```
Jason
ip msdp peer 172.16.224.1 connect-source Loopback0
ip msdp default-peer 172.16.224.1

Freddy
ip msdp peer 192.168.1.1 connect-source Loopback0
ip msdp default-peer 192.168.1.1
```

A stub AS also might want to have MSDP peering with more than one RP for the sake of redundancy, as shown in Figure 7-19. SA messages cannot just be accepted from both default peers, because there is no RPF check mechanism. Instead, SA messages are accepted from only one peer. If that peer fails, messages are then accepted from the other peer. The underlying assumption here, of course, is that both default peers are sending the same SA messages.

Figure 7-19 *Jason Is Connected to More Than One Default MSDP Peer*

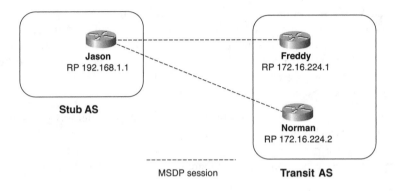

Example 7-20 shows the configuration for Jason.

Example 7-20 *Configuring Jason to Have Redundant Peering with Both Freddy and Norman*

```
ip msdp peer 172.16.224.1 connect-source Loopback0
ip msdp peer 172.16.224.2 connect-source Loopback0
ip msdp default-peer 172.16.224.1
ip msdp default-peer 172.16.224.2
```

Under normal circumstances, the active default peer is the first peer in the configuration—in this case, 172.16.224.1. SAs are not accepted from 172.16.224.2 unless 172.16.224.1 fails.

The RP in a transit AS is likely to have more than one default MSDP peer, as shown in Figure 7-20. Just listing the default peers, as was shown in the preceding example, does not work, because SAs would be accepted by only a single peer. To cause the RP to accept SA messages from multiple peers while still providing loop avoidance in the absence of a peer RPF check, BGP-style prefix lists are used. The RP then accepts SA messages from all of its default peers, but only for source prefixes allowed by each peer's associated prefix list. The underlying assumption here is that each AS is using distinct prefixes, so loop avoidance is ensured.

Figure 7-20 *The RP in the Transit AS Has Three Default MSDP Peers*

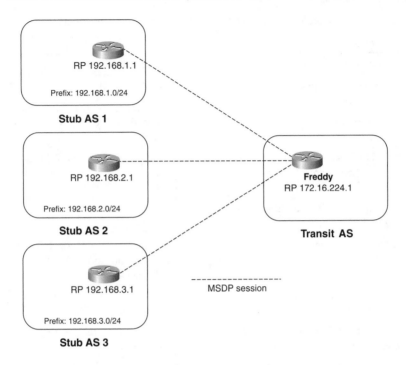

Example 7-21 shows the configuration for Freddy.

Example 7-21 *Configuring an RP to Accept SA Messages from Multiple Peers*

```
ip msdp peer 192.168.1.1 connect-source Loopback0
ip msdp peer 192.168.2.1 connect-source Loopback0
ip msdp peer 192.168.3.1 connect-source Loopback0
ip msdp default-peer 192.168.1.1 prefix-list AS1
ip msdp default-peer 192.168.2.1 prefix-list AS2
ip msdp default-peer 192.168.3.1 prefix-list AS3
!
ip prefix-list AS1 seq 5 permit 192.168.1.0/24 le 32
ip prefix-list AS2 seq 5 permit 192.168.2.0/24 le 32
ip prefix-list AS3 seq 5 permit 192.168.3.0/24 le 32
```

Command Summary

Table 7-6 lists and describes the commands discussed in this chapter.

Table 7-6   *Command Summary*

Command	Description
address-family {**ipv4** | **vpnv4**} {**multicast** | **unicast** | **vrf**}	Enables MBGP.
exit-address-family	Marks the end of the MBGP configuration stanzas.
ip mroute *source mask* [*protocol as-number*] {*rpf-address* | *type number*} [*distance*]	Configures a static mroute used for RPF checks.
ip msdp cache-sa-state [**list** *access-list-number*]	Enables SA caching.
ip msdp default-peer *ip-address* | *name* [**prefix-list** *list*]	Specifies an MSDP peer from which SA messages are accepted without performing an RPF check.
ip msdp description {*peer-name* | *peer-address*} *text*	Adds descriptive text to an MSDP peer configuration.
ip msdp filter-sa-request {*ip-address* | *name*} [**list** *access-list-number*]	Enables a filter for outgoing SA Request messages.
ip msdp mesh-group name {*ip-address* | *name*}	Designates a peer to be a member of a mesh group. SA messages from a mesh group member are not forwarded to other mesh group members.
ip msdp originator-id *type number*	Changes the default RP address used in MSDP messages.
ip msdp peer {*peer-name* | *peer-address*} [**connect-source** *type number*] [**remote-as** *as-number*]	Designates a router as an MSDP peer.
ip msdp redistribute [**list** *access-list-name*] [**asn** *aspath-access-list-number*] [**route-map** *map*]	Enables a filter for MSDP SA messages originated by the local router.
ip msdp sa-filter in {*ip-address* | *name*} [**list** *access-list-name*] [**route-map** *map-tag*]	Enables a filter for incoming MSDP SA messages.
ip msdp sa-filter out {*ip-address* | *name*} [**list** *access-list-name*] [**route-map** *map-tag*]	Enables a filter for outgoing MSDP messages.

Table 7-6   *Command Summary (Continued)*

ip msdp sa-request {*ip-address* | *name*}	Enables an RP to send MSDP SA Request messages to the designated caching peer.
ip msdp ttl-threshold {*ip-address* | *name*} *ttl*	Sets a TTL value for MSDP messages originated by the local router.
ip multicast boundary *access-list-number*	Designates an interface as a multicast boundary for administrative scoping.
ip multicast ttl-threshold *ttl-value*	Designates an interface as a multicast boundary for TTL scoping.
neighbor {*ip-address* | *name*} **activate**	Specifies an MBGP neighbor to be activated for unicast, multicast, or both.
no bgp default ipv4-unicast	Disables the default designation of all BGP neighbors as unicast so that unicast neighbors can be individually activated.
show ip msdp peer *peer-address* | *name*	Displays detailed information about MSDP peers.
show ip msdp sa-cache [*group-address* | *source-address* | *group-name* | *source-name*] [*group-address* | *source-address* | *group-name* | *source-name*] [*autonomous-system-number*]	Displays information about SA state cached in the local router.
show ip msdp summary	Displays summary information about MSDP peers.

End Notes

[1]David Meyer, "RFC 2365: Administratively Scoped IP Multicast," (Work in Progress).

[2]Tony Bates, Ravi Chandra, Dave Katz, and Yakov Rekhter, "RFC 2283: Multiprotocol Extensions for BGP-4," (Work in Progress).

[3]Dino Farinacci et al., "Multicast Source Discovery Protocol (MSDP)," draft-ietf-msdp-spec-05.txt, February, 2000.

[4]Dorain Kim, David Meyer, Henry Kilmer, and Dino Farinacci, "Anycast RP Mechanism Using PIM and MSDP," draft-ietf-mboned-anycast-rp-05.txt, January, 2000.

Looking Ahead

You have, at this point, invested a sizeable portion of your time to learning not only the ins and outs of IP routing, but also the problems presented by the growing complexity of routing in modern IP networks. Many of the solutions to these problems involve working with (or around) the limitations of IPv4 and its associated routing protocols. The next chapter shows how the newest version of the IP protocol, IPv6, has been created with the lessons of IPv4 firmly in mind. When most people think of IPv6, they think primarily of 128-bit addresses and the alleviation of the IPv4 addressing limitations. As you will see, however, IPv6 is much more. It is designed for better security, better inter-AS qualities, and better support for multicasting, while at the same time eliminating many of the unnecessary complexities of IPv4.

Review Questions

1 In the section "Multicast Scoping," a sample configuration is given for administrative scoping. The boundary at interface E0 blocks organization-local packets (destination addresses whose prefixes match 239.192.0.0/14) but passes packets with global scope. Will a packet with a group address 224.0.0.50 pass this boundary?

   _____

   _____

   _____

2 How does Cisco IOS Software handle DVMRP Prune messages on point-to-point and multiaccess interfaces that are configured to run PIM?

   _____

   _____

   _____

3 Why does Cisco IOS Software accept DVMRP Probe messages, but does not send them?

   _____

   _____

   _____

4 What is a PIM (*,*,RP) entry?

   _____

   _____

   _____

5 How does Multiprotocol BGP (MBGP) differ from normal BGP?

_____

_____

_____

6 What is the MBGP AFI?

_____

_____

_____

7 Is the following statement true or false? MSDP carries information about multicast sources and group members between RPs in different PIM domains.

_____

_____

_____

8 What is the transport protocol for MSDP?

_____

_____

_____

9 What is an MSDP SA message?

_____

_____

_____

10 How does an MSDP RP determine whether an SA was received on an RPF interface?

_____

_____

_____

11 What is SA caching?

_____

_____

_____

12 Is there an alternative to reducing join latency without enabling SA caching?

_____

_____

_____

This chapter covers the following key topics:

- **Design Goals of IPv6**—This section covers IPv6's design goals: enable scalable networks, ease configuration, and maintain security.

- **Current State of IPv6**—This section covers the standards and drafts that are available, vendor support or announced support, and customer-driven applications that will begin demanding its implementation.

- **IPv6 Packet Format**—This section covers the IPv6 packet format, which includes the large, hierarchical IPv6 addresses and headers that enable routers to efficiently process the packet.

- **IPv6 Functionality**—This section covers IPv6 functionality, including automatic router discovery, dead neighbor detection, automatic host configuration, and multicasting capabilities.

- **Transition from IPv4 to IPv6**—IPv4 will exist for a long time. This section covers transition mechanisms (including dual stacks, tunnels, and address/protocol translation) that ease the transition to IPv6 and enable coexistence.

CHAPTER 8

IP Version 6

IP version 6 (IPv6) is designed to be the new generation of the IP protocol, following IP version 4. The number 5 had already been assigned to another Internet protocol, the Internet Stream Protocol, version II, as defined in RFC 1190. A detailed description of all IPv6 components is beyond the scope of this book, but this chapter thoroughly summarizes the design goals of IPv6 and the current state of the protocol. This chapter also covers IPv6 packet format, IPv6 functionality, and methods to get from IPv4 internetworks to IPv6 internetworks. The Cisco router configurations shown in this chapter are created using beta software that is based on IOS 12.0. Commands may be modified, added, or deleted, and output may be modified in the final version of the code, although any changes will probably be minimal. Cisco has announced that the production code will be in a later version of Cisco IOS Software Release 12.1.

Design Goals of IPv6

The Internet has been a huge success, driving the success of corporate internetworks. Few businesses are without Web sites these days (URLs can even be found on the corks of wine bottles), and e-mail is as important a business tool as the telephone. But certain aspects of IPv4 place an upper limit on how large the Internet can grow. 32 bits of address space limits the number of globally routable hosts that can connect and also limits the amount of hierarchy that can be created. As you have observed throughout much of this book, scalable internetworks require hierarchical routing. Hierarchical routing must be strictly maintained to enable the network to scale beyond the uses that application developers and Internet users are dreaming of today. To maintain hierarchy, Internet-connected sites must adhere to addressing and aggregation rules. Sites connected to an ISP or exchange usually must use addresses allocated to that ISP or exchange and reallocated to the site. This means that renumbering, with all the inherent difficulties described early in Chapter 2, "Introduction to Border Gateway Protocol 4," will remain an issue.

The success of the Internet also may increase data integrity, authenticity, and confidentiality requirements.

IPv4 network designers have alleviated some of these issues using a number of different techniques. As discussed in Chapter 4, "Network Address Translation," a network may use private addresses internally, using network address translation to communicate with the

Internet or other companies, thereby mitigating the address space problem, allowing a huge number of nodes to access external internetworks. However, NAT is not always easy to implement and maintain. Some applications create excessive processing requirements on the NAT device, and other applications do not work at all. Furthermore, future Internet appliances, such as personal digital assistants, home security systems, or car maintenance computers, might require globally routable addresses so that they can be accessed from any Internet location.

The severe IPv4 hierarchy problems imposed by classful addresses were mitigated with the implementation of CIDR, as discussed in Chapter 2. CIDR enables you to group and divide more efficiently, but the total hierarchy is still limited to 32 bits of addressing space.

IPv6 addresses are so much bigger that there is enough address space for a large increase in globally routable addresses and for more layers of hierarchy. The size of the address space increased to 128 bits. Hierarchy is designed into the format of globally routable addresses.

ISPs assign a range of addresses to their clients. If the client wants to change ISPs, it most likely has to re-address its network. IPv4 network designers have implemented Dynamic Host Configuration Protocol (DHCP) to ease the burden of re-addressing PCs. DHCP works and will likely continue to be used with IPv6. IPv6 hosts can use DHCP or the built-in autoconfiguration method to configure themselves. Both methods can utilize the capability of IPv6 hosts to use the new address for new connections and to continue using the old address for existing connections. This capability to maintain two addresses ensures a smooth migration to a new network prefix.

Improve Scalability

You saw in Chapter 2 how IPv4 addresses restrict the scalability of internetworks. This section recaps those scalability problems. The first IPv4 problem is the limit of 32 bits for addressing, one of the main drivers for designing a new protocol. Pundits assumed that without intervention, IPv4 addresses would be depleted by the mid-1990s. That did not happen. NAT prolonged the life of IPv4 by allowing enterprises to use private addresses that are hidden from the public Internet. IPv6's 128 bits of address space allows many more globally routable devices to connect to the Internet. Private address space is also defined in IPv6.

Another problem with IPv4 is the large size of the Internet routing tables. CIDR was introduced to minimize the table size by introducing more hierarchy by aggregating addresses. However, many addresses cannot be aggregated. Addresses that were assigned before CIDR and addresses used by networks with certain multihomed Internet connections, for instance, cannot be aggregated.

IPv6 is designed for scalability, ease of configuration, and security, drawing from the lessons learned with IPv4. It is not designed to solve the Internet routing table size explosion. With strict allocation rules and procedures initiated from the start, and adherence to the hierarchy format for aggregation, however, table size can be contained. The goal is to achieve as much aggregation as possible, and the defined format of the globally routable address space facilitates this goal.

Ease of Configuration

IPv6 introduces mechanisms to ease host-to-router communication management and host configuration. These mechanisms are essential to the success of IPv6. As more and more people, schools, and businesses want to connect to the Internet or build their own internetworks, the tasks involved in enabling them must be simplified. Not everyone wants to become a CCIE just so he or she can figure out how to run a network. They just want the networks to work. IPv6 has automatic configuration mechanisms that enable hosts to obtain IP addresses, discover neighbors and default routers, and effectively use multiple default routers for redundancy.

Large companies connected to the Internet want the flexibility to change service providers without creating turmoil within their own networks. Renumbering networks will still be required with IPv6, but renumbering is made easier with the ability to maintain multiple addresses on all nodes and to have two different address states—one for use with active addresses and the other for use when an address is being phased out. In addition, network prefixes are advertised by routers to hosts, enabling the hosts to automatically configure themselves with IPv6 addresses. A company that needs to re-address its network because it changed ISPs can configure the routers to advertise the new prefixes as well as the old prefix. Hosts that receive the advertisement can automatically configure themselves with the new prefix information and can begin using the new addresses when new IP connections are made. Existing connections will continue to use the old address.

Security

People and businesses do not want to worry about security either. They want their data to be secure without thinking much about it. Authentication and encryption are built into IPv6. IPv6 packets can now be secured at the network layer within the network protocol.

Current State of IPv6

For most organizations, IPv6 has not been much more than a new set of letters and numbers to toss around when talking about networking. Now, however, more of the specifications are becoming finalized, many are IETF draft standards, and many more are proposed draft standards. IANA allocated address space to the regional Internet registries (RIR), and the RIRs have begun allocating address space to Internet providers. Network and end-station equipment vendors have begun releasing software that supports IPv6, or have announced near-term plans to offer support. A large test network, the 6bone, exists to allow organizations to try out their IPv6 implementations, to learn how to transition their networks, and to get used to managing them. A public production network, 6REN, also exists for research and education institutions ready to deploy production IPv6 networks. Network planners may begin to think more about IPv6 as it becomes more readily available and easier to implement. CCIE candidates should be ready to tackle IPv6 as well.

IPv6 Specification (RFCs)

The IPv6 specification is now an approved draft standard. Companies have released (or prereleased) products based on the specifications. Current draft standards include the following:

- RFC 2373: IP Version 6 Addressing Architecture
- RFC 2374: An IPv6 Aggregatable Global Unicast Address Format
- RFC 2460: Internet Protocol, Version 6 (IPv6) Specification
- RFC 2461: Neighbor Discovery for IP Version 6 (IPv6)
- RFC 2462: IPv6 Stateless Address Autoconfiguration
- RFC 2463: Internet Control Message Protocol (ICMPv6) for the Internet Protocol Version 6 (IPv6) Specification

Many components of IPv6 are currently proposed draft standards that are awaiting approval, including the following:

- RFC 1886: DNS Extensions to Support IP Version 6
- RFC 1887: An Architecture for IPv6 Unicast Address Allocation
- RFC 1981: Path MTU Discovery for IP Version 6
- RFC 2080: RIPng for IPv6
- RFC 2473: Generic Packet Tunneling in IPv6 Specification
- RFC 2526: Reserved IPv6 Subnet Anycast Addresses
- RFC 2529: Transmission of IPv6 over IPv4 Domains Without Explicit Tunnels
- RFC 2545: Use of BGP-4 Multiprotocol Extensions for IPv6 Inter-Domain Routing
- RFC 2710: Multicast Listener Discovery (MLD) for IPv6
- RFC 2740: OSPF for IPv6

There are many other proposed draft standards and related draft documents, and many more are expected in the near future, making it impractical to list them all here. You can find the RFCs at www.isi.edu or at many other RFC repositories.

Vendor Support

The protocol development of IPv6 and related components is far enough along in the standards process that vendors have committed to many development and testing projects. Cisco routers currently support IPv6 in a beta version of IOS based on version 12.1. They have announced IOS support in a later 12.1 release. Microsoft and Sun have IPv6 stacks available for end stations. Not all vendors support all IPv6 components. Some are waiting for the standards to mature; others are waiting for more customer pressure before committing the development resources to it. Upcoming large-scale applications, such as handheld wireless computers, may require IPv6, and vendors should at least have a plan for quickly implementing it. Cisco's IPv6 implementation currently supports the following features:

- RIPv6
- BGP-4+ for IPv6
- IPv6 static routes
- Traffic filtering
- Automatic and static tunnels
- EUI-64 addressing
- Neighbor discovery
- IPv6 over Ethernet, FDDI, Cisco HDLC, and ATM PVCs
- Dual-stack support for Telnet, DNS, and TFTP
- ICMPv6 and Ping
- traceroute and debug commands

Implementations

There are two IPv6 implementations for public use. One, the 6bone, is used as a testbed for IPv6 issues. Protocol implementations, IPv4 to IPv6 transitions, and operational procedures have all been tested using the 6bone network. The other network, IPv6 Research and Education Networks (6REN), provides organizations with operational IPv6 networks to transit to other IPv6 networks. Both implementations have been instrumental in the IPv6 development process, giving vendors and network architects large-scale platforms on which to test software, network configurations, and designs, and on which to gain understanding and familiarity with the protocol.

6bone

The 6bone is a worldwide IPv6 network used for testing and preproduction deployment of IPv6 products and networks. It currently supports 260 organizations in 39 countries. The

6bone is designed to look like a global, hierarchical, IPv6 network. It contains pseudo top-level (Tier I) transit providers, pseudo next-level (Tier II) transit providers, and pseudo site-level organizations. The pseudo top-level providers are interconnected organizations around the world. Top-level providers communicate with each other using IPv6 extensions to BGP-4. Next-level providers connect to a regional top-level provider, also using BGP-4, and site-level organizations connect to the next-level providers. Site-level organizations can default route to their providers or use BGP-4. Connections were originally made by tunneling packets in IPv4 and transporting them over the Internet. Gradually, native IPv6 connections are now being made. The 6bone has proven to be a very instrumental testbed for IPv6 standards and products. Now it also is being used to test transitions and operational procedures. Figure 8-1 shows the 6bone backbone.

Figure 8-1 *6bone Backbone*

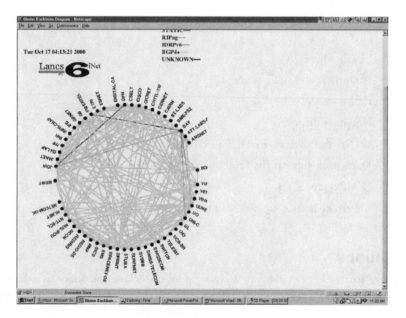

6REN

The 6REN voluntary coordination initiative is a production IPv6 network designed to provide transit IPv6 services. As stated at the www.6ren.net/overview.htm Web site, the 6REN goal is as follows:

. . .provide production IPv6 transit service to facilitate high quality, high performance, and operationally robust IPv6 networks.

The transit services are available to research and educational institutions and for-profit and not-for-profit organizations. Networks are interconnected with native IPv6 over ATM. 6REN provides connectivity to the 6bone participants as well.

IPv6 Packet Format

The IPv6 packet format includes a large, hierarchical IPv6 address and headers that enable routers to efficiently process the packet. The address is large enough to allow for considerable Internet growth and to provide many layers of hierarchy.

Some IPv4 header fields have been removed. Removal of the Options field and the requirement that all routers process the options has made the packet processing more efficient. The network options are still available; in most cases, however, the options need to be processed only by the destination node. IPv6 moves the options processing to extension headers that are processed only by the nodes that need the information.

The IPv6 address types, uses, and structure, as well as the IPv6 header, are discussed in detail in this section.

The IPv6 Address

When IP was first developed in the 1970s, the Internet world was very different. The Internet was used for research and education. An address space of 32 bits must have seemed like more than would ever be needed, at least for the lifetime of IP. The success of the Internet has been so great that IP is embedded into the operation of many businesses and homes. IP networks are integral parts of the day-to-day operations of many very successful organizations. As the organizations grow and the number of sites that want to connect to the Internet grows, the concern for a more scalable solution will grow. So many devices use (or will use in the near future) IP addresses to access internetworks that even the methods developed to prolong the depletion of IP addresses, such as NAT and CIDR, soon will not be enough. Cell phones, PDAs, e-mail appliances, home lighting systems, cars, and utility meters will all have IP addresses. The very success of IP is straining many aspects of its original design.

IPv6 addresses issues that are causing the strain. It increases the address size and defines more address hierarchy. It also defines rules governing allocation of the addresses to maintain the hierarchical aggregation capability.

Address Size

What is the appropriate size for an address that is so widely used? Should the address size be fixed or variable? Too small of an address limits scalability. Too large of an address creates too large of a header, making it difficult for routers (and people) to manage.

Variable-length addresses increase software complexity and can slow down packet processing. One proposal for the next generation of IP (IPng) suggested using network service access point (NSAP) addresses, which could vary between 1 and 20 octets in length. Another proposal suggested 64 bits of address space. Although 64 bits seemed like enough space to address IP nodes, more bits were added to account for the extra complexity that would result from the increase in the complexity of the Internet as its size increased. To allow future growth and address allocation hierarchy, 128 bits was chosen.

340,282,366,920,938,463,463,374,607,431,768,211,456 nodes can be theoretically addressed with 128 bits. If the total human population of the world is 10 billion, that's roughly $3.4 * 10^{27}$ addresses per person. Even tomorrow's on-the-go, highly connected telecommuter, with an Internet cell phone, an IP watch, a home network with routable appliances and utility meters, and a networked car won't use that many addresses.

Text Representation of Addresses

The IPv6 address is 128 bits long, written as eight 16-bit pieces, separated by colons. Each piece is represented by four hexadecimal digits. Two addresses are shown here:

- FEDC:BA98:7654:3210:FEDC:BA98:7654:3210
- 1080:0000:0000:0000:0008:0800:200C:417A

These addresses are large, capable of addressing lots of nodes and providing hierarchical flexibility, but they are not very easy to write down, let alone remember. There are ways to compress the addresses to make them a bit easier for a mere human to manipulate.

An address is very likely to have many zeros. In any 16-bit field, you can remove the leading zeros, but at least one digit must be present in every field, with one exception. Address 1 in the preceding example does not have any leading zeros in any field and cannot compact. Address 2 can compact as follows:

> 1080:0:0:0:8:800:200C:417A

You can compact multiple contiguous fields of zero even further. This is the exception to the rule that at least one digit must be present in every field. You can replace multiple fields of zeros with double colons (::). Table 8-1 shows some address compactions.

Table 8-1   *Examples of Address Compaction Show That Multiple Contiguous Fields of Zeros Can Be Compacted to ::*

Address Before Compaction	Address After Compaction
1080:0000:0000:0000:0008:0800:200C:417A	1080::8:800:200C:417A
1080:0000:0000:3245:0000:0000:200C:417A	1080:0:0:3245::200C:417A
0000:0000:0000:0000:0000:0000:0000:0001	::1
0000:0000:0000:0000:0000:0000:0000:0000	::

Trailing or leading fields of zeros can be compacted. Note that :: can replace only one set of contiguous zero fields. Multiple ::s would make the address ambiguous. For example, the incorrectly written address 1080::3245::200c:417A does not provide sufficient information about the correct position in the address of the two octets Ox3245.

You can use another form of address in certain mixed IPv6 and IPv4 modes. This form combines the colon-separated hexadecimal fields of IPv6 with the dotted-decimal notation of IPv4, as follows:

> X:X:X:X:X:X:d.d.d.d

X represents the hexadecimal digits of the IPv6 address and d.d.d.d notates the last 32 bits of the address in dotted-decimal notation. Table 8-2 shows some examples of this mixed-mode format.

Table 8-2 *Text Representation of Addresses in a Mixed IPv6 and IPv4 Environment*

Expanded Format	Compressed Format
0:0:0:0:0:0:13.1.68.3	::13.1.68.3
0:0:0:0:0:0:129.144.52.38	::129.144.52.38

The mixed IPv6/IPv4 address representation provides a method for IPv6 and IPv4 nodes to coexist on the same network. The section "Transition from IPv4 to IPv6" later in this chapter discusses the transition and coexistence methods.

Text Representation of Address Prefixes

IPv6 address prefix representation is similar to IPv4 CIDR notation. IPv6 prefix notation is as follows:

> *IPv6-address/prefix-length*

where:

> *IPv6-address* is any valid address.
> *prefix-length* is the number of contiguous bits that comprise the prefix.

The following prefixes are legal textual representations for the 56-bit prefix 200F00000000AB:

> 200F::AB00:0:0:0:0/56
> 200F:0:0:AB00::/56

Note that as with IPv6 host addresses, the double colon is used only once in each representation.

The following are not valid representations of the 56-bit prefix 200F00000000AB:

> 200F:0:0:AB/56
> 200F::AB00/56
> 200F::AB/56

The first notation is not valid because a trailing zero was dropped within one of the 16-bit fields, and the address is not a valid length. The IPv6 address on the left of the forward slash (/) must be a valid full-length or compacted IPv6 address. The second and third notations are valid compacted IPv6 addresses, but they do not expand to the correct address. Instead of 200F:0000:0000:AB00:0000:0000:0000:0000, they expand to 200F:0000:0000:0000:0000:0000:0000:AB00 and 200F:0000:0000:0000:0000:0000:0000:00AB, respectively.

Address Type Allocation

Before CIDR, the high-order bits in an IPv4 address defined its type—Class A, B, C, D, or E. The type identified a fixed-length network portion and a host portion that the owner of the address was free to use as he pleased. This was the only defined structure in an IPv4 address. IPv6 addresses have more structure defined. The structure is discussed fully in the later section "Address Structure." The high-order bits define IPv6 address types. The variable-length field comprising these bits is called the *format prefix* (FP). Table 8-3 shows the initial allocation of these prefixes.

Table 8-3   *IPv6 Prefix Allocation*

Allocation	Prefix (Binary)	Fraction of Address Space
Reserved	0000 0000	1/256
Unassigned	0000 0001	1/256
Reserved for NSAP allocation	0000 001	1/128
Reserved for IPX allocation	0000 010	1/128
Unassigned	0000 011	1/128
Unassigned	0000 1	1/32
Unassigned	0001	1/16
Aggregatable global unicast addresses	001	1/8
Unassigned	010	1/8
Unassigned	011	1/8
Unassigned	100	1/8
Unassigned	101	1/8
Unassigned	110	1/8

Table 8-3   *IPv6 Prefix Allocation (Continued)*

Unassigned	1110	1/16
Unassigned	1111 0	1/32
Unassigned	1111 10	1/64
Unassigned	1111 110	1/128
Unassigned	1111 1110 0	1/512
Link-local unicast addresses	1111 1110 10	1/1024
Site-local unicast addresses	1111 1110 11	1/1024
Multicast addresses	1111 1111	1/256

Address space is allocated for aggregatable globally routable addresses, local-use addresses, and multicast addresses. Only about 15 percent of the address space is currently allocated.

Some space is reserved. Space is reserved for future implementations of NSAP and IPX routing. A portion of the reserved space, particularly 0x00, is used for special addresses, such as the loopback and unspecified addresses, which are discussed in the next section.

Much of the space is initially unassigned. It can be utilized in the future for expansion of existing use or for new uses.

Aggregatable global unicast addresses are analogous to globally routable IPv4 IP addresses. They are assigned in blocks to Internet providers and exchanges, who then assign portions of the addresses to businesses and end users. This type of address defines multiple levels of hierarchy and aggregation. This is the largest assigned address space, and it still utilizes only 1/8 of the available addresses.

From Table 8-3, you can see that multicast addresses begin with 0xFF. An address beginning with anything else is a unicast address. Table 8-4 is a quick reference for identifying a type of IP address.

Table 8-4   *Digits that Define the Address Type*

Defining First Digits	Address Type
00	Unspecified, loopback, IPv4-compatible
2	Aggregatable global unicast
3	
FE8	Link-local
FEC	Site-local
FF	Multicast

Address Structure

IPv6 address structure is used for assignment and allocation. Packet forwarding is based on the longest matched prefix, as it is in IPv4. A unicast address may be either an aggregatable global address, a link-local, a site-local, or a special format address. An IPv6 interface may be assigned multiple addresses—unicast, anycast, or multicast. The following sections discuss individual address structure types.

Aggregatable Global Address Format

The aggregatable global addresses will be used to connect to the public Internet and for any other purpose that requires global uniqueness and routability. The address structure supports today's provider-based aggregation and a new type, exchange-based aggregation. Exchange-based aggregation allocates address space to exchanges that then subdivide the space and allocate it to their customers. An exchange is another name for a NAP, as discussed in Chapter 2. It is a Layer 2 switch that interconnects ISPs and top-level service providers. A route arbitrator might be used on an exchange to collect routing information and provide a peering point between service providers. Experience with exchange-based aggregation is yet to be accomplished. Through these aggregation points, the defined format of the aggregatable global address enables the hierarchy required to scale the Internet. The hierarchy is discussed further in the next section.

Hierarchy

Aggregatable addresses are organized into three levels of hierarchy: public, site, and interface. The public topology comprises service providers that offer public Internet transit services, and exchanges. The very top level of the public topology makes up what is called the default-free zone—the Internet routers with no default route entry in their routing tables. These sites know explicitly how to reach all other network prefixes. Site topology is local to a site or organization that does not offer public transit services, although some smaller-scale private transit services may be offered. The interface topology identifies interfaces on the network. Figure 8-2 illustrates the Internet hierarchy of aggregatable addresses.

ISP1, ISP2, ISP3, and ISP4 represent the public space. They are interconnected directly and via exchanges. Smaller ISPs—P1 and P2—and end-user sites, shown as S1 through S5, make up the site space.

The defined format of the address, detailed in the next section, reflects this hierarchy.

Figure 8-2   *Internet Hierarchy*

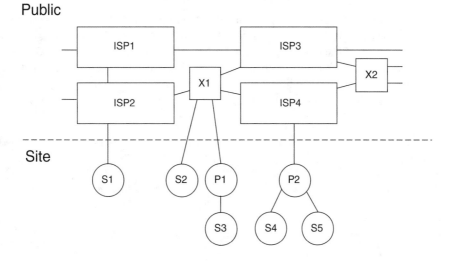

Format

Figure 8-3 displays the aggregatable global unicast address format.

Figure 8-3   *The Format of Aggregatable Global Unicast Addresses*

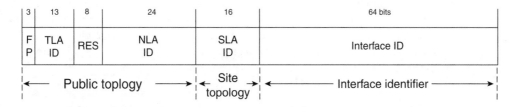

The fields that make up the public level are the FP, TLA, RES, and NLA. SLA is the site level, and interface ID is the interface level. The network portion of the address makes up the first 64 bits. The node portion is the last 64 bits.

The fields of the address are defined as follows:

- *FP* is the format prefix (001).
- *TLA ID* is the top-level aggregation identifier.
- *RES* is reserved for future use.
- *NLA ID* is the next-level aggregation identifier.

- *SLA ID* is the site-level aggregation identifier
- *Interface ID* is the interface identifier

The format prefix is binary 001, identifying the aggregatable global unicast address. Figure 8-3 shows that the FP, TLA ID, RES, and NLA ID fields comprise the public topology. SLA ID makes up the site topology, and Interface ID is the interface identifier. Both the public topology and the site topology can be subdivided to create even more levels of hierarchy. The FP, TLA, NLA, and SLA make up the network portion of the address. The interface ID is the node portion. The following sections discuss each of the fields illustrated in Figure 8-3.

Top-Level Aggregation Identifier   The top-level aggregation identifiers (TLA ID) are the top levels in the routing hierarchy. Routers in the default-free zone must have a routing entry for every TLA ID and will probably have routing entries depicting their own topology as well. The TLA ID field is 13 bits. If more TLAs are needed, another FP can be assigned, or the TLA field can expand to the right into the reserved field.

Just as a range of addresses is given by the Internet Assigned Numbers Authority (IANA) to the various regional IP registries, ranges of IPv6 TLA IDs are given to the regional IP registries around the globe. The regional IP registries in turn assign TLA IDs to large ISPs. Particularly, the large ISPs that receive TLA IDs are transit providers and exchanges.

IANA has initially allocated the TLA 0x0001. It is subdivided to provide blocks of sub-TLAs to each of the RIRs. The RIRs allocate sub-TLAs from their assigned blocks to organizations that will provide IPv6 services—TLA registries. TLA 0x0001 has 13 bits of sub-TLA, followed by 6 sub-TLA reserved bits, 13 NLA bits, 16 SLA bits, and 64 Interface ID bits. Each sub-TLA initially has up to 13 bits of NLA ID to allocate to the NLA registries. When an organization has completely allocated its NLA space, it may request more addresses. An entire sub-TLA is reserved for an organization, but only one sub-TLA is allocated at any time. If an organization needs more, it needs to justify this with engineering documentation or deployment plans. The 6 reserved bits can be used to allocate more addresses within a sub-TLA.

For example, ARIN has been allocated 2001:0400::/23. ARIN can allocate 2001:0400::/29 through 2001:05FF::/29 sub-TLAs. To encourage a slow-start addressing approach, however, the RIRs allocate addresses with a 35-bit prefix, such as 2001:0408::/35. The sub-TLA is actually 29 bits with 6 bits of reserved NLA space. VBNS has been allocated 2001:0408::/35. VBNS has 13 bits of NLA space to allocate to its customers. It can allocate the space however it chooses. It may allocate 2001:0408:0010::/40 to a smaller ISP customer. The ISP then has 2001:0408:0010::/48 through 2001:0408:001F::/48 to allocate to its customers.

Reserved   The reserved field (RES) is not currently used, except in the case of TLA 0x0001, as described in the preceding section. All bits are set to zero. Future use could include growth of the TLA ID and NLA ID.

Next-Level Aggregation Identifier   An organization allocated a TLA ID creates address hierarchy and identifies sites using the NLA ID. Organizations that receive address allocation from the NLA space are called NLA registries. This is similar to a CIDR block of IPv4 address space given to a top-level ISP, which then gives blocks of address space with longer prefixes to its customer.

An organization given a TLA has 24 bits, and an organization given a sub-TLA has 13 bits of NLA to use in allocating address space to its own customers. Its customers may be ISPs (NLA registries) or end-user subscribers. The TLA registry may use the high-order NLA bits to create hierarchy and may assign the lower-order bits to the NLA registries. NLA registries will be allocated enough address space to provide their own customers addresses. The minimum size of address space that an NLA registry can assign is a prefix of 48 bits (/48), giving the customer at least 16 bits of SLA to use in its own subnetting scheme. A site can request more than /48 addresses; however, the customer must prove the need with current deployment statistics and engineering documents or deployment plans.

Site-Level Aggregation Identifier   A site is free to create as many levels of hierarchy within the SLA-ID as is appropriate. It could have a flat numbering scheme with no further subdivision, or it could further divide the SLA ID into subnets, creating a hierarchy of SLA ID addresses.

Interface Identifier   The interface identifier is used to identify interfaces on a specific link. It is unique to the link. All addresses with high-order bits between 001 and 111, excluding multicast, must have interface IDs in EUI-64 format. Currently, only the special-format addresses, NSAP-allocated address space, and IPX allocated address space do not fall into this range.

The EUI-64 format can be derived from the interface MAC address, if one exists. An FFFE is inserted between the company ID and the node ID, and the universal/local bit is set to 1 to indicate global value (see Figure 8-4).

MAC address 0000:0C0A:2C51 is converted into EUI-64 address 0200:0CFF:FE0A:2C51 by inserting FFFE after the company identifier in the MAC and then setting the universal/local bit.[1]

Figure 8-4 *MAC-to-EUI-64 Conversion*

MAC Address: 0000:0C0A:2C51

Same MAC address in binary:

00000000 00000000 00001100 00001010 00101100 01010001

Insert FFFE between company and manufacturer assigned identifier values

00000000 00000000 00001100 <u>1111 1111 1111 1110</u> 00001010 00101100 01010001
                                             ↑

Universal/local bit set to 1 for global scope

0000000<u>1</u>0 00000000 00001100 1111 1111 1111 1110 00001010 00101100 01010001
  ↑

EUI-64 identifier:0200:0CFF:FE0A:2C51

Special-Format Addresses

Some addresses use a special format. The addresses are allocated from the reserved FP 0x00. The unspecified address, the loopback address, and the embedded IPv4 address are all examples of special-format addresses.

Unspecified

The unspecified address is made up of all zeros, 0:0:0:0:0:0:0:0. It must never be assigned to any node. It actually represents the absence of an address. One use for the unspecified address is in the source address field of an initializing host, before it has been assigned a valid address. The unspecified address must never be used as a destination address in IPv6 packets or IPv6 routing headers.

Loopback

The loopback address is 0:0:0:0:0:0:0:1. This address is analogous to the IPv4 loopback address 127.0.0.1. A node uses this address to send IP packets to itself. It can never be assigned to any physical interface. Traffic destined to the loopback address must never leave the sending node.

IPv6 with Embedded IPv4 Addresses

One transition mechanism used when migrating from IPv4 to IPv6 is the use of automatic tunnels. IPv6 packets are automatically encapsulated into IPv4 packets for transfer over the IPv4 network. This mechanism requires special-format IPv6 unicast addresses. Nodes that use this technique are dual-stack nodes running both IPv4 and IPv6. The IPv6/IPv4 node that supports automatic tunneling must be assigned an IPv6 address, with the IPv4 address embedded in the low-order 32 bits. All other bits are zero. Addresses of this type are termed *IPv4-compatible IPv6 addresses* and have the following format:

::d.d.d.d

d.d.d.d is an IPv4 dotted-decimal address. IPv4-compatible addresses and automatic tunnels are discussed further in the section "Transition from IPv4 to IPv6."

Local-Use Addresses

Two types of addresses have local significance. A link-local address is meaningful only to nodes on a single link. A site-local address is meaningful only to nodes within a site. The addresses are not globally unique. They are unique only within their respective scope.

The Link-Local Address

A link-local address is used for nodes on a single link. Autoconfiguration, neighbor discovery, nodes on a routerless link, and even routing protocols use link-local addresses. Routers must not forward packets with either source or destination link-local addresses beyond the link. Therefore, any protocol that requires sending a packet to devices on a single link and that wants to ensure that the packets do not get routed beyond the local link can use a link-local address in the IP header. A link-local address is defined by the FP 1111111010, followed by 54 zeros and the interface ID. The address contains no TLA, NLA, or SLA information. There is no hierarchical information at all. Figure 8-5 illustrates the format of the link-local address.

Figure 8-5   *Link-Local Address Format*

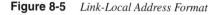

10	54	64 bits
1111111010	0	Interface ID

Every node assigns every active IPv6 interface a link-local address. They can be configured automatically, with autoconfiguration, or they can be manually configured.

The following are some examples of link-local addresses:

FE80::5ABC:01FF:FE01:1111
FE80::0060:08FF:FEB1:7EA2
FE80::200:CFF:FE0A:2C51

The Site-Local Address

A site is an organization or part of an organization. It could be a certain topological location, or it could be multiple topological locations interconnected in some way. A network configured with a site-local address is not reachable from locations outside the site. The site's edge routers must be able to keep site-local traffic within the site and are responsible for controlling the route propagation. In addition to the site-local FP and Interface ID, site-local addresses have a subnet identification field. Note, however, that no TLA or NLA IDs exist. These addresses are designed to be used within a site only; no global prefix is required. Use of these addresses is identical to the private IPv4 addresses. The addresses are not globally unique. It is recommended that you use site-local addresses, not global aggregatable addresses, on router interfaces.

The site-local address is defined by FP 1111111011 and is followed by 38 zeros, a 16-bit subnet field, and the 64-bit Interface ID, as illustrated in Figure 8-6.

Figure 8-6   *Site-Local Address Format*

10	38	16	64 bits
1111111011	0	Subnet ID	Interface ID

The subnet field can be utilized to create multiple networks within the site and to create a local hierarchy. The hierarchy can be used to aggregate addresses within the site. Site-local addresses must not be propagated beyond the site boundaries.

The following are some examples of site-local addresses:

FEC0::1:5ABC:1FF:FE01:1111
FEC0::CAB:60:8FF:FEB1:7EA2

Anycast Addresses

Anycast routing is a mechanism for addressing multiple interfaces, usually on different nodes, with the same IP address. Traffic destined to the address gets routed to the nearest node. The anycast functionality is discussed later, in the section "The Anycast Process." The anycast address has the same format as a unicast address. No special FP defines an anycast address.

Anycast addresses are assigned from the unicast address space. In fact, the addresses are taken from the Interface ID field. The Subnet-Router anycast address is predefined, and all router interfaces connected to a link must be assigned this address. It is a unicast address with an all-zero interface identifier. Figure 8-7 illustrates the Subnet-Router anycast address.

Figure 8-7   *Subnet-Router Anycast Address*

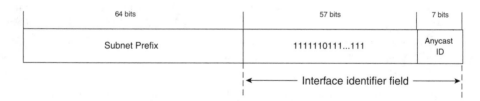

An example of a Subnet-Router anycast address is FEC0:0:0:A:: on a router interface assigned with the unicast address FEC0:0:0:A:200:CFF:FE0A:2C51.

The highest 128 interface IDs are reserved for assigned subnet anycast addresses. A reserved subnet anycast address is an anycast address that is available on every IPv6 subnet, regardless of the type or format of the prefix. Figure 8-8 illustrates the construction of reserved anycast addresses.

Figure 8-8   *Anycast Address Construction*

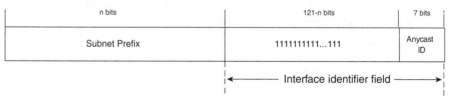

Figure 8-8 shows that the reserved anycast address space is taken completely from the Interface ID field. A reserved anycast address is reserved for every subnet. The top 128 interface IDs are reserved for anycast address allocation. The last 7 bits of the address identify the specific anycast address.

At the time of this writing, the only specified anycast address is the mobile IPv6 home-agents. It has an anycast identifier of binary 1111110. That is, on every IPv6 subnet, the address associated with the EUI-64 interface ID FDFF:FFFF:FFFF:FFFE is reserved for the mobile IPv6 home-agent anycast address. The mobile IPv6 home-agent on prefix FEC0:0:0:A::/64 uses the anycast address FEC0:0:0:A:FDFF:FFFF:FFFF:FFFE.

All the remaining anycast IDs, hexadecimal values 0-7D and 7F, are reserved for future use.

Because anycast addresses are syntactically indistinguishable from unicast addresses, an interface must be explicitly configured to recognize that its address is an anycast address.

Multicast Addresses

Multicast addresses identify groups of interfaces, each of which can contain multiple multicast addresses. Multicast addresses are distinguishable from unicast addresses because they always begin with 0xFF. There is no such thing as broadcasting at the network layer in IPv6. Broadcasting induced a lot of extra overhead on nodes that were not necessarily interested in the broadcast packet. All IP interfaces that received a broadcast packet had to process the packet to see whether it might be the intended recipient. Very often, the node was not the intended recipient. Every IPv6 interface knows the multicast groups to which it belongs. A multicast packet is processed only by those interfaces that belong to the multicast group. IPv6 uses multicasting rather than broadcasting.

IPv6 multicast addresses may be either assigned by an official addressing authority (well-known addresses) or transient—that is, locally assigned for nonglobal use. The initial assignment of IPv6 multicast addresses was based on assigned IPv4 multicast addresses. All relevant IPv4 multicast addresses are converted to IPv6 multicast addresses. You can find a complete list of the currently assigned IPv6 multicast addresses in RFC 2375. Table 8-6, shown in a moment, lists some examples.

IPv6 multicast addresses are also scoped. The addresses have a field that identifies the scope as either local to the node, local to the link, local to the site, local to the organization, or global. Transient addresses defined within a particular scope are meaningful only to nodes within that scope. The same address may be defined in a different scope, or a different network, and have a completely different meaning.

Figure 8-9 illustrates the format of a multicast address.

Figure 8-9 *Multicast Address Format*

The leading octet, 11111111, identifies this address as multicast.

flgs is a set of 4 bits. The leading 3 bits are reserved and must be set to 0. The last bit indicates whether the multicast address is an address permanently assigned by the global Internet numbering authority or whether it is not permanently assigned, known as "transient." A value of 0 in the fourth bit indicates that the multicast address is "well-known." The global Internet numbering authority assigned it.

scop is a 4-bit value used to limit the scope of the multicast address. Table 8-5 lists the values.

Table 8-5   *Multicast Address Scope Values*

Value	Description
0	Reserved
1	Node local scope
2	Link local scope
5	Site local scope
8	Organization local scope
e	Global scope
f	Reserved

Any of the scope values may exist with either well-known or transient addresses. Transient addresses within a given scope are valid only for that scope. They are meaningless under any other scope.

Group ID identifies the multicast group, either well-known or transient, within the given scope.

Table 8-6 lists some common multicast groups, along with their assigned addresses and scopes.

Table 8-6   *Some IPv6 Well-Known Multicast Addresses*

IPv6 Well-Known Multicast Address	IPv4 Well-Known Multicast Address	Multicast Group
Node-Local Scope		
FF01:0:0:0:0:0:0:1	224.0.0.1	All-nodes address
FF01:0:0:0:0:0:0:2	224.0.0.2	All-routers address
Link-Local Scope		
FF02:0:0:0:0:0:0:1	224.0.0.1	All-nodes address

continues

Table 8-6   *Some IPv6 Well-Known Multicast Addresses (Continued)*

FF02:0:0:0:0:0:0:2	224.0.0.2	All-routers address
FF02:0:0:0:0:0:0:5	224.0.0.5	OSPFIGP
FF02:0:0:0:0:0:0:6	224.0.0.6	OSPFIGP-designated routers
FF02:0:0:0:0:0:0:9	224.0.0.9	RIP routers
FF02:0:0:0:0:0:0:D	224.0.0.13	All PIM routers
Site-Local Scope		
FF05:0:0:0:0:0:0:2	224.0.0.2	All-routers address
Any Valid Scope		
FF0X:0:0:0:0:0:0:101	224.0.1.1	Network Time Protocol (NTP)
FF0X:0:0:0:0:0:0:127	224.0.1.39	cisco-rp-announce
FF0X:0:0:0:0:0:0:128	224.0.1.40	cisco-rp-discovery

Upon interface initialization and when multicast protocols and applications are initialized, nodes join the required multicast groups. Nodes join the all-nodes multicast addresses of FF01::1 and FF02::1. The address' formats indicate that the multicast addresses are well-known and have node-local and link-local scope, respectively. Routers join the all-routers multicast address of FF01::2, FF02::2, and FF05::2. These are well-known addresses with node-local, link-local, and site-local scope, respectively.

You can see from Table 8-6 that a multicast group capable of operating within multiple scopes has multiple IPv6 addresses. This is not the case with the well-known IPv4 addresses. These are not scoped. Two methods of multicast scoping with IPv4 were discussed in Chapter 5, "Introduction to IP Multicast Routing." TTL scoping requires the network administrator to set TTL thresholds on multicast boundaries. If the TTL value in a multicast packet is lower than the defined threshold when the packet reaches the boundary, the packet is discarded. One drawback to this approach is its inflexibility—an interface's TTL threshold applies to all multicast packets exiting the interface. Another drawback is that in a large network, it is difficult to predict what the correct TTL threshold value should be. The other type of scoping for IPv4, administrative scoping, defines a range of private-use multicast addresses that can be used to define scope within an enterprise. The reserved range is 239.0.0.0–239.255.255.255. Suggested scoping ranges are 239.255.0.0/16 for local or site scope and 239.192.0.0/14 for organizationwide scope. These are just suggested ranges. Enterprises are free to use the addresses as they see fit. Administrative scoping might work fine within an organization, but it cannot work globally. The addresses are for private use only.

Multicast scoping is built into all IPv6 multicast addresses. Currently, five levels of scope are defined. Link-local scope is achieved in IPv4 with TTL scoping by setting the TTL value in all link-local multicast packets to 1. The rest of the IPv6 scopes create the potential for various levels of multicast containment. Multicast applications using IPv6 can be contained within a link, site, or organization. There are reserved addresses for future scopes. Scoped, well-known multicast addresses enable multicast containment while at the same time ensuring that the same address is not used for two different multicast groups. There is no danger of two companies using the same address for two different applications and then conflicting when the two companies later decide to merge.

A particular type of multicast address is the "solicited-node" address. Solicited-node multicast addresses are used by various IPv6 functions to communicate with IPv6 nodes. The functions' use of the address is discussed in the section "IPv6 Functionality." Solicited-node multicast addresses are created and assigned for every unicast and anycast address assigned to an interface, other than the link-local address. The solicited-node multicast address is created using the last 24 bits of the interface ID and appending it to the prefix FF02:0:0:0:0:1:FF00::/104. Figure 8-10 illustrates how a solicited-node multicast address is formed.

Figure 8-10 *Solicited-Node Multicast Address Formation*

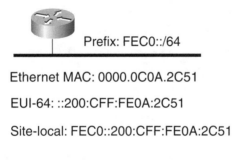

Prefix: FEC0::/64

Ethernet MAC: 0000.0C0A.2C51

EUI-64: ::200:CFF:FE0A:2C51

Site-local: FEC0::200:CFF:FE0A:2C51

Solicited-node multicast: **FF02::1:FF0A:2C51**

An interface with the MAC address 0000.0C0A.2C51 forms EUI-64 interface ID ::200:CFF:FE0A:2C51, which then creates link-local address FE80::200:CFF:FE0A:2C51. The site-local prefix FEC0::/64 on subnet 0 creates site-local address FEC0::200:CFF: FE0A:2C51. A solicited-node multicast address is formed because the interface now has a site-local address. The solicited-node address takes the last 24 bits of the interface ID, 0A:2C51, and appends it to the solicited-node prefix, forming FF02::1:FF0A:2C51.

Each interface may have multiple prefixes and multiple IPv6 addresses associated with it. The interface ID is likely the same for all addresses. Creating the solicited-node multicast address out of the final 24 bits of the interface ID minimizes the number of multicast addresses that the node must join.

Required Addresses for Nodes

Nodes are required to recognize multiple addresses as identifying themselves. IPv6 mechanisms require nodes to maintain these addresses in order to work correctly. The use of each address is discussed further with the particular IPv6 function.

A host is required to recognize the following addresses:

- The link-local address for each interface
- All assigned unicast addresses
- The loopback address
- All-nodes multicast addresses
- The solicited-node multicast address for each of its assigned unicast and anycast addresses
- The multicast addresses of all other groups to which the host belongs

In addition to all these addresses, a router also is required to recognize the following:

- The subnet-router anycast address for each of its routing interfaces
- All other anycast addresses configured on the router
- The all-routers multicast address
- Multicast addresses of all other groups to which the router belongs

Table 8-7 summarizes the address types.

Table 8-7   *Address Types and Examples*

Defining First Digits	Example	Address Type
00	::1	Unspecified
		Loopback
		IPv4-compatible
2 3	2001:0608:1000::	Aggregatable global unicast
FE8	FE80::200:CFF:FE0A:2C51	Link-local
FEC	FEC0::200:CFF:FE0A:2C51	Site-local
FF	FF02::2	Multicast
FF02:0:0:0:0:1:FF00::	FF02:0:0:0:0:1:FF0A:2c51	Solicited-node

IPv6 Header

One of the design goals of IPv6 is to improve on the IPv4 header. It is simpler, more flexible, and more efficient when using options. Some of the IPv4 fields were removed; others were renamed. The address is four times as long, but the header is only twice as large. Option encoding changed to make processing more efficient and to offer greater flexibility in the size and addition of options.

Header Format

The header is simple. It has eight fields, including the Source and Destination fields. Figure 8-11 shows the header.

Figure 8-11 *IPv6 Header Format*

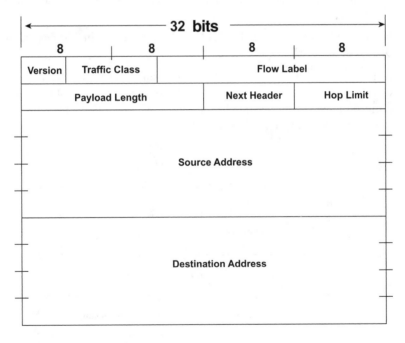

The fields in the IPv6 header format are defined as follows:

- *Version* indicates the IP version (in this case, 6).
- *Payload Length* is the length of the IP packet, excluding this header, in octets. Extension headers, discussed in the next section, are considered part of the payload and are therefore included in this length.

- *Next Header* is the value identifying the header immediately following the IPv6 header. The next header is either an upper-layer header (such as ICMP, TCP, or UDP) or it is an IPv6 extension header, as discussed in the next section.

- *Hop Limit* is decremented by each node the packet traverses. The packet is discarded if the hop limit reaches zero. Some IPv6 functions, such as Router Advertisements, Neighbor Advertisements and Solicitations, and IPv6 Redirects, are used only between devices on a single link. A technique used by IPv6 processes to validate that a packet was not sent by an off-link node (perhaps as an attempt to maliciously redirect traffic) is to require the hop limit to be set to 255, which is the maximum value for the hop limit. If the packet had traversed a router and was thus sent by an off-link node, the hop limit of the received packet would be something less than 255. An IPv6 node receiving this packet considers it invalid and drops it.

- *Source Address/Destination Address* are 128-bit fields for the IPv6 source and destination addresses.

The Traffic Class and Flow Label fields are discussed later in this chapter, in the section "Quality of Service."

Figure 8-12 shows the IPv4 header for comparison. Only the fields that require processing by every IP node in the path remain in the IPv6 header. The rest of the fields contain information that may or may not be relevant to any given IP packet. This information has been moved to extension headers in IPv6.

Figure 8-12 *IPv4 Header Format*

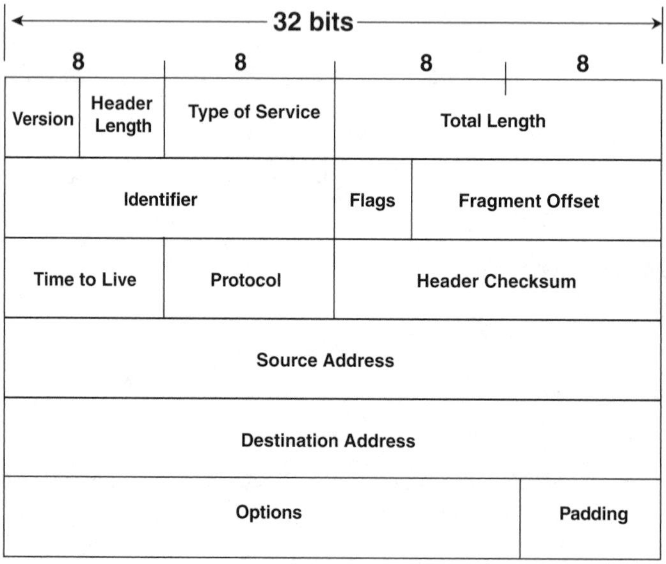

Extension Headers

Optional network layer information is not included in the IPv6 header. It is included in separate headers that are encoded and placed between the IPv6 and the upper-layer header. The extension headers are not processed by every node along the packet's delivery path, with one exception. They are examined only by the node (or nodes in the case of multicast destinations) identified in the Destination Address field of the IP header. This improves the efficiency of options processing by not requiring every IP router to process information that is perhaps intended only for the destination node. The exception is the hop-by-hop option. The hop-by-hop option contains information that is intended for every router along the delivery path.

Extension Header Order

A node determines whether it must examine and process an extension header by looking at information that is contained in the preceding header. Therefore, extension headers must be processed in the order that they appear in the packet. If they all exist in a packet, they should be in the order shown in Table 8-8. The table shows the next-header value that identifies this header. The headers should be in the order shown in Table 8-8, but they might not be, except for the hop-by-hop header, which must always immediately follow the IPv6 header, if it exists at all. Nodes are required to process the headers, regardless of the order received.

Table 8-8   *Headers and Next-Header Value*

Header	Previous Header's Next-Header Value
Hop-by-Hop Options	0
Destination Options	60
Routing	43
Fragment	44
Authentication	51
Encapsulating Security Payload	50
Destination Options	60
OSPF for IPv6	89

The Destination Options header appears twice in Table 8-8. Its meaning differs in each location. When it occurs before a routing header, the header is to be examined by the first destination that appears in the Destination field of the IPv6 header, plus by all the subsequent addresses listed in the routing header. When the Destination Options header appears without a routing header, or after the routing header, the options are to be processed only by the final destination of the packet. Figure 8-13 illustrates how the extension headers are used.

Figure 8-13 *The Use of Extension Headers*

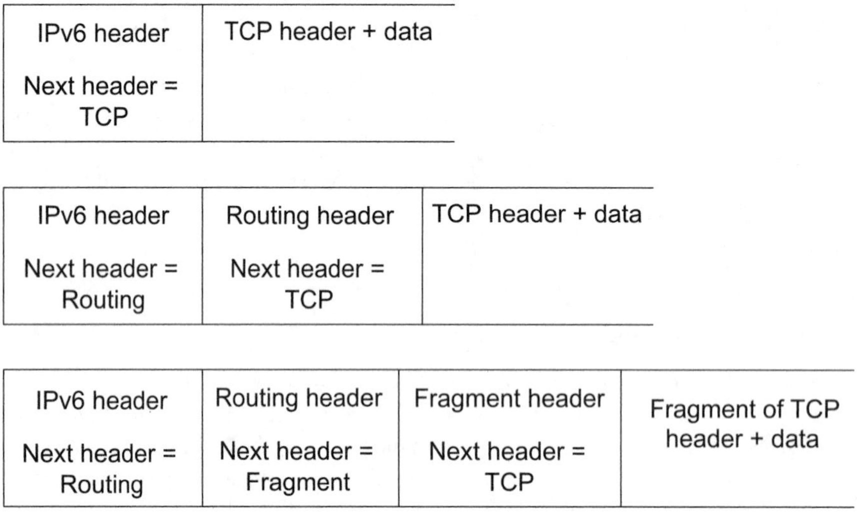

IPv6 header Next header = TCP	TCP header + data

IPv6 header Next header = Routing	Routing header Next header = TCP	TCP header + data

IPv6 header Next header = Routing	Routing header Next header = Fragment	Fragment header Next header = TCP	Fragment of TCP header + data

In each header, the next-header value identifies the following header. After reading the IPv6 header, if the processing node is not the final destination, and the next header is not the hop-by-hop header, the packet is forwarded. If the node is the destination, it processes each header in the order received.

Options

Two of the currently defined extension headers—Hop-by-Hop and Destination—are composed of a variable number of type-length-value (TLV) options. Options include a flag that indicates whether the data may change in transit. This has significance to the Authentication header. If the data may change, the Authentication header must treat the field as all zeros when computing the authentication information. Currently, only two options are defined—Pad1 and PadN. Both are used to pad the header so that the length is a multiple of eight octets, or to align subsequent options. Pad1 inserts one octet of padding into the Options area of a header. PadN inserts two or more octets.

Hop-by-Hop Options Header

Information included in the Hop-by-Hop Options header must be examined by every router along the delivery path to the destination. The Hop-By-Hop Options header must be immediately follow the IPv6 header. This enables the routers along the path to examine the header without the need to process any other extension header.

Routing Header

Addresses listed in the Routing header identify nodes that must be visited en route to the destination. The IPv6 header contains the first node to be visited, and the Routing header contains the list of remaining nodes, including the final destination.

The Routing header contains Next-Header, Length, Type, Segments Left, and Address fields. The Type field has one defined value, type 0. The Segments Left field contains the number of explicitly listed nodes yet to be visited before reaching the destination.

The Routing header is processed by the node identified in the Destination Address field of the IP header. This node examines the Routing header. If there are nodes listed that have yet to be visited, the processing node identifies the next node to visit by comparing the total number of route header nodes to the number of segments left. The next node address is placed in the IP Destination Address field, the Segments Left value is decremented, and the packet is forwarded.

Fragment Header

A source node desiring to send a packet larger than what will fit in the path MTU to the destination uses the Fragment header. The source node is responsible for fragmenting the packet if any link MTU along the path is smaller than the packet. Routers do not fragment IPv6 packets. The source node fragments the packet and sends the fragments in multiple packets, to be reassembled by the destination. The source node can use a process called MTU path discovery to determine the minimum MTU along the path to the destination node. After it has learned the minimum MTU, the source knows the maximum size packet that can traverse the path. If the source is not running the MTU path discovery process, it assumes the maximum MTU it can use is the IPv6 minimum MTU of 1280 bytes. This process is covered in detail in the section "MTU Path Discovery." All the fragments of an individual packet are marked with an Identification value that is generated by the source node.

Destination Options Header

The Destination Options header contains options that must be examined by the destination(s) of an IPv6 packet. When the Destination Options header immediately precedes the Routing header, the option is processed by each node in the Routing header. When the Destination Options header immediately precedes the Upper-Layer Protocol header, it is processed by the final destination.

Authentication

An Authentication header (AH) has been added to IPv6. Its intent is to provide integrity and authentication for IP packets. All fields in the IP packet that do not change in transit to the destination are used to calculate the authentication information. Fields or options that do change, such as the hop limit, are considered to be zero when calculating the authentication information.

Encapsulating Security Payload

Integrity and confidentiality are provided by the Encapsulating Security Payload (ESP). You can use the Authentication header in conjunction with ESP to provide authentication. ESP encrypts the data to be protected and places the encrypted data into the Data portion of the ESP header. There are two encryption modes—Tunnel mode and Transport mode. In Tunnel mode, the ESP header encrypts the entire IPv6 packet, which it places in its encrypted field. The ESP header then gets placed in a new, unencrypted IPv6 header. In Transport mode, the ESP header encrypts only the transport layer segment (TCP, UDP, ICMP), places this encrypted data into its encrypted field, and is then placed in the original packet, just before the Transport Layer Protocol header.

Security mechanisms are beyond the scope of this book. For more information about IPv6 security, refer to RFCs 2401, 2402, and 2403.

IPv6 Functionality

A number of functions designed as a part of IPv6 must be implemented by any node said to support IPv6, including the following:

- ICMPv6
- Neighbor discovery
- Stateless autoconfiguration
- Anycast
- Multicast
- MTU path discovery (recommended)

These functions are the basis of IPv6, in most cases enhancing the capabilities of IPv4.

Another feature of IPv6 is the ability to assign multiple addresses to any interface, easing the problem of prefix renumbering. Not only can any IPv6 interface have multiple addresses in multiple prefixes, but two nodes on a link also can communicate together directly, regardless of the prefix to which they belong.

This functionality is discussed in detail in this section. Cisco routers are configured and command output is examined to help you understand the IPv6 functionality.

Enabling IPv6 Capability on a Cisco Router

IPv6 (disabled by default) is enabled on the Cisco router by issuing the following global command:

```
ipv6 unicast-routing [table-count num]
```

Cisco's support enables multiple routing tables. One routing table is enabled by default. Multiple tables enable the network administrator to have more control over routing entry lookups. Longest match routing is no longer the only rule. If multiple tables are enabled, the forwarding algorithm searches the routing tables in increasing order until a usable route is found.

The next step in configuring IPv6 is to enable an IPv6 interface and enable autoconfiguration, or to configure an address. The following section discusses autoconfiguration.

The interface subcommand to enable the interface for IPv6 and configure the interface with an address is as follows:

```
ipv6 address ipv6address/prefix-length [link-local]
```

The interface subcommand to enable an interface without a specific address configured is as follows:

```
ipv6 enable
```

The router autoconfigures a link-local unicast address as part of enabling the interface.

Two routers, Falcon and Eagle, both reside on a single Ethernet link and have the configurations shown in Example 8-1.

Example 8-1   *Enabling IPv6 on Two Routers That Reside on a Single Ethernet Link*

```
Falcon
ipv6 unicast-routing
!
interface Ethernet0
 ipv6 enable
```
```
Eagle
ipv6 unicast-routing
!
interface Ethernet0
 ipv6 enable
```

Note that the configurations in Example 8-1 are identical.

The command to display the state of IPv6 on the interface, as well as relevant interface information, is as follows:

```
show ipv6 interface interface-type number
```

Example 8-2 shows partial output from the **show ipv6 interface** command, which displays the Ethernet interfaces' MAC addresses and the IPv6 state and link-local addresses automatically configured on the interfaces.

Example 8-2   *show ipv6 interface ethernet 0 Is Used to View IPv6 Interface Information*

```
Falcon#sh int e 0
Ethernet0 is up, line protocol is up
  Hardware is Lance, address is 0000.0c0a.2c51 (bia 0000.0c0a.2c51)

Falcon#show ipv6 interface ethernet 0
Ethernet0 is up, line protocol is up
  IPv6 is enabled, link-local address is FE80::200:CFF:FE0A:2C51

Eagle#sh int e 0
Ethernet0 is up, line protocol is up
  Hardware is Lance, address is 0000.0c76.5b7c (bia 0000.0c76.5b7c)

Eagle#show ipv6 interface ethernet 0
Ethernet0 is up, line protocol is up
  IPv6 is enabled, link-local address is FE80::200:CFF:FE76:5B7C
```

Notice that Falcon's MAC address 0000.0C0A.2C51 creates the link-local address FE80::200:CFF:FE0A:2C51, and Eagle's MAC address 0000.0C76.5B7C creates the link-local address FE80::200:CFF:FE76:5B7C. Also note that IPv6 is enabled.

ICMPv6

ICMPv6 is integral to IPv6. Every node that implements IPv6 must fully implement ICMPv6. ICMPv6 is a modified version of ICMP for IPv4. Error reporting and many IPv6 functions, such as MTU path discovery and neighbor discovery, utilize ICMPv6. Error messages are discussed here.

The ICMPv6 packet follows the IPv6 header or one of the extension headers and is identified by the IPv6 Next-Header value of 58 in the immediately preceding header. (This is not the same value used by IP to identify ICMP for IPv4.) Informational and error messages are identified by the high-order bit in the ICMP Type field. An error message has a zero in the high-order bit of the ICMP Type field. An ICMP error message includes as much of the offending packet as possible without making the ICMP message larger than the minimum IPv6 MTU, 1280 bytes.

The following error messages are discussed:

- Destination Unreachable
- Packet Too Big
- Time Exceeded
- Parameter Problem

Destination Unreachable errors are sent when a node cannot forward the packet for some reason other than congestion. The node sends an error message to the source of the packet, with a code indicating the following:

- No route to the destination (0)
- Access is administratively prohibited (1)
- Address unreachable (3)
- Port unreachable (4)

A node sends a Packet Too Big message when the size of the packet exceeds the MTU on the link. In IPv6, fragmentation is not performed by routers, as it is in IPv4. Only the source node performs fragmentation. The MTU of the link that caused the error is included in the packet. The Packet Too Big message is sent regardless of whether the IPv6 destination is unicast or multicast. The message is used by the MTU path discovery process.

When the IPv6 hop limit reaches zero, an ICMP Time Exceeded message is sent. A zero hop limit usually indicates a routing loop.

An ICMP Parameter Problem message is sent if a node finds a problem with part of an IP header or an extension header. A pointer to the location in the offending header is included in the error message. An error code identifies the type of problem encountered:

- Erroneous header field encountered (0)
- Unrecognized next-header type encountered (1)
- Unrecognized IPv6 option encountered (2)

Neighbor Discovery

The Neighbor Discovery (ND) protocol addresses many problems related to nodes on a single link. It provides the functionality for serverless automatic configuration, router discovery, prefix discovery, address resolution, neighbor unreachability detection, link MTU discovery, next-hop determination, and duplicate address detection. With IPv4, a combination of many protocols, including DHCP, ICMP router discovery, a routing protocol, and ARP, are required to provide only some of this functionality. ND uses ICMPv6 to perform these tasks. ND intended to improve on the IPv4 processes by integrating them all into ICMPv6, a required component of IPv6.

When a node is initialized, it must know a few things before it begins communicating:

- It must know its own address.
- It must know its own prefix information so that it can figure out how to send packets to nodes located in other prefixes.
- It must know about any routers on the link.
- It needs to know how to determine the next hop in the path to a destination.

- It needs to know how to obtain the link-level address associated with a known network layer address.

- It needs to know how large of a packet it can send.

To make communication run a lot smoother, a node should know some other things:

- It should be able to detect when a neighbor is no longer reachable so that it does not send packets to that neighbor.

- It should know about neighbors on its link.

- It should know whether the address it is trying to use is in use already by another node on the link.

- It needs to know what other prefixes are assigned to nodes on the same link.

- It should be able to redirect traffic to a better next-hop node, if one exists, for any destination.

ND defines five ICMPv6 packets to provide IPv6 nodes with the information they must and should know before communicating:

- **Router Solicitation (RS)**—Multicasted by a node when it wants routers to send a Router Advertisement immediately instead of waiting for the next scheduled advertisement. An initializing node may send the Router Solicitation so that it can immediately learn about configuration parameters and about the existence of routers on the link.

- **Router Advertisement (RA)**—Sent periodically or in response to a solicitation. Routers advertise their presence, as well as provide information necessary for a node to configure itself.

- **Neighbor Solicitation (NS)**—Enables a node to determine the link layer address of a neighbor or to determine whether the neighbor is still reachable via a cached link layer address. Also enables a node to determine whether a duplicate IP address exists on the link.

- **Neighbor Advertisement (NA)**—Sent in response to Neighbor Solicitations, or unsolicited if a node's link layer address changes.

- **Redirect**—Sent by routers to redirect traffic to a better first hop on the link.

Each message is an ICMP packet with a defining type. The ICMP packet contains type-specific information. Each type of message may also contain one or more TLV options.

ND provides the basis for stateless autoconfiguration—automatic configuration without a configuration server. Router Advertisements provide the information necessary for node configuration. Autoconfiguration is discussed fully in the section "Autoconfiguration."

Router Solicitation

Hosts send Router Solicitations when they want to receive a Router Advertisement right away—they do not want to wait for the periodic advertisement. An initializing host sends an RS so that it can quickly learn the information it needs for configuration.

An RS is an ICMP packet of type 133. Its source address is an address assigned to the sending host's interface. If no address has yet been assigned, it is the unspecified address, 0:0:0:0:0:0:0:0. The destination is typically the all-routers multicast address. The RS also may contain an option with the sender's link layer address. The link layer address must not be included if the source address is the unspecified address.

Router Advertisements

Routers advertise their presence on a link and provide the information necessary for a node to configure itself. The RA is multicast to the link-scope all-nodes multicast group.

An RA is an ICMP packet of type 134. Its source IP address is the link-local address of the sending router, and the destination address is either the address of a node that sent a Router Solicitation or the link-scope all-nodes multicast address. The hop limit must be set to 255. The hop limit is not used, in this case, to stop routers from forwarding the packet. A value of 1 ensures that the packet does not get forwarded, because a router that receives the packet decrements the hop limit and drops the packet when the hop limit reaches 0. The value of 255 ensures that no off-link device sends RAs in an attempt to disrupt traffic flow. If an off-link device does send an RA, the RA traverses a router, which automatically decrements the hop-limit value, rendering the packet invalid. One of the ways that the receiving node validates the packet is by verifying that the hop limit is 255. IPv4 does not use this method of ensuring that the packet could not possibly have traversed a router.

An RA contains a Router Lifetime. The Router Lifetime informs nodes how long they should consider the router as a default. The time is in units of seconds, with a maximum value of 18.2 hours. A value of 0 means that the router is not a default candidate and should not appear on any host's default router list.

A host receiving RAs builds a default router list. All routers that advertised RAs with non-zero valued Router Lifetimes appear in the default router list. The entry for a router's Router Lifetime value in the default list is updated with each subsequent RA received. If an RA contains a zero-valued Router Lifetime for an already listed router, the host immediately removes the router from the default list (an improvement over IPv4). IPv4 hosts have to be manually configured with default router lists. Some IPv4 hosts run a routing protocol, such as RIP, to dynamically learn this information, and some run the ICMP Router Discovery Protocol (IRDP). Neither RIP nor IRDP are implemented on all IPv4 hosts, however.

An RA also contains a Reachable Time and a Retransmit Timer. The Reachable Time informs hosts how long to assume a neighbor is alive after receiving a reachability confirmation from that neighbor. This information is used in the Neighbor Unreachability detection process. The Retransmit Timer is the time, in milliseconds, between subsequent

Neighbor Solicitation messages. It is used in the address resolution and the Neighbor Unreachability detection processes.

Two bits found in the RA packet, the Managed Address (M) bit and the Other Stateful Configuration (O) bit, inform a host how it should configure itself. If the M bit is set, the host configures its address using the stateful autoconfiguration protocol, such as DHCP, in addition to any addresses configured with stateless autoconfiguration. If the O bit is set, hosts use the stateful autoconfiguration protocol to configure other information besides the address. IPv4 hosts are manually configured to indicate whether they should learn their IP configuration information via DHCP. Automatically providing this information to hosts on a link via router advertisements minimizes the amount of static configuration information contained in hosts, easing future reconfiguration efforts. The autoconfiguration methods are discussed in the section "Autoconfiguration."

The options that may be present in the RA are the source link layer address, the MTU, and prefix information. Including the source link layer address of the router in the RA eliminates the need for hosts to perform the address resolution protocol on default routers. A router may elect not to include the link layer address. The MTU option enables centralized control of the MTU that hosts on a link use. This option is used mainly for links with a variable MTU but may be used on other links. The value is set in the router, which then enables the configuration of all the hosts on the link. The prefix information is used to inform other nodes of on-link prefixes and for address autoconfiguration. A host that knows of all the prefixes that are configured on a link forwards traffic more knowledgeably. A multihomed host can choose the closest interface to any known on-link destination prefix. A nonmultihomed host uses the prefix list to assist in next-hop detection.

The prefix information option contains data that is used for both on-link determination and stateless autoconfiguration. It contains the actual prefix and the length of the prefix, which is always from 1 to 128 bits. It also contains bits that indicate whether the prefix is to be used for on-link determination or for address configuration. When the L bit is set, you can use the prefix for on-link determination. When it is not set, you can determine no information about on-link or off-link. The A bit, when set, indicates that you can use the prefix for stateless address configuration.

The prefix option also contains a Valid Lifetime value and a Preferred Lifetime value. The Valid Lifetime indicates, in seconds, how long a prefix is valid for purposes of on-link determination. The lifetime is relative to the time the packet was sent. An advertised Valid Lifetime value of zero indicates that the prefix is no longer valid. The Preferred Lifetime is the number of seconds that the address automatically configured from the prefix can remain "preferred." A preferred address on an interface is one that any node can actively use for communication. A Preferred Lifetime of zero means the addresses configured with the prefix must be deprecated. A deprecated address is one that is used to maintain existing connections, but it should not be used to initiate new connections if a preferred address exists. A lifetime of all ones indicates infinity. You can use a prefix for both on-link determination and configuration. The two types of addresses are discussed further in the section "Autoconfiguration."

Neighbor Solicitation

Neighbor Solicitation messages are used to obtain the link layer address of a neighbor, as well as to provide link layer addresses and to verify the reachability of a neighbor. It is an ICMP packet of type 135. The source address of the IP packet is the link-local address of the soliciting node. The destination is the solicited-node multicast address associated with the target IP address in the case of link layer determination, and the unicast address of the target in the case of reachability verification. The hop limit is 255. As in the RA, a hop limit of 255 in the received NS ensures that the packet has not traversed a router. If the packet had traversed a router, the hop limit would be some value less than 255. A field indicating the target address is also included in the NS.

The source link layer address option may be included in the NS. If the NS is attempting to find a target link layer address, and the NS is therefore multicast on the link, the source link layer address must be included in the packet. This inclusion minimizes the occurrence of address resolution packets on the link.

Neighbor Advertisement

A Neighbor Advertisement is sent in response to an NS or is unsolicited to immediately propagate new information, such as a change in a node's link layer address. NA is an ICMP packet of type 136. The source address is any valid unicast address assigned to the sending interface. For solicited advertisements, the destination is the source address of the solicitation, or, if the solicitation's address is the unspecified address, it is the all-nodes multicast address. Unsolicited advertisements are typically sent to the all-nodes multicast address. The NA contains a Solicited flag (S) bit. It is set when the NA is in response to an NS. The hop limit is 255. The target address is the same target address from the solicitation. This is the address for which a link layer address is sought. For an unsolicited advertisement, this is the IP address whose link layer address has changed. The NA may include the target link layer address option. Unsolicited advertisements sent to inform nodes of the advertiser's new link layer address include this option with the value of the new link layer address. The solicited NA is analogous to the IPv4 ARP reply. The unsolicited NA, however, is an added feature. One NA multicast to the all-nodes address, informing other nodes of a link layer address change, replaces many ARP requests and replies broadcast on an IPv4 network when ARP caches time out and a new link layer address is sought for a well-used device.

Redirect

Routers send Redirect messages to inform a host of a better first hop to the destination. The better first hop could be a different router or it could be the destination itself. If the destination is a neighbor of the source, even if the source and destination nodes belong to different prefixes, the router can redirect the traffic so that they communicate directly (an enhancement of IPv4 ICMP). IPv4 ICMP Redirect messages are sent by a router when an alternative router on the same link as the source host has a better path to the destination host or network. It does not redirect traffic if the better first hop is the destination itself. This feature enables hosts on the same data link but assigned different prefixes to communicate directly, without having to hop through a router.

The Redirect message's source address is the link-local address of the router. The destination is the source address of the redirected packet. The hop limit is 255.

The target IP address and the destination address also are included in the ICMP packet. If the better first hop is a router, the target address is the link-local address of that router. If the better first hop is the actual destination, the target address is the IP address of that destination. The ICMP destination address is the destination IP address of the traffic being redirected. Note that if the better first hop is the destination itself, both these fields will contain the same address.

The Redirect message may contain the target link layer address option. This enables hosts to discover the link layer address without relying on address resolution.

Part of the IP packet that caused the Redirect message might be included as an option as well. The Redirect message includes as much of the IP packet as possible, without causing the Redirect packet to exceed 1280 bytes.

Next-Hop Discovery

A host that has a packet to send must first determine what next hop to use. If a packet was previously sent to the destination, the next hop might be stored in a destination cache. If this is the first packet to a destination, the next hop is discovered by comparing the destination address with the host's on-link prefix list. A packet to an on-link destination is sent directly to that destination node. An off-link destination is sent to a default router. An IPv4 node, however, must send all traffic destined to a subnet other than its own to a router. If the destination is on the same link as the source, but on a different subnet, the router forwards the traffic back onto the link. The traffic traverses the link twice.

Whether the next hop is the destination itself or a default router, the link layer address of the next hop must be identified.

Address Resolution

Address resolution is performed by nodes looking for a link layer address associated with a known IP address. The address resolution process uses Neighbor Solicitation and Neighbor Advertisement. A node with packets to send to a destination IP address first checks its neighbor cache to see whether an entry already exists. If it does not, the node creates an entry for the IP address, with a state of INCOMPLETE. The node then sends a Neighbor Solicitation to the solicited-node multicast address of the IP address in question. The source address of the solicitation is a unicast address and is either the source address of the node initiating the traffic or the source address of a router searching for the destination on a link remote from the source node. The packet also includes the source link-level address, if one is available.

A node that receives a Neighbor Solicitation from a unicast address, destined to an address that is assigned to its interface, responds with a Neighbor Advertisement indicating its own link-level address.

When the soliciting node receives a responding Neighbor Advertisement, it updates its neighbor cache entry with the target's link-level address and changes its state from INCOMPLETE to REACHABLE.

NOTE   For a complete description of the different possible reactions, see RFC 2461.[3]

Neighbor Unreachability Detection

If a node to which another is communicating fails, it is not very beneficial to detect the failure before the upper layers do. If a router in the path to the destination fails, however, there may be an alternative router to use, and it would be extremely helpful to be able to detect that failure before the upper-layer protocol does.

Neighbor reachability is verified in one of two ways—from hints from the upper-layer protocols or from responses to Neighbor Solicitations. Forward-direction communication must be possible for a neighbor to be reachable. Reachability is verified if forward progress is being made by an upper-layer protocol. If forward progress is being made in a TCP connection, for example, as indicated by new acknowledgements being received for data sent or by new data being received in response to a sent acknowledgement, reachability is verified. If forward progress is being made end to end, it also is being made to the next-hop router, and reachability to the router is confirmed.

Some upper-layer protocols do not provide such hints, such as UDP communications. If no verification can be received from upper-layer protocols, the node actively probes neighbors to determine their reachability state. A node sends Neighbor Solicitations to the cached link layer address of the neighbor in question and waits for Neighbor Advertisements. A node sends a Neighbor Advertisement with the solicited bit set *only* if it received a Neighbor Solicitation. If a node receives a Neighbor Advertisement with the solicited bit set, the node can be certain that its neighbor received the NS that it sent, and therefore forward-direction communication exists. These probes are sent in conjunction with traffic. If no traffic is being sent to a node, no probes are sent to the node.

A neighbor cache stores information about neighbors, including the IP address, link layer address, and reachability state. Table 8-9 lists the possible reachability states.

Table 8-9 *Neighbor Reachability States*

State	Description
INCOMPLETE	Address resolution is in progress. An NS has been sent, but no reply has yet been received.
REACHABLE	Forward-direction communication has been verified within the past 30 seconds.
STALE	An entry in the neighbor cache has not been verified as reachable within the past 30 seconds. An unsolicited Neighbor Advertisement message will add an entry to the cache for the sender of the message, with state STALE. No action is required until traffic is sent to the STALE entry.
DELAY	No reachable verification has been received within the past 30 seconds, and a packet has been sent to the specified neighbor within the past 5 seconds. If no positive confirmation is received within 5 seconds of entering DELAY state, send an NS and change the state to PROBE.
PROBE	An NS has been sent to verify reachability. No NA has yet been received.

An entry in the neighbor cache is INCOMPLETE initially. After the link layer address for the entry has been learned, and forward-direction communication has been verified, the state changes to REACHABLE. The state remains REACHABLE as long as the forward-direction communication continues to be verified.

When no reachability confirmation is received from a REACHABLE neighbor, its state changes to STALE. An unsolicited RA or NA received from a node puts an INCOMPLETE entry into the neighbor cache, which immediately transitions to STALE. An unsolicited advertisement does not provide any information about forward communication. The entries remain STALE until traffic is sent to that neighbor.

As soon as a packet is sent to the neighbor, its state changes to DELAY, and a timer is set to 5 seconds in the neighbor cache for the entry. The packet is sent to the cached link layer address, even though it is STALE. If the timer expires before any reachability confirmation is received, the state changes to PROBE. If reachability is confirmed, the state changes to REACHABLE.

Upon entering PROBE state, an NS is sent to the cached link layer address of the neighbor. Solicitations continue to be sent every second in the absence of a response, even if no additional data packets are sent. If no response is received for 1 second after three solicitations have been sent, the entry should be deleted from the cache.

Example 8-3 shows output from the **debug ipv6 icmp** and **debug ipv6 nd** commands and shows a router's neighbor cache state going from INCOMPLETE to REACHABLE, through all the intermediate states. Example 8-3 also displays the output from the **show ipv6 neighbor** command, which displays the neighbor cache. The output of the **show ipv6 neighbor** command provides the IPv6 address, its age, its link layer address (if known), its state, and the interface through which it is known.

Example 8-3   **debug** *Output Showing Neighbor Reachability State Changes*

```
Falcon#debug ipv6 icmp
ICMP packet debugging is on
Falcon#debug ipv6 nd
ICMP Neighbor Discovery events debugging is on

10:58:08: ICMPv6-ND: Received RA from FE80::200:CFF:FE76:5B7C on
  Ethernet010:58:08: ICMPv6-ND: INCMP created: FE80::200:CFF:FE76:5B7C
10:58:08: ICMPv6-ND: INCMP -> STALE: FE80::200:CFF:FE76:5B7C

Falcon#show ipv6 nei
IPv6 Address                     Age MAC Address     State Interface
FE80::200:CFF:FE76:5B7C            2 0000.0c76.5b7c STALE Ethernet0

11:01:13: ICMPv6: Received echo request from FE80::200:CFF:FE76:5B7C
11:01:13: ICMPv6: Sending echo reply to FE80::200:CFF:FE76:5B7C

11:01:13: ICMPv6-ND: STALE -> DELAY: FE80::200:CFF:FE76:5B7C

11:01:19: ICMPv6-ND: DELAY -> PROBE: FE80::200:CFF:FE76:5B7C
11:01:19: ICMPv6-ND: Sending NS for FE80::200:CFF:FE76:5B7C on Ethernet0
11:01:19: ICMPv6-ND: Received NA for FE80::200:CFF:FE76:5B7C on Ethernet0
  from FE80::200:CFF:FE76:5B7C
11:01:19: ICMPv6-ND: PROBE -> REACH: FE80::200:CFF:FE76:5B7C

Falcon#show ipv6 nei
IPv6 Address                     Age MAC Address     State Interface
FE80::200:CFF:FE76:5B7C            0 0000.0c76.5b7c REACH Ethernet0
```

Falcon receives an RA from Eagle's link-local address FE80::200:CFF:FE76:5B7C. An INCOMPLETE entry is created in Falcon's cache, which immediately turns STALE, because the RA is unsolicited. At this point, the neighbor cache is queried. The entry does indeed say the address is STALE. Eagle's link layer address is known.

A couple of minutes later, Eagle pings Falcon, as shown by the received echo request. Falcon replies to Eagle, sending the echo response to the stored link layer. Because a packet is forwarded by the router to a STALE entry, however, the router must change the state to DELAY to see whether it can verify the forward-direction communication path. The router cannot verify this with ICMP packets. So it changes the state to PROBE and sends an NS to see whether it can get reachability verification by probing Eagle. Eagle sends an NA. The **debug** does not show that the solicited bit is set in the NA. After receiving the NA and verifying communication, Falcon changes the state of Eagle's entry to REACH.

The neighbor unreachability detection process enables a host to redirect traffic to an alternative router if its default router fails. It detects the failure of the default router and then chooses another router to which to forward its traffic. Potentially, this can all occur before the upper-layer protocol or application times out. IPv4 hosts might never detect that the default router has failed. An upper-layer protocol or application will time out if the router fails. The IPv4 host will likely attempt to use the dead router to reestablish a connection. Some IPv4 hosts might know of multiple default routers and could choose the second router through which to reestablish the connection.

Default Router Selection

A host chooses one router (out of possibly many) from its default router list when the destination is off-link and there is no existing cached entry for the destination or when an existing default router appears to be failing. Normally, a default router is chosen the first time traffic to a particular destination requires it. The information is cached and used for subsequent traffic.

The default router selection process uses the default router list and the neighbor cache. Any router that is not known to be unreachable has preference when becoming the default router—that is, any router not in the INCOMPLETE state. If multiple routers are in any state other than INCOMPLETE, the router selection process either returns the same router or returns routers from this list in a round-robin fashion, depending on the implementation.

If a next-hop router appears to be failing, the neighbor unreachability detection process will detect it. If it indeed has failed, the router entry is deleted from the neighbor cache. Next-hop detection and address resolution are repeated, and an available next-hop router is used.

Case Study: Default Router Failure and Communication Recovery

A host transfers a file from a remote server using FTP. The host sends the traffic to its on-link default router. The host continues to receive ACKs for data sent, so the host knows that its default router must be reachable. In mid-session, the router fails. The host stops receiving ACKs. The host can no longer verify forward-direction communication through hints from the TCP layer, so it changes the router's state to STALE. It still attempts to send packets, so the state changes to DELAY. After 5 seconds, the host still has not received positive confirmation of the router's reachability state, so it changes the state to PROBE and sends NS. The router does not respond and therefore gets deleted from the host's neighbor cache.

The host still tries to send packets, but it no longer has a next-hop entry to which to send them. So it sees, the prefix of the destination is off-link and that retrieves a default router from its stored list. It puts the router into its neighbor cache with an INCOMPLETE state, if it does not already exist, and attempts to resolve its link layer address by sending an NS. When the new router responds with an NA, positive reachability is confirmed, and traffic begins flowing through the new router.

Duplicate Address Detection

All nodes perform duplicate address detection before assigning a unicast address to an interface. It is not performed for anycast addresses. This is performed regardless of whether the address is assigned via stateless, stateful, or manual configuration. It is performed before assigning an address to an interface and on an initializing interface. The address to be assigned to the interface is called "tentative" while the duplicate address detection process is taking place.

Before sending a solicitation, the interface joins the all-nodes multicast group to ensure that the node receives Neighbor Advertisements from any node already using the address and joins the solicited-node multicast group for the tentative address to ensure that if another node is attempting to begin using the address, both nodes will learn of each other's presence.

The node sends a Neighbor Solicitation message, with the tentative IP address as the target. The source address is the unspecified address, and the destination is the tentative address's solicited-node multicast address. By default, one solicitation is sent.

Any neighbor that is already assigned the address receives the solicitation and sends a Neighbor Advertisement in reply. The target specified in the advertisement is the tentative address. The destination address is the solicited-node address of the tentative address. If a node receives this Neighbor Advertisement, and the target address is the interface's tentative address, the address is a duplicate and must not be assigned to the interface. Some IPv4 hosts perform a duplicate address detection process before assigning an IP address to an interface. Not all do, however, allowing an interface with a duplicate address to potentially disrupt existing traffic flows.

Autoconfiguration

Because network manageability is so crucial to the success of any network, processes to facilitate it need to be built in to the protocol. Networks with hosts that have static configurations, manually entered, are difficult to manage when changes are necessary. Many tools ease the management burden of IPv4 networks, such as DHCP to minimize the amount of static configuration, but they are not required elements to the protocol. IPv6 nodes can automatically configure themselves, with or without the help of a DHCP server, making host configuration changes much easier.

Router Advertisements are used to tell hosts how to configure themselves. The RA contains two bits that tell the hosts whether to use a configuration server and, if so, whether information other than addresses should be obtained from the server. The Managed Address Configuration (M) bit, if set, tells hosts to use a stateful address configuration protocol to configure its address, such as DHCP. Stateless autoconfiguration of addresses also occurs on the host. The Other Stateful Configuration (O) bit tells the host to use the stateful configuration protocol to configure information other than the address. IPv4 hosts, on the other hand, are statically configured to use DHCP with a specific DHCP server if the IP address and other configuration are to be obtained dynamically. Otherwise, the configuration is all entered manually.

Stateless Autoconfiguration

Through a combination of what a node knows (its interface identifier) and what a router knows (the prefixes assigned to a link), a node can configure its own IP address. No server is needed to establish basic IP connectivity. This works on any multicast-capable interface.

Upon interface initialization, a node generates a link-local address for that interface. The link-local address is the interface's identifier concatenated with the well-known link-local prefix FE80::. The rightmost zeros of the link-local prefix are replaced with the interface ID, forming a 128-bit address. Note that interface IDs are typically 64 bits, but not always.

Link-local prefix FE80:0:0:0:0:0:0:0 and interface ID 200:CFF:FE0A.2C51 form link-local address FE80:0:0:0: 200:CFF:FE0A.2C51.

If the interface ID is more than 118 bits long, it cannot be concatenated with the link-local FP, which is 10 bits long. The autoconfiguration will fail, and the interface will have to be configured manually.

The node does not immediately assign the generated link-local address to the interface. First, it must determine whether a duplicate address exists. The node initiates the duplicate address detection process.

A node that learns that its generated address is not unique must be configured manually. One way to configure the node is to configure an alternate interface ID. This way, the node can still participate in the stateless autoconfiguration process and automatically configure each of its required addresses plus any assigned unicast and multicast addresses. The alternative to configuring an interface ID is to manually configure IPv6 addresses on the interface. Such a configuration could be a large administrative task, given the number of addresses that must be configured on the interface.

When the node is satisfied that no duplicate address exists, it assigns the address to the interface.

At this point, basic IP level connectivity exists. IPv6 hosts on a link with no router can now communicate with each other. No manual network layer configuration is required in the hosts to enable this communication.

Example 8-4 shows the minimal basic configurations for both Falcon and Eagle.

Example 8-4   *Minimal Basic Configurations for Falcon and Eagle to Enable IPv6 Communication*

```
Falcon
ipv6 unicast-routing
!
interface Ethernet0
 ipv6 enable
```

Example 8-4   *Minimal Basic Configurations for Falcon and Eagle to Enable IPv6 Communication (Continued)*

```
Eagle
ipv6 unicast-routing
!
interface Ethernet0
 ipv6 enable
```

Pinging Falcon's link-local address from Eagle shows that communication exists, as demonstrated by the output in Example 8-5.

Example 8-5   *Verifying Communication Between Falcon and Eagle from Falcon's Link-Local Address*

```
Eagle#ping ipv6 fe80::200:cff:fe0a:2c51
Type escape sequence to abort.
Sending 5, 100-byte ICMP Echos to FE80::200:CFF:FE0A:2C51, timeout is 2 seconds:
!!!!!
Success rate is 100 percent (5/5), round-trip min/avg/max = 60/68/80 ms
```

Both routers and hosts perform all the steps of the stateless autoconfiguration process discussed so far, to enable the basic IP connectivity. Every interface must create a link-local address. Duplicate address detection is performed for all unicast addresses prior to assigning them to an interface, regardless of whether the IPv6 address is configured via stateless autoconfiguration, stateful autoconfiguration, or manually, except as discussed in the following paragraph.

Hosts, not routers, continue the autoconfiguration process. The host sends an "all-routers" multicast solicitation to find a router on the link. All routers respond with Router Advertisements. The RA may tell the host to use stateful autoconfiguration to configure addresses and other information. The host uses the prefix information marked for address configuration to create a site-local address. To create a site-local address, the site-local FP, the prefix, and the interface ID are concatenated. A host is not required to perform the duplicate address detection process when assigning its site-local address. The theory is that the process just verified that the link-local address is unique. This means that the interface identifier is unique to the link. Because the site-local address assigns a different prefix to the same interface identifier, the site-local address is also unique. Globally aggregatable addresses are generated and assigned using the same method.

The RA also provides on-link prefix information. This information is a list of prefixes and prefix lengths, marked as on-link prefixes, that the host uses to build its prefix list. The prefix list is used by the host to determine whether a destination node is on-link or off, and therefore whether it needs to use a default router to send the traffic.

A host can configure its MTU size based on information contained in the RA also.

Stateful autoconfiguration is required to configure other information, such as the DNS server.

Use the following interface subcommands to configure a router to advertise a prefix with specific values, to set the managed configuration flag, and to set the other configuration flag:

```
ipv6 nd prefix-advertisement 2001:ABAB::/48 3000 3000 onlink autoconfig
ipv6 nd managed-config-flag
ipv6 nd other-config-flag
```

The prefix **2001:ABAB::/48** is advertised with a Valid Lifetime of **3000** seconds and a Preferred Lifetime of **3000** seconds, to be used as both an on-link advertisement and autoconfiguration.

The autoconfiguration process occurs on each interface of a node whenever the interface becomes enabled. A multihomed node performs autoconfiguration on each interface independently. An interface is enabled upon the following:

- Initialization of the interface at system startup
- The interface is re-enabled after an interface failure or after being temporarily disabled by a system administrator
- The interface attaches to a link for the first time
- The interface becomes enabled after being administratively down

Stateful Autoconfiguration

Stateful autoconfiguration may be used in conjunction with stateless autoconfiguration. DHCP provides stateful autoconfiguration for IPv4. A modified DHCP for IPv6 implementation could take advantage of a number of IPv6 features, enhancing the capabilities of DHCP.

NOTE   The Dynamic Host Configuration working group has published a draft for DHCP for IPv6 titled "draft-ietf-dhc-dhcpv6-15.txt."

A configuration server allocates addresses and other information, such as DNS server address, to requesting hosts. The addresses are associated with a Valid and Preferred Lifetime, just as are the prefixes used for stateless autoconfiguration. A server with the capability to request that all hosts revalidate their assigned addresses can use the lifetime values to renumber networks.

Renumbering

Site renumbering will still occur, even with the abundance of IP addresses. Address prefixes are strictly maintained, and an address assigned to a site might need to be recalled occasionally. Or the site might want to change ISPs, which would require a prefix change, just as it does today with IPv4 if a company changes ISPs. IPv6 was not designed to eliminate this phenomenon, but it is designed to make renumbering easier.

An address is in one of two states: preferred or deprecated. A host should always attempt to communicate using a preferred address. A deprecated address should be used only as the source address if using a preferred address will cause an existing connection to be disrupted. If two hosts have a TCP connection established using preferred addresses, for example, and one host's address changes to deprecated, if the host switches to a new preferred address, the connection will fail.

Host renumbering is simplified by the use of preferred and deprecated addresses. The time that an address remains preferred is set and modified in Router Advertisements, which are periodically sent on the link and are processed by every node on the link. New prefixes can be added to the Router Advertisements, thus adding new addresses to the interfaces, and old ones can be deprecated and removed. A similar mechanism can be used to renumber hosts using a configuration server. The server may multicast a request to all nodes, asking them to reconfirm their assigned addresses. The hosts will query the configuration server and obtain addresses with modified lifetime values, deprecating existing addresses or assigning new preferred addresses. The robustness of this renumbering mechanism depends on the Router Advertisements and stateful messages reaching all hosts on a link. Consider the following case study taken from RFC 2641.

Case Study: Renumbering a Network

A prefix is advertised with a lifetime of two months. On August 1, it is determined that the prefix must be changed and not used by September 1. The prefix advertisement can be changed so that its lifetime is two weeks, and then made smaller as the date approaches September 1, until the prefix is eventually advertised with a lifetime of zero, thereby invalidating the address. Consider, however, that a host is disconnected from the network on July 31. If it is plugged in again after September 1, it still thinks the old prefix is valid until September 30. The only way to force a host to discontinue using a prefix that was previously advertised with a long lifetime is to send an RA with a shorter lifetime. The routers must continue to send the RA with the lifetime value of zero until October 1 to ensure that any host that is disconnected before the change and reconnected before its two-month lifetime expiration does not use the invalid prefix.

In general, a router should continue to advertise a zero lifetime until such a time as any host that was disconnected, when reconnected, will not use an old prefix. Note that infinite lifetimes advertised by routers cause a problem when trying to renumber links and when hosts are connected and disconnected frequently.

Renumbering routers takes a lot of planning if communication is to be maintained. Routers communicate together, and hosts communicate with routers via the router's link-local address. This communication is independent of any assigned prefix. The nodes will therefore continue to communicate with the routers' link-local addresses, regardless of what global address is assigned to the link.

DNS implications are the same for IPv6 as they are for renumbering under IPv4. Either the new addresses need to be manually entered into the DNS databases prior to the new addresses being usable, or dynamically updated DNS servers (DDNS) should be implemented.

Routing

The preceding section discussed how an IPv6 node discovers the information required to forward a packet to neighbors and to next-hop routers if the destination is not on-link. Now routing issues are discussed to show different ways the IPv6 packet can be routed through a larger network.

MTU Path Discovery

The MTU is required to be at least 1280 bytes long on every link in an IPv6 network. However, the recommended size is 1500 bytes or larger. Any link that cannot handle a packet this large is required to provide link-level fragmentation. IP-level fragmentation is performed only by the source node, not by routers along the packet's path. Nodes are not required to implement MTU path discovery, but it is recommended. A node not implementing MTU path discovery uses an MTU equal to the minimum IPv6 MTU, 1280 bytes. A source node that implements MTU path discovery can take advantage of the largest possible packet, and possibly gain higher performance. Path discovery works for both unicast and multicast destinations.

MTU path discovery utilizes ICMP Packet Too Big error messages. A node sending traffic initially assumes the path MTU (PMTU) is equal to the MTU of its attached link. Any node along the delivery path that detects that it cannot deliver the packet over a link with a smaller MTU sends a Packet Too Big ICMP error message, which includes the size of its link MTU, and drops the big packet. The source node receives the ICMP error and reduces the size of the packets it is sending to the MTU value included in the error message. The process is likely to be repeated with nodes further down the delivery path. Figure 8-14 demonstrates the PMTU discovery.

Figure 8-14 *PMTU Discovery Process*

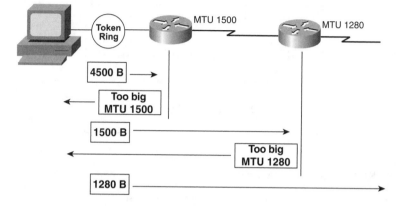

The Token Ring-connected PC begins by sending a packet of size 4500 B. The packet reaches a router with an MTU of 1500 B on the link to the delivery path. The router sends an ICMP Packet Too Big message back to the host, includes its MTU of 1500 B, and drops the original packet. The PC creates a smaller packet, of size 1500 B. The first router passes it on. The next router's link to the delivery path has an MTU of 1280 B. It sends an ICMP Packet Too Big message back to the host and drops the packet. The PC then sends a packet of size 1280 B, which is forwarded through both routers.

MTU path discovery works with multicast destination addresses as well as unicast. A multicast packet branches off into many paths. Any node along any path may send the Packet Too Big message. The minimum value of the set of PMTUs determines the size of the packets sent.

RIPng

RIPng (*ng* stands for "next generation") is based on RIP version 2 (RIP-2). None of the operational procedures, timers, or stability functions have been changed. RIPng is RIP-2, modified to support the larger IP addresses and multiple addresses on each interface of IPv6. The UDP port number for RIPng is 521. RIPng does not support both IPv4 and IPv6 and is therefore not backward-compatible with RIP-2.

NOTE   Chapter 7, "Routing Information Protocol Version 2," of *Routing TCP/IP, Volume I*, discusses RIP version 2.

Figure 8-15 shows the RIPng message format. The basic structure is very similar to RIP-2.

Figure 8-15 *RIPng Message Format*

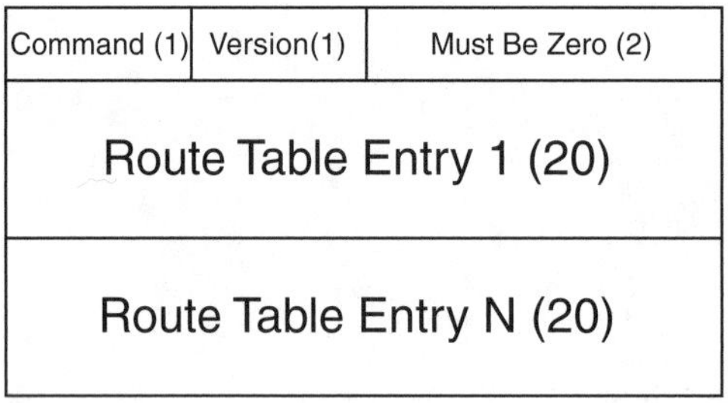

Command (1)	Version(1)	Must Be Zero (2)
Route Table Entry 1 (20)		
Route Table Entry N (20)		

The RIPng message fields are defined as follows (with lengths shown in bytes):

- *Command* is set to either 1, signifying a request, or 2, signifying a response.

- *Version* is currently 1.

The rest of the message contains the list of route table entries (RTEs). Figure 8-16 shows the format of the RTEs.

Figure 8-16 *RIPng Route Table Entry Format*

IPv6 Prefix (16)		
Route Tag (2)	Prefix Length (1)	Metric (1)

The fields in the RTE format are defined as follows:

- *IPv6 Prefix* is the 128-bit IPv6 address prefix.

- *Route Tag* is identical to RIP-2, which provides a field for tagging external routes or routes that have been redistributed into the RIPng process.

- *Prefix Length* specifies the significant part of the address prefix.

- *Metric* is the same as in RIP-2, a hop count value between 1 and 15, inclusive.

The number of routes that a RIPng update can contain depends on the link MTU, the number of octets of header information preceding the RIPng message, the size of the RIPng header, and the size of a route table entry (RTE). The formula for determining the number of RTEs in a single update is as follows:

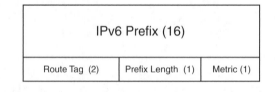

$$\#\text{RTE} = \text{Integer}\left[\frac{\text{MTU} - \text{sizeoff(ipheaders)} - \text{UDP\_header\_len} - \text{RIPng\_header\_len}}{\text{RTE\_size}}\right]$$

The number of RTEs directly relates to the link MTU and the length of the IP headers, UDP header, and RIPng header.

Each RIP-2 RTE contains a Next-Hop field associated with it, specifying a better next-hop address than the address of the advertising router. IPv6 addresses are so large that this would almost double the size of the RTE. RIPng specifies a single next-hop RTE that applies to all the following RTEs until the end of the message or until the existence of another next-hop RTE. The next-hop RTE in Figure 8-17 shows that the Route-Tag field and prefix field must contain all zeros. The metric value will be 0xFF. A value of 0:0:0:0:0:0:0:0 in the Address field indicates the next-hop is the originator of the RIPng advertisement.

Figure 8-17 *Next-Hop RTE*

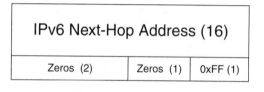

The next-hop address must be the link-local address of the next-hop router. If the address is not a link-local address, the receiver of the advertisement treats the packet as if the address prefix value is 0:0:0:0:0:0:0:0.

Periodic and triggered RIPng responses must remain local to a link—they must not traverse a router. Both periodic updates and triggered updates must have the router's link-local address as the source of the advertisement and the IPv6 hop limit equal to 255. The hop limit of 255 ensures that the advertisement has not traversed a router, because a router decrements the hop limit of every packet. The destination multicast address is the all-rip-routers multicast address FF02::9.

The Cisco router is capable of running multiple RIPng processes. The routing process is enabled as an interface subcommand:

```
ipv6 rip tag enable
```

The command must be enabled on any interface addressed with a prefix that needs to be advertised in the RIPng update. Multiple processes are distinguished by the tag. Currently, up to four processes are supported. Each process must use a unique UDP port number. A single process can use the default value, 521. The port number must be modified for subsequent processes; otherwise, the new process will not start up. The global command to modify the UDP port number and the multicast address used by RIPng is as follows:

```
ipv6 rip tag port udp-port multicast-group multicast-address
```

More than one process can use the same multicast address. If this command is not given, the default port number, 521, and the default multicast address, FF02::9, are used.

Unlike RIP-2, for which the global command **router rip** is required to enable the routing protocol, no global commands are required to enable RIPng.

Optional global commands control the entire RIPng process, affecting all configured interfaces. Global commands are available to disable or enable split-horizon and poison reverse, modify UDP port numbers and RIPng multicast addresses, change default timers, change the administrative distance, and redistribute static routes. Most of these functions are also available with RIP-2.

Table 8-10 lists the available global commands.

Table 8-10   *RIPng Global Commands*

Command	Description
[no] **ipv6 rip** *tag* **port** *udp-port* **multicast-group** *multicast-address*	Configures the RIP routing process to use the specified UDP port and multicast address.
[no] **ipv6 rip** *tag* **table** *table-number*	Assigns the specified routing table to the RIP process. Default is table 0. Note that only table 0 will be used for IPv6 unicast packet forwarding.
[no] **ipv6 rip** *tag* **distance** *distance-value*	Sets the administrative distance for this process. Default is 120.
[no] **ipv6 rip** *tag* **timers** *update expire holddown garbage-collect*	Modifies the RIPng timers for this process. The values indicate seconds. Default values are 30 180 180 120.
[no] **ipv6 rip** *tag* **redistribute static**	Advertises static routes into IPv6 as if they were directly connected.
[no] **ipv6 rip** *tag* **split-horizon**	Performs split-horizon processing of updates. This is on by default.
[no] **ipv6 rip** *tag* **poison-reverse**	Performs poison-reverse processing of updates. This is off by default.

Additional RIPng interface subcommands are also available. There are interface subcommands to initiate the advertisement of default routes on updates out the specific interface, to summarize routes advertised out the interface, to apply input and output filters to updates received or sent from the interface, and to change the metric-offset for routes received on the interface. All these functions are available with RIP-2. Table 8-11 lists the interface subcommands.

Table 8-11   *RIPng Interface Subcommands*

Command	Description
[no] **ipv6 rip** *tag* **enable**	Configures RIPng routing on an interface.
[no] **ipv6 rip** *tag* **default-information originate**	Originates the default route (0::0/0) and includes it in updates sent from this interface.

Table 8-11   *RIPng Interface Subcommands (Continued)*

[no] **ipv6 rip** *tag* **default-information only**	Originates the default route (0::0/0). Suppresses sending any routes except the default route on this interface.
[no] **ipv6 rip** *tag* **summary-address** *prefix/length*	Summarizes routing information. If the first *length* bits of a route match the given prefix, the prefix will be advertised instead. Multiple routes are thus replaced by a single route whose metric is the lowest metric of the multiple routes. You may use this command multiple times.
[no] **ipv6 rip** *tag* **input-filter** *name*	Applies a simple access list to RIP routing updates received on the interface.
[no] **ipv6 rip** *tag* **output-filter** *name*	Applies a simple access list to RIP routing updates generated on the interface.
[no] **ipv6 rip** *tag* **metric-offset** *number*	Changes the metric-offset of a route entering the routing table. Default is 1. Value may be between 1 and 16.

A simple network diagram along with the routers' configurations helps illustrate the minimal router configurations needed to run RIPng (see Figure 8-18).

Figure 8-18 *Simple RIPng Network*

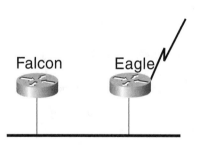

RIPng is configured on both routers, on the Ethernet link and the serial link. Example 8-6 shows the router configurations.

Example 8-6 *Configuring RIPng on Routers Falcon and Eagle*

```
Falcon
ipv6 unicast-routing
no ipv6 rip birdbath split-horizon
!
```

continues

Example 8-6 *Configuring RIPng on Routers Falcon and Eagle (Continued)*

```
!
interface Ethernet0
 no ip address
 no ip directed-broadcast
 ipv6 enable
 ipv6 address FEC0::/64 eui-64
 ipv6 address FEC0::1:0:0:0:0/64 eui-64
 ipv6 address FEC0::2:0:0:0:0/64 eui-64
 ipv6 rip birdbath enable
!
```

```
Eagle
ipv6 unicast-routing
no ipv6 rip birdbath split-horizon
 !
 !
interface Ethernet0
 no ip address
 no ip directed-broadcast
 ipv6 address FEC0::/64 eui-64
 ipv6 address FEC0::2:0:0:0:0/64 eui-64
 ipv6 address FEC0::3:0:0:0:0/64 eui-64
 ipv6 rip birdbath enable
!
interface Serial1
 ipv6 address FEC0::A:0:0:0:1/126
 ipv6 rip birdbath enable
!
```

The two routers share two common prefixes: FEC0::/64 and FEC0::2:0:0:0:0/64. Each also is configured with a third prefix. To enable the routers to advertise their noncommon prefix to each other, split-horizon has been disabled. RIPng is enabled on the Ethernet ports and on Eagle's serial1. The process name is birdbath.

Example 8-7 shows Falcon's routing table.

Example 8-7 *IPv6 Routing Table Showing RIPng-Learned Routes*

```
Falcon#show ipv6 route
IPv6 Routing Table - 9 entries
Codes: C - Connected, L - Local, S - Static, R - RIP, B - BGP
Timers: Uptime/Expires

L FE80::/64 [0/0]
  via ::, Null0, 01:37:41/never
L FEC0::200:CFF:FE0A:2C51/128 [0/0]
  via FEC0::200:CFF:FE0A:2C51, Ethernet0, 01:20:58/never
C FEC0::/64 [0/0]
  via FEC0::200:CFF:FE0A:2C51, Ethernet0, 01:20:58/never
```

Example 8-7 *IPv6 Routing Table Showing RIPng-Learned Routes (Continued)*

```
L FEC0::1:200:CFF:FE0A:2C51/128 [0/0]
   via FEC0::1:200:CFF:FE0A:2C51, Ethernet0, 01:01:36/never
C FEC0::1:0:0:0:0/64 [0/0]
   via FEC0::1:200:CFF:FE0A:2C51, Ethernet0, 01:01:36/never
L FEC0::2:200:CFF:FE0A:2C51/128 [0/0]
   via FEC0::2:200:CFF:FE0A:2C51, Ethernet0, 01:00:21/never
C FEC0::2:0:0:0:0/64 [0/0]
   via FEC0::2:200:CFF:FE0A:2C51, Ethernet0, 01:00:21/never
R FEC0::3:0:0:0:0/64 [120/2]
   via FE80::200:CFF:FE76:5B7C, Ethernet0, 00:00:08/00:02:51
R FEC0::A:0:0:0:0/126 [120/2]
   via FE80::200:CFF:FE76:5B7C, Ethernet0, 00:00:08/00:02:51
```

The routing table in Example 8-7 shows that the prefixes configured on Falcon's Ethernet port are connected. Eagle's Ethernet prefix FEC0::3:0:0:0:0/64 and serial prefix FEC0::A:0:0:0:0/126 are learned via the RIPng process.

RIPng is still a very easy protocol to implement, and the introduction of multiple processes adds a little more flexibility over RIP-2; however, the drawbacks still exist, as detailed in Chapter 7 of *Volume I*. For instance, it still has a small maximum hop count, limiting the size of network that can run the protocol.

OSPF for IPv6

OSPFv2 features many modifications designed to support the larger IPv6 address and changes in protocol semantics between IPv4 and IPv6. Cisco IOS does not yet support OSPF for IPv6. The fundamental mechanisms—flooding, DR election, area support, SPF, and so on—have remained unchanged. IPv6 OSPF operates directly over IPv6. The preceding header's next-header value is 89. The following functions have not changed in OSPF for IPv6:

- Both versions of the protocol support the same packet types—namely, Hellos, Database Description, Link-State Request, Link-State Update, and Link-State Acknowledgement packets, although some, such as the Hello packet, have been modified.

- Hello packets are exchanged to discover neighbor information.

- Adjacency selection and establishment.

- The interface state machine, including the states that interfaces traverse as well as designated router election process.

- The neighbor state machine, including the states that neighbors traverse before becoming adjacent.

- Link state database aging.

NOTE   Chapter 9, "Open Shortest Path First," of *Routing TCP/IP, Volume I*, discusses OSPF version 2.

Some mechanisms have changed. The changes result from the desire to make OSPF network-protocol-independent (and therefore more extensible), the new address format, explicitly specified flooding scope, and interface support of multiple addresses and prefixes. The OSPF protocol has become network-protocol-independent. The version number has changed from 2 to 3, and so the protocol is referred to in the remainder of this chapter as OSPFv3. This section addresses the changes made to the protocol.

Links Rather Than Subnets

IPv6 nodes communicate over links, not subnets. They can have multiple addresses and prefixes configured on interfaces connected to the link and can communicate with other nodes on the link, independent of the subnet being used. OSPFv3 focuses on links rather than subnets as OSPFv2 does. A router interface sending an OSPF packet no longer needs to reside on the same subnet as the router interface receiving the packet, because IPv6 OSPF runs per link rather than per subnet.

Addressing Semantics Removed

Addressing semantics have been removed from OSPFv2 packets and LSAs, thus creating a network-protocol-independent core within OSPFv3. This leads the way for a future multi-protocol OSPF. Many OSPFv2 packets and LSAs contain IPv4 addresses, representing router IDs, area IDs, or LSA link state IDs. OSPFv3 router IDs, area IDs, and LSA link state IDs are still expressed using 32 bits, so they cannot be represented by an IP address (although they can be represented by a portion of the address). OSPFv2 broadcast and NBMA networks list neighbors by IP address. OSPFv3 neighbors are known solely by their router IDs. Other OSPFv2 LSAs, such as Router-LSAs and Network-LSAs, contain IP addresses; the IP addresses are used to represent the network topology in the link state database. OSPFv3 Router-LSAs and Network-LSAs express topological information only; they describe the network topology in a network-protocol-independent manner. Instead of using IP addresses to identify links, IPv6 uses interface IDs. Every interface on a router is assigned a unique interface ID. Some implementations may use the MIB-II ifIndex. The MIB-II ifIndex is discussed in RFC 2233, "The Interfaces Group MIB using SMIv2." Neighbors and designated routers are identified by router IDs, which are no longer IP addresses. IPv6 addresses are contained only in the LSA payloads carried by Link-State Update packets.

LSA Flooding Scope and Unknown LSA Types

The flooding scope of LSA packets has been generalized. The LSA type determines the scope of OSPFv2 flooding. Each type is associated with its flooding scope. In OSPFv3, the flooding scope is explicitly configured in the LSA header. An OSPFv3 router that does not recognize the LSA type still knows how to flood the packet. The scope could be local-link, Area, or AS. OSPFv3 allows routers to have differing capabilities. Routers are no longer required to drop received LSAs with unknown types. Flooding scope, handling of unknown types, and LSA type are encoded in an expanded LSA Type field in the header. The upper 3 bits encode the flooding scope and the handling of unknown types. The handling bit informs the router to either flood the unknown LSA with link-local scope or to store and flood the LSA as if it were known. The router can do the latter because of the encoded flooding scope. Tables 8-12 and 8-13 display the flooding scope values and the values associated with the handling of unknown LSAs.

Table 8-12   *Flooding Scope Values and Descriptions*

Flooding Scope Value (Binary)	Description
00	Link-local scoping. Flooded only on the link it is originated on.
01	Area scoping. Flood to all routers in the originating area.
10	AS scoping. Flood to all routers in the AS.
11	Reserved.

Table 8-13   *Values Indicating the Handling of Unknown LSA Types*

Handling of Unknown LSA Value (binary)	Description
0	Treat the LSA as if it has link-local flooding scope.
1	Store and flood the LSA as if the type is understood.

Explicitly coded flooding scope facilitates the integration new OSPF features into an existing network.

Multiple OSPF Instances per Link

Multiple OSPFv3 protocol processes can run on a single link. This proves useful when multiple areas need to share a single link (see Figure 8-19). The instance ID in OSPFv3 packet headers enables this functionality.

Figure 8-19 *Two Routers Share a Link, and Two Areas Need to Run on the Single Link; Multiple OSPF Protocol Processes per Link Enables This*

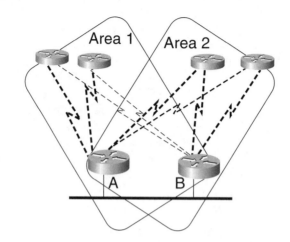

In Figure 8-19, Area 1 has four routers and Area 2 has four routers. The two remote routers in Area 1 have primary links to Router A with backup links to Router B. The two remote routers in Area 2 have just the opposite—primary links to Router B and backup links to Router A. Both Area 1 and Area 2 must run between Routers A and B over a single Ethernet link. You can accomplish this with OSPFv3, but not with OSPFv2.

Another case is when multiple companies or independent subsidiaries of a company running OSPF share a single link and use the link to communicate with each other. The link may belong to one of the companies, which uses it to connect to all independent organizations. A subset of the companies may want to peer, excluding the other companies. A more common practice is to use BGP to interconnect the independent organizations. However, an organization with OSPF expertise and no BGP expertise may dictate that the interconnecting protocol be OSPF. Figure 8-20 illustrates this scenario.

Figure 8-20 *OSPF Routers Share a Common Link; a Subset of the Routers Shares an OSPF Process*

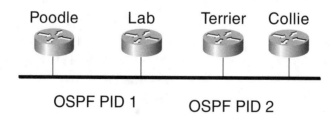

If Figure 8-20, routers Poodle and Lab peer and share a common OSPFv3 process. Routers Lab, Terrier, and Collie also peer, sharing a different OSPFv3 process. Lab's link is configured with both OSPFv3 process identifiers.

OSPF's Use of Link-Local Addresses

Because link-local addresses are configured on every active IPv6 router link, OSPFv3 uses these link-local addresses as the source address of protocol packets and as contents of the Link-LSA (described in the section "New LSAs and LSA Changes"). Link-local addresses, by definition, all share the same IPv6 prefix (FE80::/64). OSPFv3 nodes can therefore easily communicate and form adjacencies regardless of the prefix assigned for their site-local or global aggregatable addresses. Link-local addresses are used within LSAs to identify links on a router without associating the link with a particular IP address, keeping the topology information independent of the network protocol in use.

Removal of Authentication

Authentication has been removed from OSPF for IPv6. IPv6 has integrity, authenticity, and confidentiality mechanisms built in to the network layer of the protocol. OSPFv3 operates directly on top of this layer. OSPFv3 improved its efficiency by removing the authentication information from its headers. Networks that do not require routing security no longer have to process the headers. Networks that do require routing security can use the Authentication and Security Encrypting Payload extension headers at the IP layer.

New LSAs and LSA Changes

Although most of the functionality has remained unchanged, some OSPFv2 LSA fields have been modified, and LSAs have been renamed in OSPFv3. New LSAs have been added to OSPF to carry IPv6 addresses and next-hop information.

The OSPFv2 LSA header contained these fields: Age, Options, Type, Link State ID, Advertising Router, Sequence Number, Checksum, and Length. The OSPFv3 LSA removed the Options field from the header, expanded it from 8 to 24 bits, and moved it to the body of Router-LSAs, Network-LSAs, Inter-Area-Router-LSAs, and Link-LSAs. The Type field expanded to 16 bits, using the space originally occupied by the Options field. The rest of the header remains unchanged.

The LSA Type field is composed of unknown type handling, flooding scope, and LSA type bits. Figure 8-21 displays the LSA Type field.

Figure 8-21 *The OSPFv3 LSA Type Field*

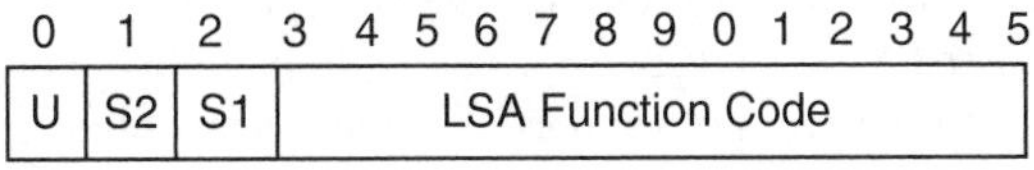

The U bit specifies the handling of unknown LSA types. S2 and S1 indicate the flooding scope.

Handling of unknown LSA types has changed. IPv4 OSPF discarded LSAs of unknown type. This discarding is undesirable in OSPFv3 because of the desire to mix routers of varying capabilities on a single link. If the designated router supports fewer options than other routers on the link, full functionality will not be available.

Table 8-14 lists the link type values for each LSA.

Table 8-14 *Link Type Values for Each OSPFv3 LSA*

LSA Function Code	Value	LSA Type
1	0x2001	Router-LSA
2	0x2002	Network-LSA
3	0x2003	Inter-Area-Prefix-LSA
4	0x2004	Inter-Area-Router-LSA
5	0x4005	AS-External-LSA
6	0x2006	Group-Membership-LSA
7	0x2007	Type-7-LSA
8	0x0008	Link-LSA
9	0x2009	Intra-Area-Prefix-LSA

From Table 8-14, you can see that the two OSPFv2 summary LSAs have been renamed, and there are two additional LSAs: Link-LSA and Intra-Area-Prefix-LSA. You also can see the flooding scope and handling of each type. All the listed types have a U bit set to 0, which indicates that if the type is unknown to any receiving router, it should treat the LSA as if it has link-local flooding scope. If the router does recognize the type, it floods the LSA according to the S2 and S1 bits. A Router-LSA type 0x2001, for instance, has S2S1 value 01 (binary). The LSA gets flooded to all routers within the area. The AS-External-LSA has a value of 10 (binary) and gets flooded to all routers in the AS.

The type-3 Network Summary-LSAs of OSPFv2 have been renamed *Inter-Area-Prefix-LSAs*. Remember that these LSAs are used by an Area Border Router to advertise networks external to an area.

Type-4 ASBR Summary-LSAs have been renamed *Inter-Area-Router-LSAs*. These LSAs are advertised by the AS boundary router and advertise ASBRs external to an area.

The LSA Options field expanded from 8 to 24 bits in OSPFv3. The field is present in Hello packets, database description packets, and certain LSAs (Router-LSAs, Network-LSAs, Inter-Area-Router-LSAs, Link-LSAs). The Options field enables routers to inform each other of their supported (or not supported) optional capabilities, allowing routers of mixed capabilities to exist within an OSPF routing domain. The action taken when routers do not support the same capabilities depends on the option.

The following 6 bits of the Options field have been defined:

- **V6**—If the bit is clear, the router participates in topology distribution but is not used to forward transit IPv6 packets.

- **E**—As in OSPFv2, E is set when the originating router is capable of accepting AS External LSA. E = 0 in all LSAs originated within a stub area. The bit also is used in Hello packets, indicating the interface's capability to send and receive AS External LSAs. Neighboring routers with mismatched E bits do not become adjacent, ensuring that all routers in an area support stub capabilities equally.

- **MC**—The bit is set when the originating router is capable of forwarding IP multicast packets. MOSPF uses this bit.

- **N**—Used only in Hello packets. A set N bit indicates the originating router's support for NSSA External LSAs. If N = 0, the originating router does not send or accept these NSSA External LSAs. Neighboring routers with mismatched N bits do not become adjacent, ensuring that all routers in an area support NSSA capabilities equally. If N = 1, E must be 0.

- **R**—A set Router bit indicates that the router is active. If the R bit is clear, an OSPF speaker can participate in topology distribution without being used to forward transit traffic. This could be used by a multihomed node that wants to participate in routing but does not want to act as a router, forwarding packets between its interfaces. The V6 bit specializes the R bit. If the R bit is set, but the V6 bit is clear, the node does not forward IPv6 datagrams, but it does forward datagrams belonging to another protocol.

- **DC**—This bit is set when the originating router is capable of supporting OSPF over demand circuits.

Comparing these bits to the 6 defined bits in the OSPFv2 Options field (T, E, MC, N/P, EA, DC), you can see that there have been some changes. Type of service (ToS) is not supported in OSPFv3, so the T bit has been replaced. The N bit is still used only in Hello packets. The P bit is part of another set of options in OSPFv3, the prefix options associated with each advertised prefix. The OSPFv2 EA bit indicates the support of External Attribute LSAs. External Attribute LSAs are proposed as an alternative to running Internal BGP (iBGP) to transport BGP information across an OSPF domain. External Attribute LSAs have not been implemented, nor have any drafts or RFCs been published. Even without the options bit to define the EA capability, however, External Attribute LSAs could still be supported by OSPFv3, as an additional LSA type, with specified flooding scope and unknown LSA type handling.

The new Link-LSA is used to exchange IPv6 prefix and address information between routers on a single link. It is also used by a router to advertise a set of options to associate with the Network-LSA that will be originated for the link. The Link-LSA provides the router's link-local address and the list of prefixes to associate with the link. The LSA is multicast to all routers on a link. The options that are advertised by the Network-LSA are the logical OR of the options sent by all routers in the Link-LSA.

There is another new LSA, called the *Intra-Area-Prefix-LSA*. This LSA carries IPv6 prefix information that in OSPFv2 was carried in Router-LSAs and Network-LSAs. It is used by a router to advertise address prefixes assigned to the router itself, such as attached stub networks and attached transit networks.

The OSPFv3 LSAs that contain prefix information always carry the prefix length, prefix options, and prefix address. The Prefix Options field is an 8-bit field describing capabilities associated with the prefix. The following four options are defined:

- **NU**—A set "no-unicast" bit excludes the prefix from unicast routing calculations.
- **LA**—The set "local-address" bit indicates that the prefix is actually an IPv6 address of the advertising router.
- **MC**—A set "multicast-capable" bit indicates that the prefix should be included in multicast routing calculations.
- **P**—The "propagate" bit is set on NSSA prefixes that should be re-advertised at the NSSA area border.

Each prefix is advertised with the 8-bit Prefix Options field that serves as input to the various routing calculations. The options could indicate that certain prefixes should be excluded or that others should not be propagated.

BGP-4 Multiprotocol Extensions

Additions made to BGP-4 are not specific to IPv6. They also include support for other protocols, such as IPX. The multiprotocol additions to BGP-4 are discussed here as they relate to IPv6. Multiprotocol BGP (MBGP) is discussed in Chapter 7, "Large-Scale IP Multicast Routing."

Three pieces of BGP-4 information are IPv4-specific:

- The next-hop attribute
- The AGGREGATOR attribute
- The network layer reachability information (NLRI)

At the time of this writing, it is assumed that every BGP-4 speaker will maintain at least one IPv4 address. The AGGREGATOR attribute will continue to use this address. Refer back to Chapter 2 for more information about the AGGREGATOR attribute. So, the additions to BGP-4 address the NEXT-HOP attribute and the NLRI. Furthermore, because the next-hop information is used to forward packets to a set of destinations and is used only when adding NLRI, not when withdrawing routes, the next-hop information has been added to the reachable NLRI updates.

Two new attributes are defined to support multiple protocols over BGP. The multiprotocol-reachable NLRI (MP-REACH-NLRI) and the multiprotocol-unreachable NLRI (MP-UNREACH-NLRI). Both attributes are optional and nontransitive, meaning that a BGP process that does not recognize the attribute can quietly ignore the Update message in which it is included and not advertise the information to its other peers.

As the name suggests, the multiprotocol-reachable NLRI attribute describes the reachable destinations. The attribute contains information about the network layer protocol to which the addresses belong and the next-hop address used to forward packets destined for the contained list of destination prefixes. Each MP-REACH-NLRI Update message includes one next-hop address and a list of associated NLRIs. The NLRI is a 2-tuple of the form <*length*/*prefix*> in which *length* is the length of the prefix and *prefix* is the reachable IPv6 address prefix.

The next hop is the address to be used by BGP speakers when forwarding packets destined to an associated address prefix. Looking back at Chapter 2, the default rules for the next-hop attribute are as follows:

- If the advertising router and receiving router are in different autonomous systems (external peers), the NEXT_HOP is the IP address of the advertising router's interface.

- If the advertising router and the receiving router are in the same autonomous system (internal peers), and the NLRI of the update refers to a destination within the same autonomous system, the NEXT_HOP is the IP address of the neighbor that advertised the route.

- If the advertising router and the receiving router are internal peers and the NLRI of the update refers to a destination in a different AS, the NEXT_HOP is the IP address of the external peer from which the route was learned.

For IPv6, the rules are more specific because of the defined scopes of IPv6 addresses. An IPv6 BGP router advertises the global address of the next-hop router, possibly followed by its link-local address. The link-local address is included only if the BGP speaker shares a common data link with both the node identified in the Next-Hop field *and* the peer to which the Update message is being sent. In all other cases, only the global address is included in the Next-Hop field.

A network diagram, router configuration, and command output illustrate that the configuration and output of commands for MBGP using IPv6 closely resemble those used for IPv4.

Figure 8-22 shows a simple BGP router topology.

Figure 8-22 *Simple BGP Network*

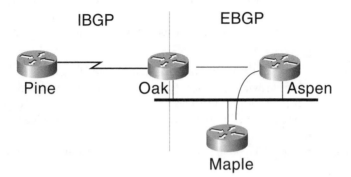

Maple and Aspen are E-BGP peers. Oak and Aspen are EBGP peers. All three routers are on the same Fast Ethernet segment. Oak and Pine are IBGP peers.

Aspen advertises NLRI, learned from Maple, to Oak. It includes Maple's address as the next-hop information, so Oak can send any traffic directly to Maple instead of making the extra hop through Aspen. Because the three routers share a Fast Ethernet segment, both Maple's global address and link-local addresses are included in the update.

Oak advertises Maple's NLRI information to Pine. The next-hop address is Maple's global address. The link-local address is removed. Example 8-8 shows the configuration of Oak and Aspen.

Example 8-8 *BGP Router Configurations*

```
Oak
interface fastethernet 0
 description Oak to Aspen (e-bgp)
 ipv6 address 200A::2:0:0:0:1/64
!
interface serial 0
 description Oak to Pine (iBGP)
 ipv6 address 200A:0:0:10::1/124
!
interface serial 1
 description IGP link
 ipv6 address 200A:0:0:1::1/124
!
router bgp 100
 neighbor 200A::2:0:0:0:2 remote-as 300
 neighbor 200A:0:0:10::2 remote-as 100
!
 address-family ipv6
 neighbor 200A::2:0:0:0:2 activate
 neighbor 200A:0:0:10::2 activate
 network 200a:0:0:1::/124
 exit-address-family
```

Example 8-8 *BGP Router Configurations (Continued)*

```
Aspen
interface fastethernet 0
 description Oak to Aspen (e-bgp)
 ipv6 address 200A::2:0:0:0:2/64
!
router bgp 300
 neighbor 200A::2:0:0:0:1 remote-as 100
 !
 address-family ipv6
 neighbor 200A::2:0:0:0:1 activate
 exit-address-family
```

Oak's FastEthernet address is 200A::2:0:0:0:1/64, as you can see in the interface subcommand, and is Aspen's EBGP neighbor. Oak also has an IGP link addressed with the 200A:0:0:1::/124 prefix. Example 8-9 displays the state of the BGP neighbors, a BGP update being sent from Oak to Aspen about the IGP prefix, and the entry in Aspen's routing table.

Example 8-9 *Output from BGP Commands*

```
Aspen#show bgp ipv6 nei
BGP neighbor is 200A::2:0:0:0:1,  remote AS 100, external link
  BGP version 4, remote router ID 172.16.255.1
  BGP state = Established, up for 00:00:18
  Last read 00:00:18, hold time is 180, keepalive interval is 60 seconds
  Neighbor capabilities:
    Route refresh: advertised and received
    Address family IPv6 Unicast: advertised and received
  Received 40 messages, 0 notifications, 0 in queue
  Sent 51 messages, 0 notifications, 0 in queue
  Route refresh request: received 0, sent 0
  Minimum time between advertisement runs is 30 seconds

 For address family: IPv6 Unicast
  BGP table version 2, neighbor version 1
  Index 1, Offset 0, Mask 0x2
  1 accepted prefixes consume 64 bytes
  Prefix advertised 0, suppressed 0, withdrawn 0

  Connections established 4; dropped 3
  Last reset 00:00:43, due to User reset
Connection state is ESTAB, I/O status: 1, unread input bytes: 0
Local host: 200A::2:0:0:0:2, Local port: 11015
Foreign host: 200A::2:0:0:0:1, Foreign port: 179
```

You can see that the information displayed from the command output is very similar to that of IPv4. In fact, because this routing protocol is MBGP, and not a new version of BGP for IPv6, the only thing that you would expect to be added to the output is the address family type denoting IPv6 and IPv6 address formats. The output shows this. The address family value has been added. The address types differ. The TCP port number is the same, 179.

The Anycast Process

Anycast is a mechanism used to route packets to one of many identically addressed nodes. The identically addressed nodes might be a group of servers offering a well-known service to clients, or a group of routers belonging to an ISP, which requires that traffic pass through one of its anycast-addressed routers. A node addresses the IP packet to the single anycast address of the group. The node learns the next hop for the address just as it would for a unicast address. If the anycast address is on-link, the node performs the address resolution process. The first response is added to the neighbor cache. If the address is off-link, the packet is forwarded to the nearest destination based on the routing protocol's measure of distance. There will be a prefix that contains the set of anycast nodes in a domain. For instance, all nodes using the anycast address FEC0::A:FDFF:FFFF:FFFF:FFFE/64 reside within the FEC0:0:0:A::/64 prefix. All these anycast nodes must be advertised as host routes within the domain addressed with this prefix. A node uses the metric of the host route to determine the closest anycast node. You can see that if there are a lot of anycast groups and anycast nodes within the groups, and the containing domains are very large, routing tables within the domain could get very large.

Although anycasting is specified in IPv6, its use is currently very restricted. There is little experience using widespread anycasting services, and there are some known complications, such as ensuring all packets for a session reach the same anycast node, or requiring the anycast nodes to share state information[4]. More issues need to be resolved as experience is gained. The only defined anycast group, other than all anycast subnet-routers, is the Mobile IPv6 home-agent address. Until solutions to the problems are agreed upon, use of anycasting is restricted to routers only.

Multicast

IPv6 uses and facilitates the use of multicasting. Multicasting is used rather than broadcasting to minimize the impact of solicitations, advertisements, updates, and so forth on multicast-capable links. IPv6 facilitates the widespread use of multicasting through its support of scoped multicast addresses and its built-in support for a data-link group membership protocol, the Listener Discovery Protocol. The Protocol Independent Multicast (PIM) routing protocol enables the IPv6 hosts on a link to join a networkwide multicast group.

Scoped Addresses

Multicast scopes have been added to the IPv6 multicast address space. Applications and uses for multicast technology can be created for global, public use, for use within an organization or site, or for use on single links. Administrative policies have to be set to identify the boundaries of sites and organizations to utilize the scopes effectively. Well-known multicast groups can be contained within the defined scopes, making the containment of these multicast applications easier to control.

Listener Discovery

Derived from IGMPv2, the Multicast Listener Discovery (MLD) protocol enables routers to discover which nodes on a link want to receive multicast packets, and to which multicast groups those nodes belong. This information is then passed on to the multicast routing protocol in use on the network, such as PIM. MLD can be broken down into two groups of functions: the host functions and the router functions.

Host Functions

Host functions are similar to the host functions of IGMPv2, discussed in Chapter 5, "Introduction to IP Multicast Routing." Two types of Report messages are defined:

- Membership Report
- Done Report

When a host first begins listening to a particular multicast address on a link, it should immediately transmit a Report to inform the router that there is a listener on the link. It sends the Report to the address of the multicast group and also includes the address in the MLD Multicast Address field within the Report packet. The source address of the report is the host's link-local address. The presence of the link-local source address prevents the packet from traveling beyond the local link.

The router periodically sends queries to determine to which multicast groups hosts on the link belong. When a host hears a general query, which does not refer to any particular multicast address, it sets its delay timer for each of the multicast addresses to which it is listening, except the link-scope all-nodes multicast address and any multicast address with scope 0 (reserved) or 1 (node-local). When the host hears a query for a particular multicast address, it sets its delay timer for that particular address only. It sets the delay timers to a random value between 0 and the Max Response Time value that is sent as part of the query. The timer for each individual address is set to a different random value.

If the host does not hear any Reports from other hosts on the link for an address before that address's timer expires, the host sends its own Report. If it does hear a Report before the timer expiration, the host stops the timer and does not send a Report. The link is therefore not flooded with Reports from every member of the group, but the presence of at least one member is known.

When the router receives a Report for a particular multicast address, if the address is not already present in the router's list of multicast addresses, the router adds it to the list and informs the network's running multicast routing protocol of the addition. If the address is already in the list, the router resets the address's timer to the Multicast Listener Interval value. If this timer expires without hearing a Report for a particular address, the address is deleted from the router's list.

Figure 8-23 is a flowchart diagramming the host functions of the MLD process.

Figure 8-23 *Host Functions of the MLD Process*

Host Function Flow

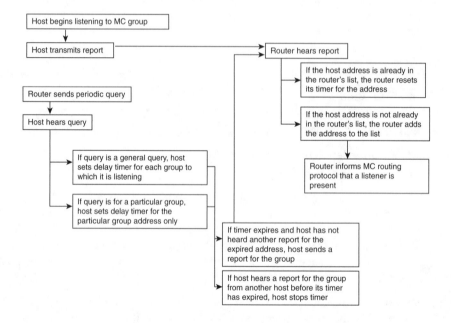

When a host is finished listening to a multicast group, it should send a Done message. This is analogous to the IGMP2 Leave message. It is sent to the link-scope all-routers multicast group FF02::2. The Multicast Address field of the message carries the address to which the host is finished listening. A host does not need to send a Done message if its last Report for the address was interrupted by a Report from another node, because there is very likely still another node on the link listening to the same multicast address.

Router Functions

The router functions of MLD also are very similar to IGMPv2, as discussed in Chapter 5. The terms differ a little. The router sends a Multicast Listener Query, of which there are two subtypes:

- General Query
- Multicast-Address-Specific Query

The concepts of a querier and a nonquerier router still exist. A router assumes the state of querier or nonquerier for each of its multicast links. As with IGMPv2, an initializing router assumes it is the querier and immediately sends a General Query. If the router hears a query message from another router, it checks the received query's IPv6 source address. If the source address is numerically less than its own, the router relinquishes the role of querier to the other router. If its own address is lower, it remains the querier.

The querier router polls each of its attached links upon startup and periodically with the General Query to discover whether any group members are present. The router's link-local address is the source address of the query. The queries are sent to the link-scope all-nodes multicast address of FF02::1.

When a querier router receives a Done message, if the address referred to in the Done message is in its multicast list, it sends a Multicast-Address-Specific Query to the multicast address to determine whether any listeners remain on the link. If no host responds within the Maximum Response Delay, the router removes the address from the list and informs the multicast routing component.

Figure 8-24 shows the process flow of the MLD router function.

Figure 8-24 *Router Functions of the MLD Process*

Router Function Flow

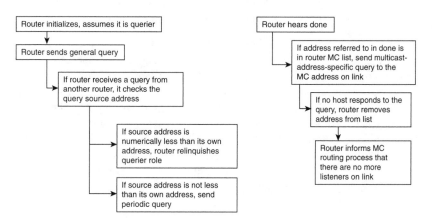

PIM Multicast Routing

As with the unicast routing protocols, multicast routing protocols are modified to support IPv6. Functionally, the protocols operate in the same manner. The modifications mainly support the larger address space. PIM is currently the only multicast routing protocol with IPv6 modifications defined. PIM and other multicast routing protocols are discussed fully in Chapter 5.

The IPv6 modifications define addresses that must be used in PIM messages and identify an area of concern involving scoped multicast addresses and the centralized bootstrap mechanism.

With IPv4, each of the different PIM messages uses multicast or unicast addresses in its Destination field and its assigned interface IP address as the source. With the advent of scoped addresses in IPv6, and the multiple addresses assigned to each link, the choice of which address to use is further defined.

Most of the messages use the global IPv6 all-PIM-routers multicast address, FF02::D, as the IPv6 destination, and the sending interface's link-local address as the source. Other messages use the specific global IPv6 unicast address of the service to which they need to communicate as the destination, and their own global unicast address as the source.

Hello messages are sent on multicast interfaces to discover PIM neighbors. The all-PIM-routers multicast address is the destination of these packets. The interface's link-local address is the source. The link-local address is therefore used in building neighbor tables and in electing the designated router.

Assert messages are sent when a multicast packet is received by a router through an interface that the router views as an outgoing interface for that (source, group) or (S, G) pair. Recall from Chapter 5 that the multicast router maintains a multicast forwarding table with upstream and downstream interfaces for each particular source destined for a particular group (the (S, G) pair). If a router receives a multicast packet on an outgoing (downstream) interface for that (S, G) pair, the packet was forwarded by another router connected to that downstream link. Figure 8-25 illustrates this.

Router SJ's multicast forwarding table for the particular (S, G) pair indicates that E0 is downstream from the source and is therefore the outgoing interface. SJ receives a multicast packet for this (S, G) pair through its Ethernet interface. Assert messages are used to determine a single PIM forwarder for the multi-access network. The Assert message is sent by SJ in Figure 8-25 on the Ethernet network to determine which of the PIM routers should be the single PIM forwarder. The messages are sent to the all-PIM-routers multicast address and are sourced from the interface's link-local address. The value of the link-local address is used to break ties in the assert process, with the numerically highest link-local address becoming the forwarder. Downstream routers save the forwarder's link-local address to resolve any future RPF requirements.

Figure 8-25 *Multicast Packet Received on Downstream Interface*

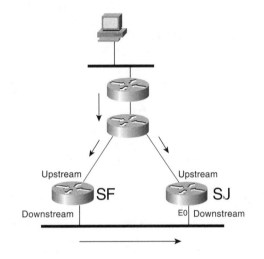

The Join/Prune, Graft, and Graft-Ack messages, which are used to build and prune the multicast routers' forwarding tables, also use the all-PIM-router multicast address as the destination and the link-local address as the source. All these messages also contain an address for the upstream neighbor. The upstream neighbor address is set to the link-local address of that neighbor. An RPF lookup is used to obtain the address. If a link-local address for the neighbor cannot be obtained, a known global address for that neighbor is used.

Another message that uses the all-PIM-router mulitcast address destination and the link-local address source is the Bootstrap message. The Bootstrap message is multicast to all PIM routers by the bootstrap router (BSR). The bootstrap router address is contained within the message. Because this address must be accessible by all PIM routers, the address is the domainwide-reachable address of the bootstrap router.

The Register and the Register Stop messages are used in PIM Sparse mode. A source designated router (DR) wanting to send traffic to a multicast group initially encapsulates the multicast packets in a Register message and sends it to the rendezvous point (RP). An RP sends a Register Stop message to the DR, telling the source to stop encapsulating the multicast packets in the Register message. These events are not necessarily sequential. Chapter 5 describes the full sequence of these events. Both the Register and the Register Stop messages address packets to the domainwide reachable unicast address of the rendezvous point router. The source address is the domainwide-reachable unicast address of the DR. The source DR obtains the RP address from the RP-set information multicast to all-PIM-routers by the bootstrap router. The RP obtains the global IPv6 address of the DR from the source address of the Register message it received from the DR.

Each candidate RP unicasts a Candidate-RP-Advertisement message to the bootstrap router. The message contains the multicast group address for which the advertising router is a candidate RP. The message also contains the IPv6 address to be used as the RP address for this router. The destination address for the Candidate-RP-Advertisement is the domainwide-reachable unicast address of the BSR. The source address is a domainwide-reachable unicast address of the candidate RP. The BSR forms the RP-set from these advertisements.

Scoped multicast addresses solve the multicast containment problem; however, they bring up an issue involved with PIM and the bootstrap mechanism. The bootstrap process is a centralized process within a PIM-SM domain. Bootstrap messages from the centralized BSR are expected to reach all PIM routers. If the PIM domain is not a subset of the multicast scoped address domain, the bootstrap mechanism will not work. Multicast packets within one scoped address domain will not traverse to a second scoped address domain. The result is that to allow the bootstrap mechanism to work, the PIM domain must be a subset of the scoped address domain, or all multiple-hop messages must use globally reachable IPv6 addresses.

Quality of Service

No quality of service (QoS) functions are built into IPv6, such as procedures that describe ways you can queue and forward differing traffic classes through routers or ways you can prioritize multiple traffic flows, but there are mechanisms that allow such protocols to work with IPv6. The two such mechanisms are the Traffic Flow and Traffic Class fields of the IPv6 header, as defined in the following sections.

Traffic Flow

Nodes initiating traffic may want to request special handling of certain traffic flows. The node can label the flow, requesting that IPv6 routers provide nondefault QoS for that flow. For instance, a call center application requires very fast response time, so the call center representative using the application can give information obtained from a server to the person on the phone as she speaks. A node may label this flow, requesting that it obtain a different QoS from other traffic.

Traffic Class

The traffic class bits in the IPv6 header are provided for source nodes and/or intermediate routers to distinguish between different classes or priorities of IP packets. The bits can be used in the same way that the IPv4 type-of-service and precedence bits are experimentally being used today. Differentiated Services (DiffServ) redefines the Traffic Class field and calls it the DS field. The definition of the DS field is the same for IPv6 as for IPv4. The leftmost 6 bits are used by the DiffServ codepoint. Packets are marked with a codepoint at the edges of a network. The codepoint determines the behavior of each router when queuing and forwarding the packet. This behavior is called the per-hop behavior (PHB).

Transition from IPv4 to IPv6

A new routing protocol cannot be implemented if there is not a clear transition methodology. The easier the transition procedures, the more likely the new protocol will be implemented. It is imperative that IPv6 interoperate with IPv4. IPv6 nodes need to communicate with IPv4 nodes, at least initially, and more likely, indefinitely. The NGTRANS IETF working group developed a number of different methodologies to facilitate the transition and to ensure compatibility.

Compatibility with IPv4 is possible in a number of different ways. A node running a dual-stack implementation fully implements both IPv4 and IPv6. It may communicate using both IPv4 and IPv6. A node could encapsulate IPv6 packets into an IPv4 header, creating a tunnel over an existing IPv4 network, allowing two IPv6 nodes to communicate. There are two tunneling mechanisms:

- Automatic tunneling
- Configured tunneling

An IPv4-compatible IPv6 address is defined such that the first 96 bits of the IPv6 address are all zero, and the remaining 32 bits compose an IPv4 address. For example, ::172.69.1.1 is an IPv4-compatible address. A node configured with an IPv4-compatible address uses automatic tunneling.

For IPv4 and IPv6 to coexist on the same network, a mechanism must be in place to resolve names to IP addresses correctly. DNS modifications have been defined to enable the DNS servers to correctly return IPv4 or IPv6 addresses (or both). The capability to do this is crucial to the success of protocol coexistence.

Or, a network address translation - protocol translation (NAT-PT) device might be implemented on the network between the IPv6 network and the IPv4 network. Dual stack is discussed first.

Dual Stacks

One way for a node to implement IPv6 and remain compatible with IPv4 nodes is to fully implement both IPv6 and IPv4. A node that fully implements both stacks is called an IPv6/IPv4 node. An IPv6/IPv4 node can communicate with IPv6 nodes using IPv6 packets and with IPv4 nodes using IPv4 packets.

An IPv6/IPv4 node must be configured with both an IPv6 and IPv4 address. The addresses may or may not be related. IPv4-compatible addresses may be viewed as single address that can be used as either an IPv6 address or an IPv4 address. The entire 128 bits represents the IPv6 address, whereas the low-order 32 bits represents the IPv4 address.

You can configure the addresses in many ways:

- You can configure the IPv6 address using stateless or stateful (DHCP for IPv6) autoconfiguration. The address can be either an IPv4-compatible address or an IPv6-only IPv6 address.

- You can use any IPv4 mechanism to acquire the node's IPv4 address.

- You can configure an IPv4-compatible address using an IPv4 configuration mechanism to acquire the IPv4 part of the address. The node then maps the IPv4 address into an IPv4-compatible address by prepending the 96-bit prefix 0:0:0:0:0:0. This method can prove particularly useful when an IPv6/IPv4 node is installed before IPv6 routers or address configuration servers are available.

A node with both an IPv4 and an IPv6 address must have some mechanism in place to determine which address to use. DNS provides this mechanism.

DNS

A new type of resource record is defined for IPv6—the *AAAA* record. This record provides name-to-IPv6 address mapping. A DNS resolver on an IPv6/IPv4 node must be able to handle both IPv4 A resource records and IPv6 AAAA resource records. When a node queries the DNS server for an address, an A record or an AAAA record is returned. The type of address returned determines the protocol that is used. If an A record is returned, the node uses its IPv4 address and the IPv4 protocol for communication with the requested destination. If an AAAA address is returned, IPv6 is used.

When an IPv4-compatible address is assigned to an IPv6/IPv4 host, both an AAAA record and an A record are defined in the DNS. The AAAA record lists the full 128-bit IPv6 address, and the A record lists the low-order 32 bits of the address. Both types are listed so that IPv6-only nodes can query the server and receive an IPv6 address and IPv4-only nodes can receive the IPv4 address.

Now, if both AAAA and A type records are listed for an IPv4-compatible address, the DNS resolver has some choices on what to return, and what it returns affects which protocol is used in the communication:

- Return only the IPv6 address to the application.

- Return only the IPv4 address to the application.

- Return both addresses to the application.

The address or the order of the addresses returned affects the type of IP traffic generated.

IPv6 Tunneled in IPv4

Most IPv6 implementations will be installed alongside IPv4 networks. IPv6 hosts will communicate over mostly IPv4 networks. IPv6 packet encapsulation into IPv4 packets supports this. You can create four types of tunnels:

- Router to router
- Host to router
- Host to host
- Router to host

IPv6/IPv4 routers can encapsulate IPv6 traffic for transmission over an IPv4 infrastructure. You can use this method for IPv6-only nodes that exist on either side of the routers, or for any communication that requires that this one segment of the end-to-end IPv6 path traverse an IPv4 network. The source node sends an IPv6 packet to an IPv6 router. This router acts as the tunnel source point, encapsulates the packet into an IPv4 packet, and sends the IPv4 packet on to the tunnel endpoint. The router at the far end of the tunnel decapsulates the packet and forwards it on toward the IPv6 destination.

IPv6/IPv4 nodes can initiate a tunnel to an IPv6/IPv4 router. This tunnel is created for the first segment of the IPv6 path. The initiating node encapsulates the IPv6 packet into an IPv4 packet and sends the IPv4 packet to the tunnel endpoint router. The endpoint router decapsulates the packet and forwards the IPv6 packet toward its final destination.

An IPv6/IPv4 host can create a tunnel to another IPv6/IPv4 host. This is a complete end-to-end tunnel. The IPv6/IPv4 source node encapsulates the IPv6 packet in an IPv4 packet and forwards the packet over an all-IPv4 network to the destination host. The destination host receives the IPv4 packet, decapsulates it, and processes the IPv6 packet.

A router-to-host tunnel is created on the final segment of the IPv6 path. A router receives an IPv6 packet and creates a tunnel so that it can forward the packet toward the destination host over the connected IPv4 network. The destination host receives the IPv4 packet, decapsulates it, and processes the IPv6 packet.

The first two methods, router to router and host to router, are not tunneled all the way to the final destination. The far endpoint of the tunnel differs from the final destination of the packet. The address of the far endpoint of the tunnel differs from the address of the final destination. An IPv4 address for the far end of the tunnel is required, and there is no way to obtain this information from the actual IPv6 destination address. These methods require configured tunnels.

In the second two methods, the far-end tunnel endpoint is the same as the final packet destination. The IPv4 address of the far end of the tunnel is contained in the low-order 32 bits of the IPv4-compatible IPv6 destination address. You can create automatic tunnels in the second two tunneling methods.

Configured Tunnels

A tunnel is created between Cisco routers by creating tunnel interfaces in the routers that border the IPv6 and IPv4 networks. The tunnel's endpoints are defined in both routers. An IPv6 subnet is created for the tunnel, and both routers are assigned IPv6 addresses. If an IPv6 dynamic routing protocol is in use, such as RIPng or BGP, the protocol is enabled on the tunnel interface. Figure 8-26 shows two IPv6 networks connected to an IPv4 network. A tunnel is configured between the IPv6 networks to enable communication.

Figure 8-26 *Network Diagram of IPv6 Networks Tunneled Over an IPv4 Network*

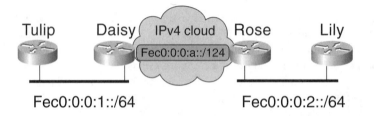

Tulip and Lily are IPv6-only routers. They communicate with each other via the IPv6-over -IPv4 tunnel between Daisy and Rose.

Example 8-10 shows the configurations of Daisy and Rose.

Example 8-10 *Configured Tunnel Router Configurations*

```
Daisy
ipv6 unicast-routing
!
interface Tunnel0
 description tunnel Daisy -> Rose
 no ip address
 no ip directed-broadcast
 ipv6 address FEC0::A:0:0:0:1/124
 ipv6 rip flowerpot enable
 tunnel source Serial1.503
 tunnel destination 172.69.255.250
 tunnel mode ipv6ip
!
interface Ethernet0
 ipv6 address FEC0::1:0:0:0:0/64 eui-64
 ipv6 rip flowerpot enable
!
interface Serial1.503 point-to-point
 ip address 172.69.255.254 255.255.255.252

Rose
ipv6 unicast-routing
```

Example 8-10 *Configured Tunnel Router Configurations (Continued)*

```
!
interface Tunnel0
 description tunnel Rose -> Daisy
 no ip address
 no ip directed-broadcast
 ipv6 address FEC0::A:0:0:0:2/124
 ipv6 rip flowerpot enable
 tunnel source Serial1.703
 tunnel destination 172.69.255.254
 tunnel mode ipv6ip
!
interface Ethernet1
 no ip address
 ipv6 address FEC0::2:0:0:0:0/64 eui-64
 ipv6 rip flowerpot enable
!
interface Serial1.703 point-to-point
 ip address 172.69.255.250 255.255.255.252
```

The tunnel interface is a generic tunnel, configured with ipv6ip mode.

The **traceroute** from Tulip to Lily in Example 8-11 shows the IPv6 packet traversing the tunnel.

Example 8-11 *Displaying the IPv6 Packet Traversing the Tunnel from Tulip to Lily*

```
Tulip#traceroute ipv6 fec0:0:0:2:210:7bff:fe3a:ce8a

Type escape sequence to abort.
Tracing the route to FEC0::2:210:7BFF:FE3A:CE8A

  1 FEC0::1:200:CFF:FE0A:2AA9 8 msec *  4 msec
  2 FEC0::A:0:0:0:2 24 msec *  16 msec
  3 FEC0::2:210:7BFF:FE3A:CE8A 28 msec *  20 msec
```

The first address is Daisy's IPv6 Ethernet address. The second address is Rose's tunnel interface address. The third address is Lily's Ethernet address.

Configured tunnels offer a straightforward way to connect two IPv6 networks over an IPv4 network.

Automatic Tunnels

An encapsulating host configured for automatic tunnels extracts the IPv4 address from the destination's IPv4-compatible IPv6 address. This IPv4 address will be the automatic tunnel endpoint. The encapsulating host must have IPv4 connectivity to the address represented in the IPv4-compatible address. The source host encapsulates the packet into an IPv4 header, with the extracted IPv4 address as the destination and the address extracted from its own IPv4-compatible address as the source. Routers between the hosts know nothing of the IPv6 payload.

Network Address Translation - Protocol Translation

Another way to allow IPv6 and IPv4 networks and hosts to coexist is with the use of network address translation - protocol translation (NAT-PT). IPv6/IPv4 routers do the translation for IPv6-only and IPv4-only hosts. When these hosts want to communicate, neither needs to know that they are not running the same version of IP. The NAT-PT-configured router does all the translation. Both source and destination addresses are translated between IPv6 and IPv4.

The same issues that exist with IPv4 NAT also exist with IPv6-to-IPv4 NAT-PT. Inbound and outbound traffic translated between IPv6 and IPv4 domains must traverse the same address translator. The address translator maintains state information about translated sessions. End-to-end security is not possible. IPSec does not work through a network address translator. Applications that carry IP addresses anywhere other than the IP header will not work unless application translation gateways are running on the translating router. DNS queries crossing the protocol domains must have request and response information within the DNS packet translated between IPv4 and IPv6.

One issue particular to translation between IPv4 and IPv6, besides the address, is the header information. IPv6 headers do not contain the same fields as IPv4 headers, as you learned in this chapter. Option handling is very different. Translating between the two domains is nontrivial, and you should use this method of coexistence only when no other method is available.

End Notes

[1]IEEE, "Guidelines for 64-Bit Global Identifier (EUI-64) Registration Authority," http://standards.ieee.org/regauth/oui/tutorials/EUI64.html (March 1997)

[2]R. Hinden and S. Deering, "RFC 2375: IPv6 Multicast Address Assignments" (Work in Progress)

[3]T. Narten, E. Nordmark, and W. Simpson, "RFC 2461: Neighbor Discovery for IP Version 6 (IPv6)" (Work in Progress)

[4]C. Partridge, T. Mendez, and W. Milliken, "RFC 1546: Host Anycasting Service" (Work in Progress)

Looking Ahead

IPv6 enables the Internet to scale to an extremely large size. It also eases host configuration management. Much of the host configuration is accomplished through router configurations. Router management, as discussed in Chapter 9, "Router Management," will be needed as much as ever, to provide secure configurations and to keep the routers running reliably and optimally.

Recommended Reading

Huitema, C. *IPv6: The New Internet Protocol.* Upper Saddle River, New Jersey: Prentice Hall PTR; 1996.

Although it's a little dated (many RFCs have become draft standards, many more have been written, some have been modified), this book offers very good technical discussions and insight into design decisions.

Review Questions

1   Which of the following are valid representations for the address 200A 0000 0000 0C00 0000 0000 0000 0000 with a 60-bit prefix?

A. 200A:0000:0000:0C/60

B. 200A::0C00:0:0:0:0/60

C. 200A:0000:0000:0C00::/60

D. 200A::0C00::/60

E. 200A:0:0:C00::/60

F. 200A::0C/60

2   For what is the address 0:0:0:0:0:0:0:0 used?

3 You configure your site border routers, connecting to an IPv6 public network, to advertise all your internal network numbers, including FEC0:0020:0:0100::/56. You get a nasty call from the IPv6 public network administrator. What is wrong?

_____

_____

_____

4 Which extension headers are processed by every IPv6 node in the path from source to destination?

_____

_____

_____

5 Which extension headers are used to specify a list of routers to visit before reaching the destination and to have each of those routers process the header?

_____

_____

_____

6 A router receives a packet larger than its outgoing link's MTU. Does it fragment the packet and forward the fragments toward the destination?

_____

_____

_____

7 If set in a Router Advertisement, what affect does the Managed bit have?

_____

_____

_____

8 If a router advertises prefix information in its RAs, how is the information used?

_____

_____

_____

9 In what two states can a host's IP address reside, and what are the roles of the two states?

_____

_____

_____

10 What information does a router advertise in its RA to tell hosts to stop using a particular prefix when initiating IP sessions?

_____

_____

_____

11 If a node has a neighbor with state DELAY, can the node send the neighbor packets?

_____

_____

_____

12 A host is not running any routing protocol. It is sending data to a remote node using a default router. The default router fails. Will the host continue to send data into the black hole of the dead router until its TCP connection fails?

_____

_____

_____

13 What are the scope values for multicast packets, and for what are they used?

_____

_____

_____

14 What Cisco router command enables IPv6 routing?

_____

_____

_____

15 What interface subcommands enable IPv6 on an interface?

_____

_____

_____

16 What commands are used to enable a RIPng process?

_____

_____

_____

17 How is the BGP-for-IPv6 process enabled between neighbors?

_____

_____

_____

Chapter Bibliography

Atkinson, R., and S. Kent, "IP Authentication Header," RFC 2402, November 1998.

Atkinson, R., and S. Kent, " IP Encapsulating Security Payload (ESP)," RFC 2403, November 1998.

Atkinson, R., and S. Kent, "Security Architecture for the Internet Protocol," RFC 2401, November 1998.

Bates, T., R. Chandra, D. Katz, and Y. Rekhter, "Multiprotocol Extensions for BGP-4", RFC 2283, February 1998.

Coltun, R., D. Ferguson, and J. Moy, "OSPF for IPv6," RFC 2740, December 1999.

Conta, A., and S. Deering, "Generic Packet Tunneling in IPv6 Specification," RFC 2473, December 1998.

Conta, A., and S. Deering, "Internet Control Message Protocol (ICMPv6) for the Internet Protocol Version 6 (IPv6) Specification," RFC 1885, December 1995.

Deering, S., and R. Hinden, "Internet Protocol, Version 6 (IPv6) Specification," RFC 1883, December 1995.

Deering, S., W. Fenner, and B. Haberman, "Multicast Listener Discovery (MLD) for IPv6," RFC 2710, October 1999.

Gilligan, R., and E. Nordmark, "Transition Mechanisms for IPv6 Hosts and Routers," RFC 1993, April 1996.

Haberman, B., H. Sandick, and G. Kump, "Protocol Independent Multicast Routing in the Internet Protocol Version 6 (IPv6)," draft-ietf-pim-ipv6-03.txt, March 2000.

Hinden, R., M. O'Dell, and S. Deering, "An Aggregatable Global Unicast Address Format," RFC 2374, July 1998.

Hinden, R., and S. Deering, "IP Version 6 Addressing Architecture," RFC 2373, July 1998.

Hinden, R., and S. Deering, "IPv6 Multicast Address Assignments", RFC 2375, July 1998.

Hinden, R., S. Deering, R. Fink, and T. Hain, "Initial IPv6 Sub-TLA ID Assignments," <draft-ietf-ipngwg-iana-tla-03.txt>, January 13, 2000.

Hubbard, K., M. Kosters, D. Conrad, D. Karrenberg, and J. Postel, "Internet Registry IP Allocation Guidelines," BCP 12, RFC 1466, November 1996.

IAB and IESG, "IPv6 Address Allocation Management," RFC 1881, December 1995.

IEEE, "Guidelines for 64-bit Global Identifier (EUI-64) Registration Authority", http://standards.ieee.org/db/oui/tutorials/EUI64.html, March 1997.

Johnson, D., and S. Deering, "Reserved IPv6 Subnet Anycast Addresses," RFC 2526, March 1999.

McCann, J., S. Deering, and J. Mogul, "Path MTU Discovery for IP version 6," RFC 1981, August 1996.

Malkin, G., and R. Minnear, "RIPng for IPv6," RFC 2080, January 1997.

Marques, P., and F. Dupont, "Use of BGP-4 Multiprotocol Extensions for IPv6 Inter-Domain Routing," RFC 2545, March 1999

Narten, T., Nordmark, E. and W. Simpson, "Neighbor Discovery for IP Version 6 (IPv6)", RFC 2461, December 1998.

Partridge, C., T. Mendez, and W. Milliken, "Host Anycasting Service," RFC 1546, November 1993.

Reynolds, J., and J. Postel, "Assigned Numbers," STD 2, RFC 1700, October 1994. (see also www.iana.org/iana/assignments.html)

Thomson, S., and C. Huitema, "DNS Extensions to support IP version 6," RFC 1886, December 1995.

Thompson, S. and T. Narten, "IPv6 Stateless Address Autoconfiguration," RFC 1971, August 1996.

Thomson, S., and T. Narten, "IPv6 Stateless Address Autoconfiguration," RFC 2462, December 1998.

Tsirtsis, G., and P. Srisuresh, "Network Address Translation - Protocol Translation (NAT-PT)," RFC 2766, February 2000.

- **Policies and Procedure Definition**—A clear policy and procedure definition is required to maintain any well-running network. Service Level Agreements, change management policies, and escalation procedures are all necessary.

- **Simple Network Management Protocol**—SNMP provides the basis for network management applications. Understanding how it works is essential if you are going to use any network management application on the network.

- **RMON**—RMON provides additional network management capabilities. Understanding how it works is essential if you are going to use any RMON-based network management application on the network.

- **Logging**—Logging the information about events that occur on Cisco routers provides a valuable resource when you are researching a network issue that may relate to the router.

- **Syslog**—Logging information to a syslog server creates a centralized repository of router event information that you can use to corrolate a network event to multiple network devices.

- **Network Time Protocol**—The Network Time Protocol synchronizes the clocks on all participating network devices, easing the corrolation of past events.

- **Accounting**—Accounting performed on network devices collects data that you can use to understand traffic flow as well as to bill network users based on the traffic flow.

- **Configuration Management**—Configuration management is the set of tools, processes, and policies used to maintain working, valid configuration files.

- **Fault Management**—Fault management systems notify the network manager of a failure somewhere in the network. The failure may be an event that causes some network services to be unavailable, or it may be an indication that performance may be affected.

- **Performance Management**—Performance management systems collect data used for trending and capacity planning.

- **Security Management**—Router security management ensures the integrity of routers. Various tools and configuration parameters are available to ensure that routers are not compromised.

- **Designing Servers to Support Management Processes**—The servers that support management processes provide the eyes into the network and therefore need to be secure, robust, and redundantly accessible to the network devices they are managing.

- **Network Robustness**—Network robustness requirements should include LANs and routing from the end node off the LAN to the rest of the network. HSRP provides default router redundancy, enabling end nodes configured with a single default gateway to utilize the robustness.

- **Lab**—The network lab is used to test plans, designs, new hardware, new operating systems, new protocols, new procedures, and so on. The lab should mirror the production network as much as possible to enable valid testing to occur.

CHAPTER 9

Router Management

So far in this book, you have read about ways to forward IP packets through networks and routers. For the packet forwarding to be successfull the networks and routers have to be healthy, in good working condition, and always available. The network and routers need to be managed, both reactively and proactively, to ensure their health. It is also important to lab test and monitor the effect of the forwarding mechanisms—the routing protocols, the network address translation, multicasting, and quality of service—to make sure that the network and routers continue to run smoothly.

This chapter covers the necessity of clear operational policies and procedures, the basics of configuring SNMP and RMON on the router to monitor the network and routers, and essentials for successful performance, fault, and security management. Also discussed are ways to maintain router availability and general concepts of lab construction and use.

Policies and Procedure Definition

It is impossible to successfully manage routers without clear policies and procedures. The policies need to document who is responsible for various levels of management and when they are responsible. They need to document when changes can be made to router configurations. The procedures document how changes are made, including describing what changes are taking place and backout and testing procedures. The procedures specify steps to follow when a more skilled engineer needs to begin working on a problem and when management needs to get involved. It also is important to have a clear plan for disseminating updated policies and procedures so that everyone involved is aware of the changes.

Policies that specify the Quality of Service (QoS) the users can expect from the network should be in place, such as round-trip delay time, a minimum amount of throughput or the amount of network availability, along with the actions that will be taken if the service is not met. These are referred to as *Service Level Agreements*. This section describes Service Level Agreements, change management policies, escalation procedures, and the necessity of keeping the policies and procedures up to date.

Service Level Agreements

Service Level Agreements (SLAs) clearly define the quality and quantity of service that is to be provided, as well as when and by whom it will be provided. They specify quality, such as guaranteed response time and throughput, as well as maximum jitter. Quantity is expressed as a percentage of network availability. SLAs identify when the network will be available, the maximum amount of time for a single outage, scheduled outages, and who is providing the service. It is important to identify who is providing the service to avoid misconceptions about realms of responsibility. Avoid finger-pointing by defining which organizations are responsible for which network components and the level of service for which each organization is responsible. The SLA must be clearly defined so that both the organization providing the SLA and the organization receiving the SLA understand and agree on the contents. SLAs could be provided by outside organizations providing services to your business, such as ISPs or companies to which you are outsourcing your network. Or, they may be provided by internal IT departments providing service to business units within the company.

The most effective SLAs are written with business objectives in mind. Consider, for example, the following SLA statements:

- Round-trip delay is less then 50ms, averaged over 1 hour, from site A to site B.
- Link availability is no less than 95%.

These SLA statements are not very useful if the business objectives require 99.9999% availability but do not need anything faster than 400ms round-trip delay. Any provider that is offering specialized QoS to particular applications, end stations, or sites will include the guaranteed level of QoS in an SLA.

An SLA does not provide any benefit if the service is not monitored. The provider guaranteeing the QoS in the SLA will need to verify that the user or application is indeed receiving that QoS. An SLA that provides end-to-end guarantees must be monitored end to end. An SLA that states the following:

> Round-trip delay is less than 200ms, averaged over 1 hour, from users at site A to servers at site B.

is measured differently from one that states the following:

> Round-trip delay is less than 100ms, averaged over 1 hour, from site border routers at site A to site border routers at site B.

Both statements may be included in a service level contract, and both should be monitored. The collected data is reported to both the service provider and the service users. Both need to read the reports to verify the SLA has been satisfied.

Change Management

A network without change management policies is likely to be a network in chaos. Change management policies state when changes can be made, who can make them, how to document and publish upcoming changes, and how and where to document completed changes.

The change management policy specifies the procedure to use when any network or system change is going to take place. This includes router configuration changes, new design implementations, IOS upgrades, or even the implementation of new network applications. There should be an electronic form to fill out with some or all of the following information:

- Who is requesting the change
- Why the change is being made
- What is the impact of the change (nondisruptive, maybe disruptive, disruptive)
- When will the change take place
- How long will it take to make the change
- How long will the change remain in effect
- What test procedures have been accomplished to test the change about to take place
- Who performed the tests
- Who will perform the change
- What are the procedures to perform the change
- What are the post-change test procedures to verify the change was successful
- What are the backout procedures

A change control board (CCB) may look at all upcoming changes for any given week and approve or disapprove changes. The CCB should include a knowledgeable representative from each group that designs, operates, maintains, and manages the network. It also should include a representative for each group that uses the network, such as the various business units within an organization. If the network is an ISP, the network user representative may be a customer service representative, responsible for the well-being of groups of customers. The CCB review process ensures that all network architects, operators, administrators, managers and customer support personnel, and network users are aware of planned activities, know of potential impacts, and have an opportunity to consider other mitigating factors before changes are applied.

The requested change must be approved by all members of the CCB and signed by all relevant parties, indicating that they are aware of the change and potential risks.

Sometimes an emergency change is required—to solve a problem, for instance. The change policy also specifies what to do in the case of an emergency. The policy specifies who can make emergency changes, under what circumstances, and how to document the changes.

It is very important to document all changes. A table identifying when a change was made, what change was made, who made it, and a reference to the change description document (such as the sample shown in Table 9-1) enables someone to go back and know what changed, in the event of a future network or router problem.

Table 9-1   *Change Policy Management Documentation*

Change Date and Time	Change Description	Change Implementer	Emergency	Change Document Location, *server.file*
6/3/00, 1:00 a.m.	Modified BGP peer on router Taos	Joe Smith	No	Pluto:changes\RtrTaos060300
5/27/00, 1:00 a.m.	Enabled custom queuing on router Aspen, on link to site Denver	Jane Anders	No	Pluto:changes\RtrAspen052700

If someone at site Denver calls the network operations center to report a problem with his connections to remote sites, and he says that the problems were first noticed early Monday morning, 5/29/00, the change log clearly shows that a change that affects Denver was made on Saturday night. This makes a clear starting point for troubleshooting the problem.

Strict change control policies should not be enforced only in enterprise networks. ISPs can benefit as much, if not more, from these policies. In enterprise networks, when changes are made that inadvertently affect a lot of people, business is disrupted, and there will be a lot of angry end users. A disruptive change made on an ISP network has the potential to affect many companies, causing a lot more disrupted business. Not only will there be a lot of angry people, these people have the option of switching to competing ISPs if they are not happy with the way the network operates. Strictly enforced policies minimize unscheduled disruptive changes and enable quicker recovery if problems are encountered.

Escalation Procedures

Clearly defined escalation procedures specify how long an engineer with a certain skill set works on a problem before handing the problem to a more skilled engineer. They specify who to turn the problem over to and how to turn it over. They also define how, when, and how often management is informed of issues, including how long a problem goes unresolved before it is brought to management's attention.

Updating Policies

No matter how well a policy is written, it eventually becomes outdated due to new technology or new organizations. The policies need to be updated to reflect changes. People who are responsible for implementing the policies and procedures need to be informed of and trained on the changes. Those whom the policies affect should be informed of all changes.

Simple Network Management Protocol

Network management software, such as CiscoWorks, uses the Simple Network Management Protocol (SNMP) to manage network devices. SNMP is the workhorse behind all those nice network diagrams, charts, and graphs. It queries the devices, collecting the data necessary to build the diagrams, charts, and graphs. SNMPv1[1] is supported on all Cisco routers. SNMPv2C is supported on all Cisco routers with IOS 11.3 or later. SNMPv2C supports bulk data transfers and more detailed error reporting than SNMPv1.

NOTE SNMPv2C consists of SNMPv2, as defined in RFCs 1902 through 1907, and SNMPv2C, as defined in RFC 1901.[2]

Overview of SNMP

SNMP consists of managers and agents. The manager collects the data; the agent provides the data.

A manager can be part of a Network Management System (NMS) such as CiscoWorks. Agents reside on the device being managed, such as the router.

A relationship is set up between the manager and the agent so that the manager can get or set information on the agent. The manager sends SNMP messages to the agent requesting data or requesting that the agent set parameters with data specified by the manager. These messages are called *gets* and *sets*, respectively. The community of managers that can request data from the agent, or request it to set parameters, is defined using access control lists and a password. The password is called a *community string*. The manager includes the community string in all get and set requests. The agent, which is preconfigured with the community string, verifies that the requesting manager is allowed to perform gets and sets and that the community string is correct. The manager can request any parameter defined in the Management Information Bases (MIBs) supported by the platform running the agent. Figure 9-1 illustrates a manager requesting link status information from a router.

The management station wants to find out the operational status of serial interface 0 on the router. The management station issues an SNMP get request, requesting the MIB variable ifEntry.ifOperStatus.1. ifEntry is the list of variables that can be polled for any interface on an agent. IfOperStatus is one of the variables. 0.1 is an index value, in this case identifying interface serial 0. The community string "restricted" is included in the get request. The router responds to the request. The response indicates that the value of the requested variable equals 1. The MIB defines ifOperStatus values 1, indicating the status is up; 2, indicating the status is down; and 3, indicating the status is testing. Link serial 0 in the figure is up.

Figure 9-1   *The Management Station Issues a Get Request, Looking for the Operational Status of the Router's Serial 0 Interface; The Router Responds with a Get Reply*

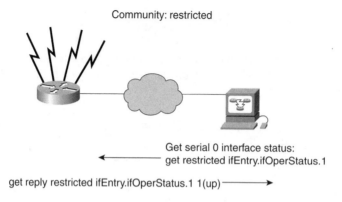

Community: restricted

Get serial 0 interface status:
get restricted ifEntry.ifOperStatus.1

get reply restricted ifEntry.ifOperStatus.1 1(up)

NOTE   MIB II is supported on all SNMP-capable routers. Interface variables are defined in MIB II. RFC 1213 defines MIB II.[3]

SNMP operates over UDP. SNMP also runs as a lower priority than other processes on the router. If the router is very busy running higher-priority tasks, SNMP messages can be dropped. Most manager configurations specify that more than one lost poll must occur before any state changes display.

SNMP enables you to collect a lot of information. Just about every statistic for every network device (and components within a device) and every protocol at all layers of the protocol stack can be gathered via SNMP. Sometimes the statistic being collected changes rapidly, and the manager is gathering information about the changing data, such as the number of errors occurring every minute on a flaky interface. It is tempting to use SNMP extensively and frequently to get the most accurate statistical data. Excessive SNMP traffic can adversely affect network performance, however, and therefore the amount of SNMP traffic needs to be carefully managed. Before you enable any management application, the amount of SNMP traffic (and other traffic, as well) generated by the application should be thoroughly understood.

Trap messages are sent by the agent to a management station. The traps are unsolicited and occur as the result of some event. The event may be a link down, a BGP connection failure, an authentication failure, or any number of other things. When the event occurs, the router sends an SNMP trap to the management station, informing the station of the event. The configuration of the management station dictates what is done with the trap. It may cause a piece of the network diagram to change colors, a message may be displayed on the screen, or an e-mail or page could be sent to a network manager.

SNMP provides the foundation for network management platforms, such as CiscoWorks.

CiscoWorks

Cisco networks can be managed with the assistance of CiscoWorks. CiscoWorks runs on top of a network management platform, such as HP OpenView, IBM NetView, or Sun Net Manager. The management platform provides general network diagrams, charts, and graphs, and CiscoWorks adds Cisco-specific entities, such as chassis views and device configuration management.

CiscoView is one of the CiscoWorks applications. CiscoView provides real-time views of networked Cisco devices. These views deliver a continuously updated physical picture of device configuration and performance conditions. The chassis views show front- and back-panel views of Cisco devices, including LED status lights. If you click a port shown in the chassis view, you can bring up a table of statistics related to the port, such as utilization, input and output errors, queue drops, collisions, and ignored packets. CiscoView also provides a dashboard-type view, which displays system performance of the Cisco device, such as memory usage, buffer usage, and CPU utilization. CiscoView is run from a centralized network management site from which you can review, reconfigure, and monitor essential device data from a simple GUI (that displays information such as dynamic status reports, performance statistics, and network inquiries) without having to physically check connections for each device, module, or port at every different or remote location.

The network management platform of choice and CiscoWorks work together to perform fault management, performance management, and configuration management. The diagrams, charts, and graphs rely mainly on SNMP to remain up to date.

The agent being managed by CiscoWorks must be configured to accept polls and to send traps to the CiscoWorks workstation.

Router Configuration for SNMP

Various global SNMP commands enable the router to be managed by CiscoWorks. All the global **snmp** commands begin with **snmp-server**. No specific one enables SNMP. The first **snmp-server** command entered enables both versions of SNMP on the router.

The router must be configured to use the same SNMP version supported by the management station.

The command to create the management community is as follows:

```
[no] snmp-server community string [view view-name] [ro | rw][access-list number]
```

The community string acts as a password between the managers and the agent. The management stations may have read-only (RO) or read/write (RW) SNMP access to the router. The CiscoWorks management station requires RW access for full manageability, specifically for the capability to set parameters, reload routers, and update configurations. SNMP is a very powerful tool. Almost all configuration and state information about the router can be read via the SNMP MIBs. Information obtained via SNMP read access could be used to learn routing tables and ARP tables, making it easier for someone to learn about specific devices and therefore specific areas of attack. SNMP write access allows configurations to be changed and links and routers to be reset. To limit which devices are allowed to read and/or write information to the router, use the *access-list* option. The list is a simple access list, specifying the address of the management station or a range of addresses with permitted management stations.

The only required command when enabling SNMP is **snmp-server community**. All the other SNMP commands are optional and provide fine-tuning of the collectable or settable information.

The **view** option in the **snmp-server community** command is used in conjunction with the following command:

```
snmp-server view view-name oid-tree {included | excluded}
```

This command limits which MIB objects an SNMP manager can access. The *oid-tree*, or Object Identifier tree, identifies the MIB subtree to be included or excluded. To identify a subtree, specify the top of the desired subtree using a text string consisting of numbers, such as 1.3.6.2.4, or the word, such as "system." Specifying system means that all MIB values in the system subtree are included or excluded. 1.3.6.2.1.2 is the numeric representation of iso.org.dod.mgmt.mib2.interfaces.

NOTE   Refer to the RFCs defining each individual MIB and to RFC 1902, "Structure of Management Information for Version 2 of the Simple Network Management Protocol (SNMPv2)," for the numeric representations of all object identifiers.

SNMP managers can send messages to users on virtual terminals and the console. The SNMP request that sends the message also specifies the action to be taken after the message has been sent, such as shut down the system. This is a very powerful tool. To enable this function, you must configure the **snmp-server system-shutdown** command. If you do not configure this command, the mechanism is not enabled.

Another powerful tool is the capability for TFTP servers to save and load configuration files via SNMP. You can limit this to servers specified in an access list using the **snmp-server tftp-server-list** *number* command, where *number* is the access list number.

The command to specify the host to which the traps are sent, and what trap types are sent, is as follows:

```
snmp-server host host [version {1 | 2c}] community-string [udp-port port] [trap-type]
```

If no *trap-type* is specified, all trap types enabled on the router are sent to the host. The version defines the SNMP version of the management station. The **udp-port** option changes the default port number.

Before any traps are sent to the specified hosts, the traps must be enabled globally. Some traps are enabled by default. Others must be enabled by the following command:

```
snmp-server enable traps trap-type trap-option
```

The **snmp-server enable traps** command enables the trap mechanism on the router for the specific traps. It does not specify a host to which to send them. Use this command to enable or disable traps of a certain type. When disabling traps, this overrides traps specified per host.

Another command is available to control traps on an interface basis. The interface subcommand to enable or disable link status traps on the configured interface is [**no**] **snmp trap link-status**. The traps are enabled on all interfaces by default.

For a host to receive traps, the host's address must be specified using the **snmp-server host** command, and the trap must be enabled globally, through either the **snmp-server enable traps** command, some other command, such as **snmp trap link-status**, or by default. Some configuration examples follow.

The configuration in Example 9-1 allows read-only access to any SNMP manager using community string "access." BGP traps are enabled and sent to hosts 172.16.1.200 and 172.16.1.201.

Example 9-1 *Allowing Read-Only Access to Any SNMP Manager and Enabling BGP Trap*

```
snmp-server community access RO
snmp-server enable traps bgp
snmp-server host 172.16.1.200 access
snmp-server host 172.16.1.201 access
```

A BGP external connection is established between routers 10.1.2.1 and 10.1.2.25. When the connection is cleared, traps are generated, as documented in Example 9-2.

Example 9-2 *Clearing BGP External Connections Generates Traps*

```
Bowler#clear ip bgp *

SNMP: Queuing packet to 172.16.1.200
SNMP: V1 Trap, ent bgp, addr 10.1.2.25
 bgpPeerEntry.14.10.1.2.1 = 00 00
 bgpPeerEntry.2.10.1.2.1 = 1
```

continues

Example 9-2 *Clearing BGP External Connections Generates Traps (Continued)*

```
SNMP: Queuing packet to 172.16.1.201
SNMP: V1 Trap, ent bgp, addr 10.1.2.25
 bgpPeerEntry.14.10.1.2.1 = 00 00
 bgpPeerEntry.2.10.1.2.1 = 1

SNMP: Packet sent via UDP to 172.16.1.200
SNMP: Packet sent via UDP to 172.16.1.201
```

Version 1 traps are sent to both trap hosts. The router's address that is sending the traps is 10.1.2.25, which is the address of the outbound interface used when sending the packet to the trap host. The value for the MIB OID bgpPeerEntry.14.10.1.2.1, which represents the last BGP error code seen by this peer, on the connection to the peer with address 10.1.2.1, is 00 00, meaning no error was seen. The OID bgpPeerEntry.2.10.1.2.1 represents the BGP peer state, as seen by this peer for the connection to peer 10.1.2.1. A value of 1 means the state is idle.

NOTE   To see a defined list of all supported Cisco MIBs, go to www.cisco.com/public/mibs/v1.

In the configuration in Example 9-3, host 172.16.1.201 has been upgraded to SNMP version 2c, and this host receives only BGP traps. 172.16.1.200 receives only TTY traps. In addition, the source IP address of all SNMP traps is configured to be the IP address of the loopback interface, 172.16.2.25.

Example 9-3 *Enabling SNMPv2C Traps and Specifying the SNMP Source IP Address*

```
snmp-server community access RO
snmp-server enable traps bgp tty
snmp-server host 172.16.1.200 access tty
snmp-server host 172.16.1.201 version 2c access bgp
snmp-server trap-source loopback 1
```

When a user logs out of the router, the router sends TTY connection traps, as indicated in Example 9-4.

Example 9-4 *Routers Send TTY Connection Traps When Users Log Out of the Router*

```
#Telnet Boxer
Trying 10.1.1.1 ... Open


User Access Verification
```

Example 9-4   *Routers Send TTY Connection Traps When Users Log Out of the Router (Continued)*

```
Password:
Boxer>logout

[Connection to Boxer closed by foreign host]

Boxer#
SNMP: Queuing packet to 172.16.1.200
SNMP: V1 Trap, ent enterprises.9, addr 172.16.2.25
 ltsLineSessionEntry.1.66.1 = 5
 tcpConnEntry.1.10.1.1.1.23.10.1.10.1.11000 = 5
 ltcpConnEntry.5.10.1.1.1.23.10.1.10.1.11000 = 958
 ltcpConnEntry.1.10.1.1.1.23.10.1.10.1.11000 = 45
 ltcpConnEntry.2.10.1.1.1.23.10.1.10.1.11000 = 87
 ltsLineEntry.18.66 =
```

The trap type is **enterprises.9**, which is generated when a router reload takes place *or* a TCP connection is closed.

ltsLineSessionEntry.1 represents the line session type. A value of 5 means a Telnet session generated the trap.

tcpConnEntry.1 represents the state of the TCP connection. The value 5 means the connection is closed. The next digits are the IP addresses of Boxer and the device that performed the Telnet into Boxer.

ltcpConnEntry.5 represents the length of time that the TCP connection was established, in hundredths of a second. So this connection was open for 9.58 seconds. The next two OIDs represent the number of bytes input for this TCP connection, and the number of bytes output for the connection—45 bytes were input, 87 output. The **ltsLineEntry.18** displays the TACACS username, if TACACS is enabled. Example 9-5 shows the SNMPv2C BGP trap sent to 172.16.1.201.

Example 9-5   *SNMPv2C BGP Trap Includes More Information Than the SNMPv1 BGP Trap*

```
SNMP: Queuing packet to 172.16.1.201
SNMP: V2 Trap
 sysUpTime.0 = 14423502
 internet.6.3.1.1.4.1.0 = bgp.7.2
 bgpPeerEntry.14.10.1.2.1 = 00 00
 bgpPeerEntry.2.10.1.2.1 = 1
```

The version 2c trap includes more information than the version 1 trap. The system uptime is the time in hundredths of a second since the network management portion of the system was last reinitialized. The **internet.6.3.1.1.4.1.0** OID, with a value of **bgp.7.2**, represents the specific trap, bgpBackwardTransition, which is generated when the connection state transitions from a higher numbered state to a lower numbered state, such as from established to idle. The traps in Example 9-6 show the BGP state entering the ESTABLISHED state.

Example 9-6 *BGP State Enters ESTABLISHED*

```
SNMP: V1 Trap, ent bgp, addr 172.16.2.25
  bgpPeerEntry.14.10.1.2.1 = 00 00
  bgpPeerEntry.2.10.1.2.1 = 6

SNMP: V2 Trap
  sysUpTime.0 = 14425396
  internet.6.3.1.1.4.1.0 = bgp.7.1
  bgpPeerEntry.14.10.1.2.1 = 00 00
  bgpPeerEntry.2.10.1.2.1 = 6
```

The **internet.6.3.1.1.4.1.0** OID with value **bgp.7.1** represents the bgpEstablished trap, and the peer entry value of 6 means the connection for the peer 10.1.2.1 is ESTABLISHED.

The configuration in Example 9-7 allows read-only access only to those IP addresses specified in access list 1, using community string "restricted." It also limits this host to view only a portion of the MIB, particularly the interface entries.

Example 9-7 *Permitting Read-Only Access to IP Addresses Specified in an Access List*

```
access-list 1 permit 172.16.1.200
snmp-server view interface_entries ifEntry included
snmp-server community restricted view interface_entries RO 1
```

No other SNMP manager can access the SNMP agent on this device with community string "restricted." If this is the only community string configured on the router, 172.16.1.200 is the only device that can read SNMP MIB variables; however, it cannot set variables. The **view** command configures the view named **interface_entries** and limits this view to the ifEntry variables only. The **community** command associates the defined view to the community string "restricted" and to access list 1.

Example 9-8 displays partial output from an SNMP walk on the ifEntry and the IP branches of the MIB.

Example 9-8 *MIB Walk on ifEntry and IP Branches of MIB Before View Restrictions Are Placed on the Router*

```
ObiWan:~# snmpwalk 172.16.1.7 restricted ifEntry
interfaces.ifTable.ifEntry.ifIndex.1 = 1
interfaces.ifTable.ifEntry.ifIndex.2 = 2
interfaces.ifTable.ifEntry.ifIndex.3 = 3
interfaces.ifTable.ifEntry.ifIndex.4 = 4
interfaces.ifTable.ifEntry.ifDescr.1 = Ethernet0
interfaces.ifTable.ifEntry.ifDescr.2 = Ethernet1
interfaces.ifTable.ifEntry.ifDescr.3 = Serial0
interfaces.ifTable.ifEntry.ifDescr.4 = Serial1
interfaces.ifTable.ifEntry.ifOperStatus.1 = down(2)
```

Example 9-8   *MIB Walk on ifEntry and IP Branches of MIB Before View Restrictions Are Placed on the Router (Continued)*

```
interfaces.ifTable.ifEntry.ifOperStatus.2 = up(1)
interfaces.ifTable.ifEntry.ifOperStatus.3 = down(2)
interfaces.ifTable.ifEntry.ifOperStatus.4 = up(1)
interfaces.ifTable.ifEntry.ifInOctets.1 = 720250042
interfaces.ifTable.ifEntry.ifInOctets.2 = 283245
interfaces.ifTable.ifEntry.ifInOctets.3 = 0
interfaces.ifTable.ifEntry.ifInOctets.4 = 761771001
interfaces.ifTable.ifEntry.ifOutOctets.1 = 779888827
interfaces.ifTable.ifEntry.ifOutOctets.2 = 228281
interfaces.ifTable.ifEntry.ifOutOctets.3 = 0
interfaces.ifTable.ifEntry.ifOutOctets.4 = 10994586

ObiWan:~# snmpwalk 172.16.1.7 restricted ip
ip.ipRouteTable.ipRouteEntry.ipRouteDest.172.16.1.0 = IpAddress: 172.16.1.0
ip.ipRouteTable.ipRouteEntry.ipRouteIfIndex.172.16.1.0 = 2
ip.ipRouteTable.ipRouteEntry.ipRouteMetric1.172.16.1.0 = 0
ip.ipRouteTable.ipRouteEntry.ipRouteNextHop.172.16.1.0 = IpAddress: 172.16.1.7
ip.ipRouteTable.ipRouteEntry.ipRouteType.172.16.1.0 = direct(3)
ip.ipRouteTable.ipRouteEntry.ipRouteProto.172.16.1.0 = local(2)
ip.ipRouteTable.ipRouteEntry.ipRouteAge.172.16.1.0 = 0
ip.ipRouteTable.ipRouteEntry.ipRouteMask.172.16.1.0 = IpAddress: 255.255.255.0
ip.ipNetToMediaTable.ipNetToMediaEntry.ipNetToMediaPhysAddress.2.172.16.1.2 =
   0:10:5a:e5:e:e3
ip.ipNetToMediaTable.ipNetToMediaEntry.ipNetToMediaPhysAddress.2.172.16.1.7 =
   0:0:c:76:5b:7d
```

NOTE   The **snmpwalk** command reads an entire branch of the MIB tree, as compared to an **snmp get**, which reads a single entry.

Example 9-9 shows the same **snmpwalk** commands after the view limitations are imposed.

Example 9-9   *MIB Walk on ifEntry and IP Branches of MIB After View Restrictions Are Placed on the Router*

```
ObiWan:~# snmpwalk 172.16.1.7 restricted ifEntry
interfaces.ifTable.ifEntry.ifIndex.1 = 1
interfaces.ifTable.ifEntry.ifIndex.2 = 2
interfaces.ifTable.ifEntry.ifIndex.3 = 3
interfaces.ifTable.ifEntry.ifIndex.4 = 4
interfaces.ifTable.ifEntry.ifDescr.1 = Ethernet0
interfaces.ifTable.ifEntry.ifDescr.2 = Ethernet1
interfaces.ifTable.ifEntry.ifDescr.3 = Serial0
interfaces.ifTable.ifEntry.ifDescr.4 = Serial1
interfaces.ifTable.ifEntry.ifOperStatus.1 = down(2)
```

continues

Example 9-9   *MIB Walk on ifEntry and IP Branches of MIB After View Restrictions Are Placed on the Router (Continued)*

```
interfaces.ifTable.ifEntry.ifOperStatus.2 = up(1)
interfaces.ifTable.ifEntry.ifOperStatus.3 = down(2)
interfaces.ifTable.ifEntry.ifOperStatus.4 = up(1)
interfaces.ifTable.ifEntry.ifInOctets.1 = 720250042
interfaces.ifTable.ifEntry.ifInOctets.2 = 334364
interfaces.ifTable.ifEntry.ifInOctets.3 = 0
interfaces.ifTable.ifEntry.ifInOctets.4 = 761771405
interfaces.ifTable.ifEntry.ifOutOctets.1 = 779888827
interfaces.ifTable.ifEntry.ifOutOctets.2 = 268919
interfaces.ifTable.ifEntry.ifOutOctets.3 = 0
interfaces.ifTable.ifEntry.ifOutOctets.4 = 10995692
End of MIB

ObiWan:~# snmpwalk 172.16.1.7 restricted ip
End of MIB
ObiWan:~# logout
```

The management station cannot read any portion of the MIB that is not explicitly included in the view definition.

RMON

Remote Monitoring (RMON) enhances the capabilities provided by SNMP by enabling a management station to view more information about the node and its interaction with other nodes.

Overview of RMON

Like SNMP, RMON functionality is used in conjunction with a management station, or a RMON console and the managed agent. RMON data is stored in tables on the router and is sent, when requested or when an event is triggered to send a trap, to the RMON console. It reduces network traffic by minimizing the amount of data needing to be polled in regular SNMP packets. The RMON engine on a router polls the SNMP MIB variables locally. There are two thresholds: a rising threshold and a falling threshold. When the value of the MIB variable crosses a threshold, RMON creates a log entry and sends an SNMP trap. No more events are generated for that threshold until the opposite threshold is crossed. If the variable value rises and crosses the rising threshold, an event is triggered. No more events are triggered until the value falls below the falling threshold.

Routers ordered without the RMON option have alarm and event capability. The RMON option, available only on 2500 and AS5200 series routers, adds the other groups—statistics, history, hosts, hostTopN, matrix, filter, and capture.

Packet capture is available only on the Ethernet interfaces of 2500 series and AS5200 series routers, and only headers are captured. Packets can be captured in one of two ways:

- **Natively**—Packets destined to the Ethernet interface of the router
- **Promiscuously**—All packets on the Ethernet segment

The packet-capture mechanism can be very data- and processor-intensive. If enabled, the router performance and network traffic should be closely monitored.

Alarms and events, combined with existing MIB variables, enable you to define areas of proactive monitoring. You can set an alarm on any MIB object that resolves to a value of type integer, counter, gauge, or timetick.

NOTE   RFC 2819 fully defines all the groups of RMON and how they interact.

Router Configuration for RMON

The command to define an alarm table entry and the variable for which the alarm is being set is as follows:

```
rmon alarm number variable interval {delta | absolute} rising-threshold value [event-number] falling-threshold value [event-number] [owner string]
```

The *number* uniquely identifies the entry in the alarm table. The *variable* is a MIB OID. The *interval* is the time between subsequent monitors of the MIB object. The **delta** or **absolute** keywords specify whether the alarm will test the change in MIB values over the specified interval or the actual MIB value. The **rising-threshold** value is the threshold at which an event is generated. If the sampled value is equal to or greater than this value, and the last sampled value was lower than this value, an event is generated. If an *event-number* is specified, this is the number of the event to trigger when the sampled value exceeds the rising threshold value. Another event is not generated until the sampled value falls below the **falling-threshold** value. The **falling-threshold** value is also a threshold at which an event is generated. If the sampled value is less than or equal to the **falling-threshold** value, and the previous sampled value was greater than this value, an event is generated. Another event is not generated until the sampled value rises above the **rising-threshold** value.

The command to add or remove an event in the RMON event table is as follows:

```
rmon event number [log] [trap community] [description string] [owner string]
```

An event defined with this command is triggered when the alarm specifies an *event-number* and the **rising** or **falling-threshold** value is met or exceeded. A log entry or an SNMP trap (or both) may be generated when the event occurs. The **snmp-server community** and **snmp-server host** commands must be configured for the community specified in the **rmon event** command before an SNMP trap is sent.

Example 9-10 shows a configuration example enabling events and alarms for a high number of output errors on an interface and high CPU on the router. The MIB OID can be entered in full, such as 1.3.6.1.2.1.2.2.1.20.4, which represents the MIBII value for ifOutErrors on index 4, or 1.3.6.1.4.1.9.2.1.58.0, which represents the Cisco CPU MIB value for the 5-minute moving average of the CPU busy percentage. The router automatically converts the OID to that shown in Example 9-10.

Example 9-10 *Enabling Events and Alarms for a High Number of Output Errors on an Interface and High CPU on the Router*

```
snmp-server community eventtrap RO
snmp-server enable traps
snmp-server host 172.16.1.2 eventtrap
snmp-server trap-source loopback 1
rmon event 1 log trap eventtrap description "High ifOutErrors"
rmon event 2 log trap eventtrap description "High 5-minute CPU" owner jsmith
rmon alarm 10 ifEntry.20.4 20 delta rising-threshold 15 1 falling-threshold 0
  owner jsmith
rmon alarm 11 lsystem.58.0 20 absolute rising-threshold 50 2 falling-threshold 25
  owner jsmith
```

RMON event 1 logs an event with the description **"High ifOutErrors"** associated with owner jsmith. The event also triggers an SNMP trap for community **eventtrap**. The event is created when an associated alarm occurs. RMON alarm number 10 is configured for the MIB variable **ifEntry.20.4**, which represents output errors on interface number 4. Interface number 4 in this case is serial interface 1. The alarm monitors the MIB variable every 20 seconds. If the value between polls rises by 15 or more, the alarm is triggered, triggering event number 1. If subsequent samples of the MIB OID indicate that there have been no output errors on the interface, the alarm is reset and can be triggered again.

Event 2 logs an event described as **"High 5-minute CPU"**. The associated alarm, alarm 11, generates an event when the value sampled with the MIB OID **lsystem.58.0** (AvgBusy5) is equal to or greater than 50. When the 5-minute average CPU busy percentage falls below 25, the alarm is reset and can be triggered again.

Example 9-11 shows an SNMP trap generated by event 1.

Example 9-11 *SNMP Trap Generated by Event 1 Defined in Example 9-10*

```
SNMP: Queuing packet to 172.16.1.2
SNMP: V1 Trap, ent rmon, addr 172.16.2.25
 alarmEntry.1.10 = 10
 alarmEntry.3.10 = ifEntry.20.4
 alarmEntry.4.10 = 2
 alarmEntry.5.10 = 20
 alarmEntry.7.10 = 15
```

RFC 2819 defines alarm entries.[4] Alarm entry 1 represents the alarm index. As indicated in Example 9-11, alarm index 10 generated this SNMP trap. Alarm entry 3 defines the object identifier being sampled. In this SNMP trap, the OID is ifEntry.20.4, the number of output errors on interface serial 1. Alarm entry 4 is the sample type. A value of 1 means the sample type is absolute. A value of 2 indicates that the sample type is delta. Alarm entry 5 is the alarm value during the last sampling period. Alarm entry 7 is the defined rising threshold. In the SNMP trap in Example 9-11, the alarm value of 20 exceeds the rising threshold of 15, and therefore the event occurred.

RMON alarms and events are viewed using the **show rmon alarms** and **show rmon events** commands.

Example 9-12 displays the output from these two commands.

Example 9-12 *Displaying RMON Alarm and Event Tables with the* **show rmon alarms** *and* **show rmon events** *Commands*

```
Bowler#show rmon event alarms
Event 1 is active, owned by jsmith
 Description is High ifOutErrors
 Event firing causes log and trap to community eventtrap, last fired 1d00h
 Current log entries:
      index       time    description
         1       1d00h    High ifOutErrors
         2       1d00h    High ifOutErrors
Event 2 is active, owned by jsmith
 Description is High 5-minute CPU
 Event firing causes log and trap to community eventtrap, last fired 1d00h
 Current log entries:
      index       time    description
         1       1d00h    High 5-minute CPU
Alarm 10 is active, owned by jsmith
 Monitors ifEntry.20.4 every 20 second(s)
 Taking delta samples, last value was 20
 Rising threshold is 15, assigned to event 1
 Falling threshold is 0, assigned to event 0
 On startup enable rising or falling alarm
Alarm 11 is active, owned by jsmith
 Monitors lsystem.58.0 every 20 second(s)
 Taking absolute samples, last value was 60
 Rising threshold is 50, assigned to event 2
 Falling threshold is 25, assigned to event 0
 On startup enable rising or falling alarm
```

The time shown in the event and alarm table is the value of sysUpTime when the event was generated. sysUpTime is the amount of time since the router was last reset. The output in Example 9-12 shows a value of 1 day and 0 hours.

Logging

When logging is enabled on a router, messages for certain events that occur on the router are created and stored. The log may reside on the router, or it may be an external log, residing on a server somewhere in the network.

Routers send output from **debug** commands and system error messages to the logging process. The logging process distributes the messages to the various logging devices and files, depending on the router configuration. Messages are sent to the logging buffer, to terminal lines, and/or to a UNIX syslog server. The logging buffer is maintained on the router. It is a circular buffer, with the oldest messages replaced by the newest messages. The oldest entry appears first when you are viewing the log.

NOTE   The syslog format is compatible with 4.3 BSD UNIX.

The following commands enable the log to be buffered, show the contents of the log, and clear the log:

- **logging buffered** [*size*]
- **show logging**
- **clear logging**

Messages sent to a syslog service are stored in files on a server. The messages are sent directly to the syslog process running on the server, which stores the messages in the appropriate files.

The **logging** *host* command enables logging to the syslog server and specifies the IP address of that server.

When you Telnet to a router, normally you do not see any log messages. To enable the router to send log messages to the Telnet session, enter the EXEC command **terminal monitor**. You do not need to enter the command if you connect to a router via the console port. The default configuration is to send logging messages to the console port.

The router will send all messages, from the debugging level to emergencies, to the Telnet session, which is extremely useful when troubleshooting problems. Log all information sent and received over the Telnet session, and you will have a good record of debugging activity and events that occurred on the router while you were connected to it.

NOTE   Log the information via the Telnet application's logging or capture facility.

Time stamps must be enabled and the clock set to make the information in the logs meaningful.

Example 9-13 displays the output of the **show logging** command with no time stamps enabled.

Example 9-13 *Output of the* **show logging** *Command*

```
Seattle#show logging
Syslog logging: enabled (0 messages dropped, 0 flushes, 0 overruns)
    Console logging: level debugging, 9 messages logged
    Monitor logging: level debugging, 0 messages logged
    Buffer logging: level debugging, 9 messages logged
    Trap logging: level informational, 13 message lines logged

Log Buffer (4096 bytes):

%LINK-5-CHANGED: Interface TokenRing0, changed state to administrative
ly down
%LINK-5-CHANGED: Interface Serial0, changed state to administratively
down
%LINK-3-UPDOWN: Interface Serial1, changed state to down
%SYS-5-CONFIG_I: Configured from console by console
```

There is no reference to the time that any of the events occurred.

Using the **service timestamps log uptime** command displays the time stamp with the time since the system was last rebooted. Example 9-14 displays the same log output with **service timestamps log uptime** enabled.

Example 9-14 *Output of the* **show logging** *Command with* **service timestamps log uptime** *Enabled*

```
Seattle#show logging
Syslog logging: enabled (0 messages dropped, 0 flushes, 0 overruns)
    Console logging: level debugging, 9 messages logged
    Monitor logging: level debugging, 0 messages logged
    Buffer logging: level debugging, 9 messages logged
    Trap logging: level informational, 13 message lines logged

Log Buffer (4096 bytes):

00:00:39: %LINK-5-CHANGED: Interface TokenRing0, changed state to administratively
down
00:00:39: %LINK-5-CHANGED: Interface Serial0, changed state to administratively
down
00:00:39: %LINK-3-UPDOWN: Interface Serial1, changed state to down
1d07h: %SYS-5-CONFIG_I: Configured from console by console
```

The events are time stamped. You can see that the first three events occurred at the same time. In fact, they all occurred 39 seconds after router startup. The fourth event occurred 1 day and 7 hours after the router startup.

To display the actual date and time, as known by the router, enter the following command:

```
service timestamps log datetime [msec] [localtime] [show-timezone]
```

This time can include milliseconds and can be displayed as the router's local time. The time zone can be displayed. Some routers do not maintain calendars, so when they reboot, their clock resets. If no network time protocol is being used, you need to set the clocks manually by using the following EXEC command:

```
clock set hh:mm:ss day month year
```

When you are recording log information from multiple routers, consistent time stamp information makes event correlation much easier. When troubleshooting problems, and looking for messages that were reported from multiple routers due to a particular event, it is useful to have all routers time stamp their messages using a single time zone—that is, do not specify **localtime**. If each router is time stamping the message with its **localtime**, you should specify **show-timezone** for clarification. Syslog daemons log the date and time in the file based on their own clocks at the time a message arrives. You can limit the messages logged by specifying the severity level of messages. Table 9-2 lists the message logging levels.

Table 9-2   *Message Logging Levels*

Message Severity Level	Value	Translation
Emergencies	0	System unusable
Alerts	1	Immediate action needed
Critical	2	Critical condition
Errors	3	Error condition
Warnings	4	Warning condition
Notifications	5	Normal but significant condition
Informational	6	Informational message only
Debugging	7	Debugging message

If you specify a level of messages to see in a particular log, you get that level and all levels above. If you specify debugging, for instance, you get all levels of messages. If you specify warnings, you also get errors, critical, alerts, and emergencies.

Specify the level using the following configuration commands:

- **logging console** *level*—Limits messages logged to the console
- **logging monitor** *level*—Limits messages logged to the terminal lines
- **logging trap** *level*—Limits messages logged to the syslog servers

Software and hardware malfunctions display at the levels warning through emergencies. Interface up/down transitions and system restart messages display at the notifications level. Reload requests and low-process stack messages display at the informational level, and **debug** output displays at the debugging level.

Example 9-15 shows the configuration of a router located in Seattle, in the Pacific time zone.

Example 9-15 *Configuring Logging of a Router in Seattle (Pacific Time Zone)*

```
service timestamp debug datetime localtime show-timezone
service timestamp log datetime localtime show-timezone
clock timezone PST -8
clock summer-time PDT recurring
logging buffered
```

The router's system clock is based on Coordinated Universal Time (UTC), which is the same as Greenwich mean time. Pacific standard time is 8 hours earlier than UTC.

Example 9-16 displays the router's log after the configuration referenced in Example 9-15 has been implemented.

Example 9-16 *Display of the Logging Buffer After the Configuration Listed in Example 9-15 Is Implemented*

```
Seattle>show logging
Syslog logging: enabled (0 messages dropped, 0 flushes, 0 overruns)
    Console logging: level debugging, 8 messages logged
    Monitor logging: level debugging, 0 messages logged
    Buffer logging: level debugging, 8 messages logged
    Trap logging: level informational, 12 message lines logged

Log Buffer (4096 bytes):

*Nov 28 16:00:39 PST: %LINK-5-CHANGED: Interface TokenRing0, changed state to
administratively down
*Nov 28 16:00:39 PST: %LINK-3-UPDOWN: Interface Serial1, changed state to down
*Nov 28 16:00:39 PST: %LINK-5-CHANGED: Interface Serial0, changed state to
administratively down
*Nov 30 12:00:39 PST: %SYS-5-CONFIG_I: Configured from console by console
```

Although the logging buffer is very useful if no syslog server is available, it has some drawbacks. Searching for an event requires either paging through the entire file or saving the file to another system and using the system's search facilities. If you are looking for a very recent event, you have to page through the entire file (or again, save the file to another system), because the oldest events display first. Logging to syslog automatically creates a file on the UNIX server, which offers better search and file maintenance techniques.

Syslog

Syslog is a process, or daemon, that runs on UNIX servers. The process collects information and stores it in log files. File management systems on the server are used to maintain the files.

Overview of Syslog

Messages are sent from various services running on the UNIX server, or from other network nodes. The service that sends the message indicates its facility type. The syslog daemon utilizes the indicated facility type when determining how to log the message. Table 9-3 lists the various facility types.

Table 9-3   *Syslog Facility Types*

Facility Type	Service
Auth	Authorization system
Cron	Cron facility
Daemon	System daemon
Kern	Kernel
Local0-7	Locally defined messages
Lpr	Printer system
Mail	Mail system
News	USENET news
Sys9-14	System use
Syslog	System log
User	User process
Uucp	UNIX-to-UNIX copy system

A syslog daemon is configured by updating a file on the server in the */etc* directory called *syslog.conf*. The syslog daemon reads this file upon startup to determine how to handle incoming messages. The file contains lines such as the following:

```
local7.debugging     /user/adm/logs/cisco.log
```

The preceding line indicates that **local7** facility messages, with level debugging or higher, will get logged to the file *cisco.log*, located in the */user/adm/logs* directory. The entries in the file are case-sensitive.

Any configuration file change requires the UNIX administrator to force the syslog daemon to reread the file.

Router Configuration for Syslog

Cisco routers use the **local7** facility by default when sending messages to a syslog server. If this facility is being used by another process sending messages to the syslog server, you can change the facility type on the Cisco router using the following configuration command:

```
logging facility facility-type
```

The router configuration in Example 9-17 enables syslog logging to the specified host. Messages with level notifications and above are logged.

Example 9-17 *Enabling Syslog Logging to a Specified Host*

```
logging 172.16.1.2
logging trap notifications
```

Include a line such as the following in the */etc/syslog.conf* file on the UNIX server:

```
local7.notice      /usr/adm/logs/cisco.log
```

NOTE	Refer to the User Manual pages for your particular server, syslog configuration file, and syslog daemon for specific information.

local7 specifies the logging facility, and **notifications** is the logging level. All information is stored in the file *cisco.log* in the */usr/adm/logs* directory. The file must already exist, and the syslog daemon must have permission to write to it. Verify that the syslog daemon is running and that it has reread the configuration file after any configuration changes.

NOTE	Processes are forced to reread configuration files with the UNIX **kill** command, along with specific signals. Refer to the UNIX system's User Manual pages for the **kill** command for details.

Some routers support the capability to send syslog messages via SNMP to the SNMP network manager. Enable this by entering the router command **snmp-server enable traps syslog** and specifying the level of logs to be sent using the command **logging history** *level*.

Example 9-18 shows a syslog message sent in an SNMP packet from the router.

Example 9-18 *A Syslog Message Generated as the Result of a Configuration Change Is Sent via SNMP*

```
Cascade#conf t
Cascade(config)#snmp-server enable traps syslog
Cascade(config)#logging history notification
Cascade(config)#^Z

SNMP: V1 Trap, ent ciscoSyslogMIB.2, addr 10.2.1.1
 clogHistoryEntry.2.65 = SYS
 clogHistoryEntry.3.65 = 6
 clogHistoryEntry.4.65 = CONFIG_I
 clogHistoryEntry.5.65 = Configured from console by console
 clogHistoryEntry.6.65 = 30249161
```

The syslog message is generated as the result of a router configuration modification. The **65** at the end of each HistoryEntry line is the index identifying the particular event. The syslog history entries range from values 1 through 6. A 2 indicates that the value of the OID is the facility that generated the message. The facility in Example 9-18 is SYS. 3 is the severity of the message. A value of 6 indicates notification. History entry 4 is a textual identification for the message type. History entry 5 is the actual text of the message. History entry 6 is the value of sysUpTime when this message was generated.

NOTE   The syslog MIB is fully defined at www.cisco.com/public/mibs/v1/
CISCO-SYSLOG-MIB-V1SMI.my.

Sending the syslog message to the SNMP management station simplifies data management by collecting the data on a single server, under a single system.

Network Time Protocol

The Network Time Protocol (NTP) enables you to synchronize system clocks with a centralized time source. Troubleshooting network problems rarely involves a single system. Searching through log files—looking for error messages that were recorded at a particular time of day as a result of a particular event—is made much simpler when all the systems potentially involved in the event use the same clock time to time stamp the error messages.

Overview of NTP

NTP synchronizes timekeeping among distributed devices. Each device makes peer associations with the time sources. The reliability of the time sources is defined by stratum levels. A stratum 1 server is directly connected to a reliable time source, such as radio clocks, GPS satellite timing receivers, or atomic clocks. Stratum 2 servers obtain their time from a stratum 1 source. The stratum 2 server may connect to a publicly available stratum 1 server via the Internet. You can find a list of public NTP servers and information about using them at www.eecis.udel.edu/~ntp/ (from the University of Delaware).

A couple of reliable NTP servers configured in an organization could associate with the stratum 2 public NTP servers and then provide time services to all the routers in the organization's network. A router can be the NTP server as well. In fact, if no Internet connection is available, or the NTP protocol is not permitted through the firewall to the Internet, routers can be configured to be the authoritative NTP server. The router uses its own system clock as the time reference. Only a router that maintains its time after a reset—a router with a calendar—can be used as an authoritative time source. Any other router will not have a valid reference clock. If NTP is running on a router with a calendar system, and the router is obtaining time via NTP, the calendar may be updated by NTP to compensate for the inherent drift in the calendar time. It may not be quite as accurate as an atomic clock, but at least all the routers in the network will have synchronized times, which eases troubleshooting problems.

NTP is very efficient. One packet per minute allows two devices to synchronize within 10 milliseconds.

Router Configuration for NTP

When configuring NTP, first create an association. Use the following commands to initiate the creation of the associations:

```
ntp server ip_address [version number] [key keyid] [source interface] [prefer]
ntp peer ip_address [version number] [key keyid] [source interface] [prefer]
```

Create a server association if this router is going to synchronize its clock to another NTP clock source. Create a peer association if this router is willing to synchronize to another device or allow another device to synchronize to it.

The default version number is 3. No authentication *keyid* is configured, and the source IP address is that of the outgoing interface, by default. The **prefer** keyword tells the IOS to prefer this peer for synchronization.

To control access to the router's NTP services, use the following command:

```
ntp access-group {query-only | serve-only | serve | peer} access-list-number
```

Use the **query-only** option to allow only NTP control queries from the listed IP addresses. Control queries are used in lieu of an SNMP management station to monitor the NTP process.

The serve-only option allows only time requests from the IP addresses listed in the access list. This router will not synchronize its clock to the remote system.

The serve option allows time requests and control queries. This system will still not synchronize its clock to the remote system.

The peer option allows both time requests and control queries, and it does allow this router to synchronize its clock to the remote system.

The configuration in Example 9-19 permits one router, Seattle, to synchronize its clock to a secondary public time source. Another router, Tacoma, in the same network as Seattle, is allowed to synchronize with Seattle.

Example 9-19 *Synchronizing the Seattle Router Clock to a Secondary Public Time Source; the Tacoma Router Synchronizes with Seattle*

```
Seattle
access-list 1 permit 172.16.0.0 0.0.255.255
access-list 2 permit 128.105.39.11
ntp access-group peer 2
ntp access-group serve 1
ntp server 128.105.39.11

Tacoma
ntp server 172.16.1.5
```

Seattle is permitted to synchronize its clock with only 128.105.39.11. Any node with an address in the range 172.16.0.0/16 can synchronize its clock with Seattle's clock.

A router can be configured as the master time source if no external time source is available. The router must have an internal calendar that maintains the date and time through a reboot or power cycle. To enable this calendar as the authoritative time source for the router, configure the **clock calendar-valid** command.

To configure the Cisco IOS Software as an NTP master clock to which peers synchronize, use the **ntp master** [*stratum*] command. Configure a high stratum number to ensure that this router does not override the clock on another system with a lower stratum number (and therefore a more reliable clock). The default stratum is 8. The router with NTP master configured still attempts to find a server with a lower stratum number. If it cannot, the router will becomes synchronized at the configured stratum number. After it has been synchronized, other systems can synchronize to it.

NTP time is UTC. If you want a router to maintain a different time zone, you can still use the following commands to maintain local time:

```
clock timezone PST -8
clock summer-time PDT recurring
```

To update a router's calendar with the time obtained via NTP, use the **ntp update-calendar** command.

The NTP protocol can use authentication. The following configuration commands enable authentication:

```
ntp authenticate
ntp authentication-key number md5 key
ntp trusted-key number
ntp server ip-address key number
```

The **ntp authenticate** command is required on both the NTP server and the router requesting time synchronization. It globally enables authentication. The **ntp authentication-key** command also is required on both routers. This command defines an authentication string and assigns it a number.

The router requesting time synchronization is configured with the **ntp trusted-key** command. This command lists key numbers that have already been defined with the **ntp authentication-key** command, which the server must include in its NTP packets, before this router will synchronize to it. The **ntp trusted-key** command is therefore only required on the client router.

The **key** *number* option must also be included in the client's **ntp server** command. This adds the key to the NTP packets from the client to the server. When the server sees the key, if the key has been defined on the server, the server includes it in its NTP packets to the client.

Authentication is enabled between Seattle and Tacoma in the configurations in Example 9-20.

Example 9-20 *Enabling Authentication Between Routers Seattle and Tacoma*

```
Seattle
ntp authenticate
ntp authentication-key 10 md5 ntpkey

Tacoma
ntp authenticate
ntp authentication-key 10 md5 ntpkey
ntp trusted-key 10
ntp server seattle key 10
```

Tacoma's **ntp server seattle key 10** command specifies that the server, Seattle, must provide key number 10 in its NTP packets, before Tacoma will synchronize its clock with Seattle's clock. Seattle sees the key 10 in the NTP packets from Tacoma. Seattle's **ntp authentication-key 10 md5 ntpkey** enables Seattle to include the authentication key 10 in its reply back to Tacoma. To illustrate the authentication, the **authentication-key** command is left out of the server's configuration. Example 9-21 displays the output of the **debug ntp packet** command. Initially, the time server, Seattle, is not configured for authentication. The client router, Tacoma, requires authentication before it will synchronize its clock with the time server.

Example 9-21 *1NTP Packet Exchange with No Authentication Key Configured on the NTP Server*

```
Seattle
ntp clock-period 17179873
ntp server 128.105.39.11

NTP: xmit packet to 172.16.1.105:
leap 3, mode 3, version 3, stratum 0, ppoll 64
rtdel 1813 (94.040), rtdsp 3E25 (242.752), refid AC100169 (172.16.1.105)
ref  BDD13136.BEAD46C0 (15:04:06.744 Eastern Thu Nov 30 2000)
org  BDD13580.2FF266EC (15:22:24.187 Eastern Thu Nov 30 2000)
rec  BDD13580.272011D4 (15:22:24.152 Eastern Thu Nov 30 2000)
xmt  BDD13580.BD318A8C (15:22:24.739 Eastern Thu Nov 30 2000)
Authentication key 10

NTP: rcv packet from 172.16.1.105 to 172.16.1.106 on Ethernet0:
leap 0, mode 4, version 3, stratum 3, ppoll 64
rtdel 0FD1 (61.783), rtdsp 080C (31.433), refid 8069270B (128.105.39.11)
ref  BDD1355B.9F07E00F (15:21:47.621 Eastern Thu Nov 30 2000)
org  BDD13580.BD318A8C (15:22:24.739 Eastern Thu Nov 30 2000)
rec  BDD13580.CB4EBD34 (15:22:24.794 Eastern Thu Nov 30 2000)
xmt  BDD13580.CB6623DA (15:22:24.794 Eastern Thu Nov 30 2000)
inp  BDD13580.C5C23E0A (15:22:24.772 Eastern Thu Nov 30 2000)
```

The debug packet transmitted from Tacoma to Seattle displays the authentication key 10. Tacoma expects this key to be included in the NTP packet received from Seattle. It is not. Therefore, as shown in Example 9-22, the NTP status remains unsynchronized.

Example 9-22 *Display of* **show ntp status** *and* **show ntp association detail** *Commands with Incorrect Authentication*

```
Tacoma#show ntp status
Clock is unsynchronized, stratum 16, no reference clock
nominal freq is 250.0000 Hz, actual freq is 249.9999 Hz, precision is 2**19
reference time is BDD13136.BEAD46C0 (15:04:06.744 Eastern Thu Nov 30 2000)
clock offset is 5.8229 msec, root delay is 94.04 msec
root dispersion is 242.74 msec, peer dispersion is 70.86 msec

Tacoma#show ntp association detail
172.16.1.105 configured, insane, invalid, unsynced, stratum 16
```

Only the first line of the **show ntp association detail** command is shown. It reveals that the peer is manually configured and that the peer did not pass a basic sanity check (authentication failed). The time is therefore invalid, the peers are unsynchronized, and the stratum level is the default level, 16.

Now, the commands **ntp authentication-key 10 md5 ntpkey** and **ntp authenticate** are added to the Seattle configuration. Examples 9-23 and 9-24 display the **debug ntp packet** and the **show ntp status** and **show ntp association detail** output, respectively.

Example 9-23 *NTP Packet Exchange with Correct Authentication Key Configured on NTP Server and Client*

```
Seattle(config)#ntp authentication
Seattle(config)#ntp authentication-key 10 md5 ntpkey
Seattle(config)#^Z

Tacoma#
NTP: xmit packet to 172.16.1.105:
leap 3, mode 3, version 3, stratum 0, ppoll 64
rtdel 1813 (94.040), rtdsp 3E25 (242.752), refid AC100169 (172.16.1.105)
ref  BDD13136.BEAD46C0 (15:04:06.744 Eastern Thu Nov 30 2000)
org  BDD13600.B85D38DF (15:24:32.720 Eastern Thu Nov 30 2000)
rec  BDD13600.B5E44B24 (15:24:32.710 Eastern Thu Nov 30 2000)
xmt  BDD13640.CED09281 (15:25:36.807 Eastern Thu Nov 30 2000)
Authentication key 10

NTP: rcv packet from 172.16.1.105 to 172.16.1.106 on Ethernet0:
leap 0, mode 4, version 3, stratum 3, ppoll 64
rtdel 10CE (65.643), rtdsp 0821 (31.754), refid 8069270B (128.105.39.11)
ref  BDD1361B.9EC9B021 (15:24:59.620 Eastern Thu Nov 30 2000)
org  BDD13640.CED09281 (15:25:36.807 Eastern Thu Nov 30 2000)
rec  BDD13640.DAE3EC4F (15:25:36.855 Eastern Thu Nov 30 2000)
xmt  BDD13640.DB1FC317 (15:25:36.855 Eastern Thu Nov 30 2000)
inp  BDD13640.D7686AD0 (15:25:36.841 Eastern Thu Nov 30 2000)
Authentication key 10
NTP: 172.16.1.105 reachable
NTP: sync change
NTP: peer stratum change
```

Seattle included the expected authentication key in its NTP packet to Tacoma. The peer became reachable within NTP, the peer status changed from unsynchronized state and the stratum changed from the default value. Example 9-24 displays the new NTP status.

Example 9-24 *Output of **show ntp status** and **show ntp association detail** After Valid Authentication*

```
Tacoma#show ntp status
Clock is synchronized, stratum 4, reference is 172.16.1.105
nominal freq is 250.0000 Hz, actual freq is 249.9999 Hz, precision is 2**19
reference time is BDD13640.D7686AD0 (15:25:36.841 Eastern Thu Nov 30 2000)
clock offset is 30.8433 msec, root delay is 98.30 msec
root dispersion is 15937.61 msec, peer dispersion is 15875.02 msec

Tacoma#show ntp association detail
172.16.1.105 configured, authenticated, our_master, sane, valid, stratum 3
```

The clock is now synchronized, the stratum changed from the default of 16 to 4, the peer has become authenticated, and the peer time is believed to be valid.

Accounting

Sometimes it proves useful to collect statistics on traffic flows, to account for network usage. This process may be useful for traffic engineering, as well as for billing network users based on usage.

You can enable basic IP accounting on router interfaces. Packet source and destination are listed, as well as the number of bytes and packets transmitted between the two nodes. NetFlow offers a more thorough accounting functionality. In addition to source, destination, packet, and byte count, protocol and AS information is included. The NetFlow data can be aggregated in various ways, including by autonomous system, by subnet prefixes, and by protocol type. NetFlow is discussed further in the section titled "NetFlow."

IP Accounting

IP accounting provides basic accounting services. Packets that traverse the router are counted and are maintained on a source/destination basis. Packets that are sourced from or destined to the router itself are not counted. The accounting occurs on outbound interfaces. IP accounting disables autonomous switching and SSE switching on the interface. Packets that pass access lists and are actually routed through the router are counted. Optionally, accounting can be enabled for packets that do not pass access lists. A large number of access list violations may indicate an attempted network attack or a misconfigured router.

You can enable accounting on outbound interfaces using the **ip accounting** command.

To display the results of enabling accounting on outbound interfaces, use the **show ip accounting** [**checkpoint**] [**access-violations**] command.

Example 9-25 displays IP accounting data collected on an Ethernet interface.

Example 9-25 *IP Accounting Is Enabled on an Ethernet Interface; the* **show ip accounting** *Command Displays Multicast Packets Being Sent Out the Interface*

```
Bowler(config)#int e 0
Bowler(config-if)#ip accounting
Bowler(config-if)#^Z
Bowler#show ip accounting
   Source           Destination            Packets              Bytes
  10.1.1.88       228.13.20.216               45                24611
```

Example 9-25 *IP Accounting Is Enabled on an Ethernet Interface; the* **show ip accounting** *Command Displays Multicast Packets Being Sent Out the Interface (Continued)*

```
Accounting data age is 0
Bowler#show ip accounting
   Source          Destination          Packets          Bytes
   10.1.1.88       224.2.127.254              1            229
   10.1.1.88       228.13.20.216            133          73689

Accounting data age is 0
Bowler#show ip accounting
   Source          Destination          Packets          Bytes
   10.1.1.88       224.2.127.254              1            229
   10.1.1.88       228.13.20.216            173          95952

Accounting data age is 0
```

IP accounting is enabled on Ethernet 0 of router Bowler. Packets routing out the Ethernet port are counted. Three subsequent displays of the accounting table show the source address 10.1.1.88 multicasting packets to both 224.2.127.254 and 228.13.20.216.

You can clear the accounting table with the **clear ip accounting** command.

IP accounting can provide valuable information about traffic exiting an interface. Note, however, that performance degradation may occur when you implement it. Because IP accounting disables autonomous switching and SSE switching on the interface, the packets will be switched through the interface using a less-efficient mechanism than may have been designed into the network. In addition, maintaining the accounting database utilizes the router's memory. Do not enable IP accounting if the router is running low on memory.

The command **ip accounting-threshold** *threshold* defines the number of entries that can be stored in an accounting database. The default value is 512 source/destination pairs. This default results in a maximum of 12,928 bytes of memory usage for each of the databases, active and check pointed. If you modify and set the threshold too high, all the available memory could be consumed.

Enabling IP accounting on an interface is a quick way to view outbound traffic by source and destination address, but there is no built-in mechanism to get the data to a server that can parse the data and make it useful over time. NetFlow provides this functionality, in addition to providing more information about the traffic flows.

NetFlow

NetFlow switching identifies traffic flows and performs switching and access list processing within a router. In addition, because the flows are identified, statistics regarding the flows can be exported to an accounting server. While the flow is active, data about the flow is maintained in a NetFlow cache. When the flow expires, it can be added to an aggregation cache and can be exported to a management station. The default size of the NetFlow cache can contain 64 K flow cache entries.

To enable NetFlow switching, use the interface subcommand **ip route-cache flow**.

To define the IP address and UDP port number of the flow collector that receives the data, use the following global commands:

```
ip flow-export destination ip-address udp-port
ip flow-export [version 1 | version 5 [origin-as | peer-as]]
```

The version number must match the version that the flow collector is expecting. **version 1** is the default.

The **origin-as** option specifies that the exported data include the BGP origin AS for the source and destination.

The **peer-as** option specifies that the exported data include the BGP peer AS of the router collecting the data, rather than the traffic's actual AS for the source and destination.

Figure 9-2 shows a simple network running BGP and collecting NetFlow data on router Hummer.

Figure 9-2 *BGP Network Running NetFlow for Flow Accounting*

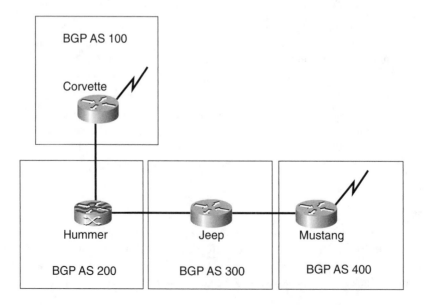

NetFlow is enabled on router Hummer. The router is configured to collect information on flows on both interfaces. Example 9-26 shows the configuration for Hummer.

Example 9-26 *Configuring Router Hummer in Figure 9-2 to Collect Information on Flows on Both Ethernet Interfaces*

```
interface Ethernet1/2
 ip address 1.1.7.5 255.255.255.0
 ip route-cache flow
!
interface Ethernet1/3
 ip address 1.1.5.5 255.255.255.0
 ip route-cache flow
!
ip flow-export version 5 peer-as
ip flow-export destination 1.1.3.250 125
```

In the configuration in Example 9-26, the data includes the peer AS, rather than the origin AS.

The **show ip flow export** command displays the data exporting parameters, whereas the **show ip cache flow** command displays the flow cache.

Example 9-27 shows the flow export parameters and a sample of the flow cache of router Hummer.

Example 9-27 *NetFlow Flow Information Displayed Using Commands* **show ip flow export** *and* **show ip cache flow**

```
Hummer#show ip flow export
Flow export is enabled
  Exporting flows to 1.1.3.250 (125)
  Exporting using source IP address 1.1.7.5
  Version 5 flow records, peer-as
  527 flows exported in 18 udp datagrams
  0 flows failed due to lack of export packet
  0 export packets were sent up to process level
  0 export packets were dropped due to no fib
  0 export packets were dropped due to adjacency issues

Hummer#show ip cache flow
IP packet size distribution (51719 total packets):
   1-32   64   96  128  160  192  224  256  288  320  352  384  416 448  480
   .131 .000 .034 .000 .000 .000 .490 .000 .000 .000 .000 .000 .000 .000 .000

    512  544  576 1024 1536 2048 2560 3072 3584 4096 4608
   .000 .000 .000 .000 .343 .000 .000 .000 .000 .000 .000

IP Flow Switching Cache, 4456704 bytes
  68 active, 65468 inactive, 1080 added
```

continues

Example 9-27 *NetFlow Flow Information Displayed Using Commands* **show ip flow export** *and* **show ip cache flow** *(Continued)*

```
    22140 ager polls, 0 flow alloc failures
    Active flows timeout in 30 minutes
    Inactive flows timeout in 15 seconds
    last clearing of statistics 00:08:35
    Protocol         Total    Flows   Packets Bytes  Packets Active(Sec) Idle(Sec)
    --------         Flows    /Sec    /Flow   /Pkt   /Sec    /Flow       /Flow
    TCP-Telnet          19    0.0        90     70    3.3      0.0        15.5
    TCP-WWW            596    1.1        40    220   46.7      0.0        15.4
    UDP-DNS            397    0.7         3     28    2.3      0.0        15.5
    Total:            1012    1.9        26    201   52.4      0.0        15.4

    SrcIf         SrcIPaddress    DstIf         DstIPaddress    Pr SrcP  DstP  Pkts
    Et1/3         1.1.2.13        Et1/2         1.1.3.13        06 0403  0015   17K
    Et1/3         1.1.2.12        Et1/2         1.1.3.12        06 042D  0017   90
    Et1/3         1.1.2.11        Et1/2         1.1.3.11        06 099E  0050   40
    Et1/3         1.1.2.21        Et1/2         1.1.3.21        11 07D3  0035    3
    Et1/3         1.1.2.21        Et1/2         1.1.3.21        11 07D2  0035    3
    Et1/3         1.1.2.21        Et1/2         1.1.3.21        11 07D1  0035    3
    Et1/3         1.1.2.21        Et1/2         1.1.3.21        11 07D0  0035    3
```

You can see how much more information is included with NetFlow than with IP accounting—packet size distribution, summary information, information by protocol, and by individual flows.

You can aggregate and group flow information in various ways: into groups based on autonomous system numbers, source and destination prefixes, and by protocol ports. Aggregation caches enable the router to aggregate some of the NetFlow data before it is exported to a flow collector. The flow data is entered in each of the enabled aggregation caches as they expire in the main NetFlow cache.

Flow aggregation uses a NetFlow version 8 aggregation cache only. Version 8 allows the aggregated caches to be exported. A version 5 main cache needs to be configured with the **peer-as** or **origin-as** option specified.

Cisco Express Forwarding (CEF) and NetFlow switching must be enabled before configuring flow aggregation. Enabling CEF populates the forwarding cache with source and destination addresses of the packets, which are used in the aggregation data.

NOTE   See Cisco Express Forwarding Overview in the 12.1 Configuration Guide, switching services configuration guide, on CCO, for more information on CEF.

Globally enabling CEF using the **ip cef** command enables CEF route-cache on all interfaces that support it. The following global command defines an aggregation cache:

```
ip flow-aggregation cache {autonomous_system | destination-prefix | prefix |
    protocol-port | source-prefix}
```

Table 9-4 documents some commands that you can apply to the cache. All these commands are entered in the aggregation cache configuration mode.

Table 9-4   cache *Commands*

Command	What It Does
cache entries *number_of_entries*	Sets the maximum number of cache entries, which ranges from 1024 to 524,288. The default is 4096.
cache timeout inactive *seconds*	Defines the number of seconds that an inactive entry remains in the cache before timing out. The range is from 10 to 600 seconds. The default is 15 seconds.
cache timeout active *minutes*	Defines the number of minutes that an active entry remains active. The range is from 1 to 60 minutes. The default is 30 minutes.
export destination *ip_address udp_port*	Specifies the export destination under the aggregation cache configuration mode, and specifies the IP address and UDP port number of the aggregation cache flow collector. This collector will receive the version 8 flow records.
enabled	Enables the aggregation cache.

AS aggregation groups flows with the same source BGP AS, destination BGP AS, input interface, and output interface. The number of flows, packets, and bytes summarized by the aggregated record is included in the exported data.

Example 9-28 shows Hummer configured with AS aggregation.

Example 9-28 *Router Hummmer from Figure 9-2 Is Configured with AS Aggregation*

```
ip cef
!
ip flow-export version 5 origin-as
ip flow-export destination 1.1.3.250 125
ip flow-aggregation cache as
 cache entries 2046
 cache timeout inactive 200
 cache timeout active 45
 export destination 1.1.3.250 9991
 enabled
!
```

Example 9-29 shows the AS aggregation cache, using the command **show ip cache flow aggregation as**.

Example 9-29 *Contents of the AS Aggregation Cache as Viewed with the Command* **show ip cache flow aggregation as**

```
Hummer#show ip cache flow aggregation as

IP Flow Switching Cache, 135048 bytes
  1 active, 2043 inactive, 3 added
  167 ager polls, 0 flow alloc failures
  Active flows timeout in 45 minutes
  Inactive flows timeout in 200 seconds

Src If      Src AS  Dst If      Dst AS  Flows   Pkts   B/Pk  Active
  Et1/3       400     Et1/2       100     357     42K    848   407.6
```

There are 357 flows associated with source interface Ethernet 1/3, source AS 400, destination interface Ethernet 1/2, and destination AS 100.

Enable prefix aggregation to take this a step further. Prefix aggregation groups traffic based on the same data as AS aggregation, source and destination BGP AS, and input and output interface, and further groups it by source and destination prefix and source and destination prefix masks.

Destination-prefix aggregation groups data flows with the same destination prefix, destination prefix mask, destination BGP AS, and output interface. Use this to examine traffic traversing a NetFlow router by destination information.

The configuration in Example 9-30 is added to Hummer.

Example 9-30 *Configuring Router Hummer from Figure 9-2 with Destination-Prefix Aggregation*

```
ip flow-aggregation cache destination-prefix
 cache entries 2046
 cache timeout inactive 200
 cache timeout active 45
 export destination 1.1.3.250 9991
 enabled
```

Example 9-31 displays the destination prefix aggregation cache.

Example 9-31 *The Destination Prefix Aggregation Cache Is Viewed with the Command* **show ip cache flow aggregation destination-prefix**

```
Hummer#show ip cache flow aggregation destination-prefix

IP Flow Switching Cache, 135048 bytes
  1 active, 2045 inactive, 1 added
```

Example 9-31 *The Destination Prefix Aggregation Cache Is Viewed with the Command* **show ip cache flow aggregation destination-prefix** *(Continued)*

```
    240 ager polls, 0 flow alloc failures
    Active flows timeout in 45 minutes
    Inactive flows timeout in 200 seconds

Dst If         Dst Prefix        Msk  AS    Flows  Pkts B/Pk  Active
  Et1/2          1.1.3.0         /24  100    324   11K  442   239.5
```

There are 324 flows associated with destination interface Ethernet 1/2, destination prefix 1.1.3.0, mask /24, and destination AS 100.

You also can examine traffic by source information, using the source-prefix aggregation scheme. This scheme groups data by source prefix, source prefix mask, source BGP AS, and input interface.

The configuration in Example 9-32 is added to Hummer.

Example 9-32 *Configuring Router Hummer from Figure 9-2 with Source-Prefix Aggregation*

```
ip flow-aggregation cache source-prefix
 cache entries 2046
 cache timeout inactive 200
 cache timeout active 45
 export destination 1.1.3.250 9991
 enabled
```

Example 9-33 shows the source prefix aggregated flows.

Example 9-33 *The Source Prefix Aggregation Cache Is Viewed with the Command* **show ip cache flow aggregation source-prefix**

```
Hummer#show ip cache flow aggregation source-prefix

IP Flow Switching Cache, 135048 bytes
  2 active, 2044 inactive, 3 added
  440 ager polls, 0 flow alloc failures
  Active flows timeout in 45 minutes
  Inactive flows timeout in 200 seconds

Src If         Src Prefix        Msk  AS    Flows  Pkts B/Pk  Active
  Et1/3          1.1.2.0         /24  400    181   4813  200   42.0
  Et1/2          1.1.7.0         /24  0      1     1    44    0.0
```

There are 181 flows associated with the source interface Ethernet 1/3, source prefix 1.1.2.0, mask /24, and source AS 400.

If you want to examine flows by traffic type, enable protocol-port aggregation. Flows with the same IP protocol, source port number, and destination port number are grouped.

To configure protocol-port aggregation, add the configuration in Example 9-34 to Hummer.

Example 9-34 *Configuring Router Hummer from Figure 9-2 with Protocol-Port Aggregation*

```
ip flow-aggregation cache protocol-port
 cache entries 2046
 cache timeout inactive 200
 cache timeout active 45
 export destination 1.1.3.250 9991
 enabled
```

Example 9-35 displays the protocol-port aggregation cache.

Example 9-35 *Protocol Port Aggregation Cache Is Viewed with the Command* **show ip cache flow aggregation protocol-port**

```
Hummer#show ip cache flow aggregation protocol-port

IP Flow Switching Cache, 135048 bytes
  14 active, 1972 inactive, 74 added
  882 ager polls, 0 flow alloc failures
  Active flows timeout in 45 minutes
  Inactive flows timeout in 200 seconds

Protocol  Source Port  Dest Port  Flows  Packets  Bytes/Packet  Active
   0x06      0x0401     0x0017      1       90         70         0.0
   0x06      0x0400     0x0017      1       90         70         0.0
   0x11      0x0404     0x0035      1        3         28         0.0
   0x11      0x0405     0x0035      1        3         28         0.0
   0x11      0x0406     0x0035      1        3         28         0.0
   0x11      0x0407     0x0035      1        3         28         0.0
   0x11      0x0400     0x0035      1        3         28         0.0
   0x11      0x0414     0x0035      1        3         28         0.0
   0x11      0x0415     0x0035      1        3         28         0.0
   0x06      0x040B     0x0050      1       40        220         0.0
   0x06      0x0408     0x0050      1       40        220         0.0
   0x06      0x0409     0x0050      1       40        220         0.0
   0x06      0x0436     0x0050      1       40        220         0.0
   0x06      0x0437     0x0050      1       40        220         0.0
```

There are 14 different protocol port flows. They are grouped by IP protocol, source ports, and destination ports.

The various aggregation caches provide a lot of flexibility with the way data about traffic flows is aggregated. This information can facilitate traffic analysis and even billing.

Table 9-5 lists the maximum number of flow records per UDP datagram and the maximum UDP packet size for each aggregation scheme.

Table 9-5 *A Listing of the Maximum Number of Flow Records and Maximum UDP Packet Sizes for Each NetFlow Aggregation Scheme*

Aggregation Scheme	Maximum Number of Flow Records per UDP Datagram	Maximum UDP Packet Size
BGP autonomous system	51	1456 bytes
Destination-prefix	44	1436 bytes
Prefix	35	1428 bytes
Protocol-port	51	1456 bytes
Source-prefix	44	1436 bytes

Cisco NetFlow FlowCollector is an application that collects and reports on the NetFlow data. FlowCollector aggregates data coming from multiple Cisco routers (and switches) exporting NetFlow data. You can filter and group the data to suit the needs of the network manager.

NOTE   You can find detailed information about Cisco FlowCollector on CCO at www.cisco.com/univercd/cc/td/doc/product/rtrmgmt/nfc/nfc_3_0/nfc_ug/index.htm.

Configuration Management

Configurations maintained in a database, downloaded from all network devices regularly (nightly, weekly), ensure that a very recent configuration can be restored to a router in need. Configuration files may need to be restored if an existing router needs to be replaced, loses its configuration, or becomes misconfigured.

CiscoWorks provides the capability to download configuration files from a router via TFTP. In fact, configuration can be downloaded from the router to any TFTP server. Many organizations use UNIX TFTP servers and Perl scripts, which are run on a regularly scheduled basis to perform their configuration management. An organization's policy may be to store configuration files for 7 days. The filenames may be *routername*.current and *routername*.1, *routername*.2, *routername*.3, and so on, representing 7 days of configurations. A simple script run nightly could copy the file *routername.N* to file *routername.N*+1 (as long as *N* is 1 through 6), copy the file *routername*.current to file *routername*.1, connect to the router to initiate the TFTP configuration file download into file *routername*.current, and log out of the router. The script could loop through a list of routers in the network.

NOTE   You can find more information about Perl in the following two books: *Learning Perl, Second Edition*, by Randal L. Schwartz, Tom Christiansen, and Steve Talbot (Editor) (O'Reilly & Associates, Inc., July 1997), and *Programming Perl*, by Larry Wall, Jon Orwant, and Tom Christiansen (O'Reilly & Associates, Inc., July 2000).

You should store old configurations for some period of time, at least a week, preferably a month, for restoring known working configurations to routers and for troubleshooting problems that may have occurred as a result of a past configuration change. With the combination of daily configuration files and change management logs, a working configuration can easily be restored to a router.

Fault Management

A dependable network requires that a fault management system be in place. Potential and existing problems need to be detected as soon as possible so that you can take immediate action to resolve the issues. A fault management system detects problems with devices and links, hopefully before end users notice the outage.

An SNMP-configured router sends traps to the management station when it detects a failure. Because SNMP uses UDP to send traps, however, there is no guarantee that the message describing the fault will reach the management station. A fault management system cannot rely solely on traps, but also must poll the routers for information about the state of lines, interfaces, and router components. In addition to polling routers for component information, the management station polls the router itself, sometimes using ICMP pings, to make sure it is accessible. To ensure that the IP address of the router is accessible via any active interface, it is a good idea to use a loopback address as the identifying IP address on the router. A management station polling or pinging the loopback address can use any available routed path to reach the router. A management station polling or pinging a nonloopback interface address on the router will declare the router inaccessible if that interface is down, even if the router can be reached via an alternative path. You should configure traps to use the loopback address as the source address of the packet, and configure the management stations to poll the router via the loopback address.

As with many protocols, a trade-off exists between how fast a management station can detect an outage and the amount of network traffic generated. If the management station misses a trap, and needs to rely on its polling or pinging to detect an outage, the outage may not be detected for quite a while. If the failed device is a router, and the management station is configured to ping the router every 5 minutes, and declare it dead if it misses three pings, it will take up to 15 minutes to detect the failure. A link or other component failure is detected sooner. The management station does not rely on the absence of a response to detect these outages, but rather asks the router for the state of the component. The router responds with the state information.

For example, Figure 9-3 shows a management station polling a router for the state of its interfaces.

Figure 9-3   *Management Station Is Polling the Router for Interface States*

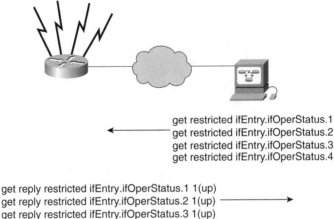

get restricted ifEntry.ifOperStatus.1
get restricted ifEntry.ifOperStatus.2
get restricted ifEntry.ifOperStatus.3
get restricted ifEntry.ifOperStatus.4

get reply restricted ifEntry.ifOperStatus.1 1(up)
get reply restricted ifEntry.ifOperStatus.2 1(up)
get reply restricted ifEntry.ifOperStatus.3 1(up)
get reply restricted ifEntry.ifOperStatus.4 2(down)

The management station polls the router for the state of its interfaces using the ifEntry.ifOperStatus object ID in the MIB. The router responds. Three interfaces are up, and one is down.

A fault management system detects failures. The failures are reported to the network operators by visual or audible alerts or are sent by e-mail or pager. The method used for sending alerts is customized to the user's environment. If someone is in front of the management console 7x24, audible and visual alerts suffice. If the console is not manned all the time, e-mail or pager alerts are sent when no one is at the console. The failure indicates link, router, or router component outages. The alerts occur after the problem has occurred. The fault management station also attempts to alert operators before failures occur.

Many times, specific events lead to a failed component. For instance, a serial line may report high error counts or carrier transitions before it fails completely. A router may report memory problems before it fails. Fault management stations maintain threshold information. When the threshold has been exceeded, an alarm is sent to the network operator. You can configure thresholds for any number of variables. To configure the values of the thresholds, the network is first baselined. The baseline takes place over a period of time, such as a week, when the network is running normally. The normal values of the variables are obtained. You then can configure thresholds at some level (say 20%) above normal.

Some MIB variables that provide useful threshold information include the following:

- Amount of free memory
- Average CPU utilization
- Buffer misses
- Interface input and output rate
- Interface input and output errors
- Interface input and output queue drops
- Interface packets ignored
- Interface resets
- Serial interface CRC, abort, and frame errors
- Frame Relay FECN/BECN
- Serial interface carrier transitions
- Ethernet collisions
- Ethernet runts, giants, and frame errors
- Token Ring line and burst errors
- Token Ring internal errors
- Token Ring token and soft errors
- Token Ring signal losses

Some of the items listed occur in a perfectly normal network. When they exceed a threshold, however, performance can be degraded, and a more serious problem may be brewing. The management station polls the routers for the value of these variables periodically. If the change in values between polling periods exceeds the threshold, an alarm is generated.

You also can use RMON for thresholding. With RMON, the management station does not have to poll for the variables. The RMON agent on the router polls the variables locally and sends a trap to the management station when the threshold is exceeded. The management station receives the trap and generates the alarm. The trade-off here is network usage versus router processing. Enabling RMON minimizes network traffic but increases the amount of processing done on the router.

Performance Management

Performance management is used for trending and capacity planning. Data is collected and analyzed. Network engineers and managers review it, looking for trends that may indicate the need to increase or decrease network capacity. Link utilization, Frame Relay FECN and BECNs, and router CPU are some items that may indicate a change in capacity is required.

Response time, measured regularly between routers on the edges of networks, as close to end users as possible, directly shows the impact of the over- or underutilized network components. It also shows the improvement when the capacity has been modified.

The performance management station is continuously collecting data. It collects data via SNMP, polling for groups of variables on regular short intervals, such as every 5 minutes. The data is stored in raw form for historical research. It also is processed and reported as minimum, maximum, and average values on an hourly basis. The data may be processed during the day for previous hours, providing almost up-to-the-minute reports and graphs, or it may be processed at some time during the night, providing reports detailing the preceding day's numbers.

The system also should report on the amount of time during the day that the values fell into certain ranges.

Consider link utilization, for example. It is helpful to know how much time during the day the utilization fell into the following ranges: 0–20%, 20–40%, 40–60%, 60–80%, 80–90%, and 90–100%.

After a few days of collecting and processing data, the system processes the data further, reporting on minimum, maximum, average per day, and ranges for the time period. If the time period is a week, the minimum, maximum, and average should be reported for each day, and the amount of time during the week spent in each range should be reported.

The performance management system needs to be up and collecting data uninterrupted. Trend analysis is meaningful on the collected data only after collecting data for an extended period of time. Projecting the trends into the future helps to determine when breaking points are likely to occur.

Flexibility makes the performance management system more valuable. Configurable time periods in which to view data, with reports as near to real time as possible, make this a very valuable tool for quickly identifying the need for capacity changes.

Security Management

If a network is to be secure, the routers themselves must be secured. Passwords are one way to control access to the routers. You can configure passwords on the routers, or you can use authentication servers such as TACACS+ or RADIUS. In addition to password protection, you should limit interactive access to the routers to necessary protocols and users. Enable only the protocols that are required for the proper functionality and manageability of the router and restrict access to the routers to those IP subnets that you know are secure. Even with access controlled, it is possible for mischievous network users to attempt to prevent the routers from functioning. Take steps to reduce the chance of these denial-of-service attacks on the routers. The next few sections discuss router configuration parameters needed to provide secure and properly functioning routers.

Password Types and Encryption

You should control all access by some authentication mechanism. If you cannot use TACACS+ or RADIUS, you should protect privileged EXEC mode router access with the **enable secret** password type. Do not use the older **enable password**, because it has a weak encryption algorithm. The **enable secret** *password* command provides better security by storing the enable secret password using a nonreversible cryptographic function. The added layer of security encryption provided proves useful in environments where the configuration file, and therefore the password, crosses the network or is stored on a TFTP server. Encrypt all passwords, including username passwords, authentication key passwords, the privileged command password, console and virtual terminal line access passwords, and BGP neighbor passwords using **service password-encryption** to prevent an onlooker from seeing passwords when you display the router configuration.

Controlling Interactive Access

You should control interactive access to the router. You can limit access to specified network numbers by using the following command:

```
access-class access-list_1-199_or_1300-2699 {in | out}
```

The *access-list* argument specifies the source network number allowed to connect to the line (with the keyword **in**), or the network number to which a connection is permitted (with the keyword **out**).

Ensure that there are no access holes by permitting only the remote access protocol desired, such as the following:

```
transport input telnet ssh
```

List the protocols that are permitted. Everything else is denied.

You should password protect all modems connected to the router, in addition to the login required on the console and auxiliary ports.

If the modems are to be used for dial-in purposes only, so administrators can access the router from home, disable the capability to use reverse Telnet to connect to the modem from the network and dial out to another location. Reverse Telnet provides the capability to specify a port number along with the IP address to connect to a device off of an asynchronous port on the router. Disable reverse Telnet on any port connected to an asynchronous terminal or modem that should not be used to dial out by issuing the **transport input none** command on the modem-connected line.

Example 9-36 illustrates a router configuration with all the access control methods discussed so far.

Example 9-36 *Controlling Interactive Access on a Router*

```
access-list 1 permit 172.16.0.0 0.0.255.255
line con 0
 transport input none
line aux 0
 transport input none
line vty 0 4
 access-class 1 in
 transport input telnet ssh
```

Telnet and Secure Shell access are the only remote protocols permitted, and those who can use the protocols to connect to the router are limited to source IP addresses in the range 172.16.0.0/16.

Minimizing Risks of Denial-of-Service Attacks

Denial-of-service (DoS) attacks deny access to some resource. Someone can perform a DoS attack in many ways. You can take some actions, however, to minimize the risks of an attack aimed at the router.

A limited number of vty ports are available on a router. Once they are all in use, no more remote sessions are permitted to the router, opening up the potential for a DoS attack. An intruder can block all vty ports, denying access to the administrator. Configure a very restrictive **access-class** command on the last vty port. Permit only a specific management station. This way, at least one port will be accessible. Configure **exec-timeout** also, to prevent idle sessions from consuming the vty indefinitely. The **service tcp-keepalives-in** command configures TCP keepalive messages on incoming connections to guard against malicious attacks and "orphaned" sessions caused by remote system crashes.

A specific DoS attack uses directed broadcasts. ICMP packets are sent to a directed broadcast address with a falsified source address, and all machines on the LAN reply, sending a large stream of traffic to the falsified source address. The real node addressed with the source IP address gets flooded with data. The command **no ip directed-broadcast** configured on all LAN interfaces thwarts this attack. **no ip directed-broadcast** is the default on IOS 12.0 and later.

IP packets with the **source-route** option specify routers that the packet must traverse between the source and destination. Return packets also must traverse the specified routers. A spoofed source address in a source-routed packet can cause a node to bypass routing tables and send data to a spoofed address. There is rarely ever a valid use for source-routed packets. Configure the routers to drop packets with the **source-route** option using the global command **no ip source-route**.

Very fast floods of packets may cause the router to spend so much time responding to interrupts from interfaces that it cannot do anything else. The command **scheduler interval** *milliseconds* tells the router to stop handling interrupts and attend to other business at regular intervals. Newer platforms may use **scheduler allocate** *interrupt-time process-time* instead.

The *interrupt-time* argument is the maximum number of microseconds the router spends on fast switching within any one network-interrupt context. The *process-time* argument is the minimum number of microseconds the router spends at the process level when network interrupts are disabled.

The routers run small servers used for diagnostic purposes. In reality, these are rarely used. The TCP services are Echo, Chargen, Discard, and Daytime. The UDP services are Echo, Chargen, and Discard. An attacker can flood traffic to these services, impacting the capability of the router to route. The following commands disable these services:

```
no service tcp-small-servers
no service udp-small-servers
```

The services are disabled by default in Cisco IOS Software Release 12.0 and later.

Some other services that should be disabled are Finger and the Async Line BOOTP Server, if they are not being used. Use the following commands to disable these services:

```
no service finger
no ip bootp server
```

The Finger service allows Finger protocol requests to the router. A Finger protocol request is equivalent to issuing a remote **show users** command, which displays information about active lines on the router.

The router offers BOOTP services to hosts connected to asynchronous lines. The command **no ip bootp server** disables these BOOTP services.

The configuration in Example 9-37 illustrates minimizing the DoS risks using the previously discussed commands.

Example 9-37 *Minimizing DoS Attacks*

```
enable secret jj15Qp
service tcp-keepalives-in
scheduler interval 500
no server tcp-small-servers
no server udp-small-servers
no service finger
no ip bootp server
no ip source-route
int e 0
 no ip directed-broadcast
access-list 10 permit 172.16.1.2
line vty 4
 access-class 10 in
 transport input telnet
```

Configure a remote authentication and authorization server, such as TACACS+, to secure the router further.

TACACS+

Terminal Access Controller Access Control System Plus (TACACS+) provides centralized validation of users attempting to gain access to routers or network access servers. A TACACS+ application resides on a server, runs as a daemon, and stores information about access privileges in a database. When a user logs in to a router configured with TACACS+, the TACACS+ client on the router and the TACACS+ daemon communicate to send the user login and password prompts and to exchange authentication and authorization information. The router also sends accounting information to the TACACS+ daemon. All communication between the router and the TACACS+ daemon is encrypted, although the communication between the user and the router may not be.

TACACS+ provides authentication, authorization, and accounting information:

- TACACS+ authentication requires the user to enter a login ID and password. The authentication service also can send messages to logged-in users, such as a request to change their password.

- TACACS+ authorization fine-tunes what the logged-in user can do. Authorization may automatically perform commands upon login, provide access control, or limit session duration. Authorization also can limit which commands a user is permitted to perform while logged in to the router.

- TACACS+ accounting collects information used for billing, auditing, and reporting and sends it to the TACACS+ server. The accounting records include information about user identities, start and stop times, executed commands, number of packets, and number of bytes. The information is useful in a security audit and for billing purposes. When TACACS+ is used to control user access to a network access server, which then enables the user to use services on the network, billing information may be desirable.

TACACS+ Authentication Configuration

The router uses AAA to enable TACACS+. The command **aaa new-model** enables AAA.

The command that defines a list of authentication methods is as follows:

```
aaa authentication login {default | list_name} group auth_type [auth_type ...]
```

The authentication methods are **tacacs+**, **radius**, **kerberos**, **local**, **line password**, **enable password**, and **none**.

After the authentication list has been defined, it is applied to lines. The keyword **default** automatically applies the list to all lines. When you are first configuring authentication, it is a good idea to specify a list name and manually apply the list to lines. By doing so, you can test your configuration in a controlled manner, without locking yourself out of the router.

To apply the list to lines, use the following commands:

```
line type number
login authentication list_name
```

You also need to specify the location of the TACACS+ server. Use the **tacacs-server host** *ip_address* command to specify the IP address of the server.

Example 9-38 demonstrates a router configuration for TACACS+ authentication.

Example 9-38 *Configuring a Router for TACACS+ Authentication*

```
aaa new-model
aaa authentication login tac tacacs+  enable
tacacs-server host 172.16.1.2

line vty 0 1
 login authentication tac
!line vty 2 4
! login authentication tac
!line con 0
! login authentication tac
!line aux 0
! login authentication tac
```

The authentication list **tac** first attempts to authenticate using the TACACS+ server, 172.16.1.2. If the server is unreachable, the second method, **enable password** authentication, is used. The second method allows access to the router in the event that the TACACS+ server becomes unreachable. The list is traversed only if a method is unavailable, not if the method returns a failure. If the TACACS+ server is down, for instance, **enable password** is used. If TACACS+ server is up, but the user ID entered is not correct, a failed message is returned and no more methods are attempted.

Notice that the authentication list in Example 9-38 is applied only to line vty 0 and 1. This is for testing purposes. If TACACS+ is misconfigured, the router can still be accessed via the other vty lines and the console port. Make sure the configuration is correct and working as you expect before applying the list to all lines. When the configuration is correct, apply the authentication to all lines.

You can define a TACACS+ shared encryption key using **tacacs-server key** *key*.

You must define the same key in the TACACS+ configuration file on the server.

You can use TACACS+ when entering the enable mode on the router as well. Use the command **aaa authentication enable default group** *auth_type* [*auth_type*].

The configuration commands in Example 9-39 are added to router Seattle to specify enable-level authentication and a TACACS+ shared key.

Example 9-39 *Specifying Enable-Level Authentication and a TACACS+ Shared Key on Router Seattle*

```
aaa new-model
aaa authentication login tac tacacs+  enable
aaa authentication enable default group  tacacs+ enable
tacacs-server host 172.16.1.2
tacacs-server key mykey
line vty 0 4
 login authentication tac
```

Example 9-40 shows the TACACS+ server configuration file that corresponds with the router configuration in Example 9-39.

Example 9-40 *TACACS+ Server Configuration File for Seattle Configuration in Example 9-39*

```
Key = "mykey"
User = agnes
{
                    login = cleartext "agnes password"
}
user = admin
{
                    login = cleartext "encrypted"
}
user = $enab15$
{
                    login = cleartext "secret"
}
```

Two regular users are configured, **agnes** and **admin**. The user **$enab15$** is used for the enable-level authentication, at privilege level 15, which is the default. A side effect of the enable authentication is that a user named **$enab15$** is created. Someone can log in to the router with this user ID, if he knows the password.

With the configuration in Example 9-39, access to the router requires a username and a password. The normal router login IDs are used only if the TACACS+ server is unreachable. The username is included in certain log messages as a result.

The following log message shows the username, the user's IP address, and the date and time of a configuration change:

```
Jun 20 16:42:32 UTC: %SYS-5-CONFIG_I: Configured from console by agnes on
  vty0 (10.1.2.25)
```

The preceding represents a very basic configuration. You can do much more with TACACS+, including defining groups and specifying privileges based on group membership using DES-encrypted passwords or using a UNIX password file.

NOTE   Refer to the TACACS+ User Guide for full implementation specifications. Passwd(5) is the supported password file type for the UNIX password file.

TACACS+ Authorization Configuration

You can configure TACACS+ to authorize what users are permitted to do on the router. Access lists can be applied, commands can be limited, or PPP and SLIP access can be permitted. A profile is set up on the TACACS+ server for each user. The profile specifies what the user is authorized to do. When the user logs in to the router, all his actions must be authorized by the contents of the user profile.

The following commands define the authorization methods list and apply the list to lines on the router:

```
aaa authorization {network | exec | commands level | reverse-access} {default | list-
name} [method1 [method2...]]
line type number
  authorization {arap | exec | commands level | reverse-access} {default | list-name}
```

The user profile must be configured on the TACACS+ server. The same warning that applied to authentication applies here. Make sure to test the authorization configuration well, and configure a user who has unrestricted access before using the default list, which gets applied to all lines and interfaces, or before applying a named list to all lines. Authorization is applied to the router as soon as the command is entered, and it affects even the existing connections. Also, the TACACS+ configuration file defaults to no authorization allowed. If TACACS+ authorization is configured on the router and applied to all lines, but nothing is specifically permitted in the configuration file, you may find yourself unable to perform any commands.

The server configuration file in Example 9-41 limits the commands available to Agnes but provides no restrictions on user Admin.

Example 9-41 *TACACS+ Server Configuration File Providing Restrictions Based on the User*

```
Key = "mykey"
User = agnes
{
        login = cleartext "agnes password"
        cmd = show {
                    permit .*
        }
}
user = admin
```

Example 9-41 *TACACS+ Server Configuration File Providing Restrictions Based on the User (Continued)*

```
{
                default service = permit
                login = cleartext "encrypted"
}
user = $enab15$
{
                login = cleartext "secret"
}
```

Agnes is permitted to perform any **show** commands. Nothing else is permitted.

Example 9-42 shows the router commands required to make use of the TACACS+ configuration in Example 9-41.

Example 9-42 *Router Authorization Configuration Associated with the TACACS+ Server Authorization in Example 9-41*

```
aaa authorization commands 1 restrict group tacacs+
aaa authorization commands 15 restrict group tacacs+
line vty 0 1
            authorization commands 1 restrict
            authorization commands 15 restrict
! line vty 2 4
!             authorization commands 1 restrict
!             authorization commands 15 restrict
```

Remember not to apply the authorization list to all vty ports until after you have fully tested it.

Like TACACS+ authentication, you can do much more with authorization. I have illustrated a very simple use of the TACACS+ authorization feature. Access lists can be applied. Autocommands can be enforced. Telnet restrictions can be applied.

TACACS+ accounting shows information about what the user connected to the router is doing.

TACACS+ Accounting Configuration

TACACS+ accounting is used to record information about user connections, including the length of their connections, commands they entered, and the destination and length of outbound connections. This information can prove useful for billing or for a security audit. You enable accounting by using AAA accounting commands on the router and by specifying the accounting filename in the TACACS+ configuration file on the server.

The following commands define the type of accounting associated with the named list:

```
aaa accounting {system | network | exec | connection | commands level} {default | list-
name} {start-stop | wait-start | stop-only | none} [method1 [method2...]]
line type number
 accounting {arap | exec | connection | commands level} {default | list-name}
```

Information about system-level events, such as the system rebooting or accounting configured, is enabled with system accounting. Information about PPP, SLIP, or ARAP sessions, including packet and byte counts, is provided with network accounting. EXEC accounting provides information about the EXEC terminal sessions on the router. The information includes username data, as well as start and stop times of the session. Connections accounting provides information about connections made from the router. The connection could be **telnet**, **LAT**, **tn3270**, **PAD**, or **rlogin**. The data includes destination address, protocol, start and stop times, username, and packets and bytes transferred. Command accounting provides information about commands entered. The commands are normally either level 1 or level 15 commands. Level 1 commands are those that you can enter at any login level. Level 15 commands are available only at the enable level. The actual command entered is recorded. Even configuration commands are recorded.

To apply the list to lines, use the line subcommand **accounting** [**type**] *list-name*.

To configure accounting on the TACACS+ server, add the command **accounting file =** *filename*, as demonstrated in Example 9-43.

Example 9-43 *Configuring Accounting on the TACACS+ Server*

```
Key = "mykey"
Accounting file = tacacs.acct
User = agnes
{
        login = cleartext "agnes password"
        cmd = show {
                   permit .*
        }
}
user = admin
{
        default service = permit
        login = cleartext "encrypted"
}
user = $enab15$
{
        login = cleartext "secret"
}
```

Example 9-44 shows the router commands that enable command and EXEC accounting.

Example 9-44 *Enabling Command and EXEC Accounting*

```
aaa accounting commands 1 default stop-only group tacacs+
aaa accounting commands 15 default stop-only group tacacs+
aaa accounting exec default start-stop group tacacs+
```

The line vty subcommands are not needed in this configuration because the default list is used. The default list is automatically applied to all lines and interfaces.

Example 9-45 shows the content of an accounting log.

Example 9-45 *The Accounting Log Shows Commands and an EXEC Record*

```
ObiWan:/tacacs# more tacacs.acct
Tue Jun 20 10:33:06 2000          172.16.1.7      agnes   tty2  10.1.2.25
stop    task_id=2       start_time=961520711   timezone=UTC service=shell
  priv-lvl=15     cmd=debug aaa accounting <cr>
Tue Jun 20 10:33:57 2000          172.16.1.7      agnes   tty3  10.1.2.25
stop    task_id=4       start_time=961520761   timezone=UTC   service=shell
  priv-lvl=15     cmd=write terminal <cr>
Tue Jun 20 10:34:08 2000          172.16.1.7      agnes   tty3  10.1.2.25
stop    task_id=5       start_time=961520773   timezone=UTC   service=shell
  priv-lvl=15     cmd=configure terminal <cr>
Tue Jun 20 10:34:22 2000          172.16.1.7      agnes   tty3  10.1.2.25
stop    task_id=6       start_time=961520786   timezone=UTC   service=shell
  priv-lvl=15     cmd=interface Serial 1 <cr>
Tue Jun 20 10:34:24 2000          172.16.1.7      agnes   tty3  10.1.2.25
stop    task_id=7       start_time=961520789   timezone=UTC   service=shell
  priv-lvl=15     cmd=shutdown <cr>

Tue Jun 20 10:34:42 2000          172.16.1.7      agnes   tty3  10.1.2.25
stop    task_id=3       start_time=961520734   timezone=UTC   service=shell
  disc-cause=1    disc-cause-ext=1020      elapsed_time=73 nas-rx-speed=0
  nas-tx-speed=0
```

The accounting log shows commands entered and an EXEC session record. From the log, you can see that Agnes shut down serial interface 1 at 10:34:24 on Tuesday, June 20. She terminated her EXEC session at 10:34:42 on the same day. Her session lasted for 73 seconds.

You can use accounting for security audits, when the need arises to see what people have been doing on the router. You also can use it for billing. Assuming that this information comes from a network access server (NAS), and the users are accessing network resources via the NAS, the data shows that Agnes was connected for 73 seconds. You could bill her for 73 seconds of network usage.

RADIUS

Remote Access Dial-In User Service (RADIUS) provides the same functionality as TACACS+, with a few differences. RADIUS is designed to be used as an authentication, authorization, and accounting server for dial-in access to a network. The RADIUS client resides on the router or NAS and communicates with a RADIUS server on the network. The main functional difference is that RADIUS does not allow users to control which commands can be executed on a router, as TACACS+ does. This makes TACACS+ a better choice for controlling access to a router if the network administrator wants to create tight control of commands available to various users.

RADIUS was developed by Livingston Enterprises. Its source code is publicly available, and there are no use restrictions. There are many server implementations, and the client is supported in many different vendor devices.

RADIUS is configured on the Cisco router in the same way that TACACS+ is enabled, via the AAA commands. A RADIUS server and a TACACS+ server may both be in the network, authenticating, authorizing, and providing accounting for the same router or NAS.

For example, a design goal may be to use the RADIUS server to authenticate users. If the RADIUS server is unavailable, the TACACS+ server authenticates. Example 9-46 shows the router configuration to enable RADIUS as the primary authentication server and TACACS+ in case of an unavailable RADIUS server.

Example 9-46 *Enabling RADIUS and TACACS+ on a Router*

```
aaa new-model
aaa authentication login remoteauth radius tacacs+  enable
tacacs-server host 172.16.1.2
radius-server host 172.16.1.2
tacacs-server key mytackey
radius-server key myradkey
line vty 0 4
 login authentication remoteauth
```

You enable RADIUS in the same way that you enable TACACS+.

Secure Shell

Secure Shell (SSH) enables a user to make a secure, encrypted connection to a router. The connection's functionality is similar to an inbound Telnet session. Unlike Telnet, the connection is encrypted, providing a huge benefit over Telnet, which sends all data between the client and server (the router, in this case) in clear text, readable by any network analyzer collecting data along the traffic's path. Telnet's method means that if you are using Telnet to access the router, the passwords that you have purposely encrypted on the router are passed in clear text over the network. SSH encrypts the connection, so no data is exchanged in clear text between the client and router. RSA authentication for the SSH connection is not supported on routers, although it is supported in some clients. Authentication is performed by user ID and password only.

SSH is supported on 7200, 75000, and 12000 series routers only, and it is supported on DES and triple DES data encryption software images only. IOS supports SSH version 1 only.

To enable SSH on a router, you must perform the following steps:

Step 1   Configure a host name and domain name on your router.

Step 2   Generate an RSA key-pair.

Step 3   Enable local or AAA authentication.

Step 4   If you are using AAA authentication, disable it on the console port.

Step 5   Configure optional SSH parameters.

Host name and domain name are configured using the following commands:

```
hostname hostname
ip domain-name domainname
```

If these commands are not configured, errors report when you generate the RSA key-pair.

SSH is automatically enabled when the RSA key-pair is generated. It is disabled when the RSA key-pair is deleted.

The command **crypto key generate rsa** generates the RSA key-pair and enables SSH. SSH can use either local authentication, enabled using the **username** command, or AAA authentication. AAA must be disabled on the console port.

The SSH parameters modify the default connection behavior. You can modify the timeout value that applies to the SSH negotiation phase or you can specify the number of authentication retries. The timeout value must not exceed 120 seconds. The default is 120. The number of retries must not exceed 5; the default is 5. Use the following command to modify the parameters:

```
ip ssh {[timeout seconds] | [authentication-retries integer]}
```

Example 9-47 demonstrates a basic SSH configuration.

Example 9-47 *SSH Configuration*

```
hostname Seattle
ip domain-name thecompany.com
crypto key generate rsa
aaa authentication login tacauth tacacs+ local enable
aaa authentication login aaanone none
username agnes password 0 agnespassword
ip ssh time-out 60
ip ssh authentication-retries 2
```

continues

Example 9-47 *SSH Configuration (Continued)*

```
tacacs-server host 172.16.1.2
tacacs-server key secret
line con 0
 login authentication aaanone
 transport input none
line aux 0
 login authentication tacauth
line vty 0 4
 login authentication tacauth
```

Note that the AAA authentication list **aaanone**, which has no AAA authentication method defined, is applied to the console port. The other authentication list, **tacauth**, is applied to all vty ports and the auxiliary port.

Designing Servers to Support Management Processes

Servers supporting management processes should be robust and secure. They have been put in place to collect and process data that is required to maintain the integrity of the network. You should place the servers in physically secure locations where they can run without being interrupted. The operating systems must be secured, and remote access to the servers should be extremely limited. Remember that the management stations have access to all the routers in the network, so the management stations must be very secure.

The sizing of the servers is based on the vendor recommendations. Use the conservative numbers to make sure that there will be enough processing power, memory, and disk space to last well into the future, even as the amount of data collected grows.

The servers need to have redundant access to the network devices. They must be able to collect data even in the event of a router or link failure. Running a network without visibility about its operating condition can be a trying experience.

Network Robustness

A robust network can withstand outages and keep applications running smoothly.

Router redundancy on LAN segments is required to maintain communication in the event of a router failure. Hosts on the IPv4 LAN, however, are very likely to rely on a single default router to communicate to hosts on a remote segment. If the default router fails, the host is not informed, and therefore sends traffic to a black hole. Router redundancy protocols, such as the Virtual Router Redundancy Protocol (VRRP) and Cisco's Hot Standby Routing Protocol (HSRP), alleviate this problem. Both protocols enable multiple routers to share a single IP address. Therefore, when hosts are configured with the IP address of the default gateway, the shared address is used. One of the routers sharing the address is active. If the active router fails, a backup resumes receiving and sending traffic. Hosts have no knowledge of the failure, or even that multiple routers are forwarding its traffic off the LAN segment. VRRP is an open standard based on Cisco's HSRP. Cisco IOS Software does not support VRRP, so this book does not discuss it. HSRP is further discussed in the following section.

NOTE   RFC 2338 defines VRRP.

HSRP

HSRP allows multiple routers on a single LAN (Ethernet, Token Ring, FDDI) or ISL-encapsulated VLAN to share an IP and MAC address. A group of routers is configured as an HSRP group. Each router in the group is configured with the group IP address and a priority. One router is active and accepts all packets being forwarded to the group IP/MAC address. If the active router fails, another router in the group becomes active and begins accepting the packets.

The router with the highest priority is considered active. The default priority is 100. If more than one router has the same priority, the one with the numerically highest IP address on the HSRP interface is active. The router with the second-highest priority is the standby router. It becomes active if the active router fails to advertise its presence or begins advertising a lower priority. Figure 9-4 illustrates HSRP.

Figure 9-4   *HSRP*

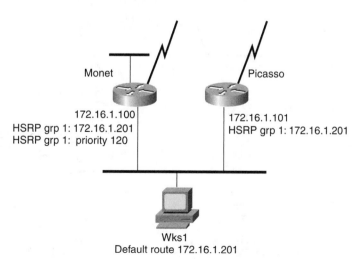

Wks1
Default route 172.16.1.201

Router Monet is configured with an interface IP address 172.16.1.100 and an HSRP group 1 IP address 172.16.1.201. Router Monet advertises an HSRP priority, for HSRP group 1, as 120. This is higher than the default priority of Picasso. Monet, therefore, is the active router for group 1. When Wks1 wants to send a packet toward its default gateway, it ARPs for the HSRP group 1 address. Monet responds with the HSRP group 1 MAC address. Wks1 then sends its packets to the HSRP group 1 MAC address, which Monet accepts.

The routers in an HSRP group exchange multicast hello packets, advertising priorities. The hello messages are exchanged over the link for which the HSRP group is configured. The routers send hello messages, by default, every 3 seconds. If the active router fails to send a hello within a configurable period of time, called the holdtime (the default holdtime is every 10 seconds), the standby router with the highest priority becomes active and begins accepting the packets destined to the group's MAC address.

Multigroup HSRP

Multigroup HSRP (MHSRP) enables an interface to be configured with multiple HSRP groups. You use MHSRP when you want to distribute the active router functionality among multiple routers on the same LAN. Some end nodes default route to the IP address of one group; other nodes default route to the IP address of a second group. If either default router fails, the other resumes the packet forwarding. MHSRP is not supported on Ethernet interfaces that are not allowed to be associated with multiple MAC addresses. (Those routers that use Lance Ethernet hardware [1000, 2500, 3000, and 4000] do not support multiple groups on a single Ethernet.) Ethernet and FDDI support up to 255 MHSRP groups. Token Ring supports up to three groups (group numbers 0, 1, 2). MHSRP is supported over Inter-Switch Link (ISL) encapsulation. Figure 9-5 illustrates MHSRP.

Figure 9-5   *MHSRP Groups Can Be Configured on Router Interfaces to Balance Load*

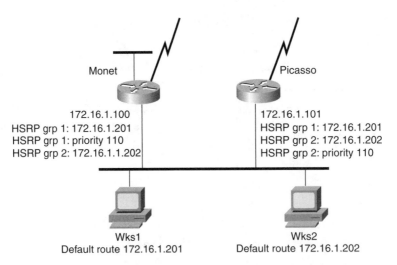

Monet
172.16.1.100
HSRP grp 1: 172.16.1.201
HSRP grp 1: priority 110
HSRP grp 2: 172.16.1.1.202

Picasso
172.16.1.101
HSRP grp 1: 172.16.1.201
HSRP grp 2: 172.16.1.202
HSRP grp 2: priority 110

Wks1
Default route 172.16.1.201

Wks2
Default route 172.16.1.202

In Figure 9-5, Monet is the active router for group 1; Picasso is the active router for group 2. Wks1 defaults to 172.16.1.201, group 1; Wks2 defaults to 172.16.1.202, group 2. If Monet stops receiving the HSRP hello messages for group 2, Monet becomes the active router for group 2 in addition to group 1.

Configuring HSRP

To enable HSRP, enter the following interface subcommand:

```
standby [group-number] ip [ip-address [secondary]]
```

You must specify the IP address on at least one router in the HSRP group. If you do not specify the IP address on a router, the address is learned via HSRP hello messages.

The following commands affect how the router participates in HSRP:

```
standby [group-number] timers hellotime holdtime
standby [group-number] priority priority [preempt [delay delay]]
standby [group-number] [priority priority] preempt [delay delay]
standby [group-number] track type number [interface-priority]
standby [group-number] authentication string
standby use-bia [scope interface]
```

The **timers** command modifies the time between hello packets and the maximum elapsed time before a standby router considers the active router dead. The default hello time is 3 seconds. The default holdtime is 10 seconds.

The **priority** and **preempt** command modifies the HSRP router's priority. **preempt** enables the router with the highest priority to take over the active role, even if the current active router is not having problems. The **delay** option causes the router to postpone preempting the active role for the specified number of seconds before becoming active. The range is from 0 to 3600 seconds. The default is 0.

A router's LAN interface may be active, and the router itself is operating fine, but the interfaces used to forward packets out of the router may have failed. In this case, packets forwarded to the router have to be redirected back to the other router, as illustrated in Figure 9-6.

The workstation sends a packet toward its default gateway, which is the active router, Monet. Monet's outbound interfaces have both failed. Monet consults its routing table and forwards the packets back onto the Ethernet and to Picasso for further forwarding.

Figure 9-6 *HSRP Without Interface Tracking*

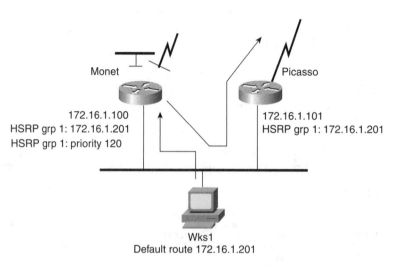

Monet

Picasso

172.16.1.100
HSRP grp 1: 172.16.1.201
HSRP grp 1: priority 120

172.16.1.101
HSRP grp 1: 172.16.1.201

Wks1
Default route 172.16.1.201

The **track** command enables HSRP to track the state of outbound interfaces, causing the router to lower its priority and possibly transition out of its active state if the interface fails. When the tracked interface fails, the router changes the priority it is advertising. If the new priority is lower than a standby router's priority, and the standby router is configured to preempt an active router with a lower priority, the standby router becomes active for the group. The router's priority for the group is decremented by the amount specified in the *interface-priority* field. The default value is 10. Multiple interfaces can be tracked. If more than one interface is tracked, and each is configured with an *interface-priority* value, when more than one interface fails, the decremented priority amount is cumulative. If no *interface-priority* value is set on tracked interfaces, and more than one goes down, the priority value is decremented by the default 10 but is not cumulative.

The **authentication** command enables the routers to include an authentication string in the HSRP messages. You must configure all routers in a group with the same authentication string, or no string at all. The first router enabled with HSRP becomes active. If the authentication strings on subsequently activated routers do not match, the newly activated routers remain in a learning state. No router becomes the standby router.

Example 9-48 shows the HSRP configurations from routers Monet and Picasso, illustrated in Figure 9-7 (single-group HSRP).

Example 9-48 *HSRP Configurations for Routers Monet and Picasso in Figure 9-7*

```
Router Monet
interface Ethernet 1
 ip address 172.16.1.100 255.255.255.0
 standby 1 priority 120 preempt delay 10
 standby 1 authentication secret
 standby 1 ip 172.16.1.201

Router Picasso
interface Ethernet 0
 ip address 172.16.1.101 255.255.255.0
 standby 1 authentication secret
 standby 1 ip
```

Figure 9-7   *Network Illustrating Single-Group HSRP*

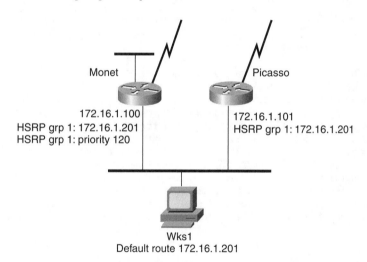

Monet

Picasso

172.16.1.100
HSRP grp 1: 172.16.1.201
HSRP grp 1: priority 120

172.16.1.101
HSRP grp 1: 172.16.1.201

Wks1
Default route 172.16.1.201

Picasso learns the IP address and timers from the HSRP function.

The output from the **show standby** command on Picasso in Example 9-49 shows the learned information.

Notice that Picasso's state is Standby, with priority 100. The active router address is 172.16.1.100, Monet. The HSRP address is 172.16.1.201. The HSRP MAC address that is associated with this address is 0000.0c07.ac01.

Example 9-49 **show standby** *Command Output Shows the IP Address and Timer Information Picasso Learns from the HSRP Function*

```
Picasso#show standby
Ethernet0 · Group 1
  Local state is Standby, priority 100
  Hellotime 3 holdtime 10
  Next hello sent in 00:00:00.340
  Hot standby IP address is 172.16.1.201
  Active router is 172.16.1.100 expires in 00:00:10
  Standby router is local
  Standby virtual mac address is 0000.0c07.ac01
  4 state changes, last state change 00:02:57
```

Pings to the HSRP address from a workstation in Example 9-50 illustrate the failure of the active router and recovery by the standby router.

Example 9-50 *Pings to the HSRP Address Indicate Active Router Failure and Standby Router Recovery*

```
ObiWan:~# ping 172.16.1.201
PING 172.16.1.201 (172.16.1.201): 56 data bytes
64 bytes from 172.16.1.201: icmp_seq=0 ttl=255 time=5.7 ms
64 bytes from 172.16.1.201: icmp_seq=1 ttl=255 time=3.5 ms
64 bytes from 172.16.1.201: icmp_seq=2 ttl=255 time=3.5 ms
64 bytes from 172.16.1.201: icmp_seq=3 ttl=255 time=3.5 ms
64 bytes from 172.16.1.201: icmp_seq=4 ttl=255 time=3.5 ms
64 bytes from 172.16.1.201: icmp_seq=5 ttl=255 time=3.4 ms
64 bytes from 172.16.1.201: icmp_seq=6 ttl=255 time=3.5 ms
64 bytes from 172.16.1.201: icmp_seq=17 ttl=255 time=3.5 ms
64 bytes from 172.16.1.201: icmp_seq=18 ttl=255 time=3.5 ms
64 bytes from 172.16.1.201: icmp_seq=19 ttl=255 time=3.5 ms
64 bytes from 172.16.1.201: icmp_seq=20 ttl=255 time=3.4 ms
64 bytes from 172.16.1.201: icmp_seq=21 ttl=255 time=3.4 ms
```

The workstation is sending pings every second. Packets 1–6 succeeded. Packets 7–16 failed. As you can see, it took 10–11 seconds for the standby router to begin accepting packets for the HSRP MAC address. The standby router stopped receiving hello messages from the active router when its LAN interface failed. It waits for its hold period of 10 seconds and then begins accepting packets.

The additions to the configuration illustrated in Example 9-51 enable HSRP interface tracking on Monet. Figure 9-8 illustrates the benefits of HSRP interface tracking. Monet's Serial 1 and Ethernet 0 lead to remote resources, which are also accessible via Picasso. The design goal is to allow workstations on the LAN to default route to Monet, as long as one or more outbound interfaces (Serial 1 and Ethernet 0) are up. If both fail, the workstations default to Picasso instead.

Example 9-51 *Enabling HSRP Interface Tracking on Router Monet*

```
Monet
interface Ethernet1
 standby 1 track Ethernet0 15
 standby 1 track Serial1 15

Picasso
interface Ethernet0
 standby 1 priority 100 preempt delay 10
```

Figure 9-8 *Network Illustrating HSRP Interface Tracking*

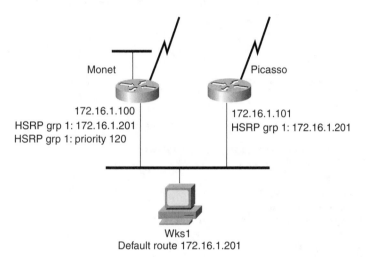

Monet · Picasso

172.16.1.100
HSRP grp 1: 172.16.1.201
HSRP grp 1: priority 120

172.16.1.101
HSRP grp 1: 172.16.1.201

Wks1
Default route 172.16.1.201

Note that Monet is tracking both Serial 1 and Ethernet 0. If only one tracked interface goes down, Monet's priority is 105, still higher than Picasso's, so Monet continues to be active. If both interfaces fail, Monet begins advertising its priority as 90 rather than 120. After waiting the preempt delay time, Picasso sends an HSRP coup message, indicating to Monet that it is taking over as the active router. Monet resigns as active router and listens for other HSRP messages to determine whether it is to become the standby router. You must add the **preempt** statement to Picasso's HSRP configuration to enable the takeover. When one of Monet's interfaces becomes active again, its priority rises to 105. Monet has **preempt** and **delay** configured, so Monet waits 10 seconds before taking over as the active router for group 1.

Configuring MHSRP

Figure 9-9 illustrates Multigroup HSRP.

Figure 9-9   *Network Illustrating MHSRP*

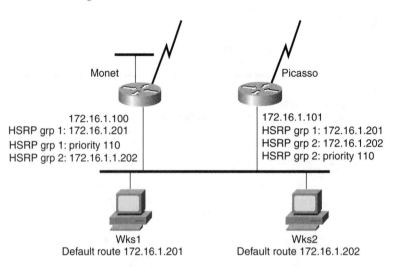

The configurations in Example 9-52 are for MHSRP on routers Monet and Picasso.

Example 9-52 *Configuring MHSRP on Routers Monet and Picasso*

```
Router Monet
interface Ethernet 1
 ip address 172.16.1.100 255.255.255.0
 standby 1 priority 120 preempt delay 10
 standby 1 authentication secret
 standby 1 ip 172.16.1.201
 standby 2 authentication secret
 standby 2 ip

Router Picasso
interface Ethernet 0
 ip address 172.16.1.101 255.255.255.0
 standby 1 authentication secret
 standby 1 ip
 standby 2 priority 120 preempt delay 10
 standby 2 authentication secret
 standby 2 ip 172.16.1.202
```

Monet is the active router for group 1, with HSRP IP address 172.16.1.201; Picasso is the active router for group 2, with HSRP IP address 172.16.1.202. To achieve load balancing, configure half the workstations on the LAN with default gateway 172.16.1.201 and the other half with default gateway 172.16.1.202.

Lab

A network lab provides a platform on which to test new configurations, IOS versions, and features.

Because a lab's purpose is to test anything new before implementing it in the live network, the lab's construction reflects the live network. An effective lab does not have to be a full-scale reproduction of the live network, but it is composed of the same type of routers, interfaces, and Cisco IOS Software. It runs the same routing protocols and routing features. Anything that is implemented in the live network can be reproduced in the lab.

The lab is isolated from the production network, but those who need to use it can easily access it. One way to keep the functionality of the lab isolated from the production network while still enabling access to the lab from the network is to use a terminal server. The terminal server's LAN interface connects to the production network. Its asynchronous ports connect to the console ports of the lab routers. Most terminal servers allow reverse Telnet connections to devices connected to their asynchronous ports. Each async port is associated with a protocol port number. If you Telnet to the IP address of the TS and specify the appropriate protocol port for the desired async port, you connect to the async device connected to that port. Figure 9-10 illustrates the interconnection of the production and lab networks using a terminal server.

Figure 9-10 *Terminal Server Provides Access to an Isolated Lab from the Production Network*

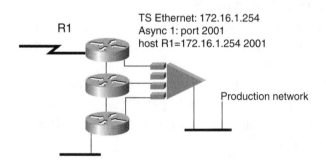

The information in Figure 9-10 shows that by Telneting to 172.16.1.254 port 2001 from the production network, the terminal server connects you to the device connected to async port 1, router R1.

A configuration entry on the terminal server associates host R1 to IP address and port number 172.16.1.254 2001. A Telnet session initiated from the terminal server to R1 connects to router R1 via async port 1.

A lab is used to test all network designs and changes taking place in the network, including configuration changes, router additions, IOS upgrades, and new feature additions. Lab testing is an integral part of a good change policy. A successful test ensures that the network change will be successful and will not present any negative surprises. The test assures business units that due diligence is being performed by the network engineers and every effort is being made to keep the network running optimally.

It is particularly important to thoroughly test new designs, feature additions, and Cisco IOS Software upgrades. These are considered major upgrades to any network.

Tests may not work out as expected, and the results may not be valid if you do not have a good test plan. A test plan describes the item to be tested and defines how it will be tested. Writing a clear test plan before beginning the test saves you time. You clarify exactly what needs to be tested, as well as define the steps necessary to perform the test. Very precisely define the steps. In fact, the plan should be so well-defined that anyone can follow it, and that any two people following the plan perform the exact same steps and get the same results.

Labs also provide an area of the network where you can just play around with the commands, testing the effect of misconfigurations and practicing troubleshooting. The lab can be used in this way for training and CCIE preparation. Only with a lab can you thoroughly experiment with configurations, break things to see what happens, and determine what symptoms identify misconfigurations. The depth of knowledge you need in the CCIE lab test requires that you have this kind of experience with Cisco IOS Software.

Recommended Reading

Marshal T. Rose, *The Simple Book*: *An Introduction to Networking Management: Revised Second Edition* (New York, NY: Simon & Schuster Trade, 1995). This book thoroughly explains SNMP.

Randal L. Schwartz, Tom Christiansen, Steve Talbot (Editor), *Learning Perl, Second Edition* (O'Reilly & Associates, Inc., July 1997).

Larry Wall, Jon Orwant, Tom Christiansen, *Programming PERL* (O'Reilly & Associates, Inc., July 2000).

End Notes

[1] J. Case et al., "RFC 1157: A Simple Network Management Protocol (SNMP)" (Work in Progress)

[2] J. Case et al., "RFC 1901: Introduction to Community-based SNMPv2" (Work in Progress)

[3] K. McCloghrie and M. Rose, "RFC 1213: Management Information Base for Network Management of TCP/IP-based internets: MIB-II" (Work in Progress)

[4] S. Waldbusser, "RFC 2819: Remote Network Monitoring Management Information Base" (Work in Progress)

Looking Ahead

This chapter concludes the in-depth look at routing TCP/IP with exterior routing protocols and other techniques used in interdomain routing. You should know this material thoroughly before taking the CCIE exam. Routing TCP/IP is not the only topic covered on the exam, however. You need to study other protocols, such as SNA, IPX, and AppleTalk. If you have not already done so, you also need to study LAN and WAN switching.

Command Summary

Table 9-6 provides a list and description of the commands discussed in this chapter.

Table 9-6   *Command Summary*

Command	Description
snmp-server community *community-string* [**view** *view-name*] [**ro** | **rw**][*access-list number*]	Defines the community string, what predefined view is available using this community string, the type of access this community string allows (ro or rw), and an associated access list, specifying the devices allowed to use this community string.
snmp-server view *view-name oid-tree* {**included** | **excluded**}	Limits which MIB objects an SNMP manager can access.
snmp-server system-shutdown	Enables an SNMP manager to send a message to users logged in to the router, and to then reboot the router, via SNMP.
snmp-server tftp-server-list *access-list_number*	Limits the capability for TFTP servers to load configuration files via SNMP to those specified in the access list.
snmp-server host *host* [**version** {**1** | **2c**}] *community-string* [**udp-port** *port*] [*trap-type*]	Specifies a host to which to send traps.
snmp-server enable traps *trap-type trap-option*	Makes traps of the listed types available for sending.
snmp trap link-status	Enables link up/down traps on the interface.
show snmp	Shows SNMP statistics.
rmon alarm *number variable interval* {**delta** | **absolute**} **rising-threshold** *value* [*event-number*] **falling-threshold** *value* [*event-number*] [**owner** *string*]	Defines an alarm and specifies when the alarm is triggered and cleared and what event the alarm triggers.

continues

Table 9-6   *Command Summary (Continued)*

Command	Description
rmon event *number* [**log**] [**trap** *community*] [**description** *string*] [**owner** *string*]	Defines an RMON event and specifies where to log the event when it is triggered by an alarm.
show rmon alarms	Displays information about the defined alarms.
show rmon events	Displays the event table.
logging buffered [*size*]	Enables buffered logging on the router and specifies the size of the log.
show logging	Displays the buffered log.
clear logging	Clears the buffered log.
logging *host*	Specifies the host name or IP address of the host that will receive syslog messages.
terminal monitor	Sends log information to the current terminal line.
service timestamps log uptime	Adds time stamps to the log.
service timestamps log datetime [**msec**] [**localtime**] [**show-timezone**]	Adds time stamps to the log.
logging console *level*	Limits messages logged to the console.
logging monitor *level*	Limits messages logged to the terminal line.
logging trap *level*	Limits messages logged to the syslog servers.
logging facility *facility-type*	Defines the facility type used when sending log messages to a syslog server.
snmp-server enable traps syslog	Enables SNMP traps for syslog messages.
logging history *level*	Specifies the level of syslog messages to be sent via SNMP.
ntp server *ip_address* [**version** *number*] [**key** *keyid*] [**source** *interface*] [**prefer**]	Creates a server association so that this router can synchronize its clock to another NTP clock source.
ntp peer *ip_address* [**version** *number*] [**key** *keyid*] [**source** *interface*] [**prefer**]	Creates a peer association so that this router can synchronize its clock to another device, or so that another device can synchronize to it.
ntp access-group {**query-only** I **serve-only** I **serve** I **peer**} *access-list-number*	Controls access to the router's NTP services.
clock calendar-valid	Enables the router's calendar as an authoritative time source.

Table 9-6   *Command Summary (Continued)*

Command	Description
ntp master [*stratum*]	Configures the IOS as an NTP master clock to which peers synchronize.
ntp update-calendar	Updates the router's calendar with the time/date learned via NTP.
ntp authenticate	Globally enables NTP authentication.
ntp authentication-key *number* **md5** *key*	Defines the NTP authentication key.
ntp trusted-key *number*	Lists key numbers, which have already been defined with the **ntp authentication-key** command, which the server must include in its NTP packets before this router will synchronize to it.
ip accounting	Enables IP accounting on an interface.
ip accounting-threshold *threshold*	Sets the maximum number of entries that can be stored in the accounting table.
show ip accounting [**checkpoint**] [**access-violations**]	Displays IP accounting data.
clear ip accounting	Clears IP accounting data.
ip route-cache flow	Enables NetFlow on an interface.
ip flow-export destination *ip-address udp-port*	Specifies the IP address and UDP port number for the host receiving NetFlow data.
ip flow-export [**version 1** | **version 5** [**origin-as** | **peer-as**]]	Specifies the NetFlow version to use when sending data to the flow collector and which AS number to send, the traffic's origin AS or the router's peer AS.
show ip flow export	Displays information about how the data is exported.
show ip cache flow	Displays the data to be exported.
ip cef	Enables CEF globally and on all interfaces that support it.
ip flow-aggregation cache {*as* | *destination-prefix* | *prefix* | *protocol-port* | *source-prefix*}	Defines an aggregated NetFlow cache.
cache entries *number_of_entries*	Specifies the maximum number of entries in the aggregated cache.

continues

Table 9-6   *Command Summary (Continued)*

Command	Description
cache timeout inactive *seconds*	Specifies the timeout value for inactive entries in the aggregated cache.
cache timeout active *minutes*	Modifies the number of minutes that an active aggregated cache entry remains active.
export destination *ip_address udp_port*	Specifies the export destination for the aggregated cache.
enabled	Enables the aggregated cache.
show ip cache flow aggregation as	Displays the AS cache data.
show ip cache flow aggregation destination-prefix	Displays the destination-prefix cache data.
show ip cache flow aggregation source-prefix	Displays the source-prefix cache data.
show ip cache flow aggregation protocol-port	Displays the protocol port cache data.
enable –secret *password*	Defines the enable-level password.
service password-encryption	Encrypts passwords when viewing the configuration.
access-class *access-list_1-199_or_1300-2699* [**in** | **out**]	Specifies an access list to use before permitting an incoming or outgoing terminal session.
transport input telnet ssh	Limits the protocols permitted to establish terminal sessions.
transport input none	Disables all terminal protocols on the configured line.
exec-timeout	Defines the timeout value for inactive terminal sessions.
service tcp-keepalives-in	Enables TCP keepalive messages on incoming connections.
no ip directed-broadcast	Disables IP directed broadcasts on interfaces.
no ip source-route	Globally disables the forwarding of packets that include source-route information.
scheduler interval *milliseconds*	Configures the interval for the router to stop handling interrupts and attend to other business.

Table 9-6   *Command Summary (Continued)*

Command	Description
scheduler allocate *interrupt-time process-time*	Defines the maximum amount of time the router spends on fast switching within any one network interrupt context, and the minimum amount of time the router spends at the process level when network interrupts are disabled.
no service tcp-small-servers	Disables the TCP small servers.
no service udp-small-servers	Disables the UDP small servers.
no service finger	Disables the Finger server.
no ip bootp server	Disables the BOOTP server.
aaa new-model	Enables AAA.
aaa authentication login {**default** | *list_name*} **group** *auth_type* [*auth_type* ...]	Defines an AAA authentication method list.
login authentication *list_name*	Specifies which defined AAA authentication method list to use when authenticating a connecting user.
tacacs-server host *ip_address*	Specifies the TACACS server.
radius-server host *ip_address*	Specifies the RADIUS server.
tacacs-server key *key*	Defines a shared key to use between the router and TACACS server.
radius-server key *key*	Defines a shared key to use between the router and RADIUS server.
aaa authentication enable default group *auth_type* [*auth_type*]	Defines the type of authentication to use for enable-level access.
aaa authorization {**network** | **exec** | **commands** *level* | **reverse-access**} {**default** | *list-name*} [*method1* [*method2*...]]	Defines an AAA authorization method list.
authorization {**arap** | **exec** | **commands** *level* | **reverse-access**} {**default** | *list-name*}	Specifies which defined AAA authorization method list to use for connecting users.
aaa accounting {**system** | **network** | **exec** | **connection** | **commands** *level*} {**default** | *list-name*} {**start-stop** | **wait-start** | **stop-only** | **none**} [*method1* [*method2*...]]	Defines an AAA accounting method list and defines what type of information to account.

continues

Table 9-6   *Command Summary (Continued)*

Command	Description
accounting {**arap**	**exec**	**connection**	**commands** *level*} {**default**	*list-name*}	Specifies which defined AAA accounting method list to use for connecting user sessions.
hostname *hostname*	Defines the router's hostname, required for RSA crypto generation.
ip domain-name *domainname*	Defines the router's domain name, required for RSA crypto generation.
crypto key generate rsa	Generates an RSA crypto key (and enables SSH).
ip ssh {[**timeout** *seconds*]	[**authentication-retries** *integer*]}	Modifies SSH parameters.
standby [*group-number*] **ip** [*ip-address* [**secondary**]]	Defines the HSRP address for the specified standby group.
standby [*group-number*] **timers** *hellotime holdtime*	Modifies the timers for the specified standby group.
standby [*group-number*] **priority** *priority* [**preempt** [**delay** *delay*]]	Modifies the priority of the router in the specified standby group. Also specifies the preemption characteristics.
standby [*group-number*] [**priority** *priority*] **preempt** [**delay** *delay*]	Specifies the preemption characteristics. Also modifies the priority of the router in the specified standby group.
standby [*group-number*] **track** *type number* [*interface-priority*]	Identifies a standby tracked interface.
standby [*group-number*] **authentication** *string*	Defines a standby authentication string.
standby use-bia [**scope interface**]	Specifies that the burnt-in address is to be used as the standby MAC address.
show standby	Displays current HSRP properties.

Review Questions

1   Explain the difference between SNMP polls and traps.

_____

_____

_____

2 If you specify the severity level of messages logged to be errors, what other levels of messages are logged?

_____

_____

_____

3 You look at a router interface and see that there are unusual traffic patterns. Normally, all traffic is inbound, but now there is outbound traffic. How can you quickly determine the source and destination of the traffic?

_____

_____

_____

Configuration Exercises

1 Configure a router to accept polls from management stations 172.16.1.2 and 172.16.1.3 only. Do not allow write access to the stations. Allow the stations to read information about the SNMP MIB II interface entries only. Allow station 172.16.1.4 to read any MIB variable and allow it to load and save configuration files via SNMP. Send logging information at the Notification level, via SNMP, to 172.16.1.4.

2 Configure the router to send an SNMP trap to 172.16.1.4 when the 5-minute average CPU exceeds 90%. Send the trap whenever the CPU goes from below 85% to above 90% in any 60-second interval.

3 Configure a router to use NTP to update its own time and date based on clock information from router 172.16.100.100. Do not allow the other router to update its clock based on information from your router.

4 Configure a NetFlow aggregation cache, grouping data based on the source and destination prefix. Use the peer AS in the data, and export the data to 172.16.1.4.

5 Configure two routers on an Ethernet segment to provide backup for each other. Router A is primary, and router B takes over when A fails. When A recovers, it becomes the primary router again. Router A has two serial links, serial 0 and serial 1, that forward traffic to various destinations. If either link fails, router B takes over as the primary router.

Bibliography

Monitoring the Router and Network. Cisco Systems – Documentation. [Web page] June, 1998; www.cisco.com/univercd/cc/td/doc/product/software/ios113ed/113ed_cr/fun_c/fcprt4/fcmonitr.htm [Accessed 24 Oct. 2000]

Troubleshooting the Router. Cisco Systems – Documentation. [Web page] October, 2000; www.cisco.com/univercd/cc/td/doc/product/software/ios113ed/113ed_cr/fun_c/fcprt4/fctroubl.htm [Accessed 24 Oct. 2000]

Synchronizing Clocks with the NTP Service. Cisco Systems – Documentation [Web page] December 1997; www.cisco.com/univercd/cc/td/doc/product/iaabu/cddm/cddm111/adguide/ntp.htm

Performing Basic System Management. Cisco Systems – Documentation [Web page] August 2000; www.cisco.com/univercd/cc/td/doc/product/software/ios121/121cgcr/fun_c/fcprt3/fcd303.htm#34418 [Accessed 24 Oct. 2000]

Configuring NetFlow Switching. Cisco Systems – Documentation [Web page] July 2000; www.cisco.com/univercd/cc/td/doc/product/software/ios121/121cgcr/switch_c/xcprt3/xcdnfc.htm#4727 [Accessed 24 Oct. 2000]

Fault Management. Cisco Systems – Documentation [Web page] December 1997; www.cisco.com/univercd/cc/td/doc/product/rtrmgmt/cwparent/cw32/cw32ug/faultmgt.htm [Accessed 24 Oct. 2000]

Performance Management. Cisco Systems – Documentation [Web page] December 1997; www.cisco.com/univercd/cc/td/doc/product/rtrmgmt/cwparent/cw32/cw32ug/perfmgmt.htm [Accessed 24 Oct. 2000]

Improving Security on Cisco Routers. Cisco Systems – Documentation [Web page] August 2000; www.cisco.com/warp/public/707/21.html, [Accessed 24 Oct. 2000]

Secure Shell Version 1 Support. Cisco Systems – Documentation [Web page] www.cisco.com/univercd/cc/td/doc/product/software/ios121/121newft/121t/121t1/sshv1.htm [Accessed 24 Oct. 2000]

Configuring TACACS+. Cisco Systems – Documentation [Web page] July 2000; www.cisco.com/univercd/cc/td/doc/product/software/ios121/121cgcr/secur_c/scprt2/scdtplus.htm#4586 [Accessed 24 Oct. 2000]

TACACS+ and RADIUS Comparison. Cisco Systems – Technical Tips [Web page] March 1999; www.cisco.com/warp/public/480/10.html [Accessed 24 Oct. 2000]

Configuring Authentication. Cisco Systems – Documentation [Web page] October 2000; www.cisco.com/univercd/cc/td/doc/product/software/ios120/12cgcr/secur_c/scprt1/scathen.htm [Accessed 24 Oct. 2000]

IP Services Commands. Cisco Systems – Documentation [Web page] September 2000; www.cisco.com/univercd/cc/td/doc/product/software/ios121/121cgcr/ip_r/iprprt1/ 1rdip.htm [Accessed 24 Oct. 2000]

Using HSRP for Fault-Tolerant IP Routing. Cisco Systems – Documentation [Web page] February 2000; www.cisco.com/univercd/cc/td/doc/cisintwk/ics/cs009.htm [Accessed 24 Oct. 2000]

Configuring IP Services. Cisco Systems – Documentation [Web page] September 2000; www.cisco.com/univercd/cc/td/doc/product/software/ios121/121cgcr/ip_c/ipcprt1/ 1cdip.htm [Accessed 24 Oct. 2000]

NetFlow Aggregation. Cisco Systems – Documentation [Web page] August 1999; www.cisco.com/univercd/cc/td/doc/product/software/ios120/120newft/120t/120t3/ netflow.htm [Accessed 24 Oct. 2000]

Cisco Network Monitoring and Event Correlation Guidelines. Cisco Systems – Documentation [Web page] July 2000; www.cisco.com/warp/public/cc/pd/wr2k/tech/ cnm_rg.htm [Accessed 24 Oct. 2000]

Guidelines for Polling MIB Variables. Cisco Systems – Documentation [Web page] September 2000; www.cisco.com/warp/public/477/Gen_NMS/38.html

Appendixes

The show ip bgp neighbors **Display**

This appendix explains the details of the large amount of information returned by the **show ip bgp** neighbors command. Some of the information is self-explanatory, and much of the information has been discussed in various chapters in this book.

Example A-1 shows a typical neighbor display, with each line numbered for easy reference. Table A-1 analyzes this sample display one line at a time.

Example A-1 *Typical Display from the* **show ip bgp neighbors** *Command*

```
TeddyBear#show ip bgp neighbors 10.100.1.1
1.  BGP neighbor is 10.100.1.1,  remote AS 6500, internal link
2.   Member of peer-group Pooh for session parameters
3.   BGP version 4, remote router ID 10.100.1.1
4.   BGP state = Established, up for 00:04:06
5.   Last read 00:00:07, hold time is 180, keepalive interval is 60 seconds
6.   Neighbor capabilities:
7.    Route refresh: advertised and received
8.    Address family IPv4 Unicast: advertised and received
9.    Address family IPv4 Multicast: advertised and received
10.   Received 7 messages, 0 notifications, 0 in queue
11.   Sent 7 messages, 0 notifications, 0 in queue
12.   Route refresh request: received 0, sent 0
13.   Minimum time between advertisement runs is 5 seconds

14.   For address family: IPv4 Unicast
15.   BGP table version 1, neighbor version 1
16.   Index 1, Offset 0, Mask 0x2
17.   Pooh peer-group member
18.   0 accepted prefixes consume 0 bytes
19.   Prefix advertised 0, suppressed 0, withdrawn 0

20.   For address family: IPv4 Multicast
21.   BGP table version 1, neighbor version 1
22.   Index 1, Offset 0, Mask 0x2
23.   0 accepted prefixes consume 0 bytes
24.   Prefix advertised 0, suppressed 0, withdrawn 0

25.   Connections established 1; dropped 0
26.   Last reset 00:04:17, due to Address family activated
```

continues

Example A-1 *Typical Display from the* **show ip bgp neighbors** *Command (Continued)*

```
27. Connection state is ESTAB, I/O status: 1, unread input bytes: 0
28. Local host: 10.100.1.2, Local port: 11012
29. Foreign host: 10.100.1.1, Foreign port: 179

30. Enqueued packets for retransmit: 0, input: 0  mis-ordered: 0 (0 bytes)

31. Event Timers (current time is 0x3ABFA00):
32. Timer          Starts    Wakeups         Next
33. Retrans           8         0            0x0
34. TimeWait          0         0            0x0
35. AckHold           7         5            0x0
36. SendWnd           0         0            0x0
37. KeepAlive         0         0            0x0
38. GiveUp            0         0            0x0
39. PmtuAger          0         0            0x0
40. DeadWait          0         0            0x0

41. iss: 2227710177  snduna: 2227710341  sndnxt: 2227710341     sndwnd:  16221
42. irs: 1632859231  rcvnxt: 1632859395  rcvwnd:        16221 delrcvwnd:    163

43. SRTT: 540 ms, RTTO: 3809 ms, RTV: 1364 ms, KRTT: 0 ms
44. minRTT: 8 ms, maxRTT: 300 ms, ACK hold: 200 ms
45. Flags: higher precedence, nagle

46. Datagrams (max data segment is 536 bytes):
47. Rcvd: 11 (out of order: 0), with data: 7, total data bytes: 163
48. Sent: 14 (retransmit: 0), with data: 7, total data bytes: 163
TeddyBear#
```

Table A-1 *Line-by-Line Explanation of* **show ip bgp neighbors** *Command Output*

Line #	Syntax	Explanation
1	**BGP neighbor is 10.100.1.1, remote AS 6500, internal link**	This line is probably the most self-explanatory of the entire display. The IP address shown is the remote end point of the TCP connection between the BGP peers. The remote peer is in AS 6500, and the peer is internal—that is, this is an IBGP connection.
2	**Member of peer-group Pooh for session parameters**	A peer group named Pooh has been configured on this router, and this neighbor is a member of the peer group.

Table A-1 *Line-by-Line Explanation of* **show ip bgp neighbors** *Command Output (Continued)*

Line #	Syntax	Explanation
3	**BGP version 4, remote router ID 10.100.1.1**	BGP-4 is running on this peering session. Recall from Chapter 2, "Introduction to Border Gateway Protocol 4," that BGP automatically negotiates the version with its peers, beginning with the most recent version supported. The BGP router ID of this peer is 10.100.1.1, which in this case is the same as the remote end point address—due to the fact that the peering is between loopback interfaces, which also are used to determine the router ID. If the peering end points were between physical interface addresses, the router ID would likely not be the same.
4	**BGP state = Established, up for 00:04:06**	The neighbor state is established, which indicates a full adjacency. The session has been up for 4 minutes and 6 seconds.
5	**Last read 00:00:07, hold time is 180, keepalive interval is 60 seconds**	BGP last read a message from this peer 7 seconds ago. The holdtime is 180 seconds, and the keepalive interval is 60 seconds. These are the default values; recall from Chapter 2 that BGP neighbors can negotiate these times.
6	**Neighbor capabilities:**	The lines indented below this line summarize the capabilities of the peer.
7	**Route refresh: advertised and received**	The local router and the peer support the BGP Soft Reset Enhancement. (The capability has been advertised by the local router and received from the peer.) This feature was released with IOS 12.0. It allows policy changes to automatically be advertised to the peer without having to configure **neighbor soft-reconfiguration**.

continues

Table A-1   *Line-by-Line Explanation of* **show ip bgp neighbors** *Command Output (Continued)*

Line #	Syntax	Explanation
8	**Address family IPv4 Unicast: advertised and received**	The local router and the peer are both running Multiprotocol BGP (MBGP). The peers have been activated to support unicast NLRI. See Chapter 7, "Large-Scale IP Multicast Routing," for a discussion of MBGP and address family indicators. As with the preceding line, the capability has been advertised to the peer and has been received from the peer.
9	**Address family IPv4 Multicast: advertised and received**	Both peers are activated to support MBGP multicast NLRI.
10	**Received 7 messages, 0 notifications, 0 in queue**	Seven BGP messages, including keepalives, have been received from this peer. No notification messages have been received, and no received messages are in the queue.
11	**Sent 7 messages, 0 notifications, 0 in queue**	Seven BGP messages, including keepalives, have been sent to this peer. No notification messages have been sent, and no messages to be sent are in the queue.
12	**Route refresh request: received 0, sent 0**	No route refresh requests (for the BGP Soft Reset Enhancement) have been received from or sent to this peer.
13	**Minimum time between advertisement runs is 5 seconds**	Update messages can be sent no closer than 5 seconds apart.
14	**For address family: IPv4 Unicast**	The indented lines beneath this line pertain to the unicast BGP routing table.
15	**BGP table version 1, neighbor version 1**	The neighbor has been updated with version 1 of the unicast BGP routing table, and the local router has been updated with version 1 of the peer's unicast BGP table.
16	**Index 1, Offset 0, Mask 0x2**	Internal indices to reference the specific peer. These fields have significance only to Cisco personnel who have access to the source code.
17	**Pooh peer-group member**	The neighbor is a member of the unicast peer group Pooh.

Table A-1 *Line-by-Line Explanation of* **show ip bgp neighbors** *Command Output (Continued)*

Line #	Syntax	Explanation
18	**0 accepted prefixes consume 0 bytes**	This line specifies how many unicast prefixes have been accepted from the peer and how many bytes of memory the prefixes have consumed. In this case, no prefixes have been received.
19	**Prefix advertised 0, suppressed 0, withdrawn 0**	No unicast prefixes have been advertised to, suppressed from, or withdrawn from this peer.
20	**For address family: IPv4 Multicast**	The indented lines beneath this line pertain to the multicast BGP routing table.
21	**BGP table version 1, neighbor version 1**	The neighbor has been updated with version 1 of the multicast BGP routing table, and the local router has been updated with version 1 of the peer's multicast BGP table.
22	**Index 1, Offset 0, Mask 0x2**	Internal indices to reference the specific peer. These fields have significance only to Cisco personnel who have access to the source code.
23	**0 accepted prefixes consume 0 bytes**	This line specifies how many multicast prefixes have been accepted from the peer and how many bytes of memory the prefixes have consumed. In this case, no prefixes have been received.
24	**Prefix advertised 0, suppressed 0, withdrawn 0**	No multicast prefixes have been advertised to, suppressed from, or withdrawn from this peer.
25	**Connections established 1; dropped 0**	A BGP connection and adjacency have been established with this peer only once, and no connection to this peer has ever been dropped.
26	**Last reset 00:04:17, due to Address family activated**	The last reset of the peer session occurred 4 minutes and 17 seconds ago, when MBGP was activated.

continues

Table A-1 *Line-by-Line Explanation of* **show ip bgp neighbors** *Command Output (Continued)*

Line #	Syntax	Explanation
27	**Connection state is ESTAB, I/O status: 1, unread input bytes: 0**	Connection state is the state of the peer connection—essentially, a repeat of the state shown on line 4. I/O status describes the internal status of the connection. Unread input bytes is the number of bytes not yet processed by BGP.
28	**Local host: 10.100.1.2, Local port: 11012**	This line is the local IP socket, consisting of the IP address and the local TCP port number.
29	**Foreign host: 10.100.1.1, Foreign port: 179**	This is the socket of the peer, consisting of the peer's IP address and TCP port. Comparing line 28 with this line, you can see that the local router initiated the TCP connection, because it uses an ephemeral port and connects to the well-known BGP port 179.
30	**Enqueued packets for retransmit: 0, input: 0 mis-ordered: 0 (0 bytes)**	The number of packets waiting in a queue for retransmit, for input, or misordered packets.
31	**Event Timers (current time is 0x3ABFA00):**	This line is the header for the event timers that follow.
32	**Timer, Starts, Wakeups, Next**	The column headers for the event timers.
33	**Retrans**	Determines how long a transmitted frame can remain unacknowledged before the Cisco IOS Software polls for an acknowledgment.
34	**TimeWait**	Determines how long the local TCP connection waits to be sure that the remote TCP host has received the acknowledgment of its connection-termination request.
35	**AckHold**	Number of times the system failed to piggyback data required on a TCP acknowledgment. Such piggybacking can significantly reduce network traffic.

Table A-1 *Line-by-Line Explanation of* **show ip bgp neighbors** *Command Output (Continued)*

Line #	Syntax	Explanation
36	**SendWnd**	Timers for sending 0 window probes. Essentially, this field reflects how often users overload the remote host with data and how long it takes users to send it. For most normal Cisco IOS Software applications, this value should be 0.
37	**KeepAlive**	Determines the frequency (in seconds) at which the Cisco IOS Software sends messages to itself (Ethernet and Token Ring) or to the other end (serial) to ensure that a network interface is alive. The **keepalive interface configuration** command is used to set this timer.
41	**iss: 2227710177 snduna: 2227710341 sndnxt: 2227710341 sndwnd: 16221**	These are sequence numbers used by the TCP connection. *iss* = The initial send sequence number. *snduna* = The send unanswered sequence number; the last sequence number the local host sent but has not received an acknowledgment for. *sndnxt* = The sequence number the local router will send next. *sndwnd* = The TCP window size of the remote peer.
42	**irs: 1632859231 rcvnxt: 1632859395 rcvwnd: 16221 delrcvwnd: 163**	These sequence numbers apply to the remote side of the TCP connection. *irs* = The initial receive sequence number. *rcvnxt* = The last receive sequence number the local router has acknowledged. *rcvwnd* = The local router's TCP window size. *delrcvwnd* = Delayed receive window— data the local host has read from the connection but has not yet subtracted from the receive window the host has advertised to the remote host. The value in this field gradually increases until it is larger than a full-sized packet, at which point it is applied to the rcvwnd field.

continues

Table A-1   *Line-by-Line Explanation of* **show ip bgp neighbors** *Command Output (Continued)*

Line #	Syntax	Explanation
43	**SRTT: 540 ms, RTTO: 3809 ms, RTV: 1364 ms, KRTT: 0 ms**	These figures pertain to the latency of the connection between the peer.
		SRTT = The calculated smooth round-trip time.
		RTTO: The round-trip timeout.
		RTV = The variance of the round-trip time.
		KRTT = The Karn round-trip time; new round-trip timeout (using the Karn algorithm). This field separately tracks the round-trip time of packets that have been retransmitted.
44	**minRTT: 8 ms, maxRTT: 300 ms, ACK hold: 200 ms**	These values are a continuation of the performance values begun on line 43.
		minRTT = The smallest recorded round-trip time.
		maxRTT = The largest recorded round-trip time.
		ACK hold = The time the local router will delay an acknowledgment so that it can piggyback data onto it.
45	**Flags: higher precedence, nagle**	IP precedence of the BGP packets.
46	**Datagrams (max data segment is 536 bytes):**	This is the header for the next two lines, which provide statistics about BGP Updates sent to and received from the peer. It also shows that the maximum TCP segment size is 536 bytes.
47	**Rcvd: 11 (out of order: 0), with data: 7, total data bytes: 163**	Statistics on received updates, including total received, datagrams with data, and total bytes.
48	**Sent: 14 (retransmit: 0), with data: 7, total data bytes: 163**	Statistics of BGP updates sent to the peer, including total sent, number of updates containing data, and total bytes.

A Regular-Expression Tutorial

This tutorial follows the excellent presentation made by Jeffrey E. F. Friedl in his book *Mastering Regular Expressions*. The book is listed as recommended reading at the end of this appendix, although almost everything you need to know about regular expressions (regex) to work with Cisco IOS Software is covered in the very first chapter of the book. Nonetheless, the book recommendation stands because you are very likely to find regular expressions useful in a wide variety of applications within the data communications and data processing industry. Friedl presents the subject clearly and with a liberal dose of humor.

Literals and Metacharacters

A typical AS_PATH filter might look like this:

```
ip as-path access-list 83 permit ^1_701_(_5646_|_1240_).*
```

The string of characters following the **permit** keyword is a regular expression. The regex is composed of *literals* and *metacharacters*. Literals are just text characters that describe what the regex will try to match. In this example, **1**, **701**, **5646**, and **1240** are literals describing autonomous system numbers.

Metacharacters are special regular-expression characters that act as operators, telling the regex how to perform matches. Table B-1 shows the metacharacters available for use with Cisco IOS; the remainder of this appendix describes how each of the metacharacters are used.

Table B-1 *Regular-Expression Metacharacters Relevant to AS_PATH Access Lists*

Metacharacter	What It Matches
.	Any single character, including white space.
[]	Any character listed between the brackets.
[^]	Any character except those listed between the brackets. (The caret is placed before the sequence of literals.)
-	(Hyphen) Any character in the range between the two literals separated by the hyphen.

continues

Table B-1   *Regular-Expression Metacharacters Relevant to AS_PATH Access Lists (Continued)*

Metacharacter	What It Matches
?	Zero or one instances of the character or pattern.
*	Zero or more instances of the character or pattern.
+	One or more instances of the character or pattern.
^	Start of a line.
$	End of a line.
|	Either of the literals separated by the metacharacter.
_	(Underscore) A comma, the beginning of the line, the end of the line, or a space.

Delineation: Matching the Start and End of Lines

Consider the following AS_PATH filter:

```
ip as-path access-list 20 permit 850
```

This filter matches any AS_PATH that includes the string **850**. Examples of matching AS_PATHs are (**850**), (23, 5, **850**, 155), and (3568, 5**850**, 310). A match is found whether the string is alone in the attribute, one of several AS numbers in the attribute, or even a part of a larger AS number in the attribute.

Suppose, however, that you want to match only an AS_PATH that contains the single AS number 850. For this, you must be able to delineate the beginning and end of a line. A caret (^) matches the beginning of a line, and a dollar sign ($) matches the end of a line. So,

```
ip as-path access-list 20 permit ^850$
```

tells the regex to match the beginning of the line, followed immediately by the string **850**, followed immediately by the end of the line.

You also can use the two metacharacters to match an empty AS_PATH:

```
ip as-path access-list 21 permit ^$
```

In this case, the regex matches the beginning of a line followed immediately by the end of the line; if any other characters exist between the beginning and end of the line, no match is made.

Bracketing: Matching a Set of Characters

Brackets enable you to specify a range of single characters. For example:

```
ip as-path access-list 22 permit ^85[0123459]$
```

This filter matches AS_PATHs with any single AS number 850, 851, 852, 853, 854, 855, or 859.

If the range of characters is contiguous, you can specify just the beginning and end character in the sequence:

```
ip as-path access-list 23 permit ^85[0-5]$
```

This filter matches the same group of AS numbers as the preceding filter, with the exception of 859.

Negating: Matching Everything Except a Set of Characters

When a caret is used inside a bracket, it negates the range specified in the bracket. As a result, the regex matches on everything except the range. For example:

```
ip as-path access-list 24 permit ^85[^0-5]$
```

This filter looks like the preceding filter, with the exception of the added caret inside the bracket, signifying "not 0–5." The regex will therefore match an AS_PATH with a single AS number in the range 856–859.

Wildcard: Matching Any Single Character

A dot (.) matches any single character. Interestingly, the single character may be a space. Consider the following filter:

```
ip as-path access-list 24 permit ^85.
```

This filter matches an AS_PATH that begins with an AS number in the range 850–859. And because the dot also matches white space, AS number 85 will match.

Alternation: Matching One of a Set of Characters

A bar (|) is used to specify an OR operation. That is, a literal on one or the other side of the bar can be matched. For example:

```
ip as-path access-list 25 permit ^(851 | 852)$
```

This filter matches an AS_PATH in which there is a single AS number, which is either 851 or 852. You may extend the OR function to check for more than two possible matches:

```
ip as-path access-list 26 permit ^(851 | 852 | 6341 | 53)$
```

Optional Characters: Matching a Character That May or May Not Be There

The question mark (?) matches zero or one instances of a literal. For example:

```
ip as-path access-list 27 permit ^(850)?$
```

This filter matches an AS_PATH in which there is either a single AS number 850 or an empty list. Note the use of parentheses here, to show that the metacharacter applies to the entire AS number. If the expression **850?** is used, the metacharacter applies only to the last character. The expression would match 85 or 850.

Repetition: Matching a Number of Repeating Characters

You can use two metacharacters to match repeating literals: The asterisk (*) matches zero or more instances of a literal, and the plus (+) matches one or more instances. For example:

```
ip as-path access-list 28 permit ^(850)*$
```

This filter matches an AS_PATH in which there are no AS numbers, or in which one or more AS numbers 850 exist. That is, the AS path could be (850), (850, 850), (850, 850, 850), and so on.

The following filter is similar, except that there must be at least one AS number 850 in the AS_PATH:

```
ip as-path access-list 29 permit ^(850)+$
```

Boundaries: Delineating Literals

The underscore (_) is used when you want to specify a string of literals and must specify their separation. Suppose, for example, that you want to match on the specific AS_PATH (5610, 148, 284, 13). The filter is as follows:

```
ip as-path access-list 30 permit ^5610_148_284_13$
```

The underscore matches a beginning of line, an end of line, a comma, or a space. Notice the difference between the preceding filter and this filter:

```
ip as-path access-list 31 permit _5610_148_284_13_
```

Because the first filter specified the beginning and end of the line, only AS_PATH (5610, 148, 284, 13) matches. In this second filter, the specified sequence must be included in the AS_PATH, but it is not necessarily the only AS numbers in the attribute. So, AS_PATHs (5610, 148, 284, 13), (23, 15, 5610, 148, 284, 13), and (5610, 148, 284, 13, 3005) all match.

Putting It All Together: A Complex Example

The real power of regular expressions comes into play when the metacharacters are used in combination to match some complex string of literals. Consider the following filter:

```
ip as-path access-list 10 permit ^(550)+_[880¦2304]?_1805_.*
```

This filter looks for AS_PATHs in which the last AS before the route was received was 550. The caret preceding that number specifies that 550 is the first number in the list. The plus sign following the number means that there must be at least one instance of 550, but there can be more. By allowing for more than one instance of the number, the filter has allowed for the possibility that AS 550 is practicing path prepending, as discussed in Chapter 3, "Configuring and Troubleshooting Border Gateway Protocol 4."

Following the one or more instances of 550, there may or may not be a single instance of either 880 or 2304. Next, there must be a single instance of 1805. The last part of the expression specifies that after 1805, the AS_PATH can consist of any number of subsequent AS numbers, including none.

Recommended Reading

Friedl, Jeffrey E. F. *Mastering Regular Expressions*. Sebastopol, California: O'Reilly & Associates; 1997.

Reserved Multicast Addresses

The following is a list of the most recent reserved multicast addresses at the time this book was written. The list is taken directly from ftp://ftp.isi.edu/in-notes/iana/assignments/multicast-addresses. For the most recent list, consult that site.

Internet Multicast Addresses

Host Extensions for IP Multicasting [RFC 1112] specifies the extensions required of a host implementation of the Internet Protocol (IP) to support multicasting. The multicast addressess are in the range 224.0.0.0 through 239.255.255.255. Current addresses are listed in the following text.

The range of addresses between 224.0.0.0 and 224.0.0.255, inclusive, is reserved for the use of routing protocols and other low-level topology discovery or maintenance protocols, such as gateway discovery and group membership reporting. Multicast routers should not forward any multicast datagram with destination addresses in this range, regardless of its TTL.

224.0.0.0	Base Address (Reserved)	[RFC1112,JBP]
224.0.0.1	All Systems on this Subnet	[RFC1112,JBP]
224.0.0.2	All Routers on this Subnet	[JBP]
224.0.0.3	Unassigned	[JBP]
224.0.0.4	DVMRP Routers	[RFC1075,JBP]
224.0.0.5	OSPFIGP OSPFIGP All Routers	[RFC2328,JXM1]
224.0.0.6	OSPFIGP OSPFIGP Designated Routers	[RFC2328,JXM1]
224.0.0.7	ST Routers	[RFC1190,KS14]
224.0.0.8	ST Hosts	[RFC1190,KS14]
224.0.0.9	RIP2 Routers	[RFC1723,GSM11]
224.0.0.10	IGRP Routers	[Farinacci]
224.0.0.11	Mobile-Agents	[Bill Simpson]
224.0.0.12	DHCP Server / Relay Agent	[RFC1884]
224.0.0.13	All PIM Routers	[Farinacci]

224.0.0.14	RSVP-ENCAPSULATION	[Braden]
224.0.0.15	all-cbt-routers	[Ballardie]
224.0.0.16	designated-sbm	[Baker]
224.0.0.17	all-sbms	[Baker]
224.0.0.18	VRRP	[Hinden]
224.0.0.19	IPAllL1ISs	[Przygienda]
224.0.0.20	IPAllL2ISs	[Przygienda]
224.0.0.21	IPAllIntermediate Systems	[Przygienda]
224.0.0.22	IGMP	[Deering]
224.0.0.23	GLOBECAST-ID	[Scannell]
224.0.0.24	Unassigned	[JBP]
224.0.0.25	router-to-switch	[Wu]
224.0.0.26	Unassigned	[JBP]
224.0.0.27	Al MPP Hello	[Martinicky]
224.0.0.28	ETC Control	[Polishinski]
224.0.0.29	GE-FANUC	[Wacey]
224.0.0.30	indigo-vhdp	[Caughie]
224.0.0.31	shinbroadband	[Kittivatcharapong]
224.0.0.32	digistar	[Kerkan]
224.0.0.33	ff-system-management	[Glanzer]
224.0.0.34	pt2-discover	[Kammerlander]
224.0.0.35	DXCLUSTER	[Koopman]
224.0.0.36-224.0.0.250	Unassigned	[JBP]
224.0.0.251	mDNS	[Cheshire]
224.0.0.252-224.0.0.255	Unassigned	[JBP]
224.0.1.0	VMTP Managers Group	[RFC1045,DRC3]
224.0.1.1	NTP Network Time Protocol	[RFC1119,DLM1]
224.0.1.2	SGI-Dogfight	[AXC]
224.0.1.3	Rwhod	[SXD]
224.0.1.4	VNP	[DRC3]
224.0.1.5	Artificial Horizons - Aviator	[BXF]
224.0.1.6	NSS - Name Service Server	[BXS2]
224.0.1.7	AUDIONEWS - Audio News Multicast	[MXF2]
224.0.1.8	SUN NIS+ Information Service	[CXM3]
224.0.1.9	MTP Multicast Transport Protocol	[SXA]
224.0.1.10	IETF-1-LOW-AUDIO	[SC3]

224.0.1.11	IETF-1-AUDIO	[SC3]
224.0.1.12	IETF-1-VIDEO	[SC3]
224.0.1.13	IETF-2-LOW-AUDIO	[SC3]
224.0.1.14	IETF-2-AUDIO	[SC3]
224.0.1.15	IETF-2-VIDEO	[SC3]
224.0.1.16	MUSIC-SERVICE	[Guido van Rossum]
224.0.1.17	SEANET-TELEMETRY	[Andrew Maffei]
224.0.1.18	SEANET-IMAGE	[Andrew Maffei]
224.0.1.19	MLOADD	[Braden]
224.0.1.20	any private experiment	[JBP]
224.0.1.21	DVMRP on MOSPF	[John Moy]
224.0.1.22	SVRLOC	[Veizades]
224.0.1.23	XINGTV	[Gordon]
224.0.1.24	microsoft-ds	<arnoldm@microsoft.com>
224.0.1.25	nbc-pro	<bloomer@birch.crd.ge.com>
224.0.1.26	nbc-pfn	<bloomer@birch.crd.ge.com>
224.0.1.27	lmsc-calren-1	[Uang]
224.0.1.28	lmsc-calren-2	[Uang]
224.0.1.29	lmsc-calren-3	[Uang]
224.0.1.30	lmsc-calren-4	[Uang]
224.0.1.31	ampr-info	[Janssen]
224.0.1.32	mtrace	[Casner]
224.0.1.33	RSVP-encap-1	[Braden]
224.0.1.34	RSVP-encap-2	[Braden]
224.0.1.35	SVRLOC-DA	[Veizades]
224.0.1.36	rln-server	[Kean]
224.0.1.37	proshare-mc	[Lewis]
224.0.1.38	dantz	[Zulch]
224.0.1.39	cisco-rp-announce	[Farinacci]
224.0.1.40	cisco-rp-discovery	[Farinacci]
224.0.1.41	gatekeeper	[Toga]
224.0.1.42	iberiagames	[Marocho]
224.0.1.43	nwn-discovery	[Zwemmer]
224.0.1.44	nwn-adaptor	[Zwemmer]
224.0.1.45	isma-1	[Dunne]
224.0.1.46	isma-2	[Dunne]

224.0.1.47	telerate	[Peng]
224.0.1.48	ciena	[Rodbell]
224.0.1.49	dcap-servers	[RFC2114]
224.0.1.50	dcap-clients	[RFC2114]
224.0.1.51	mcntp-directory	[Rupp]
224.0.1.52	mbone-vcr-directory	[Holfelder]
224.0.1.53	heartbeat	[Mamakos]
224.0.1.54	sun-mc-grp	[DeMoney]
224.0.1.55	extended-sys	[Poole]
224.0.1.56	pdrncs	[Wissenbach]
224.0.1.57	tns-adv-multi	[Albin]
224.0.1.58	vcals-dmu	[Shindoh]
224.0.1.59	zuba	[Jackson]
224.0.1.60	hp-device-disc	[Albright]
224.0.1.61	tms-production	[Gilani]
224.0.1.62	sunscalar	[Gibson]
224.0.1.63	mmtp-poll	[Costales]
224.0.1.64	compaq-peer	[Volpe]
224.0.1.65	iapp	[Meier]
224.0.1.66	multihasc-com	[Brockbank]
224.0.1.67	serv-discovery	[Honton]
224.0.1.68	mdhcpdisover	[RFC2730]
224.0.1.69	MMP-bundle-discovery1	[Malkin]
224.0.1.70	MMP-bundle-discovery2	[Malkin]
224.0.1.71	XYPOINT DGPS Data Feed	[Green]
224.0.1.72	GilatSkySurfer	[Gal]
224.0.1.73	SharesLive	[Rowatt]
224.0.1.74	NorthernData	[Sheers]
224.0.1.75	SIP	[Schulzrinne]
224.0.1.76	IAPP	[Moelard]
224.0.1.77	AGENTVIEW	[Iyer]
224.0.1.78	Tibco Multicast1	[Shum]
224.0.1.79	Tibco Multicast2	[Shum]
224.0.1.80	MSP	[Caves]
224.0.1.81	OTT (One-way Trip Time)	[Schwartz]
224.0.1.82	TRACKTICKER	[Novick]

224.0.1.83	dtn-mc	[Gaddie]
224.0.1.84	jini-announcement	[Scheifler]
224.0.1.85	jini-request	[Scheifler]
224.0.1.86	sde-discovery	[Aronson]
224.0.1.87	DirecPC-SI	[Dillon]
224.0.1.88	B1RMonitor	[Purkiss]
224.0.1.89	3Com-AMP3 dRMON	[Banthia]
224.0.1.90	imFtmSvc	[Bhatti]
224.0.1.91	NQDS4	[Flynn]
224.0.1.92	NQDS5	[Flynn]
224.0.1.93	NQDS6	[Flynn]
224.0.1.94	NLVL12	[Flynn]
224.0.1.95	NTDS1	[Flynn]
224.0.1.96	NTDS2	[Flynn]
224.0.1.97	NODSA	[Flynn]
224.0.1.98	NODSB	[Flynn]
224.0.1.99	NODSC	[Flynn]
224.0.1.100	NODSD	[Flynn]
224.0.1.101	NQDS4R	[Flynn]
224.0.1.102	NQDS5R	[Flynn]
224.0.1.103	NQDS6R	[Flynn]
224.0.1.104	NLVL12R	[Flynn]
224.0.1.105	NTDS1R	[Flynn]
224.0.1.106	NTDS2R	[Flynn]
224.0.1.107	NODSAR	[Flynn]
224.0.1.108	NODSBR	[Flynn]
224.0.1.109	NODSCR	[Flynn]
224.0.1.110	NODSDR	[Flynn]
224.0.1.111	MRM	[Wei]
224.0.1.112	TVE-FILE	[Blackketter]
224.0.1.113	TVE-ANNOUNCE	[Blackketter]
224.0.1.114	Mac Srv Loc	[Woodcock]
224.0.1.115	Simple Multicast	[Crowcroft]
224.0.1.116	SpectraLinkGW	[Hamilton]
224.0.1.117	dieboldmcast	[Marsh]
224.0.1.118	Tivoli Systems	[Gabriel]

224.0.1.119	pq-lic-mcast	[Sledge]
224.0.1.120	HYPERFEED	[Kreutzjans]
224.0.1.121	Pipesplatform	[Dissett]
224.0.1.122	LiebDevMgmg-DM	[Velten]
224.0.1.123	TRIBALVOICE	[Thompson]
224.0.1.124	UDLR-DTCP	[Cipiere]
224.0.1.125	PolyCom Relay1	[Coutiere]
224.0.1.126	Infront Multi1	[Lindeman]
224.0.1.127	XRX DEVICE DISC	[Wang]
224.0.1.128	CNN	[Lynch]
224.0.1.129	PTP-primary	[Eidson]
224.0.1.130	PTP-alternate1	[Eidson]
224.0.1.131	PTP-alternate2	[Eidson]
224.0.1.132	PTP-alternate3	[Eidson]
224.0.1.133	ProCast	[Revzen]
224.0.1.134	3Com Discp	[White]
224.0.1.135	CS-Multicasting	[Stanev]
224.0.1.136	TS-MC-1	[Sveistrup]
224.0.1.137	Make Source	[Daga]
224.0.1.138	Teleborsa	[Strazzera]
224.0.1.139	SUMAConfig	[Wallach]
224.0.1.140	Unassigned	
224.0.1.141	DHCP-SERVERS	[Hall]
224.0.1.142	CN Router-LL	[Armitage]
224.0.1.143	EMWIN	[Querubin]
224.0.1.144	Alchemy Cluster	[O'Rourke]
224.0.1.145	Satcast One	[Nevell]
224.0.1.146	Satcast Two	[Nevell]
224.0.1.147	Satcast Three	[Nevell]
224.0.1.148	Intline	[Sliwinski]
224.0.1.149	8x8 Multicast	[Roper]
224.0.1.150	Unassigned	[JBP]
224.0.1.151	Intline-1	[Sliwinski]
224.0.1.152	Intline-2	[Sliwinski]
224.0.1.153	Intline-3	[Sliwinski]
224.0.1.154	Intline-4	[Sliwinski]

224.0.1.155	Intline-5	[Sliwinski]
224.0.1.156	Intline-6	[Sliwinski]
224.0.1.157	Intline-7	[Sliwinski]
224.0.1.158	Intline-8	[Sliwinski]
224.0.1.159	Intline-9	[Sliwinski]
224.0.1.160	Intline-10	[Sliwinski]
224.0.1.161	Intline-11	[Sliwinski]
224.0.1.162	Intline-12	[Sliwinski]
224.0.1.163	Intline-13	[Sliwinski]
224.0.1.164	Intline-14	[Sliwinski]
224.0.1.165	Intline-15	[Sliwinski]
224.0.1.166	marratech-cc	[Parnes]
224.0.1.167	EMS-InterDev	[Lyda]
224.0.1.168	itb301	[Rueskamp]
224.0.1.169	rtv-audio	[Adams]
224.0.1.170	rtv-video	[Adams]
224.0.1.171	HAVI-Sim	[Wasserroth]
224.0.1.172-224.0.1.255	Unassigned	[JBP]
224.0.2.1	"rwho" Group (BSD) (unofficial)	[JBP]
224.0.2.2	SUN RPC PMAPPROC_CALLIT	[BXE1]
224.0.2.064-224.0.2.095	SIAC MDD Service	[Tse]
224.0.2.096-224.0.2.127	CoolCast	[Ballister]
224.0.2.128-224.0.2.191	WOZ-Garage	[Marquardt]
224.0.2.192-224.0.2.255	SIAC MDD Market Service	[Lamberg]
224.0.3.000-224.0.3.255	RFE Generic Service	[DXS3]
224.0.4.000-224.0.4.255	RFE Individual Conferences	[DXS3]
224.0.5.000-224.0.5.127	CDPD Groups	[Bob Brenner]
224.0.5.128-224.0.5.191	SIAC Market Service	[Cho]
224.0.5.192-224.0.5.255	Unassigned	[IANA]
224.0.6.000-224.0.6.127	Cornell ISIS Project	[Tim Clark]
224.0.6.128-224.0.6.255	Unassigned	[IANA]
224.0.7.000-224.0.7.255	Where-Are-You	[Simpson]
224.0.8.000-224.0.8.255	INTV	[Tynan]
224.0.9.000-224.0.9.255	Invisible Worlds	[Malamud]
224.0.10.000-224.0.10.255	DLSw Groups	[Lee]
224.0.11.000-224.0.11.255	NCC.NET Audio	[Rubin]

224.0.12.000-224.0.12.063	Microsoft and MSNBC	[Blank]
224.0.13.000-224.0.13.255	UUNET PIPEX Net News	[Barber]
224.0.14.000-224.0.14.255	NLANR	[Wessels]
224.0.15.000-224.0.15.255	Hewlett Packard	[van der Meulen]
224.0.16.000-224.0.16.255	XingNet	[Uusitalo]
224.0.17.000-224.0.17.031	Mercantile & Commodity Exchange	[Gilani]
224.0.17.032-224.0.17.063	NDQMD1	[Nelson]
224.0.17.064-224.0.17.127	ODN-DTV	[Hodges]
224.0.18.000-224.0.18.255	Dow Jones	[Peng]
224.0.19.000-224.0.19.063	Walt Disney Company	[Watson]
224.0.19.064-224.0.19.095	Cal Multicast	[Moran]
224.0.19.096-224.0.19.127	SIAC Market Service	[Roy]
224.0.19.128-224.0.19.191	IIG Multicast	[Carr]
224.0.19.192-224.0.19.207	Metropol	[Crawford]
224.0.19.208-224.0.19.239	Xenoscience, Inc.	[Timm]
224.0.19.240-224.0.19.255	HYPERFEED	[Felix]
224.0.20.000-224.0.20.063	MS-IP/TV	[Wong]
224.0.20.064-224.0.20.127	Reliable Network Solutions	[Vogels]
224.0.20.128-224.0.20.143	TRACKTICKER Group	[Novick]
224.0.20.144-224.0.20.207	CNR Rebroadcast MCA	[Sautter]
224.0.21.000-224.0.21.127	Talarian MCAST	[Mendal]
224.0.22.000-224.0.22.255	WORLD MCAST	[Stewart]
224.0.252.000-224.0.252.255	Domain Scoped Group	[Fenner]
224.0.253.000-224.0.253.255	Report Group	[Fenner]
224.0.254.000-224.0.254.255	Query Group	[Fenner]
224.0.255.000-224.0.255.255	Border Routers	[Fenner]
224.1.0.0-224.1.255.255	ST Multicast Groups	[RFC1190,KS14]
224.2.0.0-224.2.127.253	Multimedia Conference Calls	[SC3]
224.2.127.254	APv1 Announcements	[SC3]
224.2.127.255	SAPv0 Announcements (deprecated)	[SC3]
224.2.128.0-224.2.255.255	SAP Dynamic Assignments	[SC3]
224.252.0.0-224.255.255.255	DIS transient groups	[Joel Snyder]
225.0.0.0-225.255.255.255	MALLOC (temp - renew 1/01)	[Handley]
232.0.0.0-232.255.255.255	VMTP transient group	[DRC3]
	see single-source-multicast file	
233.0.0.0-233.255.255.255	Static Allocations (temp - renew 6/01)	[Meyer2]

239.000.000.000-239.255.255.255	Administratively Scoped	[IANA,RFC2365]
239.000.000.000-239.063.255.255	Reserved	[IANA]
239.064.000.000-239.127.255.255	Reserved	[IANA]
239.128.000.000-239.191.255.255	Reserved	[IANA]
239.192.000.000-239.251.255.255	Organization-Local Scope	[Meyer,RFC2365]
239.252.000.000-239.252.255.255	Site-Local Scope (reserved)	[Meyer,RFC2365]
239.253.000.000-239.253.255.255	Site-Local Scope (reserved)	[Meyer,RFC2365]
239.254.000.000-239.254.255.255	Site-Local Scope (reserved)	[Meyer,RFC2365]
239.255.000.000-239.255.255.255	Site-Local Scope	[Meyer,RFC2365]
239.255.002.002	rasadv	[Thaler]

There is a concept of relative addresses to be used with the scoped multicast addresses. These relative addresses are listed here:

Relative	Description	Reference
0	SAP Session Announcement Protocol	[Handley]
1	MADCAP Protocol	[RFC2730]
2	SLPv2 Discovery	[Guttman]
3	MZAP	[Thaler]
4	Multicast Discovery of DNS Services	[Manning]
5	SSDP	[Goland]
6	DHCP v4	[Hall]
7	AAP	[Hanna]
8-252	Reserved - To be assigned by the IANA	
253	Reserved	
254-255	Reserved - To be assigned by the IANA	

These addresses are listed in the Domain Name Service under MCAST.NET and 224.IN-ADDR.ARPA.

Note that when used on an Ethernet or IEEE 802 network, the 23 low-order bits of the IP Multicast address are placed in the low-order 23 bits of the Ethernet or IEEE 802 net multicast address 1.0.94.0.0.0. See the section on "IANA ETHERNET ADDRESS BLOCK."

References

[RFC1045] Cheriton, D., "VMTP: Versatile Message Transaction Protocol Specification," RFC 1045, Stanford University, February 1988.

[RFC1075] Waitzman, D., C. Partridge, and S. Deering, "Distance Vector Multicast Routing Protocol," RFC-1075, BBN STC, Stanford University, November 1988.

[RFC1112] Deering, S., "Host Extensions for IP Multicasting," STD 5, RFC 1112, Stanford University, August 1989.

[RFC1119] Mills, D., "Network Time Protocol (Version 1), Specification and Implementation," STD 12, RFC 1119, University of Delaware, July 1988.

[RFC1190] Topolcic, C., Editor, "Experimental Internet Stream Protocol, Version 2 (ST-II)," RFC 1190, CIP Working Group, October 1990.

[RFC2328] Moy, J., "OSPF Version 2," STD 54, RFC 2328, Ascend Communications, April 1998.

[RFC1723] Malkin, G., "RIP Version 2: Carying Additional Information," RFC 1723, Xylogics, November 1994.

[RFC1884] Hinden, R., and S. Deering, "IP Version 6 Addressing Architecture," RFC 1884, Ipsilon Networks, Xerox PARC, December 1995.

[RFC2114] Chiang, S. J. Lee, and H. Yasuda, "Data Link Switching Client Access Protocol," RFC 2114, Cisco, Mitsubishi, February 1997.

[RFC2365] Meyer, D., "Administratively Scoped IP Multicast," RFC 2365, University of Oregon, July 1998.

[RFC2730] Hanna, S., B. Patel, and M. Shah, "Multicast Address Dynamic Client Allocation Protocol (MADCAP)," December 1999.

People

[Adams] Chris Adams, <jc.adams@reuters.com>, July 2000.

[Albin] Jerome Albin, <albin@taec.enet.dec.com>, June 1997.

[Albright] Shivaun Albright, <shivaun_albright@hp.com>, July 1997.

[Armitage] Ian Armitage, <ian@coactive.com>, August 1999.

[Aronson] Peter Aronson, <paronson@esri.com>, August 1998.

<arnoldm@microsoft.com>

[AXC] Andrew Cherenson, <arc@SGI.COM>

[Baker] Fred Baker, <fred@cisco.com>, June 1997.

[Ballardie] Tony Ballardie, <A.Ballardie@cs.ucl.ac.uk>, February 1997.

[Ballister] Tom Ballister, <tballister@starguidedigital.com>, July 1997.

[Banthia] Prakash Banthia, <prakash_banthia@3com.com>, September 1998.

[Barber] Tony Barber, <tonyb@pipex.com>, January 1997.

[Bhatti] Zia Bhatti, <zia@netright.com>, September 1998.

[Blackketter] Dean Blackketter, <dean@corp.webtv.net>, November 1998.

[Blank] Tom Blank, <tomblank@microsoft.com>, November 1996.

[Braden] Bob Braden, <braden@isi.edu>, April 1996.

[Bob Brenner]

[Brockbank] Darcy Brockbank, <darcy@hasc.com>, December 1997.

<bloomer@birch.crd.ge.com>

[BXE1] Brendan Eic, <brendan@illyria.wpd.sgi.com>

[BXF] Bruce Factor, <ahi!bigapple!bruce@uunet.UU.NET>

[BXS2] Bill Schilit,<schilit@parc.xerox.com>

[Carr] Wayne Carr, <Wayne_Carr@ccm.intel.com>, December 1997.

[Casner] Steve Casner, <casner@isi.edu>, January 1995.

[Caughie] Colin Caughie, <cfc@indigo-avs.com>, May 2000.

[Caves] Evan Caves, <evan@acc.com>, June 1998.

[Cheshire] Stuart Cheshire, <cheshire@apple.com>, April 2000.

[Chiang] Steve Chiang, <schiang@cisco.com>, January 1997

[Cho] Joan Cho/SIAC, <jcho@siac.com>, October 1998.

[Cipiere] Patrick Cipiere, <Patrick.Cipiere@sophia.inria.fr>, February 1999.

[Tim Clark]

[Costales] Bryan Costales, <bcx@infobeat.com>, September 1997.

[Crawford] James Crawford, <jcrawford@metropol.net>, May 1998.

[Crowcroft] Jon Crowcroft, <jon@hocus.cs.ucl.ac.uk>, November 1998.

[CXM3] Chuck McManis, <cmcmanis@sun.com>

[Daga] Anthony Daga, <anthony@mksrc.com>, June 1999.

[Deering] Steve Deering, <deering@cisco.com>, October 1999.

[DeMoney] Michael DeMoney, <demoney@eng.sun.com>, April 1997.

[Dillonn] Doug Dillon, <dillon@hns.com>, August 1998.

[Dissett] Daniel Dissett, <ddissett@peerlogic.com>, December 1998.

[DLM1] David Mills, <Mills@HUEY.UDEL.EDU>

[DRC3] Dave Cheriton, <cheriton@DSG.STANFORD.EDU>

[Dunne] Stephen Dunne, <sdun@isma.co.uk>, January 1997.

[DXS3] Daniel Steinber, <Daniel.Steinberg@Eng.Sun.COM>

[Eidson] John Eidson, <eidson@hpl.hp.com>, April 1999.

[Fenner] Bill Fenner, <fenner@parc.xerox.com>, December 1997.

[Farinacci] Dino Farinacci, <dino@cisco.com>, February, March 1996.

[Felix] Ken Felix, <kfelix@pcquote.com>, August 1999.

[Flynn] Edward Flynn, <flynne@nasdaq.com>, September 1998.

[Gabriel] Jon Gabriel, <grabriel@tivoli.com>, December 1998.

[Gaddie] Bob Gaddie, <bobg@dtn.com>, August 1998.

[Gal] Yossi Gal, <yossi@gilat.com>, February 1998.

[Gibson] Terry Gibson, <terry.gibson@sun.com>, August 1997.

[Gilani] Asad Gilani, <agilani@nymex.com>, July 1997.

[Glanzer] Dave Glanzer, <dglanzer@fieldbus.org>, June 2000.

[GSM11] Gary S. Malkin, <GMALKIN@XYLOGICS.COM>

[Goland] Yaron Goland, <yarong@microsoft.com>, August 1999.

[Gordon] Howard Gordon, <hgordon@xingtech.com>

[Green] Cliff Green, <cgreen@xypoint.com>, February 1998.

[Guttman] Erik Guttman, <Erik.Guttman@eng.sun.com>, March 1998.

[Hall] Eric Hall, <ehall@ntrg.com>, August 1999, October 1999.

[Hamilton] Mark Hamilton, <mah@spectralink.com>, November 1998.

[Handley] Mark Handley, <mjh@ISI.EDU>, December 1998.

[Hanna] Stephen Hanna, <steve.hanna@sun.com>, July 2000.

[Hinden] Bob Hinden, <hinden@Ipsilon.com>, November 1997.

[Hodges] Richard Hodges, <rh@source.net>, March 1999.

[Holfelder] Wieland Holdfelder, <whd@pi4.informatik.uni-mannheim.de>, January 1997.

[Honton] Chas Honton, <chas@secant.com>, December 1997.

[IANA] IANA, <iana@iana.org>

[Iyer] Ram Iyer <ram@aaccorp.com>, March 1998.

[Jackson] Dan Jackson, <jdan@us.ibm.com>, September 1997.

[Janssen] Rob Janssen, <rob@pe1chl.ampr.org>, January 1995.

[JBP] Jon Postel, <postel@isi.edu>

[JXM1] Jim Miner, <miner@star.com>

[Kammerlander] Ralph Kammerlander, <ralph.kammerlander@khe.siemens.de>, June 2000.

[Kean] Brian Kean, <bkean@dca.com>, August 1995.

[Kerkan] Brian Kerkan, <brian@satcomsystems.com>, May 2000.

[Kittivatcharapong] Sakon Kittivatcharapong, <sakonk@cscoms.net>, May 2000.

[Koopman] Dirk Koopman, <djk@tobit.co.uk>, July 2000.

[Kreutzjans] Michael Kreutzjans, <mike@pcquote.com>, December 1998.

[KS14] Karen Seo, <kseo@bbn.com>

[Lamberg] Mike Lamberg, <mlamberg@siac.com>, February 1997.

[Lee] Choon Lee, <cwl@nsd.3com.com>, April 1996.

[Lewis] Mark Lewis, <Mark_Lewis@ccm.jf.intel.com>, October 1995.

[Lindeman] Morten Lindeman, <Morten.Lindeman@os.telia.no>, March 1999.

[Lyda] Stephen T. Lyda, <slyda@emsg.com>, February 2000.

[Lynch] Joel Lynch, <joel.lynch@cnn.com>, April 1999.

[Andrew Maffei]

[Malamud] Carl Malamud, <carl@invisible.net>, April 1998.

[Malkin] Gary Scott Malkin, <gmalkin@baynetworks.com>, February 1998.

[Mamakos] Louis Mamakos, <louie@uu.net>, March 1997.

[Manning] Bill Manning, <bmanning@isi.edu>, August 1999.

[Marocho] Jose Luis Marocho, <73374.313@compuserve.com>, July 1996.

[Marquardt] Douglas Marquardt, <dmarquar@woz.org>, February 1997.

[Marsh] Gene Marsh, <MarshM@diebold.com>, November 1998.

[Martinicky] Brian Martinicky, <Brian_Martinicky@automationintelligence.com>, March 2000.

[Meier] Bob Meier, <meierb@norand.com>, December 1997.

[Mendal] Geoff Mendal, <mendal@talarian.com>, January 1999.

[Meyer] David Meyer, <meyer@ns.uoregon.edu>, January 1997.

[Meyer2] David Meyer, <dmm@cisco.com>, June 1999 - MALLOC assignment for temp use: renew 06/2000.

[Moelard] Henri Moelard, <HMOELARD@wcnd.nl.lucent.com>, March 1998.

[Moran] Ed Moran, <admin@cruzjazz.com>, October 1997.

[John Moy] John Moy, <jmoy@casc.com>

[MXF2] Martin Forssen, <maf@dtek.chalmers.se>

[Nelson] Gunnar Nelson, <nelsong@nasd.com>, March 1999.

[Nevell] Julian Nevell, <JNEVELL@vbs.bt.co.uk>, August 1999.

[Novick] Alan Novick, <anovick@tdc.com>, August 1998.

[O'Rourke] Stacey O'Rourke, <stacey@network-alchemy.com>, August 1999.

[Parnes] Peter Parnes, <peppar@marratech.com> February 2000.

[Peng] Wenjie Peng, <wpeng@tts.telerate.com>, January 1997.

[Polishinski] Steve Polishinski, <spolishinski@etcconnect.com>, March 2000.

[Poole] David Poole, <davep@extendsys.com>, April 1997.

[Przygienda] Tony Przygienda, <prz@siara.com>, October 1999.

[Purkiss] Ed Purkiss, <epurkiss@wdmacodi.com>, September 1998.

[Querubin] Antonio Querubin, <tony@lava.net>, August 1999.

[Revzen] Shai Revzen, <shrevz@nmcfast.com>, April 1999.

[Rodbell] Mike Rodbell, <mrodbell@ciena.com>, January 1997.

[Roper] Mike Roper, <mroper@8x8.com>, September 1999.

[Guido van Rossum]

[Rowatt] Shane Rowatt, <shane.rowatt@star.com.au>, March 1997.

[Roy] George Roy, <c/o Bill Owens owens@appliedtheory.com>, October 1997.

[Rubin] David Rubin, <drubin@ncc.net>, August 1996.

[Rueskamp] Bodo Rueskamp, <br@itchigo.com>, March 2000.

[Rupp] Heiko Rupp, <hwr@xlink.net>, January 1997.

[Sautter] Robert Sautter, <rsautter@acdnj.itt.com>, August 1999.

[SC3] Steve Casner, <casner@precept.com>

[Scannell] Piers Scannell, <piers@globecastne.com>, March 2000.

[Scheifler] Bob Scheifler, <Bob.Scheifler@sun.com>, August 1998.

[Schwartz] Beverly Schwartz, <bschwart@BBN.COM>, June 1998.

[Shindoh] Masato Shindoh, <jl11456@yamato.ibm.co.jp>, August 1997.

[Shum] Raymond Shum, <rshum@ms.com>, April 1998.

[Simpson] Bill Simpson, <bill.simpson@um.cc.umich.edu> November 1994.

[Sledge] Bob Sledge, <bob@pqsystems.com>, December 1998.

[Sliwinski] Robert Sliwinski, <sliwinre@mail1st.com>, February 2000.

[Joel Snyder]

[Stanev] Nedelcho Stanev, <nstanev@csoft.bg>, May 1999.

[Stewart] Ian Stewart, <iandbige@yahoo.com>, June 1999.

[Strazzera] Paolo Strazzera, <p.strazzera@telematica.it>, June 1999.

[Sveistrup] Darrell Sveistrup, <darrells@truesolutions.net>, June 1999.

[SXA] Susie Armstrong, <Armstrong.wbst128@XEROX.COM>

[SXD] Steve Deering, <deering@PARC.XEROX.COM>

[Thaler] Dave Thaler, <dthaler@microsoft.com>, March 1999, June 2000.

[Thompson] Nigel Thompson, <nigelt@tribal.com>, January 1999.

[Timm] Mary Timm, <mary@xenoscience.com>, July 1998.

[Toga] Jim Toga, <jtoga@ibeam.jf.intel.com>, May 1996.

[Tse] Geordie Tse, <gtse@siac.com>, April 1996.

[tynan] Dermot Tynan, <dtynan@claddagh.ie>, August 1995.

[Uang] Yea Uang, <uang@force.decnet.lockheed.com> November 1994.

[Uusitalo] Mika Uusitalo, <msu@xingtech.com>, April 1997.

[van der Muelen] Ron van der Muelen, <ronv@lsid.hp.com> February 1997.

[Veizades] John Veizades, <veizades@tgv.com>, May 1995.

[Velten] Mike Velten, <mike_velten@liebert.com>, January 1999.

[Vogels] Werner Vogels, <vogels@rnets.com>, August 1998.

[Volpe] Victor Volpe, <vvolpe@smtp.microcom.com>, October 1997.

[Wacey] Ian Wacey, <iain.wacey@gefalbany.ge.com>, May 2000.

[Wallach] Walter Wallach, <walt@sumatech.com>, July 1999.

[Wang] Michael Wang, <Michael.Wang@usa.xerox.com>, March 1999.

[Wasserroth] Stephan Wasserroth, <wasserroth@fokus.gmd.de>, July 2000.

[Watson] Scott Watson, <scott@disney.com>, August 1997.
[Wei] Liming Wei, <lwei@cisco.com>, October 1998.
[Wessels] Duane Wessels, <wessels@nlanr.net>, February 1997.
[White] Peter White, <peter_white@3com.com>, April 1999.
[Wissenbach] Paul Wissenbach, <paulwi@vnd.tek.com>, June 1997.
[Wong] Tony Wong, <wongt@ms.com>, July 1998.
[Woodcock] Bill Woodcock, <woody@zocalo.net>, November 1998.
[Wu] Ishan Wu, <iwu@cisco.com>, March 2000.
[Zulch] Richard Zulch, <richard_zulch@dantz.com>, February 1996.
[Zwemmer] Arnoud Zwemmer, <arnoud@nwn.nl>, November 1996.

Answers to Review Questions

Answers to Chapter 1 Review Questions

1 What is the current version of EGP?

Answer: The current version of EGP is 2.

2 What is an EGP interior neighbor? An EGP exterior neighbor?

Answer: An EGP gateway's neighbor is interior if it is within the same AS. An exterior neighbor is in a different AS.

3 What is the primary difference between an EGP stub gateway and an EGP core gateway?

Answer: Stub gateways can advertise only networks that are interior to their own AS. Core gateways can advertise both interior and exterior networks.

4 Why does EGP use the concept of a core, or backbone, AS?

Answer: EGP has no mechanisms for detecting loops. Therefore, a loop-free topology must be engineered physically so that inter-AS traffic must traverse a backbone.

5 What is the difference between an active EGP neighbor and a passive EGP neighbor?

Answer: An active neighbor initiates the peer relationship and sends Hellos to maintain it. Passive neighbors respond to Hellos with I-Heard-You messages.

6 What is the purpose of an EGP Poll message?

Answer: A Poll message is a request to a neighbor for an Update.

7 What is an indirect, or third-party, neighbor?

Answer: An indirect neighbor is a gateway that shares a common data link with another gateway and can reach certain networks through that gateway but is not peered directly with the gateway. Rather, it learns its reachability information from yet another gateway on the data link.

8 How does EGP use its metrics to calculate the best path to a destination?

Answer: Although EGP has a metric, it has no mechanism for determining best paths. Therefore, the metric is used only for indicating an unreachable network.

Answers to Chapter 2 Review Questions

1 What is the most important difference between BGP-4 and earlier versions of BGP?

Answer: BGP-4 is classless. Earlier versions are classful.

2 What two problems was CIDR developed to alleviate?

Answer: CIDR was developed to alleviate the explosion of Internet routing tables and to slow the depletion of Class B network addresses.

3 What is the difference between classful and classless IP routers?

Answer: Classful IP routers perform routing table lookups on the major class network address first and then match the subnet. Classless IP routers ignore the class of the destination address and try to make a longest match on the address prefix.

4 What is the difference between classful and classless IP routing protocols?

Answer: Classful IP routing protocols advertise only a network or subnet address, without any information about the prefix length. As a result, routers receiving the advertisement must make certain assumptions about the address prefix. Classless IP routing protocols include information that allows the receiving router to parse the address prefix. As a result, VLSM and summarization are possible with classless protocols.

5 Given the addresses 172.17.208.0/23, 172.17.210.0/23, 172.17.212.0/23, and 172.17.214.0/23, summarize the addresses with a single aggregate, using the longest possible address mask.

Answer: 172.17.208.0/21

6 What is an address prefix?

Answer: An IP address prefix is the part of an IP address that a router considers when making routing decisions. In a classful environment, the prefix is a major class network address or one of its subnets. In a classless environment, the prefix can be any number of leading bits in the 32-bit address.

7 The routing table in Example 2-16 is taken from a classless router. To what next-hop address does the router forward packets with each of the following destination addresses?

172.20.3.5

172.20.1.67

172.21.255.254

172.16.50.50

172.16.0.224

172.16.51.50

172.17.40.1

172.17.41.1

172.30.1.1

Example 2-16 *The Routing Table for Review Question 7*

```
Stratford#show ip route
Codes: C - connected, S - static, I - IGRP, R - RIP, M - mobile, B - BGP
       D - EIGRP, EX - EIGRP external, O - OSPF, IA - OSPF inter area
       E1 - OSPF external type 1, E2 - OSPF external type 2, E - EGP
       i - IS-IS, L1 - IS-IS level-1, L2 - IS-IS level-2, * - candidate default

Gateway of last resort is not set

     172.20.0.0 is variably subnetted, 6 subnets, 2 masks
D       172.20.0.0 255.255.0.0 [90/409600] via 172.20.5.2, 00:01:50, Ethernet0
D       172.20.2.0 255.255.255.0
           [90/409600] via 172.20.6.2, 00:01:50, Ethernet1
D       172.20.3.0 255.255.255.0
           [90/5401600] via 172.20.6.2, 00:01:50, Ethernet1
C       172.20.5.0 255.255.255.0 is directly connected, Ethernet0
C       172.20.6.0 255.255.255.0 is directly connected, Ethernet1
C       172.20.7.0 255.255.255.0 is directly connected, Ethernet2
     172.16.0.0 is variably subnetted, 3 subnets, 2 masks
D       172.16.50.0 255.255.255.0
           [90/409600] via 172.20.6.2, 00:01:50, Ethernet1
D       172.16.0.0 255.255.255.0
           [90/460800] via 172.20.6.2, 00:01:51, Ethernet1
D       172.16.0.0 255.255.0.0 [90/409600] via 172.20.7.2, 00:01:51, Ethernet2
     172.17.0.0 is subnetted (mask is 255.255.255.0), 1 subnets
D       172.17.40.0 [90/2841600] via 172.20.7.2, 00:01:52, Ethernet2
D   172.16.0.0 (mask is 255.240.0.0) [90/409600] via 172.20.5.2, 00:01:52, Ethernet0
Stratford#
```

Answer:

Destination Address	Next-Hop Address
172.20.3.5	172.20.6.2
172.20.1.67	172.20.5.2
172.21.255.254	172.20.5.2
172.16.50.50	172.20.6.2

continues

(Continued)

Destination Address	Next-Hop Address
172.16.0.224	172.20.6.2
172.16.51.50	172.20.7.2
172.17.40.1	172.20.7.2
172.17.41.1	172.20.5.2
172.30.1.1	Dropped

8 Explain how summarization helps hide network instabilities.

Answer: Member addresses, or destination addresses that are summarized by an aggregate address, are not advertised past the summarization point. So if the state of one of the member addresses changes, the change is not advertised past the summarization point.

9 Explain how summarization can cause asymmetric traffic patterns.

Answer: Summarization hides the details of the internetwork behind the summarization point. If a summary address is advertised by more than one router, the routers beyond the summarization points select only the closest summarizing router.

10 Is asymmetric traffic undesirable?

Answer: The answer is subjective. Asymmetric traffic can make baselining and troubleshooting more difficult, and if the internetwork is geographically large, delay-sensitive traffic can be affected. On the other hand, the benefits of summarization might outweigh these problems.

11 What is a NAP?

Answer: A network access point is a LAN or switch through which service providers may interconnect. From the perspective of Internet traffic flow, NAPs are the hierarchically highest points in the Internet topology.

12 What is a route server?

Answer: A route server is a server with which routers may peer via some routing protocol. Each router sends its updates to the route server rather than to the other peers. The route server applies the appropriate routing policies and then sends the updates to the other peers. Route servers are useful when many routers must peer across a common data link, as in a NAP, by reducing the number of peering sessions each router must establish. This can be especially important if

the routers are using a unicast protocol such as BGP, in which a separate packet must be sent to each peer. A route server is not a router, because it performs no packet forwarding.

13 What is a provider-independent address space, and why can it be advantageous to have one?

Answer: A provider-independent address space is assigned by the regional IP address registry rather than as part of a service provider's CIDR block. It proves useful if an AS is multihomed to different service providers. It is also useful because it is portable. That is, the owner of the address space can change ISPs without having to re-address.

14 Why can it be a problem to have a /21 provider-independent address space?

Answer: Some national service providers do not accept IP prefixes longer than a /19. As a result, a /21 might not be advertised to all parts of the Internet.

15 What is a routing policy?

Answer: A routing policy is a predefined set of rules for handling incoming and outgoing routes. Typical tools for setting routing policies are redistribution, route filters, and route maps.

16 What is the underlying protocol that BGP uses to reliably connect to its neighbors?

Answer: BGP uses TCP port 179.

17 What are the four BGP message types, and how is each one used?

Answer: The four BGP message types are Open, Keepalive, Update, and Notification. Open messages are used to initially identify a BGP speaker to its neighbor and begin a peering session. Keepalives maintain the peer connection. Updates are used to advertise routes, and Notification messages advise peers of errors.

18 In what state or states can BGP peers exchange Update messages?

Answer: BGP peers can exchange Update messages only when both are in the Established state.

19 What is NLRI?

Answer: Network Layer Reachability Information is the IP address prefix or prefixes advertised in a BGP Update.

20 What is a path attribute?

Answer: A path attribute is a characteristic of a BGP route.

21   What are the four categories of BGP path attributes?

Answer: The four categories of BGP path attributes are Well-known Mandatory, Well-known Discretionary, Optional Transitive, and Optional Nontransitive.

22   What is the purpose of the AS_PATH attribute?

Answer: The AS_PATH attribute describes the AS numbers that a received Update has crossed after it left the originating router. This information can be used to determine the shortest inter-AS path, and it is also used to detect routing loops.

23   What are the different types of AS_PATH?

Answer: AS_PATH types are AS_SEQUENCE, AS_CONFED_SEQUENCE, AS_SET, and AS_CONFED_SET. AS_SEQUENCE is an ordered set of AS numbers, and AS_SET is an unordered set of AS numbers. AS_CONFED_SEQUENCE and AS_CONFED_SET are the same as AS_SEQUENCE and AS_SET but are used only within BGP confederations.

24   What is the purpose of the NEXT_HOP attribute?

Answer: The NEXT_HOP attribute describes the IP address of the next-hop router that packets should be forwarded to in order to reach the destination advertised as the NLRI in a BGP Update.

25   What is the purpose of the LOCAL_PREF attribute?

Answer: If multiple IBGP speakers are advertising the same route within an AS, the LOCAL_PREF attribute can be used to identify the preferred route. The higher the LOCAL_PREF value, the more preferred the route.

26   What is the purpose of the MULTI_EXIT_DISC attribute?

Answer: When multiple links exist between two autonomous systems, EBGP speakers can use the MED to inform the neighboring AS of the preferred link for incoming traffic.

27   What attribute or attributes are useful if a BGP speaker originates an aggregate route?

Answer: THE ATOMIC_AGGREGATE informs downstream routers that a loss of route information has occurred due to aggregation. The AGGREGATOR attribute identifies the router that originated the aggregate.

28   What is a BGP administrative weight?

Answer: A BGP administrative weight is a Cisco-specific parameter that can be assigned to routes within a single router. The higher the weight, the more preferable the route. Weights are local to the router and are not advertised to peers.

29 Given an EBGP route and an IBGP route to the same destination, which route will a BGP router prefer?

Answer: If the weights, LOCAL_PREFs, AS_PATH lengths, ORIGIN codes, and MEDs are equal, EBGP routes are preferred over IBGP routes.

30 A router has two IBGP routes to the same destination. Path A has a LOCAL_PREF of 300 and three AS numbers in the AS_PATH. Path B has a LOCAL_PREF of 200 and two AS numbers in the AS_PATH. Assuming no other differences, which path will the router choose?

Answer: LOCAL_PREF has a higher priority in the BGP decision process than AS_PATH, so path A is chosen.

31 What is route dampening?

Answer: Route dampening is a mechanism by which BGP routes are assigned a penalty for changing state. The more often the state changes (the route flaps), the greater the accumulated penalties. If the penalties exceed a certain threshold, the route is suppressed for a time. As a result, unstable routes have less adverse effect on the BGP internetwork.

32 Define the penalty, suppress limit, reuse limit, and half-life as they apply to route dampening.

Answer: The penalty is a value assigned to a route by the route-dampening mechanism each time the route changes state. The suppress limit is a threshold that, if exceeded by a route's accumulated penalties, signifies that the route should not be advertised. Reuse limit is a threshold that, if a suppressed route's accumulated penalties falls below it, signifies that the route can again be advertised. The half-life is the rate at which a route's accumulated penalties are reduced. At the end of each half-life, the penalty is reduced by half.

33 What is IGP synchronization, and why is it important?

Answer: IGP synchronization is a rule whereby a BGP router cannot advertise a transit route to an EBGP peer unless the route is found in the IGP routing table. If a BGP router forwards a transit packet to an IBGP peer via an IGP router, and the IGP router does not know the route, the packet is dropped.

34 Under what circumstances can you safely disable IGP synchronization?

Answer: You can safely turn off IGP synchronization if the IBGP peers in an AS are fully meshed, or when the AS is not a transit AS.

35   What is a BGP peer group?

Answer: A BGP peer group is a group of BGP peers that have been identified on a single router to share common routing policies. Peer groups simplify configuration by allowing route policies to be applied to the group rather than to each individual member.

36   What is a BGP community?

Answer: A BGP community is a group of routes that share common routing policies. They work by setting a common COMMUNITY attribute in the routes; peers receiving those routes can recognize the COMMUNITY attribute and apply the appropriate policy.

37   What is a route reflector? What is a route reflection client? What is a route reflection cluster?

Answer: A route reflector is similar to a route server in that it permits IBGP routers to peer with it rather than with each other. Routes from one peer are advertised, or reflected, to the other peers. As a result, the number of peering sessions is reduced from what would be required if the IBGP peers were fully meshed. Route reflectors differ from route servers in that the route reflector is also a router. A route reflection client is an IBGP router that has peered with a route reflector. A route reflection cluster is a route reflector and its clients. A cluster can have more than one route reflector, but all the clients in the cluster must be peered with all the route reflectors in the cluster.

38   What is the purpose of the ORIGINATOR_ID and the CLUSTER_LIST path attributes?

Answer: The ORIGINATOR_ID and CLUSTER_LIST attributes prevent routing loops when route reflectors are being used.

39   What is a BGP confederation?

Answer: A BGP confederation is a large AS that has been subdivided into a group of smaller autonomous systems for easier manageability.

40   Can route reflectors be used within confederations?

Answer: Yes.

41   What is the purpose of the **next-hop-self** function? Are there any reasonable alternatives to using this function?

Answer: next-hop-self tells a router to change the NEXT_HOP attribute of routes received from an external peer to its own IP address. This function is used when the IGP has no knowledge of the external next-hop address. An alternative method is to run the IGP passively on the external link so that it knows the subnet on which the external next-hop address resides.

Answers to Chapter 5 Review Questions

1 Give several reasons why replicated unicast is not a practical substitution for true multicast in a large network.

Answer: Replicated unicast places a processing burden on the source and can cause severe bottlenecks at the source interface, data link, and connected router. The source also must hold state to remember what addresses to send the replicated packets, and there must be some potentially complex mechanism for members to signal joins and leaves to the source. Finally, replicated unicast can cause queuing problems and unacceptable latency between packets.

2 What range of addresses is reserved for IP multicast?

Answer: The Class D addresses, in which the first four bits are 1110. This address range is 224.0.0.0–239.255.255.255.

3 How many subnets can be created from a single Class D prefix?

Answer: No subnets are created from a Class D prefix. IP multicast uses only single addresses, not subnets.

4 In what way do routers treat packets with destination addresses in the range 224.0.0.1–224.0.0.255 differently from other multicast addresses?

Answer: Routers do not forward packets with destination addresses in the range 224.0.0.1 through 224.0.0.255.

5 Write the Ethernet MAC addresses that correspond to the following IP addresses:

(a) 239.187.3.201

(b) 224.18.50.1

(c) 224.0.1.87

Answer:

(a) 0100.5E3B.03C9

(b) 0100.5E12.3201

(c) 0100.5E00.0157

6 What multicast IP address or addresses are represented by the MAC address 0100.5E06.2D54?

Answer: The MAC address 0100.5E06.2D54 can represent any of 32 IP addresses in which the first octet is 1 of 15 numbers in the range 224–239, the second octet is either 134 or 6, the third octet is always 45, and the last octet is always 87.

7   Why is Token Ring a poor medium for delivering multicast packets?

Answer: Token Ring is a poor medium for delivery of IP multicast packets because of the Token Ring frame's little-endian format, which prevents an easy encoding of the multicast IP address into the MAC address. Instead, either a reserved functional MAC address or a broadcast MAC address must be used, either of which can sharply reduce efficiency on the data link.

8   What is join latency?

Answer: Join latency is the time between when a host first signals a desire to join a group and the time the host begins receiving group traffic.

9   What is leave latency?

Answer: Leave latency is the time between when a host first leaves a group and the time the host is removed from the group.

10   What is a multicast DR (or querier)?

Answer: A multicast querier is the router on a subnet responsible for querying the attached hosts for group membership.

11   What device sends IGMP Query messages?

Answer: IGMP Query messages are sent by routers. If more than one router is attached to the subnet, the router with the lowest IP address is the querier.

12   What device sends IGMP Membership Report messages?

Answer: Hosts send IGMP Membership Report messages.

13   How is an IGMP Membership Report message used?

Answer: An IGMP Membership Report is sent by a host to inform the local router that it wants to join a group.

14   What is the functional difference between a General IGMP Query and a Group-Specific IGMP Query?

Answer: A router sends a General IGMP Query to discover members of any and all groups. A Group-Specific IGMP Query is sent to discover members of a specific group, usually after the reception of a Leave Group message.

15   Is IGMPv2 compatible with IGMPv1?

Answer: IGMPv2 is mostly compatible with IGMPv1, although if there is an IGMPv1 router on a subnet, all routers should be set to IGMPv1.

16   What IP protocol number signifies IGMP?

Answer: IGMP uses protocol number 2.

17 What is the purpose of the Cisco Group Membership Protocol (CGMP)?

Answer: CGMP is a protocol by which Ethernet switches can discover which ports group members are connected to and thereby avoid having to forward IP multicast frames out all ports.

18 What is the advantage of using IP Snooping rather than CGMP? What is the possible disadvantage?

Answer: Unlike CGMP, IP Snooping is not proprietary and therefore may be preferable in a mixed-vendor environment. Its potential disadvantage is that if IP Snooping is supported on a switch only in software, it can affect performance.

19 What devices send CGMP messages: routers, Ethernet switches, or both?

Answer: Only routers send CGMP messages. Switches listen for CGMP messages.

20 What is Reverse Path Forwarding?

Answer: RPF is the basic forwarding mechanism of IP multicast routing. Because the routers find the shortest paths to the source rather than the destination, when multicast packets are forwarded toward the destination (or, more accurately, away from the source), they are forwarded in the reverse direction along the shortest path.

21 How many hosts constitute a dense topology, and how many hosts constitute a sparse topology?

Answer: There is no set number differentiating sparse and dense topologies.

22 What is the primary advantage of explicit joins over implicit joins?

Answer: The primary advantage of explicit joins over implicit joins is that routers do not have to hold state for interfaces that are not upstream from any group members.

23 What is the primary structural difference between a source-based multicast tree and a shared multicast tree?

Answer: A source-based tree is rooted at the source subnet or source router, whereas a shared tree is rooted at some common rendezvous point or core and can be, by definition, shared by multiple sources.

24 What is multicast scoping?

Answer: Multicast scoping is the practice of limiting the range of certain multicast packets to a determined topological area.

25 What are the two methods of IP multicast scoping?

Answer: The two methods of IP multicast scoping are TTL scoping and administrative scoping.

26 From the perspective of a multicast router, what is meant by upstream and what is meant by downstream?

Answer: Upstream is the direction toward a multicast source, and downstream is the direction away from the source.

27 What is an RPF check?

Answer: An RPF check is a verification that a multicast packet from a particular source has arrived on the upstream interface toward that source and no other interface.

28 What is a prune? What is a graft?

Answer: A prune is the action of removing a router from a multicast tree. A graft is the action of adding a router to a multicast tree.

29 What is a prune lifetime? What happens when a prune lifetime expires?

Answer: A prune lifetime, used by implicit join protocols, is the amount of time that a router holds an interface in prune state. When a prune lifetime expires, the router again forwards packets on the interface until the downstream neighbor again requests a prune.

30 What is a route dependency? How does DVMRP signal a route dependency?

Answer: A route dependency is a dependency a router has on an upstream neighbor to forward packets for a particular group. DVMRP routers signal a route dependency by using a poison reverse route, in which the metric is the advertised hop count to the source plus 32.

31 Is DVMRP a dense-mode protocol or a sparse-mode protocol?

Answer: DVMRP is a dense-mode protocol.

32 Is MOSPF a dense-mode protocol or a sparse-mode protocol?

Answer: MOSPF is a dense-mode protocol.

33 What is the name and type number of the LSA used exclusively by MOSPF?

Answer: The LSA used exclusively by MOSPF is the Group Membership LSA, which is type 6.

34 Can an MOSPF router establish an adjacency with an OSPF router that does not support MOSPF?

Answer: Yes, although only neighbors whose MC bits are set in their Database Description packets exchange Group Membership LSAs.

35 Define the following MOSPF router types:

(a) Interarea multicast forwarder

(b) Inter-AS multicast forwarder

(c) Wildcard multicast receiver

Answer:

(a) An interarea multicast forwarder forwards IP multicast packets between areas and is similar to a unicast OSPF ABR.

(b) An inter-AS multicast forwarder forwards IP multicast packets outside of the MOSPF domain and is similar to a unicast OSPF ASBR.

(c) A wildcard multicast receiver is a router to which all multicast packets are forwarded.

36 Is CBT a dense-mode protocol or a sparse-mode protocol?

Answer: CBT is a sparse-mode protocol.

37 What are a CBT parent router and a CBT child router?

Answer: A CBT parent router is an upstream router, and a CBT child router is a downstream router.

38 Describe the two ways a CBT DR can deliver packets from a source to the core and the circumstances under which each method is used.

Answer: If a directly connected source is a member source, its packets are forwarded on the tree. If the source is a nonmember source, a tunnel to the core is created, and the packets are forwarded over the tunnel.

39 What is a PIM prune override?

Answer: A prune override is a Join message sent to an upstream router on a multiaccess network to cancel a prune requested by another router on the same network.

40 What is a PIM forwarder? How is a forwarder selected?

Answer: When multiple upstream routers are connected to the same multiaccess network and are receiving packets for the same group, the PIM forwarder is the router that forwards the packets onto the network. The forwarder is elected by

the lowest administrative distance advertised in an Assert message. If the administrative distances are equal, the lowest route metric is used. If the metrics are the same, the lowest IP address is the tiebreaker.

41   What criteria does PIM use to select a DR?

Answer: The PIM router with the highest IP address (according to the PIM Hello messages) is the DR.

42   What is a PIM SPT? What is a PIM RPT?

Answer: A shortest path tree is a source-based tree, and a rendezvous point tree is a shared tree rooted at a rendezvous point.

43   What two mechanisms are available for Cisco routers to automatically discover PIM-SM RPs?

Answer: PIM-SM RPs can be automatically discovered using either Auto-RP or the bootstrap protocol.

44   Of the mechanisms in Question 43, which should be used in multivendor router topologies?

Answer: Auto-RP may not be supported by other vendors, so bootstrap protocol should be used.

45   What is a C-RP?

Answer: A C-RP is a Candidate RP, or a router that is eligible to become an RP for either all groups or a specified set of groups.

46   What is a BSR?

Answer: When the bootstrap protocol is used, a bootstrap router advertises C-RPs throughout the PIM-SM domain in an RP-Set.

47   What is an RP mapping agent?

Answer: When Auto-RP is used, an RP mapping agent advertises group-to-RP mappings.

48   What is the difference between an (S, G) mroute entry and a (*, G) mroute entry?

Answer: An (S, G) entry refers to an SPT, whereas a (*, G) entry refers to an RPT.

49   What is the major drawback with a bidirectional CBT tree between the source and core, as opposed to a PIM-SM unidirectional tree from the RP to the source?

Answer: It is difficult to guarantee a loop-free path with bidirectional trees, because there is no distinct upstream and downstream.

50 What is PIM-SM source registration?

Answer: Source registration is a mechanism whereby a router forwards packets from a multicast source to an RP in PIM Register messages. If there is significant traffic from the source, the RP builds an SPT and then sends a Register Stop.

51 When does a Cisco router switch from a PIM-SM RPT to an SPT?

Answer: Cisco routers switch from an RPT to an SPT immediately after receiving the first packet for a particular (S, G) on the RPT, or when the arrival rate of the packets for the (S, G) exceeds a threshold specified with the command ip pim spt-threshold.

Answers to Chapter 7 Review Questions

1 In the section "Multicast Scoping," a sample configuration is given for administrative scoping. The boundary at interface E0 blocks organization-local packets (destination addresses whose prefixes match 239.192.0.0/14) but passes packets with global scope. Will a packet with a group address 224.0.0.50 pass this boundary?

Answer: Packets with a destination address of 224.0.0.50 pass this boundary only if the local router originates them. Although 224.0.0.50 is permitted by access list 10, it is in the link-local range and so is not forwarded by any next-hop router.

2 How does Cisco IOS Software handle DVMRP Prune messages on point-to-point and multiaccess interfaces that are configured to run PIM?

Answer: DVMRP Prunes are ignored on multiaccess interfaces and are processed normally on point-to-point interfaces.

3 Why does Cisco IOS Software accept DVMRP Probe messages but does not send them?

Answer: The reception of DVMRP Probes is necessary to detect DVMRP neighbors. Probes are not sent because another Cisco PIM router on a multiaccess network would mistake the originator for a DVMRP-only router.

4 What is a PIM (*,*,RP) entry?

Answer: A (*,*,RP) entry is to a PIM Multicast Border Router. MBRs are not supported by Cisco IOS.

5 How does Multiprotocol BGP (MBGP) differ from normal BGP?

Answer: MBGP is extended with two route attributes: MP_REACH_NLRI and MP_UNREACH_NLRI.

6 What is the MBGP AFI?

Answer: The AFI is the Address Family Identifier. When MBGP is used for multicasting, the AFI is always set to 1 (for IPv4), and the sub-AFI will indicate whether the related NLRI is to be used for multicast, unicast, or both.

7 Is the following statement true or false? MSDP carries information about multicast sources and group members between RPs in different PIM domains.

Answer: False. MSDP only communicates information about multicast sources, not group members.

8 What is the transport protocol for MSDP?

Answer: MSDP uses TCP port 639.

9 What is an MSDP SA message?

Answer: An SA is a Source Active message. When a source's DR registers with an RP, if the RP is running MSDP, it advertises the (S,G) pair to its peers in SA messages.

10 How does an MSDP RP determine whether an SA was received on an RPF interface?

Answer: It checks the BGP next-hop database (MBGP first, and then unicast BGP) for the correct upstream interface.

11 What is SA caching?

A: SA caching is the storage of (S,G) state information learned from SA messages. SA caching trades some memory in the router for reduced join latency. By default, SA caching is disabled in Cisco IOS Software.

12 Is there an alternative to reducing join latency without enabling SA caching?

Answer: Yes. If an MSDP peer is caching, you can configure an RP to use SA Request messages to request (S,G) information from the peer as soon as a join is received.

Answers to Chapter 8 Review Questions

1 Which of the following are valid representations for the address 200A 0000 0000 0C00 0000 0000 0000 0000 with a 60-bit prefix?

A. 200A:0000:0000:0C/60

B. 200A::0C00:0:0:0:0/60

C. 200A:0000:0000:0C00::/60

D. 200A::0C00::/60

E. 200A:0:0:C00::/60

F. 200A::0C/60

Answer: B, C, E. A is not a complete address. D is ambiguous, with two sets of ::. F doesn't expand to the correct address.

2 For what is the address 0:0:0:0:0:0:0:0 used?

Answer: This is the unspecified address. It represents the absence of an address. If this is the source address of a packet, the interface has not yet been assigned an address. It is attempting to discover whether its tentative address is being used by another node.

3 You configure your site border routers, connecting to an IPv6 public network, to advertise all your internal network numbers, including FEC0:0020:0:0100::/56. You get a nasty call from the IPv6 public network administrator. What is wrong?

Answer: FEC0:0020:0:0100::/56 is a site-local address. It must never be advertised beyond the boundaries of a site.

4 Which extension headers are processed by every IPv6 node in the path from source to destination?

Answer: Hop-by-Hop.

5 Which extension headers are used to specify a list of routers to visit before reaching the destination and to have each of those routers process the header?

Answer: Destination Options header followed by the Routing header.

6 A router receives a packet larger than its outgoing link's MTU. Does it fragment the packet and forward the fragments toward the destination?

Answer: No. It drops the packet and sends an ICMP Packet Too Big message back to the source. The source uses these ICMP packets to perform path MTU discovery. It is the sole responsibility of the source to fragment the packet.

7 If set in a Router Advertisement, what affect does the Managed bit have?

Answer: The router sends the RA to all hosts on a link. If the Managed bit is set, the hosts obtain an address from a stateful configuration server.

8 If a router advertises prefix information in its RAs, how is the information used?

Answer: Prefix information included in RAs tells hosts which prefixes are on-link and/or which prefixes to use when they autoconfigure their addresses.

9 In what two states can a host's IP address reside, and what are the roles of the two states?

Answer: Preferred and deprecated. A preferred address can be used to initiate any IP session. A deprecated address should be used only to maintain an existing connection, not to initiate a new connection, if a preferred address exists.

10 What information does a router advertise in its RA to tell hosts to stop using a particular prefix when initiating IP sessions?

Answer: Either a Valid Lifetime or Preferred Lifetime of value 0. Valid Lifetime 0 says the prefix is no longer valid. Preferred Lifetime 0 says to deprecate the prefix.

11 If a node has a neighbor with state DELAY, can the node send the neighbor packets?

Answer: Yes. A neighbor with state DELAY has not been verified reachable, but the node will send packets to its cached link layer address for the neighbor.

12 A host is not running any routing protocol. It is sending data to a remote node using a default router. The default router fails. Will the host continue to send data into the black hole of the dead router until its TCP connection fails?

Answer: No. The neighbor unreachability process, default router list, and address resolution processes will assist the host in discovering the dead router and finding a new one.

13 What are the scope values for multicast packets, and for what are they used?

Answer: Node, link, site, organization, global. The scope values are used to limit the meaning of a multicast group and to control how far a multicast packet can travel.

14 What Cisco router command enables IPv6 routing?

Answer: ipv6 unicast-routing

15 What interface subcommands enable IPv6 on an interface?

Answer: ipv6 enable, ipv6 address *address prefix* [eui-64]

16 What commands are used to enable a RIPng process?

Answer: Interface subcommand: ipv6 rip *process-name* enable

17 How is the BGP-for-IPv6 process enabled between neighbors?

Answer:

```
router bgp local-AS
 neighbor neighbor-ipv6-address remote-as remote-as-number
 !
 address-family ipv6
 neighbor neighbor-ipv6-address activate
```

Answers to Chapter 9 Review Questions

1 Explain the difference between SNMP polls and traps.

Answer: A management station requesting information from a router is polling the router. A router that sends unsolicited information about an event that occurred sends a trap.

2 If you specify the severity level of messages logged to be Errors, what other levels of messages are logged?

Answer: Emergencies, Alerts, Critical

3 You look at a router interface and see that there are unusual traffic patterns. Normally, all traffic is inbound, but now there is outbound traffic. How can you quickly determine the source and destination of the traffic?

Answer: Enable IP accounting on the interface. Use the show ip accounting command repeatedly to see which source/destination pair is sending the traffic.

Answers to Configuration Exercises

Answers to Chapter 1 Configuration Exercises

1 Autonomous System 65531 in Figure 1-14 is a core AS.

Figure 1-14 *The Internetwork for Configuration Exercise 1*

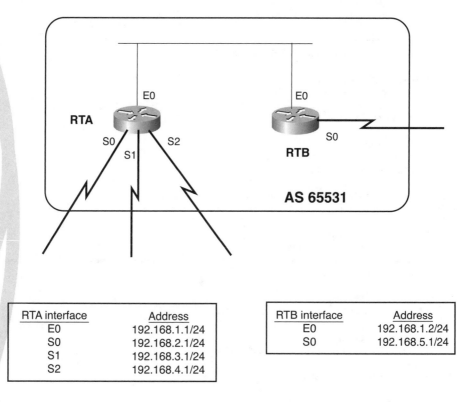

RTA interface	Address
E0	192.168.1.1/24
S0	192.168.2.1/24
S1	192.168.3.1/24
S2	192.168.4.1/24

RTB interface	Address
E0	192.168.1.2/24
S0	192.168.5.1/24

Configure EGP on RTA and RTB, with the following constraints:

— The data link interior to the AS is not advertised to any exterior neighbor.

— RTA advertises the network attached to its S1 interface to RTB; with this exception, no other inter-AS link is advertised between RTA and RTB.

— RTA and RTB advertise a default route to their exterior neighbors in addition to networks learned from other autonomous systems. Neither gateway advertises a default route to its internal neighbor.

Answer: The configurations of RTA and RTB are as follows:

```
hostname RTA
!
interface Ethernet0
 ip address 192.168.1.1 255.255.255.0
!
interface Serial0
 ip address 192.168.2.1 255.255.255.0
!
interface Serial1
 ip address 192.168.3.1 255.255.255.0
!
interface Serial2
 ip address 192.168.4.1 255.255.255.0
!
autonomous-system 65531
!
router egp 0
 network 192.168.3.0
 neighbor 192.168.1.2
 neighbor any
 default-information originate
 distribute-list 1 out Ethernet0
!
access-list 1 deny    0.0.0.0
access-list 1 permit any
```

```
hostname RTB
!
interface Ethernet0
 ip address 192.168.1.2 255.255.255.0
!
interface Serial0
 ip address 192.168.5.1 255.255.255.0
!
autonomous-system 65531
!
router egp 0
 neighbor any
 default-information originate
 distribute-list 1 out Ethernet0
```

```
!
access-list 1 deny    0.0.0.0
access-list 1 permit any
```

2 Example 1-26 shows the route table of RTC in Figure 1-15.

Example 2-26 *The Route Table of RTC in Figure 1-15*

```
RTC#show ip route
Codes: C - connected, S - static, I - IGRP, R - RIP, M - mobile, B - BGP
       D - EIGRP, EX - EIGRP external, O - OSPF, IA - OSPF inter area
       E1 - OSPF external type 1, E2 - OSPF external type 2, E - EGP
       i - IS-IS, L1 - IS-IS level-1, L2 - IS-IS level-2, * - candidate default

Gateway of last resort is not set

I    192.168.105.0 [100/8976] via 192.168.6.2, 00:01:00, Serial1
I    192.168.110.0 [100/8976] via 192.168.6.2, 00:01:00, Serial1
I    192.168.100.0 [100/8976] via 192.168.10.2, 00:01:00, Serial2
I    192.168.120.0 [100/8976] via 192.168.10.2, 00:01:01, Serial2
C    192.168.2.0 is directly connected, Serial0
C    192.168.6.0 is directly connected, Serial1
C    192.168.10.0 is directly connected, Serial2
RTC#
```

Figure 1-15 *The Internetwork for Configuration Exercise 2*

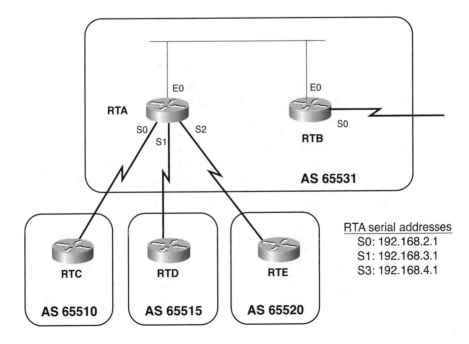

RTA serial addresses
S0: 192.168.2.1
S1: 192.168.3.1
S3: 192.168.4.1

Using redistribution, configure RTC to advertise all EGP-learned networks into AS 65510, and all internal networks except 192.168.105.0 to the core AS. Protect against route feedback by ensuring that none of the networks internal to AS 65510 are advertised back via EGP. The process ID in this configuration is the same as the local AS number.

Answer: The relevant configuration of RTC is as follows:

```
autonomous-system 65510
!
router igrp 65510
 redistribute egp 65531 metric 1544 100 255 1 1500
 network 192.168.6.0
!
router egp 65531
 redistribute igrp 65510
 neighbor 192.168.2.1
 distribute-list 10 out Serial0
 distribute-list 20 in Serial0
!
access-list 10 deny    192.168.105.0
access-list 10 permit any
access-list 20 deny    192.168.105.0
access-list 20 deny    192.168.110.0
access-list 20 deny    192.168.100.0
access-list 20 deny    192.168.120.0
access-list 20 deny    192.168.10.0
access-list 20 deny    192.168.6.0
access-list 20 permit any
```

Notice that no metric is specified for the redistribution into EGP; EGP adds a default metric of 3. In this example, the distribute-list command is used to filter routes, although a route map could also be used for the same purpose. Of particular interest is the filter that blocks internal network addresses if they are included in incoming EGP updates. Even though 192.168.105.0 is not being advertised out of the AS, the address is included in access list 20. This guards against the possibility of the network's finding its way into the EGP domain by some other means and then being routed back into AS 65510. It also guards against the possibility of a duplicate network address entering the AS.

3 Example 1-27 shows the route table of RTD in Figure 1-15.

Example 1-27 *The Route Table of RTD in Figure 1-15*

```
RTD#show ip route
Codes: C - connected, S - static, I - IGRP, R - RIP, M - mobile, B - BGP
       D - EIGRP, EX - EIGRP external, O - OSPF, IA - OSPF inter area
       E1 - OSPF external type 1, E2 - OSPF external type 2, E - EGP
       i - IS-IS, L1 - IS-IS level-1, L2 - IS-IS level-2, * - candidate default
```

Example 1-27 *The Route Table of RTD in Figure 1-15 (Continued)*

```
Gateway of last resort is not set

C    192.168.3.0 is directly connected, Serial0
C    192.168.7.0 is directly connected, Serial1
R    192.168.230.0 [120/1] via 192.168.7.2, 00:00:14, Serial1
R    192.168.200.0 [120/2] via 192.168.7.2, 00:00:15, Serial1
R    192.168.220.0 [120/1] via 192.168.7.2, 00:00:15, Serial1
R    192.168.210.0 [120/2] via 192.168.7.2, 00:00:15, Serial1
RTD#
```

Configure RTD with the following parameters:

— Only 192.168.220.0 and 192.168.230.0 are to be advertised to AS 65531.

— No routing protocol is redistributed into EGP.

— EGP is redistributed into the IGP of AS 65515.

— 192.168.3.0 is advertised into AS 65515 with a metric of 1.

— 192.168.100.0, from RTC, is advertised into AS 65515 with a metric of 1.

— 192.168.120.0, from RTC, is advertised into AS 65515 with a metric of 3.

— All other routes are advertised into AS 65515 with a metric of 5.

Answer: The relevant configuration of RTD is as follows:

```
autonomous-system 65515
!
router rip
 redistribute egp 65531 route-map EXTERNAL
 network 192.168.7.0
 network 192.168.3.0
 default-metric 5
!
router egp 65531
 network 192.168.220.0
 network 192.168.230.0
 neighbor 192.168.3.1
!
access-list 10 permit 192.168.100.0
access-list 20 permit 192.168.120.0
access-list 30 permit any
!
route-map EXTERNAL permit 10
 match ip address 10
 set metric 1
!
route-map EXTERNAL permit 20
 match ip address 20
 set metric 3
!
route-map EXTERNAL permit 30
 match ip address 30
```

4 Example 1-28 shows the route table of RTE in Figure 1-15.

Example 1-28 *The Route Table of RTE in Figure 1-15*

```
RTE#show ip route
Codes: C - connected, S - static, I - IGRP, R - RIP, M - mobile, B - BGP
       D - EIGRP, EX - EIGRP external, O - OSPF, IA - OSPF inter area
       N1 - OSPF NSSA external type 1, N2 - OSPF NSSA external type 2
       E1 - OSPF external type 1, E2 - OSPF external type 2, E - EGP
       i - IS-IS, L1 - IS-IS level-1, L2 - IS-IS level-2, * - candidate default
       U - per-user static route, o - ODR

Gateway of last resort is not set

O      192.168.125.0/28 [110/74] via 192.168.130.6, 00:01:03, Serial1
C      192.168.4.0/24 is directly connected, Serial0
       192.168.225.0/28 is subnetted, 1 subnets
O E2   192.168.225.160 [110/50] via 192.168.130.18, 00:01:04, Ethernet0
       192.168.215.0/24 is variably subnetted, 3 subnets, 3 masks
O         192.168.215.161/32 [110/65] via 192.168.130.6, 00:01:04, Serial1
O E2      192.168.215.192/26 [110/50] via 192.168.130.18, 00:01:04, Ethernet0
O E1      192.168.215.96/28 [110/164] via 192.168.130.6, 00:01:04, Serial1
       192.168.130.0/24 is variably subnetted, 7 subnets, 4 masks
D         192.168.131.192/27 [90/2195456] via 192.168.130.6, 00:16:49, Serial1
D         192.168.131.96/27 [90/409600] via 192.168.130.18, 00:16:49, Ethernet0
O         192.168.131.97/32 [110/11] via 192.168.130.18, 00:01:05, Ethernet0
D         192.168.131.64/27 [90/409600] via 192.168.130.18, 00:15:01, Ethernet0
D         192.168.131.8/30 [90/2195456] via 192.168.130.6, 00:16:49, Serial1
C         192.168.131.4/30 is directly connected, Serial1
C         192.168.131.16/28 is directly connected, Ethernet0
RTE#
```

Configure RTE with the following parameters:

— No IGP is redistributed into EGP.

— EGP is not redistributed into any IGP.

— All the internal networks of AS 65520 are advertised to AS 65531.

— The internal routers of AS 65520 can forward packets to any network advertised by RTA.

— All process IDs are the same as the AS number.

— All OSPF interfaces are in area 0.

Answer: The relevant configuration of RTE is as follows:

```
autonomous-system 65520
!
router eigrp 65520
 redistribute static
 network 192.168.130.0
```

```
 default-metric 1000 100 255 1 1500
 no auto-summary
!
router ospf 65520
 redistribute static metric 10 subnets
 network 192.168.130.4 0.0.0.3 area 0
 network 192.168.130.16 0.0.0.15 area 0
!
router egp 65531
 network 192.168.125.0
 network 192.168.131.0
 network 192.168.215.0
 network 192.168.225.0
 neighbor 192.168.4.1
!
ip route 0.0.0.0 0.0.0.0 192.168.4.1
```

5 In Figure 1-16, AS 65525 has been added to the internetwork of the previous
   exercises. RTF's Ethernet interface has an IP address of 192.168.1.3/24.

Figure 1-16 *The Internetwork for Configuration Exercise 5*

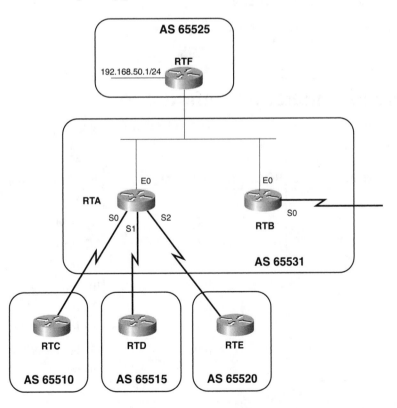

Configure this router to peer only with RTB, and make any necessary configuration changes to support third-party neighbors.

Answer: The configurations of RTF and RTB are as follows:

```
RTF
autonomous-system 65525
!
router egp 65531
 network 192.168.50.0
 neighbor 192.168.1.2
```

```
RTB
autonomous-system 65531
!
router egp 0
 neighbor 192.168.1.1
 neighbor 192.168.1.1 third-party 192.168.1.3 external
 neighbor 192.168.1.3
 neighbor 192.168.1.3 third-party 192.168.1.1
 neighbor any
 default-information originate
 distribute-list 1 out Ethernet0
!
access-list 1 deny   0.0.0.0
access-list 1 permit any
```

Answers to Chapter 3 Configuration Exercises

Table 3-4 shows the routers and addresses used for Configuration Exercises 1–13.

Table 3-4 *Routers/Addresses for Configuration Exercises 1–13*

Autonomous System	Router	Interface	IP Address/Mask
1	R1	L0	10.255.255.1/32
		S0	192.168.100.1/30
		E0	192.168.100.5/30
		E1	192.168.100.13/30
	R2	L0	10.255.255.2/32
		S0	192.168.100.9/30
		S1	192.168.100.57/30
		E0	192.168.100.6/30
		E1	192.168.100.17/30

Table 3-4   *Routers/Addresses for Configuration Exercises 1–13 (Continued)*

Autonomous System	Router	Interface	IP Address/Mask
1 *(continued)*	R3	L0	10.255.255.3/32
		S0	192.168.100.25/30
		E0	192.168.100.18/30
		E1	192.168.100.21/30
	R4	L0	10.255.255.4/32
		S0	192.168.100.29/30
		S1	192.168.100.33/30
		E0	192.168.100.22/30
		E1	192.168.100.14/30
2	R5	S0	192.168.100.2 /30
		E0	192.168.1.129/26
	R6	S0	192.168.100.10/30
		E0	192.168.1.130/26
3	R7	L0	10.255.255.7/32
		S0	192.168.100.26/30
		S1	192.168.100.41/30
		E0	192.168.100.37/30
		E1	172.16.1.1/24
4	R8	L0	10.255.255.8/32
		S0	192.168.100.30/30
		S1	192.168.100.45/30
		E0	192.168.100.38/30
		E1	172.16.2.1/24

continues

Table 3-4   *Routers/Addresses for Configuration Exercises 1–13 (Continued)*

Autonomous System	Router	Interface	IP Address/Mask
5	R9	L0	10.255.255.9/32
		S0	192.168.100.42/30
		E0	192.168.9.1/24
		E1	192.168.150.1/24
	R10	L0	10.255.255.10/32
		S0	192.168.100.46/30
		E0	192.168.10.1/24
		E1	192.168.100.53/30
		E2	192.168.150.2/24
	R11	L0	10.255.255.11/32
		S0	192.168.100.34/30
		E0	192.168.100.54/30
		E1	192.168.11.1/24
6	R12	L0	192.168.255.1/32
		S0	192.168.100.58/30
		E0	192.168.16.83/27

Table 3-4 lists the autonomous systems, routers, interfaces, and addresses used in Configuration Exercises 1–13. All interfaces of the routers are shown. For each exercise, if the table indicates that the router has a loopback interface, that interface should be the source of all IBGP connections. EBGP connections should always be between physical interface addresses unless otherwise specified in the exercise. Hint: Draw the internetwork, based on the subnets listed in the table, before attempting the exercises.

1   AS 1 in Table 3-4 is a transit AS, and the IGP is OSPF. Area 0 spans the entire AS. No networks internal to the AS are advertised outside of the AS. None of the subnets over which EBGP are run should be advertised into AS 1. Write BGP configurations for the routers in AS 1, putting all internal neighbors in a peer group called LOCAL. For R3 only, EBGP peering should be performed between loopback interfaces. Authenticate all IBGP connections with the password **ExeRCise1**.

Answer:

R1

```
router ospf 1
 network 10.255.255.1 0.0.0.0 area 0
 network 192.168.100.5 0.0.0.0 area 0
 network 192.168.100.13 0.0.0.0 area 0
!
router bgp 1
 neighbor LOCAL peer-group
 neighbor LOCAL remote-as 1
 neighbor LOCAL password 7 15371309360922372D62
 neighbor LOCAL update-source Loopback0
 neighbor LOCAL next-hop-self
 neighbor 10.255.255.2 peer-group LOCAL
 neighbor 10.255.255.3 peer-group LOCAL
 neighbor 10.255.255.4 peer-group LOCAL
 neighbor 192.168.100.2 remote-as 2
```

R2

```
router ospf 1
 network 10.255.255.2 0.0.0.0 area 0
 network 192.168.100.6 0.0.0.0 area 0
 network 192.168.100.17 0.0.0.0 area 0
!
router bgp 1
 neighbor LOCAL peer-group
 neighbor LOCAL remote-as 1
 neighbor LOCAL password 7 15371309360922372D62
 neighbor LOCAL update-source Loopback0
 neighbor LOCAL next-hop-self
 neighbor 10.255.255.1 peer-group LOCAL
 neighbor 10.255.255.3 peer-group LOCAL
 neighbor 10.255.255.4 peer-group LOCAL
 neighbor 192.168.100.10 remote-as 2
 neighbor 192.168.100.58 remote-as 6
```

R3

```
router ospf 1
 network 10.255.255.3 0.0.0.0 area 0
 network 192.168.100.18 0.0.0.0 area 0
 network 192.168.100.21 0.0.0.0 area 0
!
router bgp 1
 neighbor LOCAL peer-group
 neighbor LOCAL remote-as 1
 neighbor LOCAL password 7 15371309360922372D62
 neighbor LOCAL update-source Loopback0
 neighbor LOCAL next-hop-self
 neighbor REMOTE peer-group
 neighbor REMOTE ebgp-multihop 2
 neighbor REMOTE update-source Loopback0
```

continues

(Continued)
```
  neighbor 10.255.255.1 peer-group LOCAL
  neighbor 10.255.255.2 peer-group LOCAL
  neighbor 10.255.255.4 peer-group LOCAL
  neighbor 192.168.100.26 peer-group REMOTE
  neighbor 192.168.100.26 remote-as 3
```

R4
```
router ospf 1
  network 10.255.255.4 0.0.0.0 area 0
  network 192.168.100.14 0.0.0.0 area 0
  network 192.168.100.22 0.0.0.0 area 0
!
router bgp 1
  neighbor LOCAL peer-group
  neighbor LOCAL remote-as 1
  neighbor LOCAL password 7 15371309360922372D62
  neighbor LOCAL update-source Loopback0
  neighbor LOCAL next-hop-self
  neighbor 10.255.255.1 peer-group LOCAL
  neighbor 10.255.255.2 peer-group LOCAL
  neighbor 10.255.255.4 peer-group LOCAL
  neighbor 192.168.100.30 remote-as 4
  neighbor 192.168.100.34 remote-as 5
```

2 AS 2 in Table 3-4 is a stub (nontransit) AS, and its IGP is EIGRP. Configure the
   routers in AS 2 to speak EBGP to any external peers and to redistribute any EIGRP
   routes into BGP. Redistribute BGP-learned routes into EIGRP. Implement any
   necessary filters to prevent incorrect routes from being redistributed.

   Answer:

R5
```
router eigrp 2
  redistribute bgp 2 route-map External_Routes metric 10000 100 255 1 1500
  passive-interface Serial0
  network 192.168.1.0
  network 192.168.100.0
  no auto-summary
!
router bgp 2
  redistribute eigrp 2 route-map Internal_Routes
  neighbor 192.168.100.1 remote-as 1
!
ip as-path access-list 1 deny _2_
ip as-path access-list 1 permit .*
ip as-path access-list 2 permit ^$
!
route-map External_Routes permit 10
  match as-path 1
!
```

```
route-map Internal_Routes permit 10
 match as-path 2
```

R6
```
router eigrp 2
 redistribute bgp 2 route-map External_Routes metric 10000 100 255 1 1500
 passive-interface Serial0
 network 192.168.1.0
 network 192.168.100.0
 no auto-summary
!
router bgp 2
 redistribute eigrp 2 route-map Internal_Routes
 neighbor 192.168.100.9 remote-as 1
!
ip as-path access-list 1 deny _2_
ip as-path access-list 1 permit .*
ip as-path access-list 2 permit ^$
!
route-map External_Routes permit 10
 match as-path 1
!
route-map Internal_Routes permit 10
 match as-path 2
```

3 Networks 192.168.1.0, 192.168.2.0, 192.168.3.0, 192.168.4.0, and 192.168.5.0 exist
within AS 2. The administrator of this AS wants the neighboring AS to prefer R5 when
sending traffic to 192.168.1.0 and 192.168.3.0. The neighboring AS should prefer R6
when sending traffic to 192.168.2.0 and 192.168.4.0. In each case, the less-preferred
link serves as a backup to the more-preferred link. 192.168.5.0 is a private network
and must not be advertised to any EBGP peer. Modify the configurations written in
Exercise 2 to implement this policy.

**Answer: Note that in these configurations, the AS_PATH filters from Exercise 2
remain. Although not entirely necessary due to the access lists filtering specific
prefixes, in a real network they can act as an extra bit of insurance against the
wrong routes being advertised.**

R5
```
router eigrp 2
 redistribute bgp 2 route-map External_Routes metric 10000 100 255 1 1500
 passive-interface Serial0
 network 192.168.1.0
 network 192.168.100.0
 no auto-summary
!
router bgp 2
 redistribute eigrp 2 route-map Internal_Routes
 neighbor 192.168.100.1 remote-as 1
!
```

continues

(Continued)

```
ip as-path access-list 1 deny _2_
ip as-path access-list 1 permit .*
ip as-path access-list 2 permit ^$
!
access-list 1 permit 192.168.1.0
access-list 1 permit 192.168.3.0
access-list 2 permit 192.168.2.0
access-list 2 permit 192.168.4.0
!
route-map External_Routes permit 10
 match as-path 1
!
route-map Internal_Routes permit 10
 match ip address 1
 match as-path 2
 set metric 50
!
route-map Internal_Routes permit 20
 match ip address 2
 match as-path 2
 set metric 150
```

R6

```
router eigrp 2
 redistribute bgp 2 route-map External_Routes metric 10000 100 255 1 1500
 passive-interface Serial0
 network 192.168.1.0
 network 192.168.100.0
 no auto-summary
!
router bgp 2
 redistribute eigrp 2 route-map Internal_Routes
 neighbor 192.168.100.9 remote-as 1
!
ip as-path access-list 1 deny _2_
ip as-path access-list 1 permit .*
ip as-path access-list 2 permit ^$
!
access-list 1 permit 192.168.2.0
access-list 1 permit 192.168.4.0
access-list 2 permit 192.168.1.0
access-list 2 permit 192.168.3.0
!
route-map External_Routes permit 10
 match as-path 1
!
route-map Internal_Routes permit 10
 match ip address 1
 match as-path 2
 set metric 50
!
route-map Internal_Routes permit 20
```

```
match ip address 2
match as-path 2
set metric 150
```

4 Configure the EBGP neighbors of R5 and R6 to advertise a default route to AS 2. No other routes are to be advertised.

Answer:

```
R1
router ospf 1
 network 10.255.255.1 0.0.0.0 area 0
 network 192.168.100.5 0.0.0.0 area 0
 network 192.168.100.13 0.0.0.0 area 0
!
router bgp 1
 neighbor LOCAL peer-group
 neighbor LOCAL remote-as 1
 neighbor LOCAL password 7 15371309360922372D62
 neighbor LOCAL update-source Loopback0
 neighbor LOCAL next-hop-self
 neighbor 10.255.255.2 peer-group LOCAL
 neighbor 10.255.255.3 peer-group LOCAL
 neighbor 10.255.255.4 peer-group LOCAL
 neighbor 192.168.100.2 remote-as 2
 neighbor 192.168.100.2 default-originate
 neighbor 192.168.100.2 distribute-list 1 out
!
access-list 1 permit 0.0.0.0
access-list 1 deny any
```

```
R2
router ospf 1
 network 10.255.255.2 0.0.0.0 area 0
 network 192.168.100.6 0.0.0.0 area 0
 network 192.168.100.17 0.0.0.0 area 0
!
router bgp 1
 neighbor LOCAL peer-group
 neighbor LOCAL remote-as 1
 neighbor LOCAL password 7 15371309360922372D62
 neighbor LOCAL update-source Loopback0
 neighbor LOCAL next-hop-self
 neighbor 10.255.255.1 peer-group LOCAL
 neighbor 10.255.255.3 peer-group LOCAL
 neighbor 10.255.255.4 peer-group LOCAL
 neighbor 192.168.100.10 remote-as 2
 neighbor 192.168.100.10 default-originate
 neighbor 192.168.100.10 distribute-list 1 out
 neighbor 192.168.100.58 remote-as 6
!
access-list 1 permit 0.0.0.0
access-list 1 deny any
```

5 The administrator of AS 2's neighboring AS disagrees with part of the policy set in Exercise 2. He wants all routers in his AS to send traffic destined for 192.168.3.0 to R6, with R5 as a backup. All traffic destined for 192.168.4.0 should be sent to R5, with R6 as a backup. The rest of the policy set in Exercise 2 is acceptable. Write configurations to implement this policy.

Answer: Remember that LOCAL_PREF is considered ahead of MED in the BGP decision process. Therefore, changing the default LOCAL_PREF attributes of the appropriate routes on the appropriate routers in AS 2 overrides the routes' MEDs.

```
R1
router bgp 1
 neighbor LOCAL peer-group
 neighbor LOCAL remote-as 1
 neighbor LOCAL password 7 15371309360922372D62
 neighbor LOCAL update-source Loopback0
 neighbor LOCAL next-hop-self
 neighbor 10.255.255.2 peer-group LOCAL
 neighbor 10.255.255.3 peer-group LOCAL
 neighbor 10.255.255.4 peer-group LOCAL
 neighbor 192.168.100.2 remote-as 2
 neighbor 192.168.100.2 route-map SET_PREF in
 neighbor 192.168.100.2 default-originate
 neighbor 192.168.100.2 distribute-list 1 out
!
access-list 1 permit 0.0.0.0
access-list 1 deny any
access-list 2 permit 192.168.4.0
access-list 2 deny any
!
route-map SET_PREF permit 10
 match ip address 2
 set local-preference 200
!
route-map SET_PREF permit 20
```

```
R2
router bgp 1
 neighbor LOCAL peer-group
 neighbor LOCAL remote-as 1
 neighbor LOCAL password 7 15371309360922372D62
 neighbor LOCAL update-source Loopback0
 neighbor LOCAL next-hop-self
 neighbor 10.255.255.1 peer-group LOCAL
 neighbor 10.255.255.3 peer-group LOCAL
 neighbor 10.255.255.4 peer-group LOCAL
 neighbor 192.168.100.10 remote-as 2
 neighbor 192.168.100.10 route-map SET_PREF in
 neighbor 192.168.100.10 default-originate
```

```
 neighbor 192.168.100.10 distribute-list 1 out
 neighbor 192.168.100.58 remote-as 6
!
access-list 1 permit 0.0.0.0
access-list 1 deny any
access-list 2 permit 192.168.3.0
access-list 2 deny any
!
route-map SET_PREF permit 10
 match ip address 2
 set local-preference 200
!
route-map SET_PREF permit 20
```

6 AS 3 in Table 3-4 is a stub AS, and AS 4 is a transit AS. The IGP of both autonomous systems is OSPF, and the internal interfaces of R7 and R8 are both in area 0. Write BGP and OSPF configurations for R7 and R8, advertise the internal addresses shown in Table 3-5 to all EBGP peers, and ensure that routers in the OSPF domains can reach any external destination. Do not redistribute routes in either direction. Also, ensure that the BGP router ID of R7 is 192.168.3.254.

Answer: The route-map STUB at R7 prevents routes received from an EBGP peer from being advertised to other EBGP peers, thus making the AS nontransit. R8 has no such route filter, so AS 4 is a transit AS.

```
R7
router ospf 3
 network 10.255.255.7 0.0.0.0 area 0
 network 172.16.1.1 0.0.0.0 area 0
 default-information originate
!
router bgp 3
 bgp router-id 192.168.3.254
 network 172.16.1.0 mask 255.255.255.0
 network 172.16.3.0 mask 255.255.255.0
 network 172.17.0.0
 network 192.168.6.128 mask 255.255.255.128
 neighbor 192.168.100.25 remote-as 1
 neighbor 192.168.100.25 ebgp-multihop 2
 neighbor 192.168.100.25 update-source Loopback0
 neighbor 192.168.100.25 route-map STUB out
 neighbor 192.168.100.38 remote-as 4
 neighbor 192.168.100.38 route-map STUB out
 neighbor 192.168.100.42 remote-as 5
 neighbor 192.168.100.42 route-map STUB out
 no auto-summary
!
ip route 0.0.0.0 0.0.0.0 Null0
!
```

continues

(Continued)
```
ip as-path access-list 1 permit ^$
!
route-map STUB permit 10
 match as-path 1
```

R8
```
router ospf 4
 network 10.255.255.8 0.0.0.0 area 0
 network 172.16.2.1 0.0.0.0 area 0
 default-information originate
!
router bgp 4
 network 172.16.2.0 mask 255.255.255.0
 network 172.16.4.0 mask 255.255.255.0
 network 172.18.0.0
 network 192.168.6.0 mask 255.255.255.128
 neighbor 192.168.100.29 remote-as 1
 neighbor 192.168.100.37 remote-as 3
 neighbor 192.168.100.46 remote-as 5
 no auto-summary
!
ip route 0.0.0.0 0.0.0.0 Null0
```

Table 3-5   *Destinations Internal to AS 3 and AS 4*

AS 3	AS 4
172.16.1.0/24	172.16.2.0/24
172.16.3.0/24	172.16.4.0/24
172.17.0.0/16	172.18.0.0/16
192.168.6.128/25	192.168.6.0/25

7 Modify the configurations of Exercise 6 so that R7 and R8 speak OSPF across the link directly connecting them; remove BGP from the link. Traffic between subnets 172.16.3.0/24 and 172.16.4.0/24 should prefer this direct link and should use any EBGP links only as backup. Traffic between the other addresses internal to AS 3 and AS 4 should use the EBGP links and should use the direct link only as backup. Additionally, traffic from other autonomous systems can use the direct link as a backup route. If an EBGP link to AS 4 fails, for example, the neighboring AS can send traffic destined for AS 4 to AS 3, to be forwarded to AS4 across the direct link.

Answer:

R7
```
router ospf 3
 network 10.255.255.7 0.0.0.0 area 0
 network 172.16.1.1 0.0.0.0 area 0
```

```
    network 192.168.100.37 0.0.0.0 area 0
    default-information originate
!
router bgp 3
 bgp router-id 192.168.3.254
 network 172.16.1.0 mask 255.255.255.0
 network 172.16.3.0 mask 255.255.255.0 backdoor
 network 172.17.0.0
 network 192.168.6.128 mask 255.255.255.128
 neighbor 192.168.100.25 remote-as 1
 neighbor 192.168.100.25 ebgp-multihop 2
 neighbor 192.168.100.25 update-source Loopback0
 neighbor 192.168.100.25 route-map STUB out
 neighbor 192.168.100.42 remote-as 5
 neighbor 192.168.100.42 route-map STUB out
 no auto-summary
!
ip route 0.0.0.0 0.0.0.0 Null0
!
ip as-path access-list 1 permit ^$
!
route-map STUB permit 10
 match as-path 1
```

R8
```
router ospf 4
 network 10.255.255.8 0.0.0.0 area 0
 network 172.16.2.1 0.0.0.0 area 0
 network 192.168.100.38 0.0.0.0 area 0
 default-information originate
!
router bgp 4
 network 172.16.2.0 mask 255.255.255.0
 network 172.16.4.0 mask 255.255.255.0 backdoor
 network 172.18.0.0
 network 192.168.6.0 mask 255.255.255.128
 neighbor 192.168.100.29 remote-as 1
 neighbor 192.168.100.46 remote-as 5
 no auto-summary
!
ip route 0.0.0.0 0.0.0.0 Null0
```

8 AS 5 in Table 3-4 is a transit AS, and its IGP is IS-IS. The Level 2 area 47.0001 spans the entire AS. The internal networks are 192.168.9.0, 192.168.10.0, 192.168.11.0, and 192.168.12.0. Write IS-IS and BGP configurations for R9, R10, and R11. Ensure that all external routes are known by the routers in the IS-IS domain and that all internal networks are advertised to all EBGP peers. Do not redistribute IS-IS routes into BGP.

Answer: These configurations use next-hop-self, although alternatively you could run IS-IS in passive mode on the external interfaces.

```
R9
router isis
 net 47.0001.0000.1234.abcd.00
 is-type level-2-only
 redistribute bgp 5 metric 0 metric-type external level-2
!
router bgp 5
 network 192.168.9.0
 network 192.168.10.0
 network 192.168.11.0
 network 192.168.12.0
 neighbor LOCAL peer-group
 neighbor LOCAL remote-as 5
 neighbor LOCAL update-source Loopback0
 neighbor LOCAL next-hop-self
 neighbor 10.255.255.10 peer-group LOCAL
 neighbor 10.255.255.11 peer-group LOCAL
 neighbor 192.168.100.41 remote-as 3
```

```
R10
router isis
 net 47.0001.0000.5678.ef01.00
 is-type level-2-only
 redistribute bgp 5 metric 0 metric-type external level-2
!
router bgp 5
 network 192.168.9.0
 network 192.168.10.0
 network 192.168.11.0
 network 192.168.12.0
 neighbor LOCAL peer-group
 neighbor LOCAL remote-as 5
 neighbor LOCAL update-source Loopback0
 neighbor LOCAL next-hop-self
 neighbor 10.255.255.9 peer-group LOCAL
 neighbor 10.255.255.11 peer-group LOCAL
 neighbor 192.168.100.45 remote-as 4
```

```
R11
router isis
 net 47.0001.0000.4321.dcba.00
 is-type level-2-only
 redistribute bgp 5 metric 0 metric-type external level-2
!
router bgp 5
 network 192.168.9.0
 network 192.168.10.0
 network 192.168.11.0
 network 192.168.12.0
 neighbor LOCAL peer-group
 neighbor LOCAL remote-as 5
 neighbor LOCAL update-source Loopback0
```

```
 neighbor LOCAL next-hop-self
 neighbor 10.255.255.9 peer-group LOCAL
 neighbor 10.255.255.10 peer-group LOCAL
 neighbor 192.168.100.33 remote-as 1
```

9 Modify the configurations written in Exercise 8 so that network 192.168.12.0 is known only by AS 4, and no other autonomous system.

Answer: The network statement for 192.168.12.0 is removed from the configurations of R9 and R11 so that they do not advertise that network. At R10, the NO_EXPORT community is added to the route to 192.168.12.0 so that it is not advertised beyond AS 4.

R9
```
router isis
 net 47.0001.0000.1234.abcd.00
 is-type level-2-only
 redistribute bgp 5 metric 0 metric-type external level-2
!
router bgp 5
 network 192.168.9.0
 network 192.168.10.0
 network 192.168.11.0
 neighbor LOCAL peer-group
 neighbor LOCAL remote-as 5
 neighbor LOCAL update-source Loopback0
 neighbor LOCAL next-hop-self
 neighbor 10.255.255.10 peer-group LOCAL
 neighbor 10.255.255.11 peer-group LOCAL
 neighbor 192.168.100.41 remote-as 3
```

R10
```
router isis
 net 47.0001.0000.5678.ef01.00
 is-type level-2-only
 redistribute bgp 5 metric 0 metric-type external level-2
!
router bgp 5
 network 192.168.9.0
 network 192.168.10.0
 network 192.168.11.0
 network 192.168.12.0
 neighbor LOCAL peer-group
 neighbor LOCAL remote-as 5
 neighbor LOCAL update-source Loopback0
 neighbor LOCAL next-hop-self
 neighbor 10.255.255.9 peer-group LOCAL
 neighbor 10.255.255.11 peer-group LOCAL
 neighbor 192.168.100.45 remote-as 4
```

continues

(Continued)

```
 neighbor 192.168.100.45 send-community
 neighbor 192.168.100.45 route-map EXPORT_COMMUNITY out
!
access-list 1 permit 192.168.12.0
!
route-map EXPORT_COMMUNITY permit 10
 match ip address 1
 set community no-export
!
route-map EXPORT_COMMUNITY permit 20
```

R11
```
router isis
 net 47.0001.0000.4321.dcba.00
 is-type level-2-only
 redistribute bgp 5 metric 0 metric-type external level-2
!
router bgp 5
 network 192.168.9.0
 network 192.168.10.0
 network 192.168.11.0
 neighbor LOCAL peer-group
 neighbor LOCAL remote-as 5
 neighbor LOCAL update-source Loopback0
 neighbor LOCAL next-hop-self
 neighbor 10.255.255.9 peer-group LOCAL
 neighbor 10.255.255.10 peer-group LOCAL
 neighbor 192.168.100.33 remote-as 1
```

10 Modify the configurations written in Exercise 9 so that AS 3 and AS 4 prefer the path through AS 1 to reach network 192.168.11.0.

Answer: Network 192.168.11.0 is advertised normally by R11 but is prepended by R9 and R10.

R9
```
router isis
 net 47.0001.0000.1234.abcd.00
 is-type level-2-only
 redistribute bgp 5 metric 0 metric-type external level-2
!
router bgp 5
 network 192.168.9.0
 network 192.168.10.0
 network 192.168.11.0
 neighbor LOCAL peer-group
 neighbor LOCAL remote-as 5
 neighbor LOCAL update-source Loopback0
 neighbor LOCAL next-hop-self
 neighbor 10.255.255.10 peer-group LOCAL
```

```
 neighbor 10.255.255.11 peer-group LOCAL
 neighbor 192.168.100.41 remote-as 3
 neighbor 192.168.100.41 route-map PREPEND out
!
access-list 1 permit 192.168.11.0
!
route-map PREPEND permit 10
 match ip address 1
 set as-path prepend 5 5
!
route-map PATH permit 20
```

R10
```
router isis
 net 47.0001.0000.5678.ef01.00
 is-type level-2-only
 redistribute bgp 5 metric 0 metric-type external level-2
!
router bgp 5
 network 192.168.9.0
 network 192.168.10.0
 network 192.168.11.0
 network 192.168.12.0
 neighbor LOCAL peer-group
 neighbor LOCAL remote-as 5
 neighbor LOCAL update-source Loopback0
 neighbor LOCAL next-hop-self
 neighbor 10.255.255.9 peer-group LOCAL
 neighbor 10.255.255.11 peer-group LOCAL
 neighbor 192.168.100.45 remote-as 4
 neighbor 192.168.100.45 send-community
 neighbor 192.168.100.45 route-map EXPORT_COMMUNITY out
!
access-list 1 permit 192.168.12.0
access-list 2 permit 192.168.11.0
!
route-map EXPORT_COMMUNITY permit 10
 match ip address 1
 set community no-export
!
route-map EXPORT_COMMUNITY permit 20
 match ip address 1
 set as-path prepend 5 5
!
route-map EXPORT_COMMUNITY permit 30
```

R11
```
router isis
 net 47.0001.0000.4321.dcba.00
 is-type level-2-only
 redistribute bgp 5 metric 0 metric-type external level-2
!
```

continues

(Continued)

```
router bgp 5
 network 192.168.9.0
 network 192.168.10.0
 network 192.168.11.0
 neighbor LOCAL peer-group
 neighbor LOCAL remote-as 5
 neighbor LOCAL update-source Loopback0
 neighbor LOCAL next-hop-self
 neighbor 10.255.255.9 peer-group LOCAL
 neighbor 10.255.255.10 peer-group LOCAL
 neighbor 192.168.100.33 remote-as 1
```

11 The networks internal to AS 6 in Table 3-4 are 192.168.16.0, 192.168.17.0, 192.168.18.0, and 192.168.19.0. Write a BGP configuration for R12 that advertises these networks to the neighboring AS and that also advertises a summary route for the networks. The neighboring AS should advertise only the summary to other autonomous systems.

Answer:

```
router bgp 6
 network 192.168.16.0
 network 192.168.17.0
 network 192.168.18.0
 network 192.168.19.0
 aggregate-address 192.168.16.0 255.255.252.0
 neighbor 192.168.100.57 remote-as 1
 neighbor 192.168.100.57 send-community
 neighbor 192.168.100.57 route-map AGGREGATE out
!
access-list 101 permit ip host 192.168.16.0 host 255.255.252.0
!
route-map AGGREGATE permit 10
 match ip address 101
 set community none
!
route-map AGGREGATE permit 20
 set community no-export
```

12 Modify the most recent configuration you wrote for R12's EBGP neighbor so that the neighbor does not accept prefixes that do not belong to the aggregate being advertised by R12, does not accept prefixes longer than 24 bits, and does not accept more than five prefixes.

Answer:

```
R2
router bgp 1
 neighbor LOCAL peer-group
 neighbor LOCAL remote-as 1
 neighbor LOCAL password 7 15371309360922372D62
 neighbor LOCAL update-source Loopback0
 neighbor LOCAL next-hop-self
 neighbor 10.255.255.1 peer-group LOCAL
 neighbor 10.255.255.3 peer-group LOCAL
 neighbor 10.255.255.4 peer-group LOCAL
 neighbor 192.168.100.10 remote-as 2
 neighbor 192.168.100.10 route-map SET_PREF in
 neighbor 192.168.100.10 default-originate
 neighbor 192.168.100.10 distribute-list 1 out
 neighbor 192.168.100.58 remote-as 6
 neighbor 192.168.100.58 maximum-prefix 5
 neighbor 192.168.100.58 route-map PREFIX_LIMIT in
!
access-list 1 permit 0.0.0.0
access-list 1 deny any
access-list 2 permit 192.168.3.0
access-list 2 deny any
!
ip prefix-list AS6 seq 5 permit 192.168.16.0/22 le 24
!
route-map SET_PREF permit 10
 match ip address 2
 set local-preference 200
!
route-map SET_PREF permit 20
!
route-map PREFIX_LIMIT permit 10
 match ip address prefix-list AS6
```

13 Example 3-164 shows a BGP configuration for R7 in Table 3-4. The internal prefixes shown in Table 3-5 are advertised by OSPF.

Example 3-164 *BGP Configuration of Router R7*

```
router bgp 3
 redistribute ospf 1
 neighbor NEIGHBORS peer-group
 neighbor NEIGHBORS ebgp-multihop 2
 neighbor NEIGHBORS update-source Loopback0
 neighbor NEIGHBORS route-map EX13 out
 neighbor 10.255.255.8 remote-as 4
 neighbor 10.255.255.8 peer-group NEIGHBORS
 neighbor 10.255.255.9 remote-as 5
```

continues

Example 3-164 *BGP Configuration of Router R7 (Continued)*

```
 neighbor 10.255.255.9 peer-group NEIGHBORS
 neighbor 10.255.255.3 remote-as 1
 neighbor 10.255.255.3 peer-group NEIGHBORS
 no auto-summary
!
ip classless
ip as-path access-list 1 permit ^1 2$
!
access-list 1 permit 172.16.1.0
access-list 2 permit 172.16.3.0
!
route-map EX13 permit 10
 match ip address 1
 set as-path prepend 2
!
route-map EX13 permit 20
 match ip address 2
 set as-path prepend 1
!
route-map EX13 permit 30
 match as-path 1
 set as-path prepend 4 5
!
route-map EX13 deny 40
```

Explain the effects of route map EX13.

Answer: Term 10 of the route map matches prefix 172.16.1.0 and prepends 2 to the AS_PATH. As a result, routers in AS 2 will reject the prefix. Term 20 matches prefix 172.16.2.0 and prepends 1 to the AS_PATH, so the route is rejected by routers in AS 1. Term 30 matches routes that have an AS_PATH of [1, 2], meaning routes that are originated in AS 2 and have been advertised by AS 1. That term prepends 4 and 5 to the AS_PATH of these routes, so they are rejected by AS 4 and AS 5. Term 40 suppresses the advertisement of any other routes.

14 Router R1 in Figure 3-36 is a route reflector for routers R2, R3, and R4 and is connected to those neighbors via Frame Relay PVCs. Write a BGP configuration for R1 that provides full connectivity for the networks attached to the four routers. The cluster ID is 6500.

Figure 3-36 *The Route Reflection Cluster for Configuration Exercise 14*

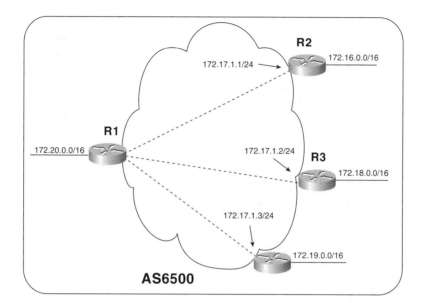

Answer:

```
router bgp 6500
 no synchronization
 bgp cluster-id 6500
 network 172.20.0.0
 neighbor 172.16.1.1 remote-as 6500
 neighbor 172.16.1.1 route-reflector-client
 neighbor 172.16.1.2 remote-as 6500
 neighbor 172.16.1.2 route-reflector-client
 neighbor 172.16.1.3 remote-as 6500
 neighbor 172.16.1.3 route-reflector-client
```

Answers to Chapter 4 Configuration Exercises

Refer to Figure 4-28 for Configuration Exercises 1–5.

Figure 4-28 *The Internetwork for Configuration Exercises 1–5*

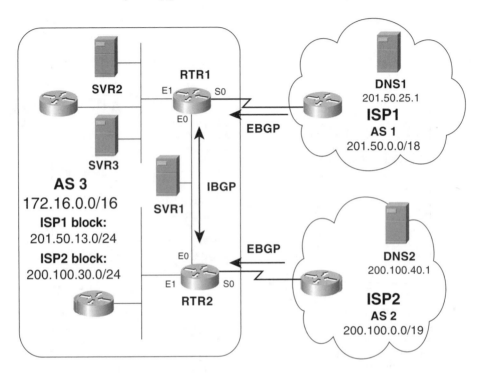

1 ISP1 in Figure 4-28 has assigned the address block 201.50.13.0/24 to AS 3. ISP2 has assigned the address block 200.100.30.0/24 to AS 3. RTR1 and RTR2 are accepting full BGP routes from the ISP routers but do not transmit any routes to the ISPs. They run IBGP between them and OSPF on all Ethernet interfaces. No routes are redistributed between BGP and OSPF. The addresses of the router interfaces are as follows:

RTR1, E0: 172.16.3.1/24

RTR1, E1: 172.16.2.1/24

RTR1, S0: 201.50.26.13/30

RTR2, E0: 172.16.3.2/24

RTR2, E1: 172.16.1.1/24

RTR2, S0: 200.100.29.241/30

SVR1 is the DNS server authoritative for AS 3; its address is 172.16.3.3. DNS1 reaches SVR1 at 201.50.13.1, whereas DNS2 reaches the same server at 200.100.30.254. Write routing and NAT configurations for RTR1 and RTR2, translating inside addresses appropriately for each ISP's assigned address block. Any inside device must be able to reach either ISP, but no packets can leave AS 3 with a private source address under any circumstance.

Answer:

```
RTR1
interface Loopback0
 ip address 172.16.255.2 255.255.255.255
!
interface Ethernet0
 ip address 172.16.3.1 255.255.255.0
 ip nat inside
!
interface Ethernet1
 ip address 172.16.2.1 255.255.255.0
 ip nat inside
!
interface Serial0
 description to ISP1
 ip address 201.50.26.13 255.255.255.252
 ip access-group 101 out
 ip nat outside
!
autonomous-system 3
!
router ospf 1
 redistribute static
 network 172.16.0.0 0.0.255.255 area 0
 default-information originate
!
router bgp 3
 neighbor 172.16.255.1 remote-as 3
 neighbor 172.16.255.1 update-source Loopback0
 neighbor 201.50.26.14 remote-as 1
!
ip nat pool ISP1Pool 201.50.13.2 201.50.13.254 netmask 255.255.255.0
ip nat inside source list 1 pool ISP1Pool
ip nat inside source static 172.16.3.3 201.50.13.1
!
ip route 0.0.0.0 0.0.0.0 201.50.26.14
ip route 201.50.0.0 255.255.192.0 201.50.26.14
!
access-list 1 permit 172.16.0.0 0.0.255.255
access-list 101 deny    ip 172.16.0.0 0.0.255.255 any
access-list 101 permit ip any any
```

```
RTR2
interface Loopback0
 ip address 172.16.255.1 255.255.255.255
!
```

continues

(Continued)

```
interface Ethernet0
 ip address 172.16.3.2 255.255.255.0
 ip nat inside
!
interface Ethernet1
 ip address 172.16.1.1 255.255.255.0
 ip nat inside

!
interface Serial0
 description to ISP2
 ip address 200.100.29.241 255.255.255.252
 ip access-group 101 out
 ip nat outside
!
autonomous-system 3
!
router ospf 1
 redistribute static
 network 172.16.0.0 0.0.255.255 area 0
 default-information originate
!
router bgp 3
 neighbor 172.16.255.2 remote-as 3
 neighbor 172.16.255.2 update-source Loopback0
 neighbor 200.100.29.242 remote-as 2
!
ip nat pool ISP2Pool 200.100.30.1 200.100.30.253 netmask 255.255.255.0
ip nat inside source list 1 pool ISP2Pool
ip nat inside source static 172.16.3.3 200.100.30.254
!
ip route 0.0.0.0 0.0.0.0 200.100.29.242
ip route 200.100.0.0 255.255.224.0 200.100.29.242
!
access-list 1 permit 172.16.0.0 0.0.255.255
access-list 101 deny ip 172.16.0.0 0.0.255.255 any
access-list 101 permit ip any any
```

2 The address of SVR2 in Figure 4-28 is 172.16.2.2, and the address of SVR3 is 172.16.2.3. Modify the configurations of Configuration Exercise 1 so that devices within ISP1's AS connect to the servers' round-robin at the address 201.50.13.3.

Answer: Notice that in addition to the new commands, ISP1Pool has been modified to no longer include the address 201.50.13.3.

```
RTR1
ip nat pool ISP1Pool 201.50.13.4 201.50.13.254 netmask 255.255.255.0
ip nat pool SVRs 172.16.2.2 172.16.2.3 netmask 255.255.0.0 type rotary
ip nat inside source list 1 pool ISP1Pool
ip nat inside source static 172.16.3.3 201.50.13.1
```

```
ip nat inside destination list 2 pool SVRs
!
access-list 1 permit 172.16.0.0 0.0.255.255
access-list 2 permit 201.50.13.3
```

3 HTTP packets sent to 200.100.30.50 from ISP2 are sent to SVR2 in Figure 4-28. SMTP packets sent to 200.100.30.50 from ISP2 are sent to SVR3. Modify the configurations of the previous exercises to implement these translations.

Answer: The IG address falls in the middle of the ISP2Pool range, so in addition to the static NAT mappings, ISP2Pool must be reconfigured.

```
RTR2
ip nat pool ISP2Pool netmask 255.255.255.0
 address 200.100.30.1 200.100.30.49
 address 200.100.30.51 200.100.30.253
ip nat inside source list 1 pool ISP2Pool
ip nat inside source static tcp 172.16.2.3 24 200.100.30.50 25 extendable
ip nat inside source static tcp 172.16.2.2 80 200.100.30.50 80 extendable
ip nat inside source static 172.16.3.3 200.100.30.254
!
access-list 1 permit 172.16.0.0 0.0.255.255
```

4 Five outside devices in Figure 4-28, 201.50.12.67–201.50.12.71, must appear to devices within AS 3 as having addresses 192.168.1.1–192.168.1.5, respectively. Add the appropriate NAT configurations to the previously created configurations.

Answer:

```
RTR1
ip nat pool ISP1Pool 201.50.13.2 201.50.13.254 netmask 255.255.255.0
ip nat pool SVRs 172.16.2.2 172.16.2.3 netmask 255.255.255.0 type rotary
ip nat inside source list 1 pool ISP1Pool
ip nat inside source static 172.16.3.3 201.50.13.1
ip nat inside destination list 2 pool SVRs
ip nat outside source static 201.50.12.71 192.168.1.5
ip nat outside source static 201.50.12.70 192.168.1.4
ip nat outside source static 201.50.12.69 192.168.1.3
ip nat outside source static 201.50.12.68 192.168.1.2
ip nat outside source static 201.50.12.67 192.168.1.1
!
access-list 1 permit 172.16.0.0 0.0.255.255
access-list 2 permit 201.50.13.1
```

5 Devices in AS 3 of Figure 4-28 with addresses in the 172.16.100.0/24 subnet should all appear to have the IG address 200.100.30.75 when sending packets to ISP2. Modify the configurations of the previous exercises to accommodate this.

Answer: The solution is to configure PAT. Unlike the PAT example shown in this chapter, however, the address to be used here is not the address of the outgoing interface. So, an address pool is configured on RTR2 that consists of a single address. Notice also that access list 1 is modified so that the IL addresses used for PAT are not translated to the ISP2Pool range.

```
RTR2
ip nat pool ISP2Pool netmask 255.255.255.0
 address 200.100.30.1 200.100.30.49
 address 200.100.30.51 200.100.30.253
ip nat pool PATPool 200.100.30.75 200.100.30.75 netmask 255.255.0.0
ip nat inside source list 1 pool ISP2Pool
ip nat inside source list 3 pool PATPool overload
ip nat inside source static tcp 172.16.2.3 24 200.100.30.50 25 extendable
ip nat inside source static tcp 172.16.2.2 80 200.100.30.50 80 extendable
ip nat inside source static 172.16.3.3 200.100.30.254
!
access-list 1 deny 172.16.100.0 0.0.0.255
access-list 1 permit 172.16.0.0 0.0.255.255
access-list 3 permit 172.16.100.0 0.0.0.255
```

6 In Figure 4-29, redundant links have been added so that RTR1 and RTR2 each have connections to both ISPs and each accepts full BGP routes from both ISPs. The address of RTR1, S1 is 200.100.29.137/30, and the address of RTR2, S1 is 201.50.26.93/30. Write configurations for the two routers, ensuring that all features added in the previous exercises still work correctly.

Figure 4-29 *The Internetwork for Configuration Exercise 6*

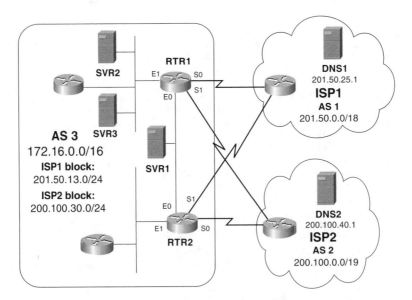

Answer:

```
RTR1
interface Loopback0
 ip address 172.16.255.2 255.255.255.255
!
interface Ethernet0
 ip address 172.16.3.1 255.255.255.0
 ip nat inside
!
interface Ethernet1
 ip address 172.16.2.1 255.255.255.0
 ip nat inside
!
interface Serial0
 description to ISP1
 ip address 201.50.26.13 255.255.255.252
 ip access-group 101 out
 ip nat outside
!
interface Serial1
 description to ISP2
 ip address 200.100.29.137 255.255.255.252
 ip access-group 101 out
 ip nat outside
!
autonomous-system 3
!
router ospf 1
 redistribute static
 network 172.16.0.0 0.0.255.255 area 0
 default-information originate
!
router bgp 3
 neighbor 172.16.255.1 remote-as 3
 neighbor 172.16.255.1 update-source Loopback0
 neighbor 200.100.29.138 remote-as 2
 neighbor 201.50.26.14 remote-as 1
!
ip nat pool ISP1Pool 201.50.13.2 201.50.13.254 netmask 255.255.255.0
ip nat pool ISP2Pool netmask 255.255.255.0
 address 200.100.30.1 200.100.30.49
 address 200.100.30.51 200.100.30.253
ip nat pool PATPool 200.100.30.75 200.100.30.75 netmask 255.255.0.0
ip nat pool SVRs 172.16.2.2 172.16.2.3 netmask 255.255.255.0 type rotary
ip nat inside source route-map ISP1 pool ISP1Pool
ip nat inside source route-map ISP2 pool ISP2Pool
ip nat inside source list 3 pool PATPool overload
ip nat inside source static tcp 172.16.2.3 24 200.100.30.50 25 extendable
ip nat inside source static tcp 172.16.2.2 80 200.100.30.50 80 extendable
ip nat inside source static 172.16.3.3 201.50.13.1
ip nat inside destination list 2 pool SVRs
```

continues

(Continued)

```
ip nat outside source static 201.50.12.71 192.168.1.5
ip nat outside source static 201.50.12.70 192.168.1.4
ip nat outside source static 201.50.12.69 192.168.1.3
ip nat outside source static 201.50.12.68 192.168.1.2
ip nat outside source static 201.50.12.67 192.168.1.1
!
access-list 1 deny 172.16.100.0 0.0.0.255
access-list 1 permit 172.16.0.0 0.0.255.255
access-list 2 permit 201.50.13.1
access-list 3 permit 172.16.100.0 0.0.0.255
access-list 4 permit 200.100.29.138
access-list 5 permit 201.50.26.14
access-list 101 deny    ip 172.16.0.0 0.0.255.255 any
access-list 101 permit ip any any
!
route-map ISP1 permit 10
 match ip address 1
 match ip next-hop 5
!
route-map ISP2 permit 10
 match ip address 1
 match ip next-hop 4
```

RTR2

```
interface Loopback0
 ip address 172.16.255.1 255.255.255.255
!
interface Ethernet0
 ip address 172.16.3.2 255.255.255.0
 ip nat inside
!
interface Ethernet1
 ip address 172.16.1.1 255.255.255.0
 ip nat inside


!
interface Serial0
 description to ISP2
 ip address 200.100.29.241 255.255.255.252
 ip access-group 101 out
 ip nat outside
!
interface Serial1
 description to ISP1
 ip address 201.50.26.93 255.255.255.252
 ip access-group 101 out
 ip nat outside
autonomous-system 3
!
router ospf 1
 redistribute static
 network 172.16.0.0 0.0.255.255 area 0
```

```
   default-information originate
!
router bgp 3
 neighbor 172.16.255.2 remote-as 3
 neighbor 172.16.255.2 update-source Loopback0
 neighbor 200.100.29.242 remote-as 2
 neighbor 201.50.26.94 remote-as 1
!
ip nat pool ISP1Pool 201.50.13.2 201.50.13.254 netmask 255.255.255.0
ip nat pool ISP2Pool netmask 255.255.255.0
 address 200.100.30.1 200.100.30.49
 address 200.100.30.51 200.100.30.253
ip nat pool PATPool 200.100.30.75 200.100.30.75 netmask 255.255.0.0
ip nat pool SVRs 172.16.2.2 172.16.2.3 netmask 255.255.255.0 type rotary
ip nat inside source route-map ISP1 pool ISP1Pool
ip nat inside source route-map ISP2 pool ISP2Pool
ip nat inside source list 3 pool PATPool overload
ip nat inside source static tcp 172.16.2.3 24 200.100.30.50 25 extendable
ip nat inside source static tcp 172.16.2.2 80 200.100.30.50 80 extendable
ip nat inside source static 172.16.3.3 200.100.30.254
ip nat inside destination list 2 pool SVRs
ip nat outside source static 201.50.12.71 192.168.1.5
ip nat outside source static 201.50.12.70 192.168.1.4
ip nat outside source static 201.50.12.69 192.168.1.3
ip nat outside source static 201.50.12.68 192.168.1.2
ip nat outside source static 201.50.12.67 192.168.1.1
!
access-list 1 deny 172.16.100.0 0.0.0.255
access-list 1 permit 172.16.0.0 0.0.255.255
access-list 2 permit 201.50.13.1
access-list 3 permit 172.16.100.0 0.0.0.255
access-list 4 permit 200.100.29.242
access-list 5 permit 201.50.26.94
access-list 101 deny ip 172.16.0.0 0.0.255.255 any
access-list 101 permit ip any any
!
route-map ISP1 permit 10
 match ip address 1
 match ip next-hop 5
!
route-map ISP2 permit 10
 match ip address 1
 match ip next-hop 4
```

Answers to Chapter 6 Configuration Exercises

1 What global Cisco IOS Software command is required to enable IP multicast routing?

Answer: ip multicast-routing

2 Show the commands that enable PIM on an interface in dense mode, sparse mode, and sparse-dense mode.

Answer:

```
ip pim dense-mode
ip pim sparse-mode
ip pim sparse-dense mode
```

3 Show the command to statically specify an RP with an address of 172.18.20.4.

Answer: ip pim rp-address 172.18.20.4

4 Write the configuration statements necessary to statically map groups 239.1.2.3 and 228.1.8.0 – 228.1.8.255 to RP 192.168.15.5, and group 239.6.7.8 to RP 192.168.20.10. Map all other groups to RP 192.168.25.1.

Answer:

```
ip pim rp-address 192.168.15.5 1
ip pim rp-address 192.168.20.10 2
ip pim rp-address 192.168.25.1
!
access-list 1 permit 239.1.2.3 0.0.0.0
access-list 1 permit 228.1.8.0 0.0.0.255
access-list 2 permit 239.6.7.8 0.0.0.0
```

5 All router interfaces shown in Figure 6-11 are running in sparse-dense mode. Show the relevant configurations in order for R1 to be the RP for only groups whose addresses begin with 226.13.0.0/24. R2 should only be the RP for groups whose addresses begin with 239.0.0.0/8. R3 is the mapping agent; ensure that the mapping agent will recognize only R1 and R2 as RPs, and only for the specified groups. All Auto-RP messages should have a TTL of 20.

Figure 6-11 *The Topology for Configuration Exercises 5–8*

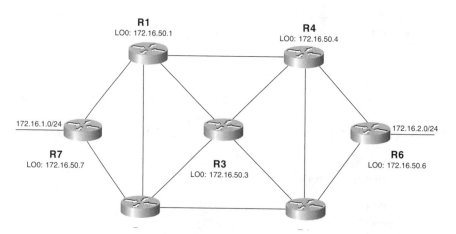

Answer:

```
R1
ip pim send-rp-announce Loopback0 scope 20 group-list 1
!
access-list 1 permit 226.13.0.0 0.0.0.255
```

```
R2
ip pim send-rp-announce Loopback0 scope 20 group-list 1
!
access-list 1 permit 239.0.0.0 0.255.255.255
```

```
R3
ip pim rp-announce-filter rp-list 10 group-list 11
ip pim rp-announce-filter rp-list 20 group-list 21
ip pim send-rp-discovery Loopback0 scope 20
!
access-list 10 permit 172.16.50.1
access-list 11 permit 226.13.0.0 0.0.0.255
access-list 20 permit 172.16.50.2
access-list 21 permit 239.0.0.0 0.255.255.255
```

6 Given the configurations of Configuration Exercise 5, suppose a source originates
traffic for group 228.23.14.135, and a member requests a join to that group. What will
happen?

**Answer: Neither R1 nor R2 is configured to become the RP for that group.
Because all interfaces are running in sparse-dense mode, however, dense mode is
invoked for the group, and an SPT is built between the source and member.**

7 Again referring to Figure 6-11, write the necessary configurations to enable the
bootstrap protocol, making R1 and R2 C-RPs for the same group addresses described
in Configuration Exercise 5. Make R3 the BSR, and make R4 a backup BSR.

Answer:

```
R1
ip pim rp-candidate Loopback0 group-list 1
!
access-list 1 permit 226.13.0.0 0.0.0.255
```

```
R2
ip pim rp-candidate Loopback0 group-list 1
!
access-list 1 permit 239.0.0.0 0.255.255.255
```

```
R3
ip pim bsr-candidate Loopback0 50
```

continues

R4
```
ip pim bsr-candidate Loopback0 0
```

---

8 Write configurations for the topology in Figure 6-11 that allow multicast load
   balancing between source 172.16.1.75 and group member 172.16.2.100. Use
   unnumbered addressing on the tunnel interfaces, referencing E0, and assume the IGP
   is advertising those addresses.

   Answer:

R6
```
interface Tunnel0
 ip unnumbered Ethernet0
 ip pim sparse-dense mode
 tunnel source Loopback0
 tunnel destination 172.16.50.7
!
ip mroute 172.16.1.75 255.255.255.255 Tunnel0
```

R7
```
interface Tunnel0
 ip unnumbered Ethernet0
 ip pim sparse-dense mode
 tunnel source Loopback0
 tunnel destination 172.16.50.6
```

9 Examine the configurations of Homburg and Porkpie shown in the case study
   "Multicast Load Sharing." Each router is running OSPF in passive mode on the tunnel
   interfaces. Why?

   **Answer: By putting the unicast protocol (in this case, OSPF) into passive mode,
   the protocol is aware of the interface addresses, necessary for the multicast RPF
   function, while at the same time preventing unicast traffic from using the tunnel.**

10 What is the purpose of the command **ip pim spt-threshold 100 group-list 25**?

   **Answer: When the arrival rate of packets for the group address or addresses
   specified in access list 25 exceeds 100 Kbps, the PIM-SM router switches from
   the shared tree to the shortest path tree.**

Answers to Chapter 9 Configuration Exercises

1 Configure a router to accept polls from management stations 172.16.1.2 and 172.16.1.3 only. Do not allow write access to the stations. Allow the stations to read information about the SNMP MIB II interface entries only. Allow station 172.16.1.4 to read any MIB variable, and allow it to load and save configuration files via SNMP. Send logging information at the Notification level, via SNMP, to 172.16.1.4.

Answer:

```
access-list 1 permit 172.16.1.2 0.0.0.1
access-list 2 permit 172.16.1.4
snmp-server view interface_entries ifEntry included
snmp-server community anystring view interface_entries RO 1
snmp-server community restricted RO 2
snmp-server tftp-server-list 2
snmp-server enable traps syslog
logging history notification
```

2 Configure the router to send an SNMP trap to 172.16.1.4 when the 5-minute average CPU exceeds 90%. Send the trap whenever the CPU goes from below 85% to above 90% in any 60-second interval.

Answer:

```
snmp-server community eventtrap RO
snmp-server enable traps
snmp-server host 172.16.1.4 eventtrap
rmon event 1 trap eventtrap description "High 5-minute CPU" owner smith
rmon alarm 10 lsystem.58.0 60 absolute rising-threshold 90 1 falling-threshold 85
owner smith
```

3 Configure a router to use NTP to update its own time and date based on clock information from router 172.16.100.100. Do not allow the other router to update its clock based on information from your router.

Answer:

```
ntp server 172.16.100.100
```

4 Configure a NetFlow aggregation cache, grouping data based on the source and destination prefix. Use the peer AS in the data, and export the data to 172.16.1.4.

Answer:

```
ip cef
!
ip flow-export version 5 peer-as
ip flow-export destination 172.16.1.4 125
ip flow-aggregation cache prefix
 cache entries 2046
 cache timeout inactive 200
 cache timeout active 45
 export destination 172.16.1.4 9991
 enabled
!
```

5 Configure two routers on an Ethernet segment to provide backup for each other.
   Router A is primary, and router B takes over when A fails. When A recovers, it
   becomes the primary router again. Router A has two serial links, serial 0 and serial 1,
   that forward traffic to various destinations. If either link fails, router B takes over as
   the primary router.

Answer:

```
Router A
interface Ethernet 0
 ip address 172.16.1.100 255.255.255.0
 standby 1 priority 120 preempt
 standby 1 ip 172.16.1.201
 standby 1 track Serial0 25
 standby 1 track Serial1 25
```

```
Router B
interface Ethernet 0
 ip address 172.16.1.101 255.255.255.0
 standby 1 ip
 standby 1 priority 100 preempt
```

Answers to Troubleshooting Exercises

Answer to Chapter 1 Troubleshooting Exercise

1 In Figure 1-17, router RTG has been added to the internetwork.

Figure 1-17 *The Internetwork for Troubleshooting Exercise 1*

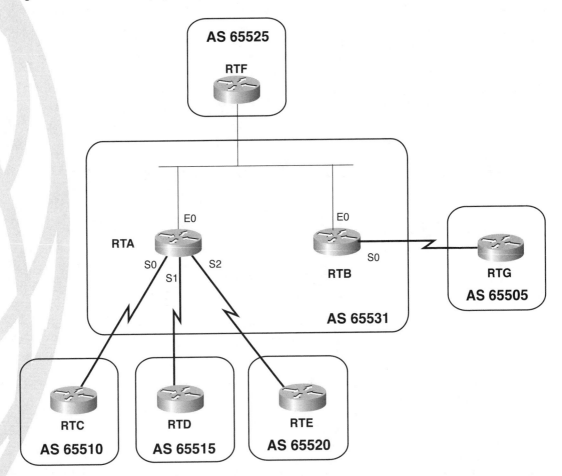

Although it is peering with RTB and exchanging reachability information, there is a configuration error. Based on the information in Example 1-29, what is the error?

Example 1-29 *The EGP Tables of RTB and RTG in Figure 1-17*

```
RTB#show ip egp
Local autonomous system is 65531

 EGP Neighbor      FAS/LAS  State    SndSeq RcvSeq Hello  Poll j/k Flags
*192.168.1.1    65531/65531 UP     4    2      6    60    180   2 Perm, Pass
*192.168.1.3    65525/65531 UP     4    2     492   60    180   2 Perm, Pass
*192.168.5.2    65505/65531 UP     3    2      33   60    180   3 Temp, Pass
 EGP Neighbor      Third Party
*192.168.1.1      192.168.1.3(e)
*192.168.1.3      192.168.1.1
RTB#
```

```
RTG#show ip egp
Local autonomous system is 65505

 EGP Neighbor      FAS/LAS  State    SndSeq RcvSeq Hello  Poll j/k Flags
*192.168.5.1    65505/65505 UP     9    36     3    60    180   4 Perm, Act
RTG#
```

Answer: The EGP configuration of RTG is router egp 65505 rather than router egp 65531.

Answers to Chapter 3 Troubleshooting Exercises

Figure 3-37 shows the internetwork diagram for Troubleshooting Exercises 1 through 6.

Figure 3-37 *The Internetwork for Troubleshooting Exercises 1 through 6*

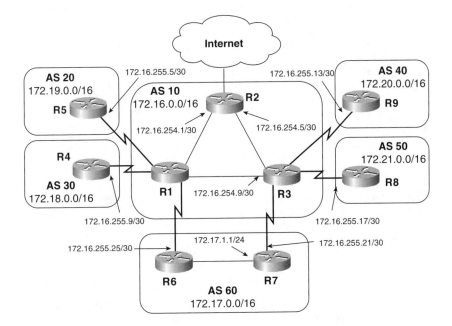

1 Example 3-165 shows the BGP configuration of router R2 in Figure 3-37.

Example 3-165 *BGP Configuration of Router R2*

```
router bgp 10
 no synchronization
 network 0.0.0.0
 neighbor 172.16.254.2 remote-as 10
 neighbor 172.16.254.2 next-hop-self
 neighbor 172.16.254.6 remote-as 10
 neighbor 172.16.254.6 next-hop-self
 no auto-summary
!
ip classless
ip route 0.0.0.0 0.0.0.0 Ethernet10
```

Example 3-166 shows the BGP table and routing table for R2. Although there are routes to the destinations in the autonomous systems shown in Figure 3-37, pings to those destinations fail. Why?

Example 3-166 *The BGP and Routing Tables of R2 in Figure 3-37*

```
R2#show ip bgp
BGP table version is 7, local router ID is 10.1.1.1
Status codes: s suppressed, d damped, h history, * valid, > best, i - internal
Origin codes: i - IGP, e - EGP, ? - incomplete
   Network          Next Hop          Metric LocPrf Weight Path
*> 0.0.0.0          0.0.0.0                0          32768 i
*>i172.17.0.0       172.16.255.21          0     100      0 60 i
*>i172.18.0.0       172.16.255.9           0     100      0 30 i
*>i172.19.0.0       172.16.255.5           0     100      0 20 i
*>i172.20.0.0       172.16.255.13          0     100      0 40 i
*>i172.21.0.0       172.16.255.17          0     100      0 50 i

R2#show ip route
Codes: C - connected, S - static, I - IGRP, R - RIP, M - mobile, B - BGP
       D - EIGRP, EX - EIGRP external, O - OSPF, IA - OSPF inter area
       E1 - OSPF external type 1, E2 - OSPF external type 2, E - EGP
       i - IS-IS, L1 - IS-IS level-1, L2 - IS-IS level-2, * - candidate default

Gateway of last resort is 0.0.0.0 to network 0.0.0.0

     10.0.0.0 255.255.255.0 is subnetted, 1 subnets
C       10.1.1.0 is directly connected, Ethernet11
B    172.20.0.0 [200/0] via 172.16.255.13, 00:01:15
B    172.21.0.0 [200/0] via 172.16.255.17, 00:01:16
     172.16.0.0 255.255.255.252 is subnetted, 2 subnets
C       172.16.254.0 is directly connected, Ethernet12
C       172.16.254.4 is directly connected, Ethernet13
B    172.17.0.0 [200/0] via 172.16.255.21, 00:01:16
B    172.18.0.0 [200/0] via 172.16.255.9, 00:00:59
B    172.19.0.0 [200/0] via 172.16.255.5, 00:00:59
S*   0.0.0.0 0.0.0.0 is directly connected, Ethernet10
R2#ping 172.17.1.1
Type escape sequence to abort.
Sending 5, 100-byte ICMP Echos to 172.17.1.1, timeout is 2 seconds:
.....
Success rate is 0 percent (0/5)
R2#
```

Answer: R2 has no routes to the next-hop addresses referenced in the BGP table. R1 and R3 must advertise routes to these addresses or use the neighbor next-hop-self command.

2 Example 3-167 shows **debug** output from routers R1 and R5 in Figure 3-37. What problem do the messages indicate?

Example 3-167 *debug Output from R1 and R5 in Figure 3-37*

```
R1#debug ip bgp
BGP debugging is on
R1#
BGP: 172.16.255.5 open active, local address 172.16.255.6
BGP: 172.16.255.5 sending OPEN, version 4
BGP: 172.16.255.5 received NOTIFICATION 2/2 (peer in wrong AS) 2 bytes 000A
BGP: 172.16.255.5 closing
```

```
R5#
6d08h: BGP: 172.16.255.6 open active, delay 28272ms
6d08h: BGP: 172.16.255.6 open active, local address 172.16.255.5
6d08h: BGP: 172.16.255.6 sending OPEN, version 4
6d08h: BGP: 172.16.255.6 OPEN rcvd, version 4
6d08h: BGP: 172.16.255.6 bad OPEN, remote AS is 10, expected 30
6d08h: BGP: 172.16.255.6 sending NOTIFICATION 2/2 (peer in wrong AS) 2 bytes 000A
6d08h: BGP: 172.16.255.6 remote close, state CLOSEWAIT
6d08h: BGP: 172.16.255.6 closing
```

Answer: R5's BGP configuration contains the statement neighbor 172.16.255.6 remote-as 30, when the statement should be neighbor 172.16.255.6 remote-as 10.

3 Example 3-168 shows the BGP tables of R1 and R3 in Figure 3-37. The first table indicates that 172.17.0.0/24 can be reached either via R6 (172.16.255.25) or R3 (172.16.254.9). Which path is R1 using, and why?

Example 3-168 *BGP Tables from R1 and R3 in Figure 3-37*

```
R1#show ip bgp
BGP table version is 8, local router ID is 172.20.7.1
Status codes: s suppressed, * valid, > best, i - internal
Origin codes: i - IGP, e - EGP, ? - incomplete

   Network          Next Hop         Metric LocPrf Weight Path
*>i0.0.0.0          172.16.254.1          0    100      0 i
*  i172.17.0.0      172.16.254.9          0    100      0 60 i
*>                  172.16.255.25         0             0 60 i
*> 172.18.0.0       172.16.255.9          0             0 30 i
*> 172.19.0.0       172.16.255.5          0             0 20 i
*>i172.20.0.0       172.16.254.9          0    100      0 40 i
*>i172.21.0.0       172.16.254.9          0    100      0 50 i
R1#
```

continues

Example 3-168 *BGP Tables from R1 and R3 in Figure 3-37 (Continued)*

```
R3#show ip bgp
BGP table version is 5, local router ID is 172.16.255.22
Status codes: s suppressed, d damped, h history, * valid, > best, i - internal
Origin codes: i - IGP, e - EGP, ? - incomplete

   Network          Next Hop          Metric LocPrf Weight Path
* i0.0.0.0          172.16.254.5           0    100      0 i
* i172.17.0.0       172.16.254.10          0    100      0 60 i
*>                  172.16.255.21          0             0 60 i
* i172.18.0.0       172.16.254.10          0    100      0 30 i
* i172.19.0.0       172.16.254.10          0    100      0 20 i
*> 172.20.0.0       172.16.255.13          0             0 40 i
*> 172.21.0.0       172.16.255.17          0             0 50 i
R3#
```

> **Answer: R1 is using the path through R6, because EBGP paths are preferred over IBGP paths.**

4 Example 3-169 shows the BGP and IGP configurations for R1, R3, R6, and R7 in Figure 3-37.

Example 3-169 *BGP and IGP Configurations for Routers R1, R3, R6, and R7*

```
R1
router bgp 10
 neighbor 172.16.254.1 remote-as 10
 neighbor 172.16.254.1 next-hop-self
 neighbor 172.16.254.9 remote-as 10
 neighbor 172.16.254.9 next-hop-self
 neighbor 172.16.255.5 remote-as 20
 neighbor 172.16.255.9 remote-as 30
 neighbor 172.16.255.25 remote-as 60

R3
router bgp 10
 neighbor 172.16.254.5 remote-as 10
 neighbor 172.16.254.5 next-hop-self
 neighbor 172.16.254.10 remote-as 10
 neighbor 172.16.254.10 next-hop-self
 neighbor 172.16.255.13 remote-as 40
 neighbor 172.16.255.17 remote-as 50
 neighbor 172.16.255.21 remote-as 60
 neighbor 172.16.255.21 next-hop-self

R6
router eigrp 60
 redistribute bgp 60 metric 1000 100 255 1 1500
 network 172.17.0.0
```

Example 3-169 *BGP and IGP Configurations for Routers R1, R3, R6, and R7 (Continued)*

```
!
router bgp 60
 network 172.17.0.0
 neighbor 172.16.255.26 remote-as 10
```

R7
```
router eigrp 60
 redistribute bgp 60 metric 1000 100 255 1 1500
 network 172.17.0.0
!
router bgp 60
 network 172.17.0.0
 neighbor 172.16.255.22 remote-as 10
```

Example 3-168 shows the BGP tables for R1 and R3. For each of the following destinations, what next-hop address does R6 use? Explain why R6 uses the addresses you name.

Destinations:

172.20.7.102

172.18.58.35

10.53.12.6

Answer:

172.20.7.102: Next-hop 172.17.1.1

172.18.58.35: Next-hop 172.16.255.26

10.53.12.6: Packet is dropped

Neither R1 nor R3 has synchronization turned off. As a result, each advertises only the addresses it has learned from EBGP neighbors. R6 has learned 172.18.0.0/24 from R1, but R1 does not advertise 172.20.0.0/24, which it learned from an IBGP neighbor. R3 advertises that route to R7, which advertises it to R6 via EIGRP. Both R1 and R3 have learned the default route from IBGP neighbor R2, so neither router advertises the default.

5 Example 3-170 shows the BGP configurations for R1 and R3 in Figure 3-37.

Example 3-170 *BGP Configurations for Routers R1 and R3*

```
R1
router bgp 10
no synchronization
aggregate-address 172.16.0.0 255.255.248.0 summary-only
neighbor 172.16.254.1 remote-as 10
```

continues

Example 3-170 *BGP Configurations for Routers R1 and R3 (Continued)*

```
neighbor 172.16.254.1 next-hop-self
neighbor 172.16.254.9 remote-as 10
neighbor 172.16.254.9 next-hop-self
neighbor 172.16.255.5 remote-as 20
neighbor 172.16.255.9 remote-as 30
neighbor 172.16.255.25 remote-as 60
```

```
R3
router bgp 10
 no synchronization
 aggregate-address 172.16.0.0 255.255.248.0 summary-only
 neighbor 172.16.254.5 remote-as 10
 neighbor 172.16.254.5 next-hop-self
 neighbor 172.16.254.10 remote-as 10
 neighbor 172.16.254.10 next-hop-self
 neighbor 172.16.255.13 remote-as 40
 neighbor 172.16.255.17 remote-as 50
 neighbor 172.16.255.21 remote-as 60
 neighbor 172.16.255.21 next-hop-self
```

The objective is to suppress all the more-specific routes and advertise only an aggregate. R8's BGP table, in Example 3-171, still shows the more-specific routes. What is wrong?

Example 3-171 *The BGP Table of R8 in Figure 3-37*

```
R8#show ip bgp
BGP table version is 163, local router ID is 172.21.1.1
Status codes: s suppressed, * valid, > best, i - internal
Origin codes: i - IGP, e - EGP, ? - incomplete

   Network          Next Hop         Metric LocPrf Weight Path
*> 0.0.0.0          172.16.255.18                      0 10 i
*> 172.17.0.0       172.16.255.18                      0 10 60 i
*> 172.18.0.0       172.16.255.18                      0 10 30 i
*> 172.19.0.0       172.16.255.18                      0 10 20 i
*> 172.20.0.0       172.16.255.18                      0 10 40 i
*> 172.21.0.0       0.0.0.0               0         32768 i
R8#
```

Answer: The mask specified in the aggregate-address command should be 255.248.0.0. The aggregate specified does not match anything in the routing tables of R1 or R3 and so is not advertised.

6 Packets from AS 60 destined for any of the other autonomous systems shown in Figure 3-37 should be forwarded across the link between R6 and R1. The link between R7 and R3 should be used only as a backup for this traffic, although packets destined

for the Internet can still use this link. To implement this policy, R3 should advertise only the default route and the aggregate 172.16.0.0/13. R1 should advertise the more-specific routes. Example 3-172 shows the configurations for R1, R3, R6, and R7.

Example 3-172 *Configurations for Routers R1, R3, R6, and R7*

```
R1
router bgp 10
no synchronization
neighbor 172.16.254.1 remote-as 10
neighbor 172.16.254.1 next-hop-self
neighbor 172.16.254.9 remote-as 10
neighbor 172.16.254.9 next-hop-self
neighbor 172.16.255.5 remote-as 20
neighbor 172.16.255.9 remote-as 30
neighbor 172.16.255.25 remote-as 60

R3
router bgp 10
 no synchronization
 aggregate-address 172.16.0.0 255.248.0.0 summary-only
 neighbor 172.16.254.5 remote-as 10
 neighbor 172.16.254.5 next-hop-self
 neighbor 172.16.254.10 remote-as 10
 neighbor 172.16.254.10 next-hop-self
 neighbor 172.16.255.13 remote-as 40
 neighbor 172.16.255.17 remote-as 50
 neighbor 172.16.255.21 remote-as 60
 neighbor 172.16.255.21 next-hop-self

R6
redistribute bgp 60 metric 1000 100 255 1 1500
 network 172.17.0.0
!
router bgp 60
 network 172.17.0.0
 neighbor 172.16.255.26 remote-as 10

R7
router eigrp 60
 redistribute bgp 60 metric 1000 100 255 1 1500
 network 172.17.0.0
!
router bgp 60
 network 172.17.0.0
 neighbor 172.16.255.22 remote-as 10
```

Example 3-173 shows R7's routing table. Has the objective been accomplished? If not, why not?

Example 3-173 *R7's Routing Table for Troubleshooting Exercise 6*

```
R7#show ip route
Codes: C - connected, S - static, I - IGRP, R - RIP, M - mobile, B - BGP
       D - EIGRP, EX - EIGRP external, O - OSPF, IA - OSPF inter area
       N1 - OSPF NSSA external type 1, N2 - OSPF NSSA external type 2
       E1 - OSPF external type 1, E2 - OSPF external type 2, E - EGP
       i - IS-IS, L1 - IS-IS level-1, L2 - IS-IS level-2, * - candidate default
       U - per-user static route, o - ODR
       T - traffic engineered route

Gateway of last resort is 172.16.255.22 to network 0.0.0.0

     172.17.0.0/24 is subnetted, 3 subnets
C       172.17.1.0 is directly connected, Ethernet0
D       172.17.3.0 [90/409600] via 172.17.1.2, 09:18:50, Ethernet0
C       172.17.2.0 is directly connected, Ethernet1
     172.16.0.0/30 is subnetted, 1 subnets
C       172.16.255.20 is directly connected, Serial0
D EX 172.19.0.0/16 [170/2611200] via 172.17.1.2, 00:19:08, Ethernet0
D EX 172.18.0.0/16 [170/2611200] via 172.17.1.2, 00:19:08, Ethernet0
B*   0.0.0.0/0 [20/0] via 172.16.255.22, 00:18:37
B    172.16.0.0/13 [20/0] via 172.16.255.22, 00:18:09
R7#
```

Answer: The objective has not been fully accomplished. The routes to 172.18.0.0/24 and 172.19.0.0/24 are correct, but the routes to 172.20.0.0 and 172.21.0.0/24 are not in the routing table. The aggregate-address command at R3 has suppressed the advertisement of more-specific routes not only to R3's EBGP peers, but also to its IBGP peers. As a result, R1 does not know about 172.20.0.0/24 and 172.21.0.0/24.

7   Reexamine Figure 3-19 and Example 3-98 and the associated discussion. Meribel advertises its local route 172.17.0.0 to its EBGP peers with an ORIGIN of Incomplete, whereas Lillehammer advertises the route back to Meribel with an ORIGIN of IGP. Will this cause Meribel to prefer the route from Lillehammer, thereby causing a routing loop?

Answer: No. Although an ORIGIN of IGP takes precedence over an ORIGIN of Incomplete in the BGP decision process, administrative weight takes precedence over ORIGIN. By default, Meribel assigns a weight of 32768 to locally originated routes and a weight of 0 to learned routes, so the local route is preferred.

8 Example 3-174 shows the configuration for the router named Colorado in Figure 3-24.

Example 3-174 *Configuration for Router Colorado in Figure 3-24*

```
router bgp 100
 network 10.1.11.0 mask 255.255.255.0
 network 10.1.12.0 mask 255.255.255.0
 neighbor CLIENTS peer-group
 neighbor CLIENTS ebgp-multihop 2
 neighbor CLIENTS update-source Loopback2
 neighbor CLIENTS filter-list 2 in
 neighbor CLIENTS filter-list 1 out
 neighbor 10.1.255.2 remote-as 200
 neighbor 10.1.255.2 peer-group CLIENTS
 neighbor 10.1.255.3 remote-as 300
 neighbor 10.1.255.3 peer-group CLIENTS
 neighbor 10.1.255.4 remote-as 400
 neighbor 10.1.255.4 peer-group CLIENTS
 neighbor 10.1.255.5 remote-as 500
 neighbor 10.1.255.5 peer-group CLIENTS
 neighbor 10.1.255.6 remote-as 600
 neighbor 10.1.255.6 peer-group CLIENTS
 no auto-summary
!
ip classless
ip route 10.1.255.2 255.255.255.255 Serial0/1.305
ip route 10.1.255.3 255.255.255.255 Serial0/1.306
ip route 10.1.255.4 255.255.255.255 Serial0/1.307
ip route 10.1.255.5 255.255.255.255 Serial0/1.308
!
ip as-path access-list 1 permit ^$
ip as-path access-list 2 permit ^[2-6]00$
```

All router IDs shown in Figure 3-24 are configured on loopback interfaces, and no routing protocol other than BGP is running on any of the routers. Assuming that all the links shown in the figure are functioning properly, are all the other five routers EBGP peers of Colorado? If not, why not?

Answer: No. Router NewHampshire is not a peer, because there is no static route entry at Colorado for 10.1.255.6/32.

9 Refer to the configuration shown in Troubleshooting Exercise 8 for router Colorado in Figure 3-24. What will be the result of removing the **no auto-summary** statement from the configuration?

Answer: Removing the statement has no effect on the topology shown in Figure 3.82, because all the router IDs and all the addresses of all the autonomous systems are subnets of 10.0.0.0.

10 Refer again to the configuration shown in Troubleshooting Exercise 8. What routes does the incoming route filter permit?

Answer: The incoming route filter refers to AS_PATH list 2. The one line of that list permits any route whose AS_PATH meets the following criteria:

- **The route's AS_PATH consists of a single AS number.**

- **The decimal representation of the AS number must be three digits.**

- **The first digit must be a number between 2 and 6, inclusive.**

- **The second and third digits must be 0s.**

11 Refer to Figure 3-24 and the configuration for router Colorado in Troubleshooting Exercise 8. What subnets, other than those local to its own AS or the inter-AS links, can a host on subnet 10.1.3.0/24 ping?

Answer: Only subnets 10.1.11.0/24, 10.1.12.0/24, and 10.1.255.1/32. The outgoing route filter at Colorado prevents its EBGP peers from learning of any routes other than local routes.

Answers to Chapter 4 Troubleshooting Exercises

1 Identify the mistake in the configuration in Example 4-33.

Example 4-33 *Configuration for Troubleshooting Exercise 1*

```
ip nat pool EX1 192.168.1.1 192.168.1.254 netmask 255.255.255.0 type match-host
ip nat pool EX1A netmask 255.255.255.240
 address 172.21.1.33 172.21.1.38
 address 172.21.1.40 172.21.1.46
ip nat inside source list 1 pool EX1
ip nat inside source static 10.18.53.210 192.168.1.1
ip nat outside source list 2 pool EX1A
!
access-list 1 permit 10.0.0.0 0.255.255.255
access-list 2 permit 192.168.2.0 0.0.0.255
```

Answer: The IG address in the static mapping overlaps with the pool EX1.

2 RTR1 in Figure 4-30 connects two internetworks with overlapping addresses.

Figure 4-30 *The Internetwork for Troubleshooting Exercise 2*

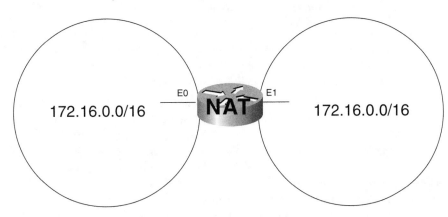

NAT is implemented on the router as configured in Example 4-34, but devices cannot communicate across the router. What is wrong?

Example 4-34 *Configuration for Troubleshooting Exercise 2*

```
interface Ethernet0
 ip address 172.16.10.1 255.255.255.0
 ip nat inside
!
interface Ethernet1
 ip address 172.16.255.254 255.255.255.0
 ip nat outside
!
router ospf 1
 redistribute static metric 10 metric-type 1 subnets
 network 10.0.0.0 0.255.255.255 area 0
!
ip nat translation timeout 500
ip nat pool NET1 10.1.1.1 10.1.255.254 netmask 255.255.0.0
ip nat pool NET2 192.168.1.1 192.168.255.254 netmask 255.255.0.0
ip nat inside source list 1 pool NET1
ip nat outside source list 1 pool NET2
!
ip classless
!
ip route 10.1.0.0 255.255.0.0 Ethernet0
ip route 192.168.0.0 255.255.0.0 Ethernet1
!
access-list 1 permit 172.16.0.0 0.0.255.255
```

Answer: The problem is not with the NAT itself, but with routing. All translations are dynamic, and there is no way for a host on either side to determine the initial address to which packets must be sent to reach the other side.

3 Refer to the configurations of Cozumel and Guaymas in Figure 4-21. If the first line of access list 1 in both configurations is removed, what is the result? Can Guaymas and Cozumel still ping each other?

Answer: When either router sends a packet to the other sourced from its E1 interface, the source address is translated to an address out of the IG pool. The two routers can still ping each other even if the source address is translated. If Cozumel pings Guaymas, for example, its source address of 10.255.13.254 might be translated to 206.100.176.50. Although Guaymas does not recognize this address as part of its directly connected subnet, it has a route to 206.100.176.0/20 pointing to Cozumel. When it sends a response to the ping, the response is forwarded to Cozumel, which translates the destination address back to 10.255.13.254.

Answers to Chapter 6 Troubleshooting Exercises

1 What is the output of Example 6-63 telling you?

Example 6-63 *The Output for Troubleshooting Exercise 1*

```
R1#
Turban#debug ip mpacket
IP multicast packets debugging is on
R1#
IP: s=192.168.14.35 (Serial0/1.307) d=228.13.20.216 len 573, mrouting disabled
IP: s=192.168.14.35 (Serial0/1.307) d=228.13.20.216 len 573, mrouting disabled
IP: s=192.168.14.35 (Serial0/1.307) d=228.13.20.216 len 573, mrouting disabled
IP: s=192.168.14.35 (Serial0/1.307) d=228.13.20.216 len 573, mrouting disabled
IP: s=192.168.14.35 (Serial0/1.307) d=228.13.20.216 len 573, mrouting disabled
IP: s=192.168.14.35 (Serial0/1.307) d=228.13.20.216 len 573, mrouting disabled
IP: s=192.168.14.35 (Serial0/1.307) d=228.13.20.216 len 573, mrouting disabled
IP: s=192.168.14.35 (Serial0/1.307) d=228.13.20.216 len 573, mrouting disabled
IP: s=192.168.14.35 (Serial0/1.307) d=228.13.20.216 len 573, mrouting disabled
IP: s=192.168.14.35 (Serial0/1.307) d=228.13.20.216 len 573, mrouting disabled
IP: s=192.168.14.35 (Serial0/1.307) d=228.13.20.216 len 573, mrouting disabled
IP: s=192.168.14.35 (Serial0/1.307) d=228.13.20.216 len 573, mrouting disabled
IP: s=192.168.14.35 (Serial0/1.307) d=228.13.20.216 len 573, mrouting disabled
```

Answer: Multicast packets are being dropped because multicast routing is not enabled on the router.

2 What is the output of Example 6-64 telling you?

Example 6-64 *The Output for Troubleshooting Exercise 2*

```
R2#
IP: s=192.168.13.5 (Ethernet0) d=227.134.14.26 len 583, not RPF interface
IP: s=192.168.13.5 (Ethernet0) d=227.134.14.26 len 583, not RPF interface
IP: s=192.168.13.5 (Ethernet0) d=227.134.14.26 len 583, not RPF interface
IP: s=192.168.13.5 (Ethernet0) d=227.134.14.26 len 583, not RPF interface
IP: s=192.168.13.5 (Ethernet0) d=227.134.14.26 len 583, not RPF interface
IP: s=192.168.13.5 (Ethernet0) d=227.134.14.26 len 583, not RPF interface
IP: s=192.168.13.5 (Ethernet0) d=227.134.14.26 len 583, not RPF interface
IP: s=192.168.13.5 (Ethernet0) d=227.134.14.26 len 583, not RPF interface
IP: s=192.168.13.5 (Ethernet0) d=227.134.14.26 len 583, not RPF interface
```

Answer: Packets for group 227.134.14.26, sourced by 192.168.13.5, are being received on interface E0. This interface is apparently not the upstream interface toward the source, however. Therefore, it is not the RPF interface, and the packets are failing the RPF check and are being dropped.

3 What is the output of Example 6-65 telling you?

Example 6-65 *The Output for Troubleshooting Exercise 3*

```
R3#debug ip mpacket
IP multicast packets debugging is on
R3#
IP: s=172.16.3.50 (Serial0.405) d=224.0.1.40 (Serial0.407) len 52, mforward
IP: s=172.16.3.50 (Ethernet0) d=224.0.1.40 len 62, not RPF interface
IP: s=172.16.3.50 (Ethernet0) d=224.0.1.39 len 62, not RPF interface
IP: s=172.16.3.50 (Serial0.405) d=224.0.1.39 (Serial0.407) len 52, mforward
```

Answer: A router at address 172.16.3.50 is both a C-RP (224.0.1.39) and a mapping agent (224.0.1.40). The Auto-RP messages are being received on interface S0.405 and are being forwarded out interface S0.407. The messages also are being received on interface E0 and are failing the RPF check. Therefore, interface S0.405 is the upstream interface to 172.16.3.50.

4 In Figure 6-12, which of the four routers is the PIM-designated router?

Figure 6-12 *The Topology for Troubleshooting Exercises 4, 5, and 6*

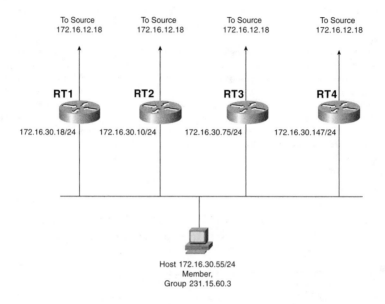

    Answer: The PIM DR is the router with the highest IP address. Therefore, RT4 is the PIM DR.

5 In Figure 6-12, which router is sending IGMPv2 queries to the group member?

    Answer: The IGMPv2 querier is the router with the lowest IP address. Therefore, RT2 is the querier.

6 Table 6-5 shows the unicast routes to source 172.16.12.18 in Figure 6-12. Which router is the PIM forwarder?

Table 6-5 *Unicast Routes to 172.16.12.18 in Figure 6-12*

Router	Next Hop	Protocol	Metric
R1	172.16.50.5	OSPF	35
R2	172.16.51.80	EIGRP	307200
R3	172.16.13.200	EIGRP	2297856
R4	172.16.44.1	OSPF	83

Answer: The PIM forwarder is the router with the lowest administrative distance. Given equal administrative distances, the forwarder is the router with the lowest metric. The administrative distance of EIGRP is 90, and the distance of OSPF is 110, so EIGRP is lower. Between the two EIGRP routes, R2's route has a lower metric, so R2 is the PIM forwarder.

7 Example 6-66 shows an RPF trace taken from the PIM domain in Figure 6-10, which is running RIP-2 as its unicast IGP. Does this trace indicate a possible problem?

Example 6-66 *The mtrace for Troubleshooting Exercise 7*

```
Sombrero#mtrace 192.168.14.35 192.168.10.8 235.1.2.3
Type escape sequence to abort.
Mtrace from 192.168.14.35 to 192.168.10.8 via group 235.1.2.3
From source (?) to destination (?)
Querying full reverse path...
 0   192.168.10.8
-1   192.168.10.1 PIM  [192.168.14.0/24]
-2   192.168.200.2 PIM  [192.168.14.0/24]
-3   192.168.201.2 PIM  [192.168.14.0/24]
-4   192.168.204.1 PIM  [192.168.14.0/24]
-5   192.168.14.35
Sombrero#
```

Answer: Yes. There are equal-cost paths between Beret and Boater via either Turban or Fez. Beret can have only one RPF neighbor, so it picks the neighbor with the highest IP address. In this case, Turban has the highest IP address, but the trace shows that the path through Fez is used. Therefore, there is an apparent problem between Beret and Turban.

INDEX

Symbols

(*, G) state, 435

Numerics

6bone, 647
6REN (IPv6 Research and Education Networks, 646–648

A

A (Address) records, 350
ABRs (area border routers), 456–457
access lists
  alternation, 817
  BGP
    filtering by AS_PATH, 219–224
    filtering by NLRI, 211–218
    filtering with route maps, 224–226
  bracketing, 817
  community lists, 276
  delineation, 816
  regular expressions, negation, 817
  wildcards, 817
accounting, 756
  IP accounting, 756–757
  NetFlow switching, 757–765
accuracy of summarization, 63
active gateways, EGP, 10
Active state (BGP), 97
adding multicast addresses to CAM table, 421
address family ipv4 command, 617
Address Length field (CBT messages), 469
address translation table
  clearing entries, 387
  NAT, 335
addresses
  IPv6, 649
    address type allocation, 652–653
    compacting, 650
    embedded IPv4 addresses, 659

IPv4 compatible, 659
  link-local addresses, 659
  loopback, 658
  site-local addresses, 660
  structure, 654–666
  text representation, 650
  unspecified, 658
leaking to Internet, 73, 339
overloading, 342
preferred, 678
prefixes, 57
reachability, maintaining during ISP
  migration, 339
resolution, ND protocol, 680–681
space depletion, 71
address-family ipv-4 command, 615
Adj-RIBs-In, 113
Adj-RIBs-Out, 113
administrative distance, BGP, 234–241
administrative scoping, 440, 594–595, 664
administrative weight, 110
  filtering multiple routes to the same destination,
    226–234
advertisements
  LSAs, OSPFv2, 701–704
  NA, 679
  ND protocol, 677–678
  RA, 677–678
advertising BGP aggregate routes, 188–195.
  See also route maps
Advertising Router fields (Group Membership
  LSAs), 460
AFI (Address Family Identifier), 606
agent (SNMP), 731–732
aggregatable global address structure, 654
  FP, 656
  interface identifier, 657
  reserved field, 656
  SLAID, 657
  TLAID, 656
  unicast format, 655
aggregate-address command, 185–188, 203, 290

C

J-K

L

N

O

P

T

CCIE Professional Development

Cisco LAN Switching

Kennedy Clark, CCIE; Kevin Hamilton, CCIE

1-57870-094-9 • AVAILABLE NOW

This volume provides an in-depth analysis of Cisco LAN switching technologies, architectures, and deployments, including unique coverage of Catalyst network design essentials. Network designs and configuration examples are incorporated throughout to demonstrate the principles and enable easy translation of the material into practice in production networks.

Advanced IP Network Design

Alvaro Retana, CCIE; Don Slice, CCIE; and Russ White, CCIE

1-57870-097-3 • AVAILABLE NOW

Network engineers and managers can use these case studies, which highlight various network design goals, to explore issues including protocol choice, network stability, and growth. This book also includes theoretical discussion on advanced design topics.

Large-Scale IP Network Solutions

Khalid Raza, CCIE; and Mark Turner

1-57870-084-1 • AVAILABLE NOW

Network engineers can find solutions as their IP networks grow in size and complexity. Examine all the major IP protocols in-depth and learn about scalability, migration planning, network management, and security for large-scale networks.

Routing TCP/IP, Volume I

Jeff Doyle, CCIE

1-57870-041-8 • AVAILABLE NOW

This book takes the reader from a basic understanding of routers and routing protocols through a detailed examination of each of the IP interior routing protocols. Learn techniques for designing networks that maximize the efficiency of the protocol being used. Exercises and review questions provide core study for the CCIE Routing and Switching exam.

Cisco Press

www.ciscopress.com

Cisco Career Certifications

Cisco CCNA Exam #640-507 Certification Guide

Wendell Odom, CCIE

0-7357-0971-8 • AVAILABLE NOW

Although it's only the first step in Cisco Career Certification, the Cisco Certified Network Associate (CCNA) exam is a difficult test. Your first attempt at becoming Cisco certified requires a lot of study and confidence in your networking knowledge. When you're ready to test your skills, complete your knowledge of the exam topics, and prepare for exam day, you need the preparation tools found in *Cisco CCNA Exam #640-507 Certification Guide* from Cisco Press.

CCDA Exam Certification Guide

Anthony Bruno, CCIE & Jacqueline Kim

0-7357-0074-5 • AVAILABLE NOW

CCDA Exam Certification Guide is a comprehensive study tool for DCN Exam #640-441. Written by a CCIE and a CCDA, and reviewed by Cisco technical experts, *CCDA Exam Certification Guide* will help you understand and master the exam objectives. In this solid review on the design areas of the DCN exam, you'll learn to design a network that meets a customer's requirements for performance, security, capacity, and scalability.

Interconnecting Cisco Network Devices

Edited by Steve McQuerry

1-57870-111-2 • AVAILABLE NOW

Based on the Cisco course taught worldwide, *Interconnecting Cisco Network Devices* teaches you how to configure Cisco switches and routers in multi-protocol internetworks. ICND is the primary course recommended by Cisco Systems for CCNA #640-507 preparation. If you are pursuing CCNA certification, this book is an excellent starting point for your study.

Designing Cisco Networks

Edited by Diane Teare

1-57870-105-8 • AVAILABLE NOW

Based on the Cisco Systems instructor-led and self-study course available worldwide, *Designing Cisco Networks* will help you understand how to analyze and solve existing network problems while building a framework that supports the functionality, performance, and scalability required from any given environment. Self-assessment through exercises and chapter-ending tests starts you down the path for attaining your CCDA certification.

Cisco Press

Cisco Press Solutions

Enhanced IP Services for Cisco Networks

Donald C. Lee, CCIE

1-57870-106-6 • **AVAILABLE NOW**

This is a guide to improving your network's capabilities by understanding the new enabling and advanced Cisco IOS services that build more scalable, intelligent, and secure networks. Learn the technical details necessary to deploy Quality of Service, VPN technologies, IPsec, the IOS firewall and IOS Intrusion Detection. These services will allow you to extend the network to new frontiers securely, protect your network from attacks, and increase the sophistication of network services.

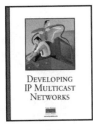

Developing IP Multicast Networks, Volume I

Beau Williamson, CCIE

1-57870-077-9 • **AVAILABLE NOW**

This book provides a solid foundation of IP multicast concepts and explains how to design and deploy the networks that will support appplications such as audio and video conferencing, distance-learning, and data replication. Includes an in-depth discussion of the PIM protocol used in Cisco routers and detailed coverage of the rules that control the creation and maintenance of Cisco mroute state entries.

Designing Network Security

Merike Kaeo

1-57870-043-4 • **AVAILABLE NOW**

Designing Network Security is a practical guide designed to help you understand the fundamentals of securing your corporate infrastructure. This book takes a comprehensive look at underlying security technologies, the process of creating a security policy, and the practical requirements necessary to implement a corporate security policy.

Cisco Press

www.ciscopress.com

Cisco Press Solutions

EIGRP Network Design Solutions
Ivan Pepelnjak, CCIE
1-57870-165-1 • AVAILABLE NOW

EIGRP Network Design Solutions uses case studies and real-world configuration examples to help you gain an in-depth understanding of the issues involved in designing, deploying, and managing EIGRP-based networks. This book details proper designs that can be used to build large and scalable EIGRP-based networks and documents possible ways each EIGRP feature can be used in network design, implmentation, troubleshooting, and monitoring.

Top-Down Network Design
Priscilla Oppenheimer
1-57870-069-8 • AVAILABLE NOW

Building reliable, secure, and manageable networks is every network professional's goal. This practical guide teaches you a systematic method for network design that can be applied to campus LANs, remote-access networks, WAN links, and large-scale internetworks. Learn how to analyze business and technical requirements, examine traffic flow and Quality of Service requirements, and select protocols and technologies based on performance goals.

Cisco IOS Releases: The Complete Reference
Mack M. Coulibaly
1-57870-179-1 • AVAILABLE NOW

Cisco IOS Releases: The Complete Reference is the first comprehensive guide to the more than three dozen types of Cisco IOS releases being used today on enterprise and service provider networks. It details the release process and its numbering and naming conventions, as well as when, where, and how to use the various releases. A complete map of Cisco IOS software releases and their relationships to one another, in addition to insights into decoding information contained within the software, make this book an indispensable resource for any network professional.

Cisco Press

www.ciscopress.com

Cisco Press Solutions

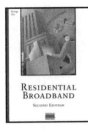

Residential Broadband, Second Edition
George Abe
1-57870-177-5 • **AVAILABLE NOW**

This book will answer basic questions of residential broadband networks such as: Why do we need high speed networks at home? How will high speed residential services be delivered to the home? How do regulatory or commercial factors affect this technology? Explore such networking topics as xDSL, cable, and wireless.

Internetworking Technologies Handbook, Second Edition
Kevin Downes, CCIE, Merilee Ford, H. Kim Lew, Steve Spanier, Tim Stevenson
1-57870-102-3 • **AVAILABLE NOW**

This comprehensive reference provides a foundation for understanding and implementing contemporary internetworking technologies, providing you with the necessary information needed to make rational networking decisions. Master terms, concepts, technologies, and devices that are used in the internetworking industry today. You also learn how to incorporate networking technologies into a LAN/WAN environment, as well as how to apply the OSI reference model to categorize protocols, technologies, and devices.

OpenCable Architecture
Michael Adams
1-57870-135-X • **AVAILABLE NOW**

Whether you're a television, data communications, or telecommunications professional, or simply an interested business person, this book will help you understand the technical and business issues surrounding interactive television services. It will also provide you with an inside look at the combined efforts of the cable, data, and consumer electronics industries' efforts to develop those new services.

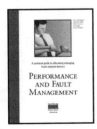

Performance and Fault Management
Paul Della Maggiora, Christopher Elliott, Robert Pavone, Kent Phelps, James Thompson
1-57870-180-5 • **AVAILABLE NOW**

This book is a comprehensive guide to designing and implementing effective strategies for monitoring performance levels and correctng problems in Cisco networks. It provides an overview of router and LAN switch operations to help you understand how to manage such devices, as well as guidance on the essential MIBs, traps, syslog messages, and show commands for managing Cisco routers and switches.

Cisco Press   **www.ciscopress.com**

Cisco Press Fundamentals

IP Routing Primer

Robert Wright, CCIE

1-57870-108-2 • **AVAILABLE NOW**

Learn how IP routing behaves in a Cisco router environment. In addition to teaching the core fundamentals, this book enhances your ability to troubleshoot IP routing problems yourself, often eliminating the need to call for additional technical support. The information is presented in an approachable, workbook-type format with dozens of detailed illustrations and real-life scenarios integrated throughout.

Cisco Router Configuration

Allan Leinwand, Bruce Pinsky, Mark Culpepper

1-57870-022-1 • **AVAILABLE NOW**

An example-oriented and chronological approach helps you implement and administer your internetworking devices. Starting with the configuration devices "out of the box;" this book moves to configuring Cisco IOS for the three most popular networking protocols today: TCP/IP, AppleTalk, and Novell Interwork Packet Exchange (IPX). You also learn basic administrative and management configuration, including access control with TACACS+ and RADIUS, network management with SNMP, logging of messages, and time control with NTP.

IP Routing Fundamentals

Mark A. Sportack

1-57870-071-x • **AVAILABLE NOW**

This comprehensive guide provides essential background information on routing in IP networks for network professionals who are deploying and maintaining LANs and WANs daily. Explore the mechanics of routers, routing protocols, network interfaces, and operating systems.

Cisco Press

www.ciscopress.com

Cisco Press Fundamentals

Internet Routing Architectures, Second Edition

Sam Halabi with Danny McPherson

1-57870-233-x • **AVAILABLE NOW**

This book explores the ins and outs of interdomain routing network design with emphasis on BGP-4 (Border Gateway Protocol Version 4)--the de facto interdomain routing protocol. You will have all the information you need to make knowledgeable routing decisions for Internet connectivity in your environment.

Voice over IP Fundamentals

Jonathan Davidson and James Peters

1-57870-168-6 • **AVAILABLE NOW**

Voice over IP (VoIP), which integrates voice and data transmission, is quickly becoming an important factor in network communications. It promises lower operational costs, greater flexibility, and a variety of enhanced applications. This book provides a thorough introduction to this new technology to help experts in both the data and telephone industries plan for the new networks.

For the latest on Cisco Press resources and Certification and

Training guides, or for information on publishing opportunities, visit

www.ciscopress.com

Cisco Press

How many computer technology books do you own?
- ❏ 1
- ❏ 2–7
- ❏ more than 7

Which best describes your job function? (check all that apply)
- ❏ Corporate Management
- ❏ Network Design
- ❏ Marketing/Sales
- ❏ Professor/Teacher
- ❏ Systems Engineering
- ❏ Network Support
- ❏ Consultant
- ❏ Other
- ❏ IS Management
- ❏ Webmaster
- ❏ Student
- ❏ Cisco Networking Academy Program Instuctor

Do you hold any computer certifications? (check all that apply)
- ❏ MCSE
- ❏ CCNP
- ❏ CCNA
- ❏ CCDP
- ❏ CCDA
- ❏ CCIE
- ❏ Other _____

Are you currently pursuing a certification? (check all that apply)
- ❏ MCSE
- ❏ CCNP
- ❏ CCNA
- ❏ CCDP
- ❏ CCDA
- ❏ CCIE
- ❏ Other _____

On what topics would you like to see more coverage?

_____
_____
_____

Do you have any additional comments or suggestions?

_____
_____
_____

Thank you for completing this survey and registration. Please fold here, seal, and mail to Cisco Press.

Routing TCP/IP, Volume II (1-57870-089-2)

Indianapolis, IN 46278-8046
P.O. Box #781046
Customer Registration—CP050227
Cisco Press

Place
Stamp
Here

ciscopress.com
Indianapolis, IN 46290
201 West 103rd Street
Cisco Press

CISCO SYSTEMS/PACKET MAGAZINE
ATTN: C. Glover
170 West Tasman, Mailstop SJ8-2
San Jose, CA 95134-1706

Place
Stamp
Here